Employment Law for Business

Tenth Edition

wn D.
nett-Alexander
y of Georgia

La
*DePau***Hartman**
ty

Contri
Robyn B

Southern Illino
Edwardsville

Mc Graw Hill

EMPLOYMENT LAW FOR BUSINESS, TENTH EDITION

Copyright ©2022 by

1 2 3 4 5 6 7 8 9 LCR 24 23 22 21

ISBN 978-1-260-73427-0 (bound edition)
MHID 1-260-73427-7 (bound edition)

ISBN 978-1-264-12608-8 (loose-leaf edition)
MHID 1-264-12608-5 (loose-leaf edition)

Portfolio Manager: *Kathleen Klehr*
Product Developer: *Alexandra Kukla*   *Clune*
Marketing Manager: *Claire McLemore*
Content Project Managers: *Amy Gehl; [V]*
Buyer: *Susan K. Culbertson*   *[h]itt*
Designer: *Matt Diamond*   *[G]etty Images*
Content Licensing Specialist: *Sh*
Cover Image: *Lisa Stokes/Mo[m]*
Compositor: *SPi Global*

[th]e end of the book are considered to be an extension of the copyright page.

All credits appearing on

[Lib]rary of Congress Cataloging-in-Publication Data

[..]n, author. | Hartman, Laura Pincus, author. |
[..]or.
Names: Bennett-A[l]siness / Dawn Bennett-Alexander, University of
Berkley, Roby[a]n, DePaul University; Robyn Berkley, Southern
Title: Employ[...]ardsville.
Georgia; [...]ion. | New York, NY : McGraw Hill LLC, [2021] |
Illinois [...]hical references and index.
Descri[...]2020025614 (print) | LCCN 2020025615 (ebook) | ISBN
In[...] (hardback) | ISBN 1260734277 (bound edition) | ISBN
Id[...]88 (loose-leaf edition) | ISBN 1264126085 (loose-leaf edition) | ISBN 9781264126101 (ebook)
[...]H: Labor laws and legislation–United States. | Discrimination
[...]ment–Law and legislation–United States. | LCGFT: Casebooks (Law)
[...]ion: LCC KF3455 .B46 2021 (print) | LCC KF3455 (ebook) | DDC 344.7301–dc23
[...]rd available at https://lccn.loc.gov/2020025614
[..]ook record available at https://lccn.loc.gov/2020025615

[..] Internet addresses listed in the text were accurate at the time of publication. The inclusion of a website does
[no]t indicate an endorsement by the authors or McGraw Hill LLC, and McGraw Hill LLC does not guarantee the
[a]ccuracy of the information presented at these sites.

mheducation.com/highered

Dedication

Brian A. Thompson
One word: *Masterpiece.*
On second thought, three: *Thank you.*

D D B-A

For those whose voices continue to be silenced by others, ours is now and always a responsibility to speak. *Kenbe la:* stand firm, stay true.

L P H

About the Authors

Mike Horn

Dawn D. Bennett-Alexander *University of Georgia*

With over fifty awards to her credit, Dawn D. Bennett-Alexander, Esq., is a tenured associate professor of Employment Law and Legal Studies at the University of Georgia's Terry College of Business. An attorney admitted to practice in the District of Columbia and six federal jurisdictions, she is a *cum laude* graduate of the Howard University School of Law and a *magna cum laude* graduate of the Federal City College, now the University of the District of Columbia. With her coauthor, she was cofounder and cochair of the Employment and Labor Law Section of the Academy of Legal Studies in Business and coeditor of the section's *Employment and Labor Law Quarterly,* past coeditor of the section's newsletter, and past president of the Southeastern Academy of Legal Studies in Business. Among other texts, she coauthored, with Linda F. Harrison, McGraw Hill's groundbreaking *The Legal, Ethical, and Regulatory Environment of Business in a Diverse Society* in 2011. Bennett-Alexander taught Employment Law in the University of North Florida's MBA program from 1982 to 1987 and has been conducting Employment Law seminars for managers and supervisors since 1983. Prior to teaching, Bennett-Alexander worked in Washington, DC, at the Federal Labor Relations Authority, the White House Domestic Council, the Federal Trade Commission, the Department of Justice Appellate Division, and the Antioch School of Law and as law clerk to the Honorable Julia Cooper Mack as Judge Mack became the first Black female in the country to be appointed a judge in a court of last resort, the D.C. Court of Appeals. Bennett-Alexander publishes widely in the Employment Law area; is a noted expert on Employment Law and Diversity, Equity and Inclusion issues; was asked to write the first-ever sexual harassment entry for *Grolier Encyclopedia;* edited the National Employee Rights Institute's definitive book on federal employment rights; has chapters in several other books including five Employment Law entries in Sage Publications' first and second editions of the *Encyclopedia of Business Ethics and Society;* has been widely quoted on TV and radio and in the print press, including *USA Today, The Wall Street Journal,* and *Fortune* magazine; and is founder of Practical Diversity, consultants on Diversity, Equity, and Inclusion as well as Employment Law issues. Among other accomplishments, Bennett-Alexander was one of only ten winners of the prestigious national Elizabeth Hurlock Beckman award for teaching excellence in 2015; presented an invited diversity paper for the Oxford Roundtable at Oxford University, Oxford, England in 2014 and the Huber Hurst Research Roundtable in 2019; was a 2000–2001 recipient of the Fulbright Senior Scholar Fellowship under which she taught at the Ghana School of Law in Ghana, West Africa; and conducted research on race and gender in employment. She has also taught in Budapest, Krakow, Austria, Prague, Australia, New Zealand, Italy, and Costa Rica. She is the recipient of the 2019 Honored Trailblazer recognition from UGA's Minority Services and Programs, 2011 University of Georgia President's Martin Luther King, Jr., Fulfilling the Dream Award, her university's highest diversity award, for her outstanding work in building bridges to understanding and unity;

the 2010 recipient of the University of Georgia's Terry College of Business inaugural Diversity Award; and the 2009 recipient of the Ernst & Young Inclusive Excellence Award for Accounting and Business School faculty. She dedicates all her research and writing to her cherished Ancestors, three daughters, and two grandchildren.

Marketing Communications Department, Questrom School of Business

Laura P. Hartman   *DePaul University (Chicago) & The School of Choice/ l'Ecole de Choix (Haiti)*

Laura Pincus Hartman is a professor *emerita* at DePaul University and executive director of the School of Choice Education Organization, a U.S.-based nonprofit that she co-founded, which oversees the School of Choice / l'Ecole de Choix, a unique trilingual elementary school in Haiti that provides high-quality leadership development education to children living in extreme conditions of poverty.

From 2015–2017, Professor Hartman also served as the inaugural director of the Susilo Institute for Ethics in the Global Economy and clinical professor of Business Ethics in the Department of Organizational Behavior. She also was an associated professor at the Kedge Business School (Marseille, France).

Professor Hartman held a number of roles at DePaul University over her almost three-decade career there, including associate vice president for Academic Affairs, Vincent de Paul Professor of Business Ethics at DePaul University's Driehaus College of Business, and director of its Institute for Business and Professional Ethics. Hartman also has taught at INSEAD (France), HEC (France), the Université Paul Cezanne Aix Marseille III, the University of Toulouse, and the Grenoble Graduate School of Business. Hartman is past president of the Society for Business Ethics, was co-chair of its Committee on International Collaborations, and established and directed its professional mentorship program.

In the private sector, concurrent to her academic work, Hartman was director of External Partnerships for Zynga.Org (2009–2012), through which Zynga players of *FarmVille, Words with Friends,* and other online games have contributed over $20 million toward both domestic and international social causes. From 2009–2011, she represented DePaul University on the Worldwide Vincentian Family's Vincentian Board for Haiti and was instrumental in the hands-on design and implementation of a micro-development, finance, and education system for people living in poverty in Haiti. Hartman is a thought leader in leadership and ethical decision making, and her work has resulted in the publication of more than 80 articles, cases, and books and demonstrates the potential for innovative and profitable partnerships to alleviate poverty while providing measurable value to all stakeholders involved.

A winner of the Microsoft CreateGOOD award at Cannes Lions (2015), named one of *Ethisphere's* 100 Most Influential People in Business Ethics, and one of *Fast Company's* Most Creative People in Business (2014), Hartman serves as an advisor to a number of start-ups and has consulted with multinational for-profits, nonprofits, and educational institutions. She was invited to BAInnovate's inaugural UnGrounded lab and has been named to *Fast Company's* "League of Extraordinary Woman."

Hartman graduated *magna cum laude* from Tufts University and received her law degree from the University of Chicago Law School. She divides her time between Haiti and Sint Maarten and has been a mother to two daughters.

Prelude to the 10th Edition

Well before our tenth edition, when we knew we would make it to that momentous and quite admirable milestone, our preliminary thoughts for the preface were all about what a milestone it was, especially in light of the fact that it had trod such new territory as a first-of-its-kind textbook that ended up creating the discipline. That is quite an accomplishment. However, as the actual time approached, those thoughts took a far back seat to the situation the country found itself in as relates to the subject matter of this text.

This has been a hard edition to write. Not because writing the book is difficult in and of itself. After all, we have been at this for nearly thirty years now and we love writing it. The difficulty came in day after day seeing all sorts of changes being made to issues addressed in the text that would have been unthinkable before. In February 2020, the FBI for the fist time deemed white supremacist groups on par with Middle Eastern terrorist groups in terms of the threat they pose to the United States.[1] Hundreds of judges have been appointed by the Trump administration, many of whose backgrounds seem to reflect a point of view akin to Trump's rather than qualifications and experience that reflect an ability to be able to listen and judge fairly and objectively based on legal principles. Trump continues to sow racial and ethnic discord. In the midst of a tremendously upsetting global pandemic in March 2020, he insisted on calling it the "China" virus rather than its scientific name, COVID-19. One of the fallouts of this characterization was people who appeared to be of Chinese ethnicity were harassed and subject to violence on our streets, including in one instance a Chinese doctor on his way to help COVID-19 patients. Trump finally announced he would no longer use the term.

In May 2020, protests as well as rioting (what MLK, Jr. called "the language of the unheard") swept across the country after yet another killing of an unarmed African American male at the hands of the police. Officer Derek Chauvin kept his knee on Floyd's neck for 8 minutes and 46 seconds while Floyd lay on his stomach on the ground, handcuffed with his hands behind his back, saying he could not breathe, in front of a crowd shouting for Chauvin to take his knee away. Trump's response was to call the protesters "THUGS" and tweet "When the looting starts, the shooting starts." Quite different than his response to heavily armed white shelter-at-home protesters on the steps of the Michigan capitol, who were, "Good people," "just angry." This attitude Trump projects inevitably finds its way into his policies and into the workplace. Legal principles such as mandatory arbitration agreements long denounced by the EEOC are now endorsed by the agency despite the principle being directly at odds with the agency's mission and declared so 22 years ago by the agency. The Department of Justice argued before the U.S. Supreme Court that Title VII should not include protection for the LGBTQ community, totally at odds with the argument of the EEOC arguing as a party in the case. We are pleased that the Court did not agree with him in its June 15 ruling in *Bostock v. Clayton County, Georgia* decision. And there have been rollbacks in other policies that were intended to give full effect to the laws the agency enforces. While employers came up with breathtaking new and creative and vigorous approaches to workplace race issues in light of the racial reckoning in the wake of the George Floyd killing, Trump ordered that the federal government cease diversity and inclusion training for federal employees and government contractors. When Wells Fargo and Microsoft announced new goals for hiring Black leaders, the Office of Federal Contract Compliance responsible for monitoring federal contracts required them to show cause why this was not illegal. The US Chamber of Commerce, joined by over 150 other profit and non-profit organizations, pushed back and in October 2020 wrote to Trump asking him to withdraw his order.

[1]Allam, Hannah, "FBI Announces That Racist Violence Is Now Equal Priority to Foreign Terrorism," National Public Radio (February 10, 2020).

It is rather unprecedented for us to make such pronouncements, but under the circumstances, we would be remiss if we did not do so. It is not *our* truth. It is *the* truth. It is not said for purposes of politics, persuasion, or denigration but rather to simply state the status of the law and present environment regarding issues this textbook addresses. Despite it all, the law exists, and we persevere and will continue to do our best to teach future employers, managers, and supervisors how to abide by the law and avoid workplace liability for unnecessary and avoidable discrimination claims.

Acting like a cloud over all of this is, at this point, the COVID-19 pandemic. As we write this prelude on October 18, 2020, our classes have been moved online since spring break in March, and they will continue online at least through the spring of 2021. Commencement and virtually every other university program has been canceled or moved to Zoom. All over the country restaurants are closed, as are movie theaters, bowling alleys, churches, and even Broadway. Anyone who can work from home is doing so. Zoom's stock spiked more than 100 percent after the COVID-19 pandemic hit, and it became the primary way meetings were held by every entity from international corporations to families, from churches to civic groups, and from entertainment to classrooms. Although there has been no national declaration of sheltering in place in the United States, scientists urged it, and more than 90 percent of the American population is under some kind of shutdown. All but nonessential venues were closed at some point. Toilet paper is difficult to find. Hospitals are running out of beds, ventilators, and personal protection equipment. Our stock markets have all but crashed. The $2 trillion virus rescue package passed by Congress was deemed insufficient as soon as it was signed. Life as we know it was at a virtual standstill. Even the EEOC paused its issuance of right to sue notices and courts are holding trials and hearings virtually. And we have no idea when things will get back to normal.

But they will. And when they do, we have no doubt that we will continue to persevere as a country, right ourselves, and bring ourselves back to our basic American values such as human dignity, equality, and appreciation of the value of a person's worth measured in what they do rather than their gender, race, ethnicity, religion, disability status, or sexual orientation or other characteristics having little or nothing to do with their qualifications for the job. That is what this law is all about. So, despite the fact that it was difficult to do, we have brought you the latest regarding the law.

We should note for you that, although COVID-19 is a huge part of our lives at the moment, it does not change the fundamental laws we discuss. There have been some impacts, and we have mentioned them where we think appropriate. But because these changes have said they were only due to and during the pandemic, we view them as temporary. So, while we note them in passing for you, we have not dwelled on them because things are moving so quickly and could change and we do not want to have them take you away from the main aspects of the law that will remain long after the pandemic is over. If there are changes in your workplace related to the virus, your employer will notify you of them.

Finally, as we write this, millions of citizens have taken to the streets across the country and even across the globe to express their concern and frustration about the country's ongoing racial inequalities further demonstrated by the killing of yet another unarmed Black man, George Floyd in Minneapolis, MN on May 25, 2020 at the hands of police officer Derek Chauvin. Deep concern for these issues by millions of people across the country was aptly represented by a note posted to his colleagues by Mark Mason, Chief Financial Officer of global Citibank. It was the first corporate response I saw. It was tremendous. The first ten lines of the post simply said, "I can't breathe." These are the words uttered by Mr. Floyd as he lay dying in the streets of Minneapolis. He went on to speak of the personal decision to speak out and why it was necessary for him to do so. He ended with a request for others to join him in contributing to organizations doing the important work of trying to make society better.

I applaud Mr. Mason for being courageous enough to take such a stand and live out the diversity, equity and inclusion values his company espouses. Nike's later "For Once, Don't Do It" anti-racism ad was awesome as well. In the days that followed, thousands of other companies followed suit and issued statements, and went beyond and sought ways to make have their organizations truly reflect the values they said they believed in. We believe that corporations play an absolutely necessary and invaluable role in helping to reflect in the workplace values that will help us all live in a more just and equitable world and I appreciate these companies taking these inclusive, cutting-edge steps to make that a reality.

In closing, while the step Mr. Mason took, as the chief financial officer for a global financial institution was one that had the potential to impact many around the globe, do not for one second think that you, too, cannot also make an impact wherever you are. Do not underestimate the seeming casual, random conversations you have with your fellow students, friends, colleagues and family members. Use them as a basis to educate, raise awareness and even advocate. People hear you. We are in this together. A win for one of us is a win for all of us. Each of us has a part to play. Play yours for all its worth. Do your part to make the world a better place.

As we have said from our very first edition, *please* do not hesitate to contact us about the book. We *love* hearing from you. And we love it that you really do email us.

Dawn D. Bennett-Alexander
Athens, GA
October 18, 2020
dawndba@gmail.com

Like Dawn, I reviewed my comments from past editions and realized that perhaps I held a bit more optimism in our social fabric than was warranted during those earlier times. But hope propels me. My hope is not necessarily grounded in abounding evidence of human goodness. Instead, I am inspired and find confidence in the resilience of those around me—how people respond when the world is not so good, to them or to others.

I see people who survive each day with intense political instability, others who manage to persevere in the face of deep conflict or baseless hatred, some who consistently speak up on behalf of those who cannot, people who fight for what is right, no matter the cost. I am in awe of their strength and the way that they wake up each morning and do it again.

What wakes you up in the morning? What keeps you awake at night? No matter what issues are important to you, we encourage you to use your voice, mobilized by education, to impact your life and the lives of others in a way that raises the quality of life for all.

Our responsibility as educators is to galvanize and motivate your response to this world and to develop (or enhance) your empathy in the face of injustice, that lingering sense of indignity even when the affront is not against ourselves. Through this text, we seek to equip you with powerful tools so that both you and those without a voice can be heard more clearly.

Many years may have passed since our first edition was published, and that first edition came out a quarter of a century after Title VII had been passed. It may seem like a great deal of time, and perhaps much has changed, but **not enough.** Whether one agrees with his politics or not, it seems fitting to begin each edition with past President Obama's words, "Change will not come if we wait for some other person, or if we wait for some other time. We are the ones we've been waiting for. We are the change that we seek."*

Be that change.

Laura Pincus Hartman
Sint Maarten, April 2020

*Barack Obama's Feb. 5 Speech. *The New York Times*, February 5, 2008.

Preface

- Can an employer terminate a female employee because male employees find her pleasing shape too distracting?
- Can an employer institute a policy prohibiting Muslim women from wearing their hijabs (head scarves)?
- Can an employer be successfully sued for "reverse discrimination" by an employee who feels harmed by the employer's affirmative action plan?
- If a disabled employee could perform the job requirements when hired, but the job has progressed and the employee is no longer able to perform, must the employer keep her on?
- Is an ex-employer liable for defamation if he gives a negative recommendation about an ex-employee to a potential employer who inquires?

These types of questions, which are routinely decided in workplaces every day, can have devastating financial and productivity consequences if mishandled by the employer. Yet few employers or their managers and supervisors are equipped to handle them well. That is why this textbook was created.

Between fiscal years 1970, when newly enacted job discrimination legislation cases started to rise, and 2019, the number of federal discrimination suits grew from fewer than 350 per year to over 70,000, reaching an all-time high in 2016 of just shy of 100,000. A major factor in this statistic is that the groups protected by Title VII of the Civil Rights Act of 1964 and similar legislation, including minorities, women, and employees over 40, now constitute over 70 percent of the total workforce. Add to that number those protected by laws addressing disability, genetic and family medical history, wages and hours, and unions; workplace environmental right-to-know laws; tort laws; and occupational safety and health laws, and the percentage increases even more. The U.S. Department of Labor alone administers more than 180 federal laws covering about 10 million employers and 125 million workers.[1]

It is good that employers and employees alike are now getting the benefits derived from having a safer, fairer workplace and one more reflective of the population. However, this is not without its attendant challenges. One of those challenges is reflected in the statistics given above. With the advent of workplace regulation by the government, particularly the Civil Rights Act of 1964, there is more of an expectation by employees of certain basic rights in the workplace. When these expectations are not met and the affected population constitutes more than 70 percent of the workforce, problems and their attendant litigation not only will arise but are likely to be numerous.

Plaintiffs generally win nearly 50 percent of lawsuits brought for workplace discrimination. The median monetary damage award is $155,000.[2] As you will soon

---

[1]https://www.dol.gov/general/aboutdol/majorlaws.

[2]"Valuing Your Case," Workplace Fairness (2017), https://www.workplacefairness.org/valuing_your_case (accessed June 5, 2017).

see, the good news is that the vast majority of the litigation and liability arising in the area covered by these statistics is completely avoidable. Many times the only difference between an employer being sued or not is a manager or supervisor who recognizes that the decision being made may lead to unnecessary litigation and thus avoids it.

When we first began this venture almost 30 years ago, we did not know if we would be able to sell enough copies of the textbook to justify even having a second edition. Luckily, we had a publisher who understood the situation and made a commitment to hang in there with us. The problem was that there was no established market for the text. There were so few classes in this area that they did not even show up as a blip on the radar screen. Actually, we only knew of two. But having worked in this area for years, we knew the need was there, even if the students, faculty, and even employers were not yet aware of it.

We convinced the publishers that "if you publish it, they will come."

And come they did. From the minute the book was first released, it was embraced. And just as we thought, classes were developed, students flooded in, and by the time the smoke cleared, the first edition had exceeded all the publisher's forecasts and expectations. The need that we knew was there really was there, and an entire discipline was created. The textbook spawned other such texts but remains the leading textbook of its kind in the country.

We cannot thank the publishers enough for being so committed to this textbook. Without their commitment, none of this would have happened. And we cannot thank professors and students enough for being there for us, supporting us, believing in the textbook and our voices, and trusting that we will honor the law and our commitment to bring the best to faculty and students.

We have seen what types of employment law problems are most prevalent in the workplace from our extensive experience in the classroom and in our research and writing as well as in conducting over the years many employment seminars for managers, supervisors, business owners, equal employment opportunity officers, human resources personnel, general counsels, and others. We have seen how management most often strays from appropriate considerations and gets into avoidable legal trouble, exposing it to potential increased liability. We came to realize that many of the mistakes were based on ignorance rather than malice. Often employers simply did not know that a situation was being handled incorrectly.

Becoming more aware of potential liability does not mean the employer is not free to make legitimate workplace decisions it deems best. It simply means that those decisions are handled appropriately in ways that lessen or avoid liability. The problem does not lie in not being able to terminate the female who is chronically late for work because the employer thinks she will sue for gender discrimination. Rather, the challenge lies in doing it in a way that precludes her from being able to file a successful gender discrimination claim. It does not mean the employer must retain her despite her failure to adequately meet workplace requirements. Rather, it means that the employer must make certain the termination is beyond reproach. If the employee has performed in a way that results in termination, this should be documentable and, therefore, defensible. Termination of the employee under such circumstances should present no problem, assuming similarly situated employees consistently have been treated the same way. The employer is free to make the management decisions necessary to run the business, but it simply does so correctly.

Knowing how to do so correctly does not just happen. It must be learned. We set out to create a textbook aimed at anyone who would or presently does manage people. Knowing what is in this book is a necessity. For those already in the workplace, your day is filled with one awkward situation after another—for which you wish you had the answers. For those in school, you will soon be in the workplace, and in the not-too-distant future you will likely be in a position managing others. We cannot promise answers to every one of your questions, but we can promise that we will provide the information and basic considerations in most areas that will help you arrive at an informed, reasonable, and defensible decision about which you can feel more comfortable. You will not walk away feeling as if you rolled the dice when you made a workplace decision and then wait with anxiety to see if the decision will backfire in some way.

In an effort to best inform employers of the reasoning behind legal requirements and to provide a basis for making decisions in "gray areas," we often provide background in relevant social or political movements, or both, as well as in legislative history and other relevant considerations. Law is not created in a vacuum, and this information gives the law context so the purpose is more easily understood. Often understanding why a law exists can help a manager make the correct choices in interpreting the law when making workplace decisions with no clear-cut answers. We have found over the years that so few people really understand what any of this is really about. They know they are not supposed to discriminate on the basis of, say, gender, but they don't always realize (1) when they are doing it and (2) why the law prohibits it. Understanding the background behind the law can give extremely important insight into areas that help with both of these issues and allow the manager to make better decisions, particularly where no clear-cut answer may be apparent.

Legal cases are used to illustrate important concepts; however, we realize that it is the managerial aspects of the concepts with which you must deal. Therefore, we took great pains to try to rid the cases of unnecessary "legalese" and procedural matters that would be more relevant to a lawyer or law student. We also follow each case with questions designed to aid in thinking critically about the issues involved from an employer's standpoint rather than from a purely legal standpoint. We understand that *how* employers make their decisions has a great impact on the decisions made. Therefore, our case-end questions are designed as critical-thinking questions to get the student to go beyond the legal concepts and think critically about management issues. This process of learning to analyze and think critically about issues from different points of view will greatly enhance students' decision-making abilities as future managers or business owners. Addressing the issues in the way they are likely to arise in life greatly enhances that ability. You may wonder why we ask questions such as whether you agree with the court's decision or what you would do in the situation. This is important in getting you to think about facts from your perspective as a potential manager or supervisor. Your thoughts matter just as much as anyone else's, and you should begin to think like a manager if you are going to be one. Nothing magical happens once you step into the workplace. You bring an awful lot of your own thoughts, preconceived notions, and prejudgments with you. Sometimes these are at odds with the law, which can lead to liability for the employer. The questions are a way to ferret out your own thoughts, to explore what is in your own head that can serve as the basis of decisions you make in the workplace. You can then make any needed adjustments to avoid liability.

It is one thing to know that the law prohibits gender discrimination in employment. It is quite another to recognize such discrimination when it occurs and govern oneself accordingly. For instance, a female employee says she cannot use a "filthy" toilet, which is the only one at the work site. The employer can dismiss the complaint, tell the employee she must use the toilet, and perhaps later be held liable for gender discrimination. Or the employer can think of what implications this may have, given that this is a female employee essentially being denied a right that male employees have in access to a usable toilet. The employer then realizes there may be a problem and is more likely to make the better decision.

This seemingly unlikely scenario is based on an actual case, which you will later read. It is a great example of how simple but unexpected decisions can create liability in surprising ways. Knowing the background and intent of a law often can help in situations where the answer to the problem may not be readily apparent. Including the law in your thinking can help the thought process for making well-founded decisions.

You may notice that, while many of our cases are extremely timely and have a "ripped from the headlines" feel to them, others are somewhat older. There are two reasons why we include those older cases. First, some of them are called "seminal" cases that created the foundation for all of the legal decisions that came afterward, so you need to be aware of them. The other reason is much more practical. Because our goal is to teach you to avoid liability in the workplace, part of our means of reaching the goal is to use fact patterns that we think do the best job of illustrating certain points. Most legal texts try to bring you *only* the latest cases. Of course, we also do that, but our primary goal is to use those cases that we think best illustrate our point. The clearest, most illustrative fact pattern might be an older case rather than a newer one. We will not include newer cases just because they are new. We provide cases that best illustrate our points for you and, if they happen to be older cases that are still good law, we will use them. We are interested in facts that will help you learn what you need to know rather than case dates. We look at the cases that have come out between editions and, if none do the job of illustrating our point better, we go with what is best geared to show you how to think through an issue.

We have made the decision to limit the number of cases in each chapter, and most chapters have three or four. Even though the subject matter from chapter to chapter may lend itself to different numbers of cases, we decided to try for consistency. Hopefully, the carefully chosen cases will still accomplish our purpose.

We also have included endnotes and boxed items from easily accessible media sources that you come across every day, such as *The New York Times, The Wall Street Journal,* and *USA Today.* The intent is to demonstrate how the matters discussed are interesting and integrated into everyday life yet can have serious repercussions for employers. In earlier editions, we opted for reading continuity and thus did not include a lot of our research material as endnotes. We have made the conscious decision to include more sources as endnotes. Hopefully, what is lost in seeing the endnote callout as you read will be balanced with the fact that you now have the resources to do further investigation on your own since you now have the resources to do so.

Much of today's litigation results from workplace decisions arising from unfortunate ideas about various groups and from lack of awareness about what may result in litigation. We do not want to take away anyone's right to think whatever he or she wants about whomever he or she wants, but we do want to teach that those thoughts may result in legal trouble when they are acted on.

Something new and innovative must be done if we are to break the cycle of insensitivity and myopia that results in spiraling numbers of unnecessary workplace lawsuits. Part of breaking this cycle is using language and terminology that more accurately reflect those considerations. We therefore, in writing the text, made a rather unorthodox move and took the offensive, creating a path rather than following one.

For instance, the term *sex* is generally used in this text to mean sex only in a purely sexual sense—which means we do not use it very much. The term *gender* is used to distinguish males from females (although we understand that gender is not necessarily binary). With the increasing use of sexual harassment as a cause of action, it became confusing to continue to speak of sex as meaning gender, particularly when it adds to the confusion to understand that sex need *not* be present in a sexual harassment claim but gender differences *are* required. For instance, to say that a claim must be based on "a difference in treatment based on sex" leaves it unclear as to whether it means gender or sexual activity. Since it actually means gender, we have made such clarifications. Also, use of the term *sex* in connection with gender discrimination cases, the majority of which are brought by women, continues to inject sexuality into the equation of women and work. This, in turn, contributes to keeping women and sexuality connected in an inappropriate setting (employment). Further, it does so at a time when there is an attempt to decrease such connections and, instead, concentrate on the applicant's qualifications for the job. The term is also confusing when a growing number of workplace discrimination claims have been brought by transgender individuals, for whom gender, sex, and sexuality intersect and can cause confusion if language is not intentional, accurate, conscious, and thoughtful.

We were utterly delighted that for the first time in the 20-year history of the text, we were comfortably using the terms *homosexual* and *sexual orientation*. We are ecstatic that society has come to a place where the negative connotations these terms once had are not as prevalent as they once were. In our previous edition, we wrote the following:

> So, too, with the term homosexuality. In this text, the term affinity orientation is used instead. The traditional term emphasizes, for one group and not others, the highly personal yet generally irrelevant issue of the employee's sexuality. The use of the term sets up those within that group for consideration as different (usually interpreted to be "less than"), when they may well be qualified for the job and otherwise acceptable. With sexuality being highlighted in referring to them, it becomes difficult to think of them in any other light. The term also

continues to pander to the historically more sensational or titillating aspects of the applicant's personal life and uses it to color her or his entire life when all that should be of interest is ability to do the job. Using more appropriate terminology will hopefully keep the focus on that ability.

Being able to see society move so far in 26 years and pass laws of protection in this area that make it easier to deal with the LGBTQ community as full human beings is heartening.

The term *disabled* or *differently abled* is used rather than *handicapped* to conform to the more enlightened view taken by the Americans with Disabilities Act of 1990. It gets away from the old notion noted by some that those who were differently abled went "cap in hand" looking for handouts. Rather, it recognizes the importance of including in employment these 40 million Americans who can contribute to the workplace despite their physical or mental condition.

There is also a diligent effort to use gender-inclusive or neutral terminology—for example, police officers rather than policemen, firefighters rather than firemen, servers rather than waiters or waitresses, and flight attendants rather than stewards or stewardesses. We urge you to add to the list and use such language in your conversations. To use different terminology for males and females performing the same job reflects a gender difference when there is no need to do so. If, as the law requires, it is irrelevant because it is the job itself on which we wish to focus, then our language should reflect this.

It is not simply a matter of terminology. Words are powerful. They convey ideas to us about the matter spoken of. To the extent we change our language to be more neutral when referring to employees, it will be easier to change our ingrained notions of the "appropriateness" of traditional employment roles based on gender, sexuality, or other largely irrelevant criteria and make employment discrimination laws more effective. Imagine a young girl who is inspired to serve and protect her community. She considers professions and yet is discouraged because she reads and hears about firemen, policemen, and other male-sounding jobs. These positions do not sound like they are oriented toward women, so instead she focuses on the roles that sound like they welcome women. That is a shame.

This conscious choice of language also is not a reflection of temporal "political correctness" considerations. It goes far beyond what terming something *politically correct* tends to do. These changes in terminology are substantive and nontrivial ones that attempt to have language reflect reality rather than have our reality shaped and limited by the language we use. Being sensitive to the matter of language can help make us more sensitive to what stands behind the words. That is an important aid in avoiding liability and obeying the law.

The best way to determine what an employer must do to avoid liability for employment decisions is to look at cases to see what courts have used to determine previous liability. This is why we have provided many and varied cases for you to consider. Much care has been taken to make the cases not only relevant, informative, and illustrative but also interesting and easy to read. There is a good mix of new cases along with the old standards that still define an area. We have assiduously tried to avoid legalese and intricate legal consideration. Instead, we emphasize the legal managerial aspects of cases—that is, what does the case mean that management should or should not do to be best protected from violating the law?

We wanted the textbook to be informative and readable—a resource to encourage critical and creative thinking about workplace issues and to sensitize you to the need for effective workplace management of these issues. We think we have accomplished our goal. We hope the text is as interesting and informative for you to read and use as it was exciting and challenging for us to write.

Modifications to the 10th Edition

Throughout the text, we have, as necessary, updated statistics and replaced in-text examples, end-of-chapter questions, and cases with the most current ones available. However, where a case represents the seminal case on a matter, we have chosen to leave that case since it is vital for students to be well versed in the legal precedent. The same is true of chapter-end questions. If they were the best to illustrate a point, we left them in. In addition to the updated statistics and figures throughout, the major changes include the following:

Chapter 1: Discusses
- New information on the costs of misclassifying a worker.
- An overview of the ABC test to determine if someone is an employee (as introduced in *Dynamex Operations v. Lee*).
- The update to section on non-competes relevant to our age of the gig economy.
- A new section on interns, trainees, and volunteers.

Chapter 2: Includes new and updated information on retaliation.

Chapter 3: Contains updated information throughout, including
- Impact of the 2016 election on the work of the EEOC.
- The EEOC's new Strategic Enforcement Plan for 2017–2022.
- The EEOC extension of the Title VII gender category to include discrimination on the basis of sexual orientation, an update on its inclusion of gender as a basis for gender identity claims, and the EEOC's new emphasis on maintaining employee access to Title VII claims.

Chapter 4: Contains
- An analysis of the use artificial intelligence (AI) tools in the recruitment and selection process to reduce even the appearance of discriminatory practices.
- Introduction of the concept of homophily in recruitment (the practice of preferring people like ourselves).
- Implications of health concerns arising from a global pandemic on recruitment and selection processes.
- Discussion of the rise of workplace violence and implications for hiring (both permanent and gig workers).
- Updates to section on drug testing to include discussion of legal marijuana use.
- Updates to section on personality testing.
- The role of social media during selection.

Chapter 5: Modifications include
- Clarification of and more background on the connection between affirmative action background and present-day vestiges.

- Update of the Dodd–Frank Wall Street Reform and Consumer Protection Act of requirement of Offices of Minority and Women's inclusion in the agencies it covers and the businesses they regulate.
- The NFL's informal extension of the Rooney Rule to cover some vacancies for offensive and defensive coordinator positions.

Chapter 6: Includes discussion of the
- Impact of the 2016 presidential election and other recent events on workplace issues.
- Increase in Asian American discrimination.
- Increase in workplace harassment claims.

Chapter 7: Updated data includes
- Brand-new section: "Latinx Discrimination: Impact of Socio-Political Environmental Factors."
- Updated statistics about immigrants in the U.S. workforce.
- Updated EEOC guidance on national origin discrimination.
- The evolving law relating to English-only rules, presented in a comprehensive manner, including expanded discussion on the costs of those policies.
- Additional discussion and clarification on discrimination based on alienage or citizenship status.
- Increasing national origin discrimination claims since September 11, 2001, and updated statistics and discussion on Middle Eastern discrimination.

Chapter 8: Contains new information on
- Increasing gender discrimination claims interpretation.
- U.S. women's soccer team pay discrimination issue and lawsuit.
- Discussion of demonstrations regarding gender issues and concerns in the country.
- Updated gender statistics.
- Claims by women terminated because they were "too hot" and updated concerted individual regional Walmart gender discrimination cases.
- Increasing technology industry gender issues and lawsuits.
- Impact of #MeToo and #TimesUp on women in the workplace.

Chapter 9: Contains
- Impact of #MeToo on sexual harassment claims being filed.
- Claims involving famous harassers such as Harvey Weinstein.
- A discussion of the new Hollywood Commission chaired by Anita Hill.
- Discussion of increased EEOC budgeting and emphasis on sexual harassment claims.

Chapter 10: Contains updated discussions on sexual orientation and gender identity, including
- President Trump's revocation of 2017 executive order calling for federal protection for LGBT employees of federal contractors.

- Discussion of the three LGBTQ cases decided by the U.S. Supreme Court in *Bostock v. Clayton County, Georgia* on June 15, 2020.
- Recent polls on LGBTQ issues and updates.
- The latest HRC Corporate Equality Index figures for corporate adoption of workplace protections and benefits for LGBTQ employees.
- Updated discussion of the Equality Act bill before Congress.

Chapter 11: Contains

- New information on increasingly different manifestations of religious discrimination in the workplace.
- The increasing ways in which religious discrimination claims are being aggressively pursued by employees.

Chapter 12: Examines

- The impact of economic downturn on older workers and the ongoing, difficult question of economics as an RFOA.
- Changes in the application of the ADEA based on size of employer.
- In greater detail the EEOC's "Final Rule on Disparate Impact and Reasonable Factors Other than Age (RFOA)."
- Analysis of the newly enacted Protecting Older Workers Against Discrimination Act (POWADA).
- Added discussion clarifying distinctions between the ADEA and Title VII.
- New section on microtargeting.
- Analysis of disparate impact changes under the ADEA.
- Updates to the "same actor" defense.

Chapter 13: Examines/Updates

- New examples of innovation in the workplace, including the hiring initiatives targeting neurodiverse candidates.
- Refreshed discussion on federal tax incentives for hiring people with disabilities.
- Updated discussion on mental impairments that qualify for protection under the ADA, including updated statistics, updated information on intellectual disabilities, and additional and refreshed information on mental illness.
- New discussion on substance abuse and alcohol, including new section on medical marijuana.
- New section on pregnancy and postpartum, including discussion of the Pregnancy Discrimination Act, which amends the ADA and discussion of postpartum depression.
- New section on service animals in the workplace.
- New section on gender dysphoria and the current legal landscape under the ADA.

Chapter 14: Contains

- Extensive updates based on significant advances in technology, information gathering, social media, monitoring, privacy, and the law that have impacted our world in general and the workplace specifically.
- New case law, examples, and end-of-chapter questions that allow the reader to have a current understanding of the environment and implications for the employment context.

Chapter 15: Discusses various labor issues such as

- Aggressive moves to weaken labor unions.
- Updated statistical information on union participation and impact.
- Student movement to unionize college athletics, graduate students.
- State passage of right-to-work laws.
- Increasing number of labor unrest and strikes.

Chapter 16: Discusses wage and benefit issues such as

- The ongoing issue of employee misclassification violations to avoid paying minimum wages and overtime pay.
- The growing concern over unpaid internships.
- New state laws restricting employer use of applicant's prior pay to determine salary.
- Increased enforcement and clarification of lactation time for nursing mothers.
- Increasing FMLA leave challenges.
- Increasing state laws regarding minimum wages even though the federal law has not changed.

As we have done with other editions, in this tenth edition we have continued to make updates and improvements that we think will help students understand the material better. We have added learning objectives for each chapter, new cases where appropriate, updated background and context information, new boxed information, up-to-the-minute legal issues, more insights, and a modified structure. We have kept the things you tell us you love and added to them.

For instance, several editions ago, a reader suggested that we address the issue of the redundancy of examining certain issues in each chapter where they are raised. Based on this excellent suggestion, which we had considered ourselves over the years, we added a "Toolkit" chapter to our eighth edition and have kept it ever since. The Toolkit chapter (Chapter 2, "The Employment Law Toolkit: Resources for Understanding the Law and Recurring Legal Concepts") introduces you to concepts that you will see throughout the text but, rather than repeat them in each chapter, we have added Toolkit icons instead. These icons will be an indication to you that the issue discussed at that point is included in the Toolkit chapter, and you can go back to that chapter and review the issue again if you would like a refresher.

As always, we *truly* welcome your feedback. We are the only textbook we know of that actually gets fan letters. Keep them coming! ☺ We urge you to email us about any thoughts you have about the text, good or bad, as well as suggestions, unclear items you don't understand, errata, or anything else you think would be helpful. Our contact information is:

Dawn D. Bennett-Alexander
University of Georgia
Terry College of Business
A413 Moore-Rooker Hall
610 South Lumpkin Street
Athens, GA 30602-6255
Email: dawndba@uga.edu

Laura P. Hartman
School of Choice / l'Ecole de Choix
(Haiti)
Email: LHartman@depaul.edu

And again as always, we hope you have as much fun reading the book as we did writing it. It really is a pleasure. Enjoy!

Acknowledgments

The authors would like to honor and thank the following individuals, without whose assistance and support this text would never have been written: McGraw Hill Higher Education editorial support for having the insight and courage to sign the first employment law text of its kind before many others were able to see the vast but undeniable merit of doing so; McGraw Hill Product Developer Allie Kukla; Content Project Manager Amy Gehl; Managing Director Tim Vertovec; Marketing Manager Claire McLemore; and Executive Portfolio Manager Kathleen Klehr. Finally, for their contributions to our tenth edition revisions, we would like to thank the scholars who have class tested and reviewed this manuscript, including the following:

Glenda Barrett
University of Maryland-University College

Walter Bogumil
University of Central Florida

Olivia Brown
West Georgia Technical College

Debra Burke
Western Carolina University

Gerald Calvasina
Salisbury University

William Carnes
University of South Florida-St. Petersburg

Carol M. Carnevale
SUNY Empire State College

Mitchell Crocker
Austin State University-Texas

Diya Das
Bryant College

Richard Dibble
New York Institute of Technology

Anthony DiPrimio
Holy Family University

Dennis R. Favaro
William Rainey Harper College

Larry Frazier
City University of Seattle

Dean Gualco
Warren National University

Tanya Hubanks
Chippewa Valley Technical College

Shumon Johnson
Columbia Southern University

Rhonda Jones
University of Maryland

Hamid Kazeroony
Inver Hills Community College

Doug Kennedy
University of Wisconsin-Stout

Dale F. Krieg
Oakland City University

Clif Koen
University of New Orleans

Jonathan Kulaga
Spring Arbor University

Cheryl Macon
Butler County Community College

Stan Malos
San Jose State University

Michael McKinney
East Tennessee State University

Liliana Meneses
University of Maryland University College

Jim Morgan
California State University, Chico

Richard O. Parry
California State University-Fullerton

John Poirier
Bryant University

Douglas Reed
Milwaukee School of Engineering

Mike Rhymes
Louisiana Tech

Stacey Scroggins
Troy University

Kathryn Seeberger
Kansas State University

Stephanie Sipe
Georgia Southern University

Laura Smagala
Carlow University

Joanie Sompayrac
University of Tennessee

Vicki Spivey
Southeastern Technical College

Lamont Stallworth
Loyola University-Chicago

Dave Stokes
MATC-Madison

Maris Stella Swift
Grand Valley State University

Cheryl Thomas
Fayetteville Tech

Jan Tucker
Warren National University

Thomas Tudor
University of Arkansas-Little Rock

Clark Wheeler
Santa Fe Community College

Glynda White
College of Southern Nevada-West Charles

Elizabeth Wilson
Georgia Southwestern State University

Bennett-Alexander: I would like to thank (1) my co-author, Laura Pincus Hartman, for her intellect, energy, support, and hard work. We don't know exactly how it's been working for nearly 30 years, but it absolutely does, and we love, love, love it. Laura, you are such a wonderful soul in the world, and it is an absolute privilege to share this gift and journey with you; (2) our publishers, editors, and other support staff who love this project as much as we do; (3) my daughters Jenniffer Dawn Bennett-Alexander Jones, Anne Alexis Bennett-Alexander, and Tess Alexandra Bennett Harrison for being my special gifts from above and for knowing that my very favorite thing in the whole world is being their Mama—even though they drive me crazy ☺; (4) my grandchildren, Makayla Anne Jones and Edward Christian Alexander Jones, who are such an absolute delight. Thank you for loving Nana so; (5) my siblings, Brenda Bennett Watkins, Dr. Gale C. Bennett Pinson, Rev. Dr. William H. Bennett II, and Barbara Jean Bennett Bethea (1939-2007), for their unwavering confidence, love, support, and laughs; (6) my BFF, linda f. harrison, who can always be counted on for whatever, including smoothing ruffled feathers and a great belly laugh. I don't know how it works, but it's been doing it for 41 (!!) years; (7) my incomparable university president, Jere W. Morehead. Where do I even start? I appreciate you more than you know in ways of which you are well aware. You make me laugh so, even as your quiet, steady, unrelenting, and total dedication to making UGA all it can be spurs me to do even more than I thought possible, and for that I thank you; (8) the thousands of managers, supervisors, employers, and employees who have shared their experiences and insights over the years; (9) my colleagues from across the country who have been so incredibly supportive of this text over the years; and, last but *certainly* not least, (10) my very favorites, my students, who are a never-ending source of utter wonder, insight, information, and fun for me. Do we have a good time *or what?*

This text is *immeasurably* richer for having the contributions of *each* of you.

DDB-A

Hartman: I have gone through a few more challenges posed by Mother Nature in the past several years than I would have anticipated, which have impacted my connectivity and working environment. However, Dawn has been patient and supportive throughout the entire time. It is her patience, along with the massive support of others, that has allowed me to continue to work at the pace I do. Dawn is a rock, and I am grateful to her.

Our lives are enriched because of the community of people who contribute to our lives and our work each day. This text is far enhanced because of the expertise of Summer Brown and Katrina Myers, who have worked on prior editions and I desperately hope continue to be by my side forever. All errors—and, *yes, we know* they are there, dear readers, so send them in—are completely our own.

LPH

Text Organization

Part 1 gives the foundations for employment law, covering introductory topics and cases to set the stage for later coverage. This initial section now includes more material to give students a more thorough grounding.

Chapter 1 provides an introduction to the employment environment and explains the freedom to contract and the current regulatory environment for employment. It also includes an expansive discussion of employment-at-will.

Chapter 2 is the Toolkit chapter that provides information on several topics that run throughout the text. Chapters thereafter that mention these issues will use a toolkit icon to notify the reader to go back to the Toolkit chapter if a refresher is needed.

Chapter 3 covers Title VII of the Civil Rights Act in order to illustrate the foundational nature this groundbreaking legislation has for employment law.

Chapter 4 introduces the reader to the regulation of the employment process, such as recruitment, selection, and hiring. In examining the variety of methods of information gathering through testing and other media, it also explores the issue of employers' access to extraordinary amounts of information via evolving technology. The chapter has been extensively updated with illustrative and supporting empirical data integrated throughout the chapter, including information relating to corporate use of employee referral programs, workplace violence, employer use of online sources for background investigation, corporate use of personality and integrity tests in the hiring process, and legislation regulating genetic testing in employment.

Part 2 covers various types of discrimination in employment, with each chapter revised to reflect recent changes.

Chapter 5 includes a discussion on recent revisions to affirmative action regulations and misuse of affirmative action, including the famous U.S. Supreme Court decision on the firefighters in New Haven, Connecticut.

Chapter 6 presents a historical overview of racism in the United States, giving students a deeper understanding of how prevalent racial discrimination still is so managers can better recognize potential liability as it arises. In addition, contemporary race issues and racial harassment are addressed.

Chapter 7 directly follows Chapter 6 in order to link and distinguish the concepts of race and national origin in U.S. laws and culture.

Chapter 8 features coverage of how gender impacts the workplace, including gender discrimination, pregnancy discrimination, gender stereotyping, workplace grooming codes, fetal protection policies, lactation break requirements, and comparable worth.

Employment Law for Business, Tenth Edition, has been revised and updated to maintain its currency amid a rapidly changing landscape in the area of employment law. Some of its content has also been streamlined to provide a more realistic opportunity for instructors to cover key concepts in one semester. Learning objectives at the start of each chapter alert instructor and students to key concepts within. Cases are found at the end of the chapter to facilitate a smoother read, with case icons inserted into the text where references are appropriate.

Chapter 9 explores the law relating to sexual harassment, clearly explaining the difference between quid pro quo and hostile environment sexual harassment as well as how to avoid employer liability in this important area.

Chapter 10 discusses developments in sexual orientation discrimination and gender identity issues and offers management tips on how to handle this quickly evolving topic.

Chapter 11 gives students up-to-date considerations on the many aspects of religious discrimination, including explanations of the legal definition of religion, points on the employer's duty to reasonably accommodate employees, and information on the correct usage of religion as a BFOQ. Issues of increasing frequency such as Muslim employee workplace conflicts are discussed and methods provided for how to handle these matters.

Chapter 12 provides a comprehensive review of age discrimination laws in the workplace and has been updated with current statistical information with regard to age discrimination and also includes comparisons of perceptions of age in the United States and other countries. Additional updates include state age discrimination laws and the legal standard prohibiting an employer from engaging in retaliatory behavior in response to an age discrimination filing.

Chapter 13 offers a complete analysis of the legal environment with regard to workers with disabilities with an expanded discussion of the legal history of protection against discrimination on the basis of disability. The chapter is comprehensive in its coverage of both the Genetic Information Non-Discrimination Act and the Americans with Disabilities Act Amendments Act (ADAAA) and offers examples to managers of ways to create more inclusive working environments.

Part 3 lays out additional regulatory processes and dilemmas in employment. Several chapters on various regulatory issues have been merged to form the final chapter.

Chapter 14 examines the roles of both the employer and the employee in connection with privacy in the workplace and has been thoroughly updated to keep step with the practically daily changes in technology and how they affect employee privacy. These developments include reference to blogging, social media, RFIDs, GPS, and expanded legal frameworks, both domestic and global.

Chapter 15 addresses collective bargaining and unions in a chapter on labor law.

Chapter 16 offers helpful information on the Fair Labor Standards Act (FLSA); the Family Medical Leave Act (FMLA), including the amendments for military families preparing for active duty or injured in active duty; the Occupational Safety and Health Act (OSHA); and the Employee Retirement Income Security Act (ERISA).

Key Features for the 10th Edition

Learning Objectives

Each chapter has active learning objectives, posted before addressing the subject matter, that give a clear picture of specifically what readers should know when they finish studying the chapter. In addition, the learning objectives are noted at the place in the chapter in which the information appears.

Learning Objectives

HAVE MET THE TEST!

Source: National Archives and Records Administration (NWDNS-44-PA-911)

After completing this chapter, you should be able to:

LO1 Recite Title VII and other laws relating to gender discrimination.

LO2 Understand the background of gender discrimination and how we know it still exists.

LO3 List the different ways in which gender discrimination is manifested in the workplace.

LO4 Analyze a situation and determine if there are gender issues that may result in employer liability.

LO5 Define fetal protection policies, gender-plus discrimination, workplace lactation issues, and gender-based logistical concerns.

LO6 Differentiate between legal and illegal grooming policies.

LO7 List common gender realities at odds with common bases for illegal work-

Opening Scenarios

Based on real cases and situations, chapter-opening scenarios introduce topics and material that illustrate the need for chapter concepts. Scenarios are then revisited throughout the chapter text as material pertinent to the opening scenario is discussed. When you encounter the scenario icon in the chapter body, return to the corresponding opening scenario to see if you can now articulate the correct way to solve the problem.

Opening Scenarios

SCENARIO 1

Scenario 1 A discount department store has a policy requiring that all male clerks be attired in coats and ties and all female clerks wear over their clothing a short loose top provided by the store, with the store's logo on the front. A female clerk complains to her supervisor that making her wear the garment is illegal gender discrimination. Is it? Why or why not?

SCENARIO 2

Scenario 2 A male applies for a position as a server for a restaurant in his hometown. The restaurant is part of a well-known regional chain named for an animal whose name is a colloquial term for a popular part of the female anatomy. Despite sev-

establishments, the male is turned down for the position, which remains vacant. The applicant is instead offered a position as a kitchen helper. The applicant notices that all servers are female and most are blonde. All servers are required to wear very tight and very short shorts, with T-shirts with the restaurant logo on the front, tied in a knot below their usually ample breasts. All kitchen help and cooks are male. The applicant feels he has been unlawfully discriminated against because he is a male. Do you agree? Why or why not?

SCENARIO 3

Scenario 3 An applicant for a position of secretary informs the employer that she is pregnant. The employer accepts her application but never seriously considers her for the position because she is preg-

Toolkit Icons

Key concepts used in several different chapters have been combined into one chapter to prevent redundancy. That chapter is Chapter 2, "The Employment Law Toolkit: Resources for Understanding the Law and Recurring Legal Concepts." Where a Toolkit chapter concept arises in a subsequent chapter a notation is made that it can be found in the Toolkit chapter, with an icon placed in the margin.

ahead will use information that is based on the same legal concepts, rath[...] repeat the information in each chapter's discussion, we explain the concept [...] this "toolkit" chapter you can use to refer back to later if necessary.

There is a corresponding toolkit icon used throughout the text. When you [...] toolkit icon, know that the text is discussing information that has been cov[...] this toolkit chapter. If you need to, refer to this chapter to refresh your recolle[...]

Part one explains how to read the cases and a couple of important co[...] to keep in mind for all legal cases. Part two provides information on the s[...] tive concept of employment-at-will, part three discusses the theoretical ba[...] all substantive employment discrimination actions, and part four describe[...] resources for searching for further legal information.

See Chapter 2 to revisit key concepts.

Case 2 **Dothard v. Rawlinson**
433 U.S. 321 (1977)

After her application for employment as an Alabama prison guard was rejected because she failed to meet the 120-pound weight and 5-foot-2-inch height requirement of an Alabama statute, the applicant sued, challenging the statutory height and weight requirements as violative of Title VII of the Civil Rights Act of 1964. The Supreme Court found gender discrimination.

Stewart, J.

***

At the time she applied for a position as a correctional counselor trainee, Rawlinson was a 22-year-old college graduate whose major course of study had been correctional psychology. She was refused employment because she failed to meet the minimum 120-pound weight requirement established by an Alabama statute. The stat-ute stated that the applicant shall not be less than five feet [...]

between genders, the district court found that when the height and weight restrictions are combined, Alabama's statutory standards would exclude 41.13% of the female population while excluding less than 1% of the male population.

In enacting Title VII, Congress required "the removal of artificial, arbitrary, and unnecessary barriers to [...]

Cases

Excerpted cases are placed at the end of the chapter rather than throughout so that reading can be accomplished without interruption. There are reference icons in the chapter when a case is discussed. There is a minimum of legalese and only facts relevant to the employment law issues are included. Each digested case has a short introductory paragraph to explain the facts and issues in the case and is followed by three critical thinking questions created to build and strengthen managerial liability-avoidance skills.

Management Tips

These boxes, included near the conclusion of each chapter, encapsulate how key concepts relate to managerial concerns. The authors offer concise tips on how to put chapter material into practice in the real world.

Management Tips *Additional Consideratio[...]*

- Always evaluate the status of your workers; do not assume independent-contractor status for any worker.
- Employment status is relevant to employer payroll and other fin[...] therefore, misclassification may be costly to the employer.
- While an employer is not liable to independent contractors for c[...] based on Title VII, the independent contractor may have other cau[...] Therefore, hiring an independent contractor is not a safe harbor f[...]
- Monitor staffing firms with which you contract for temporary or oth[...] workers to ensure that the workers are being properly paid and [...]

Key Terms

Key terms are displayed in larger boldface. The terms are also listed in the Glossary for quick reference.

independent contractor
Generally, a person who contracts with a principal to perform a task according to her or his own methods and who is not under the principal's control regarding the physical details of the work.

You just received a job offer. How do you know if you are being hire— or as an **independent contractor**? While some workers may have their classification, the actual answer may vary depending on the sta— other analysis to be applied. The courts, employers, and the goverr— to agree on one definition of "employee" and "employer," so it vari— the situation and the law being used. In addition, some statutes do— guidance. For instance, the Employee Retirement Income Secur— discussed in detail in Chapter 12) defines *employee* as "any individ— an employer."³ But, as the Supreme Court chastised the legislato— this nominal definition is "completely circular and explains nothir— tion, however, is significant for tax law compliance, and for discrimination claims. Fo— VII applies to employers and prohibits them from discriminating

Exhibits

Numerous exhibits are included throughout the text to reinforce concepts visually and to provide students with essential background information.

Exhibit 1.6 *Statutory Definitions of Employer*

The Civil Rights Act of 1866
- *Purpose:* Regulates the actions of all individuals or entities when entering into a contract to employ someone else.
- *Definition of Employer:* No requirement for a minimum number of employees in order to qualify as an employer under the CRA of 1866.
- *Other:* The Civil Rights Act of 1991 added a section to the CRA of 1866 to cover actions by the employer after the contract has been formed, including discrimination during employment or

- *Exemptions:* Government-owned corp— Indian tribes, and bona fide private mer— clubs.

Title VI of the Civil Rights Act of 1964
- *Purpose:* Applies the race, color, and origin proscriptions of Title VII to any or activity that receives federal financ— tance. Unless it falls within one of exemptions, a government contractor prohibited from discriminating on the race, color, religion, gender, or national

Exhibit 1.6 *continued*

- *Exemptions:* American employers who control foreign firms where compliance with the ADEA in connection with an American employee would cause the foreign firm to violate the laws of the country in which it is located. The ADEA, unlike Title VII, does *not* exempt Indian tribes or private membership clubs.

Title I of the Americans with Disabilities Act of 1990
- *Purpose:* Prohibits discrimination in employment against otherwise qualified individuals with disabilities who cannot perform the ar—

- *Definition of Employer:* Offers coverage— ers not necessarily based on a particul— tion of "employer" but on two distinct coverage: "enterprise coverage" and "i— coverage." *Enterprise coverage* refers to tections offered to employees who work f— businesses or organizations (i.e., "ente— that have at least two employees and d— $500,000 a year in business or that are— in certain specified industries such as— businesses providing medical or nursing—

Chapter Summaries

Each chapter closes with a summary section, giving students and instructors a tool for checking comprehension. Use this bulleted list as an aide in retaining key chapter points.

Chapter Summary
- No matter the size of your organization, as long as you have hired— to work for you, you are considered an employer and potentially subje— federal and other regulations as well as to wrongful termination lia—
- Why is the definition of "employee" important? The distinc— employees and independent contractors is crucial from a financi— Because many regulations require different responsibilities from employees and independent contractors, it is imperative that a— confident of the classification of its employees.
- How does an employer make the distinction between employees— dent contractors? The classification of employees may vary dep— statute that is to be applied or on the court in which a given cas— to be heard. However, the common thread is generally the right of t—

Guide to Reading Cases

Thank you very much to the several students who have contacted us and asked that we improve your understanding by including a guide to reading and understanding the cases. We consider the cases an important and integral part of the chapters. By viewing the court decisions included in the text, you get to see for yourself what the court considers important about a given issue. This in turn gives you as a decision maker insight into what you need to keep in mind when making decisions on similar issues in the workplace. The more you know about how a court thinks about issues that may end up in litigation, the better you can avoid it.

We provide the following in order to help you better understand the cases so that you can use them to their fullest. In order to tell you about how to view the cases, we have to give you a little background on the legal system. Hopefully, it will only be a refresher of your previous law or ethics courses.

Guide to Reading Cases

This guide gives succinct direction on how to get the most out of text cases. Terminology definitions, case citation explanations, and a walkthrough of the trial process are all included to help facilitate student comprehension.

End-of-Chapter Material

Included at the end of each chapter is a complete set of footnotes for further exploring the issues cited, as well as questions incorporating chapter concepts. Use these as tools to assess your understanding of chapter material.

Chapter-End Questions

1. In the process of its recruitment of Peters, Security Pacific inf— company was doing "just fine" and Peters would have "a long tenu— should he accept the position offered. In doing so, Security Pacif— cial losses and the substantial, known risk that the project on w— to work might soon be abandoned and Peters laid off. Peters acce— moved from New Orleans to Denver to begin his new job. Two m— laid off as a result of Security Pacific's poor financial conditio— cause of action?

2. Uber released a groundbreaking sexual assault report in 2019 revea— documented nearly 6,000 reports of sexual assault—by both driv— 2017 and 2018 as well as 19 deaths from Uber-related physical as— (not necessarily between driver and rider). How might an injur— information to support a negligent hiring claim against Uber? Wl—

INSTRUCTOR RESOURCES

INSTRUCTOR'S MANUAL

A package of supplementary materials is included in the instructor's manual.

TEST BANK AND QUIZZES

Instructors can test students using a vast bank of test and quiz questions divided by chapter.

POWERPOINTS

This edition's revised PowerPoints contain an easy-to-follow lecture outline summarizing key points for every chapter.

BUSINESS LAW NEWSLETTER

McGraw Hill Education's monthly Business Law newsletter, *Proceedings,* is designed specifically with the Business Law educator in mind. *Proceedings* incorporates "hot topics" in business law, video suggestions, an ethical dilemma, teaching tips, and a "chapter key" cross-referencing newsletter topics with the various McGraw Hill Education business law textbooks. *Proceedings* is delivered via e-mail to business law instructors each month.

McGraw Hill Connect—Online Assignments and Assessment

BUSINESS LAW APPLICATION-BASED ACTIVITIES (ABAs)

MHE Application-Based Activities are highly interactive, automatically graded online exercises that provide students a safe space to practice using problem-solving skills to apply their knowledge to realistic scenarios. Each scenario addresses key concepts and skills that students must use to work through and solve course specific problems, resulting in improved critical thinking and relevant workplace skills.

SMARTBOOK® 2.0

Available within Connect, SmartBook 2.0 is an adaptive learning solution that provides personalized learning to individual student needs, continually adapting to pinpoint knowledge gaps and focus learning on concepts requiring additional study. SmartBook 2.0 fosters more productive learning, taking the guesswork out of what to study, and helps students better prepare for class. With the ReadAnywhere mobile app, students can now read and complete SmartBook 2.0 assignments both online and off-line. For instructors, SmartBook 2.0 provides more granular control over assignments with content selection now available at the concept level. SmartBook 2.0 also includes advanced reporting features that enable instructors to track student progress with actionable insights that guide teaching strategies and advanced instruction, for a more dynamic class experience.

TEST BUILDER

Available within Connect, Test Builder is a cloud-based tool that enables instructors to format tests that can be printed or administered within a LMS. Test Builder offers a modern, streamlined interface for easy content configuration that matches course needs, without requiring a download. It provides a secure interface for better protection of content and allows for just-in-time updates to flow directly into assessments.

REMOTE PROCTORING & BROWSER-LOCKING CAPABILITIES

New remote proctoring and browser-locking capabilities, hosted by Proctorio within Connect, provide control of the assessment environment by enabling security options and verifying the identity of the student. Seamlessly integrated within Connect, these services allow instructors to control students' assessment experience by restricting browser activity, recording students' activity, and verifying students are doing their own work. Instant and detailed reporting gives instructors an at-a-glance view of potential academic integrity concerns, thereby avoiding personal bias and supporting evidence-based claims.

WRITING ASSIGNMENT

Available within McGraw Hill Connect® and McGraw Hill Connect® Master, the Writing Assignment tool delivers a learning experience to help students improve their written communication skills and conceptual understanding. As an instructor you can assign, monitor, grade, and provide feedback on writing more efficiently and effectively.

Instructors: Student Success Starts with You

Tools to enhance your unique voice

Want to build your own course? No problem. Prefer to use our turnkey, prebuilt course? Easy. Want to make changes throughout the semester? Sure. And you'll save time with Connect's auto-grading too.

65%
Less Time Grading

Laptop: McGraw Hill; Woman/dog: George Doyle/Getty Images

Study made personal

Incorporate adaptive study resources like SmartBook® 2.0 into your course and help your students be better prepared in less time. Learn more about the powerful personalized learning experience available in SmartBook 2.0 at **www.mheducation.com/highered/connect/smartbook**

Affordable solutions, added value

Make technology work for you with LMS integration for single sign-on access, mobile access to the digital textbook, and reports to quickly show you how each of your students is doing. And with our Inclusive Access program you can provide all these tools at a discount to your students. Ask your McGraw Hill representative for more information.

Padlock: Jobalou/Getty Images

Solutions for your challenges

A product isn't a solution. Real solutions are affordable, reliable, and come with training and ongoing support when you need it and how you want it. Visit **www.supportateverystep.com** for videos and resources both you and your students can use throughout the semester.

Checkmark: Jobalou/Getty Images

Students: Get Learning that Fits You

Effective tools for efficient studying

Connect is designed to make you more productive with simple, flexible, intuitive tools that maximize your study time and meet your individual learning needs. Get learning that works for you with Connect.

Study anytime, anywhere

Download the free ReadAnywhere app and access your online eBook or SmartBook 2.0 assignments when it's convenient, even if you're offline. And since the app automatically syncs with your eBook and SmartBook 2.0 assignments in Connect, all of your work is available every time you open it. Find out more at **www.mheducation.com/readanywhere**

> *"I really liked this app—it made it easy to study when you don't have your text-book in front of you."*
>
> - Jordan Cunningham, Eastern Washington University

Everything you need in one place

Your Connect course has everything you need—whether reading on your digital eBook or completing assignments for class, Connect makes it easy to get your work done.

Calendar: owattaphotos/Getty Images

Learning for everyone

McGraw Hill works directly with Accessibility Services Departments and faculty to meet the learning needs of all students. Please contact your Accessibility Services Office and ask them to email accessibility@mheducation.com, or visit **www.mheducation.com/about/accessibility** for more information.

Top: Jenner Images/Getty Images. Left: Hero Images/Getty Images. Right: Hero Images/Getty Images

Brief Contents

Contents

Chapter 13

PART THREE
REGULATION OF THE EMPLOYMENT ENVIRONMENT   767

Chapter 14

Guide to Reading Cases

Thank you very much to the several students who have contacted us and asked that we improve your understanding by including a guide to reading and understanding the cases. We consider the cases an important and integral part of the chapters. By viewing the court decisions included in the text, you get to see for yourself what the court considers important when deciding a given issue. This in turn gives you as a decision maker insight into what you need to keep in mind when making decisions on similar issues in the workplace. The more you know about how a court thinks about issues that may end up in litigation, the better you can avoid it.

We provide the following in order to help you better understand the cases so that you can use them to their fullest. In order to tell you about how to view the cases, we have to give you a little background on the legal system. Hopefully, it will only be a refresher of your previous law or civics courses.

Stare Decisis and Precedent

The American legal system is based on *stare decisis,* a system of using legal precedent. Once a judge renders a decision in a case, the decision is generally written and placed in a book called a *law reporter* and must be followed in that jurisdiction when other similar cases arise. The case thus becomes precedent for future cases.

Most of the decisions in the chapters are from federal courts since most of the topics we discuss are based on federal law. Federal courts consist of trial courts (called the "U.S. District Court" for a particular district), courts of appeal (called the "U.S. Circuit Court" for a particular circuit), and the U.S. Supreme Court. U.S. Supreme Court decisions apply to all jurisdictions, and once there is a U.S. Supreme Court decision, all courts must follow the precedent. Circuit court decisions are mandatory precedent only for the circuit in which the decision is issued. All courts in that circuit must follow the U.S. Circuit Court precedents. District court decisions (precedent) are applicable only to the district in which they were made. When courts that are not in the jurisdiction are faced with a novel issue they have not decided before, they can look to other jurisdictions to see how they handled the issue. If such a court likes the other jurisdiction's decision, it can use the approach taken by that jurisdiction's court. However, it is not bound to follow the other court's decision if that court is not in its jurisdiction.

Understanding the Case Information

With this in mind, let's take a look at a typical case included in this book. Each of the cases is an actual decision written by a judge. The first thing you will see is the *case name.* This is derived from the parties involved—the one suing (called *plaintiff* at the district court level) and the one being sued (called *defendant* at the district court level). At the court of appeals or Supreme Court level, the first name generally reflects who appealed the case to that court. It may or may not be the party who initially brought the case at the district court level. At the court of appeals level, the person who appealed the case to the court of appeals is known as the *appellant* and the other party is known as the *appellee.* At the Supreme Court level they are known as the *petitioner* and the *respondent.*

Under the case name, the next line will have several numbers and a few letters. This is called a *case citation.* A case citation is the means by which the full case can be located in a law reporter if you want to find the case for yourself in a law library or a legal database such as LEXIS/NEXIS or Westlaw. Reporters are books in which judges' case decisions are kept for later retrieval by lawyers, law students, judges, and others. Law reporters can be found in any law library, and many cases can be found on the Internet for free on websites such as Public Library of Law (plol.org) or FindLaw.com.

Take a minute and turn to one of the cases in the text. Any case will do. A typical citation would be "72 U.S. 544 (2002)." This means that you can find the decision in volume 72 of the *U.S. Supreme Court Reporter* at page 544 and that it is a 2002 decision. The U.S. reporters contain U.S. Supreme Court decisions. Reporters have different names based on the court decisions contained in them; thus, their citations are different.

The citation "43 F.3d 762 (9th Cir. 2002)" means that you can find the case decision in volume 43 of the *Federal Reporter* third series, at page 762 and that the decision came out of the U.S. Circuit Court of Appeals for the Ninth Circuit in the year 2002. The federal reporters contain the cases of the U.S. Circuit Courts of Appeal from across the country.

Similarly, the citation "750 F. Supp. 234 (S.D. N.Y. 2002)" means that you can find the case decision in volume 750 of the *Federal Supplement Reporters,* which contain U.S. district court cases, at page 234. The case was decided in the year 2002 by the U.S. District Court in the Southern District of New York.

In looking at the chapter cases, after the citation we include a short blurb on the case to let you know before you read it what the case is about, what the main issues are, and what the court decided. This is designed to give you a "heads up," rather than just dumping you into the case cold, with no background on what you are about to read.

The next line you see will have a last name and then a comma followed by "J." This is the name of the judge who wrote the decision you are reading. The "J" stands for "judge" or "justice." Judges oversee lower courts, while the term for them used in higher courts is "justices." "C. J." stands for "chief justice."

The next thing you see in looking at the chapter case is the body of the decision. Judges write for lawyers and judges, not for the public at large. As such, they use a lot of legal terms (which we call "legalese") that can make the decisions difficult for a nonlawyer to read. There are also many procedural issues included in cases, which have little or nothing to do with the issues we are providing the case to illustrate. There also may be many other issues in the case that are not relevant for our purposes. Therefore, rather than give you the entire decision of the court, we instead usually give you a shortened, excerpted version of the case containing only the information relevant for the issue being discussed. If you want to see the entire case for yourself, you can find it by using the citation provided just below the name of the case, as explained above. By not bogging you down in legalese, procedural matters, and other issues irrelevant to our point, we make the cases more accessible and understandable and much less confusing, while still giving you all you need to illustrate our point.

The last thing you will see in the chapter cases is the final decision of the court itself. If the case is a trial court decision by the district court, it will provide relief either for the plaintiff bringing the case or for the defendant against whom the case is brought.

If a defendant makes a *motion to dismiss,* the court will decide that issue and say either that the motion to dismiss is *granted* or that it is *denied.* A defendant will make a motion to dismiss when he or she thinks there is not enough evidence to constitute a violation of law. If the motion to dismiss is granted, the decision favors the defendant in that the court throws the case out. If the motion to dismiss is denied, it means the plaintiff's case can proceed to trial.

The parties also may ask the court to grant a *motion for summary judgment.* This essentially requests that the court take a look at the documentary information submitted by the parties and make a judgment based on that, as there is allegedly no issue that needs to be determined by a jury. Again, the court will either grant the motion for summary judgment or deny it. If the court grants a motion for summary judgment, it also will determine the issues and grant a judgment in favor of one of the parties. If the court dismisses a motion for summary judgment, the case proceeds to trial.

If the case is in the appellate court, it means that one of the parties did not like the trial court's decision. This party appeals the case to the appellate court, seeking to overturn the decision based on what it alleges are errors of law committed by the court below. Cases cannot be appealed simply because one of the parties did not like the facts found by the lower court. After the appellate court reviews the lower court's decision, the court of appeals will either *affirm* the lower court's decision, which means the decision is allowed to stand, or it will *reverse* the lower court's decision, which means the lower court's decision is overturned. If there is work still to be done on the case, the appellate court also will order *remand.* Remand is an order by the court of appeals to the lower court telling it to take the case back and do what needs to be done based on the court's decision.

It is also possible that the appellate court will issue a *per curiam* decision. This is merely a brief, unsigned decision by the court, rather than a long one.

Following the court's decision is a set of questions that are intended to translate what you have read in the case into issues that you would likely have to think about as a business owner, manager, or supervisor. The questions generally are included to make you think about what you read in the case and how it would impact your decisions as a manager. They are provided as a way to make you think critically and learn how to ask yourself the important questions that you will need to deal with each time you make an employment decision.

The opening scenarios, chapter cases, and case-end questions are important tools for you to use to learn to think like a manager or supervisor. Reading the courts' language and thinking about the issues in the opening scenarios and case-end questions will greatly assist you in making solid, defensible workplace decisions as a manager or supervisor.

The Regulation of the Employment Relationship

Chapter 1

The Regulation of Employment

Triangle Images/Getty Images

Learning Objectives

After completing this chapter, you should be able to:

LO1 Describe the balance between the freedom to contract and the current regulatory environment for employment.

LO2 Identify who is subject to which employment laws and understand the implication of each of these laws for both the employer and employee.

LO3 Delineate the risks to the employer caused by employee misclassification.

LO4 Explain the difference between an employee and an independent contractor and the tests that help us in that determination.

LO5 Articulate the various ways in which the concept "employer" is defined by the various employment-related regulations.

LO6 Describe the permissible parameters of non-compete agreements.

Opening Scenarios

SCENARIO 1

1) Scenario Dalia worked on a contract basis as an auto mechanic for the clients of an auto repair shop. Whenever there was too much work for the employees of the shop, Dalia would receive a call and be assigned by the shop to do specific repairs on a particular vehicle.

Dalia's specialty was rebuilding engines, and the firm would often contact her to handle complex breakdowns for which they did not have sufficient time, since she worked much faster than the other four mechanics it had on staff. When the job was completed, she was paid a commission for her work based on the amount charged to that client by the auto shop. This commission was established in advance in the contract Dalia was offered when she accepted the position.

During the time she was working, Dalia was paid weekly, was free to use the shop's garage, and also could use whatever equipment and supplies were necessary to complete the job. In order to ensure a consistent quality among all of its workers as well as to be sure that it complied with all regulations that might govern the job, the firm's head mechanic would check the car before the client was called to pick up the vehicle. This process ensured that clients saw all of the shop's workers and contractors as equivalent quality.

Dalia is laid off in the middle of a job, and she files for unemployment compensation. The shop defends the claim, arguing that she was not an employee. Was Dalia an employee or an independent contractor?

SCENARIO 2

2) Scenario Soraya worked as an administrative assistant for Illusionary Industry Inc. (III), and Raphael was her supervisor. Whenever Raphael and Soraya were alone in the office, Raphael engaged in physical contact toward Soraya that she made clear that she did not want. When he tried to kiss her or touch her, she would tell him to stop, move away from him, and even push him away at times. He continued to make sexual advances and lewd suggestive comments, all of which rose to the level of sexual harassment. Raphael even followed Soraya home one day and watched her house for over an hour from across the street. When she finally opened the door and confronted him, Raphael claimed that he had been merely on his way to a nearby market despite the fact that he lived on the other side of town near other markets.

After Soraya rejected Raphael's advances, he retaliated by writing her a poor performance review and then denied her a promotion. Soraya complained to III's Human Resources department, initially asking the department to keep her complaint confidential. However, she later informed the department that she could no longer work with Raphael. III investigated her complaint and subsequently suspended Raphael for one month with pay. Soraya appreciates III's action but remains frustrated that Raphael is simply suspended and finds that she really has no remedy against Raphael through III. She files a complaint against him with the Equal Employment Opportunity Commission. Will the EEOC case be successful? Why or why not?

SCENARIO 3

3) Scenario For two years, Mya worked for a tire supply company as an outside sales representative. Of the firm's 4,000 clients across several states in the southern United States, Mya was responsible for 100 clients, spread throughout western Texas. She visited these customers on a regular basis and maintained very close relationships with them. She was the only connection that most of these customers had with the firm, and these clients might not even have known how else to reach the firm except through Mya.

When Mya joined the firm, she signed a non-compete agreement that stipulated that, if she were to stop her relationship with the company, *she would not engage in any business of any kind with any customer of the firm for a period of two years.*

Because of her success in building client relationships, Mya is courted by a competing firm that does business all over the United States. She accepts an offer and begins to contact both her original customers and other customers of her previous employer to encourage them to change tire companies. Mya's previous employer files a cause of action for breach of the non-compete. What are her strongest arguments in her defense?

Introduction to the Regulatory Environment

How is the employer regulated? To what extent can Congress or the courts tell an employer how to run its business, whom it should hire or fire, or how it should treat its employees?

If an employer wants to hire someone to work every other hour every other week, it should be allowed to do that, as long as it can locate an employee who wants that type of job. Or if an employer requires that all employees wear a purple chicken costume throughout the workday, there is no reason why that requirement could not be enforced, as long as the employer can find employees to accept that agreement. While an employer can require that an employee wear a particular uniform, can the employer require that the employee be happy about it? Probably! A recent ruling by the Fifth Circuit Court of Appeals found that a company's handbook requirements that ". . . encouraged employees to maintain a positive work environment" and "prohibited arguing or fighting, failing to treat others with respect" were reasonable regulations set forth by an employer.[1]

The freedom to contract is crucial to freedom of the market; an employee may choose to work or not to work for a given employer, and an employer may choose to hire or not to hire a given applicant.

LO1 Describe the balance between the freedom to contract and the current regulatory environment for employment.

As a result, though the employment relationship is regulated in some important ways, Congress tries to avoid telling employers how to manage their employees or whom the employer should or should not hire. It is unlikely that Congress would enact legislation that would require employers to hire certain individuals or groups of individuals (like a pure quota system) or that would prevent employers and employees from freely negotiating the responsibilities of a given job. (See Exhibit 1.1, "Realities about the Regulation of Employment.")

Employers historically have had the right to discharge an employee whenever they wished to do so. In one example, the director of the Iowa Department of Human Services was fired the day after he sent out a large email blast to all 4,900 employees of the agency to commemorate his work anniversary and also the rapper Tupac's birthday. He chose to include lyrics from one of Tupac's

---

Exhibit 1.1 *Realities about the Regulation of Employment*

1. Generally, you do not have a right to your job.
2. This means that, once you are hired, your employer may choose to fire you, even for reasons that seem unjustified, as long as the termination is not in violation of a contract or for one of the few bases discussed in this textbook. But, basically, there are far more reasons a boss can fire you than not.
3. As an employer, you may fire someone for a good reason, for a bad reason, or even for no reason, just not for an illegal reason.
4. You may terminate someone simply because you do not get along with them. However, you must ensure that bias or perception, which might serve as the basis of a discrimination claim, is not interfering with judgment.

songs in the email as well and was fired for doing so. The lesson learned is that Title VII (or any other statute, for that matter) does not protect on the basis of music preferences.[2]

However, Congress has passed employment-related laws when it believes that there is some *imbalance of power* between the employee and the employer. For example, Congress has passed laws that require employers to pay minimum wages and avoid using certain criteria such as race or gender in reaching specific employment decisions. These laws reflect the reality that employers stand in a position of power in the employment relationship. Legal protections granted to employees seek to make the "power relationship" between employer and employee one that is fair and equitable.

Is Regulation Necessary?

See Chapter 2
to revisit key
concepts.

There are scholars who do not believe that regulation of discrimination and other areas of the employment relationship is necessary. Proponents of this view believe that the market will work to encourage employers' rational, non-biased behavior. For example, one of the main subjects of this textbook—Title VII of the Civil Rights Act of 1964 (Title VII)—prohibits discrimination based on race and gender, among other characteristics. (For detailed discussion of Title VII, see Chapter 3.) Some economists have argued that rational individuals interested in profit maximization will never hesitate to hire the most qualified applicants, regardless of their race. Decisions that are dependent on race or gender would be inefficient, they argue, since they are based on the (generally) incorrect belief that members of one class are less worthy of a job than those of another. The employers who are blind to gender or race, for instance, know that, if they were to allow their prejudices to govern or to influence their employment decisions, they may overlook the most qualified applicant because that applicant was African American or a woman. Therefore, they will not let prejudices cause them to hire less-qualified individuals and employ a less-efficient workforce.

However, opponents of this position contend that discrimination continues because often employers are faced with the choice of two *equally* qualified applicants for a position. In that case, the prejudiced employer suffers no decrease in efficiency of her or his firm as a result of choosing the white or male applicant over the minority or female applicant. In addition, human beings do not always act rationally or in ways that society might deem to be in the best interests of society as a whole. As Judge Richard Posner (retired) of the Seventh Circuit explained, "[t]he pluralism of our society is mirrored in the workplace, creating endless occasions for offense. Civilized people refrain from words and conduct that offend the people around them, but not all workers are civilized all the time."[3] Finally, given the composition of the workforce, if a biased firm chooses only from the stock of white males, it still might have a pretty qualified stock from which to choose; subsequently, it can remain awfully competitive. Therefore, economic forces do not afford absolute protection against employment discrimination where the discrimination is based on race, gender, national origin, or other protected categories.

Who Is Subject to Regulation?

LO2 Identify who is subject to which employment laws and understand the implication of each of these laws for both the employer and employee.

The issue of whether someone is an employer or employee is a critical one when it comes to regulation, but like many areas of the law, it is not one with an easy answer. (See Exhibit 1.2, "Realities about Who Is an Employee and Who Is Not.") Business decisions made in one context, for instance, may give rise to liability when there may be no liability in another (depending on factors such as the size of the business organization). In addition, defining an individual as an employee allows that person to pursue a claim that an independent contractor might not have.

In this section, we will examine who is considered to be an employer and an employee and how it is decided. These definitions are not just the concern of the employer's lawyer and accountant. Instead, concepts such as temporary help, leased workers, independent contractors, vendors, outsourcing, and staffing firms have become common elements of the employment landscape. While employers might not consider some of these workers to be employees, mere labels will not stop a court or agency from determining that the worker has been misclassified and that an employment relationship exists.[4]

Origins in Agency Law

The law relating to the employment relationship is based on the traditional law called *master and servant,* which evolved into the law of agency. It may be helpful to briefly review the fundamentals of the law of agency in order to gain a better perspective on the legal regulation of the employment relationship that follows.

In an agency relationship, one person acts on behalf of another. The actor is called the *agent,* and the party for whom the agent acts and from whom that agent derives authority to act is called the *principal.* The agent is basically a substitute appointed by the principal with power to do certain things. In the employment context, an employee is the agent of the employer, the principal. For example, if Alex hires Emma as an employee to work in his store selling paintings on his behalf, Alex would be the principal and employer, and Emma would be his agent and employee.

Exhibit 1.2   *Realities about Who Is an Employee and Who Is Not*

1. You are not an employee simply because you are paid to work.

2. Choosing how to perform your job is not a clear indicator of independent contractor status.

3. Just because you hire a worker does not mean that you are necessarily liable for anything that the employee does in the course of his or her employment.

4. If you are an employee under one statute, you are not always considered an employee under all employment-related statutes.

5. If you are considered an employer for purposes of one statute, you are not always considered an employer for all statutes.

6. It is not always better to hire someone as an independent contractor rather than as an employee.

7. A mistake in the categorization of a business's workers can be catastrophic to that business from financial and other perspectives.

In an employment–agency relationship, the employee-agent is under a specific duty to the principal to act only as *authorized.* As a rule, if an agent goes beyond her authority or places the property of the principal at risk without authority, the principal is not responsible to the third party for all loss or damage naturally resulting from the agent's unauthorized acts (while the agent remains liable to the principal for the same amount). In other words, if Alex told Emma that one of the paintings in the store should be priced at $100 and she sells it instead for $80, she would be acting without authority. Emma would be liable to Alex for his losses up to the amount authorized, $20, but Alex would still be required to sell the painting for the lower price because a customer in the store would reasonably believe the prices as marked. In addition, an agent has a duty to properly conduct herself when representing the principal and is liable for injuries resulting to the principal from her unwarranted misconduct. So, if Emma oversleeps and misses an appointment at which someone intended to purchase the painting, again she would be liable.

Throughout the entire relationship, the principal/employer has the obligation toward the agent to exercise good faith in their relationship, and the principal has to use care to prevent the agent from coming to any harm during the agency relationship. This requirement translates into the employer's responsibility to provide a safe and healthy working environment for the workers.

In addition to creating these implied duties for the employment relationship, the principal–agent characterization is important to the working relationship for other reasons, explained in the next section.

Why Is It Important to Determine Whether a Worker Is an Employee?

independent contractor
Generally, a person who contracts with a principal to perform a task according to her or his own methods and who is not under the principal's control regarding the physical details of the work.

You just received a job offer. How do you know if you are being hired as an employee or as an **independent contractor**? While some workers may have no doubt about their classification, the actual answer may vary depending on the statute, case law, or other analysis to be applied. The courts, employers, and the government are unable to agree on one definition of "employee" and "employer," so it varies depending on the situation and the law being used. In addition, some statutes do not give effective guidance. For instance, the Employee Retirement Income Security Act (ERISA, discussed in detail in Chapters 12 and 16) defines *employee* as "any individual employed by an employer."[5] But, as the Supreme Court chastised the legislators who wrote it, this nominal definition is "completely circular and explains nothing."[6] The distinction, however, is significant for tax law compliance and categorization, for benefit plans, for cost reduction plans, and for discrimination claims. For instance, Title VII applies to employers and prohibits them from discriminating against employees. It does not, however, cover discrimination against independent contractors. In addition, employers will not be liable for most torts committed by an independent contractor within the scope of the working relationship.

The definition of employee is all the more important as companies hire supplemental or contingent workers on an independent-contractor basis to cut costs. Generally, an employer's responsibilities increase when someone is an employee. This section of the chapter will discuss the varied implications of this characterization and why it is important to determine whether a worker is an employee. A later section in this chapter—"The Definition of 'Employee'"—will present the different ways to figure it out.

Employer Payroll Deductions

An employer paying an employee is subject to requirements different from those for paying an independent contractor. An employer who maintains employees has the responsibility to pay Social Security (FICA), the FICA excise tax, Railroad Retirement Tax Act (RRTA) withholding amounts, federal unemployment compensation (FUTA), IRS federal income tax withholdings, Medicare, and state taxes. In addition, it is the employer's responsibility to withhold a certain percentage of the employee's wages for federal income tax purposes.

On the other hand, an independent contractor has to pay all of these taxes on his or her own. This is usually considered to be a benefit for the employer because it is able to avoid the tax expenses and bookkeeping costs associated with such withholdings.

Benefits

When you have taken jobs in the past, were you offered a certain number of paid vacation or sick days, a retirement plan, a parking spot, a medical or dental plan? These are known as *benefits,* and they cost the employer money outside of the wages the employer must pay the employee. In an effort to attract and retain superior personnel, employers offer employees a range of benefits that generally are not required to be offered such as dental, medical, pension, and profit-sharing plans. Independent contractors have no access to these benefits.

We will discuss the Fair Labor Standards Act of 1938 (FLSA) in detail in Chapter 16 but introduce it here merely to identify it as another vital reason to ensure correct classification of workers. The FLSA was enacted to establish standards for minimum wages, overtime pay, employer record keeping, and child labor. Where a worker is considered an employee, the FLSA regulates the amount of money an employee must be paid per hour and overtime compensation. Employers may intentionally misclassify employees in order to avoid these and other costs and liabilities. A willful misclassification under FLSA may result in up to a $10,000 fine, imposed by the Department of Labor. A second violation could lead to imprisonment.

Discrimination and Affirmative Action

See Chapter 2 to revisit key concepts.

As you will learn in Chapter 3, Title VII and other related antidiscrimination statutes only protect *employees* from discrimination by employers; therefore, an independent contractor cannot hold an employer liable for discrimination on this basis, and employers are protected from some forms of discrimination and wrongful discharge claims where the worker is an independent contractor. (Coverage of employers by various statutes is discussed later in the chapter.) Status often is determinative. A regular on-air contributor to a Fox Business Network television show filed a Title VII claim against the network on the basis of sexual harassment and discrimination after she was raped and then coerced into a quid pro quo sexual relationship with a Fox anchor. However, a New York court barred her from pursuing her claims because it deemed her to be an independent contractor due to her unpaid status.[7]

Yet, as will be explored throughout this chapter, merely labeling a worker as an "independent contractor" does not protect against liability under federal antidiscrimination statutes such as Title VII. Courts and the EEOC will examine a variety of factors to determine the true meaning of the relationship between the worker and the organization. If the worker is more appropriately classified as an employee, then the label will be peeled off, allowing for antidiscrimination statutes to apply.

Additionally, the National Labor Relations Act of 1935 (NLRA) protects only employees and not independent contractors from unfair labor practices. Note, however, that independent contractors may be considered to be *employers,* so they may be subject to these regulations from the other side of the fence.

Cost Reductions

It would seem to be a safe statement that an objective of some, if not most, employers is to reduce cost and to increase profit. The regulations previously discussed require greater expenditures on behalf of employees, as does the necessity of hiring others to maintain records of the employees. In addition to avoiding those costs, hiring independent contractors also avoids the cost of overtime (the federal wage and hour laws do not apply to independent contractors), and the employer is able to avoid any work-related expenses such as tools, training, or traveling. The employer is also guaranteed satisfactory performance of the job for which the contractor was hired because it is the contractor's contractual obligation to adequately perform the contract with the employer, while the employee is generally able to quit without incurring liability (the at-will doctrine). If there is a breach of the agreement between the employer and the independent contractor, the independent contractor not only stands to lose the job but also may be liable for resulting damages. An employee is usually compensated for work completed with less liability for failure to perfectly perform. Some managers also contend that independent contractors are more motivated and, as a result, have a higher level of performance as a consequence of their freedom to control their own work and futures.

vicarious liability
The imposition of liability on one party for the wrongs of another. Liability may extend from an employee to the employer on this basis if the employee is acting within the scope of her or his employment at the time the liability arose.

In addition, the employee may actually cause the employer to have greater liability exposure. An employer has **vicarious liability** if the employee causes harm to a third party while the employee is in the course of employment. For instance, if an employee is driving a company car from one company plant to another and, in the course of that trip, sideswipes another vehicle, the employer may be liable to the owner of the other vehicle. While the employee may be required to reimburse the employer if the employer has to pay for the damages, generally the third party goes after the employer because the employee does not have the funds to pay the liability. The employer could, of course, seek repayment from the employee but, more likely, will write it off as an expense of doing business.

Questions might arise in connection with whether the worker is actually an employee of the employer and, therefore, whether the employer is liable at all, a question examined later in this chapter. For instance, if a hospital is sued for the malpractice of one of its doctors, the question of the hospital's vicarious liability will be determined based on whether the doctor is an employee or an independent contractor of the hospital. However, in certain situations, businesses will be liable for the acts of their independent contractors, including when those contractors are involved in "inherently dangerous activities."[8]

In some situations, notwithstanding the decrease in the amount of benefits that the employer must provide, independent contractors may still be more expensive to employ. This situation may exist where the employer finds that it is cheaper to have its employees perform certain types of work that are characteristically expensive to contract. Often a large firm will find it more profitable to employ a legal staff, and pay their benefits and salaries, than to employ a law firm every time a legal question arises. Or a school may find it less expensive to maintain a full janitorial staff than to employ a professional cleaning crew whenever something needs to be taken care of at the school.

The Cost of Mistakes

LO3 Delineate the risks to the employer caused by employee misclassification.

Workers and employers alike make mistakes about whether a worker is an independent contractor or an employee. If a worker is classified as an independent contractor but later is found to be an employee, the punishment by the IRS is harsh. The employer not only is liable for its share of FICA and FUTA taxes but also is subject to an additional penalty equal to 20 percent of the FICA taxes that should have been withheld. In addition, the employer is liable for 1.5 percent of the wages received by the employee.[9] These penalty charges apply if 1099 forms (records of payments to independent contractors) have been compiled for the worker and the classification is found to be a mistake by the employer. If, on the other hand, the forms have not been completed and the employer was attempting to commit fraud or intentional misconduct, the penalties increase to 40 percent of the FICA taxes and 3 percent of wages. Where the IRS determines that the worker was *deliberately* classified as an independent contractor to avoid paying taxes, the fines and penalties can easily run into six figures for even the smallest business. The IRS estimates that millions of employees are incorrectly classified each year as independent contractors.[10]

In addition to potential IRS violations, an employer may be liable for violations of the National Labor Relations Act, the Fair Labor Standards Act (FLSA), the Social Security Act, and state workers' compensation and unemployment compensation laws. The fines for each violation are substantial. In a 2018 case, the U.S. Department of Labor received a judgment against a direct mail company in Virginia for misclassifying its workers as independent contractors and for failing to pay overtime. The company was ordered to pay over $740,000 in back wages and liquidated damages to 73 employees to resolve violations of overtime and record-keeping provisions of the Fair Labor Standards Act plus $32,099 in penalties to the Department of Labor.[11]

The U.S. Department of Labor takes employee misclassification seriously and works in cooperation with the Internal Revenue Service to reduce the incidence of employee misclassification and to improve compliance with federal labor laws.[12] In addition, the DOL has signed memoranda of understanding with 45 states to share information and coordinate enforcement efforts.[13] On the federal level, the Payroll Fraud Prevention Act of 2018 was (re)introduced in Congress, for the fourth time, since it did not make it out of committee during any of the prior processes. The legislation seeks to amend the FLSA to require employers to keep records on and to notify workers of their employment or independent contractor classification as well as their right to challenge that classification. It would also increase civil penalties under the FLSA (up to $1,100 per employee for first offenders and $5,000 per employee for repeat or willful violations) on employers that misclassify employees as independent contractors.[14]

Meanwhile, many states are searching for these misclassifications through special task forces and asking for new legislation.[15] Because of the tremendous costs to a state of misclassification, Colorado has implemented a statewide crackdown on worker misclassification. The state has new, unambiguous ways to assess how workers are categorized and is using aggressive government audits. There are increased fines for businesses that misclassify, and companies are prohibited from receiving funds from state contracts after a first offense.[16] In 2018, the Government Against Misclassified Employees Operational Network (GAME ON) task force in Louisiana began ramping up its efforts to identify the misclassification of employees as independent contractors. Companies found to have willfully misclassified employees as independent contractors will have to pay taxes on the unreported wages, pay penalties of up to $1,000 per misclassified employee, and face potential imprisonment and barring from receiving state or government contracts.[17]

Why is the government so intent on ensuring that improper classification does not occur? Misclassified workers are a significant portion of the employment tax gap, but just how big a portion is unknown because the IRS's last comprehensive misclassification estimate was in 1984! At that time, the IRS found that 15 percent of employers misclassified 3.4 million workers as independent contractors, causing an estimated loss of $1.6 billion in Social Security tax, unemployment tax, and income tax. A 2017 report by the U.S. Government Accountability Office (GAO) found that noncompliance in reporting taxable wages most frequently involved how workers were classified (and whether employers had to withhold and pay employment taxes for them) to the tune of $44 billion in wage adjustments over just two years![18] Though recent nationwide data is not available, surveys across different states have estimated that worker misclassification affects 10 to 30 percent of all firms.[19] Rhode Island estimated that more than 6 percent of its workers were improperly classified as independent contractors, costing the state an estimated $50 million in uncollected income, unemployment, and other payroll taxes. A study on misclassification in Illinois showed that the state lost close to $125 million in income tax revenue over a four-year period. A New York task force investigating workplace fraud found that, in one year, misclassification cost the state more than $4.8 million in unemployment taxes alone, a significant loss when that tax revenue is needed to pay unemployment claims.[20] Misclassification is substantially higher in certain industries: construction, janitorial, transportation and warehousing, and meat and poultry processing.[21] As one scholar reported, IRS agents are told, "Go forth and find employees!" The IRS will generally attempt to "match" workers who claim to be independent contractors with their companies. If an independent contractor earned more than $10,000 from one source during a one-year period, the independent status of that individual is suspect.

While we will discuss below the process for correct worker classification, the IRS provides a small "safe harbor," called the Classification Settlement Program (CSP), through the 1978 Revenue Act for employers who have always and consistently defined a class of workers as independent contractors. Section 530 cites four criteria required to claim a worker as an independent contractor. Where these conditions have been satisfied, the employer is not liable for misclassification.

1. First, the business must have never treated the worker as an employee for the purposes of employment taxes for any period (e.g., the company has never withheld income or FICA tax from its payments).

2. Second, all federal tax returns with respect to this worker were filed consistently with the worker being an independent contractor.

3. Third, the company has treated all those in positions substantially similar to that of this worker as independent contractors.

4. Fourth, the company has a reasonable basis for treating the worker as an independent contractor. Such a reasonable basis may include a judicial precedent or published IRS ruling, a past IRS audit of the company, or long-standing industry practices, as will be discussed in greater detail later in this chapter.

In 2011, the IRS introduced the Voluntary Classification Settlement Program, which enables employers who are not currently subject to examination by the IRS, DOL, or a state agency to voluntarily reclassify their workers and to obtain substantial relief from federal payroll taxes, interest, and penalties. In both programs, the employer must agree to treat workers as employees prospectively.[22]

The Definition of "Employee"

Courts have offered various ways to determine whether a worker is an employee. Generally, the interpretation used depends on the factual circumstances presented by each case as well as which law is at issue.

An older but consistently cited case that illustrates the effect of the difference between classification as an independent contractor and as an employee is *Lemmerman v. A.T. Williams Oil Co.,*[23] where an eight-year-old boy frequently performed odd jobs for his mother's employer, the Wilco Service Station. He was paid $1 a day to stock shelves and to sweep up. One day, the boy fell and cut his hand. The boy sought damages in the form of lost wages, pain, and suffering. The main question in *Lemmerman* was whether the boy was an employee. If he was an employee, then his sole remedy was in the form of workers' compensation; however, if instead he was an independent contractor, Wilco would lose the protection of the workers' compensation limits and would be liable in tort for much higher amounts. Over a strong dissenting opinion, the court in *Lemmerman* determined that the boy actually was Wilco's employee and, therefore, could not recover beyond a standard workers' compensation claim.

Several tests have been developed and are commonly used by courts to classify employees and independent contractors. These tests include the common-law test

Scenario

of agency, which considers several factors but focuses on who has the right to control the work,[24] the Internal Revenue Service (IRS) 20-factor analysis,[25] and the economic realities analysis.[26] Several courts also use a hybrid approach, using one test that combines factors from other tests. While some courts continue to refer to all three tests as available for consideration, and therefore we will include a discussion of them here, there is a trend toward recognizing a convergence toward the common-law test.[27]

More recently, the California Supreme Court issued an opinion in *Dynamex Operations v. Lee,* in which it developed a new test called the ABC test, which we also will discuss below. While a California Supreme Court decision is not precedent for other states, this new analysis already has been adopted in Massachusetts and New Jersey, and other states have applied the test to determine unemployment compensation. So its impact is growing.[28]

The **common-law agency test** is now considered to be the leading test to determine employee status. This test originated in the master and servant law discussed at the beginning of the chapter. Using the language of those origins, since the master (employer) had control over the servant (worker), the servant was considered similar to common-law property of the master and, therefore, originally governed by property law rather than contract law. Though today we have adopted contract or agency principles to negotiate this relationship, the element of *control* has persisted in our interpretation of the distinction between an employee and an independent contractor. *The right to control remains the predominant factor.*

Under the common-law agency approach applied by the courts, the employer need not actually control the work but must merely *have the right or ability* to control the work for a worker to be classified an employee. Although this is a strong indication that the worker is an employee, other factors usually are considered. For example, sometimes the courts will review whether the worker is paid in standard wages or through an expectation of profit based on the price the worker "charges" for the job. While recent cases have applied the hybrid test under many circumstances, the common-law test is often used to determine employee status in connection with employment taxes (e.g., FUTA and FICA) as well as in federal income tax withholding.

In *Estrada v. FedEx Ground Package System, Inc.,*[29] the California Court of Appeals evaluated whether Federal Express ground package drivers were employees entitled to reimbursement for work-related expenses. The court applied the common-law test and found that they were, in fact, employees. "FedEx's control over every exquisite detail of the drivers' performance, including the color of their socks and the style of their hair, supports the trial court's conclusion that the drivers are employees, not independent contractors." In agreeing with the lower court's opinion, the Court of Appeals explained at one point that "the essence of the trial court's statement of decision is that if it looks like a duck, walks like a duck, swims like a duck, and quacks like a duck, it is a duck." One might begin to understand the magnitude of a decision such as this one when one learns that the fallout was an order by the IRS that Federal Express pay $319 million in back taxes based on the misclassification—and the *Estrada* case only applied to workers over the course of *one single year.* Although the penalty was later rescinded, the IRS finding that drivers are employees

LO4 Explain the difference between an employee and an independent contractor and the tests that help us in that determination.

common-law agency test
A test used to determine employee status; the employer must merely have the right or ability to control the work for a worker to be classified as an employee.

remained, resulting in tax liability for future years. Not all courts or circuits agree with California on this issue, however. In cases since, courts have also found in favor of FedEx, holding that the workers' ability to hire their own employees, manage multiple routes, and sell those routes without FedEx's permission, "as well as the parties' intent expressed in the contract, argues strongly in favor of independent contractor status."[30] Further, while *FedEx Home Delivery* was overturned on appeal in 2014, the reasoning in that 2014 case was overruled in *SuperShuttle DFW, Inc.,*[31] leaving the National Labor Relations Board (NLRB) interpretation of the common-law test more business friendly. Clearly, it is not a clear-cut answer.

IRS 20-factor analysis
List of 20 factors to which the IRS looks to determine whether someone is an employee or an independent contractor. The IRS compiled this list from the results of judgments of the courts relating to this issue.

The IRS does have a secondary analysis, called the **IRS 20-factor analysis**; however, even the IRS itself explains that "this Twenty Factor Test is an analytical tool and *not* the legal test used for determining worker status. The legal test is whether there is a right to direct and control the means and details of the work" (emphasis in original).[32]

Notwithstanding the IRS's own disclaimer, the following 20 factors have been continually articulated by courts, regulatory agencies, commentators, and scholars as critical to the determination of the status of an individual worker. Suffice it to say that when these factors are satisfied, courts are more likely to find "employee" status. In addition, the IRS stated that these 20 factors are not inclusive but that "every piece of information that helps determine the extent to which the business retains the right to control the worker is important." (See Exhibits 1.3, "Employee or Independent Contractor?," and 1.4, "Internal Revenue Service 'Independent Contractor or Employee?' Publication 1779.")

1. *Instructions.* A worker who is required to comply with other persons' instructions about when, where, and how to perform the work is ordinarily considered to be an employee.

Exhibit 1.3 *Employee or Independent Contractor?*

The IRS, in its training materials, offers this case study on the question of whether someone is an employee or an independent contractor:

An attorney is a sole practitioner who rents office space and pays for the following items: telephone, computer, on-line legal research database, fax machine, and photocopier. The attorney buys office supplies and pays bar dues and membership dues to three other professional organizations. The attorney has a part-time receptionist who also does the bookkeeping. The attorney pays the receptionist, withholds and pays federal and state employment taxes, and files a Form W-2

each year. For the past two years, the attorney has had only one client, a corporation with which there has been a long-standing relationship. The attorney charges the corporation an hourly rate for services and sends monthly bills detailing the work performed for the prior month. The bills include charges for cell phone bills, on-line research time, fax charges, photocopies, mailing costs, and travel costs for which the corporation has agreed to reimburse.

Is the attorney an employee?

Source: Internal Revenue Service; case modified slightly by the authors.

2. *Training.* Training a worker indicates that the employer exercises control over the means by which the result is accomplished.

3. *Integration.* When the success or continuation of a business depends on the performance of certain services, the worker performing those services is subject to a certain amount of control by the owner of the business.

4. *Personal rendering of services.* If the services must be rendered personally, the employer controls both the means and the results of the work.

5. *Hiring, supervising, and paying of assistants.* Control is exercised if the employer hires, supervises, and pays assistants.

6. *Continuing relationships.* The existence of a continuing relationship between the worker and the employer indicates an employer–employee relationship.

7. *Set hours of work.* The establishment of hours of work by the employer indicates control.

8. *Full-time requirement.* If the worker must devote full time to the employer's business, the employer has control over the worker's time. An independent contractor is free to work when and for whom she or he chooses.

9. *Work performed on the employer's premises.* Control is indicated if the work is performed on the employer's premises.

10. *Order or sequence set.* Control is indicated if a worker is not free to choose his or her own pattern of work but must perform services in the sequence set by the employer.

11. *Oral or written reports.* Control is indicated if the worker must submit regular oral or written reports to the employer.

12. *Furnishing of tools and materials.* If the employer furnishes significant tools, materials, and other equipment, an employer–employee relationship usually exists.

13. *Payment by hour, week, or month.* Payment by the hour, week, or month points to an employer–employee relationship, provided that this method of payment is not just a convenient way of paying a lump sum agreed on as a cost of a job. However, hourly pay may not be evidence that a worker is an employee if it is customary to pay an independent contractor by the hour (an attorney, for example). An independent contractor usually is paid by the job or on a straight commission.

14. *Payment of business or traveling expenses.* Payment of the worker's business or traveling expenses, or both, is indicative of an employer–employee relationship. However, this factor is less important because companies do reimburse independent contractors.

15. *Significant investment.* A worker is an independent contractor if she or he invests in facilities that are not typically maintained by employees such as the maintenance of an office rented at fair value from an unrelated party. An employee depends on the employer for such facilities.

16. *Realization of profit or loss.* A worker who can realize a profit or loss (in addition to the profit or loss ordinarily realized by employees) through management of resources is an independent contractor. The worker who cannot is generally an employee.

17. *Work performed for more than one firm at a time.* If a worker performs more than *de minimis* services for a number of unrelated persons at the same time, she or he is usually considered an independent contractor.

18. *Service made available to the general public.* A worker is usually an independent contractor if the services are made available to the general public on a regular or consistent basis.

19. *Right to discharge.* The right of the employer to discharge a worker indicates that he or she is an employee.

20. *Right to terminate.* A worker is an employee if the right to end the relationship with the principal is available at any time he or she wishes without incurring liability.

economic realities test
A test to determine whether a worker qualifies as an employee. Courts use this test to determine whether a worker is economically dependent on the business or is in business for himself or herself. To apply the test, courts look to the degree of control exerted by the alleged employer over the worker, the worker's opportunity for profit or loss, the worker's investment in the business, the permanence of the working relationship, the degree of skill required by the worker, and the extent to which the work is an integral part of the alleged employer's business.

Under the **economic realities test**, courts consider whether the worker is economically dependent on the business or, as a matter of economic fact, is in business for himself or herself. In applying the economic realities test, courts look to the degree of control exerted by the alleged employer over the worker, the worker's opportunity for profit or loss, the worker's investment in the business, the permanence of the working relationship, the degree of skill required by the worker, and the extent the work is an integral part of the alleged employer's business. Typically, all of these factors are considered as a whole with none of the factors being determinative.

In *Juino v. Livingston Parish Fire District No. 5,* a volunteer firefighter faced sexual harassment at her station. The court determined that, as a volunteer worker, Rachel Juino was not an employee and, therefore, was not protected by Title VII. In the *Juino* case, the court chose to consider whether she was paid as the threshold consideration to determine whether she was an employee. Though Juino received some indirect benefits from her volunteer work (e.g., life insurance), the court ruled that they were not significant enough to pass this first test of employment.[33] Other courts have held that pay is not the threshold condition but only one factor among others for classifying workers.[34] In short, courts must consider whether unpaid workers receive some benefit for their work when determining if they are employees. But courts vary in their rulings regarding how much weight this consideration must be given.

Finally, the ABC Test, as developed by the California Supreme Court in *Dynamex Operations v. Lee,* instructs that the worker is presumed to be an employee unless the firm is able to demonstrate three elements:

(A) that the worker is free from the control and direction of alleged employer with regard to her or his work performance, both under the contract and in fact; *and*

(B) that the worker performs work that is outside the usual course of alleged employer's business; *and*

(C) that the worker is customarily engaged in an independently established trade, occupation, or business of the same nature as the work performed.

The second prong is of particular concern for business owners who maintain a large number of independent contractors in the "gig economy"—operators who use many workers to perform small individual tasks, each of which is totally necessary for the overall business to run. Traditionally, workers in these roles have greater flexibility in hours and may even work for several business owners. The courts have not yet made a definitive decision in this arena.

The court offered examples for its third element. For instance, it explained, "when a retail store hires an outside plumber to repair a leak in a bathroom on its premises or hires an outside electrician to install a new electrical line, the services of the plumber or electrician are not part of the store's usual course of business." To the contrary, "when a clothing manufacturing company hires work-at-home seamstresses to make dresses from cloth and patterns supplied by the company that will thereafter be sold by the company, or when a bakery hires cake decorators to work on a regular basis on its custom-designed cakes, the workers are part of the hiring entity's usual business operation and . . . the workers' role within the hiring entity's usual business operations is more like that of an employee than that of an independent contractor."[35]

The *Dynamex* test has been codified into law in California, and time will tell if other jurisdictions will follow.[36]

Contingent or Temporary Workers

A *contingent worker* is one whose job with an employer is temporary, is sporadic, or differs in any way from the norm of full-time employment (this type of work also can be called *gig work*). As used by the EEOC, the term *contingent worker* includes those who are hired by an employer through a staffing firm as well as temporary, seasonal, and part-time workers and those considered to be independent contractors rather than employees.[37] In the United States, more than 40 percent of workers are employed in "alternative work arrangements," such as contingent, part-time, or gig work, according to Deloitte's 2018 Global Human Capital Trends study.[38]

When using contingent and temporary workers, an employer must be aware of the advantages and disadvantages. Although contingent or temporary workers provide a cost savings as a short-term benefit, depending on their classification, they could be entitled to protection under employment laws. It is important to be sure the classification given is the true classification. In 2019, rideshare company Uber settled with 3,600 drivers in Massachusetts and California who went to court in a class-action case seeking to be considered employees. Uber settled the six-year-old case for $20 million but will continue to classify the drivers as independent contractors—some say, at its peril.[39] California passed a law in 2019 formalizing the *Dynamex* ABC test into legislation and drastically changed the playing field for employers using contingent workers.[40] Uber and Postmates (a food delivery service app), along with two gig workers, sued the state of California within a few months of the law becoming official, claiming the law is unconstitutional. Their complaint alleges that they are "defending their fundamental liberty to pursue their chosen work as independent service providers and technology companies in the on-demand economy."[41] We will have to see how the federal courts view the classification issue around gig workers.

Interns, Trainees, and Volunteers

The past several years have seen a rise in cases filed by unpaid interns who claimed they were improperly designated "trainees" (and thus exempt from minimum wage and overtime protections), when, in fact, they should have been treated as paid employees under the FLSA and applicable state laws. The stakes in such cases can be substantial. Media giant NBCUniversal agreed to pay $6.4 million to settle a high-profile case by interns,[42] and Condé Nast signed off on a deal to pay up to $5.85 million to resolve a suit by interns who worked at *The New Yorker* and *W Magazine.*[43]

To decide whether interns, students, and trainees qualify as "employees" for purposes of wage and hour requirements, courts typically rely on multi-factor tests. These may vary by jurisdiction, but most focus on whether the nature of the relationship is educational, the economic reality of the relationship, and who primarily benefits from the work.

One of the more popular tests seen in the courts is the "primary beneficiary" test established by the Second Circuit Court of Appeals in *Glatt v. Fox Searchlight Pictures, Inc.*[44] Production and publicist interns for Fox Searchlight filed a class-action lawsuit for their work on the Oscar-winning movie *Black Swan.* The appeals court used a non-exhaustive seven-factor test to determine whether an intern/trainee is an "employee."

1. Whether it is clearly understood there is no expectation of pay;
2. Whether the internship provides formal training similar to that provided by an educational environment;
3. Whether it is tied to a formal educational program or earns academic credit;
4. Whether the internship corresponds to the academic calendar, accommodates academic commitments;
5. Whether it is limited in duration to the period it provides beneficial learning;
6. Whether the intern's work complements, rather than displaces, work by paid employees and simultaneously provides a significant educational benefit to the intern; and
7. Whether it is clearly understood that the intern is not entitled to a paid position after the internship.

True volunteers are generally not considered employees, but there are caveats. The Department of Labor states that "[i]ndividuals who volunteer or donate their services, usually on a part-time basis, for public service, religious or humanitarian objectives, not as employees and without contemplation of pay, are not considered employees of the religious, charitable or similar non-profit organizations that receive their service." The agency also notes that, under the FLSA, employees may not volunteer services to for-profit private employers. Also, individuals can volunteer for public employers, but they are not permitted to do the same work for which they are employed.[45]

Joint Employers and Staffing Firms

Title VII prohibits staffing firms from illegally discriminating against workers in assignments and opportunities for employment. Staffing firms can be considered to be employers as well, such as when they pay the worker and provide training and workers' compensation coverage.

Exhibit 1.4 *Internal Revenue Service "Independent Contractor or Employee?" Publication 1779*

Independent Contractor *or* Employee

Which are you?

For federal tax purposes, this is an important distinction. Worker classification affects how you pay your federal income tax, social security and Medicare taxes, and how you file your tax return. Classification affects your eligibility for social security and Medicare benefits, employer provided benefits and your tax responsibilities. If you aren't sure of your work status, you should find out now. This brochure can help you.

The courts have considered many facts in deciding whether a worker is an independent contractor or an employee. These relevant facts fall into three main categories: behavioral control; financial control; and relationship of the parties. In each case, it is very important to consider all the facts – no single fact provides the answer. Carefully review the following definitions.

Behavioral Control

These facts show whether there is a right to direct or control how the worker does the work. A worker is an employee when the business has the right to direct and control the worker. The business does not have to actually direct or control the way the work is done – as long as the employer has the right to direct and control the work. For example:

Instructions – if you receive extensive instructions on how work is to be done, this suggests that you are an employee. Instructions can cover a wide range of topics, for example:

• how, when, or where to do the work

• what tools or equipment to use

• what assistants to hire to help with the work

• where to purchase supplies and services

If you receive less extensive instructions about what should be done, but not how it should be done, you may be an independent contractor. For instance, instructions about time and place may be less important than directions on how the work is performed.

Training – if the business provides you with training about required procedures and methods, this indicates that the business wants the work done in a certain way, and this suggests that you may be an employee.

Financial Control

These facts show whether there is a right to direct or control the business part of the work. For example:

Significant Investment – if you have a significant investment in your work, you may be an independent contractor. While there is no precise dollar test, the investment must have substance. However, a significant investment is not necessary to be an independent contractor.

Expenses – if you are not reimbursed for some or all business expenses, then you may be an independent contractor, especially if your unreimbursed business expenses are high.

Opportunity for Profit or Loss – if you can realize a profit or incur a loss, this suggests that you are in business for yourself and that you may be an independent contractor.

Relationship of the Parties

These are facts that illustrate how the business and the worker perceive their relationship. For example:

Employee Benefits – if you receive benefits, such as insurance, pension, or paid leave, this is an indication that you may be an employee. If you do not receive benefits, however, you could be either an employee or an independent contractor.

Written Contracts – a written contract may show what both you and the business intend. This may be very significant if it is difficult, if not impossible, to determine status based on other facts.

When You Are an Employee...

■ Your employer must withhold income tax and your portion of social security and Medicare taxes. Also, your employer is responsible for paying social security, Medicare, and unemployment (FUTA) taxes on your wages. Your employer must give you a Form W-2, Wage and Tax Statement, showing the amount of taxes withheld from your pay.

■ You may deduct unreimbursed employee business expenses on Schedule A of your income tax return, but only if you itemize deductions and they total more than two percent of your adjusted gross income.

When You Are an Independent Contractor...

■ The business may be required to give you Form 1099-MISC, Miscellaneous Income, to report what it has paid to you.

■ You are responsible for paying your own income tax and self-employment tax (Self-Employment Contributions Act – SECA). The business does not withhold taxes from your pay. You may need to make estimated tax payments during the year to cover your tax liabilities.

■ You may deduct business expenses on Schedule C of your income tax return.

Michal Kowalski/Shutterstock

If a client of a staffing firm supervises, trains, and otherwise directs the worker with whom it has a continuing relationship, then perhaps the client will become an employer of the worker. In this way, *both* the staffing firm *and* the client may share liability as employers of the worker. This is called *joint and several* liability, and the worker may collect compensatory damages from either one or both of the entities combined if a wrong is proven.

Whether a contingent worker who is placed by a staffing firm with the firm's clients qualifies as an employee depends on a number of factors, including whether the staffing firm or the client retains the right to control when, where, and how the worker performs the job and whether there is a continuing relationship with the worker, among other factors. What is unique about the worker placed by a staffing firm is the potential for joint liability between the staffing firm and the client.

In a case that sought to determine liability for wage and hour violations, the Fourth Circuit Court of Appeals considered whether the right to control is necessary to create liability based on joint employment. In *Salinas v. Commercial Interiors, Inc.,*[46] Commercial Interiors was a construction firm that subcontracted drywall installers from J.I. Construction. Salinas was one of those drywall installers hired by J.I. to work for Commercial Interiors. Salinas claimed a wage dispute against both J.I. and Commercial Interiors. In finding liability based on the joint employer concept, the court held that not all outsourcing relationships would be classified as joint employers and that all relevant factors should be considered, including (but not limited to):

1. Whether the employers jointly determine, share, or allocate the power to direct, control, or supervise the worker;
2. Whether the employers jointly determine, share, or allocate the power to hire or fire the worker or modify the terms or conditions of the worker's employment;
3. The degree of permanency and duration of the relationship between the joint employers;
4. Whether, through shared management or a direct or indirect ownership interest, one joint employer controls, is controlled by, or is under common control with the other joint employer;
5. Whether the work is performed on a premises owned or controlled by one or more of the joint employers; and
6. Whether the employers jointly determine, share, or allocate responsibility over functions ordinarily carried out by an employer, such as handling payroll; providing workers' compensation insurance; paying payroll taxes; or providing the facilities, equipment, tools, or materials necessary to complete the work.[47]

The NLRB ruled that a more direct level of control needs to exist before determining a joint employment situation that places liability on both employers. In *FLRB v. Hy-land Brand Industrial Contractors, Ltd.,* two or more employers will be deemed joint employers only if there is proof that one entity actually has exercised control over essential employment terms of another entity's employees (rather than merely having reserved the right to exercise control) and has done so directly and immediately (rather than indirectly) in a manner that is not limited or routine.[48]

Courts continue to use this NLRB standard or a patchwork of factor tests to determine whether the worker is an employee or independent contractor in an outsourcing context.[49]

Further, employers may be held liable as "third-party interferers" under Title VII. For example, if an employer decides to ask its staffing firm to replace the temporary receptionist with one of another race, the receptionist could proceed with a Title VII claim against the employer because it improperly interfered with her employment opportunities with the staffing firm. Therefore, an employer using a staffing firm cannot avoid liability for discriminating against a temporary worker merely because it did not "employ" the worker.

- For reasons cited earlier in this chapter, an employer may hire someone with the intent of establishing an employment relationship or an independent-contractor relationship. A variety of protections available to the employer allow the employer some measure of control over this seemingly arbitrary categorization process. However, none will guarantee a court determination of employee or independent-contractor status.

- As in most relationships, a written document will help to identify the nature of the association between the parties and their rights and obligations, provided that the role of the worker is consistent with the duties of an employee or independent contractor. While the classification made in this document is not binding in any way on the courts or the IRS, it may serve as persuasive evidence about the parties' intentions.

- If the person is hired as an employee and it is so stipulated in the document, the written agreement may be considered an employment agreement. The employer should be careful to discuss whether the employment duration will remain at-will or for a specified time period.

- If the employer intends to hire the worker as an independent contractor, the agreement should articulate the extent of the worker's control over her or his performance and the outcome to be produced pursuant to the contract. Further, where the agreement specifies particular hours to be worked rather than a deadline for completion, it is more likely that the worker will be considered an employee.

- Included in the written agreement should be a discussion of who is responsible for the payment of income taxes and benefits and for the division of responsibility for office expenses and overhead such as tools, supplies, and office rent.

- The independent contractor should be paid on the basis of the nature of the job completed rather than the hours worked to complete it.

- No training should be offered to an independent contractor; courts hypothesize that the reason an employer would hire outside help is to reduce these costs. On the other hand, where an employer provides extensive training and support, it is likely that the employer seeks to reap a benefit from this investment in the long run through continued service of its employee.

- Where additional assistance is required, an independent contractor will be made to supply that extra assistance, while an employer would be the party to provide the aid if the worker is an employee. The employer may offer to guarantee a loan to the contractor to allow her or him to obtain the assistance, new tools, or other equipment if necessary without threatening the independent-contractor status.

- Finally, where the risk of misclassification is great—for instance, where the failure to correctly categorize the worker may result in large financial penalties—the employer may choose to obtain an advance ruling from the IRS regarding the nature of the relationship. This is accomplished through the filing of IRS Form SS-8 (see Exhibit 1.5, "IRS Form SS-8").

Exhibit 1.5 *IRS Form SS-8*

Form **SS-8** (Rev. May 2014) Department of the Treasury Internal Revenue Service	**Determination of Worker Status for Purposes of Federal Employment Taxes and Income Tax Withholding** ▶ Information about Form SS-8 and its separate instructions is at *www.irs.gov/formss8*.	OMB. No. 1545-0004 **For IRS Use Only:** **Case Number:** **Earliest Receipt Date:**

Name of firm (or person) for whom the worker performed services	Worker's name

Firm's mailing address (include street address, apt. or suite no., city, state, and ZIP code)	Worker's mailing address (include street address, apt. or suite no., city, state, and ZIP code)

Trade name	Firm's email address	Worker's daytime telephone number	Worker's email address
Firm's fax number	Firm's website	Worker's alternate telephone number	Worker's fax number
Firm's telephone number (include area code)	Firm's employer identification number	Worker's social security number	Worker's employer identification number (if any)

Note. If the worker is paid for these services by a firm other than the one listed on this form, enter the name, address, and employer identification number of the payer. ▶ --

---

Disclosure of Information

The information provided on Form SS-8 may be disclosed to the firm, worker, or payer named above to assist the IRS in the determination process. For example, if you are a worker, we may disclose the information you provide on Form SS-8 to the firm or payer named above. The information can only be disclosed to assist with the determination process. If you provide incomplete information, we may not be able to process your request. See *Privacy Act and Paperwork Reduction Act Notice* in the separate instructions for more information. **If you do not want this information disclosed to other parties, do not file Form SS-8.**

Parts I–V. All filers of Form SS-8 must complete all questions in Parts I–IV. Part V must be completed if the worker provides a service directly to customers or is a salesperson. If you cannot answer a question, enter "Unknown" or "Does not apply." If you need more space for a question, attach another sheet with the part and question number clearly identified. Write your firm's name (or worker's name) and employer identification number (or social security number) at the top of each additional sheet attached to this form.

Part I   **General Information**

1   This form is being completed by: ☐ Firm ☐ Worker; for services performed _____ to _____ .
        (beginning date)   (ending date)

2   Explain your reason(s) for filing this form (for example, you received a bill from the IRS, you believe you erroneously received a Form 1099 or Form W-2, you are unable to get workers' compensation benefits, or you were audited or are being audited by the IRS). ----------------------------

3   Total number of workers who performed or are performing the same or similar services: _____ .

4   How did the worker obtain the job? ☐ Application   ☐ Bid   ☐ Employment Agency   ☐ Other (specify) _____

5   **Attach copies of all supporting documentation (for example, contracts, invoices, memos, Forms W-2 or Forms 1099-MISC issued or received, IRS closing agreements or IRS rulings).** In addition, please inform us of any current or past litigation concerning the worker's status. If no income reporting forms (Form 1099-MISC or W-2) were furnished to the worker, enter the amount of income earned for the year(s) at issue $ _____ .
    If both Form W-2 and Form 1099-MISC were issued or received, explain why. ---

6   Describe the firm's business. --

For Privacy Act and Paperwork Reduction Act Notice, see the separate instructions.   Cat. No. 16106T   Form **SS-8** (Rev. 5-2014)

continued

Form SS-8 (Rev. 5-2014)   Page **2**

Part I   **General Information** (continued)

7   If the worker received pay from more than one entity because of an event such as the sale, merger, acquisition, or reorganization of the firm for whom the services are performed, provide the following: Name of the firm's previous owner: _____

Previous owner's taxpayer identification number: _____ Change was a: ☐ Sale ☐ Merger ☐ Acquisition ☐ Reorganization
☐ Other (specify) _____
Description of above change: _____

Date of change (MM/DD/YY): _____

8   Describe the work done by the worker and provide the worker's job title. _____

9   Explain why you believe the worker is an employee or an independent contractor. _____

10 Did the worker perform services for the firm in any capacity before providing the services that are the subject of this determination request?
☐ Yes ☐ No ☐ N/A
If "Yes," what were the dates of the prior service? _____
If "Yes," explain the differences, if any, between the current and prior service. _____

11 If the work is done under a written agreement between the firm and the worker, attach a copy (preferably signed by both parties). Describe the terms and conditions of the work arrangement. _____

Part II   **Behavioral Control** (Provide names and titles of specific individuals, if applicable.)

1   What specific training and/or instruction is the worker given by the firm? _____

2   How does the worker receive work assignments? _____

3   Who determines the methods by which the assignments are performed? _____
4   Who is the worker required to contact if problems or complaints arise and who is responsible for their resolution? _____

5   What types of reports are required from the worker? Attach examples. _____

6   Describe the worker's daily routine such as his or her schedule or hours. _____

7   At what location(s) does the worker perform services (for example, firm's premises, own shop or office, home, customer's location)? Indicate the appropriate percentage of time the worker spends in each location, if more than one. _____

8   Describe any meetings the worker is required to attend and any penalties for not attending (for example, sales meetings, monthly meetings, staff meetings). _____
9   Is the worker required to provide the services personally? . . . . ☐ Yes ☐ No
10 If substitutes or helpers are needed, who hires them? _____
11 If the worker hires the substitutes or helpers, is approval required? . . . . ☐ Yes ☐ No
If "Yes," by whom? _____
12 Who pays the substitutes or helpers? _____
13 Is the worker reimbursed if the worker pays the substitutes or helpers? . . . . . ☐ Yes ☐ No
If "Yes," by whom? _____

Form **SS-8** (Rev. 5-2014)

continued

Exhibit 1.5 *continued*

Form SS-8 (Rev. 5-2014)   Page **3**

Part III   **Financial Control** (Provide names and titles of specific individuals, if applicable.)

1   List the supplies, equipment, materials, and property provided by each party:
     The firm: ....
     The worker: ....
     Other party: ....

2   Does the worker lease equipment, space, or a facility? . . . .   ☐ **Yes**   ☐ **No**
     If "Yes," what are the terms of the lease? (Attach a copy or explanatory statement.) ....
     ....

3   What expenses are incurred by the worker in the performance of services for the firm? ....
     ....

4   Specify which, if any, expenses are reimbursed by:
     The firm: ....
     Other party: ....

5   Type of pay the worker receives: ☐ Salary   ☐ Commission   ☐ Hourly Wage   ☐ Piece Work
     ☐ Lump Sum   ☐ Other (specify)
     If type of pay is commission, and the firm guarantees a minimum amount of pay, specify amount. $ _____

6   Is the worker allowed a drawing account for advances? . . . .   ☐ **Yes**   ☐ **No**
     If "Yes," how often? ....
     Specify any restrictions. ....

7   Whom does the customer pay? . . . .   ☐ Firm   ☐ Worker
     If worker, does the worker pay the total amount to the firm? ☐ **Yes**   ☐ **No**   If "No," explain. ....

8   Does the firm carry workers' compensation insurance on the worker? . . . .   ☐ **Yes**   ☐ **No**
9   What economic loss or financial risk, if any, can the worker incur beyond the normal loss of salary (for example, loss or damage of equipment, material)? ....
     ....

10   Does the worker establish the level of payment for the services provided or the products sold? . . . .   ☐ **Yes**   ☐ **No**
     If "No," who does? ....

Part IV   **Relationship of the Worker and Firm**

1   Please check the benefits available to the worker: ☐ Paid vacations   ☐ Sick pay   ☐ Paid holidays
     ☐ Personal days   ☐ Pensions   ☐ Insurance benefits   ☐ Bonuses
     ☐ Other (specify) ....

2   Can the relationship be terminated by either party without incurring liability or penalty? . . . .   ☐ **Yes**   ☐ **No**
     If "No," explain your answer. ....

3   Did the worker perform similar services for others during the time period entered in Part I, line 1? . . . .   ☐ **Yes**   ☐ **No**
     If "Yes," is the worker required to get approval from the firm? . . . .   ☐ **Yes**   ☐ **No**

4   Describe any agreements prohibiting competition between the worker and the firm while the worker is performing services or during any later period. Attach any available documentation. ....

5   Is the worker a member of a union? . . . .   ☐ **Yes**   ☐ **No**
6   What type of advertising, if any, does the worker do (for example, a business listing in a directory or business cards)? Provide copies, if applicable. ....

7   If the worker assembles or processes a product at home, who provides the materials and instructions or pattern? ....
     ....

8   What does the worker do with the finished product (for example, return it to the firm, provide it to another party, or sell it)? ....

9   How does the firm represent the worker to its customers (for example, employee, partner, representative, or contractor), and under whose business name does the worker perform these services? ....

10   If the worker no longer performs services for the firm, how did the relationship end (for example, worker quit or was fired, job completed, contract ended, firm or worker went out of business)? ....

Form **SS-8** (Rev. 5-2014)

continued

Chapter One *The Regulation of Employment* **25**

Form SS-8 (Rev. 5-2014)	Page **4**

Part V   **For Service Providers or Salespersons.** Complete this part if the worker provided a service directly to customers or is a salesperson.

1. What are the worker's responsibilities in soliciting new customers? _____

2. Who provides the worker with leads to prospective customers? _____
3. Describe any reporting requirements pertaining to the leads. _____

4. What terms and conditions of sale, if any, are required by the firm? _____
5. Are orders submitted to and subject to approval by the firm? . . . . □ **Yes**   □ **No**
6. Who determines the worker's territory? _____
7. Did the worker pay for the privilege of serving customers on the route or in the territory? . . . . □ **Yes**   □ **No**
   If "Yes," whom did the worker pay? _____
   If "Yes," how much did the worker pay? . . . . $ _____
8. Where does the worker sell the product (for example, in a home, retail establishment)? _____

9. List the product and/or services distributed by the worker (for example, meat, vegetables, fruit, bakery products, beverages, or laundry or dry cleaning services). If more than one type of product and/or service is distributed, specify the principal one. _____

10. Does the worker sell life insurance full time? . . . . □ **Yes**   □ **No**
11. Does the worker sell other types of insurance for the firm? . . . . □ **Yes**   □ **No**
    If "Yes," enter the percentage of the worker's total working time spent in selling other types of insurance . . . . . _____ %
12. If the worker solicits orders from wholesalers, retailers, contractors, or operators of hotels, restaurants, or other similar establishments, enter the percentage of the worker's time spent in the solicitation . . . . _____ %
13. Is the merchandise purchased by the customers for resale or use in their business operations? . . . . □ **Yes**   □ **No**
    Describe the merchandise and state whether it is equipment installed on the customers' premises. _____

Sign Here ▶

Under penalties of perjury, I declare that I have examined this request, including accompanying documents, and to the best of my knowledge and belief, the facts presented are true, correct, and complete.

_____ Title ▶ _____ Date ▶ _____
Type or print name below signature.

Form **SS-8** (Rev. 5-2014)

Source: www.irs.gov/pub/irs-access/fss8_accessible.pdf.

Defining "Applicant"

Since federal regulations often require employers to track applicants on the basis of race, gender, and ethnicity, it is important to have a clear and consistent definition of who is an *applicant*. According to the EEOC's Uniform Guidelines on Employee Selection Procedures (UGESP), while the precise definition depends upon the employer's recruitment and selection procedures, in general it encompasses all individuals who indicate an interest in being considered for hiring, promotion, or other employment opportunities. This interest might be expressed by completing a written application form or by expressing interest orally, depending upon the employer's practice.

However, technology has changed the way people apply for jobs and also has raised questions about who is an applicant in the Internet age. Specific guidance was issued by the U.S. Department of Labor's Office of Federal Contract Compliance Programs through its "Internet Applicant" rule and record-keeping requirements.

According to the OFCCP, there are four criteria that define an Internet applicant (note that the OFCCP rules only apply to federal contractors):

1. The individual submits an *expression of interest* in *employment through the Internet or related electronic data technologies.*
2. The employer *considers* the individual for employment in a particular position.
3. The individual's expression of interest indicates the individual possesses the *basic qualifications* for the position.
4. The individual *does not remove* himself from the selection process at any time prior to receiving an offer or otherwise indicate that he is *no longer interested in the position.*

Considering the above standards, an email inquiry about a job does not qualify the sender as an applicant, nor does posting a résumé on a third-party job board. Where an individual does satisfy all four of the above criteria, the Internet Applicant Rule stipulates specific records that federal contractors must maintain about hiring that is done through use of the Internet (or other technologies).[50]

The Definition of "Employer"

LO5 Articulate the various ways in which the concept "employer" is defined by the various employment-related regulations.

While *employees* are hard to define, courts and regulatory agencies have not experienced great difficulty in defining the term *employer.* Depending on the applicable statute or provision, an *employer* is simply one who employs or uses others to do her or his work or to work on her or his behalf. Most statutes specifically include in this definition employment agencies, labor organizations, and joint labor–management committees.

Issues may arise where an entity claims to be a private membership club (exempt from Title VII prohibitions) or a multinational company that may or may not be subject to application of various U.S. laws. A determination also must be made whether the employer receives federal funds or maintains federal contracts for coverage under the Rehabilitation Act of 1973, among others.

Another question is whether an individual, such as a supervisor, is also considered an employer under employment-related statutes and, therefore, can be held personally liable for her or his actions. Though most statutes are silent on the issue, the majority of courts have concluded that federal antidiscrimination statutes do *not* permit the imposition of this liability.

Scenario

Therefore, in this chapter's Scenario 2, Soraya would not be able to sustain her case through the EEOC against Raphael. The court would instead find that her only cause of action would be against her employer, III. Since, in this scenario, III has a system, investigated Soraya's complaint promptly, and then took swift and decisive action against Raphael, employer III is not liable for his harassment of Soraya. Basically, an employee is entitled to an appropriate response by the employer to solve the problem, what the courts call "considerable recompense, albeit not in monetary form." In the case on which this scenario is based, the court helpfully explained the rationale for this limitation:

She has an employer who was sensitive and responsive to her complaint. She can take comfort in the knowledge that she continues to work for this company, while her harasser does not—and that the company's prompt action is likely to discourage other would-be harassers. This is precisely the result Title VII was meant to achieve.[51]

The most exacting issue is usually how many employees an employer must have in order to be subject to a given statute. It is crucial for employers to be familiar with the statutes to which they are subject and those from which they are immune. (See Exhibit 1.6 for an overview of the various statutory definitions of employer.)

Exhibit 1.6 *Statutory Definitions of Employer*

The Civil Rights Act of 1866
- **Purpose:** Regulates the actions of all individuals or entities when entering into a contract to employ someone else.
- **Definition of Employer:** No requirement for a minimum number of employees in order to qualify as an employer under the CRA of 1866.
- **Other:** The Civil Rights Act of 1991 added a section to the CRA of 1866 to cover actions by the employer after the contract has been formed, including discrimination during employment or termination.

Title VII of the Civil Rights Act of 1964
- **Purpose:** Prohibits discrimination in employment based on specified protected classes.
- **Definition of Employer:** Applies to all firms or their agents engaged in an industry affecting commerce that employ 15 or more employees for each working day in each of 20 or more weeks in the current or preceding calendar year.[1]

- **Exemptions:** Government-owned corporations, Indian tribes, and bona fide private membership clubs.

Title VI of the Civil Rights Act of 1964
- **Purpose:** Applies the race, color, and national origin proscriptions of Title VII to any program or activity that receives federal financial assistance. Unless it falls within one of several exemptions, a government contractor is also prohibited from discriminating on the bases of race, color, religion, gender, or national origin by Executive Order 11246.[2]
- **Definition of Employer:** Any government agency that receives federal funding.

Age Discrimination in Employment Act of 1967
- **Purpose:** Prohibits discrimination in employment against anyone over the age of 40.
- **Definition of Employer:** Applies to all entities or their agents that employ 20 or more employees on each working day for 20 or more weeks during the current or preceding calendar year.

[1]"Working day" is generally computed by counting the number of employees maintained on the payroll in a given week, as opposed to the number of employees who work on any one day. This calculation provides for a more expansive definition of "employer" since it includes hourly and part-time workers. *Walters v. Metropolitan Educational Enterprises, Inc.,* 72 FEP Cases (BNA) 1211 (1997). Note, however, that this form of calculation is merely the majority approach; other courts have found that part-time employees who work for any part of each day of the workweek should be counted, while part-time employees who work full days for only a portion of the workweek should not be counted.

[2]The order exempts (1) employers with contracts of less than $10,000 from the requirement to include an equal employment opportunity clause in each of their contracts; (2) contracts for work performed outside the United States by employees not recruited within the United States; (3) contracts with state and local governments by providing that the EEO requirements do not apply to any agency of that government that is not participating in the work of the contract; (4) religious educational institutions that hire only people of that religion; (5) preferences offered to Native Americans living on or near a reservation in connection with employment on or near the reservation; and (6) certain contracts on the basis of national interest or security reasons.

continued

Exhibit 1.6 *continued*

- **Exemptions:** American employers who control foreign firms where compliance with the ADEA in connection with an American employee would cause the foreign firm to violate the laws of the country in which it is located. The ADEA, unlike Title VII, does *not* exempt Indian tribes or private membership clubs.

Title I of the Americans with Disabilities Act of 1990
- **Purpose:** Prohibits discrimination in employment against otherwise qualified individuals with disabilities who cannot perform the essential functions of their jobs, with or without reasonable accommodations.
- **Definition of Employer:** The Americans with Disabilities Act (ADA) applies to all employers engaged in interstate commerce with 15 or more workers, including state and local government employers, employment agencies, labor unions, and joint labor–management committees.
- **Exemptions:** Executive agencies of the U.S. government are exempted from the ADA, but these agencies are covered instead by similar nondiscrimination requirements and additional affirmative employment requirements under section 501 of the Rehabilitation Act of 1973 (see below). Also exempted from the ADA, similar to Title VII, are corporations fully owned by the U.S. government, Indian tribes, and bona fide private membership clubs that are not labor organizations and that are exempt from taxation under the Internal Revenue Code. Religious organizations are covered by the ADA, but they may give employment preference to people of their own religion or religious organization.

The Fair Labor Standards Act of 1938
- **Purpose:** Mandates wages, hours, and ages for employment in the United States, among other labor standards.

- **Definition of Employer:** Offers coverage to workers not necessarily based on a particular definition of "employer" but on two distinct forms of coverage: "enterprise coverage" and "individual coverage." *Enterprise coverage* refers to the protections offered to employees who work for certain businesses or organizations (i.e., "enterprises") that have at least two employees and do at least $500,000 a year in business or that are involved in certain specified industries such as hospitals, businesses providing medical or nursing care for residents, schools and preschools, and government agencies. *Individual coverage* refers to the protections offered to employees if their work regularly involves them in commerce between states ("interstate commerce"). The FLSA provides coverage, even when there is no enterprise coverage, to workers who are "engaged in commerce or in the production of goods for commerce." This coverage may include workers who produce goods that will be sent out of state, who regularly make telephone calls as part of their job to persons located in other states, or who travel to other states for their jobs. Also, domestic service workers (such as housekeepers, full-time babysitters, and cooks) are normally covered by the law.

The Rehabilitation Act of 1973
- **Purpose:** Prohibits covered agencies from discriminating against otherwise qualified disabled individuals, similar to the ADA.
- **Definition of Employer:** Applies not only to all entities, programs, and activities that receive federal funds and to government contractors but also to all programs and activities of any executive agency as well as the U.S. Postal Service. A covered federal contractor is one who maintains a contract with the federal government in excess of $10,000 annually for the provision of personal property or nonpersonal services.

The "Freedom" to Contract in the Regulatory Employment Environment

In the age of increasingly complex regulations governing the workplace, the relationship between employer and employee essentially is still based on an agreement. As you will see throughout this text, terms and conditions of employment may be subject to regulation or open to contractual negotiation and either expressed or implied. Though an employer is generally free to design contract terms of any kind, the terms and conditions set by an employer cannot violate the letter or the spirit of the applicable laws we have discussed or will discuss in chapters to come.

In addition, you will learn that courts and legislatures sometimes determine that certain types of agreements between employer and employee are *unenforceable.* The focus of our discussion, therefore, is how the employment relationship is regulated, in general.

Covenants Not to Compete (Non-Compete Agreements)

LO6 Describe the permissible parameters of non-compete agreements.

non-compete agreement (or covenant not to compete)
An agreement signed by the employee agreeing not to disclose the employer's confidential information or enter into competition with the employer for a specified period of time and/or within a specified region.

One employment constraint that has received varying degrees of acceptance by different states is the **covenant not to compete** or **non-compete agreement**. While individuals in positions of trust and confidence already owe a duty of loyalty to their employers during employment, even without a non-compete agreement, a non-compete agreement usually includes prohibitions against disclosure of trade secrets, soliciting the employer's employees or customers, or entering into competition with the employer if the employee is terminated.

Non-compete agreements are pervasive in U.S workplaces. At least 27 percent of the private sector workforce in 2019 is subject to non-competes (130 million workers), compared with 18 percent in 2014.[52]

In 2018, the Workforce Mobility Act (WMA) was introduced in the U.S. Senate and the U.S. House of Representatives. However, since it was not enacted by January 2019, it failed in Congress. If it had passed, it would have abolished covenants not to compete nationwide and also would have provided the Department of Labor (DOL) with broad enforcement power. If it is reintroduced and enacted, the legislation will empower the DOL to enforce the ban through fines on employers who either fail to notify employees that non-compete agreements are illegal or who require employees to sign covenants not to compete.[53] While this act did not make it out of the Senate, Florida Senator Mark Rubio introduced the Freedom to Compete Act in January 2019, which continued to be considered at time of publication. In addition, currently all states allow employers *some* level of control over the extent to which an employer can restrict a former employee from competing.

States vary widely, from explicitly permitting non-compete agreements to permitting agreements under certain circumstances to strictly prohibiting agreements that limit for whom a former employee can work and where he or she can work. Notably, California, Colorado, Idaho, Massachusetts, Montana, North Dakota, Oklahoma, and Utah severely *restrict* the use of non-competes in their entirety.[54] Bills pending in the Vermont and New Jersey legislatures would generally ban non-competes (with limited exceptions). The Vermont bill would only permit non-competes in the context of the sale of a business or dissolution of a partnership or interest in a limited liability company.[55] Meanwhile, Georgia voters enacted a state constitutional amendment specifically expanding the enforcement of reasonable non-competes in order to make that state more economically attractive to business.[56]

In some states, certain professions are exempted from prohibitions against non-competes. For example, in certain states, prior employers can enforce non-competes against "management personnel," while they may not enforce the agreements against other types of workers; some regions instead specifically exempt security guards and physicians. In many states, an employer may restrict a past employee based on location, the length of time, and the type of work she or he may conduct, as long as the restrictions are reasonable and necessary to protect a business interest.[57] Some states restrict non-compete clauses for entire industries. For example, in 2018, Utah modified its laws to limit the enforcement of non-competes against employees in the broadcasting industry. If an employer seeks to enforce a non-compete against an employee in the broadcasting industry, the employer must confirm that (1) the employee is paid a salary of at least $913 per week, (2) the non-compete provision was part of a written employment agreement, and (3) the employee must have been terminated for cause or must have breached the employment agreement to result in termination.[58] Because of these state-by-state differences, it is critical to have **forum selection clauses** in contracts that stipulate the state law that will apply to the contract in question.

forum selection clauses
A clause in a contract that identifies the state law that will apply to any disputes that arise under the contract.

But how do you know what will be considered *reasonable* restrictions on an employee's ability to compete after the employment relationship has ended? The common law generally *prohibits* the restriction if it is more broad than necessary to protect the employer's legitimate interests or if the employer's need is outweighed by the hardship to the employee and likely injury to the public.[59] Employees also are sometimes prohibited from entering into non-compete agreements with certain groups of people, such as low-income earners. Illinois prohibits non-competes with "low-wage" employees, and there is legislation in New York City that seeks to do the same.[60] (See Exhibit 1.7, "Low-Wage Employees.")

To determine reasonableness, courts look to the location and time limitations placed on the employee's ability to compete. The definition of competition under the non-compete agreement is also relevant: Is the employee prohibited from working in any capacity with a competitor or merely restricted from entering into direct competition with the employer? Restrictions that are for an indefinite period of time or that prohibit the employee from working "anywhere in the United States" would likely be considered unreasonable. However, as an example, restricting an employee from engaging in direct competition with the employer for one year from the end of their employment relationship within the same county may be considered reasonable. Generally, in order to be considered reasonable, the restrictive covenant should not prevent the employee from earning a living of any sort under its terms.

Exhibit 1.7 *Low-Wage Employees*

The Illinois Freedom to Work Act went into force on January 1, 2017. The act bars certain Illinois employers from entering into non-compete agreements with "low-wage employees." The act defines a low-wage employee as a person who earns less than $13.01 per hour. If the federal, state, or local minimum wage is raised above $13.01, then the act applies to any person earning the minimum wage. The act prohibits employers from entering into non-competition clauses that would restrict low-wage employees from performing:

1. Any work for another employer for a specified period of time;
2. Any work in a specified geographical area; or
3. Work for another employer that is similar to such low-wage employee's work for the employer included as party to the agreement.

Source: Illinois Freedom to Work Act, 820 Ill. Comp. Stat. Ann. 90.

Scenario

It is generally accepted that a valid restrictive covenant will meet the following qualifications:

1. It protects a legitimate business interest.
2. It is ancillary to a legitimate business relationship.
3. It provides a benefit to both the employee and employer.
4. It is reasonable in scope and duration.
5. It is not contrary to the public interest.[61]

Consider the example of the rental space company WeWork, headquartered in New York. WeWork tried to enforce a very broad non-compete clause against its 3,300 employees nationwide.[62] WeWork used non-compete agreements that prohibited all employees from working for competitors after leaving the company, regardless of job duties, knowledge of confidential information, or compensation. The agreement applied not only to executive and senior staff but also to all levels of employees. After an investigation and threat of litigation by both the New York Attorney General's and the Illinois Attorney General's offices, WeWork agreed torelease over 1,400 rank-and-file employees nationwide from non-competes. These 1,400 employees included cleaners, mail associates, executive assistants, baristas, and more, some of whom were paid as little as $15 an hour. Another nearly 1,800 employees, composed of employees who were community leads, community managers, interior designers, architects, senior software engineers, and others, had their previous non-competes replaced with far less restrictive terms. These terms included a non-compete period shortened from one year to six months after employment ends; a dramatically smaller geographic restriction, from any geographic areas in which WeWork operated to just a 15-mile radius of only those WeWork locations engaged in the business lines in which the employee worked; and a much more narrowly defined scope of competition, limiting the ban to the specific business lines in which the employee worked.[63]

Management Tips *Additional Considerations*

- Always evaluate the status of your workers; do not assume employee or independent-contractor status for any worker.
- Employment status is relevant to employer payroll and other financial issues; therefore, misclassification may be costly to the employer.
- While an employer is not liable to independent contractors for discrimination based on Title VII, the independent contractor may have other causes of action. Therefore, hiring an independent contractor is not a safe harbor from liability.
- Monitor staffing firms with which you contract for temporary or other contingent workers to ensure that the workers are being properly paid and that the firm provides workers' compensation coverage.
- Since statements in an employment policy manual may be construed in some circumstances as contractual promises, review all documentation as if you will be bound to it as a contract.
- Draft non-compete agreements that strive toward reasonableness. Reasonableness requires a balance among the business interests that you seek to protect, employee interests, and the public's interest as well as a balance between a restraint that is not overly harsh or oppressive to the employee and no more broad than necessary to protect the company's legitimate interests.

A lesson learned from WeWork applies to all employers considering the use of non-compete agreements: reasonableness is measured by the realities of the industry and the nature of the employee's occupation.

As mentioned above, covenants not to compete sometimes also include provisions with regard to trade secrets or confidentiality with regard to other elements of employer intellectual property. This property might also include, for instance, customer relations and goodwill, specialized training, or particular skills unique to the workplace. The agreement often depends on what an employer considers to be trade secrets versus information in the public domain or commonly known in an industry. Confidential customer lists or customer preferences are often the source of trouble since they are usually maintained by individual workers based on professional relationships; however, most courts deem them property of the employer. Pricing, revenue, and other projections and marketing strategies are also commonly considered to be trade secrets. On the other hand, processes that are known by many in a particular industry and other information that is otherwise available through external sources are not considered to be company property. Note that customer lists, if accessible through public means, would therefore no longer fall under the rubric of trade secrets.

inevitable disclosure
Theory under which a court may prohibit a former employee from working for an employer's competitor if the employer can show that it is inevitable that the former employee will disclose a trade secret by virtue of her or his position.

Under the theory of **inevitable disclosure**, employers are protected against disclosure of trade secrets even if no non-compete applies. A court may prohibit a former employee from working for an employer's competitor if the employer can show that there is imminent threat that a trade secret will be shared. The courts look to (1) whether the employee's knowledge is exceptionally specialized and technical, (2) which would give either business (former or new) a significant advantage in the market, and (3) whether the employee could perform her or his work without it. It might be highly unlikely, if not impossible, in some instances for some of these workers to conduct their work without disclosing the trade secret.

In one of the landmark cases in the area, for instance, Continental Aviation tried to purchase a very particular type of fuel injector pump from Allis-Chalmers, one of only three companies that marketed the pump in the world. When they were unable to reach terms, Continental instead simply hired the original designer of the pump from Allis-Chalmers to design the pump for Continental. In finding inevitable disclosure and imposing an injunction that prohibited the engineer from working at Continental, the court pointed out the "virtual impossibility of Mr. Wolff [the engineer] performing all of his prospective duties for Continental to the best of his ability, without in effect giving it the benefit of Allis-Chalmers' confidential information."[64]

The Uniform Trade Secrets Act (UTSA) is a model act that strives to provide guidance to states developing statutes in this and other related areas; by 2019, 49 states and the District of Columbia had adopted its structure. New York is the only state that has not adopted the UTSA and relies on common law.[65] The UTSA provides relief in the form of monetary damages, attorney's fees, and injunctive relief for misappropriation of trade secrets and does include a provision for inevitable disclosure.

The Seventh Circuit's decision in *PepsiCo, Inc. v. Redmond*[66] is the seminal case to address inevitable disclosure after adoption of the UTSA. In that case, PepsiCo sought an injunction (a prohibition) against its employee, William Redmond, Jr., from accepting a position with a competitor, Quaker. Although Redmond had signed a confidentiality agreement relating to PepsiCo's financial goals and strategic planning, the court granted the injunction for a period of five months, concluding that "a plaintiff may prove a claim of trade secret misappropriation by demonstrating that [the] defendant's new employment will inevitably lead him to rely on the plaintiff's trade secrets."

After *PepsiCo,* the inevitable disclosure doctrine gained popularity; however, despite a workable standard presented by the Seventh Circuit, state applications of the doctrine have remained inconsistent.[67] While most states enforce it, some, like California, Kentucky, Maryland, and Massachusetts, have rejected inevitable disclosure as inconsistent with public policies favoring employee mobility.[68] Others, like Louisiana or Virginia, require actual or threatened disclosure of trade secrets or "bad faith" on behalf of the employee.[69]

Once a non-compete agreement has been found to be valid, in order to be enforceable, it must also be supported by consideration offered in a bargained-for exchange. In other words, the agreement by the employee not to compete with the employer is *only* enforceable if the employee also receives something in exchange for this agreement. Often, non-competes are signed at the time an employee is first hired, so the offer of employment on its own is considered sufficient consideration. However, if an employee is asked to sign a non-compete agreement after being hired and is not offered any additional consideration, some states do not treat continued at-will employment as sufficient.[70] It depends on the state in which the agreement is signed.[71]

Chapter Summary

- No matter the size of your organization, as long as you have hired one individual to work for you, you are considered an employer and potentially subject to numerous federal and other regulations as well as to wrongful termination liability.

- Why is the definition of "employee" important? The distinction between employees and independent contractors is crucial from a financial perspective. Because many regulations require different responsibilities from employers of employees and independent contractors, it is imperative that an employer be confident of the classification of its employees.

- How does an employer make the distinction between employees and independent contractors? The classification of employees may vary depending on the statute that is to be applied or on the court in which a given case is scheduled to be heard. However, the common thread is generally the right of the employer to control the actions of the worker. Where this is present, the worker is likely to be considered an employee. Other factors to be considered include those that are part of the economic realities test, which evaluates the economics of the employment situation. Finally, some workers may be classified statutorily as employees, making the distinction all the easier.

- Who is an "employer"? The definition of employer is generally agreed on. An employer is usually thought to be one who employs or uses others (either employees or independent contractors, or both) to do its work or to work on its behalf.

Chapter-End Questions

1. Grace Cathedral Church owns a for-profit restaurant in Ohio called Cathedral Buffet. The buffet has both employees and volunteers that staff the restaurant. Volunteers perform many of the same restaurant-related tasks as employees: cleaning, washing dishes, serving cake, chopping vegetables, and manning the cash register. However, there is one meaningful distinction between employees and volunteers. Employees receive an hourly wage; volunteers do not. The pastor often announces before his Sunday sermon that the buffet is short-handed and needs more volunteers from the parish, claiming it is the "Lord's Buffet" and that church members who repeatedly refuse to volunteer at the restaurant are at risk of "blaspheming against the Holy Ghost." The pastor never promises any compensation. Restaurant managers work around volunteers' schedules, ensuring they are free during their assigned shifts. If you were the Sixth Circuit, would you find that the volunteers are employees or independent contractors? What variables would help you in reaching your decision? [*Acosta v. Cathedral Buffet, Inc.*, 892 F.3d 819 (6th Cir. 2018).]

2. A staffing firm provides landscaping services for clients on an ongoing basis. The staffing firm selects and pays the workers, provides health insurance, and withholds taxes. The firm provides the equipment and supplies necessary to do the work. It also supervises the workers on the clients' premises. Client A reserves the right to direct the staffing-firm workers to perform particular tasks at particular times or in a specified manner, although it does not generally exercise that authority. Client A evaluates the quality of the workers' performance and regularly reports its findings to the firm. It can require the firm to remove a worker from the job assignment if it is dissatisfied. Who is the employer of the workers?

3. Uber Technologies, Inc., develops, markets, and operates the Uber app. The app allows consumers to request an Uber driver to pick them up and drop them off at the nearest location. Uber drivers use their own personal cars and are viewed by Uber as independent contractors. Uber views the app as a conduit between the transportation providers and passengers. A passenger brought action against Uber after the Uber driver stabbed the passenger following an alteration. The passenger alleged that Uber was liable for negligent hiring, training, and supervision. Should Uber be held liable for the actions of its driver? What must the passenger prove to win this case? [*Search v. Uber Techs., Inc.,* 128 F. Supp. 3d 222 (D.D.C. 2015).]

4. Former student athletes at the University of Pennsylvania sued the university and also the National Collegiate Athletic Association (NCAA), alleging that they were employees entitled to a minimum wage under the Fair Labor Standards Act. Student participation in collegiate athletics is entirely voluntary, and the court pointed out the "long tradition of amateurism in college sports [which], by definition, shows that student athletes—like all amateur athletes—participate in their sports for reasons wholly unrelated to immediate compensation." The Seventh Circuit, along with several courts in the past, ruled that student athletes are not employees. What do you think? Given the extreme amount of required time in training, the large amount of money earned by the universities where the students play, the potential for injury, and perhaps other factors you might identify, make an argument that student athletes should be viewed as employees. [*Berger v. NCAA,* 162 F.Supp.3d 845 (2016).]

5. Sandwich shop chain Jimmy John's was investigated by the New York and Illinois Attorneys General Offices for forcing its employees to sign a non-compete agreement. The non-compete agreement prohibited workers from working at any other business that sells "submarine, hero-type, deli-style, pita, and/or wrapped or rolled sandwiches" within two miles of any Jimmy John's shop in the United States during their employment and for two years thereafter. Jimmy John's agreed to stop making its employees sign the agreements as part of a legal settlement. Illinois and New York are two states that seek to protect low-wage workers from non-compete clauses. Why do you think some states are particularly concerned for low-wage workers having to sign non-compete agreements? What are the strongest arguments in favor of employers, such as Jimmy John's and others, being permitted to enforce non-compete clauses such as these?[72]

6. Licensed taxicab drivers in Boston brought an action against cab companies, alleging that they were misclassified by the companies as independent contractors. The taxicab drivers alleged that they were deprived of minimum wages, overtime pay, tips, and the protections afforded by the Wage Act.

   In Boston, the police commissioner is given the task of creating a comprehensive system of rules and regulations governing the ownership, leasing, licensing, rate setting, and operation of taxicabs in the city. In order for a qualifying taxicab to be put into service, the owner must obtain a license, called a "medallion," for each such taxicab. There are myriad requirements that must be met in order to qualify for a medallion, including being deemed "suitable" individuals by the city's inspector of carriages, obtaining adequate garage facilities within the city, and maintaining membership in an approved dispatch service or radio association, which provides 24-hour two-way communication solely and exclusively for Boston taxicabs. The radio associations, in turn, are required to provide certain enumerated dispatch services to their members and may accept payment for those services only from medallion owners.

Licensed taxicab drivers leased taxicabs and medallions from the medallion owners at flat rates, which are set by the commissioner. The contracts for leasing the taxicabs and medallions included an optional "Independent Contractor" clause, which states that the lessee is free from the control of the lessor and is not required to remit to the lessor any funds received in connection with the taxicab's operation. In 2012, licensed taxicab drivers who had signed the Independent Contractor clause filed a complaint against the cab companies, alleging that they were improperly classified as independent contractors. Should the taxicab drivers be classified as independent contractors? [*Sebago v. Boston Cab Dispatch, Inc.,* 471 Mass. 321 (2015).]

7. Twenty-five former student registered nurse anesthetists ("SRNAs") who attended a master's degree program at Wolford College, LLC, were required to participate in a clinical curriculum, which, under Florida law, was a prerequisite to obtaining their master's degrees. The students had to participate in a minimum of 550 clinical cases in a variety of surgical procedures. The patients with whom these students worked paid the hospitals or clinics for these surgical services through their health insurance or out of pocket. The students received none of that money. The students sued to receive unpaid wages and overtime under the Fair Labor Standards Act for their clinical hours. The Eleventh Circuit found it appropriate to "focus on the benefits to the student while still considering whether the manner in which the employer implements the internship program takes unfair advantage of or is otherwise abusive towards the students." Do you think the student interns were employees entitled to wages? Do you think there are scenarios where interns should *not* be entitled to wages? If the court does find that these students are entitled to wages, who then is liable: the university or the clinics? [*Schumann v. Collier Anesthesia, P.A.,* 803 F.3d 1199, 1209-12 (11th Cir. 2015).]

8. Arman was hired to drive an airport shuttle for a rental car company back and forth from the airport to the rental car company's off-site parking lot. When Arman was hired, he signed a written contract that stated specifically that he was an independent contractor. He was paid every two weeks, based on a rate per mile plus an hourly rate for waiting time. He drove the shuttle at times and to locations directed by the rental car company and was on call 24 hours a day. Was Arman an employee or an independent contractor?

9. Anthony and Philip Conway founded and operated Rochester Medical Corporation (RMC), a publicly traded medical-device company. C.R. Bard, Inc. (Bard) offered to purchase RMC at a very attractive price. Bard insisted, however, that the Conways had to sign five-year non-compete agreements. The Conways reluctantly agreed to sign the non-compete agreements, and Bard purchased RMC at the agreed-upon price. The Conways were paid tens of millions of dollars for their stock and other interests in RMC. The Conways began experiencing sellers' remorse, however, over the fact that although they had been required to sign non-compete agreements for the deal to go forward, the per-share price that they received for their stock was the same as the per-share price received by the other stockholders. The Conways filed suit, alleging that the non-compete agreements are unenforceable. Is the non-compete agreement enforceable? Do you think the non-compete was reasonable? Why or why not? [*Conway v. C.R. Bard, Inc.,* 76 F. Supp. 3d 826, 827 (D. Minn. 2015).]

10. Freedom Medical, a medical equipment company, sought an injunction to prevent three former executives and sales representatives from working for one of Freedom Medical's competitors, Med One. To maintain a competitive advantage in the health care industry, Freedom Medical developed confidential and proprietary pricing information, business plans,

and customer lists that all three former executives had access to in their former positions. Freedom Medical takes several affirmative steps to safeguard this confidential information. First, Freedom Medical requires all employees to acknowledge and agree to comply with an acceptable use policy that restricts the use of digitally stored confidential information. Second, Freedom Medical requires all employees with access to confidential information to sign restrictive covenants at the inception of their employment. The restrictive covenants prohibit unauthorized use or disclosure of confidential information. Furthermore, the restrictive covenants contain a global non-compete clause that prohibits employees from working for any competitor for a one-year period following the end of employment with Freedom Medical. All three former executives were hired as sales representatives for Med One, and two of the three stayed in the same geographic territory in which they previously worked for Freedom Medical. Freedom Medical has filed an injunction to stop them from working for Med One. Should the court issue the injunction? If so, for how long, and should there be any other restrictions? [*Freedom Med. Inc v. Whitman,* 343 F. Supp. 3d 509 (E.D. Pa. 2018).]

End Notes

1. *T-Mobile USA Inc. v. NLRB,* 5th Circuit, No. 16-60284 (July 25, 2017).
2. Foley, R., "Emails Show Iowa Official's Tupac Fixation before His Ouster," *Associated Press* (July 16, 2019), https://www.apnews.com/c7ae931fae0f4bc1a0fe3386e4b5bc38 (accessed July 24, 2019).
3. *Yuknis v. First Student, Inc.* 481 F.3d 552 (7th Cir. 2007).
4. Crosby, I.,"Avoid Misclassification Quagmires by Understanding Differences between Contractors and Employees," *Insights–DLA Piper Global Law Firm* (April 23, 2018), https://www.dlapiper.com/en/us/insights/publications/2018/04/avoid-misclassification-quagmires-by-understanding-differences-between-contractors-and-employees/ (accessed August 6, 2019).
5. 29 U.S.C.A. § 1002.
6. *Nationwide Mut. Ins. Co. v. Darden,* 503 U.S. 318 (U.S. 1992).
7. *Hughes v. Twenty-First Century Fox, Inc.,* et al., No. 1:2017cv07093–Document 60 (S.D.N.Y. 2018).
8. *N. Pointe Ins. Co. v. KB Home Jacksonville, LLC*, 2017 U.S. Dist. LEXIS 186574.
9. 26 U.S. Code § 3509.
10. Yatcilla , C., "How This IRS Program Can Help You with Employee Misclassification Penalties," *Prime Pay* (June 8, 2018), https://primepay.com/blog/how-irs-program-can-help-you-employee-misclassification-penalties (accessed March 19, 2019).
11. U.S. Department of Labor, "Virginia Direct Mail Company Pays $743,443 in Back Wages, Damages and Penalties Following U.S. Department of Labor Investigation" (2018), https://www.dol.gov/newsroom/releases/whd/whd20180817 (accessed August 6, 2019).
12. Wage and Hour Division (WHD), "Misclassification of Employees as Independent Contractors," U.S. Department of Labor, https://www.dol.gov/whd/workers/misclassification/ (accessed June 10, 2017).
13. U.S. Department of Labor, "State Enforcement and Outreach Coordination" (n.d.), https://www.dol.gov/whd/state/statecoordination.htm (accessed March 19, 2019).
14. Congress.gov, "H.R. 6189–Payroll Fraud Prevention Act of 2018," 115th Congress (2017–2018) (June 21, 2018), https://www.congress.gov/bill/115th-congress/house-bill/6189/text (accessed March 18, 2019).
15. Coalition to Promote Independent Entrepreneurs, "State Misclassification Task Forces" (2019), https://iccoalition.org/state-misclassification-task-forces/ (accessed August 6, 2019).

16. Colorado Department of Labor and Employment, "Task Force Report Pursuant to Executive Order B 2018-3 (Joint Enforcement Task Force on Payroll Fraud and Employee Misclassification in the Construction Industry)"(November 30, 2018), https://www.colorado.gov/pacific/sites/default/files/2018%20Final%20Report% 20-%20Carpenters.pdf (accessed August 6, 2019).

17. Louisiana Workforce Commission–Department of Labor,"Task Force Says 'GAME ON' in Fight to Stop Misclassifying Workers" (October 25, 2017), http://www.laworks.net/ PublicRelations/PR_PressReleaseDetails.asp?SeqNo=2169&Year=2017&Month=10 (accessed August 6, 2019).

18. U.S. Government Accountability Office, " EMPLOYMENT TAXES: Timely Use of National Research Program Results Would Help IRS Improve Compliance and Tax Gap Estimates, " (April 18, 2017), https://www.gao.gov/products/GAO-17-371 (accessed August 7, 2019).

19. Capece, M. "Size and Cost of Payroll Fraud: Survey of National and State Studies," Chicago Regional Council of Regional Council of Carpenters (November 14, 2016), https://www.carpentersunion.org/news/size-and-cost-payroll-fraud-survey-national-and-state-studies#_ftn16 (accessed August 7, 2019).

20. National Conference of State Legislatures,"Employee Misclassification," http://www.ncsl.org/research/labor-and-employment/employee-misclassification-resources.aspx#state (accessed August 7, 2019).

21. Sinroja, R., Thomason, S. and Jacobs, K., "Misclassification in California: A Snapshot of the Janitorial Services, Construction, and Trucking Industries," *Berkeley Center for Labor Research and Education* (March 11, 2019), http://laborcenter.berkeley.edu/misclassification-in-california-a-snapshot-of-the-janitorial-services-construction-and-trucking-industries/ (accessed August 7, 2019).

22. See IRS, "Voluntary Classification Settlement Program" (September 14, 2016), https://www.irs.gov/businesses/small-businesses-self-employed/voluntary-classification-settlement-program-vcsp-frequently-asked-questions (accessed August 7, 2019).

23. 318 N.C. 577, 350 S.E.2d 83 (1986).

24. See U.S. Social Security Administration, "How to Apply the Common Law Control Test in Determining an Employer/Employee Relationship," https://www.ssa.gov/section218training/advanced_course_10.htm (accessed June 25, 2020).

25. See Joint Committee on Taxation, "Present Law and Background Relating to Worker Classification for Federal Tax Purposes, IRS" (May 8, 2007), https://www.irs.gov/pub/irs-utl/x-26-07.pdf (accessed August 7, 2019).

26. See U.S. Department of Labor, "Fair Labor Standards Act Advisor: Independent Contractors," https://webapps.dol.gov/elaws/whd/flsa/docs/contractors.asp (accessed August 7, 2019).

27. *Murray v. Principal Financial Group, Inc., et al.,* 613 F.3d 943 (9th Cir. 2010).

28. *Dynamex Operations W. v. Superior Court,* 4 Cal. 5th 903 (Cal. 2018), http://www.courts.ca.gov/opinions/archive/S222732.PDF. See also Kappel, M., "The End of an Era? How the ABC Test Could Affect Your Use of Independent Contractors," *Forbes* (August 8, 2018), https://www.forbes.com/sites/mikekappel/2018/08/08/the-end-of-an-era-how-the-abc-test-could-affect-your-use-of-independent-contractors/ (accessed March 19, 2019).

29. 64 Cal. Rptr. 3d 327 (2007).

30. *FedEx Home Delivery v. NLRB,* 563 F.3d 492 (D.C. Cir. 2009).

31. 367 NLRB No. 75 (2019).

32. Department of Treasury, Internal Revenue Service, "Employee or Independent Contractor?" *Training* 3320-102 (July 1996), http://www.sjsu.edu/people/annette.nellen/website/IRS_TrainingMaterials_ECorEmployee_1996.pdf (accessed August 7, 2019).

33. 717 F.3d 431, 435 (5th Cir. 2013).

34. See *Bittermann v. Zinke,* 371 F. Supp. 3d 974 (D.N.M, 2019).

35. *Dynamex Operations W. v. Superior Court,* 4 Cal. 5th 903 (Cal. 2018), http://www.courts.ca.gov/opinions/archive/S222732.pdf.

36. Myers, J., et al., "Newsom Signs Bill Rewriting California Employment Law, Limiting Use of Independent Contractors," *LA Times* (September 18, 2019), https://www.latimes.com/california/story/2019-09-18/gavin-newsom-signs-ab5-employees0independent-contractors-california (accessed September 20, 2019).

37. See "EEOC Enforcement Guidance on Application of EEO Laws to Contingent Workers Placed by Temporary Employment Agencies and Other Staffing Firms," *EEOC Enforcement Guidance* (January 23, 2001), https://www.eeoc.gov/policy/docs/guidance-contingent.html (accessed August 8, 2019).

38. Deloitte Insights, "2018 Global Human Capital Trends," (2018), https://www2.deloitte.com/insights/us/en/focus/human-capital-trends/2018.html (accessed August 7, 2019).

39. Somerville, H., "Uber to Pay $20 Million to Settle Long-Running Legal Battle with Drivers," *Reuters* (March 12, 2019), https://www.reuters.com/article/us-uber-classaction/uber-to-pay-20-million-to-settle-long-running-legal-battle-with-drivers-idUSKBN1QT27Z (accessed August 7, 2019).

40. Ruiz-Grossman, S., "California Lawmakers Pass Bill That Could Upend Uber, Lyft Model," *HuffPost* (September 11, 2019), https://www.huffpost.com/entry/california-bill-gig-economy-uber-lyft_n_5d684281e4b06beb649b7d48 (accessed December 31, 2019).

41. Ruiz-Grossman, S., "Uber, Postmates Sue California over New Gig Economy Law," *HuffPost* (December 30, 2019), https://www.huffpost.com/entry/uber-postmates-california-lawsuit-ab-5_n_5e0aafafe4b0843d360b1f92?ncid=engmodushpmg00000006 (accessed December 31, 2019).

42. Miller, D., "NBCUniversal to Settle Suit by Former Interns for $6.4 Million," *Los Angles Times* (October 24, 2014), https://www.latimes.com/entertainment/envelope/cotown/la-et-ct-nbc-interns-lawsuit-settlement-20141024-story.html (accessed August 8, 2019).

43. Taube, A., "Condé Nast Settled Its Unpaid Internship Lawsuit—Here's How Much Each Intern Gets," *Business Insider* (November 14, 2014), https://www.businessinsider.com/conde-nast-settles-unpaid-intern-lawsuit-2014-11 (accessed August 8, 2019).

44. 791 F.3d 376 (2d Cir. 2015).

45. U.S. Department of Labor, "Fair Labor Standards Act Advisor-Volunteers," https://webapps.dol.gov/elaws/whd/flsa/docs/volunteers.asp (accessed August 8, 2019).

46. *Salinas v. Commercial Interiors, Inc.,* 848 F.3d 125 (4th Cir. 2017).

47. Ibid., at 141.

48. 365 NLRB No. 156.

49. See *Ling Nan Zheng v. Liberty Apparel Co.,* 617 F.3d 182 (2d Cir. 2010).

50. U.S. Department of Labor, "Internet Applicant Recordkeeping Rule" (n.d.), https://www.dol.gov/ofccp/regs/compliance/faqs/iappfaqs.htm (accessed March 19, 2019).

51. *Williams v. Banning,* 72 F.3d 552 (7th Cir. 1995).

52. Colvin, A. J. S., and H. Shierholz, "Noncompete Agreements," Economic Policy Institute (December 10, 2019), https://www.epi.org/publication/noncompete-agreements/ (accessed December 16, 2019).

53. Weibust, E., and A. Dunne, "Democratic U.S. Senators Seek to Abolish Non-Compete Agreements," Trading Secrets: A Law Blog on Trade Secrets, Non-Competes, and Computer Fraud (May 2, 2018), https://www.tradesecretslaw.com/2018/05/articles/legislation-2/democratic-u-s-senators-seek-to-abolish-non-compete-agreements/ (accessed August 8, 2019).

54. Seyfarth and Shaw, "50 State Desktop Reference What Businesses Need to Know about Non-Compete and Trade Secrets Law," (2017–2018), https://www.seyfarth.com/dir_docs/publications/50-State-Desktop-Reference-(2017-2018).pdf (accessed August 8, 2019); Harwath, A., "New Massachusetts Law Limits Non-Competes," Labor and Employment Law Blog (August 13, 2018), https://www.laboremploymentlawblog.com/2018/08/articles/non-competition-covenants/new-massachusetts-law-limits-non-compete/ (accessed August 8, 2019).

55. Curry, J., "The New Landscape for Non-Compete Law in 2019 and Beyond," *Baker and Donaldson* (March 13, 2019), https://www.bakerdonelson.com/the-new-landscape-for-non-compete-law-in-2019-and-beyond (accessed August 9, 2019).

56. Georgia Employment Contract Enforcement, Amendment 1 (November 2, 2010), http://www.ballotpedia.org/wiki/index.php/Georgia_Employment_Contract_Enforcement,_Amendment_1_%282010%29 (accessed August 8, 2019). For a state-by-state update, please see https://www.faircompetitionlaw.com/2019/04/22/new-trade-secret-and-noncompete-legislation-whats-already-happened-and-what-you-can-expect-for-the-rest-of-the-year-in-every-state/ (April 22, 2019, accessed October 31, 2019).

57. Legal Nature, "Are Non-Compete Agreements Enforceable in My State?" (2018), https://help.legalnature.com/articles/are-non-compete-agreements-enforceable-in-my-state#title1 (accessed August 9, 2019).

58. Fabian, S., "Utah and Idaho Limit Non-Competes and Vermont and Pennsylvania Work to Ban Them," *Sheppard Mullin: Labor and Employment Blog* (May 9, 2018), https://www.laboremploymentlawblog.com/2018/05/articles/non-competition-covenants/utah-idaho-limit-non-compete/ (accessed August 9, 2019).

59. Restatement (Second) of Contracts.

60. Curry, J., "The New Landscape for Non-Compete Law in 2019 and Beyond," *Baker and Donaldson* (March 13, 2019), https://www.bakerdonelson.com/the-new-landscape-for-non-compete-law-in-2019-and-beyond (accessed August 9, 2019).

61. Martucci, W., and J. Place, "Covenants Not to Compete," *Employment Relations Today* 21 (1998), pp. 77–83.

62. Fleishman, G., "WeWork Settles with New York, Drops Broad Employee Non-Compete Clauses," *Fortune* (September 18, 2018), https://fortune.com/2018/09/18/wework-drops-noncompete-settlement/ (accessed December 10, 2019).

63. Attorney General's Press Office, "A.G. Underwood Announces Settlement with WeWork to End Use of Overly Broad Non-Competes That Restricted Workers'Ability to TakeNewJobs," Letita James, NY Attorney General (September 18, 2018), https://ag.ny.gov/press-release/ag-underwood-announces-settlement-wework-end-use-overly-broad-non-competes-restricted (accessed August 9. 2019).

64. 255 F. Supp. 645 (E.D. Mich, 1966).

65. "Trade Secrets Act," Uniform Law Commission (2019), https://www.uniformlaws.org/committees/community-home?CommunityKey=3a2538fb-e030-4e2d-a9e2-90373dc05792 (accessed August 9, 2019).

66. 54 F.3d 1262 (7th Cir. 1995).

67. Flowers, M., "Facing the Inevitable: The Inevitable Disclosure Doctrine and the Defend Trade Secrets Act of 2016," 75 Wash. & Lee L. Rev. 2207 (2019), https://scholarlycommons. law.wlu.edu/cgi/viewcontent.cgi?article=4631&context=wlulr (accessed August 9, 2019).

68. *Id.* at 2223; see *Whyte v. Schlage Lock Co.,* 101 Cal. App. 4th 1443, 1447 (2002) and discussion infra note 105–108 (discussing California's outright rejection of the inevitable disclosure doctrine because of its impact on labor mobility).

69. Wiesner, Ryan M., "A State-by-State Analysis of Inevitable Disclosure: A Need for Uniformity and a Workable Standard," *Marquette Intellectual Property Law Review* 16, no. 1 (2012).

70. See *Allyis, Inc. v. Schroder,* 2017 Wash. App. LEXIS 490.

71. Compare *Runzheimer Int'l, Ltd. v. Friedlen,* 862 N.W.2d 879, 881 (Wis. April 30, 2015) (". . . forbearance of the right to terminate an at-will employee is lawful consideration.")

72. Reuters, "Jimmy John's Will Stop Making Low-Wage Employees Sign Non-Compete Agreements," *Fortune* (June 22, 2016), https://fortune.com/2016/06/22/jimmy-johns-non-compete-agreements/ (accessed August 9, 2019).

Cases

Opinion Letter from Acting Administrator: U.S. Department of Labor[1]

The opinion letter responds to an anonymized company requesting guidance about whether service providers working for a virtual marketplace company (VMC) are employees or independent contractors under the Fair Labor Standards Act (FSLA).

Sonderling, K.

This opinion is based exclusively on the facts you have presented. You represent that you do not seek this opinion for any party that the Wage and Hour Division (WHD) is currently investigating or for use in any litigation that commenced prior to your request.

You write on behalf of your client, a virtual marketplace company that operates in the so-called "on-demand" or "sharing" economy. Generally, a VMC is an online and/or smartphone-based referral service that connects service providers to end-market consumers to provide a wide variety of services, such as transportation, delivery, shopping, moving, cleaning, plumbing, painting, and household services. VMCs help consumers to obtain these services with greater efficiency—days, weeks, or months faster than they would outside the virtual marketplace. VMCs accomplish this through a software platform called an analytic hierarchy process—a technological structure for organizing data that uses objective criteria to match consumers to service providers.

[1] https://www.dol.gov/whd/opinion/FLSA/2019/2019_04_29_06_FLSA.pdf. The Wage and Hour Division of the Department of Labor issues guidance primarily through opinion letters. An interpretation or ruling issued by the administrator interpreting the Fair Labor Standards Act (FLSA) is an official ruling or interpretation of the Wage and Hour Division. Such rulings provide a potential good faith reliance defense for actions that may otherwise constitute violations of the FLSA. The rulings and interpretations in the letters may be affected by changes to the applicable statute or regulations. Also, from time to time they need to be updated in response to new information, such as court decisions, and the WHD may withdraw a ruling or interpretation in whole or in part.

Regarding your client specifically, before your client allows service providers to use your platform, it requires them to provide certain basic information: the service provider's name, contact information, and social security number. Service providers must also self-certify their experience and qualifications, complete a background check through an accredited third party, and complete an identity check through a different vendor. Your client also requires them to acknowledge and accept a terms of use agreement and a service agreement, which states that your client provides only a platform for connecting providers with customers and disclaims any employment relationship between your client and the service providers. Additionally, these agreements state that only the service providers, and not your client, will provide services to consumers in the virtual marketplace. The agreements also classify the service providers as independent contractors.

Your client does not interview service providers or require them to undergo training. Once the service providers begin to use its virtual platform, it provides them with information on how the virtual marketplace works, such as tips on best practices through an online resource center, and feedback from existing users (both consumers and service providers) on the level of service that 1) WHD draws the following background information from the representations that you make in your letter and 2) consumers generally expect. Your client does its entire onboarding process online and does not require service providers to review any of these materials. Your client also allows service providers to immediately begin providing work to customers once their account is activated and does not require them to report to a physical office.

Your client's platform consolidates information from a consumer's service request (such as the kind of service needed, location, and date and time) and provides that information to service providers through its virtual platform. The platform also allows its service providers to communicate with consumers—including through mobile app messaging or masked telephone calls—to exchange details about the requested service, including adjustments to the scope, price, or time. Your client allows service providers to arrange for repeat business with a consumer, including future jobs outside the virtual marketplace.

Customers using your client's platform pay service providers on a per job basis. Your client sets default prices based on the region and scope of the service provider's work and uses default price tiers that correspond to the number and type of services being offered. It also allows its service providers to request (presumably from the customer) to charge different prices based on other factors, including their work experience outside of the virtual marketplace. Finally, your client issues its service providers Form 1099s reflecting their earnings through your client's platform. Your client's service agreement allows service providers the right to, among other things: accept, reject, or ignore any service opportunity on the virtual platform; determine whether to accept any service opportunities at all; select service opportunities by time and place; determine the tools, equipment, and materials needed to deliver their services; and hire assistants or personnel.

Your client's agreement provides that it will not inspect a service provider's work for quality or rate the service provider's performance. Your client does, however, let consumers rate its service providers' performance. Your client's service agreement also allows service providers to provide their services to consumers through other means, including competing VMC platforms.

Your client does not require a service provider to accept or complete a minimum number of service opportunities. Your client designates a service provider as "inactive" if they have not taken a job for a certain period of time, but inactive service providers can reactivate their account with a telephone call or email. Your client also gives service providers the right to "multiapp"—that is, to simultaneously acquire work on a competitor VMC platform in order to determine the most desirable or profitable service opportunity available at any given time. Your client's service providers often make use of this ability to "multi-app."

Your client's service providers design their own schedules and determine exactly when, where, and how much to work in the virtual marketplace. Few of them spend full-time hours providing services through your client's platform. Service providers may consider a variety of factors when determining whether to accept work—such as, for example, fee amount, expected time, dynamic pricing in effect, location, availability of parking, traffic, and access to additional consecutive service opportunities—in order to maximize their profit or fit their work into their individual schedules. Moreover, service providers may choose between more difficult jobs that are more lucrative, and jobs with less revenue potential, according to their personal needs and profit motives. However, if a service provider cancels an accepted service opportunity without 3 sufficient notice, your client will charge a cancellation fee on behalf of the consumer. Your client collects these fees to maintain the integrity of its platform.

Your client does not impose requirements on how its service providers must perform their work, such as what transportation route to take, the order in which to clean an apartment, or the make, model, type, brand, source, or amount of their working materials. Your client is not present when the service provider works and does not monitor, supervise, or control the particulars of that work. Moreover, your client requires service providers to purchase, at their expense, all of their own supplies and equipment. Your client does not reimburse them for operating expenses, such as transportation costs, vehicles, professional certifications, or licensing.

Your client will seek to terminate its relationship only if a service provider who commits a material breach, such as: inappropriate behavior toward a consumer or the VMC; fraud; repeated canceling or rescheduling of service opportunities on short notice; or receiving an aggregate consumer rating below a certain minimum threshold. Your client will initiate this termination process only in these instances to maintain the integrity of its virtual marketplace.

GENERAL LEGAL PRINCIPLES

The FLSA applies to those workers whom the FLSA defines as "employees." An "employee" is any individual whom an employer suffers, permits, or otherwise employs to work. This definition is very broad, but it was "obviously not intended to stamp all persons as employees." *Walling v. Portland Terminal Co.,* 330 U.S. 148, 152 (1947). For example, independent contractors are not "employees." See, e.g., *Rutherford Food Corp. v. McComb,* 331 U.S. 722, 729 (1947) (recognizing that workers may be independent contractors when their work does not "in its essence . . . follow[] the usual path of an employee").

Over its history, WHD has consistently applied an interpretation of "employee" that adheres to the text of the FLSA and judicial precedent interpreting it:

An employee, as distinguished from a person who is engaged in business for himself or herself, is one who, as a matter of economic reality, follows the usual path of an employee and is dependent upon the business to which he or she renders service. The employer-employee relationship under the FLSA is tested by economic reality rather than technical concepts. It is not determined by common law standards relating to master and servant. *WHD Opinion Letter, 2002 WL 32406602, at *2 (quotation marks omitted).*

As reflected by this longstanding interpretation, the touchstone of employee versus independent contractor status has long been "economic dependence." See, e.g., *Parrish v. Premier Directional Drilling, L.P.,* 917 F.3d 369, 379–80 (5th Cir. 2019); *Saleem v. Corp. Transp. Grp., Ltd.,* 854 F.3d 131, 138–40 (2d Cir. 2017). The Supreme Court has instructed that a worker's "dependence" should be assessed "in light of the purposes of the Act." *Bartels v. Birmingham,* 332 U.S. 126, 130 (1947). Thus, for example, as "broad" as the definitions of "employ" and "employee" are, "they cannot be interpreted so as to make a person whose work serves only his own interest an employee of another person who gives him aid and instruction." *Portland Terminal,* 330 U.S. at 152.

Whether a worker is economically dependent on a potential employer is a fact-specific inquiry that is individualized to each worker. The inability of the worker to work on his or her own terms often suggests dependence. Accordingly, independent contractors are often characterized by their ability to, for example, regularly negotiate working conditions or simultaneously work for another business. When determining economic dependence, WHD considers six factors derived from Supreme Court precedent:

1. The nature and degree of the potential employer's control;

2. The permanency of the worker's relationship with the potential employer;

3. The amount of the worker's investment in facilities, equipment, or helpers;

4. The amount of skill, initiative, judgment, or foresight required for the worker's services;

5. The worker's opportunities for profit or loss; and

6. The extent of integration of the worker's services into the potential employer's business. *See Rutherford, 331 U.S. at 730; United States v. Silk, 331 U.S. 704, 716 (1947) (Social Security Act case).*

Encompassed within these factors is the worker's degree of independent organization and operation.

Other factors may also be relevant, and the appropriate weight to give to each factor depends on the facts. Additionally, "the determination of [employee status] does not depend on such isolated factors but rather upon the circumstances of the whole activity." *Rutherford,* 331 U.S. at 730. Therefore, WHD does not determine employee status by simply counting factors, but by weighing these factors in order to answer the ultimate inquiry of whether the worker is "engaged in business for himself or herself," or "is dependent upon the business to which he or she renders service." *WHD Opinion Letter,* 2002 WL 32406602.

Control. The first factor is the nature and degree of the potential employer's control. A business may have control where it, for example, requires a worker to work exclusively for the business; disavow working for or interacting with competitors during the working relationship; work against the interests of a competitor; work inflexible shifts, achieve large quotas, or work long hours, so that it is impracticable to work elsewhere; or otherwise face restrictions on or sanctions for external economic conduct, among others.

Permanency of relation. The second factor is the permanency of the worker's relationship with the potential employer. Permanence arises where a business, for example, requires a worker to agree to a fixed term of work; disavow working for or interacting with competitors after the working relationship ends; or otherwise face restrictions on or sanctions for leaving the job in order to pursue external economic opportunities, among others. Additionally, the existence of a longterm working relationship may indirectly indicate permanence.

Investment in facilities, equipment, or helpers. The third factor is the amount of the worker's investment in facilities, equipment, or helpers. If a business makes these investments and provides them to a worker, that worker may come to rely on the business to supply those investments in order to perform his or her services. That reliance could make it more difficult for the worker to pursue other economic opportunities, thereby increasing the worker's economic dependence.

Skill, initiative, judgment, and foresight required. The fourth factor is the amount of skill, initiative, judgment, and foresight required for the worker's services. In Rutherford, for example, while the business profited from the alleged independent contractors' work, the business's profits were not because of the workers' "initiative, judgment[,] or foresight," as would be expected from a "typical independent contractor." *Rutherford,* 331 U.S. at 730. Instead, the profits resulted from work that was simply "more like piecework." *Id.* This factor may also look to, for example, whether the worker has the "skills necessary to locate and manage discrete work projects [that are] characteristic of independent contractors," as opposed to skills "of the task-specific, specialized kind that form a piece of a larger enterprise." *Wilson v. Guardian Angel Nursing, Inc.,* 2008 WL 2944661, at *13 (M.D. Tenn.

2008). How the worker acquired his skill is also relevant. Among other things, if "the company provides all workers with the skills necessary to perform the job," that suggests employee status. *Keller,* 781 F.3d at 809.

Opportunity for profit and loss. The fifth factor is the worker's opportunities for profit or loss. These opportunities typically exist where the worker receives additional compensation based, not on greater efficiency, but on the exercise of initiative, judgment, or foresight (e.g., commission); has flexibility to renegotiate compensation throughout the working relationship; or has capital expenditure at risk in the job. Opportunities for profit or loss can indicate independent contractor status even if the worker is not "solely in control of [his or her] profits or losses." *Chao v. Mid-Atl. Installation Servs., Inc.,* 16 Fed. App'x 104, 107 (4th Cir. 2001) (emphasis in original).

Integrality. The sixth factor is the extent of the integration of the worker's services into the potential employer's business. For example, a worker's services are integrated into a business if they form the "primary purpose" of that business. *Werner v. Bell Family Med. Ctr.,* Inc., 529 F. App'x 541, 545 (6th Cir. 2013) (observing that an ultrasound technician was not integrated into a medical center's business because ultrasounds were not "[t]he heart of [its] business").

In short, while the FLSA has a very broad scope of coverage, it is not so broad that all workers are caught within its reach—far from it. Recognizing this limitation on coverage protects the freedom of workers to operate as independent contractors and remain outside the FLSA's scope.

OPINION

Based on the facts you provide in your letter, it appears that the service providers who use your client's virtual marketplace are independent contractors.

Your client provides a referral service. As such, it does not receive services from service providers, but empowers service providers to provide services to end-market consumers. The service providers are not working for your client's virtual marketplace; they are working for consumers through the virtual marketplace. They do not work directly for your client to the consumer's benefit; they work directly for the consumer to your client's benefit. It is therefore inherently difficult to conceptualize the service providers' "working relationship" with your client, because as a matter of economic reality, they are working for the consumer, not your client. Indeed, they are similar to certain healthcare providers who use a homecare regis-try to obtain clients—workers whom WHD has previously stated can be classified as independent contractors under appropriate circumstances. Thus, it appears that your cli-ent's service providers "do not fit any 'traditional employ-ment paradigm covered by the Act.'" *WHD Opinion Letter* FLSA2018-29, 2018 WL 6839426, at *2 (Dec. 21, 2018) (quoting *Harker v. State Use Indus.,* 990 F.2d 131, 133 (4th Cir. 1993)).

Upon consideration of "the circumstances of the whole activity," *Rutherford,* 331 U.S. at 730, WHD does not see any indication that the service providers are eco-nomically dependent on your client within the meaning of the FLSA. A discussion of the following factors dem-onstrates why.

Control. Your client does not appear to exert control over its service providers. Rather, your client gives the ser-vice providers significant flexibility, including the ability to pursue external economic opportunities.

First, your client does not impose any duties, such as strict shifts, large quotas, or long hours. Instead, your cli-ent gives them flexibility to choose if, when, where, how, and for whom they will work, and they regularly use this flexibility to their own profit and personal advantage. The service providers therefore have complete autonomy to choose the hours of work that are most beneficial to them. Indeed, your client does not even require them to perform a minimum amount of work. This freedom enables them to pursue any and all external opportunities at their lei-sure. Moreover, they are able to work full-time in your cli-ent's virtual marketplace, but most of them choose not to do so, which may indicate that they are pursuing other jobs outside your client's platform.

Your client provides its service providers the right to work simultaneously for competitors, and they routinely do so in order to maximize their profit. In fact, they will "multi-app"—that is, simultaneously run your client's vir-tual platform alongside the platform of a competitor to compare virtual opportunities in real time and pick the best opportunity on a job-by-job basis. By providing them the right to "multi-app," your client has relinquished con-trol over their external opportunities. Your client even allows service providers to cancel jobs in order to pursue external opportunities on a competitor's platform. Your client also requires service providers to pay a cancellation fee only if they cancel a job without providing the con-sumer adequate notice.

Moreover, your client does not inspect a service provider's work for quality or rate a service provider's

performance. Indeed, your client does not impose require-ments on how its service providers must perform their work, is not present when the service provider works, and does not monitor, supervise, or control the particulars of that work. Your client's lack of control weighs in favor of the service providers being in business for themselves. The service providers have complete autonomy to choose the hours of work that are most beneficial to them, may simultaneously work for competitors of your client with-out repercussions, and are subject to minimal, if any, supervision by your client. Accordingly, this factor weighs heavily in favor of independent contractor status.

Permanency of relation. Your client does not appear to have a permanent working relationship with its ser-vice providers that would be indicative of an employer-employee relationship. In fact, the service providers appear to maintain a high degree of freedom to exit the working relationship. Most importantly, your client does not restrict them from interacting with competitors, either during the relationship itself (since service provid-ers may work on multiple platforms simultaneously) or after the relationship ends.

Your letter does not indicate how long service provid-ers typically remain "active" on your client's virtual mar-ketplace. However, even assuming, in light of your client's promise that it will terminate a relationship with a service provider only for cause, that service providers maintain a lengthy working relationship with your client, they do so only "on a 'project-by-4 Your client does reserve the right to remove a service provider from its virtual marketplace if that person frequently cancels jobs without adequate notice. However, this or other neutral requirements that your client imposes—such as background and identity checks before gaining access to the platform—are less rel-evant given the general lack of control that your client exercises over when, where, how, and for whom the ser-vice providers work. This factor weighs strongly in favor of independent contractor status.

Investment in facilities, equipment, or helpers. Your client does not invest in facilities, equipment, or help-ers on behalf of its service providers. Instead, your client requires its service providers to purchase all necessary resources for their work, and your client does not reim-burse those purchases.

Your client primarily invests in its virtual referral plat-form, but those investments do not, alone, establish an employment relationship with the service providers who use that platform because they are not investments in the work the service providers perform. To be sure, the service providers rely on your client's software to quickly obtain jobs, but that reliance only marginally decreases their relative independence, because they can use similar software on competitor platforms. Overall, this factor weighs in favor of independent contractor status.

Skill, initiative, judgment, or foresight required. Your letter does not specifically identify what types of services are offered on your client's virtual marketplace. However, regardless of the specific services they perform, your client's service providers, choose between different service opportunities and competing virtual platforms and exercise managerial discretion in order to maximize their profits, thereby showing "considerable independence" from your client. See *Saleem,* 854 F.3d at 143-44. Additionally, your client's service providers do not undergo mandatory training. The fact that they do not appear to rely on your client to provide them with training also increases their economic independence. The exercise of managerial discretion and the lack of training weighs in favor of independent contractor status.

Opportunity for profit and loss. Your client's service providers do not "receive [a] predetermined amount" of compensation for their work, but instead "control[] the major determinants of profit or loss." *WHD Opinion Letter,* 2002 WL 32406602, at *2-3. Your client sets default prices, but it allows service providers to choose different types of jobs with different prices, take as many jobs as they see fit, and negotiate the price of their jobs. They can further control their profit or loss by "toggling back and forth between different" competing VMC platforms. See *Saleem,* 854 F.3d at 144. Additionally, because your client charges a fee for cancelled services, the service providers risk losing money if they do not complete a job they have accepted. These opportunities for profit or loss give them a substantial amount of control over their level of compensation, and therefore independence from your client. Moreover, service providers' flexibility to work for different platforms, choose how to perform the job, choose different jobs with different prices, negotiate the prices of their jobs, and choose whether or not cancelling a job is worthwhile indicates that their opportunity for profit or loss is driven by their own managerial skill, not simply their productivity. This factor therefore weighs in favor of independent contractor status, even though your client—by setting default prices—retains some control over their profits and losses.

Integrality. Your client's service providers are not integrated into your client's referral business. First, the service providers who use your client's virtual platform do not develop, maintain, or otherwise operate that platform; rather, they use that platform to acquire service opportunities. Your client offers a finished product to its service providers; its business operations effectively terminate at the point of connecting service providers to consumers and do not extend to the service provider's actual provision of services. In other words, the service providers are not an integral part of your client's referral service; they are consumers of that service from your client and negotiate with your client over the terms and conditions of using that service. Accordingly, they are not operationally integrated into your client's business.

Relatedly, the business's "primary purpose" is not to provide services to end-market consumers, but to provide a referral system that connects service providers with consumers. This lack of integration weighs in favor of independent contractor status.

CONCLUSION

Under the facts described in your letter, we conclude that your client's service providers are independent contractors, not employees of your client. The facts in your letter demonstrate economic independence, rather than economic dependence, in the working relationship between your client and its service providers. The FLSA therefore recognizes your client's status as independent contractors.

We trust that this letter is responsive to your inquiry.[2]

Case Questions

1. Assume for discussion purposes that the company being evaluated in this letter is Uber and the question is whether its drivers are independent contractors or employees. Do you agree with the analysis by the Department of Labor that the drivers would not be employees?

2. Why is it important for the Department of Labor to publish an opinion on this topic? What impact could it have on virtual marketplace companies such as Uber, Postmates, or Grubhub?

3. What variables would need to change in the relationship between the client and the company for the DOL to consider the clients to be employees?

[2]https://www.dol.gov/whd/opinion/FLSA/2019/2019_04_29_06_FLSA.pdf (accessed December 8, 2019). Edited for brevity.

Osborne Assocs. v. Cangemi, *2017 WL 5443146 (M.D. Fla. 2017)*

Plaintiff is a salon and spa treatment company that serviced residents of senior living facilities. Defendants were former employees of the company and had signed non-compete agreements. They began working for a competitor of the plaintiff. The court ruled the plaintiff had protectable interests in its customer relationships as well as the confidential business information it developed to further those relationships and enforced the non-competes against the defendants.

Howard, D. J.

* * *

II. Background

Over the last 25 years, Generations Salon has provided professional salon and spa services to residents in senior living facilities, personal care and assisted living communities, as well as health care and nursing centers. Generations Salon has over 300 on-site salons nationwide and services over 30,000 residents each month. . . . Generations Salon hired Defendant Sheryl Cangemi ("Cangemi") on March 2, 2016, to be its Director of Business Development. . . . Cangemi "was responsible for high level contacts with decision makers, seeking out, maintaining, and developing business relationships with senior living communities, stylists, and cosmetologists" in at least the state of Florida.

Generations Salon hired Defendant Julie Calianno ("Calianno") in March of 2016 as a Regional Operations Manager. Calianno oversaw operations in the Pennsylvania region. By virtue of their respective positions, both women had access to information relating to Generations Salon's "customers, stylists, key personnel, the terms of its contracts with senior living communities, pricing, suppliers, marketing strategies and prospective customer pipeline, among other types of information."

As a condition of employment with Generations Salon, both women signed NonCompete agreements which restricted each from:

> working in a competitive capacity for a period of one year following termination of employment; soliciting any client, customer, officer, staff, or employee of Generations Salon for her own benefit or for the benefit of a third-party that is engaged in a similar business to Generations Salon; and using or disclosing Generations Salon's confidential and proprietary information.

* * *

Cangemi left her employment with Generations Salon on January 26, 2017, and Calianno followed shortly after that. Prior to leaving Generations Salon, and unbeknownst to their employer, the women formed Silver Salons in November 2016. Neither informed Generations Salon of where she actually intended to work following her resignation, or that the two had formed Silver Salons. However, at the time they formed Silver Salons in November 2016, both Cangemi and Calianno had the intention of entering into the senior salon services industry.

By February 1, 2017, Silver Salons had already signed contracts with two communities, Bay View and Anthem Lakes. Silver Salons solicited and is now serving at least one other former client of Generations Salon – that is Rose Tree Place in Pennsylvania – and is in direct competition with Generations Salon in the senior salon services industry. [. . .] On October 10, 2017, Generations Salon filed suit against Cangemi, Calianno, and Silver Salons.

Generations Salon accuses Cangemi and Calianno of breaching the terms of their non-compete agreements, breaching their fiduciary duties . . . In particular, Generations Salon asserts that what differentiates it from its competitors is

> the information Generations Salon has developed about its customers and prospective customers, the stylists who contract with Generations Salon to perform services at the communities where Generations Salon provides services, customer pricing and discounting strategies, marketing strategies, supplier information, specific considerations relating to the resident populations at Generations Salon's customers and their respective buying habits, and a host of additional

information that is unknown and not readily ascertainable by Generations Salon's competitors, all of whom could benefit from the disclosure or use of this information.

Generations Salon considers this information to constitute its trade secrets, much of which is kept and maintained in its proprietary database (the "Stanglware" database – named after its creator, Fred Stangl). One means by which Generations Salon protects its information is by requiring employees who have access to it, like Cangemi and Calianno, to sign non-compete agreements[. . .]

* * *

Generations Salon asserts that it is necessary to enforce the non-compete agreements both women signed in order to protect Generations Salon's legitimate business interests. Specifically, Generations Salon seeks to protect its

> customers and prospective customers, the stylists who contract with Generations Salon to perform services at the communities where Generations Salon provides services, customer pricing and discounting strategies, marketing strategies, supplier information, specific considerations relating to the resident populations at Generations Salon's customers and their respective buying habits.

Likewise, Generations Salon asserts that it will suffer irreparable injury if the Defendants are not enjoined. In particular, the company claims that

> [t]he injury here is not speculative, it is already occurring [. . . .] [Cangemi and Calianno] are competing in Generations Salon's markets, in a direct capacity, in a specialized industry, and are armed with Generations Salon's confidential and trade secret information. Upon information and belief, Cangemi and Calianno have already diverted customers and independent contractors from Generations Salon, using their knowledge gained by being entrusted employees at Generations Salon.

In response, Defendants claim that their actions have not caused irreparable harm to Generations Salon. They argue that "[p]laintiff has failed to identify a single customer that Defendants have solicited or a single customer that Plaintiff has lost or stands to lose by virtue of Defendants' actions." They further assert that they

"have not solicited and do not intend to solicit Plaintiff's customers."

* * *

IV. Applicable Law

* * *

b. Non-compete agreements

i. Florida law (applicable to Cangemi's agreement)

Under Florida law, a restrictive covenant in the employment setting is valid if the employer can prove "(1) the existence of one or more legitimate business interests justifying the restrictive covenant; and (2) that the contractually specified restraint is reasonably necessary to protect the established interests of the employer." *AutoNation, Inc. v. O'Brien*, 347 F. Supp. 2d 1299, 1304 (S.D. Fla. 2004). Florida statute section 543.335 further provides that a "legitimate business interest" includes, but is not limited to:

> [t]rade secrets, as defined . . . [by state statute]; [v]aluable confidential business or professional information that otherwise does not qualify as trade secrets; [s]ubstantial relationships with specific prospective or existing customers, patients, or clients; [c]ustomer, patient, or client goodwill associated with: [a]n ongoing business or professional practice, by way of trade name, trademark, service mark, or "trade dress"; [a] specific geographic location; or [a] specific marketing or trade area; [and] [e]xtraordinary or specialized training.

* * *

V. Discussion

The threshold inquiry for the Court is whether Generations Salon has shown a likelihood of success on the merits of its claims against Cangemi and Calianno based upon the restrictive covenants. In this regard, the Court must determine whether the restrictive covenants seek to protect Generations Salon's legitimate business interests. Should the Court determine that the covenants do protect legitimate business interests, thereby permitting a presumption of irreparable harm, the Court must then consider whether Cangemi and Calianno successfully rebut that presumption. Likewise, the Court must consider the balance of harms, and whether the public interest is served by entering a preliminary injunction. [. . .]

a. Substantial likelihood of success in the enforcement of the non-compete agreements.

As relevant to this action, in Florida, a valid covenant-not-to-compete must be supported by a "one or more legitimate business interests." FLA. STAT. § 542.335(1)(b). Similarly, Pennsylvania requires that any such "restrictions imposed by the covenant are reasonably necessary for the protection of the employer. Both states take the general approach that trade secrets, confidential information, good will, customer lists, and relationships with clients, all constitute legitimate interests which can be protected by covenants-not-to-compete.

Here, Generations Salon asserts that Defendants have disclosed and used and will inevitably disclose and use [. . .] the following types of trade secret information which they learned by virtue of their respective employment with Generations Salon: (i) high level contacts with decision makers; (ii) potential customers Generations Salon has targeted and plans to target; (iii) market growth opportunities; (iv) Generations Salon's strengths and weaknesses with its customers; (v) specific products, vendors, and arrangements with third parties that may increase profitability; (vi) other information which, collectively, will result in Silver Salons being able to shortcut what it has taken Generations Salon years of labor and expense to build.

Similarly, Generations Salon asserts the non-compete agreements both women signed are necessary to protect Generations Salon's legitimate business interests in terms of its customers and prospective customers, the stylists who contract with Generations Salon to perform services at the communities where Generations Salon provides services, customer pricing and discounting strategies, marketing strategies, supplier information, specific considerations relating to the resident populations at Generations Salon's customers and their respective buying habits. . . .

For the purposes of resolving the Motion, the Court will focus on Generations Salon's contention that it possesses legitimate business interests in its relationships with current and past customers, its confidential client lists and other confidential business information, and its

goodwill. On the current record, Generations Salon's allegations of needing to protect its trade secrets, stylist lists, and supplier information, find far less support.

Cangemi and Calianno do not contest that Generations Salon has a legitimate business interest in its customer goodwill. While they assert that the identities of Generations Salon customers are not confidential, they do not dispute that Generations Salon has substantial relationships with its current and prospective customers. Florida courts have held that a "substantial relationship is more likely to exist where there is active, on-going business being conducted; exclusivity; a customer who cannot be easily identified by other competitors in the industry; and an expectation of continued business." *IDMWORKS, LLC v. Pophaly,* 192 F. Supp. 3d 1335, 1340-41 (S.D. Fla. 2016). Here, it is undisputed that Generations Salon enters into exclusive contractual relationships with its customers. It is also undisputed that Generations Salon has active ongoing relationships with its customers. Thus Generations Salon has established a legitimate business interest in its substantial relationships with its customers. . . .

Generations Salon asserts that its Stanglware data is unique in that it was "compiled" and created by the "industry" of Generations Salon, and that this data also contains non-publicly available information such as the identities of key decision makers and what "pitches" to make. Although Defendants contend that Generations Salon's alleged confidential information is generally available, the evidence before the Court does not support such a finding. While the identities of senior communities and their corporate owners is certainly information that is readily available, the identity of specific decision makers and their contact information does not appear to be so available. Indeed, an e-mail from Cangemi to Lee Weinstein shows that she could not find the phone number for a key contact for a potential customer community because the company only "list[ed] an 877# online." [. . .] Thus, the evidence before the Court at this time would support a conclusion that Generations Salon possesses confidential business information that it has compiled, is not otherwise readily available to its competitors and derives value from being confidential.

While "protection of an employer from ordinary competition is not a legitimate business interest," Evans, 178 So. 3d at 116, the evidence presented by Generations Salon suggests more than just mere competition. On this record, Generations Salon has shown a substantial likelihood of establishing that it has confidential business information entitled to protection pursuant to Florida Statute section 542.335 and Pennsylvania law.

As such, Generations Salon has established a substantial likelihood of success on its claim that the restrictive covenants it seeks to enforce are necessary to protect its legitimate business interests in its customer relationships, confidential information, and goodwill. Thus, Generations Salon satisfies the preliminary injunction requirement of showing that it is likely to succeed on the merits of its breach of contract claims against Cangemi and Calianno.

* * *

Case Questions

1. What alternative fact pattern might change the court's decision on whether Cangemi and Calianno breached their non-compete agreements?

2. If Generation Salon did not have its proprietary Stanglware database, would this case be resolved differently?

3. Is it fair to restrict Cangemi and Calianno from using their knowledge to begin their own business in this industry?

Chapter 2

The Employment Law Toolkit: Resources for Understanding the Law and Recurring Legal Concepts

Learning Objectives

After completing this chapter, you should be able to:

LO1 Understand how to read and digest legal cases and citations.

LO2 Explain and distinguish the concepts of *stare decisis* and precedent.

LO3 Evaluate whether an employee is an at-will employee.

LO4 Determine if an at-will employee has sufficient basis for wrongful discharge.

LO5 Recite and explain at least three exceptions to employment-at-will.

LO6 Distinguish between disparate impact and disparate treatment discrimination claims.

LO7 Provide several bases for employer defenses to employment discrimination claims.

LO8 Determine if there is sufficient basis for a retaliation claim by an employee.

LO9 Identify sources for further legal information and resources.

Opening Scenarios

SCENARIO 1

1
Scenario

Mark Richter is about to retire as head of sales for the company he has been with all his work life, starting out as a copper pot washer, when he closes on a deal his candy company has been trying to land for a long time. Just before Mark is to collect his substantial commission on the sale from his employer, he is terminated for no reason. Does Mark have a basis on which to sue for unlawful termination?

SCENARIO 2

2
Scenario

Jenna Zitron informs her employer that she has been summoned to serve jury duty for a week. Though rescheduling her duties is not a problem for the employer, Jenna is told by her employer that if she serves jury duty rather than trying to be relieved of it, she will be terminated. Jenna refuses to lie to the court in order to be relieved of jury

duty. She is terminated. Does Jenna have a basis on which to sue for unlawful termination?

SCENARIO 3

3
Scenario

Demetria, 5 feet, 2 inches tall, 120 pounds, applies for a position with her local police department. When the department sees that she is applying for a position as a police officer, it refuses to take her application, saying that she doesn't meet the department's requirement of being at least 5 feet, 4 inches tall and at least 130 pounds. Is the department's policy legal?

SCENARIO 4

4
Scenario

Jill, an interviewer for a large business firm, receives a letter from a consulting firm inviting her to attend a seminar on Title VII issues. Jill feels she doesn't need to go since all she does is interview applicants, who are then hired by someone else in the firm. Is Jill correct?

Introduction

We understand that while this is a legal textbook, it is not a textbook intended to create or enlighten lawyers. In fact, some of you may never have taken a law course before. Thus, we thought it might be useful to take some time up front to introduce you to helpful information that will make your legal journey easier. Throughout the text we have taken out much of the legalese that tends to stump our target readers and have tried to make the legal concepts as accessible as we can for the non-legal audience.

In this chapter, we offer several tools, both procedural and substantive, to help you navigate the text. As a procedural matter, we offer a guide to how to read cases as well as understanding what it takes to have a legally recognized cause of action. Regarding substantive issues, since several of the substantive issues you will face in the chapters ahead will use information that is based on the same legal concepts, rather than repeat the information in each chapter's discussion, we explain the concept once in this "toolkit" chapter you can use to refer back to later if necessary.

There is a corresponding toolkit icon used throughout the text. When you see the toolkit icon, know that the text is discussing information that has been covered in this toolkit chapter. If you need to, refer to this chapter to refresh your recollection.

See Chapter 2 to revisit key concepts.

Part one explains how to read the cases and a couple of important concepts to keep in mind for all legal cases. Part two provides information on the substantive concept of employment-at-will, part three discusses the theoretical bases for all substantive employment discrimination actions, and part four describes legal resources for searching for further legal information.

Guide to Reading Cases

Thank you very much to the several students who have contacted us and asked that we improve your understanding of the text by including a guide to reading and understanding the cases. We consider the cases an important and integral part of the chapters. By viewing the court decisions included in the text, you get to see for yourself what the court considers important when deciding a given issue. This in turn gives you as a decision maker insight into what you need to keep in mind when making decisions on similar issues in the workplace. The more you know about how a court thinks about issues that may end up in litigation, the better you can avoid litigation altogether.

In order to tell you about how to view the cases for better understanding, we have to give you a little background on the legal system. Hopefully, it will only be a refresher of your previous law or civics courses.

Stare Decisis and Precedent

LO2 Explain and distinguish the concepts of *stare decisis* and precedent.

stare decisis
Latin for "to stand by a decision." Process of a court using prior decisions to determine the decision for the case before it.

legal precedent
Court opinions from cases that have already been decided that are used to determine similar cases later.

law reporter
Book in which court opinions are placed.

The American legal system is based on *stare decisis,* a system of using **legal precedent** from prior cases to determine what happens in the case now before the court. Once a judge renders a decision in a case, the decision is generally written and placed in a **law reporter** and must be followed in that jurisdiction when other similar cases arise. Through the process of *stare decisis,* the case thus becomes precedent found in a court reporter when future cases arise involving that issue. It is court reporters that you usually see as the matching sets of books in law offices on TV shows and in movies. Now you know why you see them there. They are where lawyers go to find the precedent for the cases they are involved in.

Our court systems are either state or federal. State courts hear violations of state laws, which vary from state to state, while federal courts generally hear cases based on federal laws, which apply to all states. Most of the cases in our chapters are from federal courts since most of the topics we discuss are based on federal law. Federal courts consist of trial courts (called the U.S. District Court for a particular district), courts of appeal (called the U.S. Circuit Court for a particular circuit), and the U.S. Supreme Court. Trial courts have one judge and, if the parties request, a jury. The court and jury hear the witnesses testify and evaluate the evidence allowed by the judge to be presented. The jury decides facts based on the witnesses and evidence, and the judge determines the law and procedural matters. Once the decision is made, the judge writes the decision, which then becomes precedent for later cases in that jurisdiction. The circuit courts of appeal cases are appeals from the district court when one or both of the parties allege that legal error was committed by the trial court. Circuit court appeals are generally heard by three-judge panels, with one judge writing the decision for the majority of the court. If a judge wishes to do so, he or she may write a concurring opinion to go along with the majority, or, if the judge disagrees, he or she may write a dissenting opinion. These majority decisions are then precedent for all courts in that circuit, including the district courts within the circuit. If a circuit court case is particularly novel and a party disagrees with the court's decision, the party can request a rehearing *en banc,* in which all of the circuit court judges for a jurisdiction rehear the case and make a decision, rather than simply a three-judge panel. Although the U.S. Supreme Court has original jurisdiction over certain types of cases, most of its decisions are generally appeals from the circuit court alleging legal error committed by the circuit court and are heard by all (usually nine) justices of the court. Supreme Court decisions are written by one judge, with other judges either joining in the opinion if they concur or dissenting if they do not. U.S. Supreme Court decisions apply to all courts in the country.

When lower courts are faced with a novel issue they have not decided before, they can look to other jurisdictions to see how the issue was handled. If such a court likes the other jurisdiction's decision, it can use the approach taken by that jurisdiction's court. However, it is not bound to follow the other court's decision since that court is not in its jurisdiction.

States have court systems parallel to the federal court system. They vary from state to state, but generally there is also a trial court level, an intermediate court of appeals, and a state supreme court. For our purposes, the state court system works very much like the federal system in terms of appeals moving up through the appellate system, though some states have more levels. Once the case is decided by the state supreme court, it can be heard by the U.S. Supreme Court if there is a basis for appealing it to that court.

Once a case is heard by the U.S. Supreme Court, there is no other court to which it can be appealed. Under our country's constitutionally based system of checks and balances, if Congress, who passed the law the Court interpreted, believes the Court's interpretation is not in keeping with the law's intended purpose, Congress can pass a law that reflects that determination. This has been done many times. For instance, in *General Electric v. Gilbert,* 429 U.S. 125 (1976) when the U.S. Supreme Court held that it was not gender discrimination for an employer to not recognize differences based on pregnancy as a type of gender discrimination, Congress passed the Pregnancy Discrimination Act specifically including pregnancy in the definitions in Title VII of the Civil Rights Act of 1964.

Understanding the Case Information

With this in mind, let's take a look at a typical case included in this textbook. Each of the cases is an actual law case written by a judge. Choose any case to go through this exercise. The first thing you will see is the *case name.* This is derived from the parties involved—the first name is the party suing (called **plaintiff** at the district court level), and the second name is the party being sued (called **defendant** at the district court level). At the court of appeals and Supreme Court level, the first name reflects who appealed the case to that court. It may or may not be the party who initially brought the case. This means that the name of the case may be different at different levels of its history. At the court of appeals level, the person who appealed the case to the court of appeals is known as the **appellant**, and their name would be first. The other party responding to the appeal is known as the **appellee**. At the Supreme Court level, they are known as the **petitioner** and the **respondent**. Whoever brings the action at that level is the one whose name appears first in the title for that level of the case.

LO1 Understand how to read and digest legal cases and citations.

plaintiff
One who brings a civil action in court.

defendant
One against whom a case is brought.

appellant
Party who brings an appeal.

appellee
Party against whom an appeal is brought.

petitioner
Party who appeals a case to the Supreme Court.

respondent or responding party
Party against whom a case is appealed to the Supreme Court.

Under the case name, the next line will have several numbers and a few letters. This is called a *case citation*. A case citation is the means by which the full case can be located in a law reporter if you want to find the case for yourself in a law library or a digital legal database such as Lexis/Nexis or Westlaw. As mentioned, reporters are books in which judges' case decisions are kept for later retrieval by lawyers, law students, judges, and others. Law reporters can be found in any law library, and many cases can be found on the Internet for free on websites such as Public Library of Law (plol.org) or FindLaw.com. You can also just put the case name or citation into a search engine to find it.

A typical citation might be "72 U.S. 544 (2002)." This means that you can find the decision in volume 72 of the *U.S. Supreme Court Reporter* at page 544 and that it is a decision issued in 2002. Reporters have different names based on the court decisions contained in them; thus, their citations are different. For instance, the U.S. reporters contain U.S. Supreme Court decisions. *Federal Reporters* contain circuit courts of appeals decisions. *Federal Supplement Reporters* contain federal district court decisions.

The citation "43 F.3d 762 (9th Cir. 2002)" means that you can find the case decision in volume 43 of the *Federal Reporter* third series at page 762 and that the decision came out of the U.S. Circuit Court of Appeals for the Ninth Circuit in the year 2002.

Similarly, the citation "750 F. Supp. 234 (S.D.N.Y. 2002)" means that you can find the case decision in volume 750 of the *Federal Supplement Reporter* at page 234. The rest of the citation indicates that the case was decided in the year 2002 by the U.S. District Court in the Southern District of New York.

In looking at the chapter cases, after the citation we include a short paragraph to tell you what the case is about, what the main issues are that we are looking at the case for, and what the court decided. This is designed to give you a heads-up to make reading the case easier.

The next line you see will have a last name and then a comma followed by "J." (i.e., "Smith, J.") This is the name of the judge who wrote the decision you are reading. The "J" stands for *judge* or *justice*. Judges oversee lower courts, while the term for them used in higher courts is *justices*. "C.J." stands for *chief justice*.

The next thing you see in looking at the case is the body of the decision. Judges write for lawyers and judges, not for the public at large. As such, they use a lot of legal terms (called *legalese*) that can make the decisions difficult for a non-lawyer to read and understand. There are also many procedural issues included in cases, which have little or nothing to do with the issues we are illustrating for you. There also may be many other issues in the case that are not relevant for our purposes. Therefore, we usually give you a shortened, excerpted version of the case containing only relevant information, and, where necessary, we eliminate the legalese.

If you want to see the entire court opinion for yourself, you can find it by using the citation as explained above, using the legal resources provided at the end of the chapter. By not bogging you down in legalese, procedural matters, and other issues irrelevant to our point, we make the cases more accessible and understandable and much less confusing while still giving you all you need to illustrate the issue at hand.

The last thing you will see in the chapter cases is the final decision of the court. If the case is a trial court decision by the district court based on the merits of the claim, the court will provide relief either for the plaintiff or for the defendant.

Sometimes, the court does not reach the actual merits of the case, however, and the case is instead dealt with on procedural grounds. If a defendant submits to the court a **motion to dismiss**, the court will determine either that the motion to dismiss is *granted* or that it is *denied*. A defendant will make a motion to dismiss when he or she thinks there is not enough evidence in the plaintiff's complaint to constitute a violation of law. If the motion to dismiss is granted, the decision favors the defendant in that the court dismisses the case. If the motion to dismiss is denied, it means the plaintiff's case can proceed to trial. Notice that this does not mean that the ultimate issues have been decided, but only that the case can or cannot, as the case may be, proceed further. This decision can usually be appealed to the next highest court.

As a matter of procedure, the parties are also able to ask the court to grant a **motion for summary judgment**. This essentially requests that the court take a look at the documentary information submitted by the parties and make a judgment based on that, alone, as there are, they argue, no facts that need to be determined by a jury. Again, the court will either grant the motion for summary judgment or deny it. If the court grants a motion for summary judgment, it also will determine the issues and grant a judgment in favor of one of the parties. If the court dismisses a motion for summary judgment, the court has determined that there is a need for the case to proceed to trial. This, too, can be appealed.

If the case is in the appellate court, it means that one of the parties did not agree with the trial court's decision and believes that the trial court committed legal errors that should be reviewed by the next highest court. The appeal must be based on errors of law alleged to have been committed by the lower court. Cases cannot be appealed simply because one of the parties did not like the facts found in the lower court or the decision rendered by the court.

After the appellate court reviews the lower court's decision, the court of appeals will either **affirm** the lower court's decision and the decision is allowed to stand, or it will **reverse** the lower court's decision, which means the lower court's decision is overturned. If there is work still to be done on the case, the appellate court also will order **remand**. Remand is an order by the court of appeals to the lower court telling it to take the case back and do what needs to be done based on the appeal court's decision.

It is also possible that the appellate court will issue a **per curiam** decision. This is merely a brief determination by the court, rather than the usual detailed written opinion, and is not issued by a particular judge rather than a panel. Rather than seeing a judge's name, you will simply see the words *Per Curiam*.

In the textbook, following the court's decision is a set of questions we developed that is intended to translate what you have read in the case into issues that you would likely have to think about as a business owner, manager, or supervisor. The questions generally are included to make you think about what you read in the case and how it would impact your decisions as a manager. They are provided

Margin glossary

motion to dismiss
Request by a defendant for the court to dismiss the plaintiff's case.

motion for summary judgment
Defendant's request for the court to rule on the plaintiff's case based on the documents submitted, alleging that there are no triable issues of fact to be decided.

affirm
Reviewing court upholds lower court decision.

reverse
Reviewing court does not uphold the lower court's decision.

remand
Reviewing court orders lower court to take further action on a case in accordance with the reviewing court's opinion.

per curiam
Short decision by a court issued without a judge's name.

as a way to make you think critically and learn how to ask yourself the important questions that you will need to deal with each time you make a workplace decision.

The opening scenarios, chapter cases, and case-end questions are important tools for you to use to learn to think like a manager or supervisor who avoids unnecessary, embarrassing, and costly liability. Reading the courts' language and analyzing and thinking critically about the issues in the opening scenarios and case-end questions will greatly assist you in making solid, defensible workplace decisions as a business owner, manager, or supervisor.

Prima Facie Case

When a legal case is brought, it must be based on legal rights provided by the law. When an individual's legal rights have been violated, the ability to file a case on that basis is known as having a **cause of action**. Each cause of action has certain requirements that the law has determined constitute that particular cause of action. In court, if it can be shown that those requirements are met by setting forth the necessary evidence, then the plaintiff is said to have established a *prima facie case* for that cause of action. Generally, if the plaintiff is not able to present evidence to establish a *prima facie* case for his or her claim, the claim will be subject to a motion to dismiss by the defendant, generally based on a motion to dismiss discussed above, asserting that the plaintiff has not established all the elements of the claim by sufficient evidence and therefore has no basis for the court to proceed. Sometimes the court grants the defendant's motion to dismiss but allows the plaintiff leave to refile the claim, depending on what was lacking. If the plaintiff establishes a *prima facie* case, then the claim may advance to the next step in the proceedings.

cause of action
Right provided by law for a party to sue for remedies when certain legal rights are violated.

***prima facie* case**
The evidence that fits each requirement of a cause of action is present to conclude that the party alleging the violation has met all the requirements of the cause of action.

Employment-At-Will Concepts

LO3 Evaluate whether an employee is an at-will employee.

LO4 Determine if an at-will employee has sufficient basis for wrongful discharge.

Wrongful Discharge and the Employment-At-Will Doctrine

In this part of the chapter, we will examine the common law and statutes that govern the employment relationship between the employer and employee, how the two come together to form the workplace relationship, and, in some cases, how the relationship comes apart. Though it might appear strange or awkward to discuss *ending* the employment relationship so early in the book, when many of the discussions that follow involve what occurs *within* the employment environment, it is vital that we raise these issues at this point. In many of the succeeding chapters, you will read about protections offered to individuals based on their inclusion in particular classes. If we omit to mention what they might be protected *from,* the book's conversation loses a bit of its urgency. In addition, in almost all of the cases that you will read throughout this text, you will need to understand the laws that govern the employment relationship, at-will employment, and discharge in order to understand the court's judgment of the case.

The American employer–employee relationship was originally based on the English feudal system. When employers were the wealthy landowners who owned the land on which serfs (workers) toiled, employers met virtually all of the workers' needs, took care of disputes that arose, and allowed the workers to live their entire lives on the land, even after they could no longer be the productive serfs they once were. The employer took care of the employees just as parents would take care of their children.

When we moved from an agrarian to an industrialized society, the employee–employer relationship changed significantly, but some elements remained. Employees no longer worked and lived on the land owned and pretty much totally governed by an owner who took care of most issues but instead worked for a business owner, lived elsewhere, and came in to do the job, often of manufacturing some good. However, the part that remained was that the employee could be terminated at any time for any reason by the employer. By the same token, the employee also had the right to leave the employer at any time for any reason. Therefore, the relationship is called **at-will employment**.

at-will employment
An employment relationship where there is no contractual obligation to remain in the relationship; either party may terminate the relationship at any time, for any reason, as long as the reason is not prohibited by law, such as for discriminatory purposes.

Both parties are free to leave at virtually any time for any reason. If, instead, there is a contract between the parties, as either a collective bargaining agreement or an individual contract, the relationship is governed not by the will of the parties but rather by the contract. Further, government employees generally are not considered at-will employees. Limitations are imposed on the government employer through constitutionally based rules governing the terms and termination of the federal employment relationship. Thus, excluded from at-will employment are government employees, employees under a collective bargaining agreement, and employees who have an individual contract with their employer.

As you might imagine, the employment-at-will relationship has not always been considered the most balanced. Employers have had a bit of an upper hand in terms of the power, and the connection looks less and less like that familial affiliation where employment might have begun and more like the hierarchical structure present in some workplaces today. The at-will environment has spread throughout the United States as each state has sought to attract more employers by offering greater freedoms within the employment context.[1]

When equal employment opportunity legislation entered the equation, the employer's rights to hire and fire were circumscribed to a great extent. While an employer was free to terminate an employee for no particular reason, after Title VII of the Civil Rights Act of 1964, the Age Discrimination in Employment Act, the Americans with Disabilities Act, and other such legislation, it could no longer terminate (or refuse to hire or to discipline, etc.) a worker based on race, gender, religion, national origin, age, or disability. Providing protection for members of historically discriminated-against groups through such laws also had the predictable effect of making *all* employees feel more empowered in their employment relationships. While few employees sued employers for unjust dismissal before such legislation, after the legislation was passed, employees were willing to challenge employers' termination decisions in legal actions whether or not they came within the protective legislation.

With women, minorities, older employees, disabled employees, and veterans given protection under the laws, it was not long before those who were not afforded specific protection began to sue employers based on their perception that it "just wasn't fair" for an employer to be able to terminate them for any reason

compensatory damages
Money a court orders to be paid by one who harmed another to compensate for the harm done.

punitive damages
Money ordered by a court to be paid by harming party to harmed party, above the actual loss suffered, for purposes of punishing the one doing the harm and to send a message to society that the activity is not to be done.

unjust dismissal
Employee terminated from a job for a reason the law will not support. Used interchangeably with the term wrongful termination.

wrongful termination
Employee dismissed from a job for reasons the law will not support. Used interchangeably with the term unjust dismissal.

even though their termination did not violate antidiscrimination statutes. To them it was beside the point that they did not fit neatly into a protected category. They believed they had been "wronged," and they wanted their just due.

However, since our system is one of at-will employment, this is not so. We have no right to a job or to continued employment. An employer is only prohibited from terminating employees based on what the law dictates. Title VII and the other protective legislation provided reasons for which an employee could not be terminated, but if an employee cannot cite those or other legal reasons, the employer can terminate the employee. The law does not protect the employee fired because the employer did not like the employee's green socks or the way the employee chewed gum or the fact that the employee failed to land his first account after being hired. There is no recourse for these workers because the employment relationship is at-will and the employer can fire the employee for whatever reason the employer wishes, as long as it is not a violation of the law.

However, a terminated at-will employee may bring suit against the employer, seeking reinstatement or **compensatory** and **punitive damages** for the losses suffered on the basis of **unjust dismissal** or **wrongful termination**. Whether the employee wins depends on how state law has developed around this issue since it is not governed by federal law. However, if there is a legally prohibited reason for the termination, such as race or gender, the law provides its own means of pursuing those cases, discussed in the Title VII chapter.

Probably because the law also began to recognize certain basic rights in its concept of the employment relationship and because of the basic unfairness involved in some of the cases that the courts were asked to decide, courts all over the country began making *exceptions* to the at-will doctrine. Since each state is free to make its own laws governing at-will employment, the at-will doctrine developed on a state-by-state basis and varies from state to state. (See Exhibit 2.1, "Exceptions to the Doctrine of Employment-At-Will.") Congress has entertained proposals to deal with the doctrine on the federal level, but as of yet, none has been successful.

Exhibit 2.1 *Exceptions to the Doctrine of Employment-At-Will*

States vary broadly in terms of their recognition of the exceptions to the doctrine of employment-at-will. Some states recognize one or more exceptions, while others might recognize none at all. In addition, the definition of these exceptions also may vary from state to state.

- Bad faith, malicious, or retaliatory termination may serve as a violation of **public policy.**
- Termination in breach of the **implied covenant of good faith and fair dealing.**
- Termination in breach of some other implied **contract term,** such as those that might be created by employee handbook provisions (in certain jurisdictions).
- Termination in violation of the doctrine of **promissory estoppel** (where the employee reasonably relied on an employer's promise, to the employee's detriment).
- Other exceptions as determined by **statutes** (such as WARN, discussed later).

To bring uniformity, predictability, and consistency to the area, the Commission on Uniform State Laws issued in 1991 a model termination act that states may use. This model act and its status will be discussed later in the chapter.

As you can imagine, the state-by-state approach to addressing the exceptions to the at-will doctrine has created a crazy quilt of laws across the country. (See Exhibit 2.2, "State Rulings Chart.") In some states, the at-will doctrine has virtually no exceptions and, therefore, remains virtually intact. In other states, the courts have created judicial exceptions to the at-will doctrine that apply in certain limited circumstances. In still other states, the state legislature has passed laws providing legislative exceptions to the at-will doctrine. At this time, the at-will doctrine still survives as the default rule in 49 of the 50 states, with Montana remaining as the single state holdout.[2]

Exceptions to the At-Will Doctrine

LO5 Recite and explain at least three exceptions to employment-at-will.

Even though an employer can terminate an employee for any legal reason, if the reason is one that falls within an exception to the at-will doctrine, the employee can claim wrongful termination and receive either damages or reinstatement.

Though they are difficult cases for employees to prove, state courts and state legislation have been fairly consistent in holding that exceptions will be permitted where the discharge is in violation of some recognized public policy, where the employer breaches an implied covenant of good faith and fair dealing, or where an implied contract or implied promise to the employee was breached (the latter involves the legal concept of *promissory estoppel*). We will discuss each of these in more detail below.

Keep in mind that if the employee and employer have an individual contract or a collective bargaining agreement, then the employment relationship is governed by that agreement. However, the contract, of course, can be one that states simply that the relationship is at-will; that the employer's right to discharge or take any other action is at its discretion; that the relationship may be terminated at any time by either side, with or without cause; and that the employee understands the nature of this arrangement.[3] In addition, if the employer is the government, then the employment relationship regarding dismissals is governed by relevant government regulations, and those employees are not considered at-will.

2) Scenario

Violation of Public Policy

public policy
A legal concept intended to ensure that no individual lawfully does that which has a tendency to be injurious to the public or against the public good. Public policy is undermined by anything that harms a sense of individual rights.

One of the most visible exceptions to employment at-will that states are fairly consistent in recognizing, either through legislation or court cases, has been a violation of **public policy**; at least 42 states and the District of Columbia allow this exception. Violations of public policy usually arise when the employee is terminated for acts such as refusing to violate a criminal statute on behalf of the employer, exercising a statutory right, fulfilling a statutory duty, or reporting violations of statutes by an employer. States vary in terminology for the basis of a cause of action against her or his employer on this basis, and some require that the ex-employee show that the employer's actions were motivated by bad faith, malice, or retaliation.

Exhibit 2.2 State Rulings Chart

Availability of common-law exceptions to the employment-at-will doctrine on a state-by-state basis. (Implied contract includes implications through employer policies, handbooks, promises, or other representations.)

	Public Policy	Good Faith	Implied Contract		Public Policy	Good Faith	Implied Contract
Alabama	No	Yes	Yes	Montana	Yes	No	Yes
Alaska	Yes	Yes	Yes	Nebraska	Yes	No	Yes
Arizona	Yes	Yes	Yes	Nevada	Yes	Yes	Yes
Arkansas	Yes	Yes	Yes	New Hampshire	Yes	Yes	Yes
California	Yes	Yes	Yes	New Jersey	Yes	Yes	Yes
Colorado	Yes	No	Yes	New Mexico	Yes	No	Yes
Connecticut	Yes	Yes	Yes	New York	No	No	Yes
Delaware	Yes	Yes	No	North Carolina	Yes	No	No
District of Columbia	Yes	No	Yes	North Dakota	Yes	No	Yes
Florida	No	No	No	Ohio	Yes	No	Yes
Georgia	No	No	No	Oklahoma	Yes	Yes	Yes
Hawaii	Yes	No	Yes	Oregon	Yes	No	Yes
Idaho	Yes	Yes	Yes	Pennsylvania	Yes	Yes	Yes
Illinois	Yes	Yes	Yes	Rhode Island	No	No	No
Indiana	Yes	Yes	No	South Carolina	Yes	Yes	Yes
Iowa	Yes	No	Yes	South Dakota	Yes	No	Yes
Kansas	Yes	No	Yes	Tennessee	Yes	No	No
Kentucky	Yes	No	Yes	Texas	Yes	No	Yes
Louisiana	No	Yes	No	Utah	Yes	No	Yes
Maine	No	No	Yes	Vermont	Yes	Yes	Yes
Maryland	No	No	Yes	Virginia	Yes	No	Yes
Massachusetts	Yes	Yes	Yes	Washington	Yes	No	Yes
Michigan	Yes	No	Yes	West Virginia	Yes	No	Yes
Minnesota	Yes	No	Yes	Wisconsin	Yes	No	Yes
Mississippi	Yes	No	Yes	Wyoming	Yes	Yes	Yes
Missouri	Yes	No	No	**Total**	**43**	**20**	**42**

Source: National Conference of State Legislatures, "Employment At-Will Exceptions by State," https://www.ncsl.org/research/labor-and-employment/at-will-employment-exceptions-by-state.aspx (accessed January 26, 2020).

For instance, a state may have a law that says that qualified citizens must serve jury duty unless they come within one of the statutory exceptions. The employer does not want the employee to miss work just because of jury duty. The employee serves jury duty, and the employer fires the worker. The employee sues the employer for unjust dismissal. The employer counters with the at-will doctrine, which states that the employer can terminate the employee for any reason. The Jury System Improvements Act prohibits employers from discriminating based on jury service in federal courts. States vary in terms of their protection for state and local jury service. Even in states where the protection is less clear, many courts have then held that the employer's termination of the employee under these circumstances would be a violation of public policy. Terminating the employee for fulfilling that statutory duty would therefore be a violation of public policy by the employer.

In a Washington State Supreme Court case, *Gardner v. Loomis Armored, Inc.,*[4] the court ruled that an employer violated public policy when it fired an armored-truck driver after the driver left the vehicle in order to rescue a robbery hostage. In that case, the driver was making a routine stop at a bank. When he saw the bank's manager running from the bank followed by a man wielding a knife, he locked the truck's door and ran to her rescue. While the woman was saved, the driver was fired for violating his employer's policy prohibiting him from leaving his vehicle. The court held that his termination violated the public policy encouraging such "heroic conduct." Understanding the confusion sometimes left in the wake of decisions surrounding public policy (since it did not wish to create a responsibility for people to be Good Samaritans), the court explained that

> [t]his holding does not create an affirmative legal duty requiring citizens to intervene in dangerous life threatening situations. We simply observe that society values and encourages voluntary rescuers when a life is in danger. Additionally, our adherence to this public policy does nothing to invalidate [the firm's] work rule regarding drivers' leaving the trucks. The rule's importance cannot be understated, and drivers do subject themselves to a great risk of harm by leaving the driver's compartment.
> Our holding merely forbids [the firm] from firing [the driver] when he broke the rule because he saw a woman who faced imminent life-threatening harm, and he reasonably believed his intervention was necessary to save her life. Finally, by focusing on the narrow public policy encouraging citizens to save human lives from life threatening situations, we continue to protect employers from frivolous lawsuits.[5]

On the other hand, while courts often try to be sensitive to family obligations, being there for one's family is not a sufficient public policy interest, and a refusal to work overtime in consideration of those obligations was deemed a legal basis for termination. The termination of an at-will employee for meeting family obligations did not violate a public policy or any legally recognized right or duty of the employee.[6]

There is agreement among the courts that have adopted the public policy exception that the competing interests of employers and society require that this exception be recognized. However, there remains considerable disagreement in connection with *what is that public policy* and *what constitutes a violation of the policy.* It is not enough, for example, for an at-will government employee to argue that the public policy is "one of honest, open, and accountable government."[7] Such a definition, explains one court, "is inadequately defined to allow any at-will government employee who believes he was fired in violation of that policy to bring suit. The question what exactly is required by the policy of open, honest, and accountable government. . . is both difficult to define and open to debate."[8]

Whistleblowing Some states have included terminations based on whistleblowing under the public policy exception. Whistleblowing occurs when an employee reports an employer's wrongdoing. One of the most infamous cases of whistleblowing occurred when Sherron Watkins chose to speak up in connection with Enron's wrongdoings with regard to its accounting procedures.

In 1982, Congress enacted the Federal Whistleblower Statute, which prohibits retaliatory action specifically against defense contractor employees who disclose information pertaining to a violation of the law governing defense contracts. The statute is administered by the Department of Defense and is enforced solely by that department; that is, an individual who suffers retaliatory action under this statute may not bring a private, common-law suit. The statute states specifically:

> An employee of a defense contractor may not be discharged, demoted, or otherwise discriminated against as a reprisal for disclosing to a Member of Congress or an authorized official of the Department of Defense or of Justice information relating to a substantial violation of law related to a defense contract (including the competition for or negotiation of a defense contract).

Additionally, in 1989, Congress amended the Civil Service Reform Act of 1978 to include the Whistleblowers Protection Act, which expands the protection afforded to federal employees who report government fraud, waste, and abuse. The act applies to all employees appointed in the civil service who are engaged in the performance of a federal function and are supervised by a federal official. Employees of federal contractors, therefore, are not covered by the act since they are hired by the contractor and not the government itself. Of course, none of these statutes apply to other private sector workers.

Certain statutes on other subjects or specific professions include whistle-blowing protections. For example, the Health Care Worker Whistleblower Protection Act protects nurses and other health care workers from harassment, demotion, and discharge for filing complaints about workplace conditions. These complaints often report on improper patient care or business methods and can affect the patient care and staff in a positive way. The act also protects employers from disgruntled ex-employees by allowing the employer an opportunity to correct allegations and by having a compliance plan to maintain an internal file for complaints of violations. At least 25 states have implemented their own form of this act.[9]

All states and the District of Columbia also provide some additional and general form of legislative protection for whistleblowers. At least 19 of these state whistleblower protection statutes protect both public and private sector employees who report wrongdoings of their employer. Some states limit protection to the reporting of violation of federal, state, or local laws. However, an increasing number of states, including California, Colorado, and Illinois, protect the reporting of mismanagement or gross waste of public funds or of a substantial and specific

---

Exhibit 2.3   *States with Whistleblower Protection Statutes*

STATES WITH WHISTLEBLOWER PROTECTION STATUTES FOR BOTH PRIVATE AND PUBLIC EMPLOYEES

Alabama, Alaska, Arizona, Arkansas, California, Colorado, Connecticut, Florida, Hawaii, Indiana, Kentucky, Louisiana, Maine, Michigan, Minnesota, Montana, Nevada, New Hampshire, New Jersey, New Mexico, New York, North Carolina, Ohio, Oregon, Pennsylvania, Rhode Island, South Carolina, South Dakota, Tennessee, Utah, Vermont, Virginia, and Wyoming

STATES THAT OFFER SPECIAL WHISTLEBLOWER PROTECTIONS ONLY FOR PUBLIC EMPLOYEES

Delaware, District of Columbia, Georgia, Idaho, Illinois, Iowa, Kansas, Maryland, Massachusetts, Mississippi, Missouri, Nebraska, Nevada, North Dakota, Oklahoma, Texas, Washington, West Virginia, and Wisconsin

Source: Find Law, "State Whistleblower Laws," https://statelaws.findlaw.com/employment-laws/whistleblower-laws.html (accessed January 26, 2020).

---

danger to public health and safety. A few states, such as Alaska, Louisiana, Maine, and Pennsylvania, require that whistleblowing reports be made in "good faith." (See Exhibit 2.3, "States with Whistleblower Protection Statutes.")

If there is a statute permitting an employee to take certain action or to pursue certain rights, the employer is prohibited from terminating employees for engaging in such activity. Examples of this type of legislation include state statutes permitting the employee to file a workers' compensation claim for on-the-job injuries sustained by the employee. Another example is the Sarbanes–Oxley Act,[10] which primarily addresses issues relating to accountability and transparency in corporate governance (such as the issues that arose during the infamous Enron debacle). The act provides protection to employees of publicly traded companies who disclose corporate misbehavior, even if the disclosure was made only internally to management or to the board of directors and not necessarily to relevant government authorities. The *Palmateer* case at the end of the chapter is a seminal one in this area, exploring whether employees who assist law enforcement agencies should be protected as a matter of public policy.

In *Green v. Ralee Engineering Co.,*[11] decided after *Palmateer,* an employee was terminated after calling attention to the fact that parts that had failed inspection were still being shipped to purchasers. He sued for wrongful discharge, asserting a public policy exception to the at-will employment rule. The court explored whether public safety regulations governing commercial airline safety could provide a basis for declaring a public policy in the context of a retaliatory discharge action. The court found that the regulations furthered important safety policies affecting the public at large and did not merely serve either the employee's or the employer's personal or proprietary interest; "[t]here is no public policy more important or more fundamental than the one favoring the effective protection of the lives and property of citizens." The court agreed that the termination violated public policy.

Retaliatory Discharge Retaliatory discharge is a broad term that encompasses terminations in response to an employee exercising rights provided by law. We will discuss this basis for discharge later as it relates to the areas of discrimination and regulatory protections. However, the basis for the claim remains the same, which is why it is included in this toolkit. In order to protect an employee's right to protest adverse employment actions, courts are sensitive to claims of retaliation. If workers are not protected against retaliation, there would be a strong deterrent to asserting one's rights. On the other hand, if the employer's actions are legitimately based in law, the employer's actions are protected.

In order to prove a retaliatory discharge claim, an employee must show that he or she was participating in a protected activity, there was an adverse employment action toward the employee by the employer, and there is causal connection between the employee's protected activity and the adverse action taken by the employer. (See Exhibit 2.4, "Retaliatory Discharge: *Prima Facie* Case.") For instance, if an employee is given a right to serve jury duty but is terminated by the employer for doing so, with no other apparent reason for the termination, that employee has a basis for a retaliation claim.

In determining whether the adverse action is sufficient to support a claim, courts will look to an objective standard and measure whether a "reasonable employee" would view the retaliatory harm as *significant.* In *Burlington Northern & Santa Fe Railway Co. v. White,*[12] the U.S. Supreme Court reviewed the context of the retaliatory action and determined that, even though the employee received back pay for a 37-day suspension, that suspension, along with a reassignment to a job that was more physically demanding, would have "dissuaded a reasonable worker from making or supporting a charge of discrimination."[13] The case is viewed as important since it expands retaliatory discharge to include not only "ultimate" employment actions such as refusal to hire, discharge, or demotion but also any action that satisfies this new standard of "dissuasion." The impact may be that, even in cases where no violation occurred in the original decision, the court might find retaliation against the employee who complained about the alleged violation. You may wish to review the *Herawi* case at the end of the chapter, which demonstrates a fact pattern where motives for the adverse action involved are a bit more complicated since they involve several proposed justifications.

Exhibit 2.4 *Retaliatory Discharge:* Prima Facie *Case*

Participation in a **protected activity** → An **adverse employment action** → **Causal connection** between the protected activity and the adverse action

Source: EEOC, "Enforcement Guidance on Retaliation and Related Issues," *EEOC Compliance Manual* (August 25, 2016), https://www.eeoc.gov/laws/guidance/retaliation-guidance.cfm (accessed January 26, 2020).

Finally, the third element of retaliatory discharge requires a causal connection between the first two elements. Courts often require more than a simple showing of close timing; however, when the adverse employment action happens immediately after the protected activity, courts recognize that there may be no time for any other evidence to amass.[14]

It is important to understand that if an employee originally claims wrongful behavior on the part of the employer and suffers retaliation, it does not matter whether the employer proves that the original wrongful behavior actually occurred. The question is only whether there was retaliation for engaging in protected activity.

Constitutional Protections   Though perhaps it goes without saying, an employer is prohibited from terminating a worker or taking other adverse employment action against a worker on the basis of the worker's engaging in constitutionally protected activities. However—and this is a significant limitation—this prohibition applies only where the employer is a public entity or a federal contractor, since the Constitution protects against government action rather than action by private employers.

For instance, a public employer may not fire a worker for the exercise of free speech (including whistleblowing, under most circumstances) or based on a particular political affiliation. So, an employee who refuses to participate in an employer's public lobbying campaign is protected. There are exceptions in the private sector when an adverse employment action would violate some recognized expression of public policy even without state action, but, as mentioned above, these protections vary from state to state.

The concept of free speech in some societies such as the United States is so ingrained that sometimes we think we are protected in every environment when we are not. Consider the following two examples. In fall 2016, a woman posted a photo of herself giving the finger to the U.S. presidential motorcade. Her firm terminated her at-will employment based on her violation of a company policy that banned obscene content on social media. Not only was the termination upheld in a later court case, but the court found that, though the firm was a government contractor, there is no free speech public-policy exception to Virginia's at-will employment environment.

In the second case, James Damore, an engineer at Google, wrote a lengthy memo that detailed his concerns about widespread bias at Google concerning diversity and inclusion in favor of women and minorities. The memo outlined a number of "facts" to support Damore's conclusion that women are less equipped to handle the industry than men. Damore was fired from Google when his memo became public.[15]

Sundar Pichai, Google's CEO, and Danielle Brown, Vice President for Diversity, defended their decision to fire Damore based on Google's commitment to equal opportunity in the workplace. They explained that while Google was committed to the values of free speech and diverse perspectives, it had a stronger commitment to equal treatment of all employees and to a workplace free from discrimination. In their judgment, Damore's memo violated that commitment. As one former engineer asked, "You have just created a textbook hostile workplace environment. Could you imagine having to work with someone who had just publicly questioned your basic competency to do your job?"[16]

Damore filed a complaint with the National Labor Relations Board to protect his "concerted activity" to address workplace issues (rather than under a more general claim of free speech), which he subsequently withdrew. However, before that withdrawal, the NLRB found that his termination was legal based on the discriminatory nature of his statements.[17]

Breach of Implied Covenant of Good Faith and Fair Dealing

covenant of good faith and fair dealing
Implied contractual obligation to act in good faith in the fulfillment of each party's contractual duties.

Another exception to the presumption of an at-will employment relationship is the implied **covenant of good faith and fair dealing** in the performance and enforcement of the employee's work agreement. This requirement should not be confused with a requirement in some contracts of "good cause" prior to termination. A New York court defined this particular duty as follows:

> In every contract there is an implied covenant that neither party shall do anything which will have the effect of destroying or injuring the right of the other party to receive the fruits of the contract, which means that in every contract there exists an implied covenant of good faith and fair dealing. While the public policy exception to the at-will doctrine looks to the law to judge the employer's actions and deems them violations of public policy or not, the breach of implied covenant of good faith looks instead to the actions between the parties to do so.[18]

The implied covenant of good faith and fair dealing means that any agreement between the employer and the employee includes a promise that the parties will deal with each other fairly and in good faith. Imagine a situation where an employer and employee have entered into an employment contract but fail to specify why and when the employee could be terminated. Assume the employee is then terminated and the employee claims that the reason is unwarranted. The court will first look to the contract and will find that the matter is not discussed. If the situation occurs in a state that recognizes the implied covenant, the court will then look to the facts to see whether the termination is in breach of the implied covenant of good faith and fair dealing.

Only 20 states recognize this covenant as an exception to at-will employment.[19] Some states allow the cause of action but limit the damages awarded to those that would be awarded under a breach of contract claim, while other states allow the terminated employee to recover higher tort damages.

Scenario

In connection with Scenario 1, Mark Richter may have a claim against his employer for breach of the covenant of good faith and fair dealing. Mark's employer is, in effect, denying Mark the fruits of his labor.

Critics of this implied agreement argue that, where an agreement is specifically nondurational, there should be no expectation of guaranteed employment of any length. As long as both parties are aware that the relationship may be terminated at any time (which arguably would be the case if they both signed the contract), it would be extremely difficult to prove that either party acted in bad faith in terminating the relationship. Courts have supported this contention in holding that an implied contract or covenant seems to upset the balance between the employee's interest in maintaining her or his employment and the employer's interest in running its business as it sees fit. "The absence of good cause to discharge an employee does not alone give rise to an enforceable claim for breach of a condition of good faith and fair dealing." To the contrary, as mentioned, in most states, employers may terminate an individual for any reason, as long as the true reason is not contradictory to public policy, against the law, or in contravention of another agreement. The *Guz* case at the end of the chapter seeks to clarify this distinction.

Breach of Implied Contract

implied contract
A contract that is not expressed but, instead, is created by other words or conduct of the parties involved.

What happens when the employer is not violating an express contractual agreement nor the implied covenant of good faith and fair dealing yet it seems to the employee that an injustice was done? Courts might identify instead an **implied contract** from several different sources. Though primarily an implied contract arises from the acts of the parties, the acts leading to the creation of an implied contract vary from situation to situation.

Courts have found contracts implied from offhand statements made by employers during preemployment interviews, such as a statement that a candidate will become a "permanent" employee after a trial period or quotes of yearly or other periodic salaries, or statements in employee handbooks. In such cases, when the employee has been terminated in less than the time quoted as the salary (e.g., $50,000 per year), the employee may be able to maintain an action for the remainder of the salary on the theory of this establishing an implied contract for a year's duration. However, these statements must be sufficiently specific to be enforceable. In *Souders v. Mount St. Joseph Univ.,*[20] the court found that a promise that the plaintiff would remain employed as long as he worked the required volunteer hours and graduation detail is not sufficiently definite to support an implied contract that changed his at-will employment status.

Court rulings finding implied contracts based on statements of employers have caused some employers to restructure terms of agreements, employee handbooks, or hiring practices to ensure that no possible implied contract can arise. Some commentators believe that this may not result in the fairest consequence to employees.[21] The *Guz* case at the end of the chapter highlights the fact that the employer's failure to abide by those policies or documents mentioned above may be the cause of subsequent litigation and liability if an employee is harmed by the employer's failure to do so.

Some employers have tried to avoid the characterization of their employment policies or handbooks as potential contract terms by including in those documents a disclaimer such as the following:

> Our employment relationship is to be considered "at-will" as that term is defined in this state. Nothing in this policy [or handbook] shall be construed as a modification to that characterization and, where there is an apparent conflict between the statements in this policy [or handbook], the policy [or handbook] shall be construed to support a determination of an at-will relationship or shall become null.

Employers should be careful when creating an employment policy manual that includes a statement that employees will only be terminated for good cause or that employees become "permanent" employees once they successfully complete their probationary period. This type of language has been held to create binding agreements between the employer and the employee, and the employer's later termination of the employee, if inconsistent with those statements, has resulted in liability.[22]

Exception Based on Promissory Estoppel   Promissory estoppel is another exception to the at-will rule. Promissory estoppel is similar to the implied contract claim except that the promise, implied or expressed, does not rise to the level of a contract. It may be missing an element; perhaps there is no mutual consideration or some other flaw; however, promissory estoppel is still a possible exception to an employer's contention of an at-will environment. For a claim of estoppel to be successful, the plaintiff must show that the employer or prospective employer made a *promise* upon which the worker *reasonably relied* to her or his *detriment*. (See Exhibit 2.5, "Promissory Estoppel: *Prima Facie* Case.") Often the case turns on whether it was reasonable for the worker to rely on the employer's promise without an underlying contract. In addition, it is critical to have a clear and unambiguous promise.

Statutory Exceptions to Employment-At-Will   In addition to the exceptions that have been discussed in this section and any contractual constraints on discharge to which the parties might have previously agreed, a number of statutory exceptions also exist that limit the nature of employment-at-will. For instance, by legislation, an employer may not terminate an employee for exercising her or his rights to a safe working environment (Occupational Safety and Health Act), fair pay (Fair Labor Standards Act), or being pregnant (Pregnancy Discrimination Act, which amended Title VII). As you will see throughout this text, several statutes exist that serve to guide the employer away from decisions on bases that perpetuate wrongful discrimination such as decisions based on race, sex, national origin, or disability statutes.

However, though some employers have argued that the list of exceptions makes mockery of the at-will rule, the list itself is actually finite rather than limitless. Employers are, in fact, free to make business decisions based on managerial discretion outside of certain judicially limited and legislatively imposed parameters.

As discussed above, if there is no express agreement or contract to the contrary, employment is considered to be at-will; that is, either the employer or the employee may terminate the relationship at her or his discretion. Nevertheless, even where a discharge involves no statutory discrimination, breach of contract, or traditional exception to the at-will doctrine discussed above, the termination may still be considered wrongful and the employer may be liable for "wrongful

---

Exhibit 2.5 *Promissory Estoppel:* Prima Facie *Case*

The employer made a *promise* → On which the worker *reasonably relied* → To the employee's *detriment*

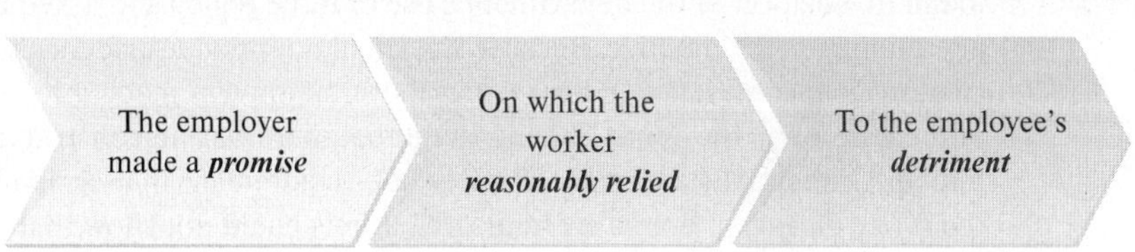

discharge," "wrongful termination," or "unjust dismissal." Therefore, in addition to ensuring that workplace policies do not wrongfully discriminate against employees and do not fall under other exceptions, the employer also must beware of situations in which the employer's policy or action in a termination can form the basis for unjust dismissal. Since such bases can be so diverse, the employer must be vigilant in its attention to this area, and employees should be fully aware of their rights, even though the relationship may be considered at-will.

Constructive Discharge

The "discharge" addressed throughout this chapter and the remainder of this text may refer either to traditional termination or to an employee's decision to leave under certain intolerable circumstances. **Constructive discharge** exists when the employee sees no alternative but to quit her or his position; that is, the act of leaving was not truly voluntary. Therefore, while the employer did not actually fire the employee, the actions of the employer caused the employee to leave. Constructive discharge usually evolves from circumstances where an employer knows that it would be wrongful to terminate an employee for one reason or another. So, to avoid being sued for wrongful termination, the employer creates an environment where the employee has no choice but to leave. If courts were to allow this type of treatment, those laws that restrict employers' actions from wrongful termination, such as Title VII, would have no effect.

According to the U.S. Supreme Court, the test for constructive discharge is whether the employer made the working conditions so intolerable that no reasonable employee should be expected to endure.[23] More specifically, the D.C. Circuit outlines the following criteria necessary for an employee to prevail on a constructive discharge claim: the plaintiff must show that:

1. Intentional discrimination existed;
2. The employer deliberately made working conditions intolerable; and
3. Aggravating factors justified the employee's conclusion that she or he had no option but to end her or his employment.[24]

Additionally, according to the D.C. Circuit, an employee must "mitigate damages by remaining on the job" unless that job creates "such an aggravated situation that a reasonable employee would be forced to resign."[25] The circumstances might present one horrendous event or a number of minor instances of hostile behavior, similar to the standard you will learn for sexual harassment later in the text.

For instance, a police officer in *Paloni v. City of Albuquerque Police Department*[26] sued her police department claiming constructive discharge after she had been found in violation of the department's use of force policy and asked to go through a retraining on the practice. Because she could not provide evidence that other officers had lost confidence in her or that the situation was made intolerable because of the retraining, the Tenth Circuit found that there was no constructive discharge. Similarly, when Allstate imposed a new job requirement that agents be present in the office during all operating hours, the agents could not show that this made the position so intolerable that they could not be expected to continue.

constructive discharge
Occurs when the employee is given no reasonable alternative but to end the employment relationship; considered an *involuntary* act on the part of the employee.

On the other hand, in *Nassar v. Univ. of Texas Southwestern Medical Center at Dallas,*[27] Dr. Nassar was subjected to such extreme harassment on the basis of race and national origin that no reasonable employee should have to tolerate within his or her working environment. Nassar, a U.S. citizen of Egyptian origin, was subject to challenges to his work that were unsupported by facts, derogatory statements from his supervisor such as "middle easterners were lazy," and alleged retaliation for his complaints when he tried to get an alternate position. Nassar was awarded more than $3.6 million in both compensatory damages and back pay and has a pending claim of up to $4 million for front pay.

Conditions that one might consider to be traditionally intolerable, such as harassment, are not required to find constructive discharge. Courts have found that a failure to accommodate a disability[28] or even an employer's offer of a severance package without a release of claims[29] (but be wary of the Older Workers Benefit Protection Act, discussed in a later chapter) is grounds for constructive discharge.

The Worker Adjustment and Retraining Notification Act

In addition to the exceptions to employment-at-will mentioned above, the Worker Adjustment and Retraining Notification (WARN) Act[30] is included in this section because it also places restrictions on an employer's management of its workforce in terms of discharging workers. Before termination, WARN requires that employers with more than 100 employees must give 60 days' advance notice of a plant closing or mass layoff to affected employees. A plant closing triggers this notice requirement if it would result in employment loss for 50 or more workers during a 30-day period.

Mass layoff is defined as employment losses at one location during any 30-day period of 500 or more workers or of 50 to 499 workers if they constitute at least one-third of the active workforce. Employees who have worked less than 6 months of the prior 12 or who work less than 20 hours a week are excluded from both computations. If an employer does not comply with the requirements of the WARN Act notices, employees can recover pay and benefits for the period for which notice was not given, up to a maximum of 60 days. All but small employers and public employers are required to provide written notice of a plant closing or mass layoff no less than 60 days in advance.

The number of employees is a key factor in determining whether the WARN Act is applicable. Only an employer who has 100 or more full-time employees or has 100 or more employees who, in the aggregate, work at least 4,000 hours per week is covered by the WARN Act. In counting the number of employees, U.S. citizens working at foreign sites, temporary employees, and employees working for a subsidiary as part of the parent company must be considered in the calculation.

There are three exceptions to the 60-day notice requirements. The first, referred to as the *faltering company* exception, involves an employer who is actively seeking capital and who in good faith believes that giving notice to the employees will preclude the employer from obtaining the needed capital. The second exception occurs when the required notice is not given due to a "sudden, dramatic, and unexpected" business circumstance not reasonably foreseen and outside the employer's control. The last exception is for actions arising out of a "natural disaster" such as a flood, earthquake, or drought.

In addition to the federal WARN Act, several states also have their own laws that put additional obligations on employers. For example, the New Jersey legislature recently amended the state's WARN Act so that it will now impose significantly stricter obligations (including potential individual liability) on employers. The law went into effect in July 2020, lengthening the notice period (from 60 days to 90 days) and expanding the definitions of "mass layoff" and "establishment." New Jersey will also be the first state to mandate severance pay to employees separated as a result of certain layoffs, transfers, or terminations of operations, regardless of whether the employer provides the requisite advance notice.[31]

Wrongful Discharge Based on Other Tort Liability

A *tort* is a violation of a duty, other than one owed when the parties have a contract. Where a termination happens because of intentional and outrageous conduct on the part of the employer and causes emotional distress to the employee, the employee may have a tort claim for a wrongful discharge in approximately half of the states in the United States. For example, in one case, an employee was terminated because she was having a relationship with a competitor's employee. The court determined that forcing the employee to choose between her position at the company and her relationship with a male companion constituted the tort of outrageous conduct.

One problem exists in connection with a claim for physical or emotional damages under tort theories: In many states, an employee's damages are limited by workers' compensation laws. Where an injury is work-related, such as emotional distress as a result of discharge, these statutes provide that the workers' compensation process is a worker's *exclusive* remedy. An exception exists where a claim of injury is based solely on emotional distress; in that situation, many times workers' compensation will be denied. Therefore, in those cases, the employee may proceed against the employer under a tort claim. If an employer seeks to protect against liability for this tort, it should ensure that the process by which an employee is terminated is respectful of the employee as well as mindful of the interests of the employer.

One tort that might result from a discharge could be a tort action for defamation, under certain circumstances. To sustain a claim for defamation, the employee must be able to show that (1) the employer made a *false and defamatory statement* about the employee, (2) the statement was *communicated* to a third party *without the employee's consent,* and (3) the communication *caused harm* to the employee. Claims of defamation usually arise where an employer makes statements about the employee to other employees or her or his prospective employers. This issue is covered in more detail in Chapter 14 relating to the employee's privacy rights and employer references.

Finally, where the termination results from a wrongful invasion of privacy, an employee may have a claim for damages. For instance, where the employer wrongfully invades the employee's privacy, searches her purse, and consequently terminates her, the termination may be wrongful.

As you can see, employment-at-will is a broad power for both the employer and the employee. However, the most likely challenge in employment-at-will is the employee being terminated rather than the employee quitting the job. There are, however, many bases upon which the employee can challenge what is perceived to be the employer's wrongful termination. If the facts of the termination fall within one of the several exceptions to employment-at-will, then the wrongful termination action can be successful for the employee. It therefore behooves the employer to make sure that there are appropriate safeguards in place that allow terminations that will not bounce back to the employer like a rubber ball.

Employment Discrimination Concepts

In part two of the chapter, we move from the concept of employment-at-will to concepts that will be visited many times in later chapters, that is, employment discrimination under Title VII of the Civil Rights Act of 1964. The chapters on Title VII constitute a good portion of this text, and it will be helpful for you to have a single chapter to which you can refer for repeating concepts throughout the other chapters. You may find it a bit awkward to be exposed to these concepts before you actually get to the chapters that explain the law itself, but we have worked to make the situation as clear as possible. For now, in reviewing the information in this section, just keep in mind something you already know: Federal law prohibits employment discrimination on the basis of race, color, gender, religion, national origin, age, disability, and genetic information.

In the chapters on Title VII, the Americans with Disabilities Act, and the Age Discrimination in Employment Act, you will find out more of the details of the law, such as to whom it applies, how cases are brought, and so on. You will discover the particulars of what is involved in avoiding costly workplace liability for each of the prohibited categories. However, for our present purposes, we will be concentrating only on the theories used to prove employment discrimination claims under the protective legislation. Since Title VII was the first comprehensive protective legislation for workplace discrimination, most of the law was developed under it, and for that reason we often refer to Title VII. However, as the age discrimination, pregnancy discrimination, and disability discrimination law were later passed, the legal considerations were applied to those categories as appropriate. So, in this part of the chapter discussing these concepts, know that the basis of the claim may vary depending on the category, but the underlying legal concepts remain applicable.

In alleging discrimination, an employee plaintiff must use one of two theories to bring suit under Title VII and other protective legislation: disparate treatment or disparate impact. The suit must fit into one theory or the other to be recognized at law. A thorough understanding of each will help employers make sounder policies that avoid litigation in the first place, help managerial and supervisory employees do a better overall job of avoiding liability, and enhance the workplace in the process. Those will be our next two topics. We will also discuss accommodation, retaliation, exhaustion of administrative remedies, and remedies available under the protective legislation, which, collectively, we tend to speak of as Title VII.

Disparate Treatment

LO6 Distinguish between disparate impact and disparate treatment discrimination claims.

disparate treatment
Treating a similarly situated employee differently because of prohibited Title VII or other employment discrimination law factors.

Disparate treatment is the theory of discrimination used in cases of individual and overt discrimination and is the one you probably think of when you think of discrimination. The employee or applicant bringing suit alleges that the employer treated the employee differently than other similarly situated employees based on a prohibited category or categories. Disparate treatment is considered intentional discrimination. However, the employee need not prove that the employer actually said that race, gender, and so on, was the reason for the decision. It is possible for it to be gathered instead from what an employer does. In disparate treatment cases, the employer's policy is discriminatory on its face, such as a policy of only hiring men to work in a warehouse facility as happened recently in a Cleveland warehouse.[32] Keep in mind that it is not the employer's subjective intent that is important. There need not be evil intent to discriminate. Claimant must simply be able to be show that the difference in treatment exists and had no other reasonable justification, leaving a prohibited category as the only remaining conclusion.

As you will see in *McDonnell Douglas Corp. v. Green,* included at the end of the chapter, the U.S. Supreme Court has developed a set of indicators creating *prima facie* case requirements that leave discrimination as the only plausible explanation when all other possibilities are eliminated. (See Exhibit 2.6, "Disparate Treatment Discrimination: *Prima Facie* Case.").

The effect of the *McDonnell Douglas* inquiries is to set up a legal test of all relevant factors that are generally taken into consideration in making employment decisions. Once those considerations have been ruled out as the reason for failure to hire the applicant, the only factor left to consider is the applicant's membership in one of the prohibited categories (e.g., race, color, gender, religion, national origin, or other protected category).

Exhibit 2.6 *Disparate Treatment Discrimination:* Prima Facie *Case*

* Employee belongs to a class protected under Title VII

* Employee applied for and was qualified for a job for which the employer was seeking applicants

* Employee was rejected and, after the rejection, the position remained open

* Employer continued to seek applicants with the rejected applicant's qualifications

The *McDonnell Douglas* Court recognized that there would be scenarios under the law other than failure to rehire involved in that case (i.e., failure to hire, promote, or train; discriminatory discipline; and so on), and its test would not be directly transferrable to them, but it could be modified accordingly. For instance, the issue may not be a refusal to rehire; it may, instead, be a dismissal or refusal to hire in the first place. In such a case, the employee would show the factors as they relate to that issue.

If an employer makes decisions in accordance with these disparate treatment requirements, it is less likely that the decisions will later be successfully challenged by the employee in court. Disparate treatment cases involve an employer's variance from the normal scheme of things, to which the employee can point to show he or she was treated differently. Employers should therefore consistently treat similarly situated employees similarly. If there are differences, ensure that they are justifiable for legitimate reasons.

Think carefully before deciding to single out an employee for a workplace action. Is the reason for the action clear? Can it be articulated? Based on the information the employer used to make the decision, is it reasonable? Rational? Is the information serving as the basis for the decision reliable? Balanced? Is the justification job-related? If the employer is satisfied with the answers to these questions, the decision is probably defensible. If not, reexamine the considerations for the decision, find its weakness, and determine what can be done to address the weakness. The employer will then be in a much better position to defend the decision and show that it is supported by legitimate, non-discriminatory reasons. In the alternative, thinking through these considerations can also show that the decision is not reasonable or justifiable but is instead based on personal issues that are inappropriate to consider in the context of the workplace. For instance, employers have refused to hire or promote qualified married females simply because the employer believes the man is, and should be, the primary breadwinner. Yep. It still happens.

For instance, let's say an employer does not hire Jane as a truck loader required to load goods onto trucks. Are the reasons for the action clear? Yes. He says it is because she is a female. Based on the information the employer is using to make the decision, is it reasonable? No, not if Jane says she can meet the lifting requirement and passes the employer's test for doing so. Is the employer's decision rational? No, it is not rational to have an applicant demonstrate that she meets the requirements the employer establishes for the job and to have the employer reject her simply because of her gender. The information serving as the basis for the employer's decision is not reliable or balanced because it is not borne out by the employer's own test results but is instead based on some idea in the employer's head about the appropriateness of women performing certain jobs. This justification is not job-related. Once the employer has these answers, it is easier to see that there is no legitimate basis for rejecting the female employee who met the job requirements established by the employer. The employer should then rethink the decision not to hire the qualified female and understand that in not hiring her, he runs the risk of an unnecessary and avoidable lawsuit.

Keep in mind that these requirements are modified to conform to the situation forming the basis of the suit, as appropriate. For instance, if it was termination rather than failure to hire or discipline rather than termination, the requirements would be adjusted accordingly.

Employer's Defense: The employer can defend by showing that the action was taken for a legitimate, non-discriminatory reason.

Employee's Counter: After the employer's defense, the employee can counter with evidence that the employer's legitimate, non-discriminatory reason was actually a mere pretext for the employer to discriminate.

Legitimate, Non-Discriminatory Reason Defense

LO7 Provide several bases for employer defenses to employment discrimination claims.

rebuttable presumption
Legal determination arising from proven evidence that can be refuted by facts to the contrary.

Even if the employee establishes all the elements of the *prima facie* case of disparate treatment, it is only a **rebuttable presumption**. That is, establishing the *prima facie* case alone does not establish that the employer discriminated against the employee. There may be some other explanation for the employer's action. As the Court stated in *McDonnell Douglas,* the employer may defend against the *prima facie* case of disparate treatment by showing that there was a legitimate, non-discriminatory reason for the decision. That reason may be virtually anything that makes sense and is not related to prohibited criteria. It is only discrimination on the basis of prohibited categories that is protected by the law. For instance, the law does not protect the category of silly people. If it can legitimately be shown that the action was taken because the employee was acting silly, then the employee has no viable claim for employment discrimination. However, if it turns out that the only silly employees terminated are those of a particular race, gender, ethnicity, and the like, then the employer may be in violation of Title VII.

Even if the employer can show a legitimate, non-discriminatory reason for the action taken against the employee, the analysis does not end there. The employee can then counter the employer's defense by showing that the legitimate, non-discriminatory reason being shown by the employer is a mere pretext for discrimination. That is, that while on its face the employer's reason may appear legitimate, there is actually something discriminatory going on. For instance, in *McDonnell Douglas,* the employer said it would not rehire Green because he engaged in unlawful activity. This is a perfectly reasonable, legitimate, non-discriminatory reason for refusing to rehire him. However, if Green could show that the employer had rehired white employees who had engaged in similar unlawful activities, then McDonnell Douglas's legitimate, non-discriminatory reason for Green's treatment would appear to be a mere pretext for discrimination since white employees who engaged in similar activities had been rehired despite their activity, but Green, who was Black, was not.

bona fide occupational qualification (BFOQ)
Permissible discrimination if legally necessary for an employer's particular business.

The Bona Fide Occupational Qualification Defense

LO7 Provide several bases for employer defenses to employment discrimination claims.

Employers also may defend against disparate treatment cases by showing that the basis for the employer's intentional discrimination is a **bona fide occupational qualification (BFOQ)** reasonably necessary for the employer's particular business. This is available only for disparate treatment cases involving gender, religion, and national origin and is not available for race or color. BFOQ is legalized discrimination and, therefore, very narrowly construed by the courts.

To have a successful BFOQ defense, the employer must be able to show that the basis for preferring one group over another goes to the essence of what the employer is in business to do and that predominant attributes of the group discriminated against are at odds with that business. (See Exhibit 2.7, "BFOQ Test.") The evidence supporting the qualification must be credible and not just the employer's opinion. The employer also must be able to show that it would be impractical to determine if each individual member of the group who is discriminated against could qualify for the position, so they are able to exclude an entire group (say, applicants over a certain age) by the employer's requirement policy.

For instance, based on expert evidence, it has been held that because bus companies and airlines are in the business of safely transporting passengers from one place to another and driving and piloting skills begin to deteriorate at a certain age, a maximum age requirement for hiring is an appropriate BFOQ for bus drivers and pilots. The employer would not have to examine each applicant over the age limit in order to use the BFOQ. Because credible research indicates that those over a certain age begin to lose the specific assets the transportation industry needs for drivers and pilots, it can exclude all applicants over that age without legal liability.

 Case 5 As you can see from *Wilson v. Southwest Airlines Company,* included at the end of the chapter, not every attempt to show a BFOQ is successful. Southwest argued that allowing only females to be flight attendants was a BFOQ. However, the court

---

Exhibit 2.7   BFOQ Test

If an employer can answer *yes* to both of these questions, there may be a legitimate basis for the employer to limit employees to one gender and use the BFOQ defense if sued for discrimination.

1. ***Does the job require that the employee be of one gender only?*** This requirement is designed to test whether gender is so essential to job performance that a member of the opposite gender simply could not do the same job. In our bunny case (discussed later), being a Playboy bunny requires being female, and a male could not be the bunny envisioned by Playboy magazine (though we understand that there are males who do a very good job of looking female).

2. ***If the answer to question 1 is yes, is that requirement reasonably necessary to the "essence" of the employer's particular business?*** This requirement is designed to ensure that the qualification being scrutinized is so important to the operation of the business that the business would be undermined if employees of the "wrong" gender were hired. Keep in mind that the BFOQ must be necessary, not just convenient. Here, having bunnies that look like the Playboy magazine bunnies is the very essence of the employer's business, not the serving of drinks.

Contrast *Southwest* with Hooters restaurants, where Hooters asserted that its business is serving spicy chicken wings. Since males can serve chicken wings just as well as females, being female is not a BFOQ for being a Hooters server. However, if Hooters had said the purpose of its business is to provide males with scantily clad female servers for entertainment purposes, as it was with the Playboy clubs, then being female could be a BFOQ.

held that the essence of the job of flight attendants is to be able to assist passengers to safety if there is an emergency and that being female was not necessary for this role. Weigh the business considerations in the case against the dictates of Title VII and think about how you would decide the issue.

Make sure that you understand the distinction the court made in *Southwest Airlines* between the essence of *what* an employer is in business to do and *how* the employer chooses to do it. People often neglect this distinction and cannot understand why business owners cannot simply hire whomever they want (or not, as the case may be) if they have a marketing scheme they want to pursue. Marketing schemes go to the "how" of the employer's business, as in how an employer chooses to conduct his or her business or attract people to it, rather than the "what" of the business, which is what the actual business itself is set up to do. Getting passengers safely from one point to another is the "what" of the flight attendant job in *Southwest.* How the airline chose to market that business to customers is another matter and has little to do with the actual purpose of the business itself. Marketing schemes are not protected by law as BFOQs are. Perhaps the Playboy Club bunnies will make it clearer.

After the success of *Playboy* magazine, Playboy opened several Playboy clubs in which the servers were dressed as Playboy bunnies. The purpose of the clubs was not to serve drinks as much as it was to extend *Playboy* magazine and its theme of beautiful women dressed in skimpy bunny costumes into another form for public consumption. *Playboy* magazine and its concept were purely for the purpose of adult male entertainment. The bunnies serving drinks were not so much drink servers as they were Playboy bunnies in the flesh rather than on a magazine page. That is what the business of the clubs was all about. Though it later chose to open up its policies to include male bunnies, being female was a defensible BFOQ for being a bunny server in a Playboy club because having female bunnies was what the club was in business to do. By contrast, having what it considers to be sexy female flight attendants was not what Southwest Airlines was in the business to do.

As you saw in *Southwest,* in order for an employer to establish a successful bona fide occupational qualification reasonably necessary for the employer's particular business that will protect the employer from liability for discrimination, the courts use a two-part test. The employer has the burden of proving that it had reasonable factual cause to believe that all or substantially all members of a particular group would be unable to perform safely and efficiently the duties of the job involved. This is most effective if the employer has consulted with an expert in the area who provides a scientific basis for the belief—for example, using a doctor who can attest to factors that applicants over 35 years of age for professional driving positions need at least 15 years to become a really competent driver but after age 50 would begin to lose physical attributes needed for safe driving. The attributes must occur so frequently within the group being screened out that it would be safe to say the group as a whole could be kept out. The two-part test must answer the following questions affirmatively: (1) Does the job require that the employee be of one gender, and (2) if yes, is that reasonably necessary to the "essence" of the employer's particular business? Keep in mind that since a BFOQ is legalized discrimination, the bar to obtaining it is set very high. (See Exhibit 2.7, "BFOQ Test.")

LO6 Distinguish between disparate impact and disparate treatment discrimination claims.

disparate/adverse impact
Deleterious effect of a facially neutral policy on a Title VII group.

facially neutral policy
Workplace policy that applies equally to all appropriate employees.

Scenario

Disparate Impact

Let us now switch gears and look at the second theory of recovery under Title VII, disparate impact. While disparate treatment is based on an employee's allegations that she or he is treated differently as an individual based on a policy that is discriminatory on its face, **disparate impact** cases are generally statistically based group cases alleging that the employer's policy, while neutral on its face (**facially neutral**), has a disparate or adverse impact on a protected group. If such a policy impacts protected groups more harshly than others, liability may be found if the employer cannot show that the requirement is a legitimate business necessity. This is why the police department's policy fails in the opening scenario. The 5-foot-2, 120-pound policy, which is neutral on its face and appears to apply regardless of gender or ethnicity, would actually screen out many more females than males and would therefore have to be shown to be job-related in order to stand. Statistically speaking, females, as a group, are slighter and shorter than males, so the policy has a disparate impact on females and could be gender discrimination in violation of Title VII. Actually, this requirement has also been determined by courts to be true of males in certain ethnic groups, such as some Latinxs and Asians, who statistically tend to be lighter and shorter than the requirement.

The disparate impact theory was set forth by the U.S. Supreme Court in 1971 in *Griggs v. Duke Power Co.,* included at the end of the chapter. *Griggs* is generally recognized as the first important case under Title VII, setting forth how Title VII was to be interpreted by courts. Even though Title VII was passed in 1964 and became effective in 1965, it was not until six years later in *Griggs* in 1971 that it was taken seriously by most employers. *Griggs* has since been codified into law by the Civil Rights Act of 1991. In *Griggs,* the employer had kept a segregated workforce before Title VII was enacted, with African American employees being consigned to only the coal-handling department, where the highest-paid coal handler made less than the lowest-paid white employee in any other department. The day after Title VII became effective, the company imposed a high school diploma requirement and passing scores on two general intelligence tests in order for employees to be able to move from coal handling to any other department. Employees working in all other departments of the company, all of whom were white, were grandfathered in and did not have to meet these requirements.

While the policy of passing scores on the exams and having a high school diploma looked neutral on its face, the impact was to effectively keep the status quo and continue to keep Blacks in coal handling and whites in the other, higher-paying, departments even though they may not have met those same requirements. The Supreme Court struck down Duke Power Company's new requirements as a violation of Title VII due to its disparate impact on African Americans. Notice the difference between the theories in the *Griggs* case involving disparate impact and the *McDonnell Douglas* case involving disparate treatment.

Griggs stood as good law from 1971 until 1989 when the U.S. Supreme Court decided *Wards Cove Packing Co. v. Atonio.*[33] In that case, the Court held that the burden was on the employee to show that the employer's policy was *not* job-related. In *Griggs* the burden was on the *employer* to show that the policy *was* job-related.

This increase in the employee's burden was taken as a significant setback in what had been considered settled civil rights law. It moved Congress to immediately call for *Griggs* and its 18-year progeny to be enacted into law so it would no longer be subject to the vagaries of whoever was sitting on the U.S. Supreme Court. The Civil Rights Act of 1991 did this.

Disparate impact cases can be an employer's nightmare. Disparate treatment is obvious on its face. It is clear when an employer's policy discriminates. Not so with a disparate impact policy that is neutral on its face. No matter how careful an employer tries to be, a policy, procedure, or **screening device** may serve as the basis of a disparate impact claim if the employer is not vigilant in watching for its indefensible disparate impact. Even the most seemingly innocuous policies can turn up unexpected cases of disparate impact. (See Exhibit 2.8, "Disparate Impact Screening Devices.") Employers must guard against analyzing policies or actions for signs of intentional discrimination yet missing those with a disparate impact. Ensure that any screening device is explainable and justifiable as a legitimate business necessity if it has a disparate impact on protected groups. Be sure to listen rather than dismiss employees who attempt to convey the negative impact a policy may have on them. This is even more important now that the EEOC has adopted its recent E-RACE initiative. The purpose of the initiative is to put a renewed emphasis on employers' hiring and promotion practices in order to eliminate even the more subtle ways in which employers can discriminate. For instance, screening applicants on the basis of "ethnic" names, arrest or conviction records, credit scores, employment and personality tests, or even wearing of natural hairstyles may have a disparate impact on applicants of color, thereby screening out qualified candidates based on race or ethnicity.

screening device
Factor used to weed out applicants from the pool of candidates.

What Constitutes a Disparate Impact?

We have talked about disparate impact in general, but we have not yet discussed what actually constitutes a disparate impact. Any time an employer uses a factor as a screening device to decide who receives the benefit of any type of employment

---

Exhibit 2.8   *Disparate Impact Screening Devices*

Court cases have determined that the following screening devices have a disparate impact:

- Credit status—gender, race.
- Arrest record—race.
- Unwed pregnancy—gender, race.
- Height and weight requirements—gender, national origin.
- Educational requirements—race.

- Marital status—gender.
- Conviction of crime unrelated to job performance—race.

Keep in mind that finding that a screening device has a disparate impact does not mean that it will automatically be struck down as discriminatory. The employer can always show that the screening device is based on a legitimate business necessity, as discussed shortly.

decision—from hiring to termination, from promotion to training, from raises to employee benefit packages—it can be the basis for disparate impact analysis.

Title VII does not mention disparate impact. On August 25, 1978, several federal agencies, including the EEOC and the Departments of Justice and Labor, adopted a set of uniform guidelines to provide standards for ruling on the legality of employee selection procedures. The Uniform Guidelines on Employee Selection Procedures takes the position that there is a 20 percent margin permissible between the outcome of the majority and the minority under a given screening device. This is known as the **four-fifths or 80 percent rule**. Disparate impact is statistically demonstrated when the selection rate for groups protected by the law is less than 80 percent, or four-fifths, that of the higher-scoring majority group.

For example, 100 women and 100 men take a promotion examination. One hundred percent of the women and 50 percent of the men pass the exam. The men have only performed 50 percent as well as the women. Since the men did not pass at a rate of at least 80 percent of the women's passage rate, the exam has a disparate impact on the men.

The four-fifths rule guideline is only a rule of thumb. The U.S. Supreme Court stated in *Watson v. Fort Worth Bank and Trust*[34] that it has never used mathematical precision to determine disparate impact. What is clear is that the employee is required to show that the statistical disparity is significant and has the effect of selecting applicants for hiring and promotion in ways adversely affecting groups protected by the law.

The terminology regarding scoring is intentionally imprecise because the "outcome" depends on the nature of the screening device. The screening device can be anything that distinguishes one employee from another for workplace decision purposes, such as a policy of hiring only ex-football players as barroom bouncers (most females would be precluded from consideration since most of them have not played football, though they may well qualify as bouncers otherwise), a minimum passing score on a written or other examination, physical attributes such as height and weight requirements, or any other type of differentiating factor. Disparate impact's coverage is very broad, and virtually any policy may be challenged if it is used as a basis for distinguishing one employee or applicant from another for any workplace decision.

If the device is a written examination, then the outcomes compared will be test scores of one group (usually whites) versus another (usually African Americans or, more recently, Latinxs). If the screening device is a no-beard policy, then the outcome will be the percentage of Black males affected by the medical condition pseudofolliculitis barbae that is exacerbated if they shave versus the percentage of white males so affected. If it is a height and weight requirement, it will be the percentage of females or members of traditionally shorter and slighter ethnic groups who can meet that requirement versus the percentage of males or majority members who can do so. The hallmark of these screening devices is that they appear neutral on their face. That is, they appear on the surface to apply equally to everyone, yet upon closer examination, they have a harsher impact on a group protected by the law. This is problematic if the criteria being used to screen out the applicants or employees is not job-related.

four-fifths or 80 percent rule
The minority group must perform at least four-fifths (80 percent) as well as the majority group under a screening device or a presumption arises that the screening device has a disparate impact on the minority group and must be shown to serve a legitimate business necessity for the employer.

Disparate Impact and Subjective Criteria

When addressing the issue of the disparate impact of screening devices, subjective and objective criteria are a concern. *Objective criteria* are factors that are able to be quantified by anyone, such as scores on a written exam. *Subjective criteria* are, instead, factors based on the evaluator's personal thoughts or ideas (e.g., a supervisor's opinion as to whether an employee being considered for promotion is "compatible with" or "a good fit for" the workplace).

Initially, it was suspected that subjective criteria could not be the basis for disparate impact claims since, until that time, the Supreme Court cases had involved only objective factors such as height and weight, educational requirements, test scores, and the like. However, in *Watson v. Fort Worth Bank,* mentioned above, the Supreme Court for the first time determined that subjective criteria also could be the basis for a disparate impact claim.

In *Watson,* a Black employee had worked for the bank for years and was constantly passed over for promotion in favor of white employees. She eventually brought suit, alleging racial discrimination in that the bank's subjective promotion policy had a disparate impact upon Black employees. The bank's policy was subjective in that promotions were based on the recommendation of a supervisor (all of whom were white). The Supreme Court held that the disparate impact analysis could indeed be used in determining illegal discrimination in subjective criteria cases.

Disparate Impact of Preemployment Interviews and Employment Applications

Quite often questions asked during idle conversational chitchat in preemployment interviews or included on job applications may unwittingly be the basis for discrimination claims. Such questions or discussions should therefore be scrutinized for their potential impact, and interviewers should be trained in potential trouble areas to be avoided. If the purpose of questions is to elicit information to be used in the evaluation process, then it makes sense for the applicant to think that if the question is asked, the employer will use the information this way. It may seem like mere innocent conversation to the interviewer, but if the applicant is rejected, then whether or not the information was gathered for discriminatory purposes, the applicant has the foundation for alleging that the information illegally impacted the decision-making process. (See Exhibit 2.8.) Only questions relevant to legal considerations for evaluating the applicant should be asked. There is virtually always a way to elicit legal, necessary information without violating the law or exposing the employer to potential liability. A chatty, untrained interviewer can innocently do an employer a world of harm.

For example, idle, friendly conversation has included questions by interviewers such as "What a beautiful head of gray hair! Is it real?" (age); "What an interesting last name. What sort of name is it?" (national origin); "Oh, just the one child? Are you planning to have more?" (gender); "Oh, I see by your engagement ring that you're getting married! Congratulations! What does your fiancé do?" (gender); "Are you planning to have a family?" (gender). These questions may seem, or even be, innocent, but they can come back to haunt an employer later. Training employees who conduct interviews is an important way to avoid liability for unnecessary discrimination claims.

Scenario

Conversation is not the only culprit. Sometimes it is job applications. Applications often ask the marital status of the applicant. Since there is often discrimination against married women holding certain jobs, this question has a potential disparate impact on married female applicants (but not married male applicants for whom this is generally not considered an issue). If the married female applicant is not hired, she can allege that it was because she was a married female. This may have nothing whatsoever to do with the actual reason for her rejection, but since the employer asked the question, the argument can be made that it did. In truth, employers often ask this question because they want to know whom to contact in case of an emergency should the applicant be hired and suffer an on-the-job emergency. Simply asking who should be contacted in case of emergency or not soliciting such information until after the applicant is hired gives the employer exactly what the employer needs without risking potential liability by asking questions about protected categories that pose a risk. That is why in opening Scenario 4, Jill, as one who interviews applicants, is in need of training, just like those who actually hire applicants.

LO7 Provide several bases for employer defenses to employment discrimination claims.

business necessity
Defense to a disparate impact case based on the employer's need for the policy as a legitimate requirement for the job.

The Business Necessity Defense

When sued by an applicant on the basis of a disparate impact claim, the employer can use the defense that the challenged policy, neutral on its face, that has a disparate impact on a group protected by law is actually job-related and consistent with **business necessity**. For instance, an applicant challenges the employer's policy of requesting credit information and demonstrates that, because of shorter credit histories, fewer women are hired than men. The employer can show that it needs the policy because the employer is in the business of handling large sums of money and that hiring only those people with good and stable credit histories is a business necessity. Business necessity is not used as a defense to a disparate treatment claim.

In a disparate impact case, once the employer provides evidence rebutting the employee's *prima facie* case by showing business necessity or other means of rebuttal, the employee can show that there is a means of addressing the issue that has less of an adverse impact than the challenged policy. If this is shown to the court's satisfaction, then the employee will prevail and the policy will be struck down. If not, the employer's policy stands.

Let's go back to our earlier example of the 100 males and 100 females who take the exam and 100 percent of the females but only 50 percent of the males pass.

Since the exam scores exhibit a disparate impact, in order to avoid liability, the employer would now be required to show that a passing score on the exam is a legitimate business necessity. If this can be shown to the satisfaction of the court, then the passing score job requirement will be permitted even though it has a disparate impact on the males. Even then the policy may still be struck down if the men can show there is a way to accomplish the employer's legitimate business necessity in using the exam without it having such a harsh impact on them.

For example, suppose a store like Sears has a 75-pound lifting requirement for applicants who apply to work as mechanics in its car repair facilities. A woman who is not hired sues on the basis of gender discrimination, saying the lifting requirement has a disparate impact on women because they generally cannot lift that much weight. The store is able to show that employees who work in the car repair facilities move heavy tools from place to place in the garage. The lifting requirement is therefore a legitimate business necessity. Though the lifting policy screens out women applying for jobs as mechanics at a higher rate than it does men, and, for argument's sake, let's say women only do 20 percent as well as men on the lifting requirement, thus not meeting the four-fifths rule, the employer has provided a legitimate, non-discriminatory reason for the lifting policy.

But suppose the applicant can counter that if the employer allowed the employee to use a rolling tool cart (which is actually sold by Sears) for the heavier tools, then the policy would not have such a harmful impact on women and would still allow Sears what it needs in terms of mechanics who are qualified to repair automobiles. Even though Sears has provided the court with a legitimate, non-discriminatory reason for its weight-lifting requirement that screened out females at a higher rate than males, it has been demonstrated that this policy can be made less harsh by allowing the use of the tool carts.

Knowing these requirements provides the employer with valuable insight into what is necessary to protect itself from liability. Even though disparate impact claims can be difficult to detect beforehand, once they are brought to the employer's attention by the employee, they can be used as an opportunity to revisit the policy. With flexible, creative, and innovative approaches, the employer is able to avoid liability in this area.

Other Defenses to Employment Discrimination Claims

Once an employee provides *prima facie* evidence that the employer has discriminated, in addition to the BFOQ, legitimate non-discriminatory reason, and business necessity defenses discussed, the employer may perhaps present evidence of other defenses:

- That the employee's evidence is not true—that is, this is not the employer's policy as alleged or it was not applied as the employee alleges, the employee's statistics regarding the policy's disparate impact are incorrect and there is no disparate impact, or the treatment the employee says she or he received did not occur.
- That the employer's "bottom line" comes out correctly (the bottom line defense). We initially said that disparate impact is a statistical theory. Unfortunately, employers have tried to avoid litigation under this theory by taking questionable measures to ensure that the relevant statistics will not exhibit a disparate impact, thinking this will insulate them from lawsuits. In an area in which they feel they may be vulnerable, such as in minorities' passing scores on a written examination, they may make decisions to use criteria that make it appear as if minorities do at least 80 percent as well as the majority, so the *prima facie* elements for a disparate impact case are not met. Rather than making sure the tests are validated and letting the chips fall where they may, this attempt at an end run around Title VII usually results in liability. The end-run approach was soundly rejected by the U.S. Supreme Court in *Connecticut v. Teal.*[35] In that

case, an employer's written test showed a disparate impact on Black employees who had already held their supervisory positions on a provisional basis for two years. Without a passing score on the written test, none of their other qualifications mattered, and they could not move forward in the promotion process no matter how well they had performed the actual job of supervisor during the provisional period. After seeing that the supervisors scores did not meet the four-fifths rule, to avoid liability, Connecticut used an unknown method to render the test scores as not having a disparate impact. The Supreme Court said this was not permissible, as it was equal employment opportunity required by law, not equal employment. Doing something to the test scores so that they no longer exhibited a disparate impact still left the Black employees without an equal opportunity for the promotions. Note that this is also very often the reason you hear someone say there are "quotas" in a workplace. They are there *not* because the law requires them—it doesn't—in fact it prohibits them—but rather because employers self-impose them to try to avoid liability. *Not* a good idea. The best policy is to have an open, fair employment process. Manipulating statistics to reach a "suitable" bottom-line outcome is *not* permitted.

Teal demonstrates that protective legislation requires equal employment *opportunity,* not simply equal *employment.* This is *extremely* important to keep in mind. It is *not* purely a "numbers game" as many employers, including the state of Connecticut, interpret the law. Under the Civil Rights Act of 1991, it is an unfair employment practice for an employer to adjust the scores of, use different cutoff scores for, or otherwise alter the results of an employment-related test on the basis of a prohibited category as was done in *Teal.*

Employers' policies should ensure that everyone has an equal chance at the job, based on qualifications. The *Teal* employees had been in their positions on a provisional basis for nearly two years before taking the examination. The employer therefore had nearly two years of actual job performance data that it could consider to determine the applicant's promotability. Instead, an exam was administered, requiring a certain score, which the employer could not show to be related to the job. Of course, the logical question is "Then why give it?" Make sure you ask yourself that question before using screening devices that may operate to exclude certain groups on a disproportional basis. If you cannot justify the device, you take an unnecessary risk by using it.

Accommodation

The next legal concept we will discuss is that of the accommodation requirement. Religious discrimination under Title VII and disability discrimination under the Americans with Disabilities Act (ADA) both require that employers attempt to accommodate workplace conflicts based on these categories. Discrimination under the law is simply prohibited on the basis of race, color, gender, national origin, religion, disability, or age. When it comes to religion and disabilities, however, the law imposes on the employer a further duty to attempt to accommodate the disability or religious conflict. For instance, the employer may expect employees to work on weekends, but a Jewish employee may be prohibited by his religion from working on his Sabbath from sundown Friday evening to Saturday evening. The employer would be required to make a serious attempt to accommodate this religious conflict. However, the employer's duty to accommodate is only to the extent that it does not cause the employer an undue hardship (which is determined on a case-by-case basis using certain specific criteria).

We only introduce you to the generalities of the concept here, but understand that the considerations are quite different for religious accommodation and accommodation of those with disabilities, and they will be discussed in their own chapters. Suffice it to say that in both cases, rather than an out-and-out prohibition against discrimination, the employer must try to accommodate conflicts, but only up to the point that it creates an undue hardship on the employer. What constitutes an undue hardship varies and will be discussed in more detail in later chapters, but the concept of trying to accommodate conflicts is present for both religion and disability discrimination.

Retaliation

LO8 Determine if there is sufficient basis for a retaliation claim by an employee.

One of the concepts that recurs throughout the chapters is retaliation. Despite the fact that Title VII has been in place for well over 50 years, there is still resistance to the law. Often, that resistance is manifested by negative actions taken toward employees who pursue their rights under the law. Title VII specifically includes provisions allowing employees to file separate claims for negative consequences they experience from their employer for pursuing their lawful rights under Title VII. This negative activity creates a separate cause of action for retaliation. Even if the substantive claim of discrimination is not proved to a court's satisfaction, the employee may still win on the retaliation claim.

In fiscal year 2018, retaliation accounted for a whopping 51.6 percent[36] of the claims filed with the EEOC, with employees winning their claims about 50 percent of the time.[37]

Retaliation can take any number of forms. For instance, an employer may be angry that an employee filed a sexual harassment claim and begin to give the employee less responsibility than before, exclude the employee from meetings in which the employee may once have been included, assign the employee to less prestigious assignments than the employee has always had, change hours to a much less desirable schedule, or even demote or terminate the employee. This is in addition to the original action that resulted in the employee suing for discrimination in the first place and, as such, is the basis for a separate cause of action against the employer for retaliation.

Noting that retaliation claims had doubled since 1991, in 1998 the EEOC issued retaliation guidelines to make clear its view on what constitutes retaliation for pursuing Title VII rights and how seriously it views such claims by employees.[38] In fiscal year 2010, at 36.3 percent, retaliation claims for the first time were the largest percentage of claims filed under the protective legislation.[39] In fiscal year 2018, retaliation claims continued to lead claims filed with EEOC.[40]

We want to make it clear: Employers are not allowed to retaliate against employees for filing workplace discrimination claims. Retaliation claims may be filed not only by the employee who filed the discrimination claim but also by others against whom the employer allegedly retaliated because of the claim; for instance, the spouse of the claimant who is terminated because her spouse filed a claim. They can be filed not only for the adverse action taken while the employee was employed but also for actions taken later to negatively impact the former employee (such as trying to block the employee's later reemployment).[41]

In the U.S. Supreme Court case of *Texas Southwestern Medical Center v. Nassar*,[42] the U.S. Supreme Court made it clear that in order to be successful in a retaliation case, the employee must prove that the employer's desire to retaliate was the but-for cause of the employer's adverse action rather than just a contributing factor. That is, the employer's adverse action would not have occurred but for the employer wishing to retaliate against the employee for filing the workplace discrimination claim. Consistent with Congress's rejection of such an approach when the law was passed in 1964, Justice Ginsburg dissented from the *Nassar* ruling as being too restrictive and called for Congress to act. The last time she did this after the Court's ruling in Lilly Ledbetter's pay discrimination case against Goodyear Tire and Rubber Company in 2007, Congress passed the Lilly Ledbetter Fair Pay Act of 2009. So far, however, the ruling has remained intact.

Just be mindful that treating an employee who has filed a workplace discrimination claim differently, less well than usual, can be problematic if an employer takes against the employee a "materially adverse" action that would dissuade a reasonable employee from making or supporting a charge of discrimination. After finding out the claim has been filed, be sure to just treat the employee as he or she has always been treated.

Exhaustion of Administrative Remedies

exhaustion of administrative remedies
Going through the EEOC administrative procedure before being permitted to seek judicial review of an agency decision.

The statutory schemes set out in the law for employment discrimination claims require that claimants first pursue their grievances within the agency created to handle such claims, the Equal Employment Opportunity Commission (EEOC). The EEOC will be discussed in detail in the Title VII chapter. All of the protective statutes provide for courts to hear employment discrimination claims only after the claimant has done all that can be done at the agency level. This is called **exhaustion of administrative remedies**. Exhaustion of administrative remedies must be shown before a court can exercise jurisdiction over handling a Title VII case.

Employment Discrimination Remedies

Title VII and other protective legislation have specific remedies available to employee claimants. Keep in mind that the tort remedies discussed in the employment-at-will part of the chapter are separate from the administrative remedies available to discrimination claimants. Employment-at-will claims of unjust dismissal are brought by employees in a court of law, while claims of workplace discrimination are brought by employees filing a claim at the EEOC. Also, these remedies are the basic ones available for winning employees, but some of the statutes may contain variations that you will learn as you read the chapters for those specific categories.

back pay
Money awarded for time an employee was not working (usually due to termination) because of illegal discrimination.

front pay
Equitable remedy of money awarded to a claimant when reinstatement is not possible or feasible.

retroactive seniority
Seniority that dates back to the time the claimant was treated illegally.

make-whole relief
Attempt to put a claimant in the position he or she would have been in had there been no discrimination.

If the employee in an EEOC case is successful, the employer may be liable for **back pay** of up to two years before the filing of the charge with the EEOC; for **front pay** for situations when reinstatement is not possible or feasible for the claimant; for reinstatement of the employee to his or her position; for **retroactive seniority**; for injunctive relief, if applicable; and for attorney fees. Until passage of the Civil Rights Act of 1991, remedies for discrimination under Title VII were limited to **make-whole relief** and injunctive relief. For instance, you could recover back pay but not recover for losing your home because you lost your income when you were illegally fired under Title VII.

The Civil Rights Act of 1991 added **compensatory damages** and **punitive damages** as available remedies. Punitive damages are permitted when it is shown that the employer's action was malicious or was done with reckless indifference to federally protected rights of the employee. They are not allowed under the disparate/adverse impact or unintentional theory of discrimination and may not be recovered from governmental employers. Compensatory damages may include future pecuniary loss as well as emotional pain, suffering, inconvenience, mental anguish, loss of enjoyment of life, and other nonpecuniary losses. (See Exhibit 2.9, "Employment Discrimination Remedies.")

There are certain limitations on the damages under the law. Gender discrimination (including sexual harassment) and religious discrimination have a $300,000 cap total on nonpecuniary (pain and suffering) compensatory and punitive damages. There is no limitation on medical compensatory damages. The cap depends on the number of employees the employer has. (See Exhibit 2.10, "Compensatory and Punitive Damages Caps.") Juries are told of the caps on liability before

Exhibit 2.9 *Employment Discrimination Remedies*

These are the basic remedies available, but as mentioned, some of the protective statutes provide additional remedies that will be discussed in those chapters.

Basic remedies
- Back pay
- Front pay
- Reinstatement
- Seniority
- Retroactive seniority
- Injunctive relief
- Compensatory damages
- Punitive damages
- Attorney fees
- Medical costs

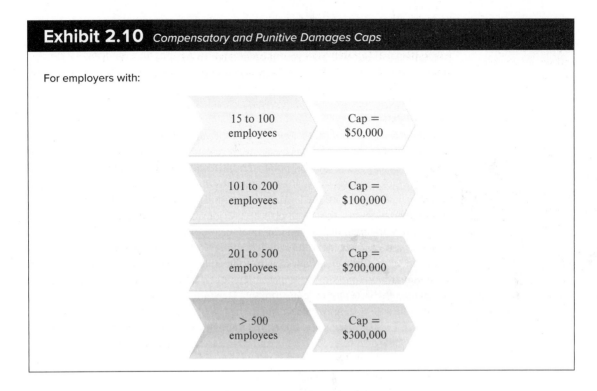

Exhibit 2.10 *Compensatory and Punitive Damages Caps*

For employers with:

15 to 100 employees	Cap = $50,000
101 to 200 employees	Cap = $100,000
201 to 500 employees	Cap = $200,000
> 500 employees	Cap = $300,000

compensatory damages
Money damages ordered by a court to be given to a party to compensate for direct losses due to an injury suffered.

punitive damages
Money over and above compensatory damages, imposed by a court to punish a defendant for willful acts and to act as a deterrent.

deciding a case. Since race and national origin discrimination cases also can be brought under 42 U.S.C. § 1981 (discussed later), which permits unlimited compensatory damages, the caps do not apply to these categories. In 2001, the U.S. Supreme Court ruled that, though compensatory damages are capped by the law, the limitations do not apply to front pay.[43]

With the 1991 Title VII amendments' addition of compensatory and punitive damages possible in Title VII cases, litigation increased dramatically. It is now more worthwhile for employees to sue and for lawyers to take the cases. The possibility of monetary damages also made it more likely that employers would settle more suits rather than risk large damage awards. Again, the best defense against costly litigation and liability is solid, consistently applied workplace policies. Lastly for the chapter, we will share with you information on how to find legal resources you can use for further exploration of issues in the text.

Additional Legal Resources

LO9 Identify sources for further legal information and resources.

One of the things students often tell us is that they found this textbook so helpful that they decided to keep it rather than sell it after the course was over. They later find it quite helpful once they enter the workplace. With this in mind, and because we also understand that the text may not cover every single issue that may be of interest to you or arise for you later, we are including a section on how to find additional legal resources once you have been exposed to the law. Our section is not exhaustive but will give you quite enough to be able to search for additional information if you need it. With the resources now available to everyone, especially online, there is no excuse not to be informed.

Law Libraries

Law libraries can be found everywhere from private law firms to public courthouses and can contain only a few necessary legal resources or vast ones. While many of these are closed to the general public, check with your local sources to be certain. If you are lucky enough to live in or near a town that has a law school, there will inevitably be a law library, and the legal world is within your reach. In addition to reporters containing law cases, there will also be law journals from around the world, legal treatises on any area of law you can imagine, books on legal issues, legal research updating sources, and local, state, federal, and international legal resources. You do not need to be a lawyer or law student to be able to access most libraries and find what you are looking for. Most institutions open their doors to everyone, and that is certainly the case at public institutions. Depending on the nature of your inquiry, you may be able to simply place a call to the law librarian and ask for help with what you need. Law librarians are incredible founts of knowledge about legal resources available, how best to access them, and where to find what you need.

The Internet

One of the most exciting things that has happened since we first began writing this textbook is the advent of the Internet and its now omnipresent use. We have rejoiced as it has expanded from a time when information was available only if you knew a website to which you could go directly to the present time when search engines can find whatever you want in seconds. This evolution has been very exciting for us to watch as the Internet includes more and more legal databases for public consumption, taking the law out of the hands of the lucky few who could access it as judges, lawyers, and law students and giving it to the public at large who could now be much more informed. Such access is imperative for an informed democratic society. If you had not thought so before, surely you did as you watched 2.5 million people around the world engage in the January 21, 2017, Women's March on Washington and Sister Marches on all seven continents, organized virtually completely online. Or in 2011 when the world watched the Arab Spring unfold in Tunisia, Egypt, and Libya and elsewhere in North Africa and the Middle East when entire countries were changed, in part, because of the ability of the masses to use social media via the Internet for organizing and disseminating information. Knowledge is powerful, and as you know, the Internet brings unbelievable legal resources right to your computer or cell phone. A few well-chosen search terms can quickly bring you exactly what you are looking for regarding your subject matter.

We will list a few websites on which you can find legal resources for free, but there are also other legal databases that cost to access. Check with your institution or employer to see if they have available for you the legal databases of Westlaw or Lexis/Nexis.

Both of these are vast full-service legal databases, but as you will see below, Lexis has limited free public access for at least the cases. In addition, many law firms maintain as part of their websites free recent information on issues they deal with. If you enter into a search engine the particular issue you wish to research, you will likely find many resources in addition to the ones listed here. At the end of the listings below, you will find two compilation resources that allow you to stay up to date by subject matter based on many of these resources created by law firms. Of course, we would welcome suggestions by students and faculty alike for resources to add to this list.

- FindLaw is a great legal research website that is easy to navigate and has extensive legal resources. http://www.public.findlaw.com
- The U.S. Supreme Court maintains a website that includes access to its decisions. http://www.supremecourt.gov/
- The Oyez Project website has easily searchable major U.S. Supreme Court decisions that include media such as the Court's oral arguments. http://www.oyez.org/
- The Government Printing Office maintains a searchable website for federal agency regulations in the Code of Federal Regulations. http://www.gpoaccess. gov/cfr/index.html
- Municode.com provides links to municipal codes all over the country in an easily searched format. http://www.municode.com/Library/Library.aspx
- LexisOne is the public website adjunct of the Lexis/Nexis legal database and provides a searchable database of free cases. http://law.lexisnexis.com/ webcenters/lexisone/
- Government Information Resources maintained by the University of Virginia provides links to administrative agency decisions and actions. http://www2.lib. virginia.edu/govtinfo/fed_decisions_agency.html
- Washlaw is a pretty comprehensive website maintained by the Washburn School of Law with free access to the public. http://www.washlaw.edu/uslaw/index.html
- The Social Science Research Network has an extensive library of journal articles and working papers on many topics, including law. http://papers.ssrn.com/sol3/ DisplayAbstractSearch.cfm
- The Directory of Open Access Journals provides links to thousands of journals, including legal journals, that do not charge for access. http://www.doaj.org/
- USA.gov is the opening portal to all types of government resources, including legal. http://www.usa.gov
- The U.S. Senate's website can access information on U.S. laws, pending bills, and other Senate business. Its Virtual Reference Desk is particularly helpful in accessing information organized around a particular topic. http://www.senate.gov/
- The website for the U.S. House of Representatives provides information on all aspects of pending and passed legislation for that body. http://www.house.gov/
- THOMAS is the Library of Congress's website that provides a wealth of information on legislation, including laws, treaties, and other legislative matters. http://thomas.loc.gov/

Management Tips

- You are always allowed to hire the best person for a job; the law merely states that you may not make this decision based on prejudice or stereotypes. In order to avoid a wrongful discharge suit and, more importantly, to ensure the ethical quality of your decisions, do not fire someone for reasons that violate basic principles of dignity, respect, or social justice.

- Make sure that your policies and procedures create a space for employees to voice any concerns and complaints. It is most effective for employees to be able to share these issues with you long before they reach a breaking point. Then make sure that everyone knows about them through appropriate training.

- You have the right to fire an employee for any reason as long as it is not for one of the specific reasons prohibited by law. On the other hand, if you do not have sufficient documentation or other evidence of the appropriate reason for your decision, a court might infer that your basis is wrongful.

- When an employee reports wrongdoing occurring at your workplace, you may not retaliate against that person. Be sure to avoid even the appearance of retaliation, as the actual motivation for employment decisions is often difficult to prove.

- Subject termination decisions to internal review. Unilateral decisions to fire an employee may lead to emotion—or the appearance of emotion—rather than reason being used to determine terminations. Additional review can protect against this consequence.

- In the event of a layoff:
  - Clearly explain to employees the reasons for the actions taken: Document all efforts to communicate with employees.
  - Prepare the managers who will deliver the message.
  - Speak plainly and do not make promises.
  - Avoid euphemisms such as "We are all family, and we will be together again someday."
  - Emphasize that the decision is not personal.
  - Know how layoffs will affect the demographic breakdown of the staff.

- Make sure employees are aware of their rights under the law regarding any protected category to which they may belong.

- Do not forget that certain protected categories must be accommodated to the extent that such accommodation does not present an undue burden on the employer.

- Check policies that appear neutral on their face for adverse impacts on protected employees.

- Discard policies that discriminate on their face.

Source: Partially adapted from Matthew Boyle, "The Not-So-Fine Art of the Layoff," *Fortune*, Mar. 19, 2001, pp. 209–210.

- The Legal Information Institute (LII) at Cornell University is one of the earliest public access legal databases formed with the intention to make the law accessible to all in an understandable way. It contains links to federal, state, and other legal resources. http://www.law.cornell.edu/
- The Congressional Research Service, which prepares reports on virtually any topic for members of Congress, maintains an open website to provide these reports to the public. http://opencrs.com/
- The Government Printing Office has a searchable database of all federal agency actions in the *Federal Register.* http://www.gpoaccess.gov/fr/index.html
- Mondaq provides legal, regulatory, and financial commentaries on recent rulings and other statutory events, organized by subject matter. You can subscribe to email alerts organized by subject matter in order to stay current on those areas of the law that interest you (and related to over 70 countries). http://www.mondaq.com/
- In association with the Association of Corporate Counsel, Lexology provides a service similar to Mondaq, with a greater focus on legal cases and their implications. http://www.lexology.com/
- Google Scholar has court opinions as well as all sorts of scholarly literature, including books, articles, and theses from universities, professional societies, and so on. http://scholar.google.com

---

Chapter Summary

- With the concepts and information provided in this chapter, not only will you be able to navigate more easily and efficiently through the subsequent chapters, but you also have resources to use if you wish to know more or even to explore your own legal issues.
- Given the possibility of unlimited compensatory and punitive damage awards in wrongful discharge actions, employers are cautioned regarding their interpretation and implementation of the at-will employment arrangement. Employees' protections from unjust dismissal are not limited to statutes prohibiting employment discrimination based on certain factors. Increasingly, employees are able to rely on promises made by the employer through, for example, the employment policy manual.
- Public policy considerations beyond antidiscrimination protections also place limits on the manner in which an employer may terminate an employment relationship. An employer is prohibited from acting in a manner that undermines public policy, however defined.
- In employment discrimination cases, employee's facts must fit within one of two bases in order to be recognized under protective employment legislation. Disparate treatment and disparate impact each have their own unique requirements.
- It is not enough for an employee to simply feel there has been discrimination; the facts must fit within the law.

- Retaliation against an employee for pursuing rights provided by the law is a separate cause of action from the underlying employer action itself and can be found even when the underlying basis is not.
- Given the rise in retaliation claims in the courts and EEOC, it is imperative that employers not take adverse action against their employees for pursuing legitimate legal claims.
- Employees must first exhaust administrative remedies before taking their discrimination claims to court.

Chapter-End Questions

1. Ron and Megan Dible needed some extra money so they decided to charge money for viewing some sexually explicit photographs and videos of themselves that they had posted on the Internet. While this was an otherwise legal act, Ron Dible was a police officer, and after the Chandler Police Department, his employer, learned of his actions, he was terminated. Is his termination in violation of his right to freedom of expression under the First Amendment? [*Dible v. City of Chandler,* 502 F.3d 1040 (9th Cir. 2007).]

2. Think about the following questions from the point of view of violation of public policy or breach of a covenant of good faith and fair dealing, and see what the outcome would be.

   a. A female child care worker alleges that she was unlawfully terminated from her position as the director of a child care facility after continually refusing to make staff cuts. The staff cuts she was asked to make resulted in violation of state regulations governing the minimum ratios between staff and child. After the employee was terminated, the employer's child care center was in violation of the staff-to-child ratio. [*Jasper v. H. Nizam, Inc.,* 764 N.W.2d 751, 2009 Iowa Sup.]

   b. A machine operator employee with a major depressive disorder intermittently takes leaves under the Family and Medical Leave Act, resulting in alleged harassment by her employer surrounding her FMLA usage as well as a transfer to various difficult machines after her return from leave. Two months after her last FMLA leave, she is terminated for "improper phone usage." [*Hite v. Vermeer Mfg. Co.,* 361 F. Supp. 2d 935 (S.D. Iowa, 2005).]

   c. A nurse is asked by her employer to sign a backdated Medicare form. She refuses and is terminated that day. As a health care provider, she is required to complete that particular form. [*Callantine v. Staff Builders, Inc.,* 271 F.3d 1124 (8th Cir. 2001).]

   d. A legal secretary to a county commissioner is terminated because of her political beliefs. [*Armour v. County of Beaver,* 271 F.3d 417 (3d Cir. 2001).]

   e. A teacher under contract is terminated after insisting that his superiors report a situation where a student was being physically abused. The teacher refused to commit an illegal act of not reporting the suspected abuse to family services. [*Keveney v. Missouri Military Academy,* 304 S.W.3d 98 (MO 2010).]

   f. A recent college graduate found a job with an office supply company as a reverse logistics analyst. Soon after being hired, he found that some practices within the department could be deemed unlawful and unethical. Three specific types of practices were written up in a formal complaint to his supervisor: (1) the issuing of monetary credits to customers without proper documentation, thus overpaying customers without returned goods; (2) the department's knowingly withholding from contract customers by underissuing credits over $25; and (3) the canceling and reissuing of pickup orders that could allow couriers to overbill the company. After his formal complaint and multiple meetings on the procedures of the department, the employee was terminated based on his insubordination and inflexibility. [*Day v. Staples Inc.,* 28 IER Cases 1121 (1st Cir. 2009).]

g.   An employee engaged in protected whistleblowing activity after filing a complaint against his employer for his termination. The employee, a licensed optician, claimed his employer was violating state statute by allowing unlicensed employees to sell optical products without a licensed optician present. There was also a complaint filed to his supervisor about the promoting and hiring of unlicensed employees. [*Dishmon v. Wal-Mart Stores Inc.,* 28 IER Cases 1393 (M.D. Tenn. 2009).]

h.   A legal secretary was hired by a law firm. The Letter of Employment stated, "In the event of any dispute or claim between you and the firm . . . including, but not limited to claims arising from or related to your employment or the termination of your employment, we jointly agree to submit all such disputes or claims to confidential binding arbitration, under the Federal Arbitration Act." On his third day of work, the employee informed his superiors that he would not agree to arbitrate disputes. He was told that the arbitration provision was "not negotiable" and that his continued employment was contingent upon signing the agreement. The employee declined to sign the agreement and was discharged. [*Lagatree v. Luce, Forward, Hamilton & Scripps,* 74 Cal. App. 4th 1005 (Cal. App. 2d Div. 1 1999).]

i.   An employee is licensed to perform certain medical procedures, but he is terminated for refusing to perform a procedure he is not licensed to perform. [*O'Sullivan v. Mallon,* 390 A.2d 149 (N.J. Super. Ct. Law Div. 1978).]

j.   An employee was fired from his job as security manager for a medical center because he was suspected of making an obscene phone call to another employee and refused to submit to voice print analysis to confirm or refute the accusation. He sued the employer for wrongful discharge, claiming that the employer's request violated public policy. A state statute prohibits an employer from requiring an employee to submit to a polygraph examination as a condition or precondition of employment. [*Theisen v. Covenant Medical Center,* 636 N.W.2d 74 (Iowa 2001).]

3.   Mariani was a licensed CPA who worked for Colorado Blue Cross and Blue Shield (BCBS) as manager of general accounting for human resources. She complained to her supervisors about questionable accounting practices on a number of occasions and was fired. She claims that her termination was in violation of public policy in favor of accurate reporting, as found in the Board of Accountancy Rules of Professional Conduct. BCBS claims that the rules are not an arbiter of public policy as ethics codes are too variable. Who is correct? [*Rocky Mountain Hospital v. Mariani,* 916 P.2d 519 (Colo. 1996).]

4.   Patricia Meleen, a chemical dependency counselor, brought charges alleging wrongful discharge, defamation, and emotional distress against the Hazelden Foundation, a chemical dependency clinic, in regard to her discharge due to her alleged sexual relations with a former patient. Hazelden's written employment policies prohibited unprofessional and unethical conduct, including sexual contact between patients and counselors. A former patient alleged that Meleen had initiated a social and sexual relationship with him within one year of his discharge. A committee appointed by Hazelden told Meleen of the allegation against her and suspended her with pay in spite of Meleen's denial that she was involved in any improper relations or sexual contact with the former patient. Hazelden offered Meleen a nonclinical position, and when she refused, she was dismissed. Is the dismissal wrongful? [*Meleen v. Hazelden Foundation,* 928 F.2d 795 (8th Cir. 1991).]

5.   Max Huber was the agency manager at Standard Insurance's Los Angeles office. He was employed as an at-will employee, and his contract did not specify any fixed duration of

guaranteed employment. Huber was discharged by the company after eight years because of his alleged negative attitude, the company's increasing expense ratio, and the agency's decreasing recruiting. Huber provided evidence that he had never received negative criticism in any of his evaluations and that his recruiting had been successful. Huber demonstrated that, even though the company had a decrease in recruitment during his employment, he himself had a net increase of contracted agents of 1,100 percent. Huber claims that he was discharged because he was asked to write a letter of recommendation about his supervisor, Canfield, whose termination was being considered. Johnson, Canfield's supervisor, was disappointed with the positive recommendation that Huber wrote because it made Canfield's termination difficult to execute. Johnson is alleged to have transferred Huber to expedite Canfield's termination, and he eventually discharged Huber in retaliation for the positive letter of recommendation. If Huber files suit, what will the result be? [*Huber v. Standard Insurance Co.,* 841 F.2d 980 (9th Cir. 1988).]

6. A new employer policy at a dental office stated that the employees were unable to leave the office except to use the restroom, even with a patient cancellation. A husband of an employee emailed the employer that he had discussed the new rules with an attorney who noted they were in violation of state law. The employer let the employee go soon after the complaint. Does the employee have a claim? [*Bonidy v. Vail Valley Ctr. for Aesthetic Dentistry, P.C.,* 186 P.3d 80 (2008 Colo.).]

7. Althea, a very popular African American deejay, had been a working for a local Christian music station for several years. The station hired a new general manager, and within a month, he terminated Althea. The reason he gave was that it was inappropriate for a Black deejay to play music on a white Christian music station. Althea sues the station. What is her best theory for proceeding?

8. An employee files a race discrimination claim against the employer under Title VII. The employee alleges that after filing a claim with the EEOC, her rating went from outstanding to satisfactory and she was excluded from meetings and important workplace communications, which made it impossible for her to satisfactorily perform her job. The court denied the race discrimination claim. Must it also deny the retaliation claim? [*Lafate v. Chase Manhattan Bank,* 123 F. Supp. 2d 773 (D. Del. 2000).]

9. Day Care Center has a policy stating that no employee can be over 5 feet 4 inches because the employer thinks children feel more comfortable with people who are closer to them in size. Does Tiffany, who is 5 feet 7 inches, have a claim? If so, under what theory could she proceed?

End Notes

1. For an expanded discussion of the evolution of the at-will environment, see Richard Bales, "Explaining the Spread of At-Will Employment as an Inter-Jurisdictional Race-to-the-Bottom of Employment Standards," *Tennessee Law Review* 75, no. 3 (2007), p. 1, http://ssrn.com/abstract=989013; Deborah A. Ballam, "Exploding the Original Myth Regarding Employment-at-Will: The True Origins of the Doctrine," *Berkeley Journal of Employment & Labor Law* 17 (1996), p. 91.

2. Bales, op. cit. 128 Wash. 2d 931, 913 P.2d 377 (1996). See also http://employeeissues.com/at_will_states.htm.

3. If the employer uses a contract to create the at-will relationship, the contract should state that the written document is their entire agreement and that only modifications in writing and signed by the employer will be valid.

4. 128 Wash. 2d 931, 913 P.2d 377 (1996).

5. Ibid., at 950 (emphasis added).

6. *Upton v. JWP Businessland,* 682 N.E.2d 1357 (Mass. 1997).

7. *Tramontozzi v. Mass. DOT,* Unpub. LEXIS 781 (Mass. App. Ct. 2016).

8. Ibid.

9. These states include Arizona, California, Colorado, Florida, Georgia, Hawaii, Illinois, Indiana, Maine, Maryland, Michigan, Minnesota, Nevada, New Jersey, New York, North Carolina, Ohio, Oregon, Texas, Utah, Vermont, Virginia, Washington, West Virginia, and Wisconsin.

10. 18 USCS § 1514A.

11. 78 Cal. Rptr. 2d 16 (Cal. 1998).

12. 126 S. Ct. 2405 (2006).

13. Ibid., at 2415.

14. *Mickey v. Zeidler Tool & Die Co., et al.,* 516 F.3d 516, 525 (6th Cir. 2008).

15. Ehrenkranz, M., "Let's Be Very Clear About What Happened to James Damore," *Gizmodo* (January 17, 2018), https://gizmodo.com/lets-be-very-clear-about-what-hap-pened-to-james-damore-1822160852 (accessed February 22, 2019).

16. Zunger, Y., "So, About This Googler's Manifesto," *Medium* (August 5, 2017), https://medium.com/@yonatanzunger/so-about-this-googlers-manifesto-1e3773ed1788 (accessed February 22, 2019).

17. Eidelson, J., "Google's Firing of Engineer James Damore Did Not Break Labor Law, NLRB Lawyer Concludes," *LA Times* (February 16, 2018), https://www.latimes.com/business/la-fi-tn-google-james-damore-20180216-story.html (accessed February 22, 2019).

18. *Kirke La Shelle Company v. The Paul Armstrong Company et al.,* 263 N.Y. 79 (1933).

19. National Conference of State Legislatures, "Employment At-Will Exceptions by State," https://www.ncsl.org/research/labor-and-employment/at-will-employment-exceptions-by-state.aspx (accessed January 26, 2020).

20. 2016 U.S. Dist. LEXIS 66649 (S.D. Ohio 2016).

21. For a more detailed discussion of the implications of these holdings, see, e.g., J. W. Fineman, "The Inevitable Demise of the Implied Employment Contract," University of Colorado Law Legal Studies Research Paper No. 07-25 (September 17, 2007), http://ssrn.com/abstract=1015136.

22. See also *Buttrick v. Intercity Alarms, LLC,* No. 08-ADMS-40004, Massachusetts District Court, Appellate Division (June 17, 2009) (held not unreasonable for the employee to regard the employee manual as a binding commitment, thus implied contract); *Quedado v. Boeing Co.,* 168 Wn. App. 363, 2 (Wash. App. 2012).

23. *Pennsylvania State Police v. Suders,* 542 U.S. 129 (2004).

24. *Carter v. George Wash. Univ.,* 180 F.Supp.2d 97 (D.D.C. 2001).

25. *Hendrix v. Napolitano,* 77 F.Supp.3d 188 (D.D.C. 2015).

26. 2006 U.S. App. LEXIS 31895 (10th Cir. May 22, 2006).

27. Tex., No. 08-1337, jury verdict, May 26, 2010.

28. *Talley v. Family Dollar Stores of Ohio,* 542 F.3d 1099 (6th Cir. 2008).

29. *Coryell v. Bank One Trust,* 2008 Ohio 2698 (C.A. 2008).

30. 29 U.S. Code § 2101.

31. New Jersey Senate Bill 3170 (S. 3170 (2019), https://www.njleg.state.nj.us/2018/Bills/S3500/3170_R3.htm (accessed January 26, 2020).

32. *EEOC v. Sherwood Food Distributors, LLC,* Civil Action No. 1:16-cv-02386 (U.S. Dist. Ct., N. Dist. OH, E. Div., Cleveland, 2016).

33. 490 U.S. 642 (1989).

34. 487 U.S. 997 (1988).

35. 457 U.S. 440 (1982).

36. "Top 10 Employment Discrimination Claims in 2016," http://www.insurancejournal.com/news/national/2017/02/08/441296.htm?print.

37. "EEOC Releases Fiscal Year 2018 Enforcement and Litigation Data," http://www.eeoc.gov/eeoc/newsroom/release/4-10-18.cfm.

38. EEOC Compliance Manual, Section 8—Retaliation," http://www.eeoc.gov/policy/docs/retal.html; "Facts about Retaliation," http://www.eeoc.gov/laws/types/facts-retal.cfm.

39. http://www.eeoc.gov/eeoc/statistics/enforcement/charges.cfm.

40. "EEOC Releases Fiscal Year 2018 Enforcement and Litigation Data" (April 10, 2019), https://www.eeoc.gov/eeoc/newsroom/release/4-10-19.cfm.

41. "Facts about Retaliation," http://www.eeoc.gov/laws/types/facts-retal.cfm.

42. No. 12-484 (S. Ct. 2013).

43. *Pollard v. E.I. du Pont de Nemours & Co.,* 532 U.S. 843 (2001).

44. We do not suggest the covenant of good faith and fair dealing has no function whatever in the interpretation and enforcement of employment contracts. The covenant prevents a party from acting in bad faith to frustrate the contract's *actual* benefits. Thus, for example, the covenant might be violated if termination of an at-will employee was a mere pretext to cheat the worker out of another contract benefit to which the employee was clearly entitled, such as compensation already earned. We confront no such claim here.

Cases

Case 1

Palmateer v. International Harvester Company,
85 Ill. 2d 124, 421 N.E.2d 876 (1981)

Ray Palmateer had worked for International Harvester (IH) for 16 years at the time of his discharge. Palmateer sued IH for retaliatory discharge, claiming that he was terminated because he supplied information to local law enforcement authorities regarding a coworker's criminal activities and for offering to assist in the investigation and trial of the coworker if necessary. The court agreed and found in favor of Palmateer.

Simon, J.

***

[The court discusses the history of the tort of retaliatory discharge in Illinois and explains that the law will not support the termination of an at-will employment relationship where the termination would contravene public policy.] But the Achilles heel of the principle lies in the definition of public policy. When a discharge contravenes public policy in any way, the employer has committed a legal wrong. However, the employer retains the right to fire workers at-will in cases "where no clear mandate of public policy is involved."

There is no precise definition of the term. In general, it can be said that public policy concerns what is right and just and what affects the citizens of the State collectively. It is to be found in the State's constitution and statutes and, when they are silent, in its judicial decisions. Although there is no precise line of demarcation dividing matters that are the subject of public policies from matters purely personal, a survey of cases in other States involving retaliatory discharge shows that a matter must strike at the heart of a citizen's social rights, duties, and responsibilities before the tort will be allowed.

It is clear that Palmateer has here alleged that he was fired in violation of an established public policy. There is no public policy more basic, nothing more implicit in the concept of ordered liberty than the enforcement of a State's criminal code. There is no public policy more important or more fundamental than the one favoring the effective protection of the lives and property of citizens.

No specific constitutional or statutory provision requires a citizen to take an active part in the ferreting out and the prosecution of crime, but public policy nevertheless favors citizen crime-fighters. Public policy favors Palmateer's conduct in volunteering information to the law enforcement agency. Palmateer was under a statutory duty to further assist officials when requested to do so.

The foundation of the tort of retaliatory discharge lies in the protection of public policy, and there is a clear public policy favoring investigation and prosecution of criminal offenses. Palmateer has stated a cause of action for retaliatory discharge.

Case Questions

1. Is there a difference between the court's protection of an employee who reports a rape by a coworker or the theft of a car and an employee who is constantly reporting the theft of the company's paper clips and pens?

2. Should the latter employee in the above question be protected? Consider that the court in Palmateer remarked that "the magnitude of the crime is not the issue here. It was the General Assembly who decided that the theft of a $2 screwdriver was a problem that should be resolved by resort to the criminal justice system."

3. What are other areas of public policy that might offer protection to terminated workers?

Herawi v. State of Alabama, Department of Forensic Sciences, *311 F. Supp. 2d 1335 (M.D. Ala. 2004)*

Herawi is an Iranian doctor whose employment was terminated. She filed a complaint against the defendant, the state Department of Forensic Sciences, alleging national origin discrimination and retaliation. The state responded that it had legitimate non-discriminatory reasons for terminating her (insubordination and poor job performance). The district court found that Herawi's national origin discrimination claim would not be dismissed on summary judgment because her supervisor's threat that she would report the doctor's national origin to law enforcement made clear that her supervisor was antagonistic toward her because of her Iranian heritage and that the timing of the doctor's termination (three weeks after complaining about the supervisor's behavior) suggested that the supervisor's apparent dislike for her national origin may have infected the process of evaluating the doctor. Herawi also prevailed against summary judgment on the retaliatory discharge claim. (Herawi also claimed hostile environment but did not succeed, and the discussion of that claim is not included below.)

Notice that Dr. Herawi is a medical doctor. She also has a PhD and is a noted researcher. The actions toward her took place just after 9/11 when feelings were running high against Iranians. As you read the excerpt, look for any actions you think may have this as a motivation for how her conduct was viewed and how poorly she was treated. After the case, several of the parties who complained about Dr. Herawi were discredited. In this age of social media and the Internet, think about how having these things (later discredited) said about you might adversely impact your career long after the case is actually over.

OPINION BY: Myron H. Thompson, J.

***

II. Factual Background

During the relevant time period, Herawi's supervisor in the Montgomery office [of the Alabama Department of Forensic Sciences] was Dr. Emily Ward. Herawi, like all state employees, was a probationary employee for her first six months on the job.

Ward was highly critical of Herawi almost immediately upon her arrival in the Montgomery office. On her first day at work, Ward accused Herawi of being inconsiderate for not offering to help her. Ward looked at Herawi with a "hatred filled stare" and mocked her by repeating her in a high-pitched voice. On or about October 22, 2001, Ward became enraged at Herawi, shouted at her, accused her of wrongdoing, and said she had enough of Herawi and that Herawi was the rudest person she had ever met. When Herawi tried to explain her actions, Ward yelled louder and said that she did not like Herawi and that no one else liked her either.

On October 24, Herawi expressed to Craig Bailey, the office director, her concerns about the way Ward was treating her. Bailey later told Herawi that, after his conversation with her, he spoke to Ward to find out if she had a problem with people of Middle Eastern descent. Bailey told Herawi that people from the Middle East were perceived as rude and aggressive.

On November 7, Ward "implied" to Herawi that she was getting calls from people asking about Herawi's background and her accent, and she threatened to expose Herawi's nationality to law enforcement agencies. Ward also said that she was getting calls from people asking who Herawi was, asking why she was there, and stating that she did not belong there.

Herawi had two more run-ins with Ward in December 2001, after Herawi had taken time off in November to visit her mother in California after the death of her father. On December 6, Ward called Herawi into her office, where Bailey yelled at Herawi, accusing her of neglecting the office after her father died and not performing enough autopsies. Bailey also questioned Herawi about whether she was looking for a job in California. On or about December 25, Herawi confronted Ward about whether Ward had spread a rumor that Herawi was looking for a job in California. [The court outlines additional, subsequent circumstances, which it discusses later in this opinion.]

On January 2, 2002, Herawi received an "employee probationary performance appraisal" and an attached narrative performance appraisal, dated November 15, 2001. The narrative performance appraisal states that Herawi "appears to be a very intelligent and dedicated Forensic Pathologist" and that she "seems to have been well trained." The narrative appraisal, however, goes on to state that "her performance has been problematic in four inter-related areas: expectations of co-workers, recognition of and subordination to authority, incessant inquisitiveness, and lack of organization." It also states that Herawi "comes across as very self-centered and projects an 'entitlement complex'"; that she "has also refused to comply with departmental regulations and/or rules if she doesn't agree with them"; and that her "work habits leave room for improvement." The narrative was signed by Ward and Downs, [J.C. Upshaw Downs, the Director of the Alabama Department of Forensic Sciences and the Chief Medical Examiner for Alabama, and others.]

Herawi brought her concerns about Ward to Downs on January 4, 2002. Herawi told Downs that Ward had threatened to expose her nationality; Herawi also told Downs that she felt confused and intimidated. Downs told Herawi that Middle Eastern people were generally facing troubles in the wake of the terrorist attacks on September 11, 2001, and that Herawi should turn the other cheek. However, Downs said he would speak to Ward.

On January 9, 2002, Downs wrote a letter to Thomas Flowers, the state personnel director, requesting that Herawi's probationary period be extended by three months. Downs wrote that Herawi "requires additional training in autopsy procedures to take a more organized approach to the process" and that she "must also learn to use the chain of command."

***

Ward alluded to Herawi's nationality again on March 7, 2002. Ward told Herawi that nobody liked her, that everybody complained about her, that she did not belong there, that should leave, and that her English was bad. After this incident, Herawi complained to Downs again on March 21, about Ward's hostility. At this meeting, Downs told Herawi that he would start an investigation, and Herawi told Downs that she had contacted a lawyer. Herawi also complained to Samuel Mitchell, the department chief of staff, on March 25.

Events came to a head on March 28, at a meeting attended by Herawi, Ward, Bailey and Steve Christian, the department's personnel manager. Herawi claims that she was terminated during the meeting and that when she met with Christian shortly after the meeting, he told her it was unofficial policy that terminated employees could submit a letter of resignation. Memoranda written by Ward, Bailey and Christian present slightly different accounts. According to Ward, she informed Herawi that the situation was not working out and that the department had not seen any improvement in the areas identified in Herawi's performance appraisal. According to Ward, before she could finish, Herawi interrupted her to say she would quit. According to Bailey, Ward requested Herawi's resignation, and Herawi agreed. According to Christian, Ward told Herawi that an offer of permanent employment would not be forthcoming and then told Herawi to speak with him later that day. When they met, according to Christian, he told her it was the department's unofficial policy to allow employees to resign to make it easier to look for work in the future.

Herawi submitted a letter of resignation on April 1, 2002. A letter from Downs, dated April 18, confirmed Herawi's "separation from employment" at the department effective April 19. Downs's letter states that the reason for Herawi's separation is that she continued "to require additional training in autopsy procedures and failure to properly use the chain of command."

III. Analysis

Herawi claims that (1) she was terminated because of her Iranian origin; (2) she was fired in retaliation for her complaints about Ward; and (3) she was harassed because of her national origin [not addressed in this excerpt]. The

Forensic Department has moved for summary judgment on the ground that its decision not to offer her a permanent position was based on legitimate, non-discriminatory reasons. The court will consider Herawi's claims in order.

A. Termination

***

IV.

Applying *McDonnell Douglas,* this court concludes that Herawi has met her *prima-facie* burden of producing "evidence adequate to create an inference that [the Forensic Department's] employment decision was based on an [illegal] discriminatory criterion." To establish a *prima-facie* case of discriminatory discharge, she must show the following: (1) she is a member of a protected class; (2) she was qualified for the position at issue; (3) she was discharged despite her qualification; and (4) some additional evidence that would allow an inference of discrimination. [The court evaluates Herawi's evidence of these elements and finds that Herawi satisfies the first three elements; it then continues in its analysis of the fourth requirement, below.]

In this case, Ward made remarks related to Herawi's national origin on three occasions. On November 7, 2001, Ward threatened to report Herawi's national origin to law enforcement agencies. On January 2, 2002, Ward told Herawi that she was getting calls asking who Herawi was and why she was working there; Ward suggested that she was getting these calls because of Herawi's accent. Finally, on March 7, 2002, Ward told Herawi that no one liked her, that she did not belong at the department, that she should leave, and that her English was bad. It is undisputed that Ward was Herawi's direct supervisor when she made these remarks and that Ward had substantial input into the ultimate decision to terminate Herawi. In fact, Ward conducted Herawi's January 2002 performance appraisal, and she wrote the four memoranda in February and March of 2002 documenting incidents involving Herawi. Given this evidence, the court is satisfied that Herawi has raised the inference that her national origin was a motivating factor in the department's decision to terminate her.

The burden thus shifts to the Forensic Department to articulate a legitimate non-discriminatory reason for its decision to fire Herawi. The department has met this "exceedingly light" burden. It asserts that Herawi was not retained because she "had problems with autopsy procedures and with the chain of command." Plainly, job performance, failure to follow instructions, and insubordination are all legitimate, non-discriminatory considerations.

Because the department has met its burden, Herawi must show that its asserted reasons are pretextual. The court finds, again, that the evidence of Ward's comments about Herawi's national origin is sufficient for Herawi to meet her burden. Comments or remarks that suggest discriminatory animus can be sufficient circumstantial evidence to establish pretext. "Whether comments standing alone show pretext depends on whether their substance, context, and timing could permit a finding that the comments are causally related to the adverse employment action at issue."

In this case, Ward's comments "might lead a reasonable jury to disbelieve [the department's] proffered reason for firing" Herawi. Ward's threat that she would report Herawi's nationality to law enforcement makes it clear that she was antagonistic towards Herawi because of Herawi's Iranian origin. Ward's later comment that Herawi did not belong in the department, made at the same time she commented on Herawi's accent, further evinced discriminatory animus. Standing alone, this might not be enough evidence to establish a genuine question of pretext, but Ward was Herawi's supervisor, conducted her performance appraisal, and wrote four memoranda containing negative evaluations of her. In this context, the evidence suggests that Ward's evident dislike for Herawi's national origin may have infected the process of evaluating Herawi. The timing of Ward's remarks reinforces this conclusion. The first incident in which Ward referred to Herawi's nationality occurred one week before the narrative performance appraisal of Herawi was written, the second incident occurred on the same day—January 2, 2002—that Ward completed the performance appraisal form, and her final remarks were made three weeks before Herawi was fired. Because of this close temporal proximity, a jury could reasonably conclude that discriminatory attitude evidence in Ward's remarks motivated the decision to fire Herawi. Accordingly, the court finds that Herawi has met her burden and that summary judgment on her termination claim is not appropriate.

B. Retaliation

Herawi contends that the Forensic Department retaliated against her for complaining to Downs and to Mitchell about Ward's conduct. The department has moved for summary

judgment, again, on the basis that its employment decision was motivated by legitimate, non-discriminatory reasons.

Under Title VII, it is an unlawful employment practice for an employer to discriminate against an employee "because [s]he has opposed any practice made an unlawful employment practice by this subchapter, or because [s]he has made a charge, testified, assisted, or participated in any manner in an investigation, proceeding, or hearing under this subchapter." The same *McDonnell Douglas* burden-shifting framework that applies to claims of discriminatory discharge applies to claims for retaliation.

The Eleventh Circuit has established broad standards for a *prima-facie* case of retaliation. An individual alleging retaliation under Title VII must establish her *prima-facie* case by demonstrating "(1) that she engaged in statutorily protected activity, (2) that an adverse employment action occurred, and (3) that the adverse action was causally related to [her] protected activities." "The causal link element is construed broadly so that a plaintiff merely has to prove that the protected activity and the negative employment action are not completely unrelated."

Herawi has established the elements of a *prima-facie* case of retaliation. First, she was engaged in protected activity on the two occasions that she spoke with Downs and on the one occasion she spoke to Mitchell. Second, Herawi was terminated. Third, Herawi satisfies the causality requirement because she was terminated only a week after her meeting with Downs and three days after her meeting with Mitchell.

Because Herawi has produced evidence sufficient to meet her *prima-facie* burden, the burden of production shifts to the Forensic Department to produce a legitimate, non-retaliatory reason for its decision. As discussed above, the department has offered legitimate reasons for its decision. The department contends that it fired Herawi because of her problems with autopsy procedure and her problems following the chain of command. The burden thus shifts to Herawi to come forward with evidence sufficient for a reasonable fact finder to conclude that the department's asserted reasons were pretext for retaliation.

Herawi has met this burden. As discussed above, Herawi has presented substantial evidence of Ward's animus towards her and thus raised a very real question about the extent to which the department's assessment of her might have been influenced by Ward's attitude. There is also evidence from which a reasonable fact finder could conclude that Ward's assessment of Herawi was infected by a retaliatory motive. In October 2001, Bailey reported to Ward that Herawi had complained to him about her, and, in January 2002, Downs spoke to Ward about Herawi's complaints. Thus, at the same time that Ward was evaluating and assessing Herawi's job performance in the fall of 2001, and the winter of 2002, she was aware that Herawi had gone to various supervisors to complain about her. The court also considers it relevant to determining pretext that Herawi was dismissed so soon after she complained to Downs and Mitchell. While temporal proximity, standing alone, may not be enough to create a genuine issue of pretext, it is a relevant factor. Thus, taking into consideration the evidence of Ward's discriminatory animus, her possible retaliatory motive, and the extreme closeness in time between Herawi's complaints and her dismissal, the court concludes that Herawi has evidence sufficient for a reasonable fact finder to conclude that the department's asserted reasons for her dismissal were pretextual.

***

IV. Conclusion

For the reasons given above, it is ORDERED as follows:

(1) The motion for summary judgment, filed by defendant Alabama Department of Forensic Sciences on November 12, 2003 (doc. no. 20), is granted with respect to plaintiff Mehsati Herawi's hostile-environment claim.

Case Questions

1. Are you persuaded by the state's evidence that it had an individual of a different national origin who was treated similarly to Herawi? If Ward (or other managers) treated everyone equally poorly, perhaps there is no national origin claim. What if Ward's defense is simply that her poor treatment of Herawi had nothing to do with national origin but that she just really did not like Herawi specifically? Would that be an acceptable defense, and could it have saved the state's case?

2. The court explains that pretext may be based on comments depending on "whether their substance, context, and timing could permit a finding that the comments are causally related to the adverse employment action at issue." What elements would you look to in order to find pretext if you were on a jury?

3. The court explains that timing alone would not be enough to satisfy the causality requirement of retaliatory discharge. Given the facts of this case, if you were in charge of the department and if Herawi truly were not performing at an acceptable level and you wished to terminate her after all of these circumstances, how might you have better protected the department from a retaliatory discharge claim?

Guz v. Bechtel National Inc.,
100 Cal. Rptr. 2d 352 (Cal. 2000)

Plaintiff John Guz, a longtime employee of Bechtel National, Inc. (BNI), was terminated at age 49 when his work unit was eliminated as a way to reduce costs. At the time he was hired and at his termination, Bechtel had a Personnel Policy (no. 1101) on the subject of termination of employment that explained that "Bechtel employees have no employment agreements guaranteeing continuous service and may resign at their option or be terminated at the option of Bechtel." Guz sued BNI and its parent, Bechtel Corporation, alleging age discrimination, breach of an implied contract to be terminated only for good cause, and breach of the implied covenant of good faith and fair dealing. The trial court found in favor of Bechtel and dismissed the action. The Court of Appeals reversed and determined that the trial should instead be permitted to proceed. Bechtel appealed to the Supreme Court of California, which in this opinion reverses the judgment of the Court of Appeals based on a finding that no *implied* contract exists and remands only for a determination of whether there are any enforceable *express* contract terms.

Baxter, J.

***

III. Implied Covenant Claim

Bechtel urges that the trial court properly dismissed Guz's separate claim for breach of the implied covenant of good faith and fair dealing because, on the facts and arguments presented, this theory of recovery is either inapplicable or superfluous. We agree.

The sole asserted basis for Guz's implied covenant claim is that Bechtel violated its established personnel policies when it terminated him without a prior opportunity to improve his "unsatisfactory" performance, used no force ranking or other objective criteria when selecting him for layoff, and omitted to consider him for other positions for which he was qualified. Guz urges that *even if his contract was for employment at-will,* the implied covenant of good faith and fair dealing precluded Bechtel from "unfairly" denying him the contract's benefits by failing to follow its own termination policies.

Thus, Guz argues, in effect, that the implied covenant can impose substantive terms and conditions beyond those to which the contract parties actually agreed. However, as indicated above, such a theory directly contradicts our conclusions in *Foley v. Interactive Data Corp.* (1988). The covenant of good faith and fair dealing, implied by law in every contract, exists merely to prevent one contracting party from unfairly frustrating the other party's right to receive the *benefits of the agreement actually made.* The covenant thus cannot "be endowed with an existence independent of its contractual underpinnings." It cannot impose substantive duties or limits on the contracting parties beyond those incorporated in the specific terms of their agreement.

. . . The mere existence of an employment relationship affords no expectation, protectable by law, that employment will continue, or will end only on certain conditions, unless the parties have actually adopted such terms. Thus if the employer's termination decisions, however arbitrary, do not breach such a substantive contract provision, they are not precluded by the covenant.

This logic led us to emphasize in *Foley* that "breach of the implied covenant cannot logically be based on a claim that [the] discharge [of an at-will employee] was made without good cause." As we noted, "[b]ecause the implied covenant protects only the parties' right to receive the benefit of their agreement, and, in an at-will relationship there is no agreement to terminate only for good cause, the implied covenant standing alone cannot be read to impose such a duty."

The same reasoning applies to any case where an employee argues that even if his employment was at-will, his arbitrary dismissal frustrated his contract benefits and thus violated the implied covenant of good faith and fair dealing. Precisely because employment at-will *allows* the employer freedom to terminate the relationship as it chooses, the employer does not frustrate the employee's contractual rights merely by doing so. In such a case, "the employee cannot complain about a deprivation of the benefits of continued employment, for the agreement never provided for a continuation of its benefits in the first instance."

At odds with *Foley* are suggestions that independent recovery for breach of the implied covenant may be available if the employer terminated the employee in "bad faith" or "without probable cause," i.e., without determining "honestly and in good faith that good cause for discharge existed." Where the employment contract itself allows the employer to terminate at-will, its motive and lack of care in doing so are, in most cases at least, irrelevant.

A number of Court of Appeal decisions since *Foley* have recognized that the implied covenant of good faith and fair dealing imposes no independent limits on an employer's prerogative to dismiss employees. . . . We affirm that this is the law.

Of course, as we have indicated above, the employer's personnel policies and practices may become *implied-in-fact terms* of the contract between employer and employee. If that has occurred, the employer's failure to follow such policies when terminating an employee is a breach of the contract itself.

A breach of the contract may also constitute a breach of the implied covenant of good faith and fair dealing. But insofar as the employer's acts are directly actionable as a breach of an implied-in-fact contract term, a claim that merely realleges that breach as a violation of the covenant is superfluous. This is because, as we explained at length in *Foley,* the remedy for breach of an employment agreement, including the covenant of good faith and fair dealing implied by law therein, is *solely contractual.* In the employment context, an implied covenant theory affords no separate *measure of recovery,* such as tort damages. Allegations that the breach was wrongful, in bad faith, arbitrary, and unfair are unavailing; there is no tort of "bad faith breach" of an employment contract.

We adhere to these principles here. To the extent Guz's implied covenant cause of action seeks to impose limits on Bechtel's termination rights *beyond* those to which the parties actually agreed, the claim is invalid. To the extent the implied covenant claim seeks simply to invoke terms to which the parties *did* agree, it is superfluous. Guz's remedy, if any, for Bechtel's alleged violation of its personnel policies depends on proof that they were contract terms to which the parties actually agreed. The trial court thus properly dismissed the implied covenant cause of action.[44]

Case Questions

1. Based on *Guz,* can the implied covenant of good faith and fair dealing apply to any conditions not actually stated in a contract? In other words, can the covenant apply to anything beyond that which is actually stated in an employment contract? If not, is there no implied covenant as long as someone is at-will without a contract?

2. Explain the distinction between the court's discussion of the covenant of good faith and fair dealing and the possibility of an implied contract term.

3. How might an employer create an "implied-in-fact term," and how could a failure to follow such policies when terminating an employee create a breach of the contract?

Case 4

McDonnell Douglas Corp. v. Green, *411 U.S. 792 (1973)*

Green, an employee of McDonnell Douglas and a Black civil rights activist, engaged with others in "disruptive and illegal activity" against his employer in the form of a traffic stall-in. The activity was done as part of Green's protest that his discharge from McDonnell Douglas was racially motivated, as were the firm's general hiring practices. McDonnell Douglas later rejected Green's reemployment application on the ground of the illegal conduct. Green sued, alleging race discrimination. The case is important because it is the first time the U.S. Supreme Court set forth how to prove a disparate treatment case under Title VII. In such cases, the employee can use an inference of discrimination drawn from a set of inquiries the Court set forth.

Powell, J.

***

The critical issue before us concerns the order and allocation of proof in a private, nonclass action challenging employment discrimination. The language of Title VII makes plain the purpose of Congress to assure equality of employment opportunities and to eliminate those discriminatory practices and devices which have fostered racially stratified job environments to the disadvantage of minority citizens.

The complainant in a Title VII trial must carry the initial burden under the statute of establishing a *prima facie* case of racial discrimination. This may be done by showing (i) that he belongs to a racial minority; (ii) that he applied and was qualified for a job for which the employer was seeking applicants; (iii) that, despite his qualifications, he was rejected; and (iv) that, after his rejection, the position remained open and the employer continued to seek applicants from persons of complainant's qualifications. The facts necessarily will vary in Title VII cases, and the specification of the *prima facie* proof required

from Green is not necessarily applicable in every respect to differing factual situations.

In the instant case, Green proved a *prima facie* case. McDonnell Douglas sought mechanics, Green's trade, and continued to do so after Green's rejection. McDonnell Douglas, moreover, does not dispute Green's qualifications and acknowledges that his past work performance in McDonnell Douglas' employ was "satisfactory."

The burden then must shift to the employer to articulate some legitimate, non-discriminatory reason for the employee's rejection. We need not attempt to detail every matter which fairly could be recognized as a reasonable basis for a refusal to hire. Here McDonnell Douglas has assigned Green's participation in unlawful conduct against it as the cause for his rejection. We think that this suffices to discharge McDonnell Douglas' burden of proof at this stage and to meet Green's *prima facie* case of discrimination.

But the inquiry must not end here. While Title VII does not, without more, compel the rehiring of Green, neither does it permit McDonnell Douglas to use Green's conduct as a pretext for the sort of discrimination prohibited by Title VII. On remand, Green must be afforded a fair opportunity to show that McDonnell Douglas' stated reason for Green's rejection was in fact pretext. Especially relevant to such a showing would be evidence that white employees involved in acts against McDonnell Douglas of comparable seriousness to the "stall-in" were nevertheless retained or rehired.

McDonnell Douglas may justifiably refuse to rehire one who was engaged in unlawful, disruptive acts against it, but only if this criterion is applied alike to members of all races. Other evidence that may be relevant to any showing of pretext includes facts as to McDonnell Douglas' treatment of Green during his prior term of employment; McDonnell Douglas' reaction, if any, to Green's legitimate civil rights activities; and McDonnell Douglas' general policy and practice with respect to minority employment.

On the latter point, statistics as to McDonnell Douglas' employment policy and practice may be helpful to a determination of whether McDonnell Douglas' refusal to rehire Green in this case conformed to a general pattern of discrimination against Blacks. The District Court may, for example, determine after reasonable discovery that "the [racial] composition of defendant's labor force is itself reflective of restrictive or exclusionary practices." We caution that such general determinations, while helpful, may not be in and of themselves controlling as to an individualized hiring decision, particularly in the presence of an otherwise justifiable reason for refusing to rehire. In short, on the retrial Green must be given a full and fair opportunity to demonstrate by competent evidence that the presumptively valid reasons for his rejection were in fact a cover up for a racially discriminatory decision. VACATED and REMANDED.

Case Questions

1. Do you think the Court should require actual evidence of discrimination in disparate treatment cases rather than permitting an inference? What are the advantages? Disadvantages?

2. Practically speaking, is an employer's burden really met after the employer "articulates" a legitimate nondiscriminatory reason for rejecting the employee? Explain.

3. Does the Court say that Green must be kept on in spite of his illegal activities? Discuss.

Case 5

Wilson v. Southwest Airlines Company,
517 F. Supp. 292 (N.D. Tex. Dallas Div. 1981)

A male sued Southwest Airlines after he was not hired as a flight attendant because he was male. The airline argued that being female was a BFOQ for being a flight attendant. The court disagreed.

Higginbotham, J.

***

Memorandum Opinion

Southwest conceded that its refusal to hire males was intentional. The airline also conceded that its height–weight restrictions would have an adverse impact on male applicants, if actually applied. Southwest contends, however, that the BFOQ exception to Title VII's ban on gender discrimination justifies its hiring only females for the public contact positions of flight attendant and ticket agent. The BFOQ window through which Southwest attempts to fly permits gender discrimination in situations where the employer can prove that gender is a "bona fide occupational qualification reasonably necessary to the normal operation of that particular business or enterprise." Southwest reasons it may discriminate against males because its attractive female flight attendants and ticket agents personify the airline's sexy image and fulfill its public promise to take passengers skyward with "love." The airline claims maintenance of its females-only hiring policy is crucial to its continued financial success.

Since it has been admitted that Southwest discriminates on the basis of gender, the only issue to decide is whether Southwest has proved that being female is a BFOQ reasonably necessary to the normal operation of its particular business.

As an integral part of its youthful, feminine image, Southwest has employed only females in the high customer contact positions of ticket agent and flight attendant. From the start, Southwest's attractive personnel, dressed in high boots and hot-pants, generated public interest and "free ink." Their sex appeal has been used to attract male customers to the airline. Southwest's flight attendants, and to a lesser degree its ticket agents, have been featured in newspaper, magazine, billboard, and television advertisements during the past 10 years. According to Southwest, its female flight attendants have come to "personify" Southwest's public image.

Southwest has enjoyed enormous success in recent years. From 1979 to 1980, the company's earnings rose from $17 million to $28 million when most other airlines suffered heavy losses.

The broad scope of Title VII's coverage is qualified by Section 703(e), the BFOQ exception. Section 703(e) states:

(e) Notwithstanding any other provision of this subchapter,

(1) It shall not be an unlawful employment practice for an employer to hire . . . on the basis of his religion, gender, or national origin in those certain instances where religion, gender, or national origin is a bona fide occupational qualification reasonably necessary to the normal operation of that particular business or enterprise.

The BFOQ defense is not to be confused with the doctrine of "business necessity" which operates only in cases involving unintentional discrimination, when job criteria which are "fair in form, but discriminatory in operation" are shown to be "related to" job performance.

This Circuit's decisions have given rise to a two step BFOQ test: (1) does the particular job under consideration require that the worker be of one gender only; and if so, (2) is that requirement reasonably necessary to the "essence" of the employer's business. The first level of inquiry is designed to test whether gender is so essential to job performance that a member of the opposite gender simply could not do the same job.

To rely on the bona fide occupational qualification exception, an employer has the burden of proving that he had reasonable cause to believe, that is, a factual basis for believing, that all or substantially all women would be unable to perform safely and efficiently the duties of the job involved. The second level is designed to assure that the qualification being scrutinized is one so important to the operation of the business that the business would be undermined if employees of the "wrong" gender were hired. . . . The use of the word "necessary" in section 703(e) requires that we apply a business necessity test, not a business convenience test. That is to say, discrimination based on gender is valid only when the essence of the business operation would be undermined by not hiring members of one gender exclusively.

Applying the first level test for a BFOQ to Southwest's particular operations results in the conclusion that being female is not a qualification required to perform successfully the jobs of flight attendant and ticket agent with Southwest. Like any other airline, Southwest's primary function is to transport passengers safely and quickly from one point to another. To do this, Southwest employs ticket agents whose primary job duties are to ticket passengers and check baggage, and flight attendants, whose primary duties are to assist passengers during boarding and deboarding, to instruct passengers in the location and use of aircraft safety equipment, and to serve passengers cocktails and snacks during the airline's short commuter flights. Mechanical, nongender-linked duties dominate both these occupations. Indeed, on Southwest's short-haul commuter flights there is time for little else. That Southwest's female personnel may perform their mechanical duties "with love" does not change the result. "Love" is the manner of job performance, not the job performed.

Southwest's argument that its primary function is "to make a profit," not to transport passengers, must be rejected. Without doubt the goal of every business is to make a profit. For purposes of BFOQ analysis, however, the business "essence" inquiry focuses on the particular service provided and the job tasks and functions involved, not the business goal. If an employer could justify employment discrimination merely on the grounds that it is necessary to make a profit, Title VII would be nullified in short order.

In order not to undermine Congress' purpose to prevent employers from "refusing to hire an individual based on stereotyped characterizations of the genders," a BFOQ for gender must be denied where gender is merely useful for attracting customers of the opposite gender, but where hiring both genders will not alter or undermine the essential function of the employer's business. Rejecting a wider BFOQ for gender does not eliminate the commercial exploitation of sex appeal. It only requires, consistent with the purposes of Title VII, that employers exploit the attractiveness and allure of a gender-integrated workforce. Neither Southwest, nor the traveling public, will suffer from such a rule. More to the point, it is my judgment that this is what Congress intended.

Case Questions

1. What should be done if, as here, the public likes the employer's marketing scheme?

2. Do you think the standards for BFOQs are too strict? Explain.

3. Should a commercial success argument be given more weight by the courts? How should that be balanced with concern for Congress's position on discrimination?

Griggs v. Duke Power Co., *401 U.S. 424 (1971)*

Until the day Title VII became effective, it was the policy of Duke Power Co. that Blacks be employed in only one of its five departments: the Labor Department. The highest-paid Black employee in the Labor Department made less than the lowest-paid white employee in any other department. Blacks could not transfer out of the Labor Department into any other department. The day Title VII became effective, Duke instituted a policy requiring new hires to have a high school diploma and passing scores on two general intelligence tests in order to be placed in any department other than Labor and a high school diploma to transfer to other departments from Labor. Two months later, Duke required that transferees from the Labor or Coal Handling Departments who had no high school diploma pass two general intelligence tests. White employees already in other departments were grandfathered in under the new policy, and the high school diploma and intelligence test requirements did not apply to them. Black employees brought this action under Title VII of the Civil Rights Act of 1964, challenging the employer's requirement of a high school diploma and the passing of intelligence tests as a condition of employment in or transfer to jobs at the power plant. They alleged that the requirements were not job-related and had the effect of disqualifying Blacks from employment or transfer at a higher rate than whites. The U.S. Supreme Court held that the act dictated that job requirements that have a disproportionate impact on groups protected by Title VII be shown to be job-related.

Burger, J.

***

We granted the writ in this case to resolve the question of whether an employer is prohibited by Title VII of the Civil Rights Act of 1964 from requiring a high school education or passing of a standardized general intelligence test as a condition of employment in or transfer to jobs when *(a)* neither standard is shown to be significantly related to successful job performance, *(b)* both requirements operate to disqualify Negroes at a substantially higher rate than white applicants, and *(c)* the jobs in question formerly had been filled only by white employees as part of a long-standing practice of giving preference to whites.

What is required by Congress [under Title VII] is the removal of artificial, arbitrary, and unnecessary barriers to employment when the barriers operate invidiously to discriminate on the basis of racial or other impermissible classifications.

The act proscribes not only overt discrimination but also practices that are fair in form, but discriminatory in operation. The touchstone is business necessity. If an employment practice which operates to exclude Negroes cannot be shown to be related to job performance, the practice is prohibited.

On the record before us, neither the high school completion requirement nor the general intelligence test is shown to bear a demonstrable relationship to successful performance of the jobs for which it was used. Both were adopted without meaningful study of their relationship to job performance ability.

The evidence shows that employees who have not completed high school or taken the tests have continued to perform satisfactorily and make progress in departments for which the high school and test criteria are now used.

Good intent or absence of discriminatory intent does not redeem employment procedures or testing mechanisms that operate as "built-in head winds" for minority groups and are unrelated to measuring job capability.

The facts of this case demonstrate the inadequacy of broad and general testing devices as well as the infirmity of using diplomas or degrees as general measures of capability. History is filled with examples of men and women who rendered highly effective performance without the conventional badges of accomplishment in terms of certificates, diplomas, or degrees. Diplomas and tests are useful servants, but Congress has mandated the commonsense proposition that they are not to become masters of reality.

Nothing in the act precludes the use of testing or measuring procedures; obviously they are useful. What Congress has forbidden is giving these devices and mechanisms controlling force unless they are demonstrably a reasonable measure of job performance. Congress has not commanded that the less qualified be measured or preferred over the better qualified simply because of minority origins. Far from disparaging job qualifications as such, Congress has made such qualifications the controlling factor, so that race, religion, nationality, and sex become irrelevant. What Congress has commanded is that any tests used must measure the person for the job and not the person in the abstract. REVERSED.

Case Questions

1. Does this case make sense to you? Why? Why not?
2. The Court said the employer's intent does not matter here. Should it? Explain.
3. What would be your biggest concern as an employer who read this decision?

Chapter **3**

Title VII of the Civil Rights Act of 1964

Learning Objectives

After completing this chapter, you should be able to:

Library of Congress Prints
and Photographs Division
[LC-DIG-ppmsca-03128]

LO1 Explain the history leading up to passage of the Civil Rights Act of 1964.

LO2 Give examples of the ways that certain groups of people were treated differently before passage of the Civil Rights Act.

LO3 Discuss what is prohibited by Title VII.

LO4 Recognize who is covered by Title VII and who is not.

LO5 State how a Title VII claim is filed and proceeds through the administrative process.

LO6 Determine if a Title VII claimant is able to proceed after receiving a no-reasonable-cause finding.

LO7 Distinguish between the various types of alternative dispute resolution used by the EEOC.

LO8 Explain the post–Civil War statutes, including what each is and what it does.

LO9 Discuss what management can do to comply with Title VII.

Opening Scenarios

SCENARIO 1

1 Jack feels he has been discriminated against
by his employer based on national origin. After
Scenario a particularly tense incident one day, Jack
leaves work and goes to his attorney and asks
the attorney to file suit against the employer for violation of Title VII of the Civil Rights Act of 1964. Will the
attorney do so?

SCENARIO 2

2 Shelly receives an anonymous tip that she is
making less money than all the other manag-
Scenario ers on her level, all of whom are male. Shelly

believes it began when she did not receive a raise
because she rejected advances by her supervisor six
years before, and the wage gap has now grown far
more than she realized. Shelly files a claim with the
EEOC. Will she prevail?

SCENARIO 3

3 When Rinson did not receive the promotion
he believed was his, he became upset. Rinson
Scenario believes he did not receive the promotion
because his boss hates him and always judges
Rinson's work harshly. If Rinson can prove this is true,
does he have a valid claim for damages under Title VII?

Statutory Basis

Title VII of the Civil Rights Act of 1964

(a) It shall be an unlawful employment practice for an employer—

    (1) to fail or refuse to hire or to discharge any individual, or otherwise to dis-
criminate against any individual with respect to his compensation, terms,
conditions, or privileges of employment, because of such individual's race,
color, religion, sex, or national origin; or

    (2) to limit, segregate, or classify his employees or applicants for employment
in any way which would deprive or tend to deprive any individual of employment opportunities or otherwise adversely affect his status as an employee,
because of such individual's race, color, religion, sex, or national origin.

Title VII of the Civil Rights Act of 1964, as amended, 42 U.S.C.A. sec. 2000e et seq., sec. 703 (a).

A Historic Rights Act

LO1 Explain the history
leading up to passage of
the Civil Rights Act of 1964.

LO2 Give examples of
the ways that certain groups
of people were treated
differently before passage
of the Civil Rights Act.

"A strong and prosperous nation secured through a fair and inclusive workplace."[1]
Such a simple statement. Who could disagree with such a vision? It is the vision
of the Equal Employment Opportunity Commission (EEOC), the federal agency
charged with enforcing laws that were created to make that statement a reality. However, not everyone agrees with that vision or realizes when they may not be acting
consistently with it. Though we have come a long way in the 55-plus years since the
law was passed creating the agency, unfortunately, much work is still to be done.
For instance, the latest EEOC figures indicate that the EEOC had a 13.6 percent
increase in sexual harassment charges from 2017 to 2018 in the wake of the #MeToo
Movement, recovering $56.6 million for sexual harassment claimants alone.[2]
Title VII of the Civil Rights Act of 1964 is the single most important piece of
legislation that has helped to shape and define employment law rights in this country. Though you likely take for granted many of its fruits without even realizing

where they came from, the act was an ambitious piece of social legislation, the likes of which had never been attempted before. Passage of the law was not an easy task. In fact, according to Robert Loevy:

> It can be said of the Civil Rights Act of 1964 that, short of a declaration of war, no other act of Congress had a more violent background—a background of confrontation, official violence, injury, and murder that has few parallels in American history.[3]

The Civil Rights Act of 1964 prohibits discrimination in education, employment, public accommodations, and the receipt of federal funds on the basis of race, color, gender, national origin, and religion. Although several categories of discrimination are included in the law, it was racial discrimination that was truly the moving force for its enactment. Since the world you live in today is so different from the one that existed when Title VII was passed, it is important for you to understand the world as it was then or the law will not seem to make much sense. We will take a few minutes to paint a picture for you. Some of the picture you may be vaguely aware of, but you may not truly understand its import.

Historical Context Leading to the Need for the Civil Rights Act of 1964

Would it surprise you to learn that the state of Mississippi ratified the Thirteenth Amendment to the U.S. Constitution abolishing slavery on February 7, 2013?[4] Nope, that is not a typo. 2013. We just wanted to let you know this history is not quite like most history you read. We know most students' eyes glaze over when the word *history* is mentioned, but not only is this history interesting, it is imperative for you to know in order to understand the law with which we will be dealing. Just bear with us for a few minutes, and we promise it will be worth your while.

The year 2019 marked the commemoration of the 400th anniversary of the arrival of "20 odd" Angolans stolen into slavery that arrived aboard the Portuguese ship the White Lion in Port Comfort, in the colony of Virginia, even before the famed Mayflower. Traded for provisions for the White Lion, this is marked as the beginning of America's entry into the Atlantic slave trade. Africans were brought to America from Africa to be slaves, period. No other role was envisioned for them. It was thus not surprising that when slavery ended 246 years later, the country struggled mightily with the idea of forging a new relationship with African Americans with whom they had no legal or social relationship other than ownership or African Americans serving their needs in the most menial ways.[5] After the Civil War ended slavery, the next 99 years saw many in the country resisting that change, learning how they could live with that change, but, in many ways, still retaining the familiar world they had always known.

The overall response to the post-slavery U.S. relationship with Blacks was Jim Crow laws. Jim Crow was the name given to a system of virtually complete and total racial segregation practiced virtually everywhere in the United States. The system was enforced through law, ironclad social custom, and, to a very great extent, terror and violence.

The separation between the races was complete. There were laws regulating the separation of Blacks and whites in every facet of life from birth to death.[6] Laws prohibited Blacks and whites from marrying, going to school together, and working together. Every facility imaginable was segregated, including movie theaters, restaurants, hospitals, cemeteries, libraries, funeral homes, doctors' waiting rooms, swimming pools, taxicabs, churches, housing developments, parks, water fountains, colleges, public transportation, recreational facilities, toilets, social organizations, and stores. Blacks could not vote, sue whites, testify against them, raise their voice to them, or even look them in the eye or stay on the sidewalk if whites came toward them. If an African American wanted to buy shoes, he or she had to bring a paper cutout of the foot rather than try the shoe on in the store. If he needed pants, he brought to the store a length of string the size of his waist. Of course it was unthinkable to allow an item purchased by an African American customer to be returned, even if it did not fit. If Blacks wanted food from a restaurant, they had to go to the back door and order it to be taken away, if the facility would serve them at all. Many men alive today recall that as young Black boys, the first few days of school were spent in book repositories taping up old, outdated, well-worn books, many with pages missing, no longer used by white schools, which could then be used by Blacks, who never received new ones. In some places it was actually illegal for Blacks to even touch books in use by white students. However, even this was for only the lucky Black students who did not have to forgo school to pick the cotton crop when it was ready for harvest.

Long after the Civil War ended, the South attempted to maintain its cheap labor force of Blacks in several ways. These included instituting prisoner lease or peonage laws that allowed Blacks without the means of making bail to be arrested for virtually anything (or, actually, nothing at all) and then "loaned out" by the sheriff to white farmers or others needing cheap labor, ostensibly under the guise of working off their bond. Accused, quickly sentenced, charged fines and fees they could never pay, and then loaned out to whoever needed them, these workers were often made to sign agreements allowing themselves to be beaten and otherwise mistreated. Without the need to protect one's investment that ownership had imposed during slavery, the mortality rate for these workers could rise as high as 60 or 70 percent, including death through beatings, starvation, and lack of medical care. This system, which provided the foundation for sharecropping as well as for chain gangs, continued pretty much unabated for the next 80 years.[7]

Sharecropping was another common means of maintaining control and having a supply of cheap labor, with the white owner of the property hiring Blacks to work the land in return for an agreed-upon share of the proceeds from the crop the worker produced. Landowners routinely cheated Blacks out of their share of the earnings so that the destitute sharecropper, often in forced debt to the landowner, would have to continue to work for the landowner.[8] Some places had laws that would not permit Blacks to work in any job other than sharecropping, leave without permission of a landowner, or even move to another farm without permission. For those Blacks who stepped out of line, the consequences were dire. Termination, being thrown off the farms and plantations (yes, there were still plantations in the early 1960s—in fact, in a trip to the Mississippi Delta in April 2013 one of the authors spoke with a high school teacher/school bus driver who said she still picks up children from working plantations today) they worked on if they challenged any decision of the owner, burning of homes, beatings, and lynchings were all common.[9]

Separation of the races was complete under Jim Crow, and Jim Crow was only outlawed in 1964, the year the Beatles descended upon America from Britain and rocked the music world. (See Exhibit 3.1, "June 1961 (Pre–Title VII) Newspaper Want Ad.") In fact, a 1965 Beatles contract auctioned off in 2011 contained a provision that the group would not perform in front of a segregated audience at the Cow Palace in Daly City, California.[10] This may not be pleasant to read, but imagine living it. It simply was the way things were and had been in the 99 years since slavery ended.[11] It is not happenstance that blues, a uniquely American genre of music known and loved around the world, was born from and created out of the raw pain of these circumstances.[12]

After World War II ended in 1945, African American veterans of World War II who had left farms, joined the military, and traveled overseas where they were

---

Exhibit 3.1   *June 1961 (Pre–Title VII) Newspaper Want Ad*

This exhibit, taken from an actual newspaper, is typical of the index to want ads from the classified section found in newspapers in the United States before Title VII was passed in 1964. Note the separate categories based on race and gender. This is no longer legal under Title VII.

INDEX TO WANT ADS	Colored Employment
Announcements	26—Help Wanted Male, Colored
	27—Employment Agency Male, Colored
1—Funeral Notices	28—Situations Wanted Male, Colored
2—Funeral Notices, Colored	29—Help Wanted Female, Colored
	30—Employment Agency Female, Colored
Male Employment	31—Situations Wanted Female, Colored
14—Male Help Wanted	
15—Male Employment Agencies	
16—Situations Wanted, Male	
17—Male, Female Help Wanted	
Female Employment	
22—Female Help Wanted	
23—Female Employment Agencies	
24—Situations Wanted, Female	

not the subject of discrimination as they were in the United States returned with a sense that if they had fought and died for their country, surely their country would now treat them as men. The country was not ready for this, and there was much violence.

Nine years later, in 1954, the doctrine of separate but equal educational facilities fell with the U.S. Supreme Court's decision in *Brown v. Topeka Board of Education*.[13] However, southern states fought the change in any number of ways, from closing down public schools entirely to creating organizations such as the White Citizens Council and the Mississippi Sovereignty Commission, a state agency of the 11 southern states specifically created to preserve Jim Crow,[14] to using public revenue to fund all-white private schools established after the Supreme Court's decision.[15]

The next year, and largely in resistance to the *Brown* decision, on August 28, 1955, Emmett Till, a young 14-year-old Black boy from Chicago, visiting his uncle in Mississippi, was dragged from his bed by white men at 2 a.m., accused of having whistled at the wife of one of the perpetrators as she stood behind the counter selling him candy at the general store the day before. Till's body was found two days later in the Tallahatchee River, tortured, beaten, and shot, with a cotton gin fan wired around his neck. When his mother, Mamie Till, insisted on having an open casket at his Chicago funeral, thousands saw what life was still like in the South for Blacks—even 14-year-old Black male children. The two men tried for his murder in September 1955 were acquitted by an all-white jury within minutes, relying heavily on the testimony of the wife, Carolyn Milam. In 2017, a book was published in which Carolyn Milam finally broke her 60-plus year silence and admitted that she lied on the stand and that nothing that Emmett Till did to her justified what happened to him.[16] Three months after the acquittal, in January 1956, and for a reported $4,000, the perpetrators' own account of the murder appeared in *Look* magazine.[17] Double jeopardy kept them from being prosecuted again for the same crime. They admitted that they had killed Till to send a message that segregation would continue in the South despite the *Brown* ruling and that they would never allow their children to go to integrated schools.

Slowly but steadily, Blacks began in earnest to challenge the system. In December 1955, Rev. Martin Luther King, Jr., agreed to lead the Montgomery Bus Boycott that began when a tired Rosa Parks refused to give up her bus seat to a white passenger. There were eventually boycotts, "freedom rides," and sit-in demonstrations for the right to nonsegregated public accommodations, transportation, municipal parks, swimming pools, libraries, and lunch counters. There were racial unrest, strife, marches, and civil disobedience on as close to a mass scale as this country has ever experienced.[18] Something had to give.

In an impressive show of how important societal considerations can be in shaping law, the 1964 Civil Rights Act was passed the year after the historic August 28, 1963 (the date of Emmett Till's death), March on Washington, which celebrated its 56th anniversary in 2019. It was at this march that the late Dr. King gave his famous "I Have a Dream" speech (http://www.americanrhetoric.com/speeches/mlkihaveadream.htm for full text and audio) on the steps of the Lincoln Memorial.

In the largest march of its kind ever held in this country until then, hundreds of thousands of people of all races, creeds, colors, and walks of life traveled from around the world to show legislators that legalized racism was no longer tolerable in a society that considered itself to be civilized.

Just two weeks later, four little Black girls were killed and 20 others injured by a bomb tossed by whites into the Sixteenth Street Baptist Church in Birmingham, Alabama, as the children donned their choir robes and prepared to sing in the choir at Sunday's church service. The country was stunned and saw in the most painful, poignant way the face of resistance to change that African Americans were facing in simply seeking the equality promised by the U.S. Constitution.

Two months later, President Kennedy, who had proposed a civil rights bill three months earlier in June 1963, was assassinated. These and other factors demonstrated in stark terms that it was time to change the status quo and move from the racially segregated Jim Crow system the country had employed in the 99 years since the end of the Civil War to something more akin to the equality the Constitution promised to all. President Kennedy's successor, President Lyndon B. Johnson of Texas, took up the fight. It was not an easy one, particularly since Johnson was a long-standing southern politician and his colleagues felt betrayed.

The 54-day Senate filibuster against the bill was led by Sen. Richard Russell (D-GA), who had the reputation of being the leader of white supremacists in the Senate and the head of the very powerful southern voting bloc. In opposing the bill, Russell famously said, "We will resist to the bitter end any measure or any movement which would have a tendency to bring about social equality and intermingling and amalgamation of the races in our southern states."[19]

The legislation eventually passed by a vote of 73–27, with 27 out of 33 Republicans voting for it and 18 segregationist Democrats voting against it. Taking only micro-movements with each pen, President Johnson used 72 commemorative ink pens to sign it into law. Later that evening, Johnson wearily said to his aide, now journalist, Bill Moyers, "We have lost the South for a long time to come."[20] Fifty-six years later, the South is still heavily Republican. We tell you this so that you can understand how the fight for civil rights was not an easy one, which is why the repercussions and vestiges are still being felt as we speak—as you will see, even more so in the past several years under a new presidential administration.

Title VII: The Legislation

The Civil Rights Act of 1964 is divided into several sections, called titles, each addressing a different aspect of the law. Title VII of the act is the title that addresses employment discrimination. Again, it is only one section of the law in a much larger piece of legislation. The Civil Rights Act of 1964 also created the legal basis for non-discrimination in education, public accommodations, and federally assisted programs. Since employment in large measure defines the availability of the other matters, the case law in Title VII of the Civil Rights Act quickly became the most important arbiter of rights under the new law. In President John F. Kennedy's original message to Congress upon proposing the bill in 1963, he stated:

"There is little value in a Negro's obtaining the right to be admitted to hotels and restaurants if he has no cash in his pocket and no job."[21]

The face of the workplace has changed dramatically since the passage of the act. Where before Title VII many jurisdictions had laws or social customs tightly limiting jobs for African Americans to those such as domestics, laborers, or other menial jobs, because of the law, more women and minorities than ever before are engaged in meaningful employment. While Title VII applies equally to everyone, because of the particular history behind the law, it gave new rights to women and minorities, who had only limited access to the workplace and limited legal recourse for job discrimination before the law. As discussed in the toolkit chapter, with the passage of Title VII, the door was opened to prohibiting job discrimination and creating expectations of fairness in employment overall. It was not long before additional federal legislation followed providing similar protection from discrimination in the workplace based on age, Vietnam veteran status, disabilities, and, later, genetic information.

Like a ripple effect, not only did the law usher in the expectations that you now have that you will be treated equally because you live in the United States and we have such laws, but antidiscrimination laws were enacted all over the world in the wake of the Civil Rights Act of 1964. The courage exhibited by African Americans and their supporters in standing up to the government and challenging long-held beliefs relegating them to second-class citizenship emboldened other groups here and around the world to challenge their treatment as well. So much so that it is now our expectation (though not necessarily the reality) for much of the world.

State and local governments passed laws paralleling Title VII and the other protective legislation. Some laws added categories such as marital status, political affiliation, sexual orientation, or receipt of public benefits as prohibited categories of discrimination. For instance, California prohibits discrimination on the basis of being a victim of domestic violence and imposed personal liability on coworkers regardless of whether the employer knew or should have known of the conduct and failed to take immediate corrective action. Washington, D.C., added personal appearance to its list of prohibited categories. Michigan is the only state that includes protection on the basis of obesity.[22]

The new expectations did not stop there. As we saw in the toolkit chapter, others not included in the coverage of the statutes came to have heightened expectations about the workplace and their role within it and were willing to pressure legislators and sue employers in pursuit of these expected rights. The exceptions created in the employment-at-will doctrine largely owe their existence to the expectations caused by Title VII. Once Title VII protected employees from unjust dismissal on the basis of discrimination, it made it easier for judges and legislators to take the step of extending it to other terminations that came to be considered as not in keeping with this evolving view of the employment relationship.

For employers, Title VII meant that the workplace was no longer a place in which decisions regarding hiring, firing, promotion, and the like could go unchallenged. Now there were prohibitions on some of the factors that had previously been a part of many employers' considerations such as race and gender (again, see, e.g., Exhibit 3.1 showing the text of an actual newspaper classified ad categorized by race and gender). Employers had been feeling the effects of federal regulation in the workplace for some time. Among other regulations, wage and hour and child labor laws governed minimum ages, wages, and permissible work hours that employers could impose, and labor laws protected collective bargaining. Now came Title VII, prohibiting certain bases an employer could use to hire or promote employees. The idea of evolving from employment-at-will to these "intrusions" into the employer's heretofore sole domain of making workplace decisions took some getting used to.

After enactment, Title VII was amended several times to further strengthen it. There were amendments in 1972 and 1978, with the passage of the Equal Employment Opportunity Act of 1972 and the Pregnancy Discrimination Act of 1978. The 1972 amendment expanded Title VII's coverage to include government employees and to strengthen the enforcement powers of the enforcing agency created by the law, the Equal Employment Opportunity Commission (EEOC). The 1978 amendment added discrimination on the basis of pregnancy as a type of gender discrimination. In addition, Title VII and other workplace protections were extended to congressional employees in the Congressional Accountability Act of 1995.

In the most far-reaching overhaul since its passage, the act was also amended by the Civil Rights Act of 1991. This amendment added jury trials, compensatory and punitive damages where appropriate, and several other provisions, further strengthening the law. (See Exhibit 3.2, "The Civil Rights Act of 1991.")

There have also been court cases that have had a profound impact on Title VII, even where federal legislation failed to do so. As discussed in the chapter on sexual orientation and gender identity, in 2012, in light of drastically changing case law interpreting Title VII's gender discrimination prohibition, the EEOC issued a determination that discrimination on the basis of being transgender is a type of gender discrimination. In 2015, the EEOC again reversed its approach in light of changing case law and interpreted Title VII's gender provision as including discrimination based on sexual orientation as well. Since the determination has not been overturned by Congress, it is the equivalent of Title VII being amended to now include this new category.

Note, however, that the Trump administration's Department of Justice is at odds with EEOC and does not agree that Title VII's prohibition on discrimination on the basis of gender includes sexual orientation and gender identity.[23] So far, EEOC has maintained its position that it does. As we write this, several cases argued on October 8, 2019,[24] about the issue are awaiting a decision at the U.S. Supreme Court that will determine which position will be upheld. It is a pretty typical example of the types of differences that can arise in interpretation of the same legislation from one administration to the next, although we must admit that this administration's changes have far exceeded those of any we have experienced in the past 25 years of authoring this textbook.

Exhibit 3.2   *The Civil Rights Act of 1991*

When the Civil Rights Act of 1991 was signed into law by President George Bush on November 21, 1991, it was the end of a fierce battle that had raged for several years over the increasingly conservative decisions of the U.S. Supreme Court in civil rights cases. The new law was a major overhaul for Title VII. The law's nearly 30-year history was closely scrutinized. It is significant for employers that, when presented the opportunity, Congress chose to strengthen the law in many ways rather than lessen its effectiveness. Among other things, the new law for the first time in Title VII cases:

- Permitted:
  - Jury trials where compensatory or punitive damages are sought.
  - Compensatory damages in religious, gender, and disability cases (such damages were already allowed for race and national origin under related legislation).
  - Punitive damages for the same (except against governmental agencies).
  - Unlimited medical expenses.
- Limited the extent to which "reverse discrimination" suits could be brought.

- Authorized expert witness fees to successful plaintiffs.
- Codified the disparate impact theory.
- Broadened protections against private race discrimination in 42 U.S.C. § 1981 cases.
- Expanded the right to bring actions challenging discriminatory seniority systems.
- Extended extraterritorial coverage of Title VII to U.S. citizens working for U.S. companies outside the United States, except where it would violate the laws of the country.
- Extended coverage and established procedures for Senate employees.
- Established the Glass Ceiling Commission.
- Established the National Award for Diversity and Excellence in American Executive Management (known as the Frances Perkins–Elizabeth Hanford Dole National Award for Diversity and Excellence in American Executive Management) for businesses who "have made substantial efforts to promote the opportunities and development experiences of women and minorities and foster advancement to management and decision-making positions within the business."

While a few other agencies have responsibilities for workplace discrimination issues, the EEOC is the lead agency for handling issues of job discrimination. The agency deals with most matters of employment discrimination arising under federal laws, including age, disability, and genetic information and family medical history. The U.S. Department of Justice handles cases involving most government agencies such as police and fire departments. The Office of Federal Contract Compliance Programs (OFCCP) enforces Executive Order 11246 prohibiting employment discrimination by those receiving government contracts and imposing affirmative action under certain circumstances we will discuss later in the text. The EEOC has implemented regulations that govern agency procedures and requirements under the law, and it provides guidelines to employers for dealing with employment discrimination laws easily accessible on its website, http://www.eeoc.gov.[25]

Most employers have come to accept the reality of Title VII. Some have gone beyond acceptance and grown to appreciate the diversity and breadth of the workplace that the law created. Most of the work at this point is in fine-tuning what it means to not discriminate in employment and keeping a reign on employers and employees who continue to engage in such activity. For instance, there has been a growing number of complaints of nooses found in Black employees' work areas, a sharp rise in retaliation claims and harassment against employees exercising their rights under the law, a growing number of class action suits regarding unequal pay and promotions for women, and a surge in discrimination against Muslims in the workplace, ranging from harassment to failure to accommodate their prayer schedules and dietary restrictions. And, of course, the #MeToo movement has had a big impact on the agency, from bringing much-needed attention to the issue of workplace sexual harassment to increased claims filed with the agency.

As the law evolved over the years as society grew and changed, the goal of the law has evolved as well. Initially, in coming from a segregated society in which African Americans and other minorities as well as women were routinely and unquestioningly excluded from jobs, the goal was to achieve entry into the workplace of those historically excluded. However, once they were there, there was a recognition that if they were treated poorly they would still be experiencing discrimination. It would not come from being excluded from the workplace altogether but from being treated unequally or unfairly once there. That is why we now have a term you have probably heard before, *diversity and inclusion* or *diversity, equity, and inclusion.* We will discuss this concept further in the next chapter, but for now, recognize that the issue is one of making Title VII's intent more realistic for those in the workplace who may need the protection of the law in more subtle ways. Getting those historically excluded into the workplace (diversity) is not the same as treating them equally or fairly once there (equity and inclusion). Keep in mind that Title VII was the vehicle for changing an entire society from what it had been during its entire existence, including excluding and castigating certain groups, to a society in which people are not judged on the basis of their race or gender or ethnicity, etc., but on their qualifications for a position in the workplace. Diversity, equity, and inclusion is an important means of supplementing Title VII so that its mission is actually met.

As the lead agency in charge of ridding the country's workplaces of illegal discrimination, over the years the EEOC has come to understand that discrimination can have many forms and manifestations, and they all greatly impact the groups the legislation has targeted for protection because of deeply rooted prejudices against them. As the agency has grown and matured, it has learned that seemingly far-removed issues can directly impact its mission. It has changed to meet those needs as they are made clear. Know, too, that the political climate and who is in power in Washington at any given time can greatly impact the EEOC's performance since such things determine agency funding and priorities. For instance, during the Obama administration, as you can see from the EEOC decisions interpreting gender as including sexual orientation and gender identity based on changing case law mentioned above, the EEOC took a much more inclusive and aggressive stance on civil rights and stamping out inequality as part of the agency's priorities. By contrast, the U.S. Department of Justice under the Trump administration argued at the U.S. Supreme Court that gender should not include sexual orientation or gender identity claims, has moved to further weaken unions, and has rolled back important mechanisms for enforcing Title VII, such as now backing mandatory arbitration agreements once very much discouraged by the EEOC.

In its 2013-2016 Strategic Enforcement Plan, the EEOC set out six areas it would pursue: (1) eliminating barriers to recruitment and hiring; (2) protecting immigrant, migrant, and other vulnerable workers; (3) addressing emerging and developing issues; (4) enforcing equal pay laws; (5) preserving access to the legal system; and (6) preventing harassment through systemic enforcement and targeted outreach.[26] Each of these has huge implications for the workplace, as well as the workforce as EEOC sets its enforcement agenda to address these areas.

In 2016, the agency updated its Strategic Enforcement Plan to encompass 2017-2021 and added a few new areas of interest including the protection of Muslim, Sikh, Middle, and southeastern Asians and Arabs or those perceived to be within these groups from increasing backlash and harassment because of recent events in the United States and abroad; the lack of diversity in technology and the increasing use of data-driven screening tools for recruitment and hiring; the lack of diversity in technology; and combatting persistent pay discrimination.[27] The 2018-2022 plan continued these efforts.

Since there is a new presidential administration, as is customary, there is also a new EEOC chair. Janet Dhillon, sworn in to head the agency on May 15, 2019, like many of this administration's appointees, comes from the corporate sector, having represented big business and employers for most of her career. Before she was appointed, on February 10, 2017, the interim appointed to the position by the administration, Victoria Lipnic, said she saw no major changes in store for the agency, but it was said that she may nudge the agency toward more employer-friendly policies. With the appointment of Dhillon as the new agency chair, this is likely to occur, given her corporate background. In fact, on December 19, 2019, it very much looked that way when Dhillon announced in a tweet[28] the rescission of a 22-year agency guidance regarding mandatory arbitration agreements. This is a term you may well have heard a lot in the wake of the recent #MeToo Movement.

The 1997 EEOC guidance set forth that mandatory arbitration agreements required to be signed by employees as a condition of employment clashed with civil rights and could harm both the individual claimant and the public interest in eradicating discrimination. As such they were frowned upon by EEOC. As a condition of being employed, such agreements require employees to forego taking their claims of workplace discrimination to the EEOC and instead require them to be heard by arbitrators (often hired by, and beholden to, the employer). Such agreements have always been criticized but have come under even more criticism recently when it came to light that many employees who had signed such agreements as a condition of employment later realized that because of the agreement they could not file sexual harassment claims with the EEOC after being harassed. Employers prefer the agreements because they save them time, money, and public embarrassment. However, the downside is that employees do not get to use the agency procedure and process envisioned and created by Congress in passing Title

VII, employers have much power while the employee has little other than walking away from employment rather than sign such an agreement in the first place, and employees are often forbidden by the agreements or documents arising therefrom from even sharing their experience of harassment.

This, of course, creates secrecy within which the harassment can continue virtually unabated. About 50 to 60 percent of U.S. employees now operate under mandatory arbitration agreements. While the chair declared that the reversal of policy in no way diminishes the agency's ability to enforce federal laws and challenge arbitration agreements, it is rather difficult to understand how it would go about this if such agreements prohibit the claimant from going to the EEOC in the first place. A boon to employers, it is not difficult to think that those who said the EEOC may become more employer-friendly under this administration may have a point.

As a part of the Obama administration's strategic enforcement plans, the EEOC moved into several new but related areas, including the "new frontier" of combating human trafficking as it relates to race, national origin, and sexual harassment.[29] In light of the enormous impact of unemployment and housing foreclosures that lingered after the 2008–2009 economic downturn, the EEOC also explored the impact of those events as well as of the use of credit histories on women, minorities, and the disabled as an unlawful employment screening device.[30] As interracial marriages increased, with the accompanying increase in multiracial employees, the agency introduced its E-RACE (Eradicating Racism and Colorism in Employment) Initiative (addressed more fully in the race chapter) to address the more subtle manifestations of color discrimination. As the growing employment impact of race and national origin of employees with arrests and convictions began to surface, in 2012 the EEOC issued enforcement guidance.[31] The agency also testified on the Paycheck Fairness Act before the Senate hearing "A Fair Share for All: Pay Equity in the New American Workplace" about the continuing pay gap between men and women in the workplace.[32] The impact on gender of what was happening to adversely impact caregivers in the graying of America was also the subject of EEOC guidance.[33] As the impact of domestic violence on the workplace experience of its victims became clear, the EEOC ventured into this area as well. When the #MeToo claims resulted in increased claims and workplace incivility and harassment, the EEOC began offering workplace civility training and also conducted a large investigation of workplace sexual harassment. As society gains more knowledge of the ways in which unlawful discrimination is manifested by workplace policies, the agency has tried to address them accordingly.

As then-EEOC Chair Naomi C. Earp said in presenting the EEOC's Performance and Accountability Report for FY 2006,

> Employment discrimination has changed fairly dramatically over the past 40 years. In the years before and immediately after Title VII was passed, discrimination was blatant and pervasive. Newspapers published sex-segregated job ads, and employers implemented or continued policies of segregating employment facilities by race,

paying female employees less than male employees, restricting employment and promotion opportunities for women and minorities, and enforcing mandatory retirement policies to force older workers out. Today, discrimination has become more subtle and thus more difficult to prove . . . [C]urrent demographic changes, such as the graying of the workforce and the increased gender and ethnic diversity of the workforce, also present new challenges and opportunities for employees, employers, and the Commission.[34]

Fifty-five-plus years after the passage of the 1964 Civil Rights Act, it is clear that the agency has maintained its mission to eradicate workplace discrimination but changed some of its tactics as it has gained experience and changed some of its emphases as it changed administrations. As mentioned, its role has also waxed and waned over the years as different presidential administrations come into power with different priorities. The EEOC's Strategic Enforcement Plan for 2013–2016 listed its first national priority as eliminating barriers in recruitment and hiring, particularly targeting "class-based intentional recruitment and hiring discrimination and facially neutral recruitment and hiring practices that impact particular groups."[35] Under the Obama administration, the agency was permitted the authority and resources to do more of the job it was created to do. Despite inevitable budget cutbacks during the recession resulting in a more focused systemic discrimination approach, the EEOC aggressively pursued the law as it was created and envisioned and reflected this in its Strategic Enforcement Plan. The new administration, on the other hand, has engaged in activity such as, despite saying that pay inequity was a priority, reversing the Obama-era order to collect pay information data from employers along with the information routinely filed in the existing employers' yearly EEO-1 workplace demographics filings in order to monitor pay equity. The reversal was blocked by a court and remains in limbo at this time, with the EEOC saying it will issue a notice of proposed rulemaking about it.[36] While the EEOC has never been particularly well funded, with some offices reporting not even being able to afford sufficient paper, more money was provided to address sexual harassment, while the current budget proposed a $23 million budget cut.

The EEOC's mission has always been conciliation-based, but it did not always seem that way. In carving out its new, untrod territory, it aggressively went after employers in order to establish its presence and place in the law (which, along with being "the feds," caused more than a little employer resentment). Once that place was firmly established, the EEOC began living up to its conciliation mission.

The EEOC now prefers to be proactive and have employers avoid litigation by thoroughly understanding the law and its requirements. The EEOC has sponsored thousands of outreach programs to teach employers and employees alike about the law; has initiated extensive mediation programs to try to handle discrimination claims quickly, efficiently, and without litigation; and maintains an informative website that makes help readily accessible for employers and employees alike. (See Exhibit 3.3, "EEOC on Call.") The new agency chair says she prefers this approach to that of litigation.

Exhibit 3.3 *EEOC on Call*

The EEOC's National Contact Center may be reached 24 hours a day at 1-800-669-4000. For the deaf or hard of hearing, the TTY number is 1-800-669-6820, or 1-844-234-5122 for the ASL Video Phone for the deaf or hard of hearing only. The EEOC can also be reached via e-mail at info@eeoc.gov. Constituents can communicate with the agency in more than 150 languages by telephone, email, and Web inquiries to obtain quick, accurate information. Additionally, through frequently asked questions posted on the EEOC's webpage and an Interactive Voice Response telephone system available 24 hours a day, customers can have their questions answered through the use of the agency's technology. But the EEOC is not just for employees inquiring about filing claims. It also serves employers, including, as of 2017, part of its website being devoted to comprehensive information and assistance for small businesses.

https://www.eeoc.gov

As the demographics and the workplace change, the EEOC has incorporated these changes into its mission. For instance, the EEOC has developed several programs targeted to the needs of specific groups such as:

- The Information Group for Asian American Rights (TIGAAR), an initiative to promote voluntary compliance with employment laws by Asian American employers and to educate Asian American employees about their workplace rights.

- In response to the growing number of retaliation and harassment claims, the EEOC's Select Task Force on the Study of Harassment in the Workplace was convened, which issued a Harassment Prevention Report with recommendations in June 2016. The report formed the basis for a proposed EEOC Guidance on Harassment, which went out for public comment on January 10, 2017.

- Programs with Sikh and Muslim communities in response to post-9/11 religious and national origin discrimination.

- The Council of Tribal Employment Rights (CTER) to work with Native Americans to eliminate workplace discrimination on or near Native American reservations, secure Native American preference agreements with employers operating on or near reservations, and process employment discrimination complaints.

- The E-RACE initiative to reinvigorate its efforts in the area of race and color discrimination, discussed in a later chapter.

- Youth@Work initiative to put renewed emphasis on discriminatory recruitment and hiring practices and discrimination against youth.

Much work, however, remains. The EEOC still receives a large number of discrimination claims. According to the latest figures, those of fiscal year 2018 issued in April 2019, the EEOC received 76,418 charges and resolved 90,558. (A portion of the resolved charges are from its backlog). (See Exhibit 3.4, "EEOC Charges for Fiscal Year 2018 by Category.") Again, while the EEOC prefers conciliation, the agency will still pursue employers when conciliation does not work to its satisfaction. The best way to avoid violations of employment discrimination laws is to know and understand their requirements. That is what the following sections and chapters will help you do.

Keep Exhibit 3.5, "Cages," in mind as you go through this section of the text. Most of us look at things microscopically. That is, we tend to see only the situation in front of us and don't give much thought to the larger picture into which it fits. But it is this larger picture within which we actually operate. It is the one the law considers when enacting legislation, the courts consider in interpreting the law and deciding cases, and thus the one an employer should consider when developing workplace policies or responding to workplace situations. Often, a situation, in and of itself, may seem to us to have little or no significance. Along with simply not being aware of issues that may seem to have little to do with our lives or experience, and we are therefore not operating with the same facts, we say, "Why are they whining about this?" "Why can't they just go along? Why are they being so sensitive?" "Why do they have to make such a big deal out of every little thing?" But we are often missing the larger picture and how this situation may fit into it. Like the birdcage in Exhibit 3.5, each thing, in and of itself, may not be a big deal, but put each of these things together, and a picture is revealed of a very different reality for those who must deal with the "wires." Again, even more so given the earlier discussion of most of us not thinking anything is wrong because it may not be a part of our own reality.

Many of the situations you see in the following chapters are "wires" that Title VII and other protective legislation try to eradicate in an effort to break down the seemingly impenetrable invisible barriers we have erected around issues of race, gender in all its manifestations, disabilities, ethnicity, religion, age, family medical history, and genetic information for generations. As you go through the cases and information, think not only about the micro picture of what is going on in front of you but also about the larger macro picture that it fits into. Sometimes what makes little sense in one setting makes perfect sense in another.

Exhibit 3.4 *EEOC Charges for Fiscal Year 2018 by Category*

In this chart you can see for yourself the latest numbers and percentages of charges filed with the EEOC in the various categories.

Retaliation: 39,469 (51.6 percent of all charges filed)

Gender: 24,655 (32.3 percent)

Disability: 24,605 (32.2 percent)

Race: 24,600 (32.2 percent)

Age: 16,911 (22.1 percent)

National Origin: 7,106 (9.3 percent)

Color: 3,166 (4.1 percent)

Religion: 2,859 (3.7 percent)

Equal Pay Act: 1,066 (1.4 percent)

Genetic Information: 220 (0.3 percent)

The percentages add up to more than 100 because some charges allege multiple bases.

EEOC Releases Fiscal Year 2018 Enforcement and Litigation Data, April 10, 2019.

Exhibit 3.5 *Cages*

Dr. Marilyn Frye of Michigan State University likens looking at discrimination issues to looking at a wire birdcage. Look at the wires closely and you can't see why a bird can't just fly around it, but look at it from further away and you see that the wire you are viewing is only one of many interconnected wires that form an impenetrable cage that keeps the bird in place. With discrimination, each little piece may not seem very significant, but put them together and they form a different existence for one group than another, which keeps the group from progressing like those without the barriers.

Source: *The Systemic Birdcage of Sexism* by Marilyn Frye. https://cpt.org/sites/default/files/2019-04/US%20-%20Bird%20Cage%20of%20Sexism.pdf.

Another way to look at it is as if it is one of those repeating-pattern "Magic Eye" stereogram pictures so popular several years ago. In fact, thanks to the wonders of the Internet, you can find some interesting ones by just typing "Magic Eye Pictures" into your search engine. Try it! It really is like magic. Just let your eyes relax, and a picture you cannot see when simply casually looking at the repeating pattern will come into focus and totally take you by surprise. Much like allowing yourself to be open to realities other than your own in order to avoid unnecessary workplace liability. If you stare at the picture the correct way, you get to see the detailed 3-D picture you'd never see by just glancing at the repeating pattern on the the surface. The picture hasn't changed, but you've looked at it in a way that now lets you see another richly detailed picture you had no idea was there.

Our point is that learning about employment discrimination will not change the reality you already know (the repeating-pattern picture you see at a glance) but will instead help you see another, richer, more detailed picture inside this one—one that will greatly assist you in being an effective manager who is less likely to be responsible for costly and embarrassing workplace discrimination claims and liability.

What does this all mean? Let's look at an example. A female who works in a garage comes in one day and there are photos of nude females all around the shop. She complains to the supervisor, and he tells her that the men like the photos and if she doesn't like it, just don't look at them. The guys she works with begin to rib her about complaining. They tell her she's a "wuss," "can't cut the mustard," and "can't hang with the big boys."

"What's the big deal?" you say. "Why didn't she just shut up and ignore the photos?"

Well, in and of itself the photos may not seem like much. But when you look at the issue in its larger context, it looks quite different. Research shows that in workplaces in which nude photos, adult language, sexual teasing, jokes, and so on, are present, women tend to be paid less and receive fewer and less-significant raises, promotions, and training. It is not unlikely that the environment that supports such photos doesn't clearly draw lines between the people in the photos and female employees in the workplace. Case after case bears it out. So the photos themselves aren't really the whole issue. It's the micro picture, the repeating-pattern picture you see at a glance in your Magic Eye picture. But the macro picture, the 3-D picture, is the objectification of women and what contributes to women being viewed as less than men and not as capable in a workplace in which they may well be just as capable as anyone else. What might have seemed like harmless joking or photos in the micro view takes on much more significance in the macro view and has much more of a potential negative impact on the work experience of the female employee who is less likely to be trained, promoted, or given a raise for which she is qualified.

Again, as you go through the following chapters, try to look at the micro as well as the macro picture—the repeating-pattern surface picture as well as the 3-D picture inside. You will also benefit from the case questions, which help you view what you have read in a larger context. Again, it is this context that will be under scrutiny when the policies of a workplace form the basis of a lawsuit. Thinking about that context beforehand and making policies consistent with it will give the employer a much greater chance of avoiding embarrassing and costly litigation. The latest available figures, those from fiscal year 2018, ending in September 2019, show that in 2018 alone, EEOC enforcement cost employers a record $505 million in relief to claimants.[37]

The Structure of Title VII

What Is Prohibited under Title VII?

LO3 Discuss what is prohibited by Title VII.

Title VII prohibits discrimination in hiring, firing, training, promotion, discipline, or other workplace decisions on the basis of an employee or applicant's race, color, gender, including sexual harassment, pregnancy discrimination, and, in the EEOC's interpretation, sexual orientation and gender identity, national origin, or religion. Included in the prohibitions are discrimination in pay, terms and conditions of employment, training, layoffs, and benefits. Virtually any workplace decision can be challenged by an applicant or employee who falls within the Title VII categories. (See Exhibit 3.6 "Title VII Provisions.")

Exhibit 3.6 *Title VII Provisions*

An employer cannot discriminate on the basis of:

- Race
- Color
- Gender, including:
  - Sexual harassment
  - Pregnancy
  - Sexual orientation (as interpreted by the EEOC)
  - Gender identity (as interpreted by the EEOC)
- Religion
- National origin

in making decisions regarding:

- Hiring
- Firing
- Training
- Discipline
- Compensation
- Benefits
- Classification
- Or other terms or conditions of employment

LO4 Recognize who is covered by Title VII and who is not.

Who Must Comply?

Title VII applies to employers, unions, and joint labor and management committees making admission, referral, training, and other decisions and to employment agencies and other similar hiring entities making referrals for employment. It applies to all private employers employing 15 or more employees and to federal, state, and local governments. (See Exhibit 3.7, "Who Must Comply.")

Who Is Covered?

Title VII applies to public (governmental) and private (nongovernmental) employees alike. Unlike labor laws that do not apply to managerial employees or wage and hour laws that exempt certain types of employees, Title VII covers all levels and types of employees. The Civil Rights Act of 1991 further extended Title VII's coverage to U.S. citizens employed by American employers outside the United States. Non-U.S. citizens are protected in the United States but not outside the United States.

Undocumented workers also are covered by the law, but after the U.S. Supreme Court's 2002 ruling in *Hoffman Plastic Compounds, Inc., v. NLRB,*[38] the EEOC reexamined its position on remedies for undocumented workers. It did so again in its most recent Strategic Enforcement Plan and reiterated its commitment to protect employees regardless of immigration status, even bringing a wage theft case against a Colorado company that hired primarily Hispanics, both documented and undocumented, then refused to adequately or consistently pay them.[39] In *Hoffman,* the Court said that U.S. immigration laws outweighed the employer's labor violations; therefore, the employee could not recover back pay for violations of the labor law. The EEOC had been treating undocumented worker claims of employment discrimination under Title VII like violations against any other worker. After *Hoffman,* the EEOC said that employment discrimination against undocumented workers is still illegal, and they will not ask employees their status in handling their discrimination claims, but *Hoffman* affected the availability of some forms of relief, such as reinstatement and back pay for periods after discharge or failure to hire.[40] The EEOC's Strategic Enforcement Plan for

Exhibit 3.7 *Who Must Comply*

- Employers engaged in interstate commerce if they have:
  - Fifteen or more employees for each working day in each of 20 or more calendar weeks in the current or preceding calendar year.
- Labor organizations of any kind that exist to deal with employers concerning labor issues engaged in an industry affecting commerce.

- Employment agencies that, with or without compensation, procure employees for employers or opportunities to work for employees.

2017–2021 revised its priority on Migrant and Other Vulnerable Workers to have district offices and other federal sector programs identify vulnerable workers and underserved communities within their areas of focused attention. The 2018–2022 plan maintained this priority.

Who Is Not Covered?

Exemptions under Title VII are limited. Title VII permits businesses operated on or around Native American reservations to give preferential treatment to Native Americans. The act specifically states that it does not apply to actions taken with respect to someone who is a member of the Communist Party or other organization required to register as a Communist-action or Communist-front organization. (Keep in mind that when Title VII was passed the country was still reeling from the McCarthy hearings investigating suspicion of Communist infiltration of the government.) The law permits religious institutions and associations to discriminate when performing their ministerial duties, which are totally defined by the organization. For instance, a Catholic priest could not successfully sue under Title VII alleging religious discrimination for not being hired to lead a Jewish synagogue. (See Exhibit 3.8 , "Employees Who Are Not Covered by Title VII.") In the case of *Petruska v. Gannon University,* included at the end of the chapter, the employee was not able to effectively bring her claim for gender discrimination because of this limitation on religious claims.

Keep in mind that the law covers what it covers and no more. In order to have a valid claim under Title VII, the employee or applicant must be able to show that he or she has been discriminated against on one of the bases in the law. If the employee cannot show this, then there is no basis for a Title VII claim. That is why in Opening Scenario 3, Rinson has no cause of action. There is no indication that the reason for the supervisor treating Rinson poorly has anything to do with any of the law's prohibited classes of race, color, gender, religion, or national origin, and so forth.

Exhibit 3.8 *Employees Who Are Not Covered by Title VII*

- Employees of employers having less than 15 employees.
- Employees whose employers are not engaged in interstate commerce.
- Non-U.S. citizens employed outside the United States.
- Employees of religious institutions, associations, or corporations hired to perform work connected with carrying on religious activities/ministerial functions.

- Members of Communist organizations.
- Employees of employers employing Native Americans living in or around Native American reservations.
- Employers who are engaged in interstate commerce but do not employ 15 or more employees for each of 20 or more calendar weeks in the current or preceding calendar year.

LO5 State how a Title VII claim is filed and proceeds through the administrative process.

claimant or charging party
The person who brings an action alleging violation of Title VII.

Filing Claims under Title VII

Nonfederal employees (federal employee claims are processed through another procedure that begins in their own agency) who believe they have experienced employment discrimination may file a charge or claim with the EEOC. An employee filing such a claim is called a **claimant** or a **charging party**. Employers should be aware that it costs an employee only time and energy to go to the nearest EEOC office and file a claim. Before doing so, you can even go online and use their tool to see if the EEOC is the agency you need to contact. If it is, you can fill out the intake questionnaire, print it out, and bring it with you to the office or mail it in. But you must come in to file a claim. However, the EEOC is constantly working to improve its technology and accessibility, with many functions now being able to be performed online, including uploading documents, checking claim status, and scheduling appointments. By law, the EEOC must in some way handle every claim it receives. This makes it even more important for employers to discourage claims and ensure the best defense when they arise by ensuring that their policies and procedures are legal, fair, and consistently applied.

However, just because filing with the EEOC is free does not mean that every employee who thinks he or she has a claim is making a beeline to the EEOC office. Filing a claim against an employer is a serious matter. Most employees work because they must do so in order to finance their lives. Doing anything to interfere with that is a shaky business. There are far more people who have legitimate claims who choose not to pursue them than those who do so or who do so for questionable reasons. You, yourself, may have had a basis for a claim and just let it go, perhaps thinking it wasn't worth the hassle and you had other more pressing matters to deal with such as school, family, or paying the rent. There are many reasons employees may choose not to pursue a claim. An employee may:

- not know their rights under the law.
- be afraid.
- fear retaliation.
- feel it is easier to just go along or to find another job.
- have valued friendships they wish to maintain.
- feel the process takes too long and feels too uncertain.
- fear the emotional cost of the proceedings.
- not wish to risk the ire of their fellow employees.
- find it too uncomfortable to remain in the workplace where they have filed claims against the employer.
- think things will get better on their own.
- believe the job market makes their present situation the best choice under the circumstances.
- not want to put their family at risk.

Keep in mind that even with the best case in the world, there are no guarantees. A claim can drag on for years, and during that time the claimant, who may have been terminated in violation of Title VII, must still eat. They must obtain other employment and, by the time the case is finished, may have moved on with their life. Keep in mind that when the U.S. Supreme Court decided the Wal-Mart[41] gender case, it had dragged on for 10 years. The decision was not even about the substantive issue of whether Wal-Mart engaged in gender discrimination against its female employees but rather whether it was correct for the trial court and court of appeals to allow the employees to be certified as a class for bringing the lawsuit. Ten years and zillions of dollars in legal fees and the case had not even been heard on the merits. So, while it may seem easy for employees to sue, the bigger concern is the ones who have legitimate cases that could have been easily avoided by the employer engaging in good workplace practices.

Regarding the ease of bringing Equal Employment Opportunity (EEO) claims, there is good news and bad news for employers. The good news is that the agency prefers alternative dispute resolution (ADR), which is a cheaper, quicker, more efficient way to resolve disputes.

The bad news for employers is that the EEOC's success rate in litigation has been at least 90 percent for years. In fiscal year 2018, the EEOC obtained $505 million in monetary benefits. No doubt owners and shareholders of companies that had to pay out this money in settlements and judgments now realize that the avoidable $505 million could have been put to more productive use.

Understanding and implementing effective workplace policies can do that. The best defense is a good offense. Avoiding trouble in the first place lessens the chances of having to deal with the EEOC and therefore the chances of being unsuccessful.

Nonfederal government employee claims must be filed within 180 days of the discriminatory event, except as noted in the next section involving 706 agencies. For federal employees, claims must be filed with their employing agency within 45 days of the event. In a significant U.S. Supreme Court case, *National Railroad Passenger Corp. (Amtrak) v. Morgan,*[42] these deadlines were made a bit more flexible by the Court for harassment cases. In the *Morgan* case, the Supreme Court said that since on-the-job harassment is part of a pattern of behavior, if a charge is filed with the EEOC within the statutory period, a jury can consider actions that occurred outside the statutory period. The violation is considered to be a continuing one, so the claimant is not limited to only evidence relating to the specific event resulting in the lawsuit. Note, however, the U.S. Supreme Court held that it was not a continuing violation each time an employer issued a paycheck based on gender-based wage discrimination. In *Ledbetter v. Goodyear Tire and Rubber Co., Inc.,*[43] discussed in more detail in the gender chapter, the Court rejected the paycheck accrual rule that would have allowed the employee to restart the statute of limitations each time she was paid based on discriminatory criteria. The Court distinguished *Morgan* by saying the act of wage discrimination was a discrete act rather than a pattern and thus did not merit the same treatment as the harassment in the *Morgan* case. Congress, however, responded by passing the Lilly Ledbetter Fair Pay Act of 2009 that adopted the paycheck accrual rule. Under that law, the 180-day statute of limitations begins to run all over again each time a paycheck is issued based on pay

Scenario **2**

discrimination. That is why in Opening Scenario 2, Shelly is still able to bring her claim even though it has been more than 180 days since the event.

The reason for the fairly short statute of limitations in Title VII is an attempt to ensure that the necessary parties and witnesses are still available and that events are not too remote to recollect accurately. Violations of Title VII may also be brought to the EEOC's attention because of its own investigation or by information provided by employers meeting their **record keeping and reporting requirements** under the law.

The filing process is somewhat different for federal employees, although the EEOC has sought to make it conform more closely to the nonfederal employee regulations.[44] Again, federal employees are protected by Title VII, but the procedures for handling their claims simply follow a different path.

State Law Interface in the Filing Process

Since most states have their own fair employment practice laws that track Title VII, they also have their own state and local enforcement agencies for employment discrimination claims. Most of these agencies contract with the EEOC to act as a **706 agency** (named for the section of the law that permits them). On the basis of a work-sharing agreement with the EEOC, these agencies receive and process claims of discrimination for the EEOC in addition to carrying on their own state business.

Title VII's intent is that claims be **conciliated** if possible. Local agencies serve as a type of screening process for the more serious cases. If the complaint is not satisfactorily disposed at this level, it may eventually be taken by the EEOC and, if necessary, litigated. State and local agencies have their own procedures, which are similar to those of the EEOC.

If there is a 706 agency in the employee's jurisdiction, the employee has 300 days rather than 180 days within which to file. If an employee files his or her claim with the EEOC when there is a 706 agency in the jurisdiction, the EEOC defers the complaint to the 706 agency for 60 days before investigating. The employee can file the complaint with the EEOC, but the EEOC sends it to the 706 agency, and the EEOC will not move on the claim for 60 days.

In further explaining the process, reference will only be made to the EEOC as the enforcing agency involved.

Proceeding through the EEOC

Within 10 days of the employee filing a claim with the EEOC, the EEOC serves notice of the charge to the employer (called **respondent** or **responding party**). The respondent must then respond to the claim. As discussed in the toolkit chapter, Title VII also includes antiretaliation provisions. It is a separate offense for an employer to retaliate against an employee for pursuing rights under Title VII. That is, once the employer is notified of the charge of workplace discrimination filed by an employee, even if the employer believes the charge to be unfounded, the employer cannot treat the employee differently, less well, because the employee filed the charge with EEOC. The EEOC may proceed to investigate the charge,

record keeping and reporting requirements
Title VII requires that certain documents must be maintained and periodically reported to the EEOC.

706 agency
State agency that handles EEOC claims under a work-sharing agreement with the EEOC.

conciliation
Attempting to reach agreement on a claim through discussion without resort to litigation.

See Chapter 2 to revisit key concepts.

respondent or responding party
Party against whom a case is appealed to the Supreme Court.

generally in a fact-finding conference between EEOC and the parties, in order to determine and define the issues set forth in the charge, determine if there are any undisputed areas that can be agreed upon and resolved or if there are disputed areas that must be pursued further. If need be, the agency has subpoena power for witnesses, testimony, records, books, correspondence, or documents in investigating the claim.

LO7 Distinguish between the various types of alternative dispute resolution used by the EEOC.

Mediation

The EEOC's approach to mediation has been very aggressive in the past few decades. In response to complaints of a tremendous backlog of cases and claims that went on for years, EEOC has adopted several important steps to try to streamline its case-handling process and make it more efficient and effective and less time-consuming for claimants. Primary among the steps is its adoption of mediation as an alternative to a full-blown EEOC investigation and litigation. In furtherance of this, the EEOC began several different programs involving mediation. In 1999, it launched the expanded mediation program discussed in the next paragraph. In 2003, in recognition that many private sector employers already have extensive mediation programs set up to handle workplace issues, the EEOC began a "referral-back" program. Private sector employment discrimination claims are referred back to participating employers for mediation by the employer's own mediation program to see if they can be resolved without going any further. The same year, the EEOC ushered in a pilot program to have local fair employment practice offices mediate claims on the EEOC's behalf. In response to the EEOC's finding that there were more employees willing to mediate than there were employers willing to do so, the EEOC instituted "universal mediation agreements," under which employers agree to have their claims mediated by the EEOC when discrimination charges are filed.

The EEOC had signed universal agreements to mediate with thousands of regional and local employers. National universal mediation agreements have been signed with such employers as Ford Motor Company, Huddle House, Inc., Ryan's Restaurant Group, Inc., Brandsmart, Cracker Barrel, and Southern Company.

Generally, the way mediation works is that, after a discrimination charge is filed by the employee and notice of the charge is given to the employer, the EEOC screens the charge to see if it is one that is appropriate for mediation. If it is appropriate for mediation, the EEOC will offer that option to the parties. Complex and weak cases are not offered mediation. Both parties are sent letters offering mediation, and the decision to participate is voluntary for both parties. Each side has 10 days to respond to the offer to mediate. If both parties elect mediation, the charge must be mediated within 60 days for in-house mediation or 45 days for external mediation. The EEOC has expanded its mediation program to allow a request for mediation at any stage of the administrative process, even after a finding of discrimination has been issued.

If the parties choose to mediate, during mediation they will have the opportunity to present their positions, express their opinions, provide information, and express their request for relief. Any information disclosed during this process is not to be

reasonable cause
EEOC finding that Title VII was violated.

no reasonable cause
EEOC finding that evidence indicates no reasonable basis to believe Title VII was violated.

right-to-sue letter
Letter given by the EEOC to claimants, notifying them of the EEOC's no-cause finding and informing them of their right to pursue their claim in court.

LO6 Determine if a Title VII claimant is able to proceed after receiving a no-reasonable-cause finding.

See Chapter 2 to revisit key concepts.

revealed to anyone, including EEOC employees. If the parties reach agreement, that agreement is as binding as any other settlement agreement. Since 1999, when its mediation program was fully implemented, the EEOC conducted thousands of mediations, with a consistent satisfaction rate of well over 90 percent.

EEOC Investigation

If the parties choose not to mediate the charge or if the mediation is not successful, the charge is referred back to the EEOC for handling. The EEOC investigates the complaint by talking with the employer and employee and any other necessary witnesses as well as viewing any documents or even visiting the workplace.

EEOC's Determination

After appropriate investigation, the EEOC makes a determination as to whether there is **reasonable cause** or no reasonable cause for the employee to charge the employer with violating Title VII. Once there has been an investigation and a cause or no-cause finding, either party can ask for reconsideration of the EEOC's decision.

No-Reasonable-Cause Finding

After investigation, if the EEOC finds there is **no reasonable cause** for the employee's discrimination complaint, the employee is given a dismissal and notice of rights, often known as a **right-to-sue letter**. If the employee wants to pursue the matter further despite the EEOC's conclusion that Title VII has not been violated, the employee is now free to do so, having exhausted the administrative remedies of the EEOC. The employee can then bring suit against the employer in federal court within 90 days of receiving the notice. (See Exhibit 3.9, "The Procedure for Bringing a Claim within the EEOC.")

Exhibit 3.9 *The Procedure for Bringing a Claim within the EEOC*

- Employee goes to the EEOC office and files the complaint.
- Agency sends a notice to the employer accused of discrimination.
- Parties receive referral to mediation (if appropriate).
- If both parties elect mediation, the charge is mediated.
- If the parties agree in mediation, the negotiated settlement is binding. Complaint is resolved and closed.
- If mediation is not successful or parties choose not to mediate, the EEOC investigates the claim.
- If the EEOC's investigation shows reasonable cause to believe discrimination has occurred, the parties meet and try to conciliate.

- If agreement is reached during conciliation, the claim is resolved and closed.
- If no agreement is reached during conciliation, the EEOC makes a determination of reasonable cause or no reasonable cause to believe discrimination occurred.
- If reasonable cause is found, the EEOC notifies the employer of the proposed remedy.
- If no reasonable cause is found, parties are notified and the charging party is issued a dismissal and the notice of rights letter.
- If the employer disagrees, then the decision is appealed to the next agency level.

Reasonable-Cause Finding

EEO investigator
Employee of the EEOC
who reviews Title VII
complaints for merit.

If the EEOC finds there is reasonable cause for the employee to charge the employer with discrimination, it will attempt to have the parties meet together and conciliate the matter. That is, the EEOC will bring the parties together in a fairly informal setting with an **EEO investigator**.

The EEO investigator sets forth what has been found during the investigation and discusses with the parties the ways the matter can be resolved. Often the employee is satisfied if the employer simply agrees to provide a favorable letter of recommendation. The majority of claims filed with the EEOC are adequately disposed of at this stage of the proceedings. If the claim is not adequately disposed of, the EEOC can take the matter further and file suit against the employer in federal district court if it is deemed justified by the EEOC and is in line with its Strategic Enforcement Plan's priorities. EEOC's 2018 Enforcement and Litigation Data issued in April 2019 indicated that EEOC had achieved a successful outcome in 95.7 percent of all district court resolutions. Not a good sign for employers. It is far better to simply comply with the law.

Judicial Review

1)
Scenario

judicial review
Court review of an
agency's decision.

de novo review
Complete new look at
an administrative case
by the reviewing court.

If no conciliation is reached, the EEOC may eventually file a civil action in federal district court. As we have seen, if the EEOC originally found no cause and issued the complaining party a right-to-sue letter, the employee can take the case to court, seeking **judicial review**. Title VII requires that courts accord EEOC decisions ***de novo* review**. A court can only take a Title VII discrimination case for judicial review after the EEOC has first disposed of the claim. Thus, in Opening Scenario 1, Jack cannot immediately file a discrimination lawsuit against his employer because he has not yet gone through the EEOC's administrative process and exhausted his administrative remedies.

Under *de novo* review, upon going to court, the case is handled entirely as if it were new, as if there had not already been a finding by the EEOC. Employees proceeding with a no-reasonable-cause letter are also free to develop the case however they wish without being bound by the EEOC's prior determination. If a party is not satisfied with the court's decision and has a basis upon which to appeal, the case can be appealed up to and including the U.S. Supreme Court, if the Court agrees to hear the case.

Before we leave the topic of judicial review, we need to discuss a matter that has become important in the area of employees' pursuing their rights under Title VII and having the right to judicial review of the EEOC's decisions. In recent years, **mandatory arbitration agreements** mentioned earlier have gained tremendously in popularity. Previously confined almost exclusively to unions and the securities industry, these agreements are entered into by employees as a condition of their employment when they are hired and stipulate that any workplace disputes, including workplace discrimination claims in violation of Title VII, will be disposed of by submitting them to arbitration rather than to the EEOC or the courts.

mandatory arbitration agreement
Agreement an employee
signs as a condition of
employment, requiring
that workplace disputes
be arbitrated rather
than litigated.

The appeal of mandatory arbitration agreements is that they greatly decrease the time and resources parties would spend by fighting workplace legal battles in court. There are at least two major drawbacks for employees: (1) When they are trying to obtain employment, applicants generally feel they have little choice about signing away their rights to go to court, and (2) once a case goes to arbitration, the arbitrator's decision is not subject to judicial review by the courts unless the decision can be shown to be arbitrary, capricious, unconstitutional, the result of fraud or collusion, or suffering some similar malady. This means that the vast majority of arbitration awards, many rendered by arbitrators with no legal background or grounding in Title VII issues, remain intact, free from review by the courts. It also means that while employers gain the advantage of having fewer cases in court, employees have the disadvantage of essentially having the courts closed to them in Title VII cases, even though Title VII provides for both an administrative process and judicial review. Arbitrators, often chosen by an employer, who want to maintain the employer's business, will rarely do so if their decisions go against the employer's interests. From the employer's viewpoint, this is in the employer's best interest.

With few downsides for employers, mandatory arbitration agreements have become so popular with employers that they are now fairly routine. Employees who come to the EEOC intending to file claims of employment discrimination are told that they cannot do so because they have entered into a mandatory arbitration agreement with their employer, which requires them to seek redress through arbitration, *not* the EEOC or the courts. This happened a few years ago in New York City to a female Citibank investment banker who was terminated because her supervisor said that her figure was too distracting to male employees.[45]

Two recent U.S. Supreme Court cases have decided important issues in this area. In *Circuit City v. Adams,*[46] the Supreme Court held that mandatory arbitration clauses requiring arbitration of workplace claims, including those under Title VII, are enforceable under the Federal Arbitration Act. In *EEOC v. Waffle House, Inc.,*[47] the Court held that even though an employee is subject to a mandatory arbitration agreement, since the EEOC is not a party to the agreement, the agreement does not prevent the EEOC from pursuing victim-specific relief such as back pay, reinstatement, and damages as part of an enforcement action.

So, the EEOC claims can be the subject of mandatory arbitration, but this does not prevent the EEOC from bringing its own enforcement action against the employer and even asking for victim-specific relief for the employee. An employer can avoid a Title VII court case by requiring mandatory arbitration of workplace claims but still may have to contend with the EEOC bringing suit on its own.

Legislation to overturn *Circuit City* and only permit voluntary arbitration agreements was introduced in both the House and Senate shortly after the decision but did not pass. Perhaps this was, at least in part, because the Supreme Court gave further indication of how it will view mandatory arbitration agreements in a later *Circuit City* case. In its initial decision, the Supreme Court required the *Circuit City* case to be remanded to the lower court for actions not inconsistent with its ruling. On remand, the court of appeals applied the Federal Arbitration Act and ruled that the employer's mandatory arbitration agreement was unconscionable and unenforceable because it was offered on a take-it-or-leave-it basis, did not require the company to arbitrate claims, limited the relief available to employees, and required employees to pay half of the arbitration costs. When the court of appeals' decision came back to the Supreme Court for review, the Court declined to hear it, leaving the court of appeals' refusal to enforce the mandatory arbitration agreement intact.[48]

Perhaps also, at least in part in response to mandatory arbitration agreements, the EEOC stepped up its mediation programs in order to provide employers with an alternative between litigation and mandatory arbitration. Since 1991 the EEOC had been moving in the direction of mediation, but the issue heated up after the Supreme Court decisions on mandatory arbitration. The EEOC's subsequent litigation alternatives heavily favoring mediation included plans aimed squarely at employers, with its adoption of the national uniform mediation agreements (NUMAs) and referral-back programs. The NUMAs specifically commit employers to mediation of Title VII claims, while the referral-back programs allow employers to use their own in-house ADR programs to attempt to settle such claims.

In 2014, the EEOC brought suit against Doherty Enterprises, Inc.,[49] owner of Panera Bread and Applebee's restaurants, for enforcing its mandatory arbitration agreements against employees, requiring them, as a condition of employment, to agree to arbitrate discrimination claims rather than going to the EEOC. The EEOC alleged that the agreement was overly broad and as such interfered with employees' rights to file discrimination claims under the law and prevented the EEOC from doing its job of oversight and eradication of workplace discrimination by shielding its actions from view behind private arbitration. Since the EEOC had made preserving access to the legal system one of its Strategic Enforcement Plan priorities, it did not seem likely to give up on the issue of mandatory arbitration agreements anytime soon.[50] However, as discussed earlier, this is a new administration. In December 2019, the EEOC reversed its position of the past 22 years that such agreements should be avoided by employers as incompatible with civil rights and instead deemed them as compatible with the law.

See Chapter 2 to revisit key concepts.

Remedies

For remedies available under Title VII, see Chapter 2, "The Employment Law Toolkit."

Jury Trials

The Civil Rights Act of 1991 also added jury trials to Title VII. From the creation of Title VII in 1964 until passage of the 1991 Civil Rights Act 27 years later, jury trials were not permitted under Title VII. Jury trials are now permitted under Title VII at the request of either party when compensatory and punitive damages are sought.

There is always less predictability about case outcomes when juries are involved. Arguing one's cause to a judge who is a trained member of the legal profession is quite different from arguing to a jury of 6 to 12 jurors, all of whom come with their own backgrounds, experiences, prejudices, and predilections and with little knowledge of the law. Employers now have even more incentive to ensure that their policies and actions are well reasoned, business-related, and justifiable—especially since the possibility of damages gives employees even more incentive to sue.

The Reconstruction Civil Rights Acts

LO8 Explain the post–Civil War statutes, including what each is and what it does.

In this chapter we have been discussing discrimination claims under Title VII of the Civil Rights Act of 1964. However, the Civil Rights Act of 1964 was not the first piece of legislation aimed at prohibiting racial discrimination. Since these other laws are still used today, the chapter would not be complete without including some mention of them. It is important to know the full range of potential employer liability for discrimination lawsuits by employees.

There are three main pre–Title VII laws. (See Exhibit 3.10, "The Reconstruction Civil Rights Acts.") Collectively, they are known as the post–Civil War statutes, or the Reconstruction Civil Rights Acts. They were passed by Congress after the Civil War ended in 1865 in an effort to provide a means of enforcing the new status of the ex-slaves as free citizens. In 1865, passage of the Thirteenth Amendment to the Constitution abolishing slavery had merely totally abolished involuntary servitude (slavery) except as punishment for crimes. Nothing on the books at that point said what that picture had to look like. In fact, largely in response to the Thirteenth Amendment, some southern states enacted "Black Codes"—mostly revisions of their pre–Civil War "Slave Codes"—that codified discrimination on the basis of race and limited the rights of the newly free slaves.[51]

Exhibit 3.10   *The Reconstruction Civil Rights Acts*

42 U.S.C. SECTION 1981. EQUAL RIGHTS UNDER THE LAW (1866)

All persons within the jurisdiction of the United States shall have the same right in every State and Territory to make and enforce contracts . . . as is enjoyed by white citizens.

42 U.S.C. SECTION 1983. CIVIL ACTION FOR DEPRIVATION OF RIGHTS (1871)

Every person who, under color of any statute, ordinance, regulation, custom, or usage, of any State or Territory, subjects, or causes to be subjected, any citizen of the United States or other person within the jurisdiction thereof to the deprivation of any rights, privileges, or immunities secured by the Constitution and laws, shall be liable to the party injured in an action at law, suit in equity, or other proper proceeding for redress.

42 U.S.C. SECTION 1985. CONSPIRACY TO INTERFERE WITH CIVIL RIGHTS—PREVENTING OFFICER FROM PERFORMING DUTIES ("KU KLUX KLAN ACT") (1871)

Depriving persons of rights or privileges . . .

(3) If two or more persons in any State or Territory conspire or go in disguise on the highway or on the premises of another, for the purpose of depriving, either directly or indirectly, any person or class of persons of the equal protection of the laws, or of equal privileges and immunities under the laws; in any case of conspiracy set forth in this section, if one or more persons engaged therein do, or cause to be done, any act in furtherance of the object of such conspiracy, whereby another is injured in his person or property, or deprived of having and exercising any rights or privileges of a citizen of the United States, the party so injured or deprived may have an action for the recovery of damages, occasioned by such injury or deprivation, against any one or more of the conspirators.

Beginning in 1866, Congress began enacting the post–Civil War statutes, understanding that without legislation providing at least minimal rights for the new status of African Americans, things would almost certainly revert to pre–Civil War status. It passed section 1981, making all African Americans born in the United States citizens and ensuring them at least the right to make and enforce contracts the same "as enjoyed by white citizens." In 1868, Congress passed the Fourteenth Amendment to make its laws applicable to the states, dictating that no state "shall make or enforce any law which shall abridge the privileges or immunities of the citizens of the United States . . . [or] deprive any person of life, liberty, or property, without due process of law, [or] deny to any person within its jurisdiction the equal protection of the laws."[52] In 1871, realizing the ongoing violent resistance to the slaves by whites, often in positions of power or in groups like the KKK, in an effort to curb it, Congress passed the KKK Act of 1871 as well as the color of state law legislation.

The three post–Civil War statutes are now codified as 42 U.S.C. sections 1981, 1983, and 1985. They prohibit discrimination on the basis of race in making and enforcing contracts, prohibit the denial of civil rights on the basis of race by someone behaving as if they are acting on behalf of the government (called **under color of state law**), and prohibit concerted activity to deny someone their rights based on race.

under color of state law
Government employee is illegally discriminating against another during performance of his or her duties.

Sections 1981 and 1983 are the laws most frequently used in the employment setting if a claim is not brought using Title VII. Since Title VII is part of a comprehensive statutory scheme to prohibit race and other discrimination, it is the preferred method of enforcing employment discrimination claims. As we have seen, a complete and comprehensive administrative structure has been set up to deal with such claims. The post–Civil War statutes do not offer such a structure. Employees bringing claims under Title VII file them with the EEOC, a federal administrative agency devoted solely to these types of claims, with an administrative structure set up to do so. Employees do not have to pay to file their claims. Employees bringing claims under the post–Civil War statutes are on their own; they must go to an attorney who understands such cases and must pay. The case is brought in a regular court of law that hears all other types of cases as well rather than an agency devoted solely to such claims.

On the other hand, the statute of limitations for the post–Civil War statutes is longer than that of Title VII. While Title VII's basic statute of limitations is 180 days from the precipitating event, the U.S. Supreme Court has ruled that the statute of limitations on race cases under section 1981 is four years.[53] In addition, the damages under section 1981 are unlimited, unlike those under Title VII that have caps.

When you put the post–Civil War statutes' limitations together with the historical context in which African Americans operated after the Civil War until passage of the Civil Rights Act in 1964, 99 years later, it makes sense that these laws were not used as much as Title VII. From the end of the Civil War until passage of the Civil Rights Act of 1964 and beyond, Jim Crow laws and iron-clad social customs segregated African Americans and denied them basic rights. This was frequently enforced through violence. Few African Americans had the money to sue. Between little bar to race discrimination in the workplace (or elsewhere), not being able to afford to bring lawsuits, and taking their lives into their hands if they tried to enforce any rights they did have under these laws, the post–Civil War statutes provided little relief to African Americans facing employment discrimination.

Still, they remain today a viable source of employer liability, and as such, you should have some exposure to them. Note also that the laws were created to address the issue of the newly freed slaves, but the language applies to anyone, so national origin cases are also brought under the statutes. By and large, most of the cases are brought under these statutes as opposed to Title VII either because the claimant was outside the Title VII statute of limitations deadline or because the claim involves a government employer.

42 U.S.C. Section 1981

Section 1981. Equal Rights under the Law

All persons within the jurisdiction of the United States shall have the same right in every State and Territory to make and enforce contracts . . . as is enjoyed by white citizens.[54]

This provision of the post–Civil War statutes has been used to a limited extent in the past as a basis for employees suing employers for racial discrimination in employment. In a case of first impression, the Second Circuit Court of Appeals held that section 1981 did not cover a race discrimination claim filed by an African American employee for actions occurring while he was on temporary work assignment in South Africa because, by its terms, the law only covers those within the jurisdiction of the United States.[55]

In 1975, the U.S. Supreme Court held that section 1981 prohibits purely private discrimination in contracts, including employment contracts. In *Patterson v. McLean Credit Union,* provided for your review, the limitations of section 1981 become evident. *Patterson* was nullified by the Civil Rights Act of 1991. The act overturned *Patterson*'s holding that section 1981 does not permit actions for racial discrimination *during* the performance of the contract, but only in *making* or *enforcing* the contract. Note that the limitation on damages the Court spoke of as part of Title VII's administrative scheme no longer applies. The Civil Rights Act of 1991 now permits recovery of compensatory and punitive damages. How do you think this squares with the Court's statement "Neither party would be likely to conciliate if there is the possibility of the employee recovering the greater damages permitted by section 1981?"

As you read the case for historical and analytical purposes, see if you can determine why Congress would want to overrule the Supreme Court's decision by enacting the 1991 legislation. *Patterson* was specifically chosen for inclusion here to demonstrate how seemingly small, insignificant actions in the workplace can accumulate and provide a solid picture of discriminatory treatment leading to employer liability. Again, vigilance pays off. Managers should curtail discriminatory activity as soon as they see it, so that it does not progress and result in costly liability.

42 U.S.C. Section 1983

Section 1983. Civil Action for Deprivation of Rights

Every person who, under color of any statute, ordinance, regulation, custom, or usage, of any State or Territory, subjects, or causes to be subjected, any citizen of the United States or other person within the jurisdiction thereof to the deprivation of any rights, privileges, or immunities secured by the Constitution and laws, shall be liable to the party injured in an action at law, suit in equity, or other proper proceeding for redress.[56]

The Civil Rights Act of 1871, codified as 42 U.S.C. section 1983, protects citizens from deprivation of their legal and constitutional rights, privileges, and immunities, under color of state law. That is, someone acting on behalf of the state cannot deprive people of their rights. For instance, if you attended a state university and a university security guard, without provocation, beats you with a nightstick during a campus demonstration about climate change or campus rape, it would give rise to such a claim. A couple of famous examples are (1) the New Jersey state troopers who were convicted in 2002 when racial profiling admittedly caused them to shoot 11 bullets into a car with four unarmed Black and Latino students, wounding three, and (2) the police officers who were videotaped beating Rodney King during his arrest in Los Angeles in 1991. While performing their duties as government employees, they were alleged to have deprived King of his rights by using excessive force and thus depriving him of his rights as if it were a legitimate part of their duties.

Section 1983 cases also arise when, for instance, a city fire department or municipal police department discriminates against an employee or applicant on the basis of race or national origin.

Neither the Fourteenth Amendment nor section 1983 may be used for discrimination by private employers. They both redress actions by government personnel. The government may not be sued without its permission because of the Eleventh Amendment to the Constitution, so the action is brought against the government official in his or her individual and official capacity.

An Important Note

One of the most prevalent misconceptions about Title VII is that all an employee must do is file a claim and the employer is automatically deemed to be liable for discrimination and the only matter to be determined is the number of zeroes on the check. This is far from the reality. Discrimination claims under Title VII and other employment discrimination legislation must be proved just as any other lawsuits. It is not enough for an employee to allege he or she is being discriminated against. The employee must offer evidence to support every aspect of the claim. As shown, at the conclusion of the chapter, in *Ali v. Mount Sinai Hospital,* not doing so has predictable results. There are many cases brought that may even seem to have merit but that do not win in the final analysis.

Many times managers do not discipline or even terminate employees with Title VII protection for fear of being sued. This is not a good strategy. It is better to simply treat them and their actions as you would those of any other similarly situated employee

Management Tips

LO9 Discuss what management can do to comply with Title VII.

Since potentially all employees can bind employers by their discriminatory actions, it is important for all employees to understand the law. This not only will greatly aid them in avoiding acts that may cause the employer liability, but it will also go far in creating a work environment in which discrimination is less likely to occur. Through training, make sure that all employees understand:

- What Title VII is.
- What Title VII requires.
- Who Title VII applies to.
- How the employees' actions can bring about liability for the employer.
- What kinds of actions will be looked at in a Title VII proceeding.
- That the employer will not allow Title VII to be violated.
- That all employees have a right to a workplace free of illegal discrimination.
- That the workplace will try hard to be inclusive, understanding that failure to include traditionally excluded groups leads to discrimination claims.
- That the workplace will use all its available resources among its personnel to attempt to determine where support is needed in order to head off problems before they become legal liabilities.
- The need for the employer to be proactive rather than reactive in the workplace to better protect the workplace from unnecessary claims of employment discrimination.
- The need for not only specific and obvious compliance with the law but also the historical reasons why certain actions can be interpreted differently by different groups and unwittingly create employer liability. Inclusion in the workplace of those historically excluded becomes important when it is clear that exclusion can serve as the basis for Title VII and other protective legislation claims.

and be consistent in doing so. There is no need to walk on eggshells. If an employee is not performing as they should, Title VII affords them no protection whatsoever just because they are in a protected class based on race, gender, national origin, and so forth. Title VII is not a job guarantee for women and minorities. Instead, it requires employers to provide them with equal employment opportunity, including termination if it is called for. No more. No less. No one can stop an employee who feels discrimination has occurred from suing. That is why the best defense an employer can have is to engage in consistency and evenhandedness that makes for a less desirable target and to have justifiable decisions to defend against the claim once sued.

In *Ali v. Mt. Sinai Hospital,* an African American employee sued her employer for race discrimination after being disciplined for violating the hospital's detailed three-page dress code requiring that dress be "conservative and in keeping with the professional image of nursing," in deference to working in the post–open heart surgery unit. Ali said enforcement of the dress code against her was discriminatory but did not show proof of this, and her case was therefore dismissed. As you read *Ali,* take note of the inadvisability of the questionable parts of the encounter between the employer and the employee. You will recognize them when you see them.

Chapter Summary

- Title VII prohibits employers, unions, joint labor–management committees, and employment agencies from discriminating in any aspect of employment on the basis of race, color, religion, gender, or national origin.
- Title VII has a full statutory scheme including a federal agency and administrative structure for bringing workplace discrimination claims.
- Where appropriate, the law allows for jury trials.
- Title VII claims can be judicially reviewed *de novo* after exhaustion of administrative remedies.
- The post–Civil War statutes add another area of potential liability for the employer and have a much longer statute of limitations and unlimited compensatory and punitive damages.
- The employer's best defense is a good offense. A strong, top-down policy of non-discrimination can be effective in setting the right tone and getting the message to managers and employees alike that discrimination in employment will not be tolerated.
- Strong policies, consistently and appropriately enforced, as well as periodic training and updating as issues emerge and even as a means of review are most helpful.
- To the extent that an employer complies with Title VII, it can safely be said that workplace productivity will benefit, as will the employer's coffers, because unlawful employment discrimination can be costly to the employer in more ways than one.

Chapter-End Questions

1. While reviewing preemployment reports as part of her job, the claimant read a report in which an applicant admitted commenting to an employee at a prior job that "making love to you is like making love to the Grand Canyon." Later, at a meeting convened by her supervisor, the supervisor read the quote and said he didn't understand it. A male subordinate said he would explain it to him later, and both chuckled. The claimant interpreted the exchange as sexual harassment and reported it internally. The claimant alleges that nearly every action after the incident constituted retaliation for her complaint, including a lateral transfer. Will the court agree? [*Clark County School District v. Breeden,* 121 S. Ct. 1508 (2001).]
2. How long does a private employee have to file a claim with the EEOC or be barred from doing so?
3. Lin Teung files a complaint with the EEOC for national origin discrimination. His jurisdiction has a 706 agency. When Teung calls up the EEOC after 45 days to see how his case is progressing, he learns that the EEOC has not yet moved on it. Teung feels the EEOC is violating its own rules. Is it?
4. Melinda wants to file a sexual harassment claim against her employer but feels she cannot do so because he would retaliate against her by firing her. She also has no money to sue him. Any advice for Melinda?

5. Saeid, a Muslim, alleges that his supervisor made numerous remarks belittling his Muslim religion, Arabs generally, and him specifically. The comments were made in general and not made in the context of a specific employment decision involving Saeid. Is this sufficient for the court to find discriminatory ill will? [*Maarouf v. Walker Manufacturing Co.,* 210 F.3d 750 (7th Cir. 2000).]

6. A construction company was sued for harassment when it failed to take seriously the complaints about offensive graffiti scrawled on rented portable toilets. The employer defended by saying (1) employees should be used to such rude and crude behavior; (2) the employer did not own or maintain the equipment, which came with graffiti already on it; (3) it took action after a formal employee complaint; and (4) the graffiti insulted everyone. Will the defenses be successful? [*Malone v. Foster-Wheeler Constructors,* 21 Fed. Appx. 470 (Westlaw) (7th Cir. 2001) (unpub. opinion).]

7. During the interview Gale had with Leslie Accounting Firm, Gale was asked whether she had any children, whether she planned to have any more children, to what church she belonged, and what her husband did for a living. Are these questions illegal? Explain.

8. True or false: Any claimant who has a cause of action for employment discrimination can bring his or her claim under the post–Civil War statutes. Explain.

9. Laurie, a lesbian and French national, was hired as a flight attendant to work in United Airlines' hub in Paris. Laurie was terminated at age 40. She sues United Airlines alleging employment discrimination on the basis of age, gender, and sexual orientation (the latter based on the Illinois Human Rights Act). The airline asks the court to dismiss Laurie's action on the basis that she does not live in the United States, so the employment protection laws do not apply to her. Will the court do so? Explain. [*Rabé v. United Airlines, Inc.,* 2011 WL677946 (7th Cir. 2011).]

10. Ted, the white coach of a local high school, has been at the school as a teacher, athletic director, and coach for 25 years. Over the years the neighborhood has changed from predominantly white to predominantly Black. When a new principal is appointed, he and Ted do not get along well at all. Ted alleges that the principal took away a good deal of his authority and publicly castigated him for the football team's performance. Ted waits too long to sue under Title VII for race discrimination but hears about section 1981. He wants to sue for race discrimination under section 1981 but thinks he cannot do so because he is white. Is Ted correct? Explain. [*Jett v. Dallas Independent School District,* 491 U.S. 701 (1989).]

End Notes

1. http://eeoc.gov/abouteeoc/plan/par/2006/index.html.

2. "EEOC Releases Fiscal Year 2018 Enforcement and Litigation Data," http://www.eeoc.gov/eeoc/newsroom/release/4-10-19.cfm.

3. Robert D. Loevy, ed., *The Civil Rights Act of 1964: The Passage of the Law that Ended Racial Segregation* (Albany: State University of New York Press, 1997), p. 40.

4. Whitaker, Morgan, "Mississippi Finally Ratifies Amendment Banning Slavery," MSNBC, February 18, 2013, http://tv.msnbc.com/2013/02/18/mississippi-finally-officially-ratifies-amendment-banning-slavery/.

5. See Stephanie McCurry, *Masters of Small Worlds: Yeoman Households, Gender Relations & the Political Culture of the Antebellum South Carolina's Low Country* (New York: Oxford University Press, 1995); and Stephanie McCurry, *Confederate Reckoning: Owners and Politics of the Civil War South* (Cambridge, MA: Harvard University Press, 2010).

6. See, e.g., Stetson Kennedy, *The Jim Crow Guide to the U.S.* (London: Lawrence & Wishart, 1959); Jerrold M. Packard, *American Nightmare: The History of Jim Crow* (New York: St. Martin's Press, 2002); Thomas Adams Upchurch, *Legislating Racism: The Billion Dollar Congress and the Birth of Jim Crow* (Lexington, KY: The University Press of Kentucky, 2004); and David K. Fremon, *Jim Crow Laws and Racism in American History,* Berkeley Heights, NJ: Enslow Publishers, 2000).

7. Douglas A. Blackmon, *Slavery by Another Name: The Re-Enslavement of Black Americans from the Civil War to World War II* (New York: Anchor Books, 2009).

8. See, e.g., Douglas A. Blackmon, *Slavery by Another Name: The Re-Enslavement of Black Americans from the Civil War to World War II* (New York: Anchor Books, 2009); and David M. Oshinsky, *Worse Than Slavery: Parchman Farm and the Ordeal of Jim Crow Justice* (New York: Free Press Paperbacks, 1996).

9. Donald L. Grant, *The Way It Was in the South: The Black Experience in Georgia* (Athens, GA: University of Georgia Press, 1993); Philip Dray, *At the Hands of Persons Unknown: The Lynching of Black America* (New York: Random House, 2002); James Allen et al., *Without Sanctuary: Lynching Photography in America* (New Mexico: Twin Palms, 2005); James W. Loewen, *Sundown Towns: A Hidden Dimension of American Racism* (New York: Touchstone, 2005); and Alex A. Alston, Jr., and James L. Dickerson, *Devil's Sanctuary: An Eyewitness History of Mississippi Hate Crimes* (Chicago: Lawrence Hill Books, 2009).

10. Diedre Woolard, "Beatles 1965 Contract Reveals the Band's Activist Side," *Luxury Lifestyle Expert* magazine (September 16, 2011), http://www.justluxe.com/lifestyle/arts/feature-1642477.php.

11. For fascinating glimpses of life at the time, see, e.g., Melton A. McLaurin, *Separate Pasts: Growing Up White in the Segregated South* (Athens, GA: University of Georgia Press, 1987); Virginia Foster Durr, *Outside the Magic Circle: The Autobiography of Virginia Foster Durr* (Tuscaloosa, AL: University of Alabama Press, 1985); Lillian Smith, *Killers of the Dream* (New York: W.W. Norton, 1949); and Leon F. Litwack, *Trouble in Mind: Black Southerners in the Age of Jim Crow* (New York: Vintage Books, 1998).

12. James A Cobb, *The Most Southern Place on Earth: The Mississippi Delta and the Roots of Regional Identity* (New York: Oxford University Press, 1992).

13. 347 U.S. 483 (1954).

14. Sovereignty Commission Online, http://mdah.state.ms.us/arrec/digital_archives/sovcom/.

15. See, e.g., Charles J. Ogletree, Jr., *All Deliberate Speed: Reflections on the First Half Century of Brown v. Board of Education* (New York: W.W. Norton, 2004); Elizabeth Jacoway, *Turn Away Thy Son: Little Rock, the Crisis That Shocked the Nation* (New York: Free Press, 2007); and Derrick A. Bell, Jr., *Race, Racism and American Law* (Boston: Little, Brown, 1980).

16. Kimble, Lindsay, "Emmett Till's Accuser Recants Part of Her Story—60 Years after His Beating Stoked Civil Rights Movement," *People Magazine* (January 27, 2017), http://people.com/crime/emmett-till-carolyn-bryant-interview/ (accessed March 7, 2017). The admission is contained in Timothy B. Tyson, *The Blood of Emmett Till* (New York: Simon & Schuster, 2017).

17. "This Day in History, Emmett Till Murderers Make Magazine Confession," The History Channel, http://www.history.com/this-day-in-history/emmett-till-murderers-make-magazine-confession/.

18. Adam Fairclough, *To Redeem the Soul of America: The Southern Christian Leadership Conference and Martin Luther King, Jr.* (Athens, GA: University of Georgia Press, 1987); Juan Williams, *Eyes on the Prize: America's Civil Rights Years, 1954–1965* (New York: Viking Press, 1987); Clive Webb, *Massive Resistance: Opposition to the Second Reconstruction* (New York: Oxford University Press, 2005); Maurice C. Daniels, *Horace T. Ward: Desegregation of the University of Georgia, Civil Rights Advocacy, and Jurisprudence* (Athens, GA: Clark Atlanta University Press, 2001); and Mark V. Tushnet, ed., *Thurgood Marshall: His Speeches, Writings, Arguments, Opinions and Reminiscences* (Chicago: Lawrence Hill Books, 2001).

19. See David C. Kozak and Kenneth N. Ciboski, eds., The American Presidency (Chicago: Nelson-Hall, 1985), http://faculty1.coloradocollege.edu/%7Ebloevy/CivilRightsActOf1964/; and Charles Whalen and Barbara Whalen, The Longest Debate: A Legislative History of the 1964 Civil Rights Act (Santa Ana, CA: Seven Locks Press, 1985).

20. See Kent B. Germany, "Lyndon Baines Johnson and Civil Rights: Introduction to the Digital Edition," http://presidentialrecordings.rotunda.upress.virginia.edu/essays?series=CivilRights.

21. John F. Kennedy.

22. Elliot-Larsens Civil Rights Act of 1976.

23. Coyle, Marcia, "EEOC Doesn't Sign Trump DOJ's Supreme Court Brief against Transgender Employees," *The National Law Journal,* law.com (August 16, 2019), https://www.law.com/nationallawjournal/2019/08/16/eeoc-doesnt-sign-trump-dojs-supreme-court-brief-against-transgender-employees/?slreturn=20191120123905; "Justice Department Urges Civil Rights Agency to Flip LGBT Stance," Daily Labor Reports (August 13, 2019), https://news.bloomberglaw.com/daily-labor-report/justice-department-urges-civil-rights-agency-to-flip-lgbt-stance.

24. *R.G. and G.R. Harris Family Funeral Homes,v. EEOC,* Docket No. 18-107. *Bostock v. Clayton County, GA,* Docket No. 17-1618. *Altitude Express v. Zarda,* Docket No. 17-1623.

25. The EEOC's regulations can be found in the Code of Federal Regulations (e.g., 29 C.F.R. § 1604.1–9, Guidelines on Discrimination Because of Sex; 29 C.F.R. § 1604.10, Guidelines on Discrimination Because of Sex, Pregnancy and Childbirth; 29 C.F.R. part 1606, Guidelines on Discrimination Because of National Origin; 29 C.F.R. part 1607, Employee Selection Procedures; 29 C.F.R. § 1613.701–707, Guidelines on Discrimination Because of Disability; 45 C.F.R. part 90, Guidelines on Discrimination Because of Age; 29 C.F.R. 1635 Regulations Under the Generic Information Nondiscrimination Act of 2008 Final Rule).

26. "Strategic Enforcement Plan 2013–2016," http://www.eeoc.gov/eeoc/plan/sep.cfm.

27. "EEOC Updates Strategic Enforcement Plan: Commission Reaffirms Priorities and Strategies for Securing Strategic Impact," https://www.eeoc.gov/eeoc/newsroom/release/10-17-16.cfm (accessed March 7, 2017).

28. https://twitter.com/USEEOC/status/1207735085669203968?ref_src=twsrc%5Etfw%7Ctwcamp%5Eembeddedtimeline%7Ctwterm%5Eprofile%3Auseeoc%7Ctwcon%5Etimelinechrome&ref_url=https%3A%2F%2Fwww.eeoc.gov%2Findex.cfm.

29. "Employment Discrimination Laws 'New Frontier' in War against Human Labor Trafficking" (January 19, 2011), http://www.eeoc.gov/eeoc/newsroom/release/1-19-11.cfm.

30. "EEOC Public Meeting Explores the Use of Credit Histories as Employment Selection Criteria" (October 20, 2010), http://www.eeoc.gov/eeoc/newsroom/release/10-20-10b.cfm.

31. "Consideration of Arrest and Conviction Records in Employment Decisions under Title VII of the Civil Rights Act of 1964" (April 25, 2012), http://www.eeoc.gov/laws/guidance/arrest_conviction.cfm.

32. "Statement of Stuart J. Ishimaru, Acting Chairman U.S. Equal Employment Opportunity Commission before the Committee on Health, Education, Labor and Pensions, U.S. Senate" (March 11, 2010), http://www.eeoc.gov/eeoc/events/ishimaru_paycheck_fairness.cfm.

33. "Enforcement Guidance: Unlawful Disparate Treatment of Workers with Caregiving Responsibilities" (May 23, 2007), http://www.eeoc.gov/policy/docs/caregiving.html.

34. https://www.eeoc.gov/eeoc/statistics/enforcement/charges.cfm.

35. http://www.eeoc.gov/eeoc/plan/sep.cfm.

36. Clarey, Katie, "EEOC May Propose Data Collection Rule in 2020," HR Drive (November 21, 2019), https://www.hrdive.com/news/eeoc-may-propose-pay-data-collection-rule-in-2020/567765/.

37. "EEOC Issues FY 2016 Performance Report" (November 16, 2016), https://www.eeoc.gov/eeoc/newsroom/release/11-16-16.cfm (accessed March 7, 2017).

38. 535 U.S. 137 (2002).

39. "EEOC Conciliates Discriminatory Wage Theft Case: Steamboat Springs Restaurant to Pay $50,000 for Failing to Pay Proper Wages to Latino Workers Because of Race or National Origin," https://www.eeoc.gov/eeoc/newsroom/release/10-4-17b.cfm (accessed March 5, 2017).

40. EEOC, "Rescission of Enforcement Guidance on Remedies Available to Undocumented Workers under Federal Employment Discrimination Laws" (June 27, 2002), http://www.eeoc.gov/policy/docs/undoc-rescind.html; "EEOC Issues Guidance on Remedies for Undocumented Workers under Federal Laws Prohibiting Employment Discrimination" (October 26, 1999), http://www.eeoc.gov/eeoc/newsroom/release/10-26-99.cfm.

41. *Dukes v. Wal-Mart,* Docket No. 10-277. For a look at the parties' briefs, oral argument points and other information on the case, see the Supreme Court of the United States blog: http://www.scotusblog.com/case-files/cases/wal-mart-v-dukes/.

42. 536 U.S. 101 (2002).

43. 550 U.S. 618, 127 S. Ct. 2162, 167 L. Ed. 2d 982, 2007 U.S. LEXIS 6295 (2007).

44. "EEOC Solicits Comments on Proposed Improvements to Federal Employee Discrimination Complaint Process" (December 22, 2009), http://www.eeoc.gov/eeoc/newsroom/release/12-21-09.cfm.

45. Elizabeth Dwoskin, "Is This Woman Too Hot to Be a Banker?" *The Village Voice News* (June 21, 2010), http://www.villagevoice.com/2010-06-01/news/is-this-woman-too-hot-to-work-in-a-bank/.

46. 532 U.S. 105 (2001).

47. 534 U.S. 279 (2002).

48. *Circuit City Stores, Inc. v. Adams,* 535 U.S. 1112 (2002).

49. *EEOC v. Doherty Enterprises, Inc.,* Civil Action No. 9:14-cv-81184-KAM (U.S. Dist. Ct. SD FL, 2015).

50. "EEOC Sues Doherty Enterprises over Mandatory Arbitration Agreement: Restaurant Franchiser Unlawfully Barred New Hires from Filing Discrimination Charges, Federal Agency Charges," https://www.eeoc.gov/eeoc/newsroom/release/9-19-14b.cfm (accessed March 7, 2017).

51. Jerrold M. Packard, *American Nightmare: The History of Jim Crow* (New York: St. Martin's Press, 2002); Thomas Adams Upchurch, *Legislating Racism: The Billion Dollar Congress and the Birth of Jim Crow* (Lexington, KY: The University Press of Kentucky, 2004); and David K. Fremon, *Jim Crow Laws and Racism in American History* (Berkeley Heights, NJ: Enslow Publishers, 2000).

52. 14th Amendment.

53. *Jones v. R.R. Donnelley & Sons Co.*, 541 U.S. 369 (2004).

54. 42 U.S.C. Section 1981.

55. *Ofori-Tenkorang v. AIG,* 460 F.3d 296 (2d Cir. 2006).

56. 42 U.S.C. Section 1983.

Cases

Case 1

Petruska v. Gannon University,
462 F.3d 294 (3d Cir. 2006)

Employee, the chaplain of a Catholic university, sued for gender-based employment discrimination in violation of, among other things, Title VII. The court dismissed the action, saying that the university, as a religious institution, was not subject to Title VII.

Smith, J.

***

Gannon University is a private, Catholic, diocesan college established under the laws of the Commonwealth of Pennsylvania. Plaintiff employee was initially hired by Gannon as Director for the University's Center for Social Concerns and in considering and accepting this position, relied upon Gannon's self-representation as an equal opportunity employer that does not discriminate on the basis of, among other things, gender.

Following [Gannon's President] Rubino's resignation [after allegations of a sexual affair with a subordinate], Gannon engaged in a campaign to cover up Rubino's sexual misconduct. Employee was vocal in opposing this and other of the Administration's policies and procedures, which she viewed as discriminatory toward females. One

such policy was [Bishop of the Roman Catholic Diocese of Erie] Trautman's willingness to allow allegedly abusive clergy to remain on campus, including at least one former Gannon priest who had been removed because of sexual misconduct directed at students.

Employee also strongly opposed the University's efforts, during the time that Rubino was coming under investigation for alleged sexual harassment of females, to limit the time frame within which victims of sexual harassment could file grievances. As Chair of the University's Institutional Integrity Committee, employee was instrumental in submitting a Middle States accreditation report which raised issues of gender-based inequality in the pay of Gannon's female employees and which was critical of the University's policies and procedures for addressing complaints of sexual harassment and other forms of discrimination. Despite pressure from the University's administration, employee refused to change those portions of the report which were critical of the University.

Employee contends that, in retaliation for the foregoing conduct and because of her gender, she was discriminated against in the terms and conditions of her employment. Believing that she was about to be fired, employee served Gannon with two weeks notice of her resignation. Employee was advised the following day that her resignation was accepted effective immediately and that she was to pack her belongings and leave the campus. Her access to the campus and to students was strictly limited thereafter. Following employee's departure, her supervisor stated on several occasions to both students and staff that a female would not be considered to replace employee as Chaplain.

The University has moved to dismiss all claims on the ground that they are barred by the so-called "ministerial exception," which is frequently applied in employment discrimination cases involving religious institutions. The ministerial exception is rooted in the First Amendment which provides that "Congress shall make no law respecting an establishment of religion, or prohibiting the free exercise thereof." Among the prerogatives protected by the Free Exercise Clause is the right of religious institutions to manage their internal affairs.

The Establishment Clause prohibits laws "respecting an establishment of religion." The Supreme Court held that a statute comports with the Establishment Clause if it has a secular legislative purpose, if its principal or primary effect neither advances nor inhibits religion, and if it does not foster an "excessive government entanglement with religion." Unconstitutional entanglement with religion may arise in situations "where a 'protracted legal process pit(s) church and state as adversaries,' and where the Government is placed in a position of choosing among 'competing religious visions.'"*

The questions presented in this case are whether applying Title VII to Gannon's decision to restructure would infringe upon its free exercise rights and whether adjudication of Petruska's Title VII claims would result in unconstitutional entanglement under the Establishment Clause. Every one of our sister circuits to consider the issue has concluded that application of Title VII to a minister-church relationship would violate—or would

risk violating—the First Amendment and, accordingly, has recognized some version of the ministerial exception. To the extent that a claim involves the church's selection of clergy—in other words, its choice as to who will perform particular spiritual functions—most of these circuits have held that the exception bars any inquiry into a religious organization's underlying motivation for the contested employment decision.

Petruska alleges that Gannon demoted and constructively discharged her from her position as University Chaplain based on her gender and retaliated against her on the basis of her opposition to sexual harassment at the University. Her discrimination and retaliation claims are premised upon Gannon's decision to restructure, a decision which Petruska argues was merely pretext for gender discrimination. It is clear from the face of Petruska's complaint, however, that Gannon's choice to restructure constituted a decision about who would perform spiritual functions and about how those function[s] would be divided. Accordingly, application of Title VII's discrimination and retaliation provisions to Gannon's decision to restructure would violate the Free Exercise Clause. For that reason, Petruska's Title VII claims should be dismissed.

The First Amendment protects a church's right to decide matters of faith and to declare its doctrine free from state interference. A church's ability to select who will perform particular spiritual functions is a necessary corollary to this right. The function of Petruska's position as University Chaplain was ministerial in nature, and therefore, her Title VII, civil claim must be dismissed. Based upon the foregoing reasons, the trial court's decision is AFFIRMED and REMANDED. [Petruska petitioned the U.S. Supreme Court to hear an appeal from this case and the Court denied the petition.]

Case Questions

1. Do you agree with the court's decision? Explain.

2. As a manager in this situation, how do you think you would have handled the chaplain's complaints?

3. Given the power that religious organizations have under Title VII, can and how do you think employment discrimination concerns can be addressed in the religious workplace?

Petruska v. Gannon University 462 F.3d 294 (3d Cir. 2006).

Patterson v. McLean Credit Union,
491 U.S. 164 (1989)

Case 2

A Black female employee alleged racial discrimination in violation of section 1981 in that she was treated differently from white employees and not promoted, on the basis of race. The Court held that section 1981 was not available to address this problem since the case did not involve the making of a contract but rather its performance.

Kennedy, J.

***

Patterson, a Black female, worked for the McLean Credit Union (MCU) as a teller and file coordinator for 10 years. She alleges that when she first interviewed for her job, the supervisor, who later became the president of MCU, told her that she would be working with all white women and that they probably would not like working with her because she was Black. According to Patterson, in the subsequent years, it was her supervisor who proved to have the problem with her working at the credit union.

Patterson alleges that she was subjected to a pattern of discrimination at MCU which included her supervisor repeatedly staring at her for minutes at a time while she performed her work and not doing so to white employees; not promoting her or giving her the usually perfunctory raises which other employees routinely received; not arranging to have her work reassigned to others when she went on vacation, as was routinely done with other employees, but rather, allowing Patterson's work to accumulate during her absence; assigning her menial, non-clerical tasks such as sweeping and dusting, while such tasks were not assigned to other similarly situated employees; being openly critical of Patterson's work in staff meetings, and that of one other Black employee, while white employees were told of their shortcomings privately; telling Patterson that it was known that "Blacks are known to work slower than whites, by nature" or, saying in one instance, "some animals [are] faster than other animals"; repeatedly suggesting that a white would be able to perform Patterson's job better than she could; unequal work assignments between Patterson and other similarly situated white employees, with Patterson receiving more work than others; having her work scrutinized more closely and criticized more severely than white employees; despite her desire to "move up and advance," being offered no training for higher jobs during her 10 years

at the credit union, while white employees were offered training, including those at the same level, but with less seniority (such employees were later promoted); not being informed of job openings, nor interviewed for them, while less senior whites were informed of the positions and hired; and when another manager recommended to Patterson's supervisor a different Black to fill a position as a data processor, the supervisor said that he did not "need any more problems around here," and would "search for additional people who are not Black."

When Patterson complained about her workload, she was given no help, and in fact was given more work and told she always had the option of quitting. Patterson was laid off after 10 years with MCU. She brought suit under 42 U.S.C. section 1981, alleging harassment, failure to promote and discharge because of her race.

None of the racially harassing conduct which McLean engaged in involved the section 1981 prohibition against refusing to make a contract with Patterson or impairing Patterson's ability to enforce her existing contract rights with McLean. It is clear that Patterson is attacking conditions of employment which came into existence after she formed the contract to work for McLean. Since section 1981 only prohibits the interference with the making or enforcement of contracts because of race, performance of the contract is not actionable under section 1981.

Section 1981's language is specifically limited to making and enforcing contracts. To permit race discrimination cases involving post-formation actions would also undermine the detailed and well-crafted procedures for conciliation and resolution of Title VII claims. While section 1981 has no administrative procedure for review or conciliation of claims, Title VII has an elaborate system which is designed to investigate claims and work toward resolution of them by conciliation rather than litigation.

This includes Title VII's limiting recovery to back pay, while section 1981 permits plenary compensatory and punitive damages in appropriate cases. Neither party would be likely to conciliate if there is the possibility of the employee recovering the greater damages permitted by section 1981. There is some overlap between Title VII and section 1981, and when conduct is covered by both, the detailed procedures of Title VII are rendered a dead letter, as the plaintiff is free to pursue a claim by bringing suit under section 1981 without resort to those statutory prerequisites.

Regarding Patterson's failure to promote claim, this is somewhat different. Whether a racially discriminatory failure to promote claim is cognizable under section 1981 depends upon whether the nature of the change in positions is such that it involved the opportunity to enter into a new contract with the employer. If so, then the employer's refusal to enter the new contract is actionable under section 1981. AFFIRMED in part, VACATED in part, and REMANDED.

Case Questions

1. Do you think justice was served in this case? Explain. Why do you think Patterson waited so long to sue?

2. If you had been the manager when Patterson was initially interviewed, would you have made the statement about whites not accepting her? Why or why not?

3. When looking at the list of actions Patterson alleged McLean engaged in, do any seem appropriate? Why do you think it was done or permitted?

Ali v. Mount Sinai Hospital, *68 Empl. Prac. Dec. (CCH) 44,188, 1996 U.S. Dist. LEXIS 8079 (S.D.N.Y. 1996)*

An African American female employee sued the employer for racial discrimination in violation of Title VII, for discriminatory enforcement of the employer's dress code. She alleged she was disciplined for violating the code but whites were not. The court found that the employee had offered no evidence of discriminatory enforcement, so the court had no choice but to find in favor of the employer.

Gershon, J.

***

It is undisputed that, at all relevant times, the Hospital had a detailed three-page dress code for all of its nursing department staff, including unit clerks. It expressly provided that "the style chosen be conservative and in keeping with the professional image in nursing" and that the "Unit clerks wear the blue smock provided by the Hospital with conservative street clothes."* The wearing of boots, among other items of dress, was expressly prohibited. With regard to hair, the dress code provided that "it should be clean and neatly groomed to prevent interference with patient care" and only "plain" hair barrettes and hairpins should be worn. As plaintiff acknowledges, "The hallmark of said code was that the staff had to dress and groom themselves in a conservative manner."

It is also undisputed that Ms. Ali violated the dress code. Ms. Ali reported to work at the CSICU wearing a red, three-quarter length, cowl-necked dress and red boots made of lycra fabric which went over her knees. Over her dress, Ms. Ali wore the regulation smock provided by the Hospital. She wore her hair in what she says she then called a "punk" style. She now calls it a "fade" style, which she describes as an "Afro hairstyle." It was shorter on the sides than on the top and was in its natural color, black. According to Dr. Shields, Ms. Ali's hair was not conservative because it "was so high" and "you noticed it right away because it was high and back behind the ears and down. It certainly caused you to look at her. It caused attention."* Deposition of Dr. Elizabeth Shields: Her hair "had to be at least three to five inches high down behind her ears." This description by Dr. Shields has not been disputed.

According to the employee, Dr. Shields approached her and asked her to look in the mirror and see what looks back at her. Ali responded that she looked beautiful.

Ms. Ali testified that Dr. Shields told her that "I belong in a zoo, and then the last thing she said was I look like I [am] . . . going to a disco or belong in a disco or something to that effect."* Dr. Shields testified: "I told her about the whole outfit. She had red boots, red dress, in the unit. This is the post open heart unit. People come out of here after just having cracked their chest. We were expected to be conservative."*

Title VII makes it an unlawful employment practice for an employer "to fail or refuse to hire or to discharge any individual, or otherwise to discriminate against any individual with respect to his compensation, terms, conditions, or privileges of employment, because of such individual's race, color, religion, sex, or national origin. . . ."* Defendants seek summary judgment dismissing the complaint on the ground that plaintiff cannot make a *prima facie* showing that they engaged in discriminatory conduct.

To establish a *prima facie* case of individualized disparate treatment from an alleged discriminatory enforcement of the dress code, plaintiff must show that she is a member of a protected class and that, at the time of the alleged discriminatory treatment, she was satisfactorily performing the duties of her position. This she has done. However, her *prima facie* showing must also include a showing that Mount Sinai Hospital had a dress code and that it was applied to her under circumstances giving rise to an inference of discrimination.

Reviewing all of the evidence submitted on the motion, employee does not raise an issue of fact as to whether the enforcement of the code against her was discriminatory. There is no dispute that employee was in violation of the dress code. Her claim is that the dress code was enforced against her but not against others, who also violated its requirements, but were not Black. The problem is the utter lack of evidence supporting this position.

Employee offers no evidence that the dress code was not enforced against other Hospital employees as it was

against her. Dr. Shields' testimony that the dress code had been enforced against other nurses was not disputed. Although Ms. Ali identified certain Caucasian women whom she believed were in violation of the code, she failed to set forth any evidence to show a lack of enforcement.

All that employee's testimony establishes is that she was unaware of the enforcement of the dress code against others. Following a full opportunity for discovery, employee has not proffered any additional evidence to support her claim of disparate treatment. On this record, there is no reason to believe that she will be able to offer at trial evidence from which a jury could reasonably conclude that there was racially discriminatory enforcement of the dress code.

It is not enough that Ms. Ali sincerely believes that she was the subject of discrimination; "[a] plaintiff is not entitled to a trial based on pure speculation, no matter how earnestly held." Summary judgment is appropriate here because employee has failed to raise an issue of fact as to whether the dress code was enforced against her under circumstances giving rise to an inference of discrimination. Motion to dismiss GRANTED.

Case Questions

1. What do you think of the way in which Ali was approached by Dr. Shields about her violation of the dress code? Does this approach seem advisable for a manager to do? What could have been done instead?

2. How much of a role do you think different cultural values played in this situation? Explain.

3. What can the employer do to avoid even the appearance of unfair enforcement of its dress policy in the future?

Ali v. Mount Sinai Hospital 68 Empl. Prac. Dec. (CCH) 44,188, 1996 U.S. Dist. LEXIS 8079 (S.D.N.Y. 1996).

Chapter 4

Legal Construction of the Employment Environment

vinnstock/123RF

Learning Objectives

After completing this chapter, you should be able to:

LO1 Explain why employers might be concerned about ensuring protections for equal opportunity during recruitment, in particular.

LO2 Describe how the recruitment environment is regulated, by both statutes and common law.

LO3 Describe the employer's opportunities during the information-gathering process to learn as much as possible about hiring the most effective worker.

LO4 Explain how the employer might be liable under the theory of negligent hiring.

LO5 Identify the circumstances under which an employer may be responsible for an employee's compelled self-publication, thus liable for defamation.

LO6 Explain the difference between testing for eligibility and testing for ineligibility and provide examples of each.

LO7 Identify the key benefits of performance appraisal structures as well as their areas of potential pitfalls.

Opening Scenarios

SCENARIO 1

1) Scenario

Ione is asked to fill two new positions at her company. The first requires complicated accounting knowledge; the second has no prerequisites, but there also is no opportunity for advancement without a college degree, preferably in marketing or English. Ione wants to hire younger workers so they will be more likely to have a long tenure at the firm. She places an advertisement in the local public university's alumni magazine, requesting résumés from "recent college graduates," business or English degrees preferred. Ione's coworker suggested that she place the advertisement in their mutual alma matter's magazine, since many of the current employees graduated from there and employees from that university have proven knowledgeable and hard-working. Ione decides not to place advertisements at this time in the alumni magazines of the two local private universities, a Jesuit in-state university, and a historically Black college that is very close to her offices and has a well-regarded business program. She figures she will get around to it if her first search is unsuccessful. Is Ione's firm subject to any liability based on this advertisement?

SCENARIO 2

2) Scenario

Wole Okri is the owner of a large apple orchard and hires about 50 young employees each season to work for him on a part-time basis to pick apples in his outdoor operation. During the past few weeks, he has noticed a suspicious smell lingering around his orchard, which he recognizes as smoke from marijuana. Because the apple pickers are required to climb high ladders and drive trucks with wagons full of apples, the orchard has a zero-tolerance policy for drugs and alcohol. The use of such substances could lead to serious injury.

Wole has no idea where to begin a search for suspects, but the smell is stronger during and just after break times and in the area where his workers gather to rest during breaks and between shifts. Can Wole simply notify his employees that they will all be required to submit to a drug test to determine who has been smoking the marijuana, or should he figure out some way to narrow down the number of "suspects" and then use the drug test only as a means of confirmation of suspicion? How could he narrow down the number?

In addition, Wole has not yet purchased computerized checkout scanners for his large retail outlet where he sells apples and other local products to the public. Therefore, all of the product prices must be input by hand to the store registers. Wole has found in the past that certain employees are able to perform this task at a much more rapid pace than others.

To maintain store efficiency, he decides to test all applicants relating to their ability to input prices into the register. After administering an on-site timed test, he finds that 12 white applicants, two Black applicants, and one Hispanic applicant are represented among the top 15 performers, in that order of performance. Wole has five positions available. Will he be subject to liability for disparate impact discrimination if he proceeds to hire the five top performers, all of whom are white?

SCENARIO 3

3) Scenario

Lominy is the supervisor of 13 employees, most of whom generally perform adequate work in conformance with company job descriptions and standards. However, he has had dilemmas in completing the annual performance reviews of two employees.

The first employee is Gordie, a young, white American male who was widowed in the past year. Since the death of his wife, who was the primary caregiver of their two young children, Gordie has had a difficult time balancing his increased familial responsibilities with his job requirements. He missed a major deadline, and the company lost an important client as a result. Gordie has received two written warnings about his inadequate performance, and a poor year-end performance appraisal would mean an automatic dismissal. However, Lominy is confident that Gordie will be able successfully to manage these two priorities in the coming year, if only given the chance.

Gordie told Lominy that his sister would be moving in "at some point soon" to help care for the children. Should Lominy draft an honest appraisal of Gordie's performance this past year with the knowledge that it would mean Gordie would lose his job according to company policy, or does he decide to use his discretion and offer a less-than-truthful assessment? Lominy thinks to himself that perhaps he could argue that it is in the company's best interest to retain this employee. He just isn't sure what lies ahead.

Lominy's dilemma is accentuated by the fact that he is to review Julietta, an Argentinian worker who holds a position similar to Gordie's. Julietta is consistently late for work and also has received two written warnings about her inadequate performance. Lominy has no idea why Julietta arrives late, and when asked, Julietta offers no justification, though Lominy recently heard office gossip that Julietta has just gotten married to her partner. If Lominy writes a performance evaluation that highlights Julietta's behavior, similar to Gordie's, and terminates Julietta but not Gordie, he is concerned about the potential for discrimination implications.

Evolution of the Employment Relationship

The people who work at a firm—its human resources—are among its most valuable assets; consequently, the utmost care must be used in their selection process. The law, therefore, permits employers a great deal of leeway in choosing and managing employees (and in their terminations, as you saw in Chapter 2). Basically, the only restrictions placed on the employment relationship are the laws that protect certain groups from employment discrimination (as will be discussed) since history has demonstrated a need for protection. As we will see, an employer is actually permitted to discriminate in employment decisions *unless* that discrimination is based on a particular category, including gender, race, religion, disability, and a few others. So, for instance, an employer looking for a salesperson is allowed to discriminate against applicants who do not get along well with others; an employer hiring a computer technician may discriminate against someone without computer training; and employers may discriminate against applicants for all sorts of other, equally permissible reasons. (See Exhibit 4.1, "Realities about Hiring Employees or Finding a Job.")

The focus of this chapter will be on the evolution of the employment relationship, from the recruitment of appropriate candidates through hiring, testing, and performance appraisals. Though the chapter will not reiterate completely the nature of Title VII regulation discussed in Chapter 3, it is difficult to discuss the regulation of this evolution without heavily drawing on those concepts. Accordingly, we

Exhibit 4.1 *Realities about Hiring Employees or Finding a Job*

1. The best way to promote workplace unity may be to seek guidance from those who do not work there.

2. If an employer places an advertisement only at limited locations within the city where hiring is to be done, it risks being accused of selective recruiting.

3. The purpose of an interview is not only for the employer to find out information about the employee. It is also for the employer to share information about itself so that the potential employee may learn whether it is the best fit for her or him.

4. While promoting from within may raise employee morale and encourage loyalty, the strategy may lead to either a real or perceived lack of diversity or discriminatory impact.

5. Though nepotism (favoring relatives and friends in hiring decisions) occurs with frequency, it has the potential to create challenges in the workplace.

will briefly mention appropriate and applicable laws as they arise, though fuller coverage will be given to these issues in the chapters that follow.

The employment relationship usually begins with recruitment. Employers use a variety of techniques to locate suitable applicants. Once the employer has a group from which to choose, information gathering begins. This stage consists of soliciting information from the applicant through forms, interviews, references, and testing. Targeting recruitment and selection has been found to be the most effective way to reduce employment discrimination charges.

Recruitment

LO1 Explain why employers might be concerned about ensuring protections for equal opportunity during recruitment, in particular.

See Chapter 2 to revisit key concepts.

Recruitment practices are particularly susceptible to claims of discrimination as barriers to equal opportunity. If applicants are denied access to employment opportunities on the basis of their membership in a protected class, they may have a claim against the potential employer for discriminatory practices.

Statutes such as Title VII of the Civil Rights Act of 1964 and others require, in part, that an employer not only recruit from a diverse audience but also design their employment announcements so that they encourage a diverse group of people to apply. How does the employer create a diverse applicant pool? Does the employer place ads in local newspapers as well as in diverse communities, advertise on social media that reach a variety of populations, ask varied groups to share the recruiting information or to encourage people to submit résumés, or ask current employees for suggestions about how to gather a broad submission pool?

Employers should review their materials with a critical eye. Does the advertisement contain gender-specific language that might discourage certain groups from applying for the position? Does it tend to speak to one particular group, one age group, one "clique," one community only? Each of these possibilities has potential hazards and *may* result in an adverse impact on a protected group even if the employer had no intent to discriminate.

Federal Statutory Regulation of Recruitment

LO2 Describe how the recruitment environment is regulated, by both statutes and common law.

See Chapter 2 to revisit key concepts.

Though a number of statutes apply to recruitment (see Exhibit 4.2, "Federal Laws Regulating Recruitment"), the EEOC has offered important guidance specific to disability-related inquiries of applicants as well as employees under the Americans with Disabilities Act, which is covered in greater detail in Chapter 13. For example, prior to an offer of employment, an employer may not ask disability-related questions or require any medical examinations, even if they seem to be related to the job. However, the EEOC's Enforcement Guidelines explain that an employer may ask whether an applicant will need a "reasonable accommodation" during the hiring process (e.g., interview, written test, job demonstration). The employer also may inquire whether the applicant will need a reasonable accommodation for the job if the employer knows that an applicant has a disability (i.e., if the disability is obvious or the applicant has voluntarily disclosed the information and the employer reasonably believes that the applicant will need a reasonable accommodation).

The employer must provide a reasonable accommodation to a qualified applicant with a disability even if it believes that it would be unable to provide this individual

Exhibit 4.2 *Federal Laws Regulating Recruitment*

TITLE VII OF THE CIVIL RIGHTS ACT OF 1964

Section 703(a)(1)

It shall be an unlawful employment practice for an employer to fail or refuse to hire. . .any individual or otherwise to discriminate against any individual with respect to his [sic] compensation, terms, conditions, or privileges of employment, because of such individual's race, color, religion, sex, or national origin.

Section 704(b)

It shall be an unlawful employment practice for an employer,. . .to print or cause to be printed or published any notice or advertisement relating to employment by such an employer indicating any preference, limitation, specification, or discrimination based on race, color, religion, sex, or national origin, except that such a notice or advertisement may indicate a preference, limitation, specification, or discrimination based on religion, sex, or national origin when religion, sex, or national origin is a bona fide occupational qualification for employment.

VOCATIONAL REHABILITATION ACT OF 1973 AND THE AMERICANS WITH DISABILITIES ACT OF 1990

The Rehabilitation Act and the Americans with Disabilities Act, which will be covered in depth in Chapter 13, protect otherwise qualified individuals with disabilities. The former regulates the employment practices of federal contractors, agencies, and employers, while the latter act applies similar standards to private sector employers of 25 (15, effective July 1993) employees or more.

The Rehabilitation Act specifically provides that, in connection with recruitment, contractors and their subcontractors who have contracts with the government in excess of $10,000 must design and commit to an affirmative action program with the purpose of providing employment opportunities to disabled applicants. Affirmative action recruitment programs may include specific recruitment plans for universities for the disabled, designing positions that will easily accommodate a disabled employee, and adjusting work schedules to conform to the needs of certain applicants.

AGE DISCRIMINATION IN EMPLOYMENT ACT OF 1967

All employers of 20 or more employees are subject to the act, which prohibits discrimination against an individual 40 years of age or older, unless age can be shown to be a bona fide occupational qualification (e.g., recruitment for new police officers might restrict applicants below age 55 due to the physical demands of the job, under the public protection exception). In addition, the act states:

Section 4(e) It shall be unlawful for an employer. . . to print or publish, or cause to be printed or published, any notice or advertisement relating to employment. . .indicating any preference, limitation, specification or discrimination based on age.

IMMIGRATION REFORM AND CONTROL ACT OF 1986

IRCA is slightly different in its regulation of recruitment. IRCA applies to all employers. IRCA's purpose is to eliminate work opportunities that attract illegal aliens to the United States. With regard to discrimination based on national origin, the act provides that all employers must determine the eligibility of each individual they intend to hire prior to the commencement of employment. In this way, IRCA condones discrimination against illegal aliens in recruitment. Note that while IRCA applies to all employers, its discrimination provisions apply only to those with four employees or more.

with a reasonable accommodation on the job if the person were eventually hired. According to the EEOC, in many instances, employers will be unable to determine whether an individual needs reasonable accommodation to perform the job based solely on a request for accommodation during the application process or whether the same type or degree of accommodation will be needed on the job as was required for the application process.

State Employment Law Regulation

Many states have enacted legislation specifically aimed at expansion of the federal statutes above. For instance, many states have human rights acts that include in their protections the prohibitions against discrimination based on marital status or affinity orientation. The statutes generally establish a state human rights commission, which hears claims brought under the state act. Several other states have enacted legislation that closely mirrors Title VII but covers a larger number of employers.[1]

Common Law: Misrepresentations and Fraud

In addition to statutes, recruitment is also governed by the common law, and one area where employers sometimes get into hot water involves statements and promises made during the recruitment process. A company representative who makes an intentional or negligent misrepresentation that encourages an applicant to take a job may be liable to that applicant for any harm that results. Misrepresentations may include claims regarding the terms of the job offer, including the type of position available, the salary to be paid, the job requirements, and other matters directly relating to the representation of the offer. (See Exhibit 4.3, "Common-Law Recruitment Violations," for elements of the *prima facie* cases.)

For example, assume that Meri is told by her employer at the time when she is hired that she will automatically receive a raise at her six-month review. Based on this representation, Meri accepts an offer. Six months pass, and she does not receive the promised raise. She may be able to sue her employer for the misrepresentation that induced her to take the job, even if she is an at-will employee working without a contract.

Why do you think Meri might pursue the claim for misrepresentation and not for fraud? For misrepresentation, the statement does not actually need to be a *false* statement; it merely needs to create a false impression. However, for fraud, Meri would need to prove an intent to deceive at the time the statement was made. Since that is a higher standard and more difficult to prove, she likely would pursue the former claim. However, employers should be aware that liability for misrepresentation attaches even where an employer is aware that the applicant is under a mistaken belief about a position or company; an employer's silence may constitute misrepresentation.

Where an employer hides certain bits of information, the employer's silence may also be considered misrepresentation. For instance, suppose an employer needs someone to serve as an assistant to the president of the company. The president has a reputation for being unpleasant to his assistants and for constantly firing them. The employer, therefore, solicits applications for a general administrative position, "with specific duties to be assigned later," knowing the hiree will spend the majority of the time working for the president.

Exhibit 4.3 *Common-Law Recruitment Violations*

Fraud	• Misrepresentation
	  ◦ ... of a material fact
	  ◦ ... with intent to deceive, or recklessness about its truth or falsity
	  ◦ ... on which the applicant reasonably relies
	  ◦ ... to her or his detriment.

Misrepresentation	• False statement.
	• True statement creating a false impression.
	• Silence where:
	  ◦ It is necessary to correct applicant's mistaken belief about material facts.
	  ◦ There is active concealment of material facts.
	  ◦ It is necessary to correct an employer's statement that was true at the time made, but which subsequently became false.

Material facts	• Statement of fact
	  ◦ ... which will influence
	  ◦ ... a reasonable person
	  ◦ ... regarding whether to enter into a contract.
	• *Note that an opinion is not a material fact because it would be generally unreasonable to rely only on the opinion of another in arriving at a decision.*

Assume that Alina applies for the job, states during her interview that she would like the position, and then says that she is glad that it is not the assistant-to-the-president position for which they were interviewing last month—phew! She explains that she had heard from a prior assistant about difficulties with the president and preferred not to work for him. She is offered the job and, even though she has an excellent offer from another company for more money, decides to take the job because she likes the culture of this work environment. Later, she is told that she will be spending a large part of her workday with the president. Alina could sue the employer for misrepresentation—and perhaps fraud—even though the employer did not respond at all to her statement about the president during the interview.

Employers also may be liable for fraud in recruitment when misstatements are used to discourage potential applicants from pursuing positions. For instance, an employer who wishes to maintain a male-dominated workforce may intentionally present an excessively negative image of the position or the company in an effort to persuade females not to apply. If all candidates are offered the same information, there may be no basis for a discrimination claim. However, if only the female applicants receive this discouraging outlook, the practice presents to the female applicants a "chilling" effect, and the employer may be subject to claims of gender discrimination.

Application of Regulation to Recruitment Practices

Advertisements

See Chapter 2 to revisit key concepts.

Statutes and the common-law claim of fraud protect applicants from discriminatory recruitment practices, ranging from a refusal to interview Latinx[2] to a job notice that is posted only in the executive suite where it will be seen primarily by white males. Assume, for instance, that an employer advertises in a newspaper that is circulated in a neighborhood that has an extremely high Asian population but does not have many other minorities represented. You, therefore, might also assume that the employer will expect to see almost all of its applications to come from Asians and few, if any, applications from other groups. While there may be no intent to discriminate, the effect of the practice will be an unbalanced workforce with a disparate impact on non-Asians.

Scenario

In connection with Scenario 1, recall that Ione is concerned about placing an advertisement requesting résumés from "recent college grads." Older workers may claim that they are discouraged from applying due to the language—they are less likely to be "recent" college grads. On the other hand, language such as this does not constitute a *per se* violation. Instead, the applicant would have to establish a *prima facie* case of age discrimination. Though terminology such as "recent college grads" seems to be a minor concern to some, courts have found that it may lead to a belief that stereotyping or pigeonholing of one gender or a certain age group in certain positions is condoned by the law. Consider Dominick's supermarket's experience when it named the second-in-command of its deli section the "Second Deli Man," notwithstanding whether the person was male or female. Maybe someone at Dominick's noticed the inconsistency this might create, but probably no one expected a class action suit by 1,500 women alleging gender discrimination! While this was only one of numerous pieces of evidence, it may have made a difference in encouraging a settlement.

Additionally, consider how the placement of Ione's advertisement may affect who is aware of the position. By failing to send it to the local historically Black college, Ione inadvertently may be discriminating against Black applicants.

Word-of-Mouth Recruiting

See Chapter 2 to revisit key concepts.

The same discriminatory effect may occur where an employer obtains its new employees or applicants only from referrals from within its own workforce, or "word-of-mouth" recruiting. Generally, most people know and recommend others similar to themselves. Word-of-mouth recruiting generally results in a workplace that looks just like the existing workplace.

This type of recruiting is not necessarily harmful as long as precautions are taken to ensure a balanced applicant pool or where it can be shown to be necessary to ensure the hiring of the most competent workers. Benefits of this type of recruitment include preliminary screening, which happens by the current employees before they even recommend the applicant for the position, and also the tendency for long-term service and loyalty among the new hires. Since they already have bonds to the company, a family attitude toward the firm (resulting in increased productivity) is more easily developed.

Where a firm uses word-of-mouth recruiting as a primary strategy, it also might make an effort to enhance the diversity of its recruiting pool by establishing an employee referral program that creates incentives for workers to recommend diverse candidates. In a particularly high-profile example of this type of program, Intel doubled its normal referral bonus "for candidates who are women, minorities, or veterans" and thereby increased its diversity hiring with 41 of new hires coming from an underrepresented group—an increase of 32 percent from the year before the implementation of the program .[3]

In fact, a recent study found that 48 percent of hires were part of an employee referral program, making employees the top source of new hires.[4] This study shows that the vast majority of respondents regard referrals as the number one source of above-average applicants. A different survey found that hiring a referred candidate takes less time and saves the company money on recruiting and advertising. Eighty-two percent of employers rated employee referrals above all other sources for generating the best return on investment. Plus there is the added benefit that 45 percent of referred hires remain at their job for at least two years after they are hired, compared with 20 percent hired from job boards.[5] But it is important to consider how this strategy might lead to liability under Title VII.

There is a significant difference between *disparate impact* and *disparate treatment* in the context of word-of-mouth recruiting. The Seventh Circuit decided two important cases in this area, one that explained the difference and one that subsequently applied it. In *EEOC v. Chicago Miniature Lamp Works*,[6] the EEOC claimed that Chicago Miniature Lamp Works discriminated against Black individuals in the recruitment and hiring of its entry-level workers because it recruited primarily through an informal word-of-mouth process. Current employees simply would tell their relatives and friends about a job. If interested, these people then would come to Miniature's office and complete an application form. Miniature did not tell or encourage its employees to recruit this way.

Between 1978 and 1981, Miniature hired 146 entry-level workers. Nine of these workers (6 percent) were Black. The trial court concluded that "the statistical probability of Chicago Miniature's hiring so few Blacks in the 1978–1981 period, in the absence of racial bias against Blacks in recruitment and hiring, is virtually zero."

The Seventh Circuit evaluated the EEOC's arguments for both discriminatory treatment and impact. It dismissed the treatment claim, since that claim requires intent, explaining that "[i]ntent means a subjective desire or wish for these discriminatory results to occur." They found no evidence whatsoever of any desire for the results. With regard to impact, the Seventh Circuit also dismissed the claims. "[A] Title VII plaintiff does not make out a case of disparate impact simply by showing that, 'at the bottom line' there is a racial imbalance in the work force." Instead, the plaintiff must identify a *particular practice* that caused the disparate impact. But in what "practice" did Miniature engage? In a seminal ruling that has been cited significantly since, the court held:

> The EEOC does not allege that Miniature affirmatively engaged in word-of-mouth recruitment of the kind where it told or encouraged its employees to refer applicants for entry-level jobs. Instead, it is uncontested that Miniature passively waited for applicants who typically learned of opportunities from current Miniature employees. The court erred in considering passive reliance on employee word-of-mouth recruiting as a particular employment practice for the purposes of disparate impact. The practices here are undertaken solely by employees.

The vital lesson from *Miniature* is the distinction in liability between acts of the general workforce and acts of the employer itself. Where workers learn of opportunities on their own and share these opportunities with those in their social networks (posting an open position notice through Twitter, for instance), *Miniature* tells us that this would not be considered a practice of the employer unless the employee was asked to do so by the employer.

The same court followed *Miniature* with its decision in *EEOC v. Consolidated Service System,* an extraordinary statement by the court, authored by Judge Posner, a noted economist, that contains some quite interesting conclusions. In that case, a janitorial firm owned by a Korean immigrant and staffed mostly by Koreans used word-of-mouth recruiting for its hires. Between 1983 and 1987, the firm hired 81 percent Korean workers, while less than 1 percent of the workforce in its surrounding community is Korean.

In this case of disparate treatment, the court basically said that just because the end result is completely askew, one should not reach the conclusion that discrimination was involved. "If the most efficient method of hiring adopted *because* it is the most efficient. . .just happens to produce a workforce whose racial or religious or ethnic or national-origin or gender composition pleases the employer, this is not intentional discrimination." The court does suggest that if the case were instead based on disparate impact, which it is not, "then the advantages of word-of-mouth recruitment would have to be balanced against its possibly discriminatory effect when the employer's current workforce is already skewed along racial or other disfavored lines."

The Seventh Circuit apparently grew frustrated with the EEOC's conception of "disparate impact," even suggesting that the defendant consider suing to recoup its fees based on *groundless* prosecution!

Promoting from Within

While promoting from within the company is not in and of itself illegal, it also has the potential for discriminatory results, depending on the process used and the composition of the employer's workforce. Some employers use a secretive process, quietly soliciting interest in a position from a few upper-level employees who have been selected based on recommendations by their supervisors. The employer then conducts interviews with the candidates and extends an offer. After the employee accepts the offer, a notice is posted announcing the promotion. If women and minorities are not well represented in a firm, this process might result in a disparate impact against them, even where the purpose of the employer is merely to locate and promote the most qualified candidate.

A process that could avoid a finding of disparate impact would be to post a notice of position availability in which all employees are offered the opportunity to compete for open positions. Ideally, the organization should also have a promotion policy that emphasizes neutral selection criteria and is very specific about performance requirements for being considered for a promotion.[7] The employer is less vulnerable to attack for discriminatory policies as long as the workforce is relatively balanced so there is equal employment opportunity.

Venue Recruiting

Employers may decide to conduct recruiting at a university or high school. Similar precautions must be taken to attract diverse applicants in a locale that may be either purposefully or unintentionally uniform. The same effect may result when an employer recruits with a preference for experienced applicants for entry-level jobs—for instance, recruiting firefighters and specifying a preference for applicants with experience in volunteer fire departments. The court held in one case that this recruitment practice was wrongful because volunteer fire departments tended in the past to be hostile to minorities and to women as firefighters. Preference for firefighters with this experience, therefore, would lead to few, if any, minorities and women being hired. Employers should be aware of the effects of the composition of their workforce on protected groups and the effects of the sources of their recruitment.

Walk-In Applicants

Recruiting may not be necessary when the company is constantly receiving unsolicited applications. Depending on the profession, potential employees may send their résumés to prospective employers in hopes of locating an open position or of persuading them to create one. While this strategy may be effective in locating employees and reducing costs of formal recruiting, the company may find that its reputation attracts only one type of employee, while others are intimidated by, unaware of, or uninterested in the firm. Equal employment opportunity is again lost.

Neutral Solicitation

While selecting an appropriate source from which to choose applicants is crucial, fashioning the process to encourage diverse applicants is also important. For instance, an advertisement that requests "recent college grads" may discourage older workers from applying and result in an adverse impact on them. Or a job announcement that states the employer is looking for "busboys" or "servicemen" may deter females from applying. Other terms that at first appear innocuous are actually discouraging to one group or another, including "draftsman," "saleswoman," "repairman," "waiter," "host," and "maid." An announcement or solicitation should invite applications from all groups and should not suggest a preference for any one class of individual.

Recruitment and Artificial Intelligence

Employers increasingly have begun to use artificial intelligence (AI) tools in the recruitment and selection process for a variety of reasons, including an effort to avoid even the appearance of discriminatory practices. There are high hopes that these tools will help to eliminate human bias from recruitment practices, but some evidence around this new technology suggests that a totally bias-free hiring process may be difficult to achieve.

One example of AI tools used in recruitment is machine learning algorithms that have candidates complete games to test for traits such as short-term memory and planning and responding to job-related tasks. Another tool uses an augmented writing platform to suggest bias-neutral language for job posts and recruiters' emails to job candidates. An area where AI has a significant impact is in anonymizing the applications of job candidates. Tools are available to redact names, photos, gender, graduation dates, and other information that may lead recruiters toward an unlawful preference for or against a candidate.

There is no doubt that AI has infiltrated a significant part of workplace practices. A recent survey from management consulting firm Korn Ferry found that 63 percent of talent acquisition professionals report that AI has changed the way recruiting is done at their organization, and 69 percent say that using AI as a sourcing tool finds higher-quality candidates.

However, the ability of any AI mechanism to eradicate bias in hiring successfully depends on whether the developers of the AI algorithms also remove any bias in the original creation of the tool. For example, Amazon discovered that a recruiting system algorithm that it was building had begun to downgrade certain résumés that included words such as "women's club" and favor male candidates when it found verbs such as "executed" and "captured." Amazon realized that the bias error was due to the fact that it was trying to build the algorithm using past résumés pulled from a 10-year period during which more men both applied and were hired than women. This process design effectively created an AI system that associated "men" with "good" or "to be hired" and downgraded traits for women. The algorithm was built using data that repeated bad habits rather than neutral, unbiased data. The recruiting system was not implemented company-wide. However, this example demonstrates that the successful use of AI in hiring depends on whether the tool is built from its inception to generate fair and balanced results as well as how recruiters and hiring managers analyze the data and act on the insights generated by the system.[8]

Information Gathering and Selection

Once the employer has recruited a group of applicants, how does the employer reach a final conclusion about whether to hire a particular applicant? The next step is for the employer to balance some additional information about the applicant—her or his experience, education, fit with the company, and other information gained through interviews, reference checks, testing, and application forms—with the needs of the company along with any negative information on the candidate discovered during the course of the information gathering. Amassing this information is a time-consuming yet important process that is subject to suspicion by applicants and others because of its potential for the invasion of privacy and discriminatory treatment. While we will discuss the extent to which an employer is prohibited from delving into private information about an employee on the basis of invasion of privacy in Chapter 14, this section will examine the information that the employer may or may not obtain during this particular stage of the employment process.

See Chapter 2 to revisit key concepts.

The Application Phase

The hiring process usually begins with an application for employment. Most of us at some point have filled out an employment application. Did you ever stop to think about whether the employer actually had a right to ask these questions? Under most circumstances, the application requests information that will serve as the basis for screening out applicants because of education or experience requirements. Questions that are business-related and used for a non-discriminatory purpose are appropriate.

The form will generally ask for name, address, educational background, work experience, and other qualifications for the position, but it may additionally request date of birth, nationality, religion, marital status, number of children, or ethnicity.

Unfortunately, research demonstrates the existence of discrimination against applicants based on assumptions about their race or national origin or membership in other protected groups. One study found that applicants with white-sounding names were 50 percent more likely to receive callbacks for interviews than applicants with African American–sounding names who were similarly qualified.[9] Another study found that job applicants in Canada with Asian names—including names of Indian, Pakistani, or Chinese origin—were 28 percent less likely to get called for an interview compared with applicants with Anglo names, even when all the qualifications were the same.[10] In the United Kingdom, a person named Adam was offered three times more interviews than someone named Mohammed in one study conducted by BBC News.[11]

Bias in recruitment also can be seen in what some workplaces call "cultural fit," a concept demonstrated when recruiters describe their ideal employee as someone they would "go to lunch with." Cultural fit most often relates to an applicant's values, behaviors, customs, interests, and even outward appearance. While familiarity is comfortable for many people, perceived cultural fit is one of the leading ways professionalism privileges the majority and those in power and disfavors the disenfranchised, minorities, and underrepresented groups.[12] A recent survey, for example, found that 84 percent of employers strongly focused on cultural fit.[13] This practice of preferring people like ourselves—whether because they look like us, sound like us, share similar backgrounds or experiences, or simply have names that seem familiar—is called **homophily**.[14]

homophily
A theory in sociology that people tend to form connections with others who are similar to them in characteristics such as socioeconomic status, values, beliefs, or attitudes.

LO3 Describe the employer's opportunities during the information-gathering process to learn as much as possible about hiring the most effective worker.

There are only a few questions that are strictly prohibited by federal law from being asked on an application and/or during the interview process. Any questions concerning disability, specific health inquiries, and workers' compensation history are either prohibited by the Americans with Disabilities Act of 1990 or strictly regulated (see Chapter 13).

It should be noted here that these regulations do not prohibit employers from asking whether workers have contracted a specific disease during times of local or global pandemics (when identified by authorities). For instance, during the 2020 COVID-19 pandemic, the EEOC updated its guidance entitled "Pandemic Preparedness in the Workplace and the Americans with Disabilities Act." It explained that, during time of pandemic where a fever is a symptom of the pending condition, employers are permitted to measure employees' body temperature. As for whether an employer may require particular testing (whether pre-employment or for existing employees) relating to the pandemic, the EEOC explains that

> [t]he ADA requires that any mandatory medical test of employees be 'job related and consistent with business necessity. Applying this standard to the current circumstances of the COVID-19 pandemic, employers may take steps to determine if employees entering the workplace have COVID-19 because an individual with the virus will pose a direct threat to the health of others. Therefore an employer may choose to administer COVID-19 testing to employees before they enter the workplace to determine if they have the virus.[15]

Employers also may ask workers whether they had COVID-19, had been tested for COVID-19, or if they were experiencing symptoms associated with COVID-19. Employers also may ask if any of their family members had been diagnosed or had symptoms. As with any other area relating to medical or other personal data, employers are cautioned to make "every effort" to keep to a minimum the number of people who have access to this information.[16]

Other questions regarding age, sex, religion, marital status, nationality, and ethnicity are not prohibited by federal statute, but they are generally considered off-limits. These answers create vulnerabilities for employers if they have access to this information, and employers are strenuously advised to avoid them. Questions involving these topics must be related to the position for which the applicant applies in order for an employer to be able to ask them. If they are not related and, even if the employer does not base its employment decision on the responses to these inquiries, if the selection process results in a disparate impact against a protected group, the employer could be liable.

Many states and local governments have their own job discrimination laws, some of which apply to smaller employers or prohibit discrimination on other grounds. For example, employers in California may not discriminate based on an applicant's political activities, HIV status, or marital status; Illinois employers may not consider an applicant's history as a survivor of domestic violence or the fact that an applicant has no permanent mailing address (or receives mail at a homeless shelter or social services agency).[17]

Nevertheless, research has shown that companies frequently violate EEOC guidelines regarding appropriate application and interview questions. You may even be thinking right now that you have answered these questions on some form in the past! The areas of inquiry that are most often violated during this phase include education (where not business-justified, where questions relate to religious affiliation of the school, and so on), arrest records, physical disabilities, pregnancy status/number of children, and age. For instance, an employer should ask if you are of a legal age to work rather than asking for your date of birth. Though there may be reason to know once hired, your date of birth provides far more information than most employers might need to know during the interview stage.

Even the most innocuous remark may be inappropriate. For instance, an employer should not really make off-the-cuff comments or ask questions about your name during an interview, other than what it is. It could be perceived as national origin discrimination. For example, someone might say, "Gosh, that's an interesting last name. How do you pronounce it? What language is that?" Imagine where the conversation might lead. Questions relating to other names by which an applicant may be known are proper, while questions regarding the origins of the applicant's surname or whether it is one's original name versus one's married name are improper. (They may be perceived as marital status discrimination, prohibited in some states.)

Moreover, while most applicants are used to filling in the response to a question regarding gender on an application, an employer actually has no right to that knowledge unless gender is a bona fide occupational qualification. As hair and eye color may lead to an inference regarding the applicant's race or color, these questions, too, may be inappropriate but not *per se* illegal. But can you imagine a position where hair or eye color would be a bona fide qualification?

The Interview

The second step in the process is usually an interview conducted by a representative of the employer. Discrimination may occur during the interview in the same manner in which it is present on application forms. An improper question on the application is just as improper in an interview.

Questions are not the only source of discrimination during an interview. In a pioneering study conducted by the Urban Institute, researchers found that Black applicants were treated more harshly during interviews than white applicants with identical qualifications.[18] Researchers submitted pairs of applications of Black and white applicants for available positions. The researchers found that Black people were treated more favorably than whites in 27 percent of the interview situations, while they were treated less favorably than whites in half of the interviews. Black applicants suffered greater abuses, including longer waiting times, shorter interviews, and being interviewed by a greater number of individuals. White applicants were more likely to receive a job offer. All of this occurred under controlled circumstances, where the applications of the pairs were kept equal in terms of qualifications and experience. A meta-analysis of 10 comparable subsequent studies, conducted in different locations and across various industries, reveals the same basic conclusion: that race matters in hiring decisions, with whites receiving on average 36 percent more callbacks than African Americans and 24 percent more callbacks than Latinxs.[19] An interview, therefore, must be nondiscriminatory not only in terms of the information solicited but also in terms of the process by which it is conducted.

There are four areas of potential problems in connection with the interview. First, the employer must ensure that the interview procedures do not discourage women, minorities, or other protected groups from continuing the process. Second, employers should be aware that all-white or all-male interviewers or interviewers who are not well trained may subject the employer to liability. Third, the training of the interviewers is crucial to avoid biased questions, gender-based remarks, and unbalanced interviews. Fourth, the evaluation of the applicant subsequent to the interview should follow a consistent and evaluative process rather than reflect arbitrary and subjective opinions.

Exhibit 4.4, "Preemployment Inquiry Guidelines," offers guidance on developing acceptable questions for an interview. Questions should be uniformly applied to all applicants.

Background or Reference Check, Negligent Hiring, and Googling Employees

Once the applicant has successfully completed the interview process, the next step for the employer is to check the applicant's background and references. This is how the employer discovers whether the information in the application and the interview is true and whether there is any additional information that might be relevant to the person's employment.

Research suggests that job candidates engage in extensive misrepresentation of academic credentials and work experience on résumés and job applications and

Exhibit 4.4 *Preemployment Inquiry Guidelines*

Subject	Acceptable	Unacceptable
Name	"Have you ever used another name?"	"What is your maiden name?"
Citizenship	"After an offer of employment, can you submit verification of your legal authorization to work in the United States?" or statement that such proof may be required after a decision is made to hire the candidate.	"Are you a U.S. citizen?"; citizenship of spouse, parents, or other relative; birthplace of applicant, applicant's parents, spouse, or other relative; requirements that applicant produce naturalization papers, alien card, etc., prior to decision to hire applicant.
National origin	Questions as to languages applicant reads, speaks, or writes, if use of a language other than English is relevant to the job for which applicant is applying.	Questions as to nationality, lineage, ancestry, national origin, descent, or parentage of applicant, applicant's parents, or spouse; "What is your native language?"; "What language do you use most?"; "How did you acquire the ability to speak [language other than English]?"
Sex, family	Statement of company policy regarding work assignment of employees who are related; name and address of parent or guardian if applicant is a minor; ability to work overtime or to travel; experience working with a certain age group.	Questions to indicate applicant's sex, marital status, number and/or ages of children or dependents; provisions for child care; "Are you pregnant?"; "Are you using birth control?"; spouse's name or contact information.
Physical or mental disability	"Can you perform [specific job-related tasks]?"; statement that employment offer may be made contingent upon passing a job-related mental or physical examination; questions about illegal drug use, missed days of work during previous year.	"Are you in good health?"; "Have you ever received workers' compensation?"; "Do you have any disabilities?"; any inquiry into the applicant's general health, medical condition, or mental/physical disability, requiring a psychological or medical examination of any applicant.
Religion	Statement by employer of regular days, hours, or shifts to be worked.	Religion or religious days observed; "Does your religion prohibit you from working weekends or holidays?"

Source: Adapted from California Department of Fair Employment and Housing, DFEH-161 (rev. 06/16), https://equity.ucla.edu/wp-content/uploads/2016/06/Questions-to-Avoid-dfeh-161.pdf (accessed September 4, 2020).

that the problem may be getting worse. While reliable statistics on résumé fraud are difficult to obtain, the best evidence comes from companies that provide employment screening services. For example, a 2018 Benchmark Report from HireRight revealed that a whopping 84 percent of employers found a lie or misrepresentation on a résumé or job application—at all levels of the organization.[20]

On the other hand, as the level of job responsibility decreases, the employer is less likely to verify all of the information provided by the applicant. But a check is crucial to verify the information that the candidate offers in the application and interview. There are some pretty basic ways to keep an eye out for these discrepancies. For instance, in the interview, do the candidate's answers sound too clean and rehearsed? It is one thing to know how you feel about something but another to repeat an answer you have memorized. On the résumé, check for overlapping dates or details that conflict. Google some of the organizations of which the candidate says that she or he has been involved in a leadership capacity to verify his or her participation. When you check references, ask those references to give you the name of someone else who has worked alongside this individual as a peer. While the candidate likely only offered the names of references who would offer glowing reviews, these second-tier names might provide a realistic capsule otherwise not available.

It is also important to ensure that there is no information that, if discovered, would disqualify the applicant from employment or could subject other employees, clients, or customers to a dangerous situation. That type of information also could subject the employer to a claim of **negligent hiring**, recognized as a cause of action in all 50 states.[21] For these reasons, employers may verify not only education and experience but also driving records, credit standing, refusals of bonds, or exclusion from government programs. An employer is liable for negligent hiring where an employee causes harm that could have been prevented if the employer had conducted a reasonable and responsible background check on the employee; in other words, when the employer knew or should have known that the worker was not fit for the job. The person injured may claim that the **negligence** of the employer placed the employee in a position where harm could result, and, therefore, the employer contributed to that harm (see Exhibit 4.5, "Grounds for Negligent Hiring Claim").

For instance, in 2019, an Illinois state appellate court affirmed a jury verdict that awarded damages of more than $54 million in a personal injury lawsuit filed against a trucking company over the negligent hiring and retention of a trucker with a "disturbing" driving record who was involved in an accident while on the job. The driver had a suspended license, was involved in four accidents in the past three years, and had been convicted of 10 traffic-related offenses, including a felony for "reckless aggravated assault" for attempting to use a tire thumper to break the headlights on a vehicle occupied by four women in 2004. The driver has initially been ruled a "no-hire" upon his application due to this history, but the company's safety director reclassified him as a "marginal candidate," and the company hired "marginal candidates" to make a profit. The court found that the company flagrantly ignored the risk this driver represented and, as such, was liable for negligently hiring him after he killed another driver in a workplace traffic incident.[22]

The frequency and severity of workplace violence have escalated over the past 10 years. Every year, nearly 2 million Americans report being victims of workplace violence, while an estimated 25 percent of workplace violence goes unreported.[23] There were 500 workplace homicides in 2017, the highest since 2010 and constituting 33 percent of all workplace fatalities.[23] When it comes to workplace violence, women are overwhelmingly victims. Seventy-two percent of homicide fatalities were women, while only 28 percent were men. Of those women, 40 percent were killed

LO4 Explain how the employer might be liable under the theory of negligent hiring.

negligent hiring
Employment of a person who causes harm that could have been prevented if the employer had conducted a reasonable and responsible background check on the employee. The standard against which the decision is measured is when the employer knew or should have known that the worker was not fit for the job.

negligence
The omission or failure to do something in the way that a reasonable or prudent person would have done the same thing or doing something that a reasonable or prudent person would not have done. Failing to raise one's standard of care to the level of care that a reasonable person would use in a given situation. In order to prove negligence, one must show that these acts or omissions resulted in damage to another person or property.

gig work
Generally refers to temporary work or work as an independent contractor. More recently, refers to work in the "gig economy," where there is an abundance of short-term "gigs"—odd jobs— available on a part-time basis. While these positions may be seen as entrepreneurial and have the potential to springboard careers, they also have the downside of offering no health insurance or other benefits.

by a relative or domestic partner *at work* compared with 2 percent of men, and 33 percent died as a result of a robbery *at work* compared with 16 percent of men.[25]

An additional wrinkle is added when a situation involves temporary or contingent workers. **Gig work** accounts for 30 percent of new jobs according to a recent report and will grow by 18.5 percent per year over the next five years, according to a report from Intuit. Intuit also reports that contingent workers of all types (temporary employees, independent contractors, project-based gig workers, and on-demand workers) make up 36 percent of the workforce and are expected to reach 43 percent by 2020.[26]

Employers often hire candidates for these positions from temporary employment agencies, which have conducted the background screening of the worker on their own. It is arguable that, as long as the employer ensures the reasonableness and diligence of these third-party checks, the employer should be sufficiently protected from liability for negligently hiring these workers. (The EEOC Guidelines suggest this framework.[27]) However, companies have become wary of this strategy since, whether the individual is an employee, independent contractor, or otherwise, that worker represents the employer's brand. (See Chapter 1 for a discussion of issues involving a gig worker's employment classification as independent contractor or employee.) Engaging in a complete screening process, particularly when access to people or sensitive material is involved, is a critical risk mitigation strategy, regardless of the worker's classification.[28]

There are several ways to ensure due diligence in checking on an applicant's references in order to insulate oneself from negligent hiring liability.

1. The employer might contact the reference in person, by telephone, by letter, or by email and request a general statement about whether the information stated in the application and interview is correct.

2. The contact might be much more specific, posing questions about the applicant's abilities and qualifications for the available position.

Exhibit 4.5 *Grounds for Negligent Hiring Claim*

Negligent hiring	To state a claim for **negligent hiring,** the plaintiff must show: • The existence of an employer–employee relationship. • The employee's incompetence or inappropriateness for the position assumed. • The employer's actual or constructive knowledge of such incompetence or inappropriateness, or the employer's ability. • That the employee's act or omission caused the plaintiff's injuries. • That the employer's negligence in hiring or retaining the employee was the proximate cause of the plaintiff's injuries • *(i.e., on investigation, the employer could have discovered the relevant information and prevented the incident from occurring).*

3. The employer may undertake an independent check of credit standing through a credit reporting agency, military service and discharge status, driving record, criminal record, or other public information to obtain the most complete information on the applicant.

There are problems inherent in each form of query:

- Most employers are willing to verify the employment of past employees, but obtaining this limited information may not necessarily satisfy the standard of care required to avoid a claim of negligent hiring.
- Certain information is not available to employers and is instead protected by state law. For instance, if an employer seeks the applicant's prior criminal arrest record or even certain convictions, some states statutorily protect disclosure of this type of information. So the employer may be subject to a claim of invasion of privacy or other statutory violations. In fact, many states and municipalities throughout the country have enacted laws that mandate the removal of criminal conviction history questions from job applications (but still allow some form of background check after conditional offers of employment). The reason for these "Ban the Box" laws is a sense that it offers previously incarcerated individuals the opportunity to obtain jobs for which they otherwise may not have been considered. One study found that Ban the Box laws increased the likelihood of a callback by 27 percent for individuals who were previously incarcerated compared with cities without the ban.[29] But these laws also provide additional burdens for employers and add additional ways for them to face liability.[30]
- There also may be the basis for a claim of disparate impact where it can be shown that those of one protected class are arrested more often than others. In that case, asking about an arrest record where the offense is not necessarily related to job performance may result in adverse impact. Note that arrests and convictions are not the same. Employers are more limited in inquiring about arrest records than about convictions relevant to the job.
- The Fair Credit Reporting Act requires that an employer notify the applicant in writing of its intention to conduct an investigative consumer report and inform the applicant of the information it seeks. It further requires the employer to obtain written authorization to obtain the report. In addition, if the employer plans to take an adverse employment action based on the report, it must notify the employee of the reporting agency and give notice that he or she can get a free copy of the report and that he or she can dispute its contents.
- The reference and background information-gathering process is a lengthy one and may be unmanageable, given the employer's position requirements.
- Past employers may not be willing to offer any further information than that the applicant worked at that company for a time. Employers have cause for concern, given the large number of defamation actions filed against employers based on references. (See Exhibit 4.6, "The ABC Company Safe Hiring Checklist"; see also Chapter 14.) Absolute truth is always a defense to defamation, but a common problem in a truth defense is that the former employer and the applicant perceive

a different version of the "truth." The key to a truth defense is to limit references to objective, verifiable, and irrefutable statements. For example, rather than saying, "He performed poorly," the reference should say, "He achieved the company quota 30 percent of the time, and the company average is 92 percent."[31]

The most effective way to avoid these potential stumbling blocks is to request that the applicant sign a statement on the application form that states that former employers are released from liability for offering references on her or his behalf. In the course of making a request for a reference from those former employers, the release should be sent to the former employer along with a copy of the applicant's entire application.

Exhibit 4.6   *The ABC Company Safe Hiring Checklist*

To be completed for every new applicant before being hired.

Applicant: _____

Position: _____

Hiring Manager: _____

Task	Yes/N or NA	Date/ Initials	Notes/ Follow-up
Application Process			
Is application complete?			
Did applicant sign and date application?			
Did applicant indicate reason for leaving prior employment?			
Any excessive cross-outs or changes seen?			
Is the application internally consistent and consistent with other information in the employer's possessions?			
Interview Process			
Did applicant explain any excessive cross-outs/changes?			
Leaving past jobs: Did applicant explain?			
Leaving past jobs: Was verbal reason consistent with reason on written application?			
Gaps in Employment: Did applicant explain?			
Employment Gaps: Are verbal explanations consistent with written application?			

continued

Task	Yes/N or NA	Date/ Initials	Notes/ Follow-up
Security Question. 1 – "Our firm has a standard drug testing policy and drug tests all applicants and perform background checks. Do you have any concerns you would like to share with me about the policy or our procedures?"			Answer:
Security Question 2 – "We also have a policy requiring criminal background checks on all finalists pursuant to all applicable rules and regulations including EEOC Guidance. Do you have any concerns you would like to share with me about the policy or our procedures?"			Answer:
Security Question 3 – "If I were to contact past employers pursuant to the release you have signed, what do you think they would tell us about you?"			Answer:
Security Question 4 – "If I were to contact past employers pursuant to the release you have signed, would any of them tell us you were terminated or were disciplined?"			Answer:
Security Question 5 – "Please explain any gaps in employment."			Answer:
Security Question 6 – "Is everything in the application and everything you told us in the hiring process true, correct, and complete?"			Answer:
Reference Checks (performed by employer or by a third party)			
Have references been checked for at least last 5–10 years, regardless of whether past employers will give details?			
Have efforts been documented?			
Discrepancies between information located and what applicant reported in application:			
a. dates/job title b. reason for leaving			
Security, Drug Screening and Background Checks			
Check with legal counsel before asking about criminal records on the employment application or in the interview process, or before using a criminal record to deny employment. When and how these inquiries can be made varies by state, county, and municipality. These regulations are generally referred to as "Ban the Box." In some jurisdictions, background checks can only be obtained post offer of employment.			
Did applicant receive a standalone background check disclosure document consistent with the federal Fair Credit Reporting Act (FCRA) and applicable state laws?			
Did applicant sign and return the background check consent document?			
Has background check been ordered?			
Did applicant receive the drug testing Chain of Custody and instructions?			

continued

Task	Yes/N or NA	Date/ Initials	Notes/ Follow-up
Have drug screening results been received and reviewed according to the policy?			
If DISQUALIFYING drug test what action was taken per drug testing policy and procedures?			Describe:
Has background check been completed?			
Has background check been reviewed for discrepancies and possible disqualifying criminal history?			
If background check not CLEAR or SATISFACTORY, what action is taken per policy and procedures including pre and post adverse action under the FCRA?			Describe:
If not CLEAR or SATISFACTORY, are there disqualifying factors based on position/company policy?			Describe:
If criminal record found, did employer analyze under EEOC three-part test and did applicant receive opportunity for an "Individualized Assessment."			Result:

Note: If in a "Ban the Box" jurisdiction, check with legal counsel before asking about criminal records in an application or an interview. Also, be aware of the U.S. Equal Employment Opportunity Commission (EEOC) rules on the use of criminal records. A criminal record should not be used to automatically eliminate a candidate.

Source: © 2007 Lester S. Rosen, Employment Screening Resources, www.ESRcheck.com, reprinted with permission.

In addition, in this environment of enhanced access to information, perhaps the standard of what a reasonable employer should do is also heightened. For instance, if people Google their blind dates as standard practice, is it really asking too much for an employer to simply Google a prospective employee to see what can be uncovered through a basic internet search? If a number of employers begin to use the internet as a method of information gathering, does that practice become the norm, thus raising the bar for other employers? The bar does seem to be rising—while a 2006 survey reported that 10 percent of employers had used social networking sites (including Facebook) to gather information on future employees,[32] by 2018 the percentage had risen seven times that level to 70 percent.[33] It is not limited to the recruitment process. Forty-eight percent of employers use a variety of social media sites to gather information on existing staff and employees, and 34 percent have used information they have discovered online to reprimand or terminate a worker.[34]

Employers must be careful when indiscriminately Googling a potential candidate because of biased algorithms already inherent in many online platforms. A study by the former chief technology officer for the U.S. Federal Trade Commission found that when a Google search is performed on a person's name, Google AdSense (the algorithm that provides targeted ads at the top of searches) is much more likely to generate ads that suggest an arrest record for persons with typical African American names (DeShawn, Darnell, Jermaine) than for typical non-Latinx white names (Geoffrey, Jill, Emma). The mere suggestion of the possibility of an arrest record—even if no such record exists—could subconsciously persuade a hiring manager to choose the "less risky" candidate.[35]

See Exhibit 4.7, "Use of Social Media in Hiring Decisions," to see some of the reasons that have both discouraged them from hiring people based on what they have found, but also encouraged some hiring decisions.

Employers should exercise caution when using online sources for background checks. While they may find valuable information about prospective employees, if they use (or appear to use) certain information, such as age, race, marital status, or other defining features of potentially protected classes, to screen job candidates, it could serve as grounds for a discrimination suit. Because social media platforms like Facebook and Instagram contain highly personal information, employers who use them to conduct background screening risk allowing hiring decisions to be affected by factors that are illegal to consider—such as medical problems or disability, marital status, or pregnancy.

Employers also are responsible for gathering information from social media about applicants in a consistent fashion. If employers have no written policy or standard approach and instead are performing social media searches in an ad hoc way, an applicant who is not hired or interviewed potentially can claim discrimination. On the other hand, if the employer uses the same search process for every candidate, it has greater protection. However, as of 2019, 26 states have enacted legislation that prohibits an employer from requesting or requiring an employee, student, or applicant to disclose her or his social media usernames or passwords, and several other states are considering similar laws.[36] Facebook itself has threatened to take legal action against companies that ask job applicants for passwords, saying such a request violates its terms of service.[37]

In considering a claim of negligent hiring and the above discussion, you might notice the inherent conflicts between the potential liability involved in hiring someone without sufficient information and the alternate liability involved in intrusion into a candidate's personal information. As we have noted, certain subjects are not acceptable areas of inquiry for employers except under specific circumstances. In addition, while the Occupational Safety and Health Act (OSHA) mandates that employers protect the workplace from "recognized" workplace safety and health hazards that are likely to cause serious injury or death, until those threats are manifested, it may be difficult to identify some of them before they enter the workplace.

Therefore, the amount of background and reference checking for an employer to shield itself from a claim of negligent hiring both should be based on a written workplace policy that applies a standard procedure across the board and maintains a zero tolerance bar for any threats of violence whatsoever but also should be sufficiently flexible to vary from situation to situation, as needed. A position that provides for absolutely no contact with clients, customers, or other employees may necessitate a quick check of the information contained on the application, while a position that requires a great deal of personal contact, such as an intensive care nurse, would require an investigation into the applicant's prior experiences and background. An employer must exercise reasonable care in hiring applicants who may pose a risk to others as a result of their employment and the employer's

Exhibit 4.7 *Use of Social Media in Hiring Decisions*

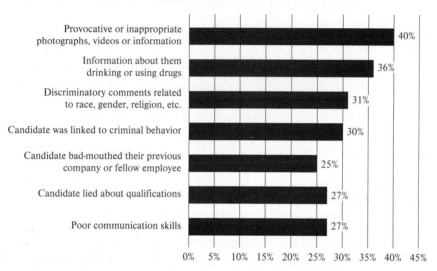

Top reasons hiring managers choose not to hire candidates

Provocative or inappropriate photographs, videos or information — 40%
Information about them drinking or using drugs — 36%
Discriminatory comments related to race, gender, religion, etc. — 31%
Candidate was linked to criminal behavior — 30%
Candidate bad-mouthed their previous company or fellow employee — 25%
Candidate lied about qualifications — 27%
Poor communication skills — 27%

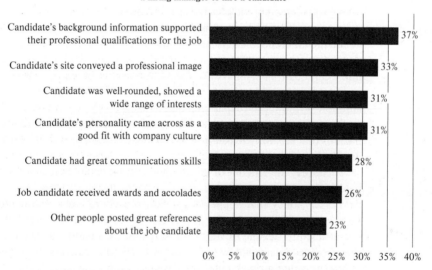

Information found online that might sway a hiring manager to hire a candidate

Candidate's background information supported their professional qualifications for the job — 37%
Candidate's site conveyed a professional image — 33%
Candidate was well-rounded, showed a wide range of interests — 31%
Candidate's personality came across as a good fit with company culture — 31%
Candidate had great communications skills — 28%
Job candidate received awards and accolades — 26%
Other people posted great references about the job candidate — 23%

Source: Adapted from CareerBuilder "More Than Half of Employers Have Found Content on Social Media That Caused Them NOT to Hire a Candidate" (August 9, 2018), https://www.prnewswire.com/news-releases/more-than-half-of-employers-have-found-content-on-social-media-that-caused-them-not-to-hire-a-candidate-according-to-recent-career-builder-survey-300694437.html (accessed October 25, 2019).

negligent failure to obtain more complete information. The standard of care to be met is what would be exercised by a reasonable employer in similar circumstances. If an employer had no means by which to learn of a dangerous propensity or if discovery of this information would place a great burden on the employer, a court is more likely to deny a claim for negligent hiring.

Reference Checks: Potential Liability for Providing References?

Due to an increasing risk of lawsuits as a result of reference checks, many employers have adopted an official policy of providing only name, position held, and salary or simply saying, "No comment." However, employers should be aware that, should an employer choose not to provide reference information on prior employees, it could face liability for injuries to the prospective employer who sought the reference or even third parties. In one case, a former employer settled for an undisclosed amount after allegedly sending an incomplete referral letter that neglected to mention that the former employee had been fired for bringing a gun to work. The employee was subsequently hired by an insurance company and went on a rampage, killing three and wounding two of his coworkers before killing himself.[38]

While employers may not have an affirmative duty to respond to a reference inquiry, those who choose to respond may be held liable for negligent misrepresentation based on misleading statements made in employment references. Therefore, while there is no affirmative duty to respond, once an employer chooses to do so, some courts have held that it creates a duty to respond fully and honestly, to avoid foreseeable harm.[39]

One possible safeguard an employer can utilize is requiring a written release from former employees before any information is released. However, the written release should be voluntary, should allow the former employee to discuss the waiver with an attorney, and should include the employee's agreement not to contest his or her termination or the contents of the personnel file. For additional guidance, see Exhibit 4.8, "Employer Strategies for Avoiding Negligent Hiring, References, and Supervision," and Exhibit 4.9, "Tips for Employer Protection."

compelled self-publication
Occurs when an ex-employee is forced to repeat the reason for her or his termination and thereby makes a claim for defamation.

Employers also can be liable for reference checks in an unexpected manner—from an ex-employee's own mouth through **compelled self-publication**. Compelled self-publication happens when an ex-employee is forced to repeat the reason for her or his termination and thereby has the basis for a claim for defamation. When the reason for the termination is allegedly defamatory (for instance, termination based on false accusations of insubordination or theft), then courts have held that self-publication can satisfy the *prima facie* requirements of defamation since the employee was compelled to publish the defamatory statement to a third person (the potential new employer) and since it was foreseeable to the employer that the employee would have to repeat the basis for termination. The tort of compelled self-publication, however, is recognized in a minority of states.[40]

LO5   Identify the circumstances under which an employer may be responsible for an employee's compelled self-publication, thus liable for defamation.

The discussion above about negligent hiring standards also applies to situations involved in negligent training, supervision, and retention. Some courts recognize a responsibility of employers in certain industries to appropriately train their employees when third parties will rely on that training, such as in the medical

Exhibit 4.8 *Employer Strategies for Avoiding Negligent Hiring, References, and Supervision*

Former Employees	
Strategy	**Considerations**
Examine state law to determine whether statutory protection is available for employers giving references. • If yes, conform reference policy for former employees to state law. • If no, develop a policy that balances the potential legal costs with the future employers' need for information regarding the former employee.	• Possible protection under General Liability Policy. • Require form signed by former employee authorizing release of information.

Current and Future Employees	
Strategy	**Considerations**
Preemployment:	
For each new hire or position change, review position to determine risk factors. Based on assessment, determine scope of necessary applicant investigation.	Risk factors include: • Contact with the public/children/infirm. • Access to employer property. • Operation of motor vehicles/dangerous equipment.
Employment application should include:	
• Statement that any misrepresentation is grounds for dismissal, no matter when discovered. • Inquiry as to any criminal convictions. • Signed permission for all former employers to release reference information, including reason for separation and eligibility for rehire. • Data on all education, certifications, and experience relevant to position.	If applicant discloses a criminal conviction, determine the nature of the crime and whether it is within the scope of job requirements or job related.
Strategy	**Considerations**
If applicant is deemed to be qualified via personal interviews, skills, or other preemployment tests, begin background check commensurate with prior review of position and risk factors.	

continued

In particular, the employer should:

- Verify all claimed credentials and certifications.
- Instigate any necessary criminal background checks.
- Send signed consent form to past employers requesting appropriate information.
- Request any other pertinent information, given job duties/responsibilities.

Where former employer does not respond, employer will need to follow up and document due diligence. Where former employer has a "no comment" reference policy, depending on position's risk factors, remind former employer of potential negligent reference issues and allow former employer opportunity to reconsider. Document due diligence.

Where negative information is received, consider risk factors, consider investigating further, or seek applicant's rebuttal to information received, and make best decision possible for all concerned.

During Employment:

If an employee exhibits any display of greater than ordinary temper or violent behavior:

- Remove employee from potentially hazardous duties (i.e., working closely with public, children, or the infirm).
- Require anger management or similar counseling before reinstatement to prior duties.

Postemployment:

When employee is terminating employment, present Reference Permission Form for employee to sign during exit interview and inform employee that factual information will be provided to future employers.

If contacted for reference of past employee:

- Provide data as prescribed by Reference Permission Form.
- Consider potential position risk factors, including risk to third parties, when deciding whether to release additional relevant factual information.

Source: S. Arsenault, D. Jessup, M. Hass, and J. Philbrick, "The Legal Implications of Workplace Violence: Negligent References, Negligent Hiring, and Negligent Supervision and Retention," *Journal of Legal Studies in Business 9* (2002), pp. 31–63. Reprinted by permission of the authors and *Journal of Legal Studies in Business.*

Exhibit 4.9 *Tips for Employer Protection*

So how does the employer protect itself?
Precaution.

During the interview process	• Obtain releases from all applicants allowing the employer to check on previous employment. • Request that all applicants obtain copies of their personnel files from previous employers.
Before a position is offered to the candidate	• Investigate the employment record, including all gaps, missing data, and positions held. • Review educational records carefully. Contact the institutions listed to verify their existence, the years attended, the course of study, and, most important, actual graduation with degree. • Check references, especially when several are reluctant to speak. This may be viewed as a warning beacon that they do not have much good to say or have no desire to support the candidate. (On the other hand, ensure that this unwillingness is not the result of a bad relationship with the person. Allow the candidate the opportunity to explain.)
After the candidate is hired	• Maintain clear, consistent policies relating to employment decisions. • Follow up on the implementation and enforcement of these policies.

environment. Negligent supervision exists where an employer fails to adequately oversee the activities of an employee who threatens violent conduct. Negligent retention occurs when the employee's conduct gives rise to employer action such as suspension or dismissal, but the employer fails to take such action and a third party suffers damages.

"After-Acquired Evidence" Defense in Wrongful Termination Suits

While the previous discussion has focused on the potential for employer mistakes, omissions, or wrongdoing, what happens when the applicant is the wrongdoer, such as when she or he includes misstatements on her or his application? An employer may fire someone for that reason. Often, this situation will come up after someone has been fired for another, allegedly wrongful reason. The "after-acquired evidence" of the misstatements is admissible to show the court that, whether or not the employer had unlawful reasons for the action, it also had this legal justification for the action. In *McKennon v. Nashville Banner Publishing Co,*[41] the court held that a discharge in violation of the Age Discrimination and Employment Act was acceptable where the employer would have terminated the employment anyway because of a breach of confidentiality.

Documentation of Failure to Hire

No federal statute or guideline requires that employers document the reasons for failing to hire any specific applicant. However, it really is in the best interests of the employer to articulate the reasons in order to avoid the presumption of inappropriate reasons. (See Exhibit 4.10, "Reasons for Not Hiring.") In addition, since a claim under Title VII or other statutes may come long after the decision was made, documentation will help an employer recall the particular reasons why a certain applicant was rejected so that she or he is not left, perhaps on a witness stand, to say, "I don't remember!"

Moreover, the individuals who originally made the decision about this candidate may no longer even be working with the firm. Finally, a firm may choose to document in order to supplement any statistical data that otherwise might prove a lack of discrimination. This paper trail may serve to prove that others who were similarly situated were treated the same way, not differently. For instance, in a gender discrimination action, the documentation may demonstrate that no one with a certain low level of experience was hired, male or female.

On the other hand, some might argue that documentation also may serve to demonstrate facts to which the employer does not want to be bound. Once the reason for failing to hire is on paper, the employer is now bound to use that, alone, as the reason for the decision. Further, while any one decision may seem appropriate, systematic documentation of these decisions may demonstrate a pattern

---

Exhibit 4.10 *Reasons for Not Hiring*

Possible Lawful Reasons for Choosing to Reject a Candidate

- No positions available.
- Not interested in positions available.
- Not qualified for positions available.
- Not qualified for position being sought.
- Better qualified persons were hired instead.
- Cannot work hours offered.
- Rejected our job offer.
- Unable to communicate effectively in the English language (if required for position).
- Obviously under the influence of drugs or alcohol during the employment interview.
- Did not return for follow-up interview or otherwise failed to complete the preemployment process.
- Employment interview revealed no interest in type of work.

- If you are looking for the most qualified candidate, make sure that you are advertising in *all* of the places where that candidate might look for employment—not just the obvious places where you are sure to find the same type of workers as those who already work for you.

- Be wary of representations about the firm that are made during recruitment interviews. While you of course want to encourage the best candidates to work for your firm, sometimes glowing accounts of life at the firm might cross the line to misrepresentations. Also, be cautious about promises made to prospective employees as these might be construed as part of the individual's contract with the firm.

- While word-of-mouth recruiting, nepotism, and promoting from within may appear on the surface to be an easy method for locating a new employee, these methods are likely to produce new employees quite similar to your present employees. Make sure that you employ additional methods to prevent discrimination in developing your applicant pool.

- Take a look at your written applicant form. Does it ask for any information that is not relevant to the candidate's potential ability to do the job? Is there any information upon which you are prohibited from basing an employment decision, such as age?

- Background checks are relevant to most positions. If you fail to conduct a check, you might be liable for any actions that you would have learned about in the check, such as previous workplace violence. From a cost–benefit perspective, conducting the check usually wins.

of adverse impact that one might not notice if nothing is ever recorded. But just because the employer can document this information more easily does not mean that it is not able to be recorded at all by others. So, in the long run, it is in the employer's best interests to document, document, document so that it is in the best position to know its own vulnerabilities and make changes, where necessary, before it is too late—and much more expensive—to do so on its own.

Employers may then discover problem areas and respond appropriately and lawfully to them once observed. As long as an employer's policies about hiring are consistently applied and are reasonable, there should be no problems—whether recorded in writing or not.

Testing in the Employment Environment

The third step beyond recruitment and information gathering is to hone in on the particular information that would tell the employer if this is the right worker to satisfy the job's essential requirements. Testing may allow the employer to do so. However, while preemployment testing can help locate ideal employees, it also may land the employer in court. Managing the risk created by use of preemployment tests requires an understanding of the types of preemployment tests used, the benefits they offer, and their possible costs beyond the monetary expenditures

preemployment testing
Testing that takes place before hiring, or sometimes after hiring but before employment in connection with such qualities as integrity, honesty, drug and alcohol use, HIV status, or other characteristics.

LO6 Explain the difference between testing for eligibility and testing for ineligibility and provide examples of each.

See Chapter 2 to revisit key concepts.

involved in testing. This balance is critical, given the high rate of résumé fraud as discussed earlier in the chapter.

Note also that, while much of this section refers to preemployment testing, the laws discussed also apply to testing throughout the employment relationship.

Preemployment testing began in the 1950s as a response to the inefficiencies that were purportedly present in American business. Since that time, preemployment testing has been considered necessary to the selection process. The majority of selection tests originally given were conducted as a means of bettering the company's position in a competitive market. Testing was seen as the answer to workplace personnel problems, ineffective hiring programs, and the inappropriate job placement of hirees. Employers believed they would be more competitive if they could test applicants to "weed out" those who failed the tests. However, many managers administered tests that had never been validated as indicators of performance or were not specifically job-related in any way. (See Exhibit 4.11, "Balancing the Interests in the Testing Debate.")

Testing in the workplace has taken two forms: tests for the purpose of finding the best individual for a position and tests to ensure that the individual is free of problems that would prevent her or him from performing the position's functions. Examples of the former include achievement tests and personality indicators. The problem with this type of eligibility test is that, while appearing facially neutral, it may have a disparate impact on a protected class. Pursuant to Title VII of the Civil Rights Act of 1964, where adverse impact has been shown, the test may still be used if it has been professionally developed and validated (discussed later in this chapter). If used properly, however, a validated test not only will determine for the employer the most appropriate applicant for the position but also may reduce the chance for discriminatory choices based on conscious or subconscious employer bias.

The latter form of examination refers to tests for ineligibility, such as for drug and alcohol abuse and other impairments that may limit an applicant's ability to perform.

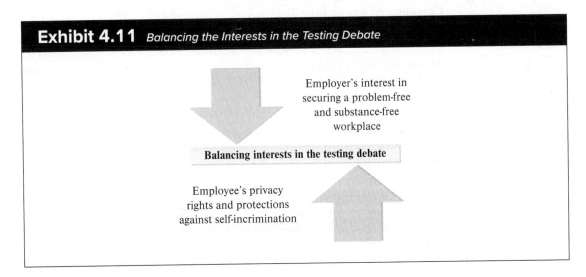

Exhibit 4.11 *Balancing the Interests in the Testing Debate*

Employer's interest in securing a problem-free and substance-free workplace

Balancing interests in the testing debate

Employee's privacy rights and protections against self-incrimination

Drug and alcohol addictions have become pervasive issues in our society, and employers are often concerned about hiring employees with a drug or alcohol addiction.

The challenges of addiction have permeated almost every facet of our lives, including the workplace. Employers have institutionalized prevention programs, not only for the safety of their workers but also in an effort to ensure high productivity and quality output. As technology has improved, impairment tests have become more efficient, less expensive, and therefore more prevalent.

In an effort to protect individual employee rights, courts do a balancing test to determine the legality of ineligibility testing. The courts weigh the conflicting interest of the employer in securing a problem-free or substance-free workplace against the privacy rights of the employee and protections against self-incrimination. The California Supreme Court ruled, for example, that a city's drug-testing program did not violate an individual's right to privacy so long as all job applicants were required to submit to suspicionless drug testing as part of a preemployment medical examination.[42] An Ohio appellate court explained that while a urinalysis drug-testing program is not a violation of privacy when applied universally and randomly, it is a violation of privacy for employers to visually monitor the collection of the sample.[43]

Since many of the protections offered to the employee come from the Constitution (Fourth Amendment protection against unreasonable searches and seizures, Fifth Amendment right against self-incrimination, and Fifth and Fourteenth Amendments' protections of due process), government employees and contractors generally receive greater protection in these areas than do employees in the private sector. However, state constitutions can be a source of protection in the private sector as well. The issue of privacy rights is more completely discussed in Chapter 14. This discussion will instead be concerned with the potential for discrimination in the course of testing procedures and requirements and the various statutes that protect against related discrimination.

Legality of Eligibility Testing

eligibility testing
Tests an employer
administers to ensure
that the potential
employee is capable and
qualified to perform
the requirements of the
position.

Eligibility testing refers to tests that an employer administers to ensure that the potential employee is capable and qualified to perform the requirements of the position. Some tests also are used to determine who is most capable among applicants. These tests may include intelligence tests, tests of physical stamina, eye exams, tests for levels of achievement or aptitude, or tests for the presence of certain personality traits. Tests for ineligibility, on the other hand, test for disqualifying factors, for example, drug and alcohol tests, polygraphs, and HIV testing.

Of course, a test may cross the line between the two. For instance, an employer may administer a preemployment, post-offer, medical exam to determine whether the applicant is sufficiently healthy to perform the job requirements. If the individual fails the medical examination, the test has determined that she or he is not qualified for the position and, therefore, the offer may be rescinded.

Employers may conduct eligibility tests for a variety of reasons. For example, the position may require a unique skill for which the employer wishes to test the applicants. Those applicants who possess that skill will continue in the application process. Or perhaps the employer may need to ensure that the applicants meet minimum standards to satisfy requirements of the position. For instance, an English language competency examination for all applicants for customer relations positions or an eye exam may be required for all potential bus drivers.

These tests, however, in their implementation may have a disparate impact on members of a protected class. To illustrate, the employer's test for English language competency would have an adverse impact on individuals of non-English-speaking origin. Where discrimination on the basis of national origin has been shown, the employer may continue to use the test only where it can establish that the requirement is a bona fide occupational qualification. For instance, the Seventh Circuit held in *Melendez v. Illinois Bell Telephone Co.*[44] that the employer's aptitude test had a disparate impact on Latinx job applicants because there was no significant correlation between an applicant's test score and his or her ability to perform the duties of an entry-level manager. The plaintiff's expert testified in that case that the aptitude tests could "predict a person's job performance only 3 percent better than chance alone." This conclusion will be discussed in more detail in Chapter 7.

Eligibility tests that have been professionally developed, such as medical licenses, are specifically exempt from claims of disparate impact, as long as the test is not designed, intended, or used to discriminate on the basis of membership in a protected class. For an eligibility test to be legally validated as an effective gauge of performance other than through this exemption, an employer must show that the test is job-related and consistent with **business necessity**.

For example, most people would agree a test of general math is probably related to successful performance as a cashier. Thus, even if this type of test had a disparate impact against a particular group, it would be allowable if the employer provided **job analysis** data supporting its claim that math skills were required to perform the job. In general, the more abstract the trait the instrument purports to test (such as "creativity"), the more difficult it becomes to establish evidence of validity. Note that a test may be challenged if a less discriminatory alternative exists.

Test Validity: Confirming Capacity to Do a Job

In 1975, the Supreme Court decided *Albemarle Paper Co. v. Moody,*[45] a seminal case with regard to test validation. In that case, Albemarle Paper imposed a requirement that those in skilled labor positions have a high school diploma and pass two tests. The Court found it a critical error that Albemarle Paper made no attempt to validate that the tests were related to the job; instead, the employer simply adopted a national norm score as a cutoff point for its new applicants. The Court held that "discriminatory tests are impermissible unless shown, by professionally acceptable methods, to be predictive of or significantly correlated with important elements of work behavior that constitute or are relevant to the job or jobs for which employees are being evaluated." Because of defects in the validation process, the court found that Albemarle was liable for discrimination for failure to evidence job relatedness of a discriminatory test process.

Scenario

Recall Wole's on-site timed test in Scenario 2 at the beginning of the chapter? He wanted to determine applicants' actual ability with regard to the specific activity

---

business necessity
Defense to a disparate impact case based on the employer's need for the policy as a legitimate requirement for the job.

job analysis
Information regarding the nature of the work associated with a job and the knowledge, skills, and abilities required to perform that work.

they would be performing in their new position. Because the test is correlated with the work that candidates would be conducting in their eventual roles, Wole could argue that he should be permitted to use the test in his selection process. The next step would be to determine whether the test is sufficiently validated. See below to figure out what type of test validation Wole would be considered to have used and whether he meets the standards of that strategy.

In 1978, the EEOC, with the assistance of several other government agencies, developed the *Uniform Guidelines on Employee Selection Procedures* as a framework for employers in connection with the determination of the proper use of tests and other selection procedures. Where a selection test has been shown to have an adverse impact on a protected class, the guidelines identify three approaches to gathering evidence of validity; the choice of **validation** strategy depends on the type of inference the user wishes to draw from the test scores. The guidelines define an adverse impact on a protected class as any procedure that has a selection rate for any group of less than 80 percent of the selection rate of the group with the highest rate.

The most traditional type of test validation is criterion-related validity. To validate using criteria, one collects data relating to job performance from a simulated exercise or on-the-job measures of performance. The test is developed using these measurements of critical work behaviors once a systematic relationship between the criteria and the test scores has been demonstrated.

The second form of validity that is identified by the guidelines is content validation. Content validation is based on a careful job analysis and definition that identifies important tasks, behaviors, and knowledge that the job requires. The test is then developed involving a representative sample of these tasks, behaviors, and knowledge. Employers should be particularly concerned with this type of validity during test construction, as there is a vulnerability toward lack of representativeness at this stage.

The third strategy to validate tests under the guidelines is construct validity, an approach that is generally most useful when the employer is seeking to measure a psychological characteristic such as reasoning ability, introversion (a personality characteristic), leadership behaviors, and others. Construct validation is a relatively technical area, dependent on inter-correlation of test items, but relevant for employers are the following considerations. First, the characteristic sought needs to be important for job performance. As with content validity, this is done through the use of careful job analysis. In addition, the characteristic should be well defined.

In a case that took more than 15 years to resolve, a New York district court invalidated a test used by the New York school system to license teachers. A class of teachers challenged the test, claiming that it was not a valid measure of qualification to teach. Further, the teachers charged, the test disparately impacted African American and Latinx test-takers, both of whom passed at a rate of 60 percent when taking it for the first time, while Caucasians passed the test at 90 percent. At trial, test developers were unable to demonstrate a significant relationship between the test content and job content. The court ruled that a proper job analysis had not been conducted prior to use of the test.[46] As this case demonstrates, if a test results in a disparate impact, its relevance to job qualifications must be substantial.

validation
Evidence that shows a test evaluates what it says it evaluates.

Integrity and Personality Tests

Because employers have been restricted in their use of polygraph tests (to be discussed in the next section), many have resorted to subjective tests that purport to measure personality, honesty, or integrity through analysis of written or oral answers to numerous questions.

As of 2018, 82 percent of companies used some sort of assessment tool as part of the hiring process.[47] Preemployment testing includes assessment of general cognitive ability and math and language skills as well as specific job-related competencies. While cognitive ability tests continue to be the most commonly used form of preemployment testing, personality and integrity tests are being used more and more frequently, although it is unclear what proportion of testing they comprise.[48]

There are a number of traits for which employers test but only general agreement that attention to detail (conscientiousness) has a strong correlation to on-the-job behavior.[49] Because of research that demonstrates that intentional faking can be successful,[50] their results have been deemed suspect by courts. However, perhaps because the tests have not been shown to have a consistently adverse impact on any one protected group, employers continue to use them to measure a wide variety of constructs, such as honesty, integrity, propensity to steal, attitude, and counter-productivity.

Personality testing is now a $500 million industry, with growth rates estimated at 10 to 15 percent annually.[51] More than 82 percent of organizations are using preemployment assessment and selection tests in their hiring process. Employers testing for job-specific skills is the most common form of assessment (59 percent), while personality assessments represent 34 percent of all the tests given.[52]

Personality or psychological tests for preemployment selection screening, however, must be used with caution. Their use pre-offer is inconsistent with the Americans with Disabilities Act. The area employers often run into problems with is when a personality or integrity test bleeds into a psychological test. Depending on the specific test and its parameters, criteria, and lines of inquiry, some courts have found tests to constitute an impermissible mental health examination under the ADA.[53] The Seventh Circuit upheld a claim against an employer on the basis of disability discrimination because of its use of one of the most popular personality tests, the Minnesota Multiphasic Personality Indicator.[54] In a class action lawsuit against the furniture rental company Rent-a-Center, the court found that the use of the screening test would likely exclude employees with mental impairments from promotions. In this case, the court noted that the ADA limits medical exams as a condition of employment; they may only be required after the offer is made and, even then, only when all entering employees are required to take the test, any medical results are maintained in a confidential manner, and the "examination or inquiry is shown to be job-related and consistent with business necessity."[55] Simply because a test is an accepted psychological measure does not make that test relevant to a particular job, nor does it validate its use in any situation.

Personality tests should not be confused with intelligence tests, which have suffered a great deal of criticism in connection with their potential for disparate impact discrimination against various minority groups. Notwithstanding these concerns, basic intelligence testing does remain one of the single best predictors of job performance across all jobs.[56]

Physical Ability Tests

Physical ability tests are administered to applicants seeking particularly physically demanding jobs in order to increase the likelihood that candidates will be able to perform the essential physical functions of the job in question. General tests of fitness may no longer be an appropriate means of testing for physical fitness for a particular position since these tests might exclude individuals who could still perform the essential functions of that position. For instance, physical ability tests in the past might have required applicants to perform sit-ups, lift weights, and run certain distances—not all of which might be required by every job. The logic of this test approach is that those who do better on these events are more physically fit and thus better able to perform the physical tasks of any job; however, as we now know, there is not always a correlation between being able to pass a physical exam and being able to perform a specific job. Today, the employer must be able to show that the physical test is related to an essential function of the job.[57]

Under current laws, physical ability testing usually results in some type of job simulation. For example, a physical ability exam for entry-level firefighters might require applicants to drag hoses, open fire hydrants, or climb ladders. Job simulations imply a content approach to test validation because the test components are direct samples of the job domain. This approach to physical ability testing is used extensively in the public sector.

But employers must be careful that their physical ability test does not have a disparate impact on women without a bona fide occupational qualification. The EEOC recently announced the implementation of the Strategic Enforcement Plan (SEP) for the next several years, which includes a continuing focus on class-based recruitment and hiring practices that discriminate against racial, ethnic, and religious groups as well as older workers, women, and people with disabilities. In 2018, the EEOC sued Hirschbach Motor Lines, which used a preemployment assessment to screen and reject applicants it believed would be unable to work as truck drivers. Applicants were tested for their ability to balance and stand on one leg, touch their toes while standing on one leg, and crawl. The company eventually agreed to pay $3.2 million to a class of female applicants after the EEOC filed a lawsuit alleging the strength and fitness tests they took impacted women disparately. Another case involving physical ability testing required by a police department resulted in a nearly $2.5 million settlement for female applicants.[58]

Medical Tests

Many employers require preemployment, post-offer medical tests to ensure that the applicant is physically capable of performing the requirements of the position. Medical examinations are prohibited only prior to the offer in order to protect against wrongful discrimination based on a discovered disability.

Medical examinations subsequent to the offer of employment but prior to the actual employment are allowed for the purpose of determining whether an employee will be able to perform the job for which she or he has been hired. The order in which the employment offer is made and the medical test is administered is important. For example, in one case, an offer was made, conditional on a drug test, medical examination, and background check. The employee happened to do the medical examination first. When the blood test uncovered the employee's HIV-positive status, the employer rescinded the offer. However, the employee prevailed in court. The court found that no medical examinations were permitted until after all of the non-medical aspects of the application process, including the background check.[59] (See Exhibit 4.12, "Timing of Testing Processes.")

All employees within the same job category must be subject to the same medical examination requirement; individual applicants may not be singled out. In addition, all information generated through the examination process must be maintained in confidential files, separate from other general personnel-related information.[60]

Subsequent to the applicant's employment, no medical examination may be required unless the test is job-related and justified by business necessity.

Legality of Ineligibility Testing

Despite the fact that the U.S. Constitution only protects employees from invasive or wrongful action by the state, an employee may make a number of possible claims against testing. For example, a U.S. District Court in Florida declared unconstitutional the City of Key West's policy requiring applicants for City jobs to be drug tested. A potential employee objected to the city's across-the-board drug testing (in other words, testing without any suspicion), and the city revoked her job offer. The court rejected the city's position that it should be permitted to categorically drug test all applicants because the city failed to demonstrate "a special need or important governmental interest" that justified the policy's Fourteenth Amendment intrusion.[61] However, a U.S. Court of Appeals found in 2018 that a substitute teacher applicant's Fourth Amendment rights were not violated by a school board's universal drug testing requirement because the applicant "had a diminished privacy interest due to the unique Fourth Amendment context of public schools and the testing was reasonable and minimal intrusion on her privacy interests."[62]

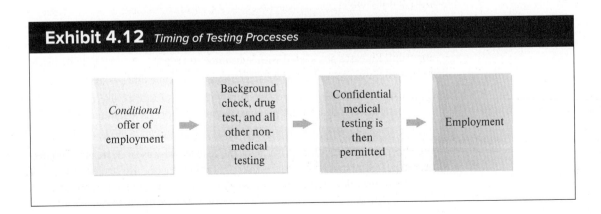

Exhibit 4.12 *Timing of Testing Processes*

Conditional offer of employment → Background check, drug test, and all other non-medical testing → Confidential medical testing is then permitted → Employment

Portions of state constitutions, state statutes, and local laws establish private-sector requirements for workplace testing. In several states, such as Connecticut, companies are not permitted to conduct random drug tests or conduct blanket drug tests. Instead, the employer must have a reasonable suspicion for believing that a particular employee is using drugs, or there must be a high risk of injury associated with the job if it is performed by someone under the influence of drugs.[63] Cities also have passed similar laws. For example, San Francisco has an ordinance that requires reasonable suspicion based on evidence of job impairment or danger to others before testing is deemed appropriate. Mandatory or random testing would not be allowed in this jurisdiction.

There is also some support for a claim of common-law invasion of privacy in connection to private sector testing, under certain circumstances.[64] We will examine the balance of rights surrounding drug testing in much greater detail when we discuss privacy issues in Chapter 14.

Generally, congruent with fundamental theories of employment law, a discharge resulting from an employee's failure to take a test for ineligibility is protected under the employment-at-will doctrine. The employment relationship is based on the consent of both parties; if the employee does not wish to be subject to various requirements or conditions of employment, the employee may refuse and leave. If the employee, for instance, is uncomfortable with the idea of random drug testing, that employee may quit and work in an environment in which she or he is more comfortable.

Drug and Alcohol Tests

One popular form of preemployment testing includes screening for drug and alcohol use. Illegal substances are prevalent in workplaces, with one recent survey concluding that a whopping 7 out of 10 Americans have used drugs while at work![65] The Bureau for Labor Statistics reports that deaths at work by unintentional overdoses due to non-medical use of drugs or alcohol increased 25 percent in 2018.[66]

The cost of substance abuse in the workplace in the form of lost productivity amounts to approximately $100 billion per year, and employees with an alcohol use disorder miss on average 34 percent more days.[67]

Additional costs to businesses of employee substance abuse are difficult to quantify but include:

1. Increased health care costs (the United States spends about $35 billion a year to treat substance use disorders and another $85 billion to treat the injuries, infections, and illnesses associated with substance use)[68];
2. Workers' compensation claims (substance abusers file nine times as many claims)[69];
3. Higher turnover (36 percent of workers with any substance use disorder and 42 percent with a prescription pain use disorder report have had more than one employer in the previous year).[70]

The enormity of these figures is one of the reasons why as of 2018, an estimated 70 percent of companies with more than 2,500 employees use drug testing, and they cover some 40 percent of all jobs, particularly in retail and construction where the rates of positive results are the highest.[71] While it might seem clear why an employer would want to ensure that its employees and contractors are not affected negatively by the use of prohibited substances (or the abuse of permitted substances), the question of whether to institute a testing program is not as easy as it might seem. Consider the costs weighed against the benefits in the next sections.

Costs of Drug Testing Programs   The basic costs of testing itself can run high when you multiply the cost of each test by the number of employees a firm chooses to test. Tests per employee can run anywhere from $30 to $200, depending on the type of test involved.[72] Additional costs mount as you consider the price of program administration, such as grievances and lawsuits. Costs also include any associated treatment and rehabilitation services offered to those workers who test positive (regardless of whether their drug use poses dangers in the workplace that would require such intervention).

Testing may also lower workplace morale and can be experienced as demeaning and degrading, particularly where it involves urine collection under direct observation. Additionally, the significant minority of Americans who are opposed to drug testing (around 40 percent) includes a large number of non-drug users who regard drug testing as an unjustified intrusion into their private lives. These potentially well-qualified candidates may be reluctant to work for a company that conducts preemployment drug testing, a particular concern where employers are recruiting from a small pool of highly skilled workers.

Most importantly, there is little empirical evidence to clearly establish a relationship between drug testing and reduced costs to employers. Many of the large, cross-industry studies that seem on their face to show the benefits of drug testing are funded by the drug-testing industry and also rely only on surveys of human resources professionals' *attitudes* toward drug testing rather than on actual cost–benefit analyses. The studies that do demonstrate an association between drug testing and savings for business are often specific to one particular industry and may not hold true beyond that context. Finally, studies suggest that drug testing might not have the intended benefits in some environments, such as discouraging drug use overall.[73]

Benefits of Drug Testing Programs   On the other hand, there are a number of reasons why an employer may want to test for drug and alcohol use. First, the employer may wish to reduce workplace injury or to provide a safer working environment. For instance, drug testing has been shown to reduce the number of workplace injuries and personal injury claims.[74] Second, an employer may use drug tests to predict employee performance or to deter poor performance. A 2018 study found that drug testing improved employee productivity, decreased absenteeism, and reduced turnover as well as employee theft and behavioral problems.[75] However, it should be noted that the validity of such studies, and the benefits of workplace drug testing broadly, are disputed.[76] Third, testing can reduce the employer's financial responsibility to the state workers' compensation system. The use of an illegal substance, which contributes to the claimant's injury, may serve as a defense to the employer's liability.

Thus, to be most effective, any workplace substance abuse program should incorporate (1) a written drug policy that has been drafted after input from employees, (2) a supervisory training program, (3) an employee education and awareness program, (4) access to an employee assistance program, and (5) a drug-testing program, where appropriate.

Federal and State Drug Testing Laws

In response to the continued problem of drugs in the workplace and injuries and accidents related to their use, former President George H. W. Bush enacted the Drug-Free Workplace Act in 1988, which authorized the drug testing (also called *biochemical surveillance,* in more legalistic terms) of federal employees under certain circumstances. It also required government service contractors with contracts of $100,000 or more to be performed within the United States to publish a statement about the act, to establish a drug-free awareness program, and to give each employee a copy of the workplace policy. (See Exhibits 4.13, "Executive Order 12564, September 15, 1986: Drug-Free Federal Workplace Act," and 4.14, "Benefits and Drawbacks of a Drug-Free Workplace Policy [DFWP].")

In response to the act, all federal agencies established individual drug-use testing programs designed to ensure the safety and security of the government and the public. For example, the Department of Defense has an employee assistance program that focuses on counseling and rehabilitation, in addition to self- and supervisory referrals to substance abuse treatment clinics. In addition, the act requires that federal contractors and grant recipients satisfy certain requirements designed to eliminate the effects of illicit drugs from the workplace. Accordingly, some federal contractors and all federal grantees have to agree that they will provide drug-free workplaces as a precondition of receiving a contract or grant from a federal agency.[77]

The act also provides that, for a drug-use testing program to be legal, federal employers must post and distribute a policy statement explaining that the unlawful manufacture, distribution, dispensation, possession, or use of controlled substances is prohibited. Discipline or sanctions against the offending employee are left to the employer's discretion. However, if a criminal conviction arises from a workplace substance abuse offense, the employer is required to administer an employment sanction or to advise and direct the employee to an approved substance abuse treatment program.

Exhibit 4.13 *Executive Order 12564, September 15, 1986: Drug-Free Federal Workplace Act*

I, Ronald Reagan, President of the United States of America, find that:

Drug use is having serious adverse effects upon a significant proportion of the national work force and results in billions of dollars of lost productivity each year;

The Federal government, as an employer, is concerned with the well-being of its employees, the successful accomplishment of agency missions, and the need to maintain employee productivity;

The Federal government, as the largest employer in the nation, can and should show the way towards achieving drug-free workplaces through a program designed to offer drug users a helping hand and, at the same time, demonstrating to drug users and potential drug users that drugs will not be tolerated in the Federal workplace.

Exhibit 4.14 *Benefits and Drawbacks of a Drug-Free Workplace Policy (DFWP)*

THE BENEFITS

- Ridding the workplace of substance abuse can improve morale, increase productivity, and create a competitive advantage.
- A comprehensive program may qualify an employer for discounts on workers' compensation and other insurance premiums.
- The prevention of a single accident or injury may pay for the entire program costs for several years.
- Some contractors may need to have a DFWP to be eligible for business.
- Many employers have successfully formulated policies that deal with ethical and privacy issues and have successfully controlled their responsibility for and the costs associated with treatment and rehabilitation benefits.
- Unions have initiated DFWPs with employers to promote good public relations and recapture work for their members.
- Having a DFWP sends a very clear message to employees, their families, and the community as to the company's position on illegal drug use.

THE DRAWBACKS

- A DFWP can increase distrust between management and workers and degrade morale and productivity in some workplaces.
- A comprehensive DFWP could add significantly to the cost of doing business.
- False accusations, misidentification of employees as drug users, unjustified dismissals, and violation of confidentiality obligations could prompt burdensome litigation.
- Identifying substance users may entail an obligation to provide costly counseling and treatment for a relapsing condition. It is not always easy to contain the financial drain, and health insurance premiums could rise.
- A DFWP, particularly one that features drug testing, can raise serious ethical and privacy issues.

- Where the workplace is organized, the employer faces additional negotiations with the union.

DRUG-FREE WORKPLACE POLICY CHECKLIST

1. What is our current company policy regarding the use of alcohol and other drugs?
2. How much of a drug or alcohol problem does our company have at the present time?
3. What is the nature of the problem (absenteeism, quality, productivity, safety, etc.)?
4. How much does this problem cost the company?
5. What type of DFWP would be most likely to improve the situation?
   a. urine testing
   b. impairment testing
   c. under the influence testing
   d. better supervision and quality control
   e. Employee Assistance Plan
   f. a combination of the above
6. If testing is involved, who will be tested?
   a. applicants
   b. employees in safety sensitive positions
   c. all employees
7. Under what circumstances will testing be done?
   a. preemployment
   b. for cause
   c. random
   d. combination
8. What will be done with those who fail the test?
9. What action will be taken regarding those who refuse to be tested?
10. What would be the costs of such a program?
11. What would be the benefits? How much would the problems described in 3 and 4 above be reduced by the program? How great is the financial benefit of the reduction?
12. Do the projected benefits justify the costs?
continued

Exhibit 4.14 *continued*

13. Which proposed components of the DFWP are cost effective?

14. How do the company's employees feel about the proposed DFWP? Would they be more supportive of another option? Have we sought their input?

15. (If the company is organized) Has the proposed DFWP been negotiated with the union?

16. Is the proposed DFWP consistent with company values?

17. Is the proposed DFWP legal in the jurisdictions where it will be implemented?

CHOOSING A POLICY

The first step in developing a policy is to decide whether to have a DFWP. Some employers may choose instead to judge employees simply on the basis of performance. Once a company has made a basic policy choice, it can consider in more detail the objectives it intends to achieve. There are a variety of possible motivations for pursuing such a program:

1. *Complying with legal requirements.* Under federal law, some employers are required to establish DFWPs, including engaging in drug (and possibly alcohol) testing.

2. *Reducing liability risks.* Having a DFWP may be viewed as assisting in the defense against certain legal actions, although DFWPs may also generate other kinds of claims.

3. *Reducing business costs due to accidents, absenteeism, and ill health.* Eliminating drug use is seen as a way to promote safety and efficiency, improve the health of the workforce and curtail use of sick leave, medical benefits, and workers' compensation.

4. *Ensuring the integrity of employees.* A potential cause of theft, pilferage, and blackmail is removed, and workers' confidence in each other is enhanced.

5. *Determining fitness for duty and corroborating evidence of misconduct.* A DFWP may help establish uniformity in standards of behavior and in discipline imposed. To establish the DFWP the employer must determine the proper balance between punitive and rehabilitative elements of the program. Being identified as a substance abuser may lead to discharge, but there may also be an attempt at rehabilitating employees and returning them to duty.

6. *Assuring public confidence in the business.* The employer prevents embarrassment by taking genuine steps to deal with employees who are affected by substance abuse.

7. *Promoting a "drug-free" society.* Many employers, seeing themselves as responsible members of society, sense a moral obligation to support law enforcement efforts against illicit drugs. NIDA has stated its "belief that the fight against illegal drugs in the workplace is critical to the nation's war against drug use." It has encouraged private employers to adopt DFWPs.

Source: ABA Section of Labor and Employment Law, *Attorney's Guide to Drugs in the Workplace* (1996).

To protect the employee's right to due process, the employer must educate the workforce of any drug/alcohol policy and testing procedures. In addition, laboratory and screening procedures must meet certain standards. In one case, *Fraternal Order of Police, Lodge No. 5 v. Tucker,*[78] the court concluded that the employees were denied due process because they were not informed of the basis of the employer's suspicion and because they were not offered the opportunity to rebut the employer's claims.

The Drug-Free Workplace Act also allows preemployment screening of job applicants. Many employers choose to implement preemployment drug testing in their workplace to avoid the costly medical care required to treat substance abuse.[79]

The Supreme Court has weighed in with regard to the government's use of drug-screening programs. For example, *National Treasury Employees Union v. Von Raab*[80] is a critical statement by the Supreme Court on the subject of drug-screening program standards for safety-sensitive positions and can be found as Case 1 at the end of this chapter. In *National Treasury Employees Union,* the Supreme Court found that suspicionless drug testing of U.S. Customs Service employees applying for promotion to positions that involved interception of illegal drugs or required them to carry firearms was reasonable under the Fourth Amendment and noted that the "government's compelling interest in safeguarding borders and public safety outweighed diminished privacy expectation in respect to intrusions occasioned by [a] urine testing program, which was carefully tailored to minimize intrusion."[81] However, in *Chandler v. Miller,*[82] the same Court held that Georgia's requirement that candidates for state office pass drug tests did not fit within the closely guarded category of constitutionally permissible suspicionless searches. More recently, the Supreme Court refused to hear former Florida Governor Rick Scott's appeal of the Eleventh Circuit's finding that his executive order requiring random drug tests for all state workers and applicants was unconstitutional. The Eleventh Circuit found the policy unconstitutional because it was overbroad and not limited to safety-sensitive positions. The Supreme Court's refusal to hear the appeal means the ruling of the Eleventh Circuit stands.[83]

State laws also govern substance abuse testing. Therefore, employers are cautioned to evaluate programs according to the laws of the state or states in which their operations are located. For instance, the laws of California include the privacy provisions of its state constitution, which, unlike most state constitutional provisions, extend to private employers. Random testing is permitted in California for those in safety-sensitive work (though that definition remains open to interpretation), and an employer is under no obligation to hire or retain individuals who fail a drug test.

Employers must also monitor local city laws when administering substance abuse testing. For example, the city of Boulder, Colorado, allows applicant testing post-offer only, and there must be reasonable suspicion based on a "clear belief of intoxication or job performance is suffering." Periodic and random testing are prohibited. This is more restrictive than the state of Colorado requires.[84]

Drug Testing and "Legal" Marijuana Use

Attitudes toward marijuana use have become more lenient over the past couple of decades. As of 2019, 33 states, the District of Columbia, Guam, Puerto Rico, and the U.S. Virgin Islands have legalized the use of marijuana for medical purposes.[85] Additionally, as of 2020, 14 states have also legalized marijuana for recreational use. Other states are expected to pass similar laws in the near future. A few cities also permit the use of marijuana.[86] Despite the recent legalization, using marijuana is still a criminal act under federal law, listed in the same category as cocaine, heroin, LSD, and ecstasy. In 2018, the U.S. Attorney General announced a policy that allows federal prosecutors to decide how to prioritize enforcement of federal marijuana laws. Specifically, the memorandum directs U.S. Attorneys to "weigh all relevant considerations, including federal law enforcement priorities set by the Attorney General, the seriousness of the crime, the deterrent effect of criminal prosecution, and the cumulative impact of particular crimes on the community."[87]

Note that testing for marijuana is *not* considered a medical test, even though several states have legalized possession and use of limited amounts of marijuana for medical purposes. The Americans with Disabilities Act of 1990 does not protect individuals who use marijuana for medical purposes. However, Arizona, Arkansas, Connecticut, Delaware, Illinois, Maine, Minnesota, Nevada, New York, Pennsylvania, and Rhode Island now have laws with explicit language with some degree of employment protection, typically prohibiting adverse action against an employee or applicant based on their status as a medical marijuana cardholder or participation in a medical marijuana program. For example, the states of Arizona and Delaware have protections in place prohibiting any punishment for medical marijuana users who are not impaired on the job, but not for recreational users.[88]

Most states that have legalized medical or recreational cannabis leave testing and decisions made thereafter up to the individual employer's discretion. A handful of states have policies in place that somehow address antidiscrimination for medical cannabis patients. Significantly fewer states require employers to carve out accommodations for these patients. Courts have upheld employers' right to discharge employees who have positive drug tests. For example, the Colorado Supreme Court held that an "employee could be terminated for his use of medical marijuana."

Employers located in states that do not offer that employee protection component to their medical marijuana law may still be liable for discrimination under the ADA. Even though a confirmed test for marijuana does not itself qualify as a disability, the underlying medical condition for which medical marijuana is used very well might be considered to be a disability.[89] An appellate court in New Jersey (a state with a medical marijuana law but without applicant/employee protections for using marijuana) argued that the medical marijuana law did not change the existing law that bars disability discrimination against applicants or employees. The plaintiff, fired for his marijuana use after it was discovered through an unrelated accident, alleged he suffered from cancer and, for that reason, used medical marijuana. The court concluded that the plaintiff should have the opportunity to prove he was fired because of his cancer and that the employer's stated reliance on his drug use was a pretext for disability discrimination.[90]

In another case, the Massachusetts Supreme Court ruled that a medical marijuana patient did indeed have the right to bring legal action against her employer for disability discrimination. While the court did not rule on whether the employer actually had discriminated, the ruling caught many employers and drug testing providers by surprise.[91] Thus, marijuana tests can still be fruitful grounds of potential liability for employers using them.

As laws on marijuana use continue to change, employers should review their substance abuse policies to ensure that their restrictions concerning marijuana use are consistent with the restrictions permitted in their respective jurisdictions. Employers should also review their job descriptions in order to ensure appropriate categorization of safety-sensitive positions or otherwise to ensure that they justify a policy against marijuana use for testing purposes. As with all types of preemployment testing, employers should be sure to treat all similarly situated employees and applicants in the same manner.[92]

Private Sector Employers and Substance Testing While the Drug-Free Workplace Act does not apply to private sector employers, for many years a large number of private employers implemented drug programs for their employees. Today, though drug use among American employees, as measured by the percentage of employees who tested positive in urine drug tests, is at a 14-year high, one study found that employee drug screening has declined. On average, only 1.47 percent of job postings in the United States mention that they require pre-employment drug tests. Even fewer jobs disclose that they require regular drug screenings during employment. On average, only 0.66 percent of job postings mention regular drug testing. Facing an aging workforce, low unemployment, and a strong economy, human resource professionals and hiring managers are having difficulty filling positions and therefore are removing any barriers that might exclude otherwise qualified people from the workplace. In addition, many employers do not see a return on investment when they weigh the costs of random and preemployment testing against the results. They express concern that random screening can hurt morale and prompt applicants and employees to look elsewhere for work.[93] However, when private employers follow the guidelines set forth in the Drug Free Workplace Act when they establish their drug screening programs, courts generally have upheld the reasonableness of those programs.

Further, on June 23, 1998, the House of Representatives passed the Drug-Free Workplace Act of 1998, aimed at providing small businesses—which often lack the resources and infrastructure to conduct employee drug tests—with financial resources and technical assistance for implementing drug-testing programs. The three purposes of the act are to (1) educate small business concerns about the advantages of a drug-free workplace, (2) provide financial incentives and technical assistance to enable small business concerns to create a drug-free workplace, and (3) assist working parents in keeping their children drug free. The Drug-Free Workplace Act of 1998 provides a $10 million grant program for nonprofit organizations that have the ability to provide technical assistance to small businesses in establishing drug-free policies.

Many states have enacted legislation designed to protect the privacy of private-sector employees.[94] These state laws vary in their approach; some states offer a great deal of protection for employees and may be classified as pro-employee (such as Connecticut, California, Minnesota, and New York), while other states allow testing after satisfaction of only modest burdens and are classified as pro-employer (such as Utah).

The Americans with Disabilities Act and Substance Testing One additional issue raised by drug and alcohol testing involves the Americans with Disabilities Act. The act, which applies to private sector employers and is discussed in much greater detail in Chapter 13, provides that individuals who currently use illegal drugs are not considered individuals with disabilities. However, if an employee or applicant is pursuing or has successfully completed a rehabilitation program and demonstrates that she or he has a disability based on prior use, she or he is covered by the act and therefore entitled to reasonable accommodation.

Polygraphs

polygraph
A lie-detecting device that measures biological reactions in individuals when questioned.

A relatively newsworthy area of testing is the **polygraph** or lie detector. An estimated 2.5 million polygraph tests are conducted in the United States every year, a system that fuels a thriving $2 billion industry.[95] It is also instructive that there are more than 2,700 polygraph examiners practicing in the United States. There are currently 25 schools of polygraph analysis accredited by the American Polygraph Association, with 13 located in the United States.[96]

A polygraph test measures three physiological indicators of arousal: rate and depth of respiration, cardiovascular activity, and perspiration. The examiner asks a structured set of questions, and the subject is evaluated as honest or deceitful based on the pattern of arousal responses. The test has been criticized, however, because stimulants other than dishonesty may produce similar effects in an individual subject.

The desire of employers to use polygraphs is perplexing when one considers the lack of evidence of their reliability. After reviewing the balance of research in connection with polygraphs, the Supreme Court in 1998 determined in *United States v. Scheffer*[96] that "[t]here is simply no consensus that polygraph evidence is reliable."

The National Academy of Sciences (NAS) conducted a subsequent comprehensive review of the research on polygraphs and found that the majority of polygraph research is "unreliable, unscientific and biased," noting that 57 of 80 studies that polygraph proponents rely on were flawed. Studies have reported accuracy ranging from 90 percent to as low as 50 percent (that is, no better than chance). The NAS report concluded that while polygraph testing may have some usefulness (resulting from subjects' belief in its reliability), there was "little basis for the expectation that a polygraph test could have extremely high accuracy."[98] Although the report urged federal agencies to stop using the tests as a screening technique, 15 agencies–from the FBI to the Postal Inspection Service–have continued or expanded their screening programs. Only the Department of Energy dramatically scaled back on screening after its own scientists protested.[99]

The NAS report also expressed concern about possible race, age, and gender biases but noted that little research had been done in the area. "We know that there's a potential effect of gender [and] race, in terms of [the] mix of polygrapher and subject," said NAS committee chairman Stephen Fienberg. "We know that context matters. And we know that there can be systematic biases." Dozens of equal opportunity complaints have been made against the FBI's polygraph screening unit, accusing examiners of racial and other biases. These kind of complaints and, later, settlements have also occurred in several police and public service departments around the country.[100]

Because of the large number of false positives and inaccuracies of the polygraph test, a loud outcry from those wrongly accused of improper behavior resulted in the enactment of the federal Employee Polygraph Protection Act (EPPA) of 1988. To a great extent, this act put an end to private sector use of the polygraph in selection and greatly restricts its use in many other employment situations.

The act provides that an employer may not:

1. Directly or indirectly require, request, suggest, or cause any employee to take or submit to any lie detector test (e.g., a polygraph, deceptograph, voice-stress

analyzer, psychological-stress evaluator, and any similar mechanical or electrical device used to render a diagnostic opinion about the honesty of an individual).

2. Use, accept, refer to, or inquire about the results of any lie detector test of any job applicant or current employee.

3. Discharge, discipline, discriminate against, or deny employment or promotion to (or threaten to take such adverse action against) any prospective or current employee who refuses, declines, or fails to take or submit to a lie detector test or who fails such a test.

However, see Exhibit 4.15 for EPPA employer exemptions as well as certain conditions under which private employers are permitted to administer a polygraph test.

The Employee Polygraph Protection Act also provides that, except in limited settlement-related circumstances, employees may not waive their rights under the act, nor is an employer allowed to offer financial incentives to employees to take the test or to waive their rights.

Violations of the act are subject to fines as high as $10,000 per violation, as well as reinstatement, employment, or promotion and the payment of back wages and benefits to the adversely affected individual. The Wage and Hour Division of the Employment Standards Administration of the Department of Labor has the authority to administer the Employee Polygraph Protection Act.

In addition to the regulations enacted by Congress, at least 27 states and the District of Columbia have statutes that either prohibit or restrict the use of polygraph examinations for use in employment decisions.[101] Where a state law is more restrictive than the federal act, the state statute governs.

Exhibit 4.15 *Employers Exempted from EPPA*

Employers exempted from EPPA:

Private employers whose primary business purpose is to provide security services.	Employers involved in the manufacture, distribution, or dispensing of controlled substances.	Federal, state, and local government employers.
Such as: the protection of nuclear power facilities; shipments or storage of radioactive or other toxic waste materials; public transport of currency, negotiable securities, precious commodities, or proprietary information.	***Such as:*** the direct access to the manufacture, storage, distribution, or sale of a controlled substance.	***Federal government may also test*** private consultants or experts under contract to the Defense Department, the National Security Agency, the Defense Intelligence Agency, the CIA, and the FBI.

Genetic Tests

genetic testing
Investigation and evaluation of an individual's biological predispositions based on the presence of a specific disease-associated gene on the individual's chromosomes.

Genetic testing is a scientific development that involves the use of laser and computer technology. Scientists make diagnostic predictions by locating a specific disease-associated gene on an individual's chromosomes. This type of testing evolved in the 1960s in connection with research regarding individuals who were "hypersusceptible" to chemicals used in certain workplaces. By testing an applicant's genes, the researchers were able to ascertain which applicants would be expected to experience negative reactions to various chemicals.

By the time the Human Genome Project was completed in 2003, which was successful in mapping all of the genes of our human genome, genetic testing was able to provide tremendous amounts of information about an individual. While this information allows us to predict and treat countless health issues, people also began to fear what others might do with this information. There was a concern that employers might require genetic testing and then treat certain individuals differently if they learned that an applicant or employee had a gene mutation that causes or increases the risk of an inherited disorder, for example. Other questions arose: If this information were uncovered during genetic testing, should the employer tell the applicant of the basis for her or his failure to be hired?

In 2008, the federal government began regulating genetic testing in employment to prevent genetic discrimination. The Genetic Information Nondiscrimination Act of 2008 (GINA) makes it illegal to discriminate against employees or job applicants on the basis of genetic information. Genetic information includes information about an individual's genetic tests and the genetic tests of an individual's family members as well as an individual's family medical history. Title II of GINA prohibits the use of genetic information in making employment decisions; restricts employers from requesting, requiring, or purchasing genetic information; and strictly limits the disclosure of genetic information. While an employer may access genetic information under a few, extremely limited exceptions under GINA (see Exhibit 4.16), an employer may never use genetic information to make an employment decision because genetic information is not seen as relevant to an individual's current ability to work.[102]

It is important to note that GINA does not protect workers in every circumstance. For example, GINA does not apply to employers who have fewer than 15 employers. It also does not cover people in the military.[103]

In addition to GINA, many states have laws that provide additional protection against genetic discrimination. As of 2019, 38 states and the District of Columbia prevent genetic discrimination in employment.[104]

One additional issue raised by genetic testing is that genetic irregularities that substantially impair a major life activity may be considered protected disabilities under the Americans with Disabilities Act and the Vocational Rehabilitation Act. A genetic test may encourage discrimination based on myths, fears, and stereotypes about genetic differences.

Unique Considerations of HIV/AIDS Testing

The Americans with Disabilities Act (ADA) and the Vocational Rehabilitation Act protect employees and job applicants from discrimination based on their

Management Tips *Testing*

- Private sector employers are *not* generally restricted by the Fourth Amendment protection against unreasonable searches. Therefore, as a private employer, you are allowed to conduct searches under a lower standard. On the other hand, common-law protections against invasions of privacy do apply in the private sector.
- You have an absolute right to determine whether someone is sufficiently healthy to do a job. The problem arises where your tests don't quite tell you that information or where you are testing for eligibility beyond the job's requirements. Make sure that your test will yield results that are relevant to the job in question.
- Health or eligibility testing should be conducted post-offer, preemployment.
- All tests should be validated; that is, they should be shown to test what they intend to test. Using an invalid test might subject you to liability.
- Restrict access to the information gained during testing. If you disclose the information to individuals who don't have a need to know it, you may be liable for an invasion of privacy or for defamation should the information turn out to be false.
- If you choose to try a polygraph test on workers, be wary of the restrictions imposed by the Employee Polygraph Protection Act.
- Since being HIV-free or AIDS-free is seldom (if ever) a BFOQ, testing for HIV is most likely to be unwarranted and a wrongful invasion of privacy.

Exhibit 4.16 *Gina Exceptions*

GINA provides six narrow exceptions to its prohibition against accessing genetic information:

1. Inadvertent acquisitions of genetic information do not violate GINA, such as in situations where a manager or supervisor overhears someone talking about a family member's illness.

2. Genetic information (such as family medical history) may be obtained as part of health or genetic services, including wellness programs, offered by the employer on a voluntary basis, if certain specific requirements are met.

3. Family medical history may be acquired as part of the certification process for FMLA leave (or leave under similar state or local laws or pursuant to an employer policy), where an employee is asking for leave to care for a family member with a serious health condition.

4. Genetic information may be acquired through commercially and publicly available documents like newspapers, as long as the employer is not searching those sources with the intent of finding genetic information or accessing sources from which they are likely to acquire genetic information (such as websites and on-line discussion groups that focus on issues such as genetic testing of individuals and genetic discrimination).

5. Genetic information may be acquired through a genetic monitoring program that monitors the biological effects of toxic substances in the workplace where the monitoring is required by law or, under carefully defined conditions, where the program is voluntary.

6. Acquisition of genetic information of employees by employers who engage in DNA testing for law enforcement purposes as a forensic lab or for purposes of human remains identification is permitted, but the genetic information may only be used for analysis of DNA markers for quality control to detect sample contamination.

Source: U.S. Equal Employment Opportunity Commission, "Genetic Information Discrimination," https://www.eeoc.gov/laws/types/genetic.cfm (accessed December 6, 2019).

There are three possible corporate approaches for testing employees for ineligibility. First, the employer may establish mandatory testing, which requires that all employees be tested for drug or alcohol use or some other form of ineligibility when they enter a specific program or at the time of their annual physical. Second, an employer may implement "probable cause" testing, where an employer tests employees only if there is suspicion of ineligibility and testing is implemented for the purpose of discovering a safety, conduct, or performance problem. Third, employers may implement random testing.

The decision about what method to use for testing will depend on the goals of the employer. Does it want to test its entire workforce? Or merely potential problem employees? Or merely test after an accident or injury where drug or alcohol use is suspected? In any case, an employer should first look carefully at state and local laws in connection with specific test-related legislation as well as at statutes regarding privacy and so on. Second, the employer should clearly articulate its policy regarding substance use, lie detectors, and other tests as well as its purpose, the procedure by which the policy is enforced, and the appeals process. Third, the policy must be consistently implemented and diligently documented. Possible human and laboratory errors must be minimized. Fourth, all positive results should be confirmed with additional tests.

HIV/AIDS status. Therefore, during the interview process, the ADA limits employers with regard to the questions they can ask surrounding an individual's medical conditions or HIV status and prohibits preemployment medical exams. As noted earlier, before making a job offer, an employer may only ask applicants whether they can perform the job with or without accommodation.

With regard to HIV, specifically, the employer may only ask about an employee's status or conduct a related exam if

1. An employee's positive HIV status would pose a direct threat to health or safety in the workplace or knowledge of the employee's status is vital for the workplace.
2. The inquiry is conducted after the employment offer.
3. The same inquiry is asked of all employees in the same job category.
4. All employees in the same job category are asked to submit to the same medical exams.

This determination must be based on an individualized assessment of the applicant's ability to safely perform essential job functions. However, arguments for HIV testing in the workplace generally have been unpersuasive. For the test to be justified, employers must demonstrate that the test serves a legitimate business purpose. Because HIV is not transmitted by casual contact of the sort that takes place in a work environment, an HIV test is improper for *most* positions. Second, the test reports only evidence the subject's past status; the test does not determine the HIV status of the individual as of the day of the examination. Therefore, unless the employer monitors and restricts the employee's off-work activities prior to the test and between testing, the inquiry is generally considered inefficient and ineffective.

The Equal Employment Opportunity Commission offers the example of a phlebotomist (someone who is trained to draw blood from a patient) who is HIV positive. The EEOC explains that this employee would not pose a direct threat to a patient based on her or his HIV status and, thus, could not be denied employment because of it. Additionally, an employer's fear about coworker reactions to a new hire's positive HIV status is not a valid reason to deny or withdraw an employment offer. Further, employers who discover that an employee has HIV/AIDS must keep this information confidential, regardless of how they obtain this information.[105]

Performance Appraisals, Evaluation, and Discipline Schemes

LO7 Identify the key benefits of performance appraisal structures as well as their areas of potential pitfalls.

See Chapter 2 to revisit key concepts.

performance appraisal
A periodic assessment of an employee's performance, usually completed by her or his immediate supervisor and reviewed, at times, by others in the company.

Once a worker is chosen and hired, the next step in the employment relationship involves its management, which might include the employee's professional development. Generally, employees want to enter organizations and rise as high as they can go, while employers want qualified employees who can handle what must be done to accomplish the job. Employees who want to succeed in their work do so by meeting their employers' expectations in an exemplary way. Success is usually documented by both sides through **performance appraisals (PAs)**. Employers wishing to have employees best suited for the job need to identify these employees for promotion, retention, transfers, training, bonuses, and raises, and they gather this necessary information through the periodic evaluation of employees. Disputes may arise when an employer's expectations of an employee are not aligned with the employee's understanding of the performance expected or offered, and they are most often brought to light through the evaluation system.

Above all, the purpose of the PA should be to identify those characteristics the employer hopes the employee will accentuate and to dissuade the employee from exhibiting characteristics not in keeping with the organization's objectives. PAs have the potential for discriminatory effect because discrimination may exist in the way the employer utilizes the evaluations as well as in the manner the appraisal is conducted.

Employers are not required to maintain poor performers. Termination as a result of inadequate work performance is justified by business considerations. It is the measure of adequacy that often results in an adverse impact or is the consequence of adverse treatment, which must be avoided by employers. (See Exhibit 4.17, "Realities about Performance Evaluations.")

Of the many ways in which an employer may assess employees' performance levels, the most efficient and effective methods are those that utilize a variety of schemes to obtain the most complete job-related information.

Exhibit 4.17 *Realities about Performance Evaluations*

---

1. An employer might be liable for giving a negative reference even when it is based on a valid performance evaluation.

2. An employer need not lower its standards or qualifications in order to accommodate an individual employee's or applicant's needs (such as a disability).

3. Performance appraisal systems, though inherently dependent on the evaluation of workers by other workers, can still rely on objective measures.

4. Performance incentive systems *can* be effective. They do not involve rewarding workers for doing the basics of their jobs but instead recognize *outstanding* performance and leadership.

5. The greater legal challenges in evaluation structures are not always found in the objectives, motivation, or incentives but often in areas of implementation, monitoring, and accountability.

Legal Implications of Performance Appraisal Systems

Given their potential for subjectivity as well as biased or skewed results, PA schemes are susceptible to abuse and criticism. It is undeniable that it is integral to the proper management of any workplace to have the ability to evaluate the performance of its employees, but concerns remain regarding the efficacy and propriety of the evaluation systems available.

Moreover, courts differ greatly in their decisions regarding similar PA methods; therefore, a rational and predictable conclusion is almost impossible about the propriety of any single method. What one is left with is merely direction.

Disparate Impact

The legal implications of PAs become relevant when their information is used as the basis for any employment-related decision. The Uniform Guidelines on Employee Selection Procedures apply to "tests and other selection procedures which are used as a basis for any employment decisions." Therefore, the guidelines regulate the design and use of PAs. Improper PA systems are those that do not fairly or adequately evaluate performance but instead perpetuate stereotypes that have an adverse impact on protected classes.

four-fifths or 80 percent rule
The minority group must perform at least four-fifths (80 percent) as well as the majority group under a screening device or a presumption arises that the screening device has a disparate impact on the minority group and must be shown to serve a legitimate business necessity for the employer.

Disparate impact may be determined by a number of methods, the most common of which is described in the guidelines as the **four-fifths rule**. The four-fifths rule holds that there is a presumption of discrimination where the selection rate (for any employment decision) of the protected group is less than 80 percent of the selection rate of the non-minority group. For example, if the number of males and females at a firm is equal, but the performance evaluation system results in promotions of 85 percent of the males and only 3 percent of the females, a court will presume discrimination. The employer could always attempt to rebut this presumption, but the default is to presume discriminatory reasons for this result.

As with other areas in which disparate impact is shown, the employer may still defend the system used. As long as the PA was sufficiently job-related, there must be some reasonable need for it and some means by which to ensure the system's objectivity and fairness. If, for example, a checklist system for appraisal is instituted, the employer must show that the person doing the checking is reasonably free of bias and that the list itself is a fair representation of what is to be expected of the reasonable or "common" employee. This is called *validation* and is strictly regulated by the guidelines.

The U.S. Supreme Court provided some guidance to employers with regard to PA systems in *Ricci v. DeStefano,*[106] a decision that demonstrated how prevention of unintentional discrimination against some employees can lead to perceived intentional discrimination against others. *Ricci* involved a test by the city of New Haven, Connecticut, for promotion of firefighters. The city subsequently learned that the test resulted in a statistically significant lower pass rate for African Americans than for other employees. Out of concern for potential liability, the city opted not to use the test for promotions. However, New Haven was then sued for discrimination by 18 firefighters (17 white and one Hispanic) who had already passed the test, claiming that they were denied their due promotions.

The court found that tossing out the test results amounted to intentional discrimination against those who did well unless the employer could demonstrate a "strong basis in evidence" that the test would lead to liability. To the contrary, as long as the test was "job related and consistent with business necessity" and the employer did not refuse to use other methods with less discriminatory impact, the employer needed to maintain the original test.

The holding in *Ricci* provides a strong incentive for employers to examine thoroughly any test before integrating it into an evaluation system. One effective strategy is to evaluate the passing rate of current successful employees in order to establish a benchmark for promotions overall.

Another example is provided by the Fifth Circuit in *Rowe v. General Motors,*[107] which reviewed a performance evaluation scheme that was based almost entirely on the recommendations of workplace foremen. The court concluded that this practice resulted in discrimination against African Americans even though, on its face, the practice appeared to be fair and there was no evidence that General Motors had an *intent* to discriminate. The court explained, "It is clearly not enough under Title VII that the procedures utilized by employers are fair *in form.* These procedures must be fair *in operation.*"

Likewise, the court explained, the intent of employers who utilize such discriminatory procedures is not controlling since "Congress directed the thrust of the Act to the *consequences* of employment practices, not simply the motivation" (emphasis added). This seminal case in this field was decided in 1972, and perhaps a different result might be reached today, depending on the circumstances of a case. However, in that case, the judge remarked, "[w]e and others have expressed a skepticism that Black persons whose positions are dependent directly on decisive recommendations from Whites can expect nondiscriminatory action."[108]

In a more recent case, two male former Yahoo! employees filed a gender discrimination case against Yahoo! for the use of their forced ranking PA system—which requires managers to rate each worker's performance using a number that compares him or her with peers. Under Yahoo!'s performance ratings process, the manager who directly supervised an employee allegedly assigned that worker a rating from 0 to 5. The ratings were called buckets and were labeled "greatly exceeds," "exceeds," "achieves," "occasionally misses," and "misses." Each quarter, a specified percentage of each department's employees would be assigned to each bucket. Then there was calibration, where higher-level management modified the employee scores up or down. Those at the bottom of the ratings were terminated, but the cutoff point for termination varied from quarter to quarter, as did the percentages assigned to each of the five buckets, and different departments would be assigned different percentages. The defendants claimed the system was subject to personal bias and that the management team at Yahoo! used it to discriminate against men in favor of women in the ranking system. The defendants also argued that when the female vice president of editorial began working at Yahoo!, less than 20 percent of the top managers in the media division were female. Three years later, more than 80 percent of the top managers were female. And of the approximately 16 senior-level editorial employees hired or promoted by her in an 18-month period, 14 of them were women.[109] The court disagreed and threw out the case in a summary judgment, arguing that the defendants had "not provided any evidence that their termination had anything to do with their gender other than their feelings that they was being discriminated against."[110]

Disparate Treatment

A PA also may result in disparate *treatment,* such as where a female employee is evaluated according to different criteria than are the male employees. An example of this type of sexual stereotyping was at issue in the *Hopkins v. Price Waterhouse* case.[111] In that case, a female accounting executive was refused a promotion to partner based on her performance evaluation. During the evaluation, the plaintiff had been told that she needed to "take a charm school course"; maintain more social grace; "walk, talk, and dress more like a woman"; use less profanity; and act less "macho."

The Supreme Court ruled in favor of the employee, even though the employer offered evidence of various non-discriminatory bases for the denial of the partnership. The Court found that, as long as the sexual stereotype and discriminatory appraisal were "motivating factors" in the employer's denial, the motive was illegitimate. This basis was incorporated into Title VII in the Civil Rights Act of 1991, which amended Title VII of the Civil Rights Act of 1964.

While most of us would claim that we rate people based on equivalent factors, research has shown, in fact, that we do not. Raters are often influenced by physical or other traits or attributes such as national origin, age, accent, and so on. Research also has shown that raters can be swayed by physical attractiveness or body type as well.

For example, a 2019 study found that there is a clear penalty to shortness. The shorter men are, relative to average, the less they earn. Men more than 20 percent shorter than average (66 inches or less) earn at least 10 percent less. Short women also earn less, but they face smaller wage penalties, about half the magnitude of short men. But tall women do out-earn their peers. Each extra inch of female height adds about 1 percent more in earnings.[112]

Research shows that obese workers earn less than their non-obese coworkers with obese women faring much worse than obese men. One study from the University of Exeter found that if a woman was 14 pounds (1 stone in the United Kingdom) heavier for no other reason than her genetics, this would lead to her having an income $1,900 (£1,500) less per year than a comparable woman of the same height who was 14 pounds lighter. Each extra pound a woman weighs knocks $165 (£125) off her annual salary.[113]

Even hair color can influence how much you earn: Research conducted by professors at the University of British Columbia's Sauder School of Business found that many women in leadership positions are blonde. Among female CEOs of S&P 500 companies (admittedly a small sample size), the percentage of blondes is 48 percent. But only 2 percent of male CEOs in the S&P 500 are blonde, according to a study they conducted. The UBC researchers explained in the presentation that blonde women leaders may come across as warmer and more attractive—and therefore more socially acceptable—than brunettes.[114] These types of biases around hair can also have racial implications. An NPR article highlighted the "Good Hair Study," conducted by Perception Institute, which reported that most people display some bias toward women of color based on their hair. White women in particular rated textured hair as "less beautiful," "less sexy/attractive," and "less professional" than smooth hair.[115] Employers can guard against this type of bias through objective and/or practical assessments.

People perceived as more attractive, for example, may be viewed as more intelligent and more competent, which could certainly have an impact on appraisers and their treatment of certain groups. Employers can guard against this type of influence through objective and/or practical assessments.

An employee disputing the PA also may prove a case using the disparate treatment analysis first articulated in *McDonnell Douglas v. Green.*[116] The employee must show that he or she

1. Is a member of a protected class.
2. Suffered an adverse employment decision as a result of a performance evaluation.
3. Was actually qualified to perform the responsibilities of the position.
4. Was replaced by someone with similar qualifications who is not a member of a protected class.

In connection with Scenario 3 where Lominy is considering his alternatives with regard to his evaluation of Gordie, Lominy must consider the disparate treatment implications of his decision. If Lominy bends the rules a bit for Gordie, in consideration of his recent life events, he may get into trouble unless he evaluates the life events that take place in the lives of *each* of his subordinates. Failure to do so would result in his treating Gordie differently, simply because he knows about Gordie's situation. While this might be fine in Gordie's mind, the next person to come along might not be so happy about it. In Scenario 3, that is just what happens. Julietta has a record similar to Gordie's. Suppose that she, too, has some difficulties in her life that have had an impact on her work performance. If Lominy does not consider these difficulties, he will be treating Julietta differently from how he treated Gordie, resulting in disparate treatment.

It is important to be aware of these issues, even where the difference in treatment is not the result of any intentional wrongful discrimination. If Lominy cannot show why there was a difference in the way he treated Gordie and Julietta, it may be difficult to prove that it was not the result of discrimination.

Defamation

Defamation takes place when one person makes an intentional false statement that harms another person.[117] Defamation can occur in connection with the publication of PAs and employers should take similar precautions to avoid liability. (See Exhibit 4.18, "Defamation by an Employer.") In this situation, faulty PAs are subject to claims of not only discrimination but also wrongful discharge or negligent evaluation.

In other words, if the employer makes a false statement during the course of an employee evaluation and that evaluation is transmitted to a third party (such as a future employer), the employee may have a claim for defamation. A false evaluation does not necessarily contain false information, but it may evaluate the employee on improper criteria (data on which the employee was told she or he would not be rated).

An evaluation also may be considered false where the rater does not include information that would explain or justify a poor appraisal, such as the fact that the employee's poor task completion rate was due to a sight disorder, which has since been corrected. Finally, a false evaluation may exist where a rater revises a prior evaluation in an attempt to justify subsequent adverse action taken against the employee. Truth is a complete defense to defamation, and truth and honesty from raters should be ensured throughout the appraisal process.

Performance Evaluations for People with Disabilities

A unique legal issue arises in connection with PAs of individuals with disabilities. An employer is not required to lower quality standards to accommodate an

---

Exhibit 4.18 *Defamation by an Employer*

Defamation: May exist where the employer:

1. States false and defamatory words concerning the employee.
2. Negligently or intentionally communicates these statements to a third party without the employee's consent.

3. Thereby subjects the employee to harm or loss of reputation.

employee with disabilities; however, it must provide reasonable accommodations to enable the employee to perform her or his essential responsibilities while not subjecting itself to an undue burden or hardship. The otherwise-qualified employee with a disability must be evaluated on reasonable job-related performance standards for the duties assigned to that position.

Discipline

As with any other area that involves actions directed toward employees, employee discipline is a sensitive domain and one that must be approached with a critical eye. Such care has both legal and business justifications. As a matter of law, if an employer can show that its discipline of an employee was for "just cause," it may be more effectively prepared to defend itself under EEO laws. In addition, there are sound business reasons for following such an approach. For example, if an employer ensures that there is "just cause" for discipline and discharge, employees are more likely to sense that they have been treated fairly, and turnover is likely to be lower. Similarly, ensuring a "just cause" disciplinary approach whenever possible may serve to create a reputation for the employer that, in turn, will act as a positive inducement for prospective employees.

Regulation of employment decisions applies to any decision, whether involving retention, promotion, and raises or demotion, termination, or other forms of discipline. All discipline decisions must be applied without discrimination and objectively administered. Discipline systems that have the purpose of educating the employee who is found to be in violation are generally considered by employees to be fairer and less arbitrary than traditional punishment-oriented systems of disciplinary action.

In general, "just cause" in discipline or discharge is determined by exploring three elements. First, one will consider whether the employee has received *due process;* that is, was the disciplinary process carried out in a fair manner? To reach this determination, it is relevant to consider the timeliness of the discipline and the adequacy of an employer's investigation, ensure that the employee is aware of the charge made and is given an opportunity to respond, and ensure that an employee is not penalized twice for the same conduct.

The second element is whether there is adequate evidence of whatever charge has been made against the employee. This inquiry depends on the reliability and weight of the evidence or proof in support of the charges. The third element is whether the penalty chosen is appropriate. Here, questions of discriminatory discipline, the proportionality of the penalty versus the employee conduct, and the length and quality of the employee's record are relevant.[118] A system that maintains consistency in application, that provides specific guidelines for attaining the varying levels of performance, and that communicates this information to employees is one likely to be deemed "fair."

Furthermore, the most effective and efficient method by which to ensure appropriate use of disciplinary action is to factually and completely document each action taken (whether such action was written or oral) and its background support. This assures employees of adequate feedback, and lawsuits will not hinge on the vagaries of a particular supervisor's memory. Where no documentation is maintained, there is no evidence that the employee was given the opportunity to redress the infraction or poor performance.

Progressive discipline involves a set of steps before a challenging employee will be terminated for poor performance. In other words, the employee is given a standardized and articulated set of "chances" to improve behavior or performance before discharge occurs. Though tailored to the needs of the workplace, these steps may begin with an oral warning, followed by a written warning, light punishment, and so on, until reaching a determination of discharge. Positive discipline refers to a progressive discipline process that involves counseling or other interventions that increase in severity or demands rather than punishments. Where either process is in place, it is critical that the process be implemented across the board and in a non-arbitrary manner in order to ensure fair treatment of all workers. Failure to impose progressive discipline systems in a standard format for all covered workers may result in potential liability for disparate treatment.[119] Where the employer does follow this process in a committed way, the process itself may be protection against liability through its consistent application to all workers.[120]

One useful measure of just cause was set forth by Arbitrator Carroll Daugherty in *Grief Bros. Cooperage Corp.,*[121] now commonly known as the Seven Tests of Just Cause (see Exhibit 4.19).

An employee who is subject to discipline has a right to request that a coworker be present as a witness during an investigatory interview. This right is not limited to employees who are union members: Nonunion employees have a right to representation under *Epilepsy Foundation of Northeast Ohio v. NLRB.*[122]

Documentation of discipline, as well as of appraisals, warnings, and commendations, should be retained in each employee's file and should be given to the employee to provide her or him with the opportunity to appeal the action.

Exhibit 4.19 *The Seven Tests of Just Cause*

1. Did the employer give to the employee forewarning of the possible or probable disciplinary consequences of the employee's conduct?

2. Was the employer's rule or managerial order reasonably related to the orderly, efficient, and safe operation of the business?

3. Did the employer, before issuing discipline, make an effort to discover whether the employee violated or disobeyed a rule or order of management?

4. Was the employer's investigation conducted fairly and objectively?

5. At the investigation, did the employer obtain substantial evidence or proof that the employee was guilty as charged?

6. Has the employer applied its rules, orders, and penalties evenhandedly and without discrimination?

7. Was the degree of discipline administered by the employer reasonable given (a) the seriousness of the employee's proven offense and (b) the record of the employee's service?

Chapter Summary

- Employers believe that freedom of contract should permit them to hire whom they please. However, such statutes as Title VII and IRCA require the employer to ensure that all qualified employees are provided with equal employment opportunity and that decisions to hire are based solely on appropriate concerns and not on prejudice or bias that is neither supported nor relevant to business necessities.

- An ethic of non-discrimination must permeate the hiring process, from advertising the position to drafting the application form to making the decision to hire.

- One of the most effective means by which an employer can protect itself from claims of discrimination in the recruitment/application process is to have a clear view of the job to be filled and the best person to fill that job (i.e., an adequate, specific job description for each position within the company).

- After the employer has conducted the analysis, it should implement those results by reviewing the written job descriptions to ensure that they are clear, specific, and in line with the analysis; all nonessential job requirements should be deleted or defined as nonessential, and minimum requirements should be listed.

- Employers are cautioned, however, that the court or enforcement agency will look first to the actual job performance and then to the description only to the extent that it accurately reflects what the employee really does in that position. If the employer fails to include a function in the description, that may be used as an admission that the function is nonessential. If the function is nonessential, it is likely that an employment decision made on that basis will be suspect.

- Employers should ensure that recruitment procedures not only seek to obtain the most diversified applicant pool by reaching diverse communities but also encourage diverse applicants through the language used and the presentation of the firm.

- Employers should establish efficient, effective procedures to guarantee that they know whom they are hiring. If an employer wants a certain type of person to fill a position, ensure that the one hired is such a person. Failure to do so may result in liability under a theory of negligent hiring.

- Employers should review their applications to ensure that they are asking only for information that is defensibly job-related or necessary to make a decision about whether to hire the candidate.

- Since employers are liable for negligent hiring based on what they knew or should have known, it is critical to do a thorough background check on each new hire. This may include new hires through employment agencies as well, since those agencies do not always conduct background checks sufficient to insulate the ultimate employer.

- Though prior employers are not obligated to provide references beyond the individual's position, salary, and dates of work, if the employer chooses to do so beyond that basic level, the reference must be complete and honest to prevent foreseeable harm.

- Testing for eligibility and ineligibility is a necessary component of the selection procedure. No employer would hire an unqualified employee if it knew the qualifications of the employee in advance of the hiring determination.

- Designing the appropriate preemployment tests in order to ensure applicants can perform the functions of the job is critical, not only to effective selection procedures but also to the prevention of liability for disparate results of your procedure.

- To keep an employer's evaluation techniques within parameters that are relatively safe from criticism, the employer should first describe precisely what is required of each position to be evaluated. An adequate description will include the following:

  1. Position title.
  2. Department or division in which the position is located.
  3. Title of supervisor (not name, as the individual may change while the supervisory position would not).
  4. Function or purpose of position.
  5. Scope of responsibility for accomplishing that purpose.
  6. Specific duties and responsibilities.
  7. Knowledge, experience, or qualifications necessary for performance of the above duties and responsibilities (the connection should be apparent or explained).
  8. Organizational relationship, persons to whom the employee should report, those employees who report to this supervisor, and those employees over whom the supervisor has direct supervisory responsibilities.

- No unwritten qualifications should exist. These may have a disparate impact on those employees outside the loop of information, pursuant to which employees learn of the "real" way of obtaining promotions and other workplace benefits.

- The employer should communicate to its employees the nature, content, timing, and weight of the performance appraisal and ensure that the employees understand each of the standards pursuant to which they will be evaluated.

- The bases for the evaluation should be specific and job- or task-defined, rather than subjective, global measures of job performance. For example, a performance measure such as "ability to finish tasks within specified time period" is preferable to "timeliness." "Suggests new approaches" would be preferable to "industrious." This is because the supervisor evaluating the individual is using baselines and vantage points such as the schedules that she or he has given the employee rather than being forced to reach a conclusion about the employee's timeliness in general.

- The employer should request justifications of ratings wherever possible. Some researchers have suggested that documentation should be required only where a rating is extreme; however, this may be construed by the court as bending over backward only in those circumstances where the rating may be questioned. To the contrary, where an employer maintains a policy that each evaluation should be documented, the consistency of treatment is a defense in itself.

- In addition to affording the employee the opportunity to be heard during the process, the employer should establish a formal appeals process, which the employee may follow subsequent to receipt of the final appraisal. This process may be

- Documentation such as written performance appraisals can be your protection against wrongful lawsuits charging discrimination. As mentioned before, you are allowed to terminate someone for any reason *except* for certain prohibited reasons. As long as you document poor or deteriorating performance, you may generally terminate an individual on that basis and have protection against claims of discrimination.

- On the other hand, if you do conduct written performance appraisals but treat workers with similar appraisals differently, you may be subject to charges of discrimination.

- Where performance appraisals are conducted by a manager on the basis of stereotypes or prejudice, you are subject to claims of either disparate treatment or disparate impact. Therefore, make sure that all supervisors undergo training in connection with non-biased reporting and evaluations that are free from prejudgments.

- Make sure that there are precautions against inappropriate disclosures. An employer may be subject to claims of privacy invasions or defamation under certain circumstances.

- If your employee manual or other materials state that you will conduct appraisals, failure to conduct them may be a problem. Make sure that you are willing to live with the claims you make regarding the regularity of appraisals and other promises.

implemented by the employer through its supervisors, a committee composed of representatives from all levels of the company, or a committee composed of the employee's peers. Under most circumstances, appeals processes act as a means to air differences and to explain misunderstandings, deterring later litigation.

Chapter-End Questions

1. In the process of its recruitment of Peters, Security Pacific informed Peters that the company was doing "just fine" and Peters would have "a long tenure" at Security Pacific should he accept the position offered. In doing so, Security Pacific concealed its financial losses and the substantial, known risk that the project on which Peters was hired to work might soon be abandoned and Peters laid off. Peters accepted the position and moved from New Orleans to Denver to begin his new job. Two months later, Peters was laid off as a result of Security Pacific's poor financial condition. Does Peters have a cause of action?

2. Uber released a groundbreaking sexual assault report in 2019 revealing that the company documented nearly 6,000 reports of sexual assault—by both drivers and passengers—in 2017 and 2018 as well as 19 deaths from Uber-related physical assaults during that time (not necessarily between driver and rider). How might an injured passenger use this information to support a negligent hiring claim against Uber? What else would the passenger need as grounds for this type of claim?

3. In Chapter 1, we discussed "Ban the Box" initiatives around the United States: legislation barring employers from asking whether applicants have been convicted of a crime. Given what you have learned in this chapter about negligent hiring liability for employers, what can employers do to protect the privacy of applicants while also protecting their customers and business? Do you agree that Ban the Box initiatives should still exist?

4. In response to a probe by the Rhode Island Commission for Human Rights, the drugstore CVS agreed to remove certain questions from its preemployment personality questionnaire for job applicants. These questions included a request to place oneself on a range from strongly agree to strongly disagree for the following statements:

   - "You change from happy to sad without any reason."
   - "You get angry more often than nervous."
   - "Your moods are steady from day to day."
   - "There's no use having close friends; they always let you down."

   CVS later decided to stop using personality tests altogether in response to scrutiny from the EEOC. Why might these questions be problematic?

5. Phillips, an African American woman, applied for a position as secretary at the Mississippi legislature as a "walk-in" applicant. Phillips worked in the same building, which was made up of approximately 80 percent African American employees. She stopped by the office one day to ask if the office was hiring clerical help. She was told that the office was, and she was given an application to fill out. After not hearing a response from the office regarding the position, she called and learned that a white woman with similar qualifications had filled the position, even though Phillips had applied before this woman. The office explained that it simply has a practice of not contacting walk-in applicants for positions. Phillips claims that this policy disfavors African American applicants who work in the building and argues therefore that the policy is illegal based on disparate impact. What result, if Phillips takes the office to court?

6. In *Pingatore v. Union Pacific Railroad Company,* a railroad employee contended that the manner in which drug and alcohol testing was administered violated his right to privacy. After several accidents and leaves from work, the employee was tested 18 times in an 11-month period. Other employees were allowed to enter and use the restroom while he was providing samples. Also, those administering the test would announce that drug testing was being performed in a specific area of the workplace. The employee contended that this damaged his reputation and led to his being called "pothead." In those 11 months, he tested negative on all tests. The Arkansas Appeals Court reasoned that employees working in a highly regulated industry such as the railroad have a lower expectation to privacy. This left the court with one question: Was the manner in which the employer conducted drug testing offensive to the reasonable person? The short answer is no. The court reasoned that because the employee did not protest the conditions under which the testing occurred, the employer had no way of knowing that its employee found the testing offensive. One's privacy in a highly regulated industry does not necessarily extend to guaranteeing complete anonymity. Do you agree with this result? How would you feel if you were tested in this manner and for this same position? [530 S.W.3d 372, 2017 Ark. App. 459 (2017).]

7. Lanie Brown, a Latinx woman, thought she would make a great police officer. She was 29 years old, was fit, and had a clean background record. Brown had military experience, including a tour of Iraq as a U.S. Marine, and her commanding officer had written her a glowing recommendation. In 2019, armed with an associate degree in criminal justice, she felt ready to apply to become an officer with the New Haven Police Department in her home state of Connecticut. Lanie sailed through the department's rigorous physical and mental tests, passing speed and agility trials and a written examination—but there was one final test. The New Haven Police Department insists that each applicant take a polygraph test. Lanie took the test with a Caucasian male polygraph examiner certified by the American Polygraph Association and was judged to have lied on the test and failed for deception about occasional marijuana use as a minor. She claimed this

was incorrect and requested a retake. The second test was with an African American male, and she passed the test. The New Haven Police Department still declined to offer her a position. Does Lanie have a claim?

8. Please respond to the following questions in connection with recruitment, selection, or employment procedures:

   a. When, if ever, may an employer ask a candidate or employee for a photograph as part of recruitment, selection, or employment procedures?

   b. May an employer ask a candidate or current employee to which organizations the individual belongs?

   c. If a contract is intended to be at-will, must it include a statement to that effect?

9. An individual contacts you in connection with a reference for one of your worst employees, who was just recently terminated for poor performance. This individual asks whether you believe the former employee will perform well in a similar position at a new company. How do you respond? Is your response different if the former employee was terminated for stealing and the individual asks whether this employee can be trusted?

10. Which of the following statements would be acceptable in a performance evaluation?

    - "Even though Jacquie was out on a few religious retreats, she exceeded June sales goals by 10 percent."

    - "Although a new, young college graduate, Spiro was very capable in leading the sales meeting."

    - "Despite time off for medical leaves, Renee was able to surpass the productivity of many of her colleagues."

    - "Though a bit tough to understand, Margeaux has received excellent reviews for her customer service."

End Notes

1. NOLO.org, "Employment Discrimination in Your State," https://www.nolo.com/legal-encyclopedia/employment-discrimination-in-your-state-31017.html (accessed October 18, 2019).

2. The authors have chosen to use the term *Latinx* as the gender-neutral plural replacement for "Latino(s) and Latina(s)." Previously, the term *Latinos* was the most often-used term to represent any gender-mixed group of Latin descent. However, that choice represents a male bias that we choose not to perpetuate. For more information and context on this term, please see Logue, J., "Latina/o/x: Many Student Groups Are Changing Their Names to Use 'Latinx' Instead of 'Latino' and 'Latina,'" *Inside Higher Ed* (December 8, 2015), https://www.insidehighered.com/news/2015/12/08/students-adopt-gender-nonspecific-term-latinx-be-more-inclusive (accessed October 19, 2019); Hayley Barrett, S., and O. Nñ, "Latinx: The Ungendering of the Spanish Language," *Latino USA* (January 29, 2016), http://latinousa.org/2016/01/29/latinx-ungendering-spanish-language/ (accessed October 19, 2019); Reichard, R., "Why We Say Latinx: Trans and Gender Non-Conforming People Explain," *Latina* (Aug. 29. 2015), http://www.latina.com/lifestyle/our-issues/why-we-say-latinx-trans-gender-non-conforming-people-explain (accessed October 19, 2019); Ramirez, T. L., and Z. Blay, "Why People Are Using The Term 'Latinx,'" *Huffington Post* (July 5, 2016), http://www.huffingtonpost.com/entry/why-people-are-using-the-term-latinx_us_57753328e4b0cc0fa136a159 (accessed October 19, 2019); and Padilla, Y., "What Does 'Latinx' Mean? A Look at the Term That's Challenging Gender Norms," *Complex* (April 18, 2016), http://www.complex.com/life/2016/04/latinx/ (accessed October 19, 2019).

3. McLarn, Samantha, "Why Referrals Might Be Hurting Your Diversity Efforts (and What You Can Do to Change That)," LinkedIn Talent Blog (April 3, 2018), https://business.linkedin.com/talent-solutions/blog/diversity/2018/why-referrals-might-be-hurting-your-diversity-efforts-and-what-you-can-do-to-change-that (accessed October 20, 2019).

4. Capelli, Peter, "Your Approach to Hiring Is All Wrong," *Harvard Business Review* (May–June 2019), https://hbr.org/2019/05/recruiting (accessed October 20, 2019).

5. Martic, Kristina, "8 Most Important Employee Referral Statistics," TalentLyft (July 6, 2018), https://medium.com/hr-blog-resources/8-most-important-employee-referral-statistics-f7c25cf41667 (accessed October 20, 2019).

6. *E.E.O.C v. Chicago Miniature Lamp Works,* 947 F.2d 292 (7th Cir. 1991).

7. Mishler, Keith, "How to Avoid Discrimination When Promoting Employees," Insperity.com, https://www.insperity.com/blog/avoid-discrimination-promoting-employees/ (accessed October 20, 2019).

8. Lewis, N., "Will AI Remove Hiring Bias?" *SHRM* (November 12, 2018), https://www.shrm.org/resourcesandtools/hr-topics/talent-acquisition/pages/will-ai-remove-hiring-bias-hr-technology.aspx (accessed November 20, 2019).

9. Bertrand, M., and S. Mullainathan, "Are Emily and Greg More Employable Than Lakisha and Jamal? A Field Experiment on Labor Market Discrimination," *The American Economic Review* 94, no. 4 (September 2004), pp. 991–1013.

10. Banerjee, R., J. Reitz, and P. Oreopolus, "Do Large Employers Treat Racial Minorities More Fairly? An Analysis of Canadian Field Experiment Data," *Canadian Public Policy* 44, no. 1 (March 2018), pp. 1–12.

11. Adesina, Z., and O. Marocico,"Is It Easier to Get a Job If You're Adam or Mohamed?," *BBC News* (February 6, 2017), https://www.bbc.com/news/uk-england-london-38751307 (accessed October 20, 2019).

12. Gray, A., "The Bias of 'Professionalism' Standards," *Stanford Social Innovation Review* (June 4, 2019), https://ssir.org/articles/entry/the_bias_of_professionalism_standards# (accessed October 21, 2019).

13. Cubiks Talent Solutions, "'Hire for Culture, Train for Skill' Recruiters Reject Candidates Based on Their Lack of Cultural Fit"(April 4, 2016), https://www.cubiks.com/insights/hire-culture-train-skill-recruiters-reject-candidates-based-their-lack-cultural-fit (accessed October 21, 2019).

14. Edo, A., N. Jacquemet, and C. Yannelis, "Language Skills and Homophilous Hiring Discrimination: Evidence from Gender and Racially Differentiated Applications," *Federal Reserve Bank of St Louis* (2013).

15. EEOC, "Pandemic Preparedness in the Workplace and the Americans with Disabilities Act," 29 CFR Part 1630, OLC Control Number EEOC-NVTA-2009-3 (as updated March 21, 2020), https://www.eeoc.gov/laws/guidance/pandemic-preparedness-workplace-and-americans-disabilities-act (accessed June 20, 2020); EEOC, "What You Should Know About COVID-19 and the ADA, the Rehabilitation Act, and Other EEO Laws," EEOC Technical Assistance Questions and Answers (June 17, 2020), https://www.eeoc.gov/wysk/what-you-should-know-about-covid-19-and-ada-rehabilitation-actand- other-eeo-laws (accessed June 20, 2020).

16. Stone, L.C., "EEOC Issues New COVID-19 Guidance For Employers," *Labor and Employment Law Blog* (April 2, 2020), https://www.laboremploymentlawblog.com/2020/04/articles/coronavirus/eeoc-webinar-guidance/ (accessed April 2, 2020).

17. Nolo.com, "Employment Discrimination in Your State"(2019), https://www.nolo.com/legal-encyclopedia/employment-discrimination-in-your-state-31017.html (accessed October 21, 2019).

18. Margery Austin Turner, Michael Fix, and Raymond J. Struyk, *Opportunities Denied, Opportunities Diminished: Discrimination in Hiring* (Washington, D.C.: Urban Institute, 1991).

19. Quillian, L., Pager, D., Hexel, L., and A. Midtboen, "Meta-Analysis of Field Experiments Shows No Change in Racial Discrimination in Hiring Over Time," *Proceedings of the National Academy of Sciences of the United States of America* 114, no. 41 (October 10, 2017), pp. 10870–75.

20. Denton, L., "Don't Panic! Background Screening Explained," *HireRight* (September 20, 2018), https://www.hireright.com/blog/background-checks/dont-panic-background-screening-explained (accessed October 22, 2019).

21. Clark, M., "How to Address Negligent Hiring Concerns," *SHRM* (February 27, 2019), https://www.shrm.org/hr-today/news/hr-magazine/spring2019/pages/how-to-address-negligent-hiring-concerns.aspx (accessed October 22, 2019).

22. *Denton v. Universal Am-Can, Ltd.,* 2019 IL App (1st) 181525, https://courts.illinois.gov/Opinions/AppellateCourt/2019/1stDistrict/1181525.pdf (accessed November 20, 2019).

23. U.S. Department of Labor, "Workplace Violence," http://www.osha.gov/SLTC/workplaceviolence/index.html (accessed October 22, 2019).

24. "2017 National Center for Victims of Crime Resource Guide: Workplace Violence Fact Sheet," https://www.ncjrs.gov/ovc_archives/ncvrw/2017/images/en_artwork/Fact_Sheets/2017NCVRW_WorkplaceViolence_508.pdf (accessed October 22, 2019).

25. Ricci, D., "Workplace Violence Statistics 2018: A Growing Problem,"*AlertFind* (2018), https://alertfind.com/workplace-violence-statistics/ (accessed October 22, 2019).

26. Maurer, R., "Know before You Hire: 2017 Employment Screening Trends," *SHRM,* (January 27, 2017), https://www.shrm.org/resourcesandtools/hr-topics/talent-acquisition/pages/2017-employment-screening-trends.aspx (accessed on October 22, 2019).

27. "EEOC Enforcement Guidance on Application of EEO Laws to Contingent Workers" (December 3, 1997).

28. Ibid.

29. Flake, D., "Do Ban-the-Box-Laws Really Work?" *Iowa Law Review* 104 (January 19, 2018), https://ssrn.com/abstract=3105433 (accessed October 22, 2019).

30. Fisch, G., and M. Goldstein, "Ban the Box" Laws & Workplace Violence: An Employer's Failure to Sufficiently Perform Background Checks Could Lead to Costly Negligence Liability," *Sheppard Mullin: Labor and Employment Law Blog* (May 31, 2018), https://www.laboremploymentlawblog.com/2018/05/articles/background-investigations/ban-the-box-negligence-hiring/ (accessed October 22, 2019).

31. FindLaw Attorney Writers, "Avoiding Defamation in the Workplace, Giving References and Disciplining Employees while Avoiding Liability,"*FindLaw,* https://corporate.findlaw.com/litigation-disputes/avoiding-defamation-in-the-workplace-giving-references-and.html (accessed October 22, 2019).

32. Duffy, E., "Employers Use Facebook in Hiring Process," *The Observer* (online) (November 1, 2006), http://media.www.ndsmcobserver.com/media/storage/paper660/news/2006/11/01/News/Employers.Use.Facebook.In.Hiring.Process-2414357.shtml (accessed August 20, 2016); see also Rupe, A. L., "Facebook Faux Pas," *Workforce Management* (March 2007).

33. Driver, S., "Keep It Clean: Social Media Screenings Gain in Popularity," *Business News Daily* (October 7, 2018), https://www.businessnewsdaily.com/2377-social-media-hiring.html (accessed October 22, 2019).

34. CareerBuilder.com, "More Than Half of Employers Have Found Content on Social Media That Caused Them NOT to Hire a Candidate, According to Recent CareerBuilder Survey" (August 9, 2019), https://www.prnewswire.com/news-releases/more-than-half-of-employers-have-found-content-on-social-media-that-caused-them-not-to-hire-a-candidate-according-to-recent-careerbuilder-survey-300694437.html (accessed October 22, 2019).

35. Bales, R., and K. Van Wezel Stone, "The Invisible Web of Work: The Intertwining of A-I, Electronic Surveillance, and Labor Law" (2019), *Berkeley Journal of Labor and Employment Law* 41, no. 1 (2020, Forthcoming), https://ssrn.com/abstract=3410655 (accessed October 22, 2019).

36. National Conference of State Legislatures, "State Social Media Privacy Laws" (May 22, 2019), http://www.ncsl.org/research/telecommunications-and-information-technology/state-laws-prohibiting-access-to-social-media-usernames-and-passwords.aspx (accessed October 22, 2019).

37. Evangelista, B., "Facebook Warns Employers over Password Requests," *San Francisco Chronicle* (March 24, 2012), http://www.sfgate.com/business/article/Facebook-warns-employers-over-password-requests-3431130.php (accessed October 22, 2019).

38. *Allstate Insurance Co. v. Jerner,* Case No. 93-09472 (Fla. Cir. Ct. 1993), cert. denied, 650 So. 2d 997 (Fla. Ct. App. 1995).

39. See *Singer v. Beach Trading Co., Inc.,* 379 N.J.Super. 63 (2005); *Davis v. Board of County Com'rs of Dona Ana County,* 127 N.M. 785 (1999); and *Randi W. v. Muroc Joint Unified School Dist.,* 14 Cal. 4th 1066 (1997).

40. For a review of the status of this tort in each state in 2019, see "MLRC 50-State Survey: Employment Libel & Privacy Law" (The Media Law Resource Center, Inc., 2019).

41. 513 U.S. 352 (1995).

42. *Loder v. City of Glendale,* 14 Cal. 4th 846 (1997).

43. *Lunsford v. Sterlite of Ohio,* L.L.C., 2018-Ohio-3437, http://www.supremecourt.ohio.gov/rod/docs/pdf/5/2018/2018-Ohio-3437.pdf (accessed November 20, 2019).

44. 79 F.3d 661, 665–69 (7th Cir. 1996).

45. 422 U.S. 405 (1975).

46. *Gulino v. New York State Educ. Dept.,* 460 F.3d 361 (3rd Cir. 2012).

47. Maurer, R.,"How to Choose Hiring Assessments That Work for You," *SHRM* (April 24, 2108), https://www.shrm.org/resourcesandtools/hr-topics/talent-acquisition/pages/how-to-choose-hiring-assessments-hr.aspx (accessed October 22, 2019).

48. Shaffer, D., and R. Schmidt, "Personality Testing in Employment," FindLaw.com, http://corporate.findlaw.com/human-resources/personality-testing-in-employment.html (accessed October 22, 2019).

49. Harper, H., "The Most Successful Personality Trait in the Workplace (and Ever!)," *WorkStyle.com* (January 29, 2019), https://www.workstyle.io/most-important-personality-trait-in-the-workplace (accessed November 20, 2019); Barrick, M. R., and M. K. Mount, "The Big Five Personality Dimensions and Job Performance: A Meta-Analysis," *Personnel Psychology* 44 (1991), pp. 1–26.

50. Fahey, G., "Faking Good and Personality Assessments of Job Applicants: A Review of the Literature," *DBS Business Review* 2 (2018), https://www.researchgate.net/

publication/329287508_Faking_Good_and_Personality_Assessments_of_Job_
applicants_A_Review_of_the_Literature (accessed November 20, 2019).

51. Goldberg, E., "Personality Tests Are the Astrology of the Office," *The New York Times* (September 17, 2019), https://www.nytimes.com/2019/09/17/style/personality-tests-office.html?auth=login-facebook&login=facebook (accessed November 20, 2019).

52. "The 2018 Talent Board North American Candidate Experience (CandE) Benchmark Research Report," *Talent Board* (2018), https://www.thetalentboard.org/wp-content/uploads/2019/02/2018_Talent-Board-NA-CandE-Research-Report_FINAL_2619.pdf (accessed November 20, 2019).

53. Smithey, J. and R. Wolfson, "Personality and Integrity Tests for Hiring and Promoting Employees," *Lexis Nexis Practice Advisor* (May 2019), https://smitheylaw.com/wp-content/uploads/2019/05/Personality-and-Integrity-Tests-for-Hiring-and-Promoting-Employees.pdf (accessed November 20, 2019).

54. *Karraker v. Rent-a-Center,* 411 F.3d 831 (7th Cir. 2005).

55. 42 U.S.C. § 12112(d)(3)(C)-(4)(A).

56. Grobelny, J.,"Predictive Validity toward Job Performance of General and Specific Mental Abilities. A Validity Study across Different Occupational Groups," *Business and Management Studies* 4, no. 3 (2018), https://www.researchgate.net/publication/326190121_Predictive_Validity_toward_Job_Performance_of_General_and_Specific_Mental_Abilities_A_Validity_Study_across_Different_Occupational_Groups (accessed November 20, 2019).

57. See, e.g., *Fuzy v. S&B Eng'rs & Constructors, Ltd.,* 332 F.3d 301 (5th Cir. 2003); and *Jeffrey v. Ashcroft,* 285 F. Supp. 2d 583 (U.S. District Ct. M.D. Pa. 2003).

58. Sparkman, D., "EEOC Cracks Down on Pre-Employment Physical Testing," *EHS Today* (July 20, 2018), https://www.ehstoday.com/health/eeoc-cracks-down-pre-employment-physical-testing (accessed November 20, 2019).

59. *Leonel v. American Airlines, Inc.,* 400 F.3d 702 (9th Cir. 2005).

60. Brown, S.,"Revisiting Disability-Related-Inquiries and Medical Examinations Under Title I of the ADA," *ADA National Network* (2018), https://adata.org/sites/adata.org/files/files/Legal%20Brief%20-%20Medical%20Exams%20and%20Employment%20final%202018.pdf (accessed November 20, 2019).

61. 24 F.Supp.3d 1219 (U.S. District Ct. S.D. Florida, 2014).

62. *Friedenberg v. Sch. Bd. of Palm Beach Cty.,* 911 F.3d 1084 (2018).

63. "Employee Drug Testing," *Justia.com* (September 2018), https://www.justia.com/employment/hiring-employment-contracts/privacy-in-employment/employee-drug-testing/ (accessed November 21, 2019).

64. *Lunsford v. Sterilite of Ohio, LLC,* 108 N.E.3d 1235 (Ohio App. 2018); *Baughman v. Wal-Mart Stores, Inc.,* 592 S.E.2d 824 (W. Va. 2003); *Twigg v. Hercules Corporation,* 406 S.E.2d 52 (W. Va. 1990).

65. Wylie, M., "Surprising Stats on Drugs in the Workplace," *Bizwomen: The Business Journals,* (January 18, 2018), https://www.bizjournals.com/bizwomen/news/latest-news/2018/01/surprising-stats-on-drugs-in-the-workplace.html (accessed November 21, 2019).

66. News Release, "National Census of Fatal Occupational Injuries in 2017," *Bureau of Labor Statistics* (December 19, 2018), https://www.bls.gov/news.release/pdf/cfoi.pdf (accessed November 20, 2019).

67. Hampton, R., and S. Murillo, "Addiction Costs Employers $100 Billion Every Year. We're Dedicated to A Better Way," *Thrive Global* (July 9, 2019), https://thriveglobal.com/

stories/addiction-costs-employers-100-billion-every-year-were-dedicated-to-a-better-way/ (accessed November 21, 2019); "Implications of Drug and Alcohol Use for Employers," *National Safety Council* (September 2019), https://www.nsc.org/work-safety/safety-topics/drugs-at-work/substances (accessed November 21, 2019).

68. National Safety Council, "Implications of Drug Use for Employers"(September 2019), https://www.nsc.org/work-safety/safety-topics/drugs-at-work/costs-for-employers (accessed November 20, 2019).

69. Aroke, H., A. Buchanan, et al., "Estimating the Direct Costs of Outpatient Opioid Prescriptions: A Retrospective Analysis of Data from the Rhode Island Prescription Drug Monitoring Program," *Journal of Managed Care & Specialty Pharmacy* 24, no. 3 (2018), pp. 214–224.

70. National Safety Council, "Implications for Drug Use for Employers," (September 2019), https://www.nsc.org/work-safety/safety-topics/drugs-at-work/costs-for-employers (accessed November 22, 2019).

71. Kleiman, M., "Is It Time to Do Away with Job Applicant Drug Testing?," *Vox* (July 30, 2018), https://www.vox.com/the-big-idea/2018/7/27/17619750/drug-testing-job-market-marijuana-opioids-cost-benefit (accessed November 22, 2019); Wylie, M.,"Surprising Stats on Drugs in the Workplace," *The Business Journals* (January 18, 2018), https://www.psychemedics.com/blog/2018/01/surprising-stats-drugs-workplace/ (accessed November 22, 2019); Davidson, P., "Retail Workers Tested Positive for Drugs at the Highest Rate Last Year, Quest Study Shows," *USA Today* (December 19, 2018), https://www.usatoday.com/story/money/2018/12/19/drug-testing-workplace-retail-had-highest-rate-positives-tests/2315373002/ (accessed November 22, 2019).

72. Nash, B., "Drug Testing Explained: Cost, Devices, Privacy and Accuracy," *North Point Recovery Blog,* https://www.northpointrecovery.com/blog/drug-testing-explained-cost-devices-privacy-accuracy/ (accessed November 22, 2019).

73. Kleiman, M.,"Is It Time to Do Away with Job Applicant Drug Testing?," *Vox* (July 30, 2018), https://www.vox.com/the-big-idea/2018/7/27/17619750/drug-testing-job-market-marijuana-opioids-cost-benefit (accessed November 22, 2019).

74. Els, C., T. D. Jackson, M. T. Milen, D. Kunyk, and S. Straube, "Random Drug and Alcohol Testing for Preventing Injury in Workers," *Cochrane Database of Systematic Reviews* no.1 (2018), https://www.cochranelibrary.com/es/cdsr/doi/10.1002/14651858.CD012921/epdf/full (accessed November 22, 2019).

75. Howell, S., "The Far-Reaching, Positive Impact of Workplace Drug Testing," *Occupational Health and Safety Magazine* (July 2018), https://ohsonline.com/Articles/2018/07/01/The-Far-Reaching-Positive-Impact.aspx?Page=1 (accessed November 22, 2019).

76. Reidy, J., and D. Hewick, "Are Employer Drug-Testing Programs Obsolete?,"*SHRM* (May 23, 2018), https://www.shrm.org/hr-today/news/hr-magazine/0618/pages/are-employer-drug-testing-programs-obsolete.aspx (accessed November 22, 2019); Pinsker, J., "The Pointlessness of the Workplace Drug Test," *The Atlantic* (June 4, 2015), https://www.theatlantic.com/business/archive/2015/06/drug-testing-effectiveness/394850/ (accessed November 22, 2019).

77. Substance Abuse and Mental Health Services Administration, "Federal Contractors and Grantees," Department of Health and Human Services, https://www.samhsa.gov/workplace/legal/federal-laws/contractors-grantees (accessed November 22, 2019).

78. 868 F.2d 74 (3d Cir. 1989).

79. National Safety Council, "Implications of Drug and Alcohol Use for Employers Alcohol," (September 2019), https://www.nsc.org/work-safety/safety-topics/drugs-at-work/substances (accessed November 25, 2019).

80. 489 U.S. 656 (1989).

81. *National Treasury Employees Union v. Von Raab,* 489 U.S. 656 (1989).

82. 520 U.S. 305 (1997).

83. *American Fed'n of State, Cnty. & Mun. Emps. Council79 v. Scott,* 717 F. 3d 851 (11th 2013), cert. denied.

84. "State by State Legal Status Guide: Workplace Drug and Alcohol Testing Laws," Alere Toxicology (August 2016), https://www.edrugtest.com/Messages_from_Admin/State-bystatelaw_Guide_89046.pdf (accessed December 3, 2019).

85. National Conference of State Legislatures, "State Medical Marijuana Laws" (October 16, 2019), http://www.ncsl.org/research/health/state-medical-marijuana-laws.aspx (accessed December 3, 2019).

86. Ibid.

87. Ibid.

88. Ayers, A., "Implications of HIPAA and Employee Confidentiality Rules on Positive Drug Test Results," *The Journal of Urgent Care Medicine* (January 1, 2018), https://www.jucm.com/implications-hipaa-employee-confidentiality-rules-positive-drug-test-results/ (accessed November 20, 2019).

89. Smith, P., "New Jersey Court Rules Employee Fired for Using Medical Marijuana May Sue for Disability Discrimination; What Does This Mean for Iowa Employers?," *Iowa Employment Law Blog* (April 10, 2019), https://www.iowaemploymentlawblog.com/2019/04/articles/disability-discrimination/new-jersey-court-rules-employee-fired-for-using-medical-marijuana-may-sue-for-disability-discrimination-what-does-this-mean-for-iowa-employers/ (accessed November 20, 2019).

90. *Wild vs. Carriage Funeral Holdings, Inc., et al.,* A-3072-17T3 (N.J. Super. Ct. App. Div. Mar. 27, 2019), https://law.justia.com/cases/new-jersey/appellate-division-published/2019/a3072-17.html (accessed November 20, 2019).

91. *Barbuto v. Advantage Sales and Marketing, LLC,* 78 N.E.3d 37 (Mass. Sup. Ct. 2017).

92. Knapp, V., "The Impact of Legalized Marijuana in the Workplace," 2015 S&H Labor & Employment Conference (April 23, 2015), https://shermanhoward.com/wp-content/uploads/2015/04/General-Session.pdf (accessed March 5, 2020).

93. Hasse, J., "Drug Testing at Work Is a Thing of the Past, Study Finds," *Forbes* (August 5, 2019), https://www.forbes.com/sites/javierhasse/2019/08/05/drug-testing-at-work/#381d1c503fa7 (accessed December 5, 2019); Reidy, J., and D. Hewick, "Are Employer Drug-Testing Programs Obsolete?," *SHRM.org* (May 23, 2018), https://www.shrm.org/hr-today/news/hr-magazine/0618/pages/are-employer-drug-testing-programs-obsolete.aspx (accessed December 5, 2019).

94. Henze, I., "Cannabis and Employment Law," National Conference of State Legislatures (October, 2019), http://www.ncsl.org/research/labor-and-employment/cannabis-employment-laws.aspx (accessed December 5, 2019).

95. Harris, M., "The Lie Generator: Inside the Black Mirror World of Polygraph Job Screenings," *Wired* (October 1, 2018), https://www.wired.com/story/inside-polygraph-job-screening-black-mirror/ (accessed December 5, 2019).

96. American Polygraph Association, "Accredited Polygraph Schools" (December 6, 2019), https://www.apapolygraph.org/accredited-programs (accessed December 7, 2019).

97. 523 U.S. 303 (1998).

98. The National Academy of Science, Board on Behavioral, Cognitive, and Sensory Sciences, *The Polygraph and Lie Detection.* Washington, DC: The National Academies Press, 2003.

99. Taylor, M., "Feds Expand Polygraph Screening, Often Seeking Intimate Facts," McClatchy (December 6, 2012), http://www.mcclatchydc.com/news/special-reports/article24741145.html (accessed December 4, 2019).

100. Harris, M., "The Lie Generator: Inside the Black Mirror World of Polygraph Job Screenings," *Wired* (October 1, 2018), https://www.wired.com/story/inside-polygraph-job-screening-black-mirror/ (accessed December 5, 2019).

101. Guerin, L., "State Laws on Polygraphs and Lie Detector Tests," NOLO (2019), http://www.nolo.com/legal-encyclopedia/state-laws-polygraphs-lie-detector-tests.html (accessed December 5, 2019).

102. U.S. Equal Employment Opportunity Commission, "Genetic Information Discrimination" (undated), https://www.eeoc.gov/laws/types/genetic.cfm (accessed December 3, 2019).

103. U.S. National Library of Medicine, "What Is Genetic Discrimination?" *Genetics Home Reference* (April 20, 2016), https://ghr.nlm.nih.gov/primer/testing/discrimination (accessed December 6, 2019).

104. National Human Genome Research Institute, "Genome Statue and Legislative Database" (2019), https://www.genome.gov/about-genomics/policy-issues/Genome-Statute-Legislation-Database (accessed December 6, 2019).

105. U.S. Equal Employment Opportunity Commission, "What You Should Know about HIV/AIDS & Employment Discrimination," https://www.eeoc.gov/eeoc/newsroom/wysk/hiv_aids_discrimination.cfm (accessed December 5, 2019).

106. 129 S. Ct. 2658 (2009).

107. 457 F.2d 348 (5th Cir. 1972).

108. Ibid.

109. Smith, A.,"Yahoo's Forced Ranking Raises Legal Questions about Ratings," *SHRM.org* (February 4, 2016), https://www.shrm.org/ResourcesAndTools/legal-and-compliance/employment-law/Pages/Yahoo-forced-ranking.aspx (accessed December 7, 2019).

110. Lee, W., "U.S. District Court Dismisses Yahoo Gender Discrimination Lawsuit," *San Francisco Chronicle* (March 14, 2018), https://www.sfchronicle.com/business/article/Yahoo-gender-discrimination-lawsuit-dismissed-12747779.php (accessed December 7, 2019).

111. 490 U.S. 228 (1989).

112. Baker, M., and K. Cornelson, "The Tall and the Short of the Returns to Height," NBER Working Paper No. w26325 (September 2019), https://ssrn.com/abstract=3461493 (accessed December 8, 2019); Schrager, A., "There Are Real Advantages to Being Tall, and It Can't Just Be Explained by Personality," *Yahoo! Finance* (October 3, 2019), https://finance.yahoo.com/news/real-advantages-being-tall-t-154838805.html (accessed December 8, 2019).

113. Moro, A., and S. Tello-Trillo, "The Impact of Obesity on Wages: The Role of Personal Interactions and Job Selection," *Labour* 33, no. 2 (June 2019), pp. 125–146, https://onlinelibrary.wiley.com/doi/abs/10.1111/labr.12145 (accessed December 7, 2019); Knapton, S., "Size Does Matter: Tall Men and Slender Women Earn More throughout Life," *The Telegraph* (March 18, 2016), https://www.telegraph.co.uk/news/science/science-news/12187872/Size-does-matter-tall-men-and-slender-women-earn-more-throughout-life.html (accessed December 8, 2019).

114. Lebowitz, S., "'It's an Ugly Fact of Life': Your Hair Can Sabotage Your Success at Work," *Business Insider* (September 4, 2018), https://www.businessinsider.com/professional-hairstyle-gender-racial-stereotypes-2018-8 (accessed December 8, 2019).

115. Bates, K., "New Evidence Shows There's Still Bias Against Black Natural Hair," *NPR-Code Switch,* (Feb 6, 2017), https://www.npr.org/sections/codeswitch/2017/02/06/512943035/new-evidence-shows-theres-still-bias-against-black-natural-hair (accessed December 7, 2019).

116. 411 U.S. 792 (1973).

117. Guerin, L., "Defamation Lawsuits: Do You Have a Case against a Former Employer?" NOLO (2016), http://www.nolo.com/legal-encyclopedia/defamation-lawsuits-do-you-have-case-against-former-employer.html (accessed December 8, 2019).

118. Note, however, that there is long-standing arbitral precedent that the decision as to the severity of a penalty is a matter of management discretion and that the exercise of that discretion should not be disturbed unless it can be shown that it was exercised in an arbitrary, capricious, or discriminatory fashion. See, e.g., *Stockham Pipe Fittings,* 1 LA 160 (1945).

119. *Chertkova v. Connecticut General Life Insurance,* 71 FEP Cases 1006 (2d Cir. 1996).

120. See *Hanchard v. Facilities Development Corporation,* 10 IER Cases 1004 (N.Y. App. 1995); *Gipson v. KAS Snacktime Company,* 71 FEP Cases 1677 (E.D. Mo. 1994).

121. 42 LA 555, 557–59 (1964).

122. 268 F.3d 1095 (D.C. Cir. 2001), cert. denied, 122 S. Ct. 2356 (2002).

Cases

National Treasury Employees Union v. Von Raab, *489 U.S. 656 (1989)*

The U.S. Customs Service implemented a drug-screening program that required urinalysis tests of service employees who wanted to be transferred or promoted to positions where there might be some contact with drugs, such as confiscation, or where the employee might have to carry a firearm or handle classified material. The program provides that the results of the test may not be turned over to any other agency without the employee's written consent. The petitioners, a federal employees' union and one of its officials, sued claiming a violation of the Fourth Amendment. The district court agreed and enjoined the program because the plan was overly intrusive without probable cause or reasonable suspicion. The court of appeals vacated the injunction, holding that this type of search was reasonable in light of its limited scope and the service's strong interest in detecting drug use among employees in certain positions. The Supreme Court affirmed in connection with positions involving contact with drugs and/or firearms but vacated and remanded the decision in regard to those positions that require handling of classified materials.

Kennedy, J.

* * *

In *Skinner v. Railway Labor Executives Assn.,* decided today, we held that federal regulations requiring employees of private railroads to produce urine samples for chemical testing implicate the Fourth Amendment, as those tests invade reasonable expectations of privacy. Our earlier cases have settled that the Fourth Amendment protects individuals from unreasonable searches conducted by the Government, even when the Government acts as an employer and, in view of our holding in *Railway Labor* that urine tests are searches, it follows that the Customs Service's drug testing program must meet the reasonableness requirement of the Fourth Amendment.

While we have often emphasized and reiterate today that a search must be supported, as a general matter, by warrant issued upon probable cause, our decision in *Railway Labor* reaffirms the longstanding principle that neither a warrant nor probable cause, nor, indeed, any measure of individualized suspicion, is an indispensable component of reasonableness in every circumstance. As we note in *Railway Labor,* our cases establish that where a Fourth Amendment intrusion serves special governmental needs, beyond the normal need for law enforcement, it is necessary to balance the individual's privacy expectations against the Government's interests to determine whether it is impractical to require a warrant or some level of individualized suspicion in the particular context.

It is clear that the Customs Service's drug testing program is not designed to serve the ordinary needs of law enforcement. Test results may not be used in criminal prosecution of the employee without the employee's consent. The purposes of the program are to deter drug use among those eligible for promotion to sensitive positions within the Service and to prevent the promotion of drug users to those positions. These substantial interests, no less than the Government's concern for safe rail transportation at issue in *Railway Labor,* present a special need that may justify departure from the ordinary warrant and probable cause requirements.

Petitioners do not contend that a warrant is required by the balance of privacy and governmental interests in this context, nor could any such contention withstand scrutiny. We have recognized that requiring the Government to procure a warrant for every work-related intrusion "would conflict with 'the common sense realization that government offices could not function if every employment decision became a constitutional matter.'"

Even where it is reasonable to dispense with the warrant requirement in the particular circumstances, a search ordinarily must be based on probable cause. . . . We think Customs employees who are directly involved in the interdiction of illegal drugs or who are required to carry firearms in the line of duty likewise have a diminished expectation of privacy in respect to intrusions occasioned by a urine test. Because successful performance of their duties depends uniquely on their judgment and dexterity, these employees cannot reasonably expect to keep from the Service personal information that bears directly on their fitness.

In sum, we believe that the Government has demonstrated that its compelling interests in safeguarding our borders and the public safety outweigh the privacy expectations of employees who seek to be promoted to positions that directly involve the interdiction of illegal drugs or who are required to carry a firearm. We hold that the testing of these employees is reasonable under the Fourth Amendment.

Case Questions

1. An approved drug use test must be conducted within reasonable parameters. In *Capua,* the court determined that a urine collection process may not be reasonable if "done under close surveillance of a government representative [as it] is likely to be a very embarrassing and humiliating experience." Courts will generally balance the employee's rights against the employer's stated basis for the test and determine whether the cause of the test is reasonable and substantial. For instance, in *Skinner v. Railway Labor Executives Assn.,* the Supreme Court stated that the railway employees had a reduced expectation of privacy due to the highly regulated nature of the industry. In addition, societal interests, such as safety and security of the railways, may outweigh the individual employee's privacy interests. When might this be the case?

2. Why do you think the Court made a distinction between positions involving contact with drugs and firearms and positions that require handling of classified materials?

Noffsinger v. SSC Niantic Operating Co., LLC, d/b/a Bride Brook Health & Rehab. Ctr., *2018*

Case 2

U.S. Dist. LEXIS 150453 (D. Conn. Sept. 5, 2018).

A federal court in Connecticut has held that refusing to hire a medical marijuana user who tested positive on a preemployment drug test violates the state's medical marijuana law. The court granted summary judgment to the applicant on her claim for employment discrimination but declined to award her attorneys' fees or punitive damages.

Meyer, D.J.

* * *

This is a case about a claim of employment discrimination on the basis of a person's use of medical marijuana as authorized under the Connecticut Palliative Use of Marijuana Act (PUMA), Conn. Gen. Stat. § 21a-408 et seq. PUMA prescribes qualifying conditions for a person to use marijuana for medicinal purposes. It also contains an anti-discrimination provision that bars an employer from refusing to hire a person or from discharging, penalizing or threatening an employee solely because of the person's status as a qualifying medical marijuana patient under state law. See Conn. Gen. Stat. § 21a-408p(b)(3). Plaintiff Katelin Noffsinger accepted a job offer from defendant SSC Niantic Operating Company, LLC d/b/a Bride Brook Health & Rehabilitation Center. But the offer was contingent on drug testing, and plaintiff told defendant that she was qualified under PUMA to use marijuana for medical purposes to treat her post-traumatic stress disorder. After her drug test came back positive for THC consistent with the use of marijuana, defendant rescinded its job offer. Plaintiff soon filed this lawsuit against defendant. I have previously ruled that PUMA creates a private right of action and that PUMA's anti-discrimination provision is not preempted by federal law. See *Noffsinger v. SSC Niantic Operating Co. LLC,* 273 F. Supp. 3d 326 (D. 2 Conn. 2017). Since then the parties have conducted discovery and have now cross-moved for summary judgment. For the reasons set forth below, I conclude that plaintiff is entitled to judgment as a matter of law in her favor on her claim of employment discrimination under PUMA.

The parties have cross-moved for summary judgment on plaintiff's claim that defendant discriminated against her in violation of PUMA when it rescinded her job offer. The statute provides in relevant part:

[U]nless required by federal law or required to obtain funding: . . . (3) No employer may refuse to hire a person or may discharge, penalize or threaten an employee solely on the basis of such person's or employee's status as a qualifying patient or primary caregiver under sections 21a-408 to 21a-408n, inclusive. Nothing in this subdivision shall restrict an employer's ability to prohibit the use of intoxicating substances during work hours or restrict an employer's ability to discipline an employee for being under the influence of intoxicating substances during work hours. Conn. Gen. Stat. § 21a-408p(b)(3).

The facts are undisputed here that plaintiff's job offer was rescinded because of her positive drug test result and that this positive drug test result stemmed from plaintiff's use of medical marijuana pursuant to her qualifying status under PUMA. Although defendant raises several arguments to avoid the grant of summary judgment, I conclude for the reasons below that all of these arguments are meritless.

First, defendant argues that it is exempt from PUMA's anti-discrimination provision because the statute allows for an exception if discrimination is "required by federal law or required to obtain federal funding." Conn. Gen. Stat. § 21a-408p(b). According to defendant, the federal Drug Free Workplace Act (DFWA) barred it from hiring plaintiff. The DFWA requires federal contractors like defendant to make a "good faith effort" to maintain a drug-free workplace by taking certain measures, such as publishing a statement regarding use of illegal drugs in the workplace and establishing a drug-free awareness program. See 41 U.S.C. § 8102. Defendant states that it adopted its substance abuse policy in order to comply with the DFWA, such that any actions it takes in accordance with that policy are outside the scope of liability under § 21a-408p. I do not agree that the DFWA required defendant to rescind plaintiff's job offer. The DFWA does not require drug testing. See *Harris v. Aerospace Testing All.,* 2008 WL 111979, at *4 (E.D. Tenn. 2008). Nor does the DFWA prohibit federal contractors from employing someone who uses illegal drugs outside of the workplace, much less an employee who uses medical marijuana outside the workplace in accordance with a program approved by state law.

That defendant has chosen to utilize a zero tolerance drug testing policy in order to maintain a drug free work environment does not mean that this policy was actually "required by federal law or required to obtain federal funding." Accordingly, I reject defendant's argument that it would violate the DFWA for it to hire someone like plaintiff who uses medical marijuana during offhours.

Case Questions

1. The Supremacy Clause of the U.S. Constitution states that if there is a conflict between federal and state law, federal law wins. Given that that the federal government still criminalizes all uses of marijuana, did the judge in this case rule correctly?

2. The Drug Free Workplace Act requires federal contractors like the defendant in this case to make a "good faith effort" to maintain a drug-free workplace. Wouldn't a zero-tolerance policy for all federally illegal drugs qualify as a "good faith effort"? Would the argument in this case change if the defendant was not a federal contractor but simply a private company in Connecticut not soliciting federal contracts?

 Case 3

Caraballo-Caraballo v. Corr. Admin.,
829 F.3d 53 (1st Cir. 2018)

Corrections Officer Vilmarie Caraballo-Caraballo filed this Title VII gender discrimination action against her employer, the Corrections Department of the Commonwealth of Puerto Rico, after she was transferred and replaced by one male employee and then, after the transfer of that employee, by a second male employee. C.O. Caraballo had a high school diploma and had worked in the Radio Communications Area for six years before being transferred to the Inmate Commissary. Her replacement had an associate's degree in computer programming and a license from a radio communications association. Caraballo's supervisor requested her return to the Radio Area but was denied with no explanation.

Lipez, C.J.

* * *

Caraballo filed a charge of gender discrimination with the EEOC and subsequently initiated this action in May 2012. Her complaint alleged that the Department's decision to transfer her and to replace her with Cordero and then Anaya was motivated by gender discrimination. The district court granted summary judgment to the Department on each claim. . . This appeal followed.

In challenging the district court's entry of summary judgment on her disparate treatment claim, Caraballo contends that the Department's initial decision to replace her with Cordero and its subsequent decision to select Anaya—instead of her—as Cordero's replacement were both based on her gender. Disparate treatment claims under Title VII are ordinarily subject to the familiar

McDonnell Douglas burden-shifting framework. The district court described Caraballo's prima facie case as requiring her to show that, "(1) she is a member of a protected class; (2) she was qualified [for the position]; (3) she suffered an adverse employment action; and (4) someone else holding similar qualifications was chosen or selected for the same position." In the ensuing discussion, we refer to the second element as the "job qualifications" element, the fourth element as the "similar qualifications" element, and the two elements collectively as the "qualifications elements."[. . .]

After reciting the elements of Caraballo's prima facie case, the court found that she had satisfied the first three elements, but failed to meet the similar qualifications element. The court compared Caraballo's credentials to Cordero's, and found Caraballo's credentials wanting. . . The court limited its analysis to this comparison of Caraballo's and Cordero's educational credentials. Relying on our decision in *Johnson,* 714 F.3d at 54, it reasoned that "[t]he qualifications [Caraballo] obtained through experience, good work, and reputation may not be used to prove her to be similarly situated to Cordero." This application of *Johnson* was incorrect.

Johnson thus stands for the straightforward proposition that where an employer requires minimum qualifications for an open position that are "reasonable on [their] face and . . . plainly legitimate," a plaintiff ordinarily cannot rely on her experience and reputation to show that she was qualified for the position if she does not possess the qualifications specified by the employer. That holding is inapposite to the similar qualifications element of the prima facie showing in Caraballo's discriminatory transfer case.

Under the *McDonnell Douglas* framework, the requirements of a plaintiff's prima facie case "can vary depending on the context and were 'never intended to be rigid, mechanized, or ritualistic.'[. . .]"

In failure to hire or promote cases, the plaintiff is ordinarily vying for an open position, for which the employer has established certain minimum qualifications. Courts thus assess the plaintiff's qualifications in light of the employer's stated job requirements. If the plaintiff does not possess the requisite qualifications, she ordinarily cannot raise an inference that her protected characteristic, rather than her lack of qualifications, accounted for the employer's failure to hire or promote her. Likewise, the plaintiff in such cases ordinarily cannot create an inference of discrimination by arguing that, on the basis of experience and reputation, she was similarly qualified as a successful applicant who did possess the qualifications specified by the employer . In discharge or transfer cases, however, the employer "has already expressed a belief that [the plaintiff] is minimally qualified," by previously "hiring the employee." *Gregory v. Daly,* 243 F.3d 687, 696 (2d Cir. 2001). Accordingly, in such cases, courts will rarely need to compare the plaintiff's credentials with the employer's stated job requirements. Instead, the plaintiff's ability to satisfy the job qualifications element will ordinarily depend on whether she was successfully performing her job at the time of her discharge or transfer, such that she did not disqualify herself by performing poorly. Likewise, the fact that the employer has already deemed the plaintiff minimally qualified undermines any basis for preventing the plaintiff from relying on her experience and reputation in establishing the similar qualifications element. As described above, we have only applied that rule to the similar qualifications element in cases such as Johnson where the plaintiff is not minimally qualified but her comparator is [. . . .]

Instead of preventing Caraballo from relying on her work experience, the district court should have compared Caraballo to Cordero "in all relevant respects." *Conward v. Cambridge Sch. Comm.,* 171 F.3d 12, 20 (1st Cir. 1999). The court must decide "whether a prudent person, looking objectively" at the plaintiff and her comparator "would think them roughly equivalent," and similarly qualified for the position. *Vélez,* 585 F.3d at 451 (quoting *Perkins v. Brigham & Women's Hosp.,* 78 F.3d 747, 752 (1st Cir. 1996))[. . . .]

By the time of her transfer, Caraballo had six years of experience working in the Radio Communications Area. Her performance during that time was so successful that her immediate supervisor, Sepúlveda, wanted her returned to the position after she was transferred. This successful tenure in the Radio Communications Area would allow a reasonable person to conclude that Caraballo's qualifications were similar— if not superior—to Cordero's, despite his better educational credentials.

Turning to Caraballo's second replacement, the district court failed to assess whether Caraballo and Anaya were similarly qualified. The record indicates that the Department transferred Anaya to the Radio Communications Area shortly after it transferred Cordero to that unit. When the Department reassigned Cordero a couple of months later, Sepúlveda asked that Caraballo be returned to her former position. Instead, the Department selected Anaya for the position. At that time, Anaya's qualifications consisted of a couple of months' experience working in the Radio Communications Area. This qualification pales in comparison to Caraballo's six years of experience in her prior position[. . . .]

Caraballo thus satisfied the similar qualifications element of her prima facie case by showing that she was similarly qualified to both Anaya and Cordero. The district court's conclusion to the contrary rested on an erroneous extension of our decision in Johnson, and on its neglect of a relevant comparator, Anaya[. . . .]

Caraballo has thus established a prima facie case of gender discrimination. She was successfully performing her position, was adversely transferred, and was twice replaced by someone whom a reasonable person could consider similarly (or less) qualified. Caraballo's satisfaction of the prima facie step of the *McDonnell Douglas* framework creates an inference of discrimination, requiring the Corrections Department to produce a legitimate, nondiscriminatory justification for its action. However, the Department's briefing before the district court did not even attempt to offer such a justification. Because Caraballo established a prima facie case of gender discrimination that her employer failed to rebut, the district court erred by granting summary judgment in the Department's favor. We thus vacate the district court's grant of summary judgment as to Caraballo's disparate treatment claim, and remand for further proceedings consistent with this opinion.

Case Questions

1. What is the distinction the court is making between what the district court did in comparing Caraballo's education credentials with Cordero's versus comparing their existing experience after employment?

2. How could a performance appraisal play a role in changing the outcome of this disparate treatment discrimination case?

Part 2

Regulation of Discrimination in Employment

Hi. Yes, we're speaking to you. Yes, we actually *do* know you're there. We think about you all the time. With each and every word we write. From the very beginning of this textbook more than 25 years ago, our *constant* thought in writing this text for you has always been: How can we say this so they "get it"? What information do they need to know in order to prevent workplace liability? What interesting cases can we choose that will best illustrate our point? What cases can we choose that will not only give them insight into how the court thinks so they will know what to consider when making workplace decisions themselves but will also demonstrate how a manager or supervisor should or should not act in this situation so he or she will not cause liability for the employer? All for you.

We have read thousands of cases, studies, journals, news, and magazine articles. Perhaps just as important, we have spoken with thousands of employers, managers, supervisors, employees, and students. We do this all with an eye toward how we can better tell you what you need to know to avoid unnecessary and preventable workplace liability.

What we've found over the years is that when it comes to the subject matter covered in this section, telling you the law is simply not enough. The subject matter of this section is much more personal than just the laws, per se. It calls upon you as managers and supervisors to make decisions that call into play your own personal narratives—that is, your worldview based on your experiences, upbringing, family, friends, and so on. As such, we would be remiss if we did not approach this area a bit differently—a way that is not geared to giving you all you need to make defensible workplace decisions. We have found through our extensive experience that it is necessary to give you not only the law but also a solid grounding in the background and history of certain areas so you will understand the issues more thoroughly and thus avoid liability because you will make better, more informed workplace decisions.

For nearly 40 years we have been on a quest to deconstruct how workplace managers make the decisions that cause liability for the employer so that we can share that information with you and prevent you from making the same mistakes when you are in that position. We hate to see employers pay out money in judgments or settlements for completely unnecessary, avoidable liability. We hate the thought of our students or readers being the cause of actions in the workplace that result in liability for the employer. All could have been so easily avoided.

The things you see in the chapters in this section reflect that. We understand that in choosing to take our approach, we may come off as sounding "preachy." What we are actually doing is stepping outside the pure law to give you better information and more context because we know from our extensive experience that this is how decisions are made and how the courts will judge them.

So, as you read the chapters in this section, keep in mind that what appears to be outside the pure law is included in order to give you what you need to be able to make better decisions in the workplace. If it seems like we're preaching, maybe we are. We are passionate about teaching you what you need to know to avoid unnecessary workplace liability about these issues. If it takes sounding preachy, we'll own it—just so you understand that the preaching comes straight from the law and research and is put there to help you better do your job for your employer.

Chapter 5

Affirmative Action

Ryan McVay/Getty Images

Learning Objectives

After completing this chapter, you should be able to:

LO1 Discuss what affirmative action is and why it was created.

LO2 Provide the results of several studies indicating why there continues to be a need to take more than a passive approach to equal employment opportunity.

LO3 Name and explain the three types of affirmative action.

LO4 Explain when affirmative action plans are required and how they are created.

LO5 List the basic safeguards put in place in affirmative action plans to minimize harm to others.

LO6 Define "reverse discrimination" and tell how it relates to affirmative action.

LO7 Explain the arguments of those opposed to affirmative action and those who support it.

LO8 Explain the concept of valuing diversity/multiculturalism/diversity, equity, and inclusion and why it is needed and give examples of ways to do it.

Opening Scenarios

SCENARIO 1

1 A union has not permitted African Americans to become a part of its ranks because of opposition from white union members. Black employees win when they sue to join. The court orders appropriate remedies. The union still resists African Americans as members. Eventually the court orders that the union admit a certain number of African Americans by a certain time or be held in contempt of court. Is this a permissible remedy under Title VII?

SCENARIO 2

2 An employer is concerned that her workplace has only a few African Americans, Latinxs, Asians, and women in upper-level management and skilled-labor jobs. Most unskilled-labor and clerical positions are held by women and minorities. The employer decides to institute a program that will increase the numbers of minorities and women in management and skilled-labor positions. Is this permissible? Do you have all the relevant facts needed to decide? Explain.

SCENARIO 3

3 An employer is found by a court to have discriminated. As part of an appropriate remedy, the employer is ordered to promote one female for every male who is promoted until the desired goal is met. Male employees who would have been next in line for promotions under the old system sue the employer, alleging "reverse discrimination" in that the new promotees are being hired on the basis of gender and the suing employees are being harmed because of their gender. Who wins, and why?

Statutory Basis

Except in the contracts exempted in accordance with Section 204 of this Order, all Government contracting agencies shall include in every Government contract hereafter entered into the following provisions:

During the performance of this contract, the contractor agrees as follows:

(1) The contractor will not discriminate against any employee or applicant for employment because of race, color, religion, sex, or national origin. The contractor will take affirmative action to ensure that applicants are employed, and that employees are treated during employment, without regard to their race, color, religion, sex, or national origin. Such action shall include, but not be limited to, the following: employment, upgrading, demotion, or transfer; recruitment or recruitment advertising; layoff or termination; rates of pay or other forms of compensation; and selection for training, including apprenticeship. [202, Executive Order 11246.]

****

If the court finds that respondent has intentionally engaged in or is intentionally engaging in an unlawful employment practice charged in the complaint, the court may enjoin the respondent from engaging in such unlawful employment practice, and order such affirmative action as may be appropriate, which may include, but is not limited to, reinstatement or hiring of employees. . . or any other equitable relief as the court deems appropriate. [Section 706(g) of Title VII of the Civil Rights Act of 1964, 42 U.S.C. § 2000e, sec. 706(g).]

****

(a) *General purpose.* An affirmative action program is a management tool designed to ensure equal employment opportunity and foster employment opportunities for individuals with disabilities. An affirmative action program institutionalizes the contractor's commitment to equality in every aspect of employment and is more than a paperwork exercise. An affirmative action program is dynamic in nature and includes measurable objectives, quantitative analyses, and internal auditing and reporting systems that measure the contractor's progress toward achieving equal employment opportunity for individuals with disabilities.

(b) *Applicability of the affirmative action program.* (1) The requirements of this subpart apply to every Government contractor that has 50 or more employees and a contract of $50,000 or more.

(2) Contractors described in paragraph (b)(1) of this section shall, within 120 days of the commencement of a contract, prepare and maintain an affirmative action program at each establishment. The affirmative action program shall set forth the contractor's policies and procedures in accordance with this part. This program may be integrated into or kept separate from other affirmative action programs.

(3) The affirmative action program shall be reviewed and updated annually by the official designated by the contractor pursuant to §60-741.44(i).

****

Under the affirmative action obligations imposed by the act, contractors shall not discriminate because of physical or mental disability and shall take affirmative action to employ and advance in employment qualified individuals with disabilities at all levels of employment, including the executive level. Such action shall apply to all employment activities set forth in §60-741.20. [41 CFR Part 60-740, 60-741.43.]

****

*2035 (a) (1) Any contract in the amount of $100,000 or more entered into by any department or agency of the United States for the procurement of personal property and nonpersonal services (including construction) for the United States, shall contain a provision requiring that the party contracting with the United States take affirmative action to employ and advance in employment qualified covered veterans. This section applies to any subcontract in the amount of $100,000 or more entered into by a prime contractor in carrying out any such contract. [Jobs for Veterans Act of 2002, 38 U.S.C.A. § 4212(a)(1).]

The Design and Unstable History

Note: Several pieces of legislation contain affirmative action provisions, but we are here primarily devoting coverage to areas covered by Title VII of the Civil Rights Act of 1964 and Executive Order 11246.

Introduction

Let's just get this out right up front in this chapter: Everyone wants to believe we live in a meritocracy and that we get what we work hard for. No one wants to be given anything just because they belong to a certain gender, race, or ethnic group. Period. Now that this is clear, let's move on.

affirmative action
Intentional inclusion of women and minorities in the workplace based on a finding of their previous exclusion.

Noise. There is a lot of it around the concept of **affirmative action**. It can be difficult to turn off the noise and determine what is real and what is not. Did you ever hear someone say, "We *have* to hire an African American" or "We *have* to hire a woman"? Such a statement is likely rooted somewhere in the concept of affirmative action. While there may be truth somewhere in the statement, it is probably far from what it appears to be. Many mistakenly think affirmative action is a law that takes qualified whites or males out of their jobs and gives the jobs to unqualified or less-qualified minorities or females or that affirmative action is an entitlement program that provides unqualified women or minorities with jobs while qualified whites or males, or both, are shut out of the workplace. According to the EEOC Compliance Manual, affirmative action is "actions appropriate to overcome the effects of past or present practices, policies, or other barriers to equal employment opportunity."[1] In fact, individuals with disabilities as well as veterans are also a part of affirmative action.

Imagine sitting at a nice upscale restaurant enjoying a great meal. At the table next to yours is what appear to be a mother and a daughter in her early twenties. Suddenly the mother raises her hand and slaps the daughter hard across the face. Everything stops. Everyone in the restaurant is shocked. You are appalled. You think the mother must be crazy for doing such a thing, and you find yourself being angry with the mother for such a violent, heartless, embarrassing public spectacle.

Imagine your surprise when you learn that from birth the daughter has sporadically suffered violent seizures that put her life in danger. She has managed to live a fairly normal life and is an honor student in her senior year of college, but occasionally, for no particular reason that doctors can discern, she will have one of these seizures. She gets a certain look in her eyes when the seizure is about to occur, and the only way it can be prevented is to immediately slap her hard across the face.

What a difference knowledge and context make. What may appear as one thing without knowing the facts and context can seem quite different when you do. We find that our students and most employees we meet during consulting dislike affirmative action. However, they rarely know what it actually is, and they know even less about its context. Seen from their experience of living in a post–Title VII world, where people think everyone is operating by the same rules in employment and not giving a lot of thought to discrimination, it makes no sense at all to have race or gender play any part whatsoever in an employment or any other decision, they think. However, once they learn what it is, why it was created, and the reality of the relevant issues, they have a better foundation upon which to base their opinion. Whether it changes their opinion (and it usually does) is up to them, but at least now they are basing that opinion on fact and reality rather than misconceptions. This is extremely important for making workplace decisions.

Affirmative Action's Misunderstandings Based on Race

Most of the anger around affirmative action stems from the issue of race. Despite the fact that white women have made the most gains under affirmative action,[2] there is still the basic view that African Americans are getting something others are not, simply because they are African American, and this makes people angry. Perhaps, as with our students and attendees at our consulting sessions, viewing affirmative action in the context of a rough timeline will give you more information and a context for the law and thus a clearer view. It puts what nowadays appears to be a ridiculously unfair legal requirement into its proper context, thus making it more understandable. You may recall some of this from our discussion on the history leading up to Title VII, but it bears repeating where necessary, in this context. Keep in mind that this is history, not a judgment of history.

1619—First slaves arrive in America. As we discussed in the Title VII chapter (Chapter 3), slavery is a way of life for African Americans, who have virtually no other role in American society for the next 246 years. Personnel are not available to constantly watch over slaves every minute of the day, so methods are developed to keep them in line without the need for constant supervision. Slave Codes, violence, and policies and actions that make them aware of their subjugation every minute of every day accomplish this mental and physical enslavement. The harshness of our system is what distinguishes the American system of slavery from others that have occurred all over the world.

1865—The Civil War ends. The war had begun four years earlier in 1861 to prevent the South from leaving the Union and establishing its own country in which slavery was permitted.

1865—The Thirteenth Amendment to the Constitution abolishes slavery.

- Shortly thereafter, Slave Codes are replaced by Black Codes.
- After federal troops, which came to the South to make sure slavery actually ended, leave 11 years later (the period called Reconstruction), the white violence against the former slaves continues, and the Ku Klux Klan (KKK) rises and enforces Jim Crow laws keeping Blacks in very much the same position they had been in during slavery.
- Jim Crow continues for the next 100 years, except for public school segregation, which is outlawed by the U.S. Supreme Court in 1954 but is met with serious violent resistance.
- Segregation is so strict that, in 1959, Alabama state librarian Emily Reed is fired for refusing to remove from the library the children's book *A Rabbit's Wedding* despite demands of state senators who say it (and other books like it) should be removed and burned because the groom was a Black bunny and the bride was a white bunny.

1964—Civil Rights Act of 1964 is passed, prohibiting discrimination on the basis of race, color, gender, religion, and national origin in employment, education, receipt of federal funds, and public accommodations.

- The country is in turmoil over African Americans not being able to vote because of remaining restrictive measures instituted after Reconstruction.
- To put this in perspective, 1964 is the year the Beatles burst onto the U.S. music scene.

1965—Civil Rights Act of 1964 becomes effective; the Voting Rights Act of 1965 is passed, allowing African Americans to vote unimpeded for the first time since Reconstruction.

- The country is to go from 346 years of treating African Americans as separate and inferior to being required by law to treat them as equals.
- The Temptations' "My Girl" is a Billboard chart-topper.

1971—First important Title VII case decided by the U.S. Supreme Court, **Griggs v. Duke Power Co.**[3]

- The case is significant because African Americans had never been equal in the United States, so few knew what this picture of equality under Title VII was actually supposed to look like. Is it enough to simply take down the omnipresent "Colored" and "white" signs? The Court said no, it would take more.
- Six years after the law takes effect, *Griggs* made clear that the new law meant equality in every way. Now the country understands that it must take Title VII seriously.
- For perspective, Janis Joplin's "Me and Bobby McGee" is a top hit for the year.

1979—First workplace affirmative action case decided by the U.S. Supreme Court.

- The Court determines that affirmative action is a viable means of effectuating the law and addressing present-day vestiges of the 346-year system that kept African Americans subjugated.
- Perspective: The Village People's hit single "Y.M.C.A." sweeps the country.

1980s—Affirmative action is hotly debated between the presidents, who are opposed, and federal agencies responsible for enforcement of the laws, some of which oppose the law. (See Exhibit 5.1, "1980s Media Statements Regarding Affirmative Action.")

See Chapter 2 to revisit key concepts.

- Employers, seeing these very public disagreements, were confused about what they were required to do but knew they were supposed to do something to bring African Americans and women into the workplace.
- Employers often simply did what they thought they needed to do to try to protect themselves from violating the new law: determined how many minorities and women they needed to prevent disparate impact discrimination suits and simply hired that number.
- This became transformed into the idea of a quota in the eyes of a society that knew little about the law.
- Note that this was not imposed by the government but came about as a result of employers trying to protect themselves and thinking this was the right way to go about it. It was, however, as hard and fast and omnipresent as any law.

Exhibit 5.1 *1980s Media Statements Regarding Affirmative Action*

After the seminal U.S. Supreme Court cases on affirmative action in 1978 and 1979, the concept of affirmative action was really shaped and molded by fallout from the Court's decisions in the 1980s. You can gather from the statements below how divisive the issue was during that time when policy was being formed. This was true even for the federal administrators and others with responsibility in the area. You can imagine why employers who were to implement the law were so confused. Think about how recent this was—there are reruns on TV that go back much further!

3/4/85. "Department of Justice is asking public sector employers to change their negotiated consent decrees [which DOJ had previously pressed for] to eliminate preferential treatment to nonvictims of discrimination." (*BNA Daily Labor Report,* No. 42.)

4/4/85. "Dept. of Justice moves to eliminate quotas called 'betrayal' by Birmingham mayor, in testimony before the Subcommittee on Civil and Constitutional Rights of the House Judiciary Committee. Cites 'remarkable progress' made in bringing blacks into the city's fire and police departments." (*BNA Daily Labor Report,* No. 74.)

5/6/85. "Challenges Mount to Department of Justice's Anti-Quota Moves." (*BNA Daily Labor Report,* No. 87.)

9/16/85. "Congress recently ordered an audit of the U.S. Civil Rights Commission and the EEOC, headed by Clarence Pendleton, Jr., and Clarence Thomas, respectively, to find out if financial and personnel troubles are hurting the way both federal panels are enforcing civil rights laws." (*Jet* magazine, p. 16.)

10/17/85. "Attorney General Meese acknowledges that review of Executive Order 11246 is proceeding at Cabinet level, but dismisses charges that Administration officials are at odds over question of affirmative action." (*BNA Daily Labor Report,* No. 201.)

11/29/85. "Majority of Senate is on record as opposing efforts by Attorney General Meese and others in Administration to alter Executive Order 11246 to prohibit goals and timetables for minority hiring." (*BNA Daily Labor Report,* No. 230.)

5/12/86. "Business Applauded for Opposing Changes in Affirmative Action Order." (*BNA Daily Labor Report,* No. 91.)

7/7/86. "Civil Rights Groups Applaud Supreme Court [for *Cleveland Firefighters and Sheet Metal Workers* decisions upholding affirmative action]; Department of Justice Vows to Continue Bid to Revise Executive Order 11246." (*BNA Daily Labor Report,* No. 129.)

7/7/86. "Labor Department says 'we don't see anything in these cases to suggest a legal necessity to change either the executive order or the OFCCP program.'" (*BNA Daily Labor Report,* No. 129.)

6/4/87. "OFCCP Enforcement Activity Scored by House Labor Staff: Alleged Lack of OFCCP Enforcement Activity Criticized by House Labor Staff." (*BNA Daily Labor Report,* No. 106.)

6/5/87. "DOL Official Defends OFCCP's Performance Against Charges of Declining Enforcement." (*BNA Daily Labor Report,* No. 107.)

7/2/89. "Civil Rights: Is Era Coming to an End? Decades of Change Called into Question by [Supreme Court] Rulings." (*Atlanta Journal and Constitution,* p. A-1.)

- At the same time, politicians took advantage of the disorganization by using tactics such as depictions of whites being fired from jobs in order to hire African Americans—something that was always illegal under the law but that fed into constituents' ignorance and worst fears.[4]

- For perspective: This is the time of Madonna's "Like a Virgin," Michael Jackson's worldwide blockbuster "Thriller," and Cindy Lauper's "Girls Just Wanna Have Fun."

2008—Maudie Hopkins, the last Civil War widow dies.[5]

2008—U.S. House of Representatives apologizes for slavery, Jim Crow, and its aftermath, joining five states that had already issued such resolutions. See Exhibit 5.2, "U.S. House of Representatives Resolution Apologizing for Slavery." The first African American president is elected (and reelected in 2012) but was said to have received more death threats than any president and, because of threats, was the first presidential candidate to be provided with Secret Service protection even before actually became the nominee.

Exhibit 5.2 *U.S. House of Representatives Resolution Apologizing for Slavery*

This is the actual text of the 2008 Congressional Resolution apologizing for slavery. The House was several times presented with the opportunity to pass such a resolution over the years, but it refused, out of fear of a call for reparations. Congress had, however, apologized for its actions toward Native Americans, to Hawaiians for overthrowing their government, and to Japanese interred in World War II internment camps, including paying them money. The resolution was presented by Rep. Steve Cohen (D-TN), the only white legislator to represent the 60 percent Black congressional district in the past 30 years.

H. Res. 194

In the House of Representatives, U.S.,

July 29, 2008

Whereas millions of Africans and their descendants were enslaved in the United States and the 13 American colonies from 1619 through 1865;

Whereas slavery in America resembled no other form of involuntary servitude known in history, as Africans were captured and sold at auction like inanimate objects or animals;

Whereas Africans forced into slavery were brutalized, humiliated, dehumanized, and subjected to the indignity of being stripped of their names and heritage;

Whereas enslaved families were torn apart after having been sold separately from one another;

Whereas the system of slavery and the visceral racism against persons of African descent upon which it depended became entrenched in the Nation's social fabric;

Whereas slavery was not officially abolished until the passage of the 13th Amendment to the United States Constitution in 1865 after the end of the Civil War;

Whereas after emancipation from 246 years of slavery, African-Americans soon saw the fleeting political, social, and economic gains they made during Reconstruction eviscerated by virulent racism, lynchings, disenfranchisement, Black Codes, and racial segregation laws that imposed a rigid system of officially sanctioned racial segregation in virtually all areas of life;

Whereas the system of de jure racial segregation known as 'Jim Crow,' which arose in certain parts of the Nation following the Civil War to create separate and unequal societies for whites and African-Americans, was a direct result of the racism against persons of African descent engendered by slavery;

Whereas a century after the official end of slavery in America, Federal action was required during the 1960s to eliminate the de jure and de facto systems of Jim Crow throughout parts of the Nation, though its vestiges still linger to this day;

Whereas African-Americans continue to suffer from the complex interplay between slavery and Jim Crow—long after both systems were formally abolished—through enormous damage and loss, both tangible and intangible, including the loss of human dignity, the frustration of careers and professional lives, and the long-term loss of income and opportunity;

Whereas the story of the enslavement and de jure segregation of African-Americans and the dehumanizing atrocities committed against them should not be purged from or minimized in the telling of American history;

Whereas on July 8, 2003, during a trip to Goree Island, Senegal, a former slave port, President George W. Bush acknowledged slavery's continuing legacy in American life and the need to confront that legacy when he stated that slavery 'was. . . one of the greatest crimes of history. . . . The racial bigotry fed by slavery did not end with slavery or with segregation. And many of the issues that still trouble America have roots in the bitter experience of other times. But however long the journey, our destiny is set: liberty and justice for all.';

Whereas President Bill Clinton also acknowledged the deep-seated problems caused by the continuing legacy of racism against African-Americans that began with slavery when he initiated a national dialogue about race;

Whereas a genuine apology is an important and necessary first step in the process of racial reconciliation;

Whereas an apology for centuries of brutal dehumanization and injustices cannot erase the past, but confession of the wrongs committed can speed racial healing and reconciliation and help Americans confront the ghosts of their past;

Whereas the legislature of the Commonwealth of Virginia has recently taken the lead in adopting a resolution officially expressing appropriate remorse for slavery and other State legislatures have adopted or are considering similar resolutions; and

Whereas it is important for this country, which legally recognized slavery through its Constitution and its laws, to make a formal apology for slavery and for its successor, Jim Crow, so that it can move forward and seek reconciliation, justice, and harmony for all of its citizens: Now, therefore, be it Resolved, *That the House of Representatives—*

1. acknowledges that slavery is incompatible with the basic founding principles recognized in the Declaration of Independence that all men are created equal;

2. acknowledges the fundamental injustice, cruelty, brutality, and inhumanity of slavery and Jim Crow;

3. apologizes to African-Americans on behalf of the people of the United States, for the wrongs committed against them and their ancestors who suffered under slavery and Jim Crow; and

4. expresses its commitment to rectify the lingering consequences of the misdeeds committed against African-Americans under slavery and Jim Crow and to stop the occurrence of human rights violations in the future.

Attest:
Clerk.

Two things should become apparent in viewing this timeline: (1) affirmative action has not been around for nearly as long as we may think, and (2) the relatively few years it has been on the country's radar screen do not constitute a very long time compared to the 345-year history that created the present-day vestiges of racial discrimination that the concept seeks to remedy.

Clearing the Air

Many people *hate* affirmative action. Most who do generally make that determination based on misconceptions about what it is. (See Exhibit 5.3, "Affirmative Action Realities.") Others simply believe it is ineffective.[6] Several points are of interest here that routinely arise in affirmative action discussions. We will address them up front and then discuss the background and need for the law as well as its provisions.

Exhibit 5.3 *Affirmative Action Realities*

Here are realities based on common misconceptions about affirmative action gathered from students, employees, managers, supervisors, and business owners over the years. See if you recognize any of them.

- Affirmative action does not require employers to remove qualified whites and males from their jobs and give these jobs to minorities and women whether or not they are qualified.
- Affirmative action does not prevent employers from hiring white males who are more qualified for the job.
- Under affirmative action, an applicant need not simply be a female or a minority to be placed in a job.
- The law takes the position that any employee who obtains a job under an affirmative action plan be qualified for the job.
- Workplace productivity and efficiency do not suffer under affirmative action plans.
- We believe we have always lived in a meritocracy in which the best person gets the job. That

simply has not always been true and operated to disadvantage minorities and women.

- There are workplaces where affirmative action is still needed to make sure job applicants have more of a level playing field.
- If a female or minority is in an applicant pool with other non-minority or female candidates, the female or minority need not automatically be hired.
- Employers are to apply to females and minorities the same job requirements they apply to males and non-minorities.
- Affirmative action is not about punishment, reparations, or slavery. As noted in Congress's apology for slavery, it is about the present-day impact of race (and gender) on minorities (and women) in the workplace.
- Minorities and females can and should be terminated from their jobs if they do not perform as required. However, their race or gender may not be the reason for the termination—their actions should be.

As you will see shortly, it is no secret in history that our system was created for the benefit of whites and has done well in that regard. Given the 345-year history between the first Africans arriving in the country in 1619 and the passage of the Civil Rights Act in 1964, it is illogical to believe that without intervention of some sort by the government, things would not continue to proceed as they were designed to do and always had. Taking a *laissez-faire,* or hands-off, approach is not illogical since it did not work in the 99 years before Title VII was passed, and 50-plus years after its passage. There are still significant differences in all facets of society, including employment, based on race and gender, the significant targets of affirmative action. Following are some of the common issues and positions regarding affirmative action, with accompanying responses.[7]

1. One of the most persistent arguments about affirmative action has little logic. The argument is that affirmative action is a bad idea because it undermines the belief that women and minorities are competent. First of all, that is not consistent with affirmative action dictates that applicants be qualified. Also, it ignores the fact that without affirmative action, it is clear that those traditionally excluded from the workplace would continue to be excluded. To take intentional

steps to address this now-unwanted exclusion and then say that those who use such steps are perceived with suspicion is self-serving. Each of us has control over what we think. If we wish to think they are less qualified than others, we can, but such a thought is not an inevitable consequence of affirmative action. Totally excluding a group of people, then realizing your error and setting up a system to address the exclusion, but then castigating those who use the system is like slapping someone and then complaining about the noise when they cry. Logically, had there been no exclusion of Blacks from the beginning, there would be no need for affirmative action to remedy that exclusion. To blame the excluded who now seek inclusion through affirmative action makes no sense.[8]

2. As President Lyndon Johnson said in endorsing the Civil Rights Act of 1964, "You do not take a person who, for years, has been hobbled by chains and liberate him, bring him up to the starting line of a race and then say, 'you are free to compete with all the others,' and still justly believe that you have been completely fair."[9] Conveniently forgetting this history and simply dismissing affirmative action that seeks to bridge that gap as more discrimination is to ignore the difference between the two very different relative positions. Blacks and women are simply not in the same position as those who benefited from a 345-year head start in the American workplace.[10]

3. Affirmative action is not a great idea for anyone concerned, but it is the best the country has managed to come up with given what it had to work with. Color-blindness is the goal of many, but the country is simply not in that place yet. To act as if it is to continue the status quo that ensures it will not be reached.

4. If a person breaks a leg, it is impossible for a doctor to repair it without causing the patient additional pain (without the use of anesthesia). Trying to repair the vestiges of a 345-year system of workplace exclusion of nonwhites presents the same problem. There will be people who feel imposed upon by it. But, as a society, it is a necessary evil if we are to get to a place of equality, just as the further pain in repairing the leg is necessary to repair it. Those who believe affirmative action is only fixing discrimination by more discrimination ignore the fact that there are laws in place that severely limit the negative impact of affirmative action. This is akin to believing that the pain from being beat up for no reason is the same as the pain from having your ruptured appendix removed. Yes, both hurt, but one at least has a good reason and is productive, while the other does not. Everyone wants to have an equal society, but to do so we must be willing to take the steps necessary to make sure it happens, and that will not always feel good to everyone. The solace comes in knowing it is addressing the problem rather than continuing to ignore it. As the country has painfully learned over the years, choosing to ignore a problem of this magnitude is not a solution. It merely continues and worsens the situation.

5. Affirmative action was created by law to address societal, endemic, persistent, systemic discrimination the country had engaged in for centuries. Interpreting it in an individual context is inappropriate. It is not the single person who believes he or she is affected that the law is about. It is the millions who will

continue to suffer if something is not done as well as the millions who continue to benefit from a system designed to exclude certain groups.[11]

6. Most of the attention is on the advantages perceived as benefiting unfairly through affirmative action programs rather than recognizing the impact of exclusion that served as the need for having affirmative action programs in the first place.

Yet and still, you are absolutely entitled to your feelings about affirmative action, whatever they are, but

- You need to know what it actually is rather than what you may have been told or gathered here and there.
- You need to know how and why it applies to the workplace.

In this chapter, we will clear up the misconceptions. We will learn what affirmative action is, what it is not, what the law requires, and whom it affects. If you are like most of our students, what you learn may surprise you. As we go through learning what affirmative action is and what it is intended to do, try to think of what you would do if you were charged with finding a solution for the problem it was created to solve. Even the proponents of affirmative action would prefer that it be unnecessary at all and tend to agree that it is far from a perfect solution. However, given what we have to deal with in ridding the workplace of the vestiges of a 345-year system that still results in discrimination, it is at least the law's attempt. Given all the factors involved, what would be your solution?

One of the first things that may come as a surprise to you about affirmative action is the fact that affirmative action does not apply to all employers. For the most part, it only applies to those with 50 or more employees who have chosen to enter into contracts with the federal government to provide the government with goods or services worth $50,000 or more. This means it covers just over 22 percent of the workforce.[12] As a part of that contract, the government requires the employer to agree not to discriminate in the workplace and, further, to engage in affirmative action if a need is established (discussed later in the chapter). Contracts are completely voluntary agreements that we can choose to enter or not. Just as each of us has the choice to contract or not with businesses whose policies we like or dislike, so too does the federal government. It has decided that it does not want to contract with businesses that discriminate against employees in violation of Title VII.

Despite what you think or may have heard, affirmative action does not require anyone to give up his or her job to someone who is not qualified to hold it. In fact, it generally does not require anyone to give up his or her job at all. It also absolutely does not require that anyone who does not meet the employer's legitimate job requirements be hired. In addition, it does not require quotas. In fact, quotas are, for the most part, illegal. If you are like most of our students, just these few facts alone go against everything you've ever heard about affirmative action.

What Is Affirmative Action?

LO1 Discuss what affirmative action is and why it was created.

At its simplest, affirmative action involves the employer taking steps to ensure equal job opportunities to traditionally excluded groups by bringing qualified women and minorities or other statutorily mandated groups into a workplace *from which it has been determined that they are excluded,* in order to make the workplace more reflective of their availability in the workforce from which the employees are drawn. This would ordinarily happen on its own in the absence of discrimination or its vestiges. Since it is not happening on its own, affirmative action helps things along. It should be noted that while Title VII does not prohibit discrimination on the basis of sexual harassment and gender identity, President Obama's 2014 Executive Order 13672 added those categories to Executive Order 11246. They were explicitly left in place by the new administration in 2017 despite, on the first day of office, removing the categories from several federal agencies.

In order for the plan of intentional inclusion of opportunity to withstand a lawsuit by those who feel wrongly impacted by it, this intentional inclusion must be premised on one of several bases we will discuss in this chapter. We should make clear that we are only using the word *qualified* here because we realize that one of the most persistent misconceptions about affirmative action is that those hired using affirmative action are unqualified. It should go without saying that anyone hired by an employer should be qualified. It is no different for hiring under an affirmative action plan, and, in fact, that is generally what occurs. Be aware that modifying women and minorities by using the word *qualified* borders on insulting, as it implies that it would be permissible to do otherwise simply because an employer is using an affirmative action plan. It is not.

The actions an employer can take to make an effort to include those historically underrepresented in the workplace include but are certainly not limited to

- Expanded outreach to groups the employer has not generally made an effort to reach.
- Recruitment of groups the employer generally has not made an attempt to recruit.
- Mentoring, management training, and development of traditionally excluded groups.
- Hiring, training, and other attempts to bring into the workplace groups that have traditionally been left out of the employment process.

The absence of these groups generally stems from attitudes about or actions toward such groups that resulted in their absence from the workplace or presence in very low numbers, at odds with their availability in the workforce. The absence can just as likely have come from simply letting the status quo continue unabated, with no particularly negative feelings or even thoughts about excluded groups. Given the history of systemic discrimination we have discussed, it is clear how and why this would occur. (See Exhibit 5.4, "Life under Jim Crow.") Since our treatment of traditionally excluded groups such as African Americans also included social exclusion, it is quite easy to grow up in a virtually homogeneous environment that does not include them or includes them only on a limited basis (for instance, you may attend school with them yet have no real interaction with them). The corollary to this is that when it is time to hire, we tend to hire those who are most familiar to us. Inevitably, this would mean exclusion of those not considered a part of our homogeneous environment. This can stem from either virtual total

Exhibit 5.4   *Life under Jim Crow*

In '64 we had a public hospital constructed, and at that hospital, Blacks were segregated by rooms. Blacks in one room, whites in another. Health, Education and Welfare came down and inspected the hospital and found out that it was segregated by race. [They] wrote a letter to the hospital telling them that they were violating federal law, and if they didn't correct the problem and admit patients to rooms regardless of color, federal funds would be withdrawn. Finally they were forced to integrate the rooms at the hospital, but the feds had to make a grand stand before that happened.

Nash General over in Nash County got around the problem by building a new hospital with all private rooms. There were no semi-private rooms in Rocky Mount. People have forgotten it now, but the reason was to get around integration. So health care was terrible.

There were two clinics staffed by white physicians and blacks could go to those clinics to see white doctors but the rules were different. You had to sit in a very, very small room bunched up together with very poor ventilation. You couldn't see out of the room very much. There was maybe an 18″ by 18″ hole that the receptionist would talk to you through. You were called by your first name. Whereas whites had this spacious, beautiful waiting room with plants and windows and the light. Black patients would always be last.

—George Kenneth Butterfield Jr.

Source: William H. Chafe, Raymond Gavins, and Robert Korstad, eds., *Remembering Jim Crow: African-Americans Tell about Life in the Segregated South* (New York: The New Press, 2001), pp. 22, 25.

social exclusion, such as between races that have little or no interaction, or exclusion from certain aspects of our existence, such as women in positions of power. If we rarely see them there, it is more difficult to imagine they could be. If you always do what you have always done, the status quo is maintained, and things remain the same. It is only through making an effort to do things differently that change occurs. Affirmative action is about trying to change what has always been done and will continue to be done without intervention. We need only look to the 99-year period of doing little or nothing between the end of the Civil War in 1865 and passage of the Civil Rights Act of 1964 to see what happens when little or nothing was done to intentionally try to impact matters. Things remained much the same.

Intentionally including employees previously excluded from a workplace is quite different from saying that workplace discrimination is prohibited. The former is the active approach required by Executive Order 11246; the latter, Title VII's passive approach.

You may wonder in this day and time, decades removed from the Civil Rights Act of 1964 prohibiting discrimination, why we would still need something like affirmative action. In order to understand why such a thing would still be needed, you must understand the basis for the law in the first place. To do so, we cannot look at the law from the perspective of today, which is how most students view it, as they sit in classrooms in which they may be surrounded by women and minorities. That is not what was going on when the law was created. It is important to look at the law in terms of what existed at the time, what the law was created to accomplish, and why.

The reason we include the "slice of life" boxes for you is to give you a flavor of what life was actually like when these laws were created. With our students we have always found that it is one thing to say, for instance, "Blacks and whites were segregated before Title VII." It is quite another for them to see a video of the 101st Airborne, with rifles at the ready, holding back crowds of screaming angry whites as nine Black teenagers surrounded by military escorts walked into a public high school being integrated three years after the *Brown v. Board of Education* decision. It can be easy to gloss over the underpinnings of the law, but if you do, you will not have any real idea of why the law was created or why we are still dealing with these issues long after their original creation. That is why we go into the historical detail we do. None of this makes sense if we don't.

It is essential to understand how divided this country was along the issues of race and gender at the time the law was passed; how thoroughly separated races and genders were (for instance, with classified ads divided into gender and race, which would likely appall you today); and how deeply held the negative views about minorities and African Americans in particular were by many in society, even legislators. It is important to understand how these issues came together and resulted in there not being the instant total embrace of groups long ostracized by society after the laws passed. (See Exhibit 5.4.) While you, personally, may not hold them, negative attitudes about those covered by affirmative action ran/run exceedingly deep and were/are closely held. You probably saw some of them surface during the 2008 presidential election and its aftermath, when the first Black president ran for office, and in the 2016 election cycle with its racial and sexist overtones when the first national female candidate for a major party ran for president. If you are like most students in your age group, you wondered what all the race fuss was about because you thought all that was over and done with long ago. Here, you get to see the genesis of some of the positions and why one need only scratch the surface to find them.

Given society's history with race and gender, it was going to take more than simply telling people not to discriminate to move the country toward what the antidiscrimination laws were created to do. Evidence of these attitudes held both then and now lies in the statistics reflected in Exhibit 5.5 ("Employment Research Findings") and other information provided in this chapter.[13]

As an example of the attitudes prevalent at the time, as you will see in the gender chapter, Howard W. Smith, a segregationist Democrat from Virginia and chairman of the powerful House Committee on Rules, promised that the civil rights bill would never emerge from his committee. Eventually it did, for reasons unrelated to the substance of the law. During the floor debate, however, Smith introduced an amendment to add the word *sex* to the bill.[14] In doing so, he said to his colleagues, who interrupted him with howls of laughter, that he was very serious about this amendment. He explained that he had received a letter from a woman in Nebraska who wanted Congress to equalize the gender ratio in the population by helping the "surplus of spinsters" obtain their "right" to happiness.[15]

Exhibit 5.5 *Employment Research Findings*

In society, tradition is as important to us as change. Change in society takes time. Take a look at the historic items below and see whether you think things have changed so significantly that affirmative action has outlived its usefulness.

- Research shows that people who hire tend to notice value more quickly in someone who looks like them.[16]

- In the suburbs, equally qualified Blacks are hired about 40 percent less than whites because of negative assumptions.[17]

- Almost 90 percent of jobs are filled through word-of-mouth rather than advertising, resulting in fewer minorities and women being able to take advantage of those networks.[18]

- In one experiment, retailers consistently chose slightly less qualified white women over more qualified Black women in entry-level positions.[19]

- When Black and white discrimination testers who are similar in qualifications, dress, and so on applied for jobs, whites were 45 percent more likely to receive job offers and 22 percent more likely to be granted interviews.[20]

- When made-up résumés were sent out in response to classified ads, with only names changed to sound more or less ethnic and addresses changed to more likely be in predominantly Black areas, white applicants were not only more likely to be granted interviews, but employers tried harder to reach them. Whites were 50 percent more likely to be chosen based only on their résumés, when the Blacks were more qualified in terms of experience and credentials.[21]

- In 2012, a female with an associate's degree had median weekly earnings of $682, while a male with only a high school diploma and no college earned $720. A female with a master's degree earned $1,125, or only $74 more than a male with a bachelor's degree, who earned $1,199. A female with a doctorate degree earned only $144 more than a male with a master's degree ($1,371 versus $1,515).[22]

- According to the Bureau of Labor Statistics, in a study released in 2013, the weekly earnings of white males was $879, white females, $710; Black males, $665; Black females, $599; Latinx males, $562, and Latinx females, $521.[23]

- In an important longitudinal study of Black and white women ages 34 to 44, only one-fifth of the gap between their wages could be explained by education and experience. The study found that while women are segregated into lower-paying jobs, the impact is greater on African American women than white women.[24]

- A comprehensive GAO study in 2003 showed a 20 percent gap in wages between males and females even when the researchers held steady for the usual factors that would cause such a difference, such as education, job tenure, race, industry, and so on. In 2008, it reported that enforcement agencies should do a better job monitoring the situation.[25]

- Women of color—African American, Latina, and Asian—are overrepresented in institutional service work, in occupations such as private household workers, cleaners, nurses' aides and licensed practical nurses, typists, file clerks, kitchen workers, hospital orderlies, and some occupations in the food packaging and textile industries. Other jobs that have disproportionate numbers of women and men of color include guards and corrections officers, mail and postal clerks, social workers, telephone operators, bus drivers, taxi drivers and chauffeurs, and some operator or laborer jobs within manufacturing.[26]

- Research indicates that as the percentage of females and the percentage of minorities in a job increase, average pay falls, even when all other factors are held steady.

- African American men with professional degrees receive 79 percent of the salary paid to white men with the same degrees and comparable jobs. African American women earn 60 percent.

- A study conducted by the U.S. Department of Labor found that women and minorities have made more progress breaking through the glass ceiling at smaller companies. Women constitute 25 percent of the managers and corporate officers in smaller establishments, while minorities represent 10 percent. But among *Fortune* 500 companies, women held 18 percent of the managerial jobs, with minorities holding 7 percent.

- The federal Glass Ceiling Commission found that white women made up close to half the workforce but held only 5 percent of the senior-level jobs in corporations. African Americans and other minorities account for less than 3 percent of top jobs (vice president and above).[27]

- The Glass Ceiling Commission found that a majority of chief executives acknowledge that the federal guidelines have been crucial in maintaining their commitment to a diverse workforce. It is estimated that only 30 to 40 percent of American companies are committed to affirmative action programs purely for business reasons, without any federal pressure. Most medium-sized and small companies, where job growth is greatest and affirmative action gains the biggest, have adopted affirmative action only grudgingly, and without guidelines, they are most likely to toss it overboard.

- Studies show that there is little correlation between what African American and white workers score on employment tests and how they perform in the workplace.

- A Census Bureau[28] survey of 3,000 businesses asked them to list the things they consider most important when hiring workers. The employers ranked test scores as 8th on a list of 11 factors. Generally speaking, job testing did not come into wide usage in the United States until after Title VII.

- The Glass Ceiling Commission research reported that stereotyping and prejudice still rule many executive suites. Women and minorities are frequently routed into career paths like customer relations and human resources, which usually do not lead to the top jobs.[29]

- Cecelia Conrad, associate professor of economics at Barnard College in New York, examined whether affirmative action plans had hurt worker productivity. She found "no evidence that there has been any decline in productivity due to affirmative action." She also found no evidence of improved productivity due to affirmative action.[30]

- A study of Standard and Poor's 500 companies found firms that broke barriers for women and minorities reported stock market records nearly 2.5 times better than comparable companies that took no action.

At the time laws for workplace equality were instituted, women and minorities were simply not an accepted part of the workplace. Congress legislating that women and minorities were not to be subjected to discrimination was going to take more than a little getting used to—especially when Congress itself was having trouble with the idea. You were able to see this scenario of lack of acceptance in stark detail in the 2016 Oscar-nominated movie *Hidden Figures.* In the drama based on actual facts, the African American women working at NASA as math computers simply were not treated the same as whites or males in the workplace. This continues in many areas for women and minorities today.

LO2 Provide the results of several studies indicating why there continues to be a need to take more than a passive approach to equal employment opportunity.

As you will see, however, affirmative action is used only when there is a *demonstrated* underrepresentation or a finding of discrimination. It is designed to remedy *present-day* employment inequities based on race or gender. It is about the past only in the sense that what happened in the past has present-day vestiges, which is why it is important for you to know about the past. Affirmative action is about remedying discrimination today, not about punishing anyone for past sins.

It makes little sense that if a system existed for 345 years, as slavery and Jim Crow did, there would be no vestiges of it just 50 years after the system ended. A very important seven-volume study in 1999 by Harvard University and the Russell Sage Foundation found that racial stereotypes and attitudes "heavily influence the labor market, with blacks landing at the very bottom."[31] The researchers found that "race is deeply entrenched in the country's cultural landscape—perhaps even more than many Americans realize or are willing to admit."[32] Attitudes such as those found by the Harvard study find their way into the workplace and lessen the chances of minority, female, and disabled applicants being chosen as employees. That, in turn, leads to the need for assistance such as affirmative action to remedy the situation. Interestingly enough, these attitudes, known as *implicit bias,* are now well documented in research and are being taken into account moving forward.

For instance, in 2011 the D.C. Courts held a judicial conference on implicit bias in the judicial process, titled "Implicit Bias: Recognizing It and Dismantling It," to "explore the neuroscience of implicit or subconscious bias and the many decision points in the judicial process that are impacted by it, ranging from jury selection to sentencing (and everything in between) to appellate decision making." The conference aimed "to help attendees overcome subconscious thoughts so that their decisions are based on fair and equal treatment that is vital to public trust and confidence in the administration of justice." "Those who have studied the subject have been quite surprised to find that their own implicit biases are much more pronounced than they ever would have imagined."[33] If this occurs with judges trained to be impartial, you can imagine what it must be like for the average manager, supervisor, or business owner without such training. Similar training is now going on all over the country.

If we could think of one thing that bothers us the most about affirmative action, it is that we believe our country is a meritocracy. We view our country to be one based on fairness and our achievement as based on the effort we put forth. Affirmative action seems to fly in the face of this because it appears that women and minorities get something without any effort when everyone else has to work for it. All they have to do is be born female or a minority, show up, and they get the job or get into schools or are granted contracts. Based on this premise, it makes perfect sense to resent affirmative action. However, as we have seen, research demonstrates this is far from reality. Despite antidiscrimination laws, minorities and women still lag in jobs, pay, and promotions. Turns out we may not be quite as much of a meritocracy as we thought we were. In this sense, you could say that affirmative action is an attempt to address this and align our idea of who we say we are with how we actually operate.

This makes sense since, as we have discussed, our history with race and gender was one of institutionalized prejudices that were manifested in laws, regulations, policies, and funding. Congress recognized as much for race when, after many failed chances to do so, it finally apologized for slavery in 2008 and recognized that "African Americans continue to suffer from the complex interplay between slavery and Jim Crow—long after both systems were formally abolished—through enormous damage and loss, both tangible and intangible, including the loss of human dignity, the frustration of careers and professional lives, and the long-term loss of income and opportunity."

Before deciding if affirmative action has outlived its usefulness, keep in mind the timeline discussed earlier and the deep-seated attitudes that result in the imbalance of one group's presence in the workplace versus another's. Also keep in mind that while African Americans, women, and other minorities were being excluded from the workplace for 345 years, those who were in the workplace gained 345 years' worth of advantages that benefited them whether they wanted them or not. The system worked the way it was intended. It was simply the way society was at the time. But once society's attitudes began changing after the Civil Rights Act of 1964, it did not mean that the entire system of privilege that had been in existence for 345 years ended. Far from it. In an example of just how long dismantling a system can take, it was not until January 2014 that a court finally ordered an end to the payments provided to, among other jurisdictions, Little Rock, Arkansas, for helping to desegregate its schools—a process that began with the 1954 *Brown v. Board of Education* case more than half a century before.[34]

We often hear that affirmative action is unfair because it seems like whites today are being punished for something they had nothing to do with since it happened so long ago. This is the "sins of the father" argument. Again, affirmative action is not about punishing anyone but rather about remedying discrimination. When a parent disciplines a child, is the parent "being mean," or is the parent training the child? It depends on perspective. The child will think the parent is being mean. The parent will see it as a parent's duty to train his or her child. Perspective makes all the difference. To have credibility, the sins-of-the-father position also must take into consideration the benefits and privileges the fathers provided for their progeny. As you have seen in piece after piece of research throughout the text, many of these privileges and benefits are still hard at work today, whether their beneficiaries are aware of it or not.

Since the passage of Title VII, it has become fashionable to think we treat everyone the same. What we may forget is that before that law came into existence, a law that has been around for more than 50 years, a system was in place that provided advantages based on race and gender for 345 years. (See Exhibit 5.4.) That system did not disappear as soon as Title VII was passed. (See Exhibit 5.6, "Institutionalizing Prejudice: The Mississippi Sovereignty Commission.") We are still struggling with it today. Recognition of this is why the courts continue to uphold the concept of affirmative action.

Exhibit 5.6 *Institutionalizing Prejudice: The Mississippi Sovereignty Commission*

This is America, and we have the right to feel however we want to about whomever we want to for whatever reasons we want to. We don't have to like everyone. Prejudice is prejudging someone before you know them and deciding you don't feel positively about them based on that prejudgment. We have a right to be prejudiced if we want to. Racism, however, is institutionalized prejudice. Racism goes beyond

(continued)

Exhibit 5.6 *continued*

the realm of mere personal feelings, becomes actualized in policies and laws that effectuate that prejudice, and acts to exclude or harm a particular group. Knowing in your head that you do not like a particular group is one thing. Acting in ways to harm or exclude that group is quite another. Prejudice is personal; racism is not. This is particularly harmful when it is the government that is doing the harming or excluding. For instance, in 1924 Virginia passed laws for involuntary sterilization aimed primarily at African Americans, and the government administrator in charge of enforcing the law was in contact with and a great admirer of German eugenics officials of Hitler's Third Reich who were exterminating Blacks as well. He even wrote to the German official about the official's work, "I hope this work is complete and not one has been missed. I sometimes regret that we have not the authority to put some measures in practice in Virginia." Virginia's involuntary sterilization law was not repealed until 1979. Yes, you read it correctly—1979.[35] California's law was repealed the same year.[36] We know it may be hard for you to believe this could ever happen in America, but it did. In many ways. But we will here give you one example so that you can understand for yourself how deeply rooted the issues are that led legislators to believe that affirmative action was necessary if the purpose of Title VII was to be fully effectuated.

In 1954 the U.S. Supreme Court outlawed racial segregation in public education. Two years later, in 1956, the Mississippi Sovereignty Commission was created to preserve segregation in the 11 southern states. The commission was charged to "protect the sovereignty of the State of Mississippi and her sister states from federal government interference." The commission, primarily an information-gathering agency, outwardly espoused racial harmony but secretly paid spies and investigators to report on civil rights activists or anyone even remotely thought to be sympathetic to the cause of racial equality. Such people were branded as racial agitators and communist infiltrators (a huge issue after the McCarthy era and during the Cold War with Russia). In addition, the commission contributed money to segregationist causes, acted as a clearinghouse for segregation

and anti–civil rights information, and circulated segregationist rhetoric and ideals. The commission was a state government commission like any other, with members of the commission appointed by the governor. The governor served as chair of the commission, and among the ex-officio members (members by reason of their office) were the lieutenant governor, the speaker of the house of representatives, and the attorney general. Commission members included state legislators and other high officials.

The commission had a budget, an executive director, and clerical staff, and its first investigators were a former FBI agent and a former chief of the Mississippi Highway Patrol. The public relations director devised projects to portray Mississippi in a favorable light. The commission was given subpoena power and had the authority to gather information and keep its files and records secret. A fine and jail time were possible for divulging the commission's secrets. Information was gathered through spying, informants, and law enforcement agencies and by working with the Citizens Counsel, a white supremacist organization.

In 1973—nearly 10 years after Title VII was passed—Governor Bill Waller vetoed funding for the commission, and it officially became defunct four years later. When the commission was officially closed in 1977, the legislature decreed that its records be sealed for 50 years, until 2027. The ACLU sued to open them and eventually won, and they were opened in 1998.* The files contained over 132,000 documents. Among them were documents that shed light on the murders of the three voting rights activists Schwerner, Chaney, and Goodman, whose story is the basis of the popular movie *Mississippi Burning*. The three were killed and buried in an earthen dam while trying to register Black voters in Mississippi.

*The records of the Mississippi Sovereignty Commission can be found online at http://mdah.state.ms.us/arlib/contents/er/sovcom/.

Sources: Mississippi History Now, http://mshistory.k12.ms.us/features/feature35/sovereignty.html; Facts about Mississippi Sovereignty Commission, http://www.mdcbowen.org/p2/bh/badco/missSov.htm.

For instance, the primary laws that set the stage for the middle class life many of us now enjoy, including things like suburbs, malls, college educations, business ownership, and so on, received their start after the Great Depression under the New Deal with passage of legislation such as the National Labor Relations Act (NLRA) in 1935, the Fair Labor Standards Act (FLSA) in 1938, and later the GI Bill (Selective Service Readjustment Act) in 1944. The NLRA allowed for the power of collective bargaining by employees to gain for employees more equitable, stable working wages and conditions. The FLSA, for the first time, guaranteed a minimum wage that could lift employees out of poverty. The GI Bill provided returning World War II veterans the right to receive financial assistance to go to college (something the vast majority of people could not afford to do) and low-interest loans for homes and businesses. It was a big part of the post–World War II boom in housing and business that created the middle class as we know it. In fact, it helped to create a housing demand so strong that suburbs were born. And, of course, malls (and, thus, life as many of us know it) were not far behind.

What does all of this have to do with institutionalized racism that serves as a foundation for the necessity of affirmative action to counteract its effects? All of this legislation was passed with the help of a very powerful southern voting bloc in Congress that was interested primarily in keeping the South as it had been since after the Civil War—segregated and in the throes of Jim Crow. The southern legislators had wide and varied views, but they were all in accord on one: the South was to remain segregated and their way of life untouched by these new laws.

In return for their votes, they received provisions in the law that guaranteed what they wanted. Seventy-five percent of African Americans in the South, and 60 percent nationwide, were agricultural workers at the time. Virtually the same was true of domestics. Those were the two top jobs African Americans were permitted to hold in the Jim Crow years. Excluding these two jobs from the minimum wage laws was one of the prices exacted by the southern legislators for their vote to pass the legislation. This meant that African Americans working as domestics and agricultural workers—the vast majority of African Americans—would not receive minimum wages and therefore would be kept in low wages that did not put them on par with whites.

We know it is probably hard for you to imagine, but at that time in our history, the idea of an African American in the South making the same wages as whites would have been unthinkable. Since many southern legislators employed agricultural workers, laborers, gardeners, caretakers, housekeepers, cooks, laundresses, and nannies to support their way of life, largely unchanged since the Civil War ended, not only would minimum wages and overtime be against their own economic interests, but it would have put the African American employees on a par with white workers, and that was, in the minds of southern legislators, unacceptable. As Rep. Martin Dies (D-TX) said, in debating the bill, "What is prescribed for one race must be prescribed for the others, and you cannot prescribe the same wages for the black man as for the white man."[37] Even if they had wanted to do it, which they did not, their constituents would never have accepted it. Minimum wages and overtime under FLSA was designed for whites.[38]

As for the labor laws, the South has always had a notoriously low rate of unionization, and now you can understand part of what accounts for that, given the political and social landscape. Since, of course, agricultural workers and domestics were not unionized, this meant the vast majority of African Americans also would not benefit from the improved working and wage provisions of the labor laws. Even where they worked with unions present, they were not permitted to join.

The GI Bill granting a host of benefits to veterans was proposed as a federally administered law. Southerners knew that if this happened, everyone would be governed by the same rules, which would mean African Americans had the same rights under the law as whites. The trade-off for the southern bloc vote to pass the laws was that administration of the law would be local. In this way, when the African American veteran wanted to use the law's college benefits to attend college, he could be told that he was not allowed to attend the college because the college was for whites only. When he went to borrow money from the local bank for a home mortgage or business loan at the favorable GI Bill rates, the local southern bank could deny the loan based on Jim Crow policies.

The Davis-Bacon Act of 1931 requiring that prevailing local wage rates be paid to workers on projects receiving federal funds of over $2,000 is another important piece of legislation born of racial protectiveness. Though historians have debated the matter and dismiss the racially derogatory statement made in Congress during the legislative debates on the bill, the reality is that it was created after Bacon of New York learned that "colored" workers had been brought to New York from Alabama to build a Veterans Administration hospital in his district because they would work for less. Of course, that mean not only that white workers were left out of the project but also that the projects he managed to get Congress to fund for his district would not employ local voters.[39]

The super boost these laws gave to create the American middle class as we know it today left the vast majority of African Americans well out of the loop. The prejudices of the southern legislators found their way into the laws, and there they remain to this day.[40] That, combined with societal attitudes and mores, virtually ensured that when the Civil Rights Act of 1964 was passed, African Americans would need more than a passive approach to realizing the law's promise. This was provided, to an extent, by affirmative action.

Efforts to eliminate affirmative action in employment, government contracts, university admissions, and other areas come primarily from those who feel it has outlived its usefulness and causes only ill will among majority employees and students. Many think of it as punishment to redress slavery and feel they should not have to bear the burden of something for which they had no responsibility and that occurred so long ago. Whites are not the only ones who complain about affirmative action. African American University of California regent and outspoken affirmative action critic Ward Connerly suggested in a *60 Minutes* interview that "Black Americans are not hobbled by chains any longer. We're free to compete. We're capable of competing. It is an absolute insult to suggest that we can't."[41] His comment ignores the fact that Blacks have always been able to compete. The insult is the mistaken belief that affirmative action is somehow a gift rather than a less-than-perfect attempt to level the playing field.

The first workplace affirmative action case did not reach the U.S. Supreme Court until 1979. Once the Court green-lighted its limited use under certain circumstances, as you saw in Exhibit 5.1 on the affirmative action statements throughout the 1980s, government agencies and officials argued about the concept, and employers were left simply confused. Note, too, that while many changes have come about since the passage of Title VII, statistics still show African Americans and other minorities lagging behind in jobs and even further behind in promotions and pay. In 2013, the Pew Research Center released a study showing that even though much has changed since the Civil Rights Act of 1964 was enacted, the fact that Black unemployment is double that of whites has not.[42] Think about this, the information we have discussed, and the research items in Exhibit 5.5, and ask yourself if it appears that everything is now equal and affirmative action has outlived its usefulness.

Throughout the chapter, keep this thought in mind: If Alaska is 99 percent Inuit (Eskimo), then, all things being equal, that will be reflected at all or most levels of its employment spectrum. All things being equal, it would look odd if Alaska is 99 percent Inuit but the Inuit hold only 5 percent of managerial-level jobs and 100 percent of the unskilled-labor jobs. Of course, the reality is that it is rare to have a workforce that has so little diversity. Among other things, there also will be differing skill levels and interests within the workforce from which the employees are drawn. However, the example is instructive for purposes of illustrating how a workplace should generally reflect the available workforce from which its employees are drawn. If there is a significant difference that cannot be accounted for otherwise, the difference between availability and representation in the workplace raises concerns. In essence, this is affirmative action. We believe that the more you understand what affirmative action actually is and what it is used for, the more likely you are to help your employer more effectively meet affirmative action obligations he or she may have under the law.

We should again note that while we have given you a good deal of background on the reasons for affirmative action, we have done so because our experience shows that lack of information about the history and context of the concept is the single biggest reason for the common misconceptions about it. It is time well spent to give you a thorough grounding. You should also note that as we have discussed and you probably know well, not everyone believes affirmative action should exist. Since affirmative action is the law and our goal is to tell you how to comply with the law in order to avoid workplace liability, we have not delved into the other side of the issue. This is not a debate. According to the Office of Federal Contract Compliance Programs responsible for enforcing Executive Order 11246, "Affirmative Action is necessary to prevent discrimination and to address stereotypical thinking and biases that still impede employment opportunity."[43] Affirmative action is presently the law and must be obeyed or the employer runs the risk of unnecessary liability.[44]

Affirmative action also arises in other contexts such as college admissions, granting of government contracts, and set-asides. However, except for historical development purposes, these are beyond the scope of this text's employment context.

LO3 Name and explain the three types of affirmative action.

There are three ways in which affirmative action obligations arise in the workplace, each of which will be explored in turn:

1. Through Executive Order 11246.
2. Judicially as a remedy for a finding of discrimination under Title VII.
3. Voluntary affirmative action established by an employer.

Affirmative Action under Executive Order 11246

Though people tend to think of affirmative action as a part of Title VII, and in fact, Title VII has an affirmative action component as part of its remedies, affirmative action actually stems from a requirement imposed by Executive Order 11246 and its amendments. Under the executive order, those employers who contract to furnish the federal government with goods and services, called *federal contractors,* must agree not to discriminate in the hiring, termination, promotion, pay, and so on, of employees on the basis of race, color, religion, gender, sexual orientation, gender identity, veteran status, disabilities, or national origin.

The first forerunner to E.O. 11246 was Executive Order 8802, signed by President Franklin D. Roosevelt on June 25, 1941. It applied only to defense contracts and was issued to combat discrimination during World War II "as a prerequisite to the successful conduct of our national defense production effort."[45] This executive order underwent several changes before the present version was signed into law by President Lyndon B. Johnson on September 24, 1965. Although it is a presidential executive order and thus could legally be taken away with the stroke of a pen, each president thereafter has allowed it to remain.

E.O. 11246 Provisions

debar
Prohibit a federal contractor from further participation in government contracts.

In addition to prohibiting discrimination in employment, for certain contracts the executive order requires that contractors who have underrepresentations of women and minorities in their workplace agree to take steps to ensure adequate representation. In cases where a federal contractor/employer refuses to remedy disparities found, his or her contract can be terminated and he or she can be **debarred** from further participation in government contracts. This is a rare occurrence since most employers eventually comply with the OFCCP's suggestions for remedying workplace disparities.

The executive order is enforced by the Office of Federal Contract Compliance Programs (OFCCP) in the Employment Standards Administration Office of the U.S. Department of Labor. The OFCCP issues extensive regulations implementing the executive order.[46] OFCCP's enforcement addresses only the employer's participation in federal government contracts and contains no provisions for private lawsuits by employees or even penalties for noncompliance by a contractor. Employees seeking relief from workplace discrimination in violation of the executive order must do so through their state's fair employment practice laws, Title VII, or similar legislation previously discussed. However, employees may file complaints with the OFCCP, which the secretary of labor is authorized to receive and investigate, and may sue the secretary to compel performance of executive order requirements. While OFCCP does not bring individual discrimination cases for employees, it does pursue employers for violations of the executive order. From October 2016 to September 2019, the latest figures available, OFCCP recovered over $81 million from employers.[47]

All contractors/employers who contract with the federal government must abide by the executive order's nondiscrimination provision. However, those who provide goods and services of $10,000 or more must agree to do even more. In addition, contractors and subcontractors agree to

- Post in conspicuous places, available to employees and applicants, notices provided by the contracting officer setting forth the provisions of the non-discrimination clause. You may have seen these in your workplace or university/college.

- Include in all the contractor's solicitations or advertisements for employees a statement that all qualified applicants will receive consideration for employment without regard to race, color, religion, gender, sexual orientation, gender identity, or national origin (although research shows that employers with such notices are just as likely to discriminate in employment as those without such notices).

- Include a statement of these obligations in all subcontracts or purchase orders, unless exempted, which will be binding on each subcontractor or vendor.

- Furnish all information and reports required by the executive order and the implementing regulations and permit access to the contractor's or subcontractor's books, records, and accounts by the contracting agency and the secretary of labor for purposes of investigation to ascertain compliance with the executive order and its regulations.

LO4 Explain when affirmative action plans are required and how they are created.

Under the implementing regulations, Executive Order 11246 increases compliance requirements based on the amount of the contract. For the smallest contracts, the employer agrees that, in addition to not discriminating in employment, it will post notices that it is an equal opportunity employer. If a contractor or subcontractor has contracts of $10,000 or more, then in addition to posting the notices, the contractor must include in all solicitations and advertisements non-discrimination language stating that "all qualified applicants will receive consideration for employment without regard to race, color, religion, sex, sexual orientation, gender identity, or national origin." If a contractor or subcontractor has 50 or more employees and a non-construction contract of $50,000 or more, the contractor must develop a written affirmative action plan for each of his or her establishments within 120 days of the beginning of the contract. Those with contracts under $10,000 are exempt from the executive order.

In 2014, OFCCP regulations expanded affirmative action obligations to disabled individuals and to veterans. The threshold amount of contracts necessary to trigger affirmative action for disabled individuals is $10,000 in government contracts and for veterans it is $100,000 in government contracts. Under the new regulations, employers must adopt hiring benchmarks for veterans based on either the national percentage of veterans in the workforce or an individualized benchmark created for the company and utilization goals for disabled individuals. The national benchmark goal is 7 percent. OFCCP launched two new databases to help employers comply. The Veterans Benchmark Database included the current benchmark as well as data for contractors wishing to create their own individualized benchmarks. The Disability and Veterans Community Resource Directory database provides information on organizations and groups that assist with training, recruiting, and hiring veterans and those with disabilities.

Affirmative Action Plans

affirmative action plan
A government contractor's plan containing placement goals for inclusion of women, minorities, veterans, and disabled individuals in the workplace and timetables for accomplishing the goals.

An **affirmative action plan** must be developed according to the rules set forth in the Code of Federal Regulations (C.F.R.) part 60-2 that effectuates the executive order. According to the regulations, "an affirmative action plan should be considered a management tool—an integral part of the way a corporation conducts its business . . . to encourage self-evaluation in every aspect of an employment by establishing systems to monitor and examine the contractor's employment decisions and compensation systems to ensure that they are free of discrimination."[48] (See Exhibit 5.7, "More Than a 'Numbers Game.'")

Exhibit 5.7 *More Than a "Numbers Game"—Major Affirmative Action Regulation Overhaul: The Dog Now Wags the Tail Rather Than Vice Versa*

Most people tend to think of affirmative action as a "numbers game" in which an employer tries to hire a certain magic number of minorities and women in order to avoid running into trouble with the "feds." That is *so* not the case. Actually, there may have been some basis for that view when set against the background of the 1980s discussed earlier. When much of the policy was hammered out, OFCCP may have seemed more interested in the bottom-line figures. But as affirmative action evolved, it became clear that numbers alone were not sufficient to accomplish what the law was designed to do. After all, it is not equal employment but rather equal employment *opportunity* that the law wanted to ensure, confident that if the opportunities were equal, that would be reflected in the bottom-line figures. With the numbers approach, OFCCP obviously found that managerial policies suffered in an attempt to achieve numbers and the intent of the law was not being met. The tail was wagging the dog rather than vice versa.

In 2000, OFCCP issued the most comprehensive set of changes to its regulations since the 1970s. Not only did the new regulations make changes in a few significant ways affirmative action plans are to be developed, such as decreasing the number of availability factors it will consider from eight to two and permitting employers to replace the previously required workforce analysis with an organization profile that is usually simpler, but it also clarified and reaffirmed basic foundations of affirmative action. In recognizing this more balanced approach, OFCCP said that "affirmative action programs contain a diagnostic component which includes a number of quantitative analyses designed to evaluate the composition of the workforce of the contractor and compare it to the composition of the relevant labor pools. Affirmative action programs also include action-oriented programs."

Probably most important, it was clear that OFCCP was moving from an approach that was perceived as being interested primarily in the mechanics of affirmative action plans submitted by employers to one in which the plan is viewed as "a management tool to ensure equal employment opportunity." The agency said that "a central premise underlying affirmative action is that, absent discrimination, over time a contractor's workforce, generally, will reflect the gender, racial and ethnic profile of the labor pools from which the contractor recruits and selects. If women and minorities are not being employed at a rate to be expected given their availability in the relevant labor pool, the contractor's affirmative action program includes specific practical steps designed to address this underutilization. Effective affirmative action programs also include internal auditing and reporting systems as a means of measuring the contractor's progress toward achieving the workforce that would be expected in the absence of discrimination."

Rather than a numbers game, OFCCP envisions affirmative action plans as a way for contractors to take the opportunity to look at their workforces and see if they are reflective of the relevant population they are drawn from and, if they determine they are not, to make a plan to work toward making that happen. This reflects the understanding that given the country's racial, ethnic, and gender history, without taking the time and opportunity to actually step back and look at the larger picture, employers may not be aware of the underrepresentation, and thus it will continue. In addressing its preferred approach, OFCCP noted that this analysis should not just be done in anticipation of reporting to OFCCP but on a regular basis as part of management of the workplace in all aspects. "An affirmative action program also ensures equal employment opportunity by institutionalizing the contractor's

commitment to equality in every aspect of the employment process. Therefore, as part of its affirmative action program, a contractor monitors and examines its employment decisions and compensation systems to evaluate the impact of those systems on women and minorities."

In this more holistic view OFCCP pronounced in its regulatory revisions, it said that "an affirmative action program is, thus, more than a paperwork exercise. An affirmative action program includes those policies, practices, and procedures that the contractor implements to ensure that all qualified applicants and employees are receiving an equal opportunity for recruitment, selection, advancement, and every other term and privilege associated with employment. Affirmative action, ideally, is a part of the way the contractor regularly conducts its business. OFCCP has found that when an affirmative action program is approached from this perspective, as a powerful management tool, there is a positive correlation between the presence of affirmative action and the absence of discrimination."

"Pursuant to these regulatory changes, OFCCP will focus its resources on the action undertaken to promote equal employment opportunity, rather than on the technical compliance."

Sources: Department of Labor, Office of Federal Contract Compliance Programs, "41 CFR Parts 60-1 and 60-2; Government Contractors, Affirmative Action Requirements; Final Rule," 165 Fed. Reg. 68021, 68021–47 (November 13, 2000), http://frwebgate.access.gpo.gov/cgi-bin/getdoc.cgi?dbname=2000_register&docid=00-28693-filed.

underrepresentation or underutilization Significantly fewer minorities or women in the workplace than relevant statistics indicate are available or their qualifications indicate they should be working at better jobs.

Affirmative action plans have both quantitative and qualitative aspects. The quantitative part of the plan examines the contractor's workplace to get a snapshot of sorts of who works there and in what capacity, as it relates to minorities and women. Minority categories include African American, Latinx, Asian/Pacific Islander, and American Indian/Alaskan Native. The qualitative part of the plan sets out a course of action for how to address any **underrepresentation or underutilization** or other problems found. Note that the executive order prohibits discrimination in employment against women, minorities, and LGBTQ employees as well as the disabled and veterans. However, the affirmative action plan requirements for each of them are not the same. When it comes to affirmative action plans, they really are primarily directed to women and minorities.

**organizational
profile**
Staffing patterns
showing organizational
units; their relationship
to each other; and
gender, race, and ethnic
composition.

job group analysis
Combines job titles with
similar content, wage
rates, and opportunities.

availability
Minorities and women
in a geographic area
who are qualified for a
particular position.

placement goal
Percentage of women
and/or minorities to
be hired to correct
underrepresentation,
based on availability in
the geographic area.

In order to get the snapshot of what the contractor's workplace looks like as it relates to minorities and/or females, employers must prepare an **organizational profile**. An organizational profile shows staffing patterns within a workplace, much like an organizational chart, showing each of the organizational units; their relationship to one another; and the gender, race, and ethnic composition of each unit. It is "one method contractors use to determine whether barriers to equal employment opportunity exist in their organization."

Another part of the snapshot is the contractor's **job group analysis**. Job group analysis combines job titles in the contractor's workplace that have similar content, wage rates, and opportunities. The job group analysis must include a list of the job titles for each job group and the percentage of minorities and the percentage of women it employs in each job group. This information is then compared to the availability of women and/or minorities for these job groups.

Now that the contractor has this snapshot of the workplace, the foundation of the affirmative action plan is laid. The purpose of the snapshot is to see if there is an underrepresentation of women and/or minorities based on the difference between their **availability** in the workforce from which employees are hired and their presence in the workplace. According to the regulation, availability is important in order to "establish a benchmark against which the demographic composition of the contractor's employees can be compared in order to determine whether barriers to equal employment opportunity may exist within particular job groups."

Availability is not based on the mere presence of women and minorities in a given geographic area. Rather, it is based on the availability of women and minorities qualified for the job under consideration.[49] Simply because women are 35 percent of the general population for a particular geographic area does not mean that they are all qualified to be doctors, professors, skilled craft workers, or managers. Availability for jobs as, for instance, managers would only consider those qualified to fill the position of managers rather than all women in the geographic area. The regulations contain resources for finding out availability for various jobs in a given geographic area.

The two factors to be used in determining availability of employees (separately for minorities and women for each job group) are (1) the percentage of minorities or women with requisite skills in the reasonable recruitment area, defined as the geographic areas from which the contractor usually seeks or reasonably could seek workers to fill the positions in question, and (2) the percentage of minorities or women among those promotable, transferable, and trainable within the contractor's organization.[50]

If the percentage of women and/or minorities employed in a job group is less than would reasonably be expected based on their availability in the area from which employees are drawn, the contractor must establish a **placement goal** that reflects the reasonable availability of women and/or minorities in the geographic area.

By regulation, placement goals, which serve as objectives "reasonably attainable by means of applying every 'good faith effort' to make all aspects of the entire affirmative action program work," do not mean that the underrepresentation is an admission or a finding of discrimination.[51] They are designed to measure progress toward achieving equal employment opportunity and "may not be rigid and inflexible quotas which must be met" nor a ceiling or floor for employing certain groups. "*Quotas are expressly forbidden.*"[52] In making decisions, employers are expressly *not* required "to hire a person who lacks qualifications to perform the job successfully, or hire a less qualified person in preference to a more qualified one."[53] In all employment decisions, the contractor must make selections in a nondiscriminatory manner.[54]

Once this quantitative part of the affirmative action plan is in place, if an underrepresentation or other problem has been found, the contractor must then develop and execute "action-oriented" programs designed to correct them. OFCCP believes that in order for the programs to be effective, they must be more than the contractor's "business as usual," which, of course, likely led to the underrepresentation in the first place. (See Exhibits 5.8, "Affirmative Actions," and 5.9, "Voluntary Affirmative Action Plan Considerations.")

Exhibit 5.8 *Affirmative Actions*

While there are guidelines as to what may or may not be legally acceptable as affirmative action designed to intentionally include traditionally excluded individuals in the workplace, there are no specific requirements about what affirmative action must be taken. As a result, employers' means of addressing affirmative action have varied greatly, some being acceptable and some not. It continues to be an ongoing battle. Following are some approaches that have been tried by employers or others. Keep in mind the Supreme Court's characterization of plans that are acceptable when viewing the ideas employers have tried. Again, because employers have used these methods does not mean they are legal. Sometimes they may simply be convenient. According to OFCCP, the best affirmative actions an employer can take are aggressive recruitment, mentoring, and training programs for qualified individuals.

- *Advertising for applicants in nontraditional sources.* Employers solicit minority and female applicants through resources such as historically African American colleges and universities; women's colleges; and minority and female civic, educational, religious, and social organizations, including the NAACP, National Urban League, La Raza, American Indian Movement, National Organization for Women, and so on.

- *One-for-one hiring, training, or promotion programs.* One traditionally excluded applicant or employee is hired, trained, or promoted for every white or male until a certain desired goal is reached. This is usually only used in long-standing, resistant cases of underrepresentation and is rarely used anymore.

- *Preferential layoff provisions.* As in *Wygant v. Jackson Board of Education,*[55] in recognition of the reality that recently hired female and minority employees would be lost if layoffs are conducted based on seniority and, thereby, affirmative action gains lost, employers institute plans that are designed to prevent the percentage of minorities and women from falling below a certain point. Some minorities and women with less seniority may be retained, while those with more are laid off. While the U.S. Supreme Court did not prohibit this approach, it did indicate an employer would have to overcome a very rigorous analysis to ensure protection of the adversely impacted employees.

- *Extra consideration.* Women and minorities are considered along with all other candidates, but extra consideration is given to their status as women and minorities because they have traditionally been excluded from the job, and all other factors being equal, they may be chosen.

(continued)

Exhibit 5.8 *continued*

- *Lower standards.* Women and minorities may be taken out of the regular pool of candidates and given different, usually less stringent, standards for qualifying for the position. Natural questions are why the higher standards are imposed if the job can be performed with lesser qualifications and why someone who is not qualified under the higher, "normal" standards should be given the job. This is *not* a good approach and would probably *not* pass judicial muster.

- *Added points.* Much like with a veteran's preference, the employer has a rating system giving points for various criteria, and women and minorities receive extra points because they are women or minorities. This was not permitted by the U.S. Supreme Court in the undergraduate admissions program at the University of Michigan. [*Grutter v. Bollinger,* 539 U.S. 306 (2003).]

- *Exam discarding.* In an effort to avoid liability for the disparate impact of an objective examination, some employers have discarded the results when minority or female candidates did not score as well as whites or males. The U.S. Supreme Court in *Ricci v. DeStefano*[56] struck down this approach. *Ricci* is included at the end of the chapter.

- *Minority or female "positions."* In an effort to meet affirmative action goals, employers create positions that are designated to be filled only by women or minorities. These positions may or may not be needed by the employer. This is not a smart approach for an employer and would not stand up in court.

Some of the approaches are more desirable than others because they are less likely to result in "reverse discrimination" suits or more likely to result in qualified minority or female employees. Affirmative action plans walk a fine line between not holding affirmative application to lower standards than other employees while, at the same time, not permitting the standards to be arbitrary and likely to unnecessarily or unwittingly screen out these candidates. The 1991 Civil Rights Act made it unlawful to "adjust the scores of, use different cutoff scores for, or otherwise alter the results of, employment related tests" on the basis of race, color, religion, gender, or national origin. That does not mean employers don't still do it. Since there are few rules, employers can be creative, within the guidelines provided by law. Now that you have seen some of the affirmative action schemes employers have tried, which seem most suited to accomplish the goals of affirmative action while having the least adverse impact on other employees? How would you design an affirmative action plan?

Exhibit 5.9 *Voluntary Affirmative Action Plan Considerations*

According to the federal regulations governing voluntary affirmative action plans:

PART 1608 AFFIRMATIVE ACTION APPROPRIATE UNDER TITLE VII OF THE CIVIL RIGHTS ACT OF 1964

Sec. 1608.3 Circumstances under which voluntary affirmative action is appropriate.

(a) Adverse effect. Title VII prohibits practices, procedures, or policies which have an adverse impact unless they are justified by business necessity. In addition, title VII proscribes

practices which "tend to deprive" persons of equal employment opportunities. Employers, labor organizations and other persons subject to title VII may take affirmative action based on an analysis which reveals facts constituting actual or potential adverse impact, if such adverse impact is likely to result from existing or contemplated practices.

(b) Effects of prior discriminatory practices. Employers, labor organizations, or other persons subject to title VII may also take affirmative action to correct the effects of prior discriminatory practices. The effects of prior discriminatory practices can be initially identified by a comparison between the employer's work force, or a part thereof, and an appropriate segment of the labor force.

(c) Limited labor pool. Because of historic restrictions by employers, labor organizations, and others, there are circumstances in which the available pool, particularly of qualified minorities and women, for employment or promotional opportunities is artificially limited. Employers, labor organizations, and other persons subject to title VII may, and are encouraged to take affirmative action in such circumstances, including, but not limited to, the following:

(1) Training plans and programs, including on-the-job training, which emphasize providing minorities and women with the opportunity, skill, and experience necessary to perform the functions of skilled trades, crafts, or professions;

(2) Extensive and focused recruiting activity;

(3) Elimination of the adverse impact caused by unvalidated selection criteria (see sections 3 and 6, Uniform Guidelines on Employee Selection Procedures (1978), 43 FR 30290; 38297; 38299 (August 25, 1978));

(4) Modification through collective bargaining where a labor organization represents employees, or unilaterally where one does not, of promotion and layoff procedures.

Source: 29 C.F.R. ch. XIV (7-1-04 Edition), § § 1608.1, 1608.3, http://www.access.gpo.gov/nara/cfr/waisidx_04/29cfr1608_04.html.

OFCCP may perform audits of contractors to determine if they are complying with the regulations and providing equal employment opportunity. To withstand an OFCCP audit, contractors must show that they have made good-faith efforts to remove any identified barriers to equal employment opportunity, expand employment opportunities, and produce measurable results. As part of an action program, contractors must

- Develop and implement internal auditing systems that periodically measure the effectiveness of their affirmative action plans, including monitoring records of all personnel activity to ensure that the contractor's non-discrimination policy is being carried out.

- Require internal reporting on a scheduled basis as to the degree to which equal employment opportunity and organizational objectives are attained.

- Review report results with all levels of management.

- Advise top management of the program's effectiveness and submit recommendations for improvement, where necessary.

corporate management compliance evaluation
Evaluations of mid- and senior-level employee advancement for artificial barriers to advancement.

In an effort to combat discrimination and exclusion, the regulations also require **corporate management compliance evaluation** designed to determine whether employees are encountering artificial barriers to advancement to mid- and senior-level corporate management. During such evaluations, special attention is given to those components of the employment process that affect advancement into these upper-level positions. The Glass Ceiling Commission found that it was easier for women and minorities to enter a business at the entry level than to progress up once there. This tool is used to address this phenomenon, which continues.

In 2010, OFCCP began developing a predictive statistical model to more accurately identify potential violators. Since the model would allow the agency to maximize limited resources and focus on the contractors and industries most likely to be found not complying with the law, it makes even more sense for employers with federal contracts to comply.[57]

Again, there is no requirement of quotas under Executive Order 11246 or under Title VII. In fact, as we saw previously, the law specifically says it is not to be interpreted as such. Virtually the only time quotas are permitted is when there has been a long-standing violation of the law and there is little other recourse. The *Sheet Metal Workers'* case, discussed shortly, demonstrated this with the union's resistance over an 18-year period, resulting in the imposition of quotas.

Placement goals to remedy underrepresentation should not be confused with quotas. As long as an employer can show a legitimate, good-faith effort to reach affirmative action placement goals, quotas are not required and will not be imposed as a remedy for underrepresentation. Again, it is equal employment opportunity that the law requires, not equal employment.

Penalties for Noncompliance

The secretary of labor or the appropriate contracting agency can impose on the employer a number of penalties for noncompliance, including

- Publishing the names of nonconforming contractors or labor unions.
- Recommending to the EEOC or the Department of Justice that proceedings be instituted under Title VII.
- Requesting that the attorney general bring suit to enforce the executive order in cases of actual or threatened substantial violations of the contractual EEO clause.
- Recommending to the Department of Justice that criminal proceedings be initiated for furnishing false information to a contracting agency or the secretary of labor.
- Canceling, terminating, or suspending the contract, or any portion thereof, for failure of the contractor or subcontractor to comply with the non-discrimination provisions of the contract (this may be done absolutely, or continuance may be conditioned on a program for future compliance approved by the contracting agency).
- Debarring the noncomplying contractor from entering into further government contracts until the contractor has satisfied the secretary that it will abide by the provisions of the order.

The secretary of labor must make reasonable efforts to secure compliance by conference, conciliation, mediation, and persuasion before requesting the U.S. attorney general to act or before canceling or surrendering a contract. While a hearing is required before the secretary can debar a contractor, it may be granted before any other sanction is imposed, if appropriate. As a practical matter, the more severe penalties are rarely used because contractors are generally not so recalcitrant toward OFCCP orders.

In making its compliance determinations for contractors' affirmative action plans, OFCCP will not make the judgment solely on whether the contractor's affirmative action goals are met, that is, "the numbers game." (See Exhibit 5.6.) That alone will not serve as a basis for sanctions under the executive order. What is important to OFCCP are the nature and extent of the contractor's good-faith affirmative action activities and the appropriateness of those activities to the problems the contractor has identified in the workplace. An assessment of compliance will be made on both statistical and nonstatistical information indicating whether employees and applicants are being treated without regard to the prohibited categories of the executive order. This is far from the law blindly requiring a certain number of places to be filled by a certain gender or race, as many think it does.

The affirmative action plan regulations clearly state that they prefer to have contractors perform ongoing monitoring of their workplaces to ensure that their policies and practices are consistent with non-discriminatory hiring, promotions, termination, pay, and other workplace considerations. An employer would do well to heed that advice and catch any small problems before they become larger ones. Careful monitoring will address this quite well. Bank of America, Dell Technologies, and Goldman Sachs found out the hard way when it was reported in October 2019 that OFCCP collected more than $21 million from them. The payouts from Dell and Goldman Sachs were the largest OFCCP had ever obtained and laid to rest the notion that the Trump administration would impose smaller enforcement fines.

Judicial Affirmative Action

judicial affirmative action

Affirmative action ordered by a court as a remedy for discrimination found by the court to have occurred rather than affirmative action arising from Executive Order 11246.

Rather than an affirmative action plan imposed by Executive Order 11246, an employee may sue alleging an employer violated Title VII, and the affirmative action arises in response to a finding of workplace discrimination by the court that it must then remedy. Title VII gives courts fairly wide latitude in redressing wrongs. When a court orders affirmative action as a means of remedying a proven violation of Title VII, it is known as **judicial affirmative action**.

In addition to agency rules and regulations, courts have played an important role in shaping the concept of affirmative action. While there are no specific requirements as to what form an affirmative action plan must take (see Exhibit 5.8), if the plan is in keeping with the requirements set forth, the employer has little to fear from suits challenging implementation of the plan, although the monetary and energy costs in dealing with them are great.

The first affirmative action case to reach the U.S. Supreme Court, *Regents of the University of California v. Bakke,*[58] involved affirmative action in medical school admissions rather than employment; however, the case is viewed as the one that opened the affirmative action debate, and much of its reasoning was used in subsequent employment cases. While endorsing the concept of affirmative action to further the educational goal of a diverse student body, the Court struck down the University of California's affirmative action plan because it set aside a certain number of places for "disadvantaged students," who could also compete for the other spaces. The Court said it was not fair for the disadvantaged group to have additional spaces open to them that were not available to others.

In *Local 28, Sheet Metal Workers v. EEOC,* included at the end of the chapter, the Court imposed one of the stiffest judicial affirmative action plans ever developed, but only after the Court's orders had repeatedly been ignored by the union. In the case, the question arose as to who can receive the benefit of affirmative action plans. Can the plan benefit individuals who were not the actual victims of the employer's discriminatory practices? The Supreme Court held that there need not be a showing of discrimination against the particular individual (employee, applicant, promotion candidate, and the like) as long as the affirmative action plan meets appropriate requirements (see Exhibit 5.9) and the individual fits into the category of employees the plan was designed to benefit. This approach recognizes that the employer's policy may result in discouraging certain people from even applying for a job because they know it would be futile, given the employer's history.

Scenario

While the notion of providing relief for nonspecific victims of discrimination may appear questionable, the *Sheet Metal Workers* case is exactly the type of situation that justifies such action. As you read the case, in addition to thinking about what the union or employer should have done, think of how you would have handled the situation if you were the court imposing the remedy. Also, think of whether you would have allowed the situation to go on for so long if you were the court. This case is the basis for Opening Scenario 1.

Would you believe that on July 21, 2015, a federal court signed an order approving an estimated $12 million settlement of back pay claims for Black and Latinx sheet metal workers in litigation against the union? Think about it. The original finding of discrimination was in 1964! The Local 28 case was in 1989; then decades later this. All to keep the Blacks and Latinx workers out of the union. Do not miss the fact that this occurred in New York, which we tend to think of as so open and diverse. This case also clearly demonstrates why Title VII applies not only to employers but to unions or other organizations that refer applicants for employment as well.

Voluntary Affirmative Action

After the Court for the first time dealt with the issue of affirmative action in the *Bakke* case, the next big questions were whether a similar analysis applied (1) if the affirmative action plan involved private rather than state action, (2) if the plan involved a workplace rather than a university admissions program, and (3) whether voluntary affirmative action plans are permissible rather than only those required by Executive Order 11246 or imposed by a court to remedy. The opportunity to have those important Title VII developmental questions answered came the year after *Bakke,* in the *United Steelworkers of America, AFL-CIO v. Weber*[59] case. The answer to all three questions was yes. No affirmative action would be permitted in the private workplace.

In *Weber,* a white employee sued under Title VII alleging race discrimination, in that the union and employer adopted a voluntary affirmative action plan reserving for African American employees 50 percent of the openings in a training program until the percentage of African American craft workers in the plant approximated the percentage of African Americans in the local labor force. The Supreme Court held that the program was permissible, in that Title VII did not prohibit voluntary race-conscious affirmative action plans undertaken to eliminate a manifest racial imbalance, the measure is only temporary, and it did not unnecessarily trample the rights of white employees.

So, in addition to affirmative action plans required by Executive Order 11246 and those imposed by a court to remedy workplace discrimination pursuant to a Title VII claim, there is also the possibility of voluntary affirmative action. Here, the employer decides to institute an affirmative action plan on his or her own, regardless of whether the employer is required to do so under the executive order and despite the fact that no one has brought a Title VII claim. Employers generally engage in voluntary affirmative action as a proactive measure to avoid discrimination claims after making a determination that there is a manifest underrepresentation of minorities and women in the workplace, generally based on previous exclusionary policies or practices. However, an employer cannot simply unilaterally decide to institute a plan out of the goodness of his or her heart and implement it. Based on *Weber,* there are strict guidelines that must be followed if the plan is to withstand a legal challenge by an affected employee alleging discrimination because of the plan's implementation. (See Exhibit 5.9.)

Many employers were surprised by *Weber* since the year before the Court struck down a voluntary affirmative action plan in *Bakke.* Both concerned affirmative action plans, but there were considerable differences beyond even employment versus school admissions. Some of these differences and the Court's reasoning got lost in news coverage. Both decisions endorsed the concept of affirmative action, but the requirements were not met in *Bakke* and were in *Weber,* thus giving different, though not inconsistent, outcomes. *Weber* is the basis for Opening Scenarios 2 and 3.

2 Scenario

After *Weber,* you now realize that in Opening Scenario 2, it is permissible for an employer to have a voluntary affirmative action plan, but certain factors must be present in order to justify the plan to a court. In Opening Scenario 2, we do not have all the relevant facts to determine if the employer can take the affirmative action measures the employer wishes. For instance, we do not know why there are such small numbers of minorities and women in upper-level management and skilled-labor jobs. We do not know if it is because there is a history of discrimination and exclusion or because there simply are not sufficient numbers of women and minorities available in the workforce from which employees are drawn.

3 Scenario

In Opening Scenario 3, we know from *Weber* that an employer can have a one-for-one affirmative action promotion plan as part of a remedy for past discrimination, and if the *Weber* requirements are met, the employer is protected from liability for discrimination against employees alleging discrimination because they are adversely impacted by implementation of the plan.

Seven years later, in the case of *Wygant v. Jackson Board of Education*[60] and consistent with the language in *Bakke* and *Weber,* the Supreme Court again upheld the concept of affirmative action, this time for protection against layoffs for public employees, though it held that the requirements of demonstrating a compelling state interest and narrowly tailoring the plan to meet the objective had not been met in this case. This answered the question of whether the Court's decision in *Bakke,* involving the admissions policy for a public university, also applied to an affirmative action plan in a public workplace. It did. It also answered the question left after *Weber* as to whether the acceptance of voluntary affirmative action in private employment also applied to public employment. It did.

Johnson v. Transportation Agency, Santa Clara County, California,[61] a 1987 Supreme Court decision discussed later, relied heavily on *Weber* to determine that, under circumstances similar to those in *Weber* but involving a public employer rather than private and gender rather than race, the employer could appropriately take gender into account under its voluntary affirmative action plan as one factor of a promotion decision. The Court said the plan, voluntarily adopted to redress a "conspicuous imbalance in traditionally segregated job categories," represented a "moderate, flexible, case-by-case approach to effecting a gradual improvement in the representation of minorities and women." Consistent with *Weber,* the plan was acceptable because

LO5 List the basic safeguards put in place in affirmative action plans to minimize harm to others.

1. It did not unnecessarily trammel male employees' rights or create an absolute bar to their advancement.

2. It set aside no positions (as did *Bakke*) for women and expressly stated that its goals should not be construed as quotas to be met.

3. It was only temporary in that it was for purposes of attaining, not maintaining, a balanced workforce.

4. There was minimal intrusion into the legitimate, settled expectations of other employees.

"Reverse Discrimination"

LO6 Define "reverse discrimination" and tell how it relates to affirmative action.

reverse discrimination
Claim brought by a majority member who feels adversely affected by the use of an employer's affirmative action plan.

So-called **reverse discrimination**[62] has often been considered the flip side of affirmative action. When an employer is taking race or gender into account under an affirmative action plan in order to achieve an affirmative action goal of including those previously excluded from the workplace, someone not in the excluded group alleges she or he is harmed.

For example, much as in *Santa Clara,* an employer finds an underrepresentation of women in managerial positions in the workplace and develops an affirmative action plan for their inclusion. As part of that plan, one qualified female employee is to be chosen for a managerial training program for each male chosen. The employer chooses one male and then one female. The male employee who feels he would have been chosen next if there were no affirmative action plan requiring a woman to be chosen sues the employer, alleging reverse discrimination. That is, but for his gender, he would have been chosen for the position the female received and instead, he alleges, he is the victim of gender discrimination in being excluded because he is male.

Reverse discrimination accounts for only about 3 percent of the charges filed with the EEOC, and most of those claims result in no-cause findings. Despite what you may have heard, reverse discrimination is not the flip side of affirmative action. Our experience has been that this misunderstanding stems from most employees having a fundamental misunderstanding of discrimination laws, how they operate, and what affirmative action is and is intended to do. Title VII and the other protective legislation protects everyone. There is no special provision for whites or males who believe they were discriminated against. Everyone is protected by the law. As a part of that protection, the remedies for proven discrimination may make others feel harmed.

As you learned in our discussion of the requirements for an employer to have an affirmative action plan, once the plan is deemed necessary because there is an underrepresentation that cannot be accounted for in virtually any way other than exclusion of certain groups, even unwittingly, then consideration of race or gender becomes a necessary part of the remedy. The law builds in protections for employees who feel they may be adversely affected by ensuring that the plan is only given protection if it complies with the legal requirements.

One of the arguments frequently made in reverse discrimination cases is that affirmative action requires the "sons to pay for the sins of the fathers" and that "slavery is over—why can't we just forget it and move on?" Affirmative action is not about something that happened 150 years ago. It is about discrimination in the workplace *today.* Also keep in mind that it is not punishment in any way but rather a *remedy* for discrimination, or its vestiges, *that has been found to exist.* As for the "sins of the fathers," keep in mind the extent to which African Americans and women were *legally* excluded from the workplace from the beginning of this country's existence until passage of the Civil Rights Act in 1964. Their intentional inclusion only began to become a significant issue in the late 1970s to early 1980s. This gave those groups who were in the workplace for all those years before a huge head start on experience, training, presence, trustworthiness, seniority, perception of appropriateness for the job, and so on, all of which made them more likely to be hired.

These factors come into play each time an applicant or employee applies for a job, promotion, training, or other workplace benefit. Without the applicant's intentionally doing anything that may ask for more favorable or less favorable consideration (depending on the group to which the applicant belongs) because of more than 345 years of ingrained history, as shown by study after study, it happens. While it may not be intentional or even conscious, it has a definite harmful impact on groups traditionally excluded from the workplace—an impact that research has proved to be present time and again. For instance, despite the anecdotal evidence of seemingly omnipresent reverse discrimination situations we may hear about from our friends or colleagues, the U.S. Department of Labor's Glass Ceiling Report found that, though antidiscrimination laws have made a significant impact in bringing women and minorities into the workplace in entry-level positions, there are still significant workplace disparities. Twenty-five years later things have not changed as much as we would like to believe. Sometimes they are not even represented there. In March 2019, Goldman Sachs announced that it wanted to increase representation in hiring entry-level analysts and associates in the Americas to 50 percent for women, 11 percent for African Americans, and 14 percent for Latinx employees. It did not set a timetable or percentages for accomplishing these goals but said it would work to improve each year. In 2017, *Forbes* magazine published the results of a McKinsey & Co. and Lean-In organization report showing women are still woefully underrepresented "at every level of seniority in the corporate pipeline from entry level to the C-suite." Women of color were shown to be the most rare and correlated with significantly more negative perceptions of their workplace fairness and personal treatment.[63] Other times women and minorities may be there but harassed or treated less well because they are not perceived as the norm for the environment.

LO7 Explain the arguments of those opposed to affirmative action and those who support it.

While we would all love to live in a colorblind society, where merit is the only factor considered in the workplace, research shows that we are not there yet. Affirmative action steps in as a measure to help remedy this situation. Nevertheless, as you can see from the *Ricci v. DeStefano* case, included at the end of the chapter, claims by those who feel they were unjustly impacted by an employer's efforts to be inclusive remain an important tool in effectuating rights under Title VII for everyone as well as further defining its parameters.

See Chapter 2 to revisit key concepts.

In *Ricci,* the city of New Haven, Connecticut, took great pains to have a test developed for the promotion of firefighters to lieutenant and captain. Since these promotions did not happen often and were a great source of pride and upward mobility for the firefighters, it was important to the city to get them right. After the test was given, the percentage of Blacks and Latinx passing the exams was considerably lower than that of whites, and under existing rules, none of the Blacks qualified for promotion, though several passed the exam. The city was concerned that the promotions based on the exam scores would be challenged by the Black firefighters as having a disparate impact upon them, so the city discarded the exam scores. Those firefighters who would have been promoted and were not sued the city, and their position was upheld by the U.S. Supreme Court.

As you will see when you read the case, it is a perfect example of why an employer should simply do the right thing and let the chips fall where they may. It is why fair and consistent rules, evenly applied, are an employer's best protection against discrimination lawsuits. The city had already done a great deal to make sure its exam was fair and reflective of what was needed for the positions. If it had simply given the exam and allowed the scores to be used, even if the Black firefighters sued based on disparate impact, they would not have been able to make their case. The city had done all it could to make sure the exam was valid, and that is what the law requires.

What the city did was, in essence, treat the situation as an affirmative action plan. As managers and supervisors, do not simply do what you think will avoid liability because you think you might be sued. Simply make defensible legal workplace policies and decisions. Not only will employees be less likely to bring lawsuits, but when they do, you will be in a better position to successfully defend against them.

Valuing Diversity/Multiculturalism/Diversity, Equity, and Inclusion

LO8 Explain the concept of valuing diversity/ multiculturalism/diversity, equity, and inclusion and why it is needed and give examples of ways to do it.

Once affirmative action plans accomplished (at least to a limited degree) their purpose of bringing heretofore excluded employees into the workplace, as we just saw, employers discovered that this, in and of itself, was not enough to provide equal opportunity conditions for keeping them there and allowing them to progress. Employees coming into workplaces not accustomed to their presence found the workplace often hostile in subtle but very real ways. There is even a term for these actions by the majority: *microaggression*. It includes things like not making eye contact with minority, female, or other employees perceived as different than the norm or not giving them other obvious signs of respect one routinely expects in a workplace; not giving them credit for ideas they propose but accepting those ideas when they come from someone in the majority; not inviting them out to lunch or office social occasions; and so forth. When experienced on a continuing basis, they create a totally different environment for these workers than for those in the majority. They also send a very strong message of noninclusion or even hostility over time.

As you can see from simply the title of this section, as the workplace evolves and we know more and grow, concepts evolve accordingly. The newest, more enlightened version of how to address the issue of making workplaces more inclusive for everyone is diversity, equity, and inclusion, or DEI. Whatever name is used, the goal is to work on ensuring that everyone in the workplace feels free to make a contribution and flourish. While equal employment opportunity under the law deals with prohibiting discrimination in the hiring of various groups, DEI is aimed at realizing the competitive advantage and business opportunity created by a workplace geared to attracting the best talent, increasing creativity, and having a globally competitive workforce. While the concept began in response to minorities and women coming into the workplace, it now includes everyone in the workplace and the very different ways that we all exist in that space. The obvious categories are those protected by law, but there are many others that can operate to make employees less productive or not the contributors they could be because of, often unintentional, subtle exclusion. (See Exhibit 5.10, "Diversity—In All Its Dimensions.") This is how it is connected to Title VII, the executive order, and other protective legislation. Lack of diversity and inclusion is also often what leads to Title VII claims. They go hand in hand, so knowing about not only the law but also the DEI aspects of the workplace makes perfect sense.

While the hostility of workplace exclusion may be subtle, the impact on female and minority work lives is not. Diverse employees find they do not move up as quickly as other, more traditional, employees. Many are not included in workplace activities, are reprimanded more often, do not receive the same opportunities, and thus have higher turnover rates. Even subtle differences in their treatment can mean the difference between progressing in the workplace and remaining stagnant or, worse, leaving.

Exhibit 5.10 *Diversity—In All Its Dimensions*

We often think of diversity only in terms of the Title VII categories or in the context of avoiding lawsuits. However, there are much bigger implications for employers and for business. Research shows that workplaces where diversity is valued and employees feel included are more productive and come up with better solutions to problems, which, in turn, makes them more competitive. The following is an example of how diversity can arise in very surprising, but productive, ways.

When the University of Georgia got a new president in 2013, like the 21 before him, he was a white male. In his first state of the union address, he said that he wanted a university in which people felt free to innovate and not be afraid to try new ideas that could help the university in all aspects of its mission.

Not long after, he decided to go to a very popular step show put on by the Black Greek organizations of the university. He had a very enjoyable time watching the lively performances and seeing his students in a way he rarely had a chance to do.

Hearing this, a few days later, the author used it in a diversity session she had been requested to conduct with some university employees. Knowing from years of conducting such sessions that attendees are likely expecting that diversity would include only the usual categories of race, gender, and so forth, and perceive the session as being for purposes of "political correctness," she needed something different that would demonstrate how important a concept diversity and inclusion is, how it has real consequences, and how it can impact situations in unexpected ways.

So, the author asked the employees if they knew the university president. They said not in a social way, but they certainly knew of him. She asked what sort of person they thought he was: formal, informal, laid back, gruff, quiet, and so on. The consensus was that he was formal. The author then asked of the vast array of university events routinely offered, what sorts of events they thought he would go to outside of the ones he would normally be required to attend. They responded probably events at the Business School (where he had been a member of the faculty) and the Law School (from which he graduated).

She then asked if they knew what a step show was. They did. She asked if it would surprise them to know that the president had attended the big step show that was held the previous Saturday night.

They gasped in unison and said yes, it would *totally* surprise them. Shock was more like it. They thought it was great.

She asked why they thought she would have told them this. They had no idea.

She then told them it was because she wanted them to realize that if the person who asked the president to attend had not invited him because he thought the president would not want to attend because he was white and the event was predominantly Black or because the president was perceived as too formal and the event was purely fun, the president would have missed out on a great time, *and* he would have missed an excellent opportunity to demonstrate that when he told the university he wanted innovative thinking, he meant it. Of course, it was also a great opportunity for all students to see that he really did care about everyone at the university as he'd said. His credibility was greatly enhanced, his experience as a minority in a majority Black setting gave him a rich experience on which he could draw in all sorts of ways going forward, and he had great laughs in the process. All because he was included even though he was diverse from most of the others at the event, in both race and persona. It was a win-win situation all around. And the president got bragging rights as the first president in UGA's history to attend such an event.

The attendees were flabbergasted—both by seeing diversity and inclusion at work in such a surprising way and by their new insight into their president.

Exhibit 5.11 *Diversity, Equity, and Inclusion Shows Up in Corporate America in the Wake of George Floyd and COVID-19*

As you no doubt have witnessed in the wake of the racial reckoning that is taking place in the United States in the wake of what has been called the double pandemic of the killing of George Floyd and many other unarmed Blacks, as well as the patently unequal impact of COVID-19 on the Black community that brought to light many of the inequalities Blacks have complained of for years, the following letter went out to employees of a large organization that addresses medical issues. It is included in this section of Diversity/Multiculturalism/Diversity, Equity and Inclusion within the Affirmative Action chapter because it is an illustration of the gap between what many think affirmative action has accomplished, and the actual reality of Black lives. It is clear that the calls ending affirmative action are premature, as the gap is not only there, but has in many ways, widened. This courageous and insightful letter is a reminder of the work still to be done that the law does not address. It is also an admirable example of the business sector stepping up to do what it can in an effort to address societal issues it is uniquely positioned to do.

MODERN HEALTHCARE

Dr. Bruce Siegel

A Legacy of Health Disparities Laid Bare by COVID-19

In early April, the U.S. surgeon general called COVID-19 "our Pearl Harbor moment, our 9/11 moment." But data from New York City suggested another analogy: It had become our Katrina moment.

City health authorities released a report showing African Americans with the disease were dying at nearly twice the rate of whites—19.8 per 100,000 lab-conSrmed COVID-19 cases compared with 10.2 for whites. The disparity was even greater for Latino victims, who were dying at a rate of 22.8 per 100,000 cases.

It's not surprising COVID-19 exacts a high toll on racial and ethnic minorities, who historically have suffered grievously from natural disasters. In 2005, Hurricane Katrina laid bare deep racial and economic rifts in New Orleans that left poor people of color stranded and without the means to reach safety. Even today, the storm's health effects linger for many poor residents who waded through toxic water and foul air as they waited for relief.

So, we could predict COVID-19 would wreak havoc on Black and Latino populations in New York City and elsewhere. What should trouble all of us is how little we achieved these past 15 years and the price we again will pay in human lives.

Essential hospitals—those central to the safety net and now on the front lines of the COVID-19 crisis—see the ill effects of racism and disparities every day among the marginalized people they serve. Deeply seated inequities in our social fabric and the broader health care system manifest in ways that put people of color in the path of COVID-19: Substandard housing and food insecurity thwart social distancing and exacerbate chronic conditions. Minorities who SII jobs in transportation and other critical infrastructure cannot stay home and, instead, are exposed to the virus. Those furloughed from hospitality and other "nonessential" positions lose paychecks and insurance coverage and the health care access these bring.

(continued)

Exhibit 5.11 *continued*

These social risks are the ingredients of a perfect storm that has been with us for centuries and that we repeatedly fail to confront. That storm rages now in New York emergency departments, rural ICUs, Navajo reservations, and countless other settings across the country.

The question for us now is whether we learn from COVID-19 or accept the status quo. There will be a desire to pull back after this storm passes, to hunker down and avoid these tough questions. That will be the exactly wrong response; one guaranteed to lead to disaster again.

Our health systems must lead through action and example. They must lead collaboration with other necessary actors—communities, cities, states, and the federal government—in possibly new and untested partnerships. They also must address the social determinants that challenge good health in their community, particularly among racial and ethnic minorities. The list is long, but not insurmountable: poverty, food insecurity, housing instability, lack of transportation, low health literacy, language barriers, and others. These are the persistent, endemic hardships that put minority populations at the back of the pack before the race begins.

But we must not stop there. We also must commit to equity, internalize it, and make it our North Star. We must live it—starting at the top and ensuring diversity in our board rooms and executive oaces. We must practice it, with culturally sensitive care and attention to race, ethnicity, and language data that can expose disparities as a Srst step to eliminating them. And we need a health care workforce that looks like America.

Our nation's leaders will need to do their part, too. Will they support a robust and sustainable safety net, based on equity, beyond just the next few months? Will they act decisively in the weeks and months ahead as millions of Americans turn to government for much-needed help? Fifteen years ago, we failed to heed the lessons of Katrina. Today, we can choose to take a different course. Our nation deserves nothing less.

Inline Play

Source URL: https://www.modernhealthcare.com/opinion-editorial/legacy-health-disparities-laid- bare-covid-19

Faced with workplaces filled with new kinds of people, employers sought answers. The search became even more immediate after the release of the Hudson Institute's "Workforce 2000" study for the U.S. Department of Labor in 1987. According to the study, the United States was about to face its largest wave of immigration since World War II, and unlike the last big wave that was 90 percent European, this one would be about 90 percent Asian and Latin American.

valuing diversity
Learning to accept and appreciate those who are different from the majority and value their contributions to the workplace.

The idea of **valuing diversity** began to take root. Valuing diversity means being sensitive to and appreciative of differences among groups outside what was thought of as the mainstream and using those differences, coupled with basic human similarities, as a positive force to increase productivity and efficiency and to avoid liability for discrimination. For the past several years, employers all over the country have sponsored workplace programs to sensitize employees to differences as well as commonalities among people in the workplace. Being made aware of these differences in various racial, ethnic, religious, and other groups and also, almost more importantly, being reminded of the similarities as human beings have helped employees learn to better deal with them. (See "Exhibit 5.15, "What Does Equity, Diversity and Inclusion Have to do with a Peach Farm? Turns Out, Everything!") Chances are, at some point in your career, you will be exposed to the concept of diversity, equity, and inclusion. It will greatly increase your value to the employer to do so. (See Exhibits 5.12, "Cultural Differences," and 5.13, "Valuing Diversity.")

Exhibit 5.12 *Cultural Differences*

Did you ever think about how much culture affects us and how we differ culturally? Not only does it impact big things like our holidays, clothing, and so on, but it shapes much smaller things.

A list of tips to travelers abroad issued by the Chinese government warned:

Don't squat when waiting for a bus or a person. Don't spit in public. Don't point at people with your fingers. Don't make noise. Don't laugh loudly. Don't yell or call to people from a distance. Don't pick your teeth, pick your nose, blow your nose, pick at your ears, rub your eyes, or rub dirt off your skin. Don't scratch, take off your shoes, burp, stretch or hum.

Exhibit 5.13 *Valuing Diversity*

This piece, written in the early days of valuing diversity, is still relevant today but also shows you the evolution of the concept. It is interesting to see how the concepts discussed in the research as speculations are now being lived as we speak. It is also interesting how even cultural gestures evolve and change over time. In this case, the simple little gesture discussed can now add to its meanings racist hate symbol after a 2017 4chan trolling campaign.[64]

Make a circle with your thumb and forefinger. What does it mean? In America we know it primarily as meaning "okay." But how many of us know that it may also mean the equivalent of "flipping someone the bird," "give me coin change," "I wish to make love with you," or "I wish you dead, as my mortal enemy?" The objective act has not changed, yet the meaning has. The interpretation the act is given depends on the cultural conditioning of the receiver. Welcome to multiculturalism. Knowing what is meant becomes a necessity in processing the act, otherwise the act has little meaning. Culture is what provides that information and, thus, meaning for virtually everything we do, say, wear, eat, value, and where and in what we live, sit, and sleep. Imagine how many other acts we engage in every day which can be misinterpreted based upon differences in cultural conditioning. Yet our cultural conditioning is rarely given much thought. Even less is given to the culture of others. That will not be true much longer.

In the fall 1992 issue of the magazine of the American Assembly of Collegiate Schools of Business, the accrediting body of schools of business, the cover story and lead article was "Teaching Diversity: Business Schools Search for Model Approaches." In the article, it stated that "without integrating a comprehensive diversity message into the entire curriculum, the most relevant management education cannot occur." Multiculturalism is learning to understand, appreciate, and value (not just "tolerate") the unique aspects of cultures different from one's own. The end product is learning to value others who may be different, for what they contribute, rather than rejecting them simply because they are different.

The concept of "culture" encompasses not only ethnicity, but also gender, age, disability, affinity orientation, and other factors which may significantly affect and in many ways, define, one's life. Multiculturalism is learning that "different from" does not

(continued)

Exhibit 5.13 *continued*

mean "less than." It is getting in touch with one's cultural conditioning and working toward inclusion, rather than conformity.

Learning to value diversity opens people up to more. A major workplace concern is maximizing production and minimizing liability. Multiculturalism and valuing diversity contribute to this. To the extent that each person, regardless of cultural differences, is valued as a contributor in the workplace, he or she is less likely to sue the employer for transgressions (or perceived transgressions) stemming from not being valued. To the extent they are valued for who they are and what they can contribute in society, they are much less likely to end up engaging in acts such as the Los Angeles riots causing death and destruction in the spring of 1992 after the Rodney King verdict.

The U.S. Department of Labor's Workforce 2000 study conducted by the Hudson Institute and released in 1987 held a few surprises that galvanized America into addressing the issue of multiculturalism. According to the widely cited study, by the year 2000 we will experience the greatest influx of immigrants since World War II. At the same time, the percentage of women entering the workforce is increasing. The net result, according to the study, is that 85% of the net growth in the workforce will be comprised of women and non-Europeans. For the first time, white males will be a minority in the workforce. This need not be viewed as a threatening circumstance, but rather an opportunity for innovation and progress.

These factors, alone, reveal that the workplace (and by implication, schools, universities, recreational facilities and everything else) will be very different from before. It will no longer do to have a white, European, male, standard of operation. Others will be pouring into the workplace and will come with talent, energy, ideas, tenacity, imagination and other contributions the United States has always held dear as the basis for the "American Dream." They will come expecting to be able to use those qualities to pursue that dream. They will come feeling that they have much to offer and are valuable for all their uniqueness and the differences they may have from "the norm." And what will happen?

There is no choice but to be prepared. It is a simple fact that the workplace cannot continue to operate in the same way and remain productive.

Studies have shown that when the same problem is given to homogeneous groups and heterogeneous groups to solve, the heterogeneous groups come up with more effective solutions. When people feel valued for who they are and what they can contribute, rather than feeling pressed into conformity as if who they are is not good enough, they are more productive. Energy and creativity can be spent on the task at hand, rather than on worrying about how well they fit into someone's idea of who they should be. A significant number of the problems we face as a society and on which is spent millions in precious tax dollars comes from rejecting multiculturalism and not valuing diversity. If people were judged for who they are and what they contribute, there would not be a need for a Civil Rights Act, affirmative action plans, riot gear, human rights commissions, etc.

There are, of course, naysayers on the topic of multiculturalism such as those who think it is just an attempt at being "politically correct." It has been said that the term "politically correct" is an attempt to devalue, trivialize, demean, and diffuse the substantive value of the issues spoken of; that once something is deemed to be an issue of "political correctness," then there is no need to worry about the real import or impact of it, because it is only a passing fad which need not be taken seriously, as it will die its own natural death soon enough.

Multiculturalism is here to stay. People have evolved to the point where it will not go away. Self-worth and valuing oneself is a lesson that it takes many a long time to learn. Once learned, it is hard to give up. And, of course, why should it be given up? Again, "different from" does not mean "less than." Learning to value others as unique human beings whose culture is [sic] an integral part of who they are, rather than something to be shed at the work or school door, and learning to value the differences rather than to try to assimilate them, will benefit everyone.

Reprinted with permission from the University of Georgia's Columns.

As the concept of valuing diversity evolved, it was then paired with the concept of inclusion. Diversity was said to be like being invited to the party, while inclusion was being asked to dance once there. As our ideas expand to include more groups, more bases for differences heretofore not addressed in the workplace, it had become clear that even simply valuing diversity is not enough. Once there, it was clear that different culture or even a difference in gender meant making changes in how things operate. For instance, male-dominated workplaces often engaged in activities like taking clients out to strip clubs or golfing while conducting business, both of which were not likely to be activities many females employees engaged in or felt comfortable doing. This put female employees at a disadvantage. They either were excluded from the business discussions if they did not go to the strip club or sat uncomfortably with naked females dancing around if they did. All just to do their job. Making employees feel included by realizing the myriad ways in which they are subtly excluded is an important tool for avoiding liability and maximizing employee productivity.

The idea of diversity and inclusion received more formal recognition in the Dodd-Frank Wall Street Reform and Consumer Protection Act of 2010.[65] While mainly a law passed in response to what were perceived as Wall Street excesses that were at least partially responsible for the U.S. financial crisis of 2007-2008, the legislation went further. Section 342 of the act required the establishment of an Office of Minority and Women Inclusion in each of the agencies responsible for enforcement under the statute within six months of the law's enactment (Department of the Treasury, Federal Deposit Insurance Corporation, Securities and Exchange Commission, Federal Housing Finance Agency, Federal Reserve banks and board, National Credit Union Administration, Comptroller of the Currency, and the Bureau of Consumer Financial Protection). The offices "shall be responsible for all matters of the agency relating to diversity in management, employment and business activities." That is, the offices are to evaluate agency adherence to equal employment in hiring and contracting.

The director of each office is required by law to develop standards for assessing the diversity policies and practices of entities regulated by the agency. Thus, the reach of the legislation is long. It covers not only the five federal agencies involved in enforcing the law but also those entities it regulates. Apparently, the assessment is more advisory and voluntary than punitive, in that there is no penalty if an assessment shows that an entity or agency fails to meet all elements of the standards developed or to reach some goal established by the standards. The five agencies came up with a set of proposed joint standards for assessing the diversity policies and procedures of entities regulated by the agencies in 2013 and have been submitting yearly annual reports to Congress as required by law since.[66]

Once the concept of diversity and inclusion was incorporated into the workplace, explored, and allowed to operate for a while, over time it became clear that bringing in diverse employees and including them may well not be enough to achieve the goal of everyone having an equal opportunity for employment as we envision it. Equity had to be a part of the picture. The concept of equity can be thought of as providing each type of employee what it is they need to best succeed rather than treating everyone the same. There is a graphic available showing three cartoon characters trying to view a soccer game being played on the other side of a wooden fence. (See Exhibit 5.14, "Equality Versus Equity.") They are three different heights. Wooden boxes are provided for them to stand on, but because the boxes are all the same and the heights are not, some can now see and others still cannot. This is equality. It did not benefit everyone, only the ones able to benefit from it. However, providing boxes that were the height necessary for each of the individual viewers to be able to see over the fence permits each of them to see. That is the concept of equity.

Again, what employers can choose to do to bring more people into their workplace who have traditionally been left out (and, without some measure to include them, would continue to be left out) is not defined in the law. But as employers have warmed up to the idea of going beyond the status quo, they have been quite innovative. Sometimes, like with the NFL's Rooney Rule (see Exhibit 5.16, "The Rooney Rule: Affirmative Action Comes to Professional Football?"), all it takes is bringing into the consideration process someone who might not necessarily otherwise be included. (See Exhibit 5.17, "The Link Between Our Nonverbal Messages and How We Treat Others. Wow! Who Knew?")

Exhibit 5.14 *Equality Versus Equity*

EQUALITY VERSUS EQUITY

In the first image, it is assumed that everyone will benefit from the same supports. They are being treated equally.

In the second image, individuals are given different supports to make it possible for them to have equal access to the game. They are being treated equitably.

In the third image, all three can see the game without any supports or accommodations because the cause of the inequity was addressed. The systemic barrier has been removed.

McGraw Hill

Exhibit 5.15 *What Does Equity, Diversity, and Inclusion Have to do With a Peach Farm? Turns Out, Everything!*

After an incredibly random conversation with a friend who lives in California about, of all things, the virtue of California peaches vs. Georgia peaches, my California friend (I live in Georgia, of course ☺) a few weeks later forwarded me the e-newsletter of his favorite fruit farm. Masumoto Farms is a family-owned business in the central California valley that grows organic fruits. Expecting to see information on their fruits and harvest times, I was blown away to find that in addition to that information, the newsletter was full of items of interest to me as someone who cares about, writes about, consults about and teaches about diversity and inclusion issues. Among other things there was an item on a recent same-sex marriage performed at the farm, a list of what the family was reading and listening to that included diverse issues, and an item about a recent online *Vogue* magazine article on the grandmother and granddaughter as part of the Day of Remembrance. I was so impressed that I wrote the owners and not only lauded them on the diversity and inclusion items provided as an absolutely totally in-context part of their newsletter but asked if they would be willing to be included in the next edition of our text to discuss their approach to diversity and inclusion, why it was important to them and why they include it was part of their farming business. Happily, they agreed. You will not only be able to see for yourself how diversity and inclusion issues show up in places you probably never thought about, but why it is important for us to know and address them.

***

The Masumoto Family Farm is a small family operation in the heart of the Central Valley of California. Our organic farm is about 80 acres and is fed by waters from the Kings River which ties us directly to the Sierra Nevada mountain range to our east. I am the fourth generation in my Japanese American family to touch the same soil that we work today.

In our fields, trees planted by my grandparents still thrive and grow luscious peaches. On their own, we hope the peaches are memorable. We work very hard to harvest our fruit as close to the peak of ripeness as possible so that when eaters find them in retail outlets, they are fragrant, juicy, and bursting with flavor. (We don't always succeed, but we never abandon our striving.) On the surface, we are in the business of growing and selling organic fruit, but for our family, being connected to the land and the legacy of our family history is a core part of who we are, why we farm, and the social and cultural work we see embedded in each bite of fruit.

A peach isn't just a peach. For us, a peach is a vehicle of connection between so many different forces in life. The peach is a result of complex interactions between ecological systems and life on the farm: think of the sunlight, the soil, the water; think of our workers, the truckers, the people we work with to get fruit from tree to eaters; think of the land itself.

If we consider just the physical location of our farm, we begin to see how our business is a result of multiple historic forces connected to identity, belonging, racism, and survival. Large sweeping historic forces shaped our land: the colonization and formation of the United States and the stealing of indigenous people's land; the commodification of land into property and parcels; the wrangling of rivers through building immense dams in the 1930s; immigration policies which restricted entry and legal citizenship based on race. My great-grandparents who immigrated from Japan were not allowed to own land in California (California Alien Land Laws of 1913 and 1920) nor become citizens only because of racist laws that isolated and targeted Asians as not worthy of the same rights as immigrants who were perceived to be white (e.g., the other side of my mixed-race family, my German immigrant side were also farmers but had no barriers to entry as did my Japanese immigrant ancestors). These large histories meant that my Japanese great-grandparents were farm workers, not farmers because they were prohibited from owning land.

My jiichan (grandfather) bought the first 40 acres of our farm in 1948, just three years after he and all our Japanese American family had been released after unjust incarceration during World War II.

(continued)

Exhibit 5.15 *continued*

My then teenage grandmother finished high school in the prison camp built without permission on Gila River Indian Community land in the desert of Arizona. No one in my family, nor the other thousands of Japanese American families, was ever treated with the basic rights of citizenship nor residency in the United States: no one was granted legal due process nor found guilty of crimes. They were imprisoned because of racism. This experience forever changed my family, and it changes who I am and how I farm.

Every day I touch our soil, I think about what it means for me to be here now. It means that our family endured and survived through tremendous racism to be here. It means that this place I call home is both full of love and also shaped by loss. (Sometimes I wonder, if my grandparents had not been incarcerated and had been granted the rights and access of white Americans of the same age, would they have pursued other careers? Where would they have lived? How would that have changed who we are?)

This is also why everything we do - from our farm newsletters, to how we interact with our employees, to the leadership we try to show in our community, to the story we tell about the peaches we grow – all of it is connected to the specificity of our farm story (diversity), the way we look at the world and the dreams we have for it (inclusion), and our unfulfilled longing for justice and healing for us and our community (equity and justice). We are not an anonymous farm; our histories are wrapped up in our passion for what we do and how we do it. The peach we grow is not the same as the peach from another farm. We farm in America and we farm as inheritors of stories and meaning, so everything we grow, even our peaches are songs of pride and longing.

Reflection from Nikiko Masumoto at the kind invitation of Professor Bennett-Alexander.

For more information on the Masumoto Family Farm: www.masumoto.com

Exhibit 5.16 *The Rooney Rule: Affirmative Action Comes to Professional Football?*

Ever wonder why so many African American football players are on the field playing extremely well yet so few end up in the front office or as coaches? The NFL eventually did. In an attempt to provide more opportunities to minorities in the consideration of NFL football coaches, the NFL adopted the Rooney Rule (named for Pittsburgh owner Dan Rooney, head of the NFL's Workplace Diversity Committee). The Rooney Rule requires a team with a vacant head coaching position to interview at least one minority candidate. The intent of the rule is to provide an opportunity for teams to look at candidates they might otherwise not interview. They are not required to hire, only to interview. The Pittsburgh Steelers interviewed former Vikings defensive coordinator Mike Tomlin when they were searching for a head coach. Tomlin ended up being the best candidate for the job and got it,

becoming the youngest head coach in the league. The Rooney Rule is still debated, with some saying it is too little to simply require that a minority candidate be interviewed and some saying it is forcing the situations and making teams just go through the motions. Tomlin received his offer the same day that, for the first time ever, two African American NFL head coaches made it to the Super Bowl. At the historic Super Bowl XLI, on February 4, 2007, Coach Tony Dungy of the Indianapolis Colts beat out Coach Lovie Smith of the Chicago Bears in what most fans referred to as one of the best games ever. Coincidentally, the BCS national championship college football game between the University of Florida Gators and the unbeaten Ohio State Buckeyes also featured a historic matchup: two African American quarterbacks. Florida's Chris Leak beat out Heisman trophy winner Troy

Smith, 41–14. In June 2009, the Rooney Rule was extended to cover general managers. In January 2013, after the NFL expressed its disappointment that no Blacks were hired for 14 open positions, the watchdog group that oversees diversity in NFL hiring asked the league to expand the rule to cover most vacancies for offensive and defensive coordinator jobs. In December 2016, the NFL said it would do so for some coordinator openings on an informal basis.[67]

Exhibit 5.17 *The Link Between Our Nonverbal Messages and How We Treat Others. Wow! Who Knew?*

Turns out we are *very* much impacted by our nonverbal messages and how we treat others. Dr. Allison Skinner, a social psychology professor at the University of Georgia, recently gained a great deal of attention for her very interesting research into racial bias and nonverbal signals. We have no doubt that you will be as fascinated as we were and that you will find it a rich source of self-reflection.

***

1. **You recently conducted some research that highlighted the impact of our nonverbal messages and how we treat others. Can you tell us what made you decide on this as a research query and what it is you found?**

I first started thinking about this research question when I learned about previous research in my field (social psychology) showing that racial biases can be influenced by nonverbal signals. These earlier studies showed that when White people in the United States observed interactions in which a White person was nonverbally cold and unfriendly toward a Black person, that increased the observer's racial biases. Reading about these findings made me wonder whether nonverbal signals just activate attitudes that we already have (e.g., racial biases) or whether people would actually form their initial attitudes toward others based on the nonverbal signals that they see others direct toward them. My findings indicated that attitudes can actually be acquired through nonverbal messages. This means that merely being exposed to someone else displaying friendlier nonverbal signals toward one person relative to another will generally lead people to favor the person who receives more positive nonverbal signals.

2. **What impact do you think your research has on issues like diversity and inclusion or diversity, equity, and inclusion in the workplace or even discrimination claims brought by employees who believe they were discriminated against in the workplace?**

My work shows that our attitudes are influenced by the nonverbal cues displayed by others around us. In terms of workplace diversity, this means that we may learn to favor certain people in the workplace over others merely because we observe coworkers/managers/employers nonverbally favoring those people. This means that even if only one or two people in a workplace have social biases (e.g., against women, people of color, people of certain religions), those biases could be subtly spread to others in the workplace via nonverbal signals.

I also found that people whose attitudes were shaped in this way tended not to be aware of what contributed to their attitudes. Only about 30 percent of participants in my study indicated that the way the individuals were treated (the thing that we experimentally manipulated in our study) influenced their attitudes. In contrast, approximately 60 percent of people reported that the way that the individuals behaved (which we held constant in our study) influenced their attitudes. Thus, not only were people no very aware of the factor that did influence their

(continued)

Exhibit 5.17 *continued*

attitudes (how the individuals were treated), they tended to misattribute their attitudes to the target individual's behavior. Thinking about this in a workplace setting, it means that people are picking up attitudes about their coworkers based on how they are treated by others but are likely unaware that they are being influenced in this way. Perhaps even more importantly, they may also attribute their attitudes to the targets of bias, believing that they are responsible for the lower quality interaction. So if an employer were less nonverbally friendly to their Black employees than they are toward their white employees, that may lead the white employees to develop negative attitudes toward the Black employees. In addition, the white employees would be more likely to think that the Black employees' behavior influenced their attitudes, than the white employer's behavior. So they may justify their attitudes, believing that they dislike the Black employees because they are rude, difficult, etc. (not a good employee). All of this presumably could have an impact on discrimination claims, because in the scenario just described, the prevailing opinion in the workplace would be that the Black employees were worse workers, and thus any negative treatment they received was based on the Black employees' attitudes and behavior, as opposed to mistreatment or discrimination on the part of the employer.

3. **Do you have any plans to take this research further?**

Yes, there are two important future directions I am currently examining in this line of work. The first is to examine whether nonverbally acquired attitudes will generalize to other members of a group. In other words, can observing nonverbal signals directed toward one member of a group (e.g., a nationality) lead observers to develop biases against the entire group. So far I have found evidence among both children and adults that the biases toward individuals can be generalized to large groups in this way. I am also examining how to limit the spread of attitudes via nonverbal signals. To do this I have looked at different messages (e.g., providing positive messages about the targets of bias) that might be provided in order to overcome the spread of nonverbal biases.

Source: Email interview with Dr. Skinner, September 16, 2019.

In an effort to promote diversity, equity, and inclusion and ensure that once employees are hired the employer maximizes the opportunity, employers do such things as

- Organize workplace affinity groups for LGBT employees, female employees, Latinx employees, and so on.
- Include diverse actors in advertising and commercials.
- Hold professional development workshops for high-potential diverse employees.
- Institute formal procedures to handle complaints from diverse employees.
- Closely monitor the progress of diverse employees along the way.
- Tie performance reviews of managers to their measurable support for diversity, equity, and inclusion.
- Organize business networking groups.
- Hold management diversity, equity, and inclusion training.
- Hold diversity, equity, and inclusion training for non-managerial employees.

Management Tips

Affirmative action can be a bit tricky. Keeping in mind these tips can help avoid liability for instituting and implementing an affirmative action plan.

- Ensure that the hiring, promotion, training, and other such processes are open, fair, and available to all employees on an equal basis, as appropriate.
- If an affirmative action plan is to be adopted voluntarily, work with the union (if there is one) and other employee groups to try to ensure fairness and get early approval from the constituencies affected to ward off potential litigation.
- Make sure voluntary affirmative action plans meet the judicial requirements of
  - Being used to redress a conspicuous imbalance in traditionally segregated job categories.
  - Being moderate, flexible, and gradual in approach.
  - Being temporary in order to attain, not maintain, a balanced workforce.
  - Not unnecessarily trammeling employees' rights or creating an absolute bar to their advancement.
  - Unsettling no legitimate, firmly rooted expectations of employees.
  - Presenting only a minimal intrusion into the legitimate, settled expectations of other employees.
- Provide training about the plan so that all employees understand its purpose and intent. Try to allay fears from the outset to ward off potential litigation. The more employees know and understand what is being done, the less likely they are to misunderstand and react adversely. Even so, keep in mind that some employees will still dislike the plan. Reiterating top-level management's commitment to equal employment opportunity will stress the seriousness of management's commitment.
- Implement periodic diversity, equity, and inclusion and related training. This not only provides a forum for employees to express their views and input about these issues, but it also provides information on learning how to deal with their coworkers as the issues arise.

- Provide mentors for diverse employees.
- Have a chief diversity officer who reports directly to the chief executive officer (CEO).
- Focus on single diversity issues such as diversity in philanthropy, recruiting, retention, supply contractors, and so on.
- Have diverse board of directors members have a "road show" to meet with diverse employees for networking.
- Take the direct approach, like Walmart did when, in 2007, it notified its 100 outside-counsel law firms that it was only going to retain firms that made a concerted effort to be inclusive of women and minorities, as evidenced by them being on the liaison committee for business with Walmart.
- Build diversity, equity, and inclusion into everything the employer does, not just Mexican food on Cinco de Mayo or remembrance of Dr. Martin Luther King during Black History Month.

- Institute scholarship and internship programs to groom diverse students or applicants for eventual hire.
- Make personal phone calls and follow-ups with diverse applicants to assure them of the seriousness of inclusion.
- Notify employees of inappropriate or exclusionary workplace behaviors toward others.
- Review workplace policies and practices and their impact on diversity.
- Make sure white males are included in the employer's concept of diversity.
- Seek the input of diverse groups in developing a workplace approach to diversity, equity, and inclusion.

Chapter Summary

- Affirmative action is intentional inclusion of women, minorities, and others traditionally excluded in the workplace after demonstrated underrepresentation of these historically disadvantaged groups.
- Affirmative action plans may arise voluntarily, as a remedy in a discrimination lawsuit, or as part of an employer's responsibilities as a contractor or subcontractor with the government.
- Understanding the historical background of why affirmative action exists is critical to a true understanding of the concept and how to avoid pitfalls in its implementation.
- Employers should conduct voluntary periodic equal employment opportunity audits to monitor their workforce for gender, minority, and other inclusion. If there is underrepresentation, the employer should develop a reasonable, nonintrusive, flexible plan within appropriate guidelines.
- Such plans should not displace nonminority employees or permit people to hold positions for which they are not qualified, simply to meet affirmative action goals. This view should not be encouraged or tolerated.
- A well-reasoned, flexible plan with endorsement at the highest levels of the workplace, applied consistently and diligently, will greatly aid in diminishing negativity surrounding affirmative action and in protecting the employer from adverse legal action.
- Diversity, equity, and inclusion have become important concepts as employers move past simply bringing women and minorities into the workplace and instead try to ensure that they are provided with the environment and tools they need to fully contribute to the workplace. Programs that promote diversity, equity, and inclusion can be an effective basis for creating a workplace that does not have affirmative action issues resulting in litigation.

18. Gertrude Exrosky, *Racism and Justice: The Case for Affirmative Action* (Ithaca, NY: Cornell University Press, 1991).

19. LeAnn Lodder et al., *Racial Preference and Suburban Employment Opportunities* (Chicago: Legal Assistance Foundation of Metropolitan Chicago and the Chicago Urban League, April 2003).

20. Benedick, Marc, Charles W. Jackson, and Victor Reinoso, "Measuring Employment Discrimination through Controlled Experiments," *Review of Black Political Economy* 25 (Summer 1994).

21. Bertrand, Marianne, and Sendhil Mullainathan, "Are Emily and Brendan More Employable Than Lakisha and Jamal? A Field Experiment on Labor Market Discrimination," http://www.economics.harvard.edu/faculty/mullainathan/files/emilygreg.pdf.

22. "Women's Earnings and Income," Equity in Business Leadership, *Catalyst* (September 18, 2013), http://www.catalyst.org/kwledge/womens-earnings-and-income.

23. Bureau of Labor Statistics, Current Population Survey, "Table 37: Median Weekly Earnings of Full-Time Wage and Salary Workers by Selected Characteristics, 2012" (2013), http://www.catalyst.org/knowledge/womens-earnings-and-income.

24. Valerie A. Rawslton and William E. Spriggs, *Pay Equity 2000: Are We There Yet?* (Washington, DC: National Urban League Institute for Opportunity and Equality, SRR-02-2001, April 2001).

25. U.S. Government Accounting Office, *Women's Earnings: Federal Agencies Should Better Monitor Their Performance in Enforcing Anti-Discrimination Laws* (August 11, 2008), http://www.gao.gov/products/A83444.

26. National Committee on Pay Equity, "Race and Pay Policy Brief," http://www.pay-equity.org/info-racebrief.html.

27. Report of the Federal Glass Ceiling Commission, *Good for Business: Making Full Use of the Nation's Human Capital,* March 1995, http://www.dol.gov/oasam/programs/history/reich/reports/ceiling.pdf.

28. Report of the Glass Ceiling Commission, "A Solid Investment: Making Full Use of the Nation's Human Capital" (November 1995), http://www.dol.gov/oasam/programs/history/reich/reports/ceiling1.pdf.

29. Ibid.

30. Conrad, Cecilia, "The Economic Cost of Affirmative Action," in M. V. Lee Badgett and Margaret Simms, eds., *Economic Perspectives on Affirmative Action* (Washington, DC: Joint Center for Political and Economic Studies, 1995).

31. *Multi-City Study on Urban Inequality* (Russell Sage Foundation Publications, 2001), http://www.icpsr.umich.edu/icpsrweb/ICPSR/studies/02535.

32. Estrin, Robin, for the Associated Press, "Study: Race Is Still Key to Chances for Success," *The Philadelphia Inquirer,* October 2, 1999. Copyright © 1999 The Philadelphia Enquirer. All rights reserved.

33. Kathryn Alfisi, "D.C. Judicial Conference Tackles Implicit Bias in Decision Making," *Washington Lawyer,* May 2011, p. 6.

34. Moritz, Rob, "Hearing Signals End to Little Rock Desegregation Case," *Arkansas News* (January 12, 2014), http://arkansasnews.com/news/arkansas/hearing-signals-end-little-rock-area-school-desegregationcase; "Pulaski County School Desegregation Case Officially Ends," Nexstar Broadcasting, Inc., Fox16.com (January 13, 2014), http://www.fox16.com/story/pulaski-co-school-desegregation-case-officiallyen/d/story/8b377UeIpEmejccogutUUg.

35. House Joint Resolution No. 607, Expressing the General Assembly's Regret for Virginia's Experience with Eugenics, 2/2/01 (House), 2/14/01 (Senate), http://leg1.state.va.us/cgi-bin/legp504.exe?011+ful+HJ607ER.

36. Stern, Alexandra Minna, "Sterilized in the Name of Public Health: Race, Immigration and Reproductive Control in Modern California," *American Journal of Public Health,* July 2005, pp. 1128–38, http://www.ncbi.nlm.nih.gov/pmc/articles/PMC1449330/.

37. Congressional Record, 75th Cong., 2d sess. (1937), 82:1388.

38. See Ira Katznelson, *When Affirmative Action Was White: An Untold History of Racial Inequality in Twentieth-Century America* (New York: W. W. Norton, 2005).

39. See David E. Bernstein, *Only One Place of Redress: African Americans, Labor Regulations and the Court from Reconstruction to the New Deal* (Durham, NC: Duke University Press, 2001).

40. Katznelson, *When Affirmative Action Was White.*

41. "Traitor or Hero?," *60 Minutes,* CBS (November 9, 1997).

42. Desliver, Drew, "Black Unemployment Rate Is Consistently Twice That of Whites," The Pew Research Center (August 21, 2013), http://www.pewresearch.org/fact-tank/2013/08/21/through-good-times-and-bad-black-unemployment-is-consistently-double-that-of-whites/.

43. "OFCCP: Facts on Executive Order 11246-Affirmative Action," http://www.dol.gov/ofccp/regs/compliance/aa.htm.

44. For fun and informative exercises about affirmative action, see http://www.understand-ingprejudice.org/demos/.

45. Executive Order 8802, Prohibition of Discrimination in the Defense Industry (May 25, 1941), http://docs.fdrlibrary.marist.edu/od8802t.html.

46. OFCCP's regulations can be found at 41 Code of Federal Regulations part 60, http://www.ogc.doc.gov/ogc/contracts/cld/regs/65fr26087.html.

47. "DOL by the Numbers," http://dol.gov.

48. Source: http://www.ogc.doc.gov/ogc/contracts/cld/regs/65fr26087.html.

49. 41 C.F.R. 60-2.14.

50. 41 C.F.R. 60-14.

51. 41 C.F.R. 60-2.16.

52. 41 C.F.R. § 60-2.16(e)(1).

53. 41 C.F.R. § 60-2.16(e)(4).

54. 41 C.F.R. § 60-2.16(e)(2).

55. 476 U.S. 267 (1986).

56. 129 5. Ct. 2658 (2009).

57. See U.S. Department of Labor's Fiscal Year 2010 Annual Performance Report at 68, http://www.dol.gov/dol/budget/2012/PDF/CBJ-2012-V1-01.pdf.

58. 438 U.S. 265 (1978).

59. 443 U.S. 193 (1979).

60. 476 U.S. 267 (1986).

61. 480 U.S. 616 (1987).

62. The reason the term "reverse discrimination" is put in quotation marks is because it is not actually a legal concept but rather an outgrowth of the implementation of affirmative action plans. *Everyone* is protected from workplace discrimination by the

antidiscrimination laws. There is only one type of discrimination recognized by law, and it applies to everyone. That discrimination is the unlawful use of prohibited criteria for making job decisions. Whether it is done in the context of an affirmative action plan or not, if it is illegal discrimination, the law does not see it as different simply because of the type of person involved or the way it arose. See EEOC Compliance Manual, Section 15, at 5. We do not use the quotation marks after the first usage.

63. Elesser, Kim, "New Study: The Broken Rung Keeping Women from Management," Kim Elesser, *Forbes* (October 16, 2019).

64. https://www.adl.org/education/references/hate-symbols/okay-hand-gesture.

65. Public Law 111-203, 124 Stat. 1376, 1541 (July 11, 2010) codified as 12 U.S. Code 5452, http://www.fdic.gov/regulations/reform/dfa_selections.html#9.

66. Proposed Interagency Policy Statement Establishing Joint Standards for Assessing the Diversity Policies and Practices of Entities Regulated by the Agencies and Request for Comment, 78 Federal Register 107 (October 25, 2013), p. 64052, https://www.federalregister.gov/articles/2013/10/25/2013-25142/proposed-interagency-policy-statement-establishing-joint-standards-for-assessing-the-diversity.

67. Maske, Mark, "Diversity Group Seeks Expansion of NFL's Rooney Rule to Cover Coordinator Jobs," *The Washington Post* (January 22, 2013), http://www.washingtonpost.com/blogs/football-insider/wp/2013/01/22/diversity-groupseeks-expansion-of-nfls-rooney-rule-to-cover-coordinator-jobs/; and Maske, Mark, "NFL Vows to Apply Rooney Rule Informally to Some Coordinator Positions," *The Washington Post* (December 21, 2016), https://www.washingtonpost.com/news/sports/wp/2016/12/21/nfl-vows-to-apply-rooney-rule-informally-to-some-coordinator-openings/?utm_term=.019ac066ed24.

Cases

Local 28, Sheet Metal Workers v. EEOC,
478 U.S. 421 (1986)

The union and its apprenticeship committee were found guilty of discrimination against Latinxs and African Americans and were ordered to remedy the violations. They were found numerous times to be in contempt of the court's order, and after 18 years the court eventually imposed fines and an affirmative action plan as a remedy. The plan included benefits to persons not members of the union. The Supreme Court held the remedies to be appropriate under the circumstances.

Brennan, J.

***

Local 28 represents sheet metal workers employed by contractors in the New York City metropolitan area. The Local 28 Joint Apprenticeship Committee (JAC) is a labor–management committee which operates a 4-year apprenticeship training program designed to teach sheet metal skills. Apprentices enrolled in the program receive training both from classes and from on-the-job work experience. Upon completing the program, apprentices become journeyman members of Local 28. Successful completion of the program is the principal means of attaining union membership.

In 1964, the New York State Commission for Human Rights determined that the union and JAC had excluded African Americans from the union and apprenticeship program in violation of state law. The Commission, among other things, found that the union had never had any Black members or apprentices, and that "admission to apprenticeship is conducted largely on a nepot[is]tic basis involving sponsorship by incumbent union members," creating an impenetrable barrier for nonwhite applicants. The union and JAC were ordered to "cease and desist" their racially discriminatory practices. Over the next 18 years and innumerable trips to court, the union did not remedy the discrimination.

To remedy the contempt and the union's refusal to comply with court orders, the court imposed a 29 percent nonwhite membership goal to be met by a certain date, and a $150,000 fine to be placed in a fund designed to increase nonwhite membership in the apprenticeship program and the union. The fund was used for a variety of purposes, including:

- Providing counseling and tutorial services to non-white apprentices, giving them benefits that had traditionally been available to white apprentices from family and friends.

- Providing financial support to employers otherwise unable to hire a sufficient number of apprentices.

- Providing matching funds to attract additional funding for job-training programs.

- Creating part-time and summer sheet metal jobs for qualified nonwhite youths.

- Extending financial assistance to needy apprentices.

- Paying for nonwhite union members to serve as liaisons to vocational and technical schools with sheet metal programs in order to increase the pool of qualified nonwhite applicants for the apprenticeship program.

The union appealed the remedy. Principally, the parties maintain that the Fund and goal exceeds the scope of remedies available under Title VII because it extends race-conscious preferences to individuals who are not the identified victims of their unlawful discrimination. They argue that section 706(g) authorizes a district court to award preferential relief only to actual victims of unlawful discrimination. They maintain that the goal and Fund violates this provision since it requires them to extend benefits to Black and Hispanic individuals who are not the identified victims of unlawful discrimination. We reject this argument and hold that section 706(g) does not prohibit a court from ordering, in appropriate circumstances, affirmative race-conscious relief as a remedy for past discrimination. Specifically, we hold that such relief may be appropriate where an employer or a labor union has engaged in persistent or egregious discrimination, or where necessary to dissipate the lingering effects of pervasive discrimination.

The availability of race-conscious affirmative relief under section 706(g) as a remedy for a violation of Title VII furthers the broad purposes underlying the statute. Congress enacted Title VII based on its determination that racial minorities were subject to pervasive and systematic discrimination in employment. It was clear to Congress that the crux of the problem was "to open employment opportunities for Negroes in occupations which have been traditionally closed to them and it was to this problem that Title VII's prohibition against racial discrimination was primarily addressed." Title VII was designed to achieve equality of employment opportunities and remove barriers that have operated in the past to favor an identifiable group of white employees over other employees. In order to foster equal employment opportunities, Congress gave the lower courts broad power under section 706(g) to fashion the most complete relief possible to remedy past discrimination.

In most cases, the court need only order the employer or union to cease engaging in discriminatory practices, and award make-whole relief to the individuals victimized by those practices. In some instances, however, it may be necessary to require the employer or union to take affirmative steps to end discrimination effectively to enforce Title VII. Where an employer or union has engaged in particularly longstanding or egregious discrimination, an injunction simply reiterating Title VII's prohibition against discrimination will often prove useless and will only result in endless enforcement litigation. In such cases, requiring a recalcitrant employer or union to hire and to admit qualified minorities roughly in proportion to the number of qualified minorities in the workforce may be the only effective way to ensure the full enjoyment of the rights protected by Title VII.

Further, even where the employer or union formally ceases to engage in discrimination, informal mechanisms may obstruct equal employment opportunities. An employer's reputation for discrimination may discourage minorities from seeking available employment. In these circumstances, affirmative race-conscious relief may be the only means available to assure equality of employment opportunities and to eliminate those discriminatory practices and devices which have fostered racially stratified job environments to the disadvantage of minority citizens. Affirmative action promptly operates to change the outward and visible signs of yesterday's racial distinctions and thus, to provide an impetus to the process of dismantling the barriers, psychological or otherwise, erected by past practices.

Finally, a district court may find it necessary to order interim hiring or promotional goals pending the development of non-discriminatory hiring or promotion procedures. In these cases, the use of numerical goals provides a compromise between two unacceptable alternatives: an outright ban on hiring or promotions, or continued use of a discriminatory selection procedure.

We have previously suggested that courts may utilize certain kinds of racial preferences to remedy past discrimination under Title VII. The Courts of Appeals have unanimously agreed that racial preferences may be used, in appropriate cases, to remedy past discrimination under Title VII. The extensive legislative history of the Act supports this view. Many opponents of Title VII argued that an employer could be found guilty of discrimination under the statute simply because of a racial imbalance in his workforce, and would be compelled to implement racial "quotas" to avoid being charged with liability. At the same time, supporters of the bill insisted that employers would not violate Title VII simply because of racial imbalance, and emphasized that neither the EEOC nor the courts could compel employers to adopt quotas solely to facilitate racial balancing. The debate concerning what Title VII did and did not require culminated in the adoption of section 703(j), which stated expressly that the statute did not require an employer or labor union to adopt quotas or preferences simply because of a racial imbalance.

Although we conclude that section 706(g) does not foreclose a court from instituting some sort of racial preferences where necessary to remedy past discrimination, we do not mean to suggest such relief is always proper. The court should exercise its discretion with an eye towards Congress' concern that the measures not be invoked simply to create a racially balanced workforce. In the majority of cases the court will not have to impose affirmative action as a remedy for past discrimination, but need only order the employer or union to cease engaging in discriminatory practices. However, in some cases, affirmative action may be necessary in order effectively to enforce Title VII, such as with persistent or egregious discrimination or to dissipate the effects of pervasive discrimination. The court should also take care to tailor its orders to fit the nature of the violation it seeks to correct.

Here, the membership goal and Fund were necessary to remedy the union and JAC's pervasive and egregious discrimination and its lingering effects. The goal was flexible and thus gives a strong indication that it was not being used simply to achieve and maintain racial balance, but rather as a benchmark against which the court could gauge the union's efforts. Twice the court adjusted the deadline for the goal and has continually approved changes in the size of apprenticeship classes to account for economic conditions preventing the union from meeting its targets. And it is temporary in that it will end as soon as the percentage of minority union members approximates the percentage of minorities in the local labor force. Similarly the fund is scheduled to terminate when the union achieves its membership goal and the court determines it is no longer needed to remedy past discrimination. Also, neither the goal nor the fund unnecessarily trammels the interests of white employees. They do not require any union members to be laid off, and do not discriminate against existing union members. While whites seeking admission into the union may be denied benefits extended to nonwhite counterparts, the court's orders do not stand as an absolute bar to such individuals; indeed a majority of new union members have been white. Many of the provisions of the orders are race-neutral (such as the requirement that the JAC assign one apprenticeship for every four journeymen workers) and the union and JAC remain free to adopt the provisions of the order for the benefit of white members and applicants. Accordingly, we AFFIRM.

Case Questions

1. Is it clear to you why a court would be able to include in its remedies those who are not directly discriminated against by an employer? Explain.

2. If you were the court and were still trying to get the union to comply with your order 18 years after the fact, what would you have done?

3. As a union official, how could you have avoided such a result?

Johnson v. Transportation Agency, Santa Clara County, California, *480 U.S. 616 (1987)*

A female was promoted over a male pursuant to an affirmative action plan voluntarily adopted by the employer to address a traditionally segregated job classification in which women had been significantly underrepresented. A male employee who also applied for the job sued, alleging it was illegal discrimination under Title VII for the employer to consider gender in the promotion process. The U.S. Supreme Court upheld the promotion under the voluntary affirmative action plan. It held that since it was permissible for a public employer to adopt such a voluntary plan, the plan was reasonable, and since the criteria for the plan had been met, gender could be considered as one factor in the promotion.

Brennan, J.

***

In December 1978, the Santa Clara County Transit District Board of Supervisors adopted an Affirmative Action Plan (Plan) for the County Transportation Agency. The Plan implemented a County Affirmative Action Plan, which had been adopted because "mere prohibition of discriminatory practices is not enough to remedy the effects of past practices and to permit attainment of an equitable representation of minorities, women and handicapped persons." Relevant to this case, the Agency Plan provides that, in making promotions to positions within a traditionally segregated job classification in which women have been significantly underrepresented, the Agency is authorized to consider as one factor the sex of a qualified applicant.

In reviewing the composition of its workforce, the Agency noted in its Plan that women were represented in numbers far less than their proportion of the County labor force in both the Agency as a whole and in five of seven job categories. Specifically, while women constituted 36.4 percent of the area labor market, they composed only 22.4 percent of Agency employees. Furthermore, women working at the Agency were concentrated largely in EEOC job categories traditionally held by women: women made up 76 percent of Office and Clerical Workers, but only 7.1 percent of Agency Officials and Administrators, 8.6 percent of Professionals, 9.7 percent of Technicians, and 22 percent of Service and Maintenance Workers. As for the job classification relevant to this case, none of the 238 Skilled Craft Worker positions was held by a woman. The Plan noted that this underrepresentation of women in part reflected the fact that women had not traditionally been employed in these positions, and that they had not been strongly motivated to seek training or employment in them "because of the limited opportunities that have existed in the past for them to work in such classifications." The Plan also observed that, while the proportion of ethnic minorities in the Agency as a whole exceeded the proportion of such minorities in the County workforce, a smaller percentage of minority employees held management, professional, and technical positions.

The Agency stated that its Plan was intended to achieve "a statistically measurable yearly improvement in hiring, training and promotion of minorities and women throughout the Agency in all major job classifications where they are underrepresented." As a benchmark by which to evaluate progress, the Agency stated that its long-term goal was to attain a workforce whose composition reflected the proportion of minorities and women in the area labor force. Thus, for the Skilled Craft category in which the road dispatcher position at issue here was classified, the Agency's aspiration was that eventually about 36 percent of the jobs would be occupied by women.

The Agency's Plan thus set aside no specific number of positions for minorities or women, but authorized the consideration of ethnicity or sex as a factor when evaluating qualified candidates for jobs in which members of such groups were poorly represented. One such job was the road dispatcher position that is the subject of the dispute in this case.

The Agency announced a vacancy for the promotional position of road dispatcher in the Agency's Roads Division. Twelve County employees applied for the promotion, including Joyce and Johnson. Nine of the applicants, including Joyce and Johnson, were deemed qualified for the job, and were interviewed by a two-person board. Seven of the applicants scored above 70 on this interview, which meant that they were certified as eligible for selection by the appointing authority. The scores awarded ranged from 70 to 80. Johnson was tied for second with a score of 75, while Joyce ranked next with a score of 73. A second interview was conducted by three Agency supervisors, who ultimately recommended that Johnson be promoted.

James Graebner, Director of the Agency, concluded that the promotion should be given to Joyce. As he testified: "I tried to look at the whole picture, the combination of her qualifications and Mr. Johnson's qualifications, their test scores, their expertise, their background, affirmative action matters, things like that. . . . I believe it was a combination of all those."

The certification form naming Joyce as the person promoted to the dispatcher position stated that both she and Johnson were rated as well qualified for the job. The evaluation of Joyce read: "Well qualified by virtue of 18 years of past clerical experience including 3½ years at West Yard plus almost 5 years as a [road maintenance worker]." The evaluation of Johnson was as follows: "Well qualified applicant; two years of [road maintenance worker] experience plus 11 years of Road Yard Clerk. Has had previous outside Dispatch experience but was 13 years ago." Graebner testified that he did not regard as significant the fact that Johnson scored 75 and Joyce 73 when interviewed by the two-person board.

Johnson filed a complaint with the EEOC alleging that he had been denied promotion on the basis of sex in violation of Title VII.

In reviewing the employment decision at issue in this case, we must first examine whether consideration of the sex of applicants for Skilled Craft jobs was justified by the existence of a "manifest imbalance" that reflected underrepresentation of women in "traditionally segregated job categories." In determining whether an imbalance exists that would justify taking sex or race into account, a comparison of the percentage of minorities or women in the employer's work force with the percentage in the area labor market or general population is appropriate in analyzing jobs that require no special expertise or training programs designed to provide expertise. Where a job requires special training, however, the comparison should be with those in the labor force who possess the relevant qualifications. The requirement that the "manifest imbalance" relate to a "traditionally segregated job category" provides assurance both that sex or race will be taken into account in a manner consistent with Title VII's purpose of eliminating the effects of employment discrimination, and that the interests of those employees not benefitting from the plan will not be unduly infringed.

It is clear that the decision to hire Joyce was made pursuant to an Agency plan that directed that sex or race be taken into account for the purpose of remedying underrepresentation. The Agency Plan acknowledged the "limited opportunities that have existed in the past," for women to find employment in certain job classifications "where women have not been traditionally employed in significant numbers." As a result, observed the Plan, women were concentrated in traditionally female jobs in the Agency, and represented a lower percentage in other job classifications than would be expected if such traditional segregation had not occurred. Specifically, 9 of the 10 Para-Professionals and 110 of the 145 Office and Clerical Workers were women. By contrast, women were only 2 of the 28 Officials and Administrators, 5 of the 58 Professionals, 12 of the 124 Technicians, none of the Skilled Craft Workers, and 1—who was Joyce—of the 110 Road Maintenance Workers. The Plan sought to remedy these imbalances through "hiring, training and promotion of . . . women throughout the Agency in all major job classifications where they are underrepresented."

The Agency adopted as a benchmark for measuring progress in eliminating underrepresentation the long-term goal of a workforce that mirrored in its major job classifications the percentage of women in the area labor market. Even as it did so, however, the Agency acknowledged that such a figure could not by itself necessarily justify taking into account the sex of applicants for positions in all job categories. For positions requiring specialized training and experience, the Plan observed that the number of minorities and women "who possess the qualifications required for entry into such job classifications is limited." The Plan therefore directed that annual short-term goals be formulated that would provide a more realistic indication of the degree to which sex should be taken into account in filling particular positions. The Plan stressed that such goals "should not be construed as 'quotas' that must be met," but as reasonable aspirations in correcting the imbalance in the Agency's workforce. These goals were to take into account factors such as "turnover, layoffs, lateral transfers, new job openings, retirements and availability of minorities, women and handicapped persons in the area workforce who possess the desired qualifications or potential for placement." The Plan specifically directed that, in establishing such goals, the Agency work with the County Planning Department and other sources in attempting to compile data on the percentage of minorities and women in the local labor force that were actually working in the job classifications constituting the Agency workforce. From the outset, therefore, the Plan sought annually to develop even more refined measures of the underrepresentation in each job category that required attention.

As the Agency Plan recognized, women were most egregiously underrepresented in the Skilled Craft job category, since none of the 238 positions was occupied by a woman. In mid-1980, when Joyce was selected for the road dispatcher position, the Agency was still in the process of refining its short-term goals for Skilled Craft Workers in accordance with the directive of the Plan. This process did not reach fruition until 1982, when the Agency established a short-term goal for that year of 3 women for the 55 expected openings in that job category—a modest goal of about 6 percent for that category.

The Agency's Plan emphasized that the long-term goals were not to be taken as guides for actual hiring decisions, but that supervisors were to consider a host of practical factors in seeking to meet affirmative action objectives, including the fact that in some job categories women were not qualified in numbers comparable to their representation in the labor force.

By contrast, had the Plan simply calculated imbalances in all categories according to the proportion of women in the area labor pool, and then directed that hiring be governed solely by those figures, its validity fairly could be called into question. This is because analysis of a more specialized labor pool normally is necessary in determining underrepresentation in some positions. If a plan failed to take distinctions in qualifications into account in providing guidance for actual employment decisions, it would dictate mere blind hiring by the numbers, for it would hold supervisors to "achievement of a particular percentage of minority employment or membership. . . regardless of circumstances such as economic conditions or the number of available qualified minority applicants. . . ."

The Agency's Plan emphatically did not authorize such blind hiring. It expressly directed that numerous factors be taken into account in making hiring decisions, including specifically the qualifications of female applicants for particular jobs. The Agency's management had been clearly instructed that they were not to hire solely by reference to statistics. The fact that only the long-term goal had been established for this category posed no danger that personnel decisions would be made by reflexive adherence to a numerical standard.

Furthermore, in considering the candidates for the road dispatcher position in 1980, the Agency hardly needed to rely on a refined short-term goal to realize that it had a significant problem of underrepresentation that required attention. Given the obvious imbalance in the Skilled Craft category, and given the Agency's commitment to eliminating such imbalances, it was plainly not unreasonable for the Agency to determine that it was appropriate to consider as one factor the sex of Ms. Joyce in making its decision. The promotion of Joyce thus satisfies the first requirement since it was undertaken to further an affirmative action plan designed to eliminate Agency workforce imbalances in traditionally segregated job categories.

We next consider whether the Agency Plan unnecessarily trammeled the rights of male employees or created an absolute bar to their advancement. The Plan sets aside no positions for women. The Plan expressly states that "[t]he 'goals' established for each Division should not be construed as 'quotas' that must be met." Rather, the Plan merely authorizes that consideration be given to affirmative action concerns when evaluating qualified applicants. As the Agency Director testified, the sex of Joyce was but one of numerous factors he took into account in arriving at his decision. The Plan thus resembles the "Harvard Plan" approvingly noted in *Regents of University of California v. Bakke,* which considers race along with other criteria in determining admission to the college. As the Court observed: "In such an admissions program, race or ethnic background may be deemed a 'plus' in a particular applicant's file, yet it does not insulate the individual from comparison with all other candidates for the available seats." Similarly, the Agency Plan requires women to compete with all other qualified applicants. No persons are automatically excluded from consideration; all are able to have their qualifications weighed against those of other applicants.

In addition, Johnson had no absolute entitlement to the road dispatcher position. Seven of the applicants were classified as qualified and eligible, and the Agency Director was authorized to promote any of the seven. Thus, denial of the promotion unsettled no legitimate, firmly rooted expectation on the part of Johnson. Furthermore, while Johnson was denied a promotion, he retained his employment with the Agency, at the same salary and with the same seniority, and remained eligible for other promotions.

Finally, the Agency's Plan was intended to attain a balanced workforce not to maintain one. The Plan contains 10 references to the Agency's desire to "attain" such a balance, but no reference whatsoever to a goal of maintaining it. The Director testified that, while the "broader goal" of affirmative action, defined as "the desire to hire, to promote, to give opportunity and training on an equitable,

non-discriminatory basis," is something that is "a permanent part" of "the Agency's operating philosophy," that broader goal "is divorced, if you will, from specific numbers or percentages." The Agency acknowledged the difficulties that it would confront in remedying the imbalance in its workforce, and it anticipated only gradual increases in the representation of minorities and women. It is thus unsurprising that the Plan contains no explicit end date, for the Agency's flexible, case-by-case approach was not expected to yield success in a brief period of time.

Express assurance that a program is only temporary may be necessary if the program actually sets aside positions according to specific numbers. This is necessary both to minimize the effect of the program on other employees, and to ensure that the plan's goals "[are] not being used simply to achieve and maintain. . . balance, but rather as a benchmark against which" the employer may measure its progress in eliminating the underrepresentation of minorities and women. In this case, however, substantial evidence shows that the Agency has sought to take a moderate, gradual approach to eliminating the imbalance in its workforce, one which establishes realistic guidance for employment decisions, and which visits minimal intrusion on the legitimate expectations of other employees. Given this fact, as well as the Agency's express commitment to "attain" a balanced workforce, there is ample assurance that the Agency does not seek to use its Plan to maintain a permanent racial and sexual balance.

In evaluating the compliance of an affirmative action plan with Title VII's prohibition on discrimination, we must be mindful of "this Court's and Congress's consistent emphasis on 'the value of voluntary efforts to further the objectives of the law.'" The Agency in the case before us has undertaken such a voluntary effort, and has done so in full recognition of both the difficulties and the potential for intrusion on males and nonminorities. The Agency has identified a conspicuous imbalance in job categories traditionally segregated by race and sex. It has made clear from the outset, however, that employment decisions may not be justified solely by reference to this imbalance, but must rest on a multitude of practical, realistic factors. It has therefore committed itself to annual adjustment of goals so as to provide a reasonable guide for actual hiring and promotion decisions. The Agency earmarks no positions for anyone; sex is but one of several factors that may be taken into account in evaluating qualified applicants for a position. As both the Plan's language and its manner of operation attest, the Agency has no intention of establishing a workforce whose permanent composition is dictated by rigid numerical standards.

We therefore hold that the Agency appropriately took into account as one factor the sex of Diane Joyce in determining that she should be promoted to the road dispatcher position. The decision to do so was made pursuant to an affirmative action plan that represents a moderate, flexible, case-by-case approach to effecting a gradual improvement in the representation of minorities and women in the Agency's workforce. Such a plan is fully consistent with Title VII, for it embodies the contribution that voluntary

employer action can make in eliminating the vestiges of discrimination in the workplace. Accordingly, the judgment of the Court of Appeals is AFFIRMED.

Case Questions

1. What do you think of the Court's decision in this case? Does it make sense to you? Why or why not?

2. If you disagree with the Court's decision, what would you as the employer have done instead?

3. Are the Court's considerations for how to institute an acceptable affirmative action program consistent with how you thought affirmative action worked? Explain.

Ricci v. DeStefano, *557 U.S. 557 (2009)*

**See Chapter 2
to revisit key
concepts.**

The City of New Haven administered an objective exam for firefighter promotions to captain and lieutenant. White candidates performed better than Blacks on the exam. Rather than risk a lawsuit by Blacks based on violation of Title VII due to disparate impact, the city discarded the results of the exam. White and Latinx employees who thought they would be able to be promoted based on their test performance sued the city for violation of, among other things, Title VII. The U.S. Supreme Court sided with the firefighters and held that fear of a disparate impact claim is not a viable basis for discriminating against the white and Latinx firefighters unless the employer can demonstrate a strong evidentiary basis that it would have been liable for disparate impact if it had not taken such action. Though the case actually is based on a disparate impact analysis, it is included here in "reverse discrimination" since the employer took the action it did in an effort to be more inclusive and not have the exam have a disparate impact upon Black candidates.

Kennedy, J.

***

Our analysis begins with this premise: The City's actions would violate the disparate-treatment prohibition of Title VII absent some valid defense. All the evidence demonstrates that the City chose not to certify the examination results because too many whites and not enough minorities would be promoted were the lists to be certified. Without some other justification, this express, race-based decisionmaking violates Title VII's command that employers cannot take adverse employment actions because of an individual's race.

Writing for a plurality in *Wygant* and announcing the strong-basis-in-evidence standard, Justice Powell recognized the tension between eliminating segregation and discrimination on the one hand and doing away with all governmentally imposed discrimination based on race on the other. The plurality stated that those "related constitutional duties are not always harmonious," and that "reconciling them requires. . . employers to act with extraordinary care." The plurality required a strong basis in evidence because "evidentiary support for the conclusion that remedial action is warranted becomes crucial when the remedial program is challenged in court by nonminority employees." An amorphous claim that there has been past discrimination. . . cannot justify the use of an unyielding racial quota."

Congress has imposed liability on employers for unintentional discrimination in order to rid the workplace of "practices that are fair in form, but discriminatory in operation." But it has also prohibited employers from taking adverse employment actions "because of " race. Applying the strong-basis-in-evidence standard to Title VII gives effect to both the disparate-treatment and disparate-impact provisions, allowing violations of one in the name of compliance with the other only in certain, narrow circumstances. The standard leaves ample room for employers' voluntary compliance efforts, which are essential to the statutory scheme and to Congress's efforts to eradicate workplace discrimination. And the standard appropriately constrains employers' discretion in making race-based decisions: It limits that discretion to cases in which there is a strong basis in evidence of disparate-impact liability, but it is not so restrictive that it allows employers to act only when there is a provable, actual violation.

Resolving the statutory conflict in this way allows the disparate-impact prohibition to work in a manner that is consistent with other provisions of Title VII, including the prohibition on adjusting employment-related test scores on the basis of race. Examinations like those administered by the City create legitimate expectations on the part of those who took the tests. As is the case with any promotion exam, some of the firefighters here invested substantial time, money, and personal commitment in preparing for the tests. Employment tests can be an important part of a neutral selection system that safeguards against the very racial animosities Title VII was intended to prevent. Here, however, the firefighters saw their efforts invalidated by the City in sole reliance upon race-based statistics.

If an employer cannot rescore a test based on the candidate's race, then it follows that it may not take the greater step of discarding the test altogether to achieve a more desirable racial distribution of promotion-eligible candidates—absent a strong basis in evidence that the test was deficient and that discarding the results is necessary to avoid violating the disparate-impact provision. Restricting an employer's ability to discard test results (and thereby discriminate against qualified candidates on the basis of

their race) also is in keeping with Title VII's express protection of bona fide promotional examinations. For the foregoing reasons, we adopt the strong-basis-in-evidence standard as a matter of statutory construction to resolve any conflict between the disparate-treatment and disparate-impact provisions of Title VII.

Nor do we question an employer's affirmative efforts to ensure that all groups have a fair opportunity to apply for promotions and to participate in the process by which promotions will be made. But once that process has been established and employers have made clear their selection criteria, they may not then invalidate the test results, thus upsetting an employee's legitimate expectation not to be judged on the basis of race. Doing so, absent a strong basis in evidence of an impermissible disparate impact, amounts to the sort of racial preference that Congress has disclaimed, and is antithetical to the notion of a workplace where individuals are guaranteed equal opportunity regardless of race.

We hold only that, under Title VII, before an employer can engage in intentional discrimination for the asserted purpose of avoiding or remedying an unintentional disparate impact, the employer must have a strong basis in evidence to believe it will be subject to disparate-impact liability if it fails to take the race-conscious, discriminatory action.

On the record before us there is no evidence—let alone the required strong basis in evidence—that the tests were flawed because they were not job-related or because other, equally valid and less discriminatory tests were available to the City. Fear of litigation alone cannot justify an employer's reliance on race to the detriment of individuals who passed the examinations and qualified for promotions. The City's discarding the test results was impermissible under Title VII.

The record in this litigation documents a process that, at the outset, had the potential to produce a testing procedure that was true to the promise of Title VII: No individual should face workplace discrimination based on race. Respondents thought about promotion qualifications and relevant experience in neutral ways. They were careful to ensure broad racial participation in the design of the test itself and its administration. As we have discussed at length, the process was open and fair.

The problem, of course, is that after the tests were completed, the raw racial results became the predominant rationale for the City's refusal to certify the results. The injury arises in part from the high, and justified, expectations of the candidates who had participated in the testing process on the terms the City had established for the promotional process. Many of the candidates had studied for months, at considerable personal and financial expense, and thus the injury caused by the City's reliance on raw racial statistics at the end of the process was all the more severe. Confronted with arguments both for and against certifying the test results—and threats of a lawsuit either way—the City was required to make a difficult inquiry. But its hearings produced no strong evidence of a disparate-impact violation, and the City was not entitled to disregard the tests based solely on the racial disparity in the results.

If, after it certifies the test results, the City faces a disparate-impact suit, then in light of our holding today it should be clear that the City would avoid disparate-impact liability based on the strong basis in evidence that, had it not certified the results, it would have been subject to disparate-treatment liability.

REVERSED AND REMANDED

Case Questions

1. What do you think of the court's decision?
2. Why do you think the Fire Department did what it did to "fix" the situation, even though it had already had the tests validated? Explain.
3. Do you understand why the candidates that received passing scores but were not promoted challenged the Fire Department's decision? Explain.

Chapter 6

Race and Color Discrimination

Learning Objectives

Source: Library of Congress, Prints & Photographs Division
[LC-USF3301-006392-M4]

After completing this chapter, you should be able to:

LO1   Discuss and give important details on the history of race discrimination and civil rights issues in the United States.

LO2   Explain the relevance of the history of civil rights to present-day workplace race and color discrimination issues.

LO3   Set forth the findings of several recent studies on race inequalities.

LO4   Identify several ways that race and color discrimination are manifested in the workplace.

LO5   Explain why national origin issues have recently been included under race discrimination claims by the EEOC and why they remain different.

LO6   Describe ways in which an employer can avoid potential liability for race and color discrimination.

Opening Scenarios

SCENARIO 1

1 Scenario Mary, an Asian employee with light skin tone, reports that her manager, Joan, who is a darker-skin-toned Asian, is saying negative things to Mary about the color of Mary's lighter skin. The comments include statements such as that Mary thinks she (Mary) is better than other employees, Mary is not as special as Mary thinks she is, and so on. Joan also constantly calls Mary "Sunshine" in a sarcastic way, which Mary takes as a reference to Mary's lighter skin. Mary is afraid that Joan will give her a bad evaluation. Mary is also embarrassed about having this constantly happen in front of other employees. Are Joan's actions more than just unprofessional behavior? Are they illegal?

SCENARIO 2

2 Scenario A Black female employee is terminated during a downsizing at her place of employment. The decision was made to terminate the two worst employees, and she was one of them.

The employer had not told the employee of her poor performance nor given her any negative feedback during evaluations to enable her to assess her performance and govern herself accordingly. In fact, there were specific orders not to give her any negative feedback. The employee sues for racial discrimination, alleging it was a violation of Title VII for the employer not to give her appropriate negative feedback during evaluations to prevent her from being put in the position of being terminated. Does the employee win? Why or why not?

SCENARIO 3

3 Scenario An employer has a "no-beard" policy, which applies across the board to all employees. A Black employee tells the employer he cannot shave without getting severe facial bumps from ingrown hairs. The employer replies that the policy is without exception and the employee must comply. The employee refuses and is later terminated. The employee brings suit under Title VII on the basis of race discrimination. Does he win? Why or why not?

Statutory Basis

It shall be an unlawful employment practice for an employer—

(1) to fail or refuse to hire or to discharge any individual, or otherwise to discriminate against any individual with respect to his compensation, terms, conditions, or privileges of employment, because of such individual's race, color . . . or

(2) to limit, segregate, or classify his employees or applicants for employment in any way which would deprive or tend to deprive any individual of employment opportunities or otherwise adversely affect his status as an employee, because of such individual's race, color . . . [Title VII of the Civil Rights Act of 1964, as amended, 42 U.S.C. § 2000e-2(a).]

Note: Not a semester goes by that white students do not ask: "Which term should we use: *Black* or *African American*?" They are unsure which term to use for fear of offending. This is particularly important for managers and supervisors. If in doubt, simply ask. Most will not mind, and it indicates respect for another's feelings, which is especially important for managers, supervisors, or business owners. Even if you do not ask, our experience has been that it rarely matters and most Blacks are not offended by the choice of one or the other. You will notice that the terms are used interchangeably throughout the text.

Surprised?

LO1 Discuss and give important details on the history of race discrimination and civil rights issues in the United States.

LO2 Explain the relevance of the history of civil rights to present-day workplace race and color discrimination issues.

LO3 Set forth the findings of several recent studies on race inequalities.

Mad Men. Hidden Figures. Remember the Titans. Green Book. *Pop culture is full of examples of discrimination from 40 and 50 years ago or more. These examples of discrimination are not only easily identifiable but also easy to dismiss as something that doesn't happen anymore, at least not in the workplace. However, the reality is that discrimination occurs every day in workplaces all over the world.*[1]

Race is the first of the prohibited categories in Title VII, the main reason for passage of the law, and it remains, even today, a factor in the lives of many employees. At the same time we can point to having elected and then reelected the country's first African American president, having had in recent years two Black attorney generals of the United States and two Black secretaries of state, having Harriet Tubman scheduled to appear on the $20 bill (then canceled by President Trump), having *Moonlight* chosen as the Oscar-winning movie of 2017 and Oprah Winfrey once again topping the *Forbes* list of the wealthiest Americans. While we may have elected our first Black president, because of the serious threats to his life, Obama had to receive Secret Service protection even before becoming president—the earliest that any candidate had ever received it.[2] Three years after that election, the Southern Poverty Law Center issued a report in 2011 that, for the first time since it began tracking hate groups in the United States, the number of groups had risen to more than 1,000.[3] In February 2020 white supremacist groups that had stepped up recruiting on college campuses around the country[4] were given by the FBI the same status as the terrorist group ISIS.[5] If you did not think race or color mattered before, you have probably come to think about it in light of our most recent election cycle. The white supremacist college recruitment stepped up after the 2016 election. Whatever peace we thought we had made with race was shown to be fragile at best. Race still matters more than many may realize. The EEOC's 2019 statistics still show that race still accounts for about one-third of the discrimination claims being filed with the agency. So much so that it might surprise you to discover the following:[6]

- Research showed that employers would rather hire a white man who had served time in prison than a Black man who had not.[7]
- When researchers sent out identical résumés for jobs listed in the newspaper, with the only difference being the names of the applicants, those with "ethnic" names like Jamal or Lakiesha received 50 percent fewer callbacks for jobs than the identical résumés with traditionally white names like Megan or Brad. This remained true even when the ethnic applicants were given zip codes that indicated that the applicant lived in an area of higher socioeconomic status.[8]
- In addition to visual profiling, researchers have found linguistic profiling—African Americans who leave messages in response to ads often never receive return calls, while whites almost always do.[9]
- A 2012 study by University of Georgia researchers published in the *Journal of Vocational Behavior* found that networking within an organization and having

a mentor, which are generally thought to promote career success, do not give African American men the same measurable benefits as whites.[10]

- An extensive meta-analysis (an analysis of studies that have been conducted) of every fieldwork experiment of hiring discrimination from 1989 through 2015 published in the *Proceedings of the National Academy of Sciences* in 2017 showed no change in racial discrimination in hiring since 1989, when such experiments became more common, for African Americans but some indication of declining discrimination against Latinxs. The results document a striking persistence of racial discrimination in U.S. labor markets. The study represented more than 55,842 applications for 26,326 positions. Since 1989, whites received on average 36 percent more callbacks than African Americans and 24 percent more than Latinxs. The study accounted for applicants' education and gender, study method, occupational groups, and local labor market conditions.[11]

- According to 2019 U.S. Census Bureau data, while white non-Hispanic women are paid 79 cents for every dollar paid to men, on average, for African American women, it is 62 cents for every dollar paid to, or $18,817 less per year, and for Hispanic women, it is only 54 cents, or $28,036 less per year.[12] For Native American women, it is 58 cents, Asian American women 90 cents. In 2008, Blacks were making about 62 cents for every dollar whites made. In 2007, it was 60 cents. In the mid-1970s it had narrowed to about 50 cents on the dollar.[13]

- During oral arguments in the *Lopez v. Gonzales*[14] and *Toledo-Flores v. United States*[15] cases that could impact thousands of immigrants, the late U.S. Supreme Court Justice Antonin Scalia made a reference to one of the parties in a case, a Mexican who had been deported back to his country, as someone unlikely to keep from drinking tequila on the chance he could return to the United States.[16] Of course you have heard worse from President Trump, but at the time such things from high officials were verboten and Scalia was a justice on the highest court in the country, and it was said in the context of a case being argued before him.

- In the 2004 elections in Alabama, voters voted to keep the Alabama constitution's language that says "separate schools shall be provided for white and colored children, and no child of either race shall be permitted to attend a school of the other race."[17] An Alabama county opened its first integrated high school in 2018, 65 years after the *Brown v. Board of Education* decision outlawed segregated schools.[18]

- A full-time paid intern hired over the phone to work at an Iowa cosmetics company as a cosmetics formulator because she was in England at the time arrived in Iowa only to be told by her supervisor that everyone would be "surprised" that she was Black. She was given no work as other white interns were despite her continually asking for it. She was fired shortly thereafter.[19]

- At Charapp Ford South, a car dealership near Pittsburgh, two Black employees who complained about constant racial harassment in the workplace allegedly found a document that suggested "ten ways to kill" African Americans. When they complained, a manager told them that "people [around here] wanted to see blacks washing cars, not selling them."[20]

- A Virginia Lowe's manager was terminated for agreeing to a white customer's request to not have a Black delivery employee.[21]

- The president of a staffing services company allegedly told Carolyn Red Bear, a Native American employee, many derogatory statements that had been made about her "ethnic" appearance, alleging that she did not "fit in" with the white community and should seek employment more consistent with the skills of Native Americans. She was terminated for refusing to comply with a directive to cut her hair, change her last name, and stop "rubbing in" her heritage.[22]

- A congressionally commissioned study by the Institute of Medicine found that "bias, prejudice, and stereotyping on the part of health care providers" contribute to African Americans being less likely than whites to receive appropriate heart medication, coronary artery bypass surgery, and kidney transplants as well as being more likely to receive a lower quality of basic clinical services such as intensive care.[23]

- Nearly half of white Bostonians surveyed said that African Americans and Hispanics are less intelligent than whites and that African Americans are harder to get along with than other ethnic groups.[24]

- A five-year, seven-volume study by the Russell Sage Foundation found that "racial stereotypes and attitudes heavily influenced the labor market, with blacks landing at the very bottom."[25]

- An Alabama Language Arts teacher was suspended after requiring her eighth graders to take a math test that included questions such as "Dwayne pimps 3 ho's. If the price is $85 per trick, how many tricks per day must each ho turn to support Dwayne's $800 per day crack habit?"[26]

- In DeKalb County, Georgia, three white and one Black employee sued for race discrimination. The Black employee alleged he was terminated because he refused to discriminate against white managers when he was told to withhold information from white employees so they would appear incompetent. The white employees alleged they were replaced with Black employees in an effort to create a "darker administration" to reflect DeKalb's racial makeup.[27]

- A 2019 Gallup Minority Rights and Relations Survey poll found that a record-high percentage of 24 percent said Blacks are treated less fairly than whites in getting health care from doctors and hospitals, while 52 percent said the same about interactions with the police. Since 2016, perceptions that Blacks are treated less fairly have increased and are at an all-time high since 1997. Twenty-eight percent say Blacks are treated less fairly in restaurants, bars, theaters, or other entertainment places, 28 percent for neighborhood shops, 30 percent for on the job, and 32 percent for downtown or in shopping malls.[28]

- The EEOC settled a case in which supervisors routinely used "egregious" ethnic slurs for African Americans, Hispanics, and Asians and said things like "It should not be against the law to shoot Mexican men, women, and children or to shoot African Americans and Chinese people" and "If I had my way I'd gas them [referring to African American employees] like Hitler did the Jews."[29]

Unfortunately, there are many, many, many more items that could be added to this list. We gave you this sampling of wide-ranging race- and ethnicity-related news items so that you can see how much racism is still a factor of life in the United States and in how many ways it can be manifested by individuals of any status. We included so many and such varied items because unless these issues are on your radar screen, you may be totally unaware of them. This is a luxury that a manager, supervisor, or business owner cannot afford.

If any of these surprises you, you are not alone. A 2001 Gallup poll reported that 76 percent of whites, *including 9 out of 10 under 30* (emphasis added because our experience shows most students think it is only older people who discriminate), thought African Americans were now being treated fairly or somewhat fairly, compared to only 38 percent of African Americans who thought so.[30] While the Gallup poll mentioned earlier showed those numbers had changed a great deal, a recent *NY Magazine* reported research finding that millennials are thought of as more racially tolerant than other generations, yet their implicit bias tests show no difference, and neither did how they thought about others racially once things went beyond the surface.[31] Given this, it makes sense that research found that three-fourths of whites had no Black friends and that while Blacks have 10 times as many Black friends as white friends, white Americans have 91 times as many white friends as Black friends.[32] It also makes sense given that much of our attitude stems from our own personal experience as well as history. The history of slavery and its aftermath represented quite a different experience for whites and Hispanics than Blacks. Hispanics, and whites of course, have their own history here as well, and you can see that reflected in the numbers.

You can see what a problem these findings would present in the workplace. Not only could discrimination be occurring, but as a manager, you could possibly not realize it. Much of the race discrimination now occurring in the workplace is not as overt as it was in the early days of Title VII (see Exhibit 6.1, "Classified Ads, 1961"), but as you can see from our opening tidbits, it is still very much a factor in employment (see Exhibit 6.6, "EEOC's Revised Race Guidance"). And, as you can also see from some of the items in our sampling, race discrimination in the workplace does not occur in a vacuum. It is part of a much larger picture of race-based discrimination in the greater society. With the history and background we've given you in previous chapters, you can understand why.

Working to get future managers and supervisors to see this larger picture in which workplace actions occur in a microcosm is a big part of what this chapter is about. The more you can see the bigger picture, the less likely you are to be a part of unnecessary claims of workplace race discrimination. That is why we can't simply tell you the law and leave it at that. The law has been in place for 50-plus years now, and race discrimination claims are still very much a part of Title VII. They have risen every decade since the law was passed and still account for over one-third of the EEOC's total claims filed. This is consistent with the research findings. What we are seeing as the Title VII system is still being fine-tuned through

Exhibit 6.1   *Classified Ads, 1961*

The exhibit below, taken from an actual newspaper classified ad section from 1961, is typical of want ads found in newspapers before Title VII was passed in 1964. For publication purposes, names and phone numbers have been omitted. It is now illegal to advertise for males, females, or racial groups. "Col." means "colored," the pre–Title VII term for African Americans.

Male Help Wanted

SOUTH ATLANTA
PERMANENT position for 2 young men 18-35, must be ambitious, high school graduate, and neat appearing. $85 week guaranteed, plus bonus. Opportunity to earn in excess of $100 per week. Must have desire to advance with company. For interview call...

ATTN YOUNG MEN
18-25, SINGLE, free to travel, New York and Florida, returns for clearing house for publishers. New car, transportation furnished. Expense account to start. Salary plus commission. We train you. Apply...

10 BOYS
14 OR OVER. Must be neat in appearance to work this summer. Salary 75 cent per hour. Will be supervised by trained student counselor. Apply...

MAN experienced in selling and familiar with the laundry and dry cleaning business needed to sell top brands of supplies to laundries and dry cleaning plants. This is an excellent opportunity for a man who is willing to work for proper rewards. Salary and comm. Reply to...

EXPERIENCED dairy man to work in modern dairy in Florida. Must be married, sober, and reliable. Salary $60 per week for 6 days with uniform, lights and water—furnished. Excellent house. Write...

SALESMEN
THIS corporation provides its salesmen with a substantial weekly drawing account. New men are thoroughly trained in the field with emphasis directed toward high-executive income bracket. Men experienced in securities, encyclopedias, and other intangibles who can stand rigid investigation, are dependable, and own late-model car. Reply to...

Situations Wanted, Female 24

SECRETARY–RECEPTIONIST (experienced). Ex-Spanish teacher desires diversified permanent position. Responsible, personable, like people, unencumbered. Can travel.

EXPERIENCED executive secretary with college degree, top skills, currently employed—seeks better position with opportunity for advancement and good salary.

SECRETARY desires typing at home, evenings, and weekends.

COLORED EMPLOYMENT

Help Wanted Male, Colored 26

CURB BOYS
DAY or night shift. No experience necessary. Good tips. Apply in person only.

HOUSEMAN, chauffeur. Must be experienced. Recent references, driver's license, health card required. Must be sober, reliable. Write...

RESTAURANT COOK
FOR frying and dinner cooking. Age 22-35. Must be sober, dependable and well-experienced. Salary $250-$275 for good man. Apply...

SOBER, experienced service station porter. No Sundays. Top pay.

PART-TIME lawn and yard maintenance man.

EXP service station porter, 6-day wk. Good sal.

KITCHEN porters, also ware washers. Apply...

Situations Wanted, Male, Col. 28

YOUNG man wants job. Short order and plain cooking, experienced.

Help Wanted, Female, Col. 29

MAID, free to travel with family, $35 to $50 week. Free room and board.

LAUNDRY MARKER—Experienced. 40 hours—pay hourly basis.

SHIRT girl. Experienced.

SHIRT girl, Experienced. Good pay. Good hours. Apply in person.

WAITRESS, experienced, for lunch counter. Over 40. Call...

Situation Wanted, Female, Col. 31

COOK-MAID (experienced)—desires Monday, Wednesday, Friday. References and health card.

MAID wants 5 days week. References.

GIRL WANTS 5 DAYS

MAID wants 5 days work. Will live-in.

MID-TEEN girl desires maid or office work.

litigation, legislation, and regulatory efforts is that supervisors and managers often do not recognize race discrimination or its effects when they occur. We do not want that to happen to you. We want to provide you with an effective and basic background in the area of race discrimination so you have the tools you need to protect your employer from liability for workplace discrimination.

Evolving Definitions of Race

LO4 Identify several ways that race and color discrimination are manifested in the workplace.

When someone says the word *race,* what do you think of? Chances are, most of us think of Black or white. We find ourselves at a rather interesting juncture regarding race claims at this point in time. For virtually the entire time Title VII has been in existence, race has been almost exclusively about African Americans and whites, with discrimination against other groups considered primarily under the national origin category. (See Exhibits 6.2, "EEOC's Revised Race/National Origin Guidance," and 6.3, "Hispanic: Race or National Origin—and Who Is Included?") As you have seen in previous chapters, the long and extensive history leading up to the passage of the Civil Rights Act and the court interpretations of it afterward reflect this.

But as the United States takes in more immigrants and they join the workforce and bring claims involving workplace discrimination, what constitutes race discrimination is changing. The term *race,* in the context of employment discrimination, is being used differently than it had been. For instance, you may recall that on April 16, 2007, Virginia Tech University senior Cho Seung-Hui shot and killed 32 people and wounded 25 others on the university campus. It was a while before police could identify the shooter. Three days later, the *Atlanta Journal and Constitution* ran a headline: "Tragedy strikes; then race enters the picture." Seung-Hui was born in Korea but was a permanent resident of the United States. According to the article, the first official identification of the Virginia Tech gunman was of his race and gender: "We do know that he was an Asian male," the university president said. It surprised us to see race (rather than national origin) used in this context. However, especially since the events of September 11, 2001, with its resulting backlash against Middle Easterners, and the simultaneous growing, visible presence of Hispanics, Southeast Asians, and other ethnicities in this country

Exhibit 6.2 *EEOC's Revised Race/National Origin Guidance*

New forms of discrimination are emerging. With a growing number of interracial marriages and families and increased immigration, racial demographics of the workforce have changed and the issue of race discrimination in America is multidimensional. Over the years, EEOC has received an increasing number of race and color discrimination charges that allege multiple or intersecting prohibited bases such as age, disability, gender, national origin, and religion.

Source: http://eeoc.gov/initiatives/e-race/why_e-race.html.

Exhibit 6.3 *Hispanic: Race or National Origin—and Who Is Included?*

Ever wonder where racial categories come from? In this interesting exhibit, you get to see (1) how a court addresses certain groups being left out of a definition of Hispanic (note especially footnote 1) and (2) how the government comes up with racial classifications and how they find their way into the mainstream. The first is an excerpt from a discrimination case; the second is a document from the U.S. Census Bureau about how Asians will be added to the minimum categories and how Hispanics will be classified in the census. While reading the document and noting all the effort and energy given to this issue, ponder the necessity of having such classifications at all.

(1)

Rocco Luiere, Jr., "the son of a Spanish mother whose parents were born in Spain," owns 75 percent of the shares in Jana-Rock Construction, Inc. Luiere and Jana-Rock bring a challenge under the Equal Protection Clause of the Fourteenth Amendment to New York's "affirmative action" statute for minority-owned businesses because the law does not include in its definition of "Hispanic" people of Spanish or Portuguese descent unless they also come from Latin America. The plaintiffs allege that by distinguishing among different subclasses of Hispanics, Article 15-A contains an explicit classification on the basis of national origin that should be subjected to strict scrutiny, and that under strict scrutiny New York's definition of "Hispanic" would fail. Applying rational basis review rather than strict scrutiny, the district court entered judgment in favor of the defendants and dismissed the complaint.

When a plaintiff challenges "racial classifications, imposed by whatever federal, state, or local governmental actor, [the classifications] must be analyzed by a reviewing court under strict scrutiny. In other words, such classifications are constitutional only if they are narrowly tailored measures that further compelling governmental interests."[1]

"The purpose of strict scrutiny is to 'smoke out' illegitimate uses of race by assuring that the legislative body is pursuing a goal important enough to warrant use of a highly suspect tool."

But once the government has shown that its decision to resort to explicit racial classifications survives strict scrutiny by being narrowly tailored to achieve a compelling interest, its program is no longer presumptively suspect. We do not think that it is appropriate to apply automatically strict scrutiny a second time in determining whether an otherwise valid affirmative action program is underinclusive for having excluded a particular plaintiff. In order to trigger strict scrutiny, such a plaintiff—like other plaintiffs with equal-protection claims—must demonstrate that his or her exclusion was motivated by a discriminatory purpose. Because the plaintiffs do not otherwise challenge the constitutional propriety of New York's race-based affirmative action program, and because Luiere and Jana-Rock cannot show that New York adopted its chosen definition of "Hispanic" for a discriminatory purpose or that its definition lacks a rational basis, we agree with the district court's judgment for the defendants and affirm.

[1]The classifications that are the subject of this appeal are based on national origin rather than race. It is undisputed, however, that principles of analysis applicable to race-based affirmative action programs are the same as those applicable to national-origin-based affirmative action programs. We therefore use the terms interchangeably.

Source: *Jana-Rock Construction, Inc. v. New York State Department of Economic Development, Division of Minority & Women's Business Development,* 438 F.3d 195 (2d Cir. 2006).

(2) RACIAL AND ETHNIC CLASSIFICATIONS USED IN CENSUS 2000 AND BEYOND

Introduction. The purpose of this document is to provide information about changes to the questions on race and Hispanic origin that have occurred for the Census 2000. These changes conform to the revisions of the standards for the classification of federal data on race and ethnicity promulgated by the Office of Management and Budget (OMB) in October 1997.

Old Standards. In response to legislative, programmatic, and administrative requirements of

(continued)

Exhibit 6.3 *continued*

the federal government, the OMB in 1977 issued Statistical Policy Directive Number 15, "Race and Ethnic Standards for Federal Statistics and Administrative Reporting." In these standards, four racial categories were established: American Indian or Alaskan Native, Asian or Pacific Islander, Black, and white. In addition, two ethnicity categories were established: Hispanic origin and Not of Hispanic origin. Although the Census Bureau has traditionally used more categories for decennial censuses, those categories collapsed into the four minimum race categories identified by the OMB, plus the category Some Other Race.

Reason for Changing the Old Standards. The racial and ethnic makeup of the country has changed since 1977, giving rise to the question of whether those standards still reflected the diversity of the country's present population. In response to this criticism, the OMB initiated a review of the Directive. This review included (1) organizing a workshop to address the issues by the National Academy of Science, (2) convening four public hearings, and (3) appointing an Interagency Committee for the Review of Racial and Ethnic Standards, which later developed a research agenda and conducted several research studies. The result of the Committee's efforts was a report describing recommended changes to the Directive. The members of the Committee included representatives of more than 30 agencies that covered the many diverse federal requirements for data on race and ethnicity. In 1997, the OMB accepted almost all of the recommendations of the Interagency Committee, resulting in changes to the standards.

What Are the New Standards and When Do They Take Effect?

In October 1997, the Office of Management and Budget (OMB) announced the revised standards for federal data on race and ethnicity. The minimum categories for race are now: American Indian or Alaska Native; Asian; Black or African-American; Native Hawaiian or Other Pacific Islander; and white. Instead of allowing a multiracial category as was originally suggested in public

and congressional hearings, the OMB adopted the Interagency Committee's recommendation to allow respondents to select one or more races when they self-identify. With the OMB's approval, the Census 2000 questionnaires also include a sixth racial category: Some Other Race. There are also two minimum categories for ethnicity: Hispanic or Latino and Not Hispanic or Latino. Hispanics and Latinos may be of any race.

How Should Hispanics or Latinos Answer the Race Question?

People of Hispanic origin may be of any race and should answer the question on race by marking one or more race categories shown on the questionnaire, including white, Black or African-American, American Indian or Alaska Native, Asian, Native Hawaiian or Other Pacific Islander, and Some Other Race. Hispanics are asked to indicate their origin in the question on Hispanic origin, not in the question on race, because in the federal statistical system ethnic origin is considered to be a separate concept from race.

What Racial Categories Will Be Used in Current Surveys and Other Data Collections by the Census Bureau?

By January 1, 2003, all current surveys must comply with the 1997 revisions to the Office of Management and Budget's standards for data on race and ethnicity, which establish a minimum of five categories for race: American Indian or Alaska Native, Asian, Black or African-American, Native Hawaiian or Other Pacific Islander, and white. Respondents will be able to select one or more of these racial categories. The minimum categories for ethnicity will be Hispanic or Latino and Not Hispanic or Latino. Tabulations of the racial categories will be shown as long as they meet agency standards for data quality and confidentiality protection. For most surveys, however, tables will show data at most for the white, Black, and Asian populations.

We would like to bring your attention to two things: (1) Notice how these categories are established by the government yet still change over the years. The term *African American* is now rarely hyphenated as it was when it began. Also, (2) think about common language use versus government categories. For instance, when it comes to the term *Latino* or *Latina* and *Hispanic,* we are now seeing the transition to *Latinx.* When these changes occur (and we have seen them quite a few times in our lifetimes), it is not at all unusual for there to be those who do not want the change and those who do. The term *Latinx* is no different. Just put the term in your online search engine and see the various opinions!

Source: U.S. Census Bureau, Population Division, Special Population Staff, http://www.census.gov/population/www/socdemo/race/racefactcb.html.

due to immigration law changes that had previously greatly restricted their entry, it is clear that there is a trend toward negative treatment of these groups that needs to be addressed.

While the first five editions of this textbook reflected the situation existing at the times they were published, the sixth edition expanded and updated the chapter on race to include discrimination against people other than the traditional groups of Black and white. This has continued for subsequent editions. Keep in mind that we always addressed workplace discrimination on the basis of ethnicity or national origin; it was simply dealt with in a separate chapter because that is the way the law handled it. There will continue to be a separate chapter on national origin discrimination, as the issues called upon in such cases have their own history and legal interpretation to which attention must be given. However, in keeping with the changing times and our rapidly changing American demographics, we will address other ethnicities in this chapter as well.

In expanding our race coverage, however, it is important that we preserve the history and background of the Civil Rights Act of 1964 so that the law can continue to be understood in its proper context; that is, the context of slavery, Jim Crow, and the fight for civil rights (and the lingering effects of each) in which it occurred. It is important that we not marginalize what has been, and continues to be, a long-standing, persistent, deeply ingrained issue in this country: discrimination against Blacks (see Exhibit 6.4, "Reality of Intentional Job Discrimination"). This is not a value judgment as to the relative importance of discrimination against one group versus another. Rather, it is a recognition of the long, tortuous, and lingering history, vestiges, and impact of traditional notions of race discrimination in the United States and the role that the quest for equality and civil rights for African Americans has played in all groups now expecting to be treated equally. The expanded notion of race will not neglect either the important basis for the law that birthed the legislation in the first place or the present-day effects that continue to persist even as other groups come into the United States and rise to become accepted as a part of our country rather than "outsiders." This is a factor that the Russell Sage/Harvard study on race mentioned in the earlier bullets in the chapter discussed.

Exhibit 6.4 *Reality of Intentional Job Discrimination*

In 2002, Alfred W. Blumrosen and Ruth G. Blumrosen, well-respected lawyers, law professors, and civil rights researchers, released an unprecedented, comprehensive, groundbreaking study of workplace discrimination called *The Reality of Intentional Job Discrimination in Metropolitan America—1999*. The objective of the Ford Foundation–funded study was "to advance the public 'sense of reality' concerning the present extent of intentional job discrimination." The study examined 160,297 EEO-1 reports supplied to the federal government by private employers with 100 or more employees and federal contractors with 50 or more employees for the period 1975–1999. It identified intentional employment discrimination by applying legal standards to statistics of the race, gender, and ethnic composition of large and medium-sized employers in the private sector. The report contained statistical information on 40 individual states as well as the nation as a whole.

The report concluded that "a substantial part of the public has erroneously assumed that intentional job discrimination is either a thing of the past, or the acts of individual 'bad apples' in an otherwise decent work environment . . . Meanwhile, thousands of employers have continued systematic restriction of qualified minority and female workers, and these workers have lost opportunities to develop and exercise the skills and abilities that would warrant higher wages." The report found that African Americans "still bear the severest brunt of this discrimination . . . Thirty-five thousand business establishments discriminated against 586,000 African Americans. Ninety percent of these black workers were affected by establishments that were so far below the average utilization that there was only a 1 in 100 chance that this happened by accident and half by 'hard core' employers who had been discriminating for at least nine years."

Source: Alfred W. Blumrosen and Ruth G. Blumrosen, *The Reality of Intentional Job Discrimination in Metropolitan America—1999*, 2002. http://www.eeo1.com/1999_NR/Title.pdf.

In taking this approach, we want to recognize that the willingness of other groups to exercise their rights under the law by using the race category rather than or in addition to the national origin category is a trend we see, note, and here reflect. The EEOC also has seen this trend and, in part because of it, launched an initiative called Eradicating Racism and Colorism from Employment (E-RACE) intended to address these changes. (See Exhibit 6.5, "EEOC's E-RACE Initiative.") As part of its revised Compliance Manual, issued in 2006, the EEOC outlined the differences between the categories of race, color, and national origin. (See Exhibits 6.6, "EEOC's Revised Race Guidance"; 6.7, "EEOC's National Origin Guidance"; and 6.11, "EEOC's Color Guidance.") The EEOC noted that the Civil Rights Act did not define race (it was understood at the time of the passage of the law, given our country's history and the recent and painful civil rights activity leading up to passage of the law, to include African Americans and whites), but in light of recent trends, the EEOC undertook to bring some understanding to the matter in a world in which things had changed since passage of the act.

Case 1

As a society, we now think of race under Title VII as a more inclusive concept. The authors applaud the EEOC's recognition of this trend and have modified our approach accordingly. In the *Alonzo v. Chase Manhattan Bank, N.A.* case, provided at the end of the chapter, you can see for yourself the struggle the courts had dealing with this issue when a Hispanic employee sued for national origin

---

Exhibit 6.5 *EEOC's E-RACE Initiative*

THE E-RACE INITIATIVE (ERADICATING RACISM AND COLORISM FROM EMPLOYMENT)

Why Do We Need E-RACE?

The most frequently filed claims with the EEOC are allegations of race discrimination, racial harassment, or retaliation arising from opposition to race discrimination. In Fiscal Year 2006, 27,238 charges alleged race-based discrimination, accounting for 36 percent of the charges filed that year.

In a 2005 Gallup poll, 31 percent of Asian Americans surveyed reported having witnessed or experienced incidents of discrimination, the largest percentage of any ethnic group, followed closely by 26 percent of African Americans, the second largest group. A December 2006 CNN poll conducted by Opinion Research Corporation revealed that 84 percent of 328 Blacks/African Americans and 66 percent of 703 non-Hispanic Whites/Caucasians think racism is a "very serious" or "somewhat serious" problem in America.

Color discrimination in employment seems to be on the rise. In Fiscal Year 1992, the EEOC received 374 charges alleging color-based discrimination. By Fiscal Year 2006, charge-filings alleging color discrimination increased to 1,241 [3166 by 2019]. A recent study conducted by a Vanderbilt University professor "found that those with lighter skin earn on average 8 to 15 percent more than immigrants with the darkest skin tone—even when taking into account education and language proficiency. This trend continued even when comparing people of the same race or ethnicity." Similarly, a 2006

University of Georgia survey revealed that a light-skinned Black male with only a bachelor's degree and basic work experience would be preferred over a dark-skinned Black male with an MBA and past managerial positions. However, in the case of Black female applicants seeking a job, "the more qualified or experienced darker-skinned woman got it, but if the qualifications were identical, the lighter-skinned woman was preferred."

Meanwhile, overt forms of race and color discrimination have resurfaced. In the past decade, some of the American workforce have witnessed nooses, KKK propaganda, and other racist insignia in the workplace. Racial stereotypes and cultural distortions continue to influence some decisions regarding hiring, discipline, evaluations, and advancement.

Finally, some facially neutral employment criteria are significantly disadvantaging applicants and employees on the basis of race and color. Studies reveal that some employers make selection decisions based on names, arrest and conviction records, employment and personality tests, and credit scores, all of which may disparately impact people of color. Further, an employer's reliance on new technology in job searches, such as video résumés, could lead to intentional race or color discrimination based on appearance or a disproportionate exclusion of applicants of color who may not have access to broadband-equipped computers or video cameras.

Collectively, these data show that racial inequality may remain a problem in the 21st century workplace.

Source: http://eeoc.gov/initiatives/e-race/index.html.

---

discrimination and then amended his complaint to include a claim for race discrimination. Compare the court's analysis about Hispanics and race in *Alonzo* to the discussion of race versus ethnicity in Exhibit 6.3, "Hispanic: Race or National Origin—and Who Is Included?" Do they seem consistent to you?

Things have certainly changed dramatically in the 55-plus years since passage of the Civil Rights Act. But keep the previously mentioned research in mind: 9 out of 10 whites under 30 believed African Americans and whites were treated equally. Millennials (born 1982 to 2003) are not as tolerant of other races as they

Exhibit 6.6   *EEOC's Revised Race Guidance*

WHAT IS "RACE" DISCRIMINATION?

Title VII prohibits employer actions that discriminate, by motivation or impact, against persons because of race. Title VII does not contain a definition of "race," nor has the Commission adopted one. For the collection of federal data on race and ethnicity, the Office of Management and Budget (OMB) has provided the following five racial categories: *American Indian or Alaska Native; Asian; Black or African-American; Native Hawaiian or Other Pacific Islander;* and *white;* and one ethnicity category, *Hispanic or Latino.* The OMB has made clear that these categories are "social-political constructs . . . and should not be interpreted as being genetic, biological, or anthropological in nature."

Title VII's prohibition of race discrimination generally encompasses:

- **Ancestry:** Employment discrimination because of racial or ethnic ancestry. Discrimination against a person because of his or her ancestry can violate Title VII's prohibition against race discrimination. Note that there can be considerable overlap between "race" and "national origin," but they are not identical. For example, discrimination against a Chinese American might be targeted at her Asian ancestry and not her Chinese national origin. In that case, she would have a claim of discrimination based on race, not national origin.

- **Physical Characteristics:** Employment discrimination based on a person's physical characteristics associated with race, such as a person's color, hair, facial features, height, and weight.

- **Race-Linked Illness:** Discrimination based on race-linked illnesses. For example, sickle cell anemia is a genetically transmitted disease that affects primarily persons of African descent. Other diseases, while not linked directly to race or ethnicity, may nevertheless have a disproportionate impact. For example, Native Hawaiians have a disproportionately high incidence of diabetes. If the employer applies facially neutral

standards to exclude treatment for conditions or risks that disproportionately affect employees on the basis of race or ethnicity, the employer must show that the standards are based on generally accepted medical criteria.

- **Culture:** Employment discrimination because of cultural characteristics related to race or ethnicity. Title VII prohibits employment discrimination against a person because of cultural characteristics often linked to race or ethnicity, such as a person's name, cultural dress and grooming practices, or accent or manner of speech. For example, an employment decision based on a person having a so-called Black accent, or "sounding white," violates Title VII if the accent or manner of speech does not materially interfere with the ability to perform job duties.

- **Perception:** Employment discrimination against an individual based on a belief that the individual is a member of a particular racial group, regardless of how the individual identifies himself. Discrimination against an individual based on a perception of his or her race violates Title VII even if that perception is wrong.

- **Association:** Employment discrimination against an individual because of his or her association with someone of a particular race. For example, it is unlawful to discriminate against a white person because he or she is married to an African American or has a multiracial child or because he or she maintains friendships or otherwise associates with persons of a certain race.

- **Subgroup or "Race Plus":** Employment discrimination against a subgroup of persons in a racial group because they have certain attributes in addition to their race. Thus, for example, it would violate Title VII for an employer to reject Black women with preschool-age children, while not rejecting other women with preschool age children.

- **"Reverse" Race Discrimination:** Title VII prohibits race discrimination against all persons, including Caucasians. A plaintiff may prove a claim of discrimination through direct or circumstantial evidence. Some courts, however, take the position that if a white person relies on circumstantial evidence to establish a reverse discrimination claim, he or she must meet a heightened standard of proof. The Commission, in contrast, applies the same standard of proof to all race discrimination claims, regardless of the victim's race or the type of evidence used. In either case, the ultimate burden of persuasion remains always on the plaintiff.

Source: EEOC Compliance Manual, Section 15-II, http://www.eeoc.gov.

Exhibit 6.7 *EEOC's National Origin Guidance*

NATIONAL ORIGIN DISCRIMINATION

Whether an employee or job applicant's ancestry is Mexican, Ukrainian, Filipino, Arab, American Indian, or any other nationality, he or she is entitled to the same employment opportunities as anyone else.

ABOUT NATIONAL ORIGIN DISCRIMINATION

National origin discrimination means treating someone less favorably because he or she comes from a particular place, because of his or her ethnicity or accent, or because it is believed that he or she has a particular ethnic background. National origin discrimination also means treating someone less favorably at work because of marriage or other association with someone of a particular nationality.

- **Employment Decisions.** Title VII prohibits any employment decision, including recruitment, hiring, and firing or layoffs, based on national origin.
- **Harassment.** Title VII prohibits offensive conduct, such as ethnic slurs, that creates a hostile work environment based on national origin. Employers are required to take appropriate steps to prevent and correct unlawful harassment. Likewise, employees are responsible for reporting harassment at an early stage to prevent its escalation.

- **Accent Discrimination.** An employer may not base a decision on an employee's foreign accent unless the accent materially interferes with job performance.
- **English Fluency.** A fluency requirement is only permissible if required for the effective performance of the position for which it is imposed.
- **English-Only Rules.** English-only rules must be adopted for non-discriminatory reasons. An English-only rule may be used if it is needed to promote the safe or efficient operation of the employer's business.

COVERAGE OF FOREIGN NATIONALS

Title VII and the other antidiscrimination laws prohibit discrimination against individuals employed in the United States, regardless of citizenship, or those working for American companies in other countries. However, relief may be limited if an individual does not have work authorization.

Source: EEOC Compliance Manual, http://www.eeoc.gov.

---

think, with three-fourths of them having no nonwhite friends. Even in the midst of legalized segregation and Jim Crow, polls showed that whites thought Blacks were treated equally. It demonstrates one of the reasons that the disappearance of race discrimination may not necessarily be as realistic in the near future as we would like to think, as per the poll mentioned above. A 2019 report from the Stanford Center on Poverty and Inequality reported that young adults are just as likely to endorse traditional racial and gender stereotypes as members of previous generations. "Little generational change has occurred on gender and racial attitudes since the Baby Boomers came of age," sociologist Sasha Shen Johfre and Aliya Saperstein wrote in the report. "More millennials endorse strongly egalitarian views than previous generations, however this trend is offset by the many millennials who maintain antivalent or traditionalist views." Between 20 and 30 percent believe Blacks are lazier than whites—the same amount as Baby Boomers and Gen Xers but lower than earlier generations.[33] Also in 2019, USC political science researchers examined 40 years of data gathered at the University of Chicago in its respected and rigorous General Social Surveys and found that racism is increasingly acceptable to most Americans and increasingly acceptable among conservatives as well as liberals and those with or without college educations. Note that the irony is that the responses of millennials drove the findings, as an affront to equality–rather like an unexpected backlash to equality– even though they also endorse strong egalitarian views.[34]

Given this landscape, employers may be less likely to respond appropriately to claims of racial discrimination from nonwhite employees and thus increase the likelihood of liability under Title VII.

In fact, researchers refer to the idea that whites think everything is fair for everyone, so nothing need be done to ensure equal opportunity anymore, as the "new racism."[35] As Congress noted in its 2008 resolution apologizing for slavery, because the United States' unique racial history involved systemic, institutionalized, legal, and social race discrimination, we are left with enough of the vestiges to account for much of the racial differences we see reflected in the items above. If managers and supervisors do not realize that vestiges remain, they are likely to run afoul of the law. We see it in case after case after case. Managers allowed things to happen in a workplace without realizing they were illegal.

See Chapter 2 to revisit key concepts.

Keep in mind that employers do not need to engage in deliberate, intentional racial discrimination in order to violate the law. That is why providing contextual information here to address these matters is so important for making workplace decisions that avoid liability. It is not difficult for you to see this situation arise from time to time. George Zimmerman shot and killed Trayvon Martin, an unarmed teenager walking home with a can of soda and a bag of Skittles. When Zimmerman was acquitted of the killing, polls showed a dramatic difference in how the situation was viewed, based on race, with 84 percent of Blacks strongly disapproving of the verdict and 51 percent of whites approving.[36] The most recent spate of killings of unarmed minority men and women by police officers, giving rise to the Black Lives Matter movement, reflected some of the same sentiment: one side totally understanding it, the other not so much. These situations arise every so often with generally the same results: totally different assessments based on race. It makes sense that these differences would manifest themselves so starkly in the polls if whites think everything is fine and Blacks are living a different reality.

Clearly much progress has been made in the area of race discrimination in the workplace since Title VII was enacted. Despite that progress, consider recent events such as:

- the Wet Seal clothing chain paying out $7.5 million in a Philadelphia-area case in which the Black store manager was terminated five days after a visiting executive director said that the manager "wasn't the right fit for the store" and she "wanted someone with blonde hair and blue eyes";[37]
- the Black Hooters server in Baltimore who was terminated after being told she could not have blonde highlights in her hair because she is Black and "Black people do not have blonde in their hair," although white employees were allowed to have highlights of any color;[38]
- the Cincinnati landlord who posted a "Whites Only" sign on the property's swimming pool to keep out a 15-year-old visiting her parents because she said the "girl used chemicals in her hair that would make the pool 'cloudy'";[39]
- or the Hoboken Police Department settling claims of "rampant" racial discrimination including coworkers posing for pictures wearing Ku Klux Klan hoods made of table napkins.[40]

So despite the progress made, clearly issues remain and they will manifest in the workplace. As mentioned earlier, the extremely comprehensive, four-year, 1,400-page study of intentional workplace discrimination released by Alfred and Ruth Blumrosen[41] found that workplace discrimination against African Americans is still the worst of all groups; "the seriousness of intentional job discrimination against black workers by major and significant industries is evident; and the 'playing field' is far from level."

There are, in fact, companies that are doing just fine, understand the impact of race in the workplace, and work to make sure they do not violate the law. *The Wall Street Journal* reported that after a study of 31,000 of its U.S. jobs showed discrepancies, Eastman Kodak Co. agreed to pay about $13 million in retroactive and current pay raises to 2,000 female and minority employees in New York and Colorado. The pay raise was not in response to a threatened lawsuit, as is generally the case. Employees had complained about it to supervisors the year before, so Kodak conducted the study and determined it would make the correction.[42]

One of the best ways we have found to address this gap in awareness that can lead to employer liability is to help you to realize and understand it by giving you some of the history of race in our country. We have found in our own classrooms that most of our students fit quite neatly into that "9 out of 10" category. They come into the course thinking everyone is treated equally and see little reason to still have discrimination lawsuits—until, that is, we show them documentaries on historical events like slavery, the Jim Crow era, and school desegregation riots leading up to its passage and discuss this and the information in this introduction. Then they get it. They are astonished at how clueless (their term, not ours) they were about it all and how little they really knew about this history yet see how important it is to know in order to understand the law, where we are today, and how it impacts their actions in the workplace. It would take volumes to do it any real justice, but we will give you the most significant highlights leading up to passage of Title VII, primarily to address racial discrimination in the workplace, so that you can see what contributes to some of the workplace situations resulting in employer liability today. We have chosen this approach because it addresses the way we have seen thousands of cases arise, both in real life and in legal decisions. We want you to learn from those lessons.

Before we do this, however, we want you to read the *Jones v. Horseshoe Casino & Hotel* case, included at the conclusion of the chapter. It is a case in which you get to see how racial discrimination can play out in the workplace. We want you to read it before you proceed to the "Background" section below so you can have some sense of why the next section is such an important one for you to be aware of.

Background of Racial Discrimination in the United States

Chances are, the *Jones* case doesn't make a lot of sense to you. You probably can't figure out why, in this day and time, an employer would do such a thing and be so open and blatant about it. You likely think that if Jones was as good a dealer as the court said, a casino would be glad to get him. This makes perfect sense if you've never really thought about or been confronted with race discrimination. That's why a bit of background is helpful. None of this makes any sense unless you understand where it comes from. The fact that this took place in Mississippi is not surprising, given the state's racial history. Keep in mind that in 2004 the people of Alabama voted to keep in their constitution racially separate schools and one county did not integrate its schools until 2018.

LO2 Explain the relevance of the history of civil rights to present-day workplace race and color discrimination issues.

History and its present-day effects account for much of the race discrimination we see manifested today. And make no mistake about it, our history regarding race has been a long, complex, and tortured one. Six months after the 2003 death of the erstwhile staunch segregationist who dedicated his life to racial segregation, South Carolina Senator Strom Thurmond, it was a national media event when a Black woman announced she was his daughter and had been privately, but not publicly, acknowledged by him all her life. She was the result of a union between Thurmond, then a 22-year-old lawyer living with his parents, and her mother, a 16-year-old maid in the household.[43] Despite the fact that the hallmark of Thurmond's career had been supporting racial segregation, including running for president on a segregationist "Dixiecrat" ticket, he had an acknowledged daughter by a Black woman and was one of the first southern legislators to hire a Black aide in the early 1970s. Complex indeed.

As you recall from the Title VII and affirmative action chapter, Africans arrived in this country in 1619, before the *Mayflower*. Their initial experience was as indentured servants. After the first 40 years or so, this changed as the need for cheap labor grew with America's rapid expansion, and slavery came into existence. While a very small number of African Americans were free, slavery as an integral and defining part of American life lasted for 247 years, until after the Civil War ended in 1865. The 11 or so years of Reconstruction were intensely hostile and violent, with whites trying desperately to regain at least some measure of the only social and economic system they had ever known. When it ended, the country saw Black Codes and Jim Crow laws legalize and codify racial discrimination all over the country into an iron cage from which Blacks could rarely escape.

During slavery, in many places, there were more slaves than whites (for instance, South Carolina had an 80 percent slave population), so absolute control was necessary in order to prevent slave uprisings, which were a major concern for whites. Without having sufficient manpower to exercise this control physically, such control had to be imposed psychologically as well. This was done quite systematically and with the intention of keeping the system of slavery in place forever. Each of the rules and regulations contained in the Slave Codes, and later, after Reconstruction, in the Black Codes, was designed to do this.

This system was all-encompassing, omnipresent, and systemic. Whether it is based in economics, religion, social custom, education, employment, recreation, social science, or even science, virtually everything was designed to support the system created to maintain a particular way of life. Even something as seemingly "objective" as medicine did not escape. For instance, "Drapetomania" was deemed an actual "medical condition" doctors ascribed to slaves who wanted to run away and be free.[44] Clearly the control was comprehensive and minutely detailed to accomplish this purpose. It is important to understand this so that you can recognize how insinuated into every aspect of life racism was in this country and why there were bound to be vestiges long after slavery ended.

When Reconstruction ended, about 11 years after the Civil War was over, the Slave Codes were, for the most part, simply renamed "Black Codes" and used virtually as if slavery had never ended. This system of laws governing Black and white relations was based on both law and social custom that was as ironclad as any law ever was. The system, adopted by either law or social custom all over the country, remained in place until the Civil Rights Act of 1964 and in some places well into the 1970s and '80s, constantly reasserting the institutionalized role of race in the United States. If you think this was a terribly long time ago, you'd probably be surprised to know that there are audio recordings of actual former slaves telling their stories of what life was like under slavery.[45] For one of your authors, it was not audiotapes, but seeing in the 1900 Census that her Grandma's household as a teen included her Grandma's grandmother, born in 1815, who was enslaved for 50 years before the Civil War freed her.

But what do we really mean by "a system" and "the institutionalized role of race"? And why can't we just all forget it and move on? Think back to the information in the prior chapters about how every facet of life was based on race. Doing so is helpful in trying to figure out why race is still such a persistent and pervasive issue in the workplace today.

Race governed every facet of life. In addition to the ways we have already set forth in earlier chapters, Blacks were routinely discriminated against by being forced to sit in the balconies of movie theaters or made to attend on days different from those when whites attended. Some fairs had designated "Negro days" as the only ones on which African Americans could attend, and some towns had "Negro days" for African Americans to shop. Rather than be seated in restaurants, they were generally sent to the back door, where they ordered their food on a take-out basis long before take-out came to be. Staying in hotels was virtually out of the question, even if they had the funds to do so. (Keep in mind that for the most part African Americans were relegated to being able to work only menial labor jobs.) The 2018 film *Green Book,* which won the Oscar for Best Picture in 2019, was about this phenomenon.

Although they paid full bus fare, in the South, African Americans had to sit in the back of the bus. They could not simply pay their fare and walk to the back of the bus, as this would mean they were in close contact with whites. Rather, they were required to pay their fare in the front, get off the bus, and reenter through the back, rain or shine. If whites wanted or needed Blacks' seats, African Americans had to give up their seats even though they were full-fare-paying passengers.

African Americans could not testify against whites in court; look whites in the eye; stay on the sidewalk when whites passed by; be called by common honor-ific titles such as "Mr.," "Mrs.," or "Miss"; or contradict anything a white person said. The simple act of registering to vote could cost an African American his or her job, family, home, or life. It was not until the Voting Rights Act of 1965 was passed the year after the Civil Rights Act, that African Americans received back their full voting rights taken away after Reconstruction. Breach of Jim Crow law or social policy by African Americans resulted in swift retribution, up to and includ-ing death—generally by lynching for males—an event that was often attended by whole families of whites, including children, and treated as a festive family outing, complete with photos, picnic baskets, postcards of the event, newspaper announce-ments ahead of time, and even special trains to the event. More than 2,000 Blacks were lynched but Congress refused to pass legislation addressing it, despite many pleas to do so. In 2005, the Senate apologized for failing to enact anti-lynching legislation for nearly 100 years, but it was not until fifteen years later in February 2020 that the U.S. House of Representatives moved to make it a federal crime with passage of the Emmett Till Antilynching bill.

In historical and societal terms, this was not that long ago. If you were not alive during that time, then most certainly your parents or grandparents were. Remem-ber that the system officially ended only in 1964, and in many places it or its effects lingered on long after—in some places, even until today. For instance, in Atlanta, retiring Black police officers suffered because of the police department's racial policy that lingered until the 1970s, which prevented Black officers from contribut-ing to a whites-only pension fund. This has resulted in hundreds of dollars a month less in pension payouts to retiring Black officers. Along with the difference in pen-sions, Black officers were not permitted to partner with white officers, were made to dress in separate dressing rooms in separate buildings, and were not permitted to arrest white suspects.[46] There are other examples of present-day vestiges:

- The EEOC filed suit against a company in Minnesota that not only fired a white employee who recommended that a Black temporary employee be hired full-time and given benefits but rejected her suggestion by "punctuating it with racist language."[47]

- In April 2019, Georgia's "Runaway Negro Creek" was finally renamed. The new name is Freedom Creek. There are many such places still remaining on official maps, named for a time reflecting their use or history as did this one.[48]

- Ava DuVernay's award-nominated Netflix documentary *13th* draws the direct connection between the abolishment of slavery under the Thirteenth Amendment to the U.S. Constitution and allowing it only as punishment for a crime and the steady move toward the mass incarceration of Black and brown men in the United States, often when they have committed no crimes.

- A North Carolina federal jury "acting as the conscience of this community" awarded $200,000 in compensatory and punitive damages to two Black truck drivers who were repeatedly subjected to "racist abuse" including supervisors and other employees referring to them as the "N-word," "monkey," "boy," and "coon" and bringing one of the Black employees a noose and saying, "This is for you. Do you want to hang from the family tree?"[49]

- Twelve white firefighters were awarded 2.5 million after not getting promotions they were scheduled for because the fire department illegally allowed promotional lists with their names on them to expire so they could promote Black firefighters instead.[50]

- TSA officers in a behavioral detection program designed to spot terrorists at Boston's Logan International Airport, and managers of similar programs nationwide, were ordered by Homeland Security to attend a special class on why racial profiling is not acceptable and is not an effective way to spot terrorists after they were investigated for stopping more Blacks and Hispanics, both of whom they thought would have more outstanding warrants or be in possession of drugs.[51]

- A New Jersey landlord settled charges with the U.S. Department of Housing and Urban Development (HUD) for violating the Fair Housing Act by refusing to show apartments or return calls of tenants after learning they were African American.[52]

- Between 2000 and 2004, 16 major insurance cases were settled, covering about 14.8 million policies sold by 90 insurance companies between 1900 and the 1980s to African Americans who were charged more, as was the custom of the day, simply because they were Black. The settlements amounted to more than $556 million. During the high-water mark for burial insurance, as it was known, American insurance companies held policies worth more than $40 billion. According to the Federal Trade Commission, some companies, like Metropolitan Life, built their businesses largely on such policies, which not only charged African Americans higher premiums but were specifically targeted to poor African Americans and often paid out less in benefits than the premiums paid in.

- The U.S. Supreme Court unanimously held that the term *boy* used by white managers at an Alabama Tyson Foods plant to refer to Black employees could, alone, be used as evidence of workplace race discrimination. Uniformly, the term was one used in the slave and Jim Crow era to refer to Black men.[53]

- In 2006 when the Delaware Masons fraternal organization signed a compact to end 150-plus years of racial separation, in 12 southern states white Masons still did not officially recognize Black Masons as their brothers.[54]

- In early 2007, nearing the 400th anniversary of the founding of Jamestown, America's first permanent English settlement and an entry point for those coming from Africa to be enslaved, the Virginia House of Delegates expressed "profound regret" for its role in the slave trade and other injustices against African Americans and Native Americans.[55] Nine members did not cast ballots. In 2001, the Virginia legislature had expressed "profound regret" for its role in the discredited "science" of eugenics that led to the sterilization of well over 6,000 Virginians between 1924 and 1979 under the Racial Integrity Act and the Sterilization Act, in the name of purifying the white race.[56] Virginia's apology was later joined by apologies in Florida,[57] Alabama,[58] North Carolina,[59] Maryland,[60] and New Jersey.[61]

- In 2008—after years of refusing to do so but after doing so for Native Americans, Japanese detention camp detainees, and Hawaiians for the overthrow of their government—the U.S. House of Representatives passed a resolution apologizing for slavery, Jim Crow, and its present-day impact on Blacks.[62] The Senate passed a similar resolution the next year.[63]

Notice that this is not dull, dry history from eons ago. This is recent. We are living the history as we speak. In fact, the last publicly known widow of a Civil War veteran died in August 2008, which is certainly in your lifetime. At the time of Maudie White Hopkins' death, the United Daughters of the Confederacy said there were still other Civil War widows living but they did not want to be known.[64]

We again provided a picture of pre-1964 life in this chapter and in this context because in order to understand why the issue still persists today, it is important to get a picture of what it meant in everyday life for all concerned. It was not until passage of the Civil Rights Act of 1964 that this country was first forced to deal with African Americans on anything even approaching an equal basis. For virtually their entire history in this country, African Americans were dealt with as inferiors, with societal laws and customs totally built around that approach. Then came the Civil Rights Act of 1964, attempting to change this 301-year history overnight. You might now understand a bit better why we have been struggling with the issue ever since.

The 2 million Irish Catholic immigrants coming to the United States beginning around 1845 went from being so reviled that store windows had signs saying "No Dogs, No Irish" to nearly 100 years later having John F. Kennedy become a revered first Irish and Catholic president of the United States. While African Americans were visibly fighting for civil rights and an end to segregation, their struggle for civil rights highlighted for other groups that they also had received poor treatment in this country. The struggle for civil rights, in part, helped some of those permitted to realize their full potential and become the successful and productive members of society they longed to be. Other groups, like Native Americans, Hispanics, and Asians, were, for various reasons, oppressed, castigated, vilified, ostracized, castigated, marginalized, and discriminated against by the greater society. They dealt with it in different ways. Asian Americans are now the minority with the highest income but also with an increasing number of discrimination claims.[65] Recent articles have wondered why Hollywood is not casting Asian actors,[66] questioned why few Asians reach top legal positions,[67] and reported that even having an Asian name can be a disadvantage.[68] Asians being locked out of full advancement in the workplace has now been referred to as the "bamboo ceiling" rather than the glass ceiling.[69] (See Exhibit 6.8, "The 'Bamboo Ceiling.'")

But a rising tide lifts all boats, so once the Civil Rights Act was passed, it benefited all groups by protecting them from discrimination. As was stated about Supreme Court Justice Thurgood Marshall, who earlier as an attorney for the NAACP argued and won the *Brown v. Board of Education* case that began to dismantle racial segregation in our country by outlawing segregated public schools, "He created a new legal landscape, where racial equality was an accepted principle. He worked in behalf of Black Americans but built a structure of individual rights that became the cornerstone of protections for all Americans."[70] (See Exhibit 6.9, "Profile: Thurgood Marshall.")

Exhibit 6.8   *The "Bamboo Ceiling"*

The U.S. Asian population includes, among others, those with roots in China, Japan, Viet Nam, the Philippines, Korea, and India. They have overtaken Hispanics as the largest group of new immigrants to the United States and have long been thought of as a "model minority" of intelligent, hard-working, quiet, compliant employees, yet they rarely make it to the top of an organization.

An April 4, 2013, a comprehensive report on Asians by the Pew Trust found that Asian Americans, who began arriving in the United States 100 years ago to be laborers, build railroads, and mine, now have a population in which nearly 50 percent have a college degree at a time when the overall rate for U.S. adults is 28 percent. Experiences among the various Asian populations differ, but in general, Asians make $16,200 more annually than the U.S. average.

Despite these positive factors, Diversity-Inc. and the Catalyst think tank found that Asian Americans fare as poorly as other minority groups when it comes to the top jobs at the nation's 500 largest companies. Only eight of those companies are led by Asian Americans, and only 2.6 percent of the seats on the corporate boards of Fortune 500 companies are held by Asian Americans. (Six African Americans are Fortune 500 CEOs, and 7.4 percent hold corporate board seats; eight Hispanics are Fortune 500 CEOs, and 3.3 percent hold corporate board seats; while nearly 87 percent of corporate board seats at the companies are held by white men.) In the federal government, Asian Americans make up 6 percent of the workforce but only 3 percent of the senior executive service.

One in five Asian Americans surveyed by Pew said "they have personally been treated unfairly in the past year because they are Asian," and one in 10 have been called an offensive name. Between 2010 and 2012, the EEOC brought 3,288 cases on behalf of workers of Asian descent. In what is known as the "perpetual foreigner" stereotype, Asian Americans in the workplace, who do not speak any Asian language, are mistaken for foreigners. This stereotype is reinforced by pop culture, where Asians were relegated to kung fu caricatures and antisocial geeks.

Source: "Pew Research's Social and Demographic Trends Project: The Rise of Asian Americans" (April 4, 2013), http://www.pewsocialtrends.org/2012/06/19/the-rise-of-asian-americans/; Thompson, Krissah, "Author, N. Va. Native Helen Wan on the 'Bamboo Ceiling,'" *The Washington Post* (February 13, 2014), http://www.washingtonpost.com/lifestyle/magazine/author-n-va-native-helen-wan-on-the-bambooceiling/2014/02/12/89cc0b76-5151-11e3-9e2c-e1d01116fd98_story.html?wpmk=MK0000200.

Exhibit 6.9   *Profile: Thurgood Marshall (1908–1993), Associate Justice of the U.S. Supreme Court, 1967–1992*

You probably have no idea how different your life would be if it had not been for Justice Thurgood Marshall. Born in Baltimore, Maryland, during the Jim Crow era, he grew up living in a segregated world. During his time at Howard University School of Law, from which he graduated in 1933, Marshall came under the notice of notable civil rights lawyers, who routinely populated the school. Marshall, by all accounts, a down-to-earth, fun-loving, brilliant, and shrewd legal mind, eventually took over as chief counsel for the NAACP after Charles Hamilton Houston, who had been dean at Howard's Law School while Marshall was there. A brilliant legal strategist, Houston had been chief legal planner for the NAACP, and when Marshall took over, realizing that the South would likely not change its laws, Marshall continued a systematic legal attack on Jim Crow segregation policies based on constitutional principles, especially the Thirteenth, Fourteenth, and Fifteenth Amendments passed after the Civil War to make real the promise of freedom for Blacks. The plan was to show how the different services and facilities provided for Blacks were far inferior to those provided for whites, resulting in second-class citizenship in violation of the constitutional equal protection laws. These cases eventually culminated in Marshall arguing and winning the 1954 *Brown v. Board of Education* case before the highest court in the land, to which he would later become the first Black to be appointed. The *Brown* case outlawed separate but equal education in public schools and was one of the most important parts of the foundation for breaking down Jim Crow laws.

Marshall was appointed to the U.S. Supreme Court in 1967 by President Lyndon B. Johnson, after having been appointed to the federal court of appeals in 1962 and as solicitor general of the United States in 1965. On the Court, Justice Marshall maintained his brilliant approach to pushing for the law to live up to its promise to provide protection for all.

Race: Putting It All Together

LO2 Explain the relevance of the history of civil rights to present-day workplace race and color discrimination issues.

As we have said before, the workplace is simply a microcosm of the larger world, so what is going on in the greater world will soon find its way into the workplace. When race has been as ingrained in a culture as it has been in the United States, it is predictable that it is taking a rather long while to rid the workplace of the vestiges of race discrimination. The effects of racially based considerations and decisions linger long after the actual intent to discriminate may have dissipated.

As we saw in the Title VII chapter, the U.S. Department of Labor Glass Ceiling Studies in 1991 and 1995 of barriers to full management participation in the workplace by women and minorities found that minorities had made strides in entering the workplace but that a "glass ceiling" exists beyond which minorities rarely progress. The study found that minorities plateau at a lower corporate level than women, who plateau at a lower level than white males. Later research has continued to find this consistently.

According to the studies, monitoring for equal access and opportunity was almost never considered a corporate responsibility or a part of the planning and developmental programs and policies of the employer nor as part of participation with regard to senior management levels. Neither employee appraisals nor total compensation systems were usually monitored. Most companies had inadequate records regarding equal employment opportunity and affirmative action responsibilities in recruitment, employment, and developmental activities for management-level positions. This has changed a great deal since then with employers, both public and private, giving more attention to the issues, but there is still far too much potential for liability.

Such factors militate against serious consideration of full participation by all sectors of the work population and prevent the employer from being presented in the best light should lawsuits arise. If an employer analyzed and monitored workplace information based on the glass ceiling considerations, much race discrimination could be discovered and addressed long before it progressed to the litigation stage. As you saw in the affirmative action chapter, that is the approach that the law would prefer employers to take so that liability can be avoided altogether.

The cases in this chapter are specifically chosen to help you learn to recognize race discrimination claims when you see them coming, before they turn into litigation. Pay particular attention to the facts in the cases and the case questions following them. They are specifically developed to make you think about the issue as a manager would so that you will be able to practice analyzing situations for potential liability as they arise and become familiar with issues in this area with which you may not have experience. After thoroughly reading and thinking about the cases, you should feel much more comfortable about being a manager or supervisor who is able to spot trouble in this area and do what needs to be done to avoid it.

General Considerations

Title VII was enacted primarily in response to discrimination against African Americans in this country, but the act applies equally to all. Although, as we saw in the chapter on affirmative action, there are times when it *appears* the law does not equally protect rights of nonminorities, this is done only in a remedial context with strict safeguards in place. The *McDonald v. Santa Fe Transportation*[71] case demonstrated that racial discrimination may occur against whites as well and is equally prohibited under Title VII. In that case, both Black and white employees stole merchandise that was being transported by the company they worked for. The white employee was terminated, while the Black employee was disciplined. The white employee sued for race discrimination and won. It may seem strange to think that it took a U.S. Supreme Court case to determine that Title VII protects whites as well as Blacks, but keep in mind the history we discussed leading up to passage of the Civil Rights Act. Race discrimination against whites was never contemplated since it was not an issue.

See Chapter 2 to revisit key concepts.

We have often heard the perception from our students and employees and employers in the business world that "all someone has to do is yell discrimination, and they win a case." This could not be further from the truth. Successfully pursuing a case takes much more. It is necessary to present credible evidence of discrimination in order to succeed. This can be done directly, by presenting evidence that the employer did or said something racially negative, or indirectly, by way of the disparate impact requirements discussed in the toolkit chapter. Much like in the Mt. Airy Hospital case of the employee wearing the red thigh-high boots in the heart patient unit in violation of the dress code and alleging she was terminated because of race, in *Phongsavane v. Potter,*[72] an Asian employee was unable to prove the discrimination she alleged and thus lost her case. She complained that she was not given as much overtime as she had wanted, and she alleged it was because she was Asian, but she gave no evidence to support the allegation, and the employer could show that the decision was not based on race. This is one of the reasons that employers who comply with the law should not overly fear Title VII claims. Either there is a viable factual basis for discrimination or there is not. If there is not, the employee's alleging discrimination does not make it true, and liability does not attach to the employer. Of course, an employer still must use resources to counter the claim, which is another reason why a "best practices" approach is always best. It lessens the likelihood that employees will file claims because they perceive fairness by the employer on an ongoing basis. This lessens the possibility of having to use precious resources to resist such claims.

Recognizing Race Discrimination

LO5 Explain why national origin issues have recently been included under race discrimination claims by the EEOC and why they remain different.

Often, one of the most difficult things for a manager is recognizing race discrimination when it presents itself. The latest EEOC statistics for fiscal year 2016 indicated that race remains one of the most frequent types of claims filed with the agency, with it being only second to retaliation claims. Many of these claims involve systemic race discrimination affecting hundreds of employees. That is, the glass ceiling is still at work, denying full workplace participation to minorities and women. Just within the past few years, the EEOC has settled class action suits with Uber for ($4.4 million), Crossmark ($2.6 million), Dollar General ($6 million), LaCantera Resort & Spa, ($2.5 million), UPS ($2.25 million), JPMorgan Chase & Co. ($55 million), Abercrombie & Fitch ($50 million), the U.S. Secret Service ($24 million), Consolidated Freightways ($2.75 million), Milgard Windows ($3.37 million), Home Depot ($5.5 million), Carl Buddig ($2.5 million), Local 28 Steelworkers' Union ($6.4 million), and Supercuts ($3.5 million). All of these cases involve widespread workplace discrimination in hiring, promotions, training, and other aspects of work life. Cases of systemic glass ceiling–type discrimination that actually go to trial are becoming increasingly rare. Even if, as was the case with JPMorgan Chase, the employer settles with the EEOC for a whopping $55 million, they still may be better off than taking the case to trial, where higher compensatory damages and punitive damages are possible, not to mention the embarrassing publicity.

Often employers are held liable for race discrimination because they treated employees of a particular race differently without even realizing that they were building a case of race discrimination for which they could ultimately be liable. Sometimes it is something seemingly small or subtle, but given the stage we are playing on, with the history we presented to you, it can be perceived as discriminatory. As the *Ricci v. DeStefano* case in Chapter 2 where the disparate impact of the

See Chapter 2 to revisit key concepts.

New York Police Department was shown or the *Vaughn v. Edel* case provided for your review demonstrates, discrimination may be established by direct evidence of discrimination by an employer even when the employer may discriminate for what it considers to be justifiable reasons. In *Vaughn,* a manager told a supervisor not to have any discussions with a Black female employee about her work because she might sue, after discovering that she asked a member of the legal staff if she thought a conversation she had with her supervisor sounded discriminatory. Two years later when she was terminated for poor performance, she sued and alleged race discrimination in that she was not given proper feedback that would have allowed her to better her performance. As you read the *Vaughn* case, think about whether you would have handled things differently to avoid the result the court reached here. *Vaughn* is the basis for Opening Scenario 2.

An employer who has not considered the issue of race may well develop and implement policies that have a racially discriminatory impact without ever intending to do so. The *Bradley v. Pizzaco of Nebraska, Inc., d/b/a Domino's Pizza*[73] "no-beard" case is a good example of this. In *Bradley,* the employer had a "no-beard" policy requiring all male employees to be clean shaven. The claimant, a Black pizza delivery driver for the company, told the employer he could not shave without severe discomfort. The employer told him it was company policy. When the employee refused, he was terminated. The employee sued for race discrimination and won. The court determined that the medical condition the employee had that caused the employee discomfort in shaving was pseudofolliculitis barbae (PFB), which occurs in about 50 percent of the Black male population and about 4 percent of the white male population. Thus, the policy that seemed totally neutral actually, in practice, had a disparate impact on Black males and had to be proved to be a business necessity if the employer was to keep the policy. The employer could not show this since being clean shaven is not a requirement for being able to drive a pizza delivery truck. It may have been a part of the company's marketing scheme, but as we saw in the toolkit chapter's discussion on BFOQs, marketing schemes are not the same as job requirements.

See Chapter 2 to revisit key concepts.

Bradley is also a good example of why disparate impact cases must be recognized if Congress's legislative intent of ridding the workplace of employment discrimination is to be at all successful. *Bradley* is the basis for Opening Scenario 3. *Bradley* also clearly demonstrates why the more an employer knows about diverse groups, the better. Here, where the employer was not aware of the impact of PFB on at least 50 percent of the Black male population and less than 4 percent of the white male population, it cost him. Such knowledge could have saved the employer from liability. *Bradley* demonstrates just how important it is to simply be able to recognize race discrimination when you see it. If you, as a manager, never had to deal with PFB (as 95 percent of the white male population and certainly all of the white female population and other ethnicities need not do), you would be blissfully unaware of the impact of your policy on 50 or so percent of the Black male population (and only about 5 percent of the white male population).

How would you avoid this situation? As a manager faced with an unfamiliar situation, your favorite eight words should be "Let me get back to you on that."

This informs the employee that you have heard her or his concern and will take it seriously. It then gives you time to find out what you need to know to make an informed decision. If it is something you do not know, ask the employee for more information, check the Internet, use resources around you, but do not simply react immediately unless you have no choice. If time is not a factor, there is no need to rush into making a decision on something about which you may be clueless that may result in unnecessary liability.

If the employer in *Bradley* had simply asked the employee to provide documentation for his condition from a reputable and reliable source, such as a dermatologist or even a barber, the outcome might have been different. Simply taking the time to treat the employee's concern as legitimate (rather than merely dismissing it because it was not something with which the manager was familiar) and trying to seek alternatives could have made all the difference.

The employer would have had a basis for providing an exception to the rule in these particular circumstances while still maintaining the general rule for other employees. While not satisfied that everyone does not have to obey the policy, the employer at least would feel satisfied that sufficient justification was provided to excuse this employee. Other employees seeing the employee treated differently would be less likely to be resentful, knowing that the difference in treatment was based on justifiable medical reasons available to anyone with the same condition.

If the employer had been flexible rather than dismissing the employee's assertions out of hand simply because it was not familiar to him, he undoubtedly could have avoided the result in this case. As a manager, make sure you try to consider all angles before making a decision. It is especially important to consider the realities of those who belong to groups with which you may not be familiar. Again, don't be afraid to seek help or information from those in a better position to know—starting with the employee for whom it is an issue. Not knowing is not a crime. We all operate out of our reality. Seeking information from someone better positioned to know may help you avoid a much bigger problem later. (For more examples of manifestations of discrimination, see Exhibit 6.10, "Names and 'Hello' Can Keep You Out.")

Another issue that is worth noting here because it has gained a tremendous amount of steam in the past year is Black natural hair in the workplace. Workplace dress codes often have provisions requiring that hair be "neat," "professional," or some variation of this language. Quite often, Black women wearing their natural hair, even when it is neatly styled, will be deemed to be at odds with the policy and they will not be hired, will be reprimanded, will be told to change it, and so on. In setting out these policies, there has been very little appreciation for the fact that Black women's natural hair in particular is not like that of white, Asian, Hispanic, or other women, so their hair will not look the same, or be styled the same. This is why it is often deemed to violate workplace grooming policies. In February 2019, New York City put in place a policy that prohibited employers from refusing to hire, firing, disciplining, or in any way treating employees adversely because of wearing their natural hair. In early July 2019, the state of California became the first to pass a similar statewide law providing workplace protection for the wearing

Exhibit 6.10 *Names and "Hello" Can Keep You Out*

Two research studies have shown just how pervasive yet subtle race discrimination can be for employees and job applicants.

In the first, researchers from the University of Chicago and MIT conducted a study in which they sent out nearly 5,000 fictional résumés in response to 1,300 newspaper ads for jobs in Chicago and Boston. To each ad they sent two sets of two résumés: one identical set had a résumé with a "traditionally Black" name and one with a "traditionally white" name; the other set of résumés had more experience, and again, one had a "traditionally Black" name and the other a "traditionally white" name. "Traditionally Black" names included Rasheed, Kareem, Leroy, Tyrone, Ebony, Kenya, LaTonya, Tanisha, Keisha, Hakim, Aisha, and Tamika. "Traditionally white" names included Greg, Jill, Allison, Emily, Laurie, Sarah, Brendan, Brad, Meredith, Kristen, Matthew, and Brett.

Applicants with "traditionally white" names received 50 percent more callbacks than those with "traditionally Black" names. The researchers found that increasing credentials resulted in a better chance of whites being called back, but not African Americans. Applicants with "traditionally white" names were called back at a rate comparable to having eight additional years of experience. The result was the same across occupations, industries, and employer size. Federal contractors or others who indicated they were equal employment opportunity employers were just as likely to discriminate as other employers, according to the researchers. Having more upscale addresses helped whites, but not African Americans. The researchers concluded that "differential treatment by race still appears to be prominent in the U.S. labor market."

In the second study, Dr. John Baugh, a professor of education and linguistics at Stanford University, presented over 300 university students recordings of voices saying a single word. The students were asked to identify the ethnicity of the speaker. Over 80 percent were able to do so correctly based solely on hearing the single word "hello."

Baugh, Black, became interested in linguistic profiling when he placed several calls in response to newspaper ads for housing; when he showed up at a property, he was always given reasons why it could not be rented to him. He suspected that the phenomenon was because he used his professional voice on the phone and the landlords thought he was white, but he showed up and was Black. He set out to investigate his suspicions. Dr. Baugh is particularly adept at voices, having grown up in Philadelphia and Los Angeles with many different dialects. He placed over 100 calls inquiring about a rental property, some using his professional voice and others his "ethnic dialects." He used the exact same sentence each time he called and only varied his voice and intonation. Dr. Baugh found that when using his "white" voice, he received 50 percent more callbacks.

After James Johnson suspected that the same thing happened to him while looking for an apartment in San Francisco, he reported it to the local fair housing agency, the Eden Council for Hope and Opportunity. Eden used five callers to inquire about housing, leaving messages. Three of the callers "sounded white," and two "sounded Black." The "white" callers' calls were returned within hours. The "Black" callers' calls were not returned. The counselor who ran the investigation said it was "pretty blatant." Shanna Smith, executive director of the National Fair Housing Alliance, says it is a familiar practice for housing, banking, and other industries, such as insurance.

Sources: Marianne Bertrand and Sendhil Mullainathan, "Are Emily and Greg More Employable Than Lakisha and Jamal? A Field Experiment on Labor Market Discrimination," 2004, http://economics.harvard.edu/faculty/mullainathan/files/emilygreg.pdf; Patrice D. Johnson, "Linguistic Profiling," *The Black Commentator* 1 (April 5, 2002), http://www.blackcommentator.com/linguistic_profiling_pr.html; Steve Osunsami, "When Voice Recognition Leads to Bias" *ABC News.com* (December 6, 2001), http://abcnews.go.com/WNT/story?id=130504&page=1; "The Color of Voice: How Inferring Race Can Become Discrimination," ABC News.com (February 6, 2002), http://abcnews.go.com/sections/Downtown/2020/downtown_linguisticsprofiling_020205.html.

of Black employees' natural hair. A few days later New York state passed such a law, followed by New Jersey. There are now similar laws pending in more than 20 states states, and several local jurisdictions have also passed similar protections. In one week in February 2020, legislatures in three states (CO, WA, and MN) introduced this legislation. The laws are called CROWN Acts (Creating a Respectful and Open World for Natural hair). Before taking an adverse action against African Americans or other employee for wearing their natural hair in the workplace, check to see if there is a regulation in place in the jurisdiction that needs to be complied with.

Chandler v. Fast Lane, Inc., provided for your review, is another unusual manifestation of racial discrimination that might well slip by a manager, just as it did in this case. In *Chandler,* the action was brought by a white manager who was trying *not* to discriminate when her company wanted her to do so. You should be aware that this also is covered by Title VII.

Racial Harassment

"No one should have to put up with racial harassment to earn a living. It does not matter whether the workplace is a warehouse or an office," said EEOC New York Regional Attorney Jeffrey Burstein.[74] The manager of the company against which EEOC filed suit had subjected Black employees to a race-based hostile work environment in a Jamaica, New York, warehouse. Blacks were called the "N-word" and "monkeys," and were assigned more difficult tasks and longer delivery routes than others. Nope, it wasn't 1950. It was 2019. It wasn't the South. It was New York. At a California construction site, workers found racist graffiti of swastikas and nooses drawn on the walls of portable johns, scrawled notes with racist epithets, insults, and other expletives and threats of lynching. The company failed to act when notified by two African American employees of this and that a white employee taunted them with a racial slur and called one of them "boy."[75] In New Orleans, an African American deck hand was subjected to similar treatment on vessels, and there was a similar reaction by management.[76] On June 14, 2018, the EEOC announced that it had filed seven racial harassment suits for similar activity.[77]

In addition to an employer being liable for race discrimination under Title VII, the employer also can be liable for workplace racial harassment. Harassment can take many forms, and claims filed with the EEOC have been increasing, particularly incidents involving nooses, the "N-word," and other racial epithets. Yes, even in this day and time. "It is shocking that such egregious and unlawful conduct toward African American employees is still occurring, even increasing, in the 21st century workplace, 50 years after enactment of the landmark Civil Rights Act of 1964," said David Grinberg of the EEOC.[78] The display of hangman's nooses became so frequent that beginning in 2007, states began amending existing laws and passing new laws banning the display of them if it was done to intimidate. For example, Connecticut and New York amended their existing laws in 2007, and Louisiana passed such a law in 2008.[79] According to the EEOC, harassment claims have more than doubled since the early 1990s and continue to rise, with race the most frequently alleged basis.[80] As then-EEOC general counsel Eric

Dreiband said, "As blatant discrimination decreases, other areas like harassment increase." African Americans, women, Hispanics, Muslims, and those perceived to be Middle Eastern have all increasingly been victims.

To hold an employer liable for racial harassment, the employee must show that the harassment was (1) unwelcome, (2) based on race, and (3) so severe or pervasive that it altered the conditions of employment and created an abusive environment and that (4) there is a basis for imposing liability on the employer. The employer is responsible for such activity if the employer himself or herself is the one who perpetrates the harassment or if it is permitted in the workplace by the employer or supervisory employees. For instance, in 2008, the EEOC announced a settlement with Lockheed Martin for $2.5 million for claims that it allowed a Black electrician to be "severely harassed," including, among other things, threatened with lynching and called the "N-word" while working on military aircraft at various places he was assigned all over the country. One of the harassers was a supervisor, and though the employer knew, no discipline was imposed, and the harassment continued unabated.[81] This was the largest settlement the EEOC had ever obtained for a single employee in a racial harassment case and one of the largest for any single employee. Then in 2016, a noose and the "N-word" led to a $3.65 million settlement for race discrimination under similar circumstances.[82] But as you saw in the opening paragraph, despite the large monetary damages imposed, these things continue to happen, and, in fact, have been increasing.

Actions for racial harassment, like those of race discrimination under Title VII, may be brought under the same alternative statutes as race discrimination, as appropriate—that is, the post–Civil War statutes, state human rights or fair employment practice laws, or constitutional provisions for public employers.

It is important to take harassment claims seriously and address them as quickly as possible. Doing so can make the difference between liability being imposed and not. In *Daniels v. WorldCom Corp.,*[83] two Black employees reported being sent racially charged emails through their work computer. The court said that racial harassment has as its basis the employer imposing on the harassed employee different terms or conditions of employment based on race. The employee is required to work in an atmosphere in which severe and pervasive harassing activity is directed at the employee because of the employee's race or color. However, here the employer took prompt, corrective remedial action to address the situation, so the court found no liability.

As *Daniels* demonstrates, the employer's best approach to racial harassment is to maintain a workplace in which such activity is not permitted or condoned in any way, to take all racial harassment complaints seriously, and to take immediate corrective action, if necessary, after investigation. An employer must do this to avoid liability. The case also demonstrates how important it is for a manager to keep up with changes that result in new and different ways to harass. In *Daniels,* the harassment was accomplished by email, but because the employer took immediate corrective action, liability was avoided. Since technology also brings about new outlets for harassment, employers must keep up with it as it changes. In 2017 it came to light that female Marines' private nude photos had been widely shared in closed Marine Facebook groups of thousands. The photos were submitted by contributors such as old boyfriends who received the photos while in a relationship and then used them when things did not work out between the couple. Female Marines not even a part of the situation reported increased harassment after the discovery.[84] Being aware of the possibility of technology ushering in new ways to harass is wise for an employer wanting to fully be aware of potential liability.

Prompt response to harassment is important. In a recent case in which the EEOC sued the employer for workplace racial harassment, the employer ended up paying a $1.8 million settlement despite the fact that in responding to the racial harassment it had called the police, photographed the "racist graffiti," offered rewards, placed undercover employees in the plant, hired handwriting analysts, sent employees to diversity training, increased plant security, and sought the help of the FBI. The graffiti continued to appear yet declined to a large extent "after the company started taking the remedial steps and the litigation was in full swing." The EEOC said that the company could have stopped the harassment earlier if it had wanted to. The company also was required to take preventive measures including adopting a policy against racial harassment and instituting camera monitoring of its facilities, training managers and employees, and periodic reporting to the EEOC on racial harassment complaints.[85]

In the *Henderson v. Irving Materials, Inc.,* case,[86] it is clear that racial harassment may be established by piecing together many things that in and of themselves may seem insignificant but, when taken together, as they must be for racial harassment, create for the harassee a very different workplace than for those not being harassed. This is extremely important for employers to keep in mind, as it may not be one big harassing act that causes liability but, rather, many small ones. That is why staying on top of things and dealing with them as they arise is important. In *Henderson,* a Black employee was subjected to a number of incidents at work, including racial epithets, threats, greasing of his truck, dead mice placed in his truck, and the buttons cut off his uniform, by two of his white coworkers. Several of the incidents were witnessed by their supervisor. The court found that though some of the events, in isolation, may not qualify as harassment, when taken in the total context of the employee's experience as the first Black hired to work there and in the greater context of race in our country, they constituted racial harassment.

A Word about Color

LO5 Explain why national origin issues have recently been included under race discrimination claims by the EEOC and why they remain different.

Detroit DJ and promoter Ulysses "DJ Lish" Barnes was totally surprised when a furor erupted over the "Light Skin Libra Birthday Bash" at Club APT he scheduled for October 2007. The plan was to allow African American women with lighter skin color to get into the party for free. An Internet blitz led him to change his mind, and he canceled the event. "I made a mistake," Barnes said. "I didn't think there would be a backlash."[87]

We can't imagine why not. As an African American, very brown at that, Barnes would certainly have been aware that skin color has a long and painful history in the African American culture, stretching back to a time when lighter Blacks were given jobs in the slave owner's home while darker Blacks worked the fields. This often resulted in better treatment for the lighter Blacks and led to resentment by darker ones. This was fueled by intentionally pitting them against each other to cause division, which meant less likelihood of slave uprisings. Later, after slavery ended, the division stuck, and for decades "the paper bag test" was used as a basis for allowing entrée to everything from schools to social organizations. If your African American skin was any darker than a brown paper bag, you were excluded. This was carried on long past the enactment of Title VII and still exists in some quarters today, either formally or informally.

Color has been a divisive issue for as long as African Americans have been in this country, and it is still with us today. As other ethnicities have joined the mix, it is clear that color is an issue with them as well. Lighter-toned Hispanics, East Asians, and Asians, among others, all have experienced serious color issues within their cultures. While you may not think that you care about color, research indicates that we tend to feel more comfortable with those most like ourselves, and one of the ways this is manifested is through color discrimination.

Now you have an idea of why color is one of the five categories included in Title VII as a prohibited basis for discrimination. (See Exhibit 6.11, "EEOC's Color Guidance.") However, despite the findings reflected in Exhibit 6.12, "Light and Dark," the first color discrimination case was not decided under Title VII until 1990.[88] The number of cases has since steadily grown, with color being one of the top 10 charges received by the EEOC in 2019.

Exhibit 6.11 *EEOC's Color Guidance*

WHAT IS "COLOR" DISCRIMINATION?

Title VII prohibits employment discrimination because of "color" as a basis separately listed in the statute. The statute does not define "color." The courts and the Commission read "color" to have its commonly understood meaning—pigmentation, complexion, or skin shade or tone. Thus, color discrimination occurs when a person is discriminated against based on the lightness, darkness, or other color characteristic of the person. Even though race and color clearly overlap, they are not synonymous. Thus, color discrimination can occur between persons of different races or ethnicities or between persons of the same race or ethnicity.

EXAMPLE 1. COLOR-BASED HARASSMENT

James, a light-complexioned African American, has worked as a waiter at a restaurant for over a year. His manager, a brown-complexioned African American, has frequently made offensive comments and jokes about James's skin color, causing him to lose sleep and dread coming in to work. James's requests that the conduct stop only intensified the abuse. James has been subjected to harassment in the form of a hostile work environment, based on his color.

EXAMPLE 2. COLOR-BASED EMPLOYMENT DECISIONS

Melanie, a brown-complexioned Latina, works as a sales clerk for a major department store. She applies for a promotion to be the Counter Manager for a major line of beauty products, but the employer denies her the promotion because the vendor prefers a "light-skinned representative" to manage its product line at this particular location. The employer has unlawfully discriminated on the basis of color.

Source: EEOC Compliance Manual, section 15-III, http://www.eeoc.gov/policy/docs/race-color.pdf.

Exhibit 6.12 *Light and Dark*

- The National Survey of Black Americans across the country, published in the *American Journal of Sociology,* found that "the fairer one's pigmentation (skin color), the higher his or her occupational standing." Researchers found that a light-complexioned Black, on average, had a 50 percent higher income than darker African Americans, regardless of educational, occupational, or family background.[1]

- We are proud to say that one of our students, psychology doctoral student (now a PhD) Dr. Matthew Harrison, received national attention (including by the EEOC; see Exhibit 6.5) when he presented at the national meeting of the Academy of Management results of a first-of-its-kind study indicating that dark-skinned African Americans face a distinct disadvantage when applying for jobs even if their résumés are better than those of lighter-skinned African Americans. Other studies had been conducted on colorism, but Dr. Harrison was the first to specifically examine how colorism operates in workplace hiring. He used the same photo but had the skin tone manipulated to dark, medium, or light with Adobe Acrobat. A light-skinned man with a bachelor's degree and minimal experience was consistently chosen for a job over a dark-skinned man with an MBA and managerial experience when evaluators were presented with their résumés.

- A law and economics professor at Vanderbilt University looked at a government survey of 2,084 legal immigrants to the United States from around the world and found that even taking into consideration virtually all other factors that could affect wages, those with the lightest skin earned an average of 8 to 15 percent more than similar immigrants with much darker skin. Economics professor Shelly White-Means of the University of Tennessee at Memphis said the study shows there is a growing body of evidence that there is a preference for whiteness in America that goes beyond race.

- Latinxs with darker skin were more commonly subjected to discrimination. 64 percent to 50 percent for lighter Latinxs.[2]

[1] **Source:** Keith, V. M., and C. Herring, "Skin Tone and Stratification in the Black Community," *American Journal of Sociology* 97, no. 3 (November 1991), pp. 760–778.

[2] **Source:** Gonzalez-Barrera Ana, Pew Research Center Fact Tank (July 2, 2019).

①
Scenario

After Title VII was enacted, the country started out with such severe race issues that it was not until later that the fine-tuning of looking at color discrimination came along—even though the color issues had been around as long as race had. Be aware that while we tend to be faced with race discrimination where the discriminator is one race and the discriminatee another, with color discrimination that is not necessarily the case. Often the discrimination is by people of the same race. In several cases, both the party alleging discrimination and the alleged perpetrator of the discrimination have been African American. Employers should not miss the possibility of this legal liability by thinking there can be no discrimination since two people of the same race are involved. This is why in Opening Scenario 1, Joan is doing more than acting unprofessionally toward Mary by constantly making comments about Mary's skin color. Joan is violating Title VII.

If you think color doesn't matter, think about whether it was a coincidence that the first-ever Black Miss America, in 1984, Vanessa Williams, was very light brown, with green eyes and long hair. Even as recently as 1984, America was not ready for Miss America to be a darker brown with short, kinky natural hair. It didn't appeal to the nation's cultural sensibilities of beauty. That is why African Americans and other ethnic groups began, and still hold, their own beauty pageants (e.g., "Miss Black America" pageant, "Miss Latina America" pageant, "Miss Asian America" pageant, etc.). It is not for purposes of self-segregation. Rather, it is to have a pageant that reflects the standards of beauty and talent that arise from and are appreciated by the group itself rather than those of the larger society that may not reflect or be able to appreciate the value of the group's own standards.

However, the reality is that it was also against the rules for nonwhites to be in the original pageants. African Americans were not allowed into the Miss America pageant until after the Civil Rights Movement in the 1960s. It was not until 1945 that they even had someone Jewish, and it was a *very* big deal when Bess Myerson won the crown. It made headlines around the world in 2019 when all five major pageant titles were won by Black women: Miss America, Miss Teen America, Miss USA, Miss Universe, and Miss World.[89]

There was a brouhaha during the 2008 presidential election when several comments were made about candidate Barack Obama only getting as far as he did as an African American presidential candidate because his skin tone was lighter than that of many African Americans. One of the statements was made by Senator Harry Reid, who was the majority leader of Obama's own Democratic Party.[90]

When several of the Hemmings who claimed to be the descendants of the 38-year-long relationship between revered U.S. President Thomas Jefferson and his slave Sally Hemmings appeared in public at a family reunion and looked just as white as many of their white Jefferson kin, there was initially widespread public disbelief. If color did not matter, this simply would not have occurred.[91]

In his book *Ace of Spades,*[92] David Matthews, who has a Jewish mother and African American father and who looks white, gives a vivid and gut-wrenching portrayal of growing up in Baltimore, Maryland, with his dad (his mother left when he was an infant), walking the tightrope of race by passing for white. He did this because even as a child, he could clearly see how much better whites were treated than African Americans, even by teachers.

Just keep it in mind as you make decisions in the workplace. As we see in Exhibit 6.13, research shows that color can matter a great deal. Whether or not you agree with the idea that color matters, the point is that skin color exists and has a value (negative or positive) in our society that may be reflected in the workplace. Make sure you are aware that Title VII prohibits discrimination on the basis of color and be mindful of the subtle, though not necessarily conscious, role it may play in how we deal with others.

Employees also can sue under the state or federal Constitution for a denial of equal protection if they work for the government or under state tort laws for defamation, intentional infliction of emotional distress, assault, or any other tort the facts support.

An employer who must remedy racial discrimination may not avoid doing so because of the possibility of a reverse discrimination suit by employees alleging they were adversely affected. If an employer institutes a judicially imposed or voluntary affirmative action plan that can withstand judicial scrutiny for the reasons set forth in the affirmative action chapter, the employer will not be liable to employees for discrimination. (See Exhibit 6.13, "Still Not Convinced?")

Management Tips

Race discrimination can seem elusive. Many of us tend to think it no longer exists or that others feel as neutral as we think we do about race. That is not necessarily so. Because a manager can be unaware of the presence of race discrimination, he or she can miss it until litigation arises. Think back to the *Patterson* case discussed in the Title VII chapter. Recall that Patterson worked for the bank for 10 years without a promotion and finally sued for race discrimination when she was laid off. Remember that many of the things Patterson alleged as part of a discriminatory pattern of treatment toward her would have been insignificant in and of themselves. However, taken together, the list becomes quite significant. Be aware of what goes on in the workplace and "don't miss the forest for the trees." The following tips may prove useful.

LO6 Describe ways in which an employer can avoid potential liability for race and color discrimination.

- Believe that race discrimination occurs and be willing to investigate it when it is alleged.
- Make sure that there is a top-down message that the workplace will not tolerate race discrimination in *any* form.
- Don't shy away from discussing race when the issue arises. Be open to learning and sharing. There are many resources you can use, including friends, podcasts, videos, YouTube, the Internet, and books on race.
- Provide a positive, nonthreatening, constructive forum for the discussion of racial issues. Don't let the only time a discussion of race arises be in the midst of an allegation of racial discrimination.
- Be aware of cultural differences that may be connected, at least in part, to race, when doing things as simple as deciding how to celebrate special events in the workplace. Be inclusive regarding where it will be held, what music will be played, what food will be served, what recreation will be offered, what clothes will be worn, and other factors. These all form a part of the atmosphere in which an employee must work and experience workplace leisure, and it all reflects the culture we know best. If people do not see themselves reflected in the workplace culture, they will not feel a part of it and will feel isolated. If they feel isolated, they are more likely to experience other factors leading to discrimination and ultimately to litigation. If this seems like a small matter to you, imagine yourself showing up at a gathering at work, and the music, decorations, food, and clothing were all Japanese. There's sushi to eat and sake to drink, and everyone is speaking Japanese. You'd probably feel a bit out of your element and would quickly realize how those seemingly simple things make a big impact. Now imagine that happening at *every* workplace party.
- When an employee reports discrimination based on race, don't let the first move be telling the employee he or she must be mistaken. Investigate it as any other workplace matter would be investigated.
- Be willing to treat the matter as a misunderstanding if it is clear that is what has taken place. There is no use in making a federal case (literally) out of a matter that could be handled much more simply. Do not, however, underplay the significance of what occurred.
- Offer support groups if there is an expressed need.
- Offer training in racial awareness and sensitivity. Courts have offered language indicating they will look more favorably on employers who do so.
- Constantly monitor events such as workplace hiring, termination, training, promotion, raises, and discipline to ensure that they are fair and even-handed. If there are differences in treatment among races, be sure they are explainable and legally justifiable.

Exhibit 6.13 *Still Not Convinced?*

We know it can be difficult to imagine that race discrimination is still an issue of grave importance when you may live in a world in which race doesn't seem to matter. Just in case you're still having trouble believing it, we ask you to consider the following.

A 2007 survey conducted by TheLadders.com, the world's largest online executive job search service, concluded that racial discrimination in the workplace is as bad now as it was 10 years ago. According to the research, 81 percent of executives had witnessed discriminatory actions in their companies, with race accounting for 42 percent of the discrimination; 54 percent say there has been no improvement in the past 10 years, and 77 percent say discrimination starts at the top.

Source: "Workplace Discrimination Starts at the Top; Found to Be Commonplace in American Business," TheLadders, February 28, 2007. Copyright ©2007 by TheLadders. All rights reserved. Used with permission. http://www.theladders.com/press/job_search_engine/workplace_discrimination_2007.2.28.

Compare this to the information from the meta-analysis research mentioned earlier in the chapter. Can you mesh the two?

Chapter Summary

See Chapter 2 to revisit key concepts.

- Title VII prohibits discrimination on the basis of race and color. This also may intersect with national origin discrimination.
- Employers must ensure that every employee has an equal opportunity for employment and advancement in the workplace, regardless of race, color, or national origin.
- Employers must be vigilant in guarding against the more stubborn, subtle manifestations of race and color discrimination.
- Racial discrimination may be by way of disparate treatment or disparate impact.
- Disparate treatment may be shown by direct or indirect evidence of discrimination.
- Disparate impact may be more difficult to discern, so employers need to closely scrutinize workplace policies and procedures to prevent unintended disparate impact leading to liability.
- Race cannot be used as a bona fide occupational qualification.

Chapter-End Questions

1. A Black firefighter alleges that each time he is transferred from one fire station to another, he must take his bed with him, on orders of the fire chief. The chief defends on the basis that it is a legitimate decision because white firefighters would not want to sleep in the same bed in which a Black firefighter slept. Is this illegal under Title VII? Explain. [Georgia newspaper article.]

2. A white college receptionist is fired when it is found that she told a Black college applicant that the applications for admissions are distinguished by race by the notation of a small *RH* in the corner of Black applicants' applications. "RH," she says, is her supervisor's term for "raisin heads," which he calls African Americans. Is the employee entitled to reinstatement? [*Jet* magazine article.]

3. It is discovered that, at a health club, the owner has been putting a notation on the application of Black membership applicants that reads "DNWAM," which means "do not want as member." In addition, the Black membership applicants are charged higher rates and are much less likely to be financed as non-Black applicants. Can the Black applicants bring a successful action under Title VII?

4. A Black female employee is told that she cannot come to work with her natural hair in locs and that if she continues to do so, she will be terminated. Does the employee have a claim under Title VII?

5. Bennie's Restaurant chain routinely hires Hispanics, but it only assigns them to the lower-paying jobs as kitchen help rather than as higher-paid servers, salad bar helpers, or managers. Bennie's says it does not discriminate because it has many Hispanic employees. If suit is brought by the Hispanic employees, who will likely win? [Based on Denny's restaurants.]

6. Five white and one Black canine unit officers sued for race discrimination when the operating procedures for their unit were drastically changed, they alleged, because the unit was "too white." Can the Black officer bring suit for race discrimination on these facts even though he is not white? [*Ginger v. District of Columbia,* 477 F. Supp. 2d 41 (D.D.C. 2007).]

7. Ken recruits applicants for several prominent companies. Often when the companies call for Ken's services, they strongly hint that they do not wish to hire Southeast Asians, so Ken never places them with those companies. Is Ken liable for illegal discrimination?

8. José and César, both Hispanic, are carpenters employed by a contractor to help build an office building in Maryland. While working, José and César discover that they are being paid less than non-Hispanic employees. In addition, they allege a hostile work environment and discriminatory terms and conditions of employment, including anti-Hispanic statements by managers and employees, segregated eating areas, and an "English-only" rule imposed by the contractor. José and César sue for race discrimination. Will they win? [*Aleman v. Chugach Support Services,* 485 F.3d 206 (4th Cir. 2007).]

9. Jill, the owner of a construction business, says her construction crew will not work if she hires Hispanic crew members, so Jill does not do so. Is this a defense to a Title VII action?

10. Sam has worked at Allied for several years with no problems. Avril is transferred into Sam's unit. Sam immediately begins having a strong allergic reaction to the perfume Avril wears each day. After having to take days off work because of his allergies, Sam asks Avril if she can tone down her perfume. Avril does so for a few days and then resumes her usual amount. Sam does not complain any further but is thinking of quitting because his allergies are so bad. He doesn't want to go any further with Avril about it because

Sam is white and Avril is Asian, and Sam thinks it might lead to race discrimination liability for his employer. Is Sam correct? [Based on student's parent's dilemma.]

End Notes

1. Isaacs, Jennifer, "Proving Title VII Discrimination in 2019," Americanbar.org, https://www.americanbar.org/groups/young_lawyers/projects/no-limits/proving-title-vii-discrimination-in-2019/.

2. "Secret Service Guards Obama, Taking Unusually Early Step," *The New York Times,* Jeff Zeleny, 5/4/2007. https://www.nytimes.com/2007/05/04/us/politics/04obama.html.

3. "Number of Hate Groups on the Rise, Report Says," CNN.com (February 23, 2011), http://articles.cnn.com/2011-02-23/us/splc.hate.groups_1_patriot-groups-southern-poverty-law-center-mark-potok?_s=PM:US.

4. Best, Tamara, "White Supremacists Step Up Recruiting on Campus, Report Says," *New York Times* (March 16, 2017).

5. Allam, Hannah, "FBI Announces That Racist Violence Is Now Equal Priority to Foreign Terrorists," NPR (February 10, 2020).

6. Ibid.

7. Pager, Devah, "The Mark of a Criminal Record," *American Journal of Sociology* 108, no. 5 (March 2003), pp. 937–75.

8. Bertrand, Marianne, and Sendhil Mullainathan, "Are Emily and Brendan More Employable Than Lakisha and Jamal? A Field Experiment on Labor Market Discrimination," http://www.economics.harvard.edu/faculty/mullainathan/files/emilygreg.pdf.

9. Rice, Patricia, "Linguistic Profiling: The Sound of Your Voice May Determine If You Get That Apartment or Not," Washington University in St. Louis Newsroom (February 2, 2006). For a fun test originally given on ABC TV's *20/20,* take a look at this website: http://www.uiowa.edu/~c103112/lingprof.html.

10. "Study: African-American Men Don't Reap Same Career Benefits from Mentoring as Caucasians" (December 19, 2011), http://www.sciencecodex.com/read/study_africanamerican_men_dont_reap_same_career_benefits_from_mentoring_as_caucasians-83423.

11. Quillian, Lincoln, Devah Pager, Ole Hexel, and Arnfinn H. Midtbøen, "Meta-Analysis of Field Experiments Shows No Change in Racial Discrimination over Time," *Proceedings of the National Academy of Sciences* (September 12, 2017), https://www.pnas.org/content/early/2017/09/11/1706255114.

12. "Wage Gap Hits African American, Latina Women Hardest, Report Shows," http://www.huffingtonpost.com/2013/01/29/wage-gap-african-american-women-infographic_n_2568838.html.

13. Derdrick Muhammad, senior organizer and research associate for the Institute for Policy Studies, "Census Shows Lingering Racial Wage Gap," *New Pittsburgh Courier* (October 11, 2010), http://www.blackvoicenews.com/news/news-wire/45111-census-shows-lingering-racial-income-gap.html. In an interesting article on the racial wage gap, Amitabh Chandra of Darmouth College's Department of Economics argues that the decrease shown in the wage gap over the years is actually greater than it appears to be because of the failure to include Black men who have left the labor market due to factors such as incarceration. See Chandra, Amitabh, "Is the Convergence of the Racial Wage Gap Illusory?" NBER Working Paper # 9476 (January 2003).

14. 127 S. Ct. 625 (2006).

15. 127 S. Ct. 638 (2006).

16. 2006 U.S. TRANS LEXIS 48.

17. Wichkham, DeWayne, "Alabama Segregation Vote Stirs Memories of Wallace," *USA Today* (December 6, 2004), http://www.usatoday.com/news/opinion/columnist/wickham/2004-12-06-wickham_x.htm.

18. Olmstead, Molly, "How Did an Alabama County Just Open Its First Integrated School?," *Slate* (August 15, 2018), https://slate.com/news-and-politics/2018/08/alabama-county-opens-first-integrated-school-in-2018-heres-why-it-took-so-long.html.

19. *EEOC v. Northwest Cosmetic Labs LLC,* consent decree Civil Action No. 10-608-CWD (D Idaho, 2011).

20. *EEOC v. Charapp Ford South,* consent decree No. 03-0171 (WD Pa. 2003), http://archive.eeoc.gov/litigation/settlements/settlement11-03.html.

21. Holley, Peter, "Black Lowe's Delivery Driver in VA Replaced by Manager after Customer Demands White Employee," *The Washington Post* (August 10, 2015), https://www.washingtonpost.com/news/morning-mix/wp/2015/08/10/black-delivery-driver-replaced-by-manager-after-lowes-customer-demands-white-employee/?utm_term=.7240df9dc699.

22. *EEOC v. Wisconsin Staffing Services, Inc., d/b/a Nicolet Staffing, Inc.,* Case No. 3:10-cv-543 (WD WI 2010).

23. "Unequal Treatment: Confronting Racial and Ethnic Disparities in Health Care," National Academies' Institute of Medicine (March 20, 2002), http://www8.nationalacademies.org/onpinews/newsitem.aspx?RecordID=10260.

24. *Boston Globe* (October 2, 1999), p. B1, http://www8.nationalacademies.org/onpinews/newsitem.aspx?RecordID=10260.

25. *Multi-City Study on Urban Inequality* (Russell Sage Foundation Publications, 2001),

26. Brown, Emma, "Alabama Teacher Disciplined for Giving Math Test about Guns, Gangs, Drugs, and Ho's," *The Washington Post* (June 1, 2016), https://www.washingtonpost.com/news/education/wp/2016/06/01/alabama-teacher-disciplined-for-giving-math-test-about-guns-gangs-drugs-and-hos/?utm_term=.e01a08212f57 (accessed March 8, 2017).

27. Scott, Jeffry, "Jones Ordered to Pay $185,000," *Atlanta Journal and Constitution* (April 1, 2010), http://www.ajc.com/news/dekalb-discrimination-suit-jones-426095.html.

28. Jones, Jeffrey M., "Americans Less Satisfied With Treatment of Minority Groups: Gallup Minority Rights and Relations Survey," Gallup.com (February 20, 2019), https://news.gallup.com/poll/246866/americans-less-satisfied-treatment-minority-groups.aspx.

29. *EEOC v. Professional Transit Management, d/b/a Springs Transit,* Case No. 06-cv-01915 (D. Colo. May 17, 2007).

30. "Gallup Poll Social Audit: Black-White Relations in the U.S.," http://www.gallup.com/poll/4627/gallup-social-audit-blackwhite-relations-us.aspx;http://media.gallup.com/GPTB/specialReports/sr010711.PDF.

31. McElwee, Sean, "Millenials Are Less Racially Tolerant Than You Think," *NY Magazine* (January 8, 2015), http://nymag.com/scienceofus/2015/01/millennials-are-less-tolerant-than-you-think.html.

32. Ingraham, Christopher, "Three-Quarters of Whites Don't Have Any Non-White Friends," *The Washington Post* (August 25, 2014), http://www.washingtonpost.com/blogs/wonkblog/wp/2014/08/25/three-quarters-of-whites-dont-have-anynon-white-friends/?tid=pm_pop (accessed March 8, 2017).

33. Jacobs, Tom, "Millennials Are No More Tolerant or Broke Than Earlier Generations," *Pacific Standard* (June 13, 2019), https://news.gallup.com/poll/246866/americans-less-satisfied-treatment-minority-groups.aspx.

34. "The U.S. is getting less tolerant of racism: Credit Milleniels," *L.A. Times,* Morley Winograd & Michael D. Hais, 8/20/2019. https://www.latimes.com/opinion/story/2019-08-19/millennials-racism-2020-campaign-usc-study.

35. Bonilla-Silva, Eduardo, *Racism without Racists: Color-Blind Racism and the Persistence of Racial Inequality in the U.S.* (Lanham, MD: Rowman & Littlefield, 2003); Bonilla-Silva, Eduardo, *White Supremacy and Racism in the Post-Civil Rights Era* (Boulder, CO: Lynne Rienner, 2001).

36. "Poll: On Zimmerman Verdict, Contrasting Views by Race," CBS News (July 23, 2013), http://www.cbsnews.com/news/poll-on-zimmerman-verdict-contrasting-views-by-race/; "Zimmerman Verdict: Poll Finds Chasm between Black and White Reactions," *The Washington Post* (July 23, 2013), http://www.washingtonpost.com/page/2010-2019/WashingtonPost/2013/07/22/National-Politics/Polling/release_252.xml?uuid5xliU2PLnEeKEZFflevhikA.

37. "Wet Seal to Pay $7.5 M in Philly-Area Discrimination Case," philly.com, (May 9, 2013), http://www.philly.com/philly/news/Wet_Seal_to_pay_75M_in_Philly-area_discrimination_case.html?c=r.

38. "Former Hooters Waitress Claims She Was Target of Racial Discrimination" (October 21, 2013), http://baltimore.cbslocal.com/video/9439521-former-hooters-waitress-claims-she-was-target-of-racial-discrimination/.

39. "Ohio Panel Rules 'Whites Only' Pool Sign Racist," CBS News (January 12, 2012), http://www.cbsnews.com/news/ohio-panel-rules-whites-only-pool-sign-racist/.

40. "Hoboken paid cop $99,000 to settle racial discrimination claims," Kathryn Brenzel, nj.com (November 20, 2013), http://www.nj.com/hudson/index.ssf/2013/11/hoboken_paid_cop_99000_to_settle_racial_discrimination_claims.html.

41. Blumrosen, Alfred, and Ruth Blumrosen, *The Reality of International Job Discrimination in Metropolitan America—1999* (Jersey City, NJ: EE01, 2002).

42. http://www.adversity.net/Kodak/02_non-lawsuit.htm.

43. Mattingly, David, "Strom Thurmond's Family Confirms Paternity Claim," CNN.com (December 16, 2003), http://articles.cnn.com/2003-12-15/us/thurmond.paternity_1_thurmond-family-essie-mae-washington-williams-carrie-butler?_s=PM:US.

44. *Diseases and Peculiarities of the Negro Race: by Dr. Cartwright (in Debow's Review),* "Africans in America," PBS.org, http://www.pbs.org/wgbh/aia/part4/4h3106t.html.

45. Berlin, Ira, Marc Favreau, and Steven F. Miller, *Remembering Slavery: African Americans Talk about Their Personal Experiences of Slavery and Emancipation* (with MP3 Audio CD) (New York: The New Press, 1998).

46. "Retired Black Police Seek Pension Parity: Retired Black Officer Lobbying to Gain Credit, Compensation for Lost Years," MSNBC (March 2, 2008), http://www.msnbc.msn.com/id/23426196/ns/us_news-life/; and Greene, Kelly, "Retired Black Cops Pressure Georgia for Pension Equity," *The Wall Street Journal* (January 16, 2006).

47. Walsh, Paul, "EEOC: Buffalo Employee Fired after Standing Up for Hiring Black Worker," *Star Tribune* (September 20, 2013), http://www.startribune.com/eeoc-buffalo-employee-fired-after-standing-up-for-hiring-black-worker/224565831/.

48. Criss, Doug, "The Name of This Georgia Waterway Was So Offensive It Was Changed to Freedom Creek," CNN (April 16, 2019), https://amp.cnn.com/cnn/2019/04/16/us/georgia-creek-renamed-trnd/index.html.

49. Cohen, Richard B., "$200,000 Jury Award: Juries Do Not Like the Use of the N-word or Nooses in the Workplace," lexology.com (February 4, 2013), http://www.lexology.com/library/detail.aspx?g=4df52158-c0fb-4379-b6a1-53f2c5c81385.

50. Chuck, Elizabeth, "White Firefighters Awarded $2.5 Million in Discrimination Case," NBC News (February 9, 2012), http://usnews.nbcnews.com/_news/2012/02/09/10362607-white-firefighters-awarded-25-million-in-discrimination-case?lite.

51. Schmidt, Michael A., "Mandatory Class for Airport Officers Accused of Profiling," *The New York Times* (April 17, 2012), http://www.nytimes.com/2012/08/18/us/mandatory-class-for-airport-officers-accused-of-profiling.html?_r=0.

52. "North Arlington Landlord Settles Discrimination Case," northjersey.com (September 26, 2013), http://www.northjersey.com/news/224265541_North_Arlington_landlord_settle_discrimination_case.html.

53. *Ash v. Tyson Foods, Inc.,* 546 U.S. 454 (2006).

54. "Masons Groups Join in 'Brotherhood,'" Tubal Cain Blog (September 18, 2006), http://tubulcain420.blogspot.com/2006/09/masons-groups-join-in-brotherhood.html; "Masonic Groups in South Struggle with Racial Separation," AP, Fox News (October 24, 2006), http://www.foxnews.com/story/2006/10/24/masonic-groups-in-south-struggle-with-racial-separation.html.

55. Klatell, James, "Virginia Assembly Apologizes for Slavery," CBS News (February 24, 2007), http://www.cbsnews.com/news/virginia-assembly-apologizes-for-slavery/.

56. "Virginia Expresses 'Regret' for Forced Sterilization of 'Mental Defectives,'" Fox News (February 15, 2001), http://www.foxnews.com/national/021501/forced_sterile.sml.

57. Cave, Damien, "Florida Legislature Apologizes for State's History of Slavery," *The New York Times* (March 27, 2008), http://www.nytimes.com/2008/03/27/us/27florida.html.

58. "Alabama Governor Joins Other States in Apologizing for Slavery," Fox News (May 31, 2007), http://www.foxnews.com/story/2007/05/31/alabama-governor-joins-other-states-in-apologizing-for-role-in-slavery/.

59. "North Carolina Senate Apologizes for Slavery," *USA Today* (April 5, 2007), http://search.yahoo.com/r/_ylt=A0LEVx_mwfJSllQAfslXNyoA;_ylu=X3oDMTEzZjEzbXB0BH NlYwNzcgRwb3MDMgRjb2xvA2JmMQR2dGlkA1ZJUDI4MF8x/SIG=1319bs6jq/EXP=1391669862/**http%3a//usatoday30.usatoday.com/news/nation/2007-04-05-nc-senate-slavery_N.htm; Robertson, Gary D., "North Carolina House Apologizes for Slavery in State," *The Washington Post* (April 12, 2007), http://www.washingtonpost.com/wp-dyn/content/article/2007/04/11/AR2007041102058.html.

60. "Maryland Issues Apology for Its Role in Slavery," NBC News (March 27, 2007), http://www.nbcnews.com/id/17813609/ns/us_news-life/t/maryland-issues-apology-its-role-slavery/#.UvLDt6WCtgI.

61. "New Jersey Officially Apologizes for Slavery," CNN (January 7, 2008), http://www.cnn.com/2008/US/01/07/nj.slavery.bill/index.html?_s=PM:US.

62. "House Apologizes for Slavery, 'Jim Crow' Injustices," CNN.com (July 29, 2008), http://www.cnn.com/2008/POLITICS/07/29/house.slavery/index.html.

63. Thompson, Kirssah, "Senate Unanimously Approves Resolution Apologizing for Slavery," *The Washington Post* (June 19, 2009), http://www.washingtonpost.com/wpdyn/content/article/2009/06/18/AR2009061803877.html.

64. "Maudie White Hopkins, 93; Was Widow of a Confederate Army Soldier," Boston.com (August 20, 2008).

65. U.S. Bureau of Labor Statistics, "Usual Weekly Earnings of Wage and Salary Workers, Fourth Quarter 2010." "Among the major race and ethnicity groups, median weekly earnings for black men working at full-time jobs were $629 per week or 73.4 percent of the median for white men ($857). The difference was less among women, as black women's median earnings ($605) were 87.1 percent of those for white women ($695). Overall, median earnings of Hispanics who worked full time ($539) were lower than those of blacks ($614), whites ($772), and Asians ($828)." http://www.bls.gov/news .release/wkyeng.nr0.htm.

66. Chow, Keith, "Why Won't Hollywood Cast Asian Actors?" *The New York Times* (April 22, 2016), https://www.nytimes.com/2016/04/23/opinion/why-wont-hollywood-cast-asian-actors.html.

67. Miller, Hayley, "Few Asians Reach Top Law Positions, Study Finds," *Huffington Post,* (January 16, 2017), http://www.huffingtonpost.com/entry/study-many-asian-americans-work-in-law-but-few-reach-top-positions_us_587d05f1e4b09281d0ebd6d9 (accessed March 8, 2017).

68. Keung, Nicholas, "Asian Job Seekers Face Disadvantages Even When They Have Higher Degrees, Study Finds," The Star.com (January 25, 2017), https://www.thestar .com/news/immigration/2017/01/25/better-education-doesnt-help-asian-job-candidates-beat-out-anglos-study.html (accessed March 8, 2017).

69. U.S. EEOC Commission Meeting of February 28, 2007, http://www.eeoc.gov/eeoc/ meetings/archive/2-28-07/transcript.html.

70. Williams, Juan, *Thurgood Marshall: American Revolutionary* (New York: Three Rivers Press, 1998), p. xiv.

71. 427 U.S. 273 (1976).

72. 2006 U.S. Dist. LEXIS 70103 (W.D. Tex. 2006).

73. 7 F3d 795 (8th Cir. 1993).

74. "Aaron's Agrees to Pay $425,000 to Settle EEOC Race Harassment Suit: Manager at Furniture Retailer Used Racist Slurs, Federal Agency Charged," EEOC Newsroom Release (June 4, 2019), https://www.eeoc.gov/eeoc/newsroom/release/6-4-19a.cfm.

75. "Air Systems Inc., Sued by EEOC for Race Harassment," 11/18/2019. https://www .eeoc.gov/eeoc/newsroom/release/11-18-19c.cfm.

76. "Artco Sued by EEOC for Racial Harassment: African American Deckhand Subjected to Racial Slurs and Noose by Co-workers, Federal Agency Charges," *Artco v. EEOC* (October15/2019), https://www1.eeoc.gov/eeoc/newsroom/release/10-15-19d.cfm.

77. "EEOC Files Seven Suits against Harassment: Agency Enforces Law in Filings around the Country," EEOC News Release (June 14, 2018), https://www.eeoc.gov/eeoc/ newsroom/release/6-14-18.cfm.

78. Tahmincioglu, Eve, "Racial Harassment Still Infecting the Workplace," MSNBC.com (January 13, 2008), http://www.msnbc.com/id/22575581/from/ET/print/1/displaymode/ 1098/ (last visited January 15, 2008).

79. Hudson, David L., "Banning the Noose," Intelligence Report, Southern Poverty Law Center (Winter 2008), http://www.splcenter.org/get-informed/intelligence-report/ browse-all-issues/2008/winter/legal-brief; Barger, Allison, "Changing State Laws to Prohibit the Display of Hangman's Nooses: Tightening the Knot around the First Amendment?" *William and Mary Bill of Rights Journal* 263, no. 17 (2008), http://

scholarship.law.wm.edu/wmborj/vol17/iss1/7, http://scholarship.law.wm.edu/cgi/viewcontent.cgi?article51018&context5wmborj&seiredir51&referer5http%3A%2F%2Fsearch.yahoo.com%2Fsearch%3Fp%3Dnoose%2Bprohibition%2Blaws%26ei%3DUTF-8%26fr%3Dclearspringsf#search5%22noose%20prohibition%20laws%22.

80. "Lockheed Martin to Pay $2.5 Million to Settle Racial Harassment Lawsuit," http://www.eeoc.gov/press/1-2-08.html (last visited February 6, 2008).

81. *EEOC v. Lockheed Martin,* CV-05-00479 (D. Hawaii 2008).

82. Gould, Tim, "Noose, 'N-Word' Lead to $3.6M Race Discrimination Settlement," HRMorning.com (August 3, 2016), http://www.hrmorning.com/noose-n-word-lead-to-3-6m-race-discrimination-settlement/(accessed March 8, 2017).

83. 1998 US Dist LEXIS 2335 (N.D. Tex. 1998).

84. Gibbons-Neff, Thomas, "'I'm Never Reenlisting': Marine Corps Rocked by Nude-Photo Scandal," *The Washington Post* (March 5, 2017), https://www.washingtonpost.com/news/checkpoint/wp/2017/03/05/im-never-reenlisting-marine-corps-rocked-by-nude-photo-scandal/?utm_term=.f7f136b44ee5.

85. *EEOC v. Scientific Colors, Inc., d/b/a Apollo Colors,* No. 99 C 1959 (N.D. Ill. 2002).

86. 329 F. Supp.2d 1002 (S.D. Indianapolis Div. 2004).

87. "Light-Skinned Party Canceled after Backlash and Threats to Sue," BET (February 11, 2008).

88. *Walker v. Secretary of the Treasury, Internal Revenue Service,* 742 F. Supp. 670 (N.D. Ga., Atl. Div. 1990).

89. "With Miss Jamaica's Miss World Win, Black Women Now Hold 5 of the World's Biggest Pageant Titles," *Time* Magazine, Tara Law, 12/15/2019. https://time.com/5750388/black-women-hold-five-beauty-pageant-titles/.

90. Zeleny, Jeff, "Reid Apologizes for Remarks on Obama's Color and Dialect," *The New York Times* (January 9, 2010), http://www.nytimes.com/2010/01/10/us/politics/10reidweb.html. See also the comment by then-Sen. Joe Biden widely understood to imply color, "Biden's Description of Obama Draws Scrutiny," CNN (January 13, 2007), http://articles.cnn.com/2007-01-31/politics/biden.obama_1_braun-and-al-sharpton-african-american-presidential-candidates-delaware-democrat?_s=PM:POLITICS.

91. "Thomas Jefferson Descendants Work to Heal Family's Past," NPR.org, Tell Me More (November 11, 2010), http://www.npr.org/templates/story/story.php?storyId=131243217 (accessed March 8, 2017).

92. David Matthews, *Ace of Spades: A Memoir* (New York: Henry Holt, 2007).

Cases

Case 1

Alonzo v. Chase Manhattan Bank, N.A.,
25 F. Supp. 2d 455 (S.D.N.Y. 1998)

A Hispanic employee sued his employer for national origin discrimination, alleging he was the only Hispanic in his unit and the only person subjected to name-calling and racial slurs because of it. After the EEOC's determination and before bringing the case to court, the employee amended the complaint to include race discrimination. The employer argued that race was not included in the original EEOC complaint; therefore, the court had no jurisdiction to hear it at this point. In holding that it was permissible to include the new category because it was within the scope of what could reasonably have been expected to grow out of the EEOC investigation, the court discussed the uncertainty of race versus national origin discrimination.

Sweet, J.

***

Whereas the term "Black," or even "Asian," does not trigger the concept of national origin or an affiliation to a particular country, the term "Hispanic" may trigger the concept of race. Thus, the allegations contained in Alonzo's EEOC charge would reasonably cause the EEOC to investigate discrimination based both on national origin and race, thereby satisfying the "reasonably related" requirement, even though he only checked the box labeled "national origin" on his EEOC charge.

Alonzo stated his belief that he was discriminated against because he is Hispanic. While the term "Black" is not associated with national origin, some courts have treated "Hispanic" as a racial category. In an oft-cited passage, the court in *Budinsky v. Corning Glass Works,* 425 F. Supp. 786 (W.D. Pa. 1977), reasoned that:

> The terms "race" and "racial discrimination" may be of such doubtful sociological validity as to be scientifically meaningless, but these terms nonetheless are subject to a commonly-accepted, albeit sometimes vague, understanding . . . On this admittedly unscientific basis, whites are plainly a "race" susceptible to "racial discrimination." Hispanic persons and Indians, like African-Americans, have been traditional victims of group discrimination, and, however inaccurately or stupidly, are frequently and even commonly subject to a "racial" identification as "non-whites."

Whether being Hispanic constitutes a race or a national origin category is a semantic distinction with historical implications not worthy of consideration here. Thus, submits Alonzo, neither he nor the EEOC employee who filled out his EEOC charge should be penalized for not checking the box marked "race." Alonzo points out that because he did not state that he was the only Hispanic from a particular country treated in a discriminatory manner, he did not confine his claim to one of national origin discrimination.

Due to Alonzo's pronouncement that he was discriminated against because he is an Hispanic, because it has not been established that the designation of being an Hispanic precludes a claim of racial discrimination, and given the uncertainty among courts as to whether "Hispanic" is better characterized as a race or a national origin, Alonzo's claims of racial discrimination are reasonably related to his claims of national origin discrimination as they fall within the reasonable scope of EEOC investigation. Accordingly, Defendants' MOTION for judgment on the pleadings regarding the claims premised on racial discrimination is DENIED.

Case Questions

1. What do you think of the court's quote from the *Budinsky* case about classification of race being stupid and inaccurate? Explain.

2. Do you think it matters whether someone's category is called "race" or "ethnicity"? Explain.

3. Do you agree with the court that the employee should not be penalized for checking the race box? Explain.

Jones v. Robinson Property Group, L.P., d/b/a Horseshoe Casino & Hotel, *427 F.3d 987 (5th Cir. 2005)*

A better-than-average Black poker dealer with a good deal of experience sued a casino for refusing to hire him over an eight-year period, alleging it was only because of his race. Based on the facts, the court agreed.

Stewart, J.

***

Ralph Jones is an African-American male living in Tunica County, Mississippi. He is a certified poker dealer who has worked in various casinos as a poker dealer and in other capacities. He has also dealt in several major poker tournaments, including the World Poker Open held at the Horseshoe Casino. It is undisputed that Jones is a well qualified poker dealer, whose dealing skills are better than the average poker dealer in Tunica County, Mississippi.

Robinson Property Group (RPG) first opened the Horseshoe Casino and Hotel in Tunica, Mississippi, in 1995. Ken Lambert has served as the poker room manager at the Horseshoe since that time.

Jones alleges that he has repeatedly sought and been refused a position with RPG. Jones first applied for a position at Horseshoe in late 1994, before the casino opened. In May 1995, Jones applied for a poker floor person and a poker dealer position at Horseshoe. Jones was not hired for either position. Two weeks later, Jones complained to Anna West, Horseshoe's Director of Human Resources, that his non-hiring was due to racism. Jones asked her whether the casino had a problem with hiring Blacks as poker dealers because he observed that there were no African Americans working at the Horseshoe as poker dealers at that time. Lambert, the poker room manager, was summoned to respond to Jones' question. Lambert responded to Jones' complaint by stating that there were no qualified African American poker dealers in Tunica County. Jones informed him that there were at least five qualified African-Americans in the area, including himself. Lambert testified that he became indignant at Jones' accusation, and he felt "misjudged" and "embarrassed." He claims that he nonetheless offered Jones a position as a poker dealer again. When Jones refused and he persisted in his racial allegations, Lambert testified that his feelings became hurt and he ended the conversation. Jones denies that he was offered a position as a poker dealer.

Between 1995 and 2002, Jones submitted applications for a poker dealer position no less than 10 times. Horseshoe has employed Jones in other departments and on a temporary basis as a poker dealer during high profile poker tournaments; however, Jones has never been hired by Horseshoe on a permanent basis. The record reveals that during the relevant time period the Horseshoe was hiring poker dealers for permanent positions. The Horseshoe generally employs a staff of 40–45 poker dealers.

***

Under Title VII, an employer cannot "fail or refuse to hire or to discharge any individual, or otherwise to discriminate against any individual with respect to his compensation, terms, conditions, or privileges of employment, because of such individual's race[.]" An employee can prove discrimination through direct or circumstantial evidence. If an employee presents credible direct evidence that discriminatory animus at least in part motivated, or was a substantial factor in the adverse employment action, then it becomes the employer's burden to prove by a preponderance of the evidence that the same decision would have been made regardless of the discriminatory animus.

***

We have previously held that "statements or documents which show on its face that an improper criterion served as a basis—not necessarily the sole basis, but a basis—for the adverse employment action are direct evidence of discrimination." When a person or persons with decision making authority evinces [sic] racial animus that may constitute direct evidence of discrimination. [sic] ("This court has implied that calling an employee a 'nigger' would be direct evidence of race discrimination.") We have also previously observed that racial epithets undoubtedly demonstrate racial animus.

***

. . . Upon extensive review of the parties' arguments and the record in this case, we find that Jones has demonstrated direct evidence of discrimination.

Mims [a poker dealer and part-time supervisor] stated that she inquired why an African American poker dealer was not hired and was told, by either Lambert or his assistant, that "they hired who they wanted to hire and there [sic] were not going to hire a Black person unless there were extenuating circumstances." She was then told by Lambert, or his assistant, that "good old white boys don't want Blacks touching their cards in their face." Sam Thomas [a former Horseshoe employee] testified that in 1995, that Lambert told him that "maybe I've been told not to hire too many Blacks in the poker room." It is incontrovertible that Lambert made the hiring decisions at Horseshoe and Presley as his assistant would have provided input, therefore, viewing the evidence in the light most favorable to Jones, the aforementioned evidence proves, without inference or presumption, that race was *a* basis in employment decisions in the poker room at Horseshoe. The evidence need not show that race was the sole basis in order to constitute

direct evidence. . . . Mims' and Thomas' testimony clearly and explicitly indicates that decision maker(s) in the poker room used race as a factor in employment decisions, which is by definition direct evidence of discrimination. Thus, we find that Jones has presented direct evidence of discrimination and accordingly, he has established a *prima facie* case of discrimination. The district court erred in granting summary judgment for RPG. We thus REVERSE and REMAND this case back to the district court for further proceedings consistent with this opinion.

Case Questions

1. Are you surprised that this is a 2005 case? Explain.
2. Given the evidence, do you understand why the lower court would have found that no race discrimination had taken place? Explain.
3. What do you think of the statements that management allegedly made? Do they seem like appropriate bases for making workplace decisions? Explain.

Vaughn v. Edel, *918 F.2d 517 (5th Cir. 1990)*

During a retrenchment, a Black female was terminated for poor performance. She alleged race discrimination in that her employer intentionally determined not to give her necessary feedback about her performance that would have helped her perform better and perhaps avoid dismissal. The court upheld the employee's claim.

Wiener, J.

***

Emma Vaughn, a Black female attorney, became an associate contract analyst in Texaco's Land Department in August of 1979. Her supervisors were Robert Edel and Alvin Earl Hatton, assistant chief contract analyst. In Vaughn's early years with Texaco, she received promotions and was the highest ranked contract analyst in the department.

The events leading to this dispute began on April 16, 1985, the day after Vaughn returned from a second maternity leave. On that day, Edel complained to Vaughn about the low volume of her prior work and the excessive number of people who visited her office. Vaughn later spoke

with Roger Keller, the head of the Land Department, about Edel's criticism of her.

In a memorandum concerning this discussion, Keller wrote that he had told Vaughn that he had been told that Vaughn's productivity "was very low"; that he "had become aware for some time of the excessive visiting by predominantly Blacks in her office behind closed doors"; and that "the visiting had a direct bearing on her productivity." Keller then told Vaughn, as he noted in his memo, that "she was allowing herself to become a Black matriarch within Texaco" and "that this role was preventing her from doing her primary work for the company and that it must stop."

Keller's remarks offended Vaughn, so she sought the advice of a friend who was an attorney in Texaco's Legal Department. Keller learned of this meeting and of Vaughn's belief that he was prejudiced. To avoid charges of race discrimination, Keller told Vaughn's supervisor, Edel, "not [to] have any confrontations with Ms. Vaughn about her work." Keller later added that "if he [Edel] was dissatisfied, let it ride. If it got serious, then see [Keller]."

Between April 1985 and April 1987 when Vaughn was fired, neither Edel nor Hatton expressed criticism of Vaughn's work to her. During this period all annual written evaluations of Vaughn's work performance (which, incidentally, Vaughn never saw) were "satisfactory." Vaughn also received a merit salary increase, though it was the minimum, for 1986. Keller testified that for several years he had intentionally overstated on Vaughn's annual evaluations his satisfaction with her performance because he did not have the time to spend going through procedures which would result from a lower rating and which could lead to termination.

In 1985–86, Texaco undertook a study to identify activities it could eliminate to save costs. To meet the cost-reduction goal set by the study, the Land Department fired its two "poorest performers," one of whom was Vaughn, as the "lowest ranked" contract analyst. The other employee fired was a white male.

In passing Title VII, Congress announced that "sex, race, religion, and national origin are not relevant to the selection, evaluation, or compensation of employees."

When direct credible evidence of employer discrimination exists, [an] employer can counter direct evidence, such as a statement or written document showing discriminatory motive on its face, "only by showing by a preponderance of the evidence that they would have acted as they did without regard to the [employee's] race."

Vaughn presented direct evidence of discrimination. Keller testified that to avoid provoking a discrimination suit he had told Vaughn's supervisor not to confront her about her work. His "Black matriarch" memorandum details the events that led Keller to initiate this policy. Keller also testified to deliberately overstating Vaughn's evaluations in order not to start the process that might eventually lead to her termination. This direct evidence clearly shows that Keller acted as he did solely because Vaughn is Black.

Although Vaughn's race may not have directly motivated the 1987 decision to fire her, race did play a part in Vaughn's employment relationship with Texaco from 1985–1987. Texaco's treatment of Vaughn was not color-blind during that period. In neither criticizing Vaughn when her work was unsatisfactory nor counseling her how

to improve, Texaco treated Vaughn differently than it did its other contract analysts because she was Black. As a result, Texaco did not afford Vaughn the same opportunity to improve her performance and perhaps her relative ranking, as it did its white employees. One of those employees was placed on an improvement program. Others received informal counseling. The evidence indicates that Vaughn had the ability to improve. As Texaco acknowledges, she was once its highest ranked contract analyst.

Had her dissatisfied supervisors simply counseled Vaughn informally, such counseling would inevitably have indicated to Vaughn that her work was deficient. Had Keller given Vaughn the evaluation that he believed she deserved, Texaco's regulations would have required his placing her on a ninety-day work improvement program, just as at least one other employee—a white male—had been placed. A Texaco employee who has not improved by the end of that period is fired.

When an employer excludes Black employees from its efforts to improve efficiency, it subverts the "broad overriding interest" of Title VII—"efficient and trusty workmanship assured through fair and racially neutral employment and personnel decisions." Texaco has never stated any reason, other than that Vaughn was Black, for treating her as it did. Had Texaco treated Vaughn in a color-blind manner from 1985–1987, Vaughn may have been fired by April 1987 for unsatisfactory work; on the other hand, she might have sufficiently improved her performance so as not to be one of the two lowest ranked employees, thereby avoiding termination in April 1987.

Because Texaco's behavior was race-motivated, Texaco has violated Title VII. Texaco limited or classified Vaughn in a way which would either "tend to deprive [her] of employment opportunities or otherwise adversely affect [her] status as an employee" in violation of the law.

Case Questions

1. Do you agree with the court's decision? Why or why not?

2. How would you have handled this matter if you were the manager?

3. What do you think of Keller's remarks about Vaughn becoming the "Black matriarch" of Texaco, "meeting behind closed doors," and "excessive meetings with predominantly Blacks"? What does it signify to you? What attitudes might it reflect that may be inappropriate in the workplace? What concern, if any, might be appropriate?

Chandler v. Fast Lane, Inc.,

868 F. Supp. 1138 (E.D. Ark., W. Div. 1994)

A white employee brought suit against her employer for constructive dismissal under Title VII and other statutes, alleging that she was forced to leave her job when the employer would not allow her to hire and promote African Americans. The employer argued that since its policies discriminated only against African Americans, the white employee had no right to sue under Title VII. The court disagreed and permitted the case to be brought.

Eisele, J.

***

In the complaint filed with the Court, Chandler (who is white) alleges that she was the victim of a discriminatory employment practice at the hands of her employers. Chandler, a former manager of employer's restaurant, claims that her employer thwarted her efforts to employ and promote African American employees, and that as a result the conditions of her employment became so intolerable that she was forced to resign. The employer argues that because they are alleged to have adopted discriminatory hiring and promotional practices targeted only at African Americans, a white person has no standing to assert a Title VII claim premised upon these policies.

It is true that only individuals whom employers are claimed to have failed or refused to hire or promote were African Americans. However, by focusing on the "fail or refuse to hire" provision of 2000e-2(a)(1), employer's argument misperceives the unlawful employment practice alleged by Chandler. Chandler does not claim that she was a target of employer's allegedly anti–African American employment practices. Rather, Chandler argues that employer's insistence that she enforce these practices violated her fundamental right to associate with African Americans, and as a consequence employer committed a separate violation by engaging in an unlawful employment practice that "otherwise discriminate[d] against an individual," namely Chandler.

Although the Court recognizes that Chandler's Title VII claim is somewhat novel, it is of the opinion that such a claim, if proven, would state a cause of action under Title VII. A white person's right to associate with African Americans is protected by Sec. 1981. Therefore, the Court concludes that an employer's implementation of an employment practice that impinges upon this right is actionable under Title VII.

Additionally, Chandler's allegations are sufficient to establish a Title VII claim under a separate provision of the statute. The relevant provision of Title VII is found in 42 U.S.C.A. § 2000e-3(a), which provides in pertinent part:

It shall be an unlawful employment practice for an employer to discriminate against any of his employees . . . because [s]he has opposed any practice made an unlawful employment practice by [Title VII].

In order to establish a *prima facie* case under the "opposition" clause of § 2000e-3(a), an employee must show: (1) that she was engaged in an opposition activity protected under Title VII; (2) that she was a victim of adverse employment action; and (3) that a causal nexus exists between these two events. The Court has no doubt that an employee who exercises her authority to promote and employ African Americans engages in protected "opposition" to her employer's unlawful employment practice which seeks to deprive African Americans of such benefits. Thus, Chandler's allegations are clearly sufficient to meet the first requirement of a § 2000e-3(a) claim. The Court further concludes that employer's insistence that Chandler enforce such an employment practice, if proven, would certainly cause an "adverse employment action" to be visited upon her. Title VII forbids an employer from requiring its employees "to work in a discriminatorily hostile or abusive environment," and included within this prohibition is the right of white employees to a work environment free from discrimination against African Americans, or any other class of persons. Indeed, subjecting an employee to such a hostile working environment may result in an actionable constructive discharge, a result that is especially likely under facts similar to those presently alleged. Under Title VII, a constructive discharge occurs whenever it is reasonably foreseeable that an employee will resign as a result of her employer's unlawful employment practice, and it is plainly foreseeable that an employee might choose to resign rather than to acquiesce in or enforce her employer's discriminatory and illegal employment practice.

The Court is therefore satisfied that employer's efforts to hinder Chandler from hiring and promoting African Americans, and their insistence that she discriminate against such persons, if proven, would result in an actionable Title VII claim. Indeed, "[u]nder the terms of § 2000e-3(a), requiring an employee to discriminate is itself an unlawful employment practice." Accordingly, it is therefore ordered that employer's motion to dismiss is DENIED.

Case Questions

1. What do you think of the employer's argument that since its policies discriminated against African Americans, the white employee should not be able to bring a suit for discrimination? Explain.

2. Do you understand the court's reasoning that the white employee was being discriminated against by not being able to hire and promote Black employees? Explain.

3. What reason can you think of as to why the employer had the policy of not hiring or promoting African Americans? Do you think it makes good economic sense? (Consider all facets of economics, including the possibility of litigation over the policies.)

Chapter 7

National Origin Discrimination

Learning Objectives

After completing this chapter, you should be able to:

LO1   Describe the impact and implications of the changing demographics of the American workforce.

LO2   Define the *prima facie* case for national origin discrimination under Title VII.

LO3   Explain the legal status surrounding "English-only policies" in the workplace.

LO4   Describe a claim for harassment based on national origin and discuss how it might be different from one based on other protected classes.

LO5   Identify the difference between citizenship and national origin.

LO6   Explain the extent of protection under the Immigration Reform and Control Act.

Opening Scenarios

SCENARIO 1

1) Scenario Carla, a partner in a law firm, recently hired a new assistant, Vladimir, who recently moved to the United States from Russia to marry his college sweetheart. Vladimir is an expert at filing and managing the firm's case management software. However, Carla has received feedback from clients that they have trouble understanding Vladimir when they speak to him on the telephone. Interacting with clients on the phone for a variety of reasons is regular part of every assistant's job; for instance, they need to schedule meetings and to inform clients of court dates. Carla is concerned that, if she continues to assign Vladimir duties similar to other assistants, her clients will be dissatisfied; some might even leave the firm. However, she is unsure about the firm's liability if she reduces Vladimir's responsibilities due to his foreign accent.

SCENARIO 2

2) Scenario Oliverio, a Mexican American high school student in California, was employed on a part-time basis at a local coffee shop. Several of his coworkers taunted him with ethnic slurs and asked him why "his people" thought they could come and steal American jobs. Oliverio did not respond to their taunts, but he did mention the comments to his manager. The manager dismissed his concerns, telling Oliverio, "If you don't like it here, then you should just go back to where you came from." Oliverio felt humiliated and angry. Soon after this exchange, Oliverio was terminated for accidentally throwing away the manager's soda bottle. Oliverio suspects that his ethnic background was the reason he was fired.

Statutory Basis

The statutory basis for protection against national origin discrimination is presented in Exhibit 7.1, "Legislation Prohibiting National Origin Discrimination." These statutes include section 703(a) of Title VII of the Civil Rights Act of 1964 and the Immigration Reform and Control Act of 1986. Additional direction can be found in the EEOC's Enforcement Guidance on National Origin Discrimination.

Chez/Casa/Fala/Wunderbar Uncle Sam

The United States of America has always considered itself to be a melting pot. Under this theory, different ethnic, cultural, and racial groups came together in the United States, but differences were melted into one homogeneous mass composed of all cultures. Recently, this characterization has been revisited, and other, more accurate terms have been proposed. They include such terms as a *salad bowl,* in which all the ingredients come together to make an appetizing, nutritious whole but each ingredient maintains its own identity, or a *stew,* in which the ingredients are blended together but maintain their distinct identity, with the common thread of living in America acting as the stew base that binds the ingredients together.

While the words on the Statue of Liberty—"Give me your tired, your poor, your huddled masses yearning to breathe free"—have always acted as a beacon to citizens of other countries to find solace on our shores, the reality once they get here, even sometimes after being here for generations, is that they are often discriminated against rather than consoled. National origin was included in Title VII's list of protected classes to ensure that employers did not make employment decisions based on preconceived notions about employees' or applicants' country of origin.

Exhibit 7.1 *Legislation Prohibiting National Origin Discrimination*

TITLE VII, CIVIL RIGHTS ACT OF 1964

Sec. 703(a)

It shall be an unlawful employment practice for an employer—

1. to fail or to refuse to hire or to discharge any individual, or otherwise to discriminate against any individual with respect to his compensation, terms, conditions, or privileges of employment, because of such individual's . . . national origin.

IMMIGRATION REFORM AND CONTROL ACT OF 1986

Sec. 274A(a)

1. It is unlawful for a person or other entity:
   A. to hire or to recruit or refer for a fee for employment in the United States an alien knowing the alien is an unauthorized alien with respect to such employment, or
   B. to hire for employment in the United States an individual without [verification of employment eligibility].

2. It is unlawful for a person or other entity, after hiring an alien for employment in accordance with paragraph (1), to continue to employ the alien in the United States knowing the alien is (or had become) an unauthorized alien with respect to such employment.

3. A person or entity that establishes that it has complied in good faith with the [verification of employment eligibility] with respect to hiring, recruiting or referral for employment of an alien in the United States has established an affirmative defense that the person or entity has not violated paragraph (1)(A).

Sec. 274(B)(a)

1. It is an unfair immigration-related practice for a person or other entity to discriminate against any individual (other than an unauthorized alien) with respect to the hiring, or recruitment or referral for a fee, of the individual for employment or the discharging of the individual from employment—
   A. because of such individual's national origin, or
   B. in the case of a protected individual [a citizen or authorized alien], because of such individual's citizenship status.

Note that section 1981 of the Civil Rights Act of 1866, as amended by the Civil Rights Act of 1991, also may apply in those circumstances where national origin is a proxy for or equivalent to race (discussed later in this chapter).[1]

Speaking of race, as we mentioned in the introduction to the chapter on race discrimination, recently there has been a sort of blending of the race and national origin categories, with employees bringing as race discrimination cases those that had traditionally been brought as national origin claims. Though the traditional distinctions in the law are becoming blurred, it is important to remember that a decision based on either attribute is illegal. Each type of claim has a unique set of case law that the courts will follow. National origin is a distinct category in this textbook because it is the way that such claims are traditionally handled and because we are reluctant to blend completely the two areas when they have quite different histories, implications, and analyses for today's employment arena.

The Changing Workforce

LO1 Describe the impact
and implications of the
changing demographics of
the American workforce.

Over the past decade, we have seen a dramatic increase in the number of immigrants
to the United States, particularly from Latin American and Asian countries. In 2017
alone, the United States was home to a record 44.4 million immigrants. In 2019,
immigrants comprised over 13.6 percent of the nation's population. The number
of immigrants is over 4.5 times higher than it was in 1960, when there were
9.7 million immigrants living in the country. At that time, immigrants made up
only 5.4 percent of the U.S. population. The growth rate is expected to continue;
the number of immigrants and their descendants in the United States is expected
to account for 88 percent of U.S. population growth through 2065.[2] By 2019, the
United States was growing by one person every 8 seconds and gaining one international migrant every 33 seconds.[3]

In 1960, 84 percent of immigrants living in the United States were born in Europe
or Canada. Since the passage of the 1965 Immigration and Naturalization Act, this
demographic has changed dramatically. As of 2017, European and Canadian immigrants made up only 13.2 percent of U.S. immigrants. Asian immigrants made up
the largest share—27.4 percent—while Mexicans immigrants comprised 25.3 percent
of U.S. immigrants. Immigrants from other Latin American countries comprised
another 25.1 percent, and 9 percent of immigrants were born in another region.[4] In
2018, there were 28.2 million foreign-born workers in the United States, compris-
ing 17.4 percent of the total labor force. Latinxs[5] accounted for 47.7 percent of the
foreign-born labor force, with Asians making up a further 25.1 percent.[6]

From 2017 to 2018, unemployment rates for foreign-born workers declined by
0.6 percent while dropping 0.4 percent for U.S.-born workers. In 2018, foreign-
born men were more likely to participate in the labor force than native-born men
(77.9 percent versus 67.3 percent). However, foreign-born women were less likely
to participate in the labor force than native-born women (54 percent compared to
57.6 percent).[7]

Despite having a slight edge in employment, the median weekly earnings of
foreign-born, full-time workers were significantly lower than their U.S.-born counterparts in 2018: $758 compared with $910 (among women, a difference of $678 to
$810 and among men, a difference of $815 versus $1007). This is likely attributable
to the fact that foreign-born workers were more likely than native-born workers to
be employed in service occupations and less likely to be employed in management,
professional, and related occupations. The earnings gap closes with higher levels
of education, and among those with a bachelors degree or higher, earnings were
slightly higher for foreign-born workers ($1,362 for foreign-born workers compared
to $1,309 for native-born workers).[8]

On its face, national origin discrimination appears to be relatively simple to determine; however, it has surprising complexities. Employers have always been uncertain of the scope of Title VII's coverage in this area and what could be used as a
defense against decisions based on national origin. (See Exhibit 7.2, "Realities about
National Origin Discrimination.") Notwithstanding this complexity, however, complaints to the EEOC based on alleged national origin discrimination have risen since

---

Exhibit 7.2 *Realities about National Origin Discrimination*

1. "Citizenship" and "national origin" are not synonymous.
2. No matter the national origin of a restaurant, it likely will still be required strictly to abide by Title VII non-discrimination principles in hiring its waitstaff.
3. The EEOC considers English-only rules applied at all times presumptively discriminatory, although courts have not always agreed.

1997. Between 1997 and 2017, complaints of discrimination on the basis of national origin grew from 6,712 to 7,106. The number of national origin complaints peaked in 2011, when there were 11,833 complaints filed.[9] The link between these two forms of complaint, particularly as they pertain to Muslim and Arab Americans after the attacks of September 11, 2001, is discussed later in the chapter.

Regulatory Overview

LO2 Define the *prima facie* case for national origin discrimination under Title VII.

national origin discrimination protection
It is unlawful for an employer to limit, segregate, or classify employees in any way on the basis of national origin that would deprive them of the privileges, benefits, or opportunities of employment.

The **national origin discrimination protection** offered by Title VII is similar to that of gender or race and is used somewhat synonymously with *ethnicity,* though they are distinguishable. In other words, Title VII makes it unlawful for employers to limit, segregate, or classify employees in any way that would deprive them of employment opportunities because of national origin. An employer may not group its employees on the basis of national origin, make employment decisions on that basis, or implement policies or programs that, though they appear not to be based on an employee's or applicant's country of origin, actually affect those of one national origin differently than those of a different group.

An employee may successfully claim discrimination on the basis of national origin if it is shown that:

1. The employee is a member of a protected class (i.e., identify the employee's national origin, including perceived national origin).
2. The employee was qualified for the position for which she or he applied or in which she or he was employed.
3. The employer made an employment decision against this employee or applicant.
4. The position was filled by someone who was not a member of the protected class.

national origin
Individual's, or her or his ancestor's, place of origin (as opposed to citizenship) or physical, cultural, or linguistic characteristics of an origin group.

We will discuss each of the above in the next few sections.

Member of the Protected Class

In connection with the first requirement, what is meant by "national origin"? While the term is not defined in Title VII, the EEOC guidelines on discrimination define **national origin** discrimination as "discrimination because an individual (or his or her ancestors) is from a certain place or has the physical, cultural, or

National origin discrimination
Defined by EEOC Guidelines on Discrimination as "discrimination because an individual (or his or her ancestors) is from a certain place or has the physical, cultural, or linguistic characteristics of a particular national origin group." Note that national origin discrimination can include discrimination by members of the same national origin group against each other.

linguistic characteristics of a particular national origin group."[10] **National origin discrimination** includes discrimination by a member of one national origin group against another member of the same group.[11]

Title VII also prohibits employer actions that discriminate based on *perceived* national origin. For instance, as you will see in *EEOC v. MVM, Inc.,*[12] included at the end of the chapter, the court found that because some employees were allegedly subject to discrimination based on the (false) belief that they were of African origin, the employees could pursue a national origin discrimination claim under Title VII. Ignorance is *not* a justification for or defense of national origin discrimination.

Note that the law provides protection against discrimination based only on country of origin (e.g., ethnicity), not based on country of *citizenship*.[13] Title VII protects employees who are not U.S. citizens from employment discrimination based on the specific categories listed, such as race, gender, ethnicity and other. However, it does not protect employees from discrimination based on their status as immigrants; citizenship status is not a protected class under the act. For example, Title VII will protect a Somali woman from gender discrimination, but it will not protect her from discrimination on the basis of her Somali citizenship. The issue of citizenship as it relates to national origin will be discussed in more detail later in this chapter.

While national origin is related to one's country of origin or that of one's ancestors, it also includes ethnic characteristics as well as physical, linguistic, or cultural traits closely associated with a national origin group. For instance, courts have held that Cajuns and people of Romani descent (sometimes referred to by the more derogatory term "gypsy"[14]) are protected under Title VII.[15] In addition, the EEOC confirms that other ethnic groups, such as Latinxs, Arabs, and Kurds, are also protected national origin groups.[16] It also may serve as the basis for a national origin discrimination claim if the employee:

- Is identified with or connected to a person of a specific national origin, such as when someone suffers discrimination because she or he is married to a person of a certain ethnic heritage.
- Is a member of an organization that is identified with a national group.
- Is a participant in a school or religious organization that is affiliated with a national origin group.
- Has a surname that is generally associated with a national origin group.
- Is perceived by an employer to be a member of a particular national origin group, whether or not the individual is in fact of that origin.

Qualification/BFOQs

The second factor that must be present for an employee to claim national origin discrimination is that the applicant or employee is *qualified* for the position. That is, the claimant must show that she or he meets the job's requirements.

Contrary to situations involving disability or religion, the employee in a national origin case must show that she or he is qualified for the position *without* the benefit of accommodation. No accommodation of one's national origin is required of employers.

For example, while an employer would be required to reasonably accommodate an employee's religious attire, there is no similar responsibility to accommodate an employee's attire of national origin, such as traditional African dress, unless it can be shown to overlap with his or her religion. (We will discuss in the section below whether courts require "accommodation" of employees' accents, like Vladimir's in our opening scenario.)

See Chapter 2 to revisit key concepts.

The employer may counter the employee's claim that she or he is otherwise qualified by showing that national origin (other than the employee's) is actually a bona fide occupational qualification (BFOQ) (discussed in Chapter 3) for the job. In other words, the employer can explain why a specific national origin is necessary for the position applied for—why that national origin is a legitimate job requirement and is reasonably necessary for the employer's particular business.

Case 4

It is important to note that customer, client, or coworker discomfort or preference in terms of national origin may not be relied upon by the employer. But, as you will see in the *Espinoza v. Farah Mfg. Co.* case at the end of the chapter, and as we discussed in the section above, citizenship is an entirely different story.

English Fluency and Speaking Other Languages in the Workplace

LO3 Explain the legal status surrounding "English-only policies" in the workplace.

Some employers choose to implement policies requiring all employees either to be fluent in English or to speak only English while in the workplace, even when employees are speaking only among themselves. Employers have also raised the question of what to do if an employee's accent interferes with his or her job performance. Fluency requirements, "English-only" policies, and accent rules raise slightly different issues, but all are becoming increasingly relevant in today's diverse workforce. In 2017, 21.3 percent of the U.S. population five years and older spoke a language other than English in the home. Over 25.6 million Americans, or 8.5 percent of the U.S. population aged five and over, spoke English less than "very well."[17]

Case 2

See Chapter 2 to revisit key concepts.

Diversity in the workplace brings many benefits, including a greater breadth of skills and life experiences among the workforce. It also may present unique challenges to employers, particularly in the form of poor communication among those who may prefer to speak in their native tongue, which might be not English but Spanish, Hindi, or Tagalog, for example. While such communication problems may cause confusion, fluency requirements may not be appropriate for some jobs, even within the same company. Severe English-only restrictions may create frustration and resentment among employees for whom English is a second language. To avoid alienating these employees, to ensure realistic and reasonable job qualifications, and to decrease the risk of litigation, employers should not permit managers to arbitrarily impose language restrictions.[18]

A job requirement that an employee must be fluent in English is legal if fluency is required to perform the work effectively. The EEOC has pointed out that the degree of fluency required varies from job to job, so blanket fluency requirements that apply equally to the customer service department, for instance, and to warehouse workers might not be legal. To best be protected from possible Title VII liability, the employer must be able to show that English fluency is required for the job and that the requirement is necessary to maintain supervisory control of the workplace. Perhaps it may be required of an employee who has significant communication with clients, or it may be justified as a BFOQ where the employee could not speak or understand English sufficiently to perform required duties.

Similarly, because an employee's accent is often associated with his or her national origin, courts closely examine employment decisions based on accent (since it may be used as a proxy for national origin discrimination). However, an employer is permitted to choose not to hire or promote an employee to a position that requires clear oral communication in English if the employee's accent substantially affects her or his ability to communicate clearly. For example, where a teacher was fluent in English but spoke with such a thick accent that her students had a difficult time understanding her, her discharge was upheld.

On the other hand, if the employee is in a job requiring little speaking and the employee can understand English, the requirement may be more difficult to defend—for instance, requiring English fluency for a janitor who talks little, has little reason to speak in order to carry out the duties of the job, and who understands what is said to her or him. In fact, in *In re Rodriguez*,[19] the court found that an employment decision based on an employee's accent and speech characteristics (where due to the employee's national origin) was *direct evidence* of employment discrimination sufficient to shift the burden of proof to the employer to articulate a legitimate non-discriminatory reason for the decision that the employer "would have terminated the [employee] had it not been motivated by discrimination." The court affirmed that "accent and national origin are inextricably intertwined."

Similarly, in *Bacchus v. Price*,[20] the court found that an employee from Guyana successfully demonstrated national origin discrimination when she alleged that remarks about her supposed "language barrier" due to her accent were unsubstantiated, since her native language was English. Her discrimination claim based on a supervisor's statements about her language skills during an interview for a promotion was permitted to go forward.

Scenario

Unlike the teacher above, in Scenario 1, Carla is considering *decreasing* Vladimir's responsibilities due to his foreign accent rather than terminating him. However, like the teacher, it is quite possible in this scenario to show that speaking clear English is a BFOQ, especially if it can be shown that clients have been complaining that they cannot understand him.

A closely related question is whether employers are permitted to implement policies requiring employees to speak only English in the workplace. These policies may be based in well-intentioned employer efforts aimed at decreasing workplace tension where multiple languages have segregated a workplace, improving employees' English, or promoting a safe and efficient workplace. The U.S. Supreme Court has not yet ruled on the lawfulness of English-only policies in the workplace, and there is disagreement by lower courts on when English-only rules are permitted.[21] Some courts have held English-only policies to be discriminatory, excessively prohibitive, and a violation of Title VII. Others have held that it is not national origin discrimination if all employees, regardless of ancestry, are prohibited from speaking anything but English on the job and that there is no statutory right to speak other languages at work. It has been held that the right to speak one's native language when the employee is bilingual is not an immutable characteristic that Title VII protects.

Garcia v. Spun Steak Co.,[22] included at the end of the chapter, is one of the most important cases on the subject. In *Garcia,* the Ninth Circuit considered an employer's policy that required bilingual workers to speak only English while on the job, though it allowed other languages to be spoken during breaks and employees' personal time. Spanish-speaking employees argued that the policy was discriminatory because it denied them the ability to express their cultural heritage, denied them a privilege of employment enjoyed by speakers of English as a first language, and created an atmosphere of inferiority and intimidation. The court rejected these arguments, stating that Title VII "does not protect the ability of workers to express their cultural heritage at the workplace" but is "concerned only with disparities in the treatment of workers." The court further argued that "Title VII is not meant to protect against rules that merely inconvenience some employees, even if the inconvenience falls regularly on a protected class."

In contrast, in *EEOC v. Premier Operator Servs., Inc.,*[23] the district court struck down an English-only policy that required all conversations on workplace premises, including those during breaks or personal time, to be in English. The court found that the defendant presented insufficient evidence to establish that there was any business necessity for the policy as implemented. The court noted that, even if it were "to assume that office 'harmony' [was] properly considered to be a business necessity that would justify an English-only policy," there was no credible evidence on the record that there was any discord among employees so as to necessitate a language-restrictive policy. The court therefore concluded that "the speak English-only policy as implemented and enforced . . . was a tool by which discrimination based on national origin was effected."

In general, though, English-only rules have been upheld. In *Pachero v. New York Presbyterian Hospital,*[24] an English-only requirement was implemented in response to complaints from patients who believed that Spanish-speaking employees were talking about them in a language that they did not understand. An employee brought suit alleging national origin discrimination under theories of a hostile work environment, disparate treatment, and disparate impact. The hospital argued that its English-only requirement was both limited and a business necessity: it helped facilitate better staff-patient relationships, and employees were permitted to speak Spanish (or any other language) when patients were not present. The court agreed and dismissed the plaintiff's case.

The courts have also summarized the types of business necessity justifications that have been upheld: In *EEOC v. Sephora USA,*[25] an English-only policy was justified as a means of improving communication with customers; in *Montes v. Vail Clinic, Inc.,*[26] the court held that an English-only policy was necessary to ensure safety for hospital patients; the court in *Roman v. Cornell University*[27] found that an English-only rule was justified to avoid or lessen interpersonal conflicts between employees; in *Long v. First Union Corp. of Virginia,*[28] the court held that an English-only policy was justified to ensure the business runs smoothly and efficiently; and the court in *Tuffa v. Flight Servs. & Sys. Inc.*[29] ruled that a policy requiring employees to read in English does not discriminate on its face and the requirement that employees pass a written test in English is not direct evidence of discrimination.

However, challenges to English-only rules are increasing, and some have resulted in large awards and settlements to affected employees. In 2001, a class-action suit filed by 18 Latinx housekeepers against the University of Incarnate Word for requiring them to speak English at all times was settled for $2.44 million.[30] In 2012, an acute care hospital in California agreed to pay $975,000 to settle a lawsuit filed by the EEOC on behalf of 70 Filipino American hospital workers, who claimed to have been harassed, humiliated, and subject to undue surveillance and discipline in relation to an English-only policy.[31] In 2018, the EEOC sued Albertsons, an American grocery company, after supervisors in a San Diego store prevented employees from speaking Spanish even during breaks. Supervisors verbally harassed Latinxs by publicly reprimanding and threatening to discipline them for violating the "no Spanish" policy.[32] In 2018, the EEOC also filed a case against Forever 21, an American clothing retailer. Three employees alleged the company prevented them from speaking Spanish at work. The retailer payed $90,000 to the former employees to settle the suit.[33]

The EEOC takes the position that English-only rules *applied at all times* or only applied to certain foreign speakers are presumptively discriminatory, although the courts have not always agreed with that approach.[34] When a rule is applied only at certain times, the EEOC recommends that it be justified by business necessity in order to avoid discrimination claims. Rules applied during work time *only* are less likely to be considered harassment and more likely to show a business necessity. When an employer is considering an English-only rule, it should take into consideration the legal implications as well as the fact that such a rule can create an atmosphere of inferiority, isolation, and intimidation that may result in a discriminatory work environment.

According to the EEOC, an employer may justify the business necessity of an English-only rule:

- For communications with customers, coworkers, or supervisors who only speak English.
- In emergencies or other situations in which workers must speak a common language to promote safety.
- For cooperative work assignments in which the English-only rule is needed to promote efficiency. For example, a taxi company was permitted to maintain an English-only policy for main office employees to prevent miscommunications during dispatch.[35]
- To enable a supervisor who only speaks English to monitor the performance of an employee whose job duties require communication with coworkers or customers.

Although in *Garcia,* the court ruled against the EEOC's guidelines, it did point out that an English-only policy may be discriminatory if it "exacerbate[s] existing tensions, combine[s] with other discriminatory behavior to contribute to discrimination, [or is] enforced in a 'draconian manner' [such] that the enforcement itself amounts to harassment."[36] In 2006, however, the EEOC's position was supported in *Maldonado v. City of Altus,*[37] where the court held that a hostile work environment might exist based solely on the employer's adoption of an English-only policy in the workplace, though this case was later overruled on other grounds. A few other district courts have accepted and applied the guidelines.[38]

In addition to federal guidelines, states are beginning to enact their own laws prohibiting English-only policies. For example, in 2018, California enacted the Fair Employment and Housing Act (FEHA), which allows English-only policies only very limited situations. Under the new rules, it is unlawful for an employer to have an English-only policy unless it is justified by business necessity. To demonstrate business necessity, the employer must prove that:

- The language requirement is needed to safely and efficiently operate the business;
- The language requirement effectively fulfills the purpose its intended to serve; and
- There is no alternative practice that would accomplish the purpose equally well with a less discriminatory impact.

Significantly, under the California law, customer preference or ease of communication with the customer are not legitimate justifications for an English-only policy. In addition, all rules must be narrowly tailored. Employers must inform workers about the specific details of their policy. English-only mandates can never be imposed during breaks or when the employee is off-duty.[39]

An employer, therefore, may properly enforce a limited, reasonable, and business-related English-only rule against an employee who can readily comply. However, if the practice of requiring only English on the job is mere pretext for discrimination on the basis of national origin (i.e., the employer imposes the rule *in order to* discriminate, or the rule produces an atmosphere of ethnic oppression), such a policy would be illegal. This is likely to be the case where an employer requires English to be spoken in all areas of the workplace, even on breaks or in discussions between employees during free time.

Adverse Employment Action and Dissimilar Treatment

The third and fourth requirements will be addressed together because they often arise together. The third element of the *prima facie* case for national origin discrimination is that the employee has suffered an **adverse employment action** by the employer's employment decision. This may include a demotion, termination, or removal of privileges afforded to other employees. The adverse effect may arise either because employees of different national origin are treated differently (disparate treatment) or because the policy, though neutral, adversely impacts those of a given national origin (disparate impact).

The fourth element requires that the employee show that her position was filled by someone who is not a member of her protected class or, under other circumstances, that those who are not members of her protected class are treated differently than she. For example, assume an Asian employee is terminated after the third time he is late for work. There is a rule that employees will be terminated if they are late for work more than twice. However, the employer does not enforce the rule against the other

adverse employment action
Any action or omission that takes away a benefit, opportunity, or privilege of employment from an employee.

employees, only against Asian employees. This would be a case of disparate treatment because the employee could show that he was treated differently from other employees who were similarly situated but not members of his protected class.

Alternatively, disparate impact has been found, for example, with physical requirements such as minimum height and weight. Such requirements may have a disparate impact on certain national origin groups as a result of genetic differences among populations and these requirements disproportionately precluded the groups from qualifying for certain jobs. These requirements violate Title VII and must be justified by business necessity. For instance, a requirement that a firefighter be at least 5 feet 7 inches tall was found to be unlawful where the average height of an Anglo man in the United States is 5 feet 8 inches, Spanish-surnamed American men average 5 feet 4½ inches, and females average 5 feet 3 inches. On the other hand, if the rule can be shown to be a business necessity, it may be allowed (such as some English fluency requirements, as discussed earlier).

**See Chapter 2
to revisit key
concepts.**

Once the employee has articulated a *prima facie* case of discrimination based on national origin, the burden falls to the employer to identify either a BFOQ or a legitimate nondiscriminatory reason (LNDR) for the adverse employment action. In *Vega v. Hempstead Union Free Sch. Dist.*,[40] included at the end of the chapter, you will have the opportunity to evaluate the bona fide occupational qualifications to teach a bilingual language class, among other questions relating to the burden of proof in a discrimination case based on national origin. (For more detailed discussions of *prima facie* cases, BFOQs, and LNDRs, please see Chapter 2.)

Harassment on the Basis of National Origin

LO4 Describe a claim for harassment based on national origin and discuss how it might be different from one based on other protected classes.

In addition to providing protection against traditional types of discrimination, Title VII also protects employees against harassment on the basis of national origin. Unfortunately, claims of national origin harassment increased from 6,712 charges filed with the EEOC in 1997 to their peak in 11,134 in 2009. National origin discrimination dropped to 7,106 charges in 2018. In 2018, 9.4 percent of all claims filed with the EEOC included a claim for national origin discrimination.[41]

Not all harassment is prohibited under Title VII, however. Similar to claims of sexual harassment, claims of national origin harassment are only actionable if the harassment was so severe or pervasive that the employee reasonably finds the workplace to be hostile or abusive. Common concerns include ethnic slurs, including insults, taunting, or ethnic epithets, such as making fun of a person's foreign accent. Additionally, workplace graffiti or other offenses based on traits such as an employee's birthplace, culture, accent, or skin color can also constitute harassment.[42]

Scenario

Comments like "Go back to where you came from," whether made by supervisors or by coworkers, are also considered harassment. Unfortunately, in the United States, President Trump has set a dangerous example for this type of discrimination. In July 2019, President Trump said that four female members of Congress should "go back" to the countries they came from rather than "loudly and viciously telling the people of the United States" how to run the government. All of the women were U.S. citizens, and only one was born outside the United States.[43] If President Trump had been the boss or supervisor of these women, he would have been liable for national origin discrimination in violation of Title VII.

In considering employer liability, the court will determine whether the activities are severe or pervasive and create an intimidating, hostile, or offensive working environment; interfere with work performance; or negatively affect job opportunities. The court will also consider how the employer responded.[44] The EEOC offers the following examples of conduct that do and do not satisfy this review:[45]

Hostile Work Environment Based on National Origin That Violates Title VII

Muhammad, who is of Pakistani descent, works for Motors, a large automobile dealership. His coworkers regularly call him "camel jockey," "the local terrorist," and "the ayatollah" and intentionally embarrass him in front of customers by claiming that he is incompetent. The EEOC finds reasonable cause to believe that the constant ridicule has made it difficult for Muhammad to do his job and has created a hostile work environment in violation of Title VII.[46]

Conduct That Does Not Create a Hostile Work Environment Based on National Origin

George, an immigrant of Haitian descent, was hired by Shipping Company as a dockworker. On his first day, George dropped a carton, prompting Bill, a coworker, to yell at him. The same day, George overheard Bill telling a coworker that foreigners are stealing jobs from Americans. Two months later, Bill confronted George after he argued with another coworker about assignments. Bill called George "lazy" and mocked his accent. Although Bill's conduct was based on national origin, standing alone, these incidents were not sufficiently severe or pervasive to create a hostile work environment in violation of Title VII.

An employer has the responsibility to prevent and correct any national origin harassment that may take place within its working environment. However, that responsibility is limited to occurrences of harassment of which the employer "knows or should have known." So, if an employee is consistently subject to abuse but never tells anyone about it (e.g., her or his employer) and the supervisors at her or his workplace have no other way of knowing the abuse is taking place, the employer *may* not be liable. In addition, if the employer finds out about the harassment and takes reasonable steps to prevent and/or correct it, the employer might also be relieved of any liability.

National origin harassment lawsuits can be costly. In 2018, SLS Hotel settled a discrimination lawsuit for $2.5 million. According to the lawsuit, Black Haitian dishwashers were wrongfully terminated on the basis of their race, color, and national origin. The Haitians were replaced by mostly light-skinned Latinxs. The supervising chefs originally had referred to the Haitian dishwashers as "slaves" and had reprimanded them for speaking Kréyol, even among themselves, while the new Latinx employees were permitted to speak Spanish. In a second case from 2019, Pape Material Handling paid $650,000 to settle a harassment lawsuit filed by Latinx employees. Pape Material Handling was charged with allowing its employees to engage in ongoing harassment against it Latinx employees, including mocking their accents and using derogatory slurs. While the Latinx employees informed the employer, the company failed to address these concerns.[47] In another 2019 case, East Coast Labor settled a lawsuit for $475,000 and provided significant equitable relief to Latinx workers at a poultry processing plant. The employees at the plant were subjected to harassment, including ethnic slurs, threats, and verbal abuse, and other abusive working conditions. They also were paid less money than promised, placed in more hazardous positions, and denied bathroom and lunch breaks and received fewer hours of work than their non-Latinx counterparts.[48]

However, as you will see from *Cortezano v. Salin Bank & Trust Co.,*[49] included at the end of the chapter, many forms of discrimination and harassment may not satisfy the *prima facie* case under Title VII. On the one hand, it is important for workers to know that they are protected, even if the adverse working conditions might not fit the traditional model under Title VII, and for employers to ensure that they are diligent in their training and sensitivity to unique cross- (and even within) cultural phenomena. On the other hand, some forms of discrimination—such as discrimination based upon citizenship status, or "alienage," as distinct from the specific nation of origin—are not prohibited under Title VII. In addition, the law remains unsettled regarding Title VII's application to cases of discrimination against a worker based on the national origin of the worker's spouse or partner.

Guidelines on Discrimination Because of Religion or National Origin

Guidelines on Discrimination Because of Religion or National Origin
Federal guidelines that apply only to federal contractors or agencies and that impose on these employers an affirmative duty to prevent discrimination.

Federal agencies or employers who enter into contracts with a government agency are required by the **Guidelines on Discrimination Because of Religion or National Origin** to ensure that individuals are hired and retained without regard to their religion or national origin.[50] These guidelines impose on the federal contractor an affirmative obligation to prevent discrimination. The provisions include the following ethnic groups: Eastern, Middle, and Southern European ancestry, including Jews, Catholics, Italians, Greeks, and Slavic groups. However, Blacks, Spanish-surnamed Americans, Asians, and Native Americans are specifically excluded from the guidelines' coverage because of their protection elsewhere in Office of Federal Contract Compliance Rules.

The guidelines provide that, subsequent to a review of the employer's policies, the employer should engage in appropriate outreach and positive recruitment activities to remedy existing deficiencies (i.e., affirmative action). Various approaches to this outreach requirement include the following:

1. Internal communication of the obligation to provide equal employment opportunity without regard to religion or national origin.
2. Development of reasonable internal procedures to ensure that the equal employment policy is fully implemented.
3. Periodic informing of all employees of the employer's commitment to equal employment opportunity for all persons, without regard to religion or national origin.

4. Enlistment of the support and assistance of all recruitment sources.

5. Review of employment records to determine the availability of promotable and transferable members of various religious and ethnic groups.

6. Establishment of meaningful contacts with religious and ethnic organizations and leaders for such purposes as advice, education, technical assistance, and referral of potential employees (many organizations send job announcements to these community groups when recruiting for positions).

7. Significant recruitment activities at educational institutions with substantial enrollments of students from various religious and ethnic groups.

8. Use of the religious and ethnic media for institutional and employment advertising.

Importantly, however, employers must not show preference for people of a specific national origin. For example, when an employment agency placed ads in a local newspaper touting that it had "lots of Mexicans," the ads were found to be in violation of Title VII because they unlawfully expressed a "preference" or "specification" for Mexicans or persons of Latin origin.[51]

Middle Eastern Discrimination after September 11, 2001, and in the Era of ISIS

In the aftermath of September 11, 2001, and following other terrorist attacks since that time by extremist groups such as the Islamic State,[52] hate crimes against individuals of Middle Eastern descent increased dramatically. Workplace discrimination complaints brought by Muslims and those of Middle Eastern descent also rose sharply. In the initial months after 9/11, the EEOC saw a 250 percent increase in the number of religion-based discrimination charges involving Muslims.

Although the number of charges directly related to September 11 has dwindled, there continues to be an increase in cases involving national origin discrimination against those with Middle Eastern backgrounds and other Muslims. In 2017, 701 such cases were filed.[53] Even well-known companies are being charged with discrimination; for example, in May 2019, three Somali women working for Amazon accused the company of creating a hostile work environment for Muslim workers and then retaliating against them for protesting working conditions.[54]

Issues of concern and questions that have arisen from these cases have centered on a few key issues. Employers may not treat workers differently because of their religious attire, such as a Muslim *hijab* (head scarf). In fact, in 2015, the Supreme Court ruled 8–1 in favor of a Muslim woman who was denied a job at an Abercrombie & Fitch store in Tulsa, Oklahoma, because she wore a headscarf. This was after an interviewer had recommended the woman for hire for a sales job. Abercrombie's dress code prohibits salespeople from wearing caps. The Court held that a job applicant seeking to prove a Title VII disparate treatment claim need only show that the need for a religious accommodation was a motivating factor in the prospective employer's adverse decision.[55] Employers also need to be sensitive to possible instances of ethnic harassment, especially that which may unfairly relate to security concerns. Finally, employers may not require individuals of one ethnic background to undergo more significant security checks or other preemployment requirements unless all applicants for that position are required to do so.

In the post–September 11 era, employers actually have a unique opportunity to raise awareness of and sensitivity to cultural diversity in the workplace. Elmer Johnson, former head of the Aspen Institute, which seeks to improve corporate leadership, has stated that corporate leaders should inspire employees and inculcate a sense of shared values.[56] Perhaps this can be achieved by reaching out to employees of Middle Eastern descent who may be experiencing fear of discrimination. Since 2001, American Muslims and those of Middle Eastern descent report experiencing increased suspicion and hostility, including verbal harassment, violent threats or intimidation, physical assault, religious profiling, and discrimination in education, employment, and housing.[57] Remaining sensitive to such employees' concerns in job assignments and work-related activities is key to their effective resolution. "Quick fixes," such as compulsory transfer to another position, must be avoided. To further promote a healthy environment at work, employers also should consider post–September 11 issues in diversity training.

It should be noted that, under certain limited circumstances, employers may reach decisions on the basis of national origin by relying on security requirements, where the security requirements are imposed "in the interest of the national security of the United States under any security program in effect pursuant to or administered under any statute of the United States or any Executive order of the President."[58] Situations in which this can be used as a justification are extremely rare.

Latinx Discrimination: Impact of Socio-Political Environmental Factors

Latinxs represent a rapidly growing minority group in the United States that has experienced an increase in discrimination over recent years. Since the 2016 presidential election, Latinxs report feeling more insecure than before 2016, as two-thirds of Latinxs report their perception that the presidential administration's policies have been harmful to Latinxs.[59]

Immediately following the 2016 election, anti-Latinx hate crimes increased 176 percent.[60] A 2017 survey found that Latinxs reported "substantial and significant personal experiences of discrimination." Specifically, 37 percent of Latinxs reported having personally experienced racial or ethnic slurs, while 33 percent described being aware of people making insensitive or offensive comments or negative assumptions about their race or ethnicity.[61] In 2018, half of the Latinxs in the United States reported that their situation had worsened over the past year.[62] Latinxs have become increasingly fearful of reporting on racially based crimes and other incidents to law enforcement.[63] Non-immigrant Latinxs and college-educated Latinxs are more likely to report individual discrimination, though it is impossible to know how many acts of discrimination are unreported.[64]

Some point to an environment that is fueled by remarks and actions of President Trump, who referred to Mexicans as "rapists" and "criminals" during his presidential campaign and then attacked a Mexican American judge for his Mexican heritage. President Trump also repeatedly promised to build a border wall along the Mexican border to keep Latinxs out, continually threatened to deport Latinxs, and locked up child migrants from Latin America in deplorable detention centers, separating babies, toddlers, and other children from their families.

Despite the political and social environment in the United States, the threat of gang violence, desperate political conditions, poverty, and effects of climate change continue to drive Latinxs northward from their homes in Central and South America. Many make the long and treacherous trek to seek asylum in the United States. In 2019, record numbers of migrants continued to cross the southern U.S. border.[65]

Discrimination against Latinxs naturally spills over into the workforce. In the context of employment, 33 percent of Latinxs reported personal discrimination on the basis of their ethnicity when applying for jobs, and 32 percent reported discrimination on the basis of pay or when considered for promotions.[66] Moreover, 76 percent of Latinxs in the U.S. workforce report repressing parts of their personas in the workplace, which they do by covering or downplaying their Latinx identity or modifying their appearance, their body language, their communication style, or their leadership presence. Latinxs who expend a lot of energy repressing their Latinx identity are more likely to strongly agree that they are being promoted quickly.[67]

Not only is workplace discrimination based on national origin illegal, as discussed in this chapter, it is bad for business. When Latinxs experience or fear discrimination and repress their identity, companies lose out on their unique insights, which may be key to tapping into the growing Latinx market, as, for example, teams with one or more members who represent the culture of the team's target end user are 158 percent more likely to understand the target audience and increase the likelihood of successfully innovating for the target audience.[68]

Moreover, the effects of discrimination go far beyond cash liabilities. Workplace discrimination can impact internal workforce productivity. Employees who experience discrimination are likely to be less productive, less motivated, less committed to the workplace, and more likely to have excess absences. Moreover, if an employee sees promotions, bonuses, and other benefits being awarded on the basis of discriminatory factors, including national origin, that employee's motivation to perform his or her best will be negatively affected. Additionally, discrimination can affect a company's ability to recruit and retain staff. If a company's voluntary turnover is high, it is likely that the company is losing skilled, competent workers. Recruiting and training staff are costly and affect productivity. Finally, discriminatory practices can negatively impact customer perception of the company, which may drive away customers and reduce profits.[69]

Citizenship and the Immigration Reform and Control Act

LO5 Identify the difference between citizenship and national origin.

As mentioned earlier in this chapter, Title VII's prohibition against discrimination on the basis of national origin does not necessarily prohibit discrimination on the basis of citizenship; this only occurs where citizenship discrimination "has the purpose or effect" of national origin discrimination or where it is pretext for national origin discrimination. In fact, non-U.S. citizens who are legally residing in and permitted to work in the United States are often restricted from access to certain government or other positions by statute. For instance, in *Foley v. Connelie,*[70] the Supreme Court held that a rule requiring citizenship was valid in connection with certain non-elected positions held by officers who participate directly in the formulation, execution, or review of broad public policy. This is called the "political function" exception for positions that are intimately related to the process of self-government. In cases where the restricted position satisfies this exception, discrimination against non-U.S. citizens who are legally allowed to reside and work in the United States is permitted. *Espinoza v. Farah Manufacturing Co.,*[71] included for your review, is the seminal case by the U.S. Supreme Court in the area of discrimination on basis of citizenship.

Another area where questions have arisen between Title VII and discrimination based on citizenship emerged in 2017 when U.S. President Trump announced his policy to *buy American and hire American.*[72] With no other context, this policy could be pretext for national origin discrimination. However, the language of the Executive Order proposes reforms designed to promote employers to hire American citizens *or* anyone else legally authorized to work in the United States under current immigration laws. A year into the program, one academic observed that, though "Trump pitched the policy as a challenge to globalist corporate hegemony in the name of the citizen worker," the policy actually "expanded fraud-based approach to governing," which fails to address core problems with acquiring worker visas and results in employers simply finding more creative ways to hire foreign workers and pay them less.[73]

Moreover, coupled with other legislation introduced by the same administration, there are additional concerns about the long-term impact of the policy to *buy American and hire American.* For example, in August 2019, the Department of Labor put forth a proposal that, if implemented, would give religious employers who seek federal contracts broad freedom to hire and fire workers. Under the new rule, closely held for-profit companies in addition to religious nonprofits will be exempt from antidiscrimination rules when it comes to religion. Additionally, companies with federal contracts may now "make employment decisions consistent with their sincerely held religious tenets and beliefs without fear of sanction by the federal government."[74] Critics fear that this rule would open the door for employers to discriminate against employees who are not Catholic, for example. Though the administration maintains that organizations must still adhere to protections for workers based on national origin, there is concern that this policy expands the religious exemption in a way that could be used to discriminate against people with different religious, cultural, or ethnic backgrounds, including discriminating against people on their national origin.

LO6 Explain the extent of protection under the Immigration Reform and Control Act.

The Immigration Reform and Control Act (IRCA), *in contrast to Title VII,* does prohibit employers in certain circumstances from discriminating against employees on the basis of their citizenship or intended citizenship. However, IRCA makes it illegal for employers to knowingly hire those not legally authorized for employment in the United States. IRCA also allows discrimination in favor of U.S. citizens as against legal aliens (non-U.S. citizens legally residing in the United States). While these individuals are guaranteed various rights pursuant to the Constitution, the law confers certain benefits only to those who are citizens and not to those who are legal residents but non-U.S. citizens. For instance, while rights pursuant to the National Labor Relations Act and Fair Labor Standards Act are provided to citizens and non-citizens alike, some government-provided benefits are limited to citizens. Also, IRCA allows employers to enact a preference for U.S. citizens if the applicants are all equally qualified. Employers may not act on this preference if the foreign national is more qualified for the position than the U.S. citizen.

Employers not subject to Title VII's prohibitions because of their small size may still be sufficiently large to be covered by IRCA's antidiscrimination provisions; those employers with four to 14 employees are prohibited from discriminating on the basis of national origin; and employers with four or more employees may not discriminate on the basis of citizenship.

Two acceptable BFOQs are statutorily allowed under IRCA:

1. English-language skill requirements that are reasonably necessary to the normal operation of the particular business or enterprise.
2. Citizenship requirements specified by law, regulation, executive order, or government contracts, along with citizenship requirements that the U.S. attorney general determines to be essential for doing business with the government.

The main difference between a proof of discrimination under Title VII and IRCA is that, in proving a case of disparate impact, Title VII does not require proof of discriminatory intent, while IRCA requires that the adverse action be knowingly and intentionally discriminatory. Therefore, innocent or negligent discrimination is a complete defense to a claim of discrimination under IRCA.

For example, consider a hypothetical firm that is interviewing for customer service representatives in its large order-processing department. It requires all applicants to speak fluent English. Ching Lee applied and was denied employment due to his accent, which some thought was heavy. It turns out that only three applicants out of 20 of Asian descent obtained jobs at the firm. The employer explained to Lee that not many Chinese applicants apply and those who do have had strong accents. It claims that customers have complained of not understanding these individuals. Does Lee have a claim under Title VII? Under IRCA? Without evidence of knowledge and intentional discrimination, the employer could survive an IRCA claim if Lee could not prove that it discriminated against him intentionally; however, such knowledge and intention are not required under Title VII, and Lee might prevail in that case.

Undocumented Workers

See Chapter 2 to revisit key concepts.

As one might imagine, identifying the precise number of undocumented immigrants in the United States is not an exact science because of fear that undocumented immigrants have in being identified (and therefore counted). In 2007, *approximately* 12 million undocumented immigrants were living in the United States, and roughly two-thirds of those individuals (8.4 million) comprised 5 percent of the nation's workforce.[75] In 2017, the number had dropped to 10.5 million undocumented immigrants. Of those, 7.6 million were in the American workforce, accounting for 4.6 percent of the workforce.[76] The Pew Research Forum reports that the number of undocumented immigrants has dropped, in part, due to a drop in unauthorized immigrants from Mexico, whose numbers decreased from 6.9 million in 2007 to 4.9 million in 2017.[77] The decline of undocumented immigrants from Mexico can be attributed to the increased efforts of the U.S. government, including through the increase of law enforcement agents at the southern border, to reduce the number of unauthorized immigrants in the United States.[78]

A section of IRCA was established to correct an unfair double standard that had previously prohibited these individuals from working in the United States but permitted employers to hire them. In other words, originally, the unauthorized worker had committed a legal wrong, but the employer who hired the worker had not! Among other things, IRCA now makes it unlawful for any person knowingly to hire, recruit, or refer for a fee any non-citizen who is not authorized to work. "Knowingly" includes that which "may be fairly inferred through notice of certain facts and circumstances which would lead a person . . . to know about a certain condition."[79] Employers are thereby denied the "ostrich" defense where they simply ignore obvious evidence to a violation. Employers are instead required to verify all newly hired employees by examining documents that identify the individual and show her or his or her authority to work in the United States using a Form I-9. (See Exhibit 7.3, "INS Employment Form and Document List.") Further, employers, recruiters, and those who refer individuals for employment are required to keep records pertaining to IRCA requirements. (For a list of employer responsibilities under IRCA, see Exhibit 7.4, "Employer Responsibilities under IRCA: Do's and Don'ts.") A violation of this provision can mean *personal liability* for corporate officers, so it is not a requirement to be taken lightly.

In 2007, in an effort to further implement these provisions, the Department of Homeland Security (DHS) announced that employers would be required to terminate all workers who used false Social Security numbers, otherwise known as a "no-match" (based on the 140,000 no-match letters received annually by employers from the Social Security Administration notifying them that the names and Social Security numbers of employees do not match the agency's records). Employers were to have 90 days in which to reconcile the no-match letters; if they could not, they were going to be forced to fire the worker or face fines of up to $10,000. With an estimated 6 million unauthorized non-U.S. citizens employed at that time, the impact on both the workforce and the economy would have been monumental, notwithstanding the claim by the Social Security Administration that 12.7 million of its records contained errors that could lead to terminations.[80] The impact in the agricultural industry alone would have been overwhelming, where estimates by the growers' associations placed undocumented workers at about 70 percent.[81] However, only five days before its implementation, a California federal judge issued an order blocking the implementation of the no-match rule based on a suit filed jointly by the American Federation of Labor and Congress of Industrial Organizations (AFL-CIO), the American Civil Liberties Union, and the National Immigration Law Center. In late

Exhibit 7.3 *INS Employment Form and Document List*

Employment Eligibility Verification
Department of Homeland Security
U.S. Citizenship and Immigration Services

USCIS
Form I-9
OMB No. 1615-0047
Expires 08/31/2019

▶ **START HERE:** Read instructions carefully before completing this form. The instructions must be available, either in paper or electronically, during completion of this form. Employers are liable for errors in the completion of this form.

ANTI-DISCRIMINATION NOTICE: It is illegal to discriminate against work-authorized individuals. Employers **CANNOT** specify which document(s) an employee may present to establish employment authorization and identity. The refusal to hire or continue to employ an individual because the documentation presented has a future expiration date may also constitute illegal discrimination.

Section 1. Employee Information and Attestation *(Employees must complete and sign Section 1 of Form I-9 no later than the **first day of employment**, but not before accepting a job offer.)*

Last Name *(Family Name)*	First Name *(Given Name)*	Middle Initial	Other Last Names Used *(if any)*

Address *(Street Number and Name)*	Apt. Number	City or Town	State	ZIP Code

Date of Birth *(mm/dd/yyyy)*	U.S. Social Security Number	Employee's E-mail Address	Employee's Telephone Number

I am aware that federal law provides for imprisonment and/or fines for false statements or use of false documents in connection with the completion of this form.

I attest, under penalty of perjury, that I am (check one of the following boxes):

☐ 1. A citizen of the United States

☐ 2. A noncitizen national of the United States *(See instructions)*

☐ 3. A lawful permanent resident   (Alien Registration Number/USCIS Number): _____

☐ 4. An alien authorized to work   until (expiration date, if applicable, mm/dd/yyyy): _____
    Some aliens may write "N/A" in the expiration date field. *(See instructions)*

Aliens authorized to work must provide only one of the following document numbers to complete Form I-9:
An Alien Registration Number/USCIS Number OR Form I-94 Admission Number OR Foreign Passport Number.

1. Alien Registration Number/USCIS Number: _____
OR
2. Form I-94 Admission Number: _____
OR
3. Foreign Passport Number: _____
    Country of Issuance: _____

QR Code - Section 1
Do Not Write In This Space

Signature of Employee	Today's Date *(mm/dd/yyyy)*

Preparer and/or Translator Certification (check one):
☐ I did not use a preparer or translator.   ☐ A preparer(s) and/or translator(s) assisted the employee in completing Section 1.
(Fields below must be completed and signed when preparers and/or translators assist an employee in completing Section 1.)

I attest, under penalty of perjury, that I have assisted in the completion of Section 1 of this form and that to the best of my knowledge the information is true and correct.

Signature of Preparer or Translator	Today's Date *(mm/dd/yyyy)*

Last Name *(Family Name)*	First Name *(Given Name)*

Address *(Street Number and Name)*	City or Town	State	ZIP Code

Employer Completes Next Page

Form I-9 11/14/2016 N

Page 1 of 3

(continued)

Exhibit 7.3 *continued*

Employment Eligibility Verification
Department of Homeland Security
U.S. Citizenship and Immigration Services

USCIS
Form I-9
OMB No. 1615-0047
Expires 08/31/2019

Section 2. Employer or Authorized Representative Review and Verification

(Employers or their authorized representative must complete and sign Section 2 within 3 business days of the employee's first day of employment. You must physically examine one document from List A OR a combination of one document from List B and one document from List C as listed on the "Lists of Acceptable Documents.")

Employee Info from Section 1	Last Name (Family Name)	First Name (Given Name)	M.I.	Citizenship/Immigration Status

List A — Identity and Employment Authorization	OR	List B — Identity	AND	List C — Employment Authorization
Document Title		Document Title		Document Title
Issuing Authority		Issuing Authority		Issuing Authority
Document Number		Document Number		Document Number
Expiration Date (if any)(mm/dd/yyyy)		Expiration Date (if any)(mm/dd/yyyy)		Expiration Date (if any)(mm/dd/yyyy)
Document Title		Additional Information		QR Code - Sections 2 & 3 Do Not Write In This Space
Issuing Authority				
Document Number				
Expiration Date (if any)(mm/dd/yyyy)				
Document Title				
Issuing Authority				
Document Number				
Expiration Date (if any)(mm/dd/yyyy)				

Certification: I attest, under penalty of perjury, that (1) I have examined the document(s) presented by the above-named employee, (2) the above-listed document(s) appear to be genuine and to relate to the employee named, and (3) to the best of my knowledge the employee is authorized to work in the United States.

The employee's first day of employment *(mm/dd/yyyy)*: _____   *(See instructions for exemptions)*

Signature of Employer or Authorized Representative	Today's Date (mm/dd/yyyy)	Title of Employer or Authorized Representative
Last Name of Employer or Authorized Representative	First Name of Employer or Authorized Representative	Employer's Business or Organization Name

Employer's Business or Organization Address (Street Number and Name)	City or Town	State	ZIP Code

Section 3. Reverification and Rehires *(To be completed and signed by employer or authorized representative.)*

A. New Name (if applicable)			**B.** Date of Rehire (if applicable)
Last Name (Family Name)	First Name (Given Name)	Middle Initial	Date (mm/dd/yyyy)

C. If the employee's previous grant of employment authorization has expired, provide the information for the document or receipt that establishes continuing employment authorization in the space provided below.

Document Title	Document Number	Expiration Date (if any) (mm/dd/yyyy)

I attest, under penalty of perjury, that to the best of my knowledge, this employee is authorized to work in the United States, and if the employee presented document(s), the document(s) I have examined appear to be genuine and to relate to the individual.

Signature of Employer or Authorized Representative	Today's Date (mm/dd/yyyy)	Name of Employer or Authorized Representative

LISTS OF ACCEPTABLE DOCUMENTS
All documents must be UNEXPIRED

Employees may present one selection from List A
or a combination of one selection from List B and one selection from List C.

LIST A	LIST B	LIST C
Documents that Establish Both Identity and Employment Authorization OR	**Documents that Establish Identity** AND	**Documents that Establish Employment Authorization**
1. U.S. Passport or U.S. Passport Card	1. Driver's license or ID card issued by a State or outlying possession of the United States provided it contains a photograph or information such as name, date of birth, gender, height, eye color, and address	1. A Social Security Account Number card, unless the card includes one of the following restrictions: (1) NOT VALID FOR EMPLOYMENT (2) VALID FOR WORK ONLY WITH INS AUTHORIZATION (3) VALID FOR WORK ONLY WITH DHS AUTHORIZATION
2. Permanent Resident Card or Alien Registration Receipt Card (Form I-551)	2. ID card issued by federal, state or local government agencies or entities, provided it contains a photograph or information such as name, date of birth, gender, height, eye color, and address	
3. Foreign passport that contains a temporary I-551 stamp or temporary I-551 printed notation on a machine-readable immigrant visa	3. School ID card with a photograph	2. Certification of Birth Abroad issued by the Department of State (Form FS-545)
4. Employment Authorization Document that contains a photograph (Form I-766)	4. Voter's registration card	3. Certification of Report of Birth issued by the Department of State (Form DS-1350)
5. For a nonimmigrant alien authorized to work for a specific employer because of his or her status: a. Foreign passport; and b. Form I-94 or Form I-94A that has the following: (1) The same name as the passport; and (2) An endorsement of the alien's nonimmigrant status as long as that period of endorsement has not yet expired and the proposed employment is not in conflict with any restrictions or limitations identified on the form.	5. U.S. Military card or draft record 6. Military dependent's ID card 7. U.S. Coast Guard Merchant Mariner Card 8. Native American tribal document 9. Driver's license issued by a Canadian government authority **For persons under age 18 who are unable to present a document listed above:**	4. Original or certified copy of birth certificate issued by a State, county, municipal authority, or territory of the United States bearing an official seal 5. Native American tribal document 6. U.S. Citizen ID Card (Form I-197) 7. Identification Card for Use of Resident Citizen in the United States (Form I-179)
6. Passport from the Federated States of Micronesia (FSM) or the Republic of the Marshall Islands (RMI) with Form I-94 or Form I-94A indicating nonimmigrant admission under the Compact of Free Association Between the United States and the FSM or RMI	10. School record or report card 11. Clinic, doctor, or hospital record 12. Day-care or nursery school record	8. Employment authorization document issued by the Department of Homeland Security

Examples of many of these documents appear in Part 8 of the Handbook for Employers (M-274).

Refer to the instructions for more information about acceptable receipts.

Exhibit 7.4   *Employer Responsibilities under IRCA: Do's and Don'ts*

Completion of Form I-9, Section 1

DO:

- Employers must ensure that new employees complete Section 1 in full before the end of their first day of work. This requirement applies to all workers hired to perform labor or services in return for wages or other remuneration.
- Review the form to ensure that the employee has fully and properly completed the form.

DO NOT:

- Do not require only certain employees to comply before the end of their first day of work; this requirement must be enforced across the board.
- Do not require employees to provide a Social Security number on Form I-9; providing a Social Security number is voluntary for all employees, *unless* the employer is participating in E-Verify. Do not even ask an employee to provide you with her or his Social Security number or with a specific document that contains the number within it, under any circumstances. To do so may constitute unlawful discrimination.

Completion of Form I-9, Section 2

DO:

- Employers must examine proper documentation from employees (one from List A **or** List B, and also with one from List C). Employers must accept the documents provided if they "reasonably appear to be genuine." This examination must be completed by the end of the new employee's third day of work. Employers must refuse acceptance of documents that do not reasonably appear to be genuine. If an employee is hired for fewer than three business days, both Sections 1 and 2 must be fully completed by the employee's first day of work.

DO NOT:

- Do not accept copies, faxes, or electronic copies of the documents. (Note: The only exception is for a certified copy of a birth certificate.)

- Do not accept expired documents.
- Do not specify which document(s) an employee must present, or require more or different documentation than the minimum necessary to avoid an unfair immigration-related employment practice.
- Do not require completion of the I-9 in the pre-offer stage.

Genuineness of documents and reporting

DO:

- Ask for help: If a document does not reasonably appear to be genuine, employers may ask for assistance from INS. If a document that reasonably appeared to be genuine is in fact not genuine, the employer will not be held responsible by the INS.

Discovering unauthorized employees

DO:

- Employers are permitted to question the employee and provide another opportunity for review of proper I-9 documentation.

DO NOT:

- If the employee is not able to provide satisfactory documentation after an opportunity to do so, the employer should not retain the employee.
- Do not make threats of reporting the employee to the INS in retaliation for discrimination complaints or other protected activity.

Discovering false documentation

DO:

- If an employee gains employment with false documentation but then later obtains and presents proper work authorization, the employer should correct the relevant information on Form I-9.
- Employers should know that personnel policies regarding provision of false information to the employer may apply.

(continued)

Exhibit 7.4 *continued*

DO NOT:

- Employers do not have to terminate an employee who presents subsequent work authorization.

"Green cards"

DO:

- Employers should be aware that "Resident Alien" cards, "Permanent Resident" cards, "Alien Registration Receipt" cards, and Forms I-551 grant permanent residence in the United States, but proof of this status may expire and cardholders must obtain new cards.
- Employers should check that unexpired "green cards" used for Form I-9 appear genuine and establish identity of the cardholder.

DO NOT:

- Employers should not accept an expired card for purposes of Form I-9.
- Employers are neither required nor permitted to reverify the employment authorization of non-US citizens who have presented one of these cards to satisfy I-9 requirements.

Social Security cards

DO:

- For purposes of payroll, employers may accept SSA cards that bear the restriction "Not Valid for Employment" from employees who satisfy I-9 requirements. Often those who initially got such a restricted SSA card proceed to permanent residence or U.S. citizenship.

DO NOT:

- Employers must not accept restricted SSA cards for purposes of I-9 requirements.

- Employers must not accept Individual Taxpayer Identification numbers for purposes of I-9 requirements.

Retention of I-9 forms

DO:

- Employers must retain an employee's Form I-9 for the duration of employment and the longer of either three years past the hire date or one year past the termination date. Forms I-9 can be retained either on paper or electronically.

DO NOT:

- While not prohibited from doing so, private employers should not store I-9 records in employee personnel files.

Official inspection of I-9 records

DO:

- All I-9 forms of current employees must be made available in their original or electronic form to an authorized official upon request. The official will give employers at least three days' advance notice before the inspection.

DO NOT:

- Employers should not leave preparation for such an inspection to the last minute. Storing I-9 records in employee personnel files makes this task unduly difficult.

Source: Adapted from U.S. Citizenship and Immigration Services, *Handbook for Employers. Instructions for Completing Form I-9 (Employment Eligibility Verification Form)* (July 2017), https://www.uscis.gov/book/export/html/59502/en (accessed September 20, 2019).

2007, the Bush administration suspended its defense of the rule, preferring to go back to the drawing board in order to respond to the judicial concerns.

In 2008, the DHS attempted to reform the program, but the proposed amendments were never enforced. When President Obama took office in early 2009, his

Secretary of Homeland Security ordered a review of the no-match policy, which the DHS rescinded later that same year. However, in 2011, the Social Security Administration (SSA) again began sending out "no-match" letters to employers but suspended the policy a year later in 2012. In 2019, the SSA once again announced that it would be issuing "no-match" letters to employers.[82] These letters are written notice issued by the SSA to an employer advising the employer that the name and Social Security Number combination reported by the employer for one or more employees does not "match" the SSA's records.

The DoJ offers a list of dos and do nots for employers who receive a no-match letter.[83]

DO:

1. Recognize that no-matches can result because of simple administrative errors.
2. Check the reported no-match information against personnel records.
3. Inform the employee of the no-match notice.
4. Ask the employee to confirm that his or her name and SSN is accurately reflected in employment records.
5. Advise employee to contact the SSA to correct and or update his or her SSA records.
6. Give the employee a reasonable period of time to address a reported no-match with the local SSA office.
7. Follow the same procedures for all employees regardless of citizenship status or national origin.
8. Periodically meet with or otherwise contact employee to learn and document the status of the employee's efforts to address and resolve the no-match.
9. Review any document the employee chooses to offer showing resolution of the no-match.
10. Submit any employer or employee corrections to the SSA.

DO NOT:

1. Assume the no-match conveys information regarding the employee's immigration status or actual work authority.
2. Use the receipt of a no-match notice alone as a basis to terminate, suspend or take other adverse action against the employee.
3. Attempt to immediately re-verify the employee's employment eligibility by requesting the completion of a new Form I-9 based solely on the no-match notice.
4. Follow different procedures for different classes of employees based on national origin or citizenship status.
5. Require the employee to produce specific I-9 documents to address the no-match.
6. Require the employee to provide a written report of SSA verification.

Another form of enforcement used by the government is to investigate employer's compliance with the Form I-9 rules. Under federal law, a Form I-9 (Employment Eligibility Verification) must be filed for every new employee regardless of citizenship, and it must be retained for three years after the date of hire or one year after the date of discharge. (See Exhibit 7.3.) Once an employer receives a Notice of Inspection from the Immigration and Customs Enforcement (ICE) Division of the Department of Homeland Security, it has three business days to provide the Form I-9s for all employees working for that employer during the stated audit period.

IRCA also established civil and criminal penalties for hiring undocumented immigrants. Employers are selected at random for compliance inspections under the General Administrative Plan (GAP) developed by the Immigration and Naturalization Services (INS), the administrative agency charged with some elements of oversight of IRCA, along with the Immigration and Customs Enforcement (ICE) Division of the Department of Homeland Security. Generally, fines are not imposed for paperwork violations alone or for employment of immigrants whose documentation status was unknown, unless the employer refused to comply or other egregious factors existed. However, enforcement has been increasing dramatically. In fiscal year 2018, ICE conducted 6,848 Notices of Inspection for I-9 audits (up from 1,691 in fiscal year 2017); criminally charged 779 employers with immigration violations (up from 139 in FY 2017); made 779 criminal and 1,525 administrative worksite-related arrests (compared to 139 and 172, respectively, in FY 2017). Also in 2018, businesses were ordered to pay more than $10.2 million in judicial fines, forfeitures and restitutions in FY18, down from $97.6 million in 2017, as the government focuses on criminal prosecution of employers.[84]

It is anticipated that ICE audits will continue to become more prevalent in the coming years. To help mitigate fines, employers should be prepared for ICE audits and, at very least, keep immigration records organized, accurate, and complete.[85]

While today's enforcement strategy has shifted to targeting employers who hire undocumented workers, the EEOC's 1999 "Enforcement Guidance on Remedies Available to Undocumented Workers," emphasized that workers' undocumented status does not justify workplace discrimination. The EEOC also set forth that employers' liability for monetary remedies irrespective of a worker's unauthorized status promotes the goal of deterring unlawful discrimination without undermining the purposes of IRCA. (Note that this guidance statement was pulled by the EEOC, but only because of an unrelated issue relating to back pay under the National Labor Relations Board.) The EEOC's position on available remedies is that unauthorized workers are entitled to the same remedies as any other worker, including back pay and reinstatement. In fact, the Ninth Circuit Court held in a 2004 ruling that discovery regarding the immigration status of plaintiffs in civil rights cases would be generally prohibited since it would otherwise have a chilling effect on filings and it could result in "countless acts of illegal and reprehensible conduct" being unreported.[86] The National Labor Relations Board took a similar position with respect to discrimination based on union activity.

However, in *Hoffman Plastic Compounds Inc. v. NLRB,*[87] the U.S. Supreme Court held that the NLRB could not award back pay to unauthorized workers who had been unlawfully discriminated against for engaging in union-organizing activities. According to the Court, to do so would contravene federal immigration policy embodied in IRCA. *Hoffman* opens the possibility that back pay will not be available to undocumented workers who have been illegally discriminated against under Title VII, the Americans with Disabilities Act (ADA), and the Age Discrimination in Employment Act (ADEA).[88]

Undocumented workers are particularly vulnerable to threats to report them to the INS. In every case in which the employer asserts that the worker is undocumented and the employer appears to have acquired that information *after* the worker complained of discrimination, the EEOC will determine whether the information was acquired through a retaliatory investigation. If the investigation is retaliatory, the employer will be liable for equitable relief as well as monetary damages without regard to the worker's actual work status. However, a worker's undocumented status may serve as a legitimate reason for an adverse employment action, although employers who knowingly employ undocumented workers could not assert this defense in a discrimination claim.[89]

The Fair Labor Standards Act also protects undocumented workers from abuse. While the Supreme Court has ruled that undocumented status bars recovery for future wages,[90] a lower court affirmed that the immigration status of employees is irrelevant to claims filed against an employer under the FLSA with respect to work already performed.[91] In 2013, a U.S. District Court in New York upheld this ruling when several workers, including some undocumented immigrants, sued under the FLSA to recover minimum and overtime wages that the employer refused to pay. In its ruling, the court explained that the text of the FLSA makes it clear that its provisions were "unambiguously" intended to apply to undocumented workers by defining the term "employee" as "any individual employed by the employer." The court went on to say that the FLSA focuses on back pay as a remedy to ensure that employers do not gain an advantage by violating immigration laws. Thus, under the FLSA, even undocumented immigrants are entitled to the statutory mandated wages for work preformed.[92]

Alternate Basis for National Origin or Citizenship Discrimination: Section 1981

While it is probably the most popular basis for the claim of discrimination based on national origin, Title VII is not the only basis for such a claim. In *St. Francis College v. Al-Khazraji*,[93] the Supreme Court held that 42 U.S.C. § 1981 addressed national origin also. In this case, a professor and U.S. citizen who was born in Iraq sued under section 1981 alleging discrimination when he was denied tenure. The Court held that, though originally designed to prohibit racial discrimination, the law also applied to "identifiable classes of persons who are subjected to intentional discrimination solely because of their ancestry or ethnic characteristics." The requirement for section 1981 actions is that employees show they were discriminated against because of their ethnic group (in this case, Arabic) and not just because of their place of origin or religion. In other words, they must show some nexus between their national origin and the major concern of section 1981, their ethnic characteristics or race.

Since *St. Francis College,* however, several courts have declined to extend section 1981 to claims of national origin discrimination. In *Gomez v. City of New York,*[94] for instance, Gomez, a former police officer with the New York City Police Department (NYPD), filed an action against the City of New York. Gomez alleged that the NYPD discriminated against her, subjected her to a hostile work environment, failed to promote her, and retaliated against her because of her gender and national origin. The NYPD filed a motion for summary judgment, arguing that Gomez failed to state her claim. The court ruled in favor of the NYPD because, according to the court, "[i]t is well-established that §1981 does not recognize claims based on gender or national origin."

In another case, *King v. Township of East Lampeter,*[95] plaintiffs sought section 1981 protection on the basis of their "Amish ethnic culture." The court denied the plaintiffs protection, distinguishing a New York case that found that Orthodox Jews were indeed protected under section 1981. The court in *King* found that Jews are a distinct race for civil rights purposes but did not find the Amish to be a similarly distinct racial group. The court did not find evidence that the Amish have an independent, separate ethnic identity beyond religious observance, so it held that they were not protected under section 1981. Interestingly, the court was persuaded by the contention that one could fail to "practice" Judaism but still be a Jew while "there is no proof of a similar population of 'non-practicing' Amish."

If projections about the increasing diversity of the U.S. population are anywhere close to accurate, then entry, development, or promotion barriers to diversity of the workplace will likely result in reductions in the business's effectiveness and productivity. For any business wishing to be on the cutting edge or simply to use its resources effectively and encourage the best performance from employees, adherence to federal requirements regarding race and national origin should be viewed as a business imperative and not merely as compliance with the law. Even when the law appears ambiguous or does not seem to provide grounds for employees to file federal claims on the basis of national origin discrimination, it is best to err on the side of caution to ensure that you do not alienate or lose employees.

The significance to managers of this protection is that there must be a complete review of all policies that may have an impact on employees or applicants of diverse national origin. As stated above, this impact may not be obvious.

Employers must be cognizant of the varying needs of employees from different backgrounds. For instance, employers may address the perceived problem of bilingual employees in a number of ways, such as offering English-as-a-second-language classes or tutors for semi-bilingual employees. Not only would this foster less isolation and exclusion of the employee, but it also would create greater confidence and less intimidation when the employees are speaking English. This type of proactive approach may prevent problems in this area before they emerge.

Management Tips

- While a specific national origin may be a BFOQ, make sure that only individuals of that origin can do the specific job since courts have a high standard for BFOQs in this area.
- An employee may have a claim for national origin discrimination if the worker is simply *perceived* to be of a certain origin, even if the individual is not, in fact, of that origin.
- While English fluency may be required, you are not allowed to discriminate because of an accent (unless the accent makes it impossible to understand the individual). However, be cautious in evaluating the requirement of the job since there may be positions that do not actually require speaking English.
- An employer may not point to customer, client, or coworker preference, comfort, or discomfort as the source of BFOQ.
- If you are a federal contractor, remember that you have additional responsibilities to engage in outreach and positive recruitment activities under the Guidelines on Discrimination Because of Religion or National Origin.
- While you are not prohibited from discriminating on the basis of citizenship under Title VII, you may be prohibited from discriminating on this basis under IRCA. Before instituting a policy, consider the implications of both statutes.
- Recognize the concerns of Middle Eastern employees in the post–September 11 era: Include the topic of ethnic diversity in any workplace diversity training. Intervene promptly in incidents of harassment. Remain sensitive and flexible. Refrain from mandatory transfers and other short-term solutions to harassment, intimidation, and discrimination.
- Be prepared for an increasingly diverse workforce. As conflict and climate crises force people in Central and South American to migrate north, more Latinx and other migrants will join the American workforce. Managers will need to respond to the changing needs of their diversifying workforce.

Chapter Summary

- Title VII of the Civil Rights Act of 1964 makes it an unlawful employment practice for employers to limit, segregate, or classify employees in any way that would deprive them of employment opportunities based on their national origin.
- An employee or applicant must show the following to be successful in a claim of discrimination based on national origin:
  1. The individual was a member of a protected class.
  2. The individual was qualified for the position at issue.
  3. The employer made an employment decision against the individual.
  4. The position was filled by someone not in a protected class.
- "National origin" refers to an individual's or an individual's ancestor's place of origin or physical, cultural, or linguistic characteristics of an origin group.
- An employer has a defense against a national origin discrimination claim if it can show that the national origin is a bona fide occupational qualification. However, in general, this is very difficult to do. An exception to the difficulty is

the requirement of English fluency, if speaking English is a substantial portion of the individual's job.

- No accommodation of a worker's national origin is required, as it would be in situations involving disability or religion.
- English-only rules applied at all times are presumptively discriminatory, according to the EEOC. If the employer is considering an English-only rule, it is recommended that the employer should
  1. Consider whether the rule is necessary.
  2. Determine if the rule is a business necessity.
  3. Consider if everybody is fluent in English.
  4. Communicate the rule to employees.
  5. Enforce the rule fairly.
- An alternative basis for national origin or citizenship discrimination is 42 U.S.C. § 1981.
- Guidelines on Discrimination Because of Religion or National Origin are federal guidelines that apply to federal contractors or agencies and impose on those employers an affirmative duty to prevent discrimination.
- The Immigration Reform and Control Act, unlike Title VII, prohibits, in certain circumstances, discrimination on the basis of citizenship. The act does allow for discrimination in favor of U.S. citizens where applicants are equally qualified.
- Two statutorily allowed BFOQs under IRCA are
  1. English-language skill requirements that are reasonably necessary.
  2. Citizenship requirements specified by law, regulation, executive order, government contracts, or requirements established by the U.S. attorney general.

| **Chapter-End Questions** | 1. Which, if any, of the following scenarios would support an employee's claim of discrimination on the basis of national origin? |

1. Which, if any, of the following scenarios would support an employee's claim of discrimination on the basis of national origin?

   a. Applicant with a speech impediment is unable to pronounce the letter "r." The applicant therefore often has difficulty being understood when speaking and is denied a position.

   b. The owner of a manufacturing facility staffed completely by Mexicans refuses employment to a white American manager because the owner is concerned that the Mexicans will only consent to supervision by and receive direction from another Mexican.

   c. An Indian restaurant seeks to fill a server position. The advertisement requests applications from qualified individuals of Indian descent to add to the authenticity of the restaurant. In the past, the restaurant found that its business declined when it used Caucasian servers because the atmosphere of the restaurant suffered. An Italian applies for the position and is denied employment.

   d. A company advertises for Japanese-trained managers because the employer has found that they are more likely to remain at the company for an extended time, to be loyal and devoted to the firm, and to react well to direction and criticism. An American applies for the position and is denied employment in favor of an equally qualified Japanese-trained applicant, who happens to also be Japanese.

2. Mateo Silva, an American citizen of Puerto Rican dissent, alleged that his employer, Service Caster Corp, subjected him to a hostile work environment and to disparate treatment because of his national origin. His supervisor repeatedly made offensive and unwelcome derogatory remarks about persons of Puerto Rican national origin. The supervisor refereed to Silva and other Puerto Rican employees as "filthy, drug-addicted, welfare recipients" who are "lazy" and "devalue" the community where they reside. When Hurricane Maria devastated the island, the supervisor told Silva that Puerto Ricans "deserved to experience devastating effects of hurricanes." After Silva complained about the supervisor's remarks, he faced threats, harassment, denial of overtime, reduced work hours, and pay reduction and was coerced to sign a document written in English that he did not understand. If Silva is an American citizen and was born in the United States, can he still make a claim of discrimination on the basis of national origin? On another issue, was the employer required to provide documents in Spanish, Silva's first language, for him to sign? [adapted from *EEOC v. Service Caster Corporation,* Civil Action No. 5:19-cv-04525-JLS).]

3. In August 2012, Hassan Snoubar began working as an operator assistant oil field worker. While employed at Halliburton Energy Services, Snoubar, who is of Syrian origin, was frequently called derogatory names, was accused of being associated with ISIS and terrorism by his supervisors and coworkers, and was forced to listen to radio broadcasts of the offensive characterizations during his workday. Snoubar later was fired in retaliation for voicing his concerns to management and human resources. Does Snoubar have a claim for discrimination against his former employer, and if so, on what basis? What are the elements of Snoubar's *prima facie* case? Do you think that playing radio broadcasts of offensive characterizations *alone* would be sufficient to constitute employment discrimination on the basis of national origin? [*EEOC v. Halliburton Energy services, Inc.,* Civil Action No. 3:18-cv-01736 (settled October 2019).]

4. Mamdouh El-Hakem was employed by BJY, Inc., for more than a year. His manager repeatedly called Mamdouh, an Arabic employee, "Manny" or "Hank" instead of his given name. His manager explained that he believed that Mamdouh would have a better opportunity for success with the firm's clients with a more Western-sounding name. However, Mamdouh made it clear during his entire time with BJY that he objected to the westernization of his name and requested repeatedly that the manager call him by his rightful moniker. Mamdouh finally sued for national origin discrimination. Does he have a claim? [*El-Hakem v. BJY, Inc.,* 415 F.3d 1068 (9th Cir. 2005).]

5. Wali Telwar, a practicing Muslim, applied for extended vacation time, using earned vacation hours, to make a pilgrimage to Mecca as required by his faith. His employer, Southern Hills Medical Center, refused to grant his request for extended leave and instructed him to either work as scheduled or resign his position and reapply. Telwar resigned and, upon returning from pilgrimage, reapplied to work at Southern Hills. He was not rehired. Does he have a case? [*EEOC v. Southern Hills Medical Center,* No. 3:07-cv-00976 (M.D. Tenn. consent decree entered April 2009).]

6. A white, non-Latinx meat cutter was fired by his supermarket employer and replaced with a Latinx worker for reasons he believes were racially motivated. Can he sue the company for national origin discrimination? Is it possible to commit national origin discrimination by favoring a Latinx person over a white, non-Latinx person? If so, what would he need to prove to satisfy a *prima facie* case and then to succeed overall? [*EEOC v. West Front Street Foods, LLC d/b/a Compare Foods,* No. 5:08-cv-102 (W.D. N.C. 2008).]

7. Latinx managers of a Florida-based tomato growing, packing, and distributing company harassed and intimidated Haitian production workers. When the Haitians complained about their treatment, the managers retaliated against them. Do the national origin anti-discrimination laws prohibit national origin discrimination by *any* group against *any other* group? Or do the laws require that the discrimination be committed by a group that is considered to represent the majority in that environment against people of color? Could the Haitians recover if their managers had been Haitian? Similarly, would the Latinxs have similar liability if the workers involved had been Latinx? [*EEOC v. LFC Agricultural, Inc., Six L's Packing Company, and Custom Pak, Inc.,* No. 2:09-cv-00636-JES-DNF (M.D. Fl. 2009).]

8. Mohamed Arafi, a naturalized U.S. citizen from Morocco, works as a valet dry cleaner for the Mandarin Oriental Hotel in Washington, D.C. In December 2010, a supervisor allegedly prohibited Arab or Muslim workers from going on floors occupied by a delegation of Israeli diplomats. The supervisor allegedly told Arafi, "You know how the Israelis are with Arabs and Muslims." Arafi says he complied with his supervisor's instructions but consequently lost out on tips. He subsequently complained to another supervisor and the hotel's director of human resources. Arafi says his work hours were cut and that his colleagues said demeaning things about Muslims to him after the incident became known to them. Arafi brought suit under Title VII, alleging disparate treatment resulting in an adverse employment action (the loss of tips) as well as retaliation. The Mandarin Hotel claimed a national security exemption. Would either of Arafi's claims be successful? Would the hotel's? [*Arafi v. Mandarin Oriental,* 867 F. Supp. 2d 66 (D.D.C. 2012).]

9. A nursing home instituted an English-only policy for its employees. Latinx employees were disciplined for violating the policy. Is the policy void on its face, or are some English-only policies acceptable under the law? Does the policy's legality depend on the type of conversation involved (i.e., whether the employee is speaking to customers or speaking to co-employees on a break)? Does the policy's legality depend on how it is enforced (i.e., Spanish-speaking employees disciplined but those speaking other foreign languages not disciplined)? [*EEOC v. Skilled Healthcare Group, Inc.,* C.D. Cal., settled in 2009; www.eeoc.gov/eeoc/newsroom/release/4-14-09.cfm]

10. Leon's Frozen Custard, a locally owned custard shop in Milwaukee, has an English-only policy that requires employees to speak only English while they are working. This includes when they speak to customers, regardless of the language spoken by the customer. The owner of Leon's explained to reporters that "any foreign language is going to be a problem. What I'm trying to avoid is when people come up here, they get waited on in a different language because there happens to be an employee who speaks that language." Is Leon's policy legal? Is speaking English a BFOQ for his employees? Do you consider Leon's policy good for business? ["Latinos v. Leon's: Is the Frozen Custard Stand's 'English Only' Policy Discriminatory?" *Fox 6* (May 18, 2016), https://www.fox6now.com/news/latinos-vs-leons-is-the-frozen-custard-stands-english-only-policy-discriminatory (accessed September 6, 2020).]

End Notes

1. See, for example, *Bisciglia v. Kenosha Unified Sch. Dist. No. 1,* 45 F.3d 223 (7th Cir. 1995).

2. Radford, Jynnah, "Key Findings about U.S. Immigrants," *Pew Research Center* (June 17, 2019), https://www.pewresearch.org/fact-tank/2019/06/17/key-findings-about-u-s-immigrants/ (accessed September 6, 2020).

3. U.S. Census Bureau, "U.S. and World Population Clock," http://www.census.gov/popclock/ (accessed September 6, 2020).

4. Radford, Jynnah and Luis Noe-Bustamante, "Facts on U.S. Immigrants, 2017," *Pew Research Center* (June 3, 2019), https://www.pewresearch.org/hispanic/2019/06/03/facts-on-u-s-immigrants-2017-data/ (accessed September 6, 2020)

5. The authors have chosen to use the term *Latinx* as the gender-neutral plural replacement for "Latino(s) and Latina(s)." Previously, the term *Latinos* was the most often-used term to represent any gender-mixed group of Latin descent. However, that choice represents a male bias that we choose not to perpetuate. For more information and context on this term, please see Logue, J., "Many Student Groups Are Changing Their Names to Use 'Latinx' Instead of 'Latino' and 'Latina,'" *Inside Higher Ed* (December 8, 2015), https://www.insidehighered.com/news/2015/12/08/students-adopt-gender-nonspecific-term-latinx-be-more-inclusive (accessed September 13, 2019); Hayley Barrett, S., and O. Nñ, "Latinx: The Ungendering of the Spanish Language," *Latino USA* (January 29, 2016), http://latinousa.org/2016/01/29/latinx-ungendering-spanish-language/ (accessed September 13, 2019); Reichard, R., "Why We Say Latinx: Trans and Gender Non-Conforming People Explain," *Latina* (August 29, 2015), http://www.latina.com/lifestyle/our-issues/why-we-say-latinx-trans-gender-non-conforming-people-explain (accessed September 13, 2019); Padilla, Y., "What Does 'Latinx' Mean? A Look at the Term That's Challenging Gender Norms," *Complex* (April 18, 2016), http://www.complex.com/life/2016/04/latinx/ (accessed September 13, 2019); Robbins, Gary, "UC San Diego Starts Referring to Latinos and Latinas as Latinx in Key Cultural Shift," *The San Diego Union-Tribune* (December 2, 2018), https://www.sandiegouniontribune.com/news/education/sd-me-latinos-latinx-20181126-story.html (accessed September 13, 2019).

6. Bureau of Labor Statistics, U.S. Department of Labor, "Labor-Force Characteristics of Foreign-Born Workers Summary" (May 16, 2019), https://www.bls.gov/news.release/forbrn.nr0.htm/labor-force-characteristics-of-foreign-born-workers-summary

7. Ibid.

8. Ibid.

9. Equal Employment Opportunity Commission, "Charge Statistics: FY 1997 to FY 2017," https://www.eeoc.gov/eeoc/statistics/enforcement/charges.cfm (accessed September 13, 2019).

10. EEOC, "EEOC Enforcement Guidance on National Origin Discrimination" (November 18, 2016), https://www.eeoc.gov/laws/guidance/national-origin-guidance.cfm#_ftnref15 (accessed September 28, 2019).

11. Ibid.

12. Civil ActionNo. TDC-17-2864 (D. Md. 2018).

13. See, for example, *Espinoza v. Farah Mfg. Co.,* 414 U.S. 86 (1973).

14. Challa, J., "Why Being 'Gypped' Hurts the Roma More Than It Hurts You," *National Public Radio* (December 30, 2013), http://www.npr.org/sections/codeswitch/2013/12/30/242429836/why-being-gypped-hurts-the-roma-more-than-it-hurts-you (accessed September 13, 2019).

15. See, for example, *Janko v. Illinois State Toll Highway Authority,* 704 F. Supp. 1531, 1532 (N.D. Ill. 1989) (finding that discrimination based on an employee's status as a Roma constitutes national origin discrimination under Title VII, which prohibits discrimination based on "ethnic distinctions commonly recognized at the time of the discrimination").

16. EEOC, "EEOC Enforcement Guidance on National Origin Discrimination"(November 18, 2016), https://www.eeoc.gov/laws/guidance/national-origin-guidance.cfm#_ftn23 (accessed September 13, 2019).

17. U.S. Census Bureau, "Selected Social Characteristics in the United States: 2013–2017 American Community Survey 5-Year Estimates https://data.census.gov (accessed September 13, 2019).

18. See Tuschman, Richard, "English-Only Policies in the Workplace: Are They Legal? Are They Smart?" *Forbes* (November 14, 2012), http://www.forbes.com/sites/richard-tuschman/2012/11/15/english-only-policies-in-the-workplace-are-they-legal-are-they-smart/#4dc3541d1802 (accessed September 28, 2019).

19. Gold v. FedEx Freight E., Inc. (In re Rodriguez), 487 F.3d 1001 (6th Cir. 2007).

20. Case No. GJH-17-1511 (D.Md. Jul. 25, 2018).

21. See Weinstein, Lauren, M. "The Role of Labor Law in Challenging English-Only Policies," *Harvard Civil Rights-Civil Liberties Law Review* 47 (2012), pp. 219–279.

22. 998 F.2d 1480, (9th Cir. July 16, 1993).

23. 113 F. Supp. 2d 1066 (N.D. Tex. 2000).

24. 593 F. Supp. 2d 599 (S.D.N.Y. 2009).

25. 419 F. Supp. 2d 408 (S.D.N.Y. 2005).

26. 497 F.3d 1160 (10th Cir. 2007).

27. 53 F. Supp. 2d 223 (N.D.N.Y. 1999).

28. 86 F.3d 1151 (4th Cir. 1996).

29. 78 F. Supp. 3d 1351, 1357 (D. Colo. 2015).

30. EEOC, "EEOC Settles English-Only Suit for $2.44 Million against University of Incarnate Word" (April 20, 2001), https://www.eeoc.gov/eeoc/newsroom/release/4-20-01.cfm (accessed September 28, 2019).

31. EEOC, "Delano Regional Medical Center to Pay Nearly $1 Million in EEOC National Origin Discrimination Suit" (September 17, 2012), https://www.eeoc.gov/newsroom/delano-regional-medical-center-pay-nearly-1-million-eeoc-national-origin-discrimination (accessed September 6, 2020).

32. Wootson Jr., Cleve R., "Feds Sue an Albertsons That Banned Hispanic Employees from Speaking Spanish, Even on Breaks," *The Washington Post* https://www.washingtonpost.com/news/post-nation/wp/2018/05/04/albertsons-no-spanish-rule-hispanic-employees-eeoc-file-lawsuit-over-language-policy/ (accessed September 6, 2020).

33. KGET, "Forever 21 Settles Suit with Employees over Alleged 'English-Only' Policy" (July 19, 2018), https://www.kget.com/news/forever-21-settles-suit-with-employees-over-alleged-english-only-policy/ (assessed July 19, 2019).

34. EEOC, "Employment Rights of Immigrants under Federal Anti-Discrimination Law," https://www.eeoc.gov/eeoc/publications/immigrants-facts.cfm (accessed August 8, 2016); see also *Garcia v. Spun Steak Co.,* 998 F.2d 1480 (9th Cir. 1993). For the contrary opinion supporting the EEOC's contention, see *EEOC v. Premier Operator Services, Inc.,* 75 F. Supp. 550 (N.D. Tex. 1999), and *EEOC v. Synchro-Start,* 29 F. Supp. 2d 911 (N.D. Ill. 1999).

35. *Gonzalo v. All Island Transportation,* No. CV-04-3452 (BMC), 2007 WL 642959, at *7 (E.D.N.Y. Feb. 26, 2007).

36. *Garcia v. Spun Steak Co.,* 998 F.2d at 1489.

37. 433 F.3d 1294 (10th Cir. 2006).

38. See, for example, *E.E.O.C. v. Premier Operator Servs., Inc.,* 113 F. Supp. 2d 1066 (N.D. Tex. 2000); and *EEOC v. Synchro–Start Prods., Inc.,* 29 F.Supp. 2d 911 (N.D. Ill. 1999).

39. See California Department of Fair Employment and Housing, "State Laws Prohibit Discrimination in the Workplace," https://www.dfeh.ca.gov/employment/ (accessed September 17, 2019); see also Vranjes, Toni, "English-Only Policies in California Are Tough to Justify," *SHRM* (October 11, 2018), https://www.shrm.org/resourcesand-tools/legal-and-compliance/state-and-local-updates/pages/english-only-policies-in-california-are-tough-to-justify.aspx (accessed September 17, 2019).

40. 801 F.3d 72 (2d Cir. 2015).

41. U.S. Equal Employment Opportunity Commission, "Charge Statistics FY 1997–2015," http://eeoc.gov/eeoc/statistics/enforcement/charges.cfm (accessed September 17, 2019).

42. EEOC, "Immigrants' Employment Rights under Federal Anti-Discrimination Laws," https://www.eeoc.gov/eeoc/publications/immigrants-facts.cfm (accessed September 18, 2019).

43. Rogers, Katie, and Nicholas Fandos, "Trump Tells Congresswomen to 'Go Back' to the Countries They Came From," *The New York Times* (July 14, 2019), https://www.nytimes.com/2019/07/14/us/politics/trump-twitter-squad-congress.html (accessed September 29, 2019).

44. EEOC, "Immigrants' Employment Rights under Federal Anti-Discrimination Laws," https://www.eeoc.gov/eeoc/publications/immigrants-facts.cfm (accessed September 18, 2019).

45. EEOC, "EEOC Enforcement Guidance on National Origin Discrimination" (November 18, 2016), https://www1.eeoc.gov//laws/guidance/national-origin-guidance.cfm?renderforprint = 1 (accessed September 17, 2019).

46. The EEOC based this example on *Amirmokri v. Baltimore Gas & Electric Co.,* 60 F.3d 1126 (4th Cir. 1995) (finding that the Iranian emigrant employed as an engineer at a nuclear power plant established a prima facie case of national origin harassment).

47. EEOC, "Pape Material Handling to Pay $650,000 to Settle EEOC National Origin Harassment Lawsuit" (May 14, 2019), https://www.eeoc.gov/eeoc/newsroom/release/5-14-19.cfm (accessed September 29, 2019).

48. EEOC, "East Coast Labor Solutions and Related Staffing Firms to Pay $475,000 to Settle EEOC National Origin and Disability Discrimination Suit" (February 19, 2019), https://www.eeoc.gov/eeoc/newsroom/release/2-19-19.cfm (accessed September 29, 2019).

49. 680 F.3d 936 (7th Cir. 2012).

50. Code of Federal Regulations, Title 41, Part 60-50, http://law.justia.com/cfr/title41/41-1.2.3.1.8.html (accessed September 17, 2019).

51. *State of Illinois v. Xing Ying Employment Agency,* 15 C 10235 (N.D. Ill 2018).

52. The authors have followed the usage at the time of publication offered by the BBC and NPR, recognizing the qualification that the identification is self-defined and may be considered to reflect expansionist ambitions. Other terms in use include ISIS ("Islamic State of Iraq and Syria") and ISIL ("Islamic State of Iraq and the Levant," meaning the whole eastern shore of the Mediterranean Sea). Jensen, E., "Islamic State, ISIS, ISIL or Daesh?" *NPR Ombudsman* (November 18, 2015), http://www.npr.org/sections/ombudsman/2015/11/18/456507131/islamic-state-isis-isil-or-daesh; Irshaid, F., "Isis, Isil, IS or Daesh? One Group, Many Names," *BBC News* (December 2, 2015), http://www.bbc.com/news/world-middle-east-27994277.

53. EEOC, "What You Should Know about the EEOC and Religious and National Origin Discrimination Involving the Muslim, Sikh, Arab, Middle Eastern and South Asian Communities," https://www.eeoc.gov/eeoc/newsroom/wysk/religion_national_origin_9-11.cfm (accessed September 18, 2019); EEOC, "National Origin-Based Charges Filed from 10/01/2000 thru 09/30/2017," http://www.eeoc.gov/eeoc/events/9-11-11_natl_origin_charges.cfm (accessed September 18, 2019).

54. Weise, Karen, "3 Muslim Workers at Amazon File Federal Discrimination Complaint," *New York Times* (May 8, 2019), https://www.nytimes.com/2019/05/08/technology/amazon-muslim-workers-complaint.html (accessed September 18, 2019).

55. *E.E.O.C. v. Abercrombie & Fitch Stores, Inc.,* 135 S. Ct. 2028 (2015).

56. See "CEOs: Human and Humane," *Corporate Counsel* (October 19, 2001).

57. Peek, Lori, *Behind the Backlash: Muslim Americans after 9/11* (New Delhi: Social Science Press, 2012 and Philadelphia: Temple University Press, 2010).

58. 42 U.S.C.A. § 2000e-2.

59. Lopez, Mark Hugo, Ana Gonzalez-Barrera, and Jens Manuel Krogstad, "More Latinos Have Serious Concerns about Their Place in America under Trump," *Pew Research Center* (October 25, 2018), https://www.pewresearch.org/hispanic/2018/10/25/more-latinos-have-serious-concerns-about-their-place-in-america-under-trump/ (accessed September 19, 2019).

60. Levin, Brian, James J. Nolan, and John David Reitzel, "New Data Shows U.S. Hate Crimes Continued to Rise in 2017," *CBS News* (June 26, 2018), https://www.cbsnews.com/news/new-data-shows-us-hate-crimes-continued-to-rise-in-2017/ (accessed September 29, 2019).

61. National Public Radio, the Robert Wood Johnson Foundation, and Harvard T. H. Chan School of Public Health, "Discrimination in America: Experiences and Views of Latinos" (October 2017), https://www.npr.org/documents/2017/oct/discrimination-latinos-final.pdf (accessed March 5, 2020).

62. Lopez, Mark Hugo, Ana Gonzalez-Barrera, and Jens Manuel Krogstad, "More Latinos Have Serious Concerns about Their Place in America under Trump," *Pew Research Forum* (October 25, 2019), https://www.pewresearch.org/hispanic/2018/10/25/more-latinos-have-serious-concerns-about-their-place-in-america-under-trump/ (accessed September 29, 2019).

63. Cambell, Brendan, Angel Mendoza, and Tessa Diestel, "Rising Hate Drives Latinos and Immigrants into Silence," The Center for Public Integrity (August 22, 2018), https://publicintegrity.org/federal-politics/rising-hate-drives-latinos-and-immigrants-into-silence/ (accessed September 29, 2019).

64. National Public Radio, the Robert Wood Johnson Foundation, and Harvard T. H. Chan School of Public Health, "Discrimination in America: Experiences and Views of Latinos" (October 2017), https://www.npr.org/documents/2017/oct/discrimination-latinos-final.pdf (accessed March 5, 2020).

65. See Dickerson, Caitlin, "Border at 'Breaking Point' as More Than 76,000 Unauthorized Migrants Cross in a Month," *New York Times* (March 5, 2019), https://www.nytimes.com/2019/03/05/us/border-crossing-increase.html (accessed September 29, 2019); see also Hersher, Rebecca, and Vanessa Quian, "3 Charts That Show What's Actually Happening along the Southern Border," *NPR* (June 22, 2018), https://www.npr.org/2018/06/22/622246815/unauthorized-immigration-in-three-graphs (accessed September 29, 2019).

66. National Public Radio, the Robert Wood Johnson Foundation, and Harvard T. H. Chan School of Public Health, "Discrimination in America: Experiences and Views of Latinos" (October 2017), https://www.npr.org/documents/2017/oct/discrimination-latinos-final.pdf (accessed March 5, 2020).

67. Allwood, Noni, and Laura Sherbin, "Latinos at Work: Unleashing the Power of Culture," Center for Talent Innovation (2016), https://lemonly.com/work/latinos-at-work-report (accessed October 13, 2019).

68. See Hewlett, Sylvia Ann, Melinda Marshall, Laura Sherbin, and Tara Gonsalves, <u>Innovation, Diversity, and Market Growth</u> (New York, NY: Center for Talent Innovation, 2013); see also Allwood, Noni, and Laura Sherbin, "Latinos at Work: Unleashing the Power of Culture," Center for Talent Innovation, 2016), https://lemonly.com/work/latinos-at-work-report (accessed October 13, 2019).

69. See Benjamin, Tia, "The Ways Discrimination Negatively Affects Businesses, http://smallbusiness.chron.com/ways-discrimination-negatively-affects-businesses-36925.html (accessed September 19, 2019).

70. 435 U.S. 291 (1978).

71. 414 U.S. 86 (1973).

72. Trump, Donald J., "Presidential Executive Order on Buy American and Hire American" (April 18, 2017), https://www.whitehouse.gov/the-press-office/2017/04/18/presidential-executive-order-buy-american-and-hire-american (accessed September 19, 2019).

73. Clark, Gabrielle, "Trump's' Buy American and Hire American' Initiative Won't Actually Help Workers," *The Washington Post* (October 10, 2018), https://www.washingtonpost.com/outlook/2018/10/10/trumps-buy-american-hire-american-initiative-wont-actually-help-workers/ (accessed September 20, 2019).

74. Baily, Sarah Pulliam, and Julie Zauzmer, "Trump Administration Proposes Protecting Federal Contractors Who Fire or Hire Workers," *The Washington Post* (August 14, 2019), https://www.washingtonpost.com/religion/2019/08/14/trump-administration-proposes-protecting-federal-contractors-who-fire-or-hire-workers-based-religious-beliefs/ (accessed September 20, 2019).

75. Pew Hispanic Center, "Unauthorized Immigrant Population: National and State Trends, 2010" (February 2011), http://www.pewhispanic.org/2011/02/01/unauthorized-immigrant-population-brnational-and-state-trends-2010/ (accessed August 7, 2016).

76. Krogstad, Jens Manuel, Jeffery S. Passel and D'vera Cohn, "5 Facts about Illegal Immigration in the U.S.," Pew Research Center (June 12, 2019), https://www.pewresearch.org/fact-tank/2019/06/12/5-facts-about-illegal-immigration-in-the-u-s/ (accessed September 20, 2019).

77. Ibid.

78. Gonzalez-Barrera, Ana, and Jens Manuel Krogstad, "What We Know about Illegal Immigrants from Mexico," The Pew Forum (June 28, 2019), https://www.pewresearch.org/fact-tank/2019/06/28/what-we-know-about-illegal-immigration-from-mexico/ (accessed September 20, 2019).

79. C.F.R. § 274a.1(1)(1).

80. Preston, J., "Revised Rule for Employers That Hire Immigrants," *The New York Times* (November 26, 2007), https://www.nytimes.com/2007/11/25/washington/25immig.html (accessed September 6, 2020).

81. Preston, J., "U.S. Set for a Crackdown on Illegal Hiring," *The New York Times* (August 8, 2007), http://www.nytimes.com/2007/08/08/washington/08immig.html?_r = 0 (accessed November 17, 2019).

82. Social Security Administration, "Employer Correction Request Notices (EDCOR)" (March 2019), https://www.ssa.gov/employer/notices.html (accessed September 20, 2019).

83. U.S. DoJ, Office of Special Council for Immigration-Related Unfair Employment Practices, "Name and Social Security Number (SSN) 'No Matches' Information for Employers," https://www.justice.gov/sites/default/files/crt/legacy/2014/12/04/Employers.pdf (accessed September 20, 2019).

84. Immigration and Customs Enforcement, "ICE worksite enforcement investigations in FY18 surge" (December 11, 2018), https://www.ice.gov/news/releases/ice-worksite-enforcement-investigations-fy18-surge (last accessed September 20, 2019).

85. John A. MacKenzie, "Workplace Immigration Issues and ICEEmployers face stiff fines from Immigration and Customs Enforcement for immigration-documents violations," *Workforce* (July 10, 2018), available at https://www.workforce.com/2018/07/10/workplace-immigration-issues-and-ice/ (last visited October 13, 2019).

86. *Rivera v. NIBCO, Inc.* 364 F.3d 1057, 1056 (9th Cir. 2004); see also *EEOC v. The Restaurant Company, d/b/a Perkins Restaurant & Bakery,* 490 F. Supp. 2d 1039 (D. Minn. 2006).

87. 535 U.S. 137 (2002).

88. See Porter, Donna Y., "Undocumented Workers Have NLRA Rights, but Not Monetary Remedies," *Employment Law Strategist* (April 2002).

89. See "Workforce Online," *CCH* (November 1999), citing "Policy Guidance: Remedies Available to Undocumented Workers under Federal Employment Discrimination Laws" (October 26, 1999), Appendix B of sec. 622, vol. II of *EEOC Compliance Manual.*

90. *Hofman Plastics Compounds v. NLRB,* 535 U.S. 137, 149 (2002).

91. *Bailon v. Seok AM No. 1 Corp.,* 2009 WL 4884340 (W.D. Wash. 2009).

92. *Colon v. Major Perry St. Corp.,* 987 F. Supp. 2d 451 (S.D.N.Y. 2013).

93. 481 U.S. 604 (1987).

94. *Gomez v. City of New York,* 2012 U.S. Dist. (E.D.N.Y. April 30, 2012).

95. 17 F. Supp. 2d 394 (E.D. Pa 1998).

Cases

Case 1 Garcia v. Spun Steak Co., 998 F.2d 1480 *(9th Cir. 1993)*

The defendant, Spun Steak Co., employs 33 workers, 24 of whom are Spanish-speaking. Two of the Spanish speakers speak no English. Plaintiffs Garcia and Buitrago are production line workers for the defendant, and both are bilingual. After receiving complaints that some workers were using their second language to harass and to insult other workers, Spun Steak enacted an English-only policy in the workplace in order to (1) promote racial harmony, (2) enhance worker safety because some employees who did not understand Spanish claimed that they were distracted by its use, and (3) enhance product quality because the USDA inspector in the plant spoke only English. The two plaintiffs received warning notices about speaking Spanish during working hours, and they were not permitted to work next to each other for two months. They filed charges with the EEOC, which found reasonable cause to believe that the defendant had violated Title VII. The district court found in favor of the employees, and Spun Steak appealed. The appellate court reversed, finding that Spun Steak did not violate Title VII in adopting the English-only rule.

O'Scannlain, J.

***

The Spanish-speaking employees do not contend that Spun Steak intentionally discriminated against them in enacting the English-only policy. Rather, they contend that the policy had a *discriminatory impact* on them because it imposes a burdensome term or condition of employment exclusively upon Hispanic workers and denies them a privilege of employment that non-Spanish-speaking workers enjoy.

The employees argue that denying them the ability to speak Spanish on the job denies them the right to cultural expression. It cannot be gainsaid that an individual's primary language can be an important link to his ethnic culture and identity. Title VII, however, does not protect the ability of workers to express their cultural heritage at the workplace. Title VII is concerned only with disparities in the treatment of workers; it does not confer substantive privileges. It is axiomatic that an employee must often sacrifice individual self-expression during working hours. Just as a private employer is not required to allow other types of self-expression, there is nothing in Title VII which requires an employer to allow employees to express their cultural identity.

Next, the Spanish-speaking employees argue that the English-only policy has a disparate impact on them because it deprives them of a privilege given by the employer to native-English speakers: the ability to converse on the job in the language with which they feel most comfortable. It is undisputed that Spun Steak allows its employees to converse on the job. The ability to converse—especially to make small talk—is a privilege of employment, and may in fact be a significant privilege of employment in an assembly-line job. It is inaccurate, however, to describe the privilege as broadly as the Spanish-speaking employees urge us to do.

The employees have attempted to define the privilege as the ability to speak in the language of their choice. A privilege, however, is by definition given at the employer's discretion; an employer has the right to define its contours. Thus, an employer may allow employees to converse on the job, but only during certain times of the day or during the performance of certain tasks. The employer may proscribe certain topics as inappropriate during working hours or may even forbid the use of certain words, such as profanity.

Here, as is its prerogative, the employer has defined the privilege narrowly. When the privilege is defined at its narrowest (as merely the ability to speak on the job), we cannot conclude that those employees fluent in both English and Spanish are adversely impacted by the policy. Because they are able to speak English, bilingual employees can engage in conversation on the job. It is axiomatic that "the language a person who is multilingual elects to speak at a particular time is . . . a matter of choice." The bilingual employee can readily comply with the English-only rule and still enjoy the privilege of speaking on the job. "There is no disparate impact" with respect to a privilege of employment "if the rule is one that the affected employee can readily observe and nonobservance is a matter of individual preference."

The Spanish-speaking employees argue that fully bilingual employees are hampered in the enjoyment of the privilege because for them, switching from one language to another is not fully volitional. Whether a bilingual speaker can control which language is used in a given circumstance is a factual issue that cannot be resolved at the summary judgment stage. However, we fail to see the relevance of the assertion, even assuming that it can be proved. Title VII is not meant to protect against rules that merely inconvenience some employees, even if the inconvenience falls regularly on a protected class. Rather, Title VII protects against only those policies that have a *significant* impact. The fact that an employee may have to catch himself or herself from occasionally slipping into Spanish does not impose a burden significant enough to amount to the denial of equal opportunity. This is not a case in which the employees have alleged that the company is enforcing the policy in such a way as to impose penalties for minor slips of the tongue. The fact that a bilingual employee may, on occasion, unconsciously substitute a Spanish word in the place of an English one does not override our conclusion that the bilingual employee can easily comply with the rule. In short, we conclude that a bilingual employee is not denied a privilege of employment by the English-only policy.

By contrast, non-English speakers cannot enjoy the privilege of conversing on the job if conversation is limited to a language they cannot speak. As applied "[t]o a person who speaks only one tongue or to a person who has difficulty using another language than the one spoken in his home," an English-only rule might well have an adverse impact. Indeed, counsel for Spun Steak conceded at oral argument that the policy would have an adverse impact on an employee unable to speak English. There is only one employee at Spun Steak affected by the policy who is unable to speak any English. Even with regard to her, however, summary judgment was improper because a genuine issue of material fact exists as to whether she has been adversely affected by the policy. She stated in her deposition that she was not bothered by the rule because she preferred not to make small talk on the job, but rather preferred to work in peace. Furthermore, there is some evidence suggesting that she is not required to comply with the policy when she chooses to speak. For example, she is allowed to speak Spanish to her supervisor. Remand is necessary to determine whether she has suffered adverse effects from the policy. It is unclear from the record whether there are any other employees who have such limited proficiency in English that they are effectively denied the privilege of speaking on the job. Whether an employee speaks such little English as to be effectively denied the privilege is a question of fact for which summary judgment is improper.

We do not foreclose the prospect that in some circumstances English-only rules can exacerbate existing tensions, or, when combined with other discriminatory behavior, contribute to an overall environment of discrimination. Likewise, we can envision a case in which such rules are enforced in such a draconian manner that the enforcement itself amounts to harassment. In evaluating such a claim, however, a court must look to the totality of the circumstances in the particular factual context in which the claim arises.

In holding that the enactment of an English-only while working policy does not inexorably lead to an abusive environment for those whose primary language is not English, we reach a conclusion opposite to the EEOC's long-standing position. The EEOC Guidelines provide that an employee meets the *prima facie* case in a disparate impact cause of action merely by proving the existence of the English-only policy. Under the EEOC's scheme, an employer must always provide a business justification for such a rule. The EEOC enacted this scheme in part because of its conclusion that English-only rules may "create an atmosphere of inferiority, isolation and intimidation based on national origin which could result in a discriminatory working environment."

We do not reject the English-only rule Guideline lightly. We recognize that "as an administrative interpretation of the Act by the enforcing agency, these Guidelines . . . constitute a body of experience and informed judgment to which courts and litigants may properly resort for guidance." But we are not bound by the Guidelines. We will not defer to "an administrative construction of a statute where there are 'compelling indications that it is wrong.'"

In sum, we conclude that the bilingual employees have not made out a *prima facie* case and that Spun Steak has not violated Title VII in adopting an English-only rule as to them. Thus, we reverse the grant of summary judgment in favor of Garcia, Buitrago, and Local 115 to the extent it represents the bilingual employees, and remand with instructions to grant summary judgment in favor of Spun Steak on their claims. A genuine issue of material fact exists as to whether there are one or more employees represented by Local 115 with limited proficiency in English who were adversely impacted by the policy. As to such employee or employees, we reverse the grant of summary judgment in favor of Local 115, and remand for further proceedings. REVERSED and REMANDED.

Case Questions

1. Do you agree with the contention that denying a group the right to speak their native tongue denies them the right to cultural expression?

2. Do employees have a "right" to cultural expression in the workplace?

3. Do you agree with the court that an English-only rule is not abusive per se to those whose primary language is not English? Do you believe that it creates a "class system" of languages in the workplace and therefore inherently places one group's language above another's?

Vega v. Hempstead Union Free Sch. Dist.,
801 F.3d 72 (2d Cir. 2015)

See Chapter 2 to revisit key concepts.

Vega, a high school math teacher, alleges that his school district and two principals discriminated against him because of his "Hispanic ethnicity" and that they retaliated against him after he complained of discrimination. The district court found that Vega had not "demonstrated that he suffered an adverse employment action" and therefore he had not "established a *prima facie* case of discrimination" and that he had failed, with respect to his claims of retaliation, "to establish an adverse action taken against him" or "a connection between the alleged retaliatory acts and his ethnicity."

The Second Circuit finds below that the retaliation claims are actionable under § 1983 and that Vega has sufficiently pleaded discrimination and retaliation claims.

CHIN, Circuit Judge

***

1. The Alleged Discrimination

Beginning in 2008, the District took a number of actions that Vega contends were discriminatory:

- Beginning in 2008, Vega was assigned an "increased percentage of students that were Spanish speaking and were not fluent in English," requiring Vega to do "twice as much work" in preparing and teaching his classes first in English and then in Spanish, without extra compensation.

- When he complained later in 2008, Vega was assigned "a mixture of bilingual classes and English classes, instead of all bilingual," and he was still not compensated for the extra preparation time.

- Vega was unable to use his regular classroom for his first period class in October 2010 and had to teach in the "excessively noisy" media center without a blackboard.

- Vega was assigned a classroom with a "University of Puerto Rico" banner above the door.

- Vega attempted to enter his students' grades into the school's computer system in October 2011, but his password had been deactivated. Vega had to use his non-Hispanic colleague's password to log into the computer system to enter his grades.

- The District twice attempted to transfer Vega out of the High School: First, on June 24, 2011, Davidson attempted to transfer Vega to the District's middle school. On July 11, 2011, Vega objected to Davidson's proposed transfer and told the Assistant Superintendent that he should not be transferred because he had a better percentage of passing students than most of his co-workers. On September 21, 2011, the District rescinded the transfer and Vega continued teaching at the High School. Second, on June 18, 2012, Vega received a letter from the District approving his transfer to the Academy of Math and Sciences—whose principal is Hispanic—even though he had never requested this transfer. Vega was never transferred.

Vega alleges that his non-Hispanic colleagues were not subjected to such actions.

2. The Alleged Retaliation

On August 8, 2011, Vega filed a charge with the Equal Employment Opportunity Commission (the "EEOC"), alleging that the District had discriminated against him based on his ethnicity in violation of Title VII. Vega amended the charge twice, first on January 4, 2012, and then on July 2, 2012, adding further allegations of discrimination.

After Vega filed his initial charge, and, in some instances, the amended charges, Defendants engaged in a number of actions that Vega alleges were retaliatory:

- For the 2011–12 school year, Vega "was assigned classes with students who [were] notoriously excessively absent." Before 2011, consistently roughly 20% of Vega's students were excessively absent, but during the 2011–12 school year, that number jumped to 75%. Chronic absence leads to poor student performance, which in turn reflects poorly on a teacher's performance.

- The District changed the curriculum for one of Vega's classes in November 2011. The District notified all non-Hispanic teachers of the curriculum change, but it did not notify Vega.

- On March 12, 2012, $738.92 was improperly deducted from Vega's paycheck for sick time, even though he had leftover sick time in his "sick day bank." Vega complained to the District's Business Office, which acknowledged the mistake, and while he was repaid a portion of the deducted amount in September, he was never repaid the full amount that was due to him.

- In February 2013, Vega received his first negative performance review in his sixteen years teaching at the High School. Artiles observed Vega's classroom performance and gave him 1.4 out of a 4-point maximum in his review. Vega was held to a different evaluation process than his colleagues, and he was the only teacher to receive a negative performance score during the evaluation period.

***

2. Pleading Standards for Discrimination Claims

We turn to the question of what a plaintiff must plead in an employment discrimination case to state a claim upon which relief may be granted.

a. Title VII

In *Littlejohn,* we held that at the pleadings stage of an employment discrimination case, a plaintiff has a "minimal burden" of alleging facts "suggesting an inference of discriminatory motivation." While we made clear that Iqbal applies to employment discrimination cases, we also clarified that Iqbal's plausibility requirement "does not affect the benefit to plaintiffs pronounced in the *McDonnell Douglas* quartet." We ruled nonetheless that the facts alleged in the complaint must provide "at least minimal support for the proposition that the employer was motivated by discriminatory intent." The question remains what a plaintiff must allege to meet this minimal burden.

The starting point is the statute. Title VII makes it unlawful for an employer "to fail or refuse to hire or to discharge any individual, or otherwise to discriminate against any individual with respect to his compensation, terms, conditions, or privileges of employment, because of such individual's race, color, religion, sex, or national origin." Title VII thus requires a plaintiff asserting a discrimination claim to allege two elements: (1) the employer discriminated against him (2) because of his race, color, religion, sex, or national origin.

As to the first element, an employer discriminates against a plaintiff by taking an adverse employment action against him. "A plaintiff sustains an adverse employment action if he or she endures a materially adverse change in the terms and conditions of employment." *Galabya v. N.Y.C. Bd. of Educ.* "An adverse employment action is one which is more disruptive than a mere inconvenience or an alteration of job responsibilities." *Terry v. Ashcroft.* "Examples of materially adverse changes include termination of employment, a demotion evidenced by a decrease in wage or salary, a less distinguished title, a material loss of benefits, significantly diminished material responsibilities, or other indices unique to a particular situation." We have held that the assignment of "a disproportionately heavy workload" can constitute an adverse employment action. *Feingold.*

As to the second element, an action is "because of" a plaintiff's race, color, religion, sex, or national origin where it was a "substantial" or "motivating" factor contributing to the employer's decision to take the action. See *Price Waterhouse v. Hopkins.* While the Supreme Court has held that a plaintiff alleging age discrimination under the Age Discrimination in Employment Act must allege "that age was the 'but-for' cause of the employer's adverse action," *Gross v. FBL Fin. Servs.,* Inc., the "motivating factor" standard still applies to discrimination claims based on race, color, religion, sex, or national origin, see *Leibowitz v. Cornell Univ.* Hence, a plaintiff in a Title VII case need not allege "but-for" causation.

Under *Iqbal* and *Twombly,* then, in an employment discrimination case, a plaintiff must plausibly allege that (1) the employer took adverse action against him and (2) his race, color, religion, sex, or national origin was a motivating factor in the employment decision.

The question remains as to what "plausibility" means in the context of employment discrimination claims. Several considerations guide the inquiry.

First, as the Supreme Court explained in *Iqbal,* a plaintiff must plead "factual content that allows the court to draw the reasonable inference that the defendant is liable for the misconduct alleged." While "detailed factual allegations" are not required, "a formulaic recitation of the elements of a cause of action will not do." *Twombly.* At the same time, the court must assume the factual allegations in the complaint to be true, "even if [they are] doubtful in fact," and a complaint may not be dismissed "based on a judge's disbelief of a complaint's factual allegations," *Neitzke v. Williams.*

Second, in making the plausibility determination, the court is to "draw on its judicial experience and common sense." *Iqbal.* Of course, the court must proceed at all times in a fair and deliberative fashion, alert to any unconscious bias that could affect decision-making. In making the plausibility determination, the court must be mindful of the "elusive" nature of intentional discrimination. See *Burdine.* As we have recognized, "clever men may easily conceal their motivations." *Robinson v. 12 Lofts Realty, Inc.* Because discrimination claims implicate an employer's usually unstated intent and state of mind, see *Meiri v. Dacon,* rarely is there "direct, smoking gun, evidence of discrimination," *Richards v. N.Y.C. Bd. of Educ.* Instead, plaintiffs usually must rely on "bits and pieces" of information to support an inference of discrimination, i.e., a "mosaic" of intentional discrimination. *Gallagher v. Delaney.* Again, as we made clear in *Littlejohn,* at the initial stage of a litigation, the plaintiff's burden is "minimal"—he need only plausibly allege facts that provide "at least minimal support for the proposition that the employer was motivated by discriminatory intent."

Finally, courts must remember that "[t]he plausibility standard is not akin to a 'probability requirement.'" *Iqbal.* On a motion to dismiss, the question is not whether a plaintiff is likely to prevail, but whether the well-pleaded factual allegations plausibly give rise to an inference of unlawful discrimination, i.e., whether plaintiffs allege

enough to "nudge[] their claims across the line from conceivable to plausible." *Twombly.*

Accordingly, to defeat a motion to dismiss or a motion for judgment on the pleadings in a Title VII discrimination case, a plaintiff must plausibly allege that (1) the employer took adverse action against him, and (2) his race, color, religion, sex, or national origin was a motivating factor in the employment decision. As we have long recognized, the "'ultimate issue' in an employment discrimination case is whether the plaintiff has met her burden of proving that the adverse employment decision was motivated at least in part by an 'impermissible reason,' i.e., a discriminatory reason." *Stratton v. Dep't for the Aging for City of N.Y.* A plaintiff can meet that burden through direct evidence of intent to discriminate, or by indirectly showing circumstances giving rise to an inference of discrimination. A plaintiff may prove discrimination indirectly either by meeting the requirements of *McDonnell Douglas* and showing that the employer's stated reason for its employment action was pretext to cover-up discrimination, or by otherwise creating a "mosaic" of intentional discrimination by identifying "bits and pieces of evidence" that together give rise to an inference of discrimination, *Gallagher.* At the pleadings stage, then, a plaintiff must allege that the employer took adverse action against her at least in part for a discriminatory reason, and she may do so by alleging facts that directly show discrimination or facts that indirectly show discrimination by giving rise to a plausible inference of discrimination.

* * * *

3. Application

We conclude that Vega pleaded a plausible discrimination claim under Title VII and § 1983, based on his allegation that the District assigned him classes with higher numbers of Spanish-speaking students and, in doing so, assigned him a disproportionate workload. None of Vega's other claims plausibly state a claim on their own, but they help create context for his discrimination claim.

Vega has plausibly alleged that his assignment to classes with increased numbers of Spanish-speaking students was an "adverse employment action" taken "because of" his Hispanic ethnicity. First, Vega alleges that he was forced to spend disproportionately more time preparing for his classes and therefore experienced a material increase in his responsibilities without additional compensation. He contends that these assignments required him to do "twice as much work" and that he was assigned class preparations on a basis that exceed "District policy." *App.* at 11. We have previously held that the assignment of "an excessive workload" as a result of "discriminatory intent," *Feingold,* can be an adverse employment action because it is "more disruptive than a mere inconvenience or an alteration of job responsibilities," *Terry.* Vega has thus plausibly alleged an adverse employment action.

Second, Vega has also plausibly alleged that the adverse action was taken "because of" his Hispanic ethnicity, that is, that his Hispanic ethnicity was a motivating factor in the employment decisions. He contends that he was assigned a large percentage of Spanish-speaking students because he is Hispanic and bilingual, while his similarly situated co-workers were not assigned additional work. Vega's other allegations of discrimination, even if they do not independently constitute adverse employment actions, provide "relevant background evidence" by shedding light on Defendant's motivation and thus bolster his claim that Defendants treated him differently because of his ethnicity. See *Nat'l R.R. Passenger Corp.; Washington v. Davis.* For example, the District placed a "University of Puerto Rico" banner outside his classroom and attempted to transfer him to a Hispanic principal's school. These actions are plausibly connected to Vega's Hispanic background and therefore provide a contextual basis for inferring discrimination. Vega has thus plausibly alleged that his Hispanic background was a "motivating factor" contributing to his being assigned extra work.

* * * *

The District may contend that Vega was assigned a disproportionate number of Spanish-speaking students solely because of his language ability, and not because of his Hispanic background, but these competing explanations are better evaluated at the summary judgment stage or beyond, and not on a motion for judgment on the pleadings.

Accordingly, the Complaint plausibly pleads under both Title VII and § 1983 that Defendants discriminated against Vega by assigning him, on or after the time-bar dates, to classes that required additional preparation because they had large numbers of Spanish-speaking students.

***

D. Pleading of Retaliation Claims

***

Here, Vega alleges that after he engaged in protected activity by filing a charge of discrimination with the EEOC in

August 2011, he was assigned more students with excessive absenteeism records (jumping from 20% to 75%), his salary was temporarily reduced, he was not notified that the curriculum for one of his classes was changed, and he received a negative performance evaluation. Each of these allegations plausibly states a claim of retaliation.

First, each of these actions "could well dissuade a reasonable worker from making or supporting a charge of discrimination." *White.* The assignment of a substantially higher number of chronically absent students could very well have adversely impacted Vega, both by making his teaching assignments more difficult and by making it more difficult for him to achieve good results. Likewise, the wrongful deduction of $738.92 from his paycheck for sick leave, the failure of the District to correct the error in full, and the failure of the District to correct the error even in part for six months surely could have had an adverse impact on Vega. Similarly, failing to notify Vega of a curriculum change could have adversely affected him by, for example, making him appear unprepared or ineffective both to his students and for his up-coming teacher evaluation, as he would have been preparing for and teaching the wrong curriculum.

Viewed in the context of his other allegations, it was plausible that the District's *92 failure to notify Vega of the curriculum change was part of their pattern of discrimination and retaliation designed to make Vega look bad. Finally, of course, a poor performance evaluation could very well deter a reasonable worker from complaining.

Second, each of these actions closely followed protected activity by Vega. His assignment of classes "for the 2011/2012 school year," must have been made shortly before the start of the school year—shortly after he filed his initial charge with the EEOC on August 8, 2011. Similarly, the District changed the curriculum for his class in November of 2011, within three months of his initial filing with the EEOC. The District made the erroneous sick leave deduction from Vega's pay check on March 2, 2012, just two months after Vega filed an addendum to his EEOC complaint on January 4, 2012, providing greater detail about his previous claims and adding new allegations of discrimination and retaliation. Vega received his poor teacher evaluation (from Artiles) in February 2013, approximately two months after he filed his *pro se* complaint in the action below, on December 12, 2012. According to Vega, this was his first negative evaluation in sixteen years of teaching at the High School. Hence, the Complaint plausibly alleges a temporal proximity for each of these actions.

Some of these actions, considered individually, might not amount to much. Taken together, however, they plausibly paint a mosaic of retaliation and an intent to punish Vega for complaining of discrimination.

CONCLUSION

We conclude that the district court erred in granting Defendants' motion for judgment on the pleadings in full and dismissing the Complaint in its entirety. For the reasons stated above, we VACATE and REMAND for further proceedings consistent with this opinion.

Case Questions

1. Who has to prove a company discriminated against an employee? Do you agree with the burden of this obligation?

2. What are the two elements that an employee must show to make a successful Title VII claim? Do you think the "motivating factor" standard is appropriate for discrimination claims based on national origin?

3. Are employers allowed to treat employees who file claims of discrimination differently after the claim has been made? What sort of actions may be construed as retaliation against an employee? How might an employer avoid actions that can be perceived as retaliation?

4. Does the school district have either a bona fide occupational qualification (BFOQ) or a legitimate nondiscriminatory reason (LNDR) for requiring Vega to teach the bilingual classes? Would it matter if Vega were the only teacher in the school with the appropriate language skills to teach these students? Would this case come out differently if three Spanish-speaking white teachers with less tenure than Vega were not required to teach any bilingual classes?

Cortezano v. Salin Bank & Trust Company,
680 F. 3d 936 (7th Circuit, 2012)

Kristi Cortezano, a U.S. citizen, was married to a Mexican citizen residing in the United States without legal authorization. While employed by Salin Bank & Trust, Cortezano assisted her husband in opening a bank account. She told her employers of her husband's unauthorized status and was subsequently fired. Cortezano filed suit against her former employer under Title VII, alleging that she was discriminated against because of her husband's national origin. Her claim was rejected, as the courts found that any discrimination that led to Cortezano's firing was not based on her husband's race or national origin but his status as an undocumented alien ("alienage").

Wood, C.J.

***

Kristi Cortezano filed suit against her former employer, Salin Bank & Trust Company, alleging national-origin discrimination based on her marriage to Javier Cortezano, a Mexican citizen whose presence in the United States was unauthorized. (We use the couple's first names to avoid confusion.) The district court granted Salin Bank's motion for summary judgment, finding that Kristi failed to establish that her firing was based on an impermissible reason. Kristi now appeals. We find that any discrimination that led to Kristi's firing was not based on Javier's race or national origin, but rather on his status as an alien

who lacked permission to be in the country. Because alienage is not a protected classification under Title VII, Kristi has no claim for relief, and so we affirm.

I

In 1997, Javier unlawfully entered the United States, where he took up residence without a valid visa or work permit. Some time later, he met Kristi and the two married in February 2001. In March 2007, Salin Bank hired Kristi as a Manager in

Training. Kristi showed promise. Less than one month later, she was promoted to Bank Sales Manager, and a few months after that she was transferred to a more profitable location.

Meanwhile, Javier attempted to start a car detailing and repair business. Given his undocumented status, he lacked a social security number to open a business banking account for his new enterprise. To open the accounts he needed, Javier obtained an individual tax identification number (ITIN). Although the exact circumstances under which Javier obtained his ITIN are murky, this appeal comes to us from a motion for summary judgment, and so we assume that Javier properly received his identification number. Kristi named Javier a joint owner on her account at Salin Bank, and with some help from Kristi, Javier used his ITIN to open two accounts of his own: a personal account, as well as a business account for his company, Cortezano Motors, Ltd. Javier's business venture floundered, unfortunately, and so in December 2007, he returned to Mexico to sort out his citizenship status.

Around that time, Kristi revealed Javier's unauthorized status to her supervisor at Salin Bank, Stacy Novotny, in connection with her request for a two-week vacation during which she planned to attend proceedings in Mexico to help Javier obtain U.S. citizenship. Novotny granted the request, and Kristi traveled to Mexico from January 24 to February 8, 2008.

After learning about Javier's situation, Novotny did not let matters lie. Instead, she called Salin Bank's security officer, Mike Hubbs, and told him that Kristi had joint accounts at the bank with a known undocumented alien. Hubbs verified that Javier was indeed on these accounts. Concerned that this arrangement might implicate laws against bank fraud, Hubbs scheduled a meeting with Novotny and Kristi for February 11, 2008.

During this meeting, Kristi admitted that Javier had illegally entered the United States. She urged, however, that he was then in Mexico trying to obtain a visa or U.S. citizenship so that he could rejoin her. Hubbs did not see this as an excuse; instead, he emphasized his concern that Javier, as an "illegal alien from Mexico," must have used fraudulent documents to open his accounts. As the meeting progressed, Hubbs's temper flared. When Novotny briefly stepped out of the room, Hubbs got in Kristi's face, screamed at her, called Javier a "piece of shit," and demanded that Kristi admit that Javier illegally opened his Salin Bank accounts. Unconvinced by Kristi's repeated statements that Javier's ITIN, other documentation, and accounts were legitimate, Hubbs informed Kristi that he would be filing an internal Suspicious Activity Report.

In the course of collecting information for his report, Hubbs emailed several Salin Bank supervisors to inform them that Javier had "gained entry into the US illegally," "illegally obtained an Indiana [Driver's License]" by providing "false identification" and used this documentation to open his accounts at Salin Bank. Hubbs's completed report harped on the fact that Javier was an "illegal alien." At this point, Salin Bank seems to have considered firing Kristi. A draft "Termination Notice," which identified Kristi's complicit behavior in Javier's alleged fraud as the reason for her firing, was circulated among the human resources department and Novotny on February 13. This notice, however, was never signed or sent to Kristi.

On February 19, Kristi and her attorney attempted to attend a scheduled meeting with Salin Bank representatives regarding the ongoing investigation. The Bank, however, refused to admit Kristi's attorney to the meeting, stating that the meeting was a "private matter" related to internal "Salin Bank business." Kristi replied that she would not attend the meeting without her attorney. At an impasse, Kristi and her attorney began to leave. One of the Salin Bank representatives called after them, telling Kristi that by walking away from the meeting she was "abandoning [her] job." Kristi left nevertheless. That afternoon, Salin Bank drafted, signed, and sent a letter to Kristi, terminating her employment for refusing to participate in the meeting.

After Kristi was fired, Hubbs reported Kristi's activity to U.S. Immigration and Customs Enforcement. He also attended, on behalf of Salin Bank, a June 4, 2008, meeting of the Fraud Financial Network, which is a loose consortium of banks in northeast Indiana with the mission of rooting out fraud. According to the minutes of that meeting, Hubbs warned the other banks that Kristi was fired for opening fraudulent accounts for Javier, an "illegal immigrant who is now back in Mexico."

On September 11, 2008, Kristi filed suit in Indiana state court, claiming that Salin Bank had blacklisted her, defamed her, and intentionally caused her emotional distress. In 2009, she amended her complaint to add a claim for employment discrimination under Title VII, 42 U.S.C. § 2000e, *et seq.* In light of the new federal claim, Salin Bank removed the case to the U.S. District Court for the Southern District of Indiana. On February 15, 2011, the district court granted Salin Bank's motion for summary judgment on all claims.

II

We review the district court's grant of summary judgment *de novo.* In order to succeed on her claim for employment discrimination under Title VII, Kristi's first task is to show that she belongs to a statutorily protected class. Here, Kristi alleges that she was discriminated against because of her marriage to a Mexican citizen whose residence in the United States was unauthorized. Although we note that several of our sister circuits have ruled that Title VII's protections apply in such cases, the answer to this question is immaterial to Kristi's case, and so we leave it for another day.

Even assuming that Title VII applies to discrimination against one's spouse, Kristi's claim falls short because it is based on Javier's alienage, which is not protected by the statute. Even reading the record in the light most favorable to Kristi, it is beyond dispute that Salin Bank's actions were motivated by the fact that Javier's presence in the United States was unauthorized. Novotny first called Hubbs because she learned that Kristi's husband was an undocumented alien. Hubbs's report repeatedly noted that Javier was "smuggled into the US illegally," had "resid[ed] in the US illegally," was an "illegal alien" and an "illegal immigrant." The report barely notes Javier's Mexican heritage, making only passing references to Javier and Kristi's trips to Mexico. Even Hubbs's tirade in his first meeting with Kristi, disagreeable as it was, emphasized Javier's unauthorized status, not his Mexican ancestry. And the *coup de grâce is the fact that after Kristi was fired, Hubbs reported his findings to federal immigration authorities.*

There are several reasons why Salin Bank might have been concerned about Kristi's assistance to Javier in opening his accounts. Even assuming that Javier's ITIN was legitimate, Salin Bank might have wanted to avoid holding accounts for people who illegally reside in the United States. It would hardly advance the bank's business to be known as a resource for such aliens. Indeed, these concerns are reflected in the unsent draft Termination Notice of February 13. Hubbs initially highlighted his concern about possible bank fraud or other violations of banking regulations, but his decision to call U.S. Immigration and Customs Enforcement, rather than local or federal banking authorities, could be seen as an effort immediately to dissociate the bank from any irregularity. The record leaves no doubt that Salin Bank's decision to fire Kristi was not taken because Javier was Mexican, but because Javier was an undocumented alien.

The question, then, is whether Title VII guards against alienage-based discrimination. It does not. Discrimination based on one's status as an immigrant might have been included within the ambit of "national origin" discrimination, but that is not the path the Supreme Court has taken. The Court instead chose almost 40 years ago to adopt a narrower definition of national origin discrimination for purposes of Title VII. See *Espinoza v. Farah Mfg. Co.* Reviewing the statute's legislative history, the Court concluded that the term "national origin" was limited to "the country from which you or your forebears came." *Espinoza,* at 89. Thus, national origin discrimination as defined in Title VII encompasses discrimination based on one's ancestry, but not discrimination based on citizenship or immigration status. *Id.* The Court thought that it would have been inconsistent for Congress to have proscribed discrimination against aliens given the "long-standing practice of requiring federal employees to be United States citizens." *Id.* at 90. In light of these conclusions, the Court explicitly held that "nothing" in Title VII "makes it illegal to discriminate on the basis of citizenship or alienage." *Espinoza,* at 95.

We acknowledge that Congress took steps to limit *Espinoza's* holding when it enacted 8 U.S.C. § 1324b in 1996. That statute addressed the subject of unfair immigration-related employment practices; it reads as follows in the relevant part:

a. Prohibition of discrimination based on national origin or citizenship status

1. General rule

    It is an unfair immigration-related employment practice for a person or other entity to discriminate against any individual *(other than an unauthorized alien,* as defined in section 1324a(h)(3) of this title) with respect to the hiring, or recruitment or referral for a fee, of the individual for employment or the discharging of the individual from employment—

    A. because of such individual's national origin, or

    B. in the case of a protected individual (as defined in paragraph (3)), because of such individual's citizenship status.

But, even apart from the fact that Kristi did not seek to rely on this statute and the fact that it is not clear that it covers spouses, she cannot overcome the statute's explicit exclusion of unauthorized aliens from its coverage. Kristi has never contested the fact that Javier was not lawfully present in the country, and as far as we can tell, that is the end of it. Any discrimination suffered by Kristi was not the result of her marriage to a Mexican, but rather the result of her marriage to an unauthorized alien. Under the circumstances, the district court correctly granted summary judgment in Salin Bank's favor on Kristi's claims under federal law.

III

[*The court then addressed Kristi's state law claims.*]

***

IV

. . . Therefore, we Remand with Instructions to strike the names of the minor children from Salin Bank's memorandum, but we Affirm the judgment of the district court in all other respects.

Case Questions

1. The court determines that Kristi was fired based on Javier's status as an undocumented immigrant, not his Mexican nationality. Do you agree that termination based upon the citizenship status ("alienage") of a worker's spouse is less unethical or wrongful than termination based on a spouse's national origin?

2. Although the court does not deem it necessary to give an opinion on the issue in this case, several district courts have ruled that Title VII prohibits discrimination against a worker based upon the national origin of the worker's spouse or partner. However, this issue remains an unsettled legal area. If you were on a jury asked to decide if Title VII should apply to spouses or partners in national origin cases, how would you rule?

3. According to the court's dicta in this opinion, workplace tirades against "illegal immigrant" (like that of Mike Hubbs, Salin Bank's security officer) may be "disagreeable," but such speech is not evidence of impermissible discrimination unless the specific national origin of the immigrant or immigrant group is referenced. Do you agree that Hubbs's comments to Kristi Cortezano about her husband's citizenship status can be clearly distinguished from Javier's Mexican national origin? Why or why not?

 Case 4

Espinoza v. Farah Manufacturing Co., *414 U.S. 86 (1973)*

Cecilia Espinoza, a lawful Mexican alien, applied for a position at Farah Manufacturing's San Antonio Division. She was denied the position, however, as a result of Farah's policy to hire only U.S. citizens. The issue to be decided by the court is whether Title VII's proscription against discrimination on the basis of national origin protects against discrimination on the basis of citizenship. The Court determines that it does not.

Marshall, J.

***

The term "national origin" on its face refers to the country where a person was born, or, more broadly, the country from which his or her ancestors came.

There are other compelling reasons to believe that Congress did not intend the term "national origin" to embrace citizenship requirements. Since 1914, the federal government itself, through Civil Service Commission regulations, has engaged in what amounts to discrimination against aliens by denying them the right to enter competitive examination for federal employment. But it has never been suggested that the citizenship requirement for federal employment constitutes discrimination because of national origin. To interpret the term "national origin" to embrace citizenship requirements would require us to conclude that Congress itself has repeatedly flouted its own declaration of

policy. This Court cannot lightly find such a breach of faith. Certainly Title VII prohibits discrimination on the basis of citizenship whenever it has the purpose or effect of discriminating on the basis of national origin. However, there is no indication in the record that Farah's policy against employment of aliens had the purpose or effect of discriminating against persons of Mexican national origin.

Douglas, J., dissenting

It is odd that the Court which holds that a State may not bar an alien from the practice of law or deny employment to aliens can read a federal statute that prohibits discrimination in employment on account of "national origin" so as to permit discrimination against aliens.

Alienage results from one condition only: being born outside the United States. Those born within the country are citizens from birth. It could not be clearer that Farah's policy of excluding aliens is *de facto* a policy of preferring those who were born in this country.

Case Questions

1. Which argument, the majority's or the dissent, do you find more compelling?

2. What implications does this case have for hiring practices in parts of the United States where immigrants are prevalent?

3. If Espinoza could show that this policy, while arguably "facially neutral," actually impacts people of Mexican origin differently than people of American origin, wouldn't Espinoza have a claim for disparate impact?

 Case 5

U.S. Equal Employment Opportunity Commission v. MVM, Inc., Civil Action No. TDC-17-2864 *(D. Ct. Md. May. 14, 2018)*

The U.S. Equal Employment Opportunity Commission filed a suit against the defendant MVM claiming that MVM discriminated against a group of African employees on the basis of national origin discrimination. MVM is a security firm that employs security guards in Maryland, and the actions subject to the suit occurred under a contract for the National Institutes of Health. Approximately half of MVM's 400 personnel are "African or foreign-born Blacks." The court evaluates a number of issues in MVM's motion to dismiss, including MVM's argument that the complaint must be dismissed because discrimination based on "perceived" national origin is not cognizable. That section is included below.

Chuang, D.J.

* * *

BACKGROUND

In October 2013, MVM appointed James Smith as the project manager for the NIH contract. In that capacity, Smith was responsible for supervising, including on matters of discipline, the security personnel at each of the four campuses. . . . Within weeks of becoming project manager, Smith began complaining that there were "too many Africans" on the NIH contract, that he was not comfortable working with foreigners, and that he "couldn't understand their accents." He also stated his intention to reduce the number of Africans, including by refusing to hire them. Following these statements, MVM managers and supervisors who reported to Smith began mistreating employees who were African or perceived to be African, telling them to "go back to Africa," ridiculing their names and accents, calling them pejorative names

such as "African faggot," and instructing them not to speak in their native dialects.

During Smith's tenure, MVM also engaged in a variety of negative actions against African and foreign-born Black security personnel, including denying them leave, forcing them to work on their scheduled days off, forcing them to work extra hours beyond their scheduled shifts, assigning them to undesirable posts, subjecting them to heightened scrutiny, disciplining them more harshly than called for by its discipline policy, intimidating and threatening them with termination, and denying them union representation so as to facilitate the imposition of discipline, suspensions, and termination without cause. MVM also obstructed employees from complying with MVM policy. For instance, in November 2014, Smith prevented Ronald Desir, a foreign-born Black employee who speaks with an accent, from renewing his security credentials in order to justify his termination. MVM also fabricated incidents of misconduct and made false accusations of poor performance, such as in December 2014, when Smith falsely accused Anthony Stephens, another foreign-born Black employee who speaks with an accent, of failing to open a garage on time in order to justify his termination. After witnessing such treatment, a number of employees complained to MVM, including to McHale, about the discriminatory treatment of Africans and those perceived to be African. MVM responded to these employees' complaints by subjecting them to the same forms of mistreatment that they alleged to be discriminatory. The EEOC alleges that at least nine employees were terminated either for discriminatory or retaliatory reasons.

Once several African or foreign-born Black employees were terminated, including union leaders and the most senior African on the NIH contract, other such employees concluded that they, too, would face termination. Because termination would negatively affect their ability to retain their security clearances and thus their future job prospects, several of these individuals decided to resign. By late 2016, as a result of terminations and resignations, the number of Africans employed on the NIH contract had decreased by approximately 29 percent.

* * *

DISCUSSION

* * *

B. Perceived National Origin

MVM seeks to dismiss those parts of the Amended Complaint alleging discrimination on the basis of "perceived" national origin, presumably those allegations made by foreign-born Black employees who were perceived to be, but were not, of African origin. MVM argues that discrimination on the basis of perceived national origin is not a cognizable claim under Title VII.

Title VII prohibits discrimination based on an individual's "race, color, religion, sex, or national origin." Although the United States Court of Appeals for the Fourth Circuit has not addressed in a published opinion whether discrimination on the basis of perceived national origin is actionable under Title VII, several other circuits have held that it is. In *EEOC v. WC&M Enterprises, Inc.,* the plaintiff was subjected to a hostile work environment, including being called "Taliban" and "Arab" in a derogatory manner, even though he was, in fact, of Indian origin.

The court held that "a party is able to establish a discrimination claim based on its own national origin even though the discriminatory acts do not identify the victim's actual country of origin." Likewise, in *Jones v. UPS Ground Freight,* the court held that "a harasser's use of epithets associated with a different ethnic or racial minority will not necessarily shield an employer from liability." (considering derogatory references to the plaintiff as "Indian" even though the plaintiff was not Indian). *Cf. Fogleman v. Mercy Hosp., Inc.,* (stating that an "employer is still discriminating on the basis of religion even if the applicant he refuses to hire is not in fact a Muslim"); *Estate of Amos ex rel. Amos v. City of Page,* (finding that a white plaintiff had standing to assert a discrimination claim under the Equal Protection Clause when he was mistakenly believed to be Native American).

A judge in this District has also concluded that Title VII bars discrimination on the basis of perceived national origin. *Arsham v. Mayor & City Council of Balt.,* (holding that Title VII covers a claim that an individual of Iranian national origin and Persian ethnicity was subjected to discrimination because she was mistakenly thought to be from the Parsee ethnic group in India). Other district courts have reached the same conclusion. *See LaRocca v. Precision Motorcars, Inc.; see also Boutros v. Avis Rent A Car Sys., LLC,* (rejecting the argument that there was no discrimination because the plaintiff, who was subjected to anti-Arab statements, was actually of Assyrian ethnicity); *Zayadeen v. Abbott Molecular, Inc.,* (holding that a plaintiff subjected to derogatory comments that he looked and sounded like an character who is of Kazakhstan national origin could advance a national origin discrimination claim even though he was, in fact, of Jordanian national origin).

In reaching this conclusion, the *WC&M* and *Arsham* courts relied in part on EEOC regulations and guidance interpreting national origin discrimination to include discrimination on the basis of perceived national origin. In 1980, the EEOC promulgated a regulation defining "national origin," which is still in effect today. *See* 29 C.F.R. § 1606.1. Under that regulation, "national origin discrimination" includes, but is not limited to, "the denial of equal employment opportunity because of an individual's, or his or her ancestor's, place of origin; or because an individual has the *physical, cultural, or linguistic characteristics of a national origin group.*" *Id.* (emphasis added). The EEOC also issued guidelines stating:

> In order to have a claim of national origin discrimination under Title VII, it is not

necessary to show that the alleged discriminator knew the *particular* national origin group to which the complainant belonged .... [I]t is enough to show that the complainant was treated differently because of his or her foreign accent, appearance, or physical characteristics. *Guidelines on Discrimination Because of National Origin, 45 Fed. Reg. 85633 (Dec. 29, 1980).*

More recently, the EEOC issued guidance stating that "Title VII prohibits employer actions that have the purpose or effect of discriminating against persons because of their real or perceived national origin." U.S. Equal Emp. Opportunity Comm'n, *Enforcement Guidance on National Origin Discrimination* (Nov. 18, 2016). Thus, the EEOC interprets Title VII to prohibit discrimination based on perceived national origin. . . .

The EEOC's interpretation is also consistent with the language of the statute, which bars discrimination based on an individual's "national origin." When an employee is subjected to discrimination on the basis of "the physical, cultural, or linguistic characteristics of a national origin group," such as a foreign accent, it is entirely reasonable to conclude that the perpetrator of the discrimination is motivated by the employee's own national origin, even if that national origin is different from the one perceived by the perpetrator. For example, if an employer harbors discriminatory animus against individuals from Pakistan, if he acts on that animus to mistreat an individual of Indian national origin who has an accent and appearance that he perceives to be those of a Pakistani, but in fact are associated with India, it is reasonable to conclude that he has discriminated on the basis of the victim's Indian origin, because the discrimination is, in fact, triggered by the victim's Indian accent and physical features. *See LaRocca v. Precision Motorcars, Inc.* (finding that an Italian American plaintiff who was subjected to anti-Mexican remarks by a manager who had "ignorantly used the wrong derogatory ethnic remark" had endured discrimination based on his Italian national origin because his "Italian characteristics," including dark brown skin, were the "foundation" of the discrimination, such that "he would not have been subject to the alleged harassment if he had not been of Italian descent").

To conclude otherwise would be to allow discrimination to go unchecked where the perpetrator is too ignorant to understand the difference between individuals from different countries or regions, and to provide causes of action against only those knowledgeable enough to target only those from the specific country against which they harbor discriminatory animus. *See Arsham* (noting that it is "fundamentally abhorrent" to shield an employer from liability based on a mistaken perception of the victim's actual national origin because the discrimination is "no less injurious to the employee"). Such a perverse result runs contrary to Congress's intent in Title VII. *See Griggs v. Duke Power Co.* ("The objective of Congress in the enactment of Title VII is plain from the language of the statute. It was to achieve equality of employment opportunities and remove barriers that have operated in the past to favor an identifiable group of white employees over other employees."). Discrimination where the employer is mistaken in his belief that an employee is of a particular national origin is just as insidious as discrimination where the employer is correct, because the culpability of the employer and the hardship suffered by the employee are the same, and the employee is adversely impacted by a characteristic that Congress has decided should be irrelevant in the employment context.First, the textual argument. Section 213(f) of the FLSA states that "[t]he provisions of sections 206, 207, 211, and 212 of [the FLSA] shall not apply with respect to any employee whose services during the workweek are performed in a workplace within a foreign country. . . ." 29 U.S.C. § 213(f). Shannon Produce argues that this section bars plaintiffs' § 215(a)(3) retaliation claim because § 213(f) "explicitly limits the FLSA to conduct that occurs within the U.S"–including retaliation.

* * *

Accordingly, the Court will deny the Motion to Dismiss to the extent it seeks dismissal of claims based on perceived national origin.

Case Questions

1. The court found that it was entirely reasonable to conclude that the perpetrator of discrimination was motivated by the employee's own national origin or perceived national origin. Do you agree with the court's ruling

2. Does Title VII protect employees who have voluntarily resigned from their positions? Why might this be important?

3. Does Title VII always protect employees who have accents? Could James Smith's complaints about his employees' accents ever have been valid?

Chapter 8

Gender Discrimination

Source: National Archives and Records Administration (NWDNS-44-PA-911)

Learning Objectives

After completing this chapter, you should be able to:

LO1 Recite Title VII and other laws relating to gender discrimination.

LO2 Understand the background of gender discrimination and how we know it still exists.

LO3 List the different ways in which gender discrimination is manifested in the workplace.

LO4 Analyze a situation and determine if there are gender issues that may result in employer liability.

LO5 Define fetal protection policies, gender-plus discrimination, workplace lactation issues, and gender-based logistical concerns.

LO6 Differentiate between legal and illegal grooming policies.

LO7 List common gender realities at odds with common bases for illegal workplace determinations.

LO8 Distinguish between equal pay and comparable worth and discuss proposed legislation.

Opening Scenarios

SCENARIO 1

1 A discount department store has a policy requiring that all male clerks be attired in coats and ties and all female clerks wear over their clothing a short loose top provided by the store, with the store's logo on the front. A female clerk complains to her supervisor that making her wear the garment is illegal gender discrimination. Is it? Why or why not?

SCENARIO 2

2 A male applies for a position as a server for a restaurant in his hometown. The restaurant is part of a well-known regional chain named for an animal whose name is a colloquial term for a popular part of the female anatomy. Despite several years of experience as a server for comparable establishments, the male is turned down for the position, which remains vacant. The applicant is instead offered a position as a kitchen helper. The applicant notices that all servers are female and most are blonde. All servers are required to wear very tight and very short shorts, with T-shirts with the restaurant logo on the front, tied in a knot below their usually ample breasts. All kitchen help and cooks are male. The applicant feels he has been unlawfully discriminated against because he is a male. Do you agree? Why or why not?

SCENARIO 3

3 An applicant for a position of secretary informs the employer that she is pregnant. The employer accepts her application but never seriously considers her for the position because she is pregnant. Is this employment discrimination?

Statutory Basis

LO1 Recite Title VII and other laws relating to gender discrimination.

It shall be an unlawful employment practice for an employer—

(1) to fail or refuse to hire or to discharge any individual, or otherwise to discriminate against any individual with respect to his compensation, terms, conditions, or privileges of employment, because of such individual's . . . sex [gender] . . . [Title VII of the Civil Rights Act of 1964, as amended. 42 U.S.C. § 2000e-2 (a).]

(1) No employer . . . shall discriminate between employees on the basis of sex by paying wages to employees . . . at a rate less than the rate at which he pays wages to employees of the opposite sex . . . for equal work on jobs the performance of which requires equal skill, effort, and responsibility, and which are performed under similar working conditions, except where such payment is made pursuant to (i) a seniority system; (ii) a merit system; (iii) a system which measures earnings by quantity or quality of production; or (iv) a differential based on any other factor other than sex. . . . [Equal Pay Act, 29 U.S.C.A. § 206(d).]

(k) The term "because of sex" or "on the basis of sex" includes, but is not limited to, because of or on the basis of pregnancy, childbirth, or related medical conditions; and women affected by pregnancy, childbirth, or related medical conditions shall be treated the same for all employment-related purposes, including receipt of benefits under fringe benefit programs, as other persons not so affected but similar in their ability or inability to work. . . . [Pregnancy Discrimination Act, 42 U.S.C. § 2000e.]

Note: Reread the Preface regarding the use of gender terminology before reading this chapter.

Does It Really Exist?

LO2 Understand the background of gender discrimination and how we know it still exists.

What does a group of 25 attorney-mediators have to do with a swimsuit calendar? Good question. The Miami-based Florida Mediation Group has probably been asking itself that same question ever since it received a good deal of flak for having its name emblazoned across one of several themed calendars given away as gifts to clients.

Of all the bases for employment discrimination we cover in class and in consulting, gender seems to be the one that is most difficult for students to believe exists. This, despite the fact that a 2010 Harris Poll of 2,227 adults surveyed online found that 7 in 10 Americans say women often do not receive the same pay as men for doing exactly the same job (a fact that still exists today), 63 percent agreed that the United States still has a long way to go to reach complete gender equality, and 74 percent believe there are more pressing issues to fix first.[1] As Stuart J. Ishimaru, then-acting chairman of the EEOC stated: "Sex discrimination against males and females alike continues to be a problem in the 21st century workplace."[2]

In 2019, *Time* magazine published a quote from 19th-century naturalist, biologist, and geologist Charles Darwin, of *Origin of Species* and evolution fame, in which he said that women were inferior because they had inferior brains and therefore did not have the right to assume a powerful role in society.[3] Did you know that in 1928, L. Frank Baum's *The Wonderful Wizard of Oz* was banned by the Chicago Public Library in part because it showed women (including witches) as leaders?[4]

So, despite tremendous gains, coming from such a different place, women, especially, have had serious obstacles to overcome to be fully accepted as full participants in society. This is especially true in the workplace. In fact, as recently as January 2014, in his State of the Union address, dismissing policies and stereotypes that prevent women and men from getting the same opportunities and salaries in the workplace, President Obama said

> Today, women make up about half our workforce. But they still make 77 cents for every dollar a man earns. That is wrong, and in 2014, it's an embarrassment. A woman deserves equal pay for equal work. She deserves to have a baby without sacrificing her job. A mother deserves a day off to care for a sick child or sick parent without running into hardship—and you know what, a father does, too. It's time to do away with workplace policies that belong in a "Mad Men" episode. This year, let's all come together—Congress, the White House, and businesses from Wall Street to Main Street—to give every woman the opportunity she deserves. Because I firmly believe when women succeed, America succeeds.[5]

It is now 2020, and this remains the state of things. New research indicates that the typical statistic that women earn 80 cents to a man's dollar is actually very much underestimated;[6] their median yearly income is $9,909 less than a man's.[7] Women make up only 6 percent of Standard & Poor 500's CEOs.[8] We understand that if you are not used to thinking that it exists, sometimes it can be difficult to recognize gender discrimination when it plays itself out in the workplace. Gender is a part of our everyday life, and so much related to it is based on stereotypes, customs, mores, and ideas that we learn from birth, given the history of how women have been perceived, as noted previously. Gender discrimination comes in many different forms. The wage gap and #MeToo may be the ways that have been uppermost in your mind because of media attention recently. That is why in this chapter we will provide many different manifestations of gender discrimination for you to examine so you can gain exposure. As a manager, supervisor, or business owner, we want you to be able to analyze fact situations in the workplace as they occur in order to determine if there is potential liability.

Suppose a woman is required by her employer to wear two-inch heels to work. Doing so causes her to develop bunions, which can only be removed by surgery. After surgery she is ordered by her doctor to wear flat shoes for two months. Her employer refuses to permit her to do so. Left with no alternative, she quits. The employer imposes no such requirement on male employees. When you realize that the employer's two-inch-heels policy cost the woman her job and that had she been male this would not have happened, it becomes more obvious that the policy is discriminatory on the basis of gender.

Remember the wires of the birdcage in Exhibit 3.5? Those wires are probably what the members of the executive board of the Miami-Dade chapter of the Florida Association of Women Lawyers were thinking of when they registered their objection to the calendar mentioned in the opening paragraph of this section. "We believe this type of advertising, whether picturing men or women, does not promote dignity in the law and is inappropriate when circulated by an organization that serves the legal community."[9]

Perhaps you got some sense of how widespread the issues are and how frustrating they can be for those who operate under them when, on January 21, 2017, you watched (or participated) as hundreds of thousands of men and women around the globe marched and demonstrated because of their anger over what they viewed as the incoming administration's refusal to even acknowledge their concerns about gender discrimination. Or perhaps you watched on March 8, 2017, International Women's Day, as again, people demonstrated around the world the need to address these pressing issues. There have been many huge marches each year since. And 2017 also marks the year the Equal Rights Amendment (ERA) was revived after not receiving the 38 states it needed for ratification by 1982. In January 2020, Virginia became the 38th state to ratify, and litigation is in process to lift the ratification deadline, which was rarely, if ever, imposed on other constitutional amendments. After all, the Madison Amendment concerning Congressional raises was passed by Congress in 1792 and was not ratified until 203 years later in 1992!

One of the takeaways from the demonstrations and the wide-ranging issues involved is how many issues gender discrimination and disparities touch and how ingrained they are. It is not difficult to discriminate on the basis of gender if an employer is not aware of or sensitive to the issues involved. (See Exhibit 8.1, "Gender-Neutral Language?" and Exhibit 8.2, "Woman/Female/Girl—What's in a Name?: The HR Girl.") Once again, as with race discrimination, vigilance pays off. This chapter will address workplace gender discrimination in general, including pregnancy discrimination, lactation policies, fetal protection policies, and equal pay. Sexual harassment, sexual orientation, and gender identity discrimination are

Exhibit 8.1 *Gender-Neutral Language?*

Attorney Harry McCall, arguing before the U.S. Supreme Court, stated, "I would like to remind you gentlemen" of a legal point. Associate Supreme Court Justice Sandra Day O'Connor asked, "Would you like to remind me, too?" McCall later referred to the Court as "Justice O'Connor and gentlemen." Associate Justice Byron White told McCall, "Just 'Justices' would be fine."*

***

According to the National Conference of State Legislatures, nearly half of states have moved to make the language in their official documents gender-neutral. Changes include replacements such as *handwriting* for *penmanship, first-year student* for *freshman,* and *outdoor enthusiast* for *sportsman.* The state of Washington finds it more difficult to replace *airman, manhole,* and *manlock.*†

MIT, USC San Diego, and University of Pottsdam linguists and cognitive scientists found that Americans were reluctant to use the word *she* in the context of a hypothetical president and that reading the word, when it referred to a future president, caused subjects "considerable disruption" in reading time. The study was based on experiments conducted during the run-up to the 2016 election. "People had difficulties reading 'she' even if the text had previously used 'she,' showing how persistent and deeply ingrained this bias is," said one of the scientists. Bennett, Jessica, "She's the Next President. Wait, Did You Read That Right?," *The New York Times* (January 24, 2020), https://www.nytimes.com/2020/01/24/us/politics/woman-president-she-her.html.

Source: *Newsweek* (November 25, 1991), p. 17.

† *Time* (February 18, 2013), p. 12.

Exhibit 8.2 *Woman/Female/Girl—What's in a Name?: The HR Girl*

Charlene Fitzpatrick and Bennett-Alexander met when they were invited to appear as panelists to discuss the issue of "Working in Male-Dominated Spaces" during an International Day of the Girl program. Intrigued that a highly qualified, vivacious, tremendously successful woman who owned her own human resources firm (and thus would clearly be in touch with gender issues) would include in her business name a term that is generally deemed to demean, belittle, and minimize women, Bennett-Alexander asked her about it. The conversation proved so productive that it is provided here for your information. Fitzpatrick's insightful response gives us lots to think about when it comes to the issue of language and gender.

***

Why is the term *girl* OK with you?
Words are exciting and spark varying feelings and emotions depending upon their use and the intention behind the use of the words. Understanding

that the word *girl* has historical significance that can be viewed as negative. It has always been used between my friends, and I like a term of endearment when we greet one another and in conversation. To me when I use the term, I feel a youthful girlie playfulness that can be serious, and depending upon the situation, it gives me a feeling of being powerful. I am sure if the term were negatively directed at me, I would have a different set of feelings and emotions regarding its meaning.

Why did you choose to use the term *girl* in naming your business?
The HR Girl was not the name of my business when it started back in 1998. I was very blessed with multiple clients and extremely busy working in my business when it began. In those early years, I did not take the time or utilize a process to develop a business name that fit me, my personality or the intention of my business. I needed to give it a name to incorporate. Because I am the face of my

(continued)

Exhibit 8.2 *continued*

company, I was often greeted as here comes HR or the HR lady. Around 2003 because of the affinity I have for the term *girl*, I began referring to myself as the HR Girl. Around 2008 it became the official name of my company. I like the name; it fit me and my personality. It describes what my company does in a succinct manner, and it was and remains memorable.

Since this is the name of your business and as such you can't explain to everyone who sees it your reasons for using the term *girl*, which has been viewed as one that demeans women by continuing to keep them viewed by the public as less than full, empowered contributors to the workplace as men are,

do you think that using the word *girl* in naming your business adds to that perception?

No, I do not. While I understand the historical significance of the term, I view it totally differently. I can and always will only be able to control my own thoughts and perceptions and do not attempt to control those of others. Those who see it and do not have the opportunity to engage with me can and will make their own choices regarding my company name. Individuals who I have the opportunity to engage with can choose to have a discussion with me or not. To date, that number of individuals who have wanted to discuss my company name has been extremely small. Specifically, the number of individuals has been less than 10 over a 10-year period.

three other types of gender discrimination and will be considered in subsequent chapters. Gender discrimination covers both males and females, but because of the unique nature of the history of gender in this country, it is females who tend to feel the negative effects of gender discrimination in the workplace more so than men, and the vast majority of EEOC gender claims are filed by women. Interestingly, however, during the 2008–2009 economic recession, more men than women lost their jobs,[10] with 78 percent of the jobs lost in the recession held by males.[11] The reason given is that the jobs women hold tend to be more stable but lower paying and that the male-dominated sectors such as construction, investment banking, and manufacturing tended to be hardest hit.[12] However, by March 2011, the Bureau of Labor Statistics reported that 90 percent of the jobs gained in the recovery had gone to men.[13] By May 2012, three years after the recovery began, women had gained only 16 percent of the new jobs created, and the workforce participation rate of women aged 45 to 54 had "dropped like a stone," with married women increasingly choosing not to work because the low-paying jobs they could get in areas like temporary help, health, leisure and hospitality, or private education simply are not worth the cost of day care, commuting, and so on.[14]

The fact is that white women are the single largest group of beneficiaries under affirmative action. Despite Charles Darwin's statement mentioned earlier that women were inferior because they had inferior brains and therefore did not have the right to assume powerful roles in society,[15] they seem to be gaining in all facets of life. The 2016 presidential cycle saw the first female selected as the presidential candidate of a major political party, and the 2020 cycle saw several female Democratic candidates. Janet Yellen headed up the U.S. Federal Reserve from 2014 to 2018 and was vice chair for four years before that, putting the world's largest economy in the hands of a woman. Three of the nine slots on the U.S. Supreme Court are held by women. Nancy Pelosi was the first female speaker of the U.S. House of Representatives. Admiral Michele Howard, retired, was the first African American four-star general, commander of a ship in the U.S. Navy, and vice chief of the Navy and commanded the Naval forces in Europe and Africa and Allied Joint Force Command Naples, captaining the *USS Porter* patrolling the international waters off the Black Sea, keeping an eye on Russian movements. Women head corporations and states, own businesses, and are members of the president's cabinet. The 2020 Super Bowl had its first female (and out lesbian) coach. The Tampa Bay Buccaneers became the first NFL team to have two female coaches. Yet when Marissa Mayer became CEO of Yahoo, it made headlines when she was chosen and pregnant. Facebook's chief operating officer, Sheryl Sandberg, was lauded for revealing she left work at 5:30 each day after becoming a parent. Beyoncé signed a $50 million endorsement deal with Pepsi. Walmart announced women-friendly plans aimed at helping women-owned businesses and workers. Women can now serve in combat, and the Navy now permits women to serve on submarines.[16]

Things seem OK. You think to yourself, who would be dumb enough to discriminate against women these days? It can be hard to believe that gender discrimination still exists when you go to school and work with so many people of both genders; you don't feel like *you* view gender as an issue, and it just seems like everything is OK. However, the 2019 EEOC statistics indicate that gender still accounts for nearly one-third, 32.4 percent, of substantive discrimination claims brought under Title VII.

At the same time we see these strides made in the gender sphere, we must keep in mind that only 30 women, 6 percent, headed up Standard & Poor's 500 companies as of March 2020, and even this can be tenuous, as 2016 saw the number decline more than 12 percent, from 24 the year before.[17]

When women now account for more than half the workforce,[18] those numbers may seem skewed.[19] See Exhibit 8.3 "Catalyst Showing Female CEOs in Fortune 500 Companies from 1995 to 2013." One factor in the way of females' progress is that even when women are imminently qualified, "male leaders tend to feel comfortable around other males, so they tend to network with, and promote, those of the same gender."[20] Also, in an issue that has grave implications in the workplace, "female leaders are caught in a Catch 22. If they adopt a command-and-control orientation, they are viewed as inappropriately masculine. If they act skillfully at solving disputes and settling conflicts, they are viewed as too feminine to be strong, directive leaders."[21]

"The Myth of the Ideal Worker: Does Doing All the Right Things Really Get Women Ahead?," a 2011 major study by renowned women's policy research group Catalyst, found that regardless of their career strategy, men seem to be paid for potential, while women seem to be paid for proven performance, and across all careers, men were more likely to reach senior executive positions than women. Men outpace women in rate of advancement and compensation growth from their first post-MBA job, and it widens to $31,258 by mid-career.[22] The Harvard

Exhibit 8.3 *Catalyst Showing Female CEOs in Fortune 500 Companies from 1995 to 2013*

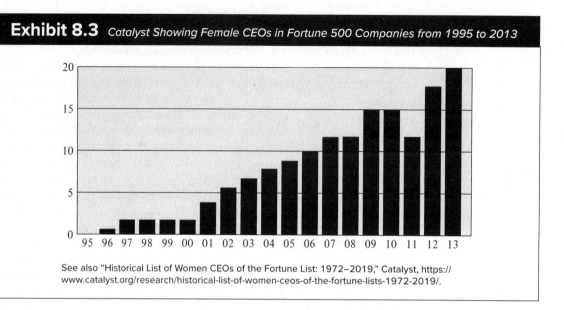

See also "Historical List of Women CEOs of the Fortune List: 1972–2019," Catalyst, https://www.catalyst.org/research/historical-list-of-women-ceos-of-the-fortune-lists-1972-2019/.

Business School class of 2013 underwent an experiment for their two years of study in which some of these issues were directly confronted and attempts made to reverse them. They noted that while all students admitted to the MBA program were similarly qualified, by the time they graduated, among other things, men had spoken in class more (where participation could be up to 50 percent of the grade), had higher grades, won more awards, and landed more prestigious jobs. By instituting new policies and procedures, a dramatic impact was made, but it remains to be seen whether it will carry over into the workplace.[23]

As a reality check, one of our female graduate students was told by an employer that if she was a man with her qualifications, he would pay her 50 percent more. Another was told she had a full-time job upon graduation in a company in which she had experienced a very successful internship, but only if she allowed the president of the company to set her up in an apartment so she could be available to him whenever he wished to have sex with her. She declined and started her job hunt all over again, not finding another job in her field until five months after she graduated. Gender discrimination is real and is not just something that happens to other people. It is real and must be addressed in the workplace. But first you have to be able to recognize it.

Even professionals can be caught off guard. In 1999, a gender-discrimination charge that started with eight female stockbrokers at Merrill Lynch alleging various forms of gender inequality, particularly economic discrimination, ballooned to 900 women and continued growing. "It's been a flood. I've been stunned. We were expecting 200–300 claims, but the calls are still coming in," said one of the lawyers representing the women. In 2004, arbitrators determined that it was standard operating procedure at Merrill Lynch to discriminate against women. It was the first time a Wall Street firm had been found to have engaged in systematic gender discrimination. Merrill Lynch spent more than $100 million settling close to 95 percent of the 900 or so claims. In subsequent press releases, the firm said this is not an accurate picture of the firm today.

Unfortunately, that was only the beginning of Wall Street's gender-based litigation. Cases continue to be brought by female employees against several Wall Street firms for the same types of discrimination that cost Merrill Lynch so much. In 2010 women filed EEOC claims against Goldman Sachs investment bank, alleging systematic discrimination against women including pay and promotions.[24] Eight years later in 2018 the judge allowed 2,300 women to proceed with their class action against one of Wall Street's largest banks. At least 58 women have joined in a 2009 suit filed by the EEOC against financial services and media company Bloomberg, founded by former New York mayor and 2020 presidential Democratic candidate hopeful Michael Bloomberg, claiming pregnancy discrimination.[25] Women at Citigroup, Inc., filed a class action for gender discrimination alleging they were laid off in the 2008 recession as part of the firm's "glass ceiling" and lesser qualified or underperforming males were retained.[26] Morgan Stanley settled a gender-bias class action suit for $46 million; Putnam Investments was sued for its "ingrained culture of chauvinism," leading to demotions and firings based on gender, a claim that has been made against many, many companies since; Smith Barney was sued for a pattern and practice of gender discrimination against its female financial consultants; and Wall Street bank Dresdner Kleinwort Wasserstein Securities, LLC, was sued for $1.4 billion by female employees who alleged they were hired as "eye candy," subjected to *Animal House*–like antics, passed over for promotions, and generally treated like second-class citizens.

Clearly, Merrill Lynch's $100 million message was not heard by all. In fact, it was not even heard by Merrill Lynch. In 2009 another group of women sued Bank of America, which acquired Merrill Lynch, alleging Bank of America had paid them substantially lower bonuses than men based on information from Merrill Lynch that BOA knew was discriminatory.[27] The next year, three female financial advisors filed a class action lawsuit against BOA Merrill Lynch alleging a pattern and practice of gender discrimination in account distributions, partnership opportunities, up-front money, pay-out rate, other benefits in its compensation plan, and opportunities for brokers to increase their income.[28] The case involving roughly 4,800 women who worked for Bank of America and its subsidiary Merrill Lynch from 2007 onward was settled for $39 million in 2013.[29] However, similar charges were made in 2016 when a senior female fixed-income banker sued BOA for $6M, alleging she was paid less than half the salary of similarly situated men there and made to feel unwelcome in their "subordinate 'bro club' of all-male syncophants."[30]

But Wall Street is hardly alone. A $100 million class action lawsuit filed by a female partner at the law firm of Chadbourne & Parke alleged an "all-male dictatorship."[31] In 2018 Microsoft's 8,600 current and former employees were denied class action status, but the Ninth Circuit is reviewing the decision on appeal. Nike was sued for gender-based pay discrepancies in 2018 and in 2019 lost its attempt to scale back the class action suit. In 2015, the EEOC contacted female directors in Hollywood to investigate gender discrimination in the television and film industry.[32] In November 2019, the courageous sexual harassment pioneer Anita Hill began heading head up the Hollywood Commission on Eliminating Sexual Harassment, and in February 2020, she said that the commission intends to "change the system that allows harassment and bias."[33] Silicon Valley and the technology industry have been having a rough time of it for the past few years as well, with several high-profile cases that have resulted in ugly publicity even when the companies end up winning the case. Venture capitalist Ellen Pao created a sensation in 2015 as the first woman to challenge the "boys club" in open court rather than settle. She alleged that she was passed over for promotions, kept out of meetings, barred from work trips, and not invited to important Kleiner Perkins events because "[i]t was said that if there were women there, the conversation would be tempered and it was because women kill the buzz."[34] Pao eventually lost her lawsuit but opened the door for other women to challenge similar treatment in other tech and other companies.

Cases have been filed for everything from a female animal handler terminated for refusing to expose her breasts to a 300-pound gorilla who had a "nipple fetish"[35]; to a female global transaction group director on track to become a managing director who sued for being terminated a month after she filed suit for gender discrimination and sexual harassment alleging she was Mommy-tracked after taking maternity leave[36]; to the Clearwater, Florida, Fire & Rescue chief being charged by the EEOC with gender discrimination for ordering the department's six female firefighters to stay away from structure fires amid reported threats that their male colleagues might not protect them[37]; to a man suing in California because there is no convenient, easy, comparable way for him to take his wife's name when they marry as it is for her to take his.[38] In June 2019, Dr. Frances Collins, head of the National Institutes of Health (NIH), said he would decline to speak at conferences that do not include enough women.[39]

intersectionality
Experiencing more than one type of discrimination at a time, e.g., that of being Black and female.

Add race to the gender mix and it gets even worse. Known as **intersectionality**, 2015 University of California at Hastings research found that while the overwhelming majority of women in science, technology, engineering, and math (STEM) fields experience sexism, women of color are put in "double jeopardy with a full 100 percent of the interviewees reporting gender bias, compared to 93 percent of white women."[40] An American Bar Association study on women of color in law firms, commissioned after a National Association for Law Placement study found that 100 percent of female minority lawyers left their jobs in law firms within eight years of being hired, found that 44 percent of the women reported being passed over for desirable assignments (compared to 2 percent for white men), 62 percent said they had been excluded from formal and informal networking opportunities (compared to 4 percent of white men), and 49 percent reported being subjected to demeaning comments or other types of harassment at their firms.[41]

Equal Pay Day is the date the average female employee has to work in order to earn as much as her white, non-Hispanic male counterpart earned by the close of the year before. For 2018, Equal Pay Day for Pacific Islander women was March 5, 2019. For white women, the date was April 2, 2019. For African American women, it was August 22, 2019. African American women are paid 61 cents for every dollar made by a white non-Hispanic male, or $23,000 a year less and more than $900,000 over the course of a 40-year career. For Hispanic women, it is 53 cents. Despite the fact that more than 70 percent of Black women are the primary breadwinners for their households, at this pace African American women would have to wait until 2130 to reach parity, according to the Institute for Women's Policy Research.[42]

Gender equality in the workplace is an ever-evolving area and does not occur in a vacuum. The issues in the workplace are only one part of a much larger environment of different, often unequal, treatment of individuals based on gender. Imagine the swimsuit calendar having bikini-clad males instead of females. Do you think it would have been received the same way? Manifestations of gender differences in society are the basis for differences in treatment in the workplace. They can be as diverse and far-flung as the group of Massachusetts teens suing the Selective Service System, arguing it is an unconstitutional violation of the Fifth and Fourteenth Amendments' Equal Protection Clause for females not to be subject to the draft just as men are, asserting that "if people want women's rights, they should want it wholeheartedly, including for women to have to fight in wars,"[43] to the protest over General Nutrition Center (GNC) dropping women from its GNC Show of Strength bodybuilding competition and replacing it with the International Federation of Body Builders (IFBB) Pro Figure competition[44]; from males suing bars for offering "Ladies' Night" discounts to women because such promotions discriminate against men[45] to the Congressional House Oversight and Government Reform Committee expressing support for the 2010 Restroom Gender Parity in Federal Building Act (H.R. 4869)[46]; from *Playboy* magazine running an article titled "Ten Conservative Women I'd Like to F—" to *Right Wing News* compiling a list of the "hottest conservative women in the news media"[47]; from Lawry's restaurant chain not allowing men to be servers because of a 1938 policy[48] to a female construction flag worker feeling compelled to wear a diaper to work because she was not allowed to find a bathroom in time at remote sites where men can find relief[49]; from female police officers being called "overtime whores"[50] to an athletic club charging men more than women[51]; from female playwrights in New York complaining at a standing-room-only town hall meeting with producers that men's plays in the 2008–2009 season were produced at four times the rate theirs were[52] to Club Med's "Ladies Fly Free" travel promotion[53]; from a temp worker alleging she was fired because she was "too hot" (such cases are on the rise)[54] to the U.S. Justice Department charging that the Chicago Fire Department discriminated against women by requiring them to pass physical tests that favored men[55]; and from female astronauts saying they have fewer opportunities to fly in space than men in part because of the strict lifetime radiation exposure restrictions[56] to the NBA facing a $3 million gender discrimination case brought by working mothers.[57] And let us not forget the female employee of Christian College who was fired for premarital sex because she was pregnant, and her job was given to her boyfriend, the father of their child[58] or the single mother who pushed the school district to end its tradition of mother–son baseball games and father–daughter dances based on a law prohibiting gender discrimination in "any and all other school functions and activities."[59] And, of course, no discussion would be complete without a mention that in 2017, the Equal Rights Amendment was revived and is being fought over as we write this. "Equality of rights shall not be denied or abridged by the United States or by any State on account of sex." Does it surprise you that something you thought was a given has been debated for decades and is still the basis of deep disagreement? Is it any surprise that without such a bedrock, foundational manifestation of this concept, the information provided would paint the picture it does? Agree with them or not, think they have merit or not, the more examples you see of how gender discrimination can be manifested, the more attuned you will be to potential liability when you view activity in the workplace that may result in Title VII violations.

Of course, it goes without saying that gender differences also find their way into the workplace through lower pay for women, even though studies show that 87 percent of men support equal pay for equal work[60]; women being consigned to lower-paid pink-collar jobs (women make up nearly half the U.S. workforce, yet almost two of every three people earning minimum wage are female)[61]; women being hassled, not promoted, or not given the same assignments and training or other opportunities as men in jobs traditionally held by men; or men not being hired for traditionally female jobs such as Hooters' servers.

Despite federal and, in some cases, state law, the need for lactation facilities for nursing mothers has become a growing area of workplace concern despite laws demanding it. Increasing male employee interest in balancing work and family also has found its way into the workplace. The first gender-based Family and Medical Leave Act (FMLA) claim involved a new father who won $40,000 after being denied appropriate FMLA leave to take care of his premature baby and seriously ill wife.[62] Many cases have followed, and paid leave is being debated, as well it should be, since the United States is one of the only developed countries without it.

In 2007, the EEOC issued guidelines on "caregiver responsibility" discrimination, also known as "caregiver bias" or "family responsibility discrimination" (FRD).[63] The EEOC issued the guidelines because it realized the growing issue of the disparate impact that the conflict between work and family had on both male and female employees, though it noted that since most caregiving responsibilities fall on women, such discrimination has a disparate impact on them. That is, because of their caregiving responsibilities, women are more likely to suffer adverse employment actions taken against them, such as diminishing workplace responsibilities, failure to be promoted or trained, exclusion from decision-making channels, or other actions stemming from the idea that if employees are also caregiving, then they are less likely to be dependable, competent employees who can live up to their full workplace responsibilities.

In 2013, the EEOC issued a new fact sheet with guidelines to employees who are victims of domestic violence, dating violence, sexual assault, and stalking, saying it could be the basis for employers' engaging in workplace violations of protective laws based on gender, sexual harassment, and disabilities.[64] Wonder what these issues have to do with gender discrimination? Women are more likely to be the victims of these issues and therefore the fallout from them, such as missed work for medical reasons and police and court follow-up as well as termination for fear the perpetrator will come to the workplace. Twenty-six state and local jurisdictions now have laws concerning domestic violence in the workplace.[65]

As women have increasingly entered the workforce since passage of Title VII, the focus of claims of gender discrimination has more recently shifted away from hiring discrimination toward on-the-job issues such as equal pay, promotions, harassment, pregnancy leave, lactation policies, caregiver responsibilities, and domestic violence. Eric S. Dreiband, former EEOC general counsel and now Assistant Attorney General for Civil Rights at the U.S. Department of Justice, stated that this reflects "new issues erupting in a diverse workforce. As blatant discrimination decreased, other areas like harassment increase."[66]

Viewed in this context, it then comes as no surprise that in the past few years, in addition to the substantial sums paid out by Wall Street for gender discrimination and claims filed for everything from the setting of car insurance rates, sexist and exclusionary language used in creating artificial intelligence and Facebook ads, teaching evaluation differences based on gender, insurance rates unnecessarily based on gender, dismissal for leaking menstrual blood at work, research discoveries such as women more sensitive to pain and differences in office thermostat temperatures, claims of differences in assignments for female movie stunt performers, and a female general counsel being made to serve cake to men:

- Platinum P.T.S. was required to pay an employee $100,000 for firing her after she requested leave to deal with a miscarriage.[67]

- The Clifford Chance law firm issued a memo called "Presentation Tips for Women," containing 163 points. Among them "wear a suit, not your party outfit," "think Lauren Bacall, not Marilyn Monroe," "don't giggle," "no one heard Hillary the day she showed cleavage," "don't tilt your head," and "pretend you're in moot court, not the high school cafeteria."[68] Big Four accounting firm Ernst & Young had complaints from employees about a similar training session in 2019.

- Novartis Pharmaceutical Corporation was ordered to pay $250 million in compensatory damages and $3.3 million in punitive damages to female sales representatives for discrimination in pay and promotions and because of pregnancy despite the fact that for the past 10 years it had been declared one of the 100 best companies by *Working Mother* magazine.[69]

- Toshiba's U.S. unit was sued by its female employees for $100 million, alleging systemic discrimination in pay and promotions and a pervasive atmosphere of women being required to be submissive to men.[70]

- A court upheld a $2 million award against Walmart to a female pharmacist who was fired for asking to be paid the same as her male colleagues.[71]

- Outback Steakhouse was made to pay $19 million to thousands of women at hundreds of its restaurants nationwide because they hit a glass ceiling and were denied favorable job assignments that were required for them to be considered for top management positions, and they could not get into the higher profit-sharing positions.[72]

- Wells Fargo Bank reached a settlement with the Office of Federal Contract Compliance Programs (OFCCP) to pay $32 million compensation for discrimination against women.[73]

- Home Depot agreed to pay $5.5 million to resolve a class action suit alleging, among other things, gender discrimination in its Colorado stores.

- The Palm Steak House agreed to a $500,000 settlement for failing to hire women to wait tables at its 29 restaurants because males, who could make up to $80,000 per year, including tips, were viewed as more prestigious.[74]

- At the time when Washington was the only state in the country that could boast that its governor was female, as were both of its U.S. senators, four of its nine state supreme court justices, and roughly a third of its state legislators, Seattle-based aeronautical giant Boeing agreed to pay $72.5 million compensation for gender-based discrimination against its female employees.

- A University of California lab agreed to pay $9.7 million to 3,200 women to whom it had paid less wages and whom it had promoted less often than male employees.

- Costco Wholesale Corp., with a workforce of 78,000, was sued by about 650 women in a class action suit alleging that the company did not announce openings for higher-paying managerial jobs, relying instead on a "tap the shoulder" policy of choosing managers. That is, top-level male managers would pick other males for high-level positions. Fewer than one in six of Costco's managers were women, while nearly 50 percent of its workforce is female.[75]

- Then, of course, there is Walmart, whose size alone puts it nearly in a class by itself. It is the world's largest retailer and the largest private employer in the United States. More than 70 percent of its hourly sales employees are women. In 2001, Walmart was sued for gender discrimination by Betty Dukes on behalf of about 1.6 million female employees. Walmart fought the issue of certifying the women as a class for 10 years, going all the way up to the U.S. Supreme Court. Both the district court and the lower court certified the class, but in *Dukes v. Wal-Mart Stores, Inc.,*[76] the U.S. Supreme Court in 2011 denied the class certification.[77] But Walmart's legal woes were not over. In June 2012, nearly 2,000 women once again sued Wal-Mart for gender discrimination. Once again alleging that Walmart systematically mistreats women in a variety of ways, including paying them less even though they may have more experience or outrank men, prohibiting women from advancing by denying them training, prohibiting them from working in departments traditionally staffed by men (positions that usually paid more), and not posting all management position openings.[78] In the aftermath, Walmart did things like announce pro-female policies and plans. The case is still not over. In July 2016, 15 years after the original suit was filed, Betty Dukes and four other women reached a confidential settlement agreement with Walmart, agreeing to dismiss their claims. The day before the agreement was filed in court, however, six other Walmart employees in the class intervened and requested that the agreement not be accepted because there were still significant issues. In February 2019, nearly 100 women filed suit accusing Walmart of abuse and discrimination in withholding raises and promotions. Some of the claims date back to the 1990s and 2000s, and the claimants say the problems still plague Walmart. Stay tuned . . .

Let's take a look at some of the statistics that might underlie these cases to see if they support the overall picture.

- Women make up 46.8 percent of the workforce, and 57 percent of women participate in the labor force.[79]

- Women earn more degrees than men and have for a long time. They have earned more bachelor degrees since 1982, more masters degrees since 1987, and more doctorates since 2006.[80]

- According to the U.S. Department of Labor, women earned 78.3 cents that of men in 2016, up from 62.3 cents in 1979 and 59 cents when the Equal Pay Act was passed in 1963. This is a 21.7 percent wage gap.[81]

- Forty-three percent of female employees work in the four most common female occupations: secretary, registered nurse, teacher, and cashier.[82] Paradoxically, a 2004 EEOC report[83] found that women have the lowest odds of being managers in nursing care facilities.

- For the fourth quarter of 2016, the median weekly salary of men was $927, while that of women was $758, or 81.8 percent of the median male salary. A 2007 report by the U.S. Census Bureau found that the gender-based wage gap is present in virtually every profession.[84]

- A March 2011 report released by the White House Commission on Women and Girls was the most comprehensive federal report on the status of women in the United States since 1963. Its statistical snapshot of women indicated that women earn 75 percent as much as men at all levels of educational attainment, with Hispanic women making 62 percent and Black women 71 percent. This is despite the fact that women have now passed men in education and are more likely than men to have college or graduate degrees. Women are also more likely to live in poverty, do more housework, and suffer depression and chronic health problems.[85]

- A study by Stephen J. Rose, an economist at the consulting firm of Macro International, Inc., and Heidi I. Hartmann, president of the Institute for Women's Policy Research, found that while the Bureau of Labor Statistics (BLS) reports that women earn about 77 percent of men's pay over the course of their careers, it is actually more like 44 percent. The researchers say the BLS statistics consider only full-time, year-round employees—a category only about 25 percent of women fit into over the course of their work life—and do not account for the roughly 75 percent of those who work only part-time at some point and dip in and out of the labor force to care for children or elderly parents. When the more accurate reality is used for calculation, the figure becomes 44 percent.[86] These differences in the way the determinations are made may account for the variations above between 75 percent and 80 percent.

- In 2019, Buffalo Wild Wings agreed to pay $30,000 to resolve three male claims that they were passed over for bartending jobs because of gender.

- A longitudinal study titled "Pipeline's Broken Promise" found that despite company-implemented diversity and inclusion programs instituted with the expectation of creating a talent pipeline where women would be poised to make rapid gains to the top, inequality remains entrenched. In the study of 4,143 MBA graduates from elite programs in the United States, Canada, Europe, and Asia, in those that companies count on for future leadership, women lagged behind men in advancement and compensation. Unless they are part of the 10 percent of women who begin their post-MBA career at mid-management or above, they do not achieve parity in position with men. They make on average $4,600 less on their initial jobs and continue to be outpaced by men in rank and salary. Men are twice as likely to hold CEO or senior executive positions and less likely to be in the lower positions where women are overrepresented. The findings held even when considering men and women without children as well as those who aspired to senior leadership positions. Needless to say, they found that, in general, men were more satisfied with their careers overall than women.[87]

- Women earn more high school diplomas, BAs, MAs, and doctorates than men, yet it is generally recognized that campuses are still predominantly male when it comes to professors, department heads, and other high-level administrators.[88]

- An American Association of University Professors' study of decades of research to cull recommendations for drawing more women into the science and technology fields found that though women have made gains, stereotypes and cultural biases are still in the way of their progress. In "Why So Few?" they found, for instance, that a female post-doctoral applicant had to publish three more papers in prestigious journals or 20 more in less prestigious journals to be judged as productive as a male applicant. The report showed that even as women earned a growing share of doctorates in the science and technology fields, they do not show up a decade later in a proportionate number of tenured faculty positions. After 310 years, Harvard tenured its first female math professor in 2010.[89]

- U.S. Department of Education data show that a year out of school, despite having earned a higher grade point average in every subject, young women will take home, on average, across professions, just 80 percent of what their male co-workers do.[90]

- Women have comprised about 50 percent of law students for over a decade and up to 45 percent of associate attorneys at the largest law firms, but only 20 percent of equity partners, 30 percent of non-equity partners, 47 percent of associates, 42 percent of non-partner-track attorneys (i.e., staff attorneys, counsel attorneys, etc.), and 3 percent of other attorneys not reflected in the above. Female associates make 89.7 percent of men's salaries and equity partners, 80 percent.[91]

- In looking at more than 3,000 global companies, Credit Suisse found that in 2015 there were 14.7 percent females, up by 54 percent since 2010.[92] The chief executive of Germany's largest bank, Deutsche Bank, said a woman on his board (there were none) would make the board "more colourful and prettier." Several European countries have instituted quotas, and others, including Germany, are considering them. In response, Deutsche Bank set proposed quotas for female participation.[93]

Given the statistics and situations we see reflected in the above items, the workplace discrimination litigation listed before it makes sense. The 1991 Civil Rights Act called for the establishment of a Glass Ceiling Commission to investigate the barriers to female and minority advancement in the workplace and suggest ways to combat the situation. In 1995, the U.S. Department of Labor released a study by the bipartisan commission. Findings were based on information obtained from independent studies, existing research, public hearings, and focus groups. The commission reported that while women have gained entry into the workforce in substantial numbers, once there they face all but invisible barriers to promotion into top ranks. "Glass ceilings" prevent them from moving up higher in the workplace. "Glass walls" prevent them from moving laterally into areas that lead to higher advancement. Research indicates that many professional women hold jobs in such areas as public relations, human resources management, and law—areas that are not prone to provide the experience management seeks when it determines promotions to higher-level positions. Since this report, other phenomena have occurred. "Glass cliffs" refer to women in leadership being brought in to help a company in desperate crisis, with the likelihood of failure being higher. "Glass escalators" refer to men entering traditionally female-dominated professions such as teaching and nursing (which accounted for nearly a third of men's job growth from 2000 to 2010)[94] and seeming to effortlessly glide to the top echelons in the workplace. Interestingly, transgender men, who have lived on both sides of the gender spectrum, have reported this to be true. They were overlooked as women and found it easier to progress in the workplace as men.[95]

The Glass Ceiling report found that segregation by both race and gender among executives and management ranks is widespread. A survey of top managers in Fortune 1000 industrial and Fortune 500 service firms found that 97 percent are white males. As part of their findings, a survey by Korn/Ferry International found that 3 to 5 percent of top managers are women. Of those, 95 percent are white, non-Hispanic. Further, women and minorities are trapped in low-wage, low-prestige, and dead-end jobs, the commission said. Not surprisingly, women polled by *The New York Times* overwhelmingly chose job discrimination as "the most important problem facing women today." Things have changed in the years since the comprehensive report was issued, but as you can see, the situation is still far from what most of us think of as a level playing field.

Our country, like many others, has a history in which women's contributions to the workplace have historically been precluded, denied, or undervalued. Prior to the 1964 Civil Rights Act, it was common for states to have laws that limited or prohibited women from working at certain jobs, under the theory that such laws were for the protection of women. Unfortunately, those jobs they were kept from tended to have higher wages. The effect was to prevent women from entering into, progressing within, or receiving higher wages in the workplace. In *Muller v. Oregon,*[96] which upheld protective legislation for women and justified them being in a class of their own for employment purposes, the U.S. Supreme Court stated that a woman must "rest upon and look to her brother for protection . . . to protect her from the greed as well as the passions of man." This is the view our laws took until the Civil Rights Act of 1964.

After women came into the workplace in unprecedented numbers out of necessity during World War II and performed traditional male jobs admirably, it became more difficult to maintain the validity of such arguments. This type of protective legislation was specifically outlawed by Title VII, and the glass ceiling, walls, cliffs, and escalators notwithstanding, women have made tremendous strides in the workplace in the fifty-five-plus years since the Civil Rights Act was passed. In evaluating those strides, keep in mind that women were virtually starting from scratch since there was little or nothing to prevent workplace discrimination before Title VII, so the barriers for women gaining entry into the workplace and the statistics reflected by that should, of course, be high.

Despite the fact that many of the strides made by women were made with the help of male judges, employers, legislators, and others, much of the cause of the inequity given is attitudinal. (See Exhibit 8.4, "Sexist Thinking.") Workplace policies generally reflect attitudes of management. In a national poll of chief executives at Fortune 1000 companies, more than 80 percent acknowledged that discrimination impedes female employees' progress, yet less than 1 percent regarded *remedying* gender discrimination as a goal that their personnel departments should pursue. In fact, when the companies' human resources officers were asked to rate their departments' priorities, women's advancement ranked last.[97] With women's income now being critical to the well-being of more than 70 percent of American families, 40 percent of primary/sole earners of households with kids, this is not a trivial issue.[98]

While the pay gap between men and women has been stubbornly resistant to closing, not all of it can be attributed to discrimination. In general, women tend to be acculturated differently, which causes differences in how they approach the workplace. A Girl Scouts study found that young women avoid leadership roles for fear they'll be labeled bossy[99]; women are four times less likely than men to negotiate a starting salary.[100] A Harvard study found that women who demand more money are perceived as "less nice."[101] In 2018, Harvard Business Review published research that said that a more recent and more detailed data set allowed them to investigate the question anew and they found women ask as often as men, they just do not get the raise. The percentage of males and females that feared the relationship with their boss or colleague was the same—14 percent. However, this was in Australia, not the United States.[102]

Exhibit 8.4 *Sexist Thinking*

An *Esquire* magazine poll asked men: "If you received $1.00 for every sexist thought you had in the past year, how much richer would you be today?" The median answer was $139.50. (We have never had a male student who didn't think the figure should be *much* higher.)

Source: *Parade Magazine* (December 1991), p. 5.

Interestingly enough, while the biggest gains under protective employment legislation in the past 55-plus years have been made by women, the truth is gender was not even originally a part of the Civil Rights Act. Gender was inserted into the civil rights bill at the last moment by Judge Howard Smith, a southern legislator and civil rights foe desperate to maintain segregation in the south who was confident that if gender was included in the bill legislating racial equality, the bill would surely be defeated. He was wrong. However, because of the ploy, there was little legislative debate on the gender category, so there is little to guide the courts in interpreting what Congress intended by prohibiting gender discrimination. To date, the EEOC has interpreted that gender discrimination also includes discrimination due to pregnancy, sexual harassment, gender identity, and sexual orientation. The pregnancy determination interpretation was turned into law through legislation (the Pregnancy Discrimination Act). The sexual harassment interpretation of gender in Title VII has long been accepted by courts as a type of gender discrimination. As you will see in the chapter on sexual orientation and gender identity, both of these are still in a precarious position, with the EEOC having determined that they are types of gender discrimination, yet no federal legislation has been enacted, the Trump administration's Department of Justice differs with the EEOC's position, and courts have rendered mixed decisions, with a case now pending at the U.S. Supreme Court.

See Chapter 2 to revisit key concepts.

The goal of a manager, supervisor, human resources employee, or business owner is to have workplace policies that maximize the potential for *every* employee to contribute to the productivity and growth of the workplace while minimizing or eliminating irrelevant, inefficient, and nonproductive policies that prevent them from doing so. The underlying consideration to keep in mind when developing, enforcing, or analyzing policies is that, no matter what we may have been taught about gender by family or cultural and societal mores, gender alone is considered by the law as irrelevant to one's ability to perform a job. By law, it is the person's *ability* to perform, *not* his or her *gender,* that must be the basis of workplace decisions. (See Exhibit 8.5, "Gender Realities.") As we shall see, there may be very limited exceptions to this rule if a bona fide occupational qualification (BFOQ) exists. It is not only the law, but it is in the best interest of any employer who is serious about maximizing production, efficiency, and profits, as well as minimizing legal liability for workplace discrimination, to recognize that gender discrimination, whether subtle or overt, is just plain bad business. After all, workplace turnover, morale, and defending against lawsuits cost the employer money, time, and energy better spent elsewhere. (See Exhibit 8.6, "Discrimination: Bad for Business and Employees.")

The aim of this chapter is to provide information about not only obvious gender discrimination but also what factors must be considered in making determinations about policies in "gray areas." This chapter provides the tools to use when developing, applying, or analyzing policies that may result in gender discrimination claims. You have already received a great start by being exposed to so very many different manifestations of gender discrimination in the pages leading here and having your eyes opened to the realities of the larger context in which gender operates around you every day.

Exhibit 8.5   *Gender Realities*

Due to the particular historical development of gender in our country, there are many stereotypes about gender that affect how those of a given gender are perceived. Here are some of the stereotypes we have actually heard from managers and supervisors. These stereotypes greatly impact how employees of a given gender are perceived in the workplace. See if any are familiar.

- Women are better suited to repetitive, fine-motor-skill tasks.
- Women are too unstable to handle jobs with a great deal of responsibility or high pressure.
- Men make better employees because they are more aggressive.
- Men do not do well at jobs requiring nurturing skills such as day care, nursing, elder care, and the like.
- When women marry, they will get pregnant and leave their jobs.
- When women are criticized at work, they will become angry or cry.
- A married woman's income is only extra family income.
- A woman who changes jobs is being disloyal and unstable.
- A woman cannot have a job that requires her to have lunch or dinner meetings with men.
- Women cannot have jobs that require travel or a good deal of time away from home.

Exhibit 8.6   *Discrimination: Bad for Business and Employees*

JURY TELLS NBA TO PAY FEMALE REFEREE $7.85 MILLION

Read what happened when a female rose to number two on the list of those in line to officiate in the NBA, only to be repeatedly passed over:

Sandra Ortiz-Del Valle sued the National Basketball Association (NBA) for gender discrimination for passing her over as a referee and handed the NBA its first discrimination case loss when the federal jury awarded Ortiz-Del Valle $7.85 million, $7 million of which was punitive damages. (The award was later reduced by a judge to $350,000.) Ortiz-Del Valle had dreamed of being an NBA referee for years but kept getting passed over. Despite documents praising Ortiz-Del Valle as being "very knowledgeable about the rules" and having "excellent basketball officiating skills" and although the evaluator said, "I would not hesitate to recommend that at sometime in the near future she be considered to enter our training program," the NBA kept giving her varying reasons for denying her the position. The NBA denied any discrimination and said she was not hired because she failed to upgrade the level of competition in her officiating schedule despite being asked to and said she was out of shape. Ortiz-Del Valle claimed she had all the qualifications to be an NBA referee, including officiating in top men's amateur and professional basketball leagues for 17 years. She was the first woman in history to officiate a men's professional basketball game. Ortiz-Del Valle said she finally sued after continuously doing everything the league asked of her and not being promoted and then seeing men she trained hired by the league. "It was like they kept moving the basket," she said.

Source: *Ortiz-Del Valle v. NBA*, 42 F. Supp. 2d 334 (S.D.N.Y. 1999). Two years before the *Ortiz* case, the NBA named Violet Palmer as the first female referee in the NBA. Palmer was the first female to reach the highest competitive tier as a referee in a major U.S. professional sport. In November 2018, the NBA promoted its fourth and fifth female referees in league history. In 2019, the Tampa Bay Buccaneers became the first NFL team with two female coaches. Twenty-one years after the *Ortiz* case, the 2020 Super Bowl boasted its first female coach.

Gender Discrimination in General

LO3 List the different ways in which gender discrimination is manifested in the workplace.

See Chapter 2
to revisit key
concepts.

Title VII and state fair-employment-practice laws regarding gender cover the full scope of the employment relationship. Unless it is a BFOQ, gender may not be the basis of any decision related to employment. This includes the following, taken from actual situations:

- *Advertising* for available positions and specifying a particular gender as being preferred (see Exhibit 8.7, "Pre–Title VII Newspaper Want Ads for Females").

- Asking questions on an *application* that are only asked of one gender. For example, for background-check purposes asking the applicant's maiden name rather than simply asking all applicants if there is another name they may have used.

- Asking questions in an *interview* that are only asked of one gender. For example, asking female interviewees if they have proper day care arrangements for their children and not asking male interviewees who also have children or asking female applicants about reproductive plans and not asking males. (Yes, people actually do such things. Quite frequently, as a matter of fact.)

Exhibit 8.7 *Pre–Title VII Newspaper Want Ads for Females*

This classified ad excerpt, taken from an actual newspaper, is typical of those found in newspapers in the United States before Title VII was passed in 1964. For publication purposes, all names and phone numbers have been omitted. Title VII made it illegal to advertise for jobs based on gender.

FEMALE EMPLOYMENT	A REFRESHING CHANGE
Female Help Wanted 23	FROM your household chores! Use those old talents of yours and become a part-time secretary. You can earn that extra money you have been needing by working when you want. XXX has temporary positions open in all locations in town and you can choose what and where you want. TOP HOURLY RATES...NO FEE
ATTRACTIVE, NEAT APPEARING, RELIABLE YOUNG LADIES FOR permanent employment as food waitresses. Interesting work in beautiful surroundings. Good salary plus tips. UNIFORMS FURNISHED. Vacation with pay. Age 21-35 years. For interview appointment phone...	
SETTLED white woman who needs home to live in.	**Opening Soon...WAITRESSES...NO EXPERIENCE NECESSARY** Will train neat, trim, and alert applicants to be coffee house and cocktail waitresses. Apply at once.
LADY to run used furniture store on...	
GIRL FRIDAY If you are a qualified executive secretary, dependable, and would like a solid connection with a growing corporation, write me your qualifications in confidence...	**CLERK FOR HOTEL** CLERK for medium-size, unusually nice motor hotel. 6-day wk. Hours 3-11. Experience not necessary. Must be mature, neat, and refined. Call...

- *Requiring one gender to work different hours or job positions* for reasons not related to their ability or availability for the job. For example, not permitting women to work at night or not giving a promotion to a woman because it involves traveling alone.

- *Disciplining* one gender for an act for which the other gender is not disciplined. For example, chastising a female employee who is late for work because of reasons related to her children while not similarly chastising a male employee who is late because of a sick dog or chastising a female employee for cursing but not a male.

LO7 List common gender realities at odds with common bases for illegal workplace determinations.

- Not taking into consideration legitimate differences between genders that can mean that treating them exactly the same may produce an undue hardship for the other, such as refusal to provide proper restroom facilities for all employees on construction sites.

- Providing or not providing *training* for one gender while doing so for another. For example, providing training opportunities for career advancement to male employees and not to similarly situated female employees.

- Establishing *seniority systems* specifically designed to give greater seniority to one gender over another. For example, instituting a new seniority system that bases seniority on how long an employee has been working for the employer rather than how long the employee has been working in a particular department with the intent that, if the employer ever needs to lay off employees for economic reasons, more males will be able to retain their positions because females have been in the workplace a shorter time and thus have less seniority.

- *Paying* employees different wages based on gender, though the job one employee performs is the same or substantially the same as another. This may also violate the Equal Pay Act, which prohibits discrimination in compensation on the basis of gender for jobs involving equal skill, effort, or responsibility.

- Providing different *benefits* for one gender than for another. For example, providing spouses of male employees with coverage for short-term disabilities, including pregnancy, while not providing female employees with similar coverage for short-term disabilities for their spouses.

- Subjecting one gender to different *terms or conditions of employment.* For example, requiring female associates in an accounting firm to dress, talk, or act "feminine" when no comparable requirement is imposed on males aspiring to partnership.

- Subjecting one gender to continual unwanted teasing, joking, comments, angry statements, or general hassling or harassment to which the other gender is not subjected.

- *Terminating* the employment of an employee of one gender for reasons that does not serve as the basis for termination for an employee of the other gender. For example, terminating a female employee for cursing or fighting on the job when males engaged in similar activity are retained.

Clearly the antidiscrimination provisions are comprehensive. The law is broad enough to cover virtually every decision or policy that could possibly be made in the workplace. The scope of antidiscrimination laws is intentionally undefined so that decisions can be made on a case-by-case basis. Some of the examples above are not illegal per se. Rather, they elicit gender or gender-related information that can form the basis of illegal gender-based employment decisions—or at least make it appear as if that is the case; therefore, it is best to simply not do them.

The law takes a case-by-case approach to gender discrimination, so it is imperative to know what factors will be considered in analyzing whether gender discrimination has occurred. To the extent that these factors are considered when developing or implementing policies, it is less likely that illegal considerations or criteria will be used in making workplace decisions and policies. (See Exhibit 8.8, "Appearance-Based Discrimination.")

Exhibit 8.8 *Appearance-Based Discrimination*

We often discriminate against others without even realizing it. Since only those things prohibited by law are considered illegal, not all discrimination is actionable. However, look at the items below and note the gender differences:

- Very attractive men and women earn at least 5 percent more per hour than people with average looks.
- Plain women earn an average of 5 percent less than women with average looks.
- Plain men earn 10 percent less than average men.
- Most employers pay overweight women 20 percent less per hour than women of average weight.
- Overweight males earn 26 percent more than underweight coworkers.
- Of men with virtually identical résumés, the taller man will be hired 72 percent of the time.
- Men who are 6 feet 2 inches or taller receive starting salaries 12 percent greater than men under 6 feet.
- Married men earn, on average, 11 percent more per hour than men who have never married.
- White women 65 pounds overweight earn 7 percent less than those of median weight; there is little adverse effect of weight on the earnings

of Hispanic women, none on Black women, and virtually none on the wages of men.

- Better-looking men get more job offers, higher starting salaries, and better raises; good-looking women get better raises but not usually better jobs or starting salaries.
- Plain women tend to attract the lowest-quality husbands (as measured by educational achievement or earnings potential); beautiful women do no better in marriage than average women; looks don't seem to affect men's marriage prospects.
- The less attractive you are, the more likely you are to receive a longer prison sentence, a lower damage award, and a lower salary.
- Over his career, a good-looking man will make about $250,000 more than his least-attractive counterpart.
- In a *Newsweek* survey, 61 percent of hiring managers said it is advantageous for a woman to show off her figure in the workplace.
- In the same survey, 57 percent of corporate managers said landing a job is harder for an unattractive candidate.
- Beauty can also be a hindrance. A study in the *Journal of Social Psychology* found that attractive women are discriminated against when applying for jobs that are considered more

(*continued*)

Exhibit 8.8 *continued*

traditionally male, such as director of finance, mechanical engineer, prison guard, tow-truck driver, construction worker, or hardware salesperson. Attractive men were not subjected to the same discrimination.

Sources: Taken from Tuttle, Cameron, *The Paranoid's Pocket Guide* (Chronicle Books, 1997); Biddle, Jeff, and Daniel Hamermesh, "Beauty and the Labor Market,"

American Economic Review 83, no. 1174 (December 1994); John Cawley, *Body Weight and Women's Labor Market Outcomes* 2, no. 1, Joint Center for Poverty Research, 2000; Lithwick, Dahlia, "Our Beauty Bias Is Unfair," *Newsweek* (June 14, 2010), p. 20; Bennett, Jessica, "The Beauty Advantage," *Newsweek* (July 26, 2010), p. 47; Johnson Mandrell, Lisa, "Workplace Discrimination: Beauty Can Be a Beast at Work," AOL Jobs Original (August 9, 2010), http://jobs.aol.com/articles/2010/08/09/discrimination-gender-beauty-study/.

Recognizing Gender Discrimination

When analyzing employment policies or practices for gender discrimination, first check to see if it is obviously so. See if the policy excludes members of a particular gender from the workplace or some workplace benefit. An example is a policy that recently appeared in a newspaper story on local restaurants. One owner said that he did not hire males as servers because he thought females were more pleasant and better at serving customers. As *Wedow v. City of Kansas City, Missouri,* demonstrates, employers may engage in obvious gender discrimination and claim to be unaware of their policies' negative legal repercussions, even though it is a workplace held in high regard such as a fire department. This case is available at the conclusion of the chapter. The difference could also arise from an employer actually trying to be protective. In 2018 a female stunt performer for movies and television shows filed a claim with the EEOC to stop the practice of "wigging." Under the theory of safety, the industry had male stunt workers don wigs and women's clothing and perform stunts rather than allowing fully capable and qualified female stunt workers to perform, thus costing them jobs and income. The industry also substituted white stunt workers for minority stunt workers.

Not all cases may be as easy to recognize as gender discrimination when making workplace decisions or policies. (See Exhibit 8.9, "Illegal or Unfair?" and Exhibit 8.10, "Real Life in the Trenches of Traditionally Male Jobs: Chela Gutierrez, Firefighter.") It is easier to realize there is gender discrimination when the policy says "no women hired as guards" than when, as with the *Dothard v. Rawlinson* case (given at the end of the chapter), there is a policy, neutral on its face, saying all applicants must meet certain height and weight requirements to be guards, yet due to their genetic differences, statistically, most women do not generally meet the requirements. In the *Dothard* case, for the first time, the U.S. Supreme Court was faced with whether Title VII's gender discrimination provision applied to a policy using the seemingly neutral criteria of height and weight restrictions, which had long been an accepted basis for screening applicants for certain types of jobs such as prison guards, police officers, and firefighters, even though there was little or no

Exhibit 8.9 *Illegal or Unfair?*

Several courts have wrestled with the issue of what constitutes gender discrimination under Title VII. One issue that has arisen several times is whether it is illegal gender discrimination under Title VII if a female who is having a relationship with a supervisor receives a job or promotion over a qualified male who applies for the position. In *Womack v. Runyon,* 77 FEP Cases 769 (11th Cir. 1998), Paul Womack, having excellent credentials, experience, and training, applied for a carrier supervisor position in Waycross, Georgia. He was unanimously selected as the best qualified candidate by a review board, but O. M. Lee, the newly appointed postmaster of Waycross, instead appointed Lee's paramour, Jeanine Bennett. In rejecting Womack's Title VII claim of gender discrimination, the court held that Title VII did not cover claims of favoritism, saying that such decisions may not be fair, but they are not illegal under Title VII. According to an EEOC policy guidance, "Title VII does not prohibit . . . preferential treatment based upon consensual romantic relationships. An isolated instance of favoritism toward a paramour . . . may be unfair, but it does not [amount to] discrimination against women or men in violation of Title VII, since both [genders] are disadvantaged for reasons other than their genders."

legitimate reason for the criteria. The Court decided that Title VII did, in fact, apply to such facially neutral policies when they screened out women (later cases extended this standard to shorter and slighter ethnicities such as Hispanics and Asians as well) at an unacceptable rate and were not shown to be directly correlated to ability to do the job. Keep in mind that if the employer can demonstrate that these are truly job requirements, then the policy can be used, but that is rarely the case.

Being one of only a few women in a traditionally male job can be daunting, and even more so when the job itself is daunting. Chela Gutierrez is a firefighter who has been at it for 15 years. She still has the everyday challenges that come with being in her position. In Exhibit 8.10, she gives an example of how her being different, being female, shows up in everyday experience. The incident itself may not seem like a big deal, but think about the cumulative effect of experiencing such things day in and day out in a job that you love but that is, by its very nature, already stressful.

Exhibit 8.10 *Real Life in the Trenches of Traditionally Male Jobs: Chela Gutierrez, Firefighter*

"Pitch Isn't the Problem"

In this piece, a female firefighter, shares the frustration of being perceived differently than her male coworkers. At first she thought she was speaking too softly to be heard but came to realize that was not the issue. She learned that as a female, what she had to say was disregarded or not taken as seriously as male input, even when it solved the problem involved. Since her focus was getting the problem taken care of, her fix was simply to let a man deliver the information.

Of the approximately 330 firefighters working at my fire department, only 10 are female. We are never assigned at a station together. They spread us out to be seen at the different stations. So, it's normal to be the only woman on the fireground.

(continued)

Exhibit 8.10 *continued*

In recruit school I learned the guys couldn't hear me on the fireground. I figured it was my pitch, so I used my diaphragm to push my voice out an octave lower when I wanted to be heard in a noisy environment. After recruit school I learned that pitch has nothing to do with it.

When I was the driver of Engine 9, we responded to the smell of gas outside a structure. We arrived on scene with another engine company and a truck company—a total of 10 firefighters. A diverse group of men and me. The only woman. Each company investigated and reported to the captain their findings.

I noticed a patch of dead grass everyone walked over. It had a concrete island curb, like there may have been a gas station there years ago. I figured there may be gas left in the underground tanks. Just like the men, I reported my observations to the captain.

He said nothing.

Other firefighters gave their reports, were acknowledged, and were sent on another task.

I reported it to him again, and nothing. It was like he couldn't hear me. Since I was the only odd thing in the mix, I pulled one of the firefighters to the side, showed him what I saw, and told him to go tell the captain.

I watched from the sideline as the captain listened intently, looked at the spot, and got everybody focused on that area.

"Gender-Plus" Discrimination

LO5 Define fetal protection policies, gender-plus discrimination, workplace lactation issues, and gender-based logistical concerns.

See Chapter 2 to revisit key concepts.

"gender-plus" discrimination
Employment discrimination based on gender and some other factor such as marital status or children.

There are some situations in which the employer may permit the hiring of women but not if there are other factors present—for example, no hiring of women who are pregnant, are married, are over a certain age, have children under a certain age, or are unmarried with children. This is **"gender-plus" discrimination**. Of course, the problem is that such policies are not neutral at all because males are not subject to the same limitations. (See Exhibit 8.11, "Breastfeeding: A Gender-Plus Issue?")

Phillips v. Martin Marietta Corp.[104] was the first Title VII case to reach the U.S. Supreme Court and is still widely cited. *Martin Marietta* involved an employer's policy of not hiring women with preschool-aged children. No such policy applied to men with such children. The Court determined that unless the employer showed a legitimate basis for making the gender-based distinction, the policy could not stand. The employer did not keep all women out of the workplace, but only those with preschool-aged children. That is the "plus" involved. The dissent in the *Martin Marietta* case filed by Justice Thurgood Marshall refused to believe there could be any basis for proof of a justification for the policy. The Court evidently took Justice Marshall's dissent seriously because in the years after *Martin Marietta* the Court has not permitted BFOQs to be used in the way Marshall warned against. Keep in mind that, while BFOQs are permitted as a lawful means of discriminating based on gender, they are *very* narrowly construed. The employer is under a heavy duty to show that the gender requirement is reasonably necessary for the employer's particular business.

Exhibit 8.11 *Breastfeeding: A Gender-Plus Issue?*

A federal judge in New York dismissed a gender discrimination and disability suit brought by Alicia Martinez, a cable television producer, alleging that after returning from maternity leave, her employer, MSNBC cable, failed to provide her with a "safe, secure, sanitary and private" place to pump breast milk during work breaks and harassed her for complaining. [*Martinez v. NBC, Inc. and MSNBC*, 49 F. Supp. 2d 305 (S.D.N.Y. 1999).]

Regarding the ADA claim, Judge Kaplan said it was "preposterous to contend a woman's body is functioning abnormally because she is lactating." As to the Title VII claim, the court said this was not "sex plus" discrimination because "to allow a claim based on sex-plus discrimination here would elevate breast milk pumping—alone—to a protected status," and that could only be done by Congress. It was not plain gender discrimination under Title VII because "the drawing of distinctions among persons of one gender on the basis of criteria that are immaterial to the other, while in given cases perhaps deplorable, is not the sort of behavior covered by Title VII."

Note that a similar argument was struck down by Congress in enacting the Pregnancy Discrimination Act, where the court determined it was not illegal gender discrimination to treat pregnant employees differently, since only females could become pregnant.

On March 23, 2010, President Obama signed into law the Patient Protection and Affordable Care Act of 2010. Among its provisions was an amendment to the Fair Labor Standards Act of 1938 that requires an employer of more than 50 employees to provide reasonable break time for an employee to express breast milk for her nursing child for one year after birth each time the employee has a need to express milk. The employer need not compensate the employee unless she is expressing milk on a regular paid break. The employer must also provide a private functional space other than a bathroom in which the employee may express the milk. If the employer has fewer than 50 employees and these requirements present an undue hardship, then the employer need not comply with this law. If state law provides stronger provisions, then the employer must comply with state law.

All 50 states, the District of Columbia, Puerto Rico and the Virgin Islands have laws allowing breastfeeding in any public or private location. Employers are taking this issue quite seriously and creating policies to address lactation.

See National Conference of State Legislatures, http://www.ncsl.org/research/health/breastfeeding-state-laws.aspx.

In 2019, at Patagonia, an outdoor clothing and gear company, an employee breastfed her baby in a meeting, and her male vice president's response and Patagonia's family-friendly workplace went viral. Why? The VP said to her in the meeting, "There's no way to measure the ROI (return on investment) on that. But I know it's huge."[103]

Gender Issues

LO4 Analyze a situation and determine if there are gender issues that may result in employer liability.

As we have seen, many issues are included under the umbrella of illegal gender discrimination. From Facebook having an EEOC claim filed in 2019 by women seeking jobs claiming Facebook's advertising technology excludes women from the users who receive their advertisements for things like truck drivers or window installers, to a Georgia woman suing her employer for terminating her for leaking menstrual blood at work, to Buffalo Wild Wings for passing over men for bartending jobs, a female general counsel having to serve men cake at a function, or

Hoboken, New Jersey, Ernst & Young employees being told in a business success training session timeworn stereotypical items about how to succeed in business such as women are affectionate, cheerful, childlike and flatterable while men are analytical and assertive, act like leaders, and have leadership abilities, to research demonstrating that female professors receive lower evaluation scores from their students because of gender-based expectations students have, they cover many different manifestations. Following are some that are most prevalent. Keep in mind that many things we take for granted and dismiss as "that's just the way things are" may actually be illegal in the workplace. That is what Justice Marshall alluded to in his dissent in the *Phillips* case, which has been followed by subsequent courts. It is extremely important to keep this in mind as managers make workplace decisions and to guard against letting such thoughts be the basis of illegal Title VII decisions that result in employer liability.

Gender Stereotyping

gender stereotypes
The assumption that most or all members of a particular gender must act a certain way.

Much discrimination on the basis of gender is in some way based on **gender stereotypes** people hold. That is, workplace decisions are based on ideas of how a particular gender should act or dress or what roles they should perform or jobs they should hold, such as the stunt workers mentioned earlier. Clearly there was a perception by the stunt coordinators or those to whom they report that men should be chosen for certain stunts even though women were qualified and available to do them. An employer may terminate a female employee who is too "abrasive" or not hire a female for a job as a welder because it is "men's work." Stereotypes generally have little or nothing to do with an individual employee's qualifications or ability to perform. Workplace decisions based on stereotypes are prohibited by Title VII. (See Exhibit 8.6, "Discrimination: Bad for Business and Employees"; Exhibit 8.12, "Stereotyped Humor"; and Exhibit 8.13, "Stereotypes.")

As *Price Waterhouse v. Hopkins* (included at the end of the chapter) demonstrates, stereotyping frequently leads to actions that form the basis of unnecessary liability for the employer. It is senseless for employers to allow managers and supervisors who hold such views to cause liability that costs the entire company

---

Exhibit 8.12 *Stereotyped Humor*

Studies have shown that activities like sexist language and jokes can impact our judgments about the group to which they refer. We need to be careful about the language we use and the ideas we convey, even through something as seemingly simple as humor. In one study of 100 college students who listened to a lecture by a female after first hearing jokes, the group who heard sexist jokes rated her in a more stereotyped way than those who heard non-sexist jokes.

In another, students exposed to sexist humor videos before being asked to make funding cuts for student organizations cut more from women's organizations.

Source: Western Carolina University, "Sexist Humor No Laughing Matter, Psychologist Says," ScienceDaily (November 7, 2007), http://www.sciencedaily.com/releases/2007/11/071106083038.htm.

Exhibit 8.13 *Stereotypes*

Do any of the following stereotypes, taken from actual cases, sound familiar? Even though women may have come a long way, such ideas are still startlingly omnipresent in the workplace. Just because you haven't heard them doesn't mean they are not operating. Keep in mind that these are taken from actual workplace situations.

- Women being included in workplace events are a "buzz kill."
- Employer would not consider "some woman" for the position, questioned applicant about future pregnancy plans, and asked whether her husband would object to her "running around the country with men."
- Women are not aggressive enough for certain jobs.

- A lesser job position was sufficient for women and no woman would be named to the higher position.
- Men are the family breadwinner.
- Once a woman gets married, she will get pregnant.
- Once a woman goes on maternity leave, she will not return to work.
- Women cannot take the pressure necessary for certain jobs.
- If a woman is away from her desk, she is in the bathroom; the man is elsewhere talking business to colleagues.
- Women are unstable and not equipped for important positions because they are too hormonal or have a menstrual period.

unnecessary loss of revenue. Gender stereotyping began as stereotyping about females, but over the years the more recent cases also used the *Price Waterhouse* case to prohibit gender stereotyping of males, particularly as it relates to effeminacy. This, in turn, eventually resulted in the EEOC interpreting Title VII's gender provision as also prohibiting discrimination on the basis of gender identity in 2012 and sexual orientation in 2015.

Grooming Codes

LO6 Differentiate between legal and illegal grooming policies.

The issue of gender stereotypes is often closely linked to that of grooming codes since the issue of grooming codes often arises in a gender context (e.g., men being prohibited from wearing earrings at work or women being required to wear makeup). It was only in 2017 that the Philippines banned companies from forcing female employees to wear high heels. Courts recognize that employers need to be able to control this aspect of the workplace, and a good deal of flexibility is permitted. In *Harper v. Blockbuster Entertainment Corporation,*[105] male employees sued for gender discrimination based on not being allowed to wear long hair, since there was no such limitation on female employees. In rejecting their claim, the court said that "distinctions in employment practices between men and women on the basis of something other than immutable or protected characteristics do not inhibit employment *opportunity* in violation of Title VII. Congress sought only to give all persons equal access to the job market, not to limit an employer's right to exercise his informed judgment as to how best to run his shop." Title VII does not prohibit an employer from using gender as a basis for reasonable grooming codes.

Note, however, that we here address grooming codes only in the context of gender discrimination. The more recent workplace issue of, for example, applicants or employees with numerous body piercings, tattoos, and the like is generally not a gender issue but, rather, one of pure dress code-based appropriate business attire as determined by the employer. Again, employers are given a good deal of leeway in setting workplace dress codes. The codes can be pretty much whatever the employer wants, unless a policy violates the law, such as being illegally discriminatory on the basis of gender. In making this determination, employers can use reasonable standards of what is generally thought to be male- or female-appropriate attire in a business setting. For instance, a Florida city council wanting to "clean up" instituted a dress code requiring employees to wear underwear and use deodorant. It also prohibited exposed underwear, clothing with "foul" language, "sexually provocative" clothes, and piercings anywhere except the ears. The one city council member who opposed the measure did so because he believed the underwear rule "takes away freedom of choice."[106]

Scenario

Courts also have upheld grooming codes that required, among other things, male supermarket clerks to wear ties, female employees to not wear pants, a female attorney to "tone down" her "flashy" attire, and male and female flight attendants to keep their weight down. Not permitted was a weight restriction policy applied only to the exclusively female category of flight attendants but not the category of male directors of passenger service when both were in-flight employees. Also not permitted was requiring male employees to wear "normal business attire" and women to wear uniforms, though both performed the same duties. The court found "there is a natural tendency to assume that the uniformed women have a lesser professional status than their male colleagues attired in normal business clothes." This is the basis for Opening Scenario 1 and the reason the female clerk made to wear the smock would have a viable claim for gender discrimination.

The wearing of the short loose top may seem like a small thing to you, and you might say to yourself, "What's the big deal? Why would anybody complain about such a little thing?" Think back to the wires of the cage. It is not the garment itself that presents the problem. Rather, as the court said above, it is how that garment positions the employee to be perceived in the workplace, especially next to someone in business attire. That perception is a large part of forming the basis of what happens in that employee's work life, affecting whether that employee receives promotions, training, raises, and so on.

When you think of business attire (keep in mind that the males with the same jobs were required to wear the "normal business attire" of coats and ties), the loose-fitting garment does not generally come to mind. If both genders were performing the same job, a female wearing the garment would not qualify as comparable to a male wearing a coat and tie. If you think she would, just turn the facts around and require the males to wear the blousy-looking short garment and the females to wear "normal business attire." Not the same picture, is it? And when you think of who should get a promotion, the employee in the garment probably doesn't come to mind as quickly as someone in business attire. Like the wires, each requirement, in and of itself, may not make a big difference, but taken together, the policies create a picture that is likely to keep the female employee on the low end of the workplace ladder and be more likely to lead to unnecessary litigation for the employer.

As a managerial exercise for yourself, try to think of why the employer would have required the garment. Why not require it for all employees if they really are all the same? What is the difference between males wearing them and females wearing them? Once you come up with a reason, ask yourself if it makes sense. Chances are it doesn't. For instance, if the garment was required to keep the employees' clothes clean, then why not protect the clothing of males as well? If it was uniformity, why not make all employees wear it rather than just females?

Being able to see and really understand this scenario goes a long way toward being able to truly grasp the big picture of how gender discrimination works and how you can think about avoiding liability when faced with your own situations as a manager.

A gender-based grooming policy that subjects one gender to different conditions of employment also would not be allowed, for instance, where the scant uniform the female lobby attendant was required to wear made her the object of lewd comments and sexual propositions from male entrants[107] or where a manager required female employees to wear skirts when the "head honcho" visited because he "liked to look at legs."

It is not a defense for an employer to argue that the employee knew about the grooming code when he or she came into the workplace. If the code is illegal, it is illegal, period. Agreeing to it makes it no less so, particularly given the unequal bargaining positions of the employer and job applicant/employee.

An interesting case arose when Harrah's Casino in Reno, Nevada, instituted a new dress code that required female employees to wear makeup. The "Personal Best" program "specified the makeup as foundation or powder, blush, lipstick and mascara, applied precisely the same way every day to match a photograph held by the supervisor." The only requirement for men was that they not wear makeup of any kind and keep their hair and nails trimmed. Darlene Jespersen, a bartender who had been employed by the casino for 21 years and had an excellent work history, was "highly offended she had to doll herself up to look like a hooker." She was terminated for failing to comply with the policy. Jespersen argued that the cosmetics cost hundreds of dollars per year and took a good deal of time to apply and therefore created an unequal burden on female employees. The Ninth Circuit Court of Appeals upheld the policy, saying, "there is no evidence in the record in support of [Jespersen's] contention that cosmetics can cost hundreds of dollars per year and that applying them requires a significant investment of time."

Can you reconcile the court's position with that of the U.S. Supreme Court in the *Price Waterhouse* decision, which held that gender stereotyping violated Title VII? Remember that the Court found gender discrimination when, among other things, Hopkins was told she must "walk more femininely, talk more femininely, dress more femininely, wear make-up, have her hair styled and wear jewelry." The Ninth Circuit said its decision did not run afoul of *Price Waterhouse* because *Price Waterhouse* did not address the specific question of whether an employer can impose sex-differentiated appearance and grooming standards on its male and female employees (presumably because the more direct issue before the Court was Hopkins's assertive/aggressive behavior, which her employers used as a large part of their rejection of her as a partner).

The full Ninth Circuit reheard the case again *en banc* (i.e., with all the judges present, not just a three-judge panel) in *Jespersen v. Harrah's Operating Co.*[108] Given the queries put to you about reconciling the case with *Price Waterhouse,* you can imagine the controversy it caused when the full court upheld the three-judge panel's decision in favor of the employer.

Customer or Employee Preferences

Frequently an employer uses gender as a basis for assigning work because of the preference of customers, clients, or other employees. You saw this in the race chapter when the Lowe's manager was terminated for honoring a customer's request to not have a Black driver deliver her purchase. Often the work to which one gender is not privy represents a loss of valuable revenue or a professionally beneficial opportunity for that employee. Such considerations may be formidable in client-driven businesses such as law, brokerages, accounting, sales, and other professions. If a customer does not wish to have a female audit his or her books, can her accounting firm legally refuse to let her service the client? Is an employer in violation of Title VII if the employer does not permit an employee of a certain gender to deal with a customer because the customer does not wish to deal with someone of that gender and the employee is thereby denied valuable work experience or earning potential? What if male employees on a construction site don't want a female to work with them?

The answer is, as it was with race, yes, the employer is in violation of Title VII and can be held liable to the employee for gender discrimination. Customer preference is *not* a legitimate and protected reason to treat otherwise-qualified employees differently based on gender.

Hooters is a successful Atlanta and Clearwater, Florida-based restaurant chain established in the 1980s known for its buffalo wings and scantily clad, generally well-endowed female servers. Hooters does not hire males as servers. The conventional wisdom is that despite Hooters' claims that it is a family restaurant and "Hooters" refers to its owl logo, "Hooters" is a not-so-subtle reference to female breasts, and the servers are likely more of a draw than the food they serve. This is further supported by the servers' outfits; the fact that Hooters is known for its "Hooters' Girls," complete with pin-up calendars, a calendar tour, and a 10-page *Playboy* magazine spread; and its "more than a mouthful" logo, which few believe refers to chicken wings or owls.

Hooters has long maintained that customers want only female servers. In 1996, in response to being sued by males for gender discrimination, Hooters launched a "no to male servers" billboard campaign featuring husky, hairy male servers clad in Hooters' attire. Despite the lawsuits brought by the EEOC and class action suits by males in Chicago and Maryland, Hooters has generally chosen to settle cases rather than litigate them, which, of course, it has the right to do as long as it is willing to foot the bill. While Hooters' serving staff is still all female, on January 31, 2017, Hooters announced that it will be hiring male servers at its new quick serve spinoff, Hoots, with counter service fashioned along the lines of Panera Bread and Chipotle's. The famous Hooters uniform will not be worn at Hoots.[109]

Scenario

The Hooters situation is the basis for Opening Scenario 2. Not a semester goes by that one of our students doesn't ask how Hooters can "get away with" hiring only female servers. The short answer is it can't. At least not legally, in its present incarnation. Hooters has the right to use gender as a BFOQ to protect its female-only server policy if it can show that the gender of its servers is a bona fide occupational qualification reasonably necessary to the particular job done by the servers rather than a marketing scheme.

For instance, the BFOQ would be defensible if Hooters declared itself to be in the business of adult entertainment rather than purely food service. Despite the fact that it maintains that it is a family restaurant that even has crayons for children to prove it, it has come to be known informally as a "breastaurant," a hybrid between a restaurant and an adult entertainment location. In fact, Hooters has been termed the "granddaddy of breastaurants." If it is a family restaurant, it means its purpose is serving food rather than adult entertainment, so either gender can serve its food and its female-only server policy violates Title VII. If it is adult entertainment, then it can have only females to "entertain." So, the way Hooters "gets away with" hiring only female servers is basically to settle lawsuits brought by males challenging its exclusionary policy. Hooters has concluded that it is worth more to keep its female-only server marketing policy and settle claims by male applicants than to change its policy. Again, that approach is something it has every right to take as long as it is willing to pay. To see the fine line Hooters walks in trying to characterize itself to avoid liability, visit its website and read the "about Hooters" section.

See Chapter 2 to revisit key concepts.

The issue of customer preference can potentially cause problems since the 1991 amendment made Title VII applicable to U.S. citizens employed by American-owned or -controlled companies doing business outside the United States. An employer in a country whose mores may not permit women to deal with men professionally must still comply with Title VII unless doing so would cause the company to actually violate the law of the country in which the business is located.

Logistical Considerations

LO5 Define fetal protection policies, gender-plus discrimination, workplace lactation issues, and gender-based logistical concerns.

In some workplaces, males and females working together can present logistical challenges—for instance, female sports reporters going into male athletes' locker rooms, female firefighters sleeping at a fire station, or lack of bathrooms at a construction site. This issue arose in the context of construction workers in the *Lynch v. Freeman* case, which is included at the conclusion of the chapter, when a female employee was told to use the same portable toilet as males. The court determined that the unclean (to put it mildly) toilets presented different challenges to males and females, resulting in gender discrimination. Note how the employer can take little for granted in making workplace decisions, as even the seemingly smallest decisions can be the basis of a time-consuming and expensive lawsuit.

Case 4

A growing logistical concern in recent years has been the matter of female employees breastfeeding or expressing their milk at work. While the benefits of breastfeeding are clear as providing the best means of giving infants, among other things, natural immunities and nutrients, women who needed to or chose to return to work before their babies were weaned from the breast had little means of continuing to provide them with the benefits of their milk when they were not available to feed them. Until very recently, it was even illegal in many states to breastfeed in public.

It was just in 2006 that a national "nurse-in" was held to protest the treatment of Emily Gillette of Santa Fe, New Mexico. Gillette was sitting aboard a Freedom Airlines (a regional airline for Delta) plane that was three hours late in taking off when she began to breastfeed her daughter. A flight attendant who told Gillette that Gillette was offending her had Gillette removed from the plane when Gillette refused to cover herself with a blanket. As mentioned earlier, 50 states plus the District of Columbia, Puerto Rico, and the Virgin Islands have passed lactation laws that make it permissible for women to breastfeed in public places without being cited for public indecency (see Exhibit 8.11, "Breastfeeding: A Gender-Plus Issue?"). As you saw in Exhibit 8.11, the Patient Protection and Affordable Care Act of 2010 amended the Fair Labor Standards Act to require that employers with 50 or more employees provide a reasonable and private place other than a restroom and breaks for new mothers to express their milk. The breaks need not be paid unless they are normal paid breaks. If the employer has fewer than 50 employees and the requirement presents an undue hardship, the employer need not comply. If state law provides more rights, the employer must comply with those. The right is given to employees who qualify for overtime under Fair Labor Standards Act laws discussed in a later chapter. A growing number of employers had already begun to provide lactation rooms for employees to be able to express milk at work and a means to keep it cool until they can take it home. As you saw earlier, Patagonia even lauded it. Doing so bought company loyalty not only from employees but from the public as well. Compare that to the woman who won $12.5 million in a breastfeeding discrimination case against KFC in 2019 because it did not provide an adequate place for her to pump her breast milk.

In sum, employers may not forgo hiring those of a certain gender because of logistical issues unless it involves an unreasonable financial burden—usually a matter difficult for an employer to prove. These challenges must be resolved in a way that does not discriminate against the employee based on gender. Generally it is not exceedingly difficult, although it may take thinking about the workplace in a different way.

Equal Pay and Comparable Worth

LO8 Distinguish between equal pay and comparable worth and discuss proposed legislation.

(1) No employer . . . shall discriminate between employees on the basis of sex by paying wages to employees . . . at a rate less than the rate at which he pays wages to employees of the opposite sex . . . for equal work on jobs the performance of which requires equal skill, effort, and responsibility, and which are performed under similar working conditions, except where such payment is made pursuant to (i) a seniority system; (ii) a merit system; (iii) a system which measures earnings by quantity

or quality of production; or (iv) a differential based on any other factor other than sex. . . . [Equal Pay Act, 29 U.S.C.A § 206(d).]

You watched it play out in 2016 when the U.S. Women's Soccer Team filed a complaint against the U.S. Soccer Federation with the Equal Employment Opportunity Commission for pay discrimination. They claimed they were paid less per game, received less for daily expenses while traveling, yet played more games than the men and had a better winning record. The federation said it was because the men's team brought in more money, but in 2015, the women's team won the World Cup and brought in more revenue. The situation drew worldwide media attention, including a piece on CBS's *60 Minutes*. In 2019, the soccer players were granted class action status in their case, an important step because in order for the class action status to be granted, the requester must show that the claims they present are held by others as well and the requesters' claims adequately represent the others who they are asking to be added to the claim to create a class action. They were successful in showing the court that there were other such claims, and class action status was granted.

Despite the statute quoted above prohibiting pay discrimination, women earn on average 78.3 cents for every dollar earned by men. The gap is even larger for minority women. (See, Exhibit 8.15, "Overall, Black and Hispanic Women Face the Biggest Pay Gap When Compared to White Men.") This is up from 60 cents in 1979. Younger women make 80 cents for every dollar a man makes in the same age group. At the rate the gender wage gap is closing, widely cited AFL-CIO research shows that women's salaries will not be equal until the year 2050.[110]

A 2003 General Accounting Office report found that the gender wage gap exists not because of less education or experience or because women get on a "mommy track" or choose low-paying professions. Instead, it concluded that discrimination is the biggest factor in the wage gap between genders.[111] Time has only borne this out in later research. In a much publicized study in May 2013, the Pew Research Center found that in a "huge leap from 50 years ago when only a handful of moms were bringing home the bacon," women are now the leading solo breadwinners in 40 percent of U.S. households, compared to 11 percent in 1960. The study also revealed that despite the fact that mothers are now equally or more educated than their husbands, a majority of fathers still earn more than their wives.[112] The gap still very much exists in 2020.

Title VII prohibits discrimination in employment including in the area of compensation, but even before Title VII there was legislation protecting employees against discrimination in compensation solely on the basis of gender. The year before Title VII was passed, the Equal Pay Act (EPA), actually part of the Fair Labor Standards Act (FLSA) governing wages and hours in the workplace, became law.

Under the act, employers subject to the minimum wage provisions of the FLSA may not use gender as a basis for paying lower wages to an employee for equal work "on jobs the performance of which requires equal skill, effort, and responsibility, and which are performed under similar working conditions." There are exceptions. Differences in wages are permitted if based on seniority or merit systems, on systems that measure earnings by quantity or quality of production, or on a differential based on "any other factor other than [gender]."

To comply with the Equal Pay Act, the employer may not reduce the wage rate of the higher-paid employees. According to Bureau of Labor Statistics figures, the pay gap that was supposed to be closed by the legislation actually widened at least nine times from one year to the next since passage of the EPA.

The EPA overlaps with Title VII's general prohibition against discrimination in employment on the basis of gender. Title VII's Bennett Amendment was passed so that the exceptions permitted by the EPA also would be recognized by Title VII. The EPA also has a longer statute of limitations (two years from the time of the alleged violation, which may be raised to three years for willful violations, rather than 180 days under Title VII, although the Lily Ledbetter Fair Pay Act may extend it even longer depending on circumstances). Perhaps due to the fact that Title VII was passed very soon after the EPA and more generally proscribed discrimination in employment, there has been less activity under the EPA than under Title VII. However, the prohibitions on pay discrimination should be considered no less important. (See Exhibit 8.14, "Equal Pay: Hardly a Dead Issue.")

Exhibit 8.14   *Equal Pay: Hardly a Dead Issue*

A 1999 national study undertaken by the AFL-CIO and the Institute for Women's Policy Research revealed very interesting insights into the issue of pay equality for over 200,000 American workers. When looking at the findings and thinking about the issue of wage equality, keep in mind that the women responding provided half or more of their families' incomes. In the years since, while some things have changed, it is pretty scary how similar the overall picture still is. See IWPR #C411 at iwpr.org, "How Equal Pay for Working Women Would Reduce Poverty and Grow the Economy" at http://www.iwpr.org/initiatives/pay-equity-and-discrimination.

- Ninety-four percent of working women described equal pay as "very important"; two of every five cited pay as the biggest problem women face at work.
- Working families lose $200 billion of income annually to the wage gap—an average yearly loss of more than $4,000 for each working woman's family because of unequal pay, even after accounting for differences in education, age, location, and the number of hours worked.
- If married women were paid the same as comparable men, their family income would rise by nearly 6 percent, and their families' poverty rates would fall from 2.1 percent to 0.8 percent.
- If single working mothers earned as much as comparable men, their family incomes would increase by nearly 17 percent, and their poverty rates would be cut in half, from 25.3 percent to 12.6 percent.
- If single women earned as much as comparable men, their incomes would rise by 13.4 percent and their poverty rates would be reduced from 6.3 percent to 1 percent.
- Working families in Ohio, Michigan, Vermont, Indiana, Illinois, Montana, Wisconsin, and Alabama pay the heaviest price for unequal pay to working women, losing an average of roughly $5,000 in family income each year.
- Family income losses due to unequal pay for women range from $326 million in Alaska to $21.8 billion in California.
- Women who work full-time are paid the least, compared with men, in Indiana, Louisiana, Michigan, Montana, North Dakota, Wisconsin, and Wyoming, where women earn less than 70 percent of men's weekly earnings.

- Women of color fare especially poorly in Louisiana, Montana, Nebraska, Oregon, Rhode Island, Utah, Wisconsin, and Wyoming, earning less than 60 percent of what men earn.

- Even where women fare best compared with men—in Arizona, California, Florida, Hawaii, Massachusetts, New York, and Rhode Island—women earn little more than 80 percent as much as men.

- Women earn the most in comparison to men—97 percent—in Washington, DC, but the primary reason women appear to fare so well is the very low wages of minority men.

- For women of color, the gender pay gap is smallest in Washington, DC; Hawaii; Florida; New

York; and Tennessee, where they earn more than 70 percent of what men overall in those states earn.

- The 25.6 million women who work in predominantly female jobs lose an average of $3,446 each per year; the 4 million men who work in predominantly female occupations lose an average of $6,259 each per year.

Sources: "Equal Pay for Working Families: National and State Data on the Pay Gap and Its Costs," 1999. https://iwpr.org/wp-content/uploads/wpallimport/files/iwpr-export/publications/C343.pdf. See also, Institute for Women's Policy Research, #C455 - "The Impact of Equal Pay on Poverty and the Economy," 4/5/2017. https://iwpr.org/publications/impact-equal-pay-poverty-economy/.

On the 50th anniversary of the Equal Pay Act, in 2013, the National Pay Equity Task Force issued an assessment of the law that found that in the latest year for which it had figures, 2011, while much progress had been made, women comprised nearly half the workforce, and many were the primary breadwinners for their families, the average woman still earned only 77 cents for every dollar earned by men and women continued to constitute a majority of employees in many low-wage sectors. For instance, 52 percent of all working women worked in service, sales, and office occupations such as secretaries, cashiers, maids, and child care workers and were an overwhelming majority in those sectors.[113] A 2017 state-by-state analysis by the National Partnership performed for Equal Pay Day found that if the gap were closed, women could afford food for 1.5 more years, 7 months of mortgage payments, 11 more months of rent, or 15 more months of child care.[114]

In *EEOC v. Colorado Seminary,*[115] the EEOC alleged that female full professors at the University of Denver's Sturm College of Law were paid less than their male counterparts. As you saw in many of the situations mentioned in the beginning of the chapter, not only is unequal pay the basis of many gender discrimination lawsuits, but often the cases are class action suits that reflect a systemic issue in the workplace. As we mentioned then, discrimination may not account for all of the wage differential, but research shows that much of it is based on gender-based ideas. That is within the employer's control and is thus something the employer can do something about to avoid liability. (See Exhibit 8.16, "Staying on Top of Gender-Based Pay Inequities.") Think back to the stereotypes given to the female employees being trained at the Hoboken, New Jersey, office of Ernst &Young earlier.

Under the EPA, it is the content of the job, not the job title or description, that controls the comparison of whether the jobs are substantially the same. For instance, if a hospital's male "orderlies" and female "aides" perform

Exhibit 8.15 *Overall, Black and Hispanic Women Face the Biggest Pay Gap When Compared to White Men*

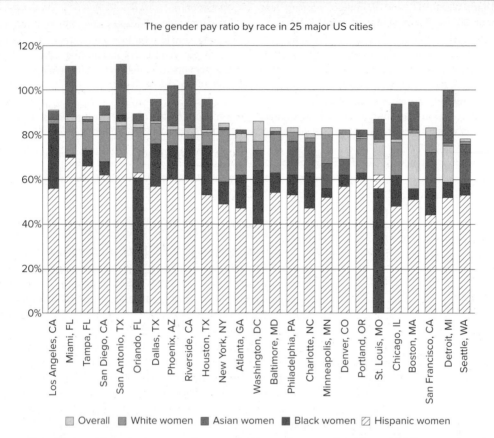

The gender pay ratio by race in 25 major US cities

Note: The overall gender gap pay ratio compares the median annual earnings of full-time, year-round female workers to male workers. The gender pay gap in dollars is the difference between median annual earnings for those two groups. Gender pay gap ratios for women self-identifying in particular racial and ethnic groups compare median annual earings for full-time, year-round female workers in those groups to full-time, year-round white male workers.

Source: Shayanne Gal/Business Insider, https://www.businessinsider.com/gender-wage-pay-gap-charts-2017-3#cities-show-an-even-bigger-discrepancy-especially-for-people-of-color-2.

substantially the same job, they should receive the same pay despite the difference in job titles.

In *County of Washington v. Gunther,*[116] the Court held that Title VII's Bennett Amendment only incorporated the four EPA exceptions into Title VII, not the

---

Exhibit 8.16 *Staying on Top of Gender-Based Pay Inequities*

The Catalyst research on MBAs discussed earlier was sponsored by many big corporations including American Express. These CEOs offered insights and suggestions on the study's findings. They included the following, and if you have been reading the chapter carefully, they should sound quite familiar:

- Don't assume that the playing field has been leveled.
- Redesign systems to correct early inequities.

- Collect and review salary growth metrics.
- Build in checks and balances against unconscious bias.
- Make assignments based on qualifications, not presumptions.

Source: Carter, Nancy M., and Christine Silva, "Pipeline's Broken Promise," Catalyst (February 24, 2010), http://www.catalyst.org/publication/372/pipelines-broken-promise.

---

comparable worth
A Title VII action for pay discrimination based on gender, in which jobs held mostly by women are compared with comparable jobs held mostly by men in regard to pay to determine if there is gender discrimination.

"substantially equal" requirement; therefore, the jobs compared in a Title VII unequal pay action need not be substantially equal.

Thus, under Title VII, employees have attempted to bring **comparable worth** cases in which higher-paid predominantly male jobs with similar value to the employer are compared in order to challenge lower wage rates for jobs held mostly by women. For instance, Minnesota has a gender pay equity law and uses outside consultants to help set wage levels. In 1982 it was determined that van drivers (predominantly male) and clerk typists (predominantly female) were comparable, yet the men earned $1,900 per month and the women $1,500 per month.[117]

Federal courts, however, have generally rejected Title VII claims based on comparable worth.

The *AFSCME v. State of Washington*[118] case was the first significant statewide case to challenge gender-based pay differences on the basis of the comparable worth theory. The state of Washington conducted studies of prevailing market rates for jobs and wages in order to determine the wages for various state jobs and found that female-dominated jobs paid lower wages than male-dominated jobs. The state then compared jobs for comparable worth and, after finding that female-dominated job salaries were generally about 20 percent less than wages in male-dominated jobs, legislated that it would begin basing its wages on comparable worth rather than the market rate over a 10-year period. State employees wanting the scheme to go into effect immediately brought a Title VII suit against the state alleging it was a violation of Title VII for the state to know of the wage differences and not remedy the situation immediately. The court held that since the state was not responsible for the market rates, it did not violate Title VII.

You can imagine the impact of the *AFSCME* decision on employers. The state had basically gotten burned by trying to do the right thing in taking it upon itself to determine if there were pay inequities based on market rates and comparable worth. When it discovered the 20 percent differential benefiting men, it made a workable plan to correct the discrepancies it found. It was then sued for not correcting the discrepancies quickly enough. If you were an employer, would you have then taken it upon yourself to go seeking discrepancies? We think not. There was no way they were going to wade into this morass of comparable worth unless they absolutely had to. Based on the court's decision, since the differential was caused by market forces rather than discrimination by the state, the state had no responsibility for the pay differential. This pretty much brought the idea of comparable worth to a halt for a long while.

Google was sued for systematically underpaying women in different career fields and not promoting them for equal work. Two class action suits were filed. In March 2019, when Google conducted a study to determine if it was paying women and minorities less, it was surprised to find that men were being paid less than women for doing similar work. This led to pay raises for thousands of male employees.

Over the years there have been many attempts at addressing the pay differentials between males and females. Few have met with significant success. Prompted by the flap over pay disparities in women's soccer in January 2000, there was a flurry of activity surrounding the issue of gender-based wage differences in the American workplace. Twenty members of the U.S. Women's Soccer Team refused to play in an Australian tournament and demanded pay equal to that of the U.S. Men's Soccer Team. The women were scheduled to be paid $3,150 per month for the most experienced player and about $250 per game. Men were to receive $5,000 per month and an additional $2,000 for the 18 players going to Australia. In the wake of the incident, at least two pieces of legislation were introduced into Congress (the Fair Pay Act and the stronger Paycheck Fairness Act) to amend the Fair Labor Standards Act to address the issue of gender-based wage disparities. In February 2000, President Clinton, accompanied by women's soccer player Michelle Akers, announced that he was seeking an Equal Pay Initiative of $27 million to close the gap between men's and women's pay, of which $10 million would be allocated to the EEOC to deal with the issue of gender-based wage violations. However, nothing much came of the flurry of activity, and the laws have yet to be enacted by Congress.

The Paycheck Fairness Act would amend the Equal Pay Act to allow, in addition to the compensatory damages now permitted by the law, punitive damages for wage discrimination; prohibit employers from retaliating against employees for disseminating wage information to other employees; create training programs to help women strengthen their negotiation skills[119]; enforce equal pay laws for federal contractors; and require the Department of Labor to work with employers to eliminate pay disparities. The Fair Pay Act seeks to end wage discrimination in female- or minority-dominated jobs by ensuring equal pay for equivalent work. This proposed law is aimed at female- and minority-dominated employees and would establish equal pay for equivalent work. Employees would be protected on the basis of race and national origin. Wage differentials would be permitted based on seniority, merit, or quantity or quality of work, and there would be exemptions for small business. The proposed law would not allow employers to pay predominantly female jobs less than predominantly male jobs if they are equivalent in value to the employer.

Another aspect of pay inequality is secrecy of the wages paid that could cause procedural issues in bringing pay discrimination lawsuits. In 2007 the U.S. Supreme Court issued its decision in the case of *Ledbetter v. Goodyear Tire and Rubber Co., Inc.*[120] Lilly Ledbetter had been the victim of illegal pay discrimination over a long period of time. The employer had a policy prohibiting discussion of salaries, so Ledbetter did not discover this until she was given an anonymous note near the time of her retirement. She then sued the employer for gender discrimination. The issue came down to whether the 180-day statute of limitations in the Civil Rights Act began to run 180 days after the initial act of discrimination, in which case she could no longer bring her claim, or whether it ran anew each time she was given a paycheck based on the discriminatory pay. The Supreme Court held that she could not sue because the statute of limitations was 180 days after the original act. The decision was roundly criticized by employees and lauded by business.

Congress immediately took issue with the Court's decision and the next month introduced the Lilly Ledbetter Fair Pay Act [H.R. (June 22, 2007)] to amend Title VII to allow the statute of limitations to start each time a paycheck is issued based on the discriminatory pay. This was the first act President Obama signed into law when he came into office in January 2009. Both the Fair Pay Act and the Paycheck Fairness Act continue to be reintroduced in Congress. Their passage does not look promising anytime soon. However, in its most recent Strategic Enforcement Plan, the EEOC has continued to identify equal pay as one of its six national priorities.

One of the things that has been found to adversely impact the wage gap is linking women's salaries in a new job to their earlier pay history. That is, when a woman is applying for a new job, she is often asked what her salary was in her prior position, and this is used in determining her pay for the new position. Since women are often underpaid, looking at their pay history and linking it to the pay for their new job rather than to what the job is worth to the employer has a detrimental impact on women's salaries. It means that this underpayment follows them throughout their careers. As a result, since the first ban in 2017, at least 34 state and local jurisdictions, as well as some employers, have banned the use of prior salary history in determining salaries. The numbers rose quickly and continue to grow, but there are also two local jurisdictions that have prohibited bans on employers asking prospective employees about present or prior salary information.

Before we leave the area of pay, it should be noted that single women with no children sometimes actually make more than men. (See Exhibit 8.17, "Not All Women Are Paid Less . . . But What a Choice.") Also, gender discrimination is not the one and only reason for wage disparities. According to a 2009 report prepared for the U.S. Department of Labor's Employment Standards Administration by the CONSAD Research Corporation, a greater percentage of women than men tend to work part-time, which tends to pay less; a greater number of women than men tend to leave the labor force for childbirth or child or elder care; women, especially working mothers, tend to value family-friendly work policies more than men; and some of the gap is explained by industry and occupations. While they believe much more research is needed, their "unambiguous" conclusion is that the gap is the result of many factors and the raw wage gap should not be used as a basis to justify corrective action since there may be nothing to correct. That is, "the difference may be almost entirely the result of the individual choices being made by both male and female workers."[121]

Employers should be aware of any pay differentials between specific males and females as well as between jobs that are held primarily by males and those held primarily by females. As indicated by the various suggestions provided in Exhibit 8.16, employers should perform periodic audits to ensure that they are not operating under gender-based pay differentials, which may lead to preventable wage discrimination litigation against the employer. It is also critically important not to allow gender stereotypes to determine pay.

Exhibit 8.17 *Not All Women Are Paid Less . . . But What a Choice*

According to a study of 2008 census data by Reach Advisors, single, childless women in their twenties working full-time who live in 39 out of the 50 biggest cities in the United States earn more than comparable men, and they match them in 8 other cities. Women 22 to 30 with no husband or children earn a median of $27,000 per year. This is 8 percent more than comparable men in the top 366 metropolitan areas. In Atlanta the difference is most pronounced, with women earning 21 percent more than comparable men. Women in their twenties who do not meet this criteria earn only 90 percent of what men do. [Notice the difference in the 90 percent figure and the 75–80 percent earnings gap figure given earlier in the chapter. The overall figure includes all women, not just those in their twenties, and thus is lower.] Researchers believe the shift is because women go to college in bigger numbers. Three-fourths of women go to college from high school, but only two-thirds

of men do. In addition, women are one and a half times more likely to go on to graduate school. It is also due to the loss of well-paying manufacturing jobs for men who did not go to college. The trend is most apparent in cities with more than a 50 percent minority population since Black and Hispanic women are more than twice as likely to earn college degrees.

The trend has interesting implications for society and the economy. Not only are male-oriented businesses such as cars and sporting goods increasingly targeting women, but builders who expected this generation to drive demand for apartments is disappointed since these women increasingly live at home with their parents.

Source: Paul Wiseman, "Young, Single, Childless Women Out-earn Male Counterparts," *USA Today* (September 1, 2010), http://www.usatoday.com/money/workplace/2010-09- 01- single-women_N.htm?csp=usat me.

Gender as a BFOQ

Title VII permits gender to be used as a bona fide occupational qualification (BFOQ) under certain limited circumstances. Under EEOC guidelines, a BFOQ may be used when there is a legitimate need for authenticity such as for the part of a female in a theater or film production. More often than not, when employers have attempted to use BFOQ as a defense to gender discrimination, courts have found the defense inapplicable. This makes sense when you consider that in the EEOC's view, the guideline for determining the appropriateness of a BFOQ is that it would be necessary for a male acting as a sperm donor or a female acting as a wet nurse (a woman who nurses someone else's baby from her own breast). That is a pretty strict guideline and provides insight into how irrelevant the EEOC considers the matter of gender in the workplace to be.

That does not only hold true for women. As we have discussed, it includes men also. In *EEOC v. Audrey Sedita, d/b/a Women's Workout World,*[122] the employer refused to hire males as managers, assistant managers, or instructors in the employer's exercise studio, even though they were used as instructors on an occasional basis. The employer alleged that since it was a women's exercise studio, being female is reasonably necessary to the employer's business. In its view, clients would want women personnel and there were privacy issues involved in seeing nudity when taking new clients around to tour the facilities. The court did not agree and said that the purpose of the operation is to provide individualized fitness and exercise instruction to the club's women members. Therefore, the employer would have to prove that it could not achieve its business purpose without engaging in single-gender hiring. The assertion that the alternatives were not feasible because of the views of its clientele and the difficulties of accommodating men in the health club were not strong enough to prove that no alternatives were feasible.

Pregnancy Discrimination

Scenario

The Pregnancy Discrimination Act (PDA) prohibits an employer from using pregnancy, childbirth, or related medical conditions as the basis for treating an employee differently than any other employee with a short-term disability if that employee can perform the job. This is why in Opening Scenario 3, it is illegal for the employer to evaluate the pregnant employee differently than it would any other. Employers illegally treat employees differently in many ways regarding pregnancy and childbirth. For instance, the employer

- Refuses to hire pregnant applicants.
- Terminates an employee on discovering the employee's pregnancy.
- Does not provide benefits to pregnant employees on an equal basis with short-term disabilities of other employees.
- Refuses to allow a pregnant employee to continue to work even though the employee wishes to do so and is physically able to do so.
- Does not provide the employee with lighter duty if needed, when such accommodations are made for employees with other short-term disabilities.

- Terminates the pregnant employee by moving her to a new job title with the same pay and then eliminates the position in a job restructuring or a reduction in force.

- Evaluates the employee as not having performed as well or as much as other employees when the basis for the evaluation is the employer's own refusal or hesitation to assign equal work to the employee because the employee is pregnant and the employer feels the need to "lighten" the employee's load, though the employee has not requested it.

- Does not permit the pregnant employee to be a part of the normal circle of office culture so she becomes less aware of matters of importance to the office or current projects, resulting in more likelihood that the employee will not be able effectively to compete with those still within the circle.

The Supreme Court determined in *General Electric Co. v. Gilbert*[123] that discrimination on the basis of pregnancy was not gender discrimination under Title VII. Two years later, Congress passed the PDA, amending Title VII's definitions to include discrimination on the basis of pregnancy. Despite the fact that women comprise nearly 50.04 percent of the workforce as of December 2019 (up from 49.7 the year before) and statistics show that about 75 percent of those of childbearing age will have children sometime during their work life, pregnancy discrimination is still a serious workplace concern.

Many employers have maternity leave policies to address this more-than-likely event, but others, particularly smaller employers, do not. Based on traditional notions about the inappropriateness of women in the workplace in general or pregnant women in particular, some employers are actually hostile to pregnant employees and run the very real risk of being sued for pregnancy discrimination.

> It didn't bother me at all that she was pregnant. But whether or not she was going to be able to spend the time to actually perform the job and to be a mom and do all that, yeah, we factored it in, sure. We were concerned.

This statement by Robert DiFazio, head of Smith Barney's equities division regarding why someone other than the pregnant applicant was promoted to head the over-the-counter sales desk, is typical of many employers' views about pregnant employees. The employee here filed a claim and the arbitration panel said, "It is hard to imagine sentiments more universally regarded as symbolic of illegal gender bias" and ruled that the remarks constituted evidence of gender discrimination. A study in the *Journal of Personality and Social Psychology* found that while "business women" were rated similar in competence to "business men" or "millionaires," women who became mothers were rated as similar in competence to the "elderly," "blind," "retarded," or "disabled."[124] That's pretty startling. But it clearly shows the impact of stereotypes in the workplace. Pregnancy is one that continues to linger.

See Chapter 2 to revisit key concepts.

The EEOC recently reported that there has been at least a 182 percent increase in the filing of pregnancy discrimination charges over the past 10 years. While the EEOC says the most common scenario in pregnancy discrimination claims is termination of the pregnant employee (like the car dealer who fired the employee for fear she'd have morning sickness and throw up in the vehicles), employers take all kinds of measures. Walmart rejected pregnant job applicants, thousands of female Verizon Wireless employees lost benefits during maternity leave, Delta Airlines fired one pregnant ramp attendant and forced another to take unpaid leave, a producer on Spelling Entertainment's *Melrose Place* fired pregnant actress Hunter Tylo on the grounds that she was "unable to play the role of a seductress," a Dallas attorney at the law firm of Jenkins & Gilchrist claimed she was constructively discharged due to her pregnancy, and a New York City police commander claims she was passed over because of her pregnancies, as does the first woman promoted within the Annapolis Fire Department, the education reporter for television station WLOX in Biloxi, a bartender at a topless bar in Long Island, a dry cleaning presser in Minneapolis, two pregnant teachers in Atlanta, an ex-*Price Is Right* model who received $8.5 million in damages, $7.7 million of which were punitive damages for refusing to allow her to return to work after taking maternity leave, and the Mississippi bar employee who was terminated because her employer said, "The baby is taking its toll on you," though she had no medical or working restrictions.

Sportswear giant Nike found itself in the news facing criticism for its maternity policies when it became known through Allyson Felix, the most decorated female Olympic track and field star, that Nike's endorsement contracts with female athletes did not provide financial protection for pregnant athletes or new mothers. Nike announced that its endorsement contracts would now not be written so as to adversely impact athletes for pregnancy and expanded to cover 18 months.[125] Even reproductive advocate Planned Parenthood found itself accused of mistreating pregnant employees by such things as ignoring an employee's entreaties and doctor's notes urging that she be allowed breaks and employees feeling that they were treated differently after becoming pregnant and even being afraid to tell their supervisors they were pregnant because of the pressure to remain at work.[126]

Sometimes the discrimination is not so blatant. In *Asmo v. Keane, Inc.*,[127] the court concluded there was pregnancy discrimination when, on a conference call with other employees and the supervisor, the employee announced being pregnant with twins and the supervisor said nothing, though everyone else congratulated her. The employee was terminated by the supervisor two months later. We specifically included these facts and some of the quick blurbs above to demonstrate to you that as a manager or supervisor, your actions matter. The court held in *Asmo* that it was clear under the circumstances, when everyone else was congratulating the employee and wishing her well, that the supervisor's silence was a clear message that the pregnancy was not acceptable. When making workplace decisions, just make sure to think about the law first and not preconceived notions all of us tend to have about the appropriateness or inappropriateness of certain groups (here, pregnant employees).

Generally speaking, if the employee is temporarily unable to perform the duties of the job because of pregnancy, then the law requires that the inability to perform be the issue, not the fact that the employee is pregnant. The employee therefore should be treated just as any other employee who is temporarily unable to perform job requirements. Whatever arrangements the employer generally makes in such circumstances must be extended to the pregnant employee. Pregnant employees are not entitled to accommodation merely because they are pregnant but rather because they need the accommodation based on a temporary necessity. The EEOC has ruled that an employer's adherence to a facially neutral sick leave policy and its consequent refusal to provide pregnant employees with a reasonable leave of absence, in the absence of a showing of business necessity, discriminates on the basis of gender because of its disproportionate impact on women.[128] The Americans with Disabilities Act Amendment Act became effective on January 9, 2009, and expanded the definition of disability under the Americans with Disabilities Act. Under the ADAAA and the EEOC regulations, an impairment can be "substantially limiting" even if it is expected to last only a limited period of time. This meant that pregnancy must be accommodated as other disabilities under the ADA.

Pregnancy can, of course, be used as a BFOQ. It is worthy to note that facing a 23 percent increase in pregnancy discrimination claims from fiscal 2005 to fiscal 2011,[129] at the end of 2012, the EEOC officially declared that pregnancy accommodation would be one of its enforcement priorities. In pursuance of that, it filed or settled five pregnancy discrimination cases in one week soon after.[130] In 2015, this effort paid off when the U.S. Supreme Court issued a favorable decision in *Young v. UPS*,[131] holding that an employer must offer pregnant employees appropriate accommodation for their pregnancies if the employer cannot justify why they offer short-term accommodation for non-pregnant employees.

Despite the fact that the Pregnancy Discrimination Act was passed decades ago in 1978 and despite the U.S. Supreme Court's decision in *Young,* discrimination against pregnant employees persists. An extensive review of post-*Young* pregnancy accommodation cases by A Better Balance, a work and family legal center, found that despite the *Young* case, over two-thirds of courts held that employers were permitted to deny accommodations to pregnant employees.[132] There is presently a bill in Congress, H.R. 2694, and one in the Georgia legislature as well, H.B. 577, attempting to address some of the serious issues still remaining for pregnant employees since passage of the Pregnancy Discrimination Act. Both bills are about the same, and much like state laws that began being enacted after the *Young* case. The federal bill is the Pregnant Workers Fairness Act; the Georgia bill is called the Working for Two bill. Both would require employers to reasonably accommodate pregnant employees and applicants, or those with childbirth or related medical conditions, unless to do so would cause undue hardship. As the law now stands, only disabilities or religious conflicts are required to be reasonably accommodated. If passed, the law would include prohibiting employers from refusing to hire pregnant applicants, forcing pregnant employees to take leave they do not need, or forcing them to take accommodations that are unnecessary for them to perform their job. As a manager, you should be aware of the ingrained ideas employees hold about pregnancy and be sure to ward off any trouble.

Given the EEOC's push to pursue pregnancy discrimination claims and the broadening of the ADA by the ADAAA to require accommodation for pregnancy, it makes little sense to engage in activity that would unnecessarily put an employer in the crosshairs for avoidable actions.

Management Tips

As you have seen from the chapter, gender discrimination can manifest itself in many forms, some of which may take the employer by surprise. Following these tips can help keep the surprises to a minimum.

- Let all employees know from the beginning that gender bias in the workplace will not be tolerated in any way. Give them examples of unacceptable behavior.
- Back up the strong gender message with appropriate enforcement as necessary.
- Take employee claims of gender discrimination or bias seriously and make adjustments as necessary.
- Promptly and thoroughly investigate all complaints, keeping privacy issues in mind.
- Don't go overboard in responding to offenses substantiated by investigation. Make sure the "punishment fits the crime."
- Conduct periodic training to keep communication lines open and to act as an ongoing reminder of the employer's antibias policy.
- Conduct periodic audits to make sure gender is not adversely affecting hiring, promotion, and raises.
- Review workplace policies to make sure there are no hidden policies or practices that could more adversely impact one gender than another.
- In dealing with gender issues, keep in mind that none of the actions need make the workplace stilted and formal. Employees can respect each other without discriminating against each other.

Fetal Protection Policies

fetal protection policies
Policies an employer institutes to protect the fetus or the reproductive capacity of employees.

The issue of **fetal protection policies** will be given attention here because of the unique gender employment problems involved. Fetal protection policies are policies adopted by an employer that limit or prohibit employees from performing certain jobs or working in certain areas of the workplace because of the potential harm presented to pregnant employees, their fetuses, or the reproductive system or capacity of employees.

The problem with these policies is that, as in the seminal case of *UAW v. Johnson Controls, Inc.,*[133] they say they are for the protection of the unborn child, but that is not the employer's duty under Title VII. In addition, they tend to only protect one group and leave the other vulnerable. In *Johnson Controls,* a group of employees challenged the employer's policy barring all women except those whose infertility was medically documented from jobs involving actual or potential lead exposure exceeding Occupational Safety and Health Administration (OSHA) standards. Included in the group was a male who wished to transfer out of the facility in order to bring up his sperm count so he and his wife could conceive. The exposure to lead lowers sperm count. Scientific evidence showed that the lead exposure had an adverse impact on the reproductive capacity of both males and females, yet the employer only limited the females from the higher-paying jobs. Thus, the Court found the policy to be illegal gender discrimination. Where fetal protection policies apply only to women and not men when both are shown to be adversely affected by the conditions or when they take away job discrimination protection from a female employee rather than letting her make her own decisions, it can violate the law.

Chapter Summary

- Discrimination on the basis of gender is illegal and not in keeping with good business practices of efficiency, maximizing resources, and avoiding unnecessary liability.

- Gender discrimination has many manifestations, including discrimination in hiring, firing, compensation, training, pregnancy, lactation issues, fetal protection policies, client preferences, dress codes, and child care leave.

- In determining whether employment policies are gender biased, look at the obvious, but also look at the subtle bias that may arise from seemingly neutral policies adversely impacting a given gender, such as height and weight requirements. Both types of discrimination are illegal.

- Where employees must be treated differently, ensure that the basis for differentiation is grounded in factors not gender based but, instead, that address the actual limitation of the employee's or applicant's qualifications.

- Dress codes are not prohibited under Title VII, but dress code differences based on gender should be reasonable and not based on limiting stereotypical ideas about gender.

- Logistical concerns of bathrooms, lactation rooms, and other such matters should be handled in a way that does not overly burden or unnecessarily exclude either gender.

- Under the PDA, employers must treat a pregnant employee who is able to perform the job just as they treat any other employee with a short-term disability.

- Because of health and other considerations, an employer may use pregnancy as a BFOQ and may have policies excluding or limiting pregnant employees if there is a reasonable business justification for such policies.

- If there are legitimate bases for treating pregnant employees differently, an employer has ample flexibility to make necessary decisions.

- Outmoded ideas regarding pregnant employees may not be the basis of denying them equal employment opportunities.

- Fetal protection policies may not operate to discriminate against employees and fail to extend to them equal employment opportunities.

Chapter-End Questions

1. A female restaurant employee is on the phone in the kitchen talking to her mother. The chef of the restaurant comes up to the employee, throws off his chef's hat, grabs both the employee's arms, and begins shaking her violently and screaming at her. She reports this to the police. She is later terminated and sues for gender discrimination. Will she win? Why or why not? [*Labonia v. Doran Assoc., LLC,* 2004 U.S. Dist. LEXIS 17025 (D. Conn. 2004).]

2. An employee says she was forced to quit her job because of her status as a mother of young children. She claimed that her female supervisor created a hostile work environment that violated Title VII. She was replaced by another mother. Does she win? [*Fuller v. GTE Corp./Contel Cellular, Inc.,* 926 F. Supp. 653 (M.D. Tenn. 1996).]

3. An employer had only one promotion to give, but he was torn between giving it to the single female and the male who had a family and, the employer thought, most needed and could best use the money. He finally decided to give the promotion to the male and told the female he gave it to the male because the male was a family man and needed the money. If the female employee sues, will she win? [*Taylor v. Runyon,* 175 F.3d 861 (11th Cir. 1999).]

4. An accounts receivable supervisor was laid off by her employer after taking an extended disability leave for pregnancy. She claimed that the employer discriminated against her on the basis of gender and ability to bear children, stating that two male employees were retained and her replacement was a childless, 40-year-old unmarried female. She files suit, alleging gender discrimination. The employer said it was a legitimate layoff. What should the court consider in determining whether the employer's argument is true? [*Leahey v. Singer Sewing Co.,* 694 A.2d 609 (N.J. Super. 1996).]

5. A female police officer becomes pregnant and, after a scuffle with an arrestee, is told by her doctor to request a light-duty assignment. The police department says it has no such positions available and that the officer must take leave until she can return to full duty, which ends up being from September to June. The female cites two male officers who were injured and did not stop working. Is this discrimination? [*Tysinger v. Police Department of the City of Zanesville,* 463 F.3d 569 (6th Cir. 2006).]

6. A cable company closed its door-to-door sales department and released all employees of that department after settling a discrimination complaint by one of the department's employees. The employee's mother, sister, and two close friends also had been employed in the department. Eighteen months later, the company resumed its door-to-door sales but refused to rehire three of the former employees connected with the employee who had previously sued. The former employees sue, alleging gender discrimination. Will they be successful in their suit? Explain. [*Craig v. Suburban Cablevision, Inc.,* 660 A.2d 505 (N.J. 1995).]

7. A power company began employing women as meter readers, and the job classification went from all-male to all-female within a few years. The labor union that represented bargaining-unit employees negotiated a new collective bargaining agreement that froze wages in the meter reader classification and lowered the wage for new hires. There was evidence that the company president made comments concerning the desirability of housewives to read meters and that he admitted the contract was unfavorable to women. A number of women in the meter reader category filed a state court lawsuit against the employer and union for gender discrimination on the basis of state law and wage discrimination under federal law. The employer argued that the federal labor law preempted the state law gender discrimination complaint; therefore, the gender complaint should be dismissed. Is the state law preempted? [*Donajkowski v. Alpena Power Co.,* 556 N.W.2d 876 (Mich. App. 1996).]

8. A female employee is terminated for slapping a male employee. The male employee is not disciplined. Is this gender discrimination? Do you know all you need to know? [*Gamboa v. American Airlines,* 170 Fed. Appx. 610, 2006 U.S. App. LEXIS 3649 (11th Cir. 2006).]

9. An employer decides to shut down one of its three plants because the employees at that plant are almost exclusively women. The males who worked at the plant and lost their

jobs as a result of the closing wish to sue for gender discrimination under Title VII. If they do, will they be successful? [*Allen v. American Home Foods, Inc.*, 644 F. Supp. 1553 (N.D. Ind. 1986).]

10. During an interview, an employer asks a female applicant questions such as whether she had children, what her child care responsibilities were, and how her family felt about her weekly commute between the business's headquarters in Virginia and the family home in New York. The employer also asked the applicant "how her husband handled the fact that [she] was away from home so much, not caring for the family" and said he had "a very difficult time" understanding why any man would allow his wife to live away from home during the workweek. Is this employer's line of questioning a violation of Title VII? Explain. [*Lettieri v. Equant, Inc.*, 478 F.3d 640 (4th Cir. 2007).]

End Notes

1. "Three in Five Americans Say U.S. Has Long Way to Go to Reach Gender Equality: Seven in 10 Americans Say Women Often Do Not Receive the Same Pay as Men for Doing Exactly the Same Job," *Harris Interactive* (August 16, 2010), http://www.harrisinteractive .com/NewsRoom/HarrisPolls/tabid/447/ctl/ReadCustom%20Default/mid/1508/ ArticleId/452/Default.aspx.

2. "Lawry's Restaurants, Inc. to Pay $1 Million for Sex Bias against Men in Hiring," EEOC press release (November 2, 2009), http://www.eeoc.gov/eeoc/newsroom/ release/11-2-09.cfm.

3. *Time* magazine (September 16, 2019), p. 68.

4. Ibid.

5. "Obama's 2014 State of the Union Address: Full Text," http://www.cbsnews.com/ news/obamas-2014-state-of-the-union-address-full-text/.

6. Institute for Women's Policy Research, https://iwpr.org/youve-heard-that-women-make-80-cents-to-mens-dollar-a-new-report-says-its-much-worse-than-that/.

7. "7 Charts that show the glaring gap between men and women's salaries in the U.S.," *Business Insider,* Sonam Sheth, Shayanna Gal, and Andy Kiersz, 8/26/019. https:// www.businessinsider.com/gender-wage-pay-gap-charts-2017-3.

8. "List: Women CEOs of the S&P 500," Catalyst (March 5, 2020), https://www.catalyst .org/research/women-ceos-of-the-sp-500/.

9. Walker, Jessica M., "Bikini Lines in the Sand: Attorney-Mediators' Swimsuit Calendar Makes Waves in Legal Community," *Miami Daily Business Review* (December 23, 2004), http://www.law.com/jsp/article.jsp?id=1103549729332.

10. Hagenbaugh, Barbara, "Men Losing Jobs at Higher Rate Than Women in Recession," *USA Today* (January 12, 2009), http://www.usatoday.com/money/economy/2009-01-11-unemployment-rate-sexes_N.htm. Apparently, there were more than simply economic consequences to men being out of work. The *London Daily Mail* Online reported the traffic at websites offering opportunities for infidelity for married men rose 25 percent during the recession. Nicholas, Sadie, "Infidelity, Inc.: The Boom in Websites Offering Illicit Encounters for Out-of-Work Highfliers and How Their Partners Cope," *London Daily Mail* (April 7, 2009), http://www.dailymail.co.uk/femail/article-1167718/ Infidelity-Inc-The-boom-websites-offering-illicit-encounters-work-high-fliers.html.

11. Eaves, Elizabeth, "In This Recession, Men Drop Out," *Forbes.com* (April 10, 2009), http://www.forbes.com/2009/04/09/employment-men-women-recession-opinions-columnists-gender-roles.html.

12. See Hagenbaugh, "Men Losing Jobs at Higher Rate Than Women in Recession"; and Blackburn, Bradley, "Women Lag behind Men in Economic Recovery: New Government Numbers Show 90 Percent of Newly Created Jobs Go to Men," ABC World News (March 21, 2011), http://abcnews.go.com/US/unemployment-recession-men-return-work-women-left-economic/story?id=13185406.

13. Blackburn, "Women Lag Behind Men in Economic Recovery: New Government Numbers Show 90 Percent of Newly Created Jobs Go to Men."

14. *Time* magazine (May 21, 2012), p. 22.

15. *Time* magazine (September 16, 2019), p. 68.

16. Bynum, Russ, "Navy to Allow Women to Serve on Submarines: Military Orders an End to One of Its Few Remaining Gender Barriers," Associated Press (April 29, 2010), http://www.msnbc.com/id/36854592/ns/us_news-militry/print/1/displaymode/1098.

17. Merelli, Annalisa, "Only 4.2 Percent of Fortune 500 Companies Are Run by Women," *Quartz* (March 7, 2017), https://qz.com/925821/how-rare-are-female-ceos-only-4-2-of-fortune-500-companies-are-run-by-women/; Cox, Josie, "International Women's Day 2017: Number of Female CEOs of Fortune 500 Companies Falls by More Than 12%," *The Independent* (March 8, 2017), http://www.independent.co.uk/news/business/news/international-womens-day-2017-female-ceo-fortune-500-companies-fall-2016-more-12-per-cent-executives-a7617771.html (accessed March 8, 2017).

18. Horsley, Scott, "Women Now Outnumber Men on U.S. Payrolls," NPR (January 10, 2020).

19. Petrecca, Laura, "Women Make Workplace Strides, But Remain on Leadership Sidelines," *USA Today* (November 13, 2013), http://www.usatoday.com/story/money/business/2013/10/12/janet-yellen-women-leadership-economy/2959761.

20. Deborah Gillis, chief operating officer for women's issues research group Catalyst, in Petrecca, "Women Make Workplace Strides, but Remain on Leadership Sidelines."

21. Don Forsyth, professor at the Jepson School of Leadership Studies at the University of Richmond, in Petrecca, "Women Make Workplace Strides, but Remain on Leadership Sidelines."

22. "Catalyst Study Explodes Myths about Why Women's Chosen Careers Lag Men's," http://www.catalyst.org/media/catalyst-study-explodes-myths-about-why-women's-careers-lag-men's.

23. Kantor, Jodi, "Harvard Business School Case Study: Gender Equity," *The New York Times* (September 7, 2013), http://www.nytimes.com/2013/09/08/education/harvard-case-study-gender-equity.html?adxnnl=1&pagewanted=all&adxnnlx=1390162196-m944YJoJSqFTYknSdGxUZQ.

24. Lattman, Peter, "3 Women Claim Bias at Goldman," *The New York Times* (September 15, 2010), http://www.nytimes.com/2010/09/16/business/16bias.html?_=ref=business&pagewanted=print.

25. Chen, David W., "Bloomberg Is Deposed in Bias Suit against Firm," *The New York Times* (May 15, 2009), http://www.nytimes.com/2009/05/15/nyregion/15bloomberg.html?_r=1.

26. "Thompson Wigdor & Gilly LLP: Class Action Gender Discrimination Charges Filed by Five Female Former Employees of Citigroup," *Women's Health Weekly* (March 12, 2009), Document WHWK000020090306e53c000fp.

27. "Bank of America Accused of Gender Discrimination at Merrill Lynch," *Workforce Management* (July 10, 2009), http://www.workforce.com/section/news/article/bank-america-accused-gender-discrimination-merrill.php.

28. Bank of America and Merrill Lynch sex discrimination lawsuit, http://bofagender lawsuit.com/.

29. Stempel, Jonathan, "Bank of America Settles Gender Bias Suit for $39M," Reuters, NBCNews (September 6, 2013), http://www.nbcnews.com/business/bank-america-settles-gender-bias-suit-39m-8C11098723.

30. Stempel, Jonathan, "Senior Female Executive at Bank of America Sues over 'Bro's Club,'" Reuters (May 17, 2016), http://www.reuters.com/article/us-bankofamerica-lawsuit-genderbias-idUSKCN0Y8226.

31. Weiss, Debra Cassens, "Partner Files $100M Class Action Against Chadbourne, Targets Pay Decisions of Male 'Dictatorship,'" *ABA Journal* (August 31, 2016), http://www.abajournal.com/news/article/ousted_partner_files_100m_gender_bias_class_action_against_chadbourne (accessed March 8, 2017).

32. Keegan, Rebecca, "The Hollywood Gender Discrimination Investigation Is On: EEOC Contacts Women Directors," latimes.com (October 2, 2015), http://www.latimes.com/entertainment/movies/moviesnow/la-et-mn-women-directors-discrimination-investigation-20151002-story.html.

33. Robb, David, "Anita Hill Says the Hollywood Commission Intends 'To Change the System' That Allows Harassment and Bias," Deadline (February 11, 2020), https://deadline.com/2020/02/anita-hill-hollywood-commission-sexual-harassment-gender-bias-1202857732/.

34. Streitfeld, David, "Ellen Pao Loses Silicon Valley Bias Case against Kleiner Perkins," *The New York Times* (March 27, 2015), https://www.nytimes.com/2015/03/28/technology/ellen-pao-kleiner-perkins-case-decision.html?_r=0 (accessed March 8, 2017).

35. "Former Gorilla Handlers Settle Lawsuit in Bosom-Baring Case," *USA Today* (December 1, 2005), http://usatoday30.usatoday.com/news/offbeat/2005-12-01-gorillacase_x.htm.

36. Stempel, Jonathan, "Deutsche Bank VP Says Fired in Retaliation for Bias Case," Reuters, *The Chicago Tribune* (September 19, 2012), http://articles.chicagotribune.com/2012-09-19/business/sns-rt-us-deutschebank-bias-lawsuitbre88i1bq-20120919_1_deutsche-bank-gender-bias-german-bank.

37. Lee, Demorris A., "Female Firefighter Claims Discrimination," *Tampa Bay Times* (September 22, 2006), http://www.sptimes.com/2006/09/22/Northpinellas/Female_firefighter_cl.shtml.

38. Ploshay, D. S., "Man Sues California to Take Wife's Last Name: Couple Fights for Gender Rights of Married Couples," Yahoo Contributor Network (January 13, 2007), http://voices.yahoo.com/man-sues-california-take-wifes-last-name-169695.html.

39. *Time* magazine (June 24, 2019), at p. 13.

40. Warner, Claire, "'Double Jeopardy' Report Shows Gender Bias against Women of Color in STEM Is Alive And Well," bustle.com (February 19, 2016), https://www.bustle.com/articles/142993-double-jeopardy-report-shows-gender-bias-against-women-of-color-in-stem-is-alive-and-well (accessed March 9, 2017).

41. *Visible Invisibility: Women of Color in Law Firms,* http://www.abanet.org/women/woc/wocinitiative.html.

42. Star, Charlett, "Does Your Company Have a Wage Gap Problem?: 4 Questions to Ask Yourself," *Business News Daily* (April2, 2019), https://www.businessnewsdaily.com/10862-wage-gap-problem.html; "Equity and Pay Discrimination," Institute for Women's Policy Research, https://iwpr.org/issue/

employment-education-economic-change/pay-equity-discrimination/; Farra, Emily, "21 Reasons to Wear Red for Equal Pay Day," *Vogue* (April2, 2019), https://www.vogue .com/article/equal-pay-day-wearing-red-fall-2019-women-designers?verso=true.

43. Thanassis, Cambanis, "Military Challenge," *The Boston Globe* (January 10, 2003), http://n1.newsbank.com/nl-serch/we/Archives?p_action=print.

44. Dobbins, Bill, "GNC Show of Strength 2003 to Exclude Female Bodybuilding: Boycott Threatened?" billdobbins.com (November 2003), http://billdobbins.com/PUBLIC/pages/coolfree/GNC-nofbb/main.html.

45. "No Longer 'Ladies Night' in New Jersey Bars," Associated Press, Fox News (June 2, 2004), http://www.foxnews.com/printer_friendly_story/0,3566,121579,00.html; McNichol, Dunstan, "Nothing Makes Up for Ladies Night Loss," *The Star-Ledger* (September 27, 2004), http://www.nj.com/news/ledger/jersey/index.ssf?/base/news-7/1096260705323880.xml.

46. Lim, Dawn, "Lawmakers Push Potty Parity," GovernmentExecutive.com (May 12, 2010). The bill called for requiring new or renovated federal buildings to have an equal number of restrooms for both genders. About half the states and many municipalities already have such laws. Branch, John, "New Ballpark Statistics: Stadium's Toilet Ratio," *The New York Times* (April 13, 2009). Many of the laws require two female restrooms for every male restroom. However, when some facilities opened up, it was found that males were waiting in line while women did not have to do so. Some laws, therefore, revised the ratio of men to women bathrooms upward. In case you think that the "potty parity" laws are silly, keep in mind that the long waits women have for bathrooms exacerbate things like urinary tract infections. In passing the laws, legislatures noted the longer time women spent in the restroom because of things like having to take their clothes up or down, having to use toilet paper, being more likely to have children with them, and so on. Note how quickly laws were changed when men had to stand in lines to address this inconvenience women had suffered forever.

47. Baird, Julia, "Too Hot to Handle: Stop Ogling Republican Women," *Newsweek* (July 12, 2010), p. 37.

48. "Lawry's Restaurant Chain Settled an EEOC Suit for Over $1M," EEOC press release, http://www.eeoc.gov.

49. Gray, Katharine, "Woman Felt Forced to Wear Diapers to Work," NBCPhiladelphia.com (November 12, 2009), http://www.nbcphiladelphia.com/news/local/150000-for-Wearing-Diapers-to-Work-69285737.html.

50. Dupis II, Roger, "Pa. Dept. Sued for 'Overtime Whores' Remark," *The Times-Tribune* (Scranton, PA) (October 25, 2009), http://www.officer.com/publication/printer.jsp?id=49020.

51. Friess, Steve, "Lower Rates for Women Are Ruled Unfair," *The New York Times* (August 13, 2008), p. A17.

52. Cohen, Patricia, "Charging Bias by Theaters, Female Playwrights to Hold Meeting," *The New York Times* (October 25, 2008), http://nytimes.com/2008/10/25/theater/25women.html.

53. Bell, Diane, "Men Win in Gender Discrimination Suit," *The San Diego Tribune* (March 25, 2008), http://www.signonsandiego.com/uniontrib/20080325/news_1m25bell.html.

54. Francescani, Chris, "Lauren Odes, Temp Worker at Native Intimates, Alleges She Was Fired for Being 'Too Hot,'" *The Huffington Post* (May 12, 2012), http://www.huffingtonpost.com/2012/05/21/lauren-odes-native-intimates_n_1534464.html.

55. Byrne, John, "City Set to Pay Nearly $2 Million for Firefighter Lawsuit," *Chicago Tribune* (September 7, 2013), http://articles.chicagotribune.com/2013-09-07/news/ct-met-chicago-firefighters-settlement-0907-20130907_1_white-job-seekers-physical-test-written-test. Corpus Christie, Texas, settled with the Justice Department for the same thing involving female police officers the year before: "Justice Department Settles Sex Discrimination Lawsuit against City of Corpus Christi, Texas, Police Department" (September 19, 2012), http://www.justice.gov/opa/pr/2012/September/12-crt-1132.html.

56. Kramer, Miriam, "Female Astronauts Said to Face Discrimination over NASA's Space Radiation Concerns," *The Huffington Post* (September 1, 2013), http://www.huffingtonpost.com/2013/09/01/female-astronauts-discrimination-radiation_n_3846118.html.

57. "NBA Forced Women with Young Children Out of Jobs: Lawsuit," *The Huffington Post* (October 23, 2012), http://www.huffingtonpost.com/2012/10/24/nba-gender-bias-lawsuit-brynn-cohn_n_2008583.html.

58. "Fired for Premarital Sex: Woman Fired, Boyfriend Gets the Job," Examiner.com (March 2, 2013), http://www.npr.org/2011/06/20/137296721/supreme-court-limits-wal-mart-discrimination-case.

59. Bidgood, Jess, "A Father-Daughter Dance Revives Charges of Discrimination," *The New York Times* (September 27, 2012), http://pandce.proboards.com/thread/65568/father-daughter-dance-revives-charges?page=1.

60. "The Shriver Report: A Woman's Nation Pushes Back from the Brink," http://shriverreport.org/special-report/a-womans-nation-pushes-back-from-the-brink/.

61. Ibid.

62. Sealey, Geraldine, "Parent Trap: Moms and Dads Starting to Sue, and Win, for Discrimination," ABCNews.com (August 29, 2004), http://abcnews.go/sections/us/dailynews/discrimination020829.html.

63. http://www.eeoc.gov/policy/docs/caregiving.html.

64. "Questions and Answers: The Application of Title VII and the ADA to Applicants or Employees Who Experience Domestic or Dating Violence, Sexual Assault, or Stalking," http://www.eeoc.gov/eeoc/publications/qa_domestic_violence.cfm.

65. http://www.workplacefairness.org/domestic-violence-workplace.

66. Masters, Brooke A., and Amy Joyce, "Costco Is the Latest Class-Action Target," *The Washington Post* (August 18, 2004), p. A01, http://www.washingtonpost.com/wp-dyn/articles/A8646-2004Aug17.html.

67. "Platinum P.T.S. to Pay $100,000 to Settle EEOC Pregnancy Discrimination Lawsuit: Oil Business Co. Fired Clerk after Requesting Leave for a Pregnancy-Related Condition, Federal Agency Charged" (August 8, 2013), http://www.eeoc.gov/eeoc/newsroom/release/8-7-13a.cfm.

68. Stockton, Chrissy, "Law Firm Sends Out Insulting 'Tips for Women' Memo (with 163 Points)," Thought Catalog (October 26, 2013), http://thoughtcatalog.com/christine-stockton/2013/10/law-firm-sends-out-insulting-tips-for-women-memo/.

69. Reuters, "Novartis Fined $250M in Sex Discrimination Suit," *The New York Times* (May 9, 2010).

70. Bray, Chad, "Toshiba's U.S. Unit Faces $100 Million Gender-Discrimination Suit," *The Wall Street Journal* (February 1, 2011), http://online.wsj.com/article/SB10001424052748703439504576116040649121656.html.

71. "Court Upholds $2M Award to WalMart Pharmacist," *The New York Times* (October 5, 2009).

72. "Outback Steakhouse to Pay $19M for Sex Bias Against Women in 'Glass Ceiling' Suit by EEOC," EEOC press release (December 29, 2009), http://www1.eeoc.gov//eeoc/newsroom/releas/12-29-09a.cfm?renderforprint=1.

73. "Wells Fargo Reaches Settlement in Gender-Bias Suit," *The Wall Street Journal,* Jennifer Hoyt Cummings, June 9, 2011. https://www.wsj.com/articles/SB10001424052702304259304576375520007891038.

74. Kuntzman, Gersh, "Steakhouse Sexism: At Risk of Litigation, a Steakhouse Chain Has Agreed to Implement Gender Training and Hire Female Servers. Could This Mean the End of Meat-Filled Men's Clubs?" *Newsweek* (January 5, 2004), http://www.msnbc.com/id/3880701/.

75. Masters and Joyce, "Costco Is the Latest Class Action Target."

76. 474 F.3d 1214 (9th Cir. 2007).

77. *Dukes v. WalMart Stores, Inc.* 603 F.3d 571 (9th Cir. 2010), http://www.ca9.uscourts.gov/datastore/opinions/2010/04/26/04-16688.pdf.

78. Totenberg, Nina, "Supreme Court Limits Wal-Mart Discrimination Case," National Public Radio News (June 20, 2011), http://www.npr.org/2011/06/20/137296721/supreme-court-limits-wal-mart-discrimination-case.

79. Bureau of Labor Statistics, "Table 3: Employment Status of the Civilian Noninstitutional Population by Age, Sex, and Race," *Current Population Survey* (2016).

80. National Center for Education Statistics, *Digest of Education Statistics,* https://nces.ed.gov/programs/digest/d15/tables/dt15_318.10.asp?current=yes.

81. U.S. Department of Labor, *Labor and Statistics: Women in the Labor Force,* https://www.dol.gov/wb/stats/stats_data.htm#earnings; U.S. Government Accounting Office, "Women in Management: Analysis of Female Managers' Representation, Characteristics and Pay," (September 28, 2010); Tanglao, Leezel, "Gender Pay Gap Report: Women Managers Still Lag Behind Men: More Women Have Higher Degrees but are Still Earning Less," ABC News (September 28, 2010), http://abcnews.go.com/print?id=11742405; and Ludden, Jeniffer, "Despite New Law, Gender Salary Gap Persists," NPR (April 19, 2010).

82. Bennett, Jessica, Jesse Ellison, and Sarah Ball, "Are We There Yet?" *Newsweek* (March 29, 2010), http://www.newsweek.com/2010/03/18/are-we-there-yet.html.

83. Equal Employment Opportunity Commission, *Glass Ceilings: The Status of Women as Officials and Managers in the Private Sector,* http://www.eeoc.gov/stats/reports/glassceiling/index.html.

84. Bureau of Labor Statistics, "Usual Weekly Earnings of Wage and Salary Workers, Fourth Quarter," (January 24, 2017), https://www.bls.gov/news.release/pdf/wkyeng.pdf.

85. http://www.whitehouse.gov/sites/default/files/rss_viewer/Women-in-America.pdf.

86. Stephen J. Rose and Heidi I. Hartmann, *Still a Man's Labor Market: The Long-Term Earnings Gap* (Washington, DC: Institute for Women's Policy Research, 2004), http://www.nd.edu/hlrc/documents/Hartmann-StillManLaborMkt.pdf (last visited February 7, 2008).

87. Carter, Nancy M., and Christine Silva, "Pipeline's Broken Promise," Catalyst (February 24, 2010), http://www.catalyst.org/publication/372/pipelines-broken-promise.

88. Will, George F., "A New Project for the Gender Police: Gallant Government Will Protect the Weaker Sex," *Newsweek* (October 4, 2010); and *AAUP Faculty Gender Equity Indicators 2006,* http://www.aaup.org/NR/rydonlyres/63396944-44BE-4ABA-9815-5792.

89. Lewin, Tamar, "Women Making Gains on Faculty at Harvard," *The New York Times* (March 12, 2010), http://www.nytimes.com/2010/03/13/education/13harvard.html; Lewin, Tamar, "Bias Called Persistent Hurdle for Women in Sciences," *The New York Times* (March 21, 2010). See also Misra, Joya, Jennifer Hickes Lundquist, Elissa Holmes, and Stephanie Agiomavritis, "The Ivory Ceiling of Service Work: Service Work Continues to Pull Women Associate Professors Away from Research, What Can Be Done?" *Academe Online* (January–February 2011), http://www.aaup.org/AAUP/pubsres/academe/2011/JF/feat/misr.htm.

90. Bennett, Ellison, and Ball, "Are We There Yet?"

91. "A Current Glance at Women and the Law," American Bar Association (January 2017), http://www.americanbar.org/content/dam/aba/marketing/women/current_glance_statistics_january2017.authcheckdam.pdf; Bureau of Labor Statistics, "Median Weekly Earnings of Full-Time Wage and Salary Workers by Detailed Occupation and Sex, 2015," http://www.bls.gov/cps/cpsaat39.htm; National Association of Women Lawyers 2019 NAWL Survey on Retention and Promotion of Women in Law Firms, https://www.nawl.org/p/cm/ld/fid=1163.

92. "Women on Corporate Boards Globally," Catalyst (January 4, 2017), http://www.catalyst.org/knowledge/women-corporate-boards-globally (accessed March 9, 2017).

93. "A Push for More Women on Corporate Boards," National Public Radio's *Morning Edition* (February 24, 2011), http://www.wbur.org/npr/133875785/a-push-for-more-women-on-corporate-boards; and "Deutsche Bank sets gender quota targets for the Management Board and top two management levels under the new German gender quota legislation," Deutsche Bank (September 30, 2015), https://www.db.com/cr/en/concrete-gender-quota-targets.htm.

94. Goudreau, Jenna, "A New Obstacle for Professional Women: The Glass Escalator," *Forbes* (May 21, 2012), http://www.forbes.com/sites/jennagoudreau/2012/05/21/a-new-obstacle-for-professional-women-the-glass-escalator/.

95. Alter, Charlotte, "Seeing Sexism from Both Sides: What Trans Men Experience," *Time* (June 27, 2016), http://time.com/4371196/seeing-sexism-from-both-sides-what-trans-men-experience/.

96. 208 U.S. 412 (1908).

97. Susan Faludi, *Backlash: The Undeclared War Against American Women* (New York: Crown, 1992), p. xiii.

98. Deveny, Kathleen, "Families Need to Man Up: The Recession's Silver Lining," *Newsweek* (December 14, 2009), p. 30; DeWolf, Mark, "12 Stats about Working Women," US. Department of Labor Blog (March 1, 2017), https://blog.dol.gov/2017/03/01/12-stats-about-working-women.

99. Thomas, Jennifer, "Girl Scouts and LeanIn.org Partner to 'Ban Bossy,'" *Patch* (March 12, 2014), http://patch.com/rhode-island/eastgreenwich/girl-scouts-and-leaninorg-partner-to-ban-bossy.

100. Lipman, Joann, "Women Are Still Not Asking for Pay Raises. Here's Why," World Economic Forum (April 12, 2018), https://www.weforum.org/agenda/2018/04/women-are-still-not-asking-for-pay-rises-here-s-why/.

101. Bennett, Ellison, and Ball, "Are We There Yet?" See also Linda Babcock and Sara Laschever, *Women Don't Ask: Negotiation and the Gender Divide* (Princeton, NJ: Princeton University Press, 2003); and Lois P. Frankel, *Nice Girls Don't Get the Corner Office: 101 Unconscious Mistakes Women Make That Sabotage Their Careers* (New York: Warner Business Books, 2004).

102. "Research: Women Ask for Raises as Often as Men but Are Less Likely to Get Them," Harvard Business Review, Benjamin Artz, Amanda Goodall, and Andrew J. Oswald, 6/25/2018. https://hbr.org/2018/06/research-women-ask-for-raises-as-often-as-men-but-are-less-likely-to-get-them.

103. "Male VP's 'ROI' Comment to Mom Breastfeeding During Meeting Goes Viral: And it's being shared for all the right reasons," *Working Woman,* Anna Cincotta, August 7, 2019. https://www.workingmother.com/patagonia-mom-breastfeeding-during-meeting-linkedin.

104. 400 U.S. 542 (1971).

105. 139 F.3d 1385 (11th Cir. 1998).

106. "City to Workers: Wear Underwear, Deodorant: New Dress Code Instructs Employees to Observe 'Strict Personal Hygiene,'" Associated Press (June 18, 2009), http://www.msnbc.msn.com/id/31424512/ns/us_news-weird_news/.

107. *EEOC v. Sage Realty Corp.,* 507 F. Supp. 599 (S.D.N.Y. 1981).

108. 444 F3d 1104 (9th Cir. 2006) (*en banc*).

109. Taylor, Kate, "Hooters Is Hiring Male Servers at its New Restaurant," *Business Insider* (January 31, 2017), http://www.businessinsider.com/hooters-hires-male-servers-at-fast-casual-2017-1. In 2018 there was speculation that the 7 percent decrease in Hooters restaurants from 2012–2016 might be because the restaurants' concept is outdated and appeals to only the most boorish of baby boomers.

110. http://www.pay-equity.org/PDFs/payequitysummarytable.pdf.

111. "Women's Earnings: Work Patterns Partially Explain Difference between Men's and Women's Earnings," http://www.maloney.house.gov/documents/olddocs/womenscaucus/2003EarningsReport.pdf.

112. Langfield, Amy, "Mom Brings Home More Bacon in Nearly 1 in 4 Homes," NBC News (May 29, 2013), http://www.nbcnews.com/business/mom-brings-home-more-bacon-nearly-1-4-homes-6C10103171.

113. "Fifty Years after the Equal Pay Act: Assessing the Past, Taking Stock of the Future," National Equal Pay Task Force (June 2013), http://www.whitehouse.gov/sites/default/files/image/image_file/equal_pay-task_force_progress_report_june_10_2013.pdf.

114. "New State-by-State Analysis Shows Terrible Toll Gender Wage Gap Takes on American Women and Families," National Partnership (April 3, 2017), https://www.nationalpartnership.org/our-impact/news-room/press-statements/for-equal-pay-day-new-state-by-state-analysis-shows-terrible-toll-gender-wage-gap-takes-on-americas-women-and-families.html.

115. Civil Action No. 1:16-cv-02471-WYD (Dist Ct. Dist CO 2016).

116. 452 U.S. 161 (1981).

117. Ludden, Jennifer, "Despite New Law, Gender Salary Gap Persists," *Morning Edition,* National Public Radio (April 19, 2010), http://www.npr.org/templates/story/story.php?storyId=125998232.

118. 770 F.2d 1401 (9th Cir. 1985).

119. Men are more than four times more likely than women to negotiate salary, which generally means higher salaries for men. This can lead women to lose more than $500,000 by age 60. Babcock, Linda, and Sara Laschever, *Women Don't Ask: Negotiation and the Gender Divide* (Princeton, NJ: Princeton University Press, 2003). See also Miller, Lee E., and Jessica Miller, *A Woman's Guide to Successful Negotiating: How to Convince, Collaborate, & Create Your Way to Agreement* (New York: McGraw-Hill, 2001);

Phyllis Mindell, *How to Say It for Women: Communicating with Confidence and Power Using the Language of Success* (Upper Saddle River, NJ: Prentice-Hall, 2001). Online tools for researching salary data preparatory to negotiating include salary.com and payscale.com. Johnson, Tory, "Take Control: How to Negotiate Your Salary," ABC News (April 24, 2007), http://abcnews.go.com/Business/TakeControlOfYourLife/Story?id=3094415&page=1.

120. 550 U.S. 618, 127 S. Ct. 2162 (2007).

121. "An Analysis of Reasons for the Disparity in Wages between Men and Women," A Report by CONSAD Research Corporation Prepared for the U.S. Department of Labor Employment Standards Administration (January 12, 2009), http://consad.com/content/reports/Gender%20Wage%20Gap%20Final%20Report.pdf (accessed January 22, 2014).

122. 755 F. Supp. 808 (N.D. IL. E.D 1991).

123. 429 U.S. 125 (1976).

124. Williams, Joan C., "How Academe Treats Mothers," *The Chronicle of Higher Education* (June 17, 2002), http://chronicle.com/article/How-Academe-Treats-Mothers/46133.

125. "Nike to End Financial Penalties for Pregnant Athletes After Backlash on Contract Protections," *Sports Illustrated,* Charlotte Carroll, 5/25/2019. https://www.si.com/olympics/2019/05/25/nike-end-financial-penalties-pregnant-athletes-contracts-maternity-protection.

126. Kitroeff, Natalie, and Jessica Silver-Greenberg, "Planned Parenthood Is Accused of Mistreating Pregnant Employees," *The New York Times* (December 20, 2018), https://www.nytimes.com/2018/12/20/business/planned-parenthood-pregnant-employee-discrimination-women.html.

127. 471 F.3d 588 (6th Cir. 2006).

128. EEOC Dec. No. 74-112, 19 FEP Cases 1817 (April 15, 1974); EEOC Guidelines, 29 C.F.R. § 1604.10(c).

129. Elmer, Vickie, "Pregnancy Discrimination Cases on the Rise," *The Washington Post* (April 8, 2012), http://www.washingtonpost.com/business/capitalbusiness/workplace-pregnancy-discrimination-cases-on-the-rise/2012/04/06/gIQALWId4S_story.html.

130. Wilkie, Christina, "Pregnancy Discrimination in the Workplace Target of New EEOC Crackdown," *The Huffington Post* (September 29, 2012), http://www.huffingtonpost.com/2012/09/29/pregnancy-discrimination-eeoc_n_1924603.html.

131. 135 S. Ct. 1338 (2015).

132. Bakst, Dina, Elizabeth Gedmark, and Sarah Brafman, "Long Overdue: It Is Time for the Federal Pregnant Workers Fairness Act," A Better Balance (May 2019), https://www.abetterbalance.org/wp-content/uploads/2019/05/Long-Overdue.pdf.

133. 499 U.S.187 (1991).

Cases

Case 1

Wedow v. City of Kansas City, Missouri
442 F.3d 441 (8th Cir. 2006)

Female firefighters were not given proper firefighting uniforms (while male firefighters were given two uniforms), which put them at risk for years; were not given restroom or shower facilities; and were otherwise not treated comparably to male firefighters. The court found that despite the fire department's arguments to the contrary, this was gender discrimination.

Hansen, J.

***

Firefighters are each issued two sets of personalized protective clothing called bunker gear, consisting of a coat, pants, boots, helmet, gloves, a tool belt, and a self-contained breathing apparatus. Two sets are necessary because if protective gear becomes wet or soiled with chemicals at one fire, there is a danger of injury from steam when the same gear must be worn at another fire that day. The protective clothing must fit properly to ensure that the body is protected from injury due to smoke, water, heat, gasoline, and chemicals and to ensure the mobility needed while fighting a fire. The City issued and required Ms. Wedow and Ms. Kline to wear ill-fitting male firefighting clothing, although female clothing and gear were available and management officials knew of sources from which female gear could be obtained. Because the protective clothing did not fit Ms. Wedow and Ms. Kline properly, they suffered injuries from fire and chemicals when the coats would not close properly, or too large hats and boots would fall off while fighting a fire. Ms. Wedow's and Ms. Kline's movements were cumbersome and restricted by pants that caused them to trip or prevented them from easily climbing ladders. Excess length in the fingers of gloves made it difficult to grip objects such as the fire hose. The City's failure to procure protective clothing tailored for women and its provision of only male-sized protective clothing to Ms. Wedow and Ms. Kline made their jobs more difficult and more hazardous than was necessary.

Despite their complaints, no one in the Fire Department made any effort to provide Ms. Kline and Ms. Wedow with adequately fitting protective clothing from 1990 through October 1998. In October 1998, the Fire Department provided Ms. Kline with one set of female-sized protective clothing, although each male firefighter is given two sets of properly fitting clothing. In late 1998,

Ms. Wedow received a female-sized pair of bunker pants and a male-sized coat; she never received a complete set of adequately fitting protective clothing during the relevant time period.

Ms. Kline and Ms. Wedow also complained of a lack of adequate restrooms, showers, and private changing facilities (referred to collectively as "facilities"). Showering at the station after fighting a fire is necessary to maintain good health when serving in 24-hour shifts. At a number of stations that Ms. Wedow and Ms. Kline visited on a daily basis as battalion chiefs, the restrooms were located in the male locker rooms with the male shower room, doors were not secure, males had the keys, and where female restrooms existed, they were unsanitary and often used as storage rooms. Food and water for the station's pet dog were kept in the women's room in two stations and sexually explicit magazines and a poster were kept in the female restroom in station 23. Most of the female restrooms that existed did not contain shower rooms and in some stations, the women's shower could be accessed only through the male bunkroom.

Department officials were aware of complaints about the facilities as early as 1993. From 1994 through 2000, the Fire Department submitted yearly budgets to the City requesting money for female locker room upgrades, and every year the City allocated money for this purpose, but the money was diverted to a whole-station upgrade at station 4, which already had a female restroom.

The City argues that it is entitled to judgment as a matter of law on the claim of disparate treatment in protective clothing and facilities because the plaintiffs failed to demonstrate that they suffered an adverse employment action. "An adverse employment action is a tangible change in working conditions that produces a material employment disadvantage." "Mere inconvenience without any decrease in title, salary, or benefits" or that results only in minor changes in working conditions does not meet this standard.

We cannot say as a matter of law that being required to work as a firefighter with inadequate protective clothing and inadequate restroom and shower facilities is a mere inconvenience. Title VII makes it unlawful to discriminate on the basis of sex with regard to the "terms, conditions, or privileges of employment" and prohibits an employer from depriving "any individual of employment opportunities or otherwise adversely affecting his status as an employee" on the basis of sex. The record amply demonstrates that the terms and conditions of a female firefighter's employment are affected by a lack of adequate protective clothing and private, sanitary shower and restroom facilities, because these conditions jeopardize her ability to perform the core functions of her job in a safe and efficient manner. The danger inherent in the job of a firefighter compounded by the need to move

and work efficiently in those dangerous circumstances, to quickly change in and out of gear, to shower for health reasons following a fire, and the need to serve in 24-hour shifts, combine to make the provision of adequate protective clothing and facilities integral terms and conditions of employment for a firefighter. JUDGMENT FOR PLAINTIFF AFFIRMED.

Case Questions

1. Are you surprised that this is a 2006 case? Why or why not?
2. How do you think the fire department should have responded when the women registered complaints about their uniforms? Explain.
3. Why do you think the fire department treated the female employees as it did?

Dothard v. Rawlinson
433 U.S. 321 (1977)

After her application for employment as an Alabama prison guard was rejected because she failed to meet the 120-pound weight and 5-foot-2-inch height requirement of an Alabama statute, the applicant sued, challenging the statutory height and weight requirements as violative of Title VII of the Civil Rights Act of 1964. The Supreme Court found gender discrimination.

Stewart, J.

***

At the time she applied for a position as a correctional counselor trainee, Rawlinson was a 22-year-old college graduate whose major course of study had been correctional psychology. She was refused employment because she failed to meet the minimum 120-pound weight requirement established by an Alabama statute. The statute stated that the applicant shall not be less than five feet two inches nor more than six feet ten inches in height, shall weigh not less than 120 pounds nor more than 300 pounds. Variances could be granted upon a showing of good cause, but none had ever been applied for by the Board and the Board did not apprise applicants of the waiver possibility.

In considering the effect of the minimum height and weight standards on this disparity in rate of hiring

between genders, the district court found that when the height and weight restrictions are combined, Alabama's statutory standards would exclude 41.13% of the female population while excluding less than 1% of the male population.

In enacting Title VII, Congress required "the removal of artificial, arbitrary, and unnecessary barriers to employment when the barriers operate invidiously to discriminate on the basis of racial or other impermissible classification." The District Court found the minimum height and weight requirements constitute the sort of arbitrary barrier to equal employment opportunity that Title VII forbids. This claim does not involve an assertion of purposeful discriminatory motive. It is asserted, rather, that these facially neutral qualification standards work in fact disproportionately to exclude women from eligibility for employment by the Alabama Board of Corrections.

We turn to Alabama's argument that they have rebutted the *prima facie* case of discrimination by showing that the height and weight requirements are job related. These requirements, they say, have a relationship to strength, a sufficient but unspecified amount of which is essential to effective job performance as a correctional counselor. In the district court, however, they failed to offer evidence of any kind in specific justification of the statutory standards.

If the job-related quality that the Board identifies is bona fide, their purpose could be achieved by adopting and validating a test for applicants that measures strength directly. But nothing in the present record even approaches such a measurement.

The district court was not in error in holding that Title VII of the Civil Rights Act of 1964 prohibits application of the statutory height and weight requirements to Rawlinson and the class she represents. AFFIRMED in part, REVERSED in part, and REMANDED.

Case Questions

1. What purpose did the height and weight requirements serve? Do you think they were made to intentionally discriminate against women?

2. How could management have avoided this outcome?

3. Does your view of illegal discrimination change now that you have seen how disparate impact claims work? Would you have been able to foresee this outcome? Explain.

Price Waterhouse v. Hopkins
490 U.S. 228 (1989)

Ann Hopkins, a female associate who was refused admission as a partner in an accounting firm, brought a gender discrimination action against the firm. The U.S. Supreme Court determined that it is a violation of Title VII for gender stereotyping to play a significant role in evaluating an employee's work performance.

Brennan, J.

***

In a jointly prepared statement supporting her candidacy, the partners in Hopkins' office showcased her successful 2-year effort to secure a $25 million contract with the Department of State, labeling it "an outstanding performance" and one that Hopkins carried out "virtually at the partner level." None of the other partnership candidates had a comparable record in terms of successfully securing major contracts for the partnership.

The partners in Hopkins' office praised her character and her accomplishments, describing her as "an outstanding professional" who had a "deft touch," a "strong character, independence, and integrity." Clients appeared to have agreed with these assessments. Hopkins "had no difficulty dealing with clients and her clients appeared to be very pleased with her work" and she "was generally viewed as a highly competent project leader who worked long hours, pushed vigorously to meet deadlines, and

demanded much from the multidisciplinary staffs with which she worked."

Virtually all of the partners' negative comments about Hopkins—even those of partners supporting her—had to do with her "interpersonal skills." Both supporters and opponents of her candidacy indicate she was sometimes "overly aggressive, unduly harsh, difficult to work with, and impatient with staff."

There were clear signs, though, that some of the partners reacted negatively to Hopkins' personality because she was a woman. One partner described her as "macho"; another suggested that she "overcompensated for being a woman"; a third advised her to take "a course at charm school." Several partners criticized her use of profanity; in response, one partner suggested that those partners objected to her swearing only "because it['s] a lady using foul language." Another supporter explained that

Hopkins "ha[d] matured from a tough-talking somewhat masculine hard-nosed manager to an authoritative, formidable, but much more appealing lady partner candidate." But it was the man who bore responsibility for explaining to Hopkins the reasons for the Policy Board's decision to place her candidacy on hold who delivered the coup de grace; in order to improve her chances for partnership, Thomas Beyer advised, Hopkins should "walk more femininely, talk more femininely, dress more femininely, wear make-up, have her hair styled, and wear jewelry."

Dr. Susan Fiske, a social psychologist and Associate Professor of Psychology at Carnegie-Mellon University, testified at trial that the partnership selection process at Price Waterhouse was likely influenced by gender stereotyping. Her testimony focused not only on the overtly gender-based comments of partners but also on gender-neutral remarks, made by partners who knew Hopkins only slightly, that were intensely critical of her. One partner, for example, baldly stated that Hopkins was "universally disliked" by staff and another described her as "consistently annoying and irritating"; yet these were people who had very little contact with Hopkins. According to Fiske, Hopkins's uniqueness (as the only woman in the pool of candidates) and the subjectivity of the evaluations made it likely that sharply critical remarks such as these were the product of gender stereotyping.

An employer who acts on the basis of a belief that a woman cannot be aggressive or that she must not be has acted on the basis of gender. Although the parties do not overtly dispute this last proposition, the placement by Price Waterhouse of "sex stereotyping" in quotation marks throughout its brief seems to us an insinuation either that such stereotyping was not present in this case or that it lacks legal relevance. We reject both possibilities. A number of the partners' comments showed gender stereotyping at work. As for the legal relevance of gender stereotyping, we are beyond the day when an employer could evaluate employees by assuming or insisting that they matched the stereotype associated with their group, for "[i]n forbidding employers to discriminate against individuals because of their gender, Congress intended to strike at the entire spectrum of disparate treatment of men and women resulting from sex stereotypes." An employer who objects to aggressiveness in women but whose positions require this trait places women in the intolerable and impermissible Catch-22: out of a job if they behave aggressively and out of a job if they don't. Title VII lifts women out of this bind.

Remarks at work that are based on gender stereotypes do not inevitably prove that gender played a part in a particular employment decision. The plaintiff must show that the employer actually relied on her gender in making its decision. In making this showing, stereotyped remarks can certainly be evidence that gender played a part. REVERSED and REMANDED.

Case Questions

1. What were Price Waterhouse's fatal flaws?
2. Does Hopkins's treatment here make good business sense? Explain.
3. How would you avoid the problems in this case?

Lynch v. Freeman
817 F.2d 380 (6th Cir. 1987)

A female carpenter's apprentice sued her employer for gender discrimination, alleging the failure to furnish adequate sanitary toilet facilities at her worksite. The court found the unsanitary facilities violated Title VII.

Lively, J.

***

The portable toilets were dirty, often had no toilet paper or paper that was soiled, and were not equipped with running water or sanitary napkins. In addition, those designated for women had no locks or bolts on the doors and one of them had a hole punched in the side.

To avoid using the toilets, Lynch began holding her urine until she left work. Within three days after starting work she experienced pain and was advised that the practice she had adopted, as well as using contaminated toilet paper, frequently caused bladder infections.

The powerhouse, which had large, clean, fully equipped restrooms, was off limits to construction workers. Lynch testified that some of the men she worked with used them regularly and were not disciplined. Knowing the restrooms were off limits, Lynch began using the powerhouse restrooms occasionally, after her doctor diagnosed her condition as cystitis, a type of urinary infection. When the infection returned Lynch began using a restroom in the powerhouse regularly and she had no further urinary tract infections. Lynch was eventually fired for insubordination in using the powerhouse toilet.

The lower court found that the toilets were poorly maintained. The cleaning was accomplished by pumping out the sewage. This process often left the toilets messy, with human feces on the floors, walls, and seats. The contractors were to scrub down the toilets afterwards, but it appears they often failed to do so. Paper covers were not provided, and the toilet paper, if any, was sometimes wet and/or soiled with urine. No running water for washing one's hands was available near the toilets, although a chemical hand cleaner could be checked out from the "gang-boxes."

The lower court found it credible that most women were inhibited from using the toilets. Further, the inhibitions described were not personal peculiarities, but that Lynch and others reasonably believed that the toilets could endanger their health. Lynch introduced credible medical expert testimony to demonstrate that women are more vulnerable to urinary tract infections than are men.

On the basis of that evidence, the court concluded that all increased danger of urinary tract infections may be linked to the practice of females holding their urine and to the use of toilets under the circumstances where the female's bacteria-contaminated hands came into contact with her external genitalia or where a female's perineal area comes into direct contact with bacteria-contaminated surfaces.

Few concerns are more pressing to anyone than those related to personal health. A *prima facie* case of disparate impact is established when a plaintiff shows that the facially neutral practice has a significantly discriminatory impact. Any employment practice that adversely affects the health of female employees while leaving male employees unaffected has a significantly discriminatory impact. The burden then shifts to the employer to justify the practice which resulted in this discriminatory impact by showing business necessity; that is, that the practice of furnishing unsanitary toilet facilities at the work site substantially promotes the proficient operation of business.

Title VII is remedial legislation, which must be construed liberally to achieve its purpose of eliminating discrimination from the workplace. Although Lynch was discharged for violating a rule, she did so in order to avoid the continued risk to her health which would have resulted from obeying the rule. The employer created an unacceptable situation in which Lynch and other female construction workers were required to choose between submitting to a discriminatory health hazard or risking termination for disobeying a company rule. Anatomical differences between men and women are "immutable characteristics," just as race, color, and national origin are immutable characteristics. When it is shown that employment practices place a heavier burden on minority employees than on members of the majority, and this burden relates to characteristics which identify them as members of the protected group, the requirements of a Title VII disparate impact case are satisfied. REVERSED and REMANDED.

Case Questions

1. Are you surprised by this outcome? Why or why not?
2. Does the outcome make sense to you? Explain.
3. What would you have done if you were the employer in this situation?

Chapter 9

Sexual Harassment

Comstock/PunchStock

Learning Objectives

After completing this chapter, you should be able to:

LO1 Discuss the background leading up to sexual harassment as a workplace issue.

LO2 Explain quid pro quo sexual harassment and give the requirements for making a case.

LO3 Explain hostile environment sexual harassment and give the requirements for making a case.

LO4 List and explain employer defenses to sexual harassment claims.

LO5 Define the reasonable victim standard and how and why it is used in sexual harassment cases.

LO6 Differentiate the sex requirement and antifemale animus in sexual harassment actions.

LO7 Explain employer liability for various types of sexual harassment claims.

LO8 Describe proactive and corrective actions an employer can take to prevent or lessen liability.

Opening Scenarios

SCENARIO 1

1 A female employee tells her supervisor that she is disturbed by the workplace display of nude pictures, calendars, and cartoons. He replies that if she is bothered, she should not look. The employee suspects this is a form of sexual harassment. Do you agree? Why or why not?

SCENARIO 2

2 An employee routinely compliments colleagues about their appearance, hair, and body. Is this sexual harassment? Why or why not?

SCENARIO 3

3 A male and female employee have engaged in a two-year consensual personal relationship, which ends. The male continues to attempt to get the female to go out with him on dates. When she does not, she is eventually fired by the male, who is her supervisor. She sues, alleging sexual harassment. Who wins, and why?

Statutory Basis

> It shall be unlawful employment practice for an employer—
>
> (1) to fail or refuse to hire or to discharge any individual, or otherwise to discriminate against any individual with respect to his compensation, terms, conditions, or privileges of employment, because of such individual's . . . sex [gender] . . . .

Title VII of the Civil Rights Act of 1964, as amended. 42 U.S.C. & 2000e2(a).

> Unwelcome sexual advances, requests for sexual favors, and other verbal or physical conduct of a sexual nature constitute sexual harassment when (1) submission to such conduct is made either explicitly or implicitly a term or condition of an individual's employment, (2) submission to or rejection of such conduct by an individual is used as the basis for employment decisions affecting such individual, or (3) such conduct has the purpose or effect of unreasonably interfering with an individual's work performance or creating an intimidating, hostile, or offensive working environment.

29 CFR § 1604.11 (a) (EEOC Sexual Harassment Guidelines).

Since Eden . . . and Counting

Introduction

Imagine your boss whacking you over the head with his naked penis and then the same day, lifting your shirt and masturbating on you while he held you down and ejaculated on you. That is precisely what happened in an Aaron's Rents case in St. Louis. The jury awarded the employee a whopping $95 million against the national rent-to-own chain. It is one of the largest, if not the largest, single sexual harassment awards in history.[1] Experience tells us that of all the chapters you will read in this book, this is probably the single most perplexing. Why in the world would someone engage in such an unnecessary act that can have such wide-ranging negative consequences for the employer? Why would an employer permit it? You will probably find yourself asking this over and over as you go through the chapter. You will likely find yourself asking how it could ever be worth it to an employer to allow an employee to do when it is so *purely* personal.

No matter what the workplace, whether employees are practicing law, serving customers, hosting a television show, being the president of the United States, running a medical clinic, coaching Olympic athletes, running a major television or movie studio, managing a restaurant, or being a professor, the fact that it is a workplace means we presume a certain standard for our interaction with coworkers. It may be loosely defined, but we know it is there. Just picture what you think your workplace will be like when you graduate. You worked long and hard to get that diploma; you shlep from one interview to another in a race to obtain a job before graduation; you step out into the workplace feeling a degree of trepidation and uncertainty but knowing that, if given a chance, you'll be able to work hard and make your dreams come true. You take a job where it is a given that you will have dignity and respect and be allowed to contribute your time and energies to the productivity of your employer. Without even giving it much thought, you may expect there to be some unpleasant personalities and even jerks in your workplace, but you still expect a certain level of decorum.

With this picture in mind, we guarantee that the following situations do not comport with your idea of a workplace you would like to step into. Keep in mind that these incidents are only a few from many, many in the past few years. They are provided in order for you to see the varied ways in which this issue manifests in the workplace so you will be more likely to recognize it when you see it and work to prevent litigation. Some of what you see may surprise you in other ways. For instance, men account for nearly one in five sexual harassment complaints filed with the EEOC.[2]

These are not easy issues to talk about, and they are not always for the faint of heart. This is especially true sitting in a class with others. But it is what it is—we are all grown-ups, and it is the law, and these things happen, so you need to know. As someone who will likely be faced with this issue as a manager, you cannot afford to be shy. Sexual harassment in the workplace happens, and more frequently than you would think, and one of the main ways the cases go further than they need to is because of the hesitation managers have in addressing the issue. Backing away from it will not help you learn what you need to in order to prevent liability. These cases are not provided for purposes of sensationalism or titillation. They are far too sad. They are cases that arise in the workplace and cause great consternation and distress not only to the harassee but also to those who witness the harassment, those who must address it, those who must pay for it, those whose family members must see their loved one suffer, and those who are employed at the workplace and are embarrassed by the negative publicity. The impact on the workplace in terms of the embarrassment, the loss of time in dealing with the issue, the cost of litigation and judgments or settlements, and the loss of productivity is simply not worth it. This is especially so for us as taxpayers who have to pay out about $1 million a year to the sexually harassed staffers of legislators on Capitol Hill.[3]

- Roger Ailes, 76-year-old chair of Fox News, stepped down in 2016 soon after anchor and reporter Gretchen Carlson accused him of sexual harassment. Reporter Megyn Kelly soon followed with similar allegations. Then others came forward. The company spent millions of dollars settling the suits. It was said that Ailes's actions had been going on for a very long time, and because of the culture at Fox and his position, he was not stopped.[4] The situation was the subject of the 2019 Oscar-nominated movie *Bombshell.*

- Powerful movie producer mogul Harvey Weinstein was sentenced to 23 years in prison in March 2020 after being convicted of the rape of two women. Dozens more had come forward with similar claims stretching back years. It was clear that in order to be able to work in the film industry, women had to comply with Weinstein's sexual demands.[5]

- Google was sued by its shareholders after it was revealed that it had paid out $105 million to two executives accused of sexual harassment. In the wake of the fiasco, Google changed its sexual harassment policy so that it no longer required employees to sign mandatory arbitration agreements giving up their right to go to court for sexual harassment claims, but arbitration was still mandatory for any other claims such as retaliation or other issues related to such claims. Sexual harassment claims are rarely brought alone, so this modification by Google was not as strong as initially thought.[6]

- In May 2019, hamburger giant McDonald's had 25 new sexual harassment lawsuits filed in 20 states (others were already pending) against it for condoning sexual harassment and retaliation against those who spoke up about it. Allegations included groping, indecent exposure, demands for sexual activity and lewd comments. Employees in 10 cities across the United States staged a mass walkout demanding action on this and wages.[7]

- Long-time CBS CEO Leslie Moonves, credited with making CBS the most-watched television network, in 2018 stepped down after 15 years due to sexual harassment allegations against him. In the wake of this, the CBS board of directors donated $20 million to organizations that work for equality for women in the workplace.[8]

- Sportswear giant Nike was sued in 2019 by female employees who sought class action status alleging the company not only systematically discriminated against female employees in terms of pay and promotions but also ignored cases of sexual harassment.[9]

- Comedian, actor, and hypocrisy critic Louis C.K. removed himself from the stage (for a while) in disgrace after five women came forward and reported that his stand-up comedy riffs about masturbation were true, as he had masturbated in front of them.[10]

- Earlier actions may later come back to haunt a person later in life and impact the workplace. In 2018, U.S. Supreme Court justice Brett Kavanaugh was severely challenged in his Senate Judiciary confirmation hearings when professor Christine Blasey Ford and others accused him of sexual misconduct in high school.[11] In 2019, a year after his confirmation to the highest court in the United States, additional allegations emerged.[12]

- Three Yale University students filed a class action lawsuit against the university alleging that the school fostered an environment where alcohol-fueled gatherings at off-campus frat houses ruled the social scene since little else exists for meeting other students.[13]

- A female Florida city commissioner who allegedly made it a habit of licking men's faces on one occasion walked up to the city manager at a gathering and licked his neck and the side of his face, slowly worked her way up from his Adam's apple, and grabbed his crotch and butt. She resigned after the state ethics panel announced that the harassee's complaint had been unanimously upheld.[14]

- *Today* show co-host icon of more than 20 years Matt Lauer was fired from NBC after allegations of inappropriate sexual behavior with a subordinate. NBC was apparently satisfied that although there had been no other complaints, this was not an isolated incident. Lauer apparently had a history of such actions, including locking his office door and sexually assaulting employees. Lauer apologized, expressing "sorrow and regret for the pain I have caused."[15]

- Fox News celebrity Bill O'Reilly settled a case with reporter Juliet Huddy for sexual harassment, with Huddy alleging that he repeatedly called her, including while on vacation, gave her a key to his hotel room, tried to kiss her, repeatedly propositioned her, and had "highly inappropriate and sexual" conversations with her, at times sounding like he was masturbating.[16]

- Not only did the director of the Federal Communications Commission's Office for Communications Business Opportunities allegedly have sex with a *Washington Post* reporter in his office, but management refused to act when a male employee repeatedly invited other male employees to watch pornography with him in the cubicle next to that of a female employee, with a male keeping watch, while the female employee would "hear groans—mmm, mmm, ahh—" in response to their viewing.[17]

- When a Deutsche Bank employee alleged that he experienced sexual harassment by his supervisor, he said top managers pressured him to rescind the claims, which took him months to bring forward for fear of no confidentiality since the bank had a policy not allowing employees to talk critically about someone unless the person was present. Its Principal No. 11: "Never say anything about a person you wouldn't say to him directly. If you do, you are a slimy weasel."[18]

- A Chicago court found for a female employee in a suit against Custom Companies, a trucking company in Northlake, Illinois, when it determined that the founder and top managers in the company engaged in "reprehensible conduct" against three female sales representatives by repeatedly touching; groping; making sexually explicit comments using lewd language; and exposing them to pornography, jokes, sexual advances, and a sexually charged atmosphere, which included making them take clients to strip clubs and other places of adult entertainment. In sharply criticizing the harassers in a 50-page memorandum opinion, among other things, the court enjoined Custom from further engaging in such activity and ordered it to send a letter to its clients notifying them of the court's decision.[19]

- A male lawyer sued his ex-firm for trying to bully him into going to an all-male weekend retreat that could involve naked participants passing around a wooden phallus in a circle and describing their sexual experiences and becoming "extremely hostile" and refusing to pay him because of his refusal.[20]

- A female employee was awarded $1.7 million after her employer spanked her in front of coworkers in what the employer called a "camaraderie-building exercise" that pitted sales teams against each other, with winners throwing pies at the losers, feeding them baby food, making them wear diapers, and spanking them.[21]

- Lutheran Medical Center in Brooklyn, New York, agreed to pay nearly $5.5 million to settle a sexual harassment case in which a hospital doctor allegedly subjected more than 50 female employees to invasive touching and intrusive questions about their sex life during mandatory physical exams. He threatened to delay or deny their employment if they did not cooperate.[22]

- A former Delta Airlines pilot filed suit alleging Delta ignored her complaints about being sexually harassed while in the cockpit, then shunned by her fellow pilots refusing to talk to her during flight operations when she reported it.[23]

- The dog groomer for a New York socialite sued for sexual harassment after repeatedly being subjected to sexual advances by his employer as he tried to train her dogs.[24]

- Burger King settled a claim for sexual harassment of seven female employees, *six of whom were high school students,* after the manager subjected them to repeated groping, vulgar sexual comments, and demands for sex. Nothing was done when this was reported to assistant managers at the restaurant or to the district manager.[25]

- A New Hampshire judge was convicted of assault on five women who were victim's advocates of his court after groping them at a conference on sexual assault and domestic violence. Late-night partying at the conference also led to the attorney general's resignation after an investigation into his inappropriate touching of a woman while dancing.[26]

We could go on, but we will stop here. You get the message. From *The Price Is Right* game show host Bob Barker[27] to governor and actor Arnold Schwarzenegger (who, after being dogged by allegations of sexual misconduct with up to 16 women during his campaign for governor of California, underwent a voluntary course in preventing sexual harassment after his election);[28] from the founder of Habitat for Humanity to conservative talk show host Bill O'Reilly (in a different case than the one above);[29] and from a sitting president (Bill Clinton, who was governor at the time the event occurred) to a candidate for the presidency who later became president (Donald Trump, who was videotaped saying "Grab 'em by the pussy" and has had many allegations and claims against him for sexual improprieties),[30] no one seems to be immune from engaging in sexual harassment. (See Exhibit 9.1, "Even a Professor. . .") Even in light of efforts like #MeToo and Times Up, sexual harassment suits are still far more frequent an occurrence than they should be or than we would like them to be, if for no other reason than they cost the employer totally unnecessary time, effort, energy, bad press, and money for purely personal reasons of the harasser.

The efforts to curtail it have paid off in some ways. After the Harvey Weinstein story broke in 2017, the #MeToo movement went viral, and more and more victims of sexual harassment were willing to come forward. It has undoubtedly had an impact. Illinois has a new mandate strengthening its law and requiring employers to conduct mandatory sexual harassment awareness and training beginning in 2020.[31] In August 2019, New York passed sweeping legislation designed to strengthen state protection for victims of sexual harassment.[32] In April 2019, the EEOC announced that in response to #MeToo, it was filing more sexual harassment cases and winning, with recovery by the agency going from $47.5 million in 2017 to nearly $70 million in 2018.[33] The agency's funding was increased in 2018 for the first time in over eight years, with about $16 million earmarked for focusing on sexual harassment claims. Sexual harassment claims filed by the EEOC increased by more than 50 percent from 2017 to 2018.9-P Headway is being made. But the[34] problem has been so dire that much still remains to be done.

Exhibit 9.1   *Even a Professor . . .*

No doubt you have heard about President Bill Clinton's sexual encounter with White House intern Monica Lewinsky. This situation involved a student who evidently resembled Ms. Lewinsky and the professor who kept reminding her of that fact in front of other students.

Inbal Hayut, a female student of political science professor Alex Young at the University of New York at New Paltz, sued Professor Young for nicknaming her "Monica" and subjecting her to harassment about it over the course of the semester. Hayut apparently resembled Monica Lewinsky, the White House intern who had an affair with then-President Bill Clinton and was much in the news at the time. Professor Young opened virtually every class session by asking Hayut in front of the entire class, "How was your weekend with Bill?" Hayut alleged that twice in class Professor Young told her, "Be quiet, Monica. I'll give you a cigar later." She asked Professor Young to stop referring to her as "Monica" but was ignored. Classmates mockingly addressed Hayut as "Monica" outside class.

Hayut said the comments affected her deeply, humiliated her in front of her classmates, and made it difficult for her to sleep or concentrate at school or work. She barely passed her courses that semester, received failing grades the next term, withdrew from the school, and had to complete a year of remedial work before she could transfer to another school.

Hayut sued the university, the professor, and several school administrators for, among other things, violating the Title IX Educational Amendments of 1972, which prohibit gender discrimination in any education program or activity receiving federal financial assistance. Professor Young, who had been teaching for 30 years, admitted making the statements but said they were a joke. He retired a month after school administrators met to decide what to do about the situation.

In the lawsuit, the school claimed the actions by Professor Young did not amount to sexual harassment. The court ruled that Professor Young, as "a teacher at a state university, was a state actor vested with considerable authority over his students." His comments were severe and pervasive enough to transcend the bounds of propriety and decency and became actionable harassment, and Hayut's academic performance suffered as a result. [*Hayut v. SUNY at New Paltz, et al.,* 352 F.3d 733 (2d Cir. 2003).]

Many of the items in the preceding list were brought as class actions. There was a time when it was thought to be unthinkable that an entire group of employees could be being harassed. Now such cases are common. In 1991, the first sexual harassment class action was approved in *Jenson v. Eveleth Taconite, Inc.*[35] Leading up to the class action certification proceedings there was much speculation in the legal community as to whether such a thing could be done or even if it really needed to be done. How frequently could there possibly be a case with so many charges that a class action suit was necessary? Unfortunately, in the years since, many such cases have been brought, involving both men and women. Few are brought to trial. The risk to the employer is too great. Sexual harassment class action trials (actual trials, not lawsuits filed) have been called "a white buffalo" by one lawyer because so few are seen.[36] Many cases are filed, but they are settled rather than litigated as a means of avoiding bad publicity and the possibility of even greater damages if the matter goes to trial. Keep in mind that rather than a quiet settlement with a non-disclosure clause, at trial the jury would hear employee after employee take the witness stand and under oath tell similar stories, generally of a grossly inappropriate-for-the-workplace, graphic sexual nature, often from the employer's offices all over the country. To think that there would be enough employees experiencing sexual harassment at a workplace to even be certified as a class action (no small feat!) ought to give you cause for concern as a future manager, supervisor, or business owner.

The *Eveleth* case became the inspiration for the Academy Award–nominated movie *North Country,* starring Charlize Theron (who was later nominated for an Oscar as best leading actress for her role in *Bombshell*), detailing the very ugly situation the employee faced in trying to do something about the sexual harassment of herself and other female employees. The film was based on the book *Class Action* by Clara Bingham and Laura Leedy Gansler.[37] In addition to the class action suits set forth above, consider these:

- CB Richard Ellis, a $1.6 billion, publicly traded commercial real estate brokerage firm with 17,000 employees in 300 offices around the world, was sued by female employees whose affidavits alleged management condoned and perpetuated discrimination and sexual harassment against women through such things as its decades-old, much-touted, annual "Fight Night" event in Atlanta. This was characterized as a "rowdy, black-tie Vegas-style boys night out of cigar smoke, boxing, and women on display." Female employees were chosen to wear evening clothes and serve them and their clients drinks and cigars. At work, female employees across the country alleged they were subjected to groping, degrading comments, and vulgar discussions about sex and women's body parts. Male employees also exposed themselves to female employees. The plaintiffs alleged daily circulation of offensive, lewd, and pornographic emails; granting or withholding permission to interface with customers based on a female employee's looks; viewing of pornographic websites and videos in the office; and the display of offensive, lewd, and pornographic pictures and calendars in the office. The real estate brokerage firm eventually settled the case for an undetermined amount that included, among other things, $3.4 million in attorney fees and a $400,000 donation to a women's real estate trade group for scholarships.[38]

- The EEOC brought a class action suit against Red Lobster in Salisbury, MD, for "egregious sexual harassment" including the culinary manager pressing his groin against them, grabbing and groping them, and making sexually offensive comments such as frequent remarks about the female employees' bodies and about his genitals.[39]

- In the EEOC's longest discrimination suit in the history of its Chicago office, a class action suit on behalf of more than 100 women against International Profit Associates, Inc., was settled with the employer admitting to "an unlawful pattern or practice of tolerating sexual harassment."[40]

- A Las Vegas real estate developer subjected a class of women to sexual propositions, touching, and even threats at gunpoint.[41]

- Merchant Management Systems Resources, Inc., subjected a class of female employees to "egregious" sexual harassment and retaliation if they complained, including sexual comments and touching up to coerced sexual intercourse.[42]

- Dial Corporation, maker of Dial soap, entered into a consent decree with the EEOC to settle a class action by 91 women who alleged that the Dial Corporation's soap factory in Montgomery, Illinois, had a sexually abusive environment for years and management either participated in the activities or did nothing when it was reported. Harassing activity included everything from grabbing female employees and fondling their breasts to sexual comments and propositions to placing a sanitary napkin doused with ketchup beside a female employee's tool box as well as a life-sized penis carved from pink soap.[43]

- Thirty-two female employees at the U.S. Mint's Denver plant, nearly one-third of the females, filed suit alleging they were subjected to sexist comments, treated more favorably if they had sex with some managers, disciplined more harshly than men, discouraged from complaining about the treatment, and ignored after they met with Mint officials. Until they met with higher authorities at the U.S. Treasury Department, the harassment continued. The Mint director was female.[44]

- In 2017 in the private Facebook group Marines United, thousands of Marines, without permission, posted nude "revenge porn" photos of fellow female Marines and others. The investigation soon spread to the Army and Navy.[45]

- In 2010, nearly 50,000 male veterans screened positive for "military sexual trauma" at the Department of Veterans Affairs, up from just over 30,000 in 2003. The Pentagon began to acknowledge the rampant problem of sexual violence as both males and females came forward in unprecedented numbers. Experts said that male-on-male assault in the military is not motivated by sexual orientation but by power, intimidation, and domination.[46]

- The EEOC sued Kraft on behalf of a class of male employees who were subjected to "egregious" same-sex harassment and retaliation by their male supervisor in Birmingham, Alabama. The employees were subjected to sexual comments and propositions, touching, grabbing, and sexual assaults by a male supervisor for Nabisco.[47]

- The EEOC filed for class action certification in an action against Federal Express Corp. for same-gender sexual harassment in Kankakee, Illinois. One of the employees alleged that he repeatedly complained to management about the harassment by another male employee, but he was told to "act like a man" and that "nothing can be done."

Can you think of a good reason an employer would watch millions of hard-earned dollars go out of a business's coffers for such unnecessary, avoidable, and totally useless actions? Impeachment of a president, resignation of multi-starred generals and other high-level military personnel, resignation of company and university presidents and long-term legislators, and embarrassing televised hearings of not one but two U.S. Supreme Court nominees all have been a part of our national consciousness and abrupt introduction to and education in the area of sexual harassment. It is frustrating to see the same thing over and over again while liability is so avoidable if employers will only take a few steps we will discuss.

LO1 Discuss the background leading up to sexual harassment as a workplace issue.

But before we do that, let's get a bit of context. Sexual harassment may have been something you are used to realizing existed, but it really is of pretty recent vintage. It seems like such a short time ago that most of us were totally unaware that the legal cause of action of sexual harassment even existed. Though it had been around for more than 10 years, most people knew very little about it. Until, that is, it was thrust into the limelight when then–University of Oklahoma law professor Anita Hill took her seat at a table before the Senate Judiciary Committee in the confirmation hearings for associate justice of the U.S. Supreme Court Clarence Thomas. Hill had worked for Thomas when he was head of the EEOC about 10 years before. When Thomas came up for confirmation, friends of Hill reported to the Judiciary Committee that she had at one time revealed to them details of unprofessional encounters with Thomas that could have amounted to sexual harassment. The committee contacted Hill and made clear that she would either testify about the matter and set the record straight herself or leave them to their own devices of discovery. Hill very reluctantly chose to testify after being subpoenaed by the Judiciary Committee, and the country hasn't been the same since. The historic situation is now the basis of the 2016 Emmy-nominated HBO docudrama *Confirmation* and the 2014 documentary *Anita: Speaking Truth to Power,* which played to packed Sundance Film Festival audiences. As previously discussed in the gender chapter, Hill was also tapped to head up the Hollywood Commission on sexual harassment in the wake of the #MeToo and Times Up movements to address the issue of sexual harassment in Hollywood.

Hill's testimony over the next several days and Thomas's barely concealed anger about it were painful for the millions of Americans who sat glued to their television sets during those unbelievable autumn days in 1991. People who had never even heard the term *sexual harassment* now had implacable opinions about it. From barber shops to executive suites and everywhere in between, *everyone* discussed the pros and cons of not only Hill's and Thomas's assertions but also the concept of sexual harassment itself. Men who had thought nothing of what they considered harmless sexually suggestive jokes, comments, gestures, propositions, and even touching suddenly felt themselves looked upon as virtual lechers. Women who had found themselves on the uncomfortable receiving end of such unwanted attentions now discovered that those attentions might be not just uncomfortable but actually illegal under Title VII. Eight months after the Hill–Thomas hearings, sexual harassment complaints filed with the EEOC increased by more than 50 percent. Ninety percent of the charges were from women. In the elections of 1992, called the "Year of the Woman," unprecedented numbers of female politicians rode the backlash wave of women who wanted to change "politics as usual" after witnessing what they perceived as the Senate's poor treatment of Hill during the hearings and Thomas's confirmation despite Hill's revelations. Ironically, at the time he engaged in the alleged activity, Thomas was head of the EEOC, the very agency charged with enforcing sexual harassment laws.

Much happened in the wake of the Hill–Thomas fiasco. Almost overnight, the country's offices and workplaces went from friendly to foul. Sexual harassment captivated the national consciousness, only there was an immediate, acerbic, often acrimonious air to it. Lines were drawn in offices, bars, schools, universities, churches, and homes all across the country, and people took their places on one side or the other and held their ground.

As you can see, sexual harassment law is not something that has been around forever or that we've grown accustomed to and learned to live with over hundreds of years or even in the 55 or so years since Title VII was born. Even though it may seem like old hat today, it is still pretty new in the legal sense. It is still evolving. The U.S. Supreme Court did not hear its first sexual harassment case until 1986, and the next one did not come until six years later in 1992. And of course, as we saw earlier, despite making it clear that sexual harassment is a type of gender discrimination and a violation of Title VII, as you can see from the recent examples, there are still too many who don't yet "get it."

Imagine, then, seeing this scenario play out all over again 26 years later in the 2017 confirmation hearings for Brett Kavanaugh to be appointed to the U.S. Supreme Court. Given what we just wrote, you would have thought that after the country's baptism by fire with the sexual harassment issue, it would have learned. But here we were again with a reluctant professor facing a nominee for the country's highest court with allegations of improprieties. Of course, a big distinguishing factor was that Thomas had been head of the EEOC when his scenario took place, while Kavanaugh was a student.

We also told you the background of sexual harassment because there is a lot of baggage that comes with the issue. Often, managers, supervisors, and employees don't recognize sexual harassment when it occurs. Our society preaches sexual permissiveness on the one hand, through music, movies, television, advertising, acculturation, and so forth, but when it comes to the workplace, the rules are different, and some people don't make the transition very well.

Despite this, is sexual harassment something with which we really should be concerned? Is it that big a deal? Well, let's take a look. In one of the first and still one of the most comprehensive studies ever conducted on the issue, the U.S. Merit Systems Protection Board in 1980 found that over 40 percent of federal employees had reported incidents of sexual harassment; seven years later, the results were nearly the same (42 percent). A survey by *Working Woman* magazine of 160 of the Fortune 500 companies showed that nearly 40 percent of the companies had received at least one sexual harassment complaint in the previous 12 months. A *New York Times* poll found that 4 of every 10 women reported having experienced sexual harassment. The *National Law Journal* reported that 60 percent of female attorneys nationally said they had experienced some form of sexual harassment. A *Parade Magazine* poll discovered that 70 percent of the women polled who served in the military said they had been sexually harassed, as had 50 percent of the women who worked in congressional offices on Capitol Hill. Despite the numbers, only about 5 percent of the incidents of sexual harassment were reported. Those who experience sexual harassment "pay all the intangible emotional costs inflicted by anger, humiliation, frustration, withdrawal, [and] dysfunction in family life."[48]

In *Robinson v. Jacksonville Shipyards, Inc.,*[49] the court found, based on expert testimony, that

[v]ictims of sexual harassment suffer stress effects from the harassment. Stress as a result of sexual harassment is recognized as a specific, diagnosable problem by the American Psychiatric Association. Among the stress effects suffered is "work performance stress," which includes distraction from tasks, dread of work, and an inability to work. Another form is "emotional stress," which covers a range of responses, including anger, fear of physical safety, anxiety, depression, guilt, humiliation, and embarrassment. Physical stress also results from sexual harassment; it may manifest itself by sleeping problems, headaches, weight changes, and other physical ailments. A study by the Working Women's Institute found that 96 percent of sexual harassment victims experienced emotional stress, 45 percent suffered work performance stress, and 35 percent were inflicted with physical stress problems.

Sexual harassment has a cumulative, eroding effect on the victim's well-being. When women feel a need to maintain vigilance against the next incidence of harassment, the stress is increased tremendously. When women feel that their individual complaints will not change the work environment materially, the ensuing sense of despair further compounds the stress.[50]

Regarding tangible costs, according to the classic 1988 MSPB update study, sexual harassment cost the federal government $267 million from May 1985 to May 1987 for losses in productivity, sick leave costs, and employee replacement costs. A *Working Woman* magazine survey found the actual cost of sexual harassment in the responding companies to be $6.7 million in low productivity, absenteeism, and employee turnover. In addition, along with the nontangible price they pay, the MSPB found that employees who are sexually harassed pay medical expenses, litigation expenses, and job search expenses and lose valuable sick leave and annual leave. In the 2016 Final EEOC Select Task Force on the Study of Harassment in the Workplace, issued after an 18-month study of the issue by a select committee that included not only lawyers but also sociologists, psychologists, trainers, and workplace representatives, the EEOC noted that what brought about the call for the study in the first place was the fact that in the 30 years since sexual harassment had been used as a cause of action, the prevalence of the incidences of the activity was still so very high. Despite this, the report found that over 90 percent of employees who experience such harassment fail to report it for, among other things, fear of not being believed or experiencing retaliation.[51]

Whether it occurs through touching, gestures, staring, jokes, emails, texts, notes, requests for dates, denials of job opportunities, negative comments based on gender, the display or showing of pornography, or some other means, sexual harassment is not just kidding or a joke or workplace fraternization. It is an illegal form of gender discrimination that violates Title VII of the 1964 Civil Rights Act. But it is not only illegal: Given the toll it takes on the workplace, it is simply not good business. Since it is purely personal on the part of the harasser, it makes little sense for an employer not to take simple steps to prevent this totally unnecessary liability. It has become even less justifiable in the face of the 1991 Civil Rights Act amending Title VII to permit jury trials and compensatory and punitive damages.

As mentioned previously, the Civil Rights Act was passed in 1964, but it was the mid- to late 1970s before courts began to seriously recognize sexual harassment as a form of gender discrimination under Title VII. In 1980, soon after the first few significant sexual harassment cases were decided, the EEOC issued guidelines on sexual harassment. The guidelines, quoted in the opening of this chapter, are not law in the sense of Title VII but carry a great deal of weight when it comes to how courts will view and analyze the issue.

Where Do Sexual Harassment Considerations Leave the Employer?

It is important to note that the intent of the law is *not* that the workplace either become totally devoid of sexuality on the one hand or be given completely over to employees who would misuse the law on the other. Consensual relationships are not forbidden under the law, and employees may date consistent with company policy. It is only when the activity directed toward an employee is *unwelcome* and imposes terms or conditions of employment different for one gender than another that it becomes a problem. For instance, a female employee might be required as a condition of employment to date her supervisor, while male employees have no such condition imposed. Most workplaces have sexual harassment policies (see Exhibit 9.2, "Example of a Sexual Harassment Policy") to govern this workplace issue. Recently, Illinois joined California, Maine, Connecticut, Delaware, New York state, and New York City to take it a step further and mandate training. The specifics vary by state, but it sends an important message to mandate the training. The EEOC recommended not only that employers have such things as policies and training but also that they go further and take a broader proactive approach that includes workplace civility training.

Exhibit 9.2 *Example of a Sexual Harassment Policy*

Often the employer doesn't really know what is appropriate to include in a sexual harassment policy. In the *Jacksonville Shipyards* case, as part of the court's order, the employer was required to adopt a sexual harassment policy, which was included in an appendix. In order for you to see what one actually looks like and make the theoretical more practical for you, it is reproduced below, with changes as appropriate to generalize the policy (rather than have it be specific to JSI). It is important to check state laws in your area, as they may vary from federal laws. For instance, some state laws mandate postings, and some do not; many begin coverage if the employer has only one employee, while others track the federal law's 15; and some specify what must be in any posting that is provided by the employer.

XYZ COMPANY SEXUAL HARASSMENT POLICY

Statement of Policy
Title VII of the Civil Rights Act of 1964 prohibits employment discrimination on the basis of race, color, gender, religion, or national origin. *Sexual harassment is included among the prohibitions.*

Sexual harassment, according to the federal Equal Employment Opportunity Commission (EEOC), consists of unwelcome sexual advances, requests for sexual favors, or other verbal or physical acts of a sexual or sex-based nature where (1) submission to such conduct is made either explicitly or implicitly a term or condition of an individual's employment; (2) an employment decision is based on an individual's acceptance or rejection of such conduct; or (3) such conduct interferes with an individual's work performance or creates an intimidating, hostile, or offensive working environment.

It is also unlawful to retaliate or take reprisal in any way against anyone who has articulated any concern about sexual harassment or discrimination, whether that concern relates to harassment of or discrimination against the individual raising the concern or against another individual.

Examples of conduct that would be considered sexual harassment or related retaliation are set forth in the Statement of Prohibited Conduct, which follows. These examples are provided to illustrate the kind of conduct proscribed by this policy; the list is not exhaustive.

XYZ Company and its agents are under a duty to investigate and eradicate any form of sexual harassment, gender discrimination, or retaliation. To further that end, XYZ Company has issued a procedure for making complaints about conduct in violation of this policy and a schedule for violation of this policy.

Sexual harassment is unlawful, and such prohibited conduct exposes not only XYZ Company but individuals involved in such conduct to significant liability under the law. Employees at all times should treat other employees respectfully and with dignity in a manner so as not to offend the sensibilities of a coworker. Accordingly, XYZ's management is committed to vigorously enforcing its Antisexual Harassment Policy at all levels within the company.

Statement of Prohibited Conduct
The management of XYZ Company considers the following conduct to represent some of the types of acts which violate XYZ's Antisexual Harassment Policy:

A. Physical assaults of a sexual nature, such as:

(1) rape, sexual battery, molestation, or attempts to commit these assaults; and

(2) intentional physical conduct, which is sexual in nature, such as touching, pinching, patting, grabbing, brushing against another employee's body, or poking another employee's body.

B. Unwanted sexual advances, propositions, or other sexual comments, such as:

(1) sexually oriented gestures, noises, remarks, jokes, or comments about a person's sexuality or sexual experience directed at or made in the presence of any employee who indicates or has indicated in any way that such conduct in his or her presence is unwelcome;

(continued)

Exhibit 9.2 *continued*

(2) preferential treatment or promise of preferential treatment to an employee for submitting to sexual conduct, including soliciting or attempting to solicit any employee to engage in sexual activity for compensation or reward; and

(3) subjecting, or threats of subjecting, an employee to unwelcome sexual attention or conduct or intentionally making performance of the employee's job more difficult because of that employee's gender.

C. Sexual or discriminatory displays or publications anywhere in XYZ's workplace by XYZ's employees, such as:

(1) displaying pictures, posters, calendars, graffiti, objects, promotional materials, reading materials, or other materials that are sexually suggestive, sexually demeaning, or pornographic, or bringing into the XYZ work environment or possessing any such material to read, display, or view at work.

A picture will be presumed to be sexually suggestive if it depicts a person of either gender who is not fully clothed or in clothes that are not suited to or ordinarily accepted for the accomplishment of routine work in and around the workplace and who is posed for the obvious purpose of displaying or drawing attention to private portions of his or her body;

(2) reading or otherwise publicizing in the work environment materials that are in any way sexually revealing, sexually suggestive, sexually demeaning, or pornographic; and

(3) displaying signs or other materials purporting to segregate an employee by gender in any area of the workplace (other than restrooms and similar semiprivate lockers/changing rooms).

D. Retaliation for sexual harassment complaints, such as:

(1) disciplining, changing work assignments of, providing inaccurate work information to, or refusing to cooperate or discuss work-related matters with any employee because that employee has complained about or resisted harassment, discrimination, or retaliation; and

(2) intentionally pressuring, falsely denying, lying about, or otherwise covering up or attempting to cover up conduct such as that described in any item above.

E. Other acts:

(1) The above is not to be construed as an all-inclusive list of prohibited acts under this policy.

(2) Sexual harassment is unlawful and hurts other employees. Any of the prohibited conduct described here is sexual harassment of anyone at whom it is directed or who is otherwise subjected to it. Each incident of harassment, moreover, contributes to a general atmosphere in which all persons who share the victim's gender suffer the consequences. Sexually oriented acts or gender-based conduct have no legitimate business purpose; accordingly, the employee who engages in such conduct should be and will be made to bear the full responsibility for such unlawful conduct.

Schedule of Penalties for Misconduct

The following schedule of penalties applies to all violations of this policy, as explained in more detail in the Statement of Prohibited Conduct.

Where progressive discipline is provided for, each instance of conduct violating the policy moves the offending employee through the steps of disciplinary action. In other words, it is not necessary for an employee to repeat the same precise conduct in order to move up the scale of discipline.

A written record of each action taken pursuant to the policy will be placed in the offending employee's personnel file. The record will reflect the conduct, or alleged conduct, and the warning given, or other discipline imposed.

A. Assault:

Any employee's first proven offense of assault or threat of assault, including assault of a sexual nature, will result in dismissal.

B. Other acts of harassment by coworkers:

An employee's commission of acts of sexual harassment, other than assault, will result in nondisciplinary oral counseling upon alleged first offense; written warning, suspension, or discharge upon the first proven offense, depending upon the nature and severity of the misconduct; and suspension or discharge upon the second proven offense, depending upon the nature and severity of the misconduct.

C. Retaliation:

Alleged retaliation against a sexual harassment complainant will result in nondisciplinary oral counseling. Any form of proven retaliation will result in suspension or discharge upon the first proven offense, depending upon the nature and severity of the retaliatory acts, and discharge upon the second proven offense.

D. Supervisors:

A supervisor's commission of acts of sexual harassment (other than assault) with respect to any employee under that person's supervision will result in nondisciplinary oral counseling upon alleged first offense, final warning or dismissal for the first offense, depending upon the nature and severity of the misconduct, and discharge for any subsequent offense.

Procedures for Making, Investigating, and Resolving Sexual Harassment and Retaliation Complaints

A. Complaints:

XYZ Company will provide its employees with convenient, confidential, and reliable mechanisms for reporting incidents of sexual harassment and retaliation. Accordingly, XYZ designates at least two employees in supervisory or managerial positions to serve as investigative officers for sexual harassment issues. The names, responsibilities, work locations, and phone numbers of each officer will be routinely and continuously posted so that an employee seeking such name can enjoy anonymity and remain inconspicuous to all of the employees in the office in which he or she works.

The investigative officers may appoint "designees" to assist them in handling sexual harassment complaints. Persons appointed as designees shall not conduct investigations until they have received training equivalent to that received by the investigative officers. The purpose of having several persons to whom complaints may be made is to avoid a situation where an employee is faced with complaining to the person, or a close associate of the person, who would be the subject of the complaint.

Complaints of acts of sexual harassment or retaliation that are in violation of the sexual harassment policy will be accepted in writing or orally, and anonymous complaints will be taken seriously and investigated. Anyone who has observed sexual harassment or retaliation should report it to a designated investigative officer. A complaint need not be limited to someone who was the target of harassment or retaliation. Only those who have an immediate need to know, including the investigative officers and/or his/her designee, the alleged target of harassment or retaliation, the alleged harasser(s) or retaliator(s), and any witnesses who will or may find out the identity of the complainant. All parties contacted in the course of an investigation will be advised that all parties involved in a charge are entitled to respect and that any retaliation or reprisal against an individual who is an alleged target of harassment or retaliation, who has made a complaint, or who has provided evidence in connection with a complaint is a separate actionable offense as provided in the schedule of penalties. This complaint process will be administered consistent with federal labor law when bargaining unit members are affected.

B. Investigations:

Each investigative officer will receive thorough training about sexual harassment and the procedures herein and will have the responsibility for investigating complaints or having an appropriately trained and designated XYZ investigator do so.

All complaints will be investigated expeditiously by a trained XYZ investigative officer or his/her designee. The investigative officer will produce a written report, which, together with the investigation file, will be shown to the complainant upon request within a reasonable time. The investigative officer is empowered to recommend remedial measures based upon the results of the investigation, and XYZ management will promptly consider and

(continued)

Exhibit 9.2 *continued*

act upon such recommendation. When a complaint is made, the investigative officer will have the duty of immediately bringing all sexual harassment and retaliation complaints to the confidential attention of the office of the president of XYZ, and XYZ's EEO officer. The investigative and EEO officers will each maintain a file on the original charge and follow up investigation. Such files will be available to investigators, to federal, state, and local agencies charged with equal employment or affirmative action enforcement, to other complainants who have filed a formal charge of discrimination against XYZ, or any agent thereof, whether that formal charge is filed at a federal, state, or local law level. The names of complainants, however, will be kept under separate file.

C. Cooperation:

An effective antisexual harassment policy requires the support and example of company personnel in positions of authority. XYZ agents or employees who engage in sexual harassment or retaliation or who fail to cooperate with company-sponsored investigations of sexual harassment or retaliation may be severely sanctioned by suspension or dismissal. By the same token, officials who refuse to implement remedial measures, obstruct the remedial efforts of other XYZ employees, and/or retaliate against sexual harassment complainants or witnesses may be immediately sanctioned by suspension or dismissal.

Procedures and Rules for Education and Training

Education and training for employees at each level of the workforce are critical to the success of XYZ's policy against sexual harassment. The following documents address such issues: the letter to be sent to all employees from XYZ's chief executive officer/president; the Antisexual Harassment Policy; Statement of Prohibited Conduct; the Schedule of Penalties for Misconduct; and Procedures for Making, Investigating, and Resolving Sexual Harassment Complaints. These documents will be conspicuously posted throughout the workplace

at each division of XYZ, on each company bulletin board, in all central gathering areas, and in every locker room. The statements must be clearly legible and displayed continuously. The antisexual harassment policy under a cover letter from XYZ's president will be sent to all employees. The letter will indicate that copies are available at no cost and how they can be obtained.

XYZ's antisexual harassment policy statement will also be included in the Safety Instructions and General Company Rules, which is issued in booklet form to each XYZ employee. Educational posters using concise messages conveying XYZ's opposition to workplace sexual harassment will reinforce the company's policy statement; these posters should be simple, eye-catching, and graffiti resistant.

Education and training include the following components:

1. *For all XYZ employees:* As part of the general orientation, each recently hired employee will be given a copy of the letter from XYZ's chief executive officer/president and requested to read and sign a receipt for the company's policy statement on sexual harassment so that they are on notice of the standards of behavior expected. In addition, supervisory employees who have attended a management training seminar on sexual harassment will explain orally at least once every six months at general meetings attended by all employees the kind of acts that constitute sexual harassment, the company's serious commitment to eliminating sexual harassment in the workplace, the penalties for engaging in harassment, and the procedures for reporting incidents of sexual harassment.

2. *For all female employees:* All women employed at XYZ will participate on company time in annual seminars that teach strategies for resisting and preventing sexual harassment. At least a half-day in length, these seminars will be conducted by one or more experienced sexual harassment educators, including one instructor with work experience in the trades

for skilled employees in traditionally male-dominated jobs.

3. *For all employees with supervisory authority of any kind over other employees:* All supervisory personnel will participate in an annual, half-day-long training session on gender discrimination. At least one-third of each session (of no less than one and one-half hours) will be devoted to education about workplace sexual harassment, including training (with demonstrative evidence) as to exactly what types of remarks, behavior, and pictures will not be tolerated in the XYZ workplace. The president of XYZ will attend the training sessions in one central location with all company supervisory employees. The president

will introduce the seminar with remarks stressing the potential liability of XYZ and individual supervisors for sexual harassment. Each participant will be informed that they are responsible for knowing the contents of XYZ's antisexual harassment policy and for giving similar presentations at meetings of employees.

4. *For all investigative officers:* The investigative officers and their designees, if any, will attend annual full-day training seminars conducted by experienced sexual harassment educators and/or investigators to educate them about the problems of sexual harassment in the workplace and the techniques for investigating and stopping it.

Sexual Harassment in General

LO4 List and explain employer defenses to sexual harassment claims.

quid pro quo sexual harassment
Sexual harassment in which the harasser requests sexual activity from the harassee in exchange for workplace benefits.

hostile environment sexual harassment
Sexual harassment in which the harasser creates an abusive, offensive, or intimidating environment for the harassee.

There are two theories on which an action for sexual harassment may be brought: **quid pro quo sexual harassment** and **hostile environment sexual harassment**. The first generally involves the employer requiring some type of sexual activity[52] from the harassee as a condition of employment or workplace benefits. The second addresses an offensive work environment to which one gender is subjected but not the other. (See Exhibit 9.3, "Wanted?") While there are two different types of sexual harassment and each has its own requirements, the U.S. Supreme Court has said that the distinction need not be rigid. In *Burlington Industries, Inc. v. Ellerth,* the supervisor made threats to the harassee but did not carry them out. The harassee brought suit on the theory of *quid pro quo sexual harassment,* but rather than deny relief because there had been no loss of a tangible job benefit necessary for quid pro quo sexual harassment, the Court said that the terms *quid pro quo* and *hostile environment* are not controlling for purposes of determining employer liability for harassment by a supervisor. Rather, they are helpful in making rough demarcations between Title VII cases in which sexual harassment threats are carried out and where they are not or are absent altogether. (See *Burlington Industries, Inc. v. Ellerth* at the end of this chapter.)

Statistically speaking, most sexual harassment takes place between males and females, with the male as the harasser and the female as the harassee. But the gender of the harasser need not be male, and the gender of the parties does not matter. Males can be sexually harassed as well. (See Exhibit 9.4, "Playing Catch-Up.") Keep in mind the statistics provided above about the incidents of male sexual harassment in the military. Unfortunately, because society views males and sex so differently from females and sex, many males do not bring cases for fear of ridicule. Males who are being sexually harassed and wish to put a stop to it often

Exhibit 9.3 *Wanted?*

One of the requirements of sexual harassment is that the activity be unwelcome. Take a look at these cases and see if this is what you think the law had in mind.

EEOC v. Bon Secours DePaul Med. Ctr., Civil Action No. 2:02cv728 (E.D. Va. 2002)

A jury awarded over $4 million to a hospital administrator who sued for retaliation under Title VII for being forced to resign when she attempted to prevent sexual harassment in the hospital's operating room. There were complaints of a nurse hugging, kissing, embracing, and rubbing doctors and other staff. The administrator verbally warned the nurse that this was inappropriate behavior. The nurse complained to doctors and staff about unfair treatment and quit. Several doctors complained about the administrator and a prominent doctor threatened to leave the hospital unless the administrator was terminated and the nurse reinstated. The administrator, given the choice to resign or be terminated for "breach of confidentiality," left. Six days later the nurse returned.

Miller v. Department of Corrections, 36 Cal. 4th 446, 115 P.3d 77 (2005)

The California Supreme Court held that an employee can sue a supervisor engaging in consensual sexual conduct with other employees when it has the effect of creating a "widespread atmosphere of sexual favoritism in the workplace." This decision forces employers to closely monitor employee relationships. While they may not constitute sexual harassment, they can be problematic in other ways.

Exhibit 9.4 *Playing Catch-Up*

In 1993, when a 10-woman, 2-man jury awarded Sabino Gutierrez more than $1 million in damages for sexual harassment by his boss, Maria Martinez, of Cal-Spas, a hot tub manufacturing company in California. It was the largest award in history for a male sexual harassee. Given the rarity of men bringing sexual harassment suits at the time (the harassing events of fondling, kissing, pressure for sex, and eventually demotion began in 1986 and continued for six years), it is almost certain that the novelty of a male suing for sexual harassment played some role in the case and jury award amount.

In the years since, however, such cases have been on the rise and are becoming more common. According to the EEOC, male victims accounted for 12 percent of claims in 1999. By 2009, a decade later, they accounted for 16.4 percent of sexual harassment claims filed with the EEOC. This uptick has been even greater since the country's 2008–2009 financial crisis resulted in a higher percentage of men losing their jobs. According to the Bureau of Labor Statistics, from September 2008 to January 2010, women lost 2.3 million jobs versus 4.4 million for men. While male victims of sexual harassment may have previously simply quit and found another job, that is not as possible in this economy. As a result, the data indicate that sexual harassment claims rose more in states with higher unemployment rates.

For years, men were hesitant to come forward about sexual harassment in the workplace because it often made them the butt of jokes. There were questions about their sexual orientation, loyalty, character, and toughness once they brought such claims forward. However, once the U.S. Supreme Court ruled in *Oncale v. Sundowner Offshore Drilling, Inc.* that males could be the victims of sexual harassment by other males in violation of Title VII's proscription on gender discrimination via sexual harassment, claims by males being sexually harassed began to increase.

Overall, only about 6 percent of sexual harassment cases are ever actually litigated in court, and the harassee wins about one-third of the time, according to a study by the American Bar Foundation.

Sources: Alissa Figueroa, "Workplace Harassment: Same-Sex Sexual Harassment Cases Are on the Rise," *The Christian Science Monitor* (July 21, 2010), http://www.csmonitor.com/Business/new-economy/2010/0721/Workplace-harassment-Same-sex-sexual-harassment-cases-are-on-the-rise; Sarah Herman, "Male Sexual Harassment on the Rise," *HRM* (June 21, 2010), http://www.hrmreport.com/news/male-sexual-harassment-claims-rising/.

find themselves the object of workplace jokes, teasing, and questioned sexuality, so they forgo filing claims. Even so, EEOC statistics show that claims by men have been increasing, beginning during the 2008–2009 recession.[53] By fiscal year 2018, 15.9 percent of sexual harassment claims were brought by men.[54]

As a final preliminary matter, the words of Title VII itself do not protect employees from discrimination on the basis of sexual orientation, but since 2015, the EEOC has interpreted it to be a type of gender discrimination due to gender stereotyping. However, well before this the U.S. Supreme Court held in *Oncale v. Sundowner Offshore Services Inc.* that even though both the harasser and the harasee are the same gender, a harassee can still bring a sexual harassment claim and be protected by Title VII.[55] Thus, there is no longer a presumption that if both parties are the same gender, the claim is not covered by Title VII, as was the case with many courts before. This is certainly in keeping with the intent and spirit of the law to protect employees in the workplace and is consistent with it.

Quid Pro Quo Sexual Harassment

LO2 Explain quid pro quo sexual harassment and give the requirements for making a case.

In quid pro quo sexual harassment, the employee is required to engage in sexual activity in exchange for workplace entitlements or benefits such as promotions, raises, or continued employment. This is the more obvious type of sexual harassment and is not generally difficult to recognize. (See Exhibit 9.5, "*Jones v. Clinton.*") In order for there to be an exchange for some workplace benefit, the harasser generally must have some sort of workplace power or position. The exchange of sex for workplace benefits will often leave a paper trail that can be followed. For instance, if an employee receives a raise, there is usually a basis for it, and the paper trail should show whether it was justified. The same is true for a promotion or more favorable hours or benefits.

In 2013, in a pair of cases brought under Title VII on other bases, the U.S. Supreme Court issued decisions with far-reaching implications for sexual harassment cases.

Exhibit 9.5 *Jones v. Clinton**

Demonstrating that no one seems to be exempt from claims of sexual harassment, in what is probably the most famous sexual harassment case in history, Paula Jones, a former Arkansas state employee, filed suit against a state trooper and a sitting president of the United States. Jones claimed that she was the victim of a sexual advance from President Bill Clinton while he was serving as governor of Arkansas prior to his presidency. The decision of whether the sexual harassment case could be brought against a sitting president went all the way to the U.S. Supreme Court, and the Court saw no impediment to Jones's bringing the suit. In the end, the Eighth Circuit Court of Appeals affirmed the district court's dismissal of Jones's case. The court held that the facts alleged by Jones, even if taken to be true, were insufficient to establish a basis for either quid pro quo or hostile work environment sexual harassment. In the court's view, the president's dropping his trousers, fondling his penis, asking Jones to kiss it, and then backing off when she said no, while boorish, was not sufficiently severe or pervasive to constitute a violation of the statute.

*138 F.3d. 758 (8th Cir. 1998).

In *Ball State University v. Vance,*[56] the Court rejected the EEOC's interpretation of who can be considered a supervisory employee for Title VII purposes. The Court determined that for Title VII purposes, a supervisor must have the ability to hire and fire rather than merely to direct work assignments, as had been the case before the Court. In the other Title VII decision issued the same day, *Texas Southwestern Medical Center v. Nassar,*[57] discussed earlier in the Toolkit Chapter section on retaliation, the Court determined that for liability to attach for retaliation under Title VII, there must be a showing that the retaliatory act would not have occurred but for the supervisor's desire to retaliate. The decisions, taken together, were interpreted by Justice Ruth Bader Ginsburg to be so wrongheaded that she took the unusual step of reading aloud in the courtroom her dissent in both cases and called on Congress to overturn the Court's decisions. It has not done so.

An employer can limit a supervisor's ability to abuse power by choosing supervisory employees carefully and having in place a system with adequate monitors and checks. It greatly decreases morale, and thus lowers workplace productivity, for other employees to witness quid pro quo harassment by the supervisor. In fact, it has even been held that the other employees witnessing such activity may bring a cause of action of their own.

Hostile Environment Sexual Harassment

LO3 Explain hostile environment sexual harassment and give the requirements for making a case.

The more difficult sexual harassment issues have been in the area of hostile environment because the activity may not be so clear-cut or leave a paper trail. Part of the difficulty lies in the fact that many of the causes that may serve as a basis for liability have historically gone unchallenged. However, a closer look at what courts have held to constitute a hostile environment lends more predictability.

To sustain a finding of hostile environment sexual harassment, it is generally required that

- The harassment be unwelcomed by the harassee.
- The harassment be based on gender.
- The harassment be sufficiently severe or pervasive to create an abusive working environment.
- The harassment affects a term, condition, or privilege of employment.
- The employer had actual or constructive knowledge of the sexually hostile working environment and took no prompt or adequate remedial action.

Scenario

In light of these requirements, it becomes clear why simply giving polite compliments as in Opening Scenario 2 is not, in and of itself, sexual harassment. Sexual harassment involves much more.

Meritor Savings Bank, FSB v. Vinson was the first sexual harassment case to reach the U.S. Supreme Court. In the case, which is provided at the conclusion of the chapter, the branch manager of a bank engaged in sexually harassing activity with the harassee, up to and including sex in the bank vault. The harassee finally took a leave of absence and was terminated for excessive leave. When she sued for sexual harassment, the employer argued that since she engaged in the sexual activity, the activity did not meet the "unwanted" requirement of the guidelines. The Supreme Court disagreed. In addition, the employer argued that since the harassee lost no raises or promotions, she lost no tangible job benefits, so it was not quid pro quo sexual harassment. Read the case and see if you can now distinguish between quid pro quo and hostile environment sexual harassment.

In *Meritor,* it is clear that the supervisor's actions changed the terms and conditions of Vinson's employment. There is a big difference between the ongoing, pervasive actions of Vinson's supervisor and merely giving someone an occasional nonsexual compliment as in Opening Scenario 2. In a hostile environment action, the activity must be more than someone committing a boorish, stupid, inappropriate act. The act must come up to the standards the courts and the EEOC have set forth for the cause of action. Contrary to what you may have been led to believe by the press or other information you've received, not every act, even if it is unwanted or offensive, will meet that standard; thus, not every act, though considered offensive by the employee, constitutes sexual harassment as set forth by law. (See Exhibit 9.5, "*Jones v. Clinton.*")

Unwelcome Activity

The basis of hostile environment sexual harassment actions is unwanted activity by the harasser. (See Exhibit 9.6, "Comparison between Quid Pro Quo and Hostile Environment Sexual Harassment.") If the activity is wanted or welcome by the harassee, it is consensual and there is no sexual harassment. If the activity started out being consensual and one employee calls a halt to it and the other continues, it can become sexual harassment at the time the activity is no longer consensual and thus is unwelcome as required, as in Opening Scenario 3.

Exhibit 9.6 *Comparison between Quid Pro Quo and Hostile Environment Sexual Harassment*

QUID PRO QUO SEXUAL HARASSMENT

- Workplace benefit promised to, given to, or withheld from harassee by harasser
- In exchange for sexual activity by harassee
- Generally accompanied by a paper trail (for example, promotion, raise, or termination paperwork)

HOSTILE ENVIRONMENT SEXUAL HARASSMENT

Activity by harasser, toward harassee that

- Is unwanted by the harassee.
- Is based on harassee's gender.
- Creates for harassee a hostile or abusive work environment.
- Unreasonably interferes with harassee's ability to do his or her job.
- Is sufficiently severe and/or pervasive.
- Affects a term or condition of harassee's employment.

3
Scenario

In making the determination of whether the harasser's activity was welcome, the actions used as a basis for the determination can be direct or indirect. For instance, in *McLean v. Satellite Technology Services, Inc.,*[58] based on the employee's previous conduct, the court had no trouble in determining that the harassee welcomed the activity of the harasser, if, in fact, it took place at all. The female employee engaged in a good deal of sexually tinged behavior at work such as pulling up her shirt to show a scar, having sexual conversations on the phone with clients even after being asked not to do so, and being away from her desk at a business conference having sex with people she met there. After being terminated upon return from the conference, she alleged that her supervisor tried to touch her leg and kiss her while they were on the business trip and she was in his room dressed in a bikini (while he was dressed in street clothes). It also demonstrates that there is more to winning a sexual harassment case than simply alleging that sexual harassment occurred.

Of course, there also may be a finding that the harassee did not welcome the activity by the harasser. Evidence can be direct, such as the harassee telling the harasser to discontinue the offending activity, or indirect, such as the harassee using body language, eye signals, and the like to show disapproval of the harasser's actions. Employees should be told to make it clear to a harasser that the activity is unwelcome; otherwise, the signals may become confused and the harasser may think his or her actions are wanted by the harassee. In Exhibit 9.7, "Wanna Fool Around?" you can see how some employers are trying to address the issue in novel ways.[59]

In another type of welcomeness issue, the Hooters restaurant chain was involved in several cases that, among other things, brought up the question of unwelcomeness parameters. As discussed in the previous chapter, Hooters is a chain of over 420 restaurants in 42 states and 29 countries. It is noted for its buffalo chicken wings and scantily clad female servers. Several lawsuits have been filed by female servers who were allegedly illegally fired or forced to quit because of sexual harassment.

The suits alleged that the environment created by management for female servers was hostile, starting with the name "Hooters," which is a slang term for women's breasts. Servers (a position for which Hooters only hires females), who are required to wear uniforms of revealing shorts and T-shirts, alleged that they were required to endure an atmosphere of sexually offensive remarks, touching, and other conduct by both management and customers. For example, the sign on entering Hooters reads, "Men: no shirt, no shoes: no service. Women: no shirt: free food."

An important issue in the lawsuits was whether, as the company argued, the women assumed the risk of the activities directed at them by agreeing to work for the company—that is, whether the conduct was welcomed by the fact that the servers worked for a company whose concept encouraged such behavior. What do you think? Should it matter if, as it turns out, the uniform requirement is illegal under Title VII? Check out the Hooters website and Wikipedia entry and see if you agree, as Hooters argued, that it is merely a neighborhood restaurant (previously it had argued it was a family restaurant), complete with a children's menu. There is at least some truth to the family restaurant claim. One of our students said his Little League baseball coach took the all-male team to Hooters to celebrate his 12th birthday and they *loved* it. The coach was his dad. :-/

Exhibit 9.7   *Wanna Fool Around? Sign on the Dotted Line, Please . . .*

In the face of increasingly expensive and embarrassing sexual harassment litigation, there have been all sorts of attempts to lessen employer liability, and, more lately, in the face of the #MeToo movement, to protect employees. Some employers have requested that if unequal employees are going to be involved in a relationship with each other, they sign what has been called a "Love Contract."* These are agreements that employees sign off on that set out their understanding that the relationship is a consensual and voluntary one and that no coercion is being used, so that the relationship is on an equal footing. Since sexual harassment is about unwelcome activity, the agreements set out that the actions on the part of the parties are, in fact, not unwelcome, but are voluntary and consensual. It also allows the parties to withdraw from the relationship at any time it becomes uncomfortable without there being any loss in the employment status, or the employment relationship. If there is an issue, the contract states that the company's sexual harassment policy will be used.

Since intimate relationships often happen without the parties thinking about it, but instead feeling drawn to each other, simply seeing the cold, explicit language written down on a sheet of paper, alone, can make parties think twice about whether they really want to enter into the relationship at all.

Similar agreements have also been used by colleges and universities in an attempt to make students much more intentional about the situations they get into with each other. This is particularly true where consent may be an issue because of the involvement of things that impair the ability to consent such as alcohol or drugs.

Often, the real impact is in having to enter into the contract in the first place. As with many contracts, there may be ways to get around having it enforced by a court. However, the true value is in making parties think twice before beginning what can become a problematic relationship.

* Teresa Butler, Littler Mendelson, Atlanta, 888- LITTLER

Severe and Pervasive Requirement

severe and/or pervasive activity
Harassing activity that is more than an occasional act or is so serious that it is the basis for liability.

One of the most troublesome problems with hostile environment is determining whether the harassing activity is **severe and/or pervasive** enough to amount to an unreasonable interference with an employee's ability to perform. (See Exhibit 9.3, "Wanted?") Built into the elements of hostile environment sexual harassment is a requirement that the offending activity be sufficiently severe and/or pervasive. That is, the activity is not an isolated occurrence that is not serious enough to warrant undue concern. The more frequent or serious the occurrences, the more likely it is that the severe and/or pervasive requirement will be met. If it is egregious enough, one time may meet the severity requirement, for example, in the case of rape.

In *Ross v. Double Diamond, Inc.*,[60] events over a two-day period were determined to meet the requirement for severity. Within hours of being hired, a female employee endured groping, sexually suggestive comments and jokes, a demand that she pull up her dress and allow her legs to be photographed, and a photo being taken up her dress as she reached across a desk to deliver a message in an all-male meeting.

Regarding the "unreasonable interference" requirement, in the U.S. Supreme Court decision in *Harris v. Forklift Systems*[61] the company owner constantly infused sexual comments and actions into the workplace by, for instance, making female employees dig in his front pockets for change or throwing it on the floor and making them bend down and pick it up so he could see their backsides. The employee finally left after the owner promised not to continue this behavior yet after she made a profitable deal and he said in front of other employees that she must have negotiated it in the Holiday Inn. The U.S. Supreme Court decided that sexual harassment claims do not require findings of severe psychological harm to be actionable. The Court said that "so long as the environment would reasonably be perceived, and is perceived, as hostile or abusive, there is no need for it also to be psychologically injurious."

Whether an environment is hostile or abusive must be determined by looking at all the circumstances. These may include the frequency of the discriminatory conduct, its severity, whether it is physically threatening or humiliating or a mere offensive utterance, and whether it unreasonably interferes with an employee's work performance. According to the Court, no single factor is determinative. (See Exhibit 9.8, "Is 'Discomfort' Enough?")

Exhibit 9.8 *Is "Discomfort" Enough?*

Students often think that merely feeling uncomfortable about something going on in the workplace is sufficient to sustain a claim under Title VII for hostile environment sexual harassment. As you can see from this situation, this is far from the case—or is it?

A male sales representative for Canon, Inc. had, as part of his territory, a store owned by a woman, his client. At a Christmas party, the female store owner/client was inappropriately touched, hugged, and kissed on the face and forehead by the sales rep's immediate supervisor. The client decided she did not want to complain about it. The sales rep complained to the company anyway. When the supervisor to whom the complaint was made called the client to discuss it as part of the investigation of the claim, the client again said she did not want to pursue the matter. When the sales rep was told this, he called the client and left a voice mail message expressing his anger at her refusal to corroborate his claims against his supervisor. In a "loud, rapid" voice, he used abusive language, told her he was "pissed off," accused her of lying to Canon, and said that he was going to "lose his f-ing job" and she needed to back up his claim of the harassment against her.

Because of the message, the client was so afraid of the sales rep that she would no longer allow him in her store. When the company found out about the voice mail message, the sales rep was fired. Canon, Inc. told him his conduct toward the client was unprofessional and unacceptable and would not be tolerated under any circumstances. The employee filed suit for retaliation under Title VII, claiming that the company terminated his employment because he complained about the sexual harassment of his client. Canon said the termination was for sufficient cause based on his actions toward the client.

As part of his claim, the employee alleged that the sexual harassment action against the client presented a hostile environment for him because he was "made uncomfortable" by his boss's alleged advances toward his client.

The court did not agree. The court said "feelings of 'discomfort' cannot support a hostile environment claim. Instead, such a claim is stated only where plaintiff alleges that the conditions of his workplace were so permeated with discriminatory intimidation, ridicule, and insult that is sufficiently severe or pervasive as to alter the conditions of the victim's employment and create an abusive working environment." [*Kunzler v. Canon, USA, Inc.,* 257 F. Supp. 3d 574 (E.D.N.Y. 2003).]

On the other hand, in the same year, the Minneapolis Public Library entered into a settlement agreement with its employees for $435,000 after the employees accused the library administration of subjecting them to a hostile environment by leaving them exposed to patrons' displays of explicit websites.

Do the two square for you?

Source: "Minneapolis Librarians Reach Settlement," University of Minnesota Silha Center for the Study of Media Ethics and Law Bulletin, Summer 2003, http://www.silha.umn.edu/news/summer2003.php?entry5200797.

Perspective Used to Determine Severity

LO5 Define the reasonable victim standard and how and why it is used in sexual harassment cases.

reasonable person standard
Viewing the harassing activity from the perspective of a reasonable person in society at large (generally tends to be the male view).

reasonable victim standard
Viewing the harassing activity from the perspective of a reasonable person experiencing the harassing activity including gender-specific sociological, cultural, and other factors.

For many years the determination of whether the harasser's activity was sufficiently severe and pervasive was generally based on a **reasonable person standard**, which is supposed to be a gender-neutral determination. That is, the activity would be judged as offensive (or not) based on whether the activity would offend a reasonable person under the circumstances. Since this "neutral" standard generally turned out to be instead a male sensibility standard, the EEOC issued a policy statement by which it required that the victim's perspective also must be considered so as not to perpetuate stereotypical notions of what behavior is acceptable to those of a given gender. This notion, labeled the "reasonable woman" or **reasonable victim standard**, has been used increasingly by courts and should be given serious consideration when evaluating harassing activity. If the victim is a male, it would, of course, be a reasonable man standard.

In *Ellison v. Brady,* provided for your review at the end of this chapter, the court adopted a reasonable woman standard for analyzing whether the harasser's behavior was severe and pervasive enough to create a hostile work environment. It explains why viewing severity and pervasiveness from this perspective may render different results. The U.S. Supreme Court has not addressed the reasonable victim versus reasonable person dichotomy as a direct issue, but in *Oncale v. Sundowner Offshore Services Inc.,*[62] the Court's first case involving same-gender sexual harassment, it said that "the objective severity of harassment should be judged from the perspective of a reasonable person *in the plaintiff's position.*" The *Ellison v. Brady* case was the basis for the movie *Hostile Advances.*

"Sexual" Requirement Explained

LO6 Differentiate the sex requirement and antifemale animus in sexual harassment actions.

While the harassment of the employee must be based on gender, it need not involve sex, requests for sexual activity, sexual comments, or other similar activity. Even today, a female entering a workplace with few or no other females is often verbally harassed about "doing men's work," "taking away the job a man should have," or simply inappropriately working at a traditionally male job. It is no coincidence that the Marines' nude photo scandal occurred in a traditionally alpha male environment. Despite the lack of sexual overtones (though the comments are obviously based on gender), this could well constitute sexual harassment. In the case of *Andrews v. City of Philadelphia,*[63] the sexual activity was only a small part of what the females who came into the traditionally male job of police officers were sub-jected to. They were called very derogatory names, their property was vandalized, their files were stolen or ripped, officers who were supposed to help them would not, their cars were vandalized, soda was poured into their typewriters, obscene phone calls were made to their unlisted numbers, a caustic substance was poured into one officer's locker and she received severe burns on her back when she put on a shirt from the locker, and pornographic material was put in their desks and male officers would gather around to see their reaction. When they reported it to their supervisor, he did nothing. Think back to the exhibit in the gender chapter about Chela Gutierrez, the female firefighter. Her supervisor refused to heed, or even act like he heard, her suggestion about where the gas leak could be coming from when she told him several times, repeating it because she thought he couldn't hear her, yet when she had a male firefighter tell him, he immediately responded and a disaster was avoided. And that is only one example of what she must endure each day.

Notice how little of what they went through conforms to what we usually think of as sexually based hostile environment. This "non sex" requirement is also one of the reasons it is better to use the term *gender* in sexual harassment discussions so that sex in the traditional sense and gender, meaning whether one is male or female, are clearly differentiated and the discussion less confusing. The *Andrews* case gives you a good example of how serious hostile sentiments can become.

antifemale animus
Negative feelings about women and/or their ability to perform jobs or functions, usually manifested by negative language and actions.

A common element of hostile environment sexual harassment cases that may lack an actual sexuality factor is **antifemale animus** exhibited by the harasser toward those of the harassee's gender. This is manifested through, for instance, the use of derogatory terms when referring to women or making negative comments about their fitness or ability to do the job. Courts also have found antifemale animus in derogatory statements to or about women in the context of their jobs, such as "women have shit for brains," "should be barefoot and pregnant," "should not be surgeons because it takes them too long to bathe and put on makeup," "could never stand up to union representatives," "are unstable when they are 'in heat' [having their menstrual cycle, said to a female doctor]," or "all she needs is a good lay." Often antifemale animus is accompanied by sexually based activity, it but need not be. A manager should not dismiss a harassee's complaint simply because it does not involve sexually related activity. (See Exhibit 9.9, "All in Good Fun? Just Joking . . .")

In analyzing hostile environment claims, keep in mind that it can also be accomplished by electronic means. Claims involving sexual harassment through workplace email, bulletin boards, chat rooms, and social websites have increased dramatically in the past few years. Think about the Marines United situation mentioned earlier. It is best to be aware of the potential for liability. Again, there need not be a sexual element involved in order for it to constitute sexual harassment. It is a good idea to have a well-enforced workplace policy giving guidelines for this kind of activity and to keep up with any technological changes that may result in new ways for liability to occur.

Exhibit 9.9 *All in Good Fun? Just Joking . . .*

A number of sexual harassment cases arise from situations having nothing to do with "sex" as we ordinarily think of it. It has to do instead with gender—more specifically, antifemale animus, or feelings against women who are in male-dominated or traditionally male jobs such as truck driving, construction, firefighting, trash collection, and so on. When males are in traditionally female jobs, they rarely are subjected to the same kind of actions directed toward them that women in traditionally male fields are. And often, when men in a traditionally female job are subjected to harassing activity, it is by other males who tease, joke, make derogatory comments, and more. Case law indicates that male nurses generally do not get hassled by female nurses or male kindergarten teachers by female kindergarten teachers.

Students, and even managers and supervisors in the workplace, often comment that "it's only joking" and that women who complain are being "overly sensitive." What they don't understand is that rarely is the ribbing or joking an isolated event. Rather, it is usually accompanied by other indicators in the workplace that one gender is being treated differently, less well, than another. Rarely will you find women progressing as they should in a workplace when the atmosphere exhibits antifemale animus through jokes, ribbing, and derogatory gender-based comments. It all goes together and creates a certain environment that is less likely to allow women to progress. The thought is parent to the act. Antifemale animus manifested through jokes, comments, and ribbing is very likely also

to be manifested in lack of full participation in the workplace for women through pay, training, discipline, and advancement. It's never "just jokes." That is why it is such a serious matter.

As a manager or supervisor, how you handle these events as they occur can make all the difference in the world for your employer. It may seem like only joking, ribbing, or all in good fun, but as a manager, you ignore it at the peril of your company. Heaped on an employee day after day, this harassing activity places upon them different terms or conditions of employment than it does other employees of the other gender who do not have to contend with this hostile environment. That violates Title VII.

The Los Angeles City Council awarded a female member of the city's canine unit $2.25 million for the harassment she suffered in the unit. She alleged the men took items from her desk and the women's locker room, used her shower and hygiene products, exposed their genitalia, made offensive and sexually explicit remarks, excluded her from training exercises and other opportunities, barred her from "cigar" meetings held to discuss training issues and practices, and blew cigar smoke in her face and that she was told another officer rubbed his penis on her phone. When she reported these events, the harassment worsened. The week before her settlement, an officer who was demoted and suffered retaliation when he defended her was awarded $3.6 million.

Source: Joanna Linn, "LAPD Officer Awarded $2.25 Million in Harassment Case," *Los Angeles Times* (November 20, 2008), http://articles.latimes.com/2008/nov/20/local/me-harass20.

Employer Liability for Sexual Harassment

LO7 Explain employer liability for various types of sexual harassment claims.

The U.S. Supreme Court has been wrestling with the issue of employer liability for sexual harassment since it decided the first case on the subject in 1986 *(Meritor,* discussed earlier in the chapter). In its *Ellerth* case, also discussed in this chapter, the Court said that it was hearing the case in order to assist in defining the relevant standards of employer liability since "Congress has left it to the courts to determine controlling agency law principles in a new and difficult area of federal law." Without trying to drag you into the legal mire that has surrounded the issue, we will give you some general rules with which to operate and leave the intricacies for the courts to continue to unravel.

Supervisor toward Employee (Tangible Employment Action)

This is generally going to be quid pro quo sexual harassment (for instance, the employee's supervisor denies the employee a raise or promotion because she refuses to have sex with him), but the courts have said that the categories are not cast in stone. An employer is strictly liable for the tangible acts of its supervisors regardless of whether the specific acts complained of were authorized or even forbidden by the employer and regardless of whether the employer knew or should have known of their occurrence. Since the supervisor is, in effect, the employer, the supervisor's acts are considered those of the employer.

The employer has a measure of control of the situation by carefully choosing supervisory employees. As discussed, in a tangible job action there is usually a paper trail involved, so it also gives the employer a measure of control by keeping up with what is going on in the workplace and monitoring for actions that may violate the law. For instance, if an employee is precipitously terminated or demoted, not given a raise if it is expected, or given a raise if none is expected, there will be a paper trail, and the law holds the employer responsible for knowing what is going on in the employer's workplace. The law says the employer cannot engage in sexual harassment, so doing so through a supervisor is tantamount to the employer doing it, and the employer is strictly liable for the harassment. You can thus see why even though Justice Ginsburg dissented mightily over the Court's decision in *Ball State University v. Vance,* the decision actually very much reflected the Court's previous positions. While the Court had not specifically said that a supervisor must have the authority to hire and fire, its language could be said to be consistent with that conclusion. However, as Justice Ginsburg noted, such a holding does not reflect the reality of the workplace since employers often have employees to whom they give important authority over other employees that falls short of the authority to hire and fire.

See Chapter 2 to revisit key concepts.

Supervisor toward Employee (No Tangible Employment Action)

If there is no tangible employment act by a supervisor, such as termination, and instead there is activity by a supervisor causing a severe and/or pervasive hostile environment resulting in harm to the harassed employee (for instance, the supervisor may constantly ask the employee out on dates and make sexual comments but still give the employee her usual raises and promotions), the employer is not strictly liable. This is also true of a constructive discharge. As you will see below, in constructive discharge, the workplace becomes so objectively unbearable that the employee has no real option except to leave. In these situations, the harassed employee can bring a claim, but there is no virtually automatic liability like there is for strict liability offenses. Here, the employer has an affirmative defense available. The employer can use the *Ellerth/Faragher* defense to show that the employer had a reasonable sexual harassment policy to prevent and address sexual harassment and the harassed employee unreasonably failed to use it. This defense is not permitted in a case where there is a tangible unfavorable job action by a supervisor.

Coworker Harassment or Third-Party Harassment of Employee

When the harassment is by (1) one employee toward another on the same level (rather than by a supervisory employee to a subordinate) or (2) someone who is not employed by the employer, such as a client or someone who comes in to service the machinery at the employer's business, the employer is liable if the employer knew or should have known of the acts of the harasser and took no immediate corrective action.

For instance, if the computer repairer comes to service computers and regularly feels the employee's legs while working with wires under the desk or makes inappropriate and suggestive sexual comments, the employer would be liable even though the repairer does not work for the employer. The employee would usually have to make the employer aware of the situation and the employer would have to take no steps to remedy the situation before liability would attach. If the employer saw what was happening and saw that the employee was clearly upset by the situation, the employer would be put on notice that something should be done and liability could attach. The same is true with coworkers. That is why it is so important for managers and supervisors to be aware of what is going on around them in the workplace and deal with it effectively. The law will hold the employer responsible through the acts of the supervisory employees who were aware and took no action to rectify the situation.

LO4 List and explain employer defenses to sexual harassment claims.

In *Faragher v. City of Boca Raton,* included for your review at the end of this chapter, the U.S. Supreme Court discussed employer liability for sexual harassment. The case involved sexual harassment of lifeguards who were stationed in a remote (from the main office) location, which resulted in less supervision of what was occurring. The Court provided employers not only with a defense they could use when sued by an employee who had not acted reasonably in seeking to avoid harm (the *Ellerth/Faragher* affirmative defense) but also with ammunition for an employee who could allege that the employer did not use reasonable measures to prevent sexual harassment.

Sometimes, the employee is not terminated but instead believes the harassment is so unbearable that he or she must quit his or her job without going through the employer's sexual harassment complaint process. This is constructive discharge. In *Pennsylvania State Police v. Suders,*[64] the Supreme Court addressed what to do if a supervisor's actions result in a constructive discharge for an employee and whether such a discharge is loss of a tangible job benefit, resulting in strict liability for the employer. The Court said that when there is no official act resulting in the constructive discharge, and thus no way for an employer to be made aware that there was an issue resulting in the constructive discharge, rather than strict liability attaching to the employer, the employer is able to use the *Ellerth* and *Faragher* affirmative defense to show how it tried to avoid liability.

1)
Scenario

In *Robinson v. Jacksonville Shipyards, Inc.,* which we mentioned earlier in the context of sexual harassment policies, the court provided important information as to how sexual harassment cases should be handled. It is the basis for Opening Scenario 1. The case involved nude pictures, magazines, plaques, and posters in the workplace. When the employee complained, she was told she simply should not look. The court said this was not an appropriate response by the employer, as this type of paraphernalia creates a hostile environment for which the law will hold the employer liable.

Remember that it is a defense to liability if an employer can show that the harassee unreasonably failed to avail himself or herself of a mechanism the employer had in place for preventing or correcting sexual harassment. Likewise, it is helpful to a harassee if he or she can show that the employer had unreasonable means of preventing or correcting sexual harassment (for instance, the only one to whom claims are reported is the harasser). This makes it more important than ever for an employer to have a strong sexual harassment policy as well as effective training, monitoring, and reporting of sexual harassment. The EEOC has determined that since harassment of any kind is the only type of discrimination carried out by a supervisor for which an employer can avoid liability, that limitation is to be narrowly construed.

Other Important Considerations

There are several other important miscellaneous matters you should be aware of that are often at issue in sexual harassment claims.

Determining the Truth of Allegations

The number one problem managers have in responding to sexual harassment complaints (other than their discomfort in dealing with such matters) is determining the truth of sexual harassment allegations. We cannot tell you how many times we have heard employers and managers say, "We don't know who to believe! How are we supposed to know who is telling the truth? We don't want to wreck someone's career if we don't have to!" Appropriate investigation should provide the employer a basis on which to decide and to appropriately respond. Both parties, as well as any witnesses, should be questioned. The investigator's objective is to find out the "who," "what," "when," "where," and "how" of the allegations as quickly and as discreetly as possible. Employees should be involved only on a "need to know" basis. When all appropriate evidence is gathered, much like the members of a jury, the employer must determine the facts. The employer bases the determination on who seems most credible, whose version of the alleged incidents is more likely to be closer to the truth, what interests the parties have in telling their version of the events, and any credible corroboration presented. The common problem of the employer's discomfort with making judgments should not, as it so often does, prevent moving quickly and appropriately on complaints. We have often seen that the main discomfort actually stems from preferring not to have to deal with the issue at all. Once it is clear that the activity may be illegal, there is no choice. It must be done. It is not a choice, any more than it would be in a rape case, which rarely has witnesses to what occurred.

The EEOC's Policy Guidance on Harassment provides insight into how credibility determinations are to be made. According to the EEOC, while none of the following is necessarily determinative, factors to consider in deciding credibility include

- *Inherent plausibility.* Is the testimony believable on its face? Does it make sense?
- *Demeanor.* Did the person seem to be telling the truth or lying?
- *Motive to falsify.* Did the person have a reason to lie?
- *Corroboration.* Is there *witness testimony* (such as testimony of eyewitnesses, people who saw the person soon after the alleged incidents or people who discussed the incidents with him or her at or around the time that they occurred) or *physical evidence* (such as written documentation) that corroborates the party's testimony?
- *Past record.* Did the alleged harasser have a history of similar behavior in the past?

We wish there was more we could tell you, but the truth is, there isn't much more that can be said. It can be uncomfortable, but investigating and making a decision must be done, and there are no special tools to do it, much like a jury has no special tools when deciding a murder case. They just come in, listen carefully to the evidence, observe carefully, and make a determination using their best judgment based on what they have taken in. There is no magic, no easy way to do it. Responding quickly, taking the matter seriously, using your best judgment to evaluate what you find, and going where the information leads you are the best tools you can use in determining the truth of the matter.

LO8 Describe proactive and corrective actions an employer can take to prevent or lessen liability.

Retaliation and Employee Privacy

Often harassees report sexual harassment and, out of fear of retaliation, want the employer to provide relief without informing the alleged harasser of the complaint or of the harassee's identity. Harassees should be informed that the alleged harasser must be told of the complaint for the employer to effectively address it but that retaliation will not be tolerated, as the law has separate retaliation provisions. Alleged harassers are not required to play hide-and-seek with claims and claimants. As uncomfortable as the claimant may be in coming forward, the alleged harasser must be notified.

According to the EEOC, there has been a dramatic increase in the number of retaliation claims in recent years. They are the number one claim reported and account for over 50 percent of claims filed. The EEOC has been clear in reiterating that it takes such cases very seriously. Courts and juries have been clear in sending the message that they do not like retaliation by employers for employees pursuing their legal rights under the law. Punitive damages are likely to be granted in such cases since retaliation, in a manner of speaking, adds insult to injury and is much more deliberate. It is important to energetically pursue retaliation claims because the law protecting employees is meaningless if those who need the law cannot use it for fear of what may happen to them if they do. Who would want to take the risk?

Corrective Action

The EEOC guidelines state that the employer must take "immediate and appropriate corrective action" to remedy sexual harassment. The most appropriate thing to do under the specific circumstance depends on the facts. Consideration should be given to such factors as the employment position of the employees, the activity involved, the duration of the actions, the seriousness of the actions, the employer's sexual harassment policy and other methods used to deter sexual harassment, the alleged harasser's prior history of sexual harassment, and so on. While the remedy must be calculated to stop the harassment and must not have the effect of punishing the harassee, neither should it be out of proportion to the act. Make sure the punishment fits the crime. Every act of sexual harassment need not result in automatic termination, the "capital punishment" of the workplace. The 2016 Task Force Report on Workplace Harassment took the position that this is why "zero tolerance" policies should be discouraged. They promote the idea that all harassing behavior is the same and should have the same consequences. That makes no sense. Telling an inappropriate off-color joke should not be treated the same as locking someone in a storeroom and sticking your hand down his or her pants. Zero tolerance policies may seem to make the issue easier to deal with, but they do little to create the sexual harassment-free workplace an employer wants.

With all this in mind, the good news is that there is now a more formalized purpose to all this. For years, courts admonished employers to take claims seriously and respond accordingly, but this had no consistent, formalized result for the employer. Employers could do the best they could and still get into trouble with the law. That is no longer so for certain cases. Through two cases you have already been introduced to in this chapter, *Faragher* and *Ellerth,* the U.S. Supreme Court created the *Ellerth/Faragher* affirmative defense we spoke of earlier, which employers can use to protect themselves from liability when they have tried to consistently obey the law. In *Burlington Industries, Inc. v. Ellerth,* the Court outlines that defense and provides employers with a good deal of control over avoiding and/or limiting liability for violations of Title VII when there is no loss of tangible job benefits because of a harasser's action. Keep in mind that the defense can only be used where there was no tangible employment action by a supervisor.

Damages and Jury Trials

See Chapter 2 to revisit key concepts.

We discussed these issues in Chapter 2, "The Employment Law Toolkit," but due to the sensitive nature of this area, we thought it was worth reiterating. Under the Civil Rights Act of 1991, based on the number of employees employed by the employer, an employee suing for sexual harassment can ask for up to $300,000 in compensatory and punitive damages (and unlimited medical damages) and request a jury trial. Both these factors greatly increase the employer's potential liability for sexual harassment and make avoiding liability for this unnecessary activity even more imperative.

As you can imagine, after the 1991 amendments allowed damages and jury trials, Title VII claims increased dramatically. It finally made economic sense to go

Sexual harassment doesn't have to be the employer's worst nightmare. Don't ever expect to have absolute control over every employee in the workplace, but following the tips below can substantially decrease the chances of a recalcitrant employee causing liability.

Seriously dealing with the issues, both in word and deed, should be the rule. The EEOC and courts take the position that the best thing an employer can do to effectively keep sexual harassment complaints to a minimum—and to minimize liability for sexual harassment complaints that do occur—is to take a preventive approach. This may include the following:

- Adopt an anti–sexual harassment policy discouraging such activity. This should be separate from the general antidiscrimination policy, and every employee should be aware of it.
- Make sure, from the top down, that all employees understand that sexual harassment in the workplace simply will not be tolerated. *Period.*
- Create and disseminate information about an effective reporting mechanism for harassees, including alternatives when the harasser is the one who would normally be the one to whom to report.
- After adopting the policy, don't let it sit in a drawer somewhere. Use it. Consistently remind employees of it.
- Provide employees with training and/or information apprising them of what sexual harassment is and of what specific activities are appropriate and inappropriate in the workplace. This will go a very long way toward decreasing potential liability for the employer.
- Ensure that reported incidents of sexual harassment are taken seriously by supervisors and others involved in reporting. Do not tell the employee to "get over it" or that it is to be expected because of where they work or the job they hold.
- Ensure that the training employees receive is effective and answers their questions and concerns and that the training is interactive and engaging.
- Keep in mind that creating an atmosphere in which sexual harassment is not tolerated is a big part of what the EEOC and courts want employers to do. Operationalize this on a real-life basis. That is, when employees engage in activity that helps to create an atmosphere that accepts harassing activity, challenge it. Don't tolerate the jokes, sneers, leers, teasing, gestures, and so forth.
- Promptly investigate all sexual harassment claims and circulate information only on a need-to-know basis.
- Keep an eye out for antifemale animus that also may constitute sexual harassment.
- If investigation warrants discipline for the harasser, ensure that immediate, appropriate corrective action is taken. Make sure the corrective action is commensurate with the policy violation. Immediate termination is not the response to every sexual harassment claim.
- Work to keep the workplace friendly and open. Having a workplace free of sexual harassment does not mean employees can't still work in a pleasant, respectful atmosphere.

through the time-consuming, arduous process of suing, for both claimants and their attorneys. Of course, this was not a welcome event for employers. In sexual harassment cases in particular, jury trials can be very damaging. The nature of the activities constituting the claim can be quite emotional for a jury to hear, not to mention the stress it puts on the employee and the embarrassment for the employer. That is why it is even more important not to let things get that far unless the employer is certain of victory—which is virtually unknown since juries are unpredictable.

In response to our country's exploding litigation dockets, the use of alternative dispute resolution, or ADR, for settling disputes went from a backwater alternative to litigation to one of the most-used methods. As we discussed in the chapter on Title VII, the EEOC has now institutionalized the use of ADR in its proceedings in several ways and has gotten employers to do the same, using their own extensive, in-house ADR resources. Among other things, the EEOC conducts mediation on appropriate claims filed with them, and in 2003, it began pilot or start-up programs for handling its own internal complaints, a program to have Fair Employment Practice Agencies mediate private-sector claims, and a program in which national employers handle claims of their employees informally before handing it over to the EEOC (if it is necessary to do so). Many attorneys and court systems now also offer ADR as a part of their services.

ADR is a much less acrimonious, expensive, time-consuming alternative that also has the bonus of not being on the public record, for the most part, or precedent setting, in the formal sense. If you are an employer or employee, it would probably be in your best interest to try this route before going to court. You have little to lose and a host of benefits to gain.

Tort and Criminal Liability

In addition to bringing an action under Title VII, harassees also may bring civil actions in state court—or, if permitted, federal court—based on state laws that also may be violated by the actions of the alleged harasser. Recall that in *Meritor,* the first sexual harassment case to come before the U.S. Supreme Court, the bank manager was alleged to have fondled the plaintiff in public, followed her to and entered the ladies' restroom with her, and engaged in unwelcome sexual intercourse, including while in the bank's vault. These acts, while constituting sexual harassment under Title VII, also could form the basis for various tort actions including:

Assault: Intentionally putting the victim in fear or apprehension, or both, of immediate unpermitted bodily touching.

Battery: Intentional unpermitted bodily touching.

Infliction of emotional distress: An intentional outrageous act that goes outside the bounds of common decency, for which the law will provide a remedy.

False imprisonment: Intentionally preventing the harassee's exit from a confined space.

Interference with contractual relations: Intentionally causing the harassee to be unable to perform her employment contract as agreed upon.

These cases are generally heard by juries, with the possible result of unlimited compensatory and punitive damages. In addition, the harasser's action could form the basis of criminal prosecution for, at a minimum, criminal assault, battery, and rape. Of course, the criminal cases would be against the harasser, rather than the employer, and would result in punishment for the harasser, rather than money damages to the harassee (unless the state has a victim assistance or restitution program). In *Miller v. Washington Workplace,*[65] the employee was assaulted and battered by her boss after simply asking for the company's sexual harassment policy!

Chapter Summary

- Consensual activity is not a violation of Title VII.
- Unwelcome sexual advances that cause one gender to work under conditions or terms of employment different from those of the other gender constitute sexual harassment for which the employer may be liable.
- Employers will be responsible only if the sexual harassment is severe and pervasive.
- Activity need not be sexual in nature to constitute sexual harassment.
- Employers should treat all sexual harassment complaints seriously and act on them quickly.
- Prevention is imperative to avoid sexual harassment claims and lessen liability. The employer must make it clear that sexual harassment will not be tolerated. This should be clearly stated and followed up and monitored by appropriate mechanisms.
- Employers need a strong anti–sexual harassment policy that is vigorously enforced.

Chapter-End Questions

1. Employer uses the "f***" word frequently in the workplace and makes statements to employee such as, in regard to an installer, he was always confused and bet that as a baby he "probably didn't know which tit to suck"; and in discussing a motorcycle seat, cupped his hands and said he would be "glad to fit employee's ass for the right size seat." Is this likely to be successful as a sexual harassment suit? [*LaPorte v. Fireplace and Patio Center, Inc.,* 2004 U.S. Dist. LEXIS 2113 (W.D. Ill. 2004).]

2. Employee, a 33-year-old unmarried male, is frequently teased by the other males in his plant about being unmarried and still living at home with his mother. Is this sexual harassment? [*Goluszek v. Smith,* 697 F. Supp. 1452 (N.D. Ill. 1988).]

3. Employee sues employer for sexual harassment because her supervisor once touched her on her back and made an "untoward" statement to her. Will she win? Explain. [*Strickland v. Sears, Roebuck and Co.,* 693 F. Supp. 403 (E.D. Va. 1988).]

4. Two employees, Marge and Ben, are having a relationship that later turns sour. When Marge does not get the promotion she goes up for, she sues the employer for sexual harassment, alleging it was committed by her ex-boyfriend Ben, who has, since their breakup, left Marge alone. Will Marge win her suit? [*Koster v. Chase Manhattan Bank,* 687 F. Supp. 848 (S.D.N.Y. 1988).]

5. Dennis comes up to his supervisor, Mae, at a Christmas party and tells Mae he wants to sue for sexual harassment. Mae asks what happened. Dennis says that Linda came over to him and tweaked his cheek and called him sweetie. Dennis pursues the case. Does he win? Why or why not? [Facts from business consulting session attendee.]

6. An employer asks an employee to go to dinner and drinks and said they could "see what happen(ed) after that." Is this enough for a sexual harassment claim? [*Mireault v. Northeast Motel Assocs., LP,* 20 Mass. L. Rep. 614; 2006 Mass. Super. LEXIS 65 (2006).]

7. A female employee has an operation on her breast, and when she returns to work, a male employee "jokingly" asks to see the scar. Actionable sexual harassment? [*Keziah v. W. M. Brown Son, Inc.,* 683 F. Supp. 542 (W.D.N.C. 1988).]

8. Joan, a female manager, asks Margaret, one of her subordinates, out on a date. When Margaret refuses, Joan becomes mean to her at work and rates Margaret's work poorly on her next evaluation. Margaret wants to bring a sexual harassment claim but feels she cannot do so since her boss is female. Is Margaret correct?

9. A truck driver trainer sexually harassed a trainee, and she brought suit for sexual harassment. The trainer claimed to have power over the trainee, but in reality, the trainer was not a supervisory employee. Is it possible for her to make her claim of quid pro quo sexual harassment if the trainer actually is not a supervisor? [*Vernarsky v. Covenant Transport, Inc.,* 2003 U.S. Dist. LEXIS 18330 (E.D. Tenn. 2003).]

10. Trudy comes to Pat, her supervisor, and tells her that Jack has been sexually harassing her by making suggestive remarks, comments, and jokes; constantly asking her for dates; and using every available opportunity to touch her. Pat has been friends with Jack for a long time and can't imagine Jack would do such a thing. Pat is hesitant to move on Trudy's complaint. What should Pat do?

End Notes

1. Mandell, Nina, "St. Louis Woman Awarded $95 Million after Former Boss Allegedly Masturbated on Her," *The New York Daily News* (June 10, 2011), http://articles.nydailynews.com/2011-06-10/news/29663292_1_verdict-harassment-runaway-jury.

2. Chandler, Michael Alison, "Men Account for Nearly 1 in 5 Complaints of Workplace Sexual Harassment with the EEOC," *The Washington Post* (April 8, 2018), https://www.washingtonpost.com/local/social-issues/men-account-for-nearly-1-in-5-complaints-of-workplace-sexual-harassment-with-the-eeoc/2018/04/08/4f7a2572-3372-11e8-94fa-32d48460b955_story.html.

3. *Newsweek* (July 26, 2010), p. 16.

4. Talbot, Margaret, "Fox News and the Repercussions of Sexual Harassment," *The New Yorker* (August 19, 2016), http://www.newyorker.com/news/daily-comment/fox-news-and-the-repercussions-of-sexual-harassment.

5. Arkin, Daniel, Adam Reiss, Erica Byfield, and Daniella Silva, "Harvey Weinstein Sentenced to 23 Years in Prison in Landmark #MeToo case," NBC News (March 11, 2020), https://www.nbcnews.com/news/us-news/harvey-weinstein-sentenced-23-years-prison-landmark-metoo-case-n1154166.

6. Carr, Flora, "Former Google Employee Hits Tech Giant with Sexual Harassment Lawsuit Alleging 'Bro Culture,'" *Fortune* (March 1, 2018), https://fortune.com/2018/03/01/google-sexual-harassment-lawsuit-bro-culture/.

7. Snider, Mike, and Zlati Meyer, "McDonald's Faces 25 New Sexual Harassment Complaints from Workers," *USA Today* (May 21, 2019), https://www.usatoday

.com/story/money/2019/05/21/mcdonalds-faces-25-new-charges-sexual-harassment-workplace/3750936002/; Haddon, Heather, "McDonald's Workers Strike to Protest Pay and Harassment Complaints," *The Wall Street Journal* (May 23, 2019), https://www.wsj.com/articles/mcdonalds-workers-strike-to-protest-pay-and-harassment-complaints-11558627417.

8. Lee, Edmund, "CBS Chief Executive Les Moonves Steps Down after Sexual Harassment Claims," *The New York Times* (September 9, 2018), https://www.nytimes.com/2018/09/09/business/les-moonves-longtime-cbs-chief-may-be-gone-by-monday.html.

9. Hsu, Tiffany, "Ex-Employees Sue Nike, Alleging Gender Discrimination," *The New York Times* (August 10, 2018), https://www.nytimes.com/2018/08/10/business/nike-discrimination-class-action-lawsuit.html.

10. Ryzik, Melena, Cara Buckley, and Jodi Kantor, "Louis C.K. Accused by 5 Women of Sexual Misconduct," *The New York Times* (November 9, 2017).

11. Cranley, Ellen, and Michelle Mark, "Here Are All the Sexual Misconduct Allegations against Brett Kavanaugh," *Business Insider* (September 27, 2018), https://www.businessinsider.com/brett-kavanaugh-sexual-assault-misconduct-allegations-2018-9.

12. Mansoor, Sanya, "Report Details New Justice Brett Kavanaugh Sexual Misconduct Claims," *Time* magazine (September 15, 2019).

13. Hartocollis, Anemona, "Women Sue Yale over a Fraternity Culture They Say Enables Harassment," *The New York Times* (February 12, 2019).

14. Scripps National, "Florida Politician Accused of Licking Faces Has Resigned," ABCActionNews (February 7, 2019), https://www.abcactionnews.com/news/national/florida-politician-accused-of-licking-faces-has-resigned.

15. "NBC Fires Matt Lauer, the Face of 'Today,'" *The New York Times,* Ellen Gabler, Jim Rutenberg, Michael M. Grynbaum, and Rachel Abrams, 11/29/2017.

16. Steel, Emily, and Michael S. Schmidt, "Fox News Settled Sexual Harassment Allegations against Bill O'Reilly, Documents Show," *The New York Times* (January 10, 2017), https://www.nytimes.com/2017/01/10/business/media/bill-oreilly-sexual-harassment-fox-news-juliet-huddy.html.

17. Campbell, Fred, "The Real Story behind the FCC Sex Scandal," *Forbes,* (October 20, 2016), https://www.forbes.com/sites/fredcampbell/2016/10/20/the-real-story-behind-the-fcc-sex-scandal/#6fd17514498c.

18. Levine, Matt, "Successful Algorithms and Rude CFOs," Bloomberg View (August 11, 2016), https://www.bloomberg.com/view/articles/2016-08-11/successful-algorithms-and-rude-cfos.

19. "Final Judgment in EEOC Sexual Harassment Case against Custom Companies Tops $1.1M: Federal Judge Cites Involvement of Top Management in Permitting Harassment and in Retaliating against Victims," EEOC press release (March 8, 2007); and *EEOC v. Custom Companies, Inc., et al.,* Nos. 02-C-3768, 03-C2293, Mem. Op. & Order (N.D. Ill. March 8, 2007).

20. "Lawyer Sues Ex-firm for Naked Male Retreat," *News.com* (September 28, 2010), http://www.news.com.au/business/business-smarts/lawyer-sues-ex-firm-for-naked-male-retreat/story-e6frfm9r-1225930875532.

21. "Woman Spanked at Work Awarded $1.7M: Alarm Company Employee Found Camaraderie-Building Exercise Humiliating," MSNBC (April 28, 2006), http://www.msnbc.msn.com/id/12534543/ns/us_news-life/.

22. Loomis, Tamara, "Record $5.5M Accord Reached in Doctor Harass Case," *Law.com* (April 10, 2003), http://www.law.com/jsp/article.jsp?id=900005534973&slreturn=1&hbxlogin=1.

23. "Ex-Delta pilot files sex discrimination suit," The Atlanta Journal & Constitution, Christopher Seward, August 23, 2013, https://www.ajc.com/business/delta-pilot-files-sex-discrimination-suit/5WNLrQvryDc4WAjrtg4xjP/.

24. "Reverse Sexual Harassment under Investigation by New York Civil Rights Violation Lawyer Following Dog Trainer's Accusations," EIN Presswire (September 9, 2011), http://www.einpresswire.com/247pr/233963.

25. "Burger King Franchise Pays $400,000 for Alleged Sexual Harassment of Teens," EEOC press release (December 6, 2004), http://www.eeoc.gov/eeoc/newsroom/release/12-6-04b.cfm.

26. Timmins, Annmarie, "Judge's Victims Feel Violated by System: 'Public Support for Him Is Cronyism,' They Say," *The Concord Monitor* (January 8, 2005), http://www.concordmonitor.com/article/judges-victims-feel-violated-by-system.

27. Keck, William, "The Time Is Right for Barker," *USA Today* (May 14, 2007), http://www.usatoday.com/life/people/2007-05-13-bob-barker_N.htm.

28. "Arnold Apologizes for 'Bad Behavior,'" Fox News (October 3, 2003), http://www.foxnews.com/story/0,2933,98883,00.html.

29. Johnson, Lauren, "O'Reilly Settles Sex Harass Suit: Lawyer for Fox News Announces Settlement with Fox Producer," CBS News (October 28, 2004), http://www.cbsnews.com/stories/2004/10/20/entertainment/main650282.shtml.

30. Garber, Megan, "Why Assault Allegations against Trump Don't Stick: E. Jean Carroll's Defamation Suit against the President Pushes Up against an Obdurate Truth: His Very Ubiquity Has Afforded Him a Kind of Impunity," *The Atlantic* (November 7, 2019), https://www.theatlantic.com/entertainment/archive/2019/11/donald-trump-e-jean-carroll-sexual-assault-defamation-suit/601561/.

31. Jimenez, Abdel, "New State Law Requires Companies to Train Employees on How to Recognize, Prevent Sexual Harassment," *The Chicago Tribune* (December 27, 2019), https://www.chicagotribune.com/business/ct-biz-illinois-law-requires-harassment-training-20191227-rgyrgwgidnfrzbpvmkjgdlpl5y-story.html.

32. "Governor Cuomo Signs Legislation Enacting Sweeping New Workplace Harassment Protection," August 12, 2019, https://www.governor.ny.gov/news/governor-cuomo-signs-legislation-enacting-sweeping-new-workplace-harassment-protections.

33. Bachman, Eric, "In Response to #MeToo, EEOC Is Filing More Sexual Harassment Lawsuits and Winning," *Forbes* (October 5, 2018).

34. "EEOC Releases Preliminary FY 2018 Sexual Harassment Data," EEOC, October 4, 2018.

35. 139 F.R.D. 657 (D. Minn. 1991).

36. Hechler, David, "A White Buffalo," *National Law Journal* (March 28, 2003).

37. Bingham, Clara, and Laura Leedy Gansler, *Class Action: The Story of Lois Jenson and the Landmark Case That Changed Sexual Harassment Law* (New York: Doubleday, 2002).

38. Chapman, Parke, "C B Richard Ellis Denies Sexual Harassment Claims," *National Real Estate Investor* (November 1, 2004), http://nreionline.com/mag/real_estate_cb_richard_ellis_16/; "Settlement: Real Estate Brokerage Harassment," *lawyersandsettlements.com* (October 16, 2007), http://www.lawyersandsettlements.com/settlements/09555/real-estate-brokerage-harassment.html.

39. "EEOC Sues Red Lobster for Sexual Harassment," EEOC press release (September 30, 2013), http://www1.eeoc.gov//eeoc/newsroom/release/9-30-13f.cfm?renderforprint=1.

40. Sachdev, Ameet, "After Nearly 10 Years, Sex-Harassment Suit May Finally Be Settled: Buffalo Grove–Based International Profit Associates Admits Pervasive Sexual Harassment in the Workplace," *Chicago Law* (February 22, 2011), http://articles.chicagotribune.com/2011-02-22/business/ct-biz-0222-chicago-law-20110222_1_eeoc-sexual-harassment-individual-class-members.

41. "Lakemont Homes to Pay $267,000 to Settle EEOC Sexual Harassment, Retaliation Suit," EEOC press release (November 30, 2011), http//www1.eeoc.gov//eeoc/newsroom/release/11-30-11.cfm?r.

42. "MMS Resources/Merchant Management Systems to Pay $365,000 to Settle EEOC Sex Harassment Suit," EEOC press release (November 21, 2011), http://www.eeoc.gov/eeoc/newsroom/release/11-21-11a.cfm.

43. "Dial Settles Sexual Harassment Lawsuit for $10M," *HR.BLR.com* (May 1, 2003), http://hr.blr.com/HR-news/Discrimination/Sexual-Harassment/Dial-Settles-Sexual-Harassment-Lawsuit-for-10M/.

44. Mulkern, Anne C., "Mint Chief: No Tolerance for Sexual Harassment," *The Carlsbad Current-Argus* (September 15, 2006), http://www.currentargus.com/ci_4339904.

45. Keller, Jared, "Nude Photo Scandal Reveals Marines' Culture of Misogyny," *Newsweek* (March 16, 2017), http://www.newsweek.com/nude-photo-scandal-exposes-marines-culture-misogyny-569104.

46. Ellison, Jesse, "The Military's Secret Shame," *Newsweek* (April 11, 2011), p. 40.

47. "EEOC Sues Kraft Foods of North America for Same Sex Harassment of Men," EEOC press release (October 25, 2002), http://www.eeoc.gov/eeoc/newsroom/release/10-25-02.cfm.

48. *Ellison v. Brady,* 924 F.2d 872, 881, n.15 (9th Cir. 1991), quoting from the MSPB update study, U.S. Merit Systems Protection Board, *Sexual Harassment in the Federal Government: An Update* (Washington, DC: U.S. Government Printing Office, 1988), p. 42.

49. 760 F. Supp. 1486, 1506–07 (M.D. Fla. 1991).

50. Ibid.

51. "EEOC Select Task Force on the Study of Harassment in the Workplace," EEOC (June 2016), https://www.eeoc.gov/eeoc/task_force/harassment/upload/report.pdf.

52. Notice that we do not use the term "sexual favors." It hardly makes sense to do so when the activity is unwanted. Making the "request" sound more palatable only masks the truth. We choose to simply call it what it is: a request for sexual activity of some kind.

53. Mattioli, Dana, "More Men Make Harassment Claims," *The Wall Street Journal* (March 23, 2010), http://online.wsj.com/article/SB10001424052748704117304575137881438719028.html.

54. "Charges Alleging Sexual Harassment FY 2010 – FY 2018." U.S. Equal Employment Opportunity Commission, eeoc.com.

55. 523 U.S. 75 (1998).

56. No. 11-556, issued June 24, 2013, http://www.supremecourt.gov/opinions/12pdf/11-556_11o2.pdf.

57. No. 12-484, issued June 24, 2013, http://www.supremecourt.gov/opinions/12pdf/12-484_o759.pdf.

58. 673 F. Supp (1458 E.D. Mo 1987).
59. Heathfield, Susan M., "The Scoop on Love Contracts: Do Dating Co-workers Need to Sign Love Contracts?" (November 13, 2018), http://humanresources.about.com/od/glossaryl/qt/love_contract.htm.
60. 672 F. Supp. 1205 (D.R.I. 1991).
61. 510 U.S. 17 (1993).
62. 523 U.S. 575 (1998).
63. 895 F.2d 1469 (3d Cir. 1990).
64. 542 U.S. 129 (2004).
65. 298 F. Supp. 2d 364 (E.D. Va 2004).

Cases

Case 1

Burlington Industries, Inc. v. Ellerth,
524 U.S. 742 (1998)

An employee claimed she was constructively discharged because of unwanted, persistent sexual advances by her supervisor. While she lost no tangible job benefit because of his actions toward her and even had a promotion during her employment, the Court held she could still bring a cause of action based on hostile environment sexual harassment. Though the employer had a sexual harassment policy, the employee did not report the harassment until a few weeks after she left. The Court said that the employee could still bring the sexual harassment action, but in cases such as this where there is no loss of tangible job benefits, the employer could use as an affirmative defense the existence of procedures for reporting and handling sexual harassment complaints and an employee's failure to use them.

Kennedy, J.

***

The employee is Kimberly Ellerth. From March 1993 until May 1994, Ellerth worked as a salesperson in one of Burlington's divisions in Chicago, Illinois. During her employment, she alleges, she was subjected to constant sexual harassment by her supervisor, one Ted Slowik.

Against a background of repeated boorish and offensive remarks and gestures which Slowik allegedly made, Ellerth places particular emphasis on three alleged incidents where Slowik's comments could be construed as threats to deny her tangible job benefits. In the summer of 1993, while on a business trip, Slowik invited Ellerth to the hotel lounge, an invitation Ellerth felt compelled to accept because Slowik was her boss. When Ellerth gave no encouragement to remarks Slowik made about her breasts, he told her to "loosen up" and warned, "you know, Kim, I could make your life very hard or very easy at Burlington."

In March 1994, when Ellerth was being considered for a promotion, Slowik expressed reservations during the promotion interview because she was not "loose enough." The comment was followed by his reaching over and rubbing her knee. Ellerth did receive the promotion; but when Slowik called to announce it, he told Ellerth, "you're gonna be out there with men who work in factories, and they certainly like women with pretty butts/legs."

In May 1994, Ellerth called Slowik, asking permission to insert a customer's logo into a fabric sample. Slowik responded, "I don't have time for you right now, Kim—unless you want to tell me what you're wearing." Ellerth told Slowik she had to go and ended the call. A day or two later, Ellerth called Slowik to ask permission again. This time he denied her request, but added something along the lines of, "are you wearing shorter skirts yet, Kim, because it would make your job a whole heck of a lot easier."

A short time later, Ellerth's immediate supervisor cautioned her about returning telephone calls to customers in a prompt fashion. In response, Ellerth quit. She faxed a letter giving reasons unrelated to the alleged sexual harassment we have described. About three weeks later, however, she sent a letter explaining she quit because of Slowik's behavior.

During her tenure at Burlington, Ellerth did not inform anyone in authority about Slowik's conduct, despite knowing Burlington had a policy against sexual harassment. In fact, she chose not to inform her immediate supervisor (not Slowik) because "it would be his duty as my supervisor to report any incidents of sexual harassment." On one occasion, she told Slowik a comment he made was inappropriate.

We must decide, then, whether an employer has vicarious liability when a supervisor creates a hostile work environment by making explicit threats to alter a subordinate's terms or conditions of employment, based on sex, but does not fulfill the threat.

Tangible employment actions are the means by which the supervisor brings the official power of the enterprise to bear on subordinates. A tangible employment decision requires an official act of the enterprise, a company act. The decision in most cases is documented in official company records, and may be subject to review by higher level supervisors. The supervisor often must obtain the imprimatur of the enterprise and use its internal processes. For these reasons, a tangible employment action taken by the supervisor becomes for Title VII purposes the act of the employer. Whatever the exact contours of the aided in the agency relation standard, its requirements will always be met when a supervisor takes a tangible employment action against a subordinate. In that instance, it would be implausible to interpret agency principles to allow an employer to escape liability.

An employer is subject to vicarious liability to a victimized employee for an actionable hostile environment created by a supervisor with immediate (or successively higher) authority over the employee. When no tangible employment action is taken, a defending employer may raise an affirmative defense to liability or damages, subject to proof by a preponderance of the evidence. The defense comprises two necessary elements: (a) that the employer exercised reasonable care to prevent and correct promptly any sexually harassing behavior, and (b) that the plaintiff employee unreasonably failed to take advantage of any preventive or corrective opportunities provided by the employer or to avoid harm otherwise.

While proof that an employer had promulgated an anti-harassment policy with complaint procedure is not necessary in every instance as a matter of law, the need for a stated policy suitable to the employment circumstances may appropriately be addressed in any case when litigating the first element of the defense. And while proof that an employee failed to fulfill the corresponding obligation of reasonable care to avoid harm is not limited to showing any unreasonable failure to use any complaint procedure provided by the employer, a demonstration of such failure will normally suffice to satisfy the employer's burden under the second element of the defense. No affirmative defense is available, however, when the supervisor's harassment culminates in a tangible employment action, such as discharge, demotion, or undesirable reassignment.

Although Ellerth has not alleged she suffered a tangible employment action at the hands of Slowik, which would deprive Burlington of the availability of the affirmative defense, this is not dispositive. In light of our decision, Burlington is still subject to vicarious liability for Slowik's activity, but Burlington should have an opportunity to assert and prove the affirmative defense to liability. AFFIRMED.

Case Questions

1. What do you think of the Court not allowing the affirmative defense if there was a tangible employment action such as a discharge, demotion, or undesirable reassignment?

2. Does it make sense to you to allow an employee to bring a sexual harassment cause of action if the employee suffered no adverse tangible employment action?

3. Do you understand why the Court would allow this affirmative defense in cases where there is no loss of tangible job benefit but not in cases where there is such a loss?

Meritor Savings Bank, FSB v. Vinson,
477 U.S. 57 (1986)

An employee alleged sexual harassment even though she lost no tangible job benefits. The Court determined that quid pro quo was not the only type of sexual harassment. For the first time, the U.S. Supreme Court determined that this kind of situation constituted hostile environment sexual harassment.

Rehnquist, J.

***

Mechelle Vinson worked at Meritor Savings Bank, initially as a teller-trainee, but was later promoted to teller, head teller, and assistant branch manager, admittedly based upon merit. Sidney Taylor was the bank branch manager and the person who hired Vinson. Vinson alleged that in the beginning Taylor was "fatherly" toward her and made no sexual advances, but eventually he asked her to go out to dinner. During the course of the meal Taylor suggested that he and Vinson go to a motel to have sexual relations. At first she refused, but out of what she described as fear of losing her job, she eventually agreed. Taylor thereafter made repeated demands upon Vinson for sexual activity, usually at the branch, both during and after business hours. She estimated that over the next several years she had intercourse with him some 40 or 50 times. In addition, she testified that Taylor fondled her in front of other employees, followed her into the women's restroom when she went there alone, exposed himself to her, and even forcibly raped her on several occasions. These activities ceased in 1977 when Vinson started going with a steady boyfriend.

Courts have applied Title VII protection to racial harassment and nothing in Title VII suggests that a hostile environment based on discriminatory *sexual* harassment should not be likewise prohibited. The Guidelines thus appropriately drew from, and were fully consistent with, the existing case law.

Of course, not all workplace conduct that may be described as "harassment" affects a "term, condition, or privilege" of employment within the meaning of Title VII. For instance, mere utterance of an ethnic or racial epithet which engenders offensive feelings in an employee would not affect the condition of employment to a sufficiently significant degree to create an abusive working environment. For sexual harassment to be actionable, it must be sufficiently severe or pervasive to alter the conditions of the victim's employment and create an abusive working environment. Vinson's allegations in this case—which include not only pervasive harassment, but also criminal conduct of the most serious nature—are plainly sufficient to state a claim for hostile environment sexual harassment.

The District Court's conclusion that no actionable harassment occurred might have rested on its earlier finding that if Vinson and Taylor had engaged in intimate or sexual relations, that relationship was a voluntary one. But the fact that sex-related conduct was "voluntary" in the sense that the complainant was not forced to participate against her will, is not a defense to a sexual harassment suit brought under Title VII. The gravamen of any sexual harassment claim is the alleged sexual advances were "unwelcome." While the question whether particular conduct was indeed unwelcome presents difficult problems of proof and turns largely on credibility determinations committed to the trier of fact, the District Court in this case erroneously focused on the "voluntariness" of Vinson's participation in the claimed sexual episodes. The correct inquiry is whether Vinson, by her conduct, indicated that the alleged sexual advances were unwelcome, not whether her participation in sexual intercourse was voluntary.

The district court admitted into evidence testimony about Vinson's "dress and personal fantasies." The court of appeals stated that testimony had no place in the litigation, on the basis that Vinson's voluntariness in submitting to Taylor's advances was immaterial to her sexual harassment claim. While "voluntariness" in the sense of consent is not a defense to such a claim, it does not follow that a complainant's sexually provocative speech or dress is irrelevant as a matter of law in determining whether she found particular sexual advances welcome. To the contrary, such evidence is obviously relevant. The EEOC Guidelines emphasize that the trier of fact must determine the existence of sexual harassment in light of "the record as a whole" and the "totality of circumstances," such as the nature of the sexual advances and the context in which the alleged incidents occurred.

In sum we hold that a claim of "hostile environment" sexual harassment gender discrimination is actionable under Title VII. AFFIRMED.

Case Questions

1. As a manager, what would you have done if Vinson had come to you with her story?

2. Under the circumstances, should it matter that Vinson "voluntarily" had sex with Taylor? That she received her regular promotions? Explain.

3. As a manager, how would you determine whom to believe?

Ellison v. Brady,
924 F.2d 872 (9th Cir. 1991)

An employee brought a sexual harassment suit because, among other things, her coworker, whom she barely knew, kept sending her personal letters. The court found that while some may think it only a small matter, viewed from the employee's perspective as a female in a society in which females are often the victims of violence, the action was offensive and a violation of Title VII.

Beezer, J.

***

The case presents the important issue of what test should be applied to determine whether conduct is sufficiently severe or pervasive to alter the conditions of employment and create a hostile working environment.

Ellison worked as a revenue agent for the IRS in San Mateo, California. During her initial training in 1984 she met Sterling Gray, another trainee also assigned to that office. The two never became friends and did not work closely together. Gray's desk was twenty feet from Ellison's, two rows behind and one row over.

In June of 1986 when no one else was in the office, Gray asked Ellison to go to lunch. She accepted. They went past Gray's house to pick up his son's forgotten lunch and Gray gave Ellison a tour of his house. Ellison alleges that after that June lunch, Gray began to pester her with unnecessary questions and hang around her desk.

On October 9, when Gray asked Ellison out for a drink after work, she declined, but suggested lunch the following week. Ellison did not want to have lunch alone with him and she tried to stay away from the office during lunch time. The next week Gray asked her out to lunch and she did not go.

On October 22, 1986, Gray handed Ellison a note written on a telephone message slip which read: "I cried over you last night and I'm totally drained today. I have never been in such constant termoil [sic]. Thank you for talking with me. I could not stand to feel your hatred for another day." Ellison was shocked at the note, became frightened and left the room. Gray followed Ellison into the hallway and demanded that she talk to him. Ellison left the building. While Gray reported this to her supervisor and asked to try to handle it herself, she asked a male co-worker to talk to Gray and tell him she was not interested in him and to leave her alone. The next day, Gray called in sick. Ellison did not work the following day, Friday, and on Monday started a four-week training session in Missouri.

While Ellison was at the training session, Gray mailed her a card and a three-page, typed, single spaced letter. Ellison described the letter as "twenty times, a hundred times weirder" than the prior note. In part, Gray wrote:

> I know that you are worth knowing with or without sex. . . . Leaving aside the hassles and disasters of recent weeks, I have enjoyed you so much over these past few months. Watching you. Experiencing you from O so far away. Admiring your style and elan. . . . Don't you think it odd that two people who have never even talked together,

alone, are striking off such intense sparks . . . I will [write] another letter in the near future.

Ellison stated that she thought Gray was "crazy. I thought he was nuts. I didn't know what he would do next. I was frightened." Ellison immediately called her supervisor and reported this and told her she was frightened and wanted one of them transferred. Gray was told many times over the next few weeks not to contact Ellison in any way. On November 24 Gray transferred to the San Francisco office. Ellison returned from Missouri in late November. After three weeks in San Francisco, Gray filed a grievance to return to San Mateo and as part of the settlement in Gray's favor, he agreed to be transferred back provided he spend four more months (a total of six months) in San Francisco and promise not to bother Ellison. When Ellison learned of Gray's request to return in a letter from her supervisor indicating Gray would return after a six-month separation, she said she was "frantic" and filed a formal sexual harassment complaint with [the] IRS. The letter to Ellison also said that they could revisit the issue if there was further need.

Gray sought joint counseling. He wrote another letter to Ellison seeking to maintain the idea that he and Ellison had a relationship.

We do not agree with the standard set forth in *Rabidue*. We believe that Gray's conduct was sufficiently severe and pervasive to alter the conditions of Ellison's employment and create an abusive working environment. We believe that, in evaluating the severity and pervasiveness of sexual harassment, we should focus on the perspective of the victim. If we examined whether a reasonable person would engage in allegedly harassing conduct, we would run the risk of reinforcing the prevailing level of discrimination. Harassers could continue to harass merely because a particular discriminatory practice was common, and victims of harassment would have no remedy.

We therefore prefer to analyze harassment from the victim's perspective. A complete understanding of the victim's view requires, among other things, an analysis of the different perspectives of men and women. Conduct that many men consider unobjectionable may offend many women. See, e.g., *Lipsett v. University of Puerto Rico*, 864 F.2d 881, 898 (1st Cir. 1988) ("A male supervisor might believe, for example, that it is legitimate for him to tell a female subordinate that she has a 'great figure' or 'nice legs.' The female subordinate, however, may find such comments offensive"); *Yates*, 819 F.2d at 637, n.2 ("men and women are vulnerable in different ways and offended

by different behavior"). See also, Ehrenreich, "Pluralist Myths and Powerless Men: The Ideology of Reasonableness in Sexual Harassment Law," 99 *Yale L. J.* 1177, 1207–1208 (1990) (men tend to view some forms of sexual harassment as "harmless social interactions to which only overly-sensitive women would object"); Abrams, "Gender Discrimination and the Transformation of Workplace Norms," 42 *Vand. L. Rev.* 1183, 1203 (1989) (the characteristically male view depicts sexual harassment as comparatively harmless amusement).

We realize that there is a broad range of viewpoints among women as a group, but we realize that many women share common concerns which men do not necessarily share. For example, because women are disproportionately victims of rape and sexual assault, women have stronger incentives to be concerned with sexual behavior. Women who are victims of mild forms of sexual harassment may understandably worry whether a harasser's conduct is merely a prelude to violent sexual assault. Men, who are rarely victims of sexual assault, may view sexual conduct in a vacuum without a full appreciation of the social setting or the underlying threat of violence that a woman may perceive.

In order to shield employers from having to accommodate the idiosyncratic concerns of the rare hypersensitive employee, we hold that a female plaintiff states a *prima facie* case of hostile environment sexual harassment when she alleges conduct that a reasonable woman would consider sufficiently severe or pervasive to alter the conditions of employment and create an abusive working environment. Of course, where male employees allege that co-workers engage in conduct which creates a hostile environment, the appropriate victim's perspective would be that of a reasonable man.

We adopt the perspective of a reasonable woman primarily because we believe that a gender-blind reasonable person standard tends to be male-biased and tends to systematically ignore the experiences of women. The reasonable woman standard does not establish a higher level of protection for women than men. Instead, a gender-conscious examination of sexual harassment enables women to participate in the workplace on an equal footing with men. By acknowledging and not trivializing the effects of sexual harassment on reasonable women, courts can work towards ensuring that neither men nor women will have to "run a gauntlet of sexual abuse in return for the privilege of being allowed to work and make a living."

We note that the reasonable woman victim standard we adopt today classifies conduct as unlawful sexual harassment even when harassers do not realize that their conduct creates a hostile working environment. Well-intentioned compliments by co-workers or supervisors can form the basis of a sexual harassment cause of action if a reasonable victim of the same gender as plaintiff would consider the comments sufficiently severe or pervasive to alter a condition of employment and create an abusive working environment. That is because Title VII is not a fault-based tort scheme. Title VII is aimed at the consequences or effects of an employment practice and not the motivation of co-workers or employers.

The facts of this case illustrate the importance of considering the victim's perspective. Analyzing the facts from the alleged harasser's viewpoint, Gray could be portrayed as a modern-day Cyrano de Bergerac wishing no more than to woo Ellison with his words. There is no evidence that Gray harbored ill-will toward Ellison. He even offered in his "love letter" to leave her alone if she wished [though he said he would not be able to forget her]. Examined in this light, it is not difficult to see why the district court characterized Gray's conduct as isolated and trivial.

Ellison, however, did not consider the acts to be trivial. Gray's first note shocked and frightened her. After receiving the three-page letter, she became really upset and frightened again. She immediately requested that she or Gray be transferred. Her supervisor's prompt response suggests that she too did not consider the conduct trivial. When Ellison learned that Gray arranged to return to San Mateo, she immediately asked to transfer and she immediately filed an official complaint.

We cannot say as a matter of law that Ellison's reaction was idiosyncratic or hyper-sensitive. We believe that a reasonable woman could have had a similar reaction. After receiving the first bizarre note from Gray, a person she barely knew, Ellison asked a co-worker to tell Gray to leave her alone. Despite her request, Gray sent her a long, passionate, disturbing letter. He told her he had been "watching" and "experiencing" her; he made repeated references to sex; and he said he would write again. Ellison had no way of knowing what Gray would do next. A reasonable woman could consider Gray's conduct, as alleged by Ellison, sufficiently severe and pervasive to alter a condition of employment and create an abusive working environment.

Sexual harassment is a major problem in the workplace. Adopting the victim's perspective ensures that courts will not "sustain ingrained notions of reasonable behavior fashioned by the offenders." Congress did not enact Title VII to codify prevailing sexist prejudices. To the contrary, "Congress designed Title VII to prevent the perpetuation of stereotypes and a sense of degradation which serve to close or discourage employment opportunities for women." We hope that over time both men and women will learn what conduct offends reasonable members of the other gender. When employers and employees internalize the standard of workplace conduct we establish today, the current gap in perception between the genders will be bridged. REVERSED and REMANDED.

Case Questions

1. Do you agree with the court's use of the "reasonable victim" standard? Explain.

2. Do you think the standard creates problems for management? If so, what are they? If not, why not?

3. Do you think Ellison was being "overly sensitive"? What would you have done if you had been the supervisor to whom she reported the incidents?

Faragher v. City of Boca Raton, *524 U.S. 775 (1998)*

Case 4

A former city lifeguard sued the city under Title VII for sexual harassment based on the conduct of her supervisors. The Supreme Court held that an employer is subject to vicarious liability under Title VII for actionable discrimination caused by a supervisor, but the employer may raise an affirmative defense that looks to the reasonableness of the employer's conduct in seeking to prevent and correct harassing conduct and to the reasonableness of the employee's conduct in seeking to avoid harm. The Court held that the employer was vicariously liable here because it failed to exercise reasonable care to prevent harassing behavior.

This case calls for identification of the circumstances under which an employer may be held liable under Title VII of the Civil Rights Act for the acts of a supervisory employee whose sexual harassment of subordinates has created a hostile work environment amounting to employment discrimination. We hold that an employer is vicariously liable for actionable discrimination caused by a supervisor but subject to an affirmative defense looking to the reasonableness of the employer's conduct as well as that of a plaintiff victim.

Souter, J.

***

Between 1985 and 1990, while attending college, petitioner Beth Ann Faragher worked part time and during the summers as an ocean lifeguard for the Marine Safety Section of the Parks and Recreation Department of respondent, the City of Boca Raton, Florida (City). During this period, Faragher's immediate supervisors were Bill Terry, David Silverman, and Robert Gordon. In June 1990, Faragher resigned. In 1992, Faragher brought an action against Terry, Silverman, and the City, asserting claims under Title VII, and Florida law. The complaint alleged that Terry and Silverman were agents of the City, and that their conduct created a "sexually hostile atmosphere" that amounted to discrimination in the "terms, conditions, and privileges" of her employment at the beach by repeatedly subjecting Faragher and other female lifeguards to "uninvited and offensive touching," by making lewd remarks, and by speaking of women in offensive terms.

Throughout Faragher's employment with the City, Terry served as Chief of the Marine Safety Division, with authority to hire new lifeguards (subject to the approval of higher management), to supervise all aspects of the lifeguards' work assignments, to engage in counseling, to deliver oral reprimands, and to make a record of any such discipline. Silverman and Gordon were captains and responsible for making the lifeguards' daily assignments, and for supervising their work and fitness training. The lifeguards and supervisors were stationed at the city beach. The lifeguards had no significant contact with higher city officials like the Recreation Superintendent.

In February 1986, the City adopted a sexual harassment policy, which it stated in a memorandum from the City Manager addressed to all employees. In May 1990, the City revised the policy and reissued a statement of it. Although the City may actually have circulated the memos and statements to some employees, it completely failed to disseminate its policy among employees of the Marine Safety Section, with the result that Terry, Silverman, Gordon, and many lifeguards were unaware of it.

Faragher did not complain to higher management about Terry or Silverman. In April 1990, however, two months before Faragher's resignation, Nancy Ewanchew, a former lifeguard, wrote to Richard Bender, the City's Personnel Director, complaining that Terry and Silverman had harassed her and other female lifeguards. Following investigation of this complaint, the City found that Terry and Silverman had behaved improperly, reprimanded them, and required them to choose between a suspension without pay or the forfeiture of annual leave.

Since our decision in *Meritor*, Courts of Appeals have struggled to derive manageable standards to govern employer liability for hostile environment harassment perpetrated by supervisory employees. While indicating the substantive contours of the hostile environments forbidden by Title VII, our cases have established few definite rules for determining when an employer will be liable for a discriminatory environment that is otherwise actionably abusive.

A "master is subject to liability for the torts of his servants committed while acting in the scope of their employment." Restatement § 219(1). This doctrine has traditionally defined the "scope of employment" as including conduct "of the kind [a servant] is employed to perform," occurring "substantially within the authorized time and space limits," and "actuated, at least in part, by a purpose to serve the master," but as excluding an intentional use of force "unexpectable by the master."

A justification for holding the offensive behavior within the scope of Terry's and Silverman's employment was well put in Judge Barkett's dissent: "[A] pervasively hostile work environment of sexual harassment is never (one would hope) authorized, but the supervisor is clearly charged with maintaining a productive, safe work environment. The supervisor directs and controls the conduct of the employees, and the manner of doing so may inure to the employer's benefit or detriment, including subjecting the employer to Title VII liability."

It is by now well recognized that hostile environment sexual harassment by supervisors (and, for that matter, co-employees) is a persistent problem in the workplace. An employer can, in a general sense, reasonably anticipate the possibility of such conduct occurring in its workplace, and one might justify the assignment of the burden of the untoward behavior to the employer as one of the costs of doing business, to be charged to the enterprise rather than the victim. As noted, developments like this occur from time to time in the law of agency.

We agree with Faragher that in implementing Title VII it makes sense to hold an employer vicariously liable for some tortious conduct of a supervisor made possible by abuse of his supervisory authority. The agency relationship affords contact with an employee subjected to a supervisor's sexual harassment, and the victim may well be reluctant to accept the risks of blowing the whistle on a superior. When a person with supervisory authority discriminates in the terms and conditions of subordinates' employment, his actions necessarily draw upon his superior position over the people who report to him, or those under them, whereas an employee generally cannot check a supervisor's abusive conduct the same way that she might deal with abuse from a co-worker. When a fellow employee harasses, the victim can walk away or tell the offender where to go, but it may be difficult to offer such responses to a supervisor, whose "power to supervise–[which may be] to hire and fire, and to set work schedules and pay rates–does not disappear . . . when he chooses to harass through insults and offensive gestures rather than directly with threats of firing or promises of promotion." Recognition of employer liability when discriminatory misuse of supervisory authority alters the terms and conditions of a victim's employment is underscored by the fact that the employer has a greater opportunity to guard against misconduct by supervisors than by common workers; employers have greater opportunity and incentive to screen them, train them, and monitor their performance.

In order to accommodate the principle of vicarious liability for harm caused by misuse of supervisory authority, as well as Title VII's equally basic policies of encouraging forethought by employers and saving action by objecting employees, we adopt the following holding in this case and in *Burlington Industries, Inc. v. Ellerth,* also decided today. An employer is subject to vicarious liability to a victimized employee for an actionable hostile environment created by a supervisor with immediate (or successively higher) authority over the employee.

When no tangible employment action is taken, a defending employer may raise an affirmative defense to liability or damages, subject to proof by a preponderance of the evidence. The defense comprises two necessary elements: (a) that the employer exercised reasonable care to prevent and correct promptly any sexually harassing behavior, and (b) that the plaintiff employee unreasonably failed to take advantage of any preventive or corrective opportunities provided by the employer or to avoid harm otherwise.

While proof that an employer had promulgated an antiharassment policy with complaint procedure is not necessary in every instance as a matter of law, the need for a stated policy suitable to the employment circumstances may appropriately be addressed in any case when litigating the first element of the defense. And while proof that an employee failed to fulfill the corresponding obligation of reasonable care to avoid harm is not limited to showing an unreasonable failure to use any complaint procedure provided by the employer, a demonstration of such failure will normally suffice to satisfy the employer's burden under the second element of the defense. No affirmative defense is available, however, when the supervisor's harassment culminates in a tangible employment action, such as discharge, demotion, or undesirable reassignment.

Applying these rules here, it is undisputed that these supervisors "were granted virtually unchecked authority" over their subordinates, "directly controll[ing] and supervis[ing] all aspects of [Faragher's] day-to-day activities." It is also clear that Faragher and her colleagues were "completely isolated from the City's higher management."

While the City would have an opportunity to raise an affirmative defense if there were any serious prospect of its presenting one, it appears from the record that any such avenue is closed. The City entirely failed to disseminate its policy against sexual harassment among the beach employees and its officials made no attempt to keep track of the conduct of supervisors like Terry and Silverman. The City's policy did not include any assurance that the harassing supervisors could be bypassed in registering complaints. Under such circumstances, we hold as a matter of law that the City could not be found to have exercised reasonable care to prevent the supervisors' harassing conduct. Unlike the employer of a small workforce, who might expect that sufficient care to prevent tortious behavior could be exercised informally, those responsible for city operations could not reasonably have thought that precautions against hostile environments in any one of many departments in far-flung locations could be effective without communicating some formal policy against harassment, with a sensible complaint procedure. REVERSED and REMANDED.

Case Questions

1. How could the city have avoided this outcome? Explain.
2. Do you think that it would have made sense for the city to consider the particulars of the circumstances here, such as that these were lifeguards, in a remote location, who by the nature of the job would be dressed in fairly little clothing, and who, because of the environment (the beach and recreational facilities), might need a different approach to sexual harassment than, say, office employees? Explain.
3. What do you think of the Court's affirmative defense given to employers and employees? What are the pros and cons?

Chapter 10

Sexual Orientation and Gender Identity Discrimination

Jill Braaten/McGraw-Hill Education

Learning Objectives

After completing this chapter, you should be able to:

LO1   Discuss the history of the modern gay rights movement.

LO2   Discuss the state of LGBTQ workplace protections before the *Bostock v. Clayton County, Georgia* case.

LO3   Understand the significance of employers being inclusive of LGBTQ employees.

LO4   Discuss how some courts have circumvented the exclusion of LGBTQ employees from Title VII coverage.

LO5   Identify whether same-gender sexual harassment is covered by Title VII.

LO6   Discuss the workplace issues involving transgender individuals.

LO7   Identify some of the employment benefits issues for LGBTQ employees.

LO8   List some ways that employers can address LGBTQ issues in the workplace.

Opening Scenarios

SCENARIO 1

1 A male employee is terminated from his employment because his employer thinks the employee's earring is too effeminate. The employee sues for sex discrimination. Does he win? Why or why not?

Scenario

SCENARIO 2

2 A male airline pilot is terminated after he puts in a request for medical leave, in accordance with company policy, to have sexual reassignment surgery to change anatomically from male to female. Is this illegal discrimination? Why or why not?

Scenario

SCENARIO 3

3 Sylvio's immediate supervisor, Leroy, has been giving Sylvio sexually suggestive looks and making sexually suggestive comments. Sylvio is feeling extremely uncomfortable about it and fears for his job. However, Sylvio thinks that because both he and Leroy are males, there can be no sexual harassment. Is Sylvio correct?

Scenario

Statutory Basis

It shall be an unlawful employment practice for an employer—

(1) to fail or refuse to hire or to discharge any individual, or otherwise to discriminate against any individual with respect to his compensation, terms, conditions, or privileges of employment, because of such individual's . . . sex. [Title VII of the Civil Rights Act of 1964, as amended. 42 U.S.C. § 2000e-2(a).]

[N]or shall any State deprive any person of life, liberty, or property, without due process of law; nor deny to any person within its jurisdiction the equal protection of the laws. [Amendment XIV of the U.S. Constitution.]

If you have been paying attention to the opening Statutory Basis section for all the other chapters, you will quickly realize that this one is quite different.

sexual orientation
Whom one is attracted to for personal and intimate relationships.

gender identity
How one identifies for male/female purposes, based on a combination of genetics and environment, including, among other things, transgender.

While sex is explicitly included in Title VII as a basis for prohibited workplace discrimination, **sexual orientation** and **gender identity** are not. However, EEOC has interpreted the prohibition on gender discrimination as including discrimination on these bases. It did so based on a 1989 U.S. Supreme Court case outlawing gender stereotyping as well as several lower court cases addressing the issue. The EEOC set forth its position in several published decisions that explained the legal basis for this determination and gave examples of what would be considered unlawful. In reaching this conclusion, the EEOC said it has not recognized any new protected characteristics under Title VII. Rather, it has applied existing Title VII precedents to gender discrimination claims raised by LGBTQ individuals.

In June 2020, the U.S. Supreme Court agreed, holding in *Bostock v. Clayton County, Georgia,* "An employer violates Title VII when it intentionally fires an individual employee based in part on sex. . . . If the employer intentionally relies in part on an individual employee's sex when deciding to discharge the employee. . . a statutory violation has occurred." *Bostock v. Clayton County, Georgia*, No. 17-1618 (U.S. Supreme Court June 15, 2020).

Out of the Closet

See Exhibit 10.1, "Terms to Know."

"Look!" the angry gentleman in the audience said gruffly as the diversity consultant walked into the room and up to the stage in preparation for conducting a training session. "Does this diversity training mean that I have to deal with *homosexuals*? Because if it does, I'm not doing it! Homosexuality is against my religion, and I just don't think it's right!"

Exhibit 10.1 *LGBTQ+ → Terms to Know**

An abbreviation for the community of people who identify as lesbian, gay, bisexual, transgender, queer, plus any other sexual or gender minority. The acronym can vary in a number of ways and often includes "I" for intersex and "A" for asexual.

AFAB/AMAB: Short for *assigned female at birth* and *assigned male at birth*. This acronym is used to describe the sex a person is first assigned based on their physical characteristics, which may or may not be different from their inner sense of gender identity.

ALLY: A person who supports the LGBTQ+ community.

ASEXUAL: A term used to describe a person who does not feel sexual attraction to others, or who has limited sexual interest or desire for others. This term should be used as an adjective, not as a noun.

BISEXUAL: A term used to describe a person who is emotionally, sexually, or romantically attracted to people of the same and other genders. This term should be used as an adjective, not as a noun.

CISGENDER: A term used to describe people whose gender identity matches the sex they were

assigned at birth. Often abbreviated to *cis*. This term should be used as an adjective, not as a noun.

CISNORMATIVITY: Cultural rules and expectations (including social, family, legal, and linguistic) that promote and assume the idea that everyone's gender identity is either female or male and that it matches their biological sex; an assumption that all people are cisgender.[1]

COMING OUT OF THE CLOSET: The process of self-acceptance and disclosure of sexual orientation or gender identity to others. People can disclose to none, some, or all of the people they know, often based on the perceived safety of their environment.

DISCLOSURE: The act or process of sharing one's sexual orientation or gender identity. In the workplace, this term is often used to refer to employees voluntarily self-identifying for the purposes of diversity and inclusion-related data collection. Disclosure policies, procedures, and laws vary across companies and countries and should be taken carefully into account.

GAY: A term used to describe a person who is primarily emotionally, sexually, or romantically

(*continued*)

Exhibit 10.1 *continued*

attracted to people of the same gender. This term is preferred over *homosexual,* which is outdated and clinical. Also, this term should be used as an adjective, not as a noun.

GENDER: The external, socially constructed rules, roles, behaviors, activities, and attributes that a society imposes on people based on their identity as a woman, man, or other alternative. Traditional gender categories are binary: woman and man; however not everyone identifies within this binary, and other categories are now accepted at some companies.

GENDER EXPANSIVE: A term used to describe people who do not identify with the woman/man gender binary, but instead identify with one of many identities on a more expansive spectrum. This term is preferred over *gender non-conforming,* which is outdated.

GENDER EXPRESSION: How people communicate their gender through appearance, behavior, grooming, and/or dress.

GENDER FLUID: A term to describe people who move between two or more gendered identities.

GENDER IDENTITY: People's inner sense of their gender, which may or may not correspond with the sex they were assigned at birth.

GENDER PERFORMANCE: The ways in which people act out their gender identity through behavior, helping to shape and reinforce their desired form of gender expression.

GENDER ROLE: Rules assigned by society that define what behaviors, thoughts, feelings, relationships, clothing, occupations, etc., are considered appropriate and inappropriate for people based on their gender.

GENDERQUEER: See *non-binary.*

HETERONORMATIVITY: Cultural rules and expectations (including social, family, legal, and linguistic) that promote a heterosexual standard of identity as the natural norm; an assumption that all people are straight.

HETEROSEXISM: The attitude that heterosexuality is the only valid sexual orientation. Heterosexismdenies, denigrates, andstigmatizes any non-heterosexual form of behavior, relationship, or community. Heterosexism often takes the form of ignoring or discriminating against LGBTQ+ people or discounting their experiences altogether.

HETEROSEXUAL: See *straight.*

HOMOPHOBIA: The hatred, hostility, disapproval, or fear of people who identify as, or are assumed to be, lesbian, gay, bisexual, transgender, or queer.

IN THE CLOSET: A term used to describe LGBTQ+ individuals who do not disclose their sexual orientation and/or gender identity to others. People can disclose to none, some, or all of the people they know. Often shortened to *closeted.*

INTERSEX: A term used to describe people whose anatomy and physiology are neither typically male nor typically female at birth, often due to chromosomal anomalies or ambiguous genitalia. This term should be used as an adjective, not as a noun.

LESBIAN: A woman who is primarily emotionally, sexually, or romantically attracted to other women.

LGBTQ+: An abbreviation for the community of people who identify as lesbian, gay, bisexual, transgender, queer, plus any other sexual or gender minority. The acronym can vary in a number of ways and often includes "I" for intersex and "A" for asexual.

NON-BINARY: Acategory for a fluidconstellation of gender identities beyond the woman/man gender binary; also called *genderqueer.*

OUT EMPLOYEE: An employee who discloses their LGBTQ+ identity to a few, some, or all of their coworkers.

PRONOUNS: Linguistic part of speech used to refer to individuals (such as she/her, he/him). Non-binary people may choose gender- neutral pronouns such as "they," "ze," or "xe." Companies may update organizational policies, procedures and/or HR systems to be inclusive of employees whose pronouns differ from the she/he binary.

QUEER: A broad term with numerous meanings. It is commonly used to describe sexual orientation and/or gender identity or gender expression that does not conform to heterosexual and cisgender norms. Historically it has been used pejoratively, but it has recently been reclaimed, particularly by younger generations, as an inclusive term for the entire LGBTQ+ community or to capture a more fluid sense of identity.

SEX: A person's biological characteristics including the internal and external sex organs, chromosomes, and hormones that make up their anatomy and physiology; sex categories are female, male, and intersex.

SEXUAL ORIENTATION: This term describes a person's innate sense of who they are emotionally, sexually, or romantically attracted to—people of the same gender, different gender, multiple genders, or some other variation.

STRAIGHT: A term used to describe a person who is primarily emotionally, sexually, or romantically attracted to people of a different gender.

TRANSGENDER: A term used to describe people who identify with the physical characteristics, roles, behaviors, and/or desires of a gender different from the one associated with the sex they were assigned at birth. This is an umbrella term that encompasses anyone who is not cisgender, from people who are gender fluid to people who undergo surgery to better align their physical body with their gender identity. Often abbreviated

to *trans.* This term should be used as an adjective, not as a noun.

TRANSITIONING: The process a transgender person goes through to change their gender presentation and/or sex characteristics to better match their gender identity. These changes can include sex reassignment surgery and/or hormone therapy. Note that not everyone who identifies as transgender will undergo a transition, or chose to transition in the same ways.

TRANSMAN: A man who was assigned female at birth (AFAB). A related term is *FTM,* short for female-to-male.

TRANSWOMAN: A woman who was assigned male at birth (AMAB). A related term is *MTF,* short for male-to-female.

TWO-SPIRIT: A contemporary Native American/First Nations/indigenous umbrella term for people within the community who embody both female and male spirits. Often, two-spirit people are honored members of the community who play an important role in spiritual gatherings. Individual tribes have their own terms in their own languages. This term is not synonymous with gay and it should not be used to refer to anyone who does not have Native American/First Nations/indigenous heritage.[2]

It has been estimated that about 4.5 percent of the U.S. population (about 11 million people) identifies as LGBTQ,[3] 88 percent of whom are employed.[4] Despite this, this employee's attitude is not unique. In no particular order, some of the events that have provoked such reactions and provide context include the following:

- An Arkansas farmer acknowledges spreading three tons of manure along the route of a gay rights parade, saying he was exercising his constitutional right to free speech.[5]
- A Mississippi high school cancels its prom after a female student wanted to bring a female date.[6]

- The day before Valentine's Day, the Kansas House passes House Bill 2453 by a vote of 74 to 29, protecting religious individuals, groups, and businesses that refuse service to same-sex couples, especially those contemplating marriage, even though the state banned same-sex marriage.[7] The measure comes after several lawsuits in other states, including one in Kentucky against a Christian T-shirt printer who refused to print T-shirts for the city's annual gay pride event,[8] one in Oregon where a Christian bakery refused to make a wedding cake for a lesbian couple,[9] and one in New Mexico where a Christian wedding photographer refused to take pictures for a lesbian wedding.[10] Claimants in jurisdictions with antidiscrimination laws in public accommodations that included sexual orientation won suits for violations of their civil rights. However, the Kansas proposal was just the opening shot fired. Shortly thereafter the Arizona house and senate passed such a measure, and it was quickly introduced in the Georgia legislature.[11] After widespread protests, Arizona Governor Jan Brewer vetoed the bill in 2014, as did Georgia's governor once the NFL threatened to boycott Atlanta for the Super Bowl.

- Shorter University requires more than 200 employees to sign a "Personal Life-style Statement" rejecting homosexuality.[12]

- In 2012, Toronto Blue Jay's shortstop Yunel Escobar plays on the field with a homophobic slur written on an eyeblack sticker (patch athletes use to reduce the sun's glare) under his eyes. The patch said, "Tu ere Maricon," for which the most common translation is "You are a faggot." In 2017, Kevin Pillar of the same team was suspended for two days for yelling a homophobic slur at Atlanta Braves pitcher Jason Mott. "This is not who I am and I will use this as an opportunity to better myself," he said.[13]

- The U.S. Treasury Department announces on August 29, 2013, that it would recognize any legally married gay couple, even in the then-37 states that did not recognize same-sex marriages. In addition, the Defense Department announced it would begin offering full spousal and family benefits to same-sex spouses of military personnel in alignment with the June 2013 U.S. Supreme Court's striking down of the Defense of Marriage Act's denial of federal marriage benefits to lawfully married same-sex couples. In Texas, Mississippi, Louisiana, and Oklahoma, the National Guard says that it would not process claims from gay couples, despite the Pentagon's authorization, without the spouses traveling to federal military installations sometimes located a long distance away.[14]

- On June 26, 2015, the U.S. Supreme Court, in *Obergefell v. Hodges,*[15] outlaws as an unconstitutional denial of equal protection state laws prohibiting same-sex marriage. Marriage between members of the same gender became legal in every state.

- In 2013, the Boy Scouts of America ended its long-standing blanket policy against admitting openly gay members but still excluded gays as Scout leaders. In 2015, it lifted the ban on gay leaders but allowed an exemption for troops with religious affiliations.[16]

- A firefighter who was allegedly harassed because he stood up for his lesbian daughter after a "condemnation of homosexuals" by his captain is forced to retire after being dunned by his captain and others even after he transferred.[17]

- Minnesota Vikings punter Chris Kluwe charges that he was released from the team because of his activism for same-sex marriage rights even though he is heterosexual.[18]

- The New York attorney general challenges the NFL for asking draft picks about their sexual orientation and enters into a settlement agreement with them in 2013 requiring, among other things, antidiscrimination posters to be placed in team locker rooms.[19]

- Republican California Governor Arnold Schwarzenegger causes an uproar when he calls Democratic legislators who oppose his budget "girlie men."[20]

- A seven-year-old is scolded and forced to write repeatedly "I will never use the word 'gay' in school again" after he told a classmate about his lesbian mom in response to a question during recess by a classmate about the boy's parents.[21]

- In 2010, after 17 years, Congress repeals "Don't Ask, Don't Tell" (DADT) for gays in the military.[22] The DADT policy permitted homosexuals to serve in the military as long as the military, which could not inquire under the policy, did not know.

- The Episcopal Church consecrates its first openly lesbian bishop in 2010.[23]

- The 2010 Census reports the number of married same-gender couples for the first time. After much back and forth about the issue, the 2020 Census will not count gays and lesbians.[24]

- In 2010, President Obama issues a memorandum for the secretary of Health and Human Services requesting that she initiate appropriate rule making and other relevant provisions of law to ensure that hospitals that participate in Medicare or Medicaid respect the rights of patients to designate visitors and not deny visitation privileges on the basis of, among other things, sexual orientation or gender identity.[25] The move came after a lesbian and the three children of her and her partner were denied visitation to see her partner, who suffered a brain aneurysm. The partner died the next day.[26]

- As part of "dirty" recruiting tactics, parents of highly sought-after female high school basketball players are told that female coaches of competing teams are lesbian in what is called the "fear of a gay boogeyman who will make their daughters choose a lesbian sexual orientation." (Partly in response, the NCAA investigated whether homophobia was a reason that the number of female head basketball coaches dropped from 79 percent in 1977 to 63 percent in 2002.)[27] In 2017, female coaches said it was still not comfortable to come out in women's college basketball.[28]

- In 2009, the American Psychological Association issues a statement that mental health professionals should not tell gay clients they can become straight through therapy.[29]

- The California governor signed into law a ban on gay conversion therapy, calling it "quackery" in 2012.[30]

- The U.S. Supreme Court rules in *Snyder v. Phelps*[31] that anti-gay protests at funerals of American soldiers are protected by the First Amendment's freedom of speech. The Court affirms the appellate court's decision that the protests with signs such as "God hates fags" were "utterly distasteful" but protected because they were related to "matters of public concern." The protests were by members of the Westboro Baptist Church in Topeka, Kansas, who contend that the death of American soldiers is God's punishment for the country's tolerance of homosexuality. They have held over 43,000 such protests since 1991.[32]

- When University of Missouri star defensive end Michael Sam returned to the university with his teammates to claim the Cotton Bowl award after announcing he was gay just before attending the NFL combine, over 2,000 people showed up in the February 2014 cold, locked arms, and turned their backs on the 14 Westboro demonstrators in an effort to support Sam and block him from even seeing the Westboro demonstrators.[33]

- Two days after unanimously requesting that the county attorney find a way to enact an ordinance banning gays and lesbians from living in the county (saying, "We need to keep them out of here"), the Rhea County, Tennessee, commissioners withdrew the request because of the outcry outside the county.[34]

- New York then-gubernatorial candidate Carl Paladino calls gay pride parades "disgusting" but lesbian sex "awesome."[35]

- Walmart, the largest private employer in the United States, joins many other employers and extends benefits to LGBTQ employees same-sex domestic partners.[36]

As you can see from this sprinkling of just a few of the things that have happened in the recent past leading up to the 2020 *Bostock* decision, LGBTQ issues push a lot of buttons in society in general, and the workplace is just a microcosm of society. Though a bit gruff, the employee's assertion that homosexuality was against his religion was a manifestation of that. We have no doubt that the employee spoke for many others when he made his statement. The good thing is that he got it out onto the table where it could be discussed, put into perspective, and fitted into what his employer wanted the program to accomplish: less exposure to unnecessary liability for violations of the law on this and other bases of discrimination. Since we understand that this sentiment is a fairly common one, let's take a bit of time up front to discuss it and give you some things to keep in mind as you go through the chapter. Just so you know, he was much comforted by what he learned in the session and said he had never thought about the issues this way before. He even said thank you! :-)

From the battle with the Boy Scouts of America over whether the Philadelphia chapter could continue to discriminate against gays and stay in the city-owned building it had been in for 80 years, paying $1 annual rent rather than the $200,000 fair market value when the city had an antidiscrimination policy, to celebrity and adoptive mother Rosie O'Donnell announcing that she is a lesbian and taking up the issue of Florida law not permitting adoptions by gays and lesbians, to whether a transgender employee can lawfully sue for the use of certain toilet facilities, to the fining of basketball superstar Kobe Bryant for calling a referee a "faggot" in the heat of a game, to the refusal of the city clerk to handle same-sex marriage license applications even after same-sex marriage became legal, the issues of sexual orientation and gender identity have been and continue to be debated and discussed not only in the United States but all across the world, in every conceivable context. The issues have vast implications for people's everyday lives. Most people need to work in order to survive, so workplaces consist of all kinds of people. That means that anything that is of any great social importance generally ends up finding its way into the workplace. The issues of sexual orientation and gender identity are no different. The increasing prominence of the issues in the workplace, arising from the legal implications and the very convoluted patchwork of rules, make it essential that we include coverage here despite the fact that the language of Title VII, as well as most of its history, did not prohibit discrimination on these bases.

Unlike the other Title VII categories, coverage of sexual orientation and gender identity is not quick or easy. Because the recognition of these categories only recently came about, it is important that we include a lot of the history because that is so much of what the country's understanding of the issues is based on. Since LGBTQ employees were not covered by Congress in the words of the statute, the law was a very, very crazy quilt of federal, state, and local laws, executive orders, and court decisions. On top of that were employers' private rules. With same-sex marriage now the law of the land, it seemed it would only be a matter of time before the issue was resolved and uniformity brought to bear either by Congress or the U.S. Supreme Court. After all, it seems rather incongruous for the Supreme Court to recognize that it is unconstitutional to discriminate regarding the issue of same-sex marriage but for Congress not to do so regarding the issue of employment discrimination. It was not at all inconceivable that a person could happily marry their soulmate on Saturday and be fired for doing so when they return to work on Monday. What was legal in Wisconsin may not have been legal in North Carolina. What was not legal in Iowa for nongovernmental employees may have been legal for government employees. What was not legal in the state of Georgia may have been legal in Atlanta. Protections or benefits denied by the federal or state government may have been granted to employees who work for a certain employer in that state. Even within the federal government, Congress had not included protections for LGBTQ employees, but the agency it created to enforce workplace discrimination laws had. The legality, protections, or rights may not have arisen from a law but from a court decision, agency determination, local ordinance, or employer. It was truly a crazy quilt of protection—or lack thereof.

Before the *Bostock* decision, there were seventeen states and the District of Columbia[37] (see Exhibit 10.2, "State Laws Banning Workplace Discrimination on the Basis of Sexual Orientation or Gender Identity") prohibited discrimination on the basis of both sexual orientation as well as gender identity. There were 29 states without protection for sexual orientation and 33 without protection on the basis of gender identity. In addition, hundreds of local ordinances and thousands of workplaces, including 91 percent of Fortune 500 companies,[38] included LGBTQ employees as part of their employment discrimination laws and policies,[39] and 2nd, 6th and the 7th Circuit Court of Appeals had determined so as well. In 2012, the EEOC began accepting complaints of gender identity discrimination as a type of gender discrimination, and as of 2015, claims of discrimination against gay,

Exhibit 10.2 *State Laws Banning Workplace Discrimination on the Basis of Sexual Orientation or Gender Identity before the U.S. Supreme Court's* Bostock *Decision Making Discrimination against LGBTQ Employees a Violation of Title VII*

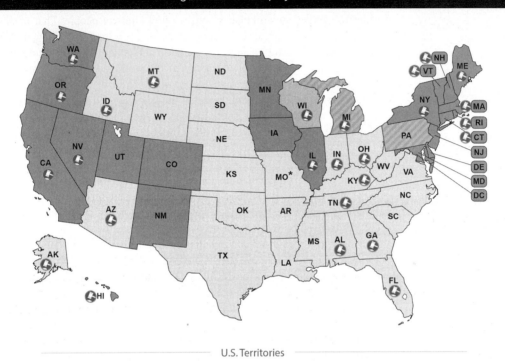

U.S. Territories

| American Samoa | Commonwealth of the Northern Mariana Islands | Guam | Puerto Rico | U.S. Virgin Islands |

Percent of Adult LGBTQ Population Covered by Laws

*Note: These percentages reflect estimates of the LGBTQ adult population living in the 50 states and the District of Columbia. Estimates of the LGBTQ adult population in the five inhabited U.S. territories are not available, and so cannot be reflected here.

47%

47% of LGBTQ population lives in states prohibiting employment discrimination based on sexual orientation and gender identity

7%

7% of LGBTQ population lives in states explicitly interpreting existing prohibition on sex discrimination to include sexual orientation and/or gender identity

2%

2% of LGBTQ population lives in states prohibiting employment discrimination based on sexual orientation only

44%

44% of LGBTQ population lives in states that do not prohibit employment discrimination based on sexual orientation or gender identity (including 5% of LGBTQ population living in states that preempt local nondiscrimination laws)

- State laws prohibiting discrimination based on sexual orientation, gender identity, or both:

California (1992) (*2003)	New Hampshire (1998)
Colorado (2007)*	New Jersey (1992) (*2007)
Connecticut (1991) (*2011)	New Mexico (2003)*
Delaware (2009) (*2013)	New York (2003)
Hawaii (1991) (*2011)	Nevada (1999) (*2011)
Illinois (2006)*	Oregon (2008)*
Iowa (2007)*	Rhode Island (1995) (*2001)
Maine (2005)*	Vermont (1991) (*2007)
Maryland (2001)	Washington (2006)*
Massachusetts (1989) (*2012)	Wisconsin (1982)*
Minnesota (1993)*	Washington, D.C. (1977) (*2006)

- An executive order prohibits discrimination in the federal civilian workforce and mandates that security clearances not be denied based on sexual orientation.
- State courts, commissions, agencies, or attorney generals have interpreted the existing law to include some protection against discrimination against transgender individuals in

Florida	New York

- In 2012, the Equal Employment Opportunity Commission determined that gender identity discrimination in employment violates Title VII's prohibition against gender discrimination; it extended this to sexual orientation in 2015.
- Hundreds of cities and counties prohibit discrimination in public and/or private employment. Jurisdictions include

Fayetteville, AR	Lawrence, KS	Portland, OR
Phoenix, AZ	Louisville, KY	Philadelphia, PA
Boulder, CO	New Orleans, LA	Charleston, SC
Wilmington, DE	Detroit, MI	Minnehaha County, SD
Broward County, FL	St. Louis, MO	Austin, TX
Atlanta, GA	Durham, NC	Salt Lake County, UT
Ames, IA	Albuquerque, NM	Alexandria, VA
Chicago, IL	New York, NY	Seattle, WA
Bloomington, IN	Toledo, OH	Morgantown, WV

*Law also includes protection based on gender identity.

Used by permission of MAP, Movement Advancement Project, https://www.lgbtmap.org/equality-maps/non_discrimination_laws

lesbian, or bisexual employees as a type of gender discrimination were accepted. New guidance and edicts come into existence virtually every day via legislatures, court opinions, agency regulations, and employer policies and guidelines. Given that, you can imagine what a crazy-quilt the issue of Title VII coverage for LGBTQ employees was before *Bostock*.

As exhibited by the gentleman in the opening paragraph (one of your authors was actually the consultant involved), sexual orientation discrimination is also one of the types of discrimination that may call into question ideas we hold dear and wish to protect. As a result, despite the *Bostock* decision, we may think of this type of discrimination differently—as more justifiable—than we do others. In order to prevent those thoughts from turning into actions that lead to litigation and avoidable liability for the employer, we must learn to view the costly and avoidable matter in its proper legal workplace perspective.

As you read the chapter, keep this thought in the front of your mind: The intent of this chapter is not to get you to "accept" anyone's sexual orientation or gender identity. This chapter is not about going against your religious beliefs, moral values, or conscience. As with our other chapter topics in the text, you are free to believe whatever you wish. Before choosing to engage in activity that may cause the employer liability for discrimination and result in your termination, however, keep in mind that this is the *employer's* workplace, not yours. Employees do not have the right to engage in personal activities that will cause unnecessary liability or embarrassing publicity for their employer. Since this is the employer's workplace, the employer is the one in charge of such things. If the employer has hired someone you don't like, for whatever reason, you have to decide what it's worth to you. Do you create trouble for the employer and run the risk of getting fired, or do you conduct yourself in a professional manner, keep your personal issues to yourself, continue to do the job you were hired to do, and collect a check? If you feel like you can't do the latter, then you are free to seek employment elsewhere. But if you choose to stay, you have no right to impose your purely personal beliefs on the workplace through the decisions you make about the acts you choose to do in a way that increases the employer's liability. If you think your beliefs do not "permit" homosexuality, then don't be LGBTQ. Don't take your LGBTQ coworker to lunch. Don't take him or her home for dinner. But refusing to work with him or her as required or otherwise treating the coworker in ways that discriminate and expose the employer to liability or negative press is simply not an option.

If this sounds like we have an agenda, then you heard us correctly. Our agenda is to protect employers from unnecessary costly liability and negative and embarrassing publicity. Our job is to make sure that if what you believe is not in sync with the law, you understand the difference and are able to do what you need to do at work to prevent unnecessary liability. As always, this chapter tries to teach you not only about the law but also about the context and history of the issue so that when you have to make workplace decisions unfamiliar to you, you understand what is involved and how the law views it. This is especially important as things in this area are changing so rapidly (see Exhibit 10.3, "Rapidly Changing Fortune 500 Sexual Orientation and Gender Identity Policy Percentages") and new issues seem to arise daily.

With that out of the way, let's explore this area and see what's here.

Despite the stereotypes of gay males as florists, designers, interior decorators, or hairstylists, a survey by the Chicago marketing research firm Overlooked Opinions[40] found that more gay males work in science and engineering than in social services, 40 percent more are employed in finance and insurance than in entertainment and

Exhibit 10.3 *Rapidly Changing Fortune 500 Sexual Orientation and Gender Identity Policy Percentages*

State law explicitly prohibits discrimination based on sexual orientation and gender identity *(21 states, 2 territories + D.C.)*

State explicitly interprets existing prohibition on sex discrimination to include sexual orientation and/or gender identity (see note) *(2 states, 0 territories)*

State law explicitly prohibits discrimination based on sexual orientation only *(1 state, 0 territories)*

No explicit prohibitions for discrimination based on sexual orientation or gender identity in state law *(26 states, 3 territories)*

State is in a federal circuit with a ruling that explicitly interprets existing federal prohibition on sex discrimination (under Title VII) to include discrimination based on sexual orientation and/or gender identity. Visit this page for more information *(26 states, 3 territories)*

	Fortune 500				
	2002	2008	2013	2014	2019
Sexual Orientation Policy	61%	88%	88%	91%	93%
Gender Identity Policy	3%	25%	57%	61%	91%

Source: HRC: The Corporate Equality Index 2020, https://assets2.hrc.org/files/assets/resources/CEI-2020.pdf?_ga=2.135933873.1249247932.1584378585-1984997810.1584378585.

Exhibit 10.4 *Heterosexual Realities Questionnaire*

The following questions provide a somewhat humorous yet insightful look at some of the more frequent assumptions surrounding gays and lesbians, which affect how they may be perceived in the workplace and society at large. The approach of reversing the questions subtly challenges commonly held heterosexually based notions.

1. What do you think caused your heterosexuality?

2. When and how did you first decide you were heterosexual?

3. Is it possible your heterosexuality is just a phase you may grow out of?

4. Is it possible your heterosexuality stems from a neurotic fear of others of the same gender?

5. Heterosexuals have histories of failures in gay relationships. Do you think you may have turned to heterosexuality out of fear of rejection?

6. If you've never slept with a person of the same gender, how do you know you wouldn't prefer that?

7. To whom have you disclosed your heterosexual tendencies? How do they react?

8. Your heterosexuality doesn't offend me as long as you don't try to force it on me. Why do you people feel compelled to seduce others into your sexual orientation?

9. Why do you insist on being so obvious and making a public spectacle of your heterosexuality by holding hands or kissing in public? Can't you just be what you are and keep it quiet?

10. How would the human race survive if everyone were heterosexual like you, considering the menace of overpopulation?

11. Why do heterosexuals place so much emphasis on sex?

12. How can you be heterosexual if you've never had sex?

Source: Adapted from Martin Rochlin, Ph.D., by Dr. Miranda Pollard, University of Georgia.

the arts, and 10 times as many work in computers as in fashion. (See Exhibit 10.4, "Heterosexual Realities Questionnaire.") Once, gays and lesbians in the workplace were virtually invisible, but diverse circumstances, some of which were provided for you earlier in the chapter, have begun to change that in dramatic ways.

You have the blessing (or curse, depending on your view) of actually living history as it relates to this issue. There have been dramatic changes in just the past 25 years or so. (That may sound like a long time to you, but it is but a blink in historical and legal terms! :-)) From never speaking the word *gay* on TV to having LGBTQ characters on nearly 50 shows in 2019, the societal landscape has changed. According to the Human Rights Campaign (HRC), the nation's largest LGBTQ advocacy group, in 2013, hundreds of major businesses signed onto historic friend-of-the-court (*amicus curiae*) briefs to the U.S. Supreme Court urging them to strike down the Defense of Marriage Act and California's Proposition 8 banning gay marriage; more than 120 businesses joined a public coalition to urge Congress to pass the Employment Non-Discrimination Act (ENDA), which would amend Title VII to prohibit workplace discrimination on the basis of sexual orientation and gender identity, and in 2019, more than 171 businesses did the same for the broader Equality Act that would extend antidiscrimination legislation past just the workplace to housing, transportation, receipt of federal funds, retail outlets and services, and juries; record numbers of businesses updated their non-discrimination policies and benefit packages ahead of the federal mandates to do so in order to support their LGBTQ employees and their families; and over 300 companies came out in support of gay marriage before the U.S. Supreme Court's historic *Obergefell* decision in 2015.[41] The number of major employers covering medically necessary reassignment surgery for transgender employees has risen to over 500, including many Fortune 500 companies, and many major employers have implemented more robust and supportive inclusion guidelines for their transitioning employees, covering 16.5 million employees. When HRC's Corporate Equality Index, the "gold standard" of corporate equality for LGBTQ treatment in the workplace, began in 2001, 13 businesses earned a score of 100 percent. In the 2020 report, the number was 571.[42] You may wonder how it happened.

These changes have all been a function of a confluence of a combination of a number of fairly recent events that really began to put LGBTQ issues on the map in a big way, including the following:

- The impact of AIDS in society and in the workplace.
- The military's "Don't Ask, Don't Tell" policy.
- The 1992 presidential election in which President Bill Clinton voiced support for gays. It was the first time a presidential candidate had dealt with the issue.
- The 1993 March on Washington for Lesbians, Gays, and Bisexuals, which brought together unprecedented numbers of participants to call for non-discrimination in employment and equity.
- Clinton's later support for the Employment Non-Discrimination Act (ENDA) prohibiting workplace discrimination against gays and lesbians, which has not yet passed.
- Clinton's appointment of over 150 gays and lesbians in his administration, including an ambassador and cabinet-level positions (see Exhibit 10.5, "Lesbian Confirmed for No. 2 HUD Post").
- Colorado's attempted constitutional ban on protection for gays and lesbians, which the U.S. Supreme Court struck down, and many other events put the issue of gays and lesbians on the national agenda for the first time.
- President Obama, in 2012, announced that he was "enlightened" about same-sex marriage and now supported the freedom to marry. When the U.S. Supreme Court issued its *Obergefell* decision upholding same-sex marriage in 2015, the White House was lit up in rainbow lights to show its support, as were iconic buildings all over the country.
- Olympic gold medal decathlete winner extraordinaire Bruce Jenner transitioned very publicly to Caitlyn Marie Jenner, taking the public on the journey with her.
- Apple CEO Tim Cook came out as gay in 2014.
- Former South Bend, Indiana, mayor Pete Buttigieg runs as the first openly gay presidential candidate for the 2020 election and made a respectable showing.

After President Clinton became the first president to ever address gay and lesbian issues, and in such a public way, 1993 was a watershed year and a turning

Exhibit 10.5 *Lesbian Confirmed for No. 2 HUD Post*

So that you can see how short a time ago things you may take for granted have occurred, take a look at this piece about the first out lesbian being appointed to a high-level federal government position.

On May 24, 1993, President Clinton's nominee for assistant secretary of housing and urban development, Roberta Achtenberg, was confirmed by the Senate 58–31 after a three-day debate. Ms. Achtenberg was a member of the San Francisco Board of Supervisors who had won numerous awards for her community service, and the Senate's vote made her the first open lesbian appointed to such a high government position.

During the Senate debate, Senator Jesse Helms (R-N.C.) brought up that Ms. Achtenberg was seen with her partner, municipal court judge Mary Morgan, kissing and hugging while leading a 1992 Gay Pride parade. The Christian Action Network sent a copy of the videotape to every member of the Senate, and senators received thousands of calls from opponents after being urged to call by TV shows like Reverend Pat Robertson's *700 Club*.

During the Senate debate, Senator Dianne Feinstein (D-Calif.), former mayor of San Francisco, said, "Today we have a chance to turn our back to prejudice. Today we can vote down the politics of hate and take a small step to make sure our government is representative of all the people it seeks to serve."*

Achtenberg resigned in 1995 to run for elected office in San Francisco. Since Achtenberg's appointment there have been several other public office holders, including the man who could be America's first openly transgender male judge, Henry Sias of Pennsylvania, joining the two female transgender judges in the United States.

*Senator Dianne Feinstein (D-Calif.),

point for gay and lesbian issues. On April 25, 1993, the Cable News Network (CNN) provided day-long national television coverage of the convergence of nearly a million people, LGBTQ and straight, on Washington, D.C., for the March on Washington for Lesbian, Gay, and Bisexual Equal Rights and Liberation. One of the largest marches ever held, it made clear that the LGBTQ community could no longer be ignored.

Since that time, states have seen a good deal of LGBTQ legislation and courts have seen cases on issues ranging from parental rights to military discharges, from domestic partner benefits (domestic partnerships preceded gay marriage as legal status for committed gay and lesbian relationships) to gay marriage, from refusal to bake a wedding cake or take photos for same-sex weddings to refusal to make T-shirts or posters for Gay Pride events, and from hate crimes legislation to protecting LGBTQ employees from workplace discrimination. Things have changed very quickly in this area, in historical terms, and continue to do so, so to avoid liability, employers must work diligently to make sure their policies are consistent with legal and other changes.

For instance, in 2009, the majority of Americans were against same-sex marriage.[43] In April 2011, a CNN poll showed that for the first time, a majority of Americans favored allowing gays and lesbians to have the same right to marry as heterosexuals. In 2013, a Gallup poll showed that 52 percent of Americans favored equal rights for such unions and would legalize gay marriage nationwide.[44] In 2015, same-sex marriage became law throughout the country. HRC began publishing its Corporate Equality Index (CEI) in 2001, rating companies on their commitment to LGBTQ issues in the workplace and beyond. That yearly index has quickly become an important indicator of a company's LGBTQ-friendly environment. Most of the Fortune 500 companies participate, as well as many other companies, and more companies join each year and use their rating status as a marketing tool. This is a huge change in such a short period, and it is an interesting indicator of employer commitment in this area. The area moves rapidly, and employers need to know about the issues.

Earning a living is a necessity for most people, as is the issue of being treated with respect, so issues related to LGBTQ employees are increasingly surfacing in the workplace and have become something that an employer will likely be called upon to deal with. There is an ever-growing realization that LGBTQ people are everywhere (and always have been) and should be judged for who they are as people and what they bring to the workplace, not for the singularly irrelevant measure of the private matter of to whom they are attracted or what body parts are under their clothing. Neither issue has any more a legitimate place in workplace considerations for LGBTQ employees than it does heterosexual employees for whom it never arises. In commenting on the first federal appellate court decision to interpret Title VII as including sexual orientation as a type of gender discrimination on April 4, 2017,[45] Greg Nevins of Lambda Legal, who represented the professor, Kimberly Hively, said, "Federal law is catching up to public opinion: 90 percent of Americans believe employees should be valued for how well they do their jobs, not who they love or what they are."[46] With the rules changing almost daily, and more state and local legislation and court decisions both for and against civil rights for gays, it had become necessary for employers to know what their potential legal liability is in this area.

A fairly recent development has been the emergence of non-discrimination policies and LGBTQ employee resource groups (ERGs, also called affinity groups, support groups, or networking groups) within the workplace. A recent meta-data review of 36 studies determined that LGBTQ-supportive policies resulted in greater job commitment, improved workplace relationships, increased job satisfaction, improved health outcomes, less discrimination, and more openness about being LGBTQ for LGBTQ employees.[47] Regarding resource groups, there are well over 2,000, including groups in hundreds of Fortune 500 companies, many colleges and universities, nonprofits, unions, and state and local governments. Ninety-seven percent of Corporate Equality Index ERGs are supported by an executive in a senior leadership position within the company.[48] Listed among such employers are Apple Computer, Digital Equipment, AT&T, Coca-Cola, IBM, Kodak, DuPont, Hewlett-Packard, Lucent Technologies, Sun Microsystems, Pacific Gas and Electric Company, Walt Disney Co., JPMorgan Chase & Co., Goldman Sachs, Merrill Lynch, and United Parcel Service, to name a few. The groups tackle such issues as workplace hostility, extending employee benefits, making sure that same-sex partners are welcome at company social functions, and generally making the workplace less threatening to the work life and workplace progress of LGBTQ employees and thus more productive for the employees and, ultimately, the employer. Since many LGBTQ employees still believe they must hide their sexual orientation or gender identity at work in order to keep their jobs, these groups have real-life implications. While these groups began before the *Bostock* decision, they are still very much needed. The long history we provided of how people feel about LGBTQ employees did not end simply because the U.S. Supreme Court held that treating them differently is a violation of Title VII. It will likely take a while before everyone is on the same page and LGBTQ employees can feel totally safe and equal in the workplace.

After a spate of gay teen suicides due to bullying caused Fort Worth City Councilman Joel Burns to give an impassioned city council speech on the difficulties facing gay youth, urging teens to know that things do get better, the YouTube video of the speech went viral.[49] PricewaterhouseCoopers, a top accounting firm, then made its own video of its gay and lesbian employees urging struggling teens to know that things do get better. Other companies did it also, such as Google and Facebook. This should give you some idea of companies' approach to this area; not only are they trying to support their LGBTQ employees, but they are also reaching beyond the workplace to their communities. For that reason, it is an issue anyone involved with employment law should be aware of.

Many companies sponsor their LGBTQ employees at events like Gay Pride Month, a nationwide celebration each June, culminating in a parade composed of many types of constituencies, including businesses. Companies provide employees with information and novelty items to be passed out to attendees or T-shirts with slogans such as "ABC Company Supports Its Gay and Lesbian Employees." (See Exhibit 10.6, "Delta Airline's Support for Its Gay Employees.") A recent poll

---

Exhibit 10.6   *Delta Air Lines' Support for Its Gay Employees*

Delta Air Lines is a great example of how business has incorporated this new and evolving approach to diversity and LGBT issues into its corporate belief system and its way of doing business. One of Delta's "Rules of the Road" core values is to embrace diverse people. Along with this, Delta offers health and travel benefits for domestic partnership and has realigned its benefits to recognize same-sex marriages. In addition to its corporate policies, Delta has established the Gay/Lesbian Employee Network (GLEN), a volunteer organization whose mission is to make Delta the best place to work by promoting inclusion, respect for differences, equal opportunity, education, and diversity in the workplace.

During the month of June, which is designated "Pride Month," Delta raised the "Rainbow Pride Flag" at the entrance of its World Headquarters in Atlanta, Ga, as well as displaying several pride flags throughout its campus. Delta also took a bold stance against legislation that would limit business from providing service to LGBT customers.

Delta is very active within the community participating in Pride events, AIDS Walk and other LGBT events in several states. Delta strives to recruit qualified employees and minority businesses by participating in conferences such as Reaching Out MBA and National Gay Lesbian Chamber of Commerce. Delta is also active with several local and national organizations such as Gay Lesbian Alliance Against Defamation (GLAAD), amfAR, Human Rights Campaign (HRC), and International Gay & Lesbian Travel Association (IGLTA).

Courtesy of Tonie D. Tobias/Delta Airlines

showed that this type of workplace support is important to 71 percent of the gays and lesbians polled. The 2020 Corporate Equality Index found that 93 percent of CEI-rated businesses met the standard of demonstrating at least three efforts of public engagement with the LGBTQ community.[50]

LO1 Discuss the history of the modern gay rights movement.

Gay Pride Month is not just a fun time. And despite what your local news coverage may choose to show, it involves not just parade participants with their behinds hanging out of leather clothing or "freaky" looking characters. It is actually the commemoration of the historic events of June 1969. Being LGBTQ is still all too often a life-threatening proposition, but it was even more so then. As a result, most in the LGBTQ community led an extremely closeted existence and often congregated in gay bars just to be sure of the relative safety of their surroundings. Since they were considered social outcasts of the highest order, they did not want to risk their own lives or embarrass their families and friends by being honest about who they were. Fearing discovery made them a very vulnerable group that rarely fought against their circumstances or abuse. They were banned from government employment because of the potential for blackmailing them to learn government secrets due to their vulnerable enforced secretive lives. Gay bars, often the only place the LGBTQ community could go and feel accepted for who they were, routinely experienced raids by police officers for no apparent reason, and the patrons were hauled off to jail for one minor infraction or another. Fearing publicity, most patrons just went quietly.

In June 1969, this changed. When plainclothes police officers raided the Stonewall Inn in New York's Greenwich Village, there was uncharacteristic resistance by the bar patrons, joined by people on the street, that resulted in a weekend of riots. The next year in New York, the first legislative hearings on LGBTQ issues were held, as was the first parade to commemorate the events at Stonewall the year before. The resistance at Stonewall in 1969 is considered the beginning of the modern LGBTQ rights movement. Over the years, the commemoration has grown and spread as more people, LGBTQ and straight, determine that being LGBTQ should not equal being vulnerable to discrimination or death. Each June there are now Gay Pride Month celebrations across the country and around the world. While in office, President Clinton issued proclamations declaring June Gay Pride Month, as do many state governors. President Bush broke with this tradition, saying he considers sexual orientation a personal matter. Every year he was in office, President Obama celebrated Gay Pride Month at the White House and issued proclamations.[51] In addition, he endorsed legislation to end workplace discrimination against LGBTQ employees, strengthened federal protection for LGBTQ employees, extended hospital visitation rights to LGBTQ partners, and endorsed same-sex marriage. He also made Stonewall a national monument.

LO3 Understand the significance of employers being inclusive of LGBTQ employees.

The Clinton administration's first U.S. Department of Transportation secretary, Federico Peña, for the first time for a federal agency, held a lunch-hour Gay Pride Day ceremony for department employees, stating, "We need to draw on the talents of everyone. It's not about special privileges. It's about equal treatment." Among many other companies, as you can see from Exhibit 10.6, Delta Air Lines also engages in such activities. For instance, in addition to those outlined in the exhibit, at its hub city hometown Atlanta's Gay Pride events, the company has not one but several booths providing information about Delta's LGBTQ support and attitudes regarding it. Each year there are many conferences held to provide guidance for human resource professionals and others needing guidance in the area.

Each October 11 is National Coming Out Day, the purpose of which is to bring attention to the forced invisibility of gays and lesbians and the importance of their being open about who they are in an effort to help dispel the myths and stereotypes society holds that have resulted from their historical silence, invisibility, and abuse. 2020's coming out day mentions included comedian and actor Niecy Nash, Illinois representative Aaron Schock, "Riverdale" star Lili Reinhart, Gray's Anatomy's Dr. Callie Torres's Sara Ramirez, actor and activist Jameela Jamil, and "Orange is the New Black" star Taylor Schilling, among others. There is also a national day of remembrance in November for transgender individuals and their supporters to bring attention to those who have been killed because of violence against transgender individuals. The situation is particularly bad for African-American transgender females.[52]

The question often arises as to why a gay person has to let people know of his or her sexual orientation. We often hear, "I don't go around telling people I'm straight, so why do they have to say they are gay?" The reason is that there is an overriding presumption that virtually everyone is heterosexual, and if the LGBTQ person does not say otherwise, he or she ends up feeding into it and living a lie. It is the default. But being honest and letting people know takes away the presumption that forces the LGBTQ employee into complicity. It also allows people to grow more accustomed to and familiar with LGBTQ employees, friends, church members, and others in their lives so that there is more information and less stereotyping. Research shows that when people know someone who is LGBTQ, they are less likely to hold negative ideas about them as a group.

The issue of LGBTQ employees in the workplace can surface in some surprising ways, making it all the more compelling for an employer to be aware of the possibilities and take them into consideration when making policy in this area. Apple (the computer company) was thinking of moving its operations to Williamson County, Texas. The city council refused to vote Apple concessions as an incentive to move there after it discovered that Apple had domestic partnership benefits for its employees. Apple refused to take away these benefits, and the city council finally voted to give Apple the concessions. The Walt Disney Company took a real beating from conservatives when it extended benefits to domestic partners of its employees. The company chose to continue the benefits. Anheuser-Busch took flak for its ads featuring two men holding hands, but the ads continued. In 2005, two weeks after dropping the protection for gays and lesbians from its legislative agenda due to threats of boycotts from religious groups, Microsoft's CEO Steve Ballmer said, "After looking at the question from all sides, I've concluded that diversity in the workplace is such an important issue for our business that it should be in our legislative agenda." Microsoft also issued an "It's Getting Better" video.[53] When Chik-fil-A's CEO made public statements opposing gay marriage, a hullabaloo arose when the LGBTQ community decided to boycott the restaurants and Chik-fil-A supporters held counterdemonstrations. Chik-fil-A eventually announced it was leaving the issue of same-sex marriage to the politicians and courts.

Marriage equality and workplace discrimination is now the law, yet the struggle still continues regarding other very important issues. Although it has calmed down for the moment, most recently, we saw the national battle over the issue of bathroom usage for transgender individuals. Part of the reality of this volatile area is that the Trump administration has rolled back protections gained in this area. For instance, Executive Order 13672, signed by President Obama in 2014, prohibits contractors doing business with the federal government from discriminating against their LGBTQ employees. Essentially, it created the equivalent of Title VII protection for LGBTQ employees of the federal government and for those employed by businesses who contract to provide goods and/or services to the federal government. The same year, Obama issued Executive Order 13673, Fair Pay and Safe Workplaces, to strengthen Executive Order 13672 by requiring federal contractors to show they have complied with various laws and executive orders regarding non-discrimination. This latter executive order was reversed by Trump. In the wake of the pressing issue over businesses refusing to serve LGBTQ individuals, on May 4, 2017, President Trump issued a "religious liberty" executive order[54] that was perceived as a basis for those who wished to do so to discriminate against LGBTQ individuals if the discriminator has a "deeply held religious belief." It also directed the IRS to use "maximum enforcement discretion" against the law preventing religious organizations from endorsing or opposing political candidates (known as the "Johnson Amendment") and provide regulatory relief for religious organizations with objections to providing health care services based on their religious beliefs (such as providing birth control in their health plans). This is widely believed to be a rollback of protections aimed at the LGBTQ community.[55] When the three cases making up the *Bostock* decision LGBTQ workplace discrimination cases were argued on October 8, 2019, the Department of Justice's position arguing that Title VII did not prohibit discrimination against LGBTQ employees made the administration's position clear. It is no wonder that studies have found that about 50 percent of LGBTQ employees feel the need to hide their true selves in the workplace.[56]

Despite this, keep in mind that employers must also obey their state and local laws and regulations, many of which preclude discrimination on this basis. For employees, this means even more vigilance in making sure to keep up with developments. As you have seen with HRC's Corporate Equality Index, the private sector has been increasing its efforts to do what the national legislature will not and has only grown in doing so over the past few years. For instance, HRC's Corporate Equality Index for 2020 had 83 new businesses ask to be included. When the CEI began in 2002, there were 13 companies that earned a top rating of 100 percent on the index. In 2020, the number was 686.

Based on the potential for increased productivity and the possibility of litigation or other business issues, some employers conclude that the safer practice is to base workplace decisions solely on an employee's ability to effectively perform the job rather than on his or her sexual orientation or gender identity. Despite the law, which now prohibits discrimination against LGBTQ employees, if the employee's *conduct* interferes with the workplace, it may well be the basis for a disciplinary action under the employer's relevant workplace policies, but this is not the same as the employee's *sexual orientation or gender identity.* The focus should not be on the employee's status as LGBTQ but, rather, on the employee's workplace performance.

While the US Supreme Court in the *Bostock* decision has, Congress has not chosen to include sexual orientation and gender identity as protected categories under Title VII of the Civil Rights Act of 1964.

Various pieces of protective legislation for LGBTQ employees have been introduced since 1974 and have never passed. The Employment Non-Discrimination Act (ENDA), introduced in every Congress since 1994 except the 109th Congress (2005–2007, under President George W. Bush), would extend Title VII's reach to include discrimination on the basis of sexual orientation and gender identity. Hundreds of corporations have formally endorsed ENDA, including NYNEX Corp., Polaroid, Bethlehem Steel Corp., Xerox, Yahoo, Kaiser Permanente, Harley-Davidson, Merrill Lynch, Quaker Oats, and Microsoft, to name a few.[57]

ENDA is not the only antidiscrimination legislation that has been proposed. The latest iteration, the Equality Act, was originally introduced in 2015 with 241 original bipartisan cosponsors, the most ever received by a piece of LGBTQ supportive legislation. If passed, the law would amend Title VII as well as several other statutes. As noted above, this is not the first time the law was introduced, but it has yet to pass. It is much broader than Title VII and ENDA, in that in addition to prohibiting workplace discrimination, it would prohibit discrimination on the basis of sexual orientation and gender identity in housing, public education, receipt of federal funds, jury service, and public accommodations and services including transportation, banking, legal services, and retail stores—in other words, all of the ways in which cases and experience demonstrate that the LGBTQ community experiences discrimination. In March 2016, the Human Rights Campaign announced the launch of its Business Coalition for the Equality Act, with the endorsement of more than 80 major employers whose revenues totaled $1.9 trillion and whose workforce employed more than 4.2 million people.[58] In just a few years the coalition has grown to include 266 companies in all 50 states, with a combined revenue of $4.9 trillion, employing more than 11.6 million people.[59]

A U.S. Government Accounting Office report on states with antidiscrimination laws for LGBTQ protection found that the laws had not generated a significant amount of litigation.

LO2 Discuss the state of LGBTQ workplace protections before the *Bostock v. Clayton County, Georgia* case.

An increase in litigation has been one of the main reasons that Congress has opposed ENDA despite the fact that the GAO study previously mentioned of states with job discrimination laws for LGBTQ employees found little, if any, increase in the number of such job discrimination lawsuits.

LGBTQ public/government employees adversely affected by an employment decision based on sexual orientation may, under appropriate circumstances, use their state constitution or the First, Fifth, or Fourteenth Amendments of the U.S. Constitution as a basis for suit as well as the constitutional right to privacy. This applies to any government employees, whether federal, state, or local. These lawsuits have traditionally been decided in the employer's favor, but recent decisions have impacted this trend and increasingly recognize LGBTQ employee protections based primarily upon equal protection of the law principles. For instance, a 2014 Ninth Circuit Court of Appeals case out of California ruled that it violated the Equal Protection Clause of the U.S. Constitution for an attorney to use peremptory strikes during jury selection (peremptory strikes permit attorneys to strike jurors for any reason except illegal ones) to strike LGBTQ prospective jurors.[60] The court determined that analyzing LGBTQ issues required heightened judicial scrutiny, which means a tougher road for those attempting to make distinctions based on sexual orientation.

If the facts warrant, LGBTQ employees also may bring civil tort actions such as intentional infliction of emotional distress, intentional interference with contractual relations, invasion of privacy, or defamation. The outcome depends on the particular circumstances, but employers should be mindful of the possibility of civil suits with unlimited damages.

Seeing how the court handles this issue in the case *Weaver v. Nebo School District,* included at the end of the chapter, is instructive in trying to shape policies consistent with its pronouncements. When a high school teacher said she was a lesbian, in response to being asked, her coaching job was taken away, and a notation was put in her personnel file. The court held that this was an unconstitutional denial of equal protection of the law.

The *Weaver* decision was mentioned in the *Romer* case,[61] in which the state of Colorado passed a constitutional provision that would have prohibited any government subdivision from passing laws protecting gays and lesbians from discrimination. This was one of the first major U.S. Supreme Court cases that challenged states' rights to pass laws restricting rights of gays and lesbians. As such, it sent an important message to states regarding their ability to exclude certain groups from constitutional protections. To some extent, this paved the way for much of what was to come, as you can see from the *Weaver* case. Note, too, that as the court mentioned, Title VII did not protect Weaver on the basis of sexual orientation, and the state did not have a law protecting her, but because she was a public school teacher, and thus a government employee, she had a cause of action for an unconstitutional denial of equal protection under the law. Of course, after the recent *Bostock* decision, we now understand that the Court recognizes that Title VII does, in fact, protect LGBTQ employees. However, this recognition would only make constitutional cases involving LGBTQ employees even stronger, should they choose to use this law.

Employers also should be aware of the possibility of several closely related matters that may arise in LGBTQ cases and cause liability based on the protected category of gender—for instance, gender stereotyping as discussed in the gender chapter. Judging employees based on stereotypical ideas about a given gender (that is, females who are "too aggressive" or "too macho" or males who are "too effeminate"), rather than on legitimate job requirements, may result in liability for gender discrimination, rather than sexual orientation, and should be avoided. Similarly, if an employer knowingly hires one group of LGBTQ employees but not another, for instance, lesbians but not gay men, this could be the basis for gender discrimination. In such a case, under Title VII, sexual orientation is clearly not an issue for the employer, since the employer knowingly hired lesbians.

So, unlike the rest of the categories we have discussed, despite the recent *Bostock* ruling interpreting Title VII as protecting LGBTQ employees, sexual orientation is not quite as settled as the other categories of employment discrimination. We are in the rare position of seeing an entirely new area of law unfold. As exciting as this is from a legal standpoint, it can have traps for the unwary employer. Sticking with only relevant qualifications and watching trends in case law and legislation at all levels will greatly aid in making policy decisions much less likely to result in liability.

Sexual Orientation as a Basis for Adverse Employment Decisions

Despite the dramatic changes that have taken place for LGBTQ employees within a short period of time, or even perhaps because of them, overall, LGBTQ employees still have significant issues with being accepted in the workplace. A recent HRC report, *The Cost of the Closet and the Rewards of Inclusion: Why the Workplace Environment for LGBT People Matters to Employers,* found that while 91 percent of Fortune 500 companies have sexual orientation antidiscrimination policies, 61 percent of Fortune 500 companies have gender identity policies, and 98 percent of global 2017 Corporate Equality Index businesses have fully inclusive, globally applicable nondiscrimination policies or codes of conduct, more than half, 53 percent, of LGBTQ workers nationwide hide who they are at work. HRC said that this "comes at a cost of inclusion and employee engagement and retention and reveals broader challenges of full inclusion in the workplace not just with respect to sexual orientation and gender identity, but along other lines of diversity such as gender, race, and ability."[62] Given the many pieces of information we have provided for you about the background and context of LGBTQ issues, the statistics should come as no surprise. This had not changed significantly when HRC did a major follow-up study in 2018, *A Workplace Divided: Understanding the Climate for LGBTQ Workers Nationwide,* in order to determine what led to these numbers. We have no reason to believe that these attitudes will change overnight, despite the recent *Bostock* decision including LGBTQ employees within Title VII's prohibition on gender discrimination. Our experience with these sorts of changes indicates that it takes several years for these issues to settle down once a decision is rendered. In fact, just look at the rest of the law. Claims are still plentiful even though the law has been on the books for the past 56+ years.

As you will see from the cases in the chapter, not all sexual orientation issues and gender identity cases arise in the same contexts. The employee may be the basis of employer concern because the employee, among other things,

- Is LGBTQ (i.e., status or orientation).
- Has primary relationships with those of the same gender (activity rather than status).

- Exhibits inappropriate workplace behavior such as detailed discussions of intimate sexual behavior or improperly propositioning others in the workplace (this is certainly not *presumed* of LGBTQ employees, and as you saw in the chapter on sexual harassment, this is most assuredly not solely an LGBTQ phenomenon).
- Wears clothing, jewelry, or makeup in violation of workplace grooming codes.
- Notifies the employer of transitioning to the opposite gender.
- Is in the presurgery adjustment stages of gender reassignment surgery.
- Undergoes gender reassignment surgery.

Note that some of the activity presents a problem no matter who the employee is. Other may be protected by law but the employer believes the employee is still not covered for the specific circumstance. An employer should not tolerate from *any* employee inappropriate workplace behavior such as improperly propositioning other employees. A distinction also should be made between *status* or *orientation* as LGBTQ, on the one hand, and, on the other, *activity* that may be inappropriate. Basing decisions and policies on an employee's actions is more defensible than basing them on his or her LGBTQ status. But even then the action should not be singled out solely based on the employee's orientation. Each of the above contexts presents its own unique issues.

On the other hand, among other things, LGBTQ employees have sued employers for things such as failure to hire; terminating employment because an employee is LGBTQ; creating for LGBTQ employees a hostile environment through calling them derogatory names; not addressing negative comments by coworkers that are reported to management or management endorsing or joining in the comments; lecturing them about their "lifestyle"; making derogatory jokes, teasing, or gesturing; changing their work schedules and/or responsibilities to be unnecessarily inconvenient or having fewer duties and responsibilities; giving them unnecessarily poor evaluations; and asking disrespectful and/or invasive and unnecessary personal questions.

As mentioned, in 2015, the EEOC announced that it was reversing years of precedent and had now determined that Title VII's gender category included discrimination on the basis of sexual orientation. Note that this was not Congress amending the law, but rather, it was being interpreted differently by the agency that had been created in Title VII of the Civil Rights Act of 1964 to enforce the law. Through a series of court decisions over the years, stemming primarily from the U.S. Supreme Court's decision in *Price Waterhouse v. Hopkins* outlawing gender stereotyping, which you saw in the gender chapter, the agency finally concluded that sexual orientation discrimination was based on gender stereotyping and is illegal. It had done a similar analysis three years before regarding gender identity, concluding in *Macy v. Holder*[63] (included for you at the end of the chapter) that gender identity discrimination is a type of gender discrimination and, thus, illegal. Consequently, although the Civil Rights Act was passed in 1964 and became effective in 1965, it was not until 2012 that the EEOC recognized gender identity as the basis for a claim of illegal discrimination and 2015 that it recognized the same for sexual orientation. As of those dates, 47 and 50 years after the effective date of the law, the EEOC began taking claims for gender identity discrimination and sexual orientation discrimination, respectively. It filed its first two sexual orientation cases on March 1, 2016.[64]

Macy is an excellent way to see how the EEOC finally came to the position it did based on the precedent established by the Supreme Court's *Price Waterhouse* decision (outlawing gender stereotyping) and *Oncale* (permitting claims for same-gender sexual harassment) decision and other federal district court decisions. The Seventh Circuit's decision in *Hively v. Ivy Tech* is also offered at the end of the chapter as an excellent read on how this federal circuit court of appeals also came to determine that sexual orientation is a type of gender discrimination prohibited by Title VII. It is imperative to read the cases to see how they came to their decisions and how doing so not only is within their authority but makes perfect sense given the precedent with which they were faced.

Of course, from what you have already read, you realize that this is not quite the entire story, since Congress has power over the EEOC and can change the law whenever it decides to do so whether it is consistent with the EEOC's position or not. The Supreme Court can also render a decision that essentially overturns both the EEOC's position and that of the Seventh Circuit. The month before the Seventh Circuit's *en banc* decision in *Hively* holding that sexual orientation is a type of gender discrimination under Title VII, a three-judge panel of the Eleventh Circuit issued a decision holding that sexual orientation is *not* covered by Title VII, although gender non-conformity is. In *Evans v. Georgia Regional Hospital,*[65] a female security guard, who, by her own admission, was more masculine in appearance than feminine, based on shoes, haircut, and so forth, alleged discrimination based on sexual orientation and gender non-conformity. The Eleventh Circuit held that based on their precedent, the claim for gender non-conformity was cognizable under Title VII, but not the claim for sexual orientation.

When federal circuit courts of appeal come to different decisions about the same law, it is called a split in the circuits. These cases are often the ones over which the U.S. Supreme Court will take jurisdiction and review when the parties file a writ of *certiorari* to ask the high court to review its decision. The Court is more likely to hear these types of cases than some other types, so that it can render a decision that puts the various positions to rest and everyone is governed by the same federal interpretation of law.

The split in the circuits is why the U.S. Supreme Court is presently reviewing the issue of whether gender discrimination includes discrimination based on sexual orientation and gender identity under Title VII. Three cases have been joined together. The Eleventh Circuit in *Bostock v. Clayton County, GA*[66] the court held that Title VII covers sexual orientation, while *Altitude Express, Inc. v. Zarda,*[67] a Second Circuit case, the court held that it did not; thus, the circuit courts of appeals were split. The Court granted the parties' *writ of certiorari* in April 2019, the case was argued on October 8, 2019, and we are awaiting the decision. Consolidated with those cases is *R.G. & G. R. Harris Funeral Homes, Inc. v. EEOC.*[68]

In *Bostock,* a gay man worked for Clayton County, Georgia, as a child welfare coordinator. Ten years later, after receiving only positive performance evaluations and numerous accolades, he began participating in a gay recreational softball league. Shortly after, he received criticism for participating in the league and for his sexual orientation and identity. Openly disparaging remarks were made about his orientation and participating in the league at a meeting at which his supervisor was present. Shortly thereafter, he was informed of an audit of the program funds he managed, and shortly after that was terminated for "conduct unbecoming of its employees." Bostock sued for violation of Title VII based on sexual orientation. His claim was dismissed, and the court of appeals upheld the dismissal on the basis that its precedent from the *Evans* case, above, did not recognize sexual orientation as a prohibited category of Title VII.

Zarda worked as a skydiving instructor, including for tandem dives. During the preparation for a tandem dive with a couple, when he was trapped in close proximity to the wife of a customer, he mentioned that he was gay in order to allay concerns about them being strapped in such close contact. He performed the jump with her. She alleged he made inappropriate contact with her and disclosed his sexual orientation to excuse his behavior. Zarda denied the claim but was terminated. Zarda claimed he was terminated solely because of his sexual orientation. The district court held that Title VII did not protect against discrimination based on sexual orientation. The Second Circuit, *en banc,* overturned the lower court and held that Title VII's prohibition on discrimination because of sex necessarily includes discrimination because of sexual orientation.

The third case consolidated for Supreme Court review involved Aimee Stephens, a funeral director of twenty years, who, after six years at the G.R. Harris Funeral Home, informed her boss that she was a transgender woman and would be transitioning by presenting as a female upon her return from vacation. Her employer fired her before she left for vacation, saying, "This is not going to work out." The Sixth Circuit held that it was unlawful gender discrimination to terminate the employee for being transgender.

As you saw in the opening statutory section, the U.S. Supreme Court determined that the employers who terminated the LGBTQ employees violated Title VII's prohibition on discrimination because of sex. The Court said that there was no way to deal with the question of what had happened to the employees without the issue of their sex being a part of the decision made about their employment.

Scenario

DeSantis v. Pacific Telephone and Telegraph Co., Inc.,[69] is one of the earliest cases about sexual orientation and Title VII. In that case, several telephone company employees brought Title VII claims when the employer terminated them because they were gay or lesbian or perceived to be so. The court's reasoning for not allowing the Title VII claims is based on the employees' status of being gay or lesbian rather than something the employees did. It is this basic approach that underlies why the employee would now be protected in Opening Scenario 1. In the *Nichols* case provided at chapter's end, this same court reversed itself to some extent, but *DeSantis* is an important historical case setting forth that Title VII did not provide protection for gays and lesbians at a time when few such cases had been brought. On the other hand, in addition to the *Bostock* case which was issued in June 2020, look at Exhibit 10.7, "New Push to Recruit Gay Students," to see how much the workplace had begun to change even 20 years before *Bostock.*

Exhibit 10.7 *New Push to Recruit Gay Students*

In a February 2000 *Wall Street Journal* article, Rachel Emma Silverman reported that Wall Street financial firms were, for the first time, targeting their recruitment toward gay and lesbian business students. Firms such as Goldman Sachs Group, Inc., J. P. Morgan & Co., and American Express Co. have gone to great lengths to woo gay students. According to the employers, the tightening labor market as well as the increasingly vocal employees of the firms caused them to use this as a tool to be or remain competitive in their recruiting efforts. The recruitment efforts include wining and dining the students at posh restaurants, co-hosting dinners for gay students, having gay and lesbian support groups in the workplace, having gay recruiting events with well-known speakers, and having discussion groups about being gay in the workplace.

Other firms, in an effort to thwart the criticism from students that they ought to be chosen for their qualifications, not their sexual orientation, declined to target gays and lesbians in recruiting. Students were clear, however, that it was important for them to feel comfortable in their workplace, including feeling comfortable about their sexual orientation. Since this time, there also have been gay and lesbian job fairs and college fairs, among other things, organized to ensure that gays and lesbians would be able to seek opportunities in settings in which they would be comfortable, given the usual hostile environment they can encounter.

Realizing the effect of *DeSantis,* which has been widely used as precedent in other jurisdictions to deny LGBTQ employees workplace discrimination protection for being LGBTQ, claimants have tried to get around the Title VII limitation by alleging some other recognized basis for discrimination under Title VII. For instance, in *Williamson v. A.G. Edwards & Sons, Inc.,*[70] a Black male employee was terminated for wearing makeup in the workplace. He sued the employer for race discrimination rather than sexual orientation discrimination. The employee alleged the employer treated him differently than white males who were allowed to wear such things. The court found no evidence that he had been treated differently based on race. The evidence the employee provided was not comparable; therefore, the comparison he made was inappropriate.

As this case indicates, sometimes an employer terminates an employee who fits into more than one category (or perceived category) of Title VII. One category may be protected and the other not, that is, in the case race is protected but not sexual orientation. Liability may still ensue. For instance, if the employee had been able to prove that the employer terminated him for wearing makeup but the employer did not terminate a white employee doing exactly the same thing, that would be race discrimination, even though being LGBTQ was not at the time a protected group. Since the basis for the discrimination was race rather than being LGBTQ, the claim would be actionable. However, as *Williamson* demonstrates, the claim must be more than a mere allegation; it must be proved. To be fully protected in the decision to terminate, an employer must be certain there are no facts that will support the other categories the employee may allege as a basis for workplace discrimination.

Regarding the makeup issue in *Williamson,* as we discussed in the gender chapter, employers are able to impose workplace dress codes as long as they do not violate Title VII. There is nothing in Title VII to prevent an employer from prohibiting men from wearing makeup in the workplace. Note that this is generally more of a transgender issue than a gay issue. The Washington State Supreme Court ruled that Boeing Company had sufficient basis for terminating a male engineer who was undergoing gender reassignment surgery. Boeing attempted to accommodate the employee by permitting him to wear "unisex" clothing, but the employee was terminated when he added pink pearls to such an outfit and insisted on using the women's bathroom. (*Boeing* is Case 5, discussed later.) Our guess is that one of the hot spots of the *Bostock* decision that will be litigated for a time to come, is the one of what is and is not appropriate dress for transitioning employees. If our experience is any gauge, we believe it will take time for those who have only known and wanted things to be one way to adjust to the new landscape. We can't imagine employees being instantly comfortable with transitioning males, for instance, showing up to work in feminine clothing and make up. Claims will arise because of their actions despite the *Bostock* decision permitting coverage of transgender employees. That is not a judgment, but simply a reality born of our experience. Just be aware and know that just because *Bostock* provides protection for gender identity does not mean everyone will be on board from June 15, 2020 (*Bostock* decision date) onward. If it is like other categories in Title VII, it will take time.

For years, male employees also tried to argue that their effeminacy should not be a basis on which employers can refuse to hire them or can terminate them from their jobs. Until recently, this argument rarely succeeded and courts routinely sided with the employer, usually using *DeSantis* for precedent. The court in *DeSantis* had stated:

> Employee Strailey contends he was terminated by the Happy Times Nursery School because the school felt that it was inappropriate for a male teacher to wear an earring to school. He claims that the school's reliance on a stereotype—that a male should have a virile, rather than an effeminate, appearance—violates Title VII. This does not fall within Title VII. We hold that discrimination because of effeminacy, like discrimination because of [sexual orientation], does not fall within the purview of Title VII.

LO4 Discuss how some courts have circumvented the exclusion of LGBTQ employees from Title VII coverage.

However, in the *Nichols* case discussed shortly, the *DeSantis* court reversed itself as it related to the issue of stereotyping and determined that under certain circumstances, Title VII permits employees claiming discrimination based on failing to fit a certain gender-based stereotype (usually effeminate men) to bring a claim based on gender stereotyping. In doing so, the court interpreted the U.S. Supreme Court's *Price Waterhouse v. Hopkins* case, discussed in the gender chapter, as being inconsistent with its *DeSantis* holding. The court said:

> *Price Waterhouse* sets a rule that bars discrimination on the basis of sex stereotypes. That rule squarely applies to preclude the harassment here. We do not imply that all gender-based distinctions are actionable under Title VII. For example, our decision does not imply that there is any violation of Title VII occasioned by reasonable regulations that require male and female employees to conform to different dress and grooming standards.
>
> The only potential difficulty arises out of a now faint shadow cast by our decision in *DeSantis* holding that discrimination based on a stereotype that a man

"should have a virile rather than an effeminate appearance" does not fall within Title VII's purview. This holding, however, predates and conflicts with the Supreme Court's decision in *Price Waterhouse*. And, in this direct conflict, *DeSantis* must lose. To the extent it conflicts with *Price Waterhouse,* as we hold it does, *DeSantis* is no longer good law.

So, by now, after seeing the progression of the case rulings from the Supreme Court's *Price Waterhouse* case up to the EEOC's 2012 and 2015 decisions to the Seventh Circuit's *Hively* case as well as the Eleventh Circuit's *Georgia Regional Hospital* case, you should have a good idea of the basis for claims of sexual orientation and gender identity under Title VII. However, you should also now realize the impact of Title VII not actually having sexual orientation language and the interplay with state laws, court decisions, executive orders, and employee policies. Clear as mud, right? :-) That is why there was such a call for uniformity.

This should also set the stage for you to now be able to understand the significance of the *Bostock* case. You saw the progression of a court thinking it was okay for an employer to not allow a male employee to wear an earring and requiring him to have a masculine appearance, to the Supreme Court's *Price Waterhouse* case outlawing gender stereotyping, to, eventually, *Bostock* concluding that treating an employee differently because of sexual orientation or gender identity violates Title VII. In *Bostock* the Court said "This Court normally interprets a statute in accord with the ordinary public meaning of its terms at the time of its enactment . . . With this in mind, our task is clear. We must determine the ordinary public meaning of Title VII's command that it is "unlawful . . . for an employer to fail or refuse to hire or to discharge any individual, or otherwise to discriminate against any individual with respect to his compensation, terms, conditions, or privileges of employment, because of such individual's race, color, religion, sex, or national origin.". . . An employer who intentionally treats a person worse because of sex—such as by firing the person for actions or attributes it would tolerate in an individual of another sex— discriminates against that person in violation of Title VII.

The *Bostock* decision only addresses the issue of Title VII and interprets its gender provision as including discrimination on the basis of sexual orientation and gender identity. But that is not the whole picture. Don't forget that Title VII only applies to employers with 15 or more employees. That leaves uncovered, employees who are employed by employers with fewer than 15 employees. They may well be covered if the state has a state fair employment practice law that lowers the number from 15 to, say, 4. However, as we saw earlier, not all states have laws that protect LGBTQ employees. Even if they do, the coverage is uneven, as some laws cover sexual orientation only, while others may also include gender identity. Some laws are only in local jurisdictions rather than the entire state. Some for state employees but not private employees. So, even though the *Bostock* case brought LGBTQ employees into the interpretation of Title VII, it is not clear exactly how it may impact other related provisions. We will just have to wait and see.

A Note about Same-Gender Sexual Harassment

LO5 Identify whether same-gender sexual harassment is covered by Title VII.

We are addressing this issue here instead of in the sexual harassment chapter because of the special development of the area and the way the law looks at this in light of Title VII itself not covering gays and lesbians. We also do it here because the background for the analyzing of sexual orientation and gender identity issues was not provided until this chapter.

When Title VII did not include a prohibition against discrimination on the basis of sexual orientation, an important legal question had been whether an employee sexually harassed by someone of the same gender could bring an action under Title VII. Some courts said no because they considered any sexual harassment between employees of the same gender to be based on sexual orientation (regardless of the nature of the harassment), and since Title VII excluded sexual orientation coverage, a harassee had no cause of action.

Other courts looked at the nature of the harassment itself and allowed a cause of action if it was not based on sexual orientation (rather than presuming that because it was between employees of the same gender it *must* be). There were many other variations on the theme. In the *Oncale v. Sundowner Offshore Services, Inc.,* case[71] the U.S. Supreme Court finally made sense of it all by saying there could be a cause of action for sexual harassment even if both parties are of the same gender, as long as it is clear that the basis for the harassment is not because the harassee is LGBTQ.

Oncale was a *huge* case. Not only had courts across the country been absolutely splintered in their approaches to the same facts (sound familiar?), but legal scholars and employers, as well as the public, debated the issue at length. The U.S. Supreme Court finally came down on the side of the intent of Title VII in striking at the full spectrum of gender-based employment discrimination. It made sense that if the issue involved was workplace harassment and discrimination, then the gender or sexual orientation of either party should not matter. That inquiry is not made in other harassment cases, and it made little sense to make it in this one. As the Court determined, the important inquiry is whether "the workplace is permeated with discriminatory intimidation, ridicule, and insult that is sufficiently severe or pervasive to alter the conditions of the victim's employment and create an abusive working environment." If so, then Title VII is violated. Clearly that happened in *Oncale*. This analysis is the basis for Opening Scenario 3.

Scenario 3

Under the *Oncale* decision, the Court preserved Title VII's exclusion of discrimination on the basis of sexual orientation by holding that the sexual harassment of an employee by someone of the same gender is prohibited unless it can be shown that it was actually based on sexual orientation. That is, if a female employee can show that a female harassed her by calling her negative names, undermining her work productivity, spreading lies about her, or negatively commenting on her personality, actions, friends, speech, or clothing, as they relate to gender, and so on, then she can bring a claim under Title VII. If, however, the harassee is a lesbian and the harassment is in the form of something such as constantly calling her a lesbian, "dyke," or other derogatory terms related to her orientation; directing teasing, joking, and comments on homosexuality toward her; or persistently asking for dates or making sexual comments, based strictly on her status as a lesbian, then the harassee would not have a cause of action under Title VII, based on *Oncale.*

The first situation is plain old sexual harassment even though the parties are both the same gender, and it is covered by Title VII. The second is harassment based on sexual orientation, and it is not covered. What the Supreme Court did is not presume that every harassment between employees of the same gender is based on sexual orientation. In a famous quote by Justice Antonin Scalia, "male or female, gay or straight, nobody should have to face sexual harassment when they go to work in the morning."

See if you can make the distinction in the *Nichols v. Azteca Restaurant Enterprises, Inc.,* case, supplied for your review at the end of this chapter, in which the court permitted a cause of action for gender harassment by an employee who was constantly harassed by his coworkers for being effeminate. Understanding Oncale is an important part of understanding the Court's progression to *Bostock* from the far different place sexual orientation was in title VII before. Understanding that the law is striking at the entire spectrum of gender-based actions makes it easier to see rather than only looking at labels like gender identity or sexual orientation. Treating employees differently in any way, whether by harassment between those of the same gender, or by firing them because an employer does not believe they act like their gender should, still involves treating them differently based on gender and that is what Title VII prohibits.

Gender Identity Discrimination

LO6 Discuss the workplace issues involving transgender individuals.

Closely related to sexual orientation, but actually quite separate, is the matter of gender identity. As you saw earlier in the chapter, some state and local laws protected sexual orientation but did not also protect gender identity. Gender identity involves how an individual identifies with gender. It encompasses several different manifestations, including sexual reassignment surgery and its stages, dressing or acting in ways consistent with a gender other than the employee's assigned gender, and being transgender. This is quite different from the issue of sexual orientation. Gays and lesbians do not feel that their body and mind are at odds. They simply prefer their significant relationships to be with people of their same gender. According to the Human Rights Campaign, the term *transgender* encompasses cross-dressers, intersexed people (formerly called hermaphrodites, or those born with both sex organs), transsexuals, and people who live substantial portions of their lives as other than their birth gender. In 2016, *The New York Times* reported that the number of transgender Americans had doubled to 1.4 million from earlier estimates based on new state and federal data.[72] As early as 2002, it was estimated that as many as 200,000 people had transitioned from their birth gender to the opposite gender during the past several years in the United States and perhaps 10,000 more do so each year.[73] A 2016 HRC survey showed that the number of Americans who know someone who is transgender increased from 22 percent in

2015 to 35 percent in 2016, as well as an increase in those who felt favorable toward transgender individuals. Sixty-six percent of those who felt favorable toward transgender individuals supported equality for them.[74]

While the term *transgender* has traditionally been used for those who have undergone gender reassignment surgery, a change in the use of the term has come with a growing awareness of the issues of transgender individuals and a greater sense of themselves than historically. It is now often used more loosely to include those who may not yet have had surgery but are living as the opposite gender. There are those within the transgender community who may have had surgery to change their gender and those who cannot afford such surgery or for other reasons may not wish to have surgery but still feel like the gender opposite their outward appearance and wish to present that to the world. They may have had some surgery and not other surgery. Whether they have or have not is totally irrelevant to their ability to do their job, and it is inappropriate to ask. Transgender employees simply want to be treated as the gender they feel themselves to be and represent themselves as.

Our students usually have a pretty hard time wrapping their heads around this issue. Unlike the other types of discrimination we have discussed, most of them are not aware of knowing anyone in this category, so they have no frame of reference for it. To them, it seems bizarre and unsettling. "Why in the world would somebody want to change their gender?" they ask. The biggest surprise for them is realizing that transgender individuals do not just decide on a whim to change their gender. See Exhibit 10.8 "Transgender: Why Did I Want to Transition?" The condition of feeling like your mind is one gender and your body is the opposite is a medical condition

---

Exhibit 10.8 *Transgender: Why Did I Want to Transition?*

This is an interesting question. The truth is, I didn't particularly have a choice. I appeared to be a man, but had this inner gender identity turmoil in that I never quite felt like everyone said a man should feel. I knew about transsexuals and cross-dressers, and presumed I was the latter for many years. Finally, I looked in the mirror and said to myself, "Oh. That explains a lot. You are a woman, and you are going to transition. Now, how can I explain this to my (soon to be) ex-wife, children, parents, brothers, other relatives, friends and coworkers." I faced what I saw as the obvious, and the obvious path. There was not a choice.

Though some believe that one can choose to be untrue to themselves; I could not. Some transgender individuals feel this strong need to transition, but choose not to because it would disrupt their marriages, relationships, careers, and so on.

They tend to have high levels of depression, and the suicide rate for transpeople is about 9 times the national average.

Because of medical insurance not covering such things, I was unable to seek necessary therapy help for another four years. But, I was able to navigate that messy, frustrating process, and begin therapy with a therapist who was an expert on transgender issues and transsexuality. Being diagnosed in 40 minutes is unusual, and even though I never presented myself as female publicly, I continued transitioning in private by doing the things that a woman would do such as wearing women's clothes, make up, hairstyles, and even doing things like female hand gestures and smiles. Transitioning was difficult. There are excellent autobiographies and therapist-written books about the process for the individual, the family, the

(continued)

Exhibit 10.8 *continued*

workplace, and for therapists, but the feeling of being alone trumps those.

I discovered that one of my old friends from undergraduate school was transsexual and living stealth (unknown). When I told her I was going to transition, she emailed back with "Uh huh. Don't do it. But you will, because you really don't have a choice. It's who you are."

I reached out to others, to activists in a campus LGBTQ faculty and staff organization, to the director of our LGBT Student Center, and my therapist, all of whom were remarkably supportive and knowledgeable while some aspects of my personal and professional life changed dramatically. I also connected with two nearby support groups.

Coming out in the workplace involved communicating with and eventually meeting several activists, and our campus director of diversity, who thankfully ran interference for me. She secured an agreement with our legal department to extend protection in the workplace to me, even though gender identity and expression are not legally protected classes. The HR director lent support in that they were ready to process forms for name and gender changes when they were necessary, and the EEOC director also lent strong support. (Interestingly enough, for students, they will update the name and gender marker in the records in advance of the legal requirements.) She also began the process of negotiating a solution to "the bathroom issue." The college provided a unisex bathroom designated for me until I fully transitioned. When I was in other buildings, I did not have that. The director of our LGBT Student Center and a campus activist did presentations at meetings with faculty, staff and doctoral students. I made my announcement that "I am transsexual and am actively transitioning. Now my friends will explain." And they did.

Coming out and actively transitioning is a difficult process. Recognizing that you will put every relationship you currently have and ever will have at risk is frightening. Having the support and caring of the administration made this process relatively smooth. When there is support at the top of an organization, the organization definitely follows. Connecting with college professor friends who transitioned before me provided valuable guidance and support. There were a few minor issues with students that I actively settled. After my first semester living full time, our director of diversity emailed me asking if everything was alright because she had heard nothing from anyone.

Sometimes I will meet on campus or elsewhere a colleague or acquaintance whom I have not seen in a while. When reintroduced, I may say, "Hi. We met when I was a man." In addition, I find it comedic when I meet a faculty member from my campus or another university who knows of my research work or books. They will often ask if I know myself or am married to myself, to which I often reply, "Oh yes. . . I used to be him."

Source: Janine Elyse Aronson, Ph.D., Professor of Management Information Systems, The University of Georgia, Athens, GA 2/19/2014. Used with permission.

recognized by the American Medical Association as gender dysphoria, also earlier called gender identity disorder. The term *transsexual* is traditionally used to describe a person who has undergone gender reassignment surgery. Though it may seem drastic to those without the condition, for transsexuals, changing their body is easy compared to living with a body that does not represent who they feel themselves to be. For them, changing their body is simply making the outside conform to the inside.

Most of us do not realize just how mental our gender is. We just take for granted that we are the way we are, period. We're male, and that's it. We're female, and that's it. The truth is a lot of what we think of as our gender is mental due to both acculturation and physiology.

If I said to males reading the text, "Paint your fingernails red and go about your day and everyone can see them," most of you would probably howl in protest, "No way!" Ever think about why? Painting your nails red doesn't change your fingers. It doesn't change who you are. It's just nail polish. Yet you don't want to do it because it just doesn't feel like you. For most of you, it would feel like it would be feminine and you feel masculine. Even if you just painted your nails red and sat in your room with no one around, you would feel uncomfortable. So much so that you would never do it. For individuals with gender dysphoria, their body looks like one gender, but their mind feels like the opposite gender and always has. For the most part, until they transition and live as the gender they feel they are, they have an overriding sense that they are in the wrong body. (The reason I asked males instead of females is because females have more flexibility in their dress. For instance, it is perfectly acceptable for females to wear nail polish or not wear colored nail polish in a business setting. For men, it is generally not acceptable to wear nail polish.)

Since most people are not familiar with this issue, you can imagine that it presents rather interesting, confusing, and, at times, complicated workplace challenges that must be addressed. As a matter of information, once someone has changed his or her gender identity and complies with state laws to do so, he or she is now legally considered to be the gender to which he or she has changed. None of that "he/she" stuff as if you don't know what to consider them once you realize they are transgender, as has happened in several cases. They are the gender they have transitioned to, again, whether you understand it or not. Depending on state law, they generally can have their identity documents reissued to be consistent with their new gender and can even have their birth certificate reissued in some jurisdictions. After surgery, they are, for all intents and purposes, the gender they transitioned to and wish to be treated that way.

That is the case for those who undergo actual surgery, but not all transgender individuals do. All transexuals are transgender, but not all transgender individuals are transsexuals. If they have not undergone surgery, this does not mean they are any less transgender. The safest thing, and the most appropriate for workplace purposes, is simply to treat the employee consistent with the way the employee presents his or her identity. Also, unless the employee is asking for time off for surgery or is him- or herself addressing the issue, it is not OK to bring it up and inquire as to whether they have had surgery. Can you imagine someone asking you such a personal question? When you think about it logically, why in the world would anyone ask such a personal question about a coworker's body parts? What is the purpose of knowing? Why is it even in a coworker's mind? The reason is usually pure curiosity, and that is not a sufficient reason to be impolite and invasive in the workplace.

It may seem a bit strange to discuss this in a legal textbook. However, we must. We tell you this because we have taught thousands of students and had thousands of attendees at consulting and training and workshop sessions, and they routinely ask these questions in order to better grasp what seems so alien a concept to them. We care about giving you the right tools to make decisions in the workplace in order to avoid unnecessary liability. Since so many of our students and seminar attendees ask the questions, we thought you might have the same ones. We also believe that providing a thumbnail sketch here gives you some means of analyzing the cases in this section. Because many people have little or no understanding of these issues when they are faced with them as managers or supervisors, they have little idea how to make legally defensible decisions. It is important to recognize that because you do not understand or "accept" gender identity issues does not mean (1) that they do not exist or (2) that you can afford to ignore the reality of handling these workplace issues.

This lack of understanding may account, at least in part, for the fact that a groundbreaking 2009 national survey of more than 6,000 transgender individuals found that 47 percent had experienced adverse job actions because of gender identity and 97 percent had experienced some form of anti-transgender harassment or discrimination on the job.[75] A 2011 joint report by the National Center for Transgender Equality and the National Gay and Lesbian Task Force found that 90 percent of transgender Americans have to deal with workplace discrimination or harassment as a result of their gender identity.[76] A 2015 US Transgender Survey found their unemployment rate to be three times the national average, and home ownership 16% as opposed to 63%.[*]

In the majority of federal jurisdictions, those who are terminated or not hired solely on the basis of sexual orientation or gender identity have no claim for relief under the words of Title VII itself, although, as we had said, the EEOC had interpreted gender to include discrimination on the basis of gender identity. Gender identity was the main reason that later iterations of ENDA have missed passage by as little as one vote. When gender identity was added to the sexual orientation antidiscrimination bill, supporters realized that they did not have enough votes for passage if discrimination on the basis of gender identity was included. The LGBTQ community chose to continue to push for the inclusive language, and it has remained that way ever since. The Senate passed ENDA for the first time in 2013, but the House failed to do so, even though polls at the time showed that 66 percent of Americans supported such a law and 56 percent supported the inclusion of transgender individuals in such a law.[77] President Obama had urged the House to pass ENDA and said he would sign it when it reached his desk,[78] but it declined to do so. By 2015, polls showed that American support for the law had grown to 70 percent.[79] Ironically, it ended up being gender identity rather than sexual orientation that the EEOC first moved to include in its interpretation of Title VII. It was not until three years later that sexual orientation was included.

Think the issues faced by transgender employees are isolated and far-fetched? In the *Boeing* case mentioned earlier, the Boeing Corporation was faced with requests for accommodating transgender employees so frequently (at least nine times) that it finally developed a carefully crafted policy. We include the case for you at the end of the chapter so you can see what that well-thought-out policy looks like—especially in the earlier days before this issue was so prevalent.

Due in part to the activity surrounding issues of sexual orientation, transgender discrimination became really active and is now one of the fastest-growing social issues. As a result, it is presenting itself more and more frequently as a workplace issue. As we saw earlier, several state and local laws included transgender employees within their antidiscrimination policies before the *Bostock* decision. According

* transequality.org

to the Human Rights Campaign, 91 percent of Fortune 500 companies include gender identity protection in their workplace antidiscrimination policies.

The argument was made by trangender persons for years, particularly those who had gender reassignment surgery, that they should be afforded the protection of Title VII because they had changed their gender status from male to female or vice versa and now are being discriminated against in employment because they had changed genders. Courts had not agreed. As stated in *Ulane v. Eastern Airlines, Inc.*,[80] the basis for Opening Scenario 2, it is not the status of the employee as a member of the gender to which he or she has been reassigned that created the issue. That is, a male who is terminated on becoming a female is not discriminated against because he is a female as contemplated by Title VII. Rather, she is discriminated against because she changed from male to female. These are considered two very different arguments, with the former being provided Title VII protection but not the latter. However, once the EEOC began accepting gender identity claims for processing, this mattered little because they were protected by law based on their gender identity as they are under the *Bostock* decision.

Ulane was the first significant case to address the matter of transgender discrimination and remained the general approach to transgender discrimination in the workplace under Title VII until the EEOC's *Macy v. Holder*[81] decision in 2012, mentioned earlier in the chapter, endorsed the lower court cases that had begun to view the issue differently. Recall that the transgender employee in *Ulane* argued that she was discriminated against because of gender, but the court held this was not the case; it held that the basis for discrimination was changing her gender from male to female, and that was not protected by Title VII.

In *Macy,* an imminently qualified job applicant who was led to believe the job was practically his given his qualifications was turned down and a lesser-qualified person hired after the employer learned that the applicant was transitioning from male to female. There had been several federal district court cases holding that discrimination on the basis of gender identity was a violation of the Equal Protection Clause of the U.S. Constitution or of Title VII through gender stereotyping, which had been outlawed by the U.S. Supreme Court in its *Price Waterhouse* decision discussed earlier and in Chapter 8, Gender Discrimination. In EEOC's view, because Title VII is a remedial law, it needed to be broadly construed to strike at the entire spectrum of ways in which discrimination is manifested. In the case of gender identity, it said there is discrimination either because the employee transitioned from one gender to the other or because the employer is uncomfortable with the employee not conforming to gender norms, and either should be actionable under Title VII as gender discrimination. Of course, this broke with the state of the law up until this time.

Employees also have argued that being transgender is a disability that must be accommodated. The "pink pearls" case, as *Jane Doe v. Boeing Company* became known, rejected that view in Washington State. It also provides great insight into how an employer can approach these issues to best provide protection against liability for discrimination. Keep in mind, while you review the case at the conclusion of the chapter, that Washington enacted a law protecting transgender individuals from workplace discrimination in 2006, but Boeing had put a policy in place several years before.

Employment Benefits

LO7 Identify some of the employment benefits issues for LGBTQ employees.

The legalization of same-sex marriage in 2015 did away with most of the benefit inequality issues that LGBTQ employees had fought for for years. While we may think of them only as add-ons to our salary, benefits can be vitally important. They can hardly be thought of as a mere add-on since they account for roughly 30 percent of employees' overall compensation.[82] It should therefore come as no surprise that this area was one of the most active regarding sexual orientation and gender identity in the workplace. With benefits accounting for nearly one-third of an employee's compensation, aside from other considerations, lack of benefits is an equal pay issue. And benefits that other employees took for granted could cause major hurdles for the LGBTQ community. For instance, before marriage equality was the law, bereavement leave routinely granted to an employee to deal with the death of a loved one was often not provided to an LGBTQ employee when his or her life partner died, even though the couple may have been together for 30 years or more. Sick leave routinely granted and, in many places, allowed to be gifted to other employees in need was often not given when the employee was LGBTQ and the family was the employee's life partner. The up to 12 weeks of unpaid leave to deal with an employee's adoption or birth of children, medical issues of the employee, the employee's spouse or children under the Family Medical Leave Act discussed in Chapter 16 was originally not available to gay and lesbian families. Now that same-sex marriage is legal, spousal benefits are available for LGB employees. Even before transgender employees were interpreted by the EEOC as having rights under Title VII, many employers chose to cover their issues related to health insurance and transitioning. Zero percent of employers offered trans-inclusive health care benefits in 2002, the year after the first issuance of the Human Rights Campaign's Corporate Equality Index. In the 2020 CEI that number was 933 of 942 employers, or 85 percent. Affirmative transgender-inclusive health care benefits and removal of all broad exclusions to coverage across plan offerings only created for employers a marginal increase, a fraction of a decimal point of cost calculations.

Management Considerations

Since the U.S. Supreme Court's decision in *Bostock*, sexual orientation and gender identity are now protected categories under Title VII.

If some action of the LGBTQ employee presents an issue, it should be dealt with as a legitimate workplace issue rather than one that arose solely because of the employee's sexual orientation or gender identity. The fact that the employee happens to be LGBTQ should not be treated as the "why," any more than it would be if the employee were heterosexual. It is irrelevant to the activity. The focus is on the conduct itself, not on the sexual orientation or gender identity of the employee. It greatly reduces the potential for liability to deal with all employees this way.

Employers who adopt a policy that treats LGBTQ employees as full contributors to the workplace should ensure that the message goes out from the very top. It is more likely to be accepted, appreciated, and understood and therefore more likely to accomplish its purpose of lessening potential liability and creating a more productive workplace. Other employees will be more likely to comport themselves consistent with the policy if it comes from the top of the hierarchy. It should be made clear that not only will the employer not discriminate against LGBTQ employees on the basis of sexual orientation or gender identity, but it will not be tolerated from other employees, particularly in the form of harassment. Keep in mind the research we learned about earlier from the professor at the University of Georgia who discovered that people can treat others poorly based on unspoken messages they receive from those they are surrounded by. Our attitudes, gestures, tone of voice, and engagement tenor can all play a part in sending a message. Make sure it is the message we intend to send.

Employers may wish to consider possible repercussions of restrictive employment policies in this area. An example of this is the Cracker Barrel restaurant chain, headquartered in Tennessee. Cracker Barrel operates a number of restaurants around the country. With no apparent motivating event, in 1991, the company announced that it would no longer employ people "whose sexual preferences fail to demonstrate normal heterosexual values which have been the foundation of families in our society." Pursuant to this policy, Cracker Barrel summarily terminated its gay and lesbian employees. After doing so, it was the subject of vigorous opposition, mainly by the gay and lesbian community. Many of Cracker Barrel's restaurants were picketed and denounced by vocal protesters. Gays and lesbians bought stock in order to have a say in its policies. Cracker Barrel later revoked the policy as overreactive. Even though the law permitted Cracker Barrel's actions, some employers may wish to avoid the controversy exhibited here, particularly if there is no pressing need to address the issue. In a complete about-face, in 2002, Cracker Barrel's board of directors voted to include gays and lesbians in its anti-discrimination policy.[83]

Case 6

Despite all the information in this chapter about how to treat LGBTQ employees now that they are protected by law, in order to prevent liability from attaching for preventable actions, a word of caution should be given. If the employer decides to create a workplace welcoming to LGBTQ employees, it is generally done under the aegis of diversity and inclusion. Employers should be aware of the religious conflicts non-LGBTQ employees have alleged based on these policies. As the *Buonanno v. AT&T Broadband, LLC* case demonstrates at the conclusion of the chapter, the employer should not trample over the rights of other employees in order to address the issue of inclusion and avoid liability. In *Buonanno,* an employee with religious objections to homosexuality was terminated for refusing to sign a workplace document pledging him to value diversity, including on the basis of LGBTQ status. The court agreed that it was wrong for the employer to terminate the employee without trying to accommodate his religious beliefs.

Management Tips

LO8 List some ways that employers can address LGBTQ issues in the workplace.

Policies and decisions in the sexual orientation and gender identity areas are rapidly evolving. The patchwork of state, federal, local, public, and private laws and policies we have discussed presents the employer with the challenge of trying to do what is required for each jurisdiction in which the employer may operate, when, in fact, the requirements may be quite different. However, conclusions can be drawn about creating policy in the midst of such seeming chaos. In order to provide the maximum protection from liability for sexual orientation–and gender identity–related issues, an employer can do several things:

- Use only relevant, work-related criteria for hiring, promotions, pay raises, discipline, training, and other workplace decisions.
- Keep inquiries about applicants' personal lives at a minimum and make sure the requested information is relevant for the job.
- Have a policy ensuring all employees respect in the workplace and ensure that all employees not only are aware of the policy and what it actually means but also realize that swift appropriate action will be taken for violators.
- No matter what the employer's policy about LGBTQ employees is, in the workplace, be sure the respect policy protects everyone from things like unsolicited negative statements about immutable and other characteristics such as race, religion, gender, gender identity, and sexual orientation.
- Take prompt action whenever there are complaints of violations of the policy or it sends the message that the policy is meaningless.
- Despite the fact that LGBTQ employees are now included in Title VII's protection, issues will arise.
- Decide what position to take on sexual orientation and gender identity–related issues for policy purposes either proactively, before the issue arises, or defensively to meet the issue when it comes about; the latter has the benefit of specificity, the former the advantage of deliberate, strategic thinking.
- Be aware of the potential impact on LGBTQ employees of workplace policies regarding issues like bereavement leave, benefits, bringing significant others to office functions, accepting personal calls during work hours, and displaying personal items at work (photos, cards, political buttons, and so forth).

Chapter Summary

- Sexual orientation and gender identity discrimination are now included in Title VII.
- Due to long-held negative attitudes or religious differences, negative issues may still arise in the workplace.
- Be prepared to treat LGBTQ employees like any other similarly situated employee to ensure fairness.
- Same-gender harassment is also a violation of Title VII.
- Base employment decisions on the person's qualifications and fitness for the job rather than on irrelevant characteristics about his or her personal life.

Chapter-End Questions

1. Employee, a skydiving instructor, generally informs his customers that he is gay so that his female customers will not feel awkward when he is strapped to them. A female's husband called the company and complained about employee doing this and employee is terminated. Does he have a cause of action under Title VII? [*Zarda v. Altitude Express,* 855 F.3d 76 (2d Cir. 2017).]

2. When the FBI learns that Mary, its FBI agent, is a lesbian, Mary is fired. Mary goes to an attorney to find out about the possibility of suing to get her job back. What does the attorney likely tell her?

3. As a manager, an employee comes to you and tells you that he has a hunch that one of the other employees is probably gay. What do you do?

4. Charlie, the manager, does not like it that Chester wears an earring and orders Chester to get rid of it or be terminated. Chester refuses. Can Charlie terminate Chester without legal liability?

5. Employee sues his employer, saying that he is being sexually harassed by gay males, who only harass young male employees. Does he have a cause of action? [*Wrightson v. Pizza Hut of America, Inc.,* 99 F.3d 138 (4th Cir. 1996).]

6. A female employee and her (now) spouse are hired as elementary teachers and receive the highest-level evaluation for the year. At the end of the school year, the principal calls the two into her office with both their résumés on the desk and says she noticed they both went to the same art school and have had the same address for 30 years, so one of them must leave, and the two must decide between them which one. One left the school, and the other is constantly harassed, publicly intimidated, and humiliated by the principal. Is this a sufficient basis for a Title VII claim? [*Boutillier v. Hartford Pub. Schools,* No. 3:2013cv01303-Doc 58 (D. Conn. 2016).]

7. A male firefighter is diagnosed with gender dysphoria seven years after coming onto the force and having no negative incidents with coworkers. As he begins to exhibit a more feminine demeanor, he begins to have administrative troubles, which he attributes to his failing to conform to gender stereotypes. Does he have a cause of action under Title VII?

8. A female assistant at a hair salon is terminated. She brings suit under Title VII, alleging that it is because she is a lesbian whose overall appearance is more male than female. The employer counters that the termination was due to poor performance; there was no dress code, and the employee was allowed to wear her hair in a Mohawk cut as long as it was styled by someone at the salon. Is the employee likely to win? [*Dawson v. Bumble & Bumble,* 398 F.3d 211 (2d Cir. 2005).]

9. Applicant applies for a position with Ace Corporation. During the interview, Ace suspects that the applicant is gay. When asked why the suspicion, Ace says that the male applicant acted effeminately. Ace decides not to hire the applicant, who is otherwise qualified. Does the applicant have a cause of action against Ace? [*Jantz v. Muci,* 759 F. Supp. 1543 (D. Kan. 1991).]

10. Maureen brings her same-gender partner of 14 years to a company picnic. One of the other employees begins treating Maureen poorly at work after realizing she is a lesbian. Does Maureen have any recourse?

End Notes

1. Amherst College Queer Resource Center, "Terms, Definitions & Labels."

2. Elton Naswood and Mattee Jim, "Mending the Rainbow: Working with the Native LGBTQ/Two Spirit Community," Powerpoint Presentation for the 13th National Indian Nations Conference, December 2012; Walter L. Williams, "The 'Two-Spirit' People of Indigenous North Americans," First People.

3. The term *LGBTQ* is used throughout the chapter, but we recognize that there are other acceptable terms. Common among them are *LGBTQ, LGBTQI,* and *LGBTQIA,* which, in our experience, are not as well known. LGBTQ is lesbian, gay, bisexual, transgender, and queer or questioning. Use of LGBTQ is not intended to exclude any other appropriate category.

4. "LGBTQ People in the Workplace," https://www.lgbtmap.org/lgbt-workers-brief.

5. "Farmer Spreads Manure along Gay Parade Route," *Shortnews* (August 2, 2004), http://www.shortnews.com/start.cfm?id=41710.

6. Parker, Suzi, and Michael Rozman, "Constance McMillen Case: Proms as Gay-Rights Battleground," *The Christian Science Monitor* (March 23, 2010), http://www.csmonitor.com/USA/Justice/2010/0323/Constance-McMillen-case-proms-as-gay-rights-battleground.

7. "Kansas House OKs Bill Allowing Refusal of Service to Same-Sex Couples," *CNN.com* (February 13, 2014), http://www.cnn.com/2014/02/13/us/kansas-bill-same-sex-services/index.html.

8. Sloan, Scott, "Commission Sides with Gay Group against Hands on Originals," *Lexington Herald-Leader* (KY) (November 26, 2012), http://www.kentucky.com/2012/11/26/2421990/city-rules-hands-on-originals.html.

9. Starnes, Todd, "Oregon Ruling Really Takes the Cake—Christian Bakery Guilty of Violating Civil Rights of Lesbian Couple," Fox News (January 21, 2014), http://www.foxnews.com/opinion/2014/01/21/christian-bakery-guilty-violating-civil-rights-lesbian-couple/.

10. Gershman, Jacob, "Photographers Discriminated against Gay Couple, Court Rules," *The Wall Street Journal* (August 22, 2013), http://blogs.wsj.com/law/2013/08/22/photographers-discriminated-against-gay-couple-court-rules/.

11. Bookman, Jay, "Georgia May Follow Arizona's Anti-Gay Lead," *The Atlanta Journal Constitution* (February 24, 2014), http://www.ajc.com/weblogs/jay-bookman/2014/feb/24/georgia-may-follow-arizonas-anti-gay-lead/.

12. Seward, Christopher, "Shorter University Requiring Staffers to Reject Homosexuality," *The Atlanta Journal-Constitution* (October 29, 2011), http://www.ajc.com/news/shorter-university-requiring-staffers-1212689.html.

13. "Blue Jay's Yunel Escobar Played Game with Homophobic Slur Written across Eyeblack," *The Star* (September 18, 2012), http://www.thestar.com/sports/baseball/2012/09/18/blue_jays_yunel_escobar_played_game_with_homophobic_slur_written_across_eye_black.html; Ley, Tom, "Kevin Pillar Suspended Two Games for Using Homophobic Slur," *Deadspin* (May 19, 2017), http://deadspin.com/kevin-pillar-suspended-two-games-for-using-homophobic-s-1795368257.

14. "Equal in Taxes, If Not in Texas," *Time* (September 16, 2013), p. 11; "The National Guard's Defiance on Civil Rights," editorial board, *The New York Times* (October 20, 2013), http://www.nytimes.com/2013/10/21/opinion/the-national-guards-defiance-on-civil-rights.html?_r=0.

15. 576 U.S. ___ , 135 S. Ct. 2584 (2015).

16. "Boy Scouts Gay Ban Controversy Highlights Growing Tug-of-War between Right and Left," *The Huffington Post* (February 9, 2013), http://www.huffingtonpost.com/2013/02/09/

boy-scouts-gay-ban-controversy_n_2648208.html; Summers, Claude, "How The Boy Scouts Tricked America into Thinking They No Longer Discriminate against Gays: BSA Lifted National Ban, but Most Troops Still Bar LGBTQ Leaders Thanks to Religious Exemption," *The New Civil Rights Movement* (October 2, 2016), http://www.thenewcivilrightsmovement.com/claude_summers/continuing_discrimination_by_the_boy_scouts_of_america.

17. Polsky, Jeffrey D., "Court Lets Firefighter Who Stood Up for Gay Daughter Proceed with Harassment Claim," *Lexology* (January 31, 2013), http://www.lexology.com/library/detail.aspx?g=f2146617-dee0-4868-a78a-3c250f7b6710.

18. "I Was an NFL Player Until I Was Fired by Two Cowards and a Bigot," *Deadspin* (January 2, 2014), http://deadspin.com /i-was-an-nfl-player-until-i-was-fired-by-two-cowards-an-1493208214.

19. http://www.rappaportlawoffice.com/blog/2013/04/nfl-new-york-reach-sexual-orientation-discrimination-agreement.shtml.

20. Broder, John M., "Schwarzenegger Calls Budget Opponents 'Girlie Men,'" *The New York Times* (July 19, 2004), http://www.nytimes.com/2004/07/19/us/schwarzenegger-calls-budget-opponents-girlie-men.html?src=pm.

21. Johnson, Lauren, "Boy, 7, Scolded for Saying 'Gay': La. Student Says Mother Is a Lesbian, Sent to Principal for Saying 'Bad Word,'" CBS News (December 1, 2003), http://www.cbsnews.com/stories/2003/12/01/national/main586293.shtml.

22. "Obama Signs Repeal of 'Don't Ask, Don't Tell' Policy," *CNN.com* (December 22, 2010), http://articles.cnn.com/2010-12-22/politics/dadt.repeal_1_repeal-openly-gay-men-president- barack-obama?_s=PM:POLITICS.

23. "Episcopal Church Consecrates First Openly Lesbian Bishop," *CNN.com* (May 15, 2010), http://articles.cnn.com/2010-05-15/us/episcopal.lesbian.bishop_1_gay-bishopscanterbury-rowan-williams-consecrated?_s=PM:US.

24. El Nasser, Haya, "Same-Sex Unions Challenge Census," *USA Today* (July 6, 2009), p. 3A; O'Hara, Mary Emily, "LGBTQ Americans Won't Be Counted in 2020 U.S. Census After All," NBC News (March 29, 2017), http://www.nbcnews.com/feature/nbc-out/lgbtq-americans-won-t-be-counted-2020-u-s-census-n739911.

25. Presidential Memorandum—Hospital Visitation (April 15, 2010), http://www.whitehouse.gov/the-press-office/presidential-memorandum-hospital-visitation.

26. "Lesbian's Case against Jackson Memorial Hospital Tossed," *The Miami Herald* (September 30, 2009), http://www.miamiherald.co/news/miami-dade/stor/1258772.html.

27. Redden, Elizabeth, "'Dirty Little Secret' in Women's Sports," *Inside Higher Ed* (April 30, 2007), https://www.insidehighered.com/news/2007/04/30/sports.

28. Ryan, Shannon, "Lesbian College Coaches Still Face Difficult Atmosphere to Come Out," *Chicago Tribune* (January 17, 2017), http://www.chicagotribune.com/sports/college/ct-lesbian-college-coaches-challenges-spt-0118-20170117-story.html.

29. Jayson, Sharon, "APA Meeting: Being Gay Isn't a Mental Illness," *USA Today* (August 10, 2009), p. 5D.

30. "California Governor OKs Ban on Gay Conversion Therapy, Calling It 'Quackery,'" CNN (October 1, 2012), http://www.cnn.com/2012/10/01/us/california-gay-therapy-ban/index.html.

31. 562 U.S. 443 (2011).

32. Barnes, Robert, "Supreme Court to Rule on Anti-Gay Protests at Military Funerals," *The Washington Post* (March 9, 2010), http://www.washingtonpost.com/wp-dyn/content/article/2010/03/08/AR2010030801578.html.

33. Reilly, Rick, "Showing How It's Done: Missouri Students Protected Michael Sam from Seeing Church Protesters," *ESPN.com* (February 18, 2014), http://espn.go.com/college-football/story/_/id/10466480/mizzou-students-display-true-spirit-supporting-michael-sam.

34. Barry, Ellen, "County Rescinds Vote to Ban Gay Residents, in the Courtroom of the 1925 'Monkey Trial,' Commissioners Retreat amid Ideological Furor," *Los Angeles Times* (March 19, 2004), http://www.commondreams.org/headlines04/0319-10.htm.

35. *Newsweek* (October 25, 2010), p. 16.

36. O'Connor, Clare, "Walmart Extends Benefits to LGBTQ Employees' Same-Sex Domestic Partners," *Forbes* (August 28, 2013), http://www.forbes.com/sites/clareoconnor/2013/08/28/walmart-extends-benefits-to-lgbt-employees-same-sex-domestic-partners/.

37. http://www.hrc.org/state-maps/employment.

38. http://www.hrc.org/issues/workplace/enda.asp.

39. Human Rights Campaign, http://www.hrc.org/laws_and_elections/enda.asp.

40. Now defunct.

41. "Corporate America Champions LGBTQ Equality in Record Numbers: Historic Numbers of Corporations Earn Top Scores in HRC's 2014 Corporate Equality Index and Come Out to Support Legal Equality," hrc.org (December 9, 2013), http://www.hrc.org/press-releases/entry/corporate-america-champions-lgbt-equality-in-record-numbers; http://www.hrc.org/blog/entry/record-breaking-year-for-corporate-equality; "Why the Equality Act?" http://www.hrc.org/resources/why-the-equality-act.

42. http://assets.hrc.org//files/assets/resources/CEI-2017-Final.pdf?_ga=2.256311819.160412852.1494984752-1357269144.1435879904.

43. "Poll: More Americans Favor Same-Sex Marriage," cnn.com (April 19, 2011), http://politicalticker.blogs.cnn.com/2011/04/19/poll-more-americans-favor-same-sex-marriage/; Gilgoff, Dan, "CNN Poll: Most Americans Oppose Gay Marriage, but Those under 35 Back It," usnews.com (May 5, 2009), http://www.usnews.com/news/blogs/god-and-country/2009/05/05/cnn-poll-most-americans-oppose-gay-marriage-but-those-under-35-back-it.

44. Saad, Lydia, "In U.S. 52% Back Law to Legalize Gay Marriage in 50 States: Americans Would Legalize Gay Marriage Nationwide, Favor Equal Rights for Such Unions," Gallup Politics (July 29, 2013), http://www.gallup.com/poll/163730/back-law-legalize-gay-marriage-states.aspx.

45. *Hively v. Ivy Technical College,* No. 5-1720 (7th Cir. April 4, 2017).

46. Williams, Pete, "LGBTQ Job Discrimination Is Prohibited by Civil Rights Law, Federal Appeals Court Rules," NBC News (April 4, 2017), http://www.nbcnews.com/feature/nbc-out/lgbt-job-discrimination-prohibited-civil-rights-law-federal-appeals-court-n742751.

47. Badgett, M. V. Lee, Laura E. Durso, Angeliki Kastanis, and Christy Mallory, "The Business Impact of LGBTQ-Supportive Sexual Orientation and Gender Identity Policies," The Williams Institute (May 2013), https://williamsinstitute.law.ucla.edu/wp-content/uploads/Business-Impact-LGBTQ-Policies-Full-May-2013.pdf.

48. Human Rights Campaign, "Establishing an Employee Resource Group," https://www.hrc.org/resources/establishing-an-employee-resource-group.

49. Ft. Worth City Council Representative Joel Burn, http://www.youtube.com/watch?v=ax96cghOnY4&feature=related; PricewaterhouseCoopers, "It Gets Better," http://www.youtube.com/watch?v=fffI4TzuIk0Google's video http://www.youtube.com/wat

ch?v=pYLs4NCgvNU&feature=relatedFacebook's video http://www.youtube.com/watch?v=iPg02qjL40g&feature=related.

50. 2020 HRC Corporate Equality Index at p. 23. https://assets2.hrc.org/files/assets/resources/CEI-2020.pdf?_ga=2.166289982.1249247932.1584378585-1984997810.1584378585.

51. "Pride at the White House," http://www.whitehouse.gov/blog/2013/06/12/pride-white-house.

52. McBride, Sarah, "HRC Releases Annual Report on Epidemic of Anti-Transgender Violence" (November 18, 2019), https://www.hrc.org/blog/hrc-releases-annual-report-on-epidemic-of-anti-transgender-violence-2019.

53. http://www.youtube.com/watch?v=DmvV-E1LEXo.

54. "Presidential Executive Order Promoting Free Speech and Religious Liberty," whitehouse.gov (May 4, 2017), https://www.whitehouse.gov/the-press-office/2017/05/04/presidential-executive-order-promoting-free-speech-and-religious-liberty.

55. Scott, Eugene, "LGBTQ Groups Condemn Trump's Religious Liberty Executive Order," CNN (May 4, 2017), http://www.cnn.com/2017/05/04/politics/lgbt-religious-liberty-executive-order/.

56. "A Workplace Divided: Understanding the Climate for LGBTQ Workers Nationwide," HRC, 2018, p. 4, https://assets2.hrc.org/files/assets/resources/AWorkplaceDivided-2018.pdf?_ga=2.199772718.1249247932.1584378585-1984997810.1584378585.

57. http://www.hrc.org/documents/Business_Coalition_for_Workplace_Fairness_-_Members.pdf.

58. http://www.hrc.org/resources/why-the-equality-act.

59. Business Coalition Equality Act, HRC, https://www.hrc.org/resources/business-coalition-for-equality.

60. *SmithKline Beecham Corp. v. Abbott Laboratories* (Nos. 11-17357, 11-17373, 9th Cir. 2014).

61. *Romer v. Evans,* 517 U.S. 620 (1996).

62. http://www.hrc.org/explore/topic/workplace.

63. EEOC App. No. 0120120821; Agency No. ATF-2011-00751 (April 20, 2012).

64. https://www.eeoc.gov/eeoc/newsroom/release/3-1-16.cfm.

65. No. 15-15234 (11th Cir. March 10, 2017).

66. (2d Cir.).

67. 883 F.3d 100 (2d Cir. 2018).

68. No. 18-107.

69. 608 F.2d 327 (9th Cir. 1979).

70. 876 F.2d 69 (8th Cir. 1998).

71. 523 U.S. 75 (1998).

72. Hoffman, Jan, "Estimate of U.S. Transgender Population Doubles to 1.4 Million," *The New York Times* (June 30, 2016), https://www.nytimes.com/2016/07/01/health/transgender-population.html?mcubz=1.

73. Conway, Lynn, "How Frequently Does Transsexualism Occur?" Artificial Intelligence, Engineering and Computer Science Department, University of Michigan (2002), ai.eecs.umich.edu/people/Conway/TST/TSprevalence.html, cited in Walworth, Janis,

"For Employers: Managing Transsexual Transitions in the Workplace," Center for Gender Sanity (2003), http://www.gendersanity.com/shrm.html. See generally, Peterson, Lee M., "Workplace Harassment against Transgender Individuals: Sex Discrimination, Status Discrimination, or Both?" *Suffolk U. L. Rev.* 227 (2002–2003), 36; and Storrow, Richard F., "Gender Typing in Stereo: The Transgender Dilemma in Employment Discrimination, *Maine L. Rev.* 118 (2002), 55:1.

74. HRC National Survey of Likely Voters, http://www.hrc.org/resources/hrc-national-survey-of-likely-voters.

75. Conway, "How Frequently Does Transsexualism Occur?" Data from the National Center for Transgender Equality and the National Gay and Lesbian Task Force found that 78 percent of transgender Americans say they have experienced workplace discrimination at some point. Testimony of Chad Griffin, president of the Human Rights Campaign, the largest LGBTQ advocacy organization in the United States, before the Health, Education, Labor and Pensions Committee on the Employment Nondiscrimination Act (ENDA) (S. 811) on June 12, 2012. "Senate HELP Committee Holds ENDA Hearings," HRC Blog (June 12, 2012).

76. "Injustice at Every Turn: A Report of the National Transgender Discrimination Survey," http://www.thetaskforce.org/downloads/reports/reports/ntds_full.pdf.

77. Malloy, Parker Marie, "Poll: Majority of Americans Support Transgender-Inclusive ENDA," *The Advocate* (December 14, 2013), http://www.advocate.com/politics/2013/12/14/poll-majority-americans-support-trans-inclusive-enda.

78. Rafter, Dan, "Pres. Obama Urges House to Pass ENDA," HRC Blog (December 4, 2013), http://www.hrc.org/blog/entry/president-obama-urges-house-to-pass-enda.

79. Wheeler, Lydia, "Poll: Seven in 10 Support LGBTQ Nondiscrimination Laws," *The Hill* (July 1, 2017), http://thehill.com/regulation/246683-poll-7-in-10-americans-support-lgbt-nondiscrimination-laws.

80. 742 F.2d 1081 (7th Cir. 1984).

81. EEOC App. NO. 0120120821; Agency No. ATF-2011-00751 (April 20, 2012).

82. 2020 Corporate Equality Index, Human Rights Campaign, p. 16, https://assets2.hrc.org/files/assets/resources/CEI-2020.pdf?_ga=2.166289982.1249247932.1584378585-1984997810.1584378585.

83. Smothers, Ronald, "Company Ousts Gay Workers, Then Reconsiders," *The New York Times* (February 28, 1991), http://www.nytimes.com/1991/02/28/us/company-ousts-gay-workers-then-reconsiders.html.

Cases

Weaver v. Nebo School District,
29 F. Supp. 2d 1279 (D. Utah 1998)

Case 1

A schoolteacher was reprimanded when she said yes when asked by a student if she was gay. Her coaching job was taken away, and a notation was put in her personnel file. The court held that treating her this way based on sexual orientation was an unconstitutional denial of equal protection.

Jenkins, J.

***

For the past 19 years, plaintiff Wendy Weaver has been a teacher at Spanish Fork High School in the Nebo School District. Ms. Weaver, a tenured faculty member since 1982, teaches psychology and physical education. Her reputation as an educator at Spanish Fork is unblemished: she has always been considered an effective and capable teacher, her evaluations range from good to excellent, and she has never been the subject of any disciplinary action. In addition to her teaching responsibilities, Ms. Weaver has served as the girls' volleyball coach since 1979. She has been effective in this endeavor, leading the team to four state championships.

Unlike her teaching position, however, Ms. Weaver's position as coach was not tenured. Instead, as is the case with all coaching positions at Spanish Fork High School, Ms. Weaver was hired as volleyball coach on a year-to-year basis. For each year she was hired as coach, Ms. Weaver received a stipend, which in her most recent year of coaching was $1,500. The practice of hiring coaches, however, is somewhat informal. It is the policy of the School District that Principal Wadley has final decision-making authority in selecting a coach. Generally, Principal Wadley finds out who has an interest, selects a coach from the interested candidates, and notifies the coach that he or she has the position. No written contract is prepared. In practice, the coach from the previous year is routinely offered the position for the following year, or, as Principal Wadley stated, "you assign them once and they stay assigned until you assign someone else."

In the late spring and early summer of 1997, Ms. Weaver began preparing for the upcoming school volleyball season—as she did in the past—by organizing two summer volleyball camps for prospective team players. As usual, these camps were to be held at Spanish Fork High School in June and July of 1997. Ms. Weaver telephoned prospective volleyball team members to inform

them of the camp schedules. One of the calls went to a senior team member. During the conversation, the team member asked Ms. Weaver, "Are you gay?" Ms. Weaver truthfully responded, "Yes." The team member then told Ms. Weaver that she would not play on the volleyball team in the fall. On July 14, 1997, the team member and her parents met with defendants Almon Mosher, Director of Human Resources for the Nebo School District, and Larry Kimball, Director of Secondary Education for the Nebo School District, and told them that Ms. Weaver told them that she is gay and that the team member decided she would not play volleyball.

In April of 1997, Gary Weaver, Ms. Weaver's ex-husband and a school psychologist for the Nebo School District, spoke with Principal Wadley about Ms. Weaver's sexual orientation. In May of 1997, Nedra Call, the Curriculum Coordinator for the School District, received two calls concerning Ms. Weaver's "lifestyle and her actions." She related the substance of these calls to defendant Mosher. Defendant Dennis Poulsen, Superintendent of the Nebo School District, also received calls about Ms. Weaver. In addition, several adults affiliated or formerly affiliated with the school contacted Principal Wadley with comments or questions about Ms. Weaver's sexual orientation. Principal Wadley held a meeting with his two assistant principals to discuss Ms. Weaver's sexual orientation. On May 22, 1997, before the phone conversation with Ms. Weaver, the team member and her mother telephoned Principal Wadley to let him know that the team member would not be playing volleyball because she was uncomfortable playing on the team knowing that Ms. Weaver is gay. On May 22nd, Principal Wadley discussed Ms. Weaver's sexual orientation with defendant Larry Kimball. Even the School Advisory Council wanted to discuss Ms. Weaver's sexual orientation.

In response to these reports, and after meeting again with the team member's family on July 14, 1997, defendants Mosher and Kimball discussed taking some action against Ms. Weaver because they felt Ms. Weaver's comments about her sexual orientation were in "violation of district policy." Several days later, on July 21, 1997, Ms. Weaver met with Principal Wadley, who informed her that she would not be assigned to coach volleyball for the 1997–98 school year. This discussion was memorialized in a letter to Ms. Weaver dated the same day but sent subsequently. The following day, Ms. Weaver was called to a meeting at the School District office and presented a letter, printed on the School District letterhead. The letter was drafted by defendant Mosher, signed by him and Larry Kimball, was reviewed by defendant Dennis Poulsen, delivered to Ms. Weaver, and placed in her personnel file. On August 8, 1997, a similar letter was issued to Gary Weaver. This letter was delivered to Mr. Weaver and placed in his personnel file.

Despite mounting evidence that gay males and lesbians suffer from employment discrimination and, as recent events in Wyoming [the brutal murder of gay college student Matthew Shepard] remind us, other more life-threatening expressions of bias, courts, including the Supreme Court, have not yet recognized a person's sexual orientation as a status that deserves heightened protection. The deep-seated prejudice on the part of some persons against the gay and lesbian community can be summed up in a single quote from ardent anti-gay activist and former entertainer Anita Bryant: "I'd rather my child be dead than be a homosexual." See Millie Ball, "I'd Rather My Child Be Dead than Homo," *The Times-Picayune,* June 19, 1977, at 3 (quoting Ms. Bryant). To date, Congress has expressly prohibited employment discrimination on the basis of race, religion, national origin, gender, age, and disability, but not sexual orientation. As of this year, eleven states and the District of Columbia offer statutory protection against discrimination on the basis of sexual orientation; thirty-nine states, including Utah, do not.

Nevertheless, the Fourteenth Amendment of the United States Constitution entitles all persons to equal protection under the law. It appears that the plain language of the Fourteenth Amendment's Equal Protection Clause prohibits a state government or agency from engaging in intentional discrimination—even on the basis of sexual orientation—absent some rational basis for so doing.

The Supreme Court has recognized that an "irrational prejudice" cannot provide the rational basis to support a state action against an equal protection challenge. "A bare desire to harm a politically unpopular group" is not a legitimate state interest. Indeed, mere negative attitudes, or fear, unsubstantiated by factors which are properly cognizable in [the circumstances], are not permissible bases for differential treatment by the government.

Supreme Court precedent has recognized that when state action reflects an animus directed at a defined minority, it cannot be supported under the Equal Protection Clause. More recently, in *Romer v. Evans,* 517 U.S. 620 (1996), the Court was called upon to examine whether an amendment to Colorado's state constitution, prohibiting any legislation or judicial action designed to protect the status of a person based on sexual orientation violated the Fourteenth Amendment. It had no trouble finding that it did. In *Romer,* the Court noted that under the ordinary deferential equal protection standard—that is, rational basis—the Court would "insist on knowing the relation between the classification adopted and the object to be obtained." It is this search for a "link" between classification and objective, noted the Court, that "gives substance to the Equal Protection Clause." In *Romer,* such a "link" was noticeably absent. Noting that the "inevitable inference" that arises from a law of this sort is that it is "born of animosity toward the class of persons affected," the Court described the amendment as "a status-based enactment divorced from any factual context from which we could discern a relationship to legitimate state interests."

The question then is whether bias concerning Ms. Weaver's sexual orientation furnishes a rational basis for the defendants' decision not to assign her as volleyball coach. The "negative reaction" some members of the community may have to homosexuals is not a proper basis for discriminating against them. So reasoned the Supreme Court in the context of race. See, e.g., *Brown v. Board of Education,* 347 U.S. 483 (1954) (declaring that racial school segregation is unconstitutional despite the widespread acceptance of the practice in the community and in the country). If the community's perception is based on nothing more than unsupported assumptions, outdated stereotypes, and animosity, it is necessarily irrational and under *Romer* and other Supreme Court precedent, it provides no legitimate support for the School District's decisions.

The record now before the court contains no job-related justification for not assigning Ms. Weaver as volleyball coach. Nor have the defendants demonstrated how Ms. Weaver's sexual orientation bears any rational relationship to her competency as teacher or coach, or her job performance as coach—a position she has held for many years with distinction. As mentioned earlier, it is undisputed that she was an excellent coach and apparently, up until the time her sexual orientation was revealed, the likely candidate for the position. Principal Wadley's decision not to assign Ms. Weaver (a decision reached after consulting with the other defendants) was based solely on her sexual orientation. Absent some rational relationship to job performance, a decision not to assign Ms. Weaver as coach because of her sexual orientation runs afoul of the Fourteenth Amendment's equal protection guarantee.

Although the Constitution cannot control prejudices, neither this court nor any other court should, directly or indirectly, legitimize them. The private antipathy of some members of a community cannot validate state discrimination. Because a community's animus towards homosexuals can never serve as a legitimate basis for state action, the defendants' actions based on that animus violate the Equal Protection Clause. Because this perceived negative reaction arose solely from Ms. Weaver's sexual orientation, and not from her abilities as coach, it does not furnish a rational job-related basis for the defendants' decision. Therefore, Ms. Weaver's motion for summary judgment is granted as to this claim.

In Ms. Weaver's second equal protection claim, she asserts that the defendants violated her rights to equal protection by imposing a viewpoint and content-based restriction on her speech. She argues that she was prohibited from discussing her sexual orientation only because she would have discussed her homosexuality, and points out that other teachers were free to discuss their heterosexual orientations.

Ms. Weaver was threatened with disciplinary action for discussing her intimate associations and sexual orientation. At the same time, no other teacher in the School District was prohibited from discussing these topics. Indeed, as the School District conceded at the hearing, no similar restriction was placed on heterosexual teachers at all. Clearly then, the School District wanted to silence Ms. Weaver's speech because of its expected pro-homosexual viewpoint. Such viewpoint-based restriction is constitutionally impermissible.

Simple as it may sound, as a matter of fairness and evenhandedness, homosexuals should not be sanctioned or restricted for speech that heterosexuals are not likewise sanctioned or restricted for. Because the School District has not restricted other teachers in speaking out on their sexual orientation, the School District has not only violated the First Amendment, but also the Fourteenth Amendment's Equal Protection Clause. In such an instance, when an equal protection claim is based on a person's exercise of a fundamental constitutional right, the proper standard of review is strict scrutiny—that is, is the restriction supported by a compelling state interest. Because the Court has concluded that the School District's actions cannot be supported on any rational basis, the District's actions obviously fail the strict scrutiny test. Ms. Weaver is granted summary judgment on this claim as well.

For the foregoing reasons, it is ordered that plaintiff's motion for summary judgment is GRANTED and defendants' motion is DENIED; that the School District shall remove the letters from plaintiff's personnel file; the School District is directed to offer the plaintiff the Spanish Fork High School girls' volleyball coaching position for the 1999–2000 school year; and the School District pay damages to the plaintiff in the sum of $1,500.

Case Questions

1. What would you have done if you had been the school administrator receiving calls in this situation?

2. Do you think the school was correct in ignoring the teacher's record?

3. Does it make a difference that this matter did not arise at the teacher's instigation but in response to a question from a student? Explain.

Macy v. Holder, *Appeal No. 0120120821 Agency No. ATF-2011-00751 (April 20, 2012)*

A male applied for a position for which he was highly qualified. He was virtually told he had the job. He informed the employer he was transitioning to female. The applicant was then informed that the position was no longer available. Believing he was told this only because the prospective employer now knew the applicant was transitioning, the applicant filed a claim alleging discrimination on the basis of gender identity as a violation of Title VII. This is the EEOC decision determining that gender identity was, in fact, actionable under Title VII as a form of gender discrimination. The case is a bit longer than usual because we believe it is important for you to see the analysis of the agency in making such a historic decision to reverse decades of precedent that opened up Title VII to an entirely new class of claimants.

***

On December 9, 2011, Complainant filed an appeal concerning her equal employment opportunity (EEO) complaint alleging employment discrimination in violation of Title VII of the Civil Rights Act of 1964 (Title VII). For the following reasons, the Commission finds that the Complainant's complaint of discrimination based on gender identity, change of sex, and/or transgender status is cognizable under Title VII and remands the complaint to the Agency for further processing.

Complainant, a transgender woman, was a police detective in Phoenix, Arizona. In December 2010 she decided to relocate to San Francisco for family reasons. According to her formal complaint, Complainant was still known as a male at that time, having not yet made the transition to being a female. Complainant's supervisor in Phoenix told her that the Bureau of Alcohol, Tobacco, Firearms and Explosives (Agency) had a position open at its Walnut Creek crime laboratory for which the Complainant was qualified. Complainant is trained and certified as a National Integrated Ballistic Information Network (NIBIN) operator and a BrassTrax ballistics investigator. Complainant discussed the position with the Director of the Walnut Creek lab by telephone, in either December 2010 or January 2011, while still presenting as a man. According to Complainant, the telephone conversation covered her experience, credentials, salary and benefits. Complainant further asserts that, following the conversation, the Director told her she would be able to have the position assuming no problems arose during her background check. The Director also told her that the position would be filled as a civilian contractor through an outside company. Complainant states that she talked again with the Director in January 2011 and asked that he check on the status of the position. According to Complainant in her formal complaint, the Director did so and reasserted that the job was hers pending completion of the background check. Complainant asserts, as evidence of her impending hire, that Aspen of DC ("Aspen"), the contractor responsible for filling the position, contacted her to begin the necessary paperwork and that an investigator from the Agency was assigned to do her background check.

On March 29, 2011, Complainant informed Aspen via email that she was in the process of transitioning from male to female and she requested that Aspen inform the Director of the Walnut Creek lab of this change. According to Complainant, on April 3, 2011, Aspen informed Complainant that the Agency had been informed of her change in name and gender. Five days later, on April 8, 2011, Complainant received an email from the contractor's Director of Operations stating that, due to federal budget reductions, the position at Walnut Creek was no longer available. According to Complainant, she was concerned about this quick change in events and on May 10, 2011, she contacted an agency EEO counselor to discuss her concerns. She states that the counselor told her that the position at Walnut Creek had not been cut but, rather, that someone else had been hired for the position. Complainant further states that the counselor told her that the Agency had decided to take the other individual because that person was farthest along in the background investigation. Complainant claims that this was a pretextual explanation because the background investigation had been proceeding on her as well. Complainant believes she was incorrectly informed that the position had been cut because the Agency did not want to hire her because she is transgender.

The EEO counselor's report indicates that Complainant alleged that she had been discriminated against based on sex, and had specifically described her claim of discrimination as "change in gender (from male to female)."

EEOC's responsibilities under Executive Order 12067 for enforcing all Federal EEO laws and leading the Federal government's efforts to eradicate workplace discrimination, require, among other things, that EEOC ensure that uniform standards be implemented defining the nature of employment discrimination under the statutes we enforce. To that end, the Commission hereby clarifies that claims of discrimination based on transgender status, also referred to as claims of discrimination based on gender identity, are cognizable under Title VII's sex discrimination prohibition, and may therefore be processed under Part 1614 of EEOC's federal sector EEO complaints process.

Title VII states that, except as otherwise specifically provided, "[a]ll personnel actions affecting [federal] employees or applicants for employment . . . shall be made free from any discrimination based on . . .sex . . . ." it is unlawful for a covered employer to "fail or refuse to hire or to discharge any individual, or otherwise to discriminate with respect to his compensation, terms, conditions, or privileges of employment," or to "limit, segregate, or classify his employees or applicants for employment in any way which would deprive or tend to deprive any individual of employment opportunities or otherwise adversely affect his status as an employee, because of such individual's . . . sex"). As used in Title VII, the term "sex" "encompasses both sex—that is, the biological differences between men and women—and gender." See *Schwenk v. Hartford,* 204 F.3d 1187, 1202 (9th Cir. 2000); see also *Smith v. City of Salem,* 378 F.3d 566, 572 (6th Cir. 2004) ("The Supreme Court made clear that in the context of Title VII, discrimination because of 'sex' includes gender discrimination."). As the Eleventh Circuit noted in *Glenn v. Brumby,* 663 F.3d 1312, 1316 (11th Cir. 2011), six members of the Supreme Court in *Price Waterhouse* agreed that Title VII barred "not just discrimination because of biological sex, but also gender stereotyping—failing to act and appear according to expectations defined by gender." As such, the terms "gender" and "sex" are often used interchangeably to describe the discrimination prohibited by Title VII. See, e.g., *Price Waterhouse v. Hopkins,* 490 U.S. 228, 239 (1989) ("Congress' intent to forbid employers to take gender into account in making employment decisions appears on the face of the statute.").

That Title VII's prohibition on sex discrimination proscribes gender discrimination, and not just discrimination on the basis of biological sex, is important. If Title VII proscribed only discrimination on the basis of biological sex, the only prohibited gender-based disparate treatment would be when an employer prefers a man over a woman, or vice versa. But the statute's protections sweep far broader than that, in part because the term "gender" encompasses not only a person's biological sex but also the cultural and social aspects associated with masculinity and femininity.

In *Price Waterhouse,* the employer refused to make a female senior manager, Hopkins, a partner at least in part because she did not act as some of the partners thought a woman should act. She was informed, for example, that to improve her chances for partnership she should "walk more femininely, talk more femininely, dress more femininely, wear make-up, have her hair styled, and wear

jewelry." The Court concluded that discrimination for failing to conform with gender-based expectations violates Title VII, holding that "[i]n the specific context of sex stereotyping, an employer who acts on the basis of a belief that a woman cannot be aggressive, or that she must not be, has acted on the basis of gender."

Although the partners at Price Waterhouse discriminated against Ms. Hopkins for failing to conform to stereotypical gender norms, gender discrimination occurs any time an employer treats an employee differently for failing to conform to any gender-based expectations or norms. "What matters, for purposes of . . . the *Price Waterhouse* analysis, is that in the mind of the perpetrator the discrimination is related to the sex of the victim." *Schwenk;* see also *Price Waterhouse,* (noting the illegitimacy of allowing "sex-linked evaluations to play a part in the [employer's] decision-making process").

When an employer discriminates against someone because the person is transgender, the employer has engaged in disparate treatment "related to the sex of the victim." See *Schwenk.* This is true regardless of whether an employer discriminates against an employee because the individual has expressed his or her gender in a non-stereotypical fashion, because the employer is uncomfortable with the fact that the person has transitioned or is in the process of transitioning from one gender to another, or because the employer simply does not like that the person is identifying as a transgender person. In each of these circumstances, the employer is making a gender-based evaluation, thus violating the Supreme Court's admonition that "an employer may not take gender into account in making an employment decision." *Price Waterhouse.*

Since *Price Waterhouse,* courts have widely recognized the availability of the sex stereotyping theory as a valid method of establishing discrimination "on the basis of sex" in many scenarios involving individuals who act or appear in gender-nonconforming ways. And since *Price Waterhouse,* courts also have widely recognized the availability of the sex stereotyping theory as a valid method of establishing discrimination "on the basis of sex" in scenarios involving transgender individuals.

For example, in *Schwenk v. Hartford,* a prison guard had sexually assaulted a pre-operative male-to-female transgender prisoner, and the prisoner sued, alleging that the guard had violated the Gender Motivated Violence Act (GMVA), 42 U.S.C. § 13981. The U.S. Court of Appeals for the Ninth Circuit found that the guard had known that the prisoner "considered herself a transsexual and that she planned to seek sex reassignment surgery in the future." According to the court, the guard had targeted the transgender prisoner "only after he discovered that she considered herself female[,]" and the guard was "motivated, at least in part, by [her] gender"—that is, "by her assumption of a feminine rather than a typically masculine appearance or demeanor." On these facts, the Ninth Circuit readily concluded that the guard's attack constituted discrimination because of gender within the meaning of both the GMVA and Title VII.

The court relied on *Price Waterhouse,* reasoning that it stood for the proposition that discrimination based on sex includes discrimination based on a failure "to conform to socially-constructed gender expectations." Accordingly, the Ninth Circuit concluded, discrimination against transgender females—i.e., "as anatomical males whose outward behavior and inward identity [do] not meet social definitions of masculinity"—is actionable discrimination "because of sex."

Similarly, in *Smith v. City of Salem,* the plaintiff was "biologically and by birth male." However, Smith was diagnosed with Gender Identity Disorder (GID), and began to present at work as a female (in accordance with medical protocols for treatment of GID). Smith's co-workers began commenting that her appearance and mannerisms were "not masculine enough." Smith's employer later subjected her to numerous psychological evaluations, and ultimately suspended her. Smith filed suit under Title VII alleging that her employer had discriminated against her because of sex, "both because of [her] gender non-conforming conduct and, more generally, because of [her] identification as a transsexual."

The district court rejected Smith's efforts to prove her case using a sex-stereotyping theory, concluding that it was really an attempt to challenge discrimination based on "transsexuality." The U.S. Court of Appeals for the Sixth Circuit reversed, stating that the district court's conclusion: "cannot be reconciled with *Price Waterhouse,* which does not make Title VII protection against sex stereotyping conditional or provide any reason to exclude Title VII coverage for non sex-stereotypical behavior simply because the person is a transsexual. As such, discrimination against a plaintiff who is a transsexual—and therefore fails to act and/or identify with his or her gender—is no different from the discrimination directed against [the plaintiff] in *Price Waterhouse* who, in sex-stereotypical terms, did not act like a woman. Sex stereotyping based on a person's gender non-conforming behavior is impermissible discrimination, irrespective of the cause of that behavior; a label, such as "transsexual" is not fatal

to a sex discrimination claim where the victim has suffered discrimination because of his or her gender non-conformity. Accordingly, we hold that Smith has stated a claim for relief pursuant to Title VII's prohibition of sex discrimination.

Finally, as the Eleventh Circuit suggested in *Glenn v. Brumby,* consideration of gender stereotypes will inherently be part of what drives discrimination against a transgendered individual. In that case, the employer testified at his deposition that it had fired Vandiver Elizabeth Glenn, a transgender woman, because he considered it "inappropriate" for her to appear at work dressed as a woman and that he found it "unsettling" and "unnatural" that she would appear wearing women's clothing. The firing supervisor further testified that his decision to dismiss Glenn was based on his perception of Glenn as "a man dressed as a woman and made up as a woman," and admitted that his decision to fire her was based on "the sheer fact of the transition." According to the Eleventh Circuit, this testimony "provides ample direct evidence" to support the conclusion that the employer acted on the basis of the plaintiff's gender non-conformity and therefore granted summary judgment to her.

In setting forth its legal reasoning, the Eleventh Circuit explained: A person is defined as transgender precisely because of the perception that his or her behavior transgresses gender stereotypes. "[T]he very acts that define transgender people as transgender are those that contradict stereotypes of gender-appropriate appearance and behavior."

There is thus a congruence between discriminating against transgender and transsexual individuals and discrimination on the basis of gender-based behavioral norms. Accordingly, discrimination against a transgender individual because of her gender-nonconformity is sex discrimination, whether it's described as being on the basis of sex or gender. *Glenn v. Brumby.*

There has likewise been a steady stream of district court decisions recognizing that discrimination against transgender individuals on the basis of sex stereotyping constitutes discrimination because of sex. Most notably, in *Schroer v. Billington,* the Library of Congress rescinded an offer of employment it had extended to a transgender job applicant after the applicant informed the Library's hiring officials that she intended to undergo a gender transition. The U.S. District Court for the District of Columbia entered judgment in favor of the plaintiff on her Title VII sex discrimination claim. According to the district court, it did not matter "for purposes of Title VII liability whether the Library withdrew its offer of employment because it perceived Schroer to be an insufficiently masculine man, an insufficiently feminine woman, or an inherently gender-nonconforming transsexual." In any case, Schroer was "entitled to judgment based on a *Price-Waterhouse*-type claim for sex stereotyping . . . ." To be sure, the members of Congress that enacted Title VII in 1964 and amended it in 1972 were likely not considering the problems of discrimination that were faced by transgender individuals. But as the Supreme Court recognized in *Oncale v. Sundowner Offshore Services, Inc.*: [S]tatutory prohibitions often go beyond the principal evil [they were passed to combat] to cover reasonably comparable evils, and it is ultimately the provisions of our laws rather than the principal concerns of our legislators by which we are governed. Title VII prohibits "discriminat[ion] . . . because of . . . sex" in . . . employment. [This] . . . must extend to [sex-based discrimination] of any kind that meets the statutory requirements. See also Newport News, 462 U.S. at 679–81 (rejecting the argument that discrimination against men does not violate Title VII despite the fact that discrimination against women was plainly the principal problem that Title VII's prohibition of sex discrimination was enacted to combat).

Although most courts have found protection for transgender people under Title VII under a theory of gender stereotyping, evidence of gender stereotyping is simply one means of proving sex discrimination. Title VII prohibits discrimination based on sex whether motivated by hostility, by a desire to protect people of a certain gender, by assumptions that disadvantage men, by gender stereotypes, or by the desire to accommodate other people's prejudices or discomfort.

While evidence that an employer has acted based on stereotypes about how men or women should act is certainly one means of demonstrating disparate treatment based on sex, "sex stereotyping" is not itself an independent cause of action. As the *Price Waterhouse* Court noted, while "stereotyped remarks can certainly be evidence that gender played a part" in an adverse employment action, the central question is always whether the "employer actually relied on [the employee's] gender in making its decision."

Thus, a transgender person who has experienced discrimination based on his or her gender identity may establish a prima facie case of sex discrimination through any number of different formulations. These different formulations are not, however, different claims of discrimination that can be separated out and investigated within different systems. Rather, they are simply different ways of describing sex discrimination.

For example, Complainant could establish a case of sex discrimination under a theory of gender stereotyping by showing that she did not get the job as an NIBIN ballistics technician at Walnut Creek because the employer believed that biological men should consistently present as men and wear male clothing. Alternatively, if Complainant can prove that the reason that she did not get the job at Walnut Creek is that the Director was willing to hire her when he thought she was a man, but was not willing to hire her once he found out that she was now a woman, she will have proven that the Director discriminated on the basis of sex. Under this theory, there would actually be no need, for purposes of establishing coverage under Title VII, for Complainant to compile any evidence that the Director was engaging in gender stereotyping.

In this respect, gender is no different from religion. Assume that an employee considers herself Christian and identifies as such. But assume that an employer finds out that the employee's parents are Muslim, believes that the employee should therefore be Muslim, and terminates the employee on that basis. No one would doubt that such an employer discriminated on the basis of religion. There would be no need for the employee who experienced the adverse employment action to demonstrate that the employer acted on the basis of some religious stereotype–although, clearly, discomfort with the choice made by the employee with regard to religion would presumably be at the root of the employer's actions. But for purposes of establishing a prima facie case that Title VII has been violated, the employee simply must demonstrate that the employer impermissibly used religion in making its employment decision.

The District Court in *Schroer* provided reasoning along similar lines: Imagine that an employee is fired because she converts from Christianity to Judaism. Imagine too that her employer testifies that he harbors no bias toward either Christians or Jews but only 'converts.' That would be a clear case of discrimination 'because of religion.' No court would take seriously the notion that 'converts' are not covered by the statute. Discrimination "because of religion" easily encompasses discrimination because of a change of religion.

Applying Title VII in this manner does not create a new "class" of people covered under Title VII–for example, the "class" of people who have converted from Islam to Christianity or from Christianity to Judaism. Rather, it would simply be the result of applying the plain language of a statute prohibiting discrimination on the basis of religion to practical situations in which such characteristics are unlawfully taken into account. See *Brumby,* (noting that "all persons, whether transgender or not" are protected from discrimination and "[a]n individual cannot be punished because of his or her perceived gender non-conformity").

Thus, we conclude that intentional discrimination against a transgender individual because that person is transgender is, by definition, discrimination "based on . . . sex," and such discrimination therefore violates Title VII.

Accordingly, the Agency's final decision declining to process Complainant's entire complaint within the Part 1614 EEO complaints process is REVERSED. The complaint is hereby REMANDED to the Agency for further processing in accordance with this decision.

Case Questions

1. This was a very important decision by the EEOC because it changed its previous position. Do you understand the agency's analysis of why it held as it did in the decision?

2. Do you understand why the prospective employer may have been concerned and made the decision it did? Explain.

3. Given the evolution of the law as set forth by the EEOC, do you agree with the EEOC's conclusion?

Hively v. Ivy Tech Community College of Indiana,
853 F. 3d 339 (7th Cir. April 4, 2017)

A female professor who taught at the college part-time was passed up for a full-time position several times because she is a lesbian. In the only federal circuit decision to interpret Title VII's protection against gender discrimination *en banc* as including discrimination on the basis of sexual orientation, the court sitting with all of its members (en banc) held for the employee. The court noted that the U.S. Supreme Court had not yet decided the issue, but it used the Court's line of reasoning in, among others, those cases permitting same-gender sexual harassment and same-sex marriage as the basis for its conclusion.

WOOD, C.J.

***

Title VII of the Civil Rights Act of 1964 makes it unlawful for employers subject to the Act to discriminate on the basis of a person's "race, color, religion, sex, or national origin . . . ." 42 U.S.C. § 2000e-2(a). For many years, the courts of appeals of this country understood the prohibition against sex discrimination to exclude discrimination on the basis of a person's sexual orientation. The Supreme Court, however, has never spoken to that question. In this case, we have been asked to take a fresh look at our position in light of developments at the Supreme Court extending over two decades. We have done so, and we conclude today that discrimination on the basis of sexual orientation is a form of sex discrimination. We therefore reverse the district court's judgment dismissing Kimberly Hively's suit against Ivy Tech Community College and remand for further proceedings.

Hively is openly lesbian. She began teaching as a part-time, adjunct professor at Ivy Tech Community College's South Bend campus in 2000. Hoping to improve her lot, she applied for at least six full-time positions between 2009 and 2014. These efforts were unsuccessful; worse yet, in July 2014 her part-time contract was not renewed. Believing that Ivy Tech was spurning her because of her sexual orientation, she filed a charge with the Equal Employment Opportunity Commission on December 13, 2013. It was short and to the point:

I have applied for several positions at IVY TECH, fulltime, in the last 5 years. I believe I am being blocked from fulltime employment without just cause. I believe I am being discriminated against based on my sexual orientation. I believe I have been discriminated against and that my rights under Title VII of the Civil Rights Act of 1964 were violated.

In light of the importance of the issue, and recognizing the power of the full court to overrule earlier decisions and to bring our law into conformity with the Supreme Court's teachings, a majority of the judges in regular active service voted to rehear this case en banc.

The question before us is not whether this court can, or should, "amend" Title VII to add a new protected category to the familiar list of "race, color, religion, sex, or national origin." Obviously that lies beyond our power. We must decide instead what it means to discriminate on the basis of sex, and in particular, whether actions taken on the basis of sexual orientation are a subset of actions taken on the basis of sex. This is a pure question of statutory interpretation and thus well within the judiciary's competence.

Our interpretive task is guided by the Supreme Court's approach in the closely related case of *Oncale v. Sundowner Offshore Servs., Inc.,* 523 U.S. 75 (1998), where it had this to say as it addressed the question whether Title VII covers sexual harassment inflicted by a man on a male victim:

> We see no justification in the statutory language or our precedents for a categorical rule excluding same-sex harassment claims from the coverage of Title VII. As some courts have observed, male-on-male sexual harassment in the workplace was assuredly not the principal evil Congress was concerned with when it enacted Title VII. But statutory prohibitions often go beyond the principal evil to cover reasonably comparable evils, and it is ultimately the provisions of our laws rather than the principal concerns of our legislators by which we are governed. Title VII prohibits "discriminat[ion] . . . because of . . . sex" in the "terms" or "conditions" of employment. Our holding that this includes sexual harassment must extend to sexual harassment of any kind that meets the statutory require ments.

The Court could not have been clearer: the fact that the enacting Congress may not have anticipated a particular application of the law cannot stand in the way of the provisions of the law that are on the books.

It is therefore neither here nor there that the Congress that enacted the Civil Rights Act in 1964 and chose

to include sex as a prohibited basis for employment discrimination (no matter why it did so) may not have realized or understood the full scope of the words it chose. Indeed, in the years since 1964, Title VII has been understood to cover far more than the simple decision of an employer not to hire a woman for Job A, or a man for Job B. The Supreme Court has held that the prohibition against sex discrimination reaches sexual harassment in the workplace, including same-sex workplace harassment, see *On cale;* it reaches discrimination based on actuarial assumptions about a person's longevity, and it reaches discrimination based on a person's failure to conform to a certain set of gender stereotypes, see *Price Waterhouse v. Hopkins,* 490 U.S. 228 (1989). It is quite possible that these interpretations may also have surprised some who served in the 88th Congress. Nevertheless, experience with the law has led the Supreme Court to recognize that each of these examples is a covered form of sex discrimination.

Any discomfort, disapproval, or job decision based on the fact that the complainant—woman or man— dresses differently, speaks differently, or dates or marries a same-sex partner, is a reaction purely and simply based on sex. That means that it falls within Title VII's prohibition against sex discrimination, if it affects employment in one of the specified ways.

Today's decision must be understood against the backdrop of the Supreme Court's decisions, not only in the field of employment discrimination, but also in the area of broader discrimination on the basis of sexual orientation. We already have discussed the employment cases, especially *Hopkins* and *Oncale.* The latter line of cases began with *Romer v. Evans,* 517 U.S. 620 (1996), in which the Court held that a provision of the Colorado Constitution forbidding any organ of government in the state from taking action designed to protect "homosexual, lesbian, or bisexual" persons, violated the federal Equal Protection Clause. *Romer* was followed by *Lawrence v. Texas,* 539 U.S. 558 (2003), in which the Court found that a Texas statute criminalizing homosexual intimacy between consenting adults violated the liberty provision of the Due Process Clause. Next came *United States v. Windsor,* 133 S.Ct. 2675 (2013), which addressed the constitutionality of the part of the Defense of Marriage Act (DOMA) that excluded a same-sex partner from the definition of "spouse" in other federal statutes. The Court held that this part of DOMA "violate[d] basic due process and equal protection principles applicable to the Federal Government."

Finally, the Court's decision in *Obergefell v. Hodges,* 135 S. Ct. 2584 (2015), held that the right to marry is a fundamental liberty right, protected by the Due Process and Equal Protection Clauses of the Fourteenth Amendment. The Court wrote that "[i]t is now clear that the challenged laws burden the liberty of same-sex couples, and it must be further acknowledged that they abridge central precepts of equality." *Id.*

It would require considerable calisthenics to remove the "sex" from "sexual orientation." EEOC concluded that such an effort cannot be reconciled with the straightforward language of Title VII. Many district courts have come to the same conclusion. Many other courts have found that gender-identity claims are cognizable under Title VII.

This is not to say that authority to the contrary does not exist. As we acknowledged at the outset of this opinion, it does. But this court sits en banc to consider what the correct rule of law is now in light of the Supreme Court's authoritative interpretations, not what someone thought it meant one, ten, or twenty years ago. The logic of the Supreme Court's decisions, as well as the common-sense reality that it is actually impossible to discriminate on the basis of sexual orientation without discriminating on the basis of sex, persuade us that the time has come to overrule our previous cases that have endeavored to find and observe that line. We hold only that a person who alleges that she experienced employment discrimination on the basis of her sexual orientation has put forth a case of sex discrimination for Title VII purposes. It was therefore wrong to dismiss Hively's complaint for failure to state a claim. The judgment of the district court is REVERSED and the case is REMANDED for further proceedings.

Case Questions

1. Do you understand why the college would not hire Kimberly Hively? Explain.

2. Do you understand the court's reasoning for the decision?

3. What would you have done had you been the college administrator who was faced with this decision? Explain.

Nichols v. Azteca Restaurant Enterprises, Inc.,
256 F.3d 864 (9th Cir. 2001)

Employee brought suit under Title VII for gender harassment directed toward him at work that the employer did little to stop. The court agreed with the employee that this constituted a violation of Title VII even though the employee was gay.

Gould, J.

***

Throughout his tenure at Azteca, Sanchez was subjected to a relentless campaign of insults, name-calling, and vulgarities. Male co-workers and a supervisor repeatedly referred to Sanchez in Spanish and English as "she" and "her." Male co-workers mocked Sanchez for walking and carrying his serving tray "like a woman," and taunted him in Spanish and English as, among other things, a "faggot" and a "f**king female whore." The remarks were not stray or isolated. Rather, the abuse occurred at least once a week and often several times a day.

This conduct violated company policy. Since 1989, Azteca has expressly prohibited sexual harassment and retaliation and has directed its employees to bring complaints regarding such conduct directly to the attention of the corporate office. Upon receipt of a complaint,

Azteca's policy is to conduct a thorough investigation, the results of which are reviewed by the company's EEO Board, which is then responsible for implementing an appropriate remedy.

In addition to this policy, Azteca has a bilingual (English and Spanish) training program about sexual harassment. This training, which all employees attend when hired, and annually thereafter, defines sexual harassment and instructs employees how to report complaints.

Under Title VII, it is unlawful for an employer "to discriminate against any individual with respect to his compensation, terms, conditions, or privileges of employment, because of . . . sex." It is by now clear that sexual harassment in the form of a hostile work environment constitutes sex discrimination.

To prevail on his hostile environment claim, Sanchez was required to establish a "pattern of ongoing and persistent harassment severe enough to alter the conditions of employment." To satisfy this requirement, Sanchez needed to prove that his workplace was "both objectively and subjectively offensive, one that a reasonable person would find hostile or abusive, and one that the victim in fact did perceive to be so." In addition, Sanchez was required to prove that any harassment took place "because of sex." The district court ruled against Sanchez on each of these elements, concluding that: (1) Sanchez's workplace was not objectively hostile; (2) Sanchez did not perceive his workplace to be hostile; and (3) the alleged conduct did not occur because of sex. We disagree with each of these conclusions and, where applicable, the clearly erroneous findings upon which they are based.

Having reviewed the record, we hold that a reasonable man would have found the sustained campaign of taunts, directed at Sanchez and designed to humiliate and anger him, sufficiently severe and pervasive to alter the terms and conditions of his employment. Indeed, even Azteca does not contend otherwise on appeal.

Assuming that a reasonable person would find a workplace hostile, if the victim "does not subjectively perceive the environment to be abusive, the conduct has not actually altered the conditions of the victim's employment, and there is no Title VII violation." We must determine whether Sanchez, by his conduct, indicated that the alleged harassment was "unwelcome."

The district court concluded that the frequent verbal abuse was not unwelcome. Although the court made no

factual finding directly on point, its determination may have been influenced by its findings that: (1) Sanchez made no complaint of sexual harassment to Serna, or anyone else from the corporate office; (2) Sanchez never sought mental health treatment; and (3) Sanchez engaged in horseplay with his male co-workers. We see the evidence another way.

The first of these findings by the district court, which forms the crux of Azteca's appeal, is clearly erroneous. It is undisputed that in May 1995 Sanchez told Serna, in considerable detail, about the fact and nature of the verbal abuse. Sanchez also complained to the Southcenter general manager and an assistant manager, though in less detail. That Sanchez complained about the frequent, degrading verbal abuse supports our conclusion that the conduct was unwelcome, as does Sanchez's unrebutted testimony to that effect. We hold that Sanchez perceived his workplace to be hostile.

Nor do the other potentially relevant findings noted above—that Sanchez never sought mental health treatment, and that he engaged in horseplay with some of his harassers—warrant a different result. As to the first, the scope of Title VII is not limited to conduct that affects a victim's psychological well-being. As to the second, the fact that not all of Sanchez's interactions with his harassers were hostile does not mean that none of them was. As any sensible person would, Sanchez drew a distinction between conduct he perceived to be objectionable, and conduct that was not. He viewed horseplay as "male bonding" and excluded it from his hostile environment claim; he viewed relentless verbal affronts as sexual harassment, and sought legal recourse for that conduct. And, in complaining to Serna about the verbal abuse, he demonstrated a subjective belief that he was being harassed.

Sexual harassment is actionable under Title VII to the extent it occurs "because of" the employee's gender. Sanchez asserts that the verbal abuse at issue was based upon the perception that he is effeminate and, therefore, occurred because of gender. In short, Sanchez contends that he was harassed because he failed to conform to a male stereotype.

At its essence, the systematic abuse directed at Sanchez reflected a belief that Sanchez did not act as a man should act. Sanchez was attacked for walking and carrying his tray "like a woman"—i.e., for having feminine mannerisms. Sanchez was derided for not having sexual intercourse with a waitress who was his friend. Sanchez's male co-workers and one of his supervisors repeatedly reminded Sanchez that he did not conform to their gender-based stereotypes, referring to him as "she" and "her." And, the most vulgar name-calling directed at Sanchez was cast in female terms. We conclude that this verbal abuse was closely linked to gender.

We hold that the verbal abuse at issue occurred because of gender. Because we hold that Sanchez has established each element of his hostile environment claim, we further hold that the conduct of Sanchez's co-workers and supervisor constituted actionable harassment under Title VII. AFFIRMED IN PART, REVERSED IN PART, and REMANDED.

Case Questions

1. Title VII does not prohibit discrimination on the basis of sexual orientation. How would you characterize this case? Do you see the discrimination as being based on sexual orientation and thus not protected by Title VII or as based on gender and thus protected by Title VII?

2. Why do you think the managers did not address the employee's complaints?

3. What would you have done differently here if you had been Sanchez's manager?

Jane Doe v. Boeing Company,
121 Wash.2d 8 (1993)

A biological male employee who was planning to have gender reassignment surgery sued his employer, Boeing, for employment discrimination, alleging an unaccommodated disability. He was discharged by Boeing for wearing "excessively" feminine attire (pink pearls) in violation of company directives. The Washington Supreme Court found that Boeing had done enough to reasonably accommodate the employee, even though it had no duty to do so under Washington's law against discrimination.

Guy, J.

***

Jane Doe was hired as a Boeing engineer in 1978. At the time of hire, Doe was a biological male and presented herself as such on her application for employment. In 1984, after years of struggling with her sexual identity, Doe concluded that she was a transsexual. Transsexualism is also known in the psychiatric and medical communities as gender dysphoria.

Doe's treating physician confirmed Doe's self-assessment and diagnosed Doe as gender dysphoric. In April 1984, Doe began hormone treatments, as prescribed by Dr. Smith, as well as electrolysis treatments. In December 1984, Doe legally changed her masculine name to a feminine name.

In March 1985, Doe informed her supervisors, management and co-workers at Boeing of her transsexualism and of her intent to have gender reassignment surgery. Doe informed Boeing of her belief that in order to qualify for gender reassignment surgery, she would have to live full time, for 1 year, in the social role of a female. Doe

based her belief on discussions with her treating psychologist and her physician about a treatment protocol for transsexuals known as the Harry Benjamin International Gender Dysphoria Standards (Benjamin Standards). Benjamin Standard 9 states: "Genital sex reassignment shall be preceded by a period of at least 12 months during which time the patient lived full-time in the social role of the genetically other sex."

Upon being notified of Doe's intentions, Boeing informed Doe that while Doe was an anatomical male, she could not use the women's rest rooms or dress in "feminine" attire. Boeing informed Doe that she could dress as a woman at work and use the women's rest rooms upon completion of her gender reassignment surgery.

While Doe was an anatomical male, Boeing permitted Doe to wear either male clothing or unisex clothing. Unisex clothing included blouses, sweaters, slacks, flat shoes, nylon stockings, earrings, lipstick, foundation, and clear nail polish. Doe was instructed not to wear obviously feminine clothing such as dresses, skirts, or frilly blouses. Boeing applied its unwritten dress policy to all employees, which included eight other transsexuals who had expressed a desire to have gender reassignment surgery while working for Boeing. Both Doe's psychologist and treating physician testified that what Doe was allowed to wear at Boeing was sufficiently feminine for Doe to qualify for gender reassignment surgery.

Between June and late September 1985, Boeing management received approximately a dozen anonymous complaints regarding Doe's attire and use of the women's rest rooms. On October 25, 1985, following the receipt of a complaint about Doe using the women's rest room, Boeing issued Doe a written disciplinary warning. The warning reiterated Boeing's position on acceptable attire and rest room use and stated that Doe's failure to comply with Boeing's directives by November 1, 1985, would result in further corrective action, including termination. During this "grace" period, Doe's compliance with Boeing's "acceptable attire" directive was to be monitored each day by Doe's direct supervisor. Doe was told that her attire would be deemed unacceptable when, in the supervisor's opinion, her dress would be likely to cause a complaint were Doe to use a men's rest room at a Boeing facility. No single article of clothing would be dispositive. Doe's overall appearance was to be assessed.

Doe's transsexualism did not interfere with her ability to perform her job duties as a software engineer at Boeing. There was no measurable decline in either her work group's performance or in Doe's own job performance. There was no testimony to indicate that Boeing's dress restrictions hindered Doe's professional development.

On November 4, 1985, the first day Doe worked after the grace period, Doe wore attire that her supervisor considered acceptable. Doe responded that she was disappointed that her attire was acceptable, and that she would "push it" the next day. By "push it," Doe testified that she meant she would wear more extreme feminine attire. The next day, Doe came to work wearing similar attire, but she included as part of her outfit a strand of pink pearls which she refused to remove. This outfit was similar to one she had been told during the grace period was unacceptable in that the addition of the pink pearls changed Doe's look from unisex to "excessively" feminine. Doe was subsequently terminated from her position at Boeing as a result of her willful violation of Boeing's directives. Doe filed a handicap discrimination action against Boeing pursuant to Washington's Law Against Discrimination (hereafter Act) RCW49.60. The trial court held that

Doe was "temporarily handicapped" under its construction of the law. The Court of Appeals reversed, finding Boeing failed to accommodate Doe. We reverse the Court of Appeals.

This case presents two issues for review. First, is Jane Doe's gender dysphoria a "handicap" under RCW 49.60.180? We hold that Doe's gender dysphoria is not a handicap under the Act. The definition of "handicap" for enforcement purposes in unfair practice cases under RCW 49.60.180, as defined in WAC 162-22-040, requires factual findings of both (1) the presence of an abnormal condition, and (2) employer discrimination against the plaintiff because of that condition. While gender dysphoria is an abnormal condition, we hold that Doe was not "handicapped" by her gender dysphoria because Boeing did not discharge her because of that condition.

Second, did Boeing have to provide Doe's preferred accommodation under RCW 49.60.180? We hold that the scope of an employer's duty to reasonably accommodate an employee's abnormal condition is limited to those steps necessary to enable the employee to perform his or her job. We hold that Boeing's actions met this standard and did not discriminate against Doe by reason of her abnormal condition.

It is uncontested that gender dysphoria is an abnormal, medically cognizable condition with a prescribed course of treatment. Assuming the presence of an abnormal condition, the next inquiry is whether the employer discriminated against the employee because of that condition. Boeing did not discriminate against Doe because of her condition. Boeing discharged Doe because she violated Boeing's directives on acceptable attire, not because she was gender dysphoric. Doe was treated in a respectful way by both her peers and supervisors at Boeing. Doe's supervisor consistently rated her work as satisfactory on her performance evaluations. While complaints were filed with Boeing management about Doe's use of the women's rest room, the record is void of any evidence that Doe suffered harassment because of her use of the rest room or because of her attire.

Inasmuch as Boeing did not discharge Doe based on her abnormal condition but on her refusal to conform with directives on acceptable attire, we must turn our attention to whether Boeing discriminated against Doe by failing to reasonably accommodate her condition of gender dysphoria.

We recognize that employers have an affirmative obligation to reasonably accommodate the sensory, mental, or physical limitations of such employees unless the employer can demonstrate that the accommodation would impose an undue hardship on the conduct of the employer's business. The issue before us is whether Boeing had a duty to accommodate Doe's preferred manner of dress prior to her gender reassignment surgery. We hold that the scope of an employer's duty to accommodate an employee's condition is limited to those steps reasonably necessary to enable the employee to perform his or her job.

Doe contends that Boeing's dress code failed to accommodate her condition and thus was discriminatory. We disagree. The record substantially supports the trial court's findings that Boeing reasonably accommodated Doe in the matter of dress by allowing her to wear unisex clothing at work. Despite this accommodation, Doe determined unilaterally, and without medical confirmation, that she needed to dress as a woman at her place of employment in order to qualify for gender reassignment surgery. We find substantial support for the trial court's finding that Doe had no medical need to dress as a woman at work in order to qualify for her surgery.

[P]laintiff's experts declined to state that any particular degree of feminine dress was required in order for plaintiff to fulfill any presurgical requirements. In fact, the evidence was uncontradicted that the unisex dress permitted by Boeing . . . would not have precluded plaintiff from meeting the Benjamin Standards presurgical requirement of living in the social role of a woman. The trial court's findings are well supported by the testimony of Doe's own treating physician and psychologist, as well as other medical evidence.

Doe argues, however, that the trial court's findings on this point are irrelevant since Boeing did not have the benefit of such medical testimony prior to enforcing its dress policy. We disagree. The trial court found that Boeing's policy on accommodation of transsexuals was developed with input from Boeing's legal, medical, personnel and labor relations departments. The Boeing medical department consulted with outside experts in the field and reviewed the literature on transsexualism. The trial court also held that Boeing has a legitimate business purpose in defining what is acceptable attire and in balancing the needs of its work force as a whole with those of Doe. The record supports the trial court's findings of fact and conclusions of law that Boeing developed and reasonably enforced a dress policy which balanced its legitimate business needs with those of its employees.

Doe further argues that, as a gender dysphoric, her perceived needs should have been accommodated. We disagree. The Act does not require an employer to offer the employee the precise accommodation he or she requests. Her perceived need to dress more completely as a woman did not impact her job performance. Doe's condition had no measurable effect on either Doe's job performance or her work group's performance. That is not to say that Doe did not have emotional turmoil over the changes that were taking place in her life, but that turmoil did not prevent her from performing her work satisfactorily. Based on the record, there was no need for any further action by Boeing to facilitate Doe in the performance of job-related tasks.

Doe also argues that Boeing failed to accommodate her unique condition because its dress policy was uniformly applied.

In determining what is a reasonable accommodation, the evaluation must begin with the job specifications and how those tasks are impacted by the abnormal condition. In the case of trauma or physical deterioration, the answers are generally apparent and the issue becomes one of whether the accommodation is reasonable, not what is the accommodation. In Doe's case, the analysis is not so simple. Doe's job performance was unchanged by reason of her condition. Based on the record, there was no accommodation that Boeing could have provided that would have aided Doe in the performance of her work. How she dressed or appeared had no impact on the physical or mental requirements of her employment responsibilities.

Doe's gender dysphoria did not impede her ability to perform her engineering duties. Therefore, Boeing had no duty to provide any further accommodation to Doe beyond what it provided for all employees. REVERSED.

Case Questions

1. What do you think the real problem was here? If you say that it was Jane trying to push too hard, explore what that really means. How responsible should the employer be for the discomfort of other employees? What about when the discomfort arises from long-held beliefs based on misinformation, which society may have taken for granted until now? Would it be different if the issue was race instead of sexual orientation (that is, employees did not want to deal with employees of other races in the workplace and were uncomfortable doing so)? Explain.

2. Are you surprised that Boeing had eight other employees to deal with on this issue? Explain. Are you surprised that an employer dealt with this issue with the depth that Boeing did? Why do you think it did so?

3. Doe evidently kept going to the female toilet, but it was the pink pearls that got her fired. Any thoughts as to why? Explain.

Buonanno v. AT&T Broadband, LLC,
313 F. Supp. 2d 1069 (D. Colo. 2004)

Employee was terminated for refusing to sign a workplace document containing language that he would "value" diversity, under the employer's diversity policy. His refusal was based on his religion rejecting homosexuality. The employee sued the employer for terminating him without trying to reasonably accommodate the employee's religious belief or practice. The court sided with the employee.

Krieger, J.

***

Buonanno is a Christian who believes that the Bible is divinely inspired. He attempts to live his life in accordance with its literal language. Because the Bible requires that he treat others as he would like to be treated, Buonanno values and respects all other AT&T employees as individuals. He never has nor would he discriminate against another employee due to differences in belief, behavior, background, or other attribute. However, his religious beliefs prohibit him from approving, endorsing, or esteeming behavior or values that are repudiated by Scripture.

In January 2001, AT&T promoted a new "Employee Handbook" that addressed "How We Work: Employee Guidelines" and "Doing What's Right: Business Integrity & Ethics Policies." AT&T maintains a "Certification Policy," which provides that "each AT&T Broadband employee must sign and return the Acknowledgment of Receipt and Certificate of Understanding form indicating that you have received a copy of the handbook and the AT&T Code of Conduct and that you will abide by our employment policies and practices." The parties agree that one of the "employment policies and practices" to which Buonanno was required to adhere is AT&T's "Diversity Policy." The Handbook, however, does not contain a single policy clearly denoted as such; instead, it contains numerous references in various locations to AT&T's philosophy and goals with regard to diversity in the workplace. The parties' references to a "Diversity

Policy" appear to be primarily referring to a section of the Handbook entitled "A Summary of Our Business Philosophy," a subsection of which is entitled "Diversity." It reads as follows:

> The company places tremendous value on the fresh, innovative ideas and variety of perspectives that come from a diverse workplace. Diversity is necessary for a competitive business advantage—and the company is competing for customers in an increasingly diverse marketplace. To make diversity work to our advantage, it's our goal to build an environment that:
>
> • Respects and values individual differences.
> • Reflects the communities we serve.
> • Promotes employee involvement in decision making.
> • Encourages innovation and differing perspectives in problem solving.
> • Allows our diverse employee population to contribute richly to our growth.
>
> We want to create a team that is diverse, committed and the most talented in America. To that end, AT&T Broadband has a "zero tolerance" policy toward any type of discrimination, harassment, or retaliation in our company. Each person at AT&T Broadband is charged with the responsibility to

fully recognize, respect and value the differences among all of us. This is demonstrated in the way we communicate and interact with our customers, suppliers and each other every day.

There was no uniform understanding at AT&T as to what comprised the company's "Diversity Policy," or, more importantly, what an employee was required to do or not do to comply with it. Buonanno questioned the meaning of the third sentence in the second paragraph of the Diversity Philosophy, which reads "Each person at AT&T Broadband is charged with the responsibility to fully recognize, respect and value the differences among all of us." (The Court will hereinafter refer to this phrase as "the challenged language.") He believed that some behavior and beliefs were deemed sinful by Scripture, and thus, that he could not "value"—that is hold in esteem or ascribe worth to—such behavior or beliefs without compromising his own religious beliefs. Buonanno was fully prepared to comply with the principles underlying the Diversity Philosophy; he recognized that individuals have differing beliefs and behaviors and he would not discriminate against or harass any person based on that person's differing beliefs or behaviors. However, he could not comply with the challenged language insofar as it apparently required him to "value" the particular belief or behavior that was repudiated by Scripture. Accordingly, if the challenged language literally required him to do so, he could not sign the Certificate of Understanding, agreeing to "abide by" such language.

No AT&T representative explored or explained the intended meaning (or any of the various interpretations) of the challenged language to Buonanno. No AT&T employee inquired as to the particulars of Buonanno's concerns, sought to devise ways to accommodate Buonanno's religious beliefs, or reassured him that the challenged language did not require him to surrender his religious beliefs. At all relevant times, Buonanno was presented with a choice between accepting the language of the Handbook without any additional clarification and signing the Certificate, or losing his employment.

AT&T's Diversity Philosophy reflects a legitimate and laudable business goal. The Court accepts AT&T's contention that allowing employees to strike piecemeal portions of the Handbook or Certification could pose an undue hardship on its business, making uniform application of company policies much more difficult. Nevertheless, had AT&T gathered more information about Buonanno's concerns before terminating his employment, it may have discovered that the perceived conflict between his beliefs and AT&T's policy was not an actual conflict at all, or that if a true conflict existed, it was possible to relieve that conflict with a reasonable accommodation.

Had [Human Resources Manager] Batliner sought more details about Buonanno's concerns, rather than steadfastly insisting that he had to agree with the ambiguous "Diversity Policy" to retain his job, she would have discovered that, but for the challenged language, Buonanno agreed with the entirety of the Handbook, including the Diversity Philosophy, the non-discrimination policy, and all other aspects of AT&T's policies and practices. His only objection was to a literal interpretation of the challenged language that required him to "value" particular behavior and beliefs of co-workers. Had Batliner followed [vice president of Human Resources for Colorado operations] Davis' instructions and engaged in a conversation through which she gathered information about Buonanno's concerns, based on her interpretation of the challenged language, she would have discovered no actual conflict between the challenged language and Buonanno's religion. If Batliner had, as directed, reported these findings back to Davis, based on Davis' interpretation of the challenged language, Buonanno's religious beliefs would not have been in conflict with the challenged language. Had Batliner reported this information to [Senior Vice President for Human Resources] Brunick, he would have observed that, like the Jewish employee who must recognize—but not adopt—the differing beliefs of his Muslim co-worker, the challenged language did not require Buonanno to actually "value" the particular conduct of his co-workers that he considered sinful. Had [Director of Employee Relations] Wilson been consulted, Buonanno's promise to recognize that there were differences between what he believed and did and what his co-workers believed and did and to treat everyone with respect regardless of their beliefs and behavior would have been sufficient to accomplish the goals of the challenged language. Had Batliner, Davis, Brunick, or Wilson ever explained that they understood the challenged language to have a figurative, rather than literal, meaning and listened to his concerns, the issue could have been resolved without any need for accommodation. Accordingly, AT&T has failed to show that it could not have accommodated Buonanno's beliefs without undue hardship.

Even assuming that—despite the testimony of Batliner, Davis, and, at times, Brunick and Wilson—AT&T intended that the challenged language be applied literally and that all employees were affirmatively required to ascribe value in the various beliefs and behaviors of their co-workers, AT&T could nevertheless have accommodated Buonanno without suffering undue hardship. Although AT&T's Diversity Philosophy confers a business advantage, AT&T did not show that the literal application of the challenged language was necessary to obtain such advantage. For example, Wilson explained the advantages conferred by the "Diversity Policy" by relating an anecdote in which homosexual employees at American Express, sensing a need for estate-planning services in the gay community, proposed the creation of a successful new targeted product. In such example, no employee at American Express was required to ascribe any "value" to the practice of homosexuality in order to capitalize on the opportunity. Rather, American Express officials simply recognized that homosexual employees had a unique perspective on ways to market the company's product. Thus, as Wilson admitted, a minor revision of the challenged language, requiring all employees company-wide to "fully recognize, respect and value that there are differences among all of us" would have "accomplished [AT&T's] goals" as set forth in the Diversity Philosophy, without imposing any apparent hardship on AT&T. Whether such

a change is characterized as clarifying AT&T's interpretation of the existing Handbook language or a reasonable accommodation for Buonanno is irrelevant.

AT&T violated Title VII by failing to engage in the required dialogue with Buonanno upon notice of his concerns and by failing to clarify the challenged language to reasonably accommodate Buonanno's religious beliefs. Accordingly, Buonanno is entitled to damages.

Case Questions

1. If you were Buonanno's manager, how would you have handled this situation?

2. Think about the issue of an employee deciding not to accept a coworker because of religious reasons. If you were the manager, how would you balance the two (workplace requirements versus religion)? What if, as in Chapter 11, the employee's religion teaches him or her to hate Blacks and Jews? Is it the same? Explain.

3. What considerations should an employer be concerned with when coming up with approaches to promote workplace cohesion and avoidance of discrimination claims?

Chapter

11

Religious Discrimination

Ingram Publishing/Getty Images

Learning Objectives

After completing this chapter, you should be able to:

LO1 Discuss the background of religious discrimination and give some contemporary issues.

LO2 Give Title VII's definition of religion for discrimination purposes.

LO3 Explain religious conflicts under Title VII and give examples.

LO4 Define religious accommodation and guidelines to its usage.

LO5 Define undue hardship as it allows an employer defense to religious discrimination claims.

LO6 Describe religious harassment and give examples.

LO7 Identify the ways in which unions and religious conflicts occur.

LO8 List some ways in which management can avoid religious discrimination conflicts.

Opening Scenarios

SCENARIO 1

1 Mohammed, a member of the Sikh religion, wears a turban as part of his religious mandate, including at work. His supervisor tells him the turban makes his coworkers uncomfortable. Must he stop wearing it?

SCENARIO 2

2 In his preemployment interview, Mosley stated that he would not work on Saturdays because that is the day of his Sabbath. As a result, he is not hired. Is this religious discrimination?

SCENARIO 3

3 Three months after coming to work for Steel Bank, Jon joins a religious group whose Sabbath is on Tuesdays. Members of the religion are not to work on the Sabbath. Jon refuses to work on Tuesdays. He is terminated. Jon sues the employer, alleging religious discrimination. The employer defends by saying that (1) Jon was not of this religion when he was hired, (2) Tuesday is not a valid Sabbath day, and (3) any religious group that celebrates a Sabbath on Tuesday is not a valid religion and the employer does not have to honor it. Are any of the employer's defenses valid?

Statutory Basis

It shall be an unlawful employment practice for an employer—

(1) to fail or refuse to hire or to discharge any individual, or otherwise to discriminate against any individual with respect to his compensation, terms, conditions, or privileges of employment, because of such individual's . . . religion . . . or

(2) to limit, segregate, or classify his employees or applicants for employment in any way which would deprive or tend to deprive any individual of employment opportunities or otherwise adversely affect his status as an employee, because of such individual's religion . . .

Title VII of the Civil Rights Act of 1964, as amended; 42 U.S.C. § 20002-2(a).

Congress shall make no law respecting an establishment of religion, or prohibiting the free exercise thereof . . . [First Amendment to the U.S. Constitution.]

This Is Not Your Parents' Religious Discrimination

LO1 Discuss the background of religious discrimination and give some contemporary issues.

- A medical services company paid out $170,000 to settle a religious discrimination suit filed by employees required to spend at least half their workdays in courses that involved Scientology religious practices such as screaming at ashtrays, staring at someone for eight hours without moving, or being connected to an "E-meter," which Scientologists believe measures religious devotion.[1]

- The owner of a logistics company took an employee to lunch and told her that she needed "to examine her walk with Jesus" and be a better Christian. She was later demoted and her job given to a younger man with no experience.[2]

- After a seven-year investigation, major shipping company J.B. Hunt entered into a settlement agreement with four of its employees to address complaints from Sikh truck drivers about religious discrimination stemming from them not being hired or being terminated when, in conformity to their religious dictates, they declined to remove their turbans or cut their hair for pre-employment drug tests when other drug tests were available that would not go against their faith.[3]

- A hospital employee sues her employer for religious discrimination when she is terminated for refusing to take a required flu shot because she said she was vegan.[4] Another employee sought EEOC guidance as to whether an employer could require verification from clergy or others who could attest that the religious belief for seeking to be excused from the flu requirement was sincerely held. (The answer was yes, an employer could seek this information.)[5]

- The EEOC sued an employer for terminating an employee of over 35 years who repeatedly told the company that the use of its new biometric hand scanner to track employee time and attendance violated his religious beliefs as an Evangelical Christian and the company refused to consider alternate means of tracking time and attendance even though it would have been easy and they were doing it for employees without fingers.[6]

- UPS settling a religious discrimination suit for $4.9 million brought by male employees prohibited from being hired or promoted if their religious practices included wearing beards or hair below collar length.[7]

- A sheriff's deputy and follower of the "Billy Graham rule" alleged religious discrimination when he was terminated because his Christian beliefs prohibited him from training women.[8]

- A Lebanese ex-Ford Motor Company PhD engineer of 15 years, who had earned a "top achiever" performance rating before his new supervisor came in, was awarded $17 million for religious discrimination after he was subjected to abuse and retaliation by being berated and criticized week after week about his English by the supervisor, a high-level executive. The employee was put into demeaning and servile positions including being asked to bring the executive's coffee and resulting in him being required to take medical leave because of the stress. Fifteen million dollars of the jury award was for punitive damages.[9]

- A Virginia company mocked a Muslim applicant during a job interview and denied her a job because she asked for two five-minute prayer breaks during the workday. When she asked if she could shorten the 90-minute lunch break, he took her to a common area and, in front of the CEO and other employees, threw his arms up in the air and said, "This is a business." He pointed to her hijab, mocked her, saying, "Religions? I don't wanna deal with that here. We don't want those shenanigans here." He then took her file, crossed out her information, and refused to hired her.[10]

- A California car dealership agreed to pay $400,000 to five Afghan American employees who were singled out in a staff meeting and called names by the general manager, who threatened to "blow them up with a grenade." When they reported this to upper management, they were met with further harassment and job scrutiny. After quitting, several joined the U.S. military.[11]

- A Home Depot employee sues his employer for terminating him after the employee refuses to stop wearing a button he had worn for over a year that said

"One nation, under God, indivisible" in honor of his brother who was in the National Guard and set to report for a second tour of duty in Iraq.[12]

- Grammy-winning musician Carlos Santana ("You've Got to Change Your Evil Ways") is sued for unjust dismissal by a former personal assistant who claims Santana and his wife made the employee visit a chiropractor to be tested for his "closeness to God." Mrs. Santana said that when prospective employees were being evaluated for hire, she had the chiropractor "calibrate" them, as the more the chiropractor "enlightened" employees through treatments, the closer to God they became and the better employees they become.[13]

- An employee sues to have the court impose an injunction allowing her to say "have a blessed day" in written communications to clients and customers.[14]

- A Starbucks server sues Starbucks for retaliation after she refuses to remove her Wiccan symbol necklace and her hours are reduced, she is not promoted or transferred, and her tardiness is scrutinized.[15] The same thing happens at Google.[16]

- An employee sues after being terminated for eating a bacon, lettuce, and tomato sandwich (BLT) at work, in violation of the "no pork or pork products" rule put in place in deference to Muslim employees and clients.[17]

- Seven female employees at Belmont Abbey College, a small Catholic institution in North Carolina, claim discrimination against them due to the college's refusal to cover prescription contraceptives in its health insurance plan.[18]

- As more Muslim employees enter the workplace, they are running into trouble as dictates of their faith conflict with workplace duties, policies, and the other non-Muslim employees there. For instance, the BBC in London found that job seekers with English-sounding names were offered three times the number of interviews as those with Muslim names.[19] And two Muslim truckers were awarded $240,000 after they were fired for refusing to deliver beer because Muslims are forbidden from handling alcohol.[20] A Muslim ExpressJet flight attendant was suspended for refusing to serve alcohol on a flight.[21] A Muslim employee in Michigan won nearly $1.2 million from a jury after being taunted, harassed, and discriminated against at work because of his religion, his race, and his long beard.[22] In Minnesota, the Metropolitan Airports Commission cracks down on Muslim taxi drivers (about one-third) for refusing to pick up passengers carrying alcohol they say violates their religion.[23]

- General Motors wins a lawsuit by an employee who wants to form a Christian group at work like other resource groups, claiming it is religious discrimination to allow those and not the Christian one. The court held that GM had no religious groups, so refusal to have a Christian one was not religious discrimination.[24]

- Pharmacists with religiously based objections to premarital sex or abortion are disciplined for refusing to fill prescriptions for birth control pills or the morning after pill.[25]

- An Indiana state police officer is terminated for refusing a casino detail, saying gambling or being around it is against his religion.[26]

- Employees whose religion requires them to "witness" or proselytize sue for the right to do so to their fellow employees in the workplace.[27]
- The New York Police Department, previously found liable for religious discrimination for banning the wearing of a turban on the job by Sikhs, decides to allow the wearing of their beards and turbans.[28] The Army also cannot require special testing of a Sikh officer.[29]
- Alabama Supreme Court Chief Justice Roy S. Moore is removed from office for refusing a court's order to remove a 5,280-pound granite carving of the Ten Commandments from the courthouse rotunda.[30]
- Oklahoma City agrees to pay $20,000 in attorney fees for two employees who filed a lawsuit over Christmas decoration policies requiring them to remove a religious decoration on a filing cabinet, remove a Bible from a break room, and cancel an annual break-room Christmas party that included an opening prayer.[31]
- A television producer is fired for complaining about the company including biblical scriptures inside paycheck envelopes and promoting office Bible study.[32]
- A soldier sues the Army, saying that his atheism led to threats in a culture that tilts heavily toward evangelical Christianity.[33]
- An AT&T employee is terminated for refusing to sign a "Certificate of Understanding" requiring him to adhere to the company's diversity policy that conflicted with the employee's religious beliefs about homosexuality.[34]
- At Hewlett-Packard, in the same situation, an employee is terminated for refusing to remove biblical scriptures he placed on an overhead bin in his workplace cubicle, hoping his LGBTQ coworkers would see them, be hurt, repent, and be saved.[35]
- Minnesota employees who bring their Bibles to the diversity session on working with LGBTQ employees sue their employers, saying punishing them for this was a violation of their constitutional rights.[36]
- The EEOC sues Grand Central Partnerships on behalf of four Grand Central Station security guards who said the policy requiring them to tuck their dreadlocks under their uniform caps discriminates against their Rastafarian beliefs.[37]
- An employee belonging to the World Church of the Creator that teaches that "all people of color are savages who should go back to Africa and the Holocaust never happened and if it did, Nazi Germany would have done the world a tremendous favor"[38] sues his employer after being terminated for giving a newspaper interview espousing these views. He wins.[39]

The face of religious discrimination has changed dramatically in just the past few years. Of course, in each of these situations, the employer argued that they had a workplace policy against religious discrimination and that they never engage in such discrimination. Without guidance, it can be difficult to know. And those were just examples of religious issues in the workplace. That doesn't even include recent issues outside the workplace that also form a part of the religious landscape. Examples include things like the "Trump effect" causing a national security concern for the military because members of the military have formed a group of extreme Christians who are harassing, bullying, and otherwise mistreating Catholics, Jews, and other religious groups;[40] the armed forces settling a lawsuit by agreeing to add to the 38 existing religious symbols it permits on military burial monuments the Wiccan pentagram symbol;[41] the speedy removal (after a "firestorm of criticism") of a New York billboard promoting a budget brand of vodka implying Jews were cheap (complete with a long-haired dog wearing a yarmulke and a smaller dog wearing a Santa hat) by stating, "Christmas quality, Hanukkah pricing";[42] the Colorado high school student who quit the high school choir over an Islamic song praising Allah included for diversity purposes;[43] the Catholic schoolteacher who was terminated because she and her husband underwent in vitro fertilization treatment, which the church said was against its teachings;[44] a New York restaurant allegedly discriminating against Jews dressed in religious garb by requiring them to pay a $25 minimum per person to sit at the bar, complete with code words to alert the maître d' of such people asking to be seated;[45] Louisiana State University administrators taking heat for removing images of the Christian crosses worn by several members of the Painted Posse fans;[46] the Kountze County, Texas, school district administrators' ban on cheerleaders holding banners bearing Bible verses during athletic events;[47] the U.S. Supreme Court case challenging the pledge of allegiance phrase "One nation under God";[48] the Supreme Court's decision on the exhibition of Ten Commandment monuments on federal or state premises;[49] the Amish challenging the use of the state-mandated bright orange triangles, whose color and shape deeply offend their religious sensibilities, on their buggies for safety purposes;[50] the University of Georgia Jewish cheerleader (one of our students) who alleged that the Christian cheerleading coach did not appoint her to the prestigious football cheering squad because she did not participate in pregame prayers or attend Bible studies held in the coach's home;[51] the female Muslim University of South Florida basketball player who voluntarily resigned from the team after the coach refused to allow her to wear a uniform with long pants, long sleeves, and a head scarf in conformity with her religious dictates;[52] on the other hand, the March 2017 issue of Oprah magazine contained a story on a new line of activewear hijabs for Muslim female basketball players.[53] There are many more we could add, but one thing is for sure: religious discrimination is no longer the backwater issue of Title VII that it once may have been perceived to be.

Religious discrimination has certainly come a long way from what was likely envisioned by our forefathers when they wrote its protection into our Constitution. As a nation of immigrants, the United States has always had a diversity of religions among its people. The immigration laws of the 1920s were intentionally designed to keep America white by favoring northern Europeans (70 percent of immigrants). In 1965, immigration reform lifted the restrictions and resulted in 10 percent European and predominantly Asian and Latin immigrants. This meant that even more types of people from around the world, each expecting the freedom of religion for which the Pilgrims left England and about which the founding fathers felt strongly enough to include in the constitution of its fledgling republic. Thus, the face of what many of us have come to expect when we think of religious discrimination has changed. (See Exhibits 11.1, "Major Religions of the World—Ranked by Number of Adherents," and 11.2, "Major Religions and Denominations in the United States.")

Exhibit 11.1 *Major Religions of the World—Ranked by Number of Adherents*

Sizes shown are *approximate estimates* and are here mainly for the purpose of ordering the groups by size, not to provide a definitive number. (This list is sociological/statistical in perspective.)

Christianity: 2.1 billion
Islam: 1.5 billion
Secular/Nonreligious/
Agnostic/Atheist:
  1.1 billion
Hinduism: 900 million
Chinese traditional
  religion: 394 million
Buddhism: 376 million
Primal-indigenous:
  300 million
African traditional
  and diasporic:
  100 million
Sikhism: 23 million
Juche: 19 million
Spiritism: 15 million
Judaism: 14 million
Baha'i: 7 million
Jainism: 4.2 million
Shinto: 4 million
Cao Dai: 4 million
Zoroastrianism: 2.6 million

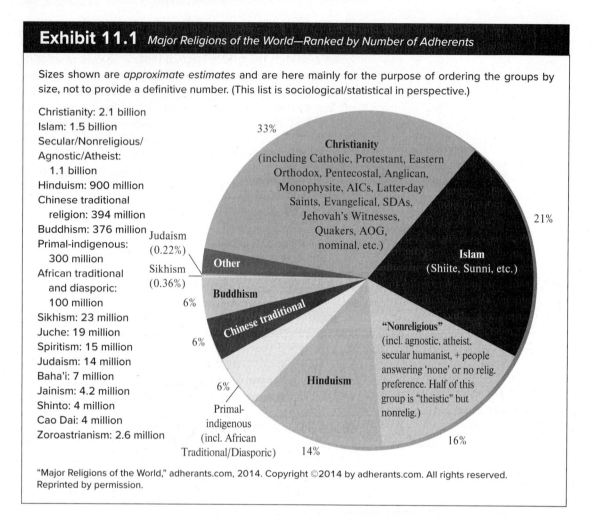

Religion has unique significance in our country's creation and development. In the 16th century, when the Catholic Church did not allow King Henry VIII to divorce his wife, Catherine of Aragon, to marry Anne Boleyn, Henry broke with Rome. This led to the establishment of a separate national church in England under the supreme headship of the king. Henry VIII was allowed to divorce Catherine (he eventually took six wives) and marry Anne, whom he ordered beheaded in 1536.

The aftermath of Henry's maneuvers was that the church became inextricably woven into the government, and religious freedom was virtually nonexistent in the government from which America was born. The right to practice religion freely and not be required to blindly accept the government's state-imposed religious beliefs was a large part of what made the Pilgrims break away from Great Britain and its Church of England more than a century later.

Exhibit 11.2 *Major Religions and Denominations in the United States*

Top Organized Religions

Christianity	76.5%
Judaism	1.3
Islam	0.5
Buddhism	0.5
Hinduism	0.4
Unitarian Universalist	0.3
Wiccan/Pagan/Druid	0.1

Largest Denominational Families

Catholic	24.5%
Baptist	16.3
Methodist	6.8
Lutheran	4.6
Pentecostal	2.1
Presbyterian	2.7
Mormon	1.3
Nondenominational Christians	1.2
Church of Christ	1.2
Episcopal/Anglican	1.7
Assemblies of God	0.5
Congregational/United Church of Christ	0.7
Seventh Day Adventist	0.3

Of course, this is only a simplified version of a very long and complex developmental process for our relationship as a country with religion. But the end product was that, rejecting the tyranny of this state-imposed religion, religious freedom was included in the U.S. Constitution, and freedom of religion has since always been highly valued and closely held and has enjoyed a protected position in American law.

Title VII embodies this protection in the employment arena by prohibiting employment discrimination based on religious beliefs or practices. While litigation on the basis of religious discrimination may not occur as frequently as some of the other categories or have as high a profile, it is just as important a concern for employers. The percentage of claims may seem small, but the more important factor is that there has been a steady increase in claims since 1993 and an absolute spike after the terrorist events of September 11, 2001. In fiscal year 2019, religious discrimination accounted for 3.7 percent of charges filed with the EEOC, which totaled 2,725 charges, compared to 33 percent for race. The numbers wax and wane over the years, but the claims are always there—and, as you can see, are certainly not in keeping with our idea of freedom from religious discrimination in the workplace.[54]

However, religious discrimination is no less important. It is clear that this issue has taken on an even more pressing note since the tragic events of September 11, 2001. According to the EEOC, federal, state, and local fair employment practice agencies documented a significant increase in the number of charges of workplace harassment and discrimination claims based on national origin (with those perceived to be of Arab and South Asian descent being the target) and religion (Muslims, Sikhs) since then. Employment discrimination claims increased by 4.5 percent from 2001 to 2002, with much of that increase coming from ethnicity and religion after 9/11. According to the Tanenbaum Center for Interreligious Understanding's annual survey of American Workers and Religion in 2013, 20 years ago the anti-Muslim discrimination primarily involved dress codes or policies on religious holidays. Today the conflicts are more personal, such as name-calling or offending jokes; they are typically based in personal prejudices between employees or between an employee and a supervisor.[55] A Carnegie Mellon University experiment involving dummy résumés and social media profiles found that between 10 and 33 percent of U.S. firms searched social networks for information on job applicants early in the hiring process and candidates whose public Facebook profiles indicated they were Muslim were less likely to be called for interviews (2 percent) than Christian applicants (17 percent).[56] We also earlier mentioned the British study, which would in all likelihood have similar results here in the United States, that applicants with Muslim-sounding names would be far less likely to have their résumés chosen for an interview. In fact, in issuing a new comprehensive directive on religious discrimination for the EEOC Compliance Manual in 2008, the EEOC noted that claims of religious discrimination had doubled between 1992 and 2007 and that as religious pluralism has increased, questions about religious discrimination have increased.[57] As Exhibit 11.3 ("It Ain't Paranoia If It's Real. . .") reflects, a 2019 Pew Research Center survey indicated that even others believed Muslims were the subject of discrimination.

But diversity consultants agree that employers who adapt and reduce conflict improve morale and performance "by attracting the best talent from a broad range of backgrounds that can help the company appeal to a larger customer base."[58] All this at a time when the Pew Research Center said that in its 2019 Religious Landscape Study that the number of atheists, agnostics, and unaffiliated rose from 17 percent in a similar study in 2009 to 26 percent in 2019. The proportion of Americans who say they are Christian has fallen from 70.6 percent in the 2014 study to 65 percent in 2019. Rates of religious attendance declined by 7 percent.[59]

Exhibit 11.3 *It Ain't Paranoia If It's Real. . .*

A March 2019 survey by the Pew Research Center found that over 50 percent of respondents believed that Muslims were being discriminated against. As the graphic shows, this is, by far, the highest percentage of the groups that were the subject of the survey.

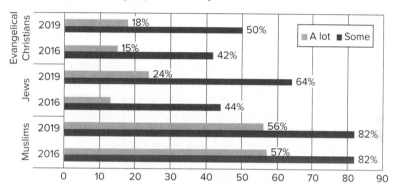

% who say there is ___ of discrimination against each group in our society

Source: Masci, David, "Most Americans Say Muslims Subject to Discrimination," Survey of U.S. adults conducted March 20–25, 2019, https://www.pewresearch.org/fact-tank/2019/05/17/many-americans-see-religious-discrimination-in-u-s-especially-against-muslims/.

Actually, the increase in litigation involving religious issues began when issues of workplace activities and harassment issues surrounding religious practices became more prominent in the late 1980s and early 1990s with the rising popularity of Fundamentalist Christianity and televangelism. Many of the Fundamentalists, commonly referred to as "born-again Christians," ran into trouble when, as an article of faith, they attempted to share their religion with others in the workplace, sometimes whether the coworker wished to have it so or not. On the other hand, Fundamentalists experienced trouble when they were mocked, teased, or otherwise singled out for their religious beliefs at work.

In fact, a survey reported that 40 percent of white evangelical Christians said they face "a lot" of discrimination and 59 percent of them say discrimination against Christians has become as big a problem as discrimination against other religious groups. "At the same time, evangelicals were the most likely to say there is little to no discrimination at work against other religions, racial, gay and lesbian and other groups."[60]

As you saw from the beginning of the chapter, these religious discrimination issues have now extended into areas surrounding the practices and dictates—and harassment—involving those of primarily Middle Eastern religions. Can a Sikh be required to remove his religiously dictated turban at work? Can a Muslim woman be terminated or even not hired for wearing a religiously dictated head covering? Must a Muslim employee be allowed to attend a midday Friday religious service or have a place provided for religion-required prayer five times a day? Can a Muslim taxi driver refuse to pick up fares that have liquor? Can a grocery store cashier refuse to touch pork, saying it is against her religion? All of these issues and those mentioned at the beginning of the chapter have arisen and continue to be a part of the post–September 11, 2001, landscape and must be addressed consistent with Title VII and other legal dictates.

Federal and state constitutional guarantees of due process, equal protection, and freedom of religion also provide protection for federal, state, and local government employees. If the employer is a governmental entity, the employer must avoid workplace policies that have the effect of tending to establish or to interfere with the practice of the employee's religion in violation of the U.S. Constitution. In determining whether the employer has discriminated on the basis of religion, the court must sometimes first address whether even deciding the issue entangles the government excessively in the practice of religion. Title VII is the only legislation specifically prohibiting religious discrimination in employment, and consideration is given to constitutional issues where necessary.

duty to reasonably accommodate
The employer's Title VII duty to try to find a way to avoid conflict between workplace policies and an employee's religious practices or beliefs.

Unlike the other categories included in Title VII, there is not an absolute prohibition against discrimination on the basis of religion. Rather, under Title VII, we see for the first time a category that has built into it a **duty to reasonably accommodate** the employee's religious conflict unless to do so would cause the employer **undue hardship**. There is no such reasonable accommodation requirement for race, gender, color, or national origin, but there is under the Americans with Disabilities Act (ADA), as we shall see in that chapter. However, the nature of the accommodation in the ADA is quite different.

undue hardship
A burden imposed on an employer, by accommodating an employee's religious conflict, that would be too onerous for the employer to bear.

To a great extent, religious organizations are exempt from the prohibitions in Title VII. As a general rule, they can discriminate so that, for instance, a Catholic church may legitimately refuse to hire a Baptist minister as its priest. Section 703(e)(2) of Title VII states that it is not an unlawful employment practice for a school, college, university, or other educational institution to hire or employ those of a particular religion if the institution is in whole or in substantial part owned, supported, controlled, or managed by that religion or by a religious corporation, association, or society or if its curriculum is directed toward the propagation of a particular religion. That is, religion is recognized as a basis for a BFOQ reasonably necessary to the normal operation of that particular business or enterprise under section 703(e)(1) of Title VII. If the church has nonsectarian activities such as running a day care center, bookstore, or athletic club, it may enjoy the same broad type of freedom to discriminate on the basis of religion since these activities may have religion or propagation of the religion as an integral part of their purpose. Employers should be cautioned that the specific facts play an important role in making this determination. In *Corporation of the Presiding Bishop of the Church of Jesus Christ of Latterday Saints v. Amos,*[61] the U.S. Supreme Court upheld the church's termination of a janitor in the church-owned gym for not paying his dues and keeping current his church affiliation card. In the Court's determination, the gym had been conceived as a manifestation of dedication to their religious beliefs that the body is a temple and the gym is a part of maintaining it, and terminating the janitor for his failure to maintain his membership in the denomination did not violate the law.

For the first time, in 2012 the U.S. Supreme Court took a close look at the "ministerial exception" to Title VII that had been granted in federal lower court decisions. In *Hosanna-Tabor Evangelical Lutheran Church and School v. EEOC,*[62] the Court unanimously determined that religious organizations have full authority to determine who their religious leaders are and to apply their religious dictates even when those dictates conflict with workplace antidiscrimination laws. In the *Tabor* case, a teacher with narcolepsy was terminated after taking leave. When she sued under the Americans with Disabilities Act, she lost. The church argued that she was a religious minister in addition to being a teacher, and as such, they had the right to fire her if they wished. The decision left open exactly which employees qualify as being within the ministerial exception. In this case, the employee was primarily a teacher, but she was also a religious leader. The fact that she only performed the primarily religious duties for a small part of her workday did not take away her status as a ministerial employee under the ministerial exception. In the high court's determination, the First Amendment's guarantee of freedom of religion shields churches and their operations from the reach of the antidiscrimination laws when the issue involves religious employees of these institutions. In their view, religious organizations are the best judge of whether ministerial employees should be terminated. To hold otherwise would create unconstitutional excessive entanglement of the government in the affairs of the religious organization.

Before Title VII, it was fairly routine for employers to be nearly as adamant about not hiring those of certain religious faiths, such as Jews, as it was about not hiring people of a certain race, ethnic background, or gender. Universities routinely imposed quotas on the number of Jewish students they would accept, just as restrictive covenants in real estate contracts routinely prohibited the sale of property to Jews, African Americans, Asians, and others. The issue has usually been more covertly handled, but it existed extensively nonetheless. Title VII was enacted to remedy such practices in the workplace, just as fair housing legislation now prohibits restrictive covenants.

Some have still not gotten the message. In 2011, a Jewish hockey player for the National Hockey League's Anaheim Ducks sued the organization for what he called a "barrage of anti-Semitic, offensive and degrading verbal attacks regarding his Jewish faith" from the head coach. The coach said he did not intend the comments to insult or hurt him in any way.[63] In 2010, the EEOC settled a case with Administaff, Inc. on behalf of two Jewish brothers for $115,000. They were called "dirty Jew" and "dumb Jew" and subjected to other anti-Semitic comments. They also had their work vehicle defaced with a swastika and were forced into a trash bin for the amusement of managers watching on surveillance cameras, calling it "throw the Jew in the Dumpster."[64] A 2009 lawsuit by two Jewish teachers contained dozens of pages describing religious discrimination by their colleagues and former principal.[65] And in 2008 two Army drill sergeants were reprimanded for

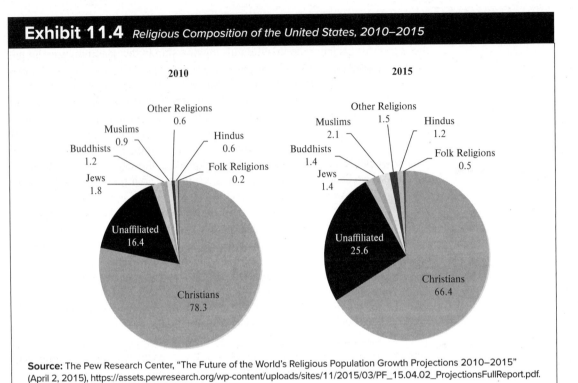

Exhibit 11.4 Religious Composition of the United States, 2010–2015

2010

Other Religions 0.6
Muslims 0.9
Hindus 0.6
Buddhists 1.2
Folk Religions 0.2
Jews 1.8
Unaffiliated 16.4
Christians 78.3

2015

Other Religions 1.5
Muslims 2.1
Hindus 1.2
Buddhists 1.4
Folk Religions 0.5
Jews 1.4
Unaffiliated 25.6
Christians 66.4

Source: The Pew Research Center, "The Future of the World's Religious Population Growth Projections 2010–2015" (April 2, 2015), https://assets.pewresearch.org/wp-content/uploads/sites/11/2015/03/PF_15.04.02_ProjectionsFullReport.pdf.

religious discrimination against a Jewish soldier who they called "Juden," the German word for Jews. They also made him remove his yarmulke religious head covering. The soldier was later beaten so badly by other soldiers that he was treated at a hospital.[66]

An employee who was constantly harassed by coworkers after converting to Islam won $5 million in punitive damages from AT&T when she was able to show constant abuse that took place after she became a Muslim. The last straw for her was when her manager snatched off her hijab and exposed her hair.[67] The EEOC sued a transport company for failing to attempt to accommodate two Muslim employees and firing them for refusing to deliver alcohol when they could have been accommodated without undue hardship.[68] Hertz suspended 34 Muslim drivers who it claimed took a longer time to pray than agreed to in their union contract.[69]

It is clear from Exhibit 11.4 ("Religious Composition of the United States, 2010–2015") that religion is going to remain with us as an important workplace issue. If history is any indication, claims will only increase as employees come to expect respectful treatment of their religious beliefs, however they come into conflict in the workplace. In addition to not hiring people of a particular religion as was often the case previously, the more frequent basis for lawsuits today is that an employee is not hired or is terminated because of some religious practice that comes into conflict with the employer's workplace policies. The employee may refuse to work on a particular day because it is the employee's Sabbath, or the employee may dress a certain way for religious reasons, may wish to take certain days off for religious holidays or observances, may need to have prayers or other religious observances that occur during work time honored, or may be asked to do something that conflicts with his or her religious beliefs. When it conflicts with the employer's policies and the employee refuses to attempt to accommodate the conflict, the employee is terminated, and Title VII comes into play.

For instance, the EEOC sued Convergys Corporation because an applicant who was a Hebrew Israelite and could not work on his Sabbath (Saturday) from sunup to sundown was told by the interviewer that unless he could work on Saturdays, the interview was over.[70] Ivy Hall Assisted Living paid an employee $43,000 in a settlement after she sued when the employer refused to allow her to wear her Muslim hijab. In fact, the employer insisted that she remove the hijab and refrain from wearing it as a condition of continued employment.[71] This latter issue has arisen in several different contexts, including an applicant who was told by Abercrombie & Fitch that the hijab she refused to take off if hired violated the Abercrombie & Fitch "Look Policy."[72] This case, *EEOC v. Abercrombie & Fitch,* went all the way up to the U.S. Supreme Court, which issued a decision in 2015 that we include for you in the case section at the end of this chapter.

In *Tyson v. Clarian Health Partners, Inc.,* the employer was faced with what to do with a Muslim employee working in the hospital who used an empty hospital room to perform her ablutions (ritual washing up) before praying in violation of hospital rules. When an employee of Sweetwater Healthcare Center who had worked most of her three years at the facility without being forced to work on Sundays told the new administrator that her religion prohibited her from working on Sundays, she was told that "God would excuse her since she worked in the healthcare field" and that she could "either report on Sundays or lose her job."[73] A similar situation resulted in a jury ward of $21.5 million for a dishwasher at the Conrad Miami hotel (previously Hilton Worldwide) who was terminated for trading shifts so she would not have to work on her Sabbath even though her manager knew of her conflict beforehand and still "demanded" that she work on Sundays.[74]

Frequently the employer discovers religious information through questions on an employment application or during a preemployment interview, either of which generally relates to notifying a religious figure or taking the employee to a particular hospital in the event of on-the-job injury. If the question is asked, the applicant has a right to think it is asked for a reason and will be taken into consideration. The employer may have the question for totally different reasons than the applicant thinks, but once the question is there, it can be left up to unintended interpretations. To eliminate the appearance of illegal consideration of religion in hiring, employers should, instead, ask such questions after hire and then simply ask who should be notified or what hospital the employee prefers.

In this chapter, we will learn what is meant by religious discrimination, what the duty to accommodate involves, and how far an employer can go in handling management considerations when religious conflict is at issue.

What Is Religion?

LO2 Give Title VII's definition of religion for discrimination purposes.

Title VII originally provided no guidance as to what it meant by the word *religion*. In the 1972 amendments to Title VII, Congress addressed the issue. In section 701, providing definitions for terms within Title VII, section (j) states: "The term 'religion' includes all aspects of religious observance and practice, as well as belief, unless an employer demonstrates that he is unable to reasonably accommodate an employee's or prospective employee's religious observance or practice without undue hardship on the conduct of the employer's business."[75]

The question frequently arises: "What if I never heard of the employee's religion? Must I still accommodate it?" The answer is based on two considerations: whether the employee's belief is closely held and whether it takes the place of religion in the employee's life. The latter requirement means that even atheism has been considered a "religion" for Title VII purposes. If the answer to both queries is yes, then the employer must accept the belief as a religious belief and attempt accommodation for conflicts.

1)
Scenario

The religious belief need not be a belief in a religious deity as we generally know it. However, courts have determined that groups like the Ku Klux Klan are political, not religious, organizations, even though their members have closely held beliefs. The employer need not previously know of, have heard of, or approve of the employee's religion in order to be required to accommodate it for Title VII purposes. Also, the employer cannot question the sincerity of the belief merely because the employer thinks the religion is strange. In *Frazee v. Illinois Department of Employment Security,*[76] the employee asserted that he could not work on the Sabbath because he was a Christian, even though he did not attend church. The U.S. Supreme Court held that the employee need not be a member of an organized religion at all. The case involves the Free Exercise Clause of the First Amendment to the U.S. Constitution, made applicable to the states by the Fourteenth Amendment, but the considerations are similar to those of Title VII. This is why in Opening Scenario 1 the Sikh need not stop wearing his religiously mandated turban simply because other employees are "uncomfortable." That is to say, they are unfamiliar with the employee's religion and religious dictates and his wearing of a turban seems strange to them.

To show you just how far this goes, think about the following quote from the October 4, 2019, *This Week* magazine, which gives news from all over the world. "A pastor of the Church of the Flying Spaghetti Monster [yes, you read that correctly] opened a local government meeting in Alaska with a prayer while wearing a colander on his head. 'I'm called to invoke the power of the true inebriated creator of the universe, the drunken tolerator of all the lesser and more recent gods, and maintainer of gravity here on earth,'[77] said 'Pastafarian' pastor Barrett Fletcher, ending his prayer with 'Ramen.'" The Church of the Flying Spaghetti Monster was formed as a satire on other religions and has won court rulings that it must be treated equally. Some politicians, Fletcher said, "seem to feel they can't do the work without being overseen by a higher authority." The organization has adherents all over the world, but in the court case here in the United States it was considered a satire rather than an actual religion. However, in some places in the United States, adherents have been permitted to do things like take drivers' license or passport photos with a colander on their head (although other jurisdictions have not permitted it, saying it was not required as a yarmulke/kippa or hijab). In Australia, however, they are allowed to perform marriages. It may seem outrageous to you, but just keep in mind that the definition of religion is very broad.

Perhaps the single most-asked question in this area is: "Must I accommodate the employee's religious conflict if the conflict did not exist when the employee was hired?" The answer is yes. The duty attaches to the conflict itself, not to when the conflict arises. The idea behind the question is that if the employer had known of the conflict, then he or she would not have hired the employee in the first place. It is illegal to use the religious conflict alone as a basis for not hiring the applicant. So, legally, it does not matter whether the conflict was present when the applicant was hired or arose later; there is still a duty on the employer to attempt to accommodate the religious conflict. The duty to accommodate, however, is only to the extent that it does not cause the employer undue hardship. What constitutes undue hardship will be discussed shortly.

The duty to accommodate only applies to religious *practices,* not religious *beliefs.* An employer is only required to accommodate a religious practice to the extent that it does not present an undue hardship on the employer, but religious beliefs do not have that limitation. That is, no matter how unorthodox or even outrageous an employee's religion may seem to the employer, the employer cannot take an adverse employment action against the employee simply because the employee holds that religious belief. In *Peterson v. Wilmur Communications, Inc.,* given at the end of the chapter, the employer was called upon to deal with a religion espousing racial separation much like the Ku Klux Klan. The court determined that the religion, as unorthodox and even as repulsive as it was, was required by Title VII to be treated just like any other religion for Title VII purposes.

Religious Conflicts

LO3 Explain religious conflicts under Title VII and give examples.

Imagine mass firings of Muslim employees who walk off the job over prayer disputes. The workers ask management to adjust their evening break time so they can pray at sunset as required; management agrees and then reverses its decision when non-Muslim employees protest. This occurred in Colorado and Nebraska, and about 200 employees were fired.[78]

Workplace conflict between employee religious practices at odds with workplace policies is probably the most frequent type of religious discrimination case there is, and as we discussed earlier, the numbers are growing. That is, it is not so much that the employer dislikes a particular religion and refuses to hire members of that religion (although there are those); rather, it is that the employee may engage in some religious practice that is not perceived to be compatible with the workplace. For instance, the employer may have a no-beard policy, but the employee's religion forbids shaving; the employer may have a policy forbidding the wearing of headgear, but the employee's religion requires the wearing of some sort of head cover; the employer may have a policy forbidding the wearing of long hair on males, but the employee's religion forbids the cutting of male hair except in certain limited circumstances; or the employer may have a policy that all employees must work on Saturdays, but the employee's religious Sabbath may be on Saturday and followers may be forbidden to work on the Sabbath.

In fact, sometimes the conflict comes not with the employee's religion but with that of the employer.

In order for an employee to proceed with a claim of religious discrimination, he must first establish a *prima facie* case by establishing that

See Chapter 2 to revisit key concepts.

1. He holds a sincere religious belief that conflicts with an employment requirement.
2. He has informed the employer of the conflict.
3. He was discharged or disciplined for failing to comply with the conflicting employment requirement.

If an employee establishes a *prima facie* case, the burden shifts to the employer to show that it offered a reasonable accommodation to the employee or that it could not reasonably accommodate the employee without incurring undue hardship.

As more and more employees come into the workplace who are not of the "traditional" religions with which an employer may be more familiar and these employees have an expectation of being accommodated in accordance with the law, employers will need to learn to effectively handle the religious conflicts that arise. The religious conflicts serving as the basis for discrimination claims have become more and more fascinating over the years. Recent conflicts have included such diverse situations as a woman suing for religious discrimination because her religion does not allow her to wear men's clothing (i.e., pants), but her employer required pants as part of her uniform[79]; a Jehovah's Witness suing Chi-Chi's Mexican restaurant for religious discrimination after being fired for not adhering to Chi-Chi's policy of all employees singing birthday songs to patrons on their birthday because the policy conflicted with her religion, which does not observe personal birthdays, believing they arise out of pagan celebrations[80]; a Jehovah's Witness suing Belk department store for being terminated when she refused to wear a Santa hat and apron because, again, her religion prohibited recognizing holidays[81]; an employee refusing to answer the telephone with the hotel's required "Happy holidays" (rather than "Merry Christmas") greeting during the Christmas season, claiming her religious beliefs prohibited her from doing so[82]; a strict vegetarian bus driver being fired for refusing to hand out coupons to riders for free hamburgers as part of a promotion between the bus company and a hamburger chain[83]; a counselor with the Centers for Disease Control and Prevention (CDC) who describes herself as a "devout Christian," who, believing that her religion prohibited her from encouraging or supporting same-sex relationships through counseling, told a lesbian seeking counseling for trust issues that the employee's counseling needs conflicted with the counselor's religious beliefs and she therefore could not provide counseling because of her own "personal values"[84]; and an employee suing Walmart for religious discrimination when it fired her for screaming at a lesbian employee that God does not accept gays, they should not "be on earth," and they will "go to hell" because they are not "right in the head."[85]

We are giving you so many of these examples because we want you to be prepared; religious conflicts come into the workplace in an awful lot of ways, and the more examples you see, the better equipped you are to make defensible workplace decisions. We are also giving you these examples because religious conflicts in the workplace are, in all likelihood, bound to arise in ways that may not at first glance seem to have anything to do with religion (the hamburger coupons and the bus driver, the "Happy holidays" greeting, the wearing of the Santa hat), but they do. The more scenarios you are exposed to, the better prepared you will be.

The key is for an employer to make sure that the basis for the employee's conflict is a religious one and then to try to work out an accommodation. Once the employer is aware of the conflict, the employer must attempt a good-faith accommodation of the religious conflict, and the employee must assist in the attempted accommodation. If none can be worked out and the employer has tried everything available that does not present an undue hardship, then the employer has fulfilled his or her Title VII obligation and there is no liability, even if the employee's religious conflict cannot be accommodated. Of course, because of the diversity of religious conflicts that are possible, there is no single set of rules that can be provided that will cover all religious conflicts.

In *Goldman v. Weinberger,*[86] for example, the issue of conflict arose in the context of the military where a rabbi's wearing of the Jewish yarmulke/kippa head covering under his military uniform violated military dress regulations. The regulation was upheld by the U.S. Supreme Court. We mention this case for several reasons. First, it presents a conflict between religious practice (wearing a kippa) and work (being a member of the military). It also allows you to understand the U.S. Supreme Court's position on matters military and how they interact with Title VII and other protective legislation. As we are discussing Title VII, students frequently ask how the military can have the rules it has, which seem to be at odds with Title VII.

Our answer is that the Court tends to view the military as being in a class all its own for most purposes. The military's need for "good order," cohesion, instant and unquestioning obedience, esprit de corps, morale, and other such interests usually results in the Court deferring to the military when there are conflicts. We also wanted to reiterate that the right to be free of religious discrimination is not absolute. There are limitations to the right where there may be overriding considerations such as the military cohesion in *Goldman* or the undue hardship on the employer under Title VII. With this said, we should also note that in 2014, the U.S. military relaxed its rules when it comes to the wearing of beards, Sikhs wearing turbans, Jews wearing yarmulkes, and Wiccans. Individual members of the armed forces can now request personal exemptions from the requirements and they will be examined on a case-by-case basis.[87]

Not every conflict involving religion will necessarily be a religious conflict recognized by the law. Think about the description of the Walmart employee who was terminated for violating Walmart's Discrimination and Harassment Prevention Policy by screaming at the lesbian employee. She was not terminated because of her religious beliefs, as she argued, but instead for violating Walmart's policy by harassing an employee. The decision to terminate was based on the employee's conduct, not on her religious beliefs.[88] In *Lumpkin v. Jordan,*[89] the legitimate non-discriminatory basis for termination was not deemed a religious conflict at all, even though it involved religion to an extent. In *Jordan,* a member of the San Francisco Human Rights Commission, who was also a minister, had religious beliefs in conflict with sexual orientation that put him at odds with the commission's work in enforcing non-discrimination laws, including on the basis of sexual orientation. The court upheld his termination despite the minister's religious beliefs, since they conflicted with the very purpose of his job and its duties.

Employer's Duty to Reasonably Accommodate

LO4 Define religious accommodation and guidelines to its usage.

Again, unlike the other categories under Title VII, the prohibition against religious discrimination is not absolute. An employer can discriminate against an employee for religious reasons if to do otherwise causes the employer undue hardship. When the employer discovers a religious conflict between the employer's policy and the employee's religion, the employer's first responsibility is to attempt accommodation. If accommodation is not possible, the employer can implement the policy even though it has the effect of discriminating against the employee on the basis of religion.

The duty to reasonably accommodate is not a static concept. Due to the nature of religious conflicts and the fact that they can arise in all types of contexts and in many different ways, there is no one single action an employer must take to show that she or he has reasonably accommodated. It depends on the circumstances and will vary from situation to situation. For example:

- The employer owns a sandwich shop. The employer's policy entitles employees to eat all the restaurant food they wish during their meal break, free of charge. An employee's religion does not allow eating meat. Aside from the meat used for sandwiches, the employer has little else, other than sandwich trimmings like lettuce and tomatoes. The employee alleges it is religious discrimination to provide the benefits of free meals that the employee cannot eat for religious reasons while other employees receive full free meals. The duty to accommodate may be as simple as the employer arranging to have peanut butter and jelly, eggs, or a variety of vegetables or pasta available for the employee.

- The employer requires employees to work six days per week. An employee cannot work on Saturdays due to a religious conflict. The accommodation may be that the employee switches days with an employee who does not wish to work on Sundays—a day that the employee with the religious conflict is available to work—or the employee switches to a job that does not require working on Saturdays.

- The employer grocery store has a policy requiring all counter clerks to be clean-shaven to present the employer's view of a "clean-cut" image to the public. An employee cannot shave for religious reasons. The accommodation may be that the employer switches the employee to a job the employee can perform that does not require public contact such as stocking shelves or handling paperwork. Or, as the case with the U.S. military and the New York police officers, the true purpose of the policy can be reexamined to see if there is an actual need for the policy and, if so, whether there are alternatives than can be used. In the case of the New York police officers, the court was able to show in the case mentioned earlier in the chapter that the clean-shaven policy that was in place for the use of gas masks and used against Hasidic Jews and Sikhs did not apply to undercover police officers. As we mentioned earlier, in December 2016, the NYPD announced a new policy allowing Sikh officers to wear their turbans and beards. Sometimes all it takes to come up with an appropriate accommodation is thinking about the issue in a different way and/or a will to want to make things work out. Our experience, reflected vividly in several of the examples of cases we have given you, indicates that often the first barrier to reaching a workable accommodation is a manager's resistance to anything outside what they consider to be their norm. Be aware that it can eventually lead to litigation.

If it can be shown that the employer reasonably accommodated or attempted to accommodate the employee, then the employer is relieved of liability. In *Wilson v. U.S. West Communications,*[90] the Catholic employee believed she should be "an instrument of God like the Virgin Mary" and wear a button showing a color photo of an 18-week fetus until abortion was outlawed. The button was offensive and disturbing to other employees for reasons unrelated to abortion such as infertility, miscarriages, and the death of a premature infant. The employer considered it a "time robber" since employees were upset and gathered to discuss it. The employer gave her the option of only wearing it in her cubicle or covering it. This was unacceptable to the employee and she sued. The court found the employer's accommodation to be reasonable but also found that the employee's claim of the problematic activity of "needing" to wear an antiabortion button with a graphic picture of a fetus on it was not based on religious requirements.

Similarly, in *EEOC v. Firestone Fibers & Textiles Company,*[91] the Fourth Circuit found that an employer met the accommodation requirements for the employee's religious beliefs prohibiting him from working on his Sabbath from sundown Friday to sundown Saturday and on seven religious holidays during the year. The employer sought an accommodation by altering the employee's Friday work shift where it could and using the collective bargaining agreement's seniority system. But the employee requested 11 additional days to observe two religious holidays and was terminated when he violated the company's attendance policy prohibiting taking over 60 hours of unpaid leave. So, too, when a Home Depot employee who wore a "One nation under God" button on his work apron, in violation of the store's policy against wearing religious buttons, was given the option to wear a company pin saying United We Stand.[92]

2)
Scenario

3)
Scenario

If an accommodation cannot be found, as *Williams v. Southern Union Gas Company*[93] demonstrates, the employer's duty is discharged. The *Williams* case involved an employee who was terminated for not working on Saturday, his Sabbath.

The court upheld the termination because it found that the employer had tried to accommodate the employee's religious conflict, but the only way it could have been done would have caused the employer undue hardship. This case is the basis for Opening Scenarios 2 and 3. The important factor is for the employer to make a good-faith attempt at an accommodation rather than simply dismissing the conflict without even trying to do so. Recall the cases mentioned previously where the Hebrew Israelite was told by the interviewer that if he could not work on Saturdays (because it was his Sabbath), the interview was over and the Muslim who requested that her 90-minute luncheon be adjusted so that she could take two 5-minute prayer breaks and was paraded out in front of the owner and others and mocked, her employment application information crossed out and the manager refused to consider her further. That sort of refusal to even try to accommodate is what the law prohibits.

Even where an employee's activity is religiously based, it need not be accommodated if doing so presents real problems for the employer. In the very interesting *Chalmers v. Tulon Company of Richmond* case, included at the end of the chapter, the employee believed it to be her religious duty to write letters to her coworkers telling them what she perceived as their religious shortcomings. When one letter led to an employee's wife thinking he had an affair, the court refused to find a basis for accommodation, even though the employee claimed she was doing what her religion dictated she do.

There have been other types of manifestations of religious dictates employers and others have had to address. In one case, a Wisconsin woman's religious leader of the Order of the Divine Will told her that a 90-year-old woman who died would come back alive if she allowed the corpse to sit on the toilet in her home. The homeowner's children were told by the religious leader that demons were destroying the corpse's appearance as she decayed in the bathroom to make it look like she would not rise from the dead. Police officers finally discovered the rotting body in the "stench filled" home.[94] A North Carolina teen's nose piercing got her suspended from school in violation of the county dress code even though she said she and her mother belonged to the Church of Body Modification, which had a clergy, statement of beliefs, and formal process for accepting new members.[95]

Employee's Duty to Cooperate in Accommodation

The U.S. Supreme Court has held that, in attempting to accommodate the employee, all that is required is that the employer attempt to make a reasonable accommodation. If one can be made, then any reasonable accommodation will do, and it need not necessarily be the most reasonable accommodation or the one the employee wants. The employee also must be reasonable in considering accommodation alternatives. The protection Title VII provides for employment discrimination on the basis of religion does not mean that the employer must resolve the conflict in the way the employee wants. In *Vargas v. Sears, Roebuck & Company*,[96] the employer attempted to accommodate the Hispanic employee's

Native American religious belief involving letting his hair grow. The employee's wearing his hair in a ponytail violated the employer's appearance policy. The employer suggested tucking the ponytail inside the employee's shirt or jacket, but the employee refused to even consider it and provided no suggestions of his own. The court held that the employee had not shown that the employer failed to attempt to accommodate the religious conflict, and the employee's termination was upheld.

The employer's only alternative may involve demoting the employee to a job without a conflict or even terminating the employee, depending on the circumstances. This is not prohibited if all other alternatives present the employer with an undue hardship. The EEOC and the courts will look to the following factors in determining whether the employer has successfully borne the burden of reasonably accommodating the employee's religious conflict:

• Whether the employer made an attempt at accommodation.
• The size of the employer's workforce.
• The type of job in which the conflict is present.
• The employer's checking with other employees to see if anyone was willing to assist in the accommodation.
• The cost of accommodation.
• The administrative aspects of accommodation.

Each factor will be considered and weighed as appropriate for the circumstances. If on balance the employer has considered the factors appropriate for the employer's particular circumstances and accommodation was not possible, there is usually no liability for religious discrimination.

What Constitutes Undue Hardship?

LO5 Define undue hardship as it allows an employer defense to religious discrimination claims.

Just as reasonable accommodation varies from situation to situation, so, too, does what constitutes undue hardship. There are no set rules about what constitutes undue hardship since each employer operates under different circumstances. What may be hardship for one employer may not be for another. What constitutes an undue hardship is addressed by the EEOC and courts on an individual basis.

It is clear, however, that the undue hardship may not be a mere inconvenience to the employer. The EEOC has provided guidelines as to what factors it will consider in deciding whether the employer's accommodation would cause undue hardship.[97] Such factors include

• The nature of the employer's workplace.
• The type of job needing accommodation.
• The cost of the accommodation.
• The willingness of other employees to assist in the accommodation.
• The possibility of transfer of the employee and its effects.

- What is done by similarly situated employers.
- The number of employees available for accommodation.
- The burden of accommodation on the union (if any).

The factors are similar to those used to determine if the employer has made reasonable accommodation. Generally, the EEOC's interpretation of what constitutes undue hardship and reasonable accommodation has been more stringent than the interpretation of undue hardship by the courts. However, since the EEOC's guidelines are simply guidelines (though strong, well-respected ones) and thus not binding and court decisions are, employers must look to the interpretation by courts in their own jurisdictions. Courts have found, among other things, that it would be an undue hardship if an employer had to violate the seniority provision of a valid collective bargaining agreement, to pay out more than a "de minimis" cost (in terms of money or efficiency) to replace a worker who has religious conflicts, or to force other employees who do not wish to do so to trade places with the employee who has a religious conflict. The U.S. Supreme Court's determination of what constitutes undue hardship was established in *Trans World Airlines, Inc. v. Hardison,* which still stands today. As you can see after reviewing the case at the end of the chapter, it did not place an unduly heavy burden on the employer.

Religion as a BFOQ

Title VII permits religion to be a bona fide occupational qualification if it is reasonably necessary to the employer's particular normal business operations. As mentioned earlier, it also specifically permits educational institutions to employ those of a particular religion if they are owned in whole or in substantial part by a particular religion. In *Pime v. Loyola University of Chicago,*[98] the court looked at whether a historically Jesuit university could have Jesuit membership as a BFOQ for philosophy professors. A Jewish professor applied to teach philosophy in a department that had passed a resolution saying the professors needed to be Jesuits. The court determined that the university could impose such a measure because essential to the mission of the university was not just to have the subject matter presented to students but to have them exposed to the particular attributes possessed by Jesuits who had actually been trained as Jesuit that was part of the basis of the university.

Religious Harassment

LO6 Describe religious harassment and give examples.

As mentioned earlier, one of the most active areas under religious discrimination lately has been religious harassment. Several factors have come together and caused many employees to decide that expressing their religious views in some way in the workplace is something they are compelled to do, by either their religious dictates or their own interpretation of them.

For instance, employees may feel they must or wish to display crosses or other religious artifacts at work; display religious brochures or material on their desk or pass them out to coworkers; hold Bible or other religious study groups during the workday; preach, teach, testify, or "witness" to their coworkers in order to practice their religion; or engage in other such activities. As mentioned earlier, after the events of September 11, 2001, there was an increase in the number of claims of religious harassment. They have continued to grow. It really is quite extraordinary. In one incident cited by the EEOC, a Muslim employee who had experienced no workplace problems before September 11, 2001, reported that afterward none of his coworkers would speak to him and that when they did, they referred to him as "the local terrorist" or "camel jockey." This has been a frequent occurrence across the country not only for Muslims but for anyone who even appeared to be of Middle Eastern descent. During and in the wake of the 2016 presidential election, claims have risen even more, with Muslims or those thought to be Muslims being aggressively harassed, even in the workplace, for no reason other than their religion. One Bed Bath & Beyond employee said that his coworkers were fine to him until they found out he was Muslim. He was then harassed, called "Terrorist," and terminated.[99] The reality is that when the Department of Homeland Security added white supremacists violence to the list of priority threats, they had perpetrated 39 of 50 domestic extremism-related murders in 2018, while jihadists were linked to only one.[100]

The New York Times reported that a survey of 743 human resource professionals by the Society for Human Resource Management indicated that the most common religion-related issues among employees are employees proselytizing (20 percent), employees feeling harassed by coworkers' religious expressions (14 percent), employees objecting to job duties (9 percent), and employees harassing coworkers for their religious beliefs (6 percent).[101]

This activity surrounding the issue of religious harassment is due, in part, to matters peripheral to workplace religious discrimination. In 1990, the U.S. Supreme Court rejected Native Americans' argument that they should be permitted the ritual use of the hallucinogenic drug peyote in their tribal religious ceremonies as a part of their First Amendment right to freedom of religion. With tremendous support from many quarters, in 1993 Congress passed the Religious Freedom Restoration Act (RFRA) in order to ensure the free exercise of religious practices. RFRA was an attempt to restore the previous status quo under which religious practices must be accommodated unless a compelling governmental interest can be demonstrated and advanced in the least restrictive manner. In 1997, the U.S. Supreme Court overturned RFRA as it related to Boerne, Texas, as giving a governmental preference for religion, in violation of the First Amendment to the Constitution.[102]

While the matter of religious practices in the workplace was not at issue in these cases or this legislation, the national attention and debate about it, along with a growing religious presence in political issues and the media, extended the religious practices issue to the workplace by extrapolation. When the religious practices were challenged, religious harassment claims rose.

Of course, with all different types of religions in the workplace, it is predictable that there would be religious conflicts and that those with religions considered out of the ordinary or with religious practices that coworkers consider extreme would be the subject of religious harassment. In addition, it is often the nonreligious employees who allege that they are being harassed by religious employees. For instance, in a case filed by information systems manager Rosamaria Machado-Wilson of DeLand, Florida, she alleged that she was fired after less than six months on the job after reporting religious harassment to the human resources office of her employer, BSG Laboratories. According to Machado-Wilson, a simple walk to the coffeepot sometimes meant "weaving past prostrate, praying co-workers and stopping for impromptu ceremonies spoken in tongues." She says she was forced to attend company prayer meetings and be baptized, employees were subjected to inquiries into and comments about their religious beliefs, and those found to be nonbelievers were fired.[103]

Of course, since Title VII prohibits religious discrimination, it also prohibits religious harassment. EEOC guidelines on liability for workplace harassment explicitly cover religious harassment. In the wake of the RFRA situation, in 1997 President Clinton issued guidelines for the religious freedom of federal employees. The purpose of the guidelines is to accommodate religious observance in the workplace as an important national priority by striking a balance between religious observance and the requirements of the workplace. Under the guidelines, employees

- Should be permitted to engage in private religious expression in personal work areas not regularly open to the public to the same extent that they may engage in nonreligious private expression.

- Should be permitted to engage in religious expression with fellow employees to the same extent that they may engage in comparable nonreligious private expression, subject to reasonable restrictions.

- Are permitted to engage in religious expression directed at fellow employees and may even attempt to persuade fellow employees of the correctness of their religious views. But employees must refrain from such expression when a fellow employee asks that it stop or otherwise demonstrates that it is unwelcome.

In order to best prevent liability for religious harassment, employers should be sure to protect employees from those religious employees who attempt to proselytize others who do not wish to be approached about religious matters as well as to protect employees with permissible religious practices who are given a hard time by those who believe differently. Making sure that employees are given comparable opportunities to use workplace time and resources for religious practices if given for secular ones is also an important consideration, as otherwise it may appear that the employer is discriminating on the basis of religion.

The *Peterson v. Hewlett-Packard Co.* case, included at the end of the chapter, sets forth the very interesting issue of what to do when an employer's workplace diversity policy is at odds with an employee's religious beliefs, to the extent that the employee who opposes the policy feels harassed. The court upheld his termination after the employer posted diversity posters that included sexual orientation and the employee placed biblical passages on the overhead bins in his office for all to see, with the goal of hurting LGBTQ employees "so they would repent."

Keep in mind here that as an employer, the employer gets to make the determinations about religion in the workplace within the confines of the law. Hopefully, they are consistent with law and promote workplace productivity. Employees who decide, for whatever reason, that they cannot abide the employer's lawful and legal policies always have the choice of either toughing it out or looking for a job that presents no such conflict. While the employer has no right to make employees choose between their religion and work, where a religious conflict does not pose an undue hardship, the employee also has no right to dictate to the employer what workplace policies must be. And, of course, harassment on the basis of religion is illegal under Title VII.

Union Activity and Religious Discrimination

LO7 Identify the ways in which unions and religious conflicts occur.

As the earlier *Hardison* case discussed, at times the religious conflicts that arise between the employee and the employer are caused by collective-bargaining agreement provisions rather than by policies unilaterally imposed by the employer. It has been determined that, even though Title VII applies the term *religion* with reference to an employer having a duty to reasonably accommodate, unions are also under a duty to reasonably accommodate religious conflicts.

The most frequent conflicts are requirements that employees be union members or pay union dues. Union membership, payment of union dues, and engaging in concerted activity such as picketing and striking conflict with some religious beliefs. Employees also have objected to the payment of union dues as violating their First Amendment right to freedom of religion and Title VII's prohibition against religious discrimination. Unions have claimed that applying the religious proscription of Title VII violates the Establishment Clause of the First Amendment to the U.S. Constitution, ensuring government neutrality in religious matters.

Courts have ruled that union security agreements requiring that employees pay union dues within a certain time after the effective date of their employment or be discharged does not violate an employee's First Amendment rights. However, it violates Title VII for an employer to discharge an employee for refusal to join the union because of his or her religious beliefs.

Employees with religious objections must be reasonably accommodated, including the possibility of the alternative of keeping their job without paying union dues. However, the union could prove undue hardship if many of the employees chose to have their dues instead paid to a nonunion, nonsectarian charitable organization chosen by the union and the employer since the impact on the union would not be insubstantial.

In *Tooley v. Martin-Marietta Corp,*[104] Seventh Day Adventists who were prohibited by their religion from becoming members of or paying a service fee to a union offered to pay an amount equal to union dues to a mutually acceptable charity. The union refused and argued that to accommodate the employees violated the Establishment Clause ensuring governmental neutrality in matters of religion. The court said that the government could legitimately enforce accommodation of religious beliefs when the accommodation reflects the obligation of neutrality in the

Management Tips

LO8 List some ways in which management can avoid religious discrimination conflicts.

One of the primary reasons employers run into trouble in this area is because they simply fail to recognize the religious conflict when an employee notifies them or refuse to adequately address it if they do. Many of the conflicts can be avoided by following a few basic rules:

- Take all employee notices of religious conflicts seriously.
- Once an employee puts the employer on notice of a religious conflict, immediately try to find ways to avoid the conflict. An employer doesn't have to accommodate if doing so would cause an undue hardship, but there *must* be an attempt at a reasonable accommodation.
- Ask the employee with the conflict for suggestions on avoiding the conflict. Employers need not take the suggestion but should allow the employee to provide input and knowledge in an area about which he or she may have more information.
- Ask other employees if they can be of assistance in alleviating the conflict (such as switching days off), but make it clear that they are not required to do so.
- Keep workplace religious comments to a minimum and do not engage in religious criticism.
- Make sure all employees understand that they are not to discriminate in any way against employees on the basis of religion.
- Once an employee expresses conflict based on religion, do not challenge the employee's religious beliefs, though it is permissible to make sure of the conflict.
- Make sure undue hardship actually exists if it is claimed.
- Revisit issues such as Christmas bonuses and Christmas parties and giving out Christmas turkeys or other gifts to see if it is more appropriate to use more inclusive language such as *holiday* to cover employees who do not celebrate the Christian holiday of Christmas. Further, revisit the issue of whether all employees are being fairly covered by such policies and events.
- Revisit the issue of granting leave for religious events and make sure it does not favor one religion over another, such as giving employees paid leave for Christmas but requiring them to take their own leave for other religious holidays such as Rosh Hashanah, Yom Kippur, or Ramadan. "Floating holidays" that they can use for whatever holiday they celebrate may make more sense and be less exclusionary.
- Make sure food at workplace events is inclusive of all employees, regardless of religion, such as having kosher (or at least nonpork or nonseafood) items for Jewish employees, having alternatives to alcoholic beverages for those who do not drink for religious reasons, having nonpork items for Muslims, and so on. Asking employees what religious dietary limitations they have or having employees bring a dish to share is an easy way to handle this. It may seem like a small, bothersome thing to deal with, but for those whose religions dictate these things, it is *very* significant. These types of things help to create (or not) a workplace that employees feel truly adheres to both the letter as well as the spirit of the law, and this, in turn, impacts an employee's perception of discrimination and feeling included, which leads to greater productivity and loyalty.

face of religious differences and does not constitute sponsorship, financial support, or active involvement of the sovereign in religious activities with which the Establishment Clause is mainly concerned. The Establishment Clause, typically applied to state legislation, such as in *Frazee,* discussed earlier, requires that the accommodation reflect a clearly secular purpose, have a primary effect that neither inhibits nor advances religion, and avoid excessive government entanglement with religion.

Whether the objection under Title VII is directed toward the employer or the union, a government employer still has a duty to reasonably accommodate the employee's religious conflict unless to do so would cause undue hardship or excessive entanglement with religion or violate the Establishment Clause.

Chapter Summary	• Employees are protected in the workplace in their right to adhere to and practice their religious beliefs, and the employer cannot discriminate against them on this basis unless to do so would be an undue hardship on the employer.
	• The employer cannot question the acceptability of an employee's religion or when or why the employee came to believe.
	• The employer should be conscious of potential religious conflicts in developing and implementing workplace policies.
	• The prohibition on religious discrimination is not absolute, as the employer has only the duty to reasonably accommodate the employee's religious conflict unless to do so would cause the employer undue hardship.
	• While the employer must make a good-faith effort to reasonably accommodate religious conflicts, if such efforts fail, the employer will have discharged his or her legal duties under Title VII.

Chapter-End Questions

1. The employer instituted a religious program in the workplace called "Onionhead" to "harness happiness" of employees. Among other things, employees were required to say "I love you," to share messages about heaven and Satan, and to burn candles to keep the devil away from the office. An employee is fired for not complying. Can employer establish an Onionhead religion? Are these practices okay for the employer to require of employees? [*EEOC v. United Health Program of America, Inc.,* 213 F. Supp. 3d 377 (E.D. NY 2016).]

2. Cynthia requested a two-week leave from her employer to go on a religious pilgrimage. The pilgrimage was not a requirement of her religion, but Cynthia felt it was a "calling from God." Will it violate Title VII if Cynthia's employer does not grant her the leave? Explain. [*Tiano v. Dillard Department Stores, Inc.,* 1998 WL 117864 (9th Cir. 1998).] Compare with a case in which the UPS Jehovah's Witness employee's supervisor denied his request for a schedule accommodation to allow him to attend the annual religious service, terminated the new employee a few days later, and placed him on a do-not-rehire list. [*EEOC v. United Parcel Service, Inc.,* Civil Action No. 2:12-cv-07334 (11/4/13).]

3. At the end of all her written communications, an employee writes, "Have a blessed day." One of the employer's most important clients requests that the employee not do so, and the employer asks the employee to stop. The employee refuses, saying it is a part of her religion. If the employee sues the employer for religious discrimination, is she likely to win? [*Anderson v. USF Logistics (IMC), Inc.,* 274 F.3d 470 (7th Cir. 2001).]

4. An employee is terminated for refusal to cover or remove his confederate flag symbols as requested by his employer. He sues the employer, claiming discrimination on the basis of his religion as a Christian and his national origin as a "Confederate Southern American." Is he likely to win? [*Storey v. Burns International Security Service,* 390 F.3d 760 (3d Cir. 2004).]

5. A Michigan Holiday Inn fired a pregnant employee because the "very Christian" staff members were very upset by her talk of having an abortion. Has the employer violated Title VII? [*Turic v. Holland Hospitality, Inc.,* No. 1-93-CV-379 (W.D. Mich. 1994).]

6. A police officer who is assigned to a casino refuses the assignment, claiming his Baptist religion prohibits him from gambling or being around gambling. Is he legitimately able to do so? [*Endres v. Indiana State Police,* 349 F.3d 922 (7th Cir. 2003).]

7. An employee police officer, a Jehovah Witness whose religion does not allow carrying weapons or celebration of Christmas, refuses to go through weapons training or to oversee a Christmas party for his job. Can he refuse to do these things and keep his job? [*Westbrook v. N. Carolina A&T State Univ.,* 51 F. Supp. 3d 612 (MD NC 2014).]

8. An employee, a Muslim, is a management trainee at an airport car rental office. As part of her religious practice, the employee wears a hijab (headscarf). She is told by her supervisor that the hijab does not match the uniforms she is required to wear, so she must stop wearing it or be transferred to another position with less customer interaction. The employee is later terminated as a part of a company cutback. She sues for religious discrimination. Does she win? Explain. [*Ali v. Alamo Rent-A-Car,* 246 F.3d 662 (4th Cir. 2001).] How about a hijab-wearing employee working as hostess at Disney's Storyteller's Café attraction, who is terminated when she refused to either work in a back area or wear a fedora over her hijab, which Disney says violates their "looks" policy and negatively affects the experience of restaurant patrons? [*Boudlal v. Disney* (U.S. Dist. Ct. for Central Dist. of CA 8/10/12).]

9. A Pentecostal nurse claims she was constructively discharged after refusing to assist in medical procedures she considered to be abortions because of her religious beliefs. She was initially transferred from labor and delivery to the newborn intensive care unit. The employee found this unacceptable because she says she would once again be forced to refuse tasks that involved allowing infants to die. The hospital invited the employee to meet with human resources and to investigate available positions, but she refused. The employee says the duty to assist in an accommodation never arose because a transfer to any other department is not a viable option since it would require her to give up her eight years of specialized training and education and undertake retraining. The employee sues for religious discrimination. Does she win? Explain. [*Shelton v. University of Medicine & Dentistry of New Jersey,* 2000 U.S. App. LEXIS 19099 (3d Cir. 2000).]

10. A Baptist-run home for troubled youngsters terminates an employee for being a lesbian. Can it do so? [*Pedreira v. Kentucky Baptist Home for Children,* 186 F. Supp. 2d 757 (W.D. Ky. 2001).] How about terminating a practicing Nazarite from Taco Bell whose religious beliefs do not allow the cutting of hair? Does it matter if the employee had worked there for seven years without cutting his hair? [*EEOC v. Family Foods, Inc.,* d/b/a Taco Bell, Civil Action No. 5:11-cv-00394 7/28/11.] What about a self-described Evangelical Christian computer specialist working for the National Aeronautics and Space Administration (NASA) Jet Propulsion Laboratory who believes in intelligent design rather than evolution, argues about it with coworkers, and passes out DVDs about it? [*Coppedge v. JPL,* Case No. BC 435600 (Superior Court of the State of CA, County of Los Angeles, 1/15/13).]

End Notes

1. "Dynamic Medical Services to Pay $170,000 to Settle EEOC Religious Discrimination Lawsuit," EEOC press release (December 23, 2013), http://www.eeoc.gov/eeoc/newsroom/release/12-23-13a.cfm.

2. Palmer, James, "Woman Wasn't Christian Enough for Employer," Courthouse News Service (April 20, 2017), http://www.courthousenews.com/woman-says-wasnt-christian-enough-employer/.

3. Weikel, Dan, "Sikh Truck Drivers Reach Accord in Religious Discrimination Case Involving a Major Shipping Company," *Los Angeles Times* (November 15, 2016), http://www.latimes.com/local/lanow/la-me-ln-sikh-truckers-20161115-story.html.

4. Myers, Amanda Lee, "Ex-Ohio Hospital Worker Sues over Flu Requirement," *The News-Herald* (January 17, 2013), http://www.news-herald.com/general-news/20130117/former-ohio-hospital-worker-sues-over-flu-shot-requirement.

5. Hammock, Bradford T., and Joseph J. Lynett, "Inquiry to Determine Employee's Religious Objection to Mandatory Vaccination Gains EEOC Counsel's Support," *Lexology* (February 5, 2013), http://www.lexology.com/library/detail.aspx?g=3a9e9308-cd85-47c9-b539-628050957f4e.

6. "EEOC Sues Consol Energy and Consolidation Coal Company for Religious Discrimination," EEOC press release (September 25, 2013), http://www.eeoc.gov/eeoc/newsroom/release/9-25-13d.cfm.

7. "UPS To Pay $4.9 Million to Settle EEOC Religious Discrimination Suit," EEOC Press Release, 12-21-2018, https://www.eeoc.gov/eeoc/newsroom/release/12-21-18b.cfm.

8. "Fired Officer Says Christian Beliefs Prohibit Him from Training Women," *HuffPost* (August 20, 2019), https://www.huffpost.com/entry/billy-graham-rule-sheriff-officer_n_5d4c2d53e4b0066eb70deaba.

9. "Ex-Ford employee Awarded $17M in Discrimination Case," *New York Post,* Associated Press (April 5, 2018), https://nypost.com/2018/04/05/ex-ford-employee-awarded-17m-in-discrimination-case/.

10. Kuruvilla, Carol, "Virginia Company Mocked Muslim Job Seeker's Religion during Interview, Lawsuit Says," *HuffPost* (September 26, 2019), https://www.huffpost.com/entry/shahin-indorewala-fast-trak-muslim-discrimination-lawsuit_n_5d8cd39fe4b0019647a4be8e.

11. "Fremont Toyota Pays $400,000 to Settle EEOC's Harassment and Retaliation Lawsuit," EEOC press release (August 7, 2012).

12. "Man Fired for God Button: Trevor Keezer Says Home Depot Fired Him over 'One Nation Under God' Pin," *The Huffington Post* (March 18, 2010), http://www.huffingtonpost.com/ 2009/10/28/trevor-keezor-florida-man_n_337875.html.

13. Horowitz, Donna, "Ex-Santana Employee Sues over Firing," *Los Angeles Times* (October 11, 2005), http://articles.latimes.com/2005/oct/11/local/me-santana11.

14. *Anderson v. U.S.F. Logistics, Inc.,* 274 F.3d 470 (7th Cir. 2001).

15. *Hedum v. Starbucks Corp.,* 546 F. Supp. 1017 (D. Or. 2008).

16. Claburn, Thomas, "Google Sued for Sexual, Religious Discrimination," *Information Week* (November 3, 2009), http://www.informationweek.com/news/services/saas/show Article.jhtml?articleID=221600072.

17. Joyner, James, "Woman Fired for Eating 'Unclean' Meat," Orlando Local6 TV (August 4, 2004), http://www.outsidethebeltway.com/_woman_fired_for_eating_unclean_meat/.

18. Reilly, Patrick J., "Look Who's Discriminating Now," *The Wall Street Journal* (August 13, 2009), http://online.wsj.com/article/SB10001424052970203863204574346833989489154.html.

19. Adesina, Zack, and Oana Marocico, "Is It Easier to Get a Job If You're Adam or Mohamed?" *BBX Inside Out* (February 6, 2017).

20. McArdle, Mairead, "Muslim Truck Drivers Fired for Refusing to Deliver Beer Awarded $240K," *CNSNews.com* (November 9, 2015).

21. Moyer, Justin Wm., "Muslim Flight Attendant Suspended for Refusing to Serve Alcohol Files Federal Complaint," *The Washington Post* (September 18, 2015), https://www.washingtonpost.com/news/morning-mix/wp/2015/09/08/muslim-flight-attendant-suspended-for-refusing-to-serve-alcohol-files-federal-complaint/?utm_term=.9f7673c3af13.

22. Baldas, Tresa, "Muslim-American Man Wins Nearly $1.2 Million in Job Discrimination Case," *DetroitFreePress* (February 20, 2014), http://www.freep.com/story/news/local/2014/02/28/muslimamerican-man-wins-nearly-12-million-in-job-discrimination-case/77152192/.

23. "Minnesota's Muslim Cabdrivers Face Crackdown," Reuters (April 17, 2007), http://www.reuters.com/article/2007/04/17/us-muslims-taxis-idUSN1633289220070417.

24. *Moranski v. General Motors Corp.,* 433 F.3d 537 (7th Cir. 2005).

25. Stein, Rob, "Pharmacists' Rights at Front of New Debate: Because of Beliefs, Some Refuse to Fill Birth Control Prescriptions," *The Washington Post* (March 28, 2005), http://www.washingtonpost.com/wp-dyn/articles/A5490-2005Mar27.html.

26. *Endres v. Indiana State Police,* 349 F.3d 922 (7th Cir. 2003). The U.S. Supreme Court declined to hear the officer's appeal.

27. *Knight v. State of Connecticut, Department of Public Health,* 275 F.3d 156 (2d Cir. 2001).

28. Castellani, Anne, "Judge Rules in Favor of Turban-Wearing Officer," CNNJustice (May 3, 2004), http://articles.cnn.com/2004-04-30/justice/turban.cop_1_turban-judge-rules-sikh?_s=PM:LAW; Shortell, David, "NYPD Changes Policy, Will Allow Officers to Wear Turbans," CNN (December 29, 2016).

29. Pérez-Peña, Richard, "Judge Says Army Can't Require Special Testing of Sikh Officer," *The New York Times* (March 4, 2016), https://www.nytimes.com/2016/03/05/us/sikh-army-captain-beard-turban.html?mcubz=1.

30. "Ten Commandments Judge Removed from Office," CNNJustice (November 4, 2003), http://articles.cnn.com/2003-11-13/justice/moore.tencommandments_1_ethics-panel-state-supreme-court-building-ethics-charges?_s=PM:LAW.

31. "City Agrees to Pay $20,000 in Fees, Clarify Rules after 2 Employees Claim Christmas Discrimination," Fox News (February 20, 2008), http://www.foxnews.com/story/0,2933,331431,00.html?sPage=fnc/us/lawcenter.

32. "Florida TV Producer Sues over Firing," *highbeam.com* (January 29, 2003), http://www.highbeam.com/doc/1P1-71355459.html.

33. Banerjee, Neela, "Soldier Sues Army, Saying His Atheism Led to Threats," *The New York Times* (April 26, 2008), http://www.nytimes.com/2008/04/26/us/26atheist.html.

34. "Worker Opposed to Gays Wins Suit," *The Washington Times* (April 7, 2004), http://www.washingtontimes.com/news/2004/apr/7/20040407-124312-3261r/.

35. *Peterson v. Hewlett-Packard, Co.,* 358 F.3d 599 (9th Cir. 2004).

36. *Altman v. Minn. Dept. of Corr.,* 251 F.3d 1199 (7th Cir. 2001).

37. Espinoza, Martin, "Order to Tuck in Dreadlocks Leads to Civil Rights Lawsuit," *The New York Times* (September 18, 2008), http://www.nytimes.com/2008/09/18/nyregion/18dreads.html.

38. *Peterson v. Wilmur Communications, Inc.,* 205 F. Supp. 1014 (E.D. Wis. 2002).

39. Ibid.

40. Burleigh, Nina, "Trump Effect Inspires Radical Christians in Military," *Newsweek* (May 22, 2017), http://www.newsweek.com/christian-fundamentalists-us-armed-forces-national-security-threat-613428.

41. "Wiccan Symbol OK on Military Headstones," *nbcnews.com* (April 23, 2007), http://www.nbcnews.com/id/18274639/ns/us_news-military/t/wiccan-symbol-ok-military-headstones/#.UvlhPP2CseY.

42. Harris, Elizabeth A., "Billboard Called Anti-Semitic Is Quickly Pulled," *The New York Times* (November 22, 2011), http://www.nytimes.com/2011/11/23/nyregion/billboard-ad-for-wodka-vodka-called-anti-semitic-is-pulled.html?_r=0.

43. "Colorado Student Quits High School Choir over Islamic Song Praising 'Allah,'" *foxnews.com* (February 15, 2012), http://www.foxnews.com/us/2012/02/15/colorado-student-reportedly-quits-choir-over-islamic-song/.

44. Remizowski, Leigh, "Teacher Who Was Fired after Fertility Treatments Sues Diocese," CNN (April 26, 2012), http://www.cnn.com/2012/04/26/us/indiana-in-vitro-lawsuit/index.html.

45. Karni, Annie, "DUMBO Restaurant the River Cafe Discriminates against Jews: Workers," *New York Post* (October 21, 2012), http://nypost.com/2012/10/21/dumbo-restaurant-the-river-cafe-discriminates-against-jews-workers/.

46. Leavines, Linnie, "LSU Apologizes for Removing Christian Cross from Photo of Students," *campusreform.org* (October 22, 2012), http://www.campusreform.org/?ID=4456.

47. Smith, Morgan, "When Faith Meets Football in East Texas," *The New York Times* (October 13, 2012), http://www.nytimes.com/2012/10/14/us/lawsuit-over-cheerleaders-bearing-bible-verses-in-kountze-texas.html?pagewanted=all&_r=0.

48. *Elk Grove Unified School District v. Newdow,* 542 U.S. 1 (2007).

49. *Van Orden v. Perry,* 545 U.S. 677 (2005) and *McCreary County v. ACLU of Kentucky,* 545 U.S. 844 (2005).

50. "Amish Buggy Bill Could Be Nearing Final Passage," Kentucky New Era (March 14, 2012), http://www.kentuckynewera.com/web/news/article_f3b6d8e2-6d76-11e1-b313-0019bb2963f4.html.

51. "UGA Cheerleading Coach Fired over Discrimination Claims," *Atlanta Journal & Constitution* via *Free Republic* (August 24, 2004), http://www.freerepublic.com/focus/f-news/1198648/posts.

52. "Muslim Basketball Player Quits USF Team," *St. Petersburg Times* (September 16, 2004), http://www.gawaher.com/topic/4040-female-muslim-basketball-player-quits-usf-team/.

53. Goldberg, Melissa, "Head Start," *Oprah Magazine* (March 2017), p. 22.

54. "EEOC Releases Fiscal Year 2019 Enforcement and Litigation Data" (January 24, 2020), https://www.eeoc.gov/eeoc/newsroom/release/1-24-20.cfm.

55. Brown, Matthew, "Religious Discrimination in the Workplace Increases with Diversity," *Deseret News* (August 31, 2013), http://www.deseretnews.com/article/865585613/Religious-discrimination-in-the-workplace-increases-with-diversity.html?pg=all.

56. Valentino-Devries, Jennifer, "Bosses May Use Social Media to Discriminate against Job Seekers: Firms Use Data They Find Early in Job Process, New Study Finds," *The Wall Street Journal* (November 20, 2013), http://online.wsj.com/news/articles/SB10001424052702303755504579208304255139392.

57. http://eeoc.gov/policy/does/religion.html.

58. Brown, "Religious Discrimination in the Workplace Increases with Diversity."

59. "In U.S., Decline of Christianity Continues at Rapid Pace" (October 17, 2019), https://www.pewforum.org/2019/10/17/in-u-s-decline-of-christianity-continues-at-rapid-pace/.

60. Brown, "Religious Discrimination in the Workplace Increases with Diversity."

61. 483 U.S. 327 (1987).

62. 565 U.S. . . ., (No. 10-553, 2012).

63. "Jewish Hockey Player Claims He Was Harassed," *CNN.com* (January 25, 2011), http://www.cnn.com/2011/US/01/25/hockey.player.lawsuit/index.html?iref=allsearch.

64. "Brothers' Religious Discrimination Suit Settled," *JTA.org* (March 18, 2010), http://www.jta.org/news/article-print/2010/03/18/1011187/lawsuit-filed-by-the-eeoc-on-behalf.html.

65. "Teachers File Discrimination Lawsuit against School District," *Bakersfield News* (May 21, 2009), http://www.turnto23.com/news/19533316/detail.html.

66. "Drill Sergeants Reprimanded for Bias, Calling Trainee 'Juden,'" *usatoday.com* (October 18, 2008), http://www.usatoday.com/news/religion/2008-10-06-jewish-soldier-n.html.

67. Gillam, Carey, "Susann Bashir, Muslim Woman, Wins $5 Million Verdict from AT&T for Discrimination," *The Huffington Post* (May 4, 2012), http://www.huffingtonpost.com/2012/05/05/muslim-woman-wins-5-million-att_n_1479884.html.

68. "EEOC Sues Star Transport, Inc., for Religious Discrimination," EEOC press release (May 29, 2013), http://eeoc.gov/eeoc/newsroom/release/5-29-13.cfm.

69. "Hertz Suspends 34 Muslim Drivers in Prayer Dispute," *The Seattle Times* (October 7, 2011), http://seattletimes.com/html.

70. "EEOC Sues Covergys Corporation for Religious Discrimination," EEOC press release (March 3, 2011), http://www.eeoc.gov/eeoc/newsroom/release/3-3-11.cfm.

71. "Ivy Hall Assisted Living Pays $43,000 to Settle Religious Discrimination Lawsuit," EEOC press release (January 29, 2010), http://www.eeoc.gov/newsroom/release/12-18-09.cfm.

72. *EEOC v. Abercrombie & Fitch Stores, Inc.,* No. 14-86, 575 U.S. __ (June 1, 2015).

73. "EEOC Sues Senior Assisted Living Company for Religious Discrimination," EEOC press release (September 29, 2011), http://www.eeoc.gov/eeoc/newsroom/release/9-29-11f.cfm.

74. Lugris, Mark, "Hotel Dishwasher Awarded $21 Million for Religious Discrimination over Being Made to Work Sundays and Then Fired for 'Misconduct,'" *Destinations* (January 18, 2019), https://www.thetravel.com/miami-hotel-dishwasher-awarded-21-million-religious-discrimination/.

75. Equal Employment Opportunity Commission.

76. 489 U.S. 829 (1989).

77. Barrett Fletcher.

78. Dvorak, Phred, "Religious-Bias Filings Up," *The Wall Street Journal* (October 16, 2008), http://online.wsj.com/article/SB122411562348138619.html.

79. "Brinks to Pay $30,000 to Peoria Area Woman for Failure to Accommodate Religious Beliefs: EEOC Suit Said Pentecostal Employee Fired for Refusal to Wear Pants as Part of Uniform," EEOC press release (January 2, 2003), http://www1.eeoc.gov//eeoc/newsroom/release/1-2-03b.cfm?renderforprint=1.

80. *EEOC v. ChiChi's Restaurant,* http://archive.eeoc.gov/abouteeoc/annual_reports/annrep96-98.html.

81. "Belk, Inc., to Pay $55,000 to Settle EEOC Religious Discrimination Suit," EEOC press release (March 16, 2011), http://www.eeoc.gov/eeoc/newsroom/release/3-16-11.cfm.

82. "Employee's Refusal to Say 'Happy Holidays' Leads to EEOC Complaint," *Business Management Daily* (April 19, 2009), http://www.businessmanagementdaily.com/articles/ 17858/1/Refusal-to-say-Happy-holidays-leads-to-EEOC-complaint/Page1.html#.

83. Haldane, David, "Dismissed Bus Driver Files Federal Complaint: Labor: The Vegetarian Who Refused to Hand Out Hamburger Coupons to Riders for OCTA Cites Religious Discrimination," *Los Angeles Times* (June 11, 1996), http://articles.latimes.com/1996-06-11/local/me-13909_1_bus-driver.

84. Zackin, Martha, "Religious Discrimination or Legitimate Business Decisions? It Depends.," Mintz Levin Employment Matters Blog (February 14, 2012), http://www.employmentmattersblog.com/2012/02/religious-discrimination -or-legitimate-business-decision-it-depends/.

85. *Tanisha Matthews v. WalMart,* 10-2242 (7th Cir. 2011) (unpublished opinion); "Court: Wal-Mart Firing of Anti-Gay Employee Not Religious Harassment," *Chicago Sun Times* (April 6, 2007), http://www.suntimes.com/4693324-417/court-wal-mart-firing-of-anti-gay-employee-not-religious-harassment.html.

86. 475 U.S. 503 (1986).

87. "Sikhs in U.S. Military Now Allowed to Wear Turbans," *Yahoonews* (January 23, 2014), http://in.news.yahoo.com/sikhs-us-military-now-allowed-wear-turbans-052736692.html.

88. *Tanisha Matthews v. WalMart,* 10-2242 (7th Cir. 2011).

89. 49 Cal. App. 4th 1223 (1996).

90. 58 F.3d 1337 (8th Cir. 1995).

91. 515 F.3d 307 (4th Cir. 2008).

92. Skoloff, Brian, "Fla. Man Says Home Depot Fired Him over God Button," *Atlanta Journal & Constitution* (October 28, 2009), http://www.ajc.com/business/fla-man-says-home-175481.html.

93. 529 F.2d 483 (10th Cir. 1976).

94. "Wis. Woman Pleads No Contest in Toilet Corpse Case," *comcast.net* (November 18, 2008), http://www.nbcnews.com/id/27779731/ns/us_news-crime_and_courts/t/woman-pleads-no-contest-toilet-corpse-case/.

95. Breen, Tom, "NC Teen: Nose Ring More Than Fashion, It's Faith," *yahoo.com* (September 16, 2010), http://news.yahoo.com/s/ap/us_rel_piercing_church/print.

96. 1998 U.S. Dist. LEXIS 21148 (E.D. Mich. 1998).

97. 29 C.F.R. § 1605.1. *City of Boerne, Texas v. Flores,* 521 U.S. 507 (1997).

98. 803 F.2d 351 (7th Cir. 1986).

99. Richards, Kimberly, "Muslim Man Fired from Bed Bath & Beyond Says He Was Called 'Terrorist,'" *The Huffington Post* (November 9, 2015), http://www.huffingtonpost.com/entry/muslim-man-fired-bed-bath-beyond_us_5640aed2e4b0b24aee4add11.

100. "Noted," *The Week* (October 4, 2019), citing *The Atlantic.com.*

101. Chartrand, Sabra, "Protecting Freedom of Religion in the Workplace," *The New York Times* (June 8, 1997), http://partners.nytimes.com/library/jobmarket/060897sabra.html.

102. *City of Boerne, Texas v. Flores,* 521 U.S. 507 (1997); and *Rosamaria D. Machado-Wilson v. BSG Laboratories, Inc.,* Case No. 98-106601 CIDL (Cir. Ct., 7th Jud. Cir., Volusia County, Fla., 1998).

103. *Rosamaria D. Machado-Wilson v. BSG Laboratories, Inc.,* Case No. 98-106601 CIDL (Cir. Ct., 7th Jud. Cir., Volusia County, Fla., 1998).

104. 648 F.2d 1239 (9th Cir. 1981).

Cases

Peterson v. Wilmur Communications, Inc.,
205 F. Supp. 2d 1014 (E.D. Wis. 2002)

An employee, a member of a religious group that believed in white supremacy, was demoted when a newspaper article was published giving his religious views. The court held that though the employee's belief was similar to groups such as the KKK, which were political groups not given protection under Title VII, this was a religion that required Title VII protection and the employee could not be demoted simply for having this religious belief.

Adelman, J.

***

Plaintiff/employee, Christopher Lee Peterson, is a follower of the World Church of the Creator, an organization that preaches a system of beliefs called Creativity, the central tenet of which is white supremacy. Creativity teaches that all people of color are "savage" and intent on "mongrelizing the White Race," that African-Americans are subhuman and should be "shipped back to Africa"; that Jews control the nation and have instigated all wars in this century and should be driven from power, and that the Holocaust never occurred, but if it had occurred, Nazi Germany "would have done the world a tremendous favor."

Creativity considers itself to be a religion, but it does not espouse a belief in a God, afterlife, or any sort of supreme being. "Frequently Asked Questions about CREATIVITY," a publication available on the World Church of the Creator's website, characterizes such beliefs as unsubstantiated "nonsense about angels and devils and gods and . . . silly spook craft" and rejects them in favor of "the Eternal Laws of Nature, about which [Creators say] the White Man does have an impressive fund of knowledge." The White Man's Bible, one of Creativity's two central texts, offers a vision of a white supremacist utopian world of "beautiful, healthy [white] people," free of

disease, pollution, fear, and hunger. This world can only be established through the degradation of all non-whites. Thus, Creativity teaches that Creators should live their lives according to the principle that what is good for white people is the ultimate good and what is bad for white people is the ultimate sin. According to The White Man's Bible, the "survival" of white people must be ensured "at all costs." Employee holds these beliefs and, in June 1998, became a "reverend" in the World Church of the Creator.

In 2000, employee was employed by employer Wilmur Communications, Inc., as a Day Room Manager, a position which entailed supervising eight other employees, three of whom were not white. On Sunday, March 19, 2000, an article appeared in the *Milwaukee Journal Sentinel* discussing the World Church of the Creator, interviewing employee, and describing his involvement in the church and beliefs. The article included a photograph of him holding a tee-shirt bearing a picture of Benjamin Smith, who, carrying a copy of The White Man's Bible, had targeted African-American, Jewish and Asian people in a two-day shooting spree in Indiana and Illinois before shooting himself in the summer of 1999. The caption under the photograph read "Rev. C. Lee Peterson of

Milwaukee holds a T-shirt commemorating Benjamin Smith, who killed two people and wounded nine others before shooting himself in a two-day spree last summer."*

When employee arrived at work the next day, his supervisor and the president of the company, Dan Murphy, suspended him without pay. Two days later, employee received a letter from Murphy demoting him to the position of "telephone solicitor," a position with lower pay and no supervisory duties. During his six years of employment at Wilmur Communications, employee had been disciplined once for a data entry error but had never been disciplined for anything else.

Title VII makes it unlawful for an employer to "discriminate against any individual with respect to his compensation, terms, conditions, or privileges of employment, because of such individual's . . . religion."* The statute defines "religion" to include "all aspects of religious observance and practice, as well as belief." § 2000e(j).

A test has emerged to determine whether beliefs are a religion for purposes of Title VII. Rather than define religion according to its content, the test requires the court should find beliefs to be a religion if they "occupy the same place in the life of the [individual] as an orthodox belief in God holds in the life of one clearly qualified."* To satisfy this test, the employee must show that the belief at issue is "'sincerely held' and 'religious' in his [or her] own scheme of things." In evaluating whether a belief meets this test, courts must give "great weight" to the employee's own characterization of his or her beliefs as religious.

To be a religion under this test, a belief system need not have a concept of a God, supreme being, or afterlife. Courts also should not attempt to assess a belief's "truth" or "validity." So long as the belief is sincerely held and is religious in the employee's scheme of things, the belief is religious regardless of whether it is "acceptable, logical, consistent, or comprehensible to others." Once an employee establishes that his or her beliefs are a religion, the employee must offer evidence that his or her religion "played a motivating role" in the adverse employment action at issue. An employee can meet this burden by presenting direct evidence of the employer's discriminatory intent, the method that employee has chosen here, or by the indirect method.

The parties hotly dispute whether Creativity is a religion under Title VII. Thus, as an initial matter, I must determine whether employee's beliefs are "sincerely held" and "religious in his own scheme of things."

Here, the first prong is undisputed. Employee states that he has "a sincere belief" in the teachings of Creativity

and employer offers no contrary evidence. Thus, employee meets the first prong of the test.

The second prong is also undisputed. Employee considers his beliefs religious and considers Creativity to be his religion. I must give "great weight" to that belief. In addition, Creativity plays a central role in employee's life. Employee has been a minister in the World Church of the Creator for more than three years.

Employee states that he "work[s] at putting [the teachings of Creativity] into practice every day." Thus, all the evidence conclusively reveals that the teachings of Creativity are "religious" in employee's "own scheme of things." These beliefs occupy for employee a place in his life parallel to that held by a belief in God for believers in more mainstream theistic religions. Thus, Creativity "functions as" religion for employee. Employee has met his initial burden of showing that his beliefs constitute a "religion" for purposes of Title VII.

Employer argues that the World Church of the Creator cannot be a religion under Title VII because it is similar to other white supremacist organizations that have been found to be political organizations and not religions. To be sure, Creativity shares some of the white supremacist beliefs of the KKK and the National Socialist White People's Party. However, the fact that employee's beliefs can be characterized as political does not mean they are not also religious. Thus, employee could share the beliefs of political organizations yet still establish that his beliefs function as religion for him.

Employer also argues that Creativity's beliefs cannot be religious because they are immoral and unethical, and EEOC regulations define religious beliefs as "moral or ethical beliefs as to what is right and wrong." The EEOC regulation means that "religion" under Title VII includes belief systems which espouse notions of morality and ethics and supply a means of distinguishing right from wrong. Creativity has these characteristics. Creativity teaches that followers should live their lives according to what will best foster the advancement of white people and the denigration of all others. This precept, although simplistic and repugnant to the notions of equality that undergird the very non-discrimination statute at issue, is a means for determining right from wrong. Thus, employer's argument must be rejected. Employee has shown that Creativity functions as religion in his life; thus, Creativity is for him a religion regardless of whether it espouses goodness or ill. Employer's argument is again rejected.

Having established that Creativity is for employee a religion, the employee must offer evidence that his religion played a motivating role in the adverse employment action, in this case his demotion. Employee argues that Murphy's letter of demotion provides direct evidence that he was demoted because of his religion. The letter of demotion from Murphy plainly states that employee was being demoted because of his membership in the World Church of the Creator and his white supremacist beliefs. Thus, employee's beliefs caused employer to demote him and employer is, therefore, liable.

Employee's motion for summary judgment on the issue of liability must be GRANTED. Employer's motion for summary judgment is DENIED.

Case Questions

1. What would you have done if you were the employer who saw this news article? Why?
2. Does the court's decision surprise you? Explain.
3. If you were the employer, what would you do if the employee mistreated nonwhite employees in the workplace?

Peterson v. Wilmur Communications, Inc. 205 F. Supp. 2d 1014 (E.D. Wis. 2002)

Case 2

Chalmers v. Tulon Company of Richmond,
101 F.3d 1012 (4th Cir. 1996)

The supervisory employee sued for religious discrimination and a failure to accommodate after being terminated for sending employees letters at home about their personal and religious lives. One employee received the letter while ill at home on leave after delivering a baby out of wedlock, and the other employee's wife opened the letter and became distraught because she thought the references in the letter meant her husband was having an affair. The court held that there was no duty to accommodate the terminated employee's religious practice of sending such letters.

Motz, J.

***

Chalmers, a supervisor, has been a Baptist all of her life, and in June 1984 became an evangelical Christian. At that time, she accepted Christ as her personal savior and determined to go forth and do work for him. As an evangelical Christian, Chalmers believes she should share the gospel and looks for opportunities to do so.

Chalmers felt that her supervisor, LaMantia, respected her, generally refraining from using profanity around her, while around other employees who did not care, "he would say whatever he wanted to say." She felt that she and LaMantia had a "personal relationship" and that she could talk to him. Chalmers stated that "in the past we have talked about God." Chalmers further testified that "starting off" she and LaMantia had discussed religion about "everytime he came to the service center . . . maybe every three months" but "then, towards the end maybe not as frequently." LaMantia never discouraged these conversations, expressed discomfort with them, or

indicated that they were improper. In one of these conversations, LaMantia told Chalmers that three people had approached him about accepting Christ.

Two or three years after this conversation, Chalmers "knew it was time for [LaMantia] to accept God." She believed LaMantia had told customers information about the turnaround time for a job when he knew that information was not true. Chalmers testified that she was "led by the Lord" to write LaMantia and tell him "there were things he needed to get right with God, and that was one thing that . . . he needed to get right with him."*

Accordingly, on Labor Day, September 6, 1993, Chalmers mailed the following letter to LaMantia at his home:

> Dear Rich:
>
> The reason I'm writing you is because the Lord wanted me to share somethings [sic] with you.

After reading this letter you do not have to give me a call, but talk to God about everything.

One thing the Lord wants you to do is get your life right with him. The Bible says in Romans 10:9vs that if you confess with your mouth the Lord Jesus and believe in your heart that God hath raised him from the dead, thou shalt be saved. vs 10—For with the heart man believeth unto righteousness, and with the mouth confession is made unto salvation. The two verse are [sic] saying for you to get right with God now.

The last thing is, you are doing somethings [sic] in your life that God is not please [sic] with and He wants you to stop. All you have to do is go to God and ask for forgiveness before it's too late.

I wrote this letter at home so if you have a problem with it you can't relate it to work.

I have to answer to God just like you do, so that's why I wrote you this letter. Please take heed before it's too late.

In his name,

Charita Chalmers*

On September 10, 1993, when Chalmers' letter arrived at LaMantia's home, he was out of town on Tulon business and his wife opened and read the letter in his absence. Mrs. LaMantia became distraught, interpreting the references to her husband's improper conduct as indicating that he was committing adultery. In tears, she called Chalmers and asked her if LaMantia was having an affair with someone in the New Hampshire area where LaMantia supervised another Tulon facility. Mrs. LaMantia explained that three years before she and LaMantia had separated because of his infidelity. Chalmers told Mrs. LaMantia that she did not know about any affair because she was in the Richmond area. When Mrs. LaMantia asked her what she had meant by writing that there was something in LaMantia's life that "he needed to get right with God," Chalmers explained about the turnaround time problem. Mrs. LaMantia responded that she would take the letter and rip it up so LaMantia could not read it. Chalmers answered, "Please don't do that, the Lord led me to send this to Rich, so let him read it." The telephone conversation then ended.

Mrs. LaMantia promptly telephoned her husband, interrupting a Tulon business presentation, to accuse him of infidelity. LaMantia, in turn, called the Richmond office and asked to speak with Chalmers; she was in back and by the time she reached the telephone, LaMantia had hung up. Chalmers then telephoned the LaMantias'

home and, when she failed to reach anyone, left a message on the answering machine that she was sorry "if the letter offended" LaMantia or his wife and that she "did not mean to offend him or make him upset about the letter."

LaMantia also telephoned Craig A. Faber, Vice President of Administration at Tulon. LaMantia told Faber that the letter had caused him personal anguish and placed a serious strain on his marriage. LaMantia informed Faber that he felt he could no longer work with Chalmers. LaMantia recommended that Tulon management terminate Chalmers' employment.

While investigating LaMantia's complaint, Faber discovered that Chalmers had sent a second letter, on the same day as she sent the letter to LaMantia, to another Tulon employee. That employee, Brenda Combs, worked as a repoint operator in the Richmond office and Chalmers was her direct supervisor. Chalmers knew that Combs was convalescing at her home, suffering from an undiagnosed illness after giving birth out of wedlock. Chalmers sent Combs the following letter:

Brenda,

You probably do not want to hear this at this time, but you need the Lord Jesus in your life right now.

One thing about God, He doesn't like when people commit adultery. You know what you did is wrong, so now you need to go to God and ask for forgiveness.

Let me explain something about God. He's a God of Love and a God of Wrath. When people sin against Him, he will allow things to happen to them or their family until they open their eyes and except [sic] Him. God can put a sickness on you that no doctor could ever find out what it is. I'm not saying this is what happened to you, all I'm saying is get right with God right now. Romans 10:9;10vs says that is [sic] you confess with your mouth the Lord Jesus and believe in your heart that God has raised him from the dead thou shalt be saved. For with the heart man believeth unto righteousness; and with the mouth confession is made unto salvation. All I'm saying is you need to invite God into your heart and live a life for Him and things in your life will get better.

That's not saying you are not going to have problems but it's saying you have someone to go to.

Please take this letter in love and be obedient to God.

In his name,

Charita Chalmers*

Upon receiving the letter Combs wept. Faber discussed the letter with Combs who told him that she had been "crushed by the tone of the letter." Combs believed that Chalmers implied that "an immoral lifestyle" had caused her illness and found Chalmers' letter "cruel." Combs, in a later, unsworn statement, asserted that although the letter "upset her" it did not "offend" her or "damage her working relationship" with Chalmers.

Faber consulted with other members of upper management and concluded that the letters caused a negative impact on working relationships, disrupted the workplace, and inappropriately invaded employee privacy. On behalf of Tulon, Faber then sent Chalmers a memorandum, informing her that she was terminated from her position. The memorandum stated in relevant part:

We have decided to terminate your employment with Tulon Co. effective today, September 21, 1993. Our decision is based on a serious error in judgment you made in sending letters to LaMantia and Combs, which criticized their personal lives and beliefs. The letters offended them, invaded their privacy, and damaged your work relationships, making it too difficult for you to continue to work here.

We expect all of our employees to show good judgment, especially those in supervisory positions, such as yours. We would hope you can learn from this experience and avoid similar mistakes in the future.*

As a result of the preceding events, Chalmers filed suit, alleging that Tulon discriminated against her based on her religion, in violation of Title VII. She contended that her letter writing constituted protected religious activity that Tulon, by law, should have accommodated with a lesser punishment than discharge.

In a religious accommodation case, an employee can establish a claim even though she cannot show that other (unprotected) employees were treated more favorably or cannot rebut an employer's legitimate, non-discriminatory reason for her discharge. This is because an employer must, to an extent, actively attempt to accommodate an employee's religious expression or conduct even if, absent the religious motivation, the employee's conduct would supply a legitimate ground for discharge.

Tulon's proffered reasons for discharging Chalmers—because her letters, which criticized her fellow employees' personal lives and beliefs, invaded the employees' privacy, offended them and damaged her working relationships—are legitimate and non-discriminatory.

To establish a *prima facie* religious accommodation claim, a plaintiff must establish that: "(1) he or she has a bona fide religious belief that conflicts with an employment requirement; (2) he or she informed the employer of this belief; (3) he or she was disciplined for failure to comply with the conflicting employment requirement."*

Chalmers has alleged that she holds bona fide religious beliefs that caused her to write the letters. Tulon offers no evidence to the contrary. The parties agree that Tulon fired Chalmers because she wrote the letters. Accordingly, Chalmers has satisfied the first and third elements of the *prima facie* test. However, in other equally important respects, Chalmers' accommodation claim fails.

Chalmers concedes that she did not expressly notify Tulon that her religion required her to write letters like those at issue here to her co-workers, or request that Tulon accommodate her conduct. Nonetheless, for several reasons, she contends that such notice was unnecessary in this case.

Initially, Chalmers asserts that Tulon never explicitly informed her of a company policy against writing religious letters to fellow employees at their homes and so she had "no reason to request an accommodation." However, companies cannot be expected to notify employees explicitly of all types of conduct that might annoy co-workers, damage working relationships, and thereby provide grounds for discharge. Chalmers implicitly acknowledged in the letters themselves that they might distress her co-workers. Moreover, she conceded that, as a supervisor, she had a responsibility to "promote harmony in the workplace."

Although a rule justifying discharge of an employee because she has disturbed co-workers requires careful application in the religious discrimination context (many religious practices might be perceived as "disturbing" to others), Chalmers, particularly as a supervisor, is expected to know that sending personal, distressing letters to co-workers' homes, criticizing them for assertedly ungodly, shameful conduct, would violate employment policy. Accordingly, the failure of the company to expressly forbid supervisors from disturbing other employees in this way provides Chalmers with no basis for failing to notify Tulon that her religious beliefs require her to write such letters.

Alternatively, Chalmers contends that the notoriety of her religious beliefs within the company put it on notice of her need to send these letters. In her view, Chalmers satisfied the notice requirement because Tulon required "only enough information about an employee's religious needs to permit the employer to understand the existence of a conflict between the employee's religious practices and the employer's job requirements."*

Knowledge that an employee has strong religious beliefs does not place an employer on notice that she might engage in any religious activity, no matter how unusual. Chalmers concedes that she did not know of any other employee who had ever written distressing or judgmental letters to co-workers before, and that nothing her co-workers had said or done indicated that such letters were acceptable. Accordingly, any knowledge Tulon may have possessed regarding Chalmers' beliefs could not reasonably have put it on notice that she would write and send accusatory letters to co-workers' homes.

Chalmers appears to contend that because Tulon was necessarily aware of the religious nature of the letters after her co-workers received them and before her discharge, Tulon should have attempted to accommodate her by giving her a sanction less than a discharge, such as a warning. This raises a false issue. There is nothing in Title VII that requires employers to give lesser punishments to employees who claim, after they violate company rules (or at the same time), that their religion caused them to transgress the rules.

Part of the reason for the advance notice requirement is to allow the company to avoid or limit any "injury" an employee's religious conduct may cause. Additionally, the refusal even to attempt to accommodate an employee's religious requests, prior to the employee's violation of employment rules and sanction, provides some indication, however slight, of improper motive on the employer's part. The proper issue, therefore, is whether Chalmers made Tulon aware, prior to her letter writing, that her religious beliefs would cause her to send the letters. Since it is clear that she did not, her claims fail.

In sum, Chalmers has not pointed to any evidence that she gave Tulon—either directly or indirectly—advance notice of her need for accommodation. For this reason, Chalmers has failed to establish a *prima facie* case of discrimination under the religious accommodation theory.

If we had concluded that Chalmers had established a *prima facie* case, Chalmers' religious accommodation claim would nonetheless fail. This is so because Chalmers' conduct is not the type that an employer can possibly accommodate, even with notice.

Chalmers concedes in the letters themselves that she knew the letters to her co-workers, accusing them of immoral conduct (in the letter to Combs, suggesting that Combs' immoral conduct caused her illness), might cause them distress. Even if Chalmers had notified Tulon expressly that her religious beliefs required her to write such letters, i.e., that she was "led by the Lord" to write them, Tulon was without power under any circumstances to accommodate Chalmers' need.

Typically, religious accommodation suits involve religious conduct, such as observing the Sabbath, wearing religious garb, etc., that result in indirect and minimal burdens, if any, on other employees. An employer can often accommodate such needs without inconveniencing or unduly burdening other employees.

In a case like the one at hand, however, where an employee contends that she has a religious need to impose personally and directly on fellow employees, invading their privacy and criticizing their personal lives, the employer is placed between a rock and a hard place. If Tulon had the power to authorize Chalmers to write such letters, and if Tulon had granted Chalmers' request to write the letters, the company would subject itself to possible suits from Combs and LaMantia claiming that Chalmers' conduct violated their religious freedoms or constituted religious harassment. Chalmers' supervisory position at the Richmond office heightens the possibility that Tulon (through Chalmers) would appear to be imposing religious beliefs on employees.

Thus, even if Chalmers had notified Tulon that her religion required her to send the letters at issue here to her co-workers, Tulon would have been unable to accommodate that conduct.

We do not in any way question the sincerity of Chalmers' religious beliefs or practices. However, it is undisputed that Chalmers failed to notify Tulon that her religious beliefs led her to send personal, disturbing letters to her fellow employees accusing them of immorality. It is also undisputed that the effect of a letter on one of the recipients, LaMantia's wife, whether intended or not, caused a co-worker, LaMantia, great stress and caused him to complain that he could no longer work with Chalmers. Finally, it is undisputed that another employee, Combs, told a company officer that Chalmers' letter upset her (although she later claimed that her working relationship with Chalmers was unaffected). Under these facts, Chalmers cannot establish a religious accommodation claim. Accordingly, the district court's order granting summary judgment to Tulon is AFFIRMED.

Case Questions

1. Is there any way the employer could have avoided this situation? Explain.

2. If the employee had initially told the employer of her plan to write the letters and the employer had told her not to send them, would the outcome be any different if she had done so anyway?

3. What would you have done if your employee's wife called as Mrs. LaMantia did?

Chalmers v. Tulon Company of Richmond 101 F.3d 1012 (4th Cir. 1996)

Trans World Airlines, Inc. v. Hardison,
432 U.S. 63 (1977)

The employer was unable to accommodate the employee's religious conflict of working on the Sabbath without undue hardship. The Court set forth the guidelines for determining what constitutes undue hardship.

White, J.

***

The employee, Hardison, was employed by Trans World Airlines (TWA), in a department that operated 24 hours a day throughout the year in connection with an airplane maintenance and overhaul base. Hardison was subject to a seniority system in a collective bargaining agreement between TWA and the International Association of Machinists & Aerospace Workers (union), whereby the most senior employees have first choice for job and shift assignments as they become available, and the most junior employees are required to work when enough employees to work at a particular time or in a particular job to fill TWA's needs cannot be found.

Because Hardison's religious beliefs prohibit him from working on Saturdays, attempts were made to accommodate him, and these were temporarily successful mainly because on his job at the time he had sufficient seniority regularly to observe Saturday as his Sabbath. But when he sought, and was transferred to, another job where he was asked to work Saturdays and where he had low seniority, problems began to arise. TWA agreed to permit the union to seek a change of work assignments, but the union was not willing to violate the seniority system, and Hardison had insufficient seniority to bid for a shift having Saturdays off. After TWA rejected a proposal that Hardison work only four days a week on the ground that this would

impair critical functions in the airline operations, no accommodation could be reached, and Hardison was discharged for refusing to work on Saturdays.

We hold that TWA, which made reasonable efforts to accommodate Hardison's religious needs, did not violate Title VII, and each of the Court of Appeals' suggested alternatives would have been an undue hardship within the meaning of the statute as construed by the EEOC guidelines. The employer's statutory obligation to make reasonable accommodation for the religious observances of its employees, short of incurring an undue hardship, is clear, but the reach of that obligation has never been spelled out by Congress or by EEOC guidelines. With this in mind, we turn to a consideration of whether TWA has met its obligation under Title VII to accommodate the religious observances of its employees.

The Court of Appeals held that TWA had not made reasonable efforts to accommodate Hardison's religious needs. In its view, TWA had rejected three reasonable alternatives, any one of which would have satisfied its obligation without undue hardship. First, within the framework of the seniority system, TWA could have permitted Hardison to work a four-day week, utilizing in his place a supervisor or another worker on duty elsewhere. That this would have caused other shop functions to suffer was insufficient to amount to undue hardship in the opinion of the Court of Appeals. Second, also within the bounds of the collective-bargaining contract the company could have filled Hardison's Saturday shift from other available personnel competent to do the job, of which the court said there were at least 200. That this would have involved premium overtime pay was not deemed an undue hardship. Third, TWA could have arranged a "swap between Hardison and another employee either for another shift or for the Sabbath days." In response to the assertion that this would have involved a breach of the seniority provisions of the contract, the court noted that it had not been settled in the courts whether the required statutory accommodation to religious needs stopped short of transgressing seniority rules, but found it unnecessary to decide the issue because, as the Court of Appeals saw the record, TWA had not sought, and the union had therefore not declined to entertain, a possible variance from the seniority provisions of the collective-bargaining agreement. The company had simply left the entire matter to the union steward who the Court of Appeals said "likewise did nothing."

We disagree with the Court of Appeals in all relevant respects. It is our view that TWA made reasonable efforts to accommodate and that each of the suggested alternatives would have been an undue hardship within the meaning of the statute as construed by the EEOC guidelines.

It might be inferred from the Court of Appeals' opinion and from the brief of the EEOC in this Court that TWA's efforts to accommodate were no more than negligible. The findings of the District Court, supported by the record, are to the contrary. In summarizing its more detailed findings, the District Court observed:

> "TWA established as a matter of fact that it did take appropriate action to accommodate as required by Title VII. It held several meetings with plaintiff at which it attempted to find a solution to plaintiff's problems. It did accommodate plaintiff's observance of his special religious holidays. It authorized the union steward to search for someone who would swap shifts, which apparently was normal procedure."*

It is also true that TWA itself attempted without success to find Hardison another job. The District Court's view was that TWA had done all that could reasonably be expected within the bounds of the seniority system.

We are also convinced, contrary to the Court of Appeals, that TWA itself cannot be faulted for having failed to work out a shift or job swap for Hardison. Both the union and TWA had agreed to the seniority system; the union was unwilling to entertain a variance over the objections of men senior to Hardison; and for TWA to have arranged unilaterally for a swap would have amounted to a breach of the collective-bargaining agreement.

Hardison and the EEOC insist that the statutory obligation to accommodate religious needs takes precedence over both the collective-bargaining contract and the seniority rights of TWA's other employees. We agree that neither a collective-bargaining contract nor a seniority system may be employed to violate the statute, but we do not believe that the duty to accommodate requires TWA to take steps inconsistent with the otherwise valid agreement. Collective bargaining, aimed at effecting workable and enforceable agreements between management and labor, lies at the core of our national labor policy, and seniority provisions are universally included in these contracts. Without a clear and express indication from Congress, we cannot agree with Hardison and the EEOC that an agreed-upon seniority system must give way when necessary to accommodate religious observances.

The Court of Appeals also suggested that TWA could have permitted Hardison to work a four-day week if necessary in order to avoid working on his Sabbath. Recognizing that this might have left TWA short-handed on the one shift each week that Hardison did not work, the court still concluded that TWA would suffer no undue hardship if it were required to replace Hardison either with supervisory personnel or with qualified personnel from other departments. Alternatively, the Court of Appeals suggested that TWA could have replaced Hardison on his Saturday shift with other available employees through the payment of premium wages. Both of these alternatives would involve costs to TWA, either in the form of lost efficiency in other jobs or higher wages.

To require TWA to bear more than a de minimis cost in order to give Hardison Saturdays off is an undue hardship. Like abandonment of the seniority system, to require TWA to bear additional costs when no such costs are incurred to give other employees the days off that they want would involve unequal treatment of employees on the basis of their religion. By suggesting that TWA should incur certain costs in order to give Hardison Saturdays off the Court of Appeals would in effect require TWA to finance an additional Saturday off and then to choose the employee who will enjoy it on the basis of his religious beliefs. While incurring extra costs to secure a replacement for Hardison might remove the necessity of compelling another employee to work involuntarily in Hardison's place, it would not change the fact that the privilege of having Saturdays off would be allocated according to religious beliefs. While the cost may seem small for one employee compared to TWA's resources, TWA may have many employees who need such accommodation.

Case Questions

1. In your opinion, were the alternatives suggested by the court of appeals viable for TWA? Why or why not?

2. Does it seem inconsistent to prohibit religious discrimination yet say that collective bargaining agreements cannot be violated to accommodate religious differences? Explain.

3. If you had been Hardison's manager and he came to you with this conflict, how would you have handled it? Does that change now that you have seen the Court's decision? If so, how?

Trans World Airlines, Inc. v. Hardison 432 U.S. 63 (1977)

Peterson v. Hewlett-Packard Co., *358 F.3d 599 (9th Cir. 2004)*

The employee sued the employer for religious discrimination and alleged religious harassment after being terminated for repeatedly refusing to remove biblical passages he posted in his workplace cubicle, easily seen by all, in response to employer's workplace diversity posters that included sexual orientation. The court upheld the termination, concluding that the employer was not required to go along with the employee's admitted goal of hurting gay and lesbian employees in an effort to get them to "repent and be saved."

Reinhardt, J.

***

In this religious discrimination action under Title VII of the Civil Rights Act of 1964, Richard Peterson claims that his former employer, the Hewlett-Packard Company, engaged in disparate treatment by terminating him on account of his religious views and that it failed to accommodate his religious beliefs.

The conflict between Peterson and Hewlett-Packard arose when the company began displaying "diversity posters" in its Boise office as one component of its workplace diversity campaign. The first series consisted of five posters, each showing a photograph of a Hewlett-Packard employee above the caption "Black," "Blonde," "Old," "Gay," or "Hispanic." Posters in the second series included photographs of the same five employees and a description of the featured employee's personal interests, as well as the slogan "Diversity is Our Strength."

Peterson describes himself as a "devout Christian," who believes that homosexual activities violate the commandments contained in the Bible and that he has a duty "to expose evil when confronted with sin." In response to the posters that read "Gay," Peterson posted two Biblical scriptures on an overhead bin in his work cubicle. The scriptures were printed in a typeface large enough to be visible to co-workers, customers, and others who passed through an adjacent corridor.

***

Peterson's direct supervisor removed the scriptural passages after consulting her supervisor and determining that they could be offensive to certain employees, and that the posting of the verses violated Hewlett-Packard's policy prohibiting harassment. Throughout the relevant period, Hewlett-Packard's harassment policy stated as follows: "Any comments or conduct relating to a person's race, gender, religion, disability, age, sexual orientation, or ethnic background that fail to respect the dignity and feeling [sic] of the individual are unacceptable."*

Over the course of several days after Peterson posted the Biblical materials, he attended a series of meetings with Hewlett-Packard managers, during which he and they tried to explain to each other their respective positions. Peterson explained that he meant the passages to communicate a message condemning "gay behavior." The scriptural passages, he said, were "intended to be hurtful. And the reason [they were] intended to be hurtful is you cannot have correction unless people are faced with truth."* Peterson hoped that his gay and lesbian co-workers would read the passages, repent, and be saved.

In these meetings, Peterson also asserted that Hewlett-Packard's workplace diversity campaign was an initiative to "target" heterosexual and fundamentalist Christian employees at Hewlett-Packard, in general, and him in particular. Ultimately, Peterson and the managers were unable to agree on how to resolve the conflict. Peterson proposed that he would remove the offending scriptural passages if Hewlett-Packard removed the "Gay" posters; if, however, Hewlett-Packard would not remove the posters, he would not remove the passages. When the managers rejected both options, Peterson responded: "I don't see any way that I can compromise what I am doing that would satisfy both [Hewlett- Packard] and my own conscience." He further remonstrated: "as long as [Hewlett-Packard] is condoning [homosexuality] I'm going to oppose it. . . ."*

Peterson was given time off with pay to reconsider his position. When he returned to work, he again posted the scriptural passages and refused to remove them. After further meetings with Hewlett-Packard managers, Peterson was terminated for insubordination.

Following receipt of a right to sue notice from the EEOC, Peterson filed a complaint alleging religious discrimination in violation of Title VII and the Idaho Human Rights Act. Both parties moved for summary judgment. The district court granted Hewlett-Packard's motion and denied Peterson's. We affirm.

Title VII makes it unlawful for an employer "to discharge any individual . . . because of such individual's . . . religion[.]" "The term 'religion' includes all aspects of religious observance and practice, as well as belief, unless an employer demonstrates that he is unable to reasonably accommodate to an employee's . . . religious observance or practice without undue hardship on the conduct of the employer's business."* Our analysis of Peterson's religious discrimination claims under the Idaho Human Rights Act is the same as under Title VII.

A claim for religious discrimination under Title VII can be asserted under several different theories, including disparate treatment and failure to accommodate. In arguing that Hewlett-Packard discriminated against him on account of his religious beliefs, Peterson relies on both these theories.

Peterson has the burden of establishing a *prima facie* case by showing that (1) he is a member of a protected class; (2) he was qualified for his position; (3) he experienced an adverse employment action; and (4) similarly situated individuals outside his protected class were treated more favorably, or other circumstances surrounding the adverse employment action give rise to an inference of discrimination. It is with respect to the fourth requirement that Peterson's case fails.

Initially, we address Peterson's argument that Hewlett-Packard's workplace diversity campaign was "a crusade to convert fundamentalist Christians to its values," including the promotion of "the homosexual lifestyle." The undisputed evidence shows that Hewlett-Packard carefully developed its campaign during a three-day diversity conference at its Boise facility in 1997 and subsequent planning meetings in which numerous employees participated. The campaign's stated goal—and no evidence suggests that it was pretextual—was to increase tolerance of diversity. Peterson may be correct that the campaign devoted special attention to combating prejudice against homosexuality, but such an emphasis is in no manner unlawful. To the contrary, Hewlett-Packard's efforts to eradicate discrimination against homosexuals in its workplace were entirely consistent with the goals and objectives of our civil rights statutes generally.

In addition to Peterson's allegations about the general purposes of the diversity initiative, he asserts that the campaign that Hewlett-Packard conducted, as well as "the entire disciplinary process" that it initiated in response to his posting of the scriptural passages, constituted "an inquisition serving no other purpose than to ferret out the extremity of Peterson's views on homosexuality." According to Peterson, Hewlett-Packard managers harassed him in order to convince him to change his religious beliefs. However, the evidence that Peterson cites in support of this theory shows that Hewlett-Packard managers acted in precisely the opposite manner. In numerous meetings, Hewlett-Packard managers acknowledged the sincerity of Peterson's beliefs and insisted that he need not change them. They did not object to Peterson's expression of his anti-gay views in a letter to the editor that was published in the *Idaho Statesman*—a letter in which Peterson stated that Hewlett-Packard was "on the rampage to change moral values in Idaho under the guise of diversity," and that the diversity campaign was a "platform to promote the homosexual agenda." Nor did the Hewlett-Packard managers prohibit him from parking his car in the company lot even though he had affixed to it a bumper sticker stating, "Sodomy is Not a Family Value." All that the managers did was explain Hewlett-Packard's diversity program to Peterson and ask him to treat his co-workers with respect. They simply requested that he remove the posters and not violate the company's harassment policy—a policy that was uniformly applied to all employees. No contrary inference may be drawn from anything in the record.

Peterson also maintains that the disciplinary proceedings and his subsequent termination stand in marked contrast to Hewlett-Packard's treatment of three other groups of similarly situated employees. Peterson compares himself, first, to the employees who hung the diversity posters. He argues that these posters were intended "to make people uncomfortable so they would think again about diversity and change their actions to be more positive." He likens these actions to his own intentions to make his "scriptures [] hurtful so that people would repent (change their actions) and experience the joys of being saved." This comparison fails because the employees who hung the diversity posters were simply communicating the views of Hewlett-Packard as they were directed to do by management, whereas Peterson was expressing his own personal views which contradicted those of management. Moreover, unlike Peterson's postings, the company's workplace diversity campaign did not attack any group of employees on account of race, religion, or any other important individual characteristic. To the contrary, Hewlett-Packard's initiative was intended to promote tolerance of the diversity that exists in its workforce. Hewlett-Packard's failure to fire employees for following management's instructions to hang the posters prepared by management provides no evidence of disparate treatment.

Second, Peterson compares himself with other employees who posted religious and secular messages and symbols in their work spaces. Yet Peterson failed to present any evidence that the posters in other Hewlett-Packard employees' cubicles were intended to be "hurtful" to, or critical of, any other employees or otherwise violated the company's harassment policy. In fact, the only posters

in other employees' work spaces that Peterson identified were of "Native American dream catchers," "New Age pictures of whales," and a yinyang symbol.

Third, Peterson argues that he was similarly situated to the network group of homosexual employees that Hewlett-Packard permitted to organize in the workplace and advertise in the company's email and its newsletter. Yet Peterson failed to present any evidence that communications from this network group were, let alone were intended to be, hurtful to any group of employees. Nor does anything in the record indicate that Hewlett-Packard permitted or would have permitted any network group or any individual employee to post messages of either a secular or religious variety that demeaned other employees or violated the company's harassment policy.

In short, we conclude that Peterson's evidence does not meet the threshold for defeating summary judgment in disparate treatment cases. Peterson offered *no* evidence, circumstantial or otherwise, that would support a reasonable inference that his termination was the result of disparate treatment on account of religion. Viewing the record in the light most favorable to Peterson, it is evident that he was discharged, not because of his religious beliefs, but because he violated the company's harassment policy by attempting to generate a hostile and intolerant work environment and because he was insubordinate in that he repeatedly disregarded the company's instructions to remove the demeaning and degrading postings from his cubicle.

Peterson also appeals the district court's rejection of his failure-to-accommodate theory of religious discrimination. An employee who fails to raise a reasonable inference of disparate treatment on account of religion may nonetheless show that his employer violated its affirmative duty under Title VII to reasonably accommodate employees' religious beliefs. To establish religious discrimination on the basis of a failure-to-accommodate theory, Peterson must first set forth a *prima facie* case that (1) he had a bona fide religious belief, the practice of which conflicts with an employment duty; (2) he informed his employer of the belief and conflict; and (3) the employer discharged, threatened, or otherwise subjected him to an adverse employment action because of his inability to fulfill the job requirement. If Peterson makes out a *prima facie* failure-to-accommodate case, the burden then shifts to Hewlett-Packard to show that it "initiated good faith efforts to accommodate reasonably the employee's religious practices or that it could not reasonably accommodate the employee without undue hardship."*

As we explain below, it is readily apparent that the only accommodations that Peterson was willing to accept would have imposed undue hardship upon Hewlett-Packard. Therefore, we will assume *arguendo* that Peterson could establish a *prima facie* case that his posting of the anti-gay scriptural passages stemmed from his religious beliefs that homosexual activities "violate the commandments of God contained in the Holy Bible" and that those same religious beliefs imposed upon him "a duty to expose evil when confronted with sin." We make that assumption with considerable reservations, however, because we seriously doubt that the doctrines to which Peterson professes allegiance compel any employee to engage in either expressive or physical activity designed to hurt or harass one's fellow employees.

An employer's duty to negotiate possible accommodations ordinarily requires it to take "some initial step to reasonably accommodate the religious belief of that employee." Peterson contends that the company did not do so in this case even though Hewlett-Packard managers convened at least four meetings with him. In these meetings, they explained the reasons for the company's diversity campaign, allowed Peterson to explain fully his reasons for his postings, and attempted to determine whether it would be possible to resolve the conflict in a manner that would respect the dignity of Peterson's fellow employees. Peterson, however, repeatedly made it clear that only two options for accommodation would be acceptable to him, either that (1) both the "Gay" posters and anti-gay messages remain, or (2) Hewlett-Packard remove the "Gay" posters and he would then remove the anti-gay messages. Given Peterson's refusal to consider other accommodations, we proceed to evaluate whether one or both of the "acceptable" accommodations would have imposed undue hardship upon Hewlett-Packard, or to determine whether Hewlett-Packard carried its burden of showing that no reasonable accommodation was possible.

As we explain further below, Peterson's first proposed accommodation would have compelled Hewlett-Packard to permit an employee to post messages intended to demean and harass his co-workers. His second proposed accommodation would have forced the company to exclude sexual orientation from its workplace diversity program. Either choice would have created undue hardship for Hewlett-Packard because it would have inhibited its efforts to attract and retain a qualified, diverse workforce, which the company reasonably views as vital to its commercial success; thus, neither provides a reasonable accommodation.

With respect to Peterson's first proposal, an employer need not accommodate an employee's religious beliefs if doing so would result in discrimination against his co-workers or deprive them of contractual or other statutory rights. Nor does Title VII require an employer to accommodate an employee's desire to impose his religious beliefs upon his co-workers.

That is not to say that accommodating an employee's religious beliefs creates undue hardship for an employer merely because the employee's co-workers find his conduct irritating or unwelcome. Complete harmony in the workplace is not an objective of Title VII. If relief under Title VII can be denied merely because the majority group of employees, who have not suffered discrimination, will be unhappy about it, there will be little hope of correcting the wrongs to which the Act is directed. While Hewlett-Packard must tolerate some degree of employee discomfort in the process of taking steps required by Title VII to correct the wrongs of discrimination, it need not accept the burdens that would result from allowing actions that demean or degrade, or are designed to demean or degrade, members of its workforce. Thus, we conclude that Peterson's first proposed accommodation would have created undue hardship for his employer.

The only other alternative acceptable to Peterson—taking down all the posters—would also have inflicted undue hardship upon Hewlett-Packard because it would have infringed upon the company's right to promote diversity and encourage tolerance and good will among its workforce. The Supreme Court has acknowledged that "the skills needed in today's increasingly global marketplace can only be developed through exposure to widely diverse people, cultures, ideas, and viewpoints."* These values and good business practices are appropriately promoted by Hewlett-Packard's workplace diversity program. To require Hewlett-Packard to exclude homosexuals from its voluntarily adopted program would create undue hardship for the company.

Because only two possible accommodations were acceptable to Peterson and implementing either would have imposed undue hardship upon Hewlett-Packard, we conclude that the company carried its burden of showing that no reasonable accommodation was possible, and we therefore reject Peterson's failure-to-accommodate claim.

Peterson failed to raise a triable issue of fact that his termination from employment at Hewlett-Packard was on account of his religious beliefs. The ruling of the district court is therefore AFFIRMED.

Case Questions

1. Do the employer's actions here seem reasonable to you (both those in response to diversity and those in response to the employee's reaction)?

2. Would you have balanced the two sides here the same as the court? Explain.

3. How would you design a diversity program that no employee would have problems with?

Peterson v. Hewlett-Packard Co. 358 F.3d 599 (9th Cir. 2004)

Case 5

EEOC v. Abercrombie & Fitch,
575 U.S. ___; 135 S. Ct. 2028 (2015)

A 17-year-old interviewed for a position at Abercrombie & Fitch clothing store wearing a headscarf. Her interviewer was impressed with the applicant but mentioned to the manager that the applicant wore a scarf and that she thought the scarf was for religious reasons. The district manager said their policy did not permit wearing "caps" and declined to hire her. The applicant sued for religious discrimination and won. The Court determined that Title VII's prohibition on the employer to not discriminate in employment on the basis of religion to the extent it did not cause an undue hardship applied even though the applicant did not inform the employer of the need for accommodation.

Scalia, J.

***

Abercrombie & Fitch Stores, Inc., operates several lines of clothing stores, each with its own "style." Consistent with the image Abercrombie seeks to project for each store, the company imposes a Look Policy that governs its employees' dress. The Look Policy prohibits "caps"—a term the Policy does not define—as too informal for Abercrombie's desired image.

Samantha Elauf is a practicing Muslim who, consistent with her understanding of her religion's requirements, wears a headscarf. She applied for a position in an Abercrombie store, and was interviewed by Heather Cooke, the store's assistant manager. Using Abercrombie's ordinary system for evaluating applicants, Cooke gave Elauf a rating that qualified her to be hired; Cooke was concerned, however, that Elauf's headscarf would conflict with the store's Look Policy.

Cooke sought the store manager's guidance to clarify whether the headscarf was a forbidden "cap." When this yielded no answer, Cooke turned to Randall Johnson, the district manager. Cooke informed Johnson that she believed Elauf wore her headscarf because of her faith.

Johnson told Cooke that Elauf's headscarf would violate the Look Policy, as would all other headwear, religious or otherwise, and directed Cooke not to hire Elauf.

The EEOC sued Abercrombie on Elauf's behalf, claiming that its refusal to hire Elauf violated Title VII. Abercrombie's primary argument is that an applicant cannot show disparate treatment without first showing that an employer has "actual knowledge" of the applicant's need for an accommodation. We disagree. Instead, an applicant need only show that his need for an accommodation was a motivating factor in the employer's decision.

The rule for disparate treatment claims based on a failure to accommodate a religious practice is straightforward: An employer may not make an applicant's religious practice, confirmed or otherwise, a factor in employment decisions. For example, suppose that an employer thinks (though he does not know for certain) that a job applicant may be an orthodox Jew who will observe the Sabbath, and thus be unable to work on Saturdays. If the applicant actually requires an accommodation of that religious practice, and the employer's desire to avoid the prospective accommodation is a motivating factor in his decision, the employer violates Title VII.

A request for accommodation, or the employer's certainty that the practice exists, may make it easier to infer motive, but is not a necessary condition of liability. *Reversed and remanded.*

Case Questions

1. Do you understand the Court's reasoning? Explain.

2. If you were the employer who was not told of the religious conflict but you were held responsible for it, how would you feel?

3. Is question 2 really a fair question if the employer even suspected that the scarf may have been for religious reasons? Do you understand why it would make no difference under the law if the employer knew or did not know? Explain.

Chapter 12

Age Discrimination

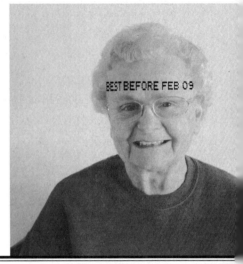

Learning Objectives

After completing this chapter, you should be able to:

LO1 Differentiate the reality of the value that an older worker could bring to the workplace from the bias that permeates some of our perception of them.

LO2 Describe the history of the protection of older workers in the United States.

LO3 Distinguish the ADEA from state-based age discrimination laws.

LO4 Identify the legal options available to an employee who believes that she or he has experienced age discrimination.

LO5 Articulate the *prima facie* case of discrimination based on age.

LO6 Describe the bona fide occupational qualification defenses available to employers under the ADEA.

LO7 Explain the difference between situations where disparate impact and disparate treatment apply in connection with age discrimination.

LO8 Analyze factual circumstances when employer economic concerns may justify adverse action against particular groups of workers.

LO9 Recognize necessary elements to establish pretext under the ADEA.

LO10 Define the parameters of a valid waiver of ADEA rights.

Opening Scenarios

SCENARIO 1

1 In an effort to reduce costs across the board, a new technology firm seeks to hire recent graduates who have little experience. The firm would be paying them wages above its competition even if it offered them one-half the salaries of its present staff members who are over age 50. Should the company terminate those older employees and hire these new, less-expensive workers? What if one or more of the older employees were willing to accept a 50 percent pay cut? Is the company permitted to make the 50 percent pay cut a condition of remaining on the job for the older employees?

SCENARIO 2

2 Beth, an employer, wants to hire someone for a strenuous job that requires a great deal of training, which will take place over the course of several years. The applicant who appears most qualified is 58 years old; however, Beth is concerned that the applicant will not be able to handle the physical demands of the position in the long run.

Further, she is concerned that the applicant will only continue working for several more years before she retires. Does Beth hire the applicant anyway? What advice would you give Beth?

SCENARIO 3

3 Airi worked as a food scientist at a once-prestigious chain restaurant for over 25 years before the restaurant filed for bankruptcy in the wake of an *E. coli* outbreak and she was laid off. Fifty-year-old Airi then applied for an entry-level position at local ice cream factory in Columbus, Ohio, which has 20 other employees. Alfonso is the factory's 31-year-old CEO and founder. He is impressed by Airi's credentials and understands that Airi had no involvement in the food contamination. But he is concerned that Airi's years of experience make her overqualified for the position. Alfonso thinks that a professional at Airi's stage of her career will not be comfortable taking direction from him or his partners, who are either Alfonso's age or younger. What advice would you give Alfonso?

Statutory Basis

The statutory basis is presented in Exhibit 12.1, "Age Discrimination in Employment Act."

Exhibit 12.1 *Age Discrimination in Employment Act*

Sec. 4 (a) It shall be unlawful for an employer—

1. to fail or refuse to hire or to discharge any individual or otherwise discriminate against any individual with respect to his compensation, terms, conditions, or privilege of employment, because of such individual's age;

2. to limit, segregate, or classify his employees in any way which would deprive or tend to deprive any individual of employment opportunity or otherwise adversely affect his status as an employee, because of such individual's age; or

3. to reduce the wage rate of any employee in order to comply with this chapter.

Source: 20 U.S.C. § 623.

Oldie . . . but Goldie?

Scenario

America has a culture in which youth is valued, but it is not that way in all cultures throughout the world. For instance, the Japanese revere age and believe that age brings wisdom and insight that young people simply have not yet obtained. In the United States, the general perception is that youth means energy, imagination, and innovation, while age means decreasing interest, lack of innovation and imagination, and even a lower-quality worker. Information technology (IT) companies, like some of the social media and mobile application ("app") start-ups clustered in Silicon Valley, have been accused of stereotyping "older" IT workers for not having the energy and innovation mindset needed to develop products for the younger demographic that they want to attract.[1] In fact, the average age of a developer in 2018 was 28 years old.[2] This bias toward young people is reinforced by the tone at the top—just consider what Facebook's CEO Mark Zuckerberg once told a Stanford University audience: "I want to stress the importance of being young and technical. Young people are just smarter. Why are most chess masters under 30?[3]

You can see Zuckerberg's inclination played out in hiring statistics. GenXers (born 1964–1980) are hired for IT jobs at a rate that is 33 percent lower than their workforce representation, and Baby Boomers (born 1946–1963) are hired at a rate that is 60 percent lower.[4] In fact, Facebook, LinkedIn, and Google ran targeted ads in 2017 recruiting workers that systematically excluded workers over the age of 40.[5]

As we can see, Facebook is not the only tech firm that might be looking for younger workers. Brian Reid, a former Google executive who was 54 years old when he was fired from the company, alleged that he was told by coworkers that his "ideas were 'obsolete' and 'too old to matter,' that he was 'slow,' 'fuzzy,' 'sluggish,' and 'lethargic,' and that he did not 'display a sense of urgency' and "lack[ed] energy.'"[6] Google settled Reid's age discrimination lawsuit for an undisclosed amount after a 2010 California Supreme Court ruling affirmed that these comments were sufficient grounds for the suit to move forward.[7] It is clear that age discrimination is still a problem for workers over the age of 40.

LO1 Differentiate the reality of the value that an older worker could bring to the workplace from the bias that permeates some of our perception of them.

The scenarios at the beginning of this chapter illustrate circumstances that are present in many workplaces. While statistics show that older workers are more reliable, harder working, and more committed and have less absenteeism than younger workers—all characteristics that employers *say* they value—the general perception of older workers as employees is exactly the opposite. A 2019 study examining age discrimination in the workplace found that 21 percent of workers over the age of 40 have experienced discrimination in the workplace due to their age. Respondents in that study believed that they were most likely to experience discrimination around the age of 51.[8] Older women have a double disadvantage since the unemployment rates for women ages 55 and older (2.6 percent) tend to be higher than the rates for men of the same age (2.2 percent).[9] Further, while older workers have lower unemployment rates overall, when they do lose their jobs, they also have a far more difficult time finding new jobs. For instance, in December 2019, 25.1 percent of unemployed workers over 55 years old had been unemployed for 27 weeks or longer, compared to 19 percent of workers ages 25 to 54.[10]

While we mentioned earlier that some cultures value qualities that come with older age, these negative perceptions also are not limited only to the United States, of course. A 2018 survey of nearly 900 HR practitioners in Australia found that 30 percent of Australian employers are reluctant to hire workers over a certain age. For over 60 percent of the respondents, that age is 50 and older.[11] Similar to the United States, 79 percent of Australian workers ages 55 and older have difficulty finding work. When they do find work, it is not secure, nor do those jobs necessarily use the skills those workers have to offer.

Some countries impose a mandatory age of retirement. For instance, in 2018 the Japanese Supreme Court reaffirmed that mandatory retirement is still legal. Japan's highest court found that employers may require employees to retire and then continue to offer them fixed term contracts with less favorable terms.[12] Similarly, in 2007, the 13-judge European Union Court of Justice upheld mandatory retirement age at 65.[13] And, as we will discuss, while the United States does not have universal mandatory retirement, *per se,* the ADEA and certain states do permit select exceptions linked to some professions such as air traffic controllers.

Contrary to common perceptions, older workers actually are now more likely to remain on the job than their counterparts earlier in this century. More Americans ages 65 and older are working than at any time since the turn of the century. In 2019, 19.6 percent of Americans ages 65 and older—nearly 10.3 million people—were employed full- or part-time.[14] This marks a notable jump since 1999 when just 11.9 percent—or 3.8 million people—ages 65 and older were still working.[15] From 1999 to 2019, the portion of the workforce that was 55 to 64 grew from 9.8 to 16.8 percent.[16] Older workers (55 and older) are expected to make up 25.9 percent of the workforce by 2022.[17] In addition, the number of workers between the ages of 35 and 44 is expected to increase between 2012 and 2022, but at a much slower pace than the rate for older workers.[18] This eventuality presents a workforce challenge since a smaller proportion of young workers are entering the market relative to the larger proportion of older workforce reaching retirement eligibility.[19] As a result, for many employers, the number one concern is how to attract and retain new talent.

Yet many companies are not actively working to recruit or retain older workers. *Forbes* reported in 2019 that older workers were experiencing longer unemployment than were younger workers.[20] The acting chair of the EEOC explained the phenomenon in this way:

> [D]espite these dramatic changes, today's older workers still confront unfounded and outdated assumptions about age and ability and age discrimination persists. Despite decades of research finding that age does not predict ability or performance, employers often fall back on precisely the ageist stereotypes the ADEA was enacted to prohibit.[21]

Employee rights attorney Kristin Alden suggests that "[a]ge discrimination is so pervasive that people don't even recognize it's illegal."[22]

In addition to the perception that older workers may be less capable, some employers perceive that older employees are more expensive to retain because they have greater experience and seniority. As a result of seniority, some workers may have received a salary increase each year, for example. The employer may determine that it could reduce costs by terminating older employees, who have more experience than may be necessary to perform the requirements of the position, and then hiring younger, less-experienced employees. However, the economic bias against older workers is not well founded in fact. (See Exhibit 12.2, "Realities about Older Workers and Age Discrimination.")

Research demonstrates that, "for virtually all jobs in virtually all circumstances, workers with more experience are almost always better performers. Any negative effects of age on performance are so minor as to be irrelevant."[23] In connection with hiring, in fact, *age-based compensation cost differences are exceptionally low.* Moreover, a 2009 survey of HR managers in U.S. state agencies found "late-career employees were perceived most positively by state agencies with regard to having low turnover rates, having a strong work ethic, being reliable, and being loyal to the agency in comparison to the early- and mid-career employees."[24] A report issued by the Center for Retirement Research in 2019 reinforces the research findings from this 2009 report.[25]

As a result of some subtle changes in perception and a change in economic conditions over the past few years, there is some good news for older workers. Jen Schramm from the AARP Public Policy Institute argues that a tight labor

Exhibit 12.2 *Realities about Older Workers and Age Discrimination*

1. In a reduction in force caused by economic factors, employers should be aware of the impact of terminations based on salary since older workers may be higher paid than others on average due to job seniority.

2. Just because most people in a certain age group might have a common weakness, it cannot be generalized that *all* in that group have the weakness, so age may not be used as a job qualification.

3. Employees have no claim under the Age Discrimination in Employment Act for discrimination on the basis of their youth, only on the basis of age 40 and older.

4. Under most circumstances, employees are not required to retire at age 65 in the United States.

5. The following are **mere myths about older employees:** As workers, they:

   • Are not hard workers.
   • Will get tired more easily than younger workers.
   • Are less able to perform than younger workers.
   • Do not understand technology.
   • Do not want to travel too much and are generally more stubborn and uninterested in learning.
   • Make too much money since pay often is based on seniority and not performance.
   • Are just marking time before they can retire.

6. The following are **mere myths about younger employees:** As workers, they:

   • Have it easy; they never suffer discrimination.
   • Always win the job when competing against older workers.
   • Have a lower unemployment rate than older workers.
   • Can easily find jobs since older workers are retiring all the time.

market encourages employers to look at nontraditional applicants such as older workers. As a result, the unemployment rate for 55 and older workers appears to be decreasing, along with the average duration of unemployment. However, these positive reports should be tempered with clear evidence that older workers still face discrimination.[26]

Further, it is arguable that *some* younger workers may indeed be better qualified than *some* older workers for certain types of positions at the moment that the younger workers enter the workforce. An employer might believe that it is easier to rely on a generalization such as this one about a group of workers when hiring and then choose a younger worker on that basis to cut down on time-consuming individual decisions. However, hiring based on a generalization rather than an individual decision is what gives rise to a possible claim for wrongful discrimination! In this chapter, we will discuss older employees, their legal rights under the laws that protect them, and the most effective way for employers to end up with the most qualified workforce while respecting those laws.

Please note that, at the time this chapter is being written, our world is facing a serious economic downturn. To be perfectly frank, given the reality of publication timelines, we do not yet know the totality of the impact of this downturn on the employment landscape in the short or long term. The financial implications could be severe or mild, and as a result, vulnerable employee populations, such as older workers, may be hard-hit. Positive trajectories, such as the one mentioned earlier, could take a significant and severe turn for the worst.

Regulation: Age Discrimination in Employment Act

Age Discrimination in Employment Act
Prohibits discrimination in employment on the basis of age; applies to individuals who are at least 40 years old. Individuals who are not yet 40 years old are not protected by the act and *may* be discriminated against on the basis of their age.

Baseless discrimination against older workers occurs with such consistency that Congress was compelled to enact legislation to protect older workers from discrimination to prevent increased unemployment for those over 40. In 1967, Congress enacted the **Age Discrimination in Employment Act (ADEA)** for the express purpose of "promot[ing the] employment of older people based on their ability rather than age [and prohibiting] arbitrary age discrimination in employment." The act applies to employment by public and private employers, by unions and employment agencies, and by foreign companies with more than 20 workers that are located in the United States. In fact, in 2018, the Supreme Court ruled unanimously that the ADEA applies to businesses with 20 employees or more and also to state and local subdivisions, even if they have fewer than 20 employees.[27] Thus, employees in small local governmental entities now are guaranteed ADEA protection.

Age discrimination complaints filed with the EEOC rose dramatically in the years leading up to the 2009 recession. Between 1999 and 2019, the number of age-based complaints peaked in 2008 at the beginning of the recession and stayed elevated until 2016. Between 2016 and 2019, claims then decreased by approximately 25 percent, from 20,857 to 15,573.[28] (See Exhibit 12.3, "EEOC Charge Statistics, Age Discrimination Charges [1999–2019].")

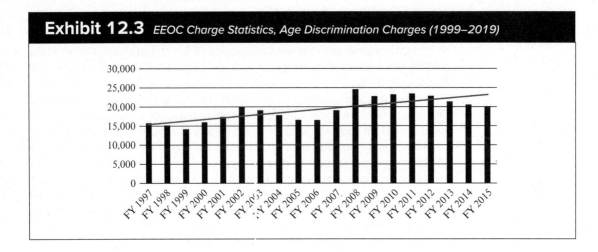

Exhibit 12.3   *EEOC Charge Statistics, Age Discrimination Charges (1999–2019)*

The percent of all EEOC complaints based on age also grew substantially during this period, from 18.3 to 21.4 percent of all complaints filed. Although there was a 7 percent drop in filings in 2009, there was a slight increase in the number of claims over the subsequent two years (1 and 2 percent, respectively), followed by several years of decreased filings (except for 2016). This comes as a surprise, given the increase in ADEA enforcement efforts by the EEOC.[29] It is possible that the decreasing number of age discrimination filings may reflect a change in the economic conditions after the 2009 recession, but it also may reflect changes in state statutes as well as arbitration that is designed to address the issue before it heads to court.[30]

Originally, the ADEA covered employees between the ages of 40 and 65. However, the upper limit was extended to age 70 in 1978 and then later removed completely (with a few exceptions, discussed below). The limit was removed because it was acknowledged that an 80-year-old might be just as qualified for a position as a 30-year-old and that older person should have the opportunity to prove her or his qualifications and earn the job. It also is important to recognize that the act will become all the more critical as advances in health care allow people to live longer and more vital lives in their old age. Many people today feel healthy enough to work long beyond the age at which most people used to retire.

Courts and Congress have recognized that there is a trade-off for the required employment of qualified older workers. In *Graefenhain v. Pabst Brewing Co.*,[31] the court said:

LO2   Describe the history of the protection of older workers in the United States.

> Although the ADEA does not hand federal courts a roving commission to review business judgments, the ADEA *does* create a cause of action against business decisions that merge with age discrimination. Congress enacted the ADEA precisely because many employers or younger business executives act as if they believe that there are good business reasons for discriminating against older employees. Retention of senior employees who can be replaced by younger lower-paid people frequently competes with other values, such as profits or conceptions of economic

efficiency. The ADEA represents a choice among these values. It stands for the propositions that this is a better country for its willingness to pay the costs for treating older employees fairly.

Distinctions between ADEA and Title VII

See Chapter 2 to revisit key concepts.

You may wonder why age was not merely included as an amendment to Title VII since the laws have several similarities. Both are enforced by the EEOC and also through private actions. However, discrimination based on age is substantively different from discrimination based on the factors covered by Title VII in three important ways.

1. The ADEA is more lenient than Title VII regarding the latitude afforded employers' reasons for adverse employment decisions. The ADEA allows an employer to rebut a *prima facie* case of age discrimination by identifying any "reasonable factor other than age" (RFOA) that motivated the decision. (For a more general discussion of a *prima facie* case, please see Chapter 3.)

2. An older worker still can pursue a claim, even if the employer treated another older worker well. In other words, a 62-year-old is not prohibited from filing a claim when fired simply because her replacement was 58 (that is, the replacement worker also is in the same protected class).

3. The ADEA protects *only* those employees who are over 40 from discrimination. In other words, unlike Title VII, there is no protection from "reverse" discrimination. Therefore, an individual under 40 cannot file a claim under the act based on the claim that she was discriminated against because of her youth. The Supreme Court made sure that this element was clear when it held in 2014 that the ADEA does not protect workers over 40 who were discriminated against in favor of an even older worker with regard to employment. As Justice Souter noted in *General Dynamics Land Systems, Inc. v. Cline,*[32] "The law does not mean to stop an employer from favoring an older employee over a younger one . . . The enemy of 40 is 30, not 50."

LO3 Distinguish the ADEA from state-based age discrimination laws.

Note, however, that certain state laws or precedents may allow for a loophole with item number 3 in the preceding list. A younger worker's "reverse discrimination" claim might be permitted to proceed under *state* age discrimination statutes. These states include Maryland, Michigan, Minnesota, New Jersey, and Oregon. Under those state laws, all workers are protected from age discrimination, regardless of their age. Employers may defend employment decisions if those decisions are based on a bona fide occupational qualification. In one Maryland case, the Division of Corrections (DOC) required that corrections officers must be at least 21 years old. The age claim was rejected, and eventually the age required was lowered to 18 years.[33]

As we mentioned earlier, as of 2020, there has been a slight upward trend in hiring and retaining older workers. (Though also see Exhibit 12.4, "The Times They Are a Changin', or Not?" for an alternate perspective.) The AARP reported that some businesses have been taking actions to recruit older workers actively and are using innovative programs to do so.[34] Goldman Sachs's "Returnship" program provides mentorship and training for older individuals who have taken a career break of longer than two years. Encore offers a six-month to one-year fellowship for workers over 50 to work at a nonprofit. Massachusetts General Hospital recruits from an organization called Operation A.B.L.E. and provides employment opportunities to applicants over 45 years old. AARP also sponsors an Employer Pledge Program in which employers affirm the value of experienced workers and are committed to developing diversity in organizations, including older workers.[35] *The Christian Science Monitor*'s words still ring true today: "Far from being a drag on the economy, so-called gray labor will be key to America's competitiveness in coming years. Mature workers can bring major productivity gains to U.S. businesses—if we can make changes to better tap their talent."[36]

Exhibit 12.4 *The Times They Are a Changin', or Not?*

Air Canada pilots recently had their age discrimination case appeal dismissed by the Federal Court of Appeal in Canada.[37] While Canada's Human Rights Commission had repealed the mandatory retirement provision for federally regulated workplaces in 2012, the employees who filed the initial claim in 2011 challenging the mandatory retirement age[38] were caught in a difficult place. The initial court ruling was that the pilots could not prove that the situation of Canadian airlines had changed enough to justify a change in the retirement age. Despite the change in the mandatory retirement age that followed their suit, because of their collective bargaining agreement and because the change in the mandatory retirement provision was not retroactive, the pilots had no recourse once the provisions changed in 2012 and lost their appeal. While pilots now are not held to the mandatory retirement age, those who challenged the laws in the Canadian Human Rights Tribunal could not take advantage of the change in the law.

While it may seem that mandatory retirement is outdated, clearly some countries and industries are struggling with how to deal with this issue. For example, as of 2018, the average life expectancy of Canadians was 84 for men and 87 for women, but the average retirement age is age 63. The Ontario Human Rights Commission states that "age discrimination is not taken as seriously as other forms of discrimination, even though it may have the same economic, social, and psychological impact

as any other type of discrimination."[39] Attorney Christina Catenacci explains, "Older persons make significant contributions to society and it is important to combat ageism by using inclusive planning and design which reflects the circumstances of persons of all ages. In order to ensure that physical, attitudinal, and systematic barriers are avoided, age diversity should be reflected in design stages for policies, programs, services, and facilities."[40]

A number of government officials advocate overturning mandatory retirement provisions. On the occasion of revoking mandatory retirement in the UK, Employment Relations minister Ed Davey said that "retirement should be a matter of choice rather than compulsion—people deserve the freedom to work for as long as they want and are able to do so."[41] However, as you will see throughout the cases and examples in this chapter, perhaps that conclusion is not so universally accepted.

A company called Age UK surveyed attitudes toward age and seniority across 28 European countries and found that the overwhelming preference was for a younger rather than an older boss. As we have seen, various countries view age and seniority quite differently and even have conflicting perceptions within each country. For example, as we mentioned at the start of the chapter, in Japan, older workers are revered and are expected to be high ranking in their companies. However, they also are discouraged from switching careers later in life due to negative, entrenched attitudes about careers and aging. In African countries, as well as in China, Korea, and Greece, older workers are honored and celebrated. In fact, in Greece, you are not considered "old" until you have hit 68, whereas in Britain, you are already old by the time you are 59.[42]

Ultimately, the United States may be able to learn from those countries that embrace their older workers as it struggles with questions of age discrimination.

Another restriction on the ADEA's protection comes from the U.S. Supreme Court's 2000 decision in *Kimel v. Florida Board of Regents.*[43] In *Kimel,* state employees alleged that their state employers had discriminated against them on the basis of age in violation of the ADEA. Under the U.S. Constitution's Eleventh Amendment, states cannot be sued by citizens of another state. Federal courts have interpreted the Eleventh Amendment to extend immunity to states not consenting to being sued by their citizens. The U.S. Supreme Court determined that, while Congress intended to allow state employees to sue their state employers under the ADEA, this attempt exceeded Congressional authority. Therefore, in almost half the states (specifically those that have not waived sovereign immunity), state employees are not able to sue their state employers under the ADEA.

It is not yet settled whether state employees with age discrimination grievances in those states have alternative claims to those provided by the ADEA. Federal courts are split on the validity of age discrimination claims under workers' rights to equal protection under the U.S. Constitution's Fourteenth Amendment. Importantly, while states are immune from claims for money damages under the ADEA, claimants suing state officials for equal protection violations under the Fourteenth Amendment are not bound by this limitation. The First, Fourth, Fifth, Ninth, and Tenth Circuits have taken the position that the existence of the ADEA's regulatory scheme demonstrates congressional intent to limit age discrimination claims to the ADEA. This position would prevent state employees from turning to other paths, such as the Fourteenth Amendment.

However, the Seventh Circuit rejected this argument in a 2012 case, affirming the right of Harvey N. Levin, a terminated Illinois assistant attorney general, to sue state law enforcement officials for an alleged equal protection age discrimination violation.[44] Though the Supreme Court accepted the Seventh Circuit case on appeal in 2013, the issue remains unsettled, since the Court dismissed the case after oral arguments without comment.[45]

To ensure that appropriate and adequate information exists as to hiring practices in connection with age, the act has specific record-keeping provisions for employers. Employers are required to maintain the following information for three years for each employee and applicant, where applicable:

- Name
- Address
- Date of birth

- Occupation
- Rate of pay
- Compensation earned each week

Employers are required to maintain the following information for one year for each employee, including both regular and temporary workers:

- Job applications, résumés, or other employment inquiries in answer to ads or notices, plus records about failure or refusal to hire
- Records on promotion, demotion, transfer, selection for training, layoff, recall, disciplinary action, or discharge of any employee
- Job orders given to agencies or unions for recruiting personnel for job openings
- Test papers
- Results of physical exams that are considered in connection with any personnel action
- Advertisements or notices relating to job openings, promotions, training programs, or opportunities for overtime

The ADEA also addresses discrimination in the provision of benefits. Specifically, employers are held to an equal-benefit/equal-cost rule. Under the rule, employers can comply with the ADEA either by providing equal benefits to workers of all ages or by spending an equal amount to purchase the benefits. In recognizing that it may cost more to provide equivalent benefits to older workers, Congress was striving to encourage the hiring of older workers.

State Law Claims

We discussed in the prior section how some states provide a different environment for workers with regard to age discrimination. State laws regarding protection against discrimination on the basis of age vary widely, and in some cases, states provide additional protections greater than those provided by the ADEA.

State law provisions generally follow the federal guidelines in the ADEA, prohibiting age discrimination for those 40 and older. While some states maintain the requirement for employers with 20 or more employees (e.g., Alabama or Nebraska), others have stricter requirements, and some have no size limit at all for employers (e.g., North Dakota or Oklahoma). A handful of states include protection for individuals ages 18 and older, and several protect only up to age 70. Both Minnesota and New Jersey, however, have provisions for those employers subject to the federal ADEA regarding mandatory retirement only in limited circumstances. An additional nine states have age discrimination statutes with no qualifying age restrictions. Only one state, South Dakota, has no state law regarding age discrimination; thus, employers in that state are subject to the ADEA. In both Arkansas and Mississippi, private employers are subject to the ADEA, while both states maintain separate provisions for age discrimination against public employees. Exhibit 12.5, "Summary of State Law Provisions for Age Discrimination," provides a summary of the state law provisions.[46]

Exhibit 12.5 *Summary of State Law Provisions for Age Discrimination*

40 Years and Older	18 Years and Older
Alabama	Utah
Arizona	Virginia
Arkansas (Public Employees Only)	Washington
California	West Virginia
Colorado	Wisconsin
Connecticut[1]	Wyoming
Delaware	District of Columbia
Georgia	Iowa
Idaho	Minnesota (18–70)
Illinois	New Jersey (18–70)
Indiana (40–75)	New York
Kansas	Oregon
Kentucky	Vermont
Louisiana	
Massachusetts	**No Qualifying Age**
Missouri (40–70)	Alaska
Nebraska	Florida
Nevada	Hawaii
New Mexico[2]	Maine
North Carolina[3]	Maryland
(Private Employees Only)	Michigan
North Dakota	Mississippi (Public Employees Only)
Ohio	Montana
Oklahoma	New Hampshire
Pennsylvania	North Carolina[3] (Public Employees Only)
Rhode Island	
South Carolina	
Tennessee	**No State Law**
Texas	South Dakota

[1] Connecticut law does not specify an age limit for covered employees. However, a federal district court using federal discrimination statutes for guidance has ruled that the state statute only protects individuals who are 40 years of age or older [*Guglietta v. Meredith Corp.*, 301 F. Supp. 2d 209 (D. Conn. 2004)].

[2] The NM Human Rights Act does not define the protected age class. However, the New Mexico Supreme Court has ruled that, in employment discrimination cases, the act's age discrimination provisions apply to individuals who are at least 40 years of age [*Cates v. Regents of the N.M. Inst. of Mining & Tech.*, 124 N.M. 633 (1998)].

[3] In North Carolina, there is no age limitation for private employers provided in the state law. However, to prevail in a civil action brought under the act, an individual must meet the standards for evidence required under the federal Age Discrimination in Employment Act (ADEA). For public employers, the NC Discrimination in Public Employment Act requires equal employment protection without any qualifying age indicated.

In general, most states have expanded their protections in this arena over the past decade. However, given the trend toward narrowing protections for older workers based on court rulings, it is possible that many states may retract those provisions. Further, under the Trump administration, the EEOC continued a more "aggressive litigation" tactic, attempting to narrow equal employment protections rather than broaden them, so it remains unclear whether age discrimination laws at both the state and federal levels will continue to narrow in the future.[47]

Employees who live in states with state age discrimination protections greater than those provided by the ADEA may choose to file a state law claim rather than a federal law claim. If a state offers greater protections than the ADEA, those protections typically provide any combination of the following:

1. **Broader application:** State age discrimination laws often apply to a wider range of employers. The ADEA applies to employers with 20 or more employees. Some state laws, however, apply to all employers in the state, while others apply to employers with 2, 5, 10, or 15 employees. Thus, employees who may be prevented from filing an ADEA claim because the law does not apply to their employer might still have a remedy under state law.

2. **Broader remedies:** State age discrimination laws sometimes allow a wider range of damages. For example, an employee can recover back wages and attorney's fees under the ADEA. However, under some state laws, an employee can also recover damages for emotional distress as well as punitive damages, both of which are not permitted under the ADEA. Punitive damages are those designed to punish the employer for its actions. Thus, an employee who believes that the employer's actions were particularly horrible may opt to file a state law claim to try to collect punitive and/or emotional distress damages.

3. **More time to file:** States often provide longer filing periods. In a federal age discrimination case, two filing deadlines are important. The first is the 180 days after the discrimination occurs that the employee has to file a complaint with the EEOC. Where state or local age discrimination laws exist, the deadline can be pushed back to 300 days. The second deadline is the amount of time to file a suit once the regulatory body evaluates the claim and gives the go-ahead to file suit, which is 90 days in complaints involving the EEOC. Many state laws give employees a longer time to file suit after getting the go-ahead. Thus, an employee who has waited too long to file a claim under the ADEA might still be able to file a state law claim.

The difference between state law coverage and the ADEA can be seen in a 2016 decision by the Eleventh Circuit in the case of *Villarreal v. R.J. Reynolds.*[48] In that case, the circuit court held that the ADEA only applies to employees and not to job applicants. The Eleventh Circuit covers the states of Alabama, Florida, and Georgia. However, since all three states have antidiscrimination protection laws that include not only coverage for age but also the broader protection for discrimination in *hiring decisions,* job applicants in those states also are covered. The case was appealed to the U.S. Supreme Court, but it declined to review the decision, leaving the issue open to interpretation by lower courts and the Circuits. The Seventh Circuit reached a similar ruling in 2019, citing the Eleventh Circuit case and holding that the ADEA does not cover job applicants.[49] While the Seventh Circuit covers Wisconsin, Illinois, and Indiana, both Wisconsin and Indiana state laws explicitly protect job applicants from age discrimination, and Illinois courts historically have interpreted its laws to protect applicants, though its law is less clear on the subject.

LO4 Identify the legal options available to an employee who believes that she or he has experienced age discrimination.

An employee who believes that his or her employer has engaged in age discrimination has several options to try to correct the wrong. The first step often is to file a complaint with the employer, using the employer's internal grievance procedures. Some companies have extensive internal grievance procedures, which may involve arbitration or some other type of mediation, though of course since they are not required, some employers have no procedures at all.

If filing a grievance does not bring resolution, the employee has several legal options:

- File a complaint with the federal Equal Employment Opportunity Commission.
- File a complaint with the state equivalent of the EEOC (if one exists).
- File a lawsuit in federal court under the ADEA.
- File a lawsuit in state court under state age discrimination laws.

These legal options are not exclusive—pursuing one option does not prevent the employee from later pursuing one or more of the other options.

As previously mentioned, the deadline for filing a complaint with the EEOC is 180 days from when the discrimination occurred, which is extended to 300 days if the state has age discrimination laws and an administrative agency to oversee age discrimination complaints. Note, however, that using the employer's internal grievance procedure does not affect the EEOC timing. Thus, if the grievance procedure drags out, the employee might be forced to file within the 180 days even if the employer's grievance procedure has not run its course. So, the employee could file an internal grievance, then file a complaint with the state agency (within however many days the state allows), and then file an EEOC complaint within 300 days. Or the employee could have skipped the complaint process entirely and filed suit right away; employees are not required to go through the grievance process before filing suit.

The use of the 300-day window may vary in practical application, depending on whether the discrimination was one single discriminatory act versus ongoing harassment (also known as a hostile working environment). In 2019, the Second Circuit ruled that the 300-day limitation period does not apply to the background evidence of age discrimination.[50] The court ruled that, for hostile working environment cases showing a pattern of harassment over a period of time, as long as at least one event occurred within 300 days of filing the claim, the court may consider events that occurred outside of the 300-day limit as background acts.

When the EEOC receives a complaint, it has several possible responses. (State procedures are generally similar.) It could dismiss the complaint if it believes that the charges have no merit, or it could investigate the charges. If it investigates the charges, the EEOC can either bring suit on the employee's behalf if it believes that the charges have merit or give the employee what is called a right-to-sue letter if it believes that the charges lack the merit needed to file suit. Once the employee receives the right-to-sue letter, she or he has 90 days to file suit against the employer in her or his own name.

Employee's *Prima Facie* Case: Disparate Treatment

LO5 Articulate the *prima facie* case of discrimination based on age.

See Chapter 2 to revisit key concepts.

Suppose that an employee believes that she or he has experienced age discrimination based on an adverse employer action (a pay cut, bad performance review, demotion, or otherwise). For our purposes, let us assume that the employee has completed the employer's complaint process and now has decided to file a federal lawsuit under the ADEA. Two types of discrimination exist under the ADEA: disparate treatment and disparate impact. As is discussed in greater detail in Chapter 3, disparate treatment occurs when the discrimination is directed at the employee, to the exclusion of other employees. The employee is treated differently from other employees because of age. The employee does not have to be the only one affected, but the action must be directed at that employee. One example is where the employer chooses not to hire the employee because of her or his age. Disparate impact, on the other hand (discussed in more detail later in this chapter), involves actions that are not directed at the employee because of her or his age but instead have an unfair impact on older workers in general.

The employee filing an action against the employer under the ADEA based on disparate treatment must prove age discrimination by using the method of proof for Title VII cases originally set forth in *McDonnell Douglas Corp. v. Green* and later adapted to age discrimination claims under the ADEA. Under this approach, an employee must establish the following four elements to persuade the court that she or he has a claim for age discrimination:

1. The employee is in the protected class.
2. She or he suffered an **adverse employment action** (was terminated or demoted or other negative employment impact).
3. The employee was doing her or his job well enough to meet her or his employer's legitimate expectations.
4. Others not in the protected class were treated more favorably.

adverse employment action
Any action or omission that takes away a benefit, opportunity, or privilege of employment from an employee.

Member of the Protected Class

To satisfy the first requirement of the *prima facie* case under the ADEA, the employee must merely show that she or he is 40 years old or older.

Adverse Employment Action

The element requires that the employee demonstrate that the employer made an employment decision that adversely affected the employee. This may include a decision not to hire the applicant or to terminate the employee.

Qualified for the Position

qualified for the position
Able to meet the employer's legitimate job requirements.

To prove the third requirement, the employee or applicant must prove that he or she was **qualified for the position**. If the employee or applicant is not qualified, then the employer's decision would be justified and the claimant's claim fails. The position requirements, however, must be legitimate requirements and not merely devised for the purpose of terminating or refusing to hire older workers. Courts have allowed claimants to meet this requirement simply by showing that the employee never was told that her or his performance was unacceptable. The qualifications requirement is not a difficult one. Courts even have held that the fact that the employee was hired in the first place indicates that he or she has the basic qualifications.

Dissimilar Treatment

In connection with the fourth requirement for a *prima facie* case of age discrimination—almost always the most difficult element to prove—the employee or applicant must show that she or he was treated differently from other employees who are not in the protected class. This might require an employer to explain its actions if it terminates (or refuses to hire) an older qualified employee while simultaneously hiring younger employees. For instance, where an employer terminates a 57-year-old worker and hires, in her place, a 34-year-old employee and the 57-year-old employee can show that she remains qualified for her position, the employer must defend its decision.

The courts have struggled to develop consistent rules that can be applied in these situations. What if an 80-year-old is fired and replaced by a 78-year-old? Is this discriminatory action? The usual ADEA case is filed where an older employee is replaced by (or not hired in favor of) a *much* younger employee. However, the Supreme Court held in *O' Connor v. Consolidated Coin Caterers*[51] that a plaintiff can state a claim as long as she or he is replaced by someone younger, even if the replacement also is a member of the protected class—in other words, even if the replacement also is 40 years old or older.

Another provision of the ADEA requires special attention: section 4(e) makes it unlawful to "print or publish or cause to be printed or published, any notice or advertisement . . . indicating any preference, limitation, specification, or discrimination, based on age." The court in *Hodgson v. Approved Personnel Serv., Inc.*[52] found that, in determining whether an advertisement had a discriminatory effect on older individuals, "the discriminatory effect of an advertisement is determined not by 'trigger words' but rather by its context." That is, the ad is not considered discriminatory because of a particular word or words but rather because of the intent of the ad to discriminate against older individuals.

Microtargeting
Microtargeting is a form of marketing in which advertisers target a particular age demographic and show tailored advertisements to each age category. The term also may be used for other forms of extremely tailored marketing based on groups.

The question of intent also has implications for advertisements that potential applicants cannot see. Recall our discussion of Facebook, LinkedIn, and Google in the beginning of this chapter when we discussed targeted advertising. In March 2019, Facebook settled a case for $5 million brought by the ACLU and the Communication Workers of America (CWA). The plaintiffs claimed age discrimination based on a recruitment practice known as **microtargeting**. Microtargeting allows advertisers to target the age demographic they want by only showing ads to those in specific age categories. While this may sound efficient, in effect it removes access to job opportunities for those workers who may not fit the desired demographic and are older than 40, in violation of the ADEA. As one of the CWA's attorneys explained, "This settlement takes away digital tools that advertisers can use to deny equal opportunity."[53] The implication here is that employers cannot use technology to hide ads from potential job applicants.

The use of certain trigger words like *girl* or *young* may establish an ADEA violation under most circumstances, so the context of the statement is important to determine its discriminatory effect. For instance, the use of *recent college graduate* is not discriminatory if a personnel agency merely intended to identify those *services* that it offered to that specific class of individuals. (See Exhibit 12.6, "Ageist Language.") The EEOC specifically explains as follows:

> The ADEA generally makes it unlawful to include age preferences, limitations, or specifications in job notices or advertisements. A job notice or advertisement may specify an age limit only in the rare circumstances where age is shown to be a "bona fide occupational qualification" (BFOQ) reasonably necessary to the normal operation of the business.[54]

Experience caps also are under scrutiny. In *Kleber v. CareFusion Corp.,*[55] Kleber challenged CareFusion's experience cap (3 to 7 years of relevant experience) as unlawful under the ADEA. While Kleber's claim was rejected by the Seventh Circuit, the court's decision was based on Kleber's standing as an *applicant,* not as an existing employee looking for a transfer or promotion. It is unclear how the court might rule if an older employee (40 years and older) looking for a transfer might fare under experience caps.[56]

Exhibit 12.6 *Ageist Language*

Though courts look beyond the words themselves when assessing the discriminatory effect of particular words or phrases on older workers, certain language has often been found to suggest ageist intent. The EEOC Interpretive Rules offer the following guidance:

> When help wanted notices or advertisements contain terms and phrases such as "age 25 to 35," "young," "boy," "girl," "college student," "recent college graduate," or others of a similar nature, such a term or phrase discriminates against the employment of older people, and will be considered in violation of the act. Such specifications as

"age 40 to 50," "age over 50," or "age over 65" are also considered to be prohibited. Where such specifications as "retired person" or "supplement your pension" are intended and applied so as to discriminate against others within the protected group, they, too, are regarded as prohibited unless one of the exceptions applies.

Examples of language cited by the EEOC as evidence of age discrimination in recent lawsuits include the following:

- Rental Pro terminated the employment of a 52-year-old man because of his age. The company's owner sought "younger and peppier" employees and wanted to bring "young blood" into the company, the agency alleged.[1]

- At Ohio State University, a university administrator called some of the veteran teachers "an extraordinarily change-averse population of people almost all of whom are over 50, contemplating retirement (or not), and it's like herding hippos." Two teachers, Julianne Taffe and Kathryn Moon, reached a settlement, receiving offers to return to their jobs as well as back pay and legal fees, along with agreement by Ohio State to review its policies and guidelines on age discrimination.[2]

- The City of Milpitas was required to pay a $140,000 fine and to provide other relief to settle an age discrimination lawsuit after the city failed to hire qualified applicants over age 50 who scored higher than the person hired. Instead, the city hired a younger applicant, age 39, for the position of executive secretary to the city manager.[3]

Alternatively, it is important to note that alleged ageist language alone is not always sufficient to argue a case of age discrimination. The U.S. District Court in *Chisolm v. 7-Eleven, Inc.* found that the alleged ageist language used by the hiring manager was insufficient to create a triable issue of fact when Chisolm was not hired for a position. The court argued that, even though he used words like *energy* and *enthusiasm*, these words were not sufficient to support a claim of age discrimination.[4]

[1] Civil Action No. 6:15-cv-00154-GFVT, filed in U.S. District Court for the Eastern District of Kentucky, London Division (2016).

[2] Smola. J., "Two Women Who Won Age Discrimination Settlement Sue Ohio State for Public Records" (July 23, 2019), https://www.dispatch.com/news/20190722/two-women-who-won-age-discrimination-settlement-sue-ohio-state-for-public-records (accessed February 22, 2020).

[3] Civil Action No. 5:15-cv-04444, filed in U.S. District Court for the Northern District of California.

[4] *Chisolm v. 7-Eleven, Inc.,* 383 F.Supp.3d 1032 (2019).

Burden Shifting No More

See Chapter 2 to revisit key concepts.

The motivations behind employment actions, such as a dismissal, are often difficult to determine. Prior to 2009, once the employee presented evidence of the employer's wrongful actions, the burden of proof shifted to the employer to present a legitimate nondiscriminatory reason (LNDR) for its actions, similar to the process in other discrimination case. There often are many reasons that enter into an employer's decisions, and at that time, the employee had to prove that age discrimination was the *motivating factor* (one of many, perhaps) in the employer's adverse decision. Then the employer was given the opportunity to prove that it would have come to the same decision even if there were no discrimination present—the employer was permitted to demonstrate that there was some non-discriminatory motivation, such as poor performance or a legitimate business necessity—the LNDR.

Case 2

However, in 2009, the U.S. Supreme Court modified this process through its holding in *Gross v. FBL Financial Services Inc.,*[57] included at the end of this chapter. In that case, the court ruled that age discrimination cases under the ADEA now require proof that the employer would not have made this decision *"but for"* the employee's age. Further, the burden of proof does *not* shift to the employer, so the employer no longer must demonstrate that it would have made the same decision regardless of age. In other words, where there are several reasons for the termination, the employee no longer can simply show that age was a "motivating factor;" it must be the "but for" factor.

The *Gross* decision caused quite a stir, with commentators interpreting the ruling to mean that disparate treatment age discrimination claims would be far more difficult to prove. Whether that comes to pass remains to be seen, but efforts were launched in the aftermath of *Gross* to undo the decision. Jack Gross was called to testify before Congress, and bills have been introduced twice in both the House and Senate to legislatively overturn the decision.[58] Finally, the U.S. House of Representatives passed HR 1230 Protecting Older Workers Against Discrimination Act (POWADA) in January 2020,[59] rejecting the ruling under *Gross* and reinstating the standard that plaintiffs must show age was one of a number of *motivating factors* rather than "but for." An identical bill is pending in the Senate.[60]

The lower courts have been left to implement *Gross* and to answer related questions not raised in the case. Generally speaking, subsequent lower court answers to open questions have softened its impact. For example, does *Gross* require that age discrimination be the *only* factor? The Tenth Circuit has said no; *Gross* can be interpreted to mean that other factors can be present as long as age is the factor that made the difference.[61] Does the *McDonnell Douglas* burden-shifting approach still have any relevance in ADEA disparate treatment cases? Surprisingly, perhaps, soon after the *Gross* decision, eight circuits—the First, Second, Third, Fourth, Fifth, Sixth, Seventh, and Tenth—all said yes. According to the Tenth Circuit,[62] summarizing the opinions of the other seven circuits, *Gross* held only that the burden of *persuasion* never shifts. *McDonnell Douglas,* on the other hand, shifts only the burden of *production.* Under those appellate court opinions, at some point after the employee has met the "but for" requirement, the burden shifts to the employer to produce evidence of a non-discriminatory justification for the action.

The burden of persuading the judge or jury that the employer is guilty of age discrimination, however, always rests with the employee. The distinction between burden of proof and burden of production can be difficult to draw. Still, continuing the trend, the Eighth Circuit joined its brethren the following year in affirming the continued relevance of *McDonnell* in the wake of *Gross.*[63] The Ninth Circuit also followed suit.[64] The Supreme Court has not yet granted review on either case from the Eighth or Ninth Circuits.

The impact of *Gross* has extended beyond the ADEA. In a 2013 case, *University of Texas Southwestern Medical Center v. Nassar,* the Supreme Court decided that the "but for" causation standard applies not only to adverse employment actions in ADEA cases but to Title VII retaliation plaintiffs as well.[65] Prior to *Nassar,* the courts were divided as to whether Title VII retaliation claims were required to meet the mixed-motive standard of Title VII discrimination claims, or a more stringent "but for" causation standard. Resolving the issue, the Supreme Court determined in *Nassar* that it is insufficient for a Title VII plaintiff to show that retaliation contributed to an adverse employment action. Instead, as in post–*Gross* ADEA suits, the Court found that plaintiffs must show that the action would not have happened absent retaliation, a significantly higher burden.

Like *Gross, Nassar* was a contentious 5–4 decision viewed by many as setting a higher bar for employees with grievances to demonstrate that their rights had been violated and offering greater protections for employers against employee lawsuits. However, while firmly establishing federal standards, *Gross* and *Nassar* offer little guidance to lower courts regarding the proper framework for state age discrimination and employer retaliation cases. It is possible that employees will not turn away from the courts but rely more heavily upon state statutes and less upon federal statutes like the ADEA and Title VII. Although it is too early to tell if these Supreme Court decisions will result in fewer lawsuits or a trend toward increased use of state-level age discrimination statutes, there are some indications that state protections could blunt the impact of *Gross.*[66] For example, in a post–*Gross* Massachusetts case, the district court instructed the jury to apply the "but for" standard to a plaintiff's assertion that her employer had violated the ADEA, and the mixed-motive framework to her claim regarding violation of a state anti-discrimination statute. The jury found for the plaintiff on the state claim, though not the ADEA charge. On appeal to the First Circuit, the defendant argued that, under *Gross,* the stricter standard should apply to the state statute as well. The court rejected this argument, holding that the mixed-motive analysis remains valid for state-level claims under *Gross.*[67]

In *National Association of African American-Owned Media v. Charter Communications, Inc.*, the Ninth Circuit reversed lower court decisions that recognized mixed motive claims.[68] The case was heard by the U.S. Supreme Court in November 2019, and as of the date of publication, results are still pending.[69]

However, in 2020, the Supreme Court did address the public sector provision of the ADEA and concluded that the public sector (including all federal employers) is held to a higher standard than other employers. Therefore, if you work in the public sector, according to *Babb v. Wilkie,* you only need to show that age was one factor among many that led to a negative employment decision.[70]

Employer's Defenses

Bona Fide Occupational Qualification

LO6 Describe the bona fide occupational qualification defenses available to employers under the ADEA.

If an employer is sued for age discrimination, it may claim that age is a bona fide occupational qualification, a BFOQ. (See Chapter 2 for a more general discussion of BFOQs.) In fact, age is one of the most consistently applied BFOQs. The employer's proof that a bona fide occupational qualification exists under the ADEA is slightly different and less exacting than under Title VII. Title VII requires that the employer demonstrate that the essence of the business requires the exclusion of the members of a protected class and all or substantially all of the members of that class are unable to perform adequately in the position in question. When demonstrating a BFOQ under the ADEA, the EEOC follows the requirements of Title VII but adds one further possibility for the employer's proof—see item 3 below. According to the EEOC, to demonstrate a BFOQ in an age discrimination case brought under the ADEA, an employer must prove that:

See Chapter 2 to revisit key concepts.

1. The age limit is reasonably necessary to the essence of the employer's business; and either

Scenario

2. All or substantially all of the individuals over that age are unable to perform the job's requirements adequately; or
3. Some of the individuals over that age possess a disqualifying trait that cannot be ascertained *except* by reference to age.

The third element of the proof allows an employer to exclude an older worker from a position that may be unsafe if held by *some* older workers. This defense would only be accepted by a court where there is no way to individually assess the safety potential of a given applicant or employee.

For example, assume there existed a medical disorder that was prevalent among those over 80 and was not discoverable under standard medical investigation. Assume also that this medical condition caused its sufferers to lose consciousness without any warning. An employer who refused to place those over 80 in the position of a school bus driver would satisfy the proof of a BFOQ. Note that it is not enough for an employer to simply believe (subjectively) that there is a condition related to age that supports a BFOQ. The decision must be based on competent expert evidence of a connection between age and the component of the job affected (see Exhibit 12.7 "Employer's Defenses").

When Congress passed the 1986 amendments to the ADEA prohibiting **mandatory retirement** on the basis of age for most workers, it included several temporary exemptions, notably one for tenured faculty in higher education. That exemption expired December 31, 1993. Since that time, mandatory retirement has been limited to two circumstances.

mandatory retirement
Employee must retire upon reaching a specified age. Deemed illegal by the 1986 amendments to the ADEA, with few exceptions.

1. A small number of high-level employees with substantial executive authority can be subjected to compulsory retirement at age 65 or beyond if the individual will receive a company pension of $44,000 or more. This exception is a very narrow one and does not allow for compulsory retirement policies for midlevel managers. Perhaps this exception is narrowly confined to those with decision-making authority based on stereotypes that the majority of powerful executives tend to be over 40, with wealth and opportunity that make a mandatory retirement policy less burdensome.

Exhibit 12.7 *Employer's Defenses*

The employer may defend its actions in one of several ways. The act states:

It shall not be unlawful for an employer
(1) to take any action otherwise prohibited where age is a bona fide occupational qualification reasonably necessary to the normal operation of the particular business, or where the differentiation is based on reasonable factors other than age.

(2) to observe the terms of a bona fide seniority system or any bona fide employee benefit plan such as a retirement, pension, or insurance plan.

(3) to discharge or otherwise discipline an individual for good cause.

2. Persons in two specific occupations, police officers and firefighters, have been subject to mandatory retirement. However, age is not necessarily a BFOQ in these occupations.

Voluntary retirement plans are, however, permitted and are discussed later in this chapter.

As mentioned above, an employer cannot simply decide on a BFOQ and base these employment decisions on age-related stereotypes; the employer must make decisions based on credible evidence. As demonstrated in *Western Air Lines, Inc. v. Criswell,* included at the end of the chapter, an airline attempted to defend its mandatory retirement policy for flight engineers over the age of 60 as a BFOQ. This defense ultimately failed because individual determinations of health could help achieve the airline's goal of safe transportation of passengers in a less restrictive manner.

Western Airlines' policy apparently was based on the Federal Aviation Administration's original "Age 60 Rule," which prohibited people at or over the age of 60 from acting as pilots or co-pilots.[71] Interestingly, while the FAA requires individual pilot medical certifications and a semiannual exam of pilots, it maintained the Age 60 Rule until 2007, when then-President Bush signed a bill raising the mandatory retirement age to 65, bringing the United States into alignment with international rules. At the time of its passage, the legislation was praised for keeping more experienced pilots in the cockpit longer, for easing the challenge brought on by a pilot shortage, but also for its requirement that pilots over 60 be accompanied by a younger copilot on international flights.

Similarly, with regard to medical issues relating to pandemics, employers are not permitted to exclude older workers who they perceive to be (or who might actually be) at a higher risk of complications if they contract the disease. In the same regard, however, at the time of publication, no case law or statute requires employers to grant requests from workers to telecommute *simply* on the basis of their age.

Employee's *Prima Facie* Case: Circumstances Involving Claims of Disparate Impact

LO7 Explain the difference between situations where disparate impact and disparate treatment apply in connection with age discrimination.

See Chapter 2 to revisit key concepts.

We now turn to disparate impact. Disparate treatment, as discussed in Chapter 2, occurs where an employee is treated differently from other employees because she or he is a member of a protected class. Disparate impact, on the other hand, exists where an employer's policy or rule, though not discriminatory on its face, affects one group differently from another.

For example, a rule that requires all bus drivers to have 20/20 vision may have the effect of limiting the number of older workers who can be bus drivers. We can agree that this rule is indeed discriminatory since it distinguishes between those who have good vision and those who do not. The question is whether the rule is wrongfully discriminatory, in violation of the ADEA. If the rule is justified by business reasons, it may not be a violation.

Because of the close connection between the *prima facie* cases and the employer defenses, we will discuss the case of disparate impact at this juncture and then

Exhibit 12.8 *Proving a Case of Age Discrimination*

DISPARATE TREATMENT

Step One: Employee's *prima facie* case

1. The employee is in the protected class.
2. She or he was terminated or demoted.
3. The employee was doing her or his job well enough to meet her employer's legitimate expectations.
4. Others not in the protected class were treated more favorably.

Step Two: Employer defenses

1. Bona fide occupational qualification.

Step Three: Employee may evidence pretext for employer actions.

DISPARATE IMPACT

Step One: Employee's *prima facie* case

1. A facially neutral policy or rule is imposed by an employer,
2. Which has a different effect on an older group of workers.
3. No intent to discriminate is necessary.

Step Two: Employer defenses

1. Reasonable factor other than age (RFOA):
   a. Economic concerns.
   b. Seniority.

---

reasonable factor other than age (RFOA)

A defense to a *prima facie* claim of age discrimination, offered by employers. May include any requirement that does not have an adverse impact on older workers as well as those factors that do adversely affect this protected class but are shown to be job-related. For example, if an employee is not performing satisfactorily and is terminated, her failure to meet reasonable performance standards would constitute a reasonable factor other than age.

return to the employee's burden of evidencing pretext shortly, but let us review where we are in the case process to help you to navigate where we are at the moment! (See Exhibit 12.8, "Proving a Case of Age Discrimination").

In mid-2005, the Supreme Court reached a decision in *Smith v. City of Jackson*[72] that resolved this issue—one that had caused a distinct split in the circuit courts. In that case, police and public safety officers employed by the city of Jackson, Mississippi, argued that the city had given senior officers lower salary increases than those offered to younger officers. The city had adopted this salary plan "to attract and retain qualified people, provide incentive for performance, maintain competitiveness with other public sector agencies and ensure equitable compensation to all employees regardless of age, sex, race and/or disability." The appellate court held that disparate impact claims are categorically unavailable under the ADEA.

While the Supreme Court reversed the appellate court and held that disparate impact claims are actionable under the ADEA, the court found against the officers because the city based its decision on **reasonable factors other than age (RFOA)**. "The RFOA provision provides that it shall not be unlawful for an employer 'to take any action otherwise prohibited under [the act] . . . where the differentiation is based on reasonable factors other than age discrimination . . . .' In most disparate treatment cases, if an employer in fact acted on a factor other than age, the action would not be prohibited under [the act] in the first place."

One of the important elements of the *Smith* decision is that the Court found that disparate impact should be interpreted much more *narrowly* under the ADEA compared to Title VII. Under Title VII, if the employee evidences disparate impact, the employer is required to justify its decisions or processes by evidencing that they are both job-related and consistent with business necessity, usually considered to be a higher and more exacting standard than an RFOA.

In evaluating the city's salary plan, the Supreme Court concluded that reliance on seniority and rank is unquestionably reasonable given the city's goal of raising employees' salaries to match those in surrounding communities. The court explained again that the analysis in this ADEA case was different from an analysis under Title VII: "While there may have been other reasonable ways for the City to achieve its goals, the one selected was not unreasonable. Unlike the business necessity test, which asks whether there are other ways for the employer to achieve its goals that do not result in a disparate impact on a protected class, the reasonableness inquiry includes no such requirement." The court therefore decided that the city's decision was based on a "reasonable factor other than age" that responded to the city's legitimate goal of retaining police officers.

Scenario

In Opening Scenario 2, the applicant's age appears to be of some concern; however, the real issue is whether the applicant can do the strenuous job. If it can be shown that the applicant can perform all the necessary job functions, he should be hired because he is the most qualified. In the future, if he becomes unable to meet the demands of the job, his termination would be a result of his lack of ability, not his age. Furthermore, regarding the concerns about the applicant leaving after a few years, *any* employee can leave an employer at any time unless there is a contract. This is not a concern with older individuals only.

Economic Concerns

LO8 Analyze factual circumstances when employer economic concerns may justify adverse action against particular groups of workers.

Would a company's desire to cut payroll costs constitute a reasonable factor other than age? Often, a reduction in force may adversely impact older workers since older workers also tend to have more seniority, which often also translates to higher salaries (though not always). To reduce costs, a firm may choose to cut its workforce based on salary amounts in order to have the greatest budget impact. Based on *City of Jackson,* discussed above, it is crucial that these termination decisions be made on the basis of a clear and objective standard so that the RFOA defense remains available to the employer.

Scenario

This issue is unique to ADEA discrimination claims because it does not cost more necessarily to hire someone of one race or ethnicity than another. But, in many cases, it *may be* more expensive to hire or to retain older workers.

Courts do not favor this justification for the termination of older workers. For example, the Massachusetts Appeals Court in *Porio v. Department of Revenue*[73] reversed a lower court ruling, explaining that an employee's claim of disparate impact can move forward even if an employer has legitimate budgetary considerations for its reduction in force. "The existence of a legitimate need to reduce the workforce does not resolve which positions should be cut . . . Porio is alleging that DOR responded to its legitimate budgetary constraints in a manner that was driven by an age-based bias against its older employers." Courts have consistently upheld the RFOA standard established under *City of Jackson* regarding pay cuts to long-tenured employees with higher salaries.[74]

In deciding which positions to be cut and trying to ensure that there is no age-based bias, employers are directed by the courts to develop and implement a clear procedure for terminations. Courts suggest that objective criteria should be used to determine the individuals who will be discharged and that the entire position be eliminated. For instance, a district court in Georgia held that a county that completely eliminated a particular position for budgetary reasons was not in violation of the ADEA. In addition, the employer's decision not to relocate the employee to another open position also was not in violation of the ADEA. The court explained, "the ADEA simply provides that a discharged employee who applies for a job he is qualified for and which is available at the time of his termination must be considered for that job along with all other candidates, and cannot be denied the position based upon his age." The employee was *not* the most qualified person for the other position; therefore, the employer had no obligation to hire him in the other position.[75]

The Supreme Court's 2008 decision *Meacham v. Knolls Atomic Power Laboratory* (included at the end of the chapter) further clarified that the burden of proving the RFOA is on the employer's shoulders in these cases, since it is an "affirmative defense."[76] In other words, the burden is on the employer to prove that age was not a factor in the decision. In *Meacham,* the employer (Knolls) had implemented a downsizing program to reduce its workforce in response to economic pressures. The company laid off 31 workers, 30 of whom (including the plaintiff, Meacham) were over 40 years old. Meacham claimed that the reduction had a disparate impact on older workers, since the outcome could not have happened by chance.

The lower court had ruled for Knolls, finding that Meacham had not met the plaintiff's burden of establishing that no reasonable factor other than age existed to explain the disparate impact on older workers. The Supreme Court overturned this ruling, holding that Meacham did not have to show that Knolls' action was unreasonable. Rather, the Court stated, Knolls was responsible for demonstrating the presence of reasonable, non-age-based causes for its action. In other words, the *Meacham* decision states unequivocally that the employer has the burden of persuasion in disparate impact age discrimination cases; hence the term *affirmative defense.*

What Is an RFOA?

When taken together, *City of Jackson* and *Meacham* definitively establish that the employer is responsible for establishing the RFOA defense; however, both employers and courts have struggled to determine *what exactly constitutes an RFOA.* If an employer makes an employment decision that negatively affects older workers, how does it know if that decision will be found to be both "reasonable" and non-age-based by a court? What standards are courts to apply when assessing employer claims regarding RFOAs?

With such questions in mind, the EEOC issued its "Final Rule on Disparate Impact and Reasonable Factors Other Than Age (RFOA)," in March 2012, a regulatory framework that answers these questions and clarifies the practical effects of the Supreme Court's two general rulings for the employer's RFOA defense.[77] The Final Rule has two purposes:

1. It creates consistency between the existing regulation and the Supreme Court's holding that the standard to which an employer will be held in defending an

ADEA disparate impact claim is RFOA, rather than business necessity (a higher standard).

2. It further describes the RFOA defense for employees, employers, and those who enforce and implement the ADEA.

The EEOC's updated ruling defines an RFOA as a basis for an employment decision that is "objectively reasonable when viewed from the position of a prudent employer mindful of its responsibilities under the ADEA under like circumstances." The EEOC explains that an employment practice is based on an RFOA "when it was reasonably designed and administered to achieve a legitimate business purpose in light of the circumstances, including its potential harm to older workers."

In assessing reasonableness, the EEOC lists the following five considerations as relevant:

1. The extent to which the factor is related to the employer's stated business purpose;

2. The extent to which the employer defined the factor accurately and applied the factor fairly and accurately, including the extent to which managers and supervisors were given guidance or training about how to apply the factor and avoid discrimination;

3. The extent to which the employer limited supervisors' discretion to assess employees subjectively, particularly where the criteria that the supervisors were asked to evaluate are known to be subject to negative age-based stereotypes;

4. The extent to which the employer assessed the adverse impact of its employment practice on older workers; and

5. The degree of the harm to individuals within the protected age group, in terms of both the extent of injury and the numbers of persons adversely affected and the extent to which the employer took steps to reduce the harm, in light of the burden of undertaking such steps.

In its guidance provided to interpret each of these considerations, the EEOC stresses that RFOAs do *not* need to meet the rigorous "business necessity" test used in Title VII cases. For example, the method that an employer chooses to achieve its business purpose should be given more weight when evaluating an RFOA claim than the content of the purpose itself, since the purpose need only meet the relatively low standard of "reasonableness." In a similar vein, the second consideration recommends that an employer's RFOA defense show that the factor has been defined "accurately" and applied "fairly and accurately." However, the EEOC points out that the employer need not show that the factor has been validated by studies or other formal means typically required to establish a "business necessity" defense, but only that "their choices are reasonable."

Importantly, unless or until the courts choose to affirm the regulatory framework of the EEOC's Final Rule, an employer is not required by law to satisfy each of the five considerations in order to mount a successful RFOA defense. The EEOC notes that "the defense could be established absent one or more of the considerations, and . . . there could even be a situation in which the defense is met, absent any of the considerations. Similarly, the defense is not automatically established merely because one or more of the considerations are present."[78]

With these caveats in mind, the EEOC does not address how the Final Rule affect an employer's daily business practices. However, courts continue to reinforce the message that the burden is on the employer when raising the RFOA defense. For instance, in 2015, the Court noted that, since the RFOA is an affirmative defense, the party raising it not only needs to produce evidence regarding the defense but also must persuade the fact finder of its merit.[79]

Reductions in Force (RIFs)

At their crux, *City of Jackson* and *Meacham* require that the employer prove that age was *not* a factor in a decision that disproportionately harms older workers. But how do you really know whether economic pressures or age bias is motivating an employer's decision to fire or lay off an employee?

Interestingly, one of the hurdles for a worker in stating a claim for discrimination based on a reduction in force is the fourth prong of the traditional *prima facie* case. When an RIF occurs, no one replaces the employee, so there is no one "similarly situated." Therefore, in the event of a RIF, age discrimination may be proven where:

- The employer refuses to allow the discharged (or demoted) employee to bump others with less seniority, and
- The employer hires younger workers when the jobs become available after the employee was discharged (or demoted) at the prior salary of the older worker.

One question that often emerges during a RIF is whether an employer is permitted to offer (or should offer) to reduce the salary of a protected employee in order to respond to its economic challenges. In this way, the employer could retain the older worker, and continue to cut costs. While this may seem a creative option, section 4(a)(3) of the ADEA specifically states that it is "unlawful for any employer . . . to reduce the wage rate of any employee in order to comply with this Act." Strangely, though striving to be clear, in light of *City of Jackson* and *Meacham,* this prohibition remains vague. An employer may argue that it was not reducing the wage rate to comply with the ADEA but, in compliance with the requirements of this line of jurisprudence, for some RFOA such as reducing costs. For example, the Third Circuit held in *Bryan v. Gov't of the Virgin Islands* that a 3 percent pay cut for older workers was acceptable under the ADEA because the employer applied the reduction based on credited years of service rather than age in an effort to reduce payroll and to increase solvency.[80]

Scenario

What if an employee who is told that she is to be laid off for economic reasons voluntarily offers to reduce her salary? The law is unsettled, but the Second Circuit reversed a lower court decision and held instead that rejecting such an offer might indeed constitute age discrimination. In *Carras v. MGS 728 Lex,*[81] a chief financial officer was told that he was being terminated for financial reasons. He then offered to take a pay cut to $60,000. The company rejected his offer, laid him off, replaced him with a younger person, and paid the new person more than $60,000. The former CFO convinced the appellate court that rejection of his offer might be an indication that economic reasons were not the real motivation.

In many circumstances, if an employer seeks cost-cutting alternatives and applies them on the basis of economics rather than age, courts are more likely to look favorably on these decisions. For example, employers may see fit to offer workers early retirement opportunities, a temporary shutdown of certain units, part-time schedules, or job-sharing programs as well as pay reductions (when applied across the board).[82]

On final point about disparate impact under the ADEA was clarified by the Third Circuit in *Karlo, et al. v. Pittsburgh Glass Works, LLC.* In that case, the holding made it easier for subgroups of employees to claim age discrimination based on disparate impact. The court found that, in some circumstance, some (older) groups of workers might experience a disproportionate adverse impact under a reduction in force.[83] Therefore, the court held that an ADEA disparate-impact case may proceed by alleging discrimination against only a portion—a subset—of the protected group (such as workers over a certain age, such as 60). Prior to *Karlo,* claims could only move forward if the impact was against the entire 40 and over age group. The *Karlo* decision created a split with the Second, Sixth, and Eighth Circuits, putting the burden on employers to be more careful and exacting in their statistical analyses for disparate impact.

Defenses Based on Benefit Plans and Seniority Systems

The ADEA specifically excludes bona fide retirement plans that distinguish based on age but are "not a subterfuge to evade the purpose of [the] Act." "Subterfuge" refer to plans that are merely schemes designed to get around the requirements of the ADEA or the Older Workers' Benefit Protection Act (discussed below). The effect of the 1978 and 1986 amendments to the ADEA was to prohibit any involuntary retirement plans when they are imposed on the sole basis of an employee's age.

To qualify as a bona fide voluntary retirement plan allowed by the act, the plan must be truly voluntary. Some employees have argued that a decision cannot be considered "voluntary" if they are given only a short time to decide whether to accept the retirement option. But a short time period to reach a decision does not necessarily mean the decision is involuntary. The determination of what qualifies as a bona fide plan must be made on a case-by-case basis.

Courts have held that early retirement plans offered by employers are not bona fide pursuant to the act *if a reasonable person would have felt compelled to resign under similar circumstances.*[84] However, even after several court decisions have further clarified the questions of voluntariness and subterfuge, employers are left without much direction in terms of the formulation of early retirement programs and other means of providing benefits.

"Same Actor" Defense

A majority of circuit courts have adopted a defense called the "same actor inference" in age discrimination claims. The circuit courts have applied various weights of strength or value of the defense when the person who does the hiring and firing are the same "actor." These courts have held that when the same person—"actor"—both hires and fires a worker protected by the ADEA, it is reasonable to presume that the employee's age was not a motivating factor in the decision. After all, why would someone hire an older worker in the first place if they held discriminatory beliefs about older workers?

The Fourth Circuit reasoned that "claims that the employer animus exists in termination but not in hiring seem irrational. From the standpoint for the putative discriminator, it hardly makes sense to hire workers from a group one dislikes (thereby incurring the psychological costs of associating with them), only to fire them once they are on the job."[85]

However, as the Washington Court of Appeals pointed out in a 2013 case involving a state age discrimination law, the same-actor defense has the potential to be manipulated by an employer. In *Lodis v. Corbis Holdings, Inc.,*[86] the employer promoted an employee, then immediately gave that employee a negative review in his new position and terminated him. The court refused to extend the same-actor defense to the defendant out of concern that doing so would permit employers to use promotion followed by termination as a means to avoid a charge of retaliation.

In a case involving age discrimination and retaliation, *Vaughan v. Anderson Reg'l Med. Ctr,*[87] the Third Circuit found that, although a strong inference does exist under the same actor defense, inference does not require an automatic finding that there was no discrimination. Therefore the court rejected the motion for summary judgment. The Court also found that the "same actor" inference offered by the employer was immaterial because it was persuaded by Vaughan's claim that the person who both hired and fired her was unduly influenced by a third party who was hostile against her based on age. *Vaughan* illustrates that extenuating factors may have an impact on these decisions.

Retaliation

The ADEA prohibits retaliation,[88] which usually occurs when an employer takes an adverse employment action against an employee in response to an age discrimination complaint filed by that employee. Adverse employment actions may include a dismissal, a denial of a promotion, a demotion, a suspension or other negative repercussions. The protection is quite broad and protects not only the person filing the complaint but also includes any other employee who may have participated in the claim. For example, the ADEA also protects an employee who may be a witness in support of the employee's allegations. If the employer retaliates against that employee, the employer violates the ADEA.

While, originally, some legal analysts thought that the ADEA might not protect federal employees from retaliation because the public sector language in the ADEA was different from the private sector language,[89] the Supreme Court dispelled any confusion on that issue in *Gomez-Perez v. Potter.*[90] In that case, the U.S. Supreme Court ruled that federal and private-sector employees have the same protection from retaliation under the ADEA, reversing the First Circuit, which had previously found no similar rights. However, the EEOC clarified that "the 'but-for' standard does not apply because the relevant federal sector statutory provisions do not employ the same language on which the Court based its holding in *Nasser*," thus affirming that retaliation is prohibited if it was a motivating factor when considering federal employers.[91] In 2009, the Supreme Court addressed the issue of causation in a case involving employer discrimination under the ADEA. In *Gross v. FBL Financial Services, Inc.,*[92] the Court concluded that the ADEA requires proof that the prohibited criterion was the but-for cause of the prohibited conduct.

punitive damages
Money over and above compensatory damages, imposed by a court to punish a defendant for willful acts and to act as a deterrent.

Punitive damages are those designed to punish the employer (rather than compensating the employee) and are often significantly higher in amount. Interestingly, while punitive damages generally are unavailable in ADEA-based claims, circuit courts are splits as to their availability in retaliation claims.[93] For example, the Fifth Circuit has ruled that punitive and compensatory damages are not available for retaliation claims under the ADEA.[94] The ADEA requires that the employer's conduct be willful in order to award punitive damages to the plaintiff,[95] which the U.S. Supreme Court has said means "the employer either knew or showed reckless disregard for the matter of whether its conduct was prohibited by the statute."[96]

Employee's *Prima Facie* Case: Proof of Pretext

LO9 Recognize necessary elements to establish pretext under the ADEA.

Let us return now to the standard *prima facie* case of discrimination. Assume that the employee has demonstrated the required four elements of that case and that the employer has demonstrated an RFOA or other affirmative defense. The next step in proving a case of discrimination is for the employee to show that the reason or defense is *pretextual.* When a claim is pretextual, it means that it is not the true reason for the action. In other words, there is some underlying motivation that the employer has not admitted. To prove that the offered reason is pretext for an actual case of age discrimination, the employee does not need to show that age was the *only* factor motivating the employment decision, but only that age was a *determining* factor.

Where there is direct evidence of discrimination, proof of pretext is not required. This may occur where the employer admits to having based the employment decision on the employee's age or when a representative of the employer says that it would be cheaper to hire younger applicants. You would not think that an employer would actually admit something so directly; but in *Mauer v. Deloitte & Touche, LLP,*[97] a supervisor gave a speech where he explained that the firm would get rid of poor performers just like you prune a blueberry bush. He explained that you cut off "older branches to make room for younger ones." The court held that the supervisor's statement was direct evidence of age discrimination.

The question of what constitutes direct evidence is not always clear. Despite the similarity between statements made by employers, however, statements regarding an applicant's or employee's race are taken more seriously than those about age. For instance, most courts would rule in the employee's favor if it were determined that she was not hired pursuant to the manager's statement "I don't want any more Blacks in my unit." But it is questionable whether this same employer would be held guilty if the manager states, "We need some new ideas in this unit. Let's hire younger analysts." The statement may be viewed as merely descriptive.

An employee also may be able to show pretext by proving that the offered reasons for the adverse employment action have no basis in fact, the offered reasons did not actually motivate the adverse employment action, or the offered reasons are insufficient to motivate the adverse action taken.

For example, consider the 2019 decision by the Fourth Circuit in *Westmoreland v. TWC Admin. LLC.*[98] In that case, the court upheld Westmoreland's assertion that her firing was due to age and that the employer's stated reasons for firing her were pretextual. Westmoreland was 61 years old, had worked for TWC for over 30 years, was a good performer, and had only committed two minor infractions before the incident in question. TWC alleged that she was fired because she modified the date on an evaluation form for one of her subordinates. Initially, she was told by her boss that it was considered a minor infraction and not to worry. The court found that it was an isolated incident and also that lesser sanctions were available to TWC. Westmoreland was subsequently fired and escorted off the premises by an employee who had made prior age-related remarks. Westmoreland also was replaced with a 37-year-old employee who previously had been her subordinate. The court held in favor of Westmoreland and stated that TWC's change in classification of her offense from a minor incident to one necessitating termination gave rise to "suspicion of mendacity" regarding their rationale for firing her.

The U.S. Supreme Court held in *Reeves v. Sanderson Plumbing Products*[99] that a jury may infer pretext if the employer's explanation for an adverse employment action is false. In October 1995, after working for Sanderson Plumbing for 40 years, 57-year-old Reeves was terminated. As a supervisor, Reeves had been responsible for keeping attendance records of his employees. After his department reportedly suffered a downturn in productivity due to tardiness and absenteeism, the department's records were audited by the firm. The firm then claimed that Reeves and two other managers had made numerous errors in timekeeping, though it discharged only one other manager along with Reeves.

Reeves brought a claim under the ADEA against his former employer, presenting evidence that he had in fact maintained accurate records of the employees under his supervision. Reeves then argued that the employer's reasons for firing him were merely a pretext for age discrimination and evidenced age-related comments made to him by his supervisor. The U.S. Supreme Court stated in its opinion that, once the employer's rationalization has been eliminated, discrimination may well be the most likely alternative explanation for the adverse employment action.[100]

The *Reeves* decision, therefore, rejected what has become known as the "pretext plus" standard. Courts cannot require employees both to show pretext and also to produce additional evidence of discrimination. No additional evidence is necessary to show discrimination because, once the pretext has been shown, an inference can be made that the action was done for discriminatory reasons.[101] It is important to emphasize that the inference itself must be reasonable. Applying the *Reeves* decision in a 2013 case, the Fifth Circuit elaborated this point: "although a plaintiff may have set forth sufficient evidence to reject the defendant's proffered explanation, it may still present a circumstance where 'no rational factfinder could conclude that the action was discriminatory.'"[102]

In addition, an adverse action taken by a non-biased decision maker but based on information from another worker who has a discriminatory motive still satisfies a *prima facie* case. In other words, if someone takes an adverse action against an employee based on what appears to be a reasonable factor, the employer will be

"cat's paw" theory of liability
An employer may be liable for discrimination if it takes an adverse action against an employee based on what appears to be a reasonable factor, but the decision actually is grounded in bias and/or a discriminatory motive. Liability attaches even if a decision has a legitimate non-discriminatory reason but is influenced by a biased third party.

liable if the basis of that decision is actually grounded in bias and a discriminatory motive.[103] This concept of liability is called the **"cat's paw" theory.**

The Eleventh Circuit addressed the impact of the *Gross* decision on this type of liability in a 2013 age discrimination case.[104] Post–*Gross,* the court ruled that an employee asserting a "cat's paw" theory of liability must show that age bias is the "but for" cause of the adverse action, not just one of the motivating factors of the decision. The employee also may show that pretext exists where the employer presents conflicting rationales for the adverse employment action.[105]

Employee's *Prima Facie* Case: Hostile Environment Based on Age

Some circuit courts have recognized a cause of action under the ADEA based on a hostile environment involving age harassment. The Sixth Circuit ruled on *Crawford v. Medina General Hosp.,*[106] in which Crawford claimed hostile environment based on ageist remarks consistently made by her supervisor such as "old people should be seen and not heard" and "I don't think women over 55 should be working." Crawford also alleged that, in addition to the disparaging remarks, the older women are "not included in anything," such as parties and information about minor changes in office procedures, and that the supervisor would customarily call the young people into her office to question them about what the older people were doing "and then she encourages them to go out and confront those people."[107]

The Sixth Circuit found that it was a "relatively uncontroversial proposition that such a theory is viable under the ADEA"[108] and, since that time, the Fifth, Eighth, and Eleventh Circuits and some district courts have applied the same theory.[109] The court then articulated the *prima facie* case for hostile environment under the act:

1. The employee is 40 years old or older.
2. The employee was subjected to harassment, either through words or actions, based on age.
3. The harassment had the effect of unreasonably interfering with the employee's work performance and creating an objectively intimidating, hostile, or offensive work environment.
4. There exists some basis for liability on the part of the employer.[110]

Other circuit courts, including the First, Second, and Fourth Circuits, have also allowed hostile work environment claims based on age discrimination under the ADEA.[111] While several other districts have followed,[112] many other courts have refused to expand the ADEA to include a hostile environment claim without express statutory language.

It is important to note here that plaintiffs are not limited to claims for hostile work environments that occurred only within a 300-day filing window. In the *Davis-Garett v. Urban Outfitters*[113] case, noted earlier, the Second Circuit ruled that only one qualifying discriminatory act has to occur within the 300-day window to establish a claim of hostile working environment, but past events (outside of the

300-day window) may also be considered to make the case for a sustained pattern of hostile working environment.

The Seventh Circuit's 2019 ruling in *Kleber v. CareFusion Corp.* may have implications for hostile working environment cases. Although the Circuit ruled that applicants are not explicitly protected under the plain language of the ADEA, commentators have argued that "even if Congress meant to limit ADEA to current employees, it seems like an organization that actively sought to hire only young people would create a hostile work environment for any existing over-40s in the company."[114] It remains to be seen if just such an argument is made.

Note that, if a hostile environment age harassment claim becomes more universally recognized, the impact may go significantly further than a solely age discrimination claim. Consider the impact on constructive discharge. A worker subject to age harassment may be reasonable in quitting, based on the intolerable working condition, which then could give rise to a claim of constructive discharge based on age harassment.

Waivers under the Older Workers' Benefit Protection Act of 1990

waiver
The intentional relinquishment of a known right.

In 1990, Congress enacted the Older Workers' Benefit Protection Act (OWBPA), amending section 4(f) of the ADEA. The OWBPA addresses the legality and enforceability of early retirement incentive programs (the act refers to them as "exit incentive programs") and of **waivers** of rights under the ADEA. It also prohibits age discrimination in connection with employee benefits. Basically, the act involves situations where employees are offered amounts of money through retirement plans as incentives for leaving a company. In that way, the company avoids actually terminating an older worker and, thereby, would not otherwise (in theory) be held liable under the ADEA.

LO10 Define the parameters of a valid waiver of ADEA rights.

Many companies may also request that older workers sign a waiver that states that they give up the right to later challenge the plan through an age discrimination claim. Once the waiver is signed and the worker accepts the benefits under the plan, the company would like to believe it is safe from all possible claims of discrimination. If a waiver complies with the requirements under the ADEA/OWBPA, the employer can use it as an affirmative defense to an ADEA claim. The burden, however, is on the employer to prove that the waiver is valid under the OWBPA. This is not necessarily always the case, as will be discussed below.

The OWBPA codifies the EEOC's "equal cost principal," requiring firms to provide benefits to older workers that are at least equal to those provided to younger workers, unless the cost of their provision to older workers *greatly* exceeds the cost of provision to younger workers. Therefore, a firm may only offer different benefits to older and younger workers if it costs a significant amount more to provide those benefits to older workers. This section amends section 4 of the ADEA, which provides that adverse employment actions taken in observance of the terms of a bona fide employee benefit plan are partially exempt from question.

In connection with employee waivers of their rights to file discrimination actions under the ADEA, the OWBPA requires that every waiver must be "knowing and voluntary" to be valid. In order to satisfy this requirement, the waiver must meet all of the following requirements:

1. The waiver must be written in a manner calculated to be understood by an average employee.

2. The waiver must specifically refer to ADEA rights or claims (but may refer to additional acts, such as Title VII or applicable state acts).

3. The waiver only affects those claims or rights that have arisen prior to the date of the waiver (i.e., the employee is not waiving any rights that will be acquired after signing the waiver).

4. The waiver of rights to claims may only be offered in exchange for some consideration in addition to anything to which the individual is already entitled. (This usually involves inclusion in an early retirement program.)

5. The employee must be advised in writing to consult with an attorney prior to execution of the waiver. (This does not mean that the employee must consult with an attorney; the employee must merely be advised of the suggestion.)

6. The employee must be given a period of 21 days in which to consider signing a waiver and an additional 7 days in which to revoke the signature. Note that where a waiver is offered in exchange for an early retirement plan, as opposed to some other consideration, the individual must have 45 days in which to consider signing the agreement.

7. If the waiver is executed in connection with an exit incentive (early retirement) or other employment termination program, the employer must inform the employee in writing of the exact terms and inclusions of the program. This information must be sufficient for the employee to test the impact of the selection decision made; in other words, does the decision about inclusion in the program have any discriminatory impact?[115]

The waiver may not prohibit the employee from filing a claim with the EEOC or participating in investigations by the EEOC. Therefore, the employee may testify on another's behalf if requested. The purpose of these provisions is basically to ensure that the employee entered into the agreement that waived her or his rights knowingly and voluntarily based on the "totality of the circumstances." Courts are serious about enforcing these provisions in order to protect stridently the rights of workers, which was the original intent of the act.

In one case,[116] the court held that an ADEA waiver was completely invalid based on the fact that the employer used vague language—such as referring to "specific organizations" within the corporation rather than identifying them by name—in describing the eligibility criteria for the RIF. In another case, the court tossed out waivers because the employer simply misstated the number of workers terminated in the RIF (154 instead of 152) and did not properly disclose job titles.[117]

A 2016 case found that a separation agreement was unenforceable because "the waiver provisions did not comply with the minimum requirement that defendant provide terminated employees with job classification and age information of the non-terminated in a manner calculated to be understood by the average employee."[118] In a 2017 case, the Eighth Circuit ruled that General Mills' motion to compel arbitration of ADEA claims by laid-off workers should have been granted because the release outlining arbitration was "knowing and voluntary."[119] This decision opened the door for arbitration to be compelled under the ADEA. Another case in federal court in Pennsylvania held that an employee could sue for age discrimination because the severance agreement was not valid under the OWPBA.[120] The court found that the employer did not provide enough information about the RIF to enable the employee to make an informed decision about the right to sue.

Based on the Supreme Court's decision in *Oubre v. Entergy Operations, Inc.,* if an employee signs a defective waiver, the employee is *not* required to give back any benefits received under the defective waiver. In addition, if the employer offers to individually negotiate the waiver (as opposed to offering a standard form to the employee on a take-it-or-leave-it basis), this may be able to serve as proof to the court that the employee knew what he was doing when he signed the document. Because the court's explanation of this holding is so critical, it has been included at the end of the chapter.

Following *Oubre,* the Ninth Circuit ruled against Sandra Harmon, an employee who was laid off from Johnson & Johnson as part of a RIF.[121] Upon termination, Harmon signed a waiver that violated OWBPA's notification requirements. She later filed suit, alleging that she was selected for termination because of her age. Though the court recognized that the waiver was defective, it found that Johnson & Johnson had shown that the termination was economically motivated by the RIF, not by discriminatory motives. Despite the defective waiver, the court granted summary judgment to the employer.

Employers may use general waivers as an attempt to avoid all employment-related liability in contexts other than layoffs, though they should be careful that their waivers do not have a disparate impact on protected classes of people. For example, Allstate Insurance decided to transform its 15,200-member sales force from regular employees to independent contractors. To remain as contractors, the agents were required to sign a release stating that they would not sue Allstate. Those agents who refused to sign the waivers were dismissed. Ninety percent of these agents were over the age of 40. In October 2004, the EEOC filed a suit against Allstate alleging it engaged in age discrimination against its agents. The case finally settled, with Allstate agreeing to pay $4,500,000, which was paid to the approximately 90 former employees, in addition to significant remedial relief.[122]

Moreover, employers must beware of asking employees to sign waivers that are considered *too general,* such as a document that contains a general release and a covenant not to sue, since courts may find that they are so ambiguous that they do not constitute a knowing and voluntary waiver of the employee's right to sue under the ADEA. In *Thomforde v. International Business Machines Corp.,*[123] the court found the agreement unclear because it failed to explain how the release and the covenant not to sue were related since it used the terms interchangeably and because it failed to explain the agreement sufficiently to the employee.

After the Supreme Court decision in *Oubre,* the EEOC issued a notice of proposed rule making to address the issues raised in that case. After receiving comments, the EEOC published its final regulation setting forth its interpretation of the waiver provisions of the OWBPA. This regulation became effective on January 10, 2001.[124] The regulation makes clear that employees cannot be required to "tender back" the consideration received under an ADEA waiver agreement before being permitted to challenge the waiver in court. Further, the contract principle of ratification does not apply to ADEA waivers. The EEOC also recognized that covenants not to sue operate as waivers in the ADEA context. Therefore, the OWBPA's requirements and these rules apply to such agreements as well.[125]

A firm must be cautious because individual negotiations may lead to slightly different agreements with various employees and varying benefits among similar employees may constitute a violation of the Employee Retirement Income Security Act (ERISA).

The OWBPA also contains the following provisions in connection with early retirement plans, 29 U.S.C. § 623:

1. Employers may set a minimum age as a condition of eligibility for normal or early retirement benefits.
2. A benefit plan may provide a subsidized benefit for early retirement.
3. A benefit plan may provide for Social Security supplements in order to cover the time period between the time when the employee leaves the firm and the time when the employee is eligible for Social Security benefits.
4. While severance pay cannot vary based on the employee's age, the employer may offset the payments made by the value of any retiree health benefits received by an individual eligible for immediate pension.

Thus, while an employer may not actually discriminate in the amount of the payments offered by the retirement plan on the basis of age, these provisions actually seem to allow for inconsistent payments to older and younger workers, under certain circumstances.

Note that no provision of the OWBPA prohibits an employer from revoking a retirement offer *while* the employee is considering it. So, for example, a firm could offer an employee a retirement package in a separation agreement; then, while the employee considers it, the firm could revoke it and offer a less attractive package. This could be abused, of course, if it is interpreted as a threat to encourage the worker to decide earlier than the 21-day limit.

The Use of Statistical Evidence

Courts allow the use of statistical evidence to prove discrimination on the basis of age, though it is generally more useful in disparate impact cases than it is in disparate treatment cases. However, the Tenth Circuit in *Heward v. Western Electric Co.*[126] explained the similarities in the application of statistics in disparate impact cases and disparate treatment cases:

> The significance of companywide statistics is heightened in disparate *impact* cases because plaintiffs need only demonstrate statistically that particular companywide

practices in actuality operate or have the effect of excluding members of the protected class. However, even in a disparate *treatment* class action or "pattern and practice" suit, only gross statistical disparities make out a *prima facie* case of discrimination.

In either case, statistical evidence is meticulously examined to ensure that the statistics shed some light on the case. There is a great deal of skepticism relating to statistical evidence in age discrimination cases precisely because of the fact that older workers are likely to be replaced by younger workers, merely as a result of attrition of the workforce. This is not true in cases brought under Title VII based on race or gender discrimination; therefore, statistics may be slightly more relevant to a determination under Title VII because they may represent pure discrimination.

Where statistics are used to prove discriminatory effect, the Supreme Court has offered some guidance about their use. The Supreme Court has considered percentage comparisons and standard deviation analyses of those comparisons: "As a general rule, . . . if the difference between the expected value and the observed number is greater than two or three standard deviations, then the hypothesis that the [selection process] was random would be suspect."[127] In addition, the Court cautioned that the usefulness or weight of statistical evidence depends on all of the surrounding facts and circumstances, and, specifically, "when special qualifications are required to fill particular jobs, comparisons to the general population (rather than to the smaller group of individuals who possess the necessary qualifications) may have little probative value."

Remedies

equitable relief
Relief that is not in the form of money damages, such as injunctions, reinstatement, and promotion. Equitable relief is based on concepts of justice and fairness.

liquidated damages
Liquidated damages limit awards to a predetermined amount. As used in the ADEA, liquidated damages are equal to the unpaid wage and are available in cases involving "willful violations" of the statute.

The court may award a variety of remedies to a successful employee-plaintiff in an age discrimination action. However, where money damages such as back pay (what the employee would have received but for the violation) or front pay (which includes a reasonable and expected amount of compensation for work that the employee would have performed until the time of her expected retirement) are ascertainable and adequately compensate the employee for damages incurred, the court may *not* grant other **equitable relief**. Compensation for pain and suffering or emotional distress is not available under the ADEA.[128] Forms of equitable relief include reinstatement, promotions, and injunctions.

If an employee-plaintiff proves that the employer-defendant "willfully violated" the ADEA, then the court is also allowed to award **liquidated damages** in an amount equal to unpaid wage liability.[129] Suffice it to say that, by contrast, violations of the ADEA need not, therefore, be otherwise willful. As one has often heard, "ignorance of the law is no excuse," and the same holds true here. In fact, it has been tested in court. The employer's defense that its hiring managers had not been trained concerning bias and admitted their ignorance on the issues was no defense to an ADEA action in *Mathis v. Phillips Chevrolet, Inc.*[130]

Employee Retirement Income Security Act

In 1974, Congress passed the Employee Retirement Income Security Act (ERISA), which regulates private employee benefit plans. While ERISA specifically governs the operation of retirement plan provisions and other benefits and is therefore relevant to the issue of age discrimination, a complete discussion of its implications is found in Chapter 16.

In short, ERISA's purpose is to protect employees from wrongful denial of all types of benefits, including retirement or pension benefits. Prior to ERISA's enactment, employers were able to discriminate against certain employees in their determination of eligibility for pension benefits and the amount of time one must work for the employer to be eligible for benefits. In addition, many employees suffered from the loss of their benefits when companies underwent management reorganizations or when the company decided to terminate the plan only a short time before the employees' benefits were to vest. Other employees lost their benefits when they became sick and were forced to quit their job prior to the time at which their pension rights vested.

ERISA prevents these problems by regulating the determination of who must be covered by pension plans, vesting requirements, and the amount that the employer must invest for the benefit of its employees. In an effort to encourage compliance with this provision, ERISA also requires complete disclosure of the administration of the plan. Further, ERISA stipulates that an employee may not be excluded from a plan on account of age, as long as she or he is at least 21 years of age and is a full-time employee with at least one year of service.[131] As of September 30, 2019, title I of ERISA expanded the definition of employer and clarified the circumstances under which an employer group or association or a professional employer organization is considered an employer for the purpose of ERISA. These amendments expand access to affordable quality retirement saving options through multiple employer workplace retirement plans.

ERISA does have some negative side effects. It has made the provision of benefit plans more costly for employers. In addition, no federal law requires that employers offer retirement plans.

One recent development involving ERISA involves arbitration. In 2019, the Ninth Circuit struck down a 35-year-old precedent[132] and held that ERISA cases are able to go to arbitration. The court held that "because there was an arbitration provision in the plan document, the plan itself had consented to arbitration." As a result, if the ERISA plan states that arbitration is required to resolve issues pertaining to ERISA issues, the parties involved must use arbitration to resolve claims.

The arbitration provision also is important because it binds individuals to the plan's *individual* arbitration requirement. Previously, plan participants were permitted to bring claims on behalf of the plan or a class of participants, which greatly reduced the cost of litigation. Now, if plan terms require individual arbitration, then the individual no longer has this right and must instead submit to individual arbitration.

Another development involves the ERISA's statute of limitations—the time within which someone is permitted to file a claim under ERISA. In 2019, the U.S. Supreme Court agreed to hear a case regarding the time when the statute of limitations begins. The Ninth Circuit found that the statute of limitations begins when the plaintiff has "actual knowledge" of an ERISA violation or is told of wrongdoing.[133] This ruling departs from the majority of other circuits that have addressed this issue.

Distinctions among Benefit Plans

Can an employer simply decide to lower the amounts of benefits it offers its employees? Yes, as long as it is in line with requirements of ERISA. However, those reductions must be made across the board; the OWBPA limits the distinctions that an employer may make on the basis of age to only those that are justified by "age-based cost differences."

Many firms also have seniority systems that award benefits on the basis of seniority. Because experience seniority is often balanced in favor of older workers, not as many problems arise as a result of these systems. Those not themselves based in age discrimination are valid. In other words, those systems that disadvantage employees as they age are not protected by the ADEA.

Section 510 of ERISA provides protection against retaliation for those who exercise their rights under ERISA and plaintiffs often find that age discrimination claims are complementary to their ERISA claims because similar factual scenarios may strengthen a plaintiff's case.[134] The advantage to the plaintiff comes in the form of cost-based termination decisions. While the ADEA does not provide an employee with a claim for termination based solely on cost, Section 510 of ERISA does offer relief as long as a benefit plan is involved. Employers may consider these issues as they make decisions involving terminations for employees aged 40 or above.

Management Considerations

Generalizations such as "older people have poorer vision" or "workers over 50 are less motivated than younger workers" may appear to be grounded in fact based on the experiences of many firms. But considering these prejudiced principles during recruitment or retention of employees may cause more problems for the company than it prevents. As with other areas of protection against wrongful discrimination, managers are not precluded by the ADEA from hiring or retaining the most qualified individual; the act specifically requires that the employer do just that.

The employer may be losing a valuable and completely qualified employee simply because it incorrectly believes that all individuals over a certain age are not qualified for the available position. Instead of relying on vague generalizations concerning all individuals of advanced years, employers would do better to reevaluate the true requirements of the position then test for those characteristics.

For instance, if an employee must have 20/20 vision to safely drive a taxicab, the taxi company will hire the most qualified individuals if it chooses the most competent and experienced from the pool of applicants and subjects these individuals to a vision test. In that way, the employer is sure to locate those workers who are, actually, the most *qualified* for the position while not excluding an older worker based on a preconceived idea about failing vision. Or if a position on an assembly line requires great dexterity and speed of movement, the employer should choose the most qualified applicants and allow them to perform the functions required of the position. If the older worker performs adequately, that applicant should be evaluated with no regard to age.

In addition, employers may inadvertently discriminate against older workers and, in doing so, hurt themselves and their firm by failing to train and develop their older workers. Often older workers are not considered for continuous learning or other development because "they're on their way out, anyway." Managers should pay attention to the basis for decision making and selection in connection with training and development opportunities.

Several problems are unique to the employer's defense of a claim of discrimination as a result of an RIF. These problems arise as a result of the difficulty of complete documentation of employee performance.

First, employers generally do not retain intricate written analyses of performance. Consequently, when asked what are the particular problems associated with the employment of this individual, the employer must rely on the subjective oral reports of its supervisors or managers. The jury is then not only faced with the question of whether the adverse action was justified but also with whether the recollection of the managers is correct or merely fabricated for purposes of the litigation. In addition, the employer should ensure that the performance appraisals that *are* recorded reflect an objective evaluation of the employee's performance at that time. The evaluator must exercise caution in the area of the employee's future potential because this is an area that may be related to age and comments may be suspect.

Second, managers and supervisors will likely evaluate an employee as compared to other employees. Therefore, a rating of "good" may be the worst rating given in a department. When the RIF later requires that certain employees be discharged, the employer is left with the obligation to justify the termination of an individual who, in fact, never received a poor evaluation. This is not a sympathetic position.

Third, employers should consider the processes involved in RIF decisions. Any individual or team responsible for these decisions should have an RIF plan, document the decision rule(s), and implement those decision rules objectively across all candidates involved in the RIF. Documentation is key to support a RIF decision in order to demonstrate that age is not a consideration.

Finally, the employer may make a decision based on some factor other than performance, such as the fact that a retained employee's wife is in the hospital or that the discharged worker had the opportunity to participate in an early retirement program, while the retained worker could not. Superior care should be exercised in reaching a conclusion regarding terminations where these issues serve as the bases for retention and discharge because many determining factors could be viewed as age based.

It is in both the employer's and the employee's interest to ensure that the employee periodically receives an objective, detailed performance appraisal. In this way, the employer protects against later claims that the employee was not informed of the employer's dissatisfaction with her or his work, and the employee can guarantee that the employer may only use valid justifications for its discharge decisions.

Management Tips

See Chapter 2 to revisit key concepts.

- Any job requirement on the basis of age must be subject to your highest scrutiny. There are extremely few BFOQs allowed on the basis of age alone. Instead, consider what you are actually concerned about and test for that characteristic. For instance, if you are concerned about the eyesight of your applicants or workers, conduct vision tests rather than follow a presumption that older workers will always be disqualified because of their eyesight.

- Reductions in force are prone to problems in connection with age discrimination as a result of higher salaries paid to older and more experienced workers. Review all termination decisions carefully in order to ensure fair and balanced procedures. Document your decision process in detail.

- Prior to implementing a RIF, study and document the forces that led to the decision and consider using an employee committee to help plan for the RIF.

- Terminating an older worker and replacing her or him with another worker who is over 40 does not protect you from a charge of age discrimination.

- Even though "accommodation" is most often associated with disability discrimination, it can apply to age discrimination claims. Managers should be trained to understand that failing to consider possible accommodations to age could be evidence of age discrimination.

- Review all recruiting literature to remove all age-based classifications like "looking for young upstarts to help build growing business."

- You may not terminate an older worker on the basis of age; if you must terminate a worker who is 40 or over, ensuring that you have appropriate documentation to justify dismissal creates a safe harbor.

- In drafting a waiver of discrimination claims for older workers to sign upon termination, review the form to ensure compliance with the OWBPA.

- Employers should neither permit nor encourage age-based remarks, comments, or jokes to avoid liability under the ADEA for age-related harassment. Anti-harassment policies and procedures should encompass age and all prohibited factors.

- Employers should be sensitive about the inclination in the past to single out workers over 40 for medical exams.

- Employees may consider whether their age discrimination claims also involved violations of ERISA (or vice versa). When making termination decisions, employers should consider the implications of both ERISA and the ADEA before implementing a decision process.

- Beware the situation where an older worker laid off for economic reasons offers to take a pay cut, especially if the offered pay cut is less than what would be paid to a younger replacement. The law is unsettled as to whether these circumstances constitute age discrimination.

- Remember that retaliation for filing a claim of age discrimination is forbidden, not just against the employee filing the claim but against anyone who supported the claim, such as by testifying.

- The chances of retaliation occurring can be reduced by proper management training and by making sure that all employee handbooks adequately address the issue.

Chapter Summary

- Employees are protected against discrimination on the basis of their age under the ADEA, unless age is a bona fide occupational qualification.
- Employees who believe that they are victims of age discrimination have available to them a wide array of choices under both state and federal law.
- To prove a case of age discrimination, the employees must show that
  1. They are 40 years of age or older.
  2. They suffered an adverse employment decision.
  3. They are qualified for the position (either that they meet the employer's requirements or that the requirements are not legitimate).
  4. They were replaced by someone younger.
- Once the employee has presented this information, the employer may defend its decision by showing that
  1. Age requirement of a job is a bona fide occupational qualification. This can be done by showing
     a. The age limit is reasonably necessary to the employer's business and
     b. All or a substantial number of people over that age are unable to perform the requirements of the job adequately; or
     c. Some of the people over that age possess a trait that disqualifies them for the position and it cannot be ascertained except by reference to age.
  2. The decision was made based on some reasonable factor other than age.
  3. The employee was not qualified for the position.
  4. The decision to leave was because of a voluntary retirement plan.
  5. The "same actor" defense may be used in some courts. The presumption is that when the same person hires and fires a worker protected by the ADEA, there is a permissible inference that the employee's age was not a motivating factor in the decision to terminate.
- Once the employer presents its defense, the employee will have the opportunity to prove that this defense is mere pretext for the actual discrimination that exists.
- The *Gross* decision seemingly altered the burden-shifting requirement, but subsequent lower court rulings have suggested that the shifting does still apply in age discrimination cases.
- The ADEA prohibits retaliation, against the employee who alleges age discrimination and any other employee who assists the employee in her or his claim.
- Federal courts are split as to whether an employer can terminate an older employee due to economic considerations.
- Benefit plans and seniority systems cannot be created for the purpose of evading the ADEA or the OWBPA.
- The OWBPA amended section 4(f) of the ADEA and places restrictions where employers offer employees amounts of money through retirement plans as incentives for leaving the company.

- The Employee Retirement Income Security Act (ERISA) regulates private employee benefit plans. It governs the operation of welfare and retirement plan provisions. (See Chapter 16 for a further discussion of ERISA.)
- A variety of remedies are available to those discriminated against due to their age.
- A reduction in force (RIF) occurs when a company is forced to downscale its operations to address rising costs or the effects of a recession. When an individual is terminated pursuant to a bona fide RIF, the employer's actions are protected. In the event of an RIF, age discrimination may be proven when

    1. The employer refuses to allow a discharged or demoted employee to bump others with less seniority.
    2. The employer hires younger workers when jobs become available.

Chapter-End Questions

1. In 2004, Lanita Thomas quit her job with United Airlines to work for Clay Lacy Aviation as a personal flight attendant on the Gulf Stream jet owned by retired NBA player Earvin "Magic" Johnson. Thomas says she worked an average of 10 to 12 hours per day, often catering to Johnson's very particular preflight requests, such as squeezing the plane's stock of Red Vine licorice regularly to ensure that it was soft. Thomas, who was over 40, took time off due to an injury in 2010 and was temporarily replaced by a "substantially younger" flight attendant. When she returned to work, she alleges that Johnson's demeanor was "less cordial" and "more standoffish and dismissive" for several months. According to Thomas, on September 6, 2010, she arrived at the plane seven minutes late, after being delayed at a deli where she was purchasing specialty food items requested by Johnson. Two weeks later, Johnson fired her for being late to the September 6 flight. Thomas alleges that Johnson immediately hired the younger flight attendant who had replaced her earlier in the year and points to this action as evidence that the "tardiness" argument was a pretext for age discrimination. In October 2012, she filed suit against Magic Johnson Entertainment and Clay Lacy Aviation for several charges, including age discrimination and wrongful termination. If you were the judge in this case, would you find that Thomas has sufficient evidence of discrimination for her claim to survive summary judgment and reach trial?

2. In 2013, Metz Culinary Management, Inc. took over the nutrition service at St. Mary's Health System. As part of the contractual agreement between St. Mary's and Metz, Metz was required to retain all food service staff, including the plaintiff, Dennis Bouyea. Not long after the management transition, Farrow became Bouyea's direct supervisor and was alleged to have made age-related comments and to have questioned why older individuals remained in entry-level positions. Metz denies direct comments but does admit that he mentioned that the salad prep workers topped the pay scale and that Metz could probably replace two salad people with one chef to save money. While Metz originally had some severe financial difficulties, by 2015, it met and exceeded budget targets at St. Mary's. Bouyea had received stellar evaluations in the past, and in February 2015, Farrow gave Bouyea a generally positive review. However, in April 2015, Farrow set a 60-day target for Bouyea to hit budget and a 30-day target to hit other performance goals. He also began actively recruiting for a replacement for Bouyea, who subsequently was fired in June 2015. At the time, Bouyea was 58, and his replacement was 51. Metz also had terminated another manager who was 35 but had put that employee on a

performance improvement plan, unlike Bouyea, who was terminated without being given a chance to improve. In the year that followed Bouyea's termination, six other employees over the age of 40 either were terminated or resigned. Given the case facts, do you believe that Bouyea has a claim under the ADEA or the Metz has an LNDR? [*Bouyea v. Metz Culinary Management Inc.,* Case Number 2:17-cv-00214, (D. Me. 2018).]

3. In two instances, Darden Restaurants did not hire applicants who were 52 and 49 years old and instead hired many less experienced applicants outside the protected age group. Darden's hiring officials told the unsuccessful applicants in the protected age group that they were too experienced, that they were looking for "fresh" employees and not "old white guys," and that they wanted a "youthful image." The EEOC alleged that a sampling of hiring data nationwide showed that Darden's hiring of applicants in the protected age group was significantly below the expected hiring of applicants in that age group based on the applications submitted to them and/or local Census data. Did these facts constitute a violation of the ADEA? [*Equal Employment Opportunity Comm'n v. Darden Restaurants, Inc.,* 143 F. Supp. 3d 1274, 1282–83 (S.D. Fla. 2015).]

4. Richard Pisoni, Darren Lindsey, and Mark Cameron worked for the Illinois State Police as members of its SWAT team. At the time of the incidents, all were over 40 and had worked in this division since at least 1999. Beginning in 2010, Trooper Charles Tolbert began to harass the older members of the SWAT team by isolating and criticizing them. Those younger team members who chose not to join Tolbert were ostracized. Cameron raised this issue with his boss Kollins on several occasions, and he said that he would take care of it. Later, during the debriefing of a problem during a training exercise, the team ignored the violation and instead the younger members complained that "Pisoni was overwhelmed and needed to leave the team." Complaints were made regularly to remove Tolbert from the group because of his actions but no action was taken. Additional comments were heard being made by the younger members of the SWAT team including "old need to go" and that they wanted to make the SWAT team a "younger, quicker team" and a "younger, more athletic team." Eventually, the three older team members transferred from their positions with the SWAT team to positions with lower pay and less benefits. What must the plaintiffs prove to sustain a claim for constructive discharge/demotion? Will they succeed? [*Pisoni, et al. v. State of Illinois,* Case No. 12-CV-678-SMY-DGW (S.D. Ill. 2018).]

5. Carol Lorenz was employed by Tyson Foods, Inc., in Cherokee, Iowa, from October 1985 until December 6, 2012, when her employment was terminated. She was 62 years old at the time of her discharge. Tyson acknowledges that Lorenz performed her job duties competently but notes that her record included some behavioral and attendance issues. For instance, in October 2012, Lorenz signed a Management Support Attendance Notification that itemized three alleged instances of tardiness during 2012. The document notes that Lorenz was just one attendance notification short of being discharged. On December 5, 2012, Lorenz was late again, this time by *less than two minutes.* She contends that she stubbed her toe that morning with enough force to make her believe she may have broken it. She did not call Tyson to report that she would be late but did explain the situation when she arrived. The following day, Lorenz was advised that she was being discharged because she had exceeded the maximum allowed tardiness. Lorenz had worked for Tyson for 27 years at the time her employment was terminated. Lorenz alleges that the tardiness was a pretext for age discrimination. Does she have a claim under the ADEA? What must she show to determine that her firing was a pretext for age discrimination? [*Lorenz v. Tyson Foods, Inc.,* 147 F. Supp. 3d 792 (N.D. Iowa 2015).]

6. In August, 2010, Dr. Brett Steele was hired as an associate professor at the National Defense University's College of International Security Affairs. Dr. Steele was 47 at the time of his hiring to a three-year contract, the first year of which was a probationary period. He was highly sought after to teach key courses in his area of expertise and finally agreed to take the position after being asked several times. During his probationary period he had disagreements with his supervisors over teaching methods and curricular decisions. Dr. Steele was not using the approved syllabus nor teaching concepts on certain subjects. While he agreed to conform to the university's expectations, he alleges that his supervisor made age-related comments such as "[young colleagues] are such a breath of fresh are, [and] are eager to please" while older workers are "stubborn [and] difficult to work with." At this same time, the college encountered budgetary challenges and determined that it would have to terminate three of its six probationary faculty, including Dr. Steele. The college did not inform Dr. Steele of the reasons for his termination. Instead of accepting termination, Dr. Steele chose to resign to avoid a negative mark on his employment record. In the semester following Steele's resignation, three other faculty were hired to take over his teaching responsibilities, one under the age of 40 and two older than 40. The college also hired two new associate professors in another area, both under the age of 40, and later permanently hired another young professor, also younger than Dr. Steele, who taught most of Dr. Steele's courses. Steele filed a complaint in the U.S. District Court of D.C., which granted summary judgment to the college, stating that the budgetary cuts were a legitimate reason for the termination. He appealed, and the D.C. Circuit Court remanded, holding that his firing may be pretextual. What result do you anticipate on remand? [*Steele v. Mattis,* 2018 WL 3893169 (D.C. Cir. Aug. 10, 2018).]

7. In 2018, the Sixth Circuit Court of Appeals upheld a mandatory retirement age of 70 for judges in Michigan. While some other states require retirement around that same age, other states have either raised or completely removed age restrictions. Michigan state court judge Michael Theile, who was 70 in 2019 and up for reelection in 2020, sued the State of Michigan, arguing that its mandatory retirement age was unconstitutional. Although he lost his case, do you agree with mandatory retirement for judges based on the discussion in the chapter, particularly given the fact that people are living longer and healthier lives? What positions do you believe warrant mandatory retirement and at what age? Consider that no age limit exists for other Michigan state officials, nor are federal judges subject to forced retirement at a specified age. Do these facts impact your answer?

8. In 2012, a New Jersey jury issued a verdict in an age discrimination suit filed against Passaic County prosecutor James Avigliano. Six detectives with a total of 150 years of law enforcement between them were laid off by Avigliano's office during a time of significant budget cuts in 2008. The detectives alleged that Avigliano had targeted them for forced retirement because of their age. As older, longtime employees, the six had significant pensions. The defense argued that the detectives' pensions were a reasonable basis for requiring their early retirement. "[I]t had nothing to do with age," the defense attorney told the jury. "Avigliano had to make a hard choice—a choice he didn't want to make. He asked these guys to retire. They had benefits packages." Given the extent of the necessary budget cuts, by laying off longtime employees with medical benefits and pensions, the defense argued, "fewer employees would have to be let go, and they'd have a safe landing." The plaintiffs' lawyer contended that targeting people for layoffs because they have pensions to fall back on is itself discriminatory, according to state

discrimination statutes. In addition, such targeting is bad public policy. "What incentive is there, then, to pay your dues?" the plaintiff's attorney asked the jury. "We want the most experienced people on the streets." How would you decide the case, if you were on this jury? What is your own judgment of Avigliano's "hard choice?" Do you view his rationale for laying off older workers as "bad public policy" or the least harmful choice in light of economic pressures?

9. LeRoy Arthur Hilde, age 51 and retirement-eligible, claims that the City of Eveleth violated the ADEA when it failed to promote him to chief of police. Hilde, who had been on the force for 29 years, was the city's only lieutenant and the second-highest rank in the department when he applied to be chief of police. A three-member commission controls hiring, promoting, discharging, and suspending the city police employees. Between 1990 and 2012, the commission promoted internally and never sought outside applications for vacancies. The commissioners agreed that Hilde was an excellent lieutenant. The commission's protocol for hiring the chief was to score three criteria: weighted years of service, training and employment, and an interview.

Before the interview, Hilde received the highest score for weighted years of service but the lowest score of the finalists on training-and-employment. At the end of the interview phase, Hilde and another person, aged 43, had tied scores. Because a city officer with at least three years of service is retirement-eligible at 50, Hilde's age made him retirement-eligible, while the other candidate had at least seven years before he could retire. Hilde never told the commissioners he was seeking retirement or would not be committed to the position. In a meeting with the unsuccessful candidates, the commissioner said that Hilde's eligibility for retirement "might have" been a factor in the commission's decision to hire the other employee. Does Hilde have an age discrimination case against the city? What might the city have done to prevent the law suit? [*Hilde v. City of Eveleth,* 777 F.3d 998 (8th Cir. 2015).]

10. The ADEA prohibits an employer from firing an employee for being old. However, in the wake of the *Gross* decision, can an employee be fired for being "old and ugly"? Though the question may sound frivolous, an Oklahoma property management company made precisely this argument in a 2013 age discrimination case. Recall that *Gross* states that the ADEA does not authorize "mixed-motive" age discrimination claims; age must be the deciding ("but for") cause of the adverse employment action. Toni Strength, a 53-year-old employee of Kanbar Property Management, was terminated by Kanbar CEO Sukhi Ghuman in 2010. Though Strength was told that her position was being eliminated, this was not true. The EEOC maintains that Strength was fired as a result of her age and filed suit against Kanbar on her behalf. Key to the EEOC's case was testimony from several individuals who alleged that Ghuman said that he had fired Strength because "she was older and he did not believe she had the ability to meet potential tenants and entertain existing clients after work"; he wanted someone younger and prettier for the position; and she was "old and ugly," adding "who would want to lease from her?" During summary judgment proceedings, Kanbar argued that these statements do not demonstrate that age was the deciding cause of Ghuman's actions. Rather, they exhibit mixed motives: "ageism" and "lookism." Although ageist motives are prohibited by the ADEA, "lookism" is not an actionable charge. Therefore, Kanbar proposed, Ghuman's alleged statements do not prevent summary judgment in the company's favor. Has Kanbar presented a sufficient case that the EEOC's age discrimination claim should not survive summary judgment [*E.E.O.C. v. Kanbar Prop. Mgmt., L.L.C.,* No. 12-CV-00422-JED-TLW, 2013 WL 4512671 (N.D. Okla. Aug. 23, 2013)]?

End Notes

1. See Eadicicco, L., "Silicon Valley's Obsession with Youth, Summed Up in One Chart," *Business Insider* (April 13, 2015), http://www.businessinsider.com/silicon-valley-age-programmer-2015-4 (accessed March 8, 2020).

2. Stack Overflow, "Developer Survey Results 2018" (2018), https://insights.stackoverflow.com/survey/2018 (accessed March 14, 2020).

3. Kanishege, T., "Is Silicon Valley's Youth Movement Just Age Discrimination?" *CIO.com* (August 19, 2013), http://www.cio.com/article/738398/Is_Silicon_Valley_s_Youth_Movement_Really_Just_Age_Discrimination_html (accessed October 11, 2016).

4. Visier, Inc., "Visier Insights Report: The Truth about Ageism in the Tech Industry" (September 2017), https://www.visier.com/wp-content/uploads/2017/09/Visier-Insights-AgeismInTech-Sept2017.pdf (accessed March 7, 2020).

5. Angwin, J., Scheiber, N., and Tobin, A., "Facebook Job Ads Raise Concerns about Age Discrimination" (December 20, 2017), *The New York Times,* Section A, Page 1, https://www.nytimes.com/2017/12/20/business/facebook-job-ads.html (accessed March 7, 2020).

6. *Reid v. Google, Inc.* 50 Cal.4th 512 (2010).

7. Glantz, Aaron, "Old Techies Never Die; They Just Can't Get Hired as an Industry Moves On," *The New York Times* (January 28, 2012), p. A23, https://www.nytimes.com/2012/01/29/us/bay-area-technology-professionals-cant-get-hired-as-industry-moves-on.html (accessed March 7, 2020).

8. The Hiscox Group, "Hiscox Ageism in the Workplace Study" (June 2019), https://www.hiscox.com/documents/2019-Hiscox-Ageism-Workplace-Study.pdf (accessed February 6, 2020).

9. AARP, "AARP PPI Employment Data Digest" (December 2019), https://www.aarp.org/content/dam/aarp/ppi/2020/01/december-2019-emplyment-data-digest.pdf (accessed February 6, 2020).

10. Ibid.

11. Patterson, K., "Work Still to Be Done Ending Age Discrimination in the Workplace" (January 24, 2019), http://www.humanrights.gov.au/about/news/work-still-be-done-ending-age-discrimination-workplace (accessed February 8, 2020).

12. Puckett, B., "Japan: Supreme Court Rules on Mandatory Retirement" (June 2019), https://ogletree.com/international-employment-update/articles/june-2019/japan/2019-06-04/japan-supreme-court-rules-on-mandatory-retirement/ (accessed February 6, 2020).

13. "Age Discrimination Widely Sanctioned Internationally," *agediscriminationinemployment.com* (April 23, 2016), https://www.agediscriminationinemployment.com/age-discrimination-widely-sanctioned-internationally/ (accessed February 18, 2020).

14. U.S. Bureau of Labor Statistics, "Labor Force Statistics from the Current Population Survey" (2019), https://www.bls.gov/cps/cpsaat03.pdf (accessed February 9, 2020).

15. U.S. Bureau of Labor Statistics, "Labor Force Statistics from the Current Population Survey" (January 22, 2020), https://www.bls.gov/cps/cps_aa1995_1999.htm (accessed on February 9, 2020).

16. Bureau of Labor Statistics, U.S. Department of Labor, "Share of Labor Force Projected to Rise for People Age 55 and Over and Fall for Younger Age Groups," *The Economics Daily* (January 24, 2014), https://www.bls.gov/opub/ted/2014/ted_20140124.htm (accessed February 18, 2020).

17. Ibid.

18. Toossi, Mitra, "Labor Force Projections to 2022: The Labor Force Participation Rate Continues to Fall," *Monthly Labor Review, U.S. Bureau of Labor Statistics* (December 2013), https://doi.org/10.21916/mlr.2013.40 (accessed February 18, 2020).

19. For an analysis of population statistics and the aging workforce, see Ibid.

20. Weller, C., "Even amid Low Unemployment, Many Workers Struggle to Find a Job," *Forbes* (October 8, 2019), https://www.forbes.com/sites/christianweller/2019/10/08/even-amid-low-unemployment-many-workers-still-struggle-finding-a-job/#6a643e4d4de2 (accessed February 9, 2020).

21. Lipnic, V., "The State of Age Discrimination and Older Workers in the U.S. 50 Years after the Age Discrimination in Employment Act (ADEA)" (June 2018), https://www.eeoc.gov/eeoc/history/adea50th/upload/report.pdf (accessed February 9, 2020).

22. Kita, J., "Workplace Age Discrimination Still Flourishes in America" (December 30, 2019), https://www.aarp.org/work/working-at-50-plus/info-2019/age-discrimination-in-america.html (accessed February 9, 2020).

23. Cappelli, Peter and Bill Novelli, *Managing the Older Worker: How to Prepare for the New Organizational Order* (Boston: Harvard Business School Publishing, 2010), p. 27.

24. Besen, E., and T. McNamara, "Attitudes Toward Workers of Different Career Stages," State Issue Brief No. 03, Sloan Center on Aging & Work at Boston College (July 2009), http://www.bc.edu/content/dam/files/research_sites/agingandwork/pdf/publications/SIB03_Attitudes.pdf (accessed February 18, 2020).

25. Center for Retirement Research, "The Business Case for Older Workers" (February 2019), https://crr.bc.edu/wp-content/uploads/2019/02/The-Business-Case-for-Older-Workers.pdf (accessed February 9, 2020).

26. Eisenberg, R., "Good News (Mostly) for Workers and Job Hunters over 50" *Marketwatch* (November 25, 2018), https://www.marketwatch.com/story/good-news-mostly-for-workers-and-job-hunters-over-50-2018-10-4 (accessed February 9, 2020).

27. *Mount Lemmon Fire District v. Guido, 586 US ___ (2018).*

28. U.S. Equal Employment Opportunity Commission, "Charge Statistics FY 1997 through FY 2019," https://www.eeoc.gov/eeoc/statistics/enforcement/charges.cfm (accessed February 9, 2020).

29. Teachout, R. S., "EEOC FY 2019 Enforcement Data Shows Continuing Decrease in Overall Charges" (January 29, 2020), https://www.xperthr.com/news/eeocfy-2019-enforcement-data-shows-continuing-decrease-in-overall-charges/43073/ (accessed February 18, 2020).

30. In 2009, the number of age-based complaints actually dropped 7 percent, to 22,778, surprising many analysts. (See, for example, Workplace Prof, "New EEOC Statistics Show Age Discrimination Complaints are . . . Down?" [November 12, 2009], https://lawprofessors.typepad.com/laborprof_blog/2009/11/page/3/ [accessed March 14, 2020].) Among the reasons offered were (1) a prolonged economic downturn in which fewer age discrimination-eligible workers were still employed; (2) greater reliance on state age discrimination laws, which sometimes allow a wider range of damages than the federal law; (3) greater reliance on arbitration; and (4) a recent U.S. Supreme Court decision that tightened the screws on certain types of age discrimination suits (more on that later in this chapter).

31. 827 F.2d 13, n. 8 (7th Cir. 1987) overruled on other grounds by *Coston v. Plitt Theatres*, *Inc.*, 860 F.2d 834 (7th Cir. 1988).

32. *General Dynamics Land Systems, Inc. v. Cline,* 540 U.S. 581, 591 (2004).

33. Thatcher Law Firm, "Can Someone Be the Victim of Age Discrimination in Their 20s?" (March 6, 2019), https://www.thatcherlaw.com/blog/2019/03/can-someone-be-the-victim-of-age-discrimination-in-their-20s.shtml (accessed February 19, 2020).

34. Emling, S., "Good News for Job Seekers over 50" (April 4, 2018), https://www.aarp.org/work/working-at-50-plus/info-2018/older-workers-programs.html (accessed February 10, 2020).

35. AARP, "Employer Pledge Program" (n.d.), https://www.aarp.org/work/job-search/employer-pledge-companies/ (accessed February 10, 2020).

36. Kaslow, A., and P. Tate, "US Economy's Hidden Asset: Older Workers," *The Christian Science Monitor* (February 14, 2011), http://www.csmonitor.com/Commentary/Opinion/2011/0214/US-economy-s-hidden-asset-older-workers (accessed February 18, 2020).

37. Catenacci, C., "Federal Court of Appeals Dismisses Air Canada Pilots' Appeal Regarding Mandatory Retirement at Age 60" (September 3, 2019), Newstext Blogs, First Reference Talks (accessed February 10, 2020).

38. *Gregg v. Air Canada Pilots Association,* 2017 FC 506 (CHRT 2017).

39. Catenacci, C., "Federal Court of Appeal Dismisses Air Canada Pilots' Appeal Regarding Mandatory Retirement at Age 60," *Blogs, First Reference Talks* (September 3, 2019), https://blog.firstreference.com/federal-court-of-appeal-dismisses-air-canada-pilots-appeal-regarding-mandatory-retirement-at-age-60/#.Xmz3fqhKiwc (accessed February 10, 2020).

40. Ibid.

41. Press Association, "Default Retirement Age Scrapped," *The Guardian U.K.* (September 30, 2011), https://www.theguardian.com/money/2011/sep/30/default-retirement-age-scrapped (accessed October 14, 2016).

42. Bryant, S., "Understanding Cultural Differences" (November 12, 2018), https://countrynavigator.com/blog/global-talent/age-seniority (accessed February 10, 2020).

43. 528 U.S. 62 (2000).

44. *Levin v. Madigan,* 692 F.3d 607 (7th Cir. 2012).

45. *Madigan v. Levin,* 134 S. Ct. 2, 187 L. Ed. 2d 1 (2013). In its dismissal, the Court stated only that *certiorari* had been "improvidently granted" to the case.

46. BLR, "Age Discrimination: What You Need to Know" (2020), https://www.blr.com/HR-Employment/Discrimination/Age-Discrimination (accessed February 22, 2020).

47. Carsen, J., "EEOC Continued 'Aggressive Litigation' under Trump—but Changes May Be on the Horizon" (January 8, 2020), http://www.hrdive.com/news/eeoc-continued-aggressive-litigation-under-trump-but-changes-may-bepon/569917/ (accessed February 14, 2020).

48. *Villarreal v. R.J. Reynolds Tobacco Co., Pinstripe, Inc.,* 2016 WL5800001 (11th Cir. 2016).

49. *Kleber v. CareFusion Corp.,* 914 F. 3d 480 (7th Cir 2019).

50. *Davis-Garett v. Urban Outfitters, Inc.,* No. 17-3371 (2d Cir. 2019).

51. 517 U.S. 308 (1996).

52. 529 F.2d 760 (4th Cir. 1975).

53. Terrell, K., "Facebook Reaches Settlement in Age Discrimination Lawsuits" (March 20, 2019), https://www.aarp.org/work/working-at-50-plus/info-2019/facebook-settles-discrimination-lawsuits.html (accessed February 22, 2020).

54. U.S. Equal Employment Commission, "Facts about Age Discrimination," http://www.eeoc.gov/facts/age.pdf (October 20, 2016).

55. *Kleber v. CareFusion Corp.,* No. 17-1206 (7th Cir. 2019).

56. Jones, K., "Insight: Capping Years of Experience in Job Postings—Employers Beware," *Bloomberg Law* (February 26, 2019), https://news.bloomberglaw.com/daily-labor-report/insight-capping-years-of-experience-in-job-postings-employers-beware (accessed February 22, 2020).

57. 557 U.S. 167 (2009).

58. Directly responding to the *Gross* decision, members of the House and Senate sympathetic to the *Gross* minority introduced the Protecting Older Workers Against Discrimination Act (POWADA) in 2012. The proposed act would have reversed *Gross,* making it clear that the "motivating factor" framework applies to all antidiscrimination and antiretaliation laws involving race, sex, national origin, religion, age, and disability. Though POWADA was not passed, the bill was reintroduced in 2013 by legislators responding to the *Nassar* decision discussed below.

59. Protecting Older Workers Against Discrimination Act, H.R. 1230, 116th Congress (2020).

60. Barnes, P., "Finally, U.S. House Will Address Disastrous U.S. Supreme Court Ruling on Age Discrimination," *Forbes* (January 13, 2020), https://www.forbes.com/sites/patriciagbares/2020/01/13/finally-us-house-will-address-disastrous-us-supreme-court-ruling-on-age-discrimination/#4e2722115efd (accessed February 22, 2020).

61. *Jones v. Oklahoma City Pub. Sch.,* 617 F.3d 1273 (10th Cir. 2010).

62. Ibid., at 1278.

63. *Haigh v. Gelita USA, Inc.,* 632 F.3d 464 (8th Cir. 2011).

64. *Hill v. Boeing Co.,* 765 F. Supp. 2d 1208 (C.D. Cal. 2011).

65. *Univ. of Texas Sw. Med. Ctr. v. Nassar,* 133 S. Ct. 2517 (2013).

66. For additional examples of post–*Gross* and post–*Nassar* cases that affirm the mixed-motive standard for claims involving state and local statutes, see Judish, Julia E., Ellen Connelly Cohen, and Keith D. Hudolin, "Impact of Supreme Court Pro-Employer Title VII Decisions Blunted by State Laws," Pillsbury Winthrop Shaw Pittman LLP (July 8, 2013), http://www.pillsburylaw.com/publications/impact-of-supreme-court-pro-employer-title-vii-decisions-blunted-by-state-laws#page=1 (accessed February 18, 2020).

67. *Diaz v. Jiten Hotel Management, Inc.,* 704 F.3d 150, 155 (1st Cir. 2012).

68. *National Association of African American-Owned Media v. Charter Communications, Inc.,* No. 17-55723 (9th Cir. 2018), http://cdn.ca9.uscourts.gov/datastore/opinions/2018/11/19/17-55723.pdf (accessed March 8, 2020).

69. *Comcast Corporation v. National Association of African American-Owned Media, et al.,* No. 18-1711.

70. *Babb v Wilkie,* No.18-882 (April 6, 2020), https://www.supremecourt.gov/opinions/19pdf/18-882_3ebh.pdf (accessed April 7, 2020).

71. See 14 C.F.R. § 121.383(c).

72. 544 U.S. 228 (2005).

73. *Porio vs. Department of Revenue, 80 Mass. App. Ct. 57 (*2011).

74. *Bryan v Gov't of the Virgin Islands,* 916 F.3d 242 (3d Cir. 2019).

75. *Johnson v. Unified Gov't of Athens-Clarke Cty.,* No. 3:13-CV-143 (CAR), 2016 WL 4499452, at 6 (M.D. Ga. August 26, 2016).

76. 554 U.S. 84 (2008).

77. This rule became effective on April 30, 2012. The Final Rule amended the Commission' prior RFOA regulation, 29 C.F.R. § 1625.7. For the complete ruling, as well an analysis of its prior stages of development, see "Disparate Impact and Reasonable Factors Other Than Age under the Age Discrimination in Employment Act," *Federal Register: The Daily Journal of the American Government* (March 30, 2012), https://www.federalreg-ister.gov/articles/2012/03/30/2012-5896/disparate-impact-and-reasonable-factors-other-than-age-under-the-age-discrimination-in-employment#h-19 (accessed February 18, 2020). For a brief overview of the key components of the ruling, see "Questions and Answers on EEOC Final Rule on Disparate Impact and 'Reasonable Factors Other Than Age' under the Age Discrimination in Employment Act of 1967," U.S. Equal Employment Opportunity Commission, http://www.eeoc.gov/laws/regulations/adea_rfoa_qa_final_rule.cfm (accessed February 18, 2020).

78. EEOC, "Questions and Answers on EEOC Final Rule on Disparate Impact and 'Reasonable Factors Other Than Age' under the Age Discrimination in Employment Act of 1967" (n.d.), https://www.eeoc.gov/laws/regulations/adea_rfoa_qa_final_rule.cfm (accessed March 17, 2020).

79. *Bader v. Air Line Pilots Ass'n,* 113 F. Supp. 3d 990, 997 (N.D. Ill. 2015).

80. *Bryan v. Gov't of the Virgin Islands,* 916 F. 3d 242 (3d Cir. 2019).

81. No 07-4480 (2d Cir. 2008).

82. Back, Jean Ohman, "Avoiding Discrimination Claims as the Result of a Reduction in Force" (March 22, 2019), https://www.schwabe.com/newsroom-publications-avoiding-discrimination-claims-as-the-result-of-a-reduction-in-force (accessed March 18, 2020).

83. *Karlo v. Pittsburgh Glass Works, LLC.,* 849 F. 3d 61 (3rd Cir. 2017).

84. *Loucks v. Bd. of Educ. of Middle Cty. Sch. Dist. No. 11,* 879 F. Supp. 2d 281 (E.D.N.Y. 2012); *Paolillo v. Dresser Indus., Inc.,* 821 F.2d 81, 84 (2d Cir.1987); and *Auerbach v. Board of Educ. of Harborfields Central School Dist.,* 136 F.3d 104 (2d Cir. 1998). For a more recent application of the "reasonable person" standard, see *Embrico v. U.S. Steel Corp.,* No. 05-5495, 2007 WL 2326862 (3d Cir. Aug. 16, 2007).

85. *Proud v. Stone,* 945 F.2d 796 (4th Cir. 1991).

86. 292 P. 3d 779 (2013).

87. *Vaughan v. Anderson Reg'l Med. Ctr.,* 2018 U.S. Dist.

88. Section 623(d) of the ADEA says, "It shall be unlawful for an employer to discriminate against any of his employees . . . because such individual . . . has made a charge, testified, assisted, or participated in any manner in an investigation, proceeding, or litigation."

89. Section 633(a) says only that personnel "shall be made free from any discrimination based on age." No mention is made of individuals who participate in an investigation, as there is in section 623(d).

90. 128 S. Ct. 1931 (2008).

91. U.S. EEOC, "EEOC Enforcement Guidance on Retaliation and Related Issues" (August 25, 2016), https://www.eeoc.gov/laws/guidance/retaliation-guidance.cfm (accessed February 24, 2020).

92. 129 S. Ct. 2343 (2009).

93. *Forster v. Deere & Co.,* 925 F. Supp. 2d 1056, 1062 (N.D. Iowa 2013).

94. *Vaughan v. Anderson Reg'l Med Ctr.,* 849 F.3d 588 (5th Cir. 2017).

95. *Trans World Airlines, Inc. v. Thurston,* 469 U.S. 111 (1985).

96. See *Hazen Paper Company v. Biggins,* 507 U.S. 604 (1993).

97. 752 F. Supp. 2d 819, 822 (S.D. Ohio 2010).

98. *Westmoreland v. TWC Admin. LLC,* 924 F.3d 718 (4th Cir 2019).

99. *Reeves v. Sanderson Plumbing Products, Inc.,* 530 U.S. 133 (2000).

100. Ibid., at 134.

101. See, for example, *Jones,* the 2010 10th Circuit decision, *supra,* at pp. 13–14.

102. *Churchill v. Texas Dep't of Criminal Justice,* 539 F. App'x 315 (5th Cir. 2013).

103. *Cariglia v. Hertz Equipment Rental Corporation,* 363 F.3d 77 (1st Cir. 2004).

104. *Sims v. MVM, Inc.,* 704 F.3d 1327 (11th Cir. 2013).

105. *Christensen v. Titan Distribution, Inc.,* 481 F.3d 1085 (8th Cir. 2007).

106. 96 F.3d 830 (6th Cir. 1996).

107. Ibid., at 833.

108. Ibid., at 834.

109. *Dediol v. Best Chevrolet, Inc.,* 655 F.3d 435 (5th Cir. 2011); *Smith v. Kmart Corporation,* 1996 WL 780490 (E.D. Wash. 1996); *Lewis v. Federal Prison Industries, Inc.,* 786 F.2d 1537 (11th Cir. 1986); *Kelewae v. Jim Meagher Chevrolet, Inc.,* 952 F.2d 1052 (8th Cir. 1992); *City of Billings v. State Human Rights Commission,* 209 Mont. 251 (1984).

110. *Crawford,* 96 F.3d at 834–35.

111. *Collazo v. Nicholson,* 535 F.3d (1st Cir. 2008); *Kassner v. 2nd Ave. Delicatessen Inc.,* 496 F.3d 229 (2d Cir. 2007); and *Burns v. AAF-McQuay, Inc.,* 166 F.3d 292, 294 (4th Cir. 1999).

112. See, e.g., *Jones v. SmithKline Beecham Corp.,* 309 F. Supp. 2d 343 (N.D.N.Y. 2004); *Lacher v. West,* 147 F. Supp. 2d 538 (N.D. Tex. 2001); *Jackson v. R.I. Williams & Associates, Inc.,* Civ. A. No. 98-1741, 1998 WL 316090 (E.D. Pa. 1998); *Tumolo v. Triangle Pacific Corp.,* 46 F. Supp. 2d 410, 412 (E.D. Pa. 1999); *Ricci v. Applebee's Northeast, Inc.,* 301 F. Supp. 81 (D. Me. 2004); and *Lacher v. Principi,* 2002 WL 1033089 (W.D. Tex. 2002). In addition, while the Tenth Circuit has not expressly recognized a cause of action for hostile work environment under the ADEA, it has decided a case where the plaintiff raised the issue before the district court. See *McKnight v. Kimberly Clark Corp.,* 149 F.3d 1125, 1129 (10th Cir. 1998) (deciding a hostile work environment claim under the ADEA but not addressing the apparent lack of authority for raising such a theory). In light of the *McKnight* case, the court in *Ellison v. Sandia National Laboratories,* 192 F. Supp. 2d 1240 (D.N.M. 2002), assumed without deciding that an employee may assert a hostile work environment claim under the ADEA.

113. *Davis-Garett v. Urban Outfitters, Inc.* 921 F.3d 30 (2nd Cir. 2019).

114. Lucas, S., "7th Circuit Court: Age Discrimination in Hiring Is Legal," *Inc.* (January 25, 2019), https://www.inc.com/suzanne-lucas/7th-circuit-court-age-discrimination-in-hiring-is-legal.html (accessed February 24, 2020).

115. *Burlison v. McDonald's Corp.,* 455 F.3d 1242 (11th Cir. 2006).

116. *Ribble v. Kimberly-Clark Corp.,* No. 09-C-643, 2012 WL 589252 (E.D. Wis. Feb. 22, 2012).

117. *Peterson v. Seagate USLLC,* 534 F.Supp. 2d 996 (D.MN 2008).

118. *Behr v. AADG, Inc.,* No. 14-CV-3075-CJW, 2016 WL 4119692, at *16 (N.D. Iowa July 29, 2016).

119. *McLeod v. General Mills, Inc.,* No. 15-3540,2017 WL 1363797 (8th Cir. 2017).

120. *Ray v. AT&T, Inc.,* No. 18-3303 (E.D. PA. 2019).

121. *Harmon v. Johnson & Johnson,* 549 F. App'x 687 (9th Cir. 2013).

122. U.S. Equal Employment Opportunity Commission, "Allstate to Pay $4.5 Million to Settle Age Bias Suit" (September 11, 2009), https://www.eeoc.gov/eeoc/newsroom/release/9-11-09a.cfm (accessed February 18, 2020).

123. 406 F.3d 500 (8th Cir. 2005).

124. 29 C.F.R. § 1625.

125. See Kiren Dosanjh, "Old Rules Need Not Apply: The Prohibition of Ratification and 'Tender Back' in Employees' Challenges to ADEA Waivers," *Journal of Legal Advocacy and Practice* 3, no. 5 (2001).

126. No. 83-2293, 1984 WL 15666 (10th Cir. July 3, 1984).

127. *Cooper v. Asplundh Tree Expert Co.,* 836 F.2d 1544 (10th Cir. 1988).

128. *Commissioner of Internal Revenue v. Schleier,* 515 U.S. 323, 115 S. Ct. 2159 (1995).

129. 29 U.S.C. § 626(b).

130. *Mathis v. Phillips Chevrolet, Inc.,* 269 F.3d 771 (7th Cir. 2001).

131. U.S. Department of Labor, "Employee Benefits Security Administration" (n.d.), https://www.dol.gov/agencies/ebsa/about-ebsa/our-activities/resource-center/faqs (accessed February 18, 2020).

132. *Dorman v. Charles Schwab Corp.,* 934 F. 3d 1107 (9th Cir, 2019); *Dorman v. Charles Schwab Corp.,* 780 Fed. App'x 510 (9th Cir. 2019).

133. *Sulyma v. Intel Corp. Investment Policy Committee,* 909 F.3d 1069 (9th Cir. 2018), *cert* granted 139 S.Ct. 2692 (2019).

134. Findlaw, "ERISA Discrimination Claims May Complicate an Age Claim" (2020), https://corporate.findlaw.com/human-resources/erisa-discrimination-claims-may-complicate-an-age-claim.html (accessed March 7, 2020).

Cases

Western Air Lines, Inc. v. Criswell,
472 U.S. 400 (1985)

Case 1

This case is a seminal Supreme Court decision examining whether age ever is permitted to serve as a BFOQ. Western Air Lines requires that its flight engineers, who are members of the cockpit crew but do not operate flight controls unless both the pilot and the copilot become incapacitated, retire at age 60. At the time of the case, Federal Aviation Administration regulation prohibited anyone from acting as a pilot or copilot after they had reached the age of 60. The respondents in this case include both pilots who were denied reassignment to the position of flight engineers at age 60 and flight engineers who were forced to retire at that age. The airline argued that the age 60 retirement requirement is a BFOQ reasonably necessary to the safe operation of the business. The lower court instructed the jury as follows: The airline could establish age as a BFOQ only if "it was highly impractical for [petitioner] to deal with each [flight engineer] over age 60 on an individualized basis to determine his particular ability to perform his job safely" and that some flight engineers "over 60 possess traits of a physiological, psychological or other nature which preclude safe and efficient job performance that cannot be ascertained by means other than knowing their age." The Supreme Court evaluated whether this instruction was appropriate and determined that it correctly stated the law.

Stevens, J.

***

The evidence at trial established that the flight engineer's "normal duties are less critical to the safety of flight than those of a pilot." The flight engineer, however, does have critical functions in emergency situations and, of course, might cause considerable disruption in the event of his own medical emergency.

The actual capabilities of persons over age 60, and the ability to detect diseases or a precipitous decline in their faculties, were the subject of conflicting medical testimony. Western's expert witness, a former FAA [Federal Aviation Administration] deputy federal air surgeon, was especially concerned about the possibility of a "cardiovascular event," such as a heart attack. He testified that "with advancing age the likelihood of onset of disease increases and that in persons over age 60 it could not be predicted whether and when such diseases would occur."

The plaintiff's experts, on the other hand, testified that physiological deterioration is caused by disease, not aging, and that "it was feasible to determine on the basis of individual medical examinations whether flight deck crew members, including those over age 60, were physically qualified to continue to fly." Moreover, several large commercial airlines have flight engineers over age 60 "flying the line" without any reduction in their safety record.

Throughout the legislative history of the ADEA, one empirical fact is repeatedly emphasized: the process of psychological and physiological degeneration caused by aging varies with each individual. "The basic research in the field of aging has established that there is a wide range of individual physical ability regardless of age." As a result, many older workers perform at levels equal or superior to their younger colleagues.

In 1965, the secretary of labor reported to Congress that despite these well-established medical facts, "there is persistent and widespread use of age limits in hiring that in a great many cases can be attributed only to arbitrary discrimination against older workers on the basis of age and regardless of ability." Two years later, the president recommended that Congress enact legislation to abolish arbitrary age limits on hiring. Such limits, the president declared, have a devastating effect on the dignity of the individual and result in a staggering loss of human resources vital to the national economy.

The legislative history of the 1978 amendments to the ADEA makes quite clear that the policies and substantive provisions of the act apply with especial force in the case of mandatory retirement provisions. The House Committee on Education and Labor reported: "Increasingly, it is being recognized that mandatory retirement based solely upon age is arbitrary and that chronological age alone is a poor indicator of ability to perform a job."

In *Usery v. Tamiami Trail Tours, Inc.,* the court of appeals for the Fifth Circuit was called upon to evaluate the merits of a BFOQ defense to a claim of age discrimination. Tamiami Trail Tours had a policy of refusing to hire persons over age 40 as intercity bus drivers. At trial, the bus company introduced testimony supporting its theory that the hiring policy was a BFOQ based upon safety considerations—the need to employ persons who have a low risk of accidents. The court concluded that "the job qualifications which the employer invokes to justify his discrimination must be *reasonably necessary* to the essence of his business—here, the safe transportation of bus passengers from one point to another. The greater the safety factor, measured by the likelihood of harm and the probable severity of that harm in case of an accident, the more stringent may be the job qualifications designed to insure safe driving."

In the absence of persuasive evidence supporting its position, Western nevertheless argues that the jury should have been instructed to defer to "Western's selection of job qualifications for the position of flight engineer that are reasonable in light of safety risks." This proposal is plainly at odds with Congress's decision, in adopting the ADEA, to subject management decisions to a test of objective justification in a court of law. The BFOQ standard adopted in the statute is one of "reasonable necessity," not reasonableness.

In adopting that standard, Congress did not ignore the public interest in safety. That interest is adequately reflected in instructions that track the language of the statute. When an employer establishes that a job qualification has been carefully formulated to respond to documented concerns for public safety, it will not be overly burdensome to persuade a trier of fact that the qualification is "reasonably necessary" to safe operation of the business. The uncertainty implicit in the concept of managing safety risks always makes it "reasonably necessary" to err on the side of caution in a close case . . . . Since the instructions in this case would not have prevented the airline from raising this contention to the jury in closing argument, we are satisfied that the verdict is a consequence of a defect in Western's proof, rather than a defect in the trial court's instructions.

Case Questions

1. What is the basis for the determination that an employer should or should not be required to test applicants on an individual basis?

2. Should an employer have available as a defense that the cost of the tests would impose a great burden on the employer? Why or why not?

3. What is the distinction the *Criswell* opinion makes between "reasonable necessity" and "reasonableness"?

Case 2

Gross v. FBL Financial Services, Inc.,
557 U.S. 167 (S.Ct. 2009)

Gross began working for FBL in 1971. In 2003, when Gross was 54, he was reassigned from his position as claims administration director to the position of claims project coordinator. His previous position was renamed to claims administration manager and was given to a younger employee whom Gross had previously supervised. Although his pay remained the same, Gross considered the change a demotion and sued FBL for age discrimination. Gross introduced evidence at trial that the decision was at least partly based on age. FBL's defense was that the move was part of a restructuring and that the new position was a better fit for Gross's skills. The trial court gave the jury an instruction that it should find for Gross if it found that "age was a motivating factor." It also instructed the jury that it should find for FBL if it found, by a preponderance of the evidence, that FBL would have demoted him regardless of age. The jury found in Gross's favor, and FBL appealed. The Eighth Circuit reversed the decision and sent the case back for trial. The U.S. Supreme Court reviews the Eighth Circuit's ruling.

Thomas, J.

***

The parties have asked us to decide whether a plaintiff must "present direct evidence of discrimination in order to obtain a mixed-motive instruction in a non-Title VII discrimination case." . . . Before reaching this question, however, we must first determine whether the burden of persuasion ever shifts to the party defending an alleged mixed-motives discrimination claim brought under the ADEA. We hold that it does not. Petitioner relies on this Court's decisions construing Title VII for his interpretation of the ADEA. Because Title VII is materially different with respect to the relevant burden of persuasion, however, these decisions do not control our construction of the ADEA.

***

In *Price Waterhouse* . . . the Court . . . determined that once a "plaintiff in a Title VII case proves that [the plaintiff's membership in a protected class] played a motivating part in an employment decision, the defendant may avoid a finding of liability only by proving by a preponderance of the evidence that it would have made the same decision even if it had not taken [that factor] into account." . . . But as we explained in *Desert Palace, Inc. v. Costa,* 539 U.S. 90, 94–95 (2003), Congress has since amended Title VII by explicitly authorizing discrimination claims in which an improper consideration was "a motivating factor" for an adverse employment decision.

***

This Court has never held that this burden-shifting framework applies to ADEA claims. And, we decline to do so now. When conducting statutory interpretation, we "must be careful not to apply rules applicable under one statute to a different statute without careful and critical examination."

***

We cannot ignore Congress' decision to amend Title VII's relevant provisions but not make similar changes to the ADEA. . . . As a result, the Court's interpretation of the ADEA is not governed by Title VII decisions such as *Desert Palace* and *Price Waterhouse.*

***

Our inquiry therefore must focus on the text of the ADEA to decide whether it authorizes a mixed-motives age discrimination claim. It does not . . . The words "because of" mean "by reason of: on account of." . . . Thus, the ordinary meaning of the ADEA's requirement that an employer took adverse action "because of" age is that age was the "reason" that the employer decided to act. . . . It follows, then, that under §623(a)(1), the plaintiff retains the burden of persuasion to establish that age was the "but-for" cause of the employer's adverse action.

***

We hold that a plaintiff bringing a disparate-treatment claim pursuant to the ADEA must prove, by a preponderance of the evidence, that age was the "but-for" cause of the challenged adverse employment action. The burden of persuasion does not shift to the employer to show that it would have taken the action regardless of age, even when a plaintiff has produced some evidence that age was one motivating factor in that decision.

Justice Stevens, with whom Justice Souter, Justice Ginsberg, and Justice Breyer join, dissenting

The "but-for" causation standard endorsed by the Court today was advanced in Justice Kennedy's dissenting opinion in *Price Waterhouse v. Hopkins,* 490 U.S. 228, 279 (1989), a case construing identical language in Title VII of the Civil Rights Act of 1964 . . . Not only did the Court reject the but-for standard in that case, but so too did Congress when it amended Title VII in 1991. Given this unambiguous history, it is particularly inappropriate for the Court, on its own initiative, to adopt an interpretation of the causation requirement in the ADEA that differs from the established reading of Title VII. I disagree not only with the Court's interpretation of the statute, but also with its decision to engage in unnecessary lawmaking. I would simply answer the question presented by the certiorari petition and hold that a plaintiff need not present direct evidence of age discrimination to obtain a mixed-motives instruction.

The Court asks whether a mixed-motives instruction is ever appropriate in an ADEA case. As it acknowledges, this was not the question we granted certiorari to decide.

***

Unfortunately, the majority's inattention to prudential Court practices is matched by its utter disregard of our precedent and Congress' intent.

***

We recognized [in *Price Waterhouse*] that the employer had an affirmative defense: It could avoid a finding of liability by proving that it would have made the same decision even if it had not taken the plaintiff's sex into account. . . . But this affirmative defense did not alter the meaning of "because of." As we made clear, when "an employer considers both gender and legitimate factors at the time of making a decision, that decision was 'because of' sex." . . . We readily rejected the dissent's contrary assertion. "To construe the words 'because of' as colloquial shorthand for 'but-for' causation," we said, "is to misunderstand them." . . . Today, however, the Court interprets the words "because of" in the ADEA "as colloquial shorthand for 'but-for' causation."

***

The Court's resurrection of the but-for causation standard is unwarranted. *Price Waterhouse* repudiated that standard 20 years ago, and Congress' response to our decision further militates against the crabbed interpretation the Court adopts today. The answer to the question the Court has elected to take up—whether a mixed-motives jury instruction is ever proper in an ADEA case—is plainly yes.

***

The Court's endorsement of a different construction of the same critical language in the ADEA and Title VII is both unwise and inconsistent with settled law. The but-for standard the Court adopts was rejected by this Court in *Price Waterhouse* and by Congress in the Civil Rights Act of 1991. Yet today the Court resurrects the standard in an unabashed display of judicial lawmaking. I respectfully dissent.

Case Questions

1. Do you agree with the dissent that the majority opinion in *Gross* completely alters the burden-shifting framework adopted in *Price Waterhouse?*

2. Is the *Gross* opinion likely to make recovery by employees more difficult in age discrimination cases, as many commentators have suggested?

3. Appellate court decisions subsequent to *Gross* have drawn a distinction between a burden of proof, which does not shift, and a burden of production, which does. In your opinion, what is the difference, and how is it relevant to the employee's age discrimination case?

Meacham v. Knolls Atomic Power Laboratory, *554 U.S. 84 (2008)*

During a reduction in force, employer Knolls instructed its managers to score their subordinates on "performance," "flexibility," and "critical skills." Along with points for years of service, these scores were used to identify individuals who would be terminated. Of the 31 workers who were fired, 30 workers were 40 or over, and petitioner Meacham was one of those 30. Meacham filed a claim under the ADEA based on evidence that these numbers could not have happened by chance. He also was able to demonstrate that the most discretionary elements of the scoring system had the most significant alignment with the outcomes.

Meacham was successful on his disparate-impact claim at both the district and appellate court levels. However, the Supreme Court vacated the Second Circuit's holding and remanded based on *Smith v. City of Jackson,* which had been decided in the meantime.

The Second Circuit reversed its earlier decision and found in favor of Knolls, since originally it had applied the "business necessity" rather than a "reasonableness" standard to examine the employer's reliance on factors other than age in its decisions. It also had shifted the burden of persuasion to Meacham and found that he had not satisfied that element of the case.

The Supreme Court granted certiorari and finds that employers defending disparate impact claims under the ADEA bear *both* the burden of production and the burden of persuasion for the "reasonable factors other than age" (RFOA) affirmative defense. The case is vacated and remanded.

Souter, J.

A provision of the Age Discrimination in Employment Act of 1967 (ADEA) creates an exemption for employer actions "otherwise prohibited" by the ADEA but "based on reasonable factors other than age" (RFOA). The question is whether an employer facing a disparate-impact claim and planning to defend on the basis of RFOA must not only produce evidence raising the defense but also persuade the factfinder of its merit. We hold that the employer must do both.

***

I

The ADEA's general prohibitions against age discrimination are subject to a separate provision creating exemptions for employer practices "otherwise prohibited under subsections (a), (b), (c), or (e)." The RFOA exemption is listed in §623(f) alongside one for bona fide occupational qualifications (BFOQ): "It shall not be unlawful for an employer . . . to take any action otherwise prohibited under subsections (a), (b), (c), or (e) . . . where age is a bona fide occupational qualification reasonably necessary to the normal operation of the particular business, or where the differentiation is based on reasonable factors other than age . . . ."

Given how the statute reads, with exemptions laid out apart from the prohibitions (and expressly referring to the prohibited conduct as such), it is no surprise that we have already spoken of the BFOQ and RFOA provisions as being among the ADEA's "five affirmative defenses." . . .

. . . [W]e find it impossible to look at the text and structure of the ADEA and imagine that the RFOA clause works differently from the BFOQ clause next to it. Both exempt otherwise illegal conduct by reference to a further item of proof, thereby creating a defense for which the burden of persuasion falls on the "one who claims its benefits," the "party seeking relief," and here, "the employer."

* * *

B

Knolls ventures that, regardless, the RFOA provision should be read as mere elaboration on an element of liability. Because it bars liability where action is taken for reasons "other than age," the argument goes, the provision must be directed not at justifying age discrimination by proof of some extenuating fact but at negating the premise of liability under §623(a)(2), "because of age."

The answer to this argument, however, is *City of Jackson,* where we confirmed that the prohibition in §623(a)(2) extends to practices with a disparate impact, inferring

this result in part from the presence of the RFOA provision at issue here. We drew on the recognized distinction between disparate-treatment and disparate-impact forms of liability, and explained that "the very definition of disparate impact" was that "an employer who classifies his employees without respect to age may still be liable under the terms of this paragraph if such classification adversely affects the employee because of that employee's age." We emphasized that these were the kinds of employer activities, "otherwise prohibited" by §623(a)(2), that were mainly what the statute meant to test against the RFOA condition: because "[i]n disparate-impact cases . . . the allegedly 'otherwise prohibited' activity is not based on age," it is "in cases involving disparate-impact claims that the RFOA provision plays its principal role by precluding liability if the adverse impact was attributable to a nonage factor that was 'reasonable.'"

Thus, in *City of Jackson,* we made it clear that in the typical disparate-impact case, the employer's practice is "without respect to age" and its adverse impact (though "because of age") is "attributable to a nonage factor"; so action based on a "factor other than age" is the very premise for disparate-impact liability in the first place, not a negation of it or a defense to it. The RFOA defense in a disparate-impact case, then, is not focused on the asserted fact that a non-age factor was at work; we assume it was. The focus of the defense is that the factor relied upon was a "reasonable" one for the employer to be using. Reasonableness is a justification categorically distinct from the factual condition "because of age" and not necessarily correlated with it in any particular way: a reasonable factor may lean more heavily on older workers, as against younger ones, and an unreasonable factor might do just the opposite.

* * *

III

* * *

Identifying a specific practice is not a trivial burden, and it ought to allay some of the concern raised by Knolls's *amici,* who fear that recognizing an employer's burden of persuasion on an RFOA defense to impact claims will encourage strike suits or nudge plaintiffs with marginal cases into court, in turn inducing employers to alter business practices in order to avoid being sued. It is also to the point that the only thing at stake in this case is the gap between production and persuasion; nobody is saying that even the burden of production should be placed on the plaintiff. And the more plainly reasonable the employer's "factor other than age" is, the shorter the step for that employer from producing evidence raising the defense, to persuading the factfinder that the defense is meritorious. It will be mainly in cases where the reasonableness of the non-age factor is obscure for some reason, that the employer will have more evidence to reveal and more convincing to do in going from production to persuasion.

That said, there is no denying that putting employers to the work of persuading factfinders that their choices are reasonable makes it harder and costlier to defend than if employers merely bore the burden of production; nor do we doubt that this will sometimes affect the way employers do business with their employees. But at the end of the day, *amici*'s concerns have to be directed at Congress, which set the balance where it is, by both creating the RFOA exemption and writing it in the orthodox format of an affirmative defense. We have to read it the way Congress wrote it.

As we have said before, Congress took account of the distinctive nature of age discrimination, and the need to preserve a fair degree of leeway for employment decisions with effects that correlate with age, when it put the RFOA clause into the ADEA, "significantly narrow[ing] its coverage." And as the outcome for the employer in *City of Jackson* shows, "it is not surprising that certain employment criteria that are routinely used may be reasonable despite their adverse impact on older workers as a group." In this case, we realize that the Court of Appeals showed no hesitation in finding that Knolls prevailed on the RFOA defense, though the court expressed its conclusion in terms of Meacham's failure to meet the burden of persuasion. Whether the outcome should be any different when the burden is properly placed on the employer is best left to that court in the first instance. The judgment of the Court of Appeals is vacated, and the case is remanded for further proceedings consistent with this opinion.

It is so ordered.

Case Questions

1. How might you have directed Knolls to have modified its evaluation structure to have avoided this claim in the first place?

2. What is the difference between the burden of production and the burden of persuasion?

3. Justice Souter writes that employers might alter their business practices in order to avoid being sued and that "this will sometimes affect the way employers do business with their employees." What do you think he meant by these statements, and if you were an employer, what changes might you now implement as a result of this ruling?

Oubre v. Entergy Operations, Inc.,
522 U.S. 422, 118 S. Ct. 838 (1998)

See Chapter 2 to revisit key concepts.

In this case that continues to be cited for its important conclusion, the Supreme Court evaluates the differences between a standard written contract and a release and waiver subject to the OWBPA. The latter is subject to specific requirements under the OWBPA, as employer Entergy Operation learns below.

Dolores Oubre worked as a scheduler at a power plant in Louisiana run by Entergy Operations, Inc. In 1994, she received a poor performance rating. Oubre's supervisor met with her on January 17, 1995, and gave her the option of either improving her performance during the coming year or accepting a voluntary arrangement for her severance. She received a packet of information about the severance agreement and had 14 days to consider her options, during which time she consulted with attorneys. On January 31, Oubre decided to accept. She signed a release, in which she "agree[d] to waive, settle, release, and discharge any and all claims, demands, damages, actions, or causes of action . . . that I may have against Entergy. . . ." In exchange, she received six installment payments over the next four months, totaling $6,258.

Kennedy, J.

***

Oubre filed this suit against Entergy alleging constructive discharge on the basis of her age in violation of the ADEA and state law. She has not offered or tried to return the $6,258 to the employer, nor is it clear she has the means to do so. The lower court agreed with the employer that Oubre had ratified the defective release by failing to return or offer to return the monies she had received. The Court of Appeals affirmed judgment for the employer and the Supreme Court reverses.

***

The statutory command [of the OWBPA] is clear: An employee "may not waive" an ADEA claim unless the waiver or release satisfies the OWBPA's requirements. The policy of the Older Workers' Benefit Protection Act is likewise clear from its title: It is designed to protect the rights and benefits of older workers. The OWBPA implements Congress' policy via a strict, unqualified statutory stricture on waivers, and we are bound to take Congress at its word. Congress imposed specific duties on employers who seek releases of certain claims created by statute. Congress delineated these duties with precision and without qualification: An employee "may not waive" an ADEA claim unless the employer complies with the statute. Courts cannot with ease presume ratification of that which Congress forbids.

. . . The statute creates a series of prerequisites for knowing and voluntary waivers and imposes affirmative duties of disclosure and waiting periods. The OWBPA governs the effect under federal law of waivers or releases on ADEA claims and incorporates no exceptions or qualifications. The text of the OWBPA forecloses the employer's defense, notwithstanding how general contract principles would apply to non-ADEA claims.

The rule proposed by the employer (that the employee must first give back monies received before avoiding the release) would frustrate the statute's practical operation as well as its formal command. In many instances a discharged employee likely will have spent the monies received and will lack the means to tender their return. These realities might tempt employers to risk noncompliance with the OWBPA's waiver provisions, knowing it will be difficult to repay the monies and relying on ratification. We ought not to open the door to an evasion of the statute by this device.

Oubre's cause of action arises under the ADEA, and the release can have no effect on her ADEA claim unless it complies with the OWBPA. In this case, both sides concede the release the employee signed did not comply with the requirements of the OWBPA. Since Oubre's release did not comply with the OWBPA's stringent safeguards, it is unenforceable against her insofar as it purports to waive or release her ADEA claim. As a statutory matter, the release cannot bar her ADEA suit, irrespective of the validity of the contract as to other claims.

In further proceedings in this or other cases, courts may need to inquire whether the employer has claims for restitution, recoupment, or setoff against the employee, and these questions may be complex where a release is effective as to some claims but not as to ADEA claims. We need not decide those issues here, however. It suffices to hold that the release cannot bar the ADEA claim because it does not conform to the statute. Nor did the employee's mere retention of monies amount to a ratification equivalent to a valid release of her ADEA claims, since the retention did not comply with the OWBPA any more than the original release did. The statute governs the effect of the release on ADEA claims, and the employer cannot invoke the employee's failure to tender back as a way of excusing its own failure to comply. REVERSED and REMANDED.

Case Questions

1. Do you think the fact that an attorney was consulted before the acceptance of the offer is relevant in this case to determine whether the waiver was knowing and voluntary?

2. As an employer, what should you do to ensure the waiver an individual will be signing is valid?

3. Why do you think an employer must follow such strict guidelines when creating a waiver? Do you think the guidelines are correct? How would you change them?

Chapter 13

Disability Discrimination

Image Source/Getty Images

Learning Objectives

After completing this chapter, you should be able to:

LO1 Identify the current environment for disabled workers in today's workplaces.

LO2 Identify the challenges inherent in drafting, interpreting, and enforcing a disability antidiscrimination statute.

LO3 Outline the *prima facie* case for discrimination under the Americans with Disabilities Act of 1990 (ADA) and the ADA Amendments Act of 2008 (ADAAA), paralleled by section 504 of the Vocational Rehabilitation Act of 1973.

LO4 Describe the term *disability* as it is defined by the ADA and offer examples of covered disabilities or disabilities that may not be covered.

LO5 Explain how someone could be covered by the ADA when they are not at all disabled, under the provision for "perception of impairment."

LO6 Define *major life activity* and *substantially limited* according to court decisions under the ADA.

LO7 Describe how employers can determine the reasonableness of any proposed accommodation.

LO8 Outline the burden-shifting framework of the ADA.

LO9 Describe the defenses available to employers under the ADA.

LO10 Describe how the law treats mental or intellectual disabilities under the ADA.

LO11 Identify the distinctions between employer liability based on workers' compensation and liability based on the ADA.

Opening Scenarios

SCENARIO 1

1) Scenario Alex was just hired as a sales manager at an online furniture company. They showed up for their first day of work with their service animal, a brown labradoodle. Alex's boss, Xavier, is disturbed about the presence of a dog in the workplace. He thinks it will be a distraction. Moreover, Xavier was once bitten in the face by a dog and is now very fearful of them. He recently read an article in which the creator of labradoodles likened this particular breed of dogs to "Frankenstein's monster," so he does not want such a creature in his office. Can Xavier tell Alex that they cannot bring the dog to work? Under the ADA, what are Alex's rights? How should Xavier discuss this with Alex?

SCENARIO 2

2) Scenario Xinyue is the chief marketing and communications officer, making roughly $115,000 per year, of a firm of about 50 employees. It has been a lean year for her firm. Product orders from customers have slowed down, and due to ongoing trade wars, commodity prices for the firm's materials are up. Sabrina, the human resources director, is considering laying off Xinyue. Because Xinyue is the chief officer and has been at the firm for 29 years, she makes about $35,000 more than the deputy clerk, who has about 15 years less experience than Xinyue. Sabrina knows that laying off Xinyue and giving her responsibilities to the very competent deputy clerk will save the company money. Also, Xinyue has been distracted at work lately, and Sabrina thinks that the deputy might bring fresh ideas, which are desperately needed to revive the company in the changing economy.

However, Xinyue is the sole supporter of her parents, both of whom have declining health with her mother suffering from dementia and her father having just completed cancer treatment. Her spouse was recently laid off, and the loss of income has put a severe strain on the family finances. Though her spouse is filing an ADA claim against his boss for her termination, it will likely not bring a settlement anytime soon. If Xinyue loses her job, they will probably lose their home. Sabrina knows of Xinyue's circumstances but is trying not to let her circumstances or the company's interests in firing the highest paid associate influence her decision. What should Sabrina do?

SCENARIO 3

3) Scenario Enkhtuyaa Davaadorj is responsible for filling a vacant position at her advertising firm. The position requires good interpersonal and communication skills, the ability to use the firm's advertising software, the ability to develop advertising campaigns and pitch them to clients, and travel on an as-needed basis. An applicant sits before her during an interview for the vacant position. Enkhtuyaa is relatively confident that the applicant satisfies the first three criteria, and she was quite impressed with the applicant's portfolio. However, Enkhtuyaa is concerned about the fourth requirement, traveling on an as-needed basis, because the applicant is morbidly obese and bound to a wheelchair. Enkhtuyaa fears that the applicant may have difficulty traveling and also that certain airlines may even require the applicant to have a second seat on a flight, which could cost the firm extra money. Further, Enkhtuyaa is concerned that the applicant may develop health risks in the future, possibly even associated with this required travel.

A second applicant's performance evaluations come from the applicant's previous employer and are slightly lower than those received by the first applicant, but the second applicant informs Enkhtuyaa that she is looking forward to the traveling. Does Enkhtuyaa hire the first applicant, even though she believes that the wheelchair and obesity may pose a problem with travel and other areas, or does she hire the second candidate?

Statutory Basis

Americans with Disabilities Act of 1990, ¶ 602, § 102

No covered entity shall discriminate against a qualified individual with a disability because of the disability of such individual in regard to job application procedures, the hiring, advancement, or discharge of employees, employee compensation, job training, and other terms, conditions, and privileges of employment.

Vocational Rehabilitation Act of 1973, ¶ 504 § 794

> No otherwise qualified individual with a disability in the United States . . . shall, solely by reason of her or his disability, be excluded from the participation in, be denied the benefits of, or be subjected to discrimination under any program or activity receiving Federal financial assistance or under any program or activity conducted by any Executive agency.

Removing Old Barriers

LO1 Identify the current environment for disabled workers in today's workplaces.

While Title VII assured certain groups of protection from discrimination in employment decisions, workers with disabilities continued to face the frustration of physical and attitudinal employment barriers long after the passage of Title VII—employers refused to hire disabled people for fear that they would not be able to perform at the same level as other employees, or employers had concerns about challenges based on the attitudes of coworkers. Disabled applicants found that they were required to prove themselves and their abilities to a much greater extent than did able-bodied applicants.

According to census data, approximately 61 million Americans, or about one in four, have one or more physical or mental disabilities (see Exhibit 13.1, "What Is in a Name?").[1] At this same time, decades after the American with Disabilities Act (ADA) was signed into law in 1990, only 19.1 percent of people with disabilities were employed, compared with 66.3 percent for those without disabilities.[2] Working-age adults with disabilities typically earn less: In 2017, the median annual earnings for people with disabilities ages 16 and over who worked full-time was $40,353, compared with $45,449 for those with no disability.[3] People who have disabilities are less likely to work full-time year-round and are less likely than people without disabilities to earn a full-time wage.[4]

Exhibit 13.1 *What Is in a Name?*

Throughout this chapter, we will use *disabled people* or *people with disabilities* to refer to individuals who have different abilities than the norm in the workplace. In the past, these individuals have been called *handicapped,* among other terms. The origins of that word were originally mistakenly connected to the term "cap in hand," referring to those who begged in the streets with their caps in hand on behalf of disabled veterans after a brutal war in England in 1504 during the reign of King Henry VII.

However, the correct etymology, in fact, is a lottery game from the 1600s, "hand-in-cap." The game involved a comparison between two items to be bartered between traders. Where the items were of unequal value, the amount of difference was placed into a cap, shortened to "hand i'cap." The term later came to reference any means by which people created an equalization such as in balancing wagers at horse tracks or casinos.

Today, *handicap* can be offensive because it stresses a lack of ability or area in need of compensation, thus perpetuating discrimination or discriminatory perception. Indeed, even the term *disability* has been criticized in favor of *less abled or differently abled.* However, because that latter terms seem to accentuate further an absence or exclusion rather than a neutral or positive perception, we have opted for the currently common usage, *disabled (people)* or *(people) with disabilities.*

Just as earnings are lower for people with disabilities, poverty rates are higher. In 2017, 29.6 percent of working-age people with disabilities were living in poverty, compared with 13.2 percent of people with no disability.[5] In 2018, nearly 10 million workers with disabilities received Social Security benefits.[6] The burden of supporting those living in poverty has a significant impact on the rest of the population. However, since research shows that many people with disabilities are able to work but have been kept out of the workplace because of misperceptions, this burden could be reduced.

Indeed, research has shown that the performance of a disabled worker, when properly placed, equals and may even surpass that of an able-bodied worker, as she or he overcomes the effects of disability—both real or perceived. Employers have yet to recognize the potential lost by their underutilization of this valuable resource. Instead, many employment decisions regarding disabled applicants are grounded in naïve prejudice. Often, managers reach inaccurate conclusions related to the scope of the disabled applicant's abilities and are apprehensive regarding the perceived costs of employing a disabled person. For instance, an employer who invites an applicant to her office for an interview based on a stellar résumé may be surprised to discover that the applicant is blind. The employer may immediately jump to the conclusion that this blind applicant is not qualified for the position, which requires a great deal of reading. If it overlooks this candidate, however, the employer may be losing an excellent worker merely because it failed to recognize possible ways in which it might be able to accommodate the disability, allowing the applicant to make a meaningful contribution to the staff. In fact, many disabled workers are capable of performing the essential requirements of their positions with little or no accommodation on the part of their employer. (See Exhibit 13.2, "Innovations Break Stereotypes" and also Exhibit 13.3, "Changing Mindsets.")

Exhibit 13.2 *Innovations Break Stereotypes*

A distribution center in Connecticut opened by Walgreens in 2007 is the company's safest, most productive warehouse. "Our facility in Connecticut has been 20 percent more productive than our others, with lower absenteeism, lower turnover and an excellent safety record," says Walgreens President and CEO Greg Wasson.[1]

What makes this particular location noteworthy is that over 40 percent of workers at the center have either a physical or cognitive disability. The center is part of an innovative program established by Walgreens (and now also in place at Home Depot, McDonald's, Walmart, and elsewhere) to design positions and tasks that can be performed by individuals with disabilities.

The idea began when Walgreens was evaluating new technology that could make its next round of distribution centers far more automated than in the past. Walgreens made the workplace disability-friendly with innovations such as switching from text- to image-based equipment and instructions without sacrificing on costs or efficiency. "One thing we found is they can all do the job," says Randy Lewis, a senior vice president of distribution and logistics at Walgreens, which is based in Deerfield, Illinois.

The facility was designed with a few modifications oriented toward helping people with cognitive disabilities adapt to the operations. For example, instead of naming pick zones by long strings of numbers,

(continued)

Walgreens named them after animals, vegetables, and snack foods to help workers find stock locations more easily. Thus, instead of going to "aisle 2, rack 3," employees will go to the "pizza zone."[2]

The program has been around long enough to generate data, which reveal its continued success. For instance, a study of Walgreens distribution centers by the American Society of Safety Engineers found that workers with disabilities had a turnover rate 48 percent lower than that of the nondisabled population, with medical costs 67 percent lower and time-off expenses 73 percent lower.[3]

Walgreens is not the only company innovating to employ differently abled employees. The tight labor market has prompted companies like Microsoft and Goldman Sachs to look to neurodivergent individuals—including people with autism, Asperger's syndrome, attention deficit and hyperactivity disorder (ADHD), dyslexia, and other cognitive differences—to fill their hiring needs.[4]

Though Microsoft has long hired people with disabilities through its typical recruitment and hiring processes, it is now working with the nonprofit organization Specialisterne to launch an initiative specifically to hire more neurodivergent candidates. Changing the recruiting and interview process is especially important, as, for example, people with autism, anxiety disorders, or other cognitive differences may struggle with typical intense interview processes despite potentially being qualified for the job.[5]

Goldman Sachs launched its Neurodiversity Hiring Initiative in April 2019. The eight-week paid program provides neurodiverse people training, coaching, mentoring, which is meant to build their technical skill-building and professional development. Goldman Sachs, and others like them, are starting to realize that recruiting and hiring neurodivergent people will bring more creativity, attention to detail, problem-solving and other attributes to the workforce.[6] Though it is too soon to measure the success of this program, there is reason to believe that it will lead to a more diverse, talented workforce.

Sources: [1] "CEOs, Major Companies and Government Officials Launch Public-Private Initiative to Remove Obstacles to Employing People with Disabilities" (June 18, 2012), http://news.delaware.gov/2012/06/18/employing-people-with-disabilities/ (accessed January 6, 2020).

[2] Maloney, David, "Ready, Willing, and Disabled," *DC Velocity* (September 15, 2016), https://www.dcvelocity.com/articles/20160915-ready-willing-and-disabled/ (accessed January 6, 2020).

[3] Cain, Sara, "The Debate behind Disability Hiring," *Fast Company* (November 26, 2012), http://www.fastcompany.com/3002957/disabled-employee-amendment (accessed October 9, 2020).

[4] Gwen Moran, "As Workers Become Harder to Find, Microsoft and Goldman Sachs Hope Neurodiverse Talent Can Be the Missing Piece" (December 7, 2019), https://fortune.com/2019/12/07/autism-aspergers-adhd-dyslexia-neurodiversity-hiring-jobs-work/ (accessed January 6, 2020).

[5] Holmes, Dane, "Embracing Neurodiversity," Goldman Sachs (April 2, 2019), https://www.goldmansachs.com/careers/blog/posts/dane-holmes-embracing-neurodiversity.html (accessed January 20, 2020); Goldman Sachs, "Neurodiveristy Hiring Initiative," https://www.goldmansachs.com/careers/professionals/neurodiversity-hiring-initiative.html (accessed January 20, 2020).

[6] Holmes, Dane, "Embracing Neurodiversity," Goldman Sachs (April 2, 2019), https://www.goldmansachs.com/careers/blog/posts/dane-holmes-embracing-neurodiversity.html (accessed January 20, 2020); Goldman Sachs, "Neurodiveristy Hiring Initiative," https://www.goldmansachs.com/careers/professionals/neurodiversity-hiring-initiative.html (accessed January 20, 2020).

To ensure that an employer is reaping the greatest benefit from its applicant pool, the employer should be "disability-blind" and evaluate each applicant on the basis of their competence. This is true during all stages of employment, including the interview, hiring, employee relations, transfer requests, performance reviews, disciplinary decisions, and termination decisions.

In order to ensure that the recruitment and selection process, in particular, remains objective as to ability, an employer's appropriate line of questioning could include "is there any reason that you might not be able to perform the essential functions of this

---

Exhibit 13.3 *Changing Mindsets*

Lance Cpl. Matias Ferreira lost both of his legs in Afghanistan in 2011. However, since the time he came to the United States from Uruguay at age six, Ferreira dreamed of being a police officer. In 2017, he fulfilled that dream and became the first double amputee to serve as a fully active police officer.

"This is someone who served our nation, paid a significant sacrifice, and is now able to overcome adversity in a tremendous way," Police Commissioner Timothy Sini said. "He's done a terrific job as a recruit in the academy, both physically, academically and in his leadership to the other recruits, and he's going to make a fine officer." Ferreira was

required to go through precisely the same training and testing as any other recruit.

Elected by his colleagues as class president, Ferreira uses humor about his situation. "A lot of guys are like, 'What happens if one of your legs break?'" he said. "'I'm sorry to say, but if I break my leg, I go in the trunk, I put on a new one. If you break your leg, you're out for a couple months, my friend.'"

Sources: Fuller, N., "Double amputee who served in Afghanistan joins Suffolk police," Newsday (October 9, 2020), http://www.newsday.com/long-island/suffolk/matias-ferreira-double-amputee-to-join-suffolk-county-police-1.13307522.

---

position, with or without reasonable accommodation?" During times of a global or local pandemic (as identified by appropriate authorities), however, employers are permitted to ask direct questions. As discussed in Chapter 4, employers may ask workers whether they have the particular virus or illness, such as during the COVID-19 pandemic in 2020. They also may ask whether workers or applicants have been tested for it, or if they are experiencing symptoms associated with the virus. Employers are permitted to ask whether any of the worker's family members have been diagnosed or have had symptoms, as well. As with any other area relating to medical or other personal data, employers are cautioned to make "every effort" to keep to a minimum the number of people who have access to this information.

Regulation

Section 503 of the Vocational Rehabilitation Act

Section 503 of the Rehabilitation Act
Prohibits discrimination against otherwise-qualified individuals with disabilities by any program or activity receiving federal assistance. Requires affirmative action on the part of federal contractors and agencies to recruit, hire, and train disabled workers.

In an effort to stem discrimination against disabled employees and applicants, Congress enacted the Vocational Rehabilitation Act of 1973, which applies to the government and any firm that does business with the government. Section 504 of the act prohibits discrimination against otherwise qualified individuals with disabilities by any program or activity receiving federal assistance. The Rehabilitation Act aims to remove those burdens that people with disabilities confront specifically because they have disabilities, so that they are left facing only the challenges normally faced by employees or applicants who are not disabled. **Section 503** of the act further requires that where a federal department or agency enters into a contract that exceeds $10,000 annually, the contractor is required to take *affirmative action* to employ and promote qualified disabled individuals.[7] Where a contractor or subcontractor has 50 or more employees and contracts of $50,000 or more, it is required to have an affirmative action program at each establishment. Federal contractors, therefore, must take proactive steps to change their hiring policies, to recruit disabled employees, to train disabled employees so they are likely to advance, and to assist in their accommodation should they experience surmountable difficulties in their position.

The Rehabilitation Act's additional requirement of federal employers or contractors to employ and to advance disabled workers may include proactive steps to recruit disabled employees, modification of personnel practices to meet the needs of the disabled workforce such as special training for individuals who will be interviewing disabled applicants, and/or the training of supervisors and managers to provide a strong internal support and an environment in which a disabled employee would feel welcome.

Unfortunately, since it only applies to the government and federal contractors, the Vocational Rehabilitation Act is insufficient to prevent discrimination against private-sector employees and is inconsistently enforced against federal employers. Congress passed other statutes relating to discrimination against disabled people after the Rehabilitation Act, but on a segmented basis. For example, disabled veterans were protected by one statute, and mine workers who had contracted black lung disease were protected by another; private-sector employers remained virtually immune from prosecution in this regard.

To help address these shortcomings, the U.S. Department of Labor's Office of Federal Contract Compliant Programs made changes to the regulations implementing Section 503. The new regulations establish a nationwide 7 percent utilization goal for qualified individuals with disabilities. Contractors must document the number of individuals with disabilities who apply for jobs and the number who are hired and also report that information to the government. Contractors must also invite applicants to self-identify as individuals with disabilities both in the pre- and post-offer stages.[8] The rule applies to those contractors with at least 50 employees and a government contract or $50,000 or more.[9] The new regulations went into effect in March 2014.

Americans with Disabilities Act

Americans with Disabilities Act
Extends Rehabilitation Act protection to employees in the private sector, with few modifications.

Prior to passage of the **Americans with Disabilities Act (ADA)** in 1992, there was limited legal protection against disability discrimination. Congress had passed the Vocational Rehabilitation Act of 1973, but that law applied only to federal employees and those who contracted with the federal government. Title VII of the Civil Rights Act of 1964, which prohibited employment discrimination, was on the books, but disability was not one of the listed protected classes. On the other hand, however, most states had laws that explicitly prohibited disability discrimination, so those in the private sector who were victims of disability discrimination could seek legal protection in state court if their state had such laws, but that was their only recourse.

In 1992, Congress passed the ADA, which was seen by many disability advocates as the "Declaration of Independence" or "Emancipation Proclamation" for people with disabilities because it applied nationwide and extended legal protections to private employers. As it exists today, the ADA applies to all employers with

Exhibit 13.4 *Not Just* Americans *with Disabilities*

On December 13, 2006, the United Nations unanimously adopted the *Convention on Rights of Persons with Disabilities.* The convention provided protections for the one billion people, or 15 percent of the world's population, who experience some form of disability, many of whom are denied opportunities to work because of their disabilities. The convention challenges people to understand disability as a human rights issue, by addressing many areas where obstacles might arise, such as physical access to buildings, transportation, and access to information. The convention also aims to reduce stigma and discrimination, which can be why people with disabilities are excluded from employment.

The convention came into force on May 3, 2008, and as of December 2019 had 163 signatories and 181 state parties. The convention prohibits discrimination against disabled workers in all forms of employment and also requires proactive efforts to create opportunities for people with disabilities in mainstream workplaces. At its adoption, outgoing UN Secretary-General Kofi Annan stressed, "Today promises to be the dawn of a new era—an era in which disabled people will no longer have to endure the discriminatory practices and attitudes that have been permitted to prevail for all too long. This convention is a remarkable and forward-looking document."

Economic loss as a result of social and labor force exclusion of otherwise able workers costs the global economy between 3 and 7 percent of each country's gross domestic product each year!

Sources: International Labour Organization, "The price of excluding people with disabilities from the workplace" (Dec. 1, 2010), https://www.ilo.org/skills/pubs/WCMS_149529/lang–en/index.htm (accessed December 22, 2019); United Nations, Convention on the Rights of Persons with Disabilities, https://www.un.org/development/desa/disabilities/convention-on-the-rights-of-persons-with-disabilities.html (accessed December 17, 2019); World Health Organization, "Why is the Convention on the Rights of Persons with Disabilities important?" (September 2013), https://www.who.int/features/qa/67/en/; (accessed December 17, 2019); World Health Organization, "Disability and health," (January 16, 2019); https://www.who.int/en/news-room/fact-sheets/detail/disability-and-health; (accessed December 17, 2019).

at least 15 employees (25, originally), and its protections extend to private, state, and local government employees. Because the approach taken by the ADA was largely borrowed from the Vocational Rehabilitation Act of 1973, the protections are now similar for private, federal, state, and local disabled employees. (See also Exhibit 13.4, "Not Just *Americans* with Disabilities.") Even today, however, a majority of employers are unsure about many applications of the act. (See Exhibit 13.5, "Realities about Disability Discrimination.")

In 1998, the first report of the Presidential Task Force on the Employment of Adults with Disabilities released some disturbing findings on the effects of the ADA. The task force concluded that "enforcement mechanisms of the ADA have not proven sufficient to begin narrowing the gap in employment rates between people with and without disabilities. Enforcement of existing legislation . . . is clearly inadequate."[10]

In an executive order later in 1998, President Clinton allocated funding to implement the task force's recommendations to help disabled adults find jobs.[11] In furtherance of these initiatives, in 2004, President George W. Bush established the New Freedom Initiative, designed to "help Americans with disabilities by increasing access to assistive technologies, expanding educational opportunities, increasing the ability of Americans with disabilities to integrate into the workforce,

Exhibit 13.5 *Realities About Disability Discrimination*

1. Employers may not question applicants about specific disabilities, only about their ability to engage in specific business-related activities.
2. An employer may have to alter the working environment in order to accommodate a disabled applicant or employee.
3. Employees with disabilities have no more rights to their jobs than do nondisabled applicants.
4. If someone does not have a disability but others believe she or he does, that person is protected against discrimination based on that misperception.
5. HIV status may be considered a disability under the ADA.
6. The definition of disability under the ADA is not limited only to physical disabilities.
7. Employers are not required to provide *any possible* accommodations requested by employees with disabilities.
8. The need for a reasonable accommodation for a preemployment test does not automatically disqualify an applicant from a job.

and promoting increased access into daily community life."[12] For example, the New Freedom Initiative established the Workforce Recruitment Program for college students with disabilities, an effort to help employers identify qualified temporary and permanent employees from a variety of fields.

The Obama administration also sought to improve employment opportunities for people with disabilities in both the public and private sectors. In July 2010, President Obama issued Executive Order 13548 requiring federal agencies to develop specific plans for hiring people with disabilities and committing the federal government to hire 100,000 people with disabilities over five years. By the end of 2014, the federal government had almost 250,000 non-seasonal, full-time permanent employees with disabilities, including approximately 115,000 new hires at all levels since 2011.[13]

Under President Trump the federal government has continued to hire people with disabilities. In 2017, the federal government had a net gain of 18,054 employees with disabilities. In October 2018, President Trump recognized National Disability Employment Awareness Month and renewed the commitment to "creating an environment of opportunity" for people with disabilities. However, despite this public show of support, in 2017 the federal government also fired 2,626 full-time employees with disabilities, a 24 percent increase from 2016. Data from the EEOC shows that people with disabilities were fired at almost two times the rate of people without disabilities. Since 2017, there has also been a 20 percent increase in disability discrimination complaints filed by federal employees of cabinet-level agencies.[14]

While Congress was busy trying to implement effective antidiscrimination rules, employers were similarly busy trying to figure out how to comply with the ADA, and the courts were at work trying to interpret it. For employers, the ADA has proven to be different from any other antidiscrimination law because the ADA imposes a duty on employers to accommodate a particular class of individuals and this duty does not apply to other protected classes, with the exception of religious belief; however, that duty to accommodate is far less extensive. The accommodation requirement, as we will discuss in more detail later in this chapter, has caused a great deal of confusion about what the law expects from employers. Prior to 2009, the Supreme Court narrowly interpreted the protections afforded by the ADA,[15] which is opposite from how courts have responded to other antidiscrimination laws, where they have basically interpreted protections as broadly as possible. As a result, the success rates of disabled employees who sued their employers under the ADA have been generally lower than success rates for other types of employees.[16]

In 2008, largely in response to the general dissatisfaction with progress for disabled workers, Congress passed the ADA Amendments Act (ADAAA),[17] which sought to right some of the perceived wrongs in the way the law was written and the way it was being interpreted. In essence, by broadening and clarifying definitions of terms used in the ADA, the ADAAA mandates that the ADA be broadly rather than narrowly interpreted.[18] The ADAAA therefore allows courts to disregard the Supreme Court's previous narrow interpretation of "disability" and has opened the door for new claims of discrimination based on less severe and even temporary disabilities. For example, in 2013, the Seventh Circuit Court of Appeals found that "[u]nder the 2008 amendments, a person with an impairment that substantially limits a major life activity, or a record of one, is disabled, even if the impairment is 'transitory and minor' (defined as lasting six months or less),"[19] ruling that an employee's episode of "very high" blood pressure and intermittent blindness substantially impaired two major life activities—his circulatory function and eyesight—making it a covered disability under the new amendment.

A review of court decisions since the ADAAA reveals that the ADAAA has met its goal of expanding the definition of "disability," thereby making it easier for employees to file cases, and the predicted wave of frivolous lawsuits has not yet materialized. However, despite these gains, some federal courts have interpreted the ADAAA in an uneven and inconsistent manner.[20]

Why Prohibiting Disability Discrimination Is So Difficult

LO2 Identify the challenges inherent in drafting, interpreting, and enforcing a disability antidiscrimination statute.

To understand why the disability discrimination laws have been so difficult to implement, imagine you are the staff attorney on a subcommittee charged with writing a new law to prohibit disability discrimination. Your first step would be to define a "disability." When most people think of a disabled person, they think of someone who is sightless, hearing-impaired, or in a wheelchair. However, under your definition, would you include any of the following conditions: depression, nicotine addiction, a disfiguring birthmark, neuroses, perfume allergy, AIDS, obesity, alcoholism, carpal tunnel syndrome, post-traumatic stress disorder, chronic fatigue syndrome, Internet addiction, migraine headaches, mild epilepsy with rare seizures, or being really short? What about someone who is denied a job because she has to care for a disabled person at home? What about someone who is simply perceived to be disabled by fellow workers? How do you define "disability" neither too narrowly nor too broadly? (See Exhibit 13.6, "DIS·ABIL·I·TY: Noun.")

Exhibit 13.6   *DIS·ABIL·I·TY: NOUN*

- A physical or mental impairment that substantially limits one or more major life activities (sometimes referred to in the regulations as an "actual disability"), or
- a record of a physical or mental impairment that substantially limited a major life activity ("record of"), or

- when an employer takes an action prohibited by the ADA because of an actual or perceived impairment that is not both transitory and minor ("regarded as").

42 U.S.C. 12102(1)-(2)

These definitional hurdles are just the beginning of the difficulties, as we shall see. The ADAAA contains a surprisingly long list of new terms, each of which has spawned its own debate about what that particular term means.

There is the additional challenge of how to manage employers who prefer to deny a job to a disabled person if hiring that person will cause the employer to spend extra money, perhaps to acquire specially equipped bathrooms or modified computer monitors or even to incur costs associated with days off for things such as doctor's appointments. Do you create a statute that requires employers to make the accommodation? If so, what extent of accommodation is fair to expect of employers? Accommodations can involve facilities—bathroom modifications, entrance ramps, special parking spaces, computer equipment—but what about the myriad other types of accommodations, such as time off for medical treatments, accommodations for guide dogs, paid human assistants, and asking fellow employees to cover some job tasks for the disabled employee? How much accommodation is too much accommodation, and where do you draw the line?

When you begin to consider all the implications of disability discrimination laws, you begin to get a sense of why all the parties involved—those who wrote the laws, the administrative bodies that handle employee discrimination complaints, the courts that interpret the laws, disabled advocates, people with disabilities, and employers—have struggled mightily to understand and define what constitutes disability discrimination.

See Chapter 2 to revisit key concepts.

hostile work environment
A work environment in which harassment of an employee exists to such an extent that a reasonable employee would dread or fear going to work.

The Statutory Structure of the ADA

The ADA combines some features of other antidiscrimination laws with some entirely new features. Similar to other antidiscrimination statutes, the ADA prohibits both disparate treatment discrimination and disparate impact discrimination.[21] (For a more detailed discussion of both disparate treatment and disparate impact, please see Chapter 2.)

A third type of discrimination, also found in other antidiscrimination laws, is based on a **hostile work environment**. Typically, however, discrimination is not found unless the employer takes some employment action against the protected person, such as firing, demoting, or refusing to hire. Some courts, however, have found an implied right of the employee to be free from a hostile work environment, even in the absence of any employment action. For example, a hostile work environment could be created if fellow employees made fun of an employee's disability or otherwise created an intolerable situation at work. Some courts have imposed a duty on employers to end such teasing and to create an environment that is free from the hostility. With regard to the ADA, whether the hostile work environment exists depends upon the circuit in which you work. Some circuits have recognized the right, while others have not. (For more on the hostile work environment, see the section "Disability Harassment" later in this chapter.)

To further complicate matters, employees can allege a pattern or practice of discrimination. Pattern-or-practice cases are tried in two stages. Stage one requires proof that the discrimination has been a regular procedure or policy. The employer must then prove that the evidence provided by the employees was inaccurate or insignificant. Proof can be met by showing numerous examples of discrimination, by using statistics, or by using anecdotal evidence from which discrimination can be inferred. For example, the party filing suit against a charter school for allegedly discriminating against disabled students was able to show a pattern and practice by providing 12 examples of disabled children who were either disenrolled or denied enrollment.[22] At this point, if the employees succeed, the court will grant equitable relief, usually ordering that the policy be stopped. Stage two consists of individual employees proving individual harm, armed with the stage-one finding that the policy was discriminatory.

ADA and Rehabilitation Act protection
As long as an individual with a disability is otherwise qualified for a position, with or without reasonable accommodation, the employer may not make an adverse employment decision solely on the basis of the disability.

If, on the other hand, an employment policy is facially discriminatory, the proof is different. In that case, the employee needs to prove only that the policy was illegal because the employer is not contesting the fact that it is discriminatory.

With those basic ideas in mind, let us turn to the actual requirements necessary to prove disability discrimination.

The *Prima Facie* Case for Disability Discrimination

LO3 Outline the *prima facie* case for discrimination under the Americans with Disabilities Act of 1990 (ADA) and the ADA Amendments Act of 2008 (ADAAA), paralleled by section 504 of the Vocational Rehabilitation Act of 1973.

ADA and Rehabilitation Act protection means that, generally, as long as the applicant or employee is otherwise qualified for the position, with or without reasonable accommodation, the employer is prohibited from making any adverse employment decision solely on the basis of the disability. For example, as long as an employee is able to adequately perform, an employer may not terminate the employee merely for using a walker to facilitate mobility. An employee may be able to claim discrimination on the basis of her or his disability if the employee can prove, in addition to the fact that the ADA applies to her or his employer, the following (see also Exhibit 13.7, "Proving a Case of Disability Discrimination"):

1. She or he is disabled.
2. She or he is otherwise qualified for the position.
3. If an accommodation is required, the accommodation is reasonable.
4. She or he suffered an adverse employment decision such as a termination or demotion.

Exhibit 13.7 *Proving a Case of Disability Discrimination*

Disparate Treatment

Step One: Employee's *prima facie* case → He or she is disabled → She or he is otherwise qualified for the position → If accommodation is necessary, the accommodation is reasonable. → He or she suffered an adverse employment decision such as a termination or demotion.

Step Two: Employer defenses → Legitimate nondiscriminatory reason → Lack of notice of accommodation → Accommodation creates undue hardship

Step Three: Employee may evidence pretext for employer actions

Disparate Impact

Step One: Employee's *prima facie* case → A facially neutral policy or rule is imposed by an employer → Which has a different effect on a disabled group of workers → No intent to discriminate is necessary

Step Two: Employer defenses → Business necessity

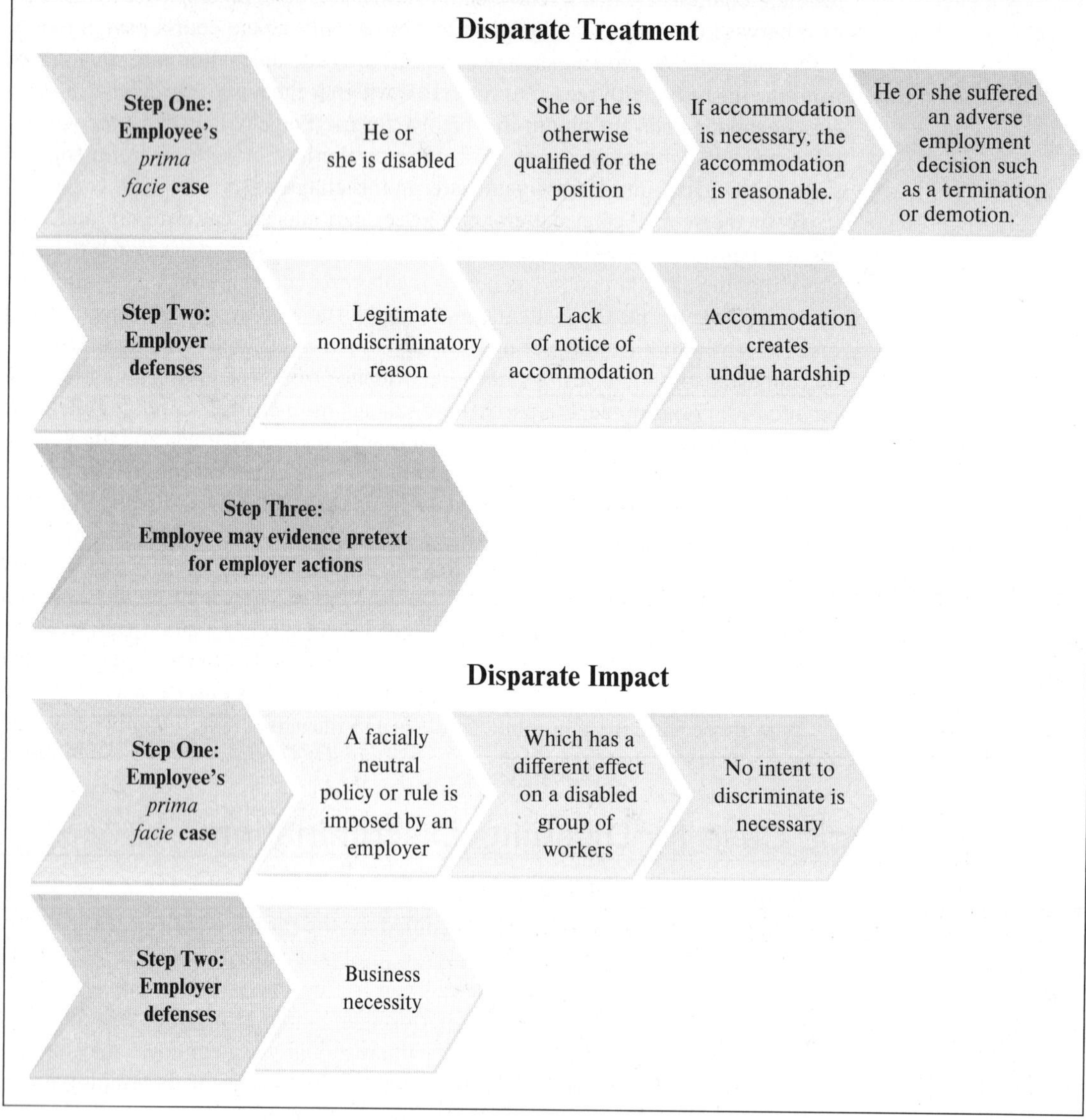

Employers should keep in mind that there are state laws as well as the federal laws that protect employees from discrimination. Employees filing claims based on a disability may find greater relief in state courts, applying state laws. In some states, damages are higher for disability discrimination under state laws, and claims are easier to prove than in federal courts applying the federal laws, although this may change as courts apply the broader interpretations mandated by Congress in the ADAAA.[23]

The key to understanding the *prima facie* approach established by the ADA is to have clarity surrounding the definitions of the terms used in the act. As we shall see shortly, the definition of *disabled* creates two new terms that must be defined: *major life activity* and *substantially limits.* The second element, that the employee be otherwise qualified for the position, requires an understanding of what is meant by *otherwise qualified.* That definition will in turn, as we shall see, require an understanding of the definition for *essential functions.* And, finally, the third element requires that the employer *reasonably accommodate* the employee, the ADA term that probably has caused the most trouble in terms of its definition and one that, in turn, requires an understanding of what is meant by *undue hardship.* It can get complicated. Let us tackle the terms one at a time.

Disability

LO4 Describe the term *disability* as it is defined by the ADA and offer examples of covered disabilities or disabilities that may not be covered.

disability
A physical or mental impairment that substantially limits one or more major life activities (sometimes referred to in the regulations as an "actual disability"), or a record of a physical or mental impairment that substantially limited a major life activity ("record of"), or when an employer takes an action prohibited by the ADA because of an actual or perceived impairment that is not both transitory and minor ("regarded as"). *42 U.S.C. §§ 12102(1)-(2).*

In our earlier analysis, we touched on the difficulties inherent in defining the term *disability.* The amendments to the ADA define **disability** as "a physical or mental impairment that substantially limits one or more major life activities (sometimes referred to in the regulations as an 'actual disability'), or a record of a physical or mental impairment that substantially limited a major life activity ('record of'), or when an employer takes an action prohibited by the ADA because of an actual or perceived impairment that is not both transitory and minor ('regarded as')."[24]

Three important points are worth noting about the choice the drafters made when defining disability. First, there are three separate possibilities for triggering ADA protection. Second, disability is determined not on the basis of the name or diagnosis of the employee's impairment but instead on the basis of the *effect* the impairment has on the disabled person's life. Third, the definition contains no definitive list of impairments that are considered to be disabilities (although some states have laws that mandate that certain conditions be considered disabilities). Courts are directed to reach determinations on a case-by-case basis. Examples of impairments that subsequently have been considered *not* to be disabilities include predisposition to an illness or disease, personality traits such as a quick temper (unless part of an underlying psychological disorder), or advanced age.

The first prong in the definition of disability refers to a physical or mental impairment that substantially limits one or more of the major life activities of an individual. This definition of disability itself opens up the need for further definitions. What is meant by "substantially limits"? And what constitutes a "major life activity"? The original drafters of the ADA left those definitions to the courts and to the Equal Employment Opportunity Commission, though in passing the ADAAA, Congress expanded the definitions originally offered by the courts and the EEOC.

Before we move forward to examine the terms *major life activities* and *substantially limits* found in the first definition, let us address the second and third prongs in the definition of disability. One of the most well-known cases discussing a "record" of impairment, the second prong of the definition, is *School Board of Nassau County v. Arline,*[25] decided under the Vocational Rehabilitation Act.[26] In the *Arline* case, the record of impairment was found in the employee's 1957 hospitalization for tuberculosis. Tuberculosis was such a serious illness in 1957 that anyone who had it was acknowledged to have an illness that interfered with a major life activity, namely, breathing.

LO5 Explain how someone could be covered by the ADA when they are not at all disabled, under the provision for "perception of impairment."

The third prong is being regarded as having such an impairment, which is a curious part of the definition of disability because it suggests that someone who is not disabled can still be covered under the ADA as long as she or he is perceived by the employer as being disabled. For example, an employee with hepatitis C might be perceived incorrectly as being incapable of functioning while, in fact, no symptoms of the disease are manifested or inhibiting.

Congress included an employee who is perceived as being disabled in the definition of disability because it was concerned with discrimination stemming from simple prejudice and also from "archaic attitudes and laws" and from "the fact that the American people are simply unfamiliar [with] and insensitive to the difficulties confront[ing] individuals with disabilities." (See Exhibit 13.8, "Attitudinal Barriers.")

Exhibit 13.8 *Attitudinal Barriers*

People with disabilities encounter many different forms of attitudinal barriers:

Inferiority. Because a person may be impaired in one of life's major functions, some people believe that individual is a "second-class citizen." However, most people with disabilities have skills that make the impairment moot in the workplace.

Pity. People feel sorry for the person with a disability, which tends to lead to patronizing attitudes. People with disabilities generally don't want pity and charity, just equal opportunity to earn their own way and live independently.

Hero worship. People consider someone with a disability who lives independently or pursues a profession to be brave or "special" for overcoming a disability. But most people with disabilities do not want accolades for performing day-to-day tasks. The disability is there; the individual has simply learned to adapt by using his or her skills and knowledge, just as everybody adapts to being tall, short, strong, fast, easy-going, bald, blonde, etc.

Ignorance. People with disabilities are often dismissed as incapable of accomplishing a task without the opportunity to display their skills. In fact, people with quadriplegia can drive cars and have children. People who are blind can tell time on a watch and visit museums. People who are deaf can play baseball and enjoy music. People with developmental disabilities can be creative and maintain strong work ethics.

The Spread Effect. People may assume that an individual's disability negatively affects other senses, abilities, or personality traits or that the total person is impaired. For example, many people shout at people who are blind or don't expect people using wheelchairs to have the intelligence to speak for themselves. Focusing on the person's abilities rather than his or her disability counters this type of prejudice.

Stereotypes. The other side of the spread effect is the positive and negative generalizations people form about disabilities. For example, many believe that all people who are blind are great musicians or have a keener sense of smell and hearing, that all people who use wheelchairs are docile or compete in paralympics, that all people with developmental disabilities are innocent and sweet-natured, that all people with disabilities are sad and bitter. Aside from diminishing the individual and his or her abilities, such prejudice can set too high or too low a standard for individuals who are merely human.

Backlash. Many people believe individuals with disabilities are given unfair advantages, such as easier work requirements. Employers need to hold people with disabilities to the same job standards as coworkers, though the means of accomplishing the tasks may differ from person to person. The Americans with Disabilities Act (ADA) does not require special privileges for people with disabilities, just equal opportunities.

Denial. Many disabilities are "hidden," such as learning disabilities, psychiatric disabilities, epilepsy, cancer, arthritis, and heart conditions. People tend to believe that these are not bona fide disabilities needing accommodation. The ADA defines "disability" as an impairment that "substantially limits one or more of the major life activities." Accommodating "hidden" disabilities that meet the above definition can keep valued employees on the job and open doors for new employees.

Fear. Many people are afraid that they will "do or say the wrong thing" around someone with a disability. They therefore avert their own discomfort by avoiding the individual with a disability. As with meeting a person from a different culture, frequent encounters can raise the comfort level.

Breaking Down Barriers
Unlike physical and systematic barriers, attitudinal barriers that often lead to illegal discrimination cannot be overcome simply through laws. The best remedy is familiarity, getting people with and without disabilities to mingle as coworkers, associates, and social acquaintances. In time, most of the attitudes will give way to comfort, respect, and friendship.

Tips for interacting with people with disabilities:

- Listen to the person with the disability. Do not make assumptions about what that person can or cannot do.
- When speaking with a person with a disability, talk directly to that person, not through his or her companion. This applies whether the person has a mobility impairment or a mental impairment, is blind, or is deaf and uses an interpreter.
- Extend common courtesies to people with disabilities as you would anyone else. Shake hands or hand over business cards. If the person cannot shake your hand or grasp your card, they will tell you. Do not be ashamed of your attempt, however.
- If the customer has a speech impairment and you are having trouble understanding what he or she is saying, ask the person to repeat rather than pretend you understand. The former is respectful and leads to accurate communication; the latter is belittling and leads to embarrassment.
- Offer assistance to a person with a disability, but wait until your offer is accepted before you help.
- It is okay to feel nervous or uncomfortable around people with disabilities, and it's okay to admit that. It is human to feel that way at first. When you encounter these situations, think "person" first instead of disability; you will eventually relax.

Source: United States Department of Labor, Office of Disability Employment Policy, https://www.dol.gov/odep/# (accessed December 17, 2019).

In 2008, the ADAAA clarified that a plaintiff is regarded as having an impairment if she or he can demonstrate that "he or she has been subjected to an action prohibited under [the ADA] because of an actual or perceived physical or mental impairment, whether or not the impairment limits or is perceived to limit a major life activity."[27]

In 2016, the Tenth Circuit affirmed that "to establish a *prima facie* case of discrimination under the ADAAA, a plaintiff must show that (1) he is disabled as defined under the ADAAA; (2) he is qualified, with or without reasonable accommodation by the employer, to perform the essential functions of the job; and (3) he was discriminated against because of his disability."[28] Other circuit courts have applied this criterion.[29]

In another case, a man was fired from a Delaware software company based on a perceived disability. The man had a record of opiate addiction and had participated in physician-supervised medication-assisted treatment (MAT) since 2009. In February 2017, the man took leave and voluntarily admitted himself to an inpatient treatment facility to eliminate the need for MAT. The man successfully completed the inpatient treatment and returned to work. When he disclosed the reason for his leave, the company fired him because his employer regarded him as disabled even though he was perfectly capable of performing the job.[30]

Violations where the employer perceives the employee as disabled are somewhat confusing because they appear counterintuitive to the real world; the courts seem to be asking employers to accommodate disabilities that do not actually exist. But, when viewed in light of the effort to remove stereotypes so that they do not negatively impact otherwise able employees, the decisions make more sense. If an employer insists on pursuing a faulty prejudice, then it cannot later claim the employee is not disabled and have it both ways. For example, in the 2015 case *Horsham v. Fresh Direct,*[31] the court held that, where an employee suffers from or is regarded as suffering from a disability within the meaning of the ADA, the employee does not even have to prove the disability in the first place. That element of the *prima facie* case is taken as already established.

One final element of the "perceived as" disability relates to someone who is perceived as disabled based on her or his association or relationship with someone who has a disability, whether or not the employee or applicant has a disability herself or himself. Again, the purpose of this extension of the ADA protection is to prevent stereotypes from adversely impacting individuals who associate with disabled individuals, such as a child, partner, or parent. The EEOC guidelines on the issue offers the following example:

> An employer is interviewing applicants for a computer programmer position. The employer determines that one of the applicants, Arnold, is the best qualified but is reluctant to offer him the position because Arnold disclosed during the interview that he has a child with a disability. The employer violates the ADA if it refuses to hire Arnold based on its belief that his need to care for his child will have a negative impact on his work attendance or performance.[32]

A claim of associational discrimination under the ADA must prove one of three theories:

1. The employer fears that the employee may contract the disability (such as a disease) or have a genetic predisposition to develop the disability,
2. The employer believes the association will impose increased costs (such as medical premiums); or
3. The employer assumes the employee's performance will be impaired because of association with a person with a disability (for example, by being distracted at work or having to take leave to care for the relative).

Interestingly, the ADA does *not* require that the employer reasonably accommodate the worker since it is not the worker who has the disability. Therefore, if, in

LO6 Define *major life activity* and *substantially limited* according to court decisions under the ADA.

impairment
"Any physiological disorder or condition . . . affecting one or more of the following body systems: neurological; musculoskeletal; special sense organs; respiratory, including speech organs; cardiovascular; reproductive; digestive; genitourinary; hemic and lymphatic; skin; and endocrine; or any mental or psychological disorder" that substantially limits one of life's major activities. [From the EEOC regulations.]

major life activities
"[F]unctions such as caring for one's self, performing manual tasks, walking, seeing, hearing, speaking, breathing, learning and working" as well as "the operation of a major bodily function." [From the EEOC regulations.]

the end, the association with the disabled child or parent does, in fact, have a negative impact on performance or attendance that interferes with the essential functions of the position, then the employer is permitted to terminate the worker. However, it cannot prejudge the worker based on a stereotype beforehand.[33]

Major Life Activity

Not surprisingly, the Supreme Court originally interpreted the terms **impairment** and **major life activity** narrowly, including only those activities that are of "central importance to most people's daily lives."[34] Then the ADAAA came along and expanded what is meant by a major life activity, although it did not provide its own definition. Instead, the ADAAA provided the following nonexhaustive list of examples of major life activities: caring for oneself, performing manual tasks, seeing, hearing, eating, sleeping, walking, standing, lifting, bending, speaking, breathing, learning, reading, concentrating, thinking, communicating, and working.[35] Importantly, the ADAA also extended the definition of major life activities to include bodily functions, such as immune system functions, reproductive functions, respiratory and circulatory functions, normal cell growth, and bladder and bowel functions.[36]

Some employers have expressed concern that the ADAAA ultimately may sanction a "bootstrap" theory of coverage. In other words, if an employer denies a position to an applicant because of an impairment, the candidate can use that denial to prove that the impairment qualifies for protection under the ADA since now the individual is perceived to be disabled. This argument was not traditionally accepted by the courts, yet some commentators warn that this may be where the ADAAA's impact could be felt in the near future.

Since the passing of the ADAAA, courts have expanded the scope of what constitutes a disability. For example, cancer in remission was not originally considered a disability under the ADA. Yet the court in *Showers v. Endoscopy Ctr. of Cent. Pennsylvania, LLC* held otherwise.[37] In that case, the employer argued that since the employee had recovered from her cancer surgery by the time of her termination, the employee was not disabled within the meaning of the ADA. The court notes, however, that there can be little doubt that cancer, even while in remission, is a disability under the ADAAA.[38]

In *Summers v. Altarum Inst., Corp.,*[39] a former employee brought an action against his former employer, alleging that his termination violated the ADA. The employee was a senior analyst, whose work required him to travel to client offices. One day, while exiting a commuter train on his way to a client's office, the employee fell and injured himself. The accident left the employee unable to walk for seven months and he was told by his doctor that, without surgery, pain medication, and physical therapy, he "likely" would be unable to walk for far longer. The Fourth Circuit held that the ADA and its implementing regulations make clear that such an impairment can constitute a disability, that the "employee's allegations were sufficient to plead he had a disability," and that it was reasonable for the EEOC to include temporary impairments in its definition of impairment.

Since the ADAAA came into effect, courts have been asked to explore whether migraines constitute a disability,[40] though some contend that it is difficult to prove that migraines limit a major life activity of working. For example, in *Allen v. South-Crest Hosp.,*[41] the court found that the employee failed to establish that migraines substantially affected a major life activity of caring for herself and ruled that it did not constitute a disability under the ADAAA. However, the court did clarify that, with the proper documentation, migraines could be considered a disability. Courts also have found that the following constitute disabilities: depression, [42] carpal tunnel syndrome, [43] HIV-positive status, [44] irritable bowel syndrome,[45] and a back injury.[46]

There remains a tension between the application of the law by the courts and the courts' tendency to defer to Congress's intent that the law be applied liberally, imposing a light burden on plaintiffs and broadening the definition of "disability" under the ADAAA. For example, in *Gesegnet v. J.B. Hunt Transp., Inc.,* the court doubted that the medical and personal evidence was sufficient to show an actual inability to perform a basic function of life. Yet the court relied on "the broad definition of disability Congress intended" and assumed that the employee had a disability under the ADAAA.[47] As legal scholar Tess O'Brien-Heinzen suggests, the long-term effects of the ADAAA remain to be seen, since the burden of proof shifts back to the defendant after a *prima facie* showing of disability is accepted, and courts will demand more evidence from both parties as cases proceed through the legal process.

Courts have also faced difficulty in determining what constitutes a major life activity. For example, consider the dilemma faced by some courts regarding an impairment that substantially limits interactivity with others. The First Circuit has held that "getting along with others" is not a major life activity under the ADA,[48] whereas the Ninth Circuit has found that "interacting with others" is a major life activity.[49] Other circuits eschew answering the question as to whether "interacting with others" is, in itself, a "major life activity" within the meaning of the ADA.[50] The impact of this confusing legal landscape for employers confronted with impairment claims that have not yet been clearly defined by the courts is discussed later in this chapter, in the section titled "Mental Impairments."

Substantially Limited

The standard to be applied to determine whether a worker is disabled is whether she or he is **substantially limited** in a major life activity. In a 2002 case, *Toyota Motor Manufacturing, Kentucky, Inc. v. Williams,*[51] the U.S. Supreme Court articulated a demanding standard for the terms *substantially limited* and *major life activity* in defining disability under the ADA. It held that "an individual must have an impairment that prevents or severely restricts the individual from doing activities that are of central importance to most people's daily lives"[52] and was seen as highly restrictive.

A specific consequence of the ADAAA was to overrule the narrow standard articulated by the *Toyota* decision, which had resulted in a denial of protection for many individuals with impairments such as cancer, diabetes, and epilepsy. In enacting the ADAAA, Congress explained that "the question of whether an individual's impairment is a disability under the ADA should not demand extensive analysis"[53] and thus made it easier for an individual seeking protection to establish that he or she has a disability by ensuring that the definition of disability should be construed more broadly.

substantially limited
An individual does not need to have an impairment that prevents or severely or significantly restricts a major life activity to be considered to be "substantially limited," nor does the impairment need to last for a set period of time. Multiple impairments that, together, substantially restrict a major life activity may also constitute a disability.

The EEOC has emphasized that the term *substantially limited* now requires a lower degree of functional limitation than the standard previously applied by the courts. An impairment does not need to prevent or severely or significantly restrict a major life activity to be considered substantially limiting, nor does it need to last for a set duration of time. Multiple impairments that together substantially restrict a major life activity may also constitute a disability. The ADAAA sets a lower standard that provides broad coverage, so that the burden of showing that an impairment limits one's ability to perform common activities is not onerous. In other words, the term *substantially limits* is not meant to be a demanding standard. The new regulations also make clear that, contrary to what many employers had assumed, an impairment need not last at least six months to qualify as substantially limiting. However, the regulations do not provide any guidance as to how long the impairment must last to qualify. Moreover, an impairment that is episodic or in remission is a disability if it would substantially limit a major life activity *when active.* Nonetheless, not every impairment will constitute a disability under the ADAAA. The determination of whether an impairment substantially limits a major life activity requires an individualized assessment, as was true prior to the ADAAA.

Another important effect of the ADAAA was largely to invalidate the "mitigating measures" rule, imposed by the U.S. Supreme Court in *Sutton v. United Air Lines Inc.,*[54] which held that the determination of whether a person has a disability must consider any mitigating or corrective measures that can be used to offset the impairment. The most obvious example, and the one at issue in Sutton, was to consider that an employee with poor vision was not disabled because the impairment could be corrected with glasses. The mitigating measures rule was extended to include medications and even an individual's own natural or learned ability to compensate for the effects of an impairment. Following *Sutton,* numerous individuals with fairly severe physical or cognitive impairments were found not to have a disability under the ADA. After the 2008 amendments, with the exception of "ordinary eyeglasses or contact lenses," the determination of whether an impairment substantially limits a major life activity is to be made without regard to the ameliorative effects of mitigating measures, such as medication or hearing aids.

Courts have also determined that a disability must substantially limit an individual's ability to participate in a major life activity generally, not just in a specific work environment. A person who is substantially limited in performing the unique aspects of a single, specific job will not be deemed substantially limited in the major life activity of working. In *Thomas v. Avon Prods., Inc.,*[55] the court held that migraine headaches caused by exposure to chemicals in the working environment did not constitute a disability. In *Allen v. SouthCrest Hosp.,*[56] the Tenth Circuit found that, even after the passing of the ADAAA, a discharged employee is still required "to demonstrate that she was substantially limited in performing class of jobs or broad range of jobs in various classes as compared to most people with comparable training, skills, and abilities in order to show that her alleged migraine headaches substantially limited major life activity of working, as would support finding that she was disabled within [the ADAAA]."[57]

Otherwise Qualified

The acts state that an employer may not terminate or refuse to hire an employee with a disability who is "otherwise qualified" to perform the essential requirements of his or her position. The determination of a position's essential functions ensures that disabled people are not disqualified simply because they may have difficulty in performing tasks that bear only a marginal relationship to a particular job. At the same time, employers are protected from liability where a worker is unable to perform the essential functions of a job and are able to most effectively utilize their human resources.

In one case, the court held that a civilian employee of the Navy failed to establish that she was qualified for her position due to her chronic fatigue syndrome. The court noted that "the accommodation plaintiff seeks is simply to be allowed to work only when her illness permits." The court held that the employee was not otherwise qualified because she was not prepared to pull her full weight. In addition, an employer may not consider the possibility that an employee or applicant will become disabled or unqualified for the position in the future. If the applicant or employee is qualified *at the time the adverse employment action is taken,* the employer has violated the acts.[58] Courts "weigh heavily the employer's judgment regarding whether a job function is essential."[59] However, though courts usually give deference to an employer's adoption of qualifications based on its judgment and experience, courts caution that "an employer may not turn every condition of employment which it elects to adopt into a job function, let alone an essential job function, merely by including it in a job description."[60]

It is important to note that the ADA amendments prohibit the use of any qualification test or other selection criteria to determine whether someone is "otherwise qualified" based on that individual's unmitigated or uncorrected disability, unless it can be shown that it is a business necessity.

Direct Threat

Where the claim of disability is based on a disease, the court in the *Arline* case (discussed earlier) held that the determination of whether an individual is "otherwise qualified" should be based on the following factors:

- The nature of the risk (how the disease is transmitted).
- The duration of the risk (how long the carrier is infectious).
- The severity of the risk (potential harm to third parties).
- The probability that the disease will be transmitted and will cause varying degrees of harm.

HIV and AIDS have presented questions to employers, and therefore to the courts, with regard to the ADA. The Supreme Court's decision in the *Arline* case is important because it serves, by implication, as a proclamation that the act safeguards the rights of employees with HIV or AIDS. Subsequent to *Arline,* the Supreme Court decided *Bragdon v. Abbott,*[61] in which it held that HIV represented an impairment that *substantially limits* reproduction and that reproduction is a *major life activity* under the ADA. The 2008 amendments further clarified that

HIV/AIDS is a covered disability. *Horgan v. Simmons,*[62] one of the first cases to apply the ADAAA to a HIV discrimination case, involved an employee who was terminated the day after disclosing his HIV status. Horgan's employer argued that HIV was not a disability since it was not a "limitation of a major life activity." However, the court rejected this argument, given the clarification of congressional intent and the explicit inclusion of the functioning of the immune system as a major life activity in the ADA Amendments Act.

The Department of Justice has clarified that individuals with HIV have physical impairments that substantially limit one or more major life activities or major bodily functions and are, therefore, protected by the ADAAA. This coverage protects people regardless of whether they present symptoms and even if the person is merely *regarded as* having HIV or AIDS. Moreover, the ADA protects persons who are discriminated against because they have a known association or relationship with an individual who has HIV.[63] This clarification is especially significant, given the fact that there were 1.1 million Americans living with HIV in 2016[64] and that the majority of people who are infected with HIV are between the ages of 15 to 49 and are employed.

The issue of the *level of risk* the disabled employee poses to herself or to others is crucial to the determination of whether the applicant is otherwise qualified for the position. The standard for balancing the risk of harm to others against the employer's duties under the acts is whether the employer can show that there is a *direct threat* to the health and safety of the potential employee or others. For example, as it has been shown that HIV is not transmitted through casual contact but only through intimate contact, it is extremely unlikely that a showing of reasonable probability of infection can be made. Therefore, employers who take adverse employment actions based on the unreasonable complaints or fears of co-employees or customers relating to HIV would violate either the Rehabilitation Act or the ADA.

For example, Gregory Packaging, Inc., had to pay $125,000 to settle a disability discrimination lawsuit brought by the EEOC. Gregory Packing had fired an employee after learning he was HIV positive. According to the EEOC's lawsuit, the employee worked as a machine operator in the packaging department. Despite his good job performance and demonstrated ability to perform his job in a safe manner, Gregory Packaging admitted that it terminated the employee because of his HIV status. The company acknowledged that the employee's continued employment after he became HIV positive did not pose a threat to the health or safety of him or others.[65]

Recent medical advances and changes in our understanding of when HIV can be transmitted have resulted in evolving views on whether there is a substantial risk of transmitting the virus. For example, in the 1998 case *Estate of Mauro By & Through Mauro v. Borgess Med. Ctr.,* the court found that a surgical technician with HIV posed a direct threat to the health and safety of others and thus was not "otherwise qualified" for such position under the ADA or Rehabilitation Act.[66] Since then, the EEOC sued a nursing home facility alleging that it violated the ADA when it fired a licensed practical nurse after learning that the employee was HIV positive. In May 2014, the company entered into a consent decree that requires it to pay $90,000 in relief and conduct ADA training, maintain records of discrimination complaints, and provide reports to the EEOC.[67] Though this case was settled out of court, there is a sense that enforcement agencies are considering the negligible chance of transferring HIV in certain circumstances—during surgery, for example—thereby increasing the standard for the level of risk. For example, the EEOC provides the following example:

> Sue, a phlebotomist who draws blood, has HIV. Since the best available medical evidence indicates that HIV-positive healthcare workers in this type of position do not pose a direct threat to patient safety if they adhere to standard precautions, she does not pose a direct threat based on her HIV-positive status.[68]

The question of *direct threat* is not only whether the employee poses a threat to others but also whether continued work will pose a direct threat to the employee. This was the question faced by the Supreme Court in *Chevron USA v. Echazabal,*[69] where Chevron refused to employ Echazabal because exposure to toxins at its refinery would have aggravated Echazabal's hepatitis C. Chevron defended itself on the basis of the direct threat that employment would pose to Echazabal's health. The Ninth Circuit disagreed with Chevron, holding that this was an inappropriate inquiry in the context of hiring and was only relevant to the context of ongoing employment.[70] The Supreme Court reversed the Ninth Circuit, rejecting the restrictive language and reaffirming the direct-threat defense for the employer. The court warned employers, however, that the defense is *only available* when based on "reasonable medical judgment and an individualized assessment" of the circumstances.

A 2013 case, *Keith v. County of Oakland,*[71] powerfully makes the point that employers must be careful to avoid hiring decisions based on stereotypes and generalizations and instead conduct an individualized assessment of the circumstances, including evaluating whether a physician's recommendation is itself reasonable and not discriminatory. Keith successfully completed training as a lifeguard with a variety of accommodations. He was offered a job as a lifeguard with Oakland County, conditional upon a physical. At the physical, the doctor stopped the exam upon realizing Keith was deaf, stating that a deaf person cannot be a lifeguard. Although the county had made individualized inquiries throughout the training process and even proposed certain accommodations for Keith's employment, it then rescinded the offer. A district court awarded summary judgment to the county but was subsequently overturned by the Sixth Circuit after evidence from experts who, unlike those relied upon by the county in its decision-making process, had experience regarding the ability of deaf individuals to serve as lifeguards. In fact, the world record for most lives saved by a lifeguard (over 900 in his career) is held by a deaf man.[72]

essential functions of a position
Those tasks that are fundamental, not marginal or unnecessary, to the fulfillment of the position's objectives. The employer may not take an adverse employment action against a disabled employee based on the disability where the individual can perform the essential functions of the position.

Essential Functions

For an employer to determine whether a worker or applicant is otherwise qualified for a position, the employer must first ascertain the **esessential functions** of that position. For example, some companies require that all employees have a driver's license "in case of emergencies." While this is a meritorious request, the ability to drive is not always a basic requirement of the positions themselves but instead is marginal to the objectives of each position. An applicant who cannot drive because of a disability is otherwise qualified for the position unless the position specifically has driving as its integral purpose, such as a taxi driver or delivery person.

The term *essential* refers to those tasks that are fundamental, and not marginal or unnecessary, to fulfillment of the position's objectives. Often this determination depends on whether removing the function would fundamentally change the job. Disabled people may not be disqualified simply because they may have difficulty in performing tasks that bear only a marginal relationship to a particular job. How does an employer determine what job tasks are considered essential? Employers may not include in their job descriptions responsibilities that are incidental to the actual job or duties that are not generally performed by someone in this position. The employer must look not to the means of performing a function but instead to the function desired to be accomplished. Some employers are shocked to find that an individual with disabilities may discover innovative and novel means to accomplish the same task. On the other hand, some individuals cannot perform the essential functions of their jobs no matter what accommodation they might request. For instance, in one case, as a result of his disability, a corrections officer did not have the physical ability to restrain inmates during an emergency. The court held that this ability was an essential function of his position and that therefore he was not qualified under the ADA.[73]

Is the frequency with which a task must be performed relevant to determining whether it is an "essential function"? In *Adair v. City of Muskogee*,[74] a city firefighter brought an action against the City of Muskogee, alleging that his termination violated the ADA. To determine whether a particular function is essential, the court considered:

1. The employer's judgment as to which functions are essential;
2. Written job descriptions;
3. The time spent performing the particular function;
4. The consequences if the individual cannot perform the function;
5. Any collective-bargaining agreement;
6. The work experience of those in the position in the past; and
7. The current work experience of those in similar positions.[75]

Despite the requirement that firefighters must be able to rescue-drag or carry victims weighing up to 200 pounds to safety, the employee was only able to lift 105 pounds occasionally and 90 pounds frequently. The court found that his employment by the city as a firefighter not only would place that particular firefighter at substantial risk, but that he may be unable to rescue someone else. The court further rejected the employee's argument that he should be excused from the lifting requirement because he had never been required to lift 200 pounds during the four years he had been on the job. Therefore, because the firefighting function and these other requirements are essential whenever the need arises, regardless of how frequent they may be, the court found that the city had not violated the ADA in terminating the employee.

One of the more perplexing issues to have developed since the ADA's inception is attendance. While the EEOC has viewed attendance as being an important but not an essential function of a job, allowing for a waiver of attendance policies as a reasonable accommodation, some courts have disagreed. In addition, courts have held that employees with erratic, unexplained absences are not protected, even if the attendance issues are due to a disability.[76]

In *E.E.O.C. v. Ford Motor Co.,*[77] the Sixth Circuit Court of Appeals' addresses the question of whether attendance is an essential element of the plaintiff's position and whether a request for telecommuting should be accommodated by an employer. This case tests the limits of an employer's attendance policy. Just how essential is showing up for work on a predictable basis? In the case of a resale buyer with irritable bowel syndrome, the Sixth Circuit concluded that attendance really is essential!

The concept of essential functions under the ADA and the Rehabilitation Act differs slightly from the job-relatedness requirement for selection criteria under Title VII. Under Title VII, an employer has a defense to a claim of discrimination if it can show that the basis for the discrimination was the employee's failure to satisfy job-related requirements. Under the ADA and the Rehabilitation Act, however, the court will look one step further. The requirement may be job-related, but the court will look to whether that requirement is also consistent with business necessity. In addition, courts disfavor employers who make general exclusions on the basis of business necessity unless it can be shown that all or substantially all of the individuals who satisfy that category of disability could not do the job or the exclusion is justified by the high personal or financial risk involved, which cannot be protected against. For example, a general prohibition against epileptics in the workforce in *Duran v. City of Tampa* was ruled unlawful, though some courts have found that epilepsy does not qualify for disability protections under ADA.[78]

Reasonable Accommodation

An applicant or employee is otherwise qualified for the position if, with or without **reasonable accommodation**, the worker can perform the essential functions of the position. Reasonable accommodation in this context generally means the removal of unnecessary restrictions or barriers. Reasonable accommodation is further defined as a modification that does not place an *undue burden* or *hardship* on the employer. The reasonableness of the accommodation may be determined by looking to the size of the employer, the cost to the employer, the type of employer, and the impact of the accommodation on the employer's operations. It is important to understand that each case will be determined by looking to the *particular* job responsibilities as they are impacted by the employee's or applicant's *particular* disability. Courts have referred to this inquiry as one that is "fact intensive and case specific."

Research shows that reasonable accommodation expenses are normally quite low. An ongoing study by the Job Accommodation Network of 2,744 employers across a range of industry sectors and sizes found that 58 percent of employers who had provided accommodations needed by their employees cost nothing. Another 37 percent had a one-time cost of typically around $400 more than what they would pay for a new employee without a disability, and 4 percent reported an annual ongoing cost or a combination of one-off and ongoing costs. The majority of employers, 74 percent, that had implemented accommodations reported that the accommodation was effective or extremely effective. The employers reported multiple benefits, including (1) allowing the company to retain a valued employee,

LO7 Describe how employers can determine the reasonableness of any proposed accommodation.

3 Scenario

reasonable accommodation
An accommodation to the individual's disability that does not place an undue burden or hardship (courts use the language interchangeably) on the employer. The reasonableness of the accommodation may be determined by looking to the size of the employer, the cost to the employer, the type of employer, and the impact of the accommodation on the employer's operations. It is important to understand that each case will be determined by looking to the *particular* job responsibilities as they are impacted by the employee's or applicant's *particular* disability. Courts have referred to this inquiry as one that is "fact intensive and case specific."

(2) increasing the employee's productivity, and (3) eliminating the costs of training a new employee.[79] (See also Exhibits 13.9, "Reasonable Accommodation," and 13.10, "Cost Guidelines for Reasonable Accommodations.") These are strikingly low compared with the potential costs of defending a complaint filed with the EEOC for failure to provide reasonable accommodation.

An example of a reasonable accommodation is allowing an employee with diabetes flexibility in break time. For instance, in one case, the employee was permitted to change the employer's highly structured break schedule so that she could take more frequent, shorter breaks.[80] In a situation where an employer has two applicants for an open position, one who requires frequent breaks to attend to her diabetes and another who has no disability, that employer is not permitted to choose the applicant without a disability solely because of the need to modify the break time for the other applicant (that is, the obligation to provide a reasonable accommodation). But what if the diabetes poses a significantly greater burden than merely adapting break time?

In that situation, the position for which the disabled applicant applied required a great deal of traveling. Unless there is some reason to believe that the disabled applicant would not be able to travel, the employer must afford her the opportunity. While accommodation may be necessary to allow her to travel, such as a modified schedule to allow her more time to get from one place to another, such accommodation would generally be considered reasonable and required.

Exhibit 13.9 *Reasonable Accommodation*

How far does the employer have to go for the disabled employee or applicant? The EEOC has defined "reasonable accommodation" in its regulations as follows:

1. The term "reasonable accommodation" means:

   i. Any modification or adjustment to a job application process that enables a qualified individual with a disability to be considered for the position such qualified individual desires, and which will not impose an undue hardship on the covered entity's business; or

   ii. Any modification or adjustment to the work environment, or to the manner or circumstances under which the position held or desired is customarily performed, that enables a qualified individual with a disability to perform the essential functions of that position, and which will not impose an undue hardship on the operation of the covered entity's business; or

   iii. Any modification or adjustment that enables a covered entity's employee with a disability to enjoy the same benefits and privileges of employment as are enjoyed by its other similarly situated employees without disabilities.

2. Reasonable accommodation may include but is not limited to:

   i. Making facilities used by employees readily accessible to and usable by individuals with disabilities, and

   ii. Job restructuring; part-time or modified work schedules; reassignment to a vacant position; acquisition or modification of equipment or devices; appropriate adjustment or modification of examinations, training materials, or policies; the provision of readers or interpreters; and other similar accommodations for individuals with disabilities.

29 C.F.R. 1630.2(o).

Exhibit 13.10 *Cost Guidelines for Reasonable Accommodations*

The Job Accommodation Network (JAN) is a free service of the Office of Disability Employment Policy of the U.S. Department of Labor. JAN identifies possible disabilities and then makes suggestions for possible accommodations. The following are just two examples of accommodations for workers with various disabilities. *Please check JAN's website for an extensive list of disabilities and proposed accommodations.*

RESPIRATORY AILMENTS (ALLERGIES)

Avoiding Environmental Triggers

It may be helpful to:

- Maintain a clean and healthy work environment.
- Provide air purification.
- Condition, heat, dehumidify, or add moisture to the air as appropriate.
- Provide additional rest breaks for the individual to get fresh air or take medication.
- Create a smoke- and fragrance-free work environment.
- Consider an alternative work arrangement such as work from home.
- Allow for alternative work arrangements when construction is taking place.
- Use alternative pest management practices.
- Implement a flexible leave policy.
- Allow for alternative means of communication such as telephone, email, instant messaging, fax, or memos.

Accessibility Accommodations

It may be necessary to address access concerns for an individual who has difficulty approaching the work facility, moving around the facility, getting to work, or traveling as an essential job function.

- Modify the work site to make it accessible.
- Provide an accessible parking space with an unobstructed and easily traveled path into the workplace.
- Provide an entrance free of steps with doors that open automatically or that have a maximum opening force of five pounds.

- Provide an accessible route of travel to and from work areas used by the individual throughout the work environment.
- Consider providing a scooter or motorized cart for the employee to use for long distances if the employee does not already use a mobility aid.
- Move the individual's workstation closer to equipment, materials, and rooms the individual uses frequently.
- Modify the workstation to accommodate a wheelchair, scooter, or the use of oxygen therapy equipment.
- Arrange the workstation so materials and equipment are within reach range.
- Provide restrooms that are easily accessed from the individual's workstation.
- Review emergency evacuation procedures.

DEPRESSION

Maintaining Stamina

- Allow flexible scheduling.
- Allow longer or more frequent work breaks.
- Provide additional time to learn new responsibilities.
- Provide self-paced workload.
- Provide backup coverage for when the employee needs to take breaks.
- Allow time off for counseling.
- Allow use of supported employment and job coaches.
- Allow employee to work from home during part of the day or week.
- Allow the employee breaks for meditation or other practices that help deter the effects of depression.

Maintaining Concentration

- Reduce distractions in the work area.
- Provide space enclosures or a private office, especially if the office uses an open office design.
- Allow for use of white noise or environmental sound machines.

(continued)

Exhibit 13.10 *continued*

- Allow the employee to wear headphones to play soothing music.
- Increase natural lighting or provide full spectrum lighting.
- Allow the employee to work from home and provide necessary equipment.
- Plan for uninterrupted work time.
- Allow for frequent breaks.
- Divide large assignments into smaller tasks and goals.
- Restructure job to include only essential functions.

Interacting with Coworkers

- Educate all employees on their right to accommodations.
- Provide sensitivity training to co-workers and supervisors.
- Do not mandate that employees attend work-related social functions.
- Encourage all employees to move non-work-related conversations out of work areas.

Difficulty Handling Stress and Emotions

- Provide praise and positive reinforcement.
- Refer to counseling and employee assistance programs.
- Allow telephone calls during work hours to doctors and others for needed support and provide private space for employees to make such calls.
- Allow the presence of a support animal.
- Allow the employee to take breaks as needed.

Attendance Issues

- Provide flexible leave for health problems.
- Provide a self-paced workload and flexible hours.
- Allow employee to work from home.
- Provide part-time work schedule.
- Allow employee to make up time.

Source: Adapted from: Job Accommodation Network, Office of Disability Employment Policy, U.S. Department of Labor, http://www.jan.wvu.edu (accessed December 17, 2019).

Importantly, as noted previously, each case will be determined by looking to the *particular* job responsibilities as they are impacted by the employee or applicant's *particular* disability. Courts have referred to this inquiry as one that is "fact intensive and case specific." An accommodation need not be the best possible solution, but it must be sufficient to meet the needs of the individual with the disability. An employee who suffers from a congenital upper respiratory disease may be unable to maintain consistent stamina or a high degree of effort throughout an entire workday. The requirement of reasonable accommodation does not mean that the employer must create a new job, modify a full-time position to create a part-time position, or modify the essential functions of the job. However, the fact that a proposed accommodation conflicts with an employer's other workplace rules and policies does not necessarily mean that it is unreasonable.

Employers are not expected to accommodate employees by eliminating an essential function of the job, lowering a production standard that applies to all employees, or providing personal use items such as a prosthetic limb or a hearing aid. Employers are certainly permitted to make those accommodations, but they are not required to do so under the ADA.

With regard to workplace policies on reassignments, courts have held that an employer does not have to promote a disabled employee to a vacant position in order to accommodate a disability, even if the disability was a result of a work-related incident. In reaching this conclusion in a 2017 case included at the end of this chapter, *Brown v. Milwaukee Bd. of Sch. Dirs, Inc.,*[81] the Seventh Circuit ruled that because Assistant Principal Sherlyn Brown could no longer be "in the vicinity of potentially unruly students" after badly injuring her knee while restraining a student and because all students are "potentially" unruly, the Milwaukee school district was not liable for failing to move her to a position requiring such proximity or for failing to promote her as an accommodation. In other words, an employer is not required to change a job description or promote an employee who is no longer able to fulfill the essential functions of the job. This follows the Seventh Circuit's finding that "an employer is not required to provide a disabled employee with an accommodation that is ideal from the employee's perspective, only an accommodation that is reasonable."[82] Similarly, the Eleventh Circuit ruled that a hospital did not have to reassign a disabled nurse to another unit without having to compete against other candidates, as this would have violated the hospital's best-qualified applicant policy.[83] Meanwhile, the Sixth Circuit found that if a position that would accommodate the employee with a disability was not open, there is no obligation under the ADA.[84]

Scenario 3 presents an issue of reasonable accommodation and concerns the definition of essential functions of a position. Our earlier discussion of the scenario in this chapter presumed that travel was simply part of the job requirements. If travel is an *essential function* of the position, Enkhtuyaa Davaadorj may be able to justify "ability to travel" as a qualification for employment. Even if it is a valid requirement, the wheelchair-bound and obese applicant may be perfectly able and willing to travel. Enkhtuyaa should simply lay out the requirements of the position and then ask both applicants if there is any reason why either individual would not be able to perform these functions, with or without reasonable accommodation. The first applicant may need some accommodation, and that applicant's reasonableness will need to be considered. For example, the firm might allow the applicant to hold digital conference calls with clients rather than asking her to take long airplane rides, which might prevent the future health complications or discomfort that Enkhtuyaa fears. However, at least one circuit court has ruled that denying employment because the employer believes the applicant could or would develop health risks in the future is not a violation under the ADAAA.

Undue Hardship

Employers are not required to accommodate disabled employees if the accommodation would impose an undue hardship on the employer. The concept of undue hardship is not limited to financial difficulty but also may include any accommodation that would be unduly extensive, substantial, or disruptive or that would fundamentally alter the nature or operation of the business.

While employers also may attempt to show that they took an adverse employment action based on their fears relating to future absences or higher insurance costs, an undue hardship, or more than a *de minimis* cost that the employer should not have to bear, these are not acceptable defenses to a claim of discrimination. In fact, courts have gone out of their way to explain the nature of the concept of undue hardship. In *Kilcullen v. New York State Department of Transportation,*[85] the court explained that it means more than the term *readily achievable,* which is used in Title III governing the requirement to alter existing public accommodations. Readily achievable means "easily accomplishable and able to be carried out without much difficulty or expense," the court said. "The duty to provide reasonable accommodation, by contrast, is a much higher standard than the duty to remove barriers in existing buildings (if removing the barriers is readily achievable) and creates a more substantial obligation on the employer."[86]

Undue hardship may be determined by examining the following factors:

- Nature and cost of the accommodation;
- Overall financial resources of the facility involved in the accommodation;
- Overall size of the employer; and
- Type of operation of the employer.[87]

The EEOC guidelines add another requirement: the impact of the accommodation on the ability of the other employees to do their jobs and on the facility to conduct its business.[88]

Undue hardship under the ADA is distinct from the duty to provide reasonable accommodation under Title VII in cases of religious discrimination such as *Trans World Airlines, Inc. v. Hardison,*[89] discussed in Chapter 11. In that case, the court held that accommodations to religious beliefs need not be provided if the cost was more than a *de minimis* expense to the employer. Thus, the court held, "the definition of undue hardship in the ADA is intended to convey a significant, as opposed to a *de minimis,* or insignificant, obligation on the part of employers."[90] As an example, in a case dealing with an employer's concern that an obese employee would cost the employer higher health care amounts in the future, the New York high court held that this was not a valid defense even though obese people, as a class, *are* at a greater risk for certain health problems than others. Another case, *EEOC v. Convergys Customer Management Group, Inc.,*[91] examines whether permitting breach of a punctuality policy constitutes reasonable accommodation or undue hardship for an employer. In general, though, the question of whether an accommodation creates an undue hardship for the employer is a fact at issue, which is left to the jury.[92]

The appendix to the EEOC's ADA regulations suggests the following hypothetical situations as examples of the weight to be given to each of the factors in an "undue hardship" determination:

> [A] small day care center might not be required to expend more than a nominal sum, such as that necessary to equip a telephone for use by a secretary with impaired hearing, but a large school district might be required to make available a teacher's aide to a blind applicant for a teaching job. Further, it might be considered reasonable to require a state welfare agency to accommodate a deaf employee by providing an

interpreter while it would constitute an undue hardship to impose that requirement on a provider of foster care services.[93]

In addition, where the cost of the accommodation would result in an undue hardship and outside funding is not available, the disabled employee or applicant should be given the option of paying the portion of the cost that constitutes an undue hardship. (See Exhibit 13.11, "Factors in Undue Hardship.")

Reasonable Accommodation and the Contingent Worker

Employment through staffing firms and temporary agencies offers individuals with disabilities unique opportunities to move into the workforce. In 2019, a tight labor market prompted employers, including staffing firms, to turn to workers with disabilities to fill their needs.[94] In December 2000, the EEOC issued its Enforcement Guidance "Application of the ADA to Contingent Workers Placed by Temporary Agencies and Other Staffing Firms,"[95] which remains current and applicable today. Only the staffing firm must provide reasonable accommodations for the application process before any client has been identified as a prospective employer. However, if an employer requests an applicant through the staffing firm, both the staffing firm and the prospective employer must provide reasonable accommodation.

When a staffing firm and its clients are joint employers of an individual with a disability, both are obligated to provide reasonable accommodation at the workplace. Of course, this obligation does not extend to undue hardship. Further, the staffing firm and its clients must have notice of the need for accommodation.

Exhibit 13.11   *Factors in Undue Hardship*

In connection with the definition of "undue hardship," the EEOC regulations direct the following:

In determining whether an accommodation would impose an undue hardship on the employer, factors to be considered include:

i. The nature and cost of the accommodation, taking into consideration the availability of tax credits and deductions, and/or outside funding.

ii. The overall financial resources of the facility or facilities involved in the provision of the reasonable accommodation, the number of people employed at such a facility, and the effect on expenses and resources.

iii. The overall financial resources of the covered entity, the overall size of the covered entity with respect to the number of its employees, and the number, type, and location of its facilities.

iv. The type of operation or operations of the covered entity, including the composition, structure, and functions of the workforce of such entity, and the geographic separateness and administrative or fiscal relationship of the facility or facilities in question to the covered entity.

v. The impact of the accommodation upon the operation of the facility, including the impact on the ability of other employees to perform their duties, and the impact on the facility's ability to conduct business.

29 C.F.R. 167; 1630.2(p)(2).

In order to ease the financial burden of providing accommodation, the Internal Revenue Service offers several federal tax incentives to eligible small businesses (those with either 30 or fewer full-time employees or $1 million or less in gross receipts in the preceding tax year) that make these accommodations. First, they can take advantage of the Disabled Access Tax Credit—50 percent of eligible expenditures over $250 (but not over $10,000) made to provide access to the workplace for disabled workers.[96] Second, any business may be eligible for the Barrier Removal Tax Deduction, which is a deduction for removing architectural or transportation barriers to disabled workers in the firm, up to $15,000 per year.[97] Eligible small businesses can take *both* of these deductions.

Furthermore, the Work Opportunity Credit provides eligible employers with tax credits ranging from $1,200 to $9,600, based on the employee hired and the length of employment. The employee must be a member of a "targeted group," which includes individuals from groups that consistently have faced significant barriers to employment. An employee with a disability is one of the targeted groups for the Work Opportunity Credit.[98] Firms that hire workers who are "vocational rehabilitation referrals" certified by local employment agencies will be allowed a tax credit under the Work Opportunity Tax Credit.[99]

The Legal Process

LO8 Outline the burden-shifting framework of the ADA.

If an employee believes that she or he is the subject of discrimination on the basis of disability, the typical first step is to file a complaint with the employer, using the employer's internal grievance procedures. If the employee expects the employer to make accommodations for his or her disability, as we will discuss in greater detail later, notice to the employer is essential. Employers are under no obligation to accommodate until they have been notified. If the internal grievance process does not resolve the problem, the employee has several legal options: file a complaint with the federal Equal Employment Opportunity Commission, file a complaint with the state equivalent of the EEOC (if one exists), file a lawsuit in federal court under the ADA, or file a lawsuit in state court under state disability discrimination laws. For a more complete discussion on the employee's options, see the equivalent process discussed in greater detail with regard to age discrimination in Chapter 12.

Burden of Proof

See Chapter 2 to revisit key concepts.

In disparate treatment cases, assuming that suit is filed under the ADA, the courts analyze the case based on the same burden-shifting analysis used in other types of discrimination. For a detailed discussion of this analysis, see Chapter 3. First set forth by the U.S. Supreme Court in *McDonnell Douglas Corp. v. Green,*[100] the burden-shifting analysis provides that once the employee meets her or his requirements for establishing a *prima facie* case of disability discrimination, the employer has the opportunity to establish a legitimate non-discriminatory reason (LNDR) for the employment action. Once the employer meets that requirement, the analysis shifts back to the employee, who has the right to establish that the non-discriminatory reason was merely a pretext for discrimination.

For example, in *Ferrari v. Ford Motor Co.,*[101] an employee brought action against Ford, alleging disability discrimination under the ADA. The employee showed that he was addicted to opioids and argued that his addiction was why he was temporarily bypassed for a skilled trades apprenticeship. However, Ford demonstrated that it did not regard the employee's opioid use as a disability. To the contrary, it believed that the employee had been cleared to work in any job that did not require ladder climbing or working at heights. The court found that the employer in good faith believed that the employee did not have a disability and that it had another LNDR reason for not selecting the employee. The employee was unable to prove otherwise, and the court found that employee did not have a legitimate claim for employment discrimination under the ADA.

Employment actions are often driven by a combination of motives. In these so-called mixed-motives cases, employees historically have been required only to establish that discrimination was one of the motivating factors. In 2009, however, the U.S. Supreme Court, in *Gross v. FBL Financial Servs., Inc.,*[102] raised the ante on employees in age discrimination cases by ruling that they had to prove that the employment action would not have taken place *but for the discrimination.* (For a more complete discussion of the *Gross* case, see Chapter 12.)

In 2010, the Seventh Circuit ruled that the language of the ADA and the Age Discrimination in Employment Act (ADEA) were similar enough to justify extending the *Gross* analysis to disability discrimination cases. *Serwatka v. Rockwell Automation Inc.*[103] involved an employee's claim that she was fired from her job because her employer regarded her as disabled even though she contended that she was able to perform the essential functions of the job. The trial court, in finding for the employee, treated the case as a mixed-motives case that combined both legitimate and discriminatory reasons for the firing. The Seventh Circuit, however, reversed the lower court's decision and ordered judgment in favor of the employer on the ground that the *Gross* decision means that mixed-motives cases no longer exist under the ADA. In 2012, in *Palmquist v. Shinseki*[104] and *Lewis v. Humboldt Acquisition Corp.,*[105] both the First and Sixth Circuit Courts of Appeals followed the same reasoning to exclude mixed-motive cases from the ADA.

In 2015, however, the Seventh Circuit backtracked on its previous decision, stating that "it is an open question whether the but-for standard we announced in *Serwatka* survived the amendment to the ADA." This statement left the question open for future courts to answer.[106] A year later, the First Circuit also avoided the question, noting that the answer would not affect the outcome of the case at hand.[107] That same year, in *Oehmke v. Medronic, Inc.,* the Eighth Circuit found that, even under the more relaxed mixed-motive standard, the employer was entitled to summary judgment, leaving open the question of whether a mixed-motive standard should be applied to ADA claims.[108]

Efforts are under way legislatively to overturn *Gross.* For the time being, at least in the First, Sixth, and Seventh Circuits (which encompass Kentucky, Michigan, Ohio, Tennessee, Wisconsin, Illinois, Indiana, Maine, Massachusetts, New Hampshire, Rhode Island, and Puerto Rico), mixed-motives cases do not exist under the ADA. Employees must prove that discrimination was *the* reason for the employment action, which is often difficult to do.[109]

Requests for Accommodation and Employer Responses: Process

As mentioned previously, an employee who needs the employee to make an accommodation must notify the employer of that need. The EEOC offers lengthy Enforcement Guidance to provide assistance to employers to help them better navigate and understand the EEOC's and the courts' perceptions and expectations concerning the employment of disabled individuals. The guidance clarifies how a disabled individual can request reasonable accommodations and how employers can reasonably accommodate such requests.

According to the Enforcement Guidance, when an ADA situation first arises, the disabled employee must provide notice to the employer of her or his disability and any resulting limitations. Courts have recognized that an employee has the initial duty to inform her or his employer of a disability before ADA liability is triggered for failing to provide an accommodation. An employee cannot keep secret her or his disability and then later sue for failure to accommodate. Nor are employers expected to be clairvoyant.

What suffices as a request for an accommodation? According to the EEOC guidance, in requesting reasonable accommodation an employee "may use 'plain English' and need not mention the ADA or use the phrase 'reasonable accommodation.'"[110] The courts also have concluded that an employee who merely tells his supervisor that "his pain prevented him from working and that he requested leave under the Family and Medical Leave Act (FMLA)" is protected by the ADA.[111] A request simply asking for continued employment can be a sufficient request for accommodation; the employee does not need to request a specific accommodation.[112] Nothing in the ADA requires an individual to use legal terms or to anticipate all of the possible information an employer may need in order to provide a reasonable accommodation. The ADA avoids a formulaic approach in favor of an interactive discussion between the employer and the individual with a disability, after the individual has requested a change due to a medical condition. However, some courts have required that individuals initially provide detailed information in order to trigger protection under the act.

In addition, the EEOC encourages employers to be receptive to any relevant information or requests they receive from a third party acting on the disabled individual's behalf because the reasonable accommodation process presumes open communication (in order to help the employer make an informed decision). The essence of the reasonable accommodation concept requires an employer to go out of its way to maintain a disabled employee's employment. It is an interactive process; it requires participation by both the employee and the employer. As part of that interactive process, once the employer's responsibilities are triggered by appropriate notice from the employee, the employer may want to take the lead. The employer may want to initiate informal discussions about the need for and the scope of any possible accommodation. Communication is essential. The object is to identify the precise limitations resulting from the disability and potential reasonable accommodations that could overcome those limitations.[113]

The EEOC and the courts have been tough on employers who have not been promptly receptive and responsive to disability situations. When determining whether there has been an unnecessary delay in responding to ADA situations, the courts consider these relevant factors: (1) the reason(s) for the delay, (2) the length of the delay, (3) how much the individual with a disability and the employer each contributed to the delay, (4) what the employer was doing during the delay, and (5) whether the required accommodation was simple or complex to provide.[114] Employers who do not respond expeditiously to an employee's requests tend to suffer greater legal consequences.

Employee's Responsibility for "Interactive Process": Identification and Request for Reasonable Accommodation

Once an employee learns that she or he will need some form of accommodation in order to perform the essential functions of her or his position, the burden is on the employee to make a request for the accommodation. As mentioned above, except in unusual circumstances, an employee does not have a claim under the ADA for an employer's failure to accommodate unless that employee has made a request for reasonable accommodation that has been denied. Once the employee has made the request for accommodation, she or he has the responsibility to work with the employer to determine the most effective and efficient means by which to meet these needs. "The federal regulations implementing the ADA describe an informal, interactive process through which the employer and employee identify the precise limitations resulting from the disability and potential reasonable accommodations that could overcome those limitations."[115] This requirement of interaction would usually include meeting with the worker, obtaining as much information as possible about the condition, discussing alternatives, considering accommodations, and documenting the process.

In one case, after restructuring its staffing system nationwide, Kohl's suddenly required one of its full-time employees to work unpredictable hours, differing from her previously predictable shifts, which started no earlier than 9:00 am and ended no later than 7:00 pm. After the restructuring, the employer worked more "swing shifts," which included night shifts followed by an early shift the next day. The employee informed her supervisor that working erratic shifts was "aggravating her diabetes and endangering her health," and she obtained a written doctor's request to switch back to regular day shift hours. During a meeting to discuss her concerns with HR and her supervisor, the employee became agitated and walked out of the meeting, putting her keys on the table and then cleaning out her locker and leaving the building, refusing to discuss possible accommodations with her supervisor. The court found that the employee's failure to cooperate in the interactive process with the employer precluded the employer's liability for failing to provide reasonable accommodations.[116]

Further, the EEOC's Enforcement Guidance on reasonable accommodations specifically states that employers have a right to request medical documentation of disabilities in order to best satisfy their duty to reasonably accommodate. The Enforcement Guidance, however, specifies that an employer may only request such "reasonable documentation" as is needed to establish that the employee has a disability that necessitates reasonable accommodation. Thus, in most situations, an employer cannot request a person's complete medical records or information pertaining to a disability other than the one for which accommodation is requested.

Employer Defenses

LO9 Describe the defenses available to employers under the ADA.

See Chapter 2 to revisit key concepts.

Once the employee puts forth a *prima facie* case of disability discrimination, the burden shifts to the employer under the *McDonnell Douglas* analysis to establish an LNDR for the employment action. The burden to prove disability discrimination always remains with the employee,[117] but the employer now has an opportunity to present evidence of an LNDR for the employment action. (See Chapter 2 for a more detailed discussion of LNDRs.)

In a disparate treatment case, one of the employer's defenses is to establish that the employment action was taken for a reason other than disability discrimination. LNDRs might include the employee's poor performance or economic necessity. In hiring and promotion cases, the employer can try to establish that the employee was unqualified for the position. (For more on what constitutes being unqualified, see the discussion above on the definition of *otherwise qualified.*)

Disability discrimination cases present employers with two additional defenses that do not exist in other types of discrimination because of the accommodation requirement. Employees are required to give notice to their employers of the need for accommodation. An employer's first defense, therefore, is that it did not receive notice from the employee of a need to accommodate the disability. Because no specific requirements apply to the notice, employers must be extremely careful in evaluating whether they received notice. Even a casual remark by an employee to a supervisor might constitute notice under the right circumstances.

For example, in *Enica v. Principi,*[118] a case brought in the First Circuit against the Department of Veterans Affairs under the Rehabilitation Act, the First Circuit evaluated whether a nurse disabled from polio met her notice requirements with regard to her claim that her employer failed to accommodate her disability. At some point during her employment, she told her employer that she was having trouble walking long distances. That communication, which triggered a series of conversations back and forth about possible solutions, satisfied the ADA notice requirement, the court said. But her claim for failure to accommodate her disability that related to actions *prior* to that communication was dismissed because she had suffered in silence without ever letting her employer know of her need for accommodation.

See Chapter 2 to revisit key concepts.

However, in another case, decided by the Sixth Circuit, an employee who suffered from acute stress reaction brought an action against his former employer. The employee alleged that he was terminated because of his disability and denied reasonable accommodation in violation of the ADA. The court found that the employee's blanket requests for human resources to review his medical records, for a meeting to discuss employment conditions, or to be placed in a new position all were insufficient to amount to an "accommodation request" under the ADA. The court found that these requests are not the same as requests to be accommodated. The employee also failed to let HR know that he was requesting a new position because of his disability.[119]

Certain types of disabilities do not require notice if, by their nature, they are so obvious that the employer should be on notice that the employee might need an accommodation. An employee who uses a wheelchair would be one example.

If an employer receives notice of or is able to easily identify the need for accommodation, the employer is obligated to provide reasonable accommodation. Now that we have defined the terms used in the ADA in detail, this concept should be more clear. Examples of reasonable accommodation might include modifying the work schedule, restructuring the job, providing leave, and reassigning the employee to a different position.[120] The second accommodation-related defense available to an employer, therefore, is that the proposed accommodation is unreasonable because it places an undue hardship or burden on the employer. (For more detail, see the preceding sections, which discuss the definitions of *reasonable accommodation* and *undue hardship.*)

qualification standards
The EEOC regulations define qualification standards as "the personal and professional attributes, including the skill, experience, education, physical, medical, safety and other requirements established . . . as requirements which an individual must meet in order to be eligible for the position held or desired."

Disparate impact cases, on the other hand, will involve a **qualification standard**, a rule that applies across the board to all employees. In those cases, the employer may defend with a claim of business necessity, [121] by explaining that the qualification standard was dictated by business requirements. Note that this is different from the bona fide occupational qualification (BFOQ) defense, which applies in some other antidiscrimination cases and which *does not apply* in disability discrimination cases.[122]

The business necessity defense requires the employer to demonstrate all of the following:

1. The qualification standard is job-related (it fairly measures the individual's actual ability to perform the essential functions of the job).

2. The standard is consistent with business necessity (it substantially promotes the business's needs).

3. Performance cannot be accomplished by reasonable accommodation (no reasonable accommodation would cure the deficiency *or* the accommodation would pose an undue hardship on the employer).[123]

Therefore, whenever an employer implements a qualification standard for a job, it must make sure that the standard is tied to the job and is necessary. A trucking company, for example, has every right to demand that applicants for truck driving positions have the required trucker's license and the necessary truck driving experience. But employers need to be careful to ensure that the qualification standard is related to an essential job function.

For example, a firefighter was terminated by the city after an accident unrelated to his work left him with vision only in one eye. The employee sued the city and its fire chief, alleging disability discrimination and retaliation in violation of the ADA. In this case, there was no genuine dispute as to whether the city relied on the employee's disability in making the adverse employment decision against him. Because of his disability, the employee was unable to drive any fire apparatus under emergency lights, and the issue in question was whether this was an essential function of a firefighter.

The city relied on the National Fire Protection Association (NFPA) guideline, which stated that operating fire apparatus or other vehicles in an emergency mode

See Chapter 2
to revisit key
concepts.

with emergency lights and sirens was an essential job task of a firefighter. The fire chief testified that the city "has always used and relied on the [NFPA] guidelines as a standard for [the city's] firefighters." However, there was no evidence that these guidelines or any other similar ones had ever been enforced by the city. The case was remanded to resolve the factual dispute as to whether the city had ever "adopted" the NFPA guidelines or if the city's reference to the NFPA was mere pretext.[124]

In another example, an emergency medical technician (EMT) had a tumultuous affair with her married coworker that began to unravel, and the employee became increasingly emotional at work. After the employee had a personal altercation with a coworker, her supervisor expressed concern regarding her "immoral" sexual conduct and demanded that she undergo psychological counseling. When the EMT refused, she was fired. The court held that the ADA prohibits an employer from "requir[ing] a medical examination . . . unless such examination or inquiry is shown to be job-related and consistent with business necessity." The employer therefore bears the burden of proving that a medical examination is job-related and consistent with business necessity by demonstrating that "(1) the employee requests an accommodation; (2) the employee's ability to perform the essential functions of the job is impaired; or (3) the employee poses a direct threat to himself or others."[125] The court further explained that the business-necessity standard cannot be satisfied by an employer's bare assertion that a medical examination was merely convenient or expedient. Rather, an employer that requires a medical examination must have a reasonable belief based on objective evidence that the employee's behavior threatens a vital function of the business. The burden was not on the employee to prove that she was not a safety threat.[126]

In contrast, however, the court upheld the business necessity defense in the context of diabetes in *Atkins v. Salazar,* [127] a 2011 Fifth Circuit case. The National Park Service (NPS) issued a new standard in 1999 stating that "[a]ny condition affecting normal hormonal/metabolic functioning and response that is likely to adversely affect safe and efficient job performance is generally disqualifying." Atkins, who was employed as a park ranger by NPS, suffered from Type I diabetes. Under the new standard, he was found unqualified and eventually given a non-law enforcement position as a staff ranger. Atkins filed suit under the Rehabilitation Act, which incorporates the standards of the ADA. Critical issues for the Fifth Circuit included the relation of the NPS standard to "the specific skills and physical requirements of the sought-after position," the standard's consistency with promotion of NPS business needs, and "the magnitude of possible harm" of a medical event considered alongside "the probability of such an occurrence." The court found that the NPS standard was job-related for a park ranger position and consistent with business necessity, given that "hypoglycemic events may have serious consequences for a law enforcement officer." Finally, the court found that "no reasonable accommodation would cure the problems posed by a park ranger with 'uncontrolled' diabetes like Atkins, at least not without inflicting 'undue hardship' on NPS."[128]

Mental Impairments

LO10 Describe how the law treats mental or intellectual disabilities under the ADA.

The issue of how to handle mental impairments has been a concern for employers and employees alike, especially because of the scope and nature of mental impairments and also the number of people who suffer from them. Under the ADA, a mental impairment is any mental or psychological disorder; these include intellectual disabilities, organic brain syndrome, mental illness, and specific learning disabilities. In the United States, approximately 6.5 million people have an intellectual disability.[129] Additionally, the National Institute for Mental Health estimates that approximately one in five adults in the United States receives mental health services in a given year (46.6 million people). Of these people, approximately 1 in 25 adults—or 11.2 million adults—experiences serious mental illness in any given year that substantially interferes with or limits one or more major life activities.[130]

The EEOC's "Questions & Answers about Persons with Intellectual Disabilities in the Workplace and the Americans with Disabilities Act"[131] addresses specific issues raised in connection with intellectual disabilities. The EEOC defines intellectual disability as anyone with an IQ of below 70–75, with significant limitations in adaptive skill areas as expressed in conceptual, social, and practical adaptive skills; and with a disability that originated before the age of 18. "Adaptive skill areas" refers to basic skills needed for everyday life, including communication, self-care, home living, social skills, leisure, health and safety, self-direction, functional academics (reading, writing, basic math), and work. This is similar to the ADA's concept of major life activities, discussed elsewhere in this chapter. The individual also must meet the traditional requirements of the ADA in that the impairment must limit major life activities, the individual must have had a record of such an impairment, or the individual must be perceived as having such an impairment.[132]

Employers should have a process in place to obtain and evaluate appropriate medical information from an employee requesting accommodation for a mental impairment. The employer can request further information, beyond a doctor's note, by requesting permission from the employee to have the company doctor review his or her medical records. The company can then verify that the accommodation is medically necessary to enable the employee to do the job.

The EEOC's guidelines offer examples of reasonable accommodations that may be offered to an intellectually disabled applicant or employee, including providing a reader or interpreter, demonstrating what the job requires, replacing a written test with an expanded interview or other measurement technique, restructuring a position, providing slower-paced training, job coaching, modifying a work schedule, providing modified equipment, and relocating a workstation to reduce distractions. Employers are cautioned to be on the lookout for harassment of individuals with intellectual disabilities, since about 20 percent of discrimination claims involve harassment or unfair treatment at work.[133]

Mental illness also may require accommodation by employers. Mental illness is defined by the National Institute of Mental Health as "a mental, behavioral, or emotional disorder."[134] A mental illness may range in impact, varying from no impairment to mild, moderate, and even severe impairment. Severe mental illness is defined as "as a mental, behavioral, or emotional disorder resulting in serious functional impairment, which substantially interferes with or limits one or more major life activities."[135]

Several mental illnesses, such as depression, bipolar disorder, anxiety disorders, post-traumatic stress disorder, substance abuse disorders, and psychotic disorders, can meet the definition of a disability under the ADA. Accommodations for people with such disabilities may include altered break and work schedules, permission to work from home, and leaves of absence. For certain disorders, more creative solutions may be useful, such as quite office spaces or devices that create a less noisy work environment and change in supervisory methods, such as written instructions from a supervisor.[136]

Does a mere "inability to get along with others" constitute a disability? Many circuits, including the First Circuit, have found that it does not.[137] The Eleventh Circuit also found that the employer's failure to accommodate an employee's request to move his office to a remote location because of his inability to get along with others did not violate the ADA because getting along with others was an essential function of the job.[138] The Second Circuit also found that an employee's request for an accommodation of no contact with any coworkers and his two supervisors, based on the psychiatrist's evaluation that the employee's return to the workplace posed a risk of workplace violence or suicide, was unreasonable as a matter of law.[139]

However, the Ninth Circuit disagrees, holding that a covered disability exists where the employee can evidence a pattern of withdrawal, consistently high levels of hostility, and failure to communicate when necessary.[140] Yet the court has cautioned that while interacting with others is a major life activity, that does not mean that any cantankerous person will be deemed substantially limited in a major life activity.[141] The court further distinguished that a person whose "interpersonal problems existed almost exclusively in his interactions with his peers and subordinates," but not with his supervisors, did suffer a substantial limitation on his ability to interact with others and was, therefore, not protected by the ADA.[142]

Individuals who are subject to mental impairments that may give rise to violence as a result of their disability may be subject to protection under the ADA. In addition, employers have a general duty under the Occupational Safety and Health Act to provide a place of employment "free from recognized hazards that are causing or are likely to cause death or serious physical harm to . . . employees."[143] For a more detailed discussion of the growing issue of violence in the workplace, please see Chapter 16.

Disability Harassment

The ADA prohibits workplace harassment when it creates a hostile environment against disabled workers. (See Exhibit 13.12, "Prohibitions under the ADA.") The number of cases brought on this basis is increasing, and there is evidence of a trend toward greater reporting and enforcement of the prohibition.[144] However, recent cases suggest that there is some limitation to what constitutes a hostile work environment. For example, the First Circuit held that "simple teasing, offhand

Exhibit 13.12 *Prohibitions under the ADA*

Employers may not reach any employment decision on the basis of individual's disability.

Employers may not classify an applicant or employee because of a disability in a way that adversely affects her or his opportunities or status.

Employers may not make presumptions about what a class of disabled individuals may or may not be able to do.

Employers may not impose standards or criteria that discriminate against or screen out employees or applicants on the basis of their disability, unless those criteria can be shown to be job-related and consistent with business necessity.

Employers may not discriminate against qualified disabled applicants or employees in recruitment, hiring, promotion, training, layoff, pay, termination, position assignment, leave policies, or benefits.

comments, and isolated incidents (unless extremely serious) will not amount to discriminatory changes in the terms and conditions of employment to establish an objectively hostile or abusive work environment."[145]

The U.S. Supreme Court has yet to address the parameters of what conduct amounts to harassment under the ADA. However, lower courts recognize that there is a cause of action for a harassment claim based on a person's disability and have relied on the Title VII sexual harassment framework to determine whether the person with a disability was subjected to a hostile work environment. Under the ADA, a plaintiff must establish the following five factors to successfully assert a harassment claim:

1. The plaintiff is a qualified individual with a disability protected by the ADA.
2. The plaintiff was subject to unwelcome harassment.
3. The harassment was based on plaintiff's disability.
4. The harassment was sufficiently severe or pervasive to alter a term, condition, or privilege of employment.
5. The employer knew or should have known of the harassment and failed to take prompt, remedial action.

In cases under the Rehabilitation Act, the plaintiff must show that the employer was the recipient of federal funds.

As with sexual harassment cases, the fourth element in the *prima facie* case is often the most challenging to prove. In cases where there is some tangible injury, courts are more likely to find that harassment has occurred. In a 2012 case, *Davis v. Vermont, Dept. of Corrections,*[146] a prison guard who sustained an injury to his groin was harassed by his coworkers and inmates and received threatening messages after his supervisors circulated offensive emails referring to his injury. He was also injured in a training session because one of the supervisors who sent the offensive emails failed to supervise the training. Although courts normally do not hold prison officials responsible for the conduct of inmates, in this case inmates only knew about the plaintiff's injury because his supervisors disclosed it. In another case, *Schwarzkopf v. Brunswick Corp.,*[147] a fitness equipment fabricator was subjected to constant derogatory comments about his mental health after disclosing that he suffered from depression and an anxiety disorder. His supervisor began calling him "stupid," "idiot," "dumb," a "mental case," and "incompetent" on a daily basis, said he needed to put a shock collar on him because of his forgetfulness, and made a slashing motion across his throat. The hostile environment forced the plaintiff to take medical leave to recover from the anxiety. In both cases, the courts found harassment had occurred.

What courts have accepted as evidence of a hostile work environment, however, has varied greatly among jurisdictions. One court held that an employer's failure to engage in an interactive process after receiving a request for accommodation constituted harassment.[148] Another dismissed a claim by a plaintiff who had been restrained and photographed in his underwear by coworkers during an epileptic seizure, arguing that even though this could be considered offensive and humiliating, it was not tantamount to a hostile work environment because the plaintiff could not prove that the other employees intended to ridicule him on account of his disability.[149]

Please see Exhibit 13.12 for an overview of the parameters for an employer in decision-making regarding employees with disabilities.

Additional Responsibilities of Employers in Connection with Health-Related Issues

LO11 Identify the distinctions between employer liability based on workers' compensation and liability based on the ADA.

"No Fault" Liability: Workers' Compensation

In addition to liability under the ADA, employer liability with regard to health issues also can arise in connection with workers' compensation. It is important to keep in mind that liability based on workers' compensation is distinct from liability based on the ADA: Just as an injury at work does not necessarily lead to workers' compensation liability, workers' compensation liability does not instantaneously result in an employer's obligation under the ADA. The purposes of the two statutes are distinct as well. Workers' compensation is a statutory scheme to provide no-fault insurance for lost wages and medical expenses resulting from work-related injuries. The ADA is a federal antidiscrimination statute designed to protect individual rights to equal employment opportunity.

negligence
The omission or failure to do something in the way that a reasonable or prudent person would have done the same thing or doing something that a reasonable or prudent person would not have done. Failing to raise one's standard of care to the level of care that a reasonable person would use in a given situation. In order to prove negligence, one must show that these acts or omissions resulted in damage to another person or property.

no-fault
Liability for injury imposed regardless of fault.

A Remedial History: Purpose of Workers' Compensation

Suppose you work in an office and one morning you come in, turn on the computer, and receive an electrical shock that severely jolts you, nearly knocking you off your chair.

Think of the repercussions of this, financial and otherwise. Now imagine adding this: suing your employer to recover for the losses you suffered as a result of the injury on the job. Among other things, you must find a suitable attorney; find a means of paying the attorney at a time when you are least able because of your injury; take time away from work to deal with the attorney and your injuries; wait for a court date, which may be a year or more away; and have the attorney gather evidence to support your claim that the employer is responsible for your injury.

When you finally get to court, you are subject to the results of the more formidable resources that the employer can probably afford and also defenses that would prevent the employer from being liable for your injuries. Among other things, the employer may allege it was your **negligence** that caused the injury or that it was the fault of some other employee.

In the end, after all of your time, energy, and expense, you may lose. Or you may get much less of a judgment than you anticipated. Just when you need it most, you also could lose your job because you sued your employer. You would lose benefits to which your job may entitle you, such as health insurance.

Bleak scenario, isn't it? That is the reason for a system of state and federal workers' compensation statutes. That scenario was the reality in the workplace before such **no-fault** statutes were enacted to address primarily the issues of lost wages and medical expenses incurred in work-related injuries. The main reason for the statutes was to reduce the troublesome scenario the employee had to go through at such a difficult time, but the statutes are not unbalanced. There are benefits for employers as well.

With workers' compensation statutes, employees trade off potentially higher damages awarded after litigation against the certainty of smaller benefits provided immediately. Also included in the statutory scheme is the guarantee of protection from employer retaliation for filing workers' compensation claims and the employer's inability to use the usual defenses against the employee to avoid liability for workplace injuries. The employee gets less in terms of benefits, but the benefits they are allowed are certain if the workers' compensation requirements are met. The employer gains freedom from lawsuits for workplace injuries and the certainty of how much such injuries will cost.

The overall effect is intended to make the workplace more efficient and to assist in the marketplace, since increased accidents mean lost time and lower production. Since workers' compensation statutes are remedial in nature, they are usually broadly construed to permit recovery where possible.

General Statutory Scheme

Workers' compensation plans basically provide compensation for time away from work and medical expenses related to on-the-job injuries. Employers pay into the system, which is administered by a state workers' compensation agent. Each state has a *schedule of benefits,* which tells how long an employee is to receive benefits (generally for a certain number of weeks) and the amount of benefits for a particular injury. The schedules also provide for the employee's death or loss of the use of a limb. Employers usually arrange the payment of their workers' compensation contributions by taking out insurance or self-insuring. Self-insuring involves employers paying into a private fund of their own, while taking out insurance may be done through private or state insurance policies.

The amounts and time periods of benefit coverage vary from state to state. Non-permanent injury benefit schedule amounts are usually based on some percentage of the employee's weekly wages. There is a limitation on the amount to be received; and, once it is reached, the employer's statutory duty is fulfilled. Generally, in exchange for this immediate nonlitigated payment benefit, the employee does not sue the employer. However, there are states where employees may (under limited circumstances) sue the employer in addition to receiving workers' compensation benefits.

For instance, Florida has determined that, in sexual harassment cases, the workers' compensation statute will not be the exclusive remedy because of the overwhelming public policy against workplace sexual harassment. In *Ramada Inn Surfside and Adjusto, Inc. v. Swanson,*[150] the court found that "[a]pplying the exclusivity rule of workers' compensation to preclude any and all tort liability effectively would abrogate this policy, undermine the Florida Human Rights Act, and flout Title VII of the Civil Rights Act of 1964."[151]

In concluding that workers' compensation should no longer be the exclusive remedy for workplace sexual harassment injuries, the court noted that

> workers' compensation is directed essentially at compensating a worker for lost resources and earnings. This is a vastly different concern than is addressed by the sexual harassment laws. While workplace injuries rob a person of resources, sexual harassment robs the person of dignity and self esteem. Workers' compensation addresses purely economic injury; sexual harassment laws are concerned with a much more intangible injury to personal rights. To the extent these injuries are separable, we believe that they both should be, and can be, enforced separately.[152]

Workers' compensation statutes in some form or another have now been adopted in all states. A small minority of states have made them optional but, in doing so, generally prohibit employers who do not become a part of the state's workers' compensation plan from using the common-law defenses if the employer is sued by the employee for negligence.

There is also federal coverage under other legislation, including the Federal Employers' Liability Act of 1908. This act limited the common-law defenses an employer could use rather than replacing virtually the entire common-law approach to on-the-job injuries with a no-fault system. Later, the Federal Employee's Compensation Act of 1916 provided a workers' compensation scheme for U.S. civil employees. The Longshore and Harbor Workers Service Compensation Act supplements state workers' compensation laws by providing benefits for employees in maritime employment.

Coverage in this arena is of vital importance as unsafe working conditions are not simply vestiges of days long ago or workplaces one reads about in *other* countries but instead remain present and current throughout the United States. (For a comparison of workplace fatalities between men and women, see Exhibit 13.13, "Workplace Fatalities Discriminate.")

Exhibit 13.13 *Workplace Fatalities Discriminate*

In 2018, men performed 56 percent of the hours worked by the American workforce. However, out of 5,250 workplace fatalities in that same year, men comprised 92 percent of those workplace fatalities.

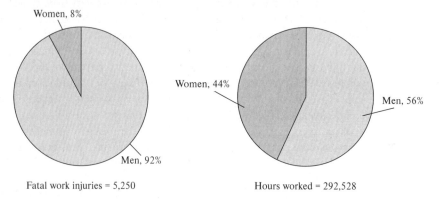

Women, 8%

Men, 92%

Fatal work injuries = 5,250

Women, 44%

Men, 56%

Hours worked = 292,528

A disproportionate share of fatal work injuries involved men relative to their hours worked in 2018.

Source: U.S. Bureau of Labor Statistics, Census of Fatal Occupational Injuries (CFOI)-Current and Revised Data," (December 17, 2019) https://www.bls.gov/iif/oshcfoi1.htm#rates (accessed January 27, 2020).

"Out of or in the Course of" Employment

One of the most frequently litigated areas of workers' compensation is whether the accident injuring an employee arose out of or in the course of employment. An injury that occurs at work is not necessarily work-related. For instance, if a diabetic employee goes into a coma while at work, this may have nothing whatsoever to do with work except that it occurred there. Though workers' compensation statutes are remedial, and generally an attempt is made to find compensation for injured employees, the statutory requirements must still be met.

"Arising out of or in the course of" employment generally requires the employee's injury to be one that has a causal connection with the employee's employment ("arise out of employment") and may involve the time, place, and circumstances of the accident ("sustained in the course of employment") or both, depending on the state. An employee can be injured off the premises and still have a valid workers' compensation claim if the employee was in the course of employment, just as she may receive an injury on the work premises and not be covered because it did not arise out of employment.

For the most part, the system works. However, it is not without flaws. A common problem employers have is that they may routinely respond to inquiries from the workers' compensation office without giving them the closer inspection they deserve. Contributions for larger employers are based on their injury record, so premium contributions, which must be paid by the employer, increase when claims are filed. Without investigation of claims, unwarranted claims slip through, and this unnecessarily increases the employer's contribution. However, it is the experience of the industry as a whole that serves as the basis for premiums; thus, this may not be as crucial for smaller companies. Employer attention to workplace safety can greatly reduce accidents and resulting premiums and claims.

Workers' compensation is big business. An employer must be vigilant about providing a safe workplace and training so preventable workplace accidents are minimized. Some states are taking this very seriously. The California Corporate Criminal Liability Act may impose fines of up to $1 million on corporations for failure to notify employees of a "serious concealed danger" in the workplace. In addition, managers also may be fined and criminally prosecuted if they actually knew of a workplace condition that created a substantial probability of death, great bodily harm, or serious exposure to a hazardous substance. Again, employers also should keep a close watch on claims to ensure that only valid claims are permitted.

Protection of Coworkers

tort
A private (civil) wrong against a person or her or his property.

The employer of an employee with a contagious disability may be liable to coworkers of the employee based on a variety of common-law **tort** theories. While the only remedy available to the employee for common workplace injury is workers' compensation (discussed above), the employer may be additionally liable to its employee for any intentional torts. The employer has both a statutory duty to provide a safe work environment according to federal regulations and a similar common-law duty to refrain from an intentional wrong against the employee. This type of tort liability may arise based on the response of the employer to the news that an employee has a contagious disease. If the employer reacts in a manner that causes the employee severe emotional distress by its outrageous conduct, the employer would be liable in tort.

In addition, unwarranted invasions of privacy, breaches of confidentiality, and defamation have been held to be bases for actions against employers. A tortious invasion of privacy occurs where the employer intentionally intrudes into an employee's private affairs and the court finds that the intrusion would be highly offensive to a reasonable person.

How does this issue arise? Predictably, several cases have been filed by employees who work with HIV-positive employees. Usually, the case will surface after the employee has made requests for additional protections. Pursuant to the Occupational Safety and Health Act, an employer must provide a safe workplace for its employees, free from conditions reasonably believed in good faith to be hazardous. Where an employer knowingly and willfully disregards the safety of its employees, the employer will be liable.

In California, for instance, a group of nurses requested gloves and masks when treating AIDS patients. The nurses were denied protection based on the California Labor Commission's finding that there was no health danger from working in an AIDS ward without protective clothing. The employees' fears must be based on an honest, good faith, and reasonable belief that their safety is threatened.

While the court in the California case evaluated the health risk posed by patients rather than employees, the logic is the same. Since the employer is required to protect both its employees covered by the ADA, and all of its employees who may be covered by the National Labor Relations Act and/or the Occupational Safety and Health Act, the only answer must be the complete education of the workforce to preclude any "good-faith" belief that the employee with AIDS presents a health danger when under practically any circumstances imaginable, the employee does not.

Retaliatory Discharge and Remedies Available

The ADA prohibits discrimination against anyone who "made a charge, testified, assisted, or participated in any manner in an investigation, proceeding, or hearing."[153] Interference, coercion, and intimidation are similarly forbidden.[154]

To establish a retaliation claim, the employee must demonstrate three elements:

**See Chapter 2
to revisit key
concepts.**

1. A protected activity (such as opposition to discrimination or participation in a complaint process).
2. An adverse action by the employer against the employee.
3. Some causal connection between the protected activity and the adverse action.[155]

No jury trial and no punitive or compensatory damages are allowed in an ADA retaliation suit, which means that the remedy is limited to equitable relief, such as reinstatement if you were fired.[156]

Genetic Testing

Advances in technology now allow employers to discover a great deal of information about their employees through the process of genetic screening—sometimes more information than the employee actually wants to know about herself or himself. **Genetic testing** "identifies changes in chromosomes, genes, or proteins. The results of a genetic test can confirm or rule out a suspected genetic condition or help determine a person's chance of developing or passing on a genetic disorder."[157] Genetic tests exist for thousands of diseases, and research is under way for hundreds more.[158] Though many people express a desire to learn about their genetic information, a majority (92 percent) also prefer that it is not collected because of fears of discrimination on the basis of what is uncovered. In this way, genetic information differs from other medical information in that society has historically justified discrimination on this basis and the information gathered also includes data about one's blood relatives in addition to oneself.[159]

genetic testing
Investigation and evaluation of an individual's biological predispositions based on the presence of a specific disease-associated gene on the individual's chromosomes.

Some courts have interpreted the ADA as prohibiting genetic discrimination in the workplace, and in 2008, Congress passed the Genetic Information Nondiscrimination Act (GINA), which prohibits employers with 15 or more employees from both requesting genetic testing and considering someone's genetic background in taking any employment action, such as hiring, firing, or promoting. GINA's stated purpose was to free employees to seek genetic counseling without having to worry that their employers might use the results against them. Prior to GINA, the EEOC had argued that the ADA protected employees against the use of genetic information by employers, though this argument was largely untested by the courts.[160] In addition, many states had passed laws prohibiting genetic discrimination in the workplace. Though many of these state statutes and much of the evolving case law in this area were superseded by GINA, it is important to note that GINA sets a floor of minimum protection against genetic discrimination; it does not preempt state laws with stricter protections.

Because "genetic information" is broadly defined in GINA, employers generally are forbidden from asking employees about their family histories for reasons other than certification. Thus, for example, a supervisor could run afoul of GINA if she or he asked an employee why the employee is requesting family medical leave. In fact, in its final regulations under GINA, the EEOC clarifies that no specific intent is required to violate GINA—a violation may occur unintentionally.[161] However, there is an exception for "inadvertent discoveries," that is, those bits of information that the employer might learn simply by overhearing them or in response to a general question of the employee.

In addition to its protection against discrimination on the basis of an individual's genetic information, GINA provides a series of privacy provisions that prohibit the collection of genetic information except where health or genetic services are offered by the employer, where an employer needs certain information to comply with the certification provisions of the Family and Medical Leave Act of 1993 (FMLA) or with state family and medical leave laws, where an employer learns the information through publicly available documentation, or where necessary to monitor the effects of toxic substances in the workplace (when authorized by the employee or as required by law).

Though advocates argue that protecting individuals in this manner provides benefits of genetic testing without fear of the discriminatory implications, opponents of the law are concerned that employers would now be prohibited from protecting workers with a genetic predisposition to certain diseases from accepting certain dangerous positions. This specific issue was not addressed in GINA, and courts will have to negotiate whether a legitimate business necessity would allow employers to make decisions based on genetic information.

A new arena of possible legal concern for employers involves the overlap of GINA with the Affordable Care Act (ACA), the comprehensive health care reform legislation signed into law by President Obama in 2010. Like GINA, the ACA prohibits group health plans and individual health insurance providers from differentiating between insured individuals in terms of premiums or eligibility based on genetic information. Also, provisions of both GINA and the ACA address the topic of employee wellness programs, although with different focus. GINA makes a limited allowance for such programs to lawfully collect genetic information about an employee under strict conditions designed to protect employee privacy. The ACA encourages—without mandating—employee wellness programs while regulating the financial incentives that businesses may provide to induce employee participation. Though the ACA explicitly prohibits wellness programs from requiring genetic information from employees or discriminating on the basis of such information voluntarily provided, it does not address privacy issues.

Though the sections of the ACA regulating access to and use of employee genetic information by insurers and wellness programs do not amend or explicitly contradict provisions of GINA, the ACA does not reference the earlier legislation, either. Though there has been scant litigation on the topic, the D.C. District Court has acknowledged the complex interactions between GINA and the ACA and suggested that the ACA amends and complements HIPAA.[162]

Family and Medical Leave Act and the ADA: Distinctions

As discussed in Chapter 16, the Family and Medical Leave Act provides eligible employees with leave based on certain circumstances. The FMLA intersects with the ADA in that both require a covered employer to grant leave based on medical reasons. The ADA's reach is slightly broader as the ADA applies to private employers of 15 or more employees while the FMLA covers private employers with 50 or more employees.

In addition, the coverage provided by the two acts differs slightly in terms of the circumstances under which each applies. Under the FMLA, an employee may take advantage of the act in connection with a "serious health condition." This is defined as "an illness, injury or physical or mental condition that involves . . . inpatient care . . . or continuing treatment by a health care provider."[163] Of course, those conditions that are covered by this definition might not constitute disabilities under the ADA. The clearest example of this divergence is in the case of pregnancy. Pregnant women qualify for leave under the FMLA, but normal circumstances of pregnancy are not considered disabilities under the ADA.

In addition, in March 2020, Congress enacted the Families First Coronavirus Response Act (FFCRA), which provides public health emergency leave under the FMLA. Division C of the Act covers situations where a worker is unable to work or telecommute because they need to care for a child because that child's school or place of care has been closed due to a public health emergency related to COVID-19 (coronavirus). Under those conditions, employers with fewer than 500 employees are must offer the worker leave.[164] There are two exceptions: The Secretary of Labor is permitted to restrict certain health care providers and emergency responders from taking leave under the bill; and it also may issue regulations exempting certain small business with fewer than 50 employees if compliance would jeopardize the viability of the business.

Another distinction between the two acts is the extent of the leave. The FMLA (and also the FFCRA) provide for up to 12 weeks of leave per year for covered conditions. The ADA does not identify a specific duration for leaves due to disabilities. In some cases, where leaves for more than 12 weeks would not constitute an undue burden on the employer, a leave for an extended period may be considered to be reasonable accommodation. Under both the FMLA and the FFCRA, an employee is entitled to return to the same or equivalent position as that which she or he left when taking the leave. Under the ADA, the employee may request additional leave even after an employer informs the employee that her or his position may no longer be available (or that it would constitute an undue burden to keep it available). If this happens, the employer is obligated to try to find a vacant position for the worker at an equivalent level or, if not available, at a lower level.

It is important to note that the FFCRA grants significant power to employers in the health care industry during times of crisis. Under the FFCRA, employers of "health care providers" can decide that their workers are prohibited from taking FMLA leave or paid sick leave (in other words, are not eligible) under the FMLA. The purpose of this power is to ensure that there is not a shortage of health care workers during a pandemic or other heath emergency. Employees may still opt for unpaid leave if a medical professional affirms that she or he needs such FMLA leave. Employers would be wise to ensure that they use an objective, non-discriminatory criteria when they determine which employees shall receive paid leave and which employees will not.[165]

Management Considerations

See Chapter 2 to revisit key concepts.

As discussed in Chapter 4, employers are restricted in their preemployment inquiries with regard to disabilities, and those restrictions should now be much clearer in their origins and implications. Medical examinations may only be required after the employment offer has been extended and only where all employees in that position category are subject to similar examinations. Employment may then be conditioned on passing the test. However, as previously stated, where the withdrawal of the offer is based on the discovery of a disability, that disability must be related to adequate performance of the job or business necessity, and there must exist no reasonable accommodation. All information obtained through medical examinations must be kept confidential by the employer. The employer should therefore establish separate files for this information and restrict access to them.

The ADA apparently treats testing differently based on when the test is given. As mentioned above, no medical testing is allowed pre-offer unless it relates specifically to job performance. Once the offer has been made but prior to employment, some testing might be acceptable. Once hired and employed, employers are far more restricted in terms of testing and the decisions that may be based on the results of testing. In *Rowles v. Automated Production Systems, Inc.,*[166] the plaintiff was a worker who had been given an offer conditioned on a drug test. The worker, an epileptic, took medication to prevent seizures. Upon learning that this particular medication was on the list of prohibited drugs for which he would be tested, he refused to take the drug test and was fired. Rowles filed a claim under the ADA asserting a violation since the firm prohibited the use of legally prescribed drugs without any showing that testing for these drugs was job-related or a business necessity.

The district court judge in *Rowles* held that since the policy prohibited the use of physician-prescribed medication, the policy was in direct violation of the ADA. In so holding, the judge granted partial summary judgment but still required the employee to show that the termination resulted from the illegal policy.

Not all preemployment inquiry issues are so clear. Imagine a situation where the interviewer notices an apparent disability that might interfere with the applicant's job performance. However, when asked if he can perform the essential functions of the position, the applicant replies that he can. The ADA is unclear as to whether the interviewer can inquire further about the applicant's disability given this response. (See Exhibit 13.14, "Preemployment Questions.")

Many firms have adopted educational programs so their managers become more aware of the needs of disabled employees. In this way, firms can better prevent problems from arising once the disabled employee joins the workforce. This is of even greater necessity given the ADA's prohibition on pre-offer medical examinations. A company may not require a medical examination before an offer has been extended, though it may make a verbal inquiry about whether the applicant is capable of performing the essential functions of the position in question. Only after that time may a company require an examination. Because of this prohibition, many firms employ disabled employees who did not appear to be disabled at the time the offer was extended.

Firms are also developing policies of direct referral of disabled employees to specially designated personnel directors. This director or counselor is aware of job possibilities and would be in the best position to suggest job content modifications and redesign potential. After assignment or reassignment, the counselor usually checks on the employee to ensure that the requirements of the position are appropriate to the needs of the employee and that the employee is satisfying the needs of the firm. In addition, many firms conduct periodic reviews of their position descriptions to ensure that they encompass the essential functions of the position as well as a review of their job application forms and procedures, facilities, personnel programs, and policies.

Employers should be aware that the Internal Revenue Service offers a Targeted Jobs Tax Credit to employers against five-year wages paid to newly hired workers with disabilities, among others who have difficulty obtaining employment. The program is administered by the U.S. Department of Labor.

Exhibit 13.14 *Preemployment Questions*

Examples of questions that may *not* be asked of an applicant for a position:

1. Please list any disabilities.
2. Have you ever filed a workers' compensation claim, and on what basis?
3. Do you have any disability(ies) that may prevent you from performing the requirements of this position?
4. How did you become disabled?

See Chapter 2 to revisit key concepts.

5. How often do you expect to miss work as a result of this disability?

Examples of questions that *may* be asked:

1. This job requires that you [be present for eight hours a day, five days a week], [lift 150-pound bags], [stand for long periods of time]. Can you meet this requirement?
2. If the employer is aware of the disability, the employer may ask how the applicant intends to perform the essential functions of the position with or without accommodation.
3. The employer may request documentation of the need for a requested accommodation.

Employers should also be aware of ADA regulations enacted by the Department of Justice, which went into effect in 2012. The new regulations require employers to continue to remove barriers of access within employee work areas, if readily achievable. The rules apply to work areas only and not to areas such as bathrooms and break rooms. In essence, employers are required to make all "circulation paths," which are those areas for getting into and out of cubicles, desks, and other work areas, accessible to disabled employees.

For many employers, an important concern in interpreting the ADA is not necessarily how to respond in connection with applicants or employees who have disabilities that our society currently recognizes as substantially limiting major life activities, such as some impairments to sight, hearing, or access. Instead, the concern may be how to create an integrated response to common conditions that might not readily be considered disabilities but that might qualify as such under some circumstances, including obesity, substance use and abuse, allergies, pregnancy and postpartum complications, gender dysphoria, and the need for a service animal.

Obesity

Scenario

The global economic impact of obesity is an estimated $2 trillion a year, or 2.8 percent of the global gross domestic product (GDP), due to increased medical costs, absenteeism, and reduced productivity.[167] Obesity may also be the source of unlawful discrimination on the basis of disability, although the circumstances under which obesity is considered a disability have caused confusion for employers and courts and are an evolving area of case law under the ADAAA.

Prior to the 2008 amendments to the ADA, obesity generally was not recognized as a disability. The EEOC guidelines at the time stated that, "except in rare circumstances, obesity is not considered a disabling impairment." Most courts held that unless the employee could prove that his or her obesity was caused by some underlying physiological condition such as diabetes or a hormonal imbalance, obesity did not qualify as a disability and could not form the basis of an ADA claim.[168]

The ADAAA signaled Congressional intent that disability be construed broadly, making it easier for plaintiffs to prove they have covered disabilities, and obesity-related disabilities are no exception. Recent case law, however, reveals the difficulty of employees in filing claims for discrimination based on obesity.

In a 2019 case, *Shell v Burlington Northern Santa Fe Railway Co.,*[169] the Seventh Circuit Court of Appeals found that the ADA does not apply to a situation where an employer refuses to hire an applicant that it fears will develop an impairment. Specifically, the employer did not hire someone with a BMI of 40 or greater because the employer believed that someone with class III obesity could unexpectedly experience a debilitating health episode and lose consciousness while operating dangerous equipment. The employer was granted summary judgment because the applicant failed to establish that the employer regarded him as having a disability or that he was otherwise disabled. In other words, his obesity was not a disability that qualified him for protection under the ADAAA.

In *Richardson v. Chicago Transit Authority,*[170] the Seventh Circuit similarly ruled on whether an obese employee qualified for protection under the ADA. Mark Richardson began working as a part-time bus driver for the Chicago Transit Authority (CTA) in 1993. From 1999 to 2010, he worked full-time. He weighed 350 pounds in January 2005 and 566 pounds in May 2009. When Richardson attempted to return to work after being out with the flu in 2010, the CTA's third-party medical provider found that the plaintiff "had uncontrolled hypertension and influenza, weighed over 400 pounds," and Richardson was placed on temporary assignment. Later the CTA determined that he could not perform all of the standard operating procedures on the CTA buses because the seats were not designed to accommodate drivers who weighed over 400 pounds. Richardson was eventually fired in 2012 after he was unable to resume his usual duties. The court employed what it considers to be a "natural reading" of the EEOC guidelines and concluded that obesity, even extreme obesity, that is not the result of an underlying physiological disease or disorder does not qualify as an impairment under the ADA. Several other courts, including the Second, Sixth, and Eighth Circuit Courts and many district courts, have made similar rulings, while the Ninth Circuit has sidestepped the question of whether obesity is a disability.[171]

Not all claims have failed, however. In 2011, a Louisiana treatment center agreed to pay $125,000 to settle a lawsuit filed by the EEOC on behalf of a deceased woman who had been fired because of severe obesity. The settlement came after a federal judge in Louisiana denied the defendant's motions for summary judgment that obesity is not an impairment under the ADA. The court held that severe obesity is an impairment within the meaning of the ADA and, moreover, when an employee is severely obese, there is no requirement that the obesity be based on a physiological cause.[172]

Thus, employers who stereotype morbidly or severely obese people and who then base employment decisions on these assumptions may be found liable under the ADA. Furthermore, if an employer merely regards an overweight employee or applicant as morbidly obese, that individual would be protected from disparate treatment based on that perception. Even if a mildly obese person is not considered impaired, related medical conditions may be considered impairments within the meaning of the ADA.

Additionally, Title VII protections against discrimination based on gender may be relevant where an overweight woman is subject to different treatment or standards than an overweight man.

Substance Use and Abuse
Alcohol
It is evident that employers must establish cohesive guidelines to ensure their compliance in the area of disability discrimination. Alcoholism is a covered disability under both the ADA and the Rehabilitation Act, and guidelines were established by the courts several decades ago in connection with claims by alcoholic employees who alleged a disability due to their alcoholism, including a five-step directive designed to assist employers in responding to alcoholic employees (see Exhibit 13.15).[173]

Exhibit 13.15 *Five-Step Directive to Respond to Alcoholic Employees*

1. If the employer suspects alcoholism, she must inform the employee of counseling services.

2. If the alcoholism continues, the employer must give the employee a "firm choice" between treatment and discipline.

3. The employer must then provide the employee the opportunity to complete outpatient treatment.

4. If this is unsuccessful, the employer must provide the employee the opportunity to complete an inpatient treatment.

5. Only if the first four steps fail can the employer legally discharge the employee. Employers are advised to follow similar directives in connection with the hiring, retention, and termination of employees with other addiction disabilities.

It is important to separate *alcoholism* from *alcohol-related misconduct,* which is not universally protected under the statutes by the courts. Employers have every right to establish workplace policies and to discipline workers who fail to meet those standards. If an alcoholic employee cannot meet the basic requirements of the job, the employer has the right to fire them, although drawing the line between alcoholism and alcohol-related misconduct is not always easy. Consider, for instance, the employee who oversleeps and misses work because of her or his alcoholism. Some courts would consider an adverse action because of this "alcoholic-related misconduct," *not "because of the disability."*[174] Other courts find to the contrary and instead hold that firing the employee for being late, for instance, would be *"because of the disability."*[175] In that case, the employer could not fire the employee for being late because that would be the same as firing the employee for being an alcoholic. This conflict between the circuits has not yet been resolved.

On the other hand, in *Kennedy v. Glen Mills School,*[176] a federal court in Pennsylvania dismissed a claim of disability discrimination on the basis of alcoholism by an employee who had an accident while driving his work car under the influence of alcohol. The employee was terminated in accordance with the school's zero tolerance policy on drugs and alcohol. The employee brought suit for disability discrimination and failure to accommodate his alleged alcoholism, and the court dismissed his claims, specifically holding that he had failed to prove that alcoholism substantially limited one or more major life activity. Furthermore, there was no record that he was disabled, and the school did not regard him as such, having never been informed of his alcoholism. Thus, his claim did not constitute an ADA disability, nor did it trigger a duty for the school to engage in an interactive process to identify potential accommodations.

Conditions that occur as a result of the alcoholism may also qualify for ADA protection. Thus, someone who has cirrhosis of the liver because of the alcoholism may qualify for protection. Also, remember that while alcoholism is covered by the ADA, some state disability statutes explicitly exempt alcoholism from legal protection.[177]

Smoking

The issue of smoking in the workplace also presents some questions. Many, if not all, states have enacted legislation banning smoking in the workplace environment. An employer is forced to balance the rights of smokers without violating the laws intended to protect nonsmokers. But is nicotine dependence or withdrawal a disability? Is the addiction a substantial impairment of major life activities? Does smoking create a physiological or a psychological dependency requiring the employer to provide a reasonable accommodation for smokers? The answer has not been fully decided, but one is hard-pressed to imagine a case with a strong employee argument. Congress remains silent on this issue, and the Supreme Court has not had a case on point.

Drug Use and Abuse

Drug addiction is also an issue that employers are now facing with regard to disabilities, but it is treated somewhat differently than alcoholism. Current drug users are not protected by the ADA, but *former* illicit drug users as well as those who use prescription medications unlawfully, including individuals who either are participating in or have completed a drug rehabilitation program, are protected by the ADA.

Courts have recognized that, under certain circumstances, drug addiction *may* constitute a disability under the ADA and the federal Rehabilitation Act. As with all disabilities, the former drug users must demonstrate that they have a disability; that is, they must show that the past drug use limits a major life activity, and it must have been sufficiently severe to be considered a drug addiction. An employee who is a recovering addict no longer using drugs may use the past drug addiction to argue that he or she has a disability based on a record of such an impairment or perception of impairment. This perception may be due to stereotypes about past drug use that lead someone to believe that someone is a current user (stereotypes such as "once a user, always a user") or erroneous beliefs based on false positives during employer drug testing. Recovered drug abusers can also be expected to meet performance and behavior standards.

The best an employer can do at this time is to amend its drug and alcohol policies to require disclosure of drugs that are being used in addition to treatment. An employee could be required to disclose use in the same way it requires disclosure of the side effects of prescription drugs. Perhaps the worker also could be moved to a position that is less sensitive to its effects. Finally, the employer could grant the worker a leave during the time she or he requires use of the drug. If an employer suspects impairment that could make the worker unqualified for the position, the worker can be tested based on that reasonable suspicion (such as slurred speech, attitude, involvement in an accident, or odor).

It is also important to recall the Supreme Court's decision in *Raytheon Co. v. Hernandez,* discussed earlier in this chapter, which held that disparate impact claims are available to workers who test positive for illegal drug use. In that case, the worker was fired after a positive result on a drug test. The employer had a no-rehire policy, but the Court left open the possibility that individuals with disabilities may be entitled to differential treatment under facially neutral policies. Accordingly, recovering drug addicts and/or recovering alcoholics may claim that they should not be covered by such a policy. Based on *Raytheon,* policies may be suspect if they automatically bar reemployment after a positive drug or alcohol test or for other possible consequences of a covered disability or if they change the conditions of work for those who have tested positive or exhibit these effects. On the other hand, as long as the employer can justify decisions based on business necessity or job-relatedness, its decisions are more likely to be defensible.

Medical Marijuana

As of 2019, marijuana for medicinal purposes is legal in 33 states and Washington, D.C.[178] Under federal law, however, marijuana is still considered to be an illegal drug, and the law provides no exceptions for medical use. As a result, medical marijuana is *not* protected under the ADA. In *James v. City of Costa Mesa,*[179] the Ninth Circuit agreed that the ADA defined "illegal drug use" by reference to federal, not state, law. Thus, because the doctor-recommended marijuana use in that case was permitted by state law but was simultaneously prohibited by federal law, it was an illegal use of drugs for purposes of the ADA. Therefore, the plaintiffs' federally prescribed medical marijuana use is not protected under the ADA.

In addition to permitting medical marijuana, 11 states and Washington, D.C., also permit recreational marijuana use.[180] In June 2019, Congress voted overwhelmingly to prevent the Department of Justice from interfering with state marijuana laws, including those allowing recreational use, cultivation, and sales.[181] As more and more states vote to legalize marijuana use, it will be important to stay informed on this topic.

Allergies

Those with allergies can be disabled under the ADA if their allergy interferes with a major life activity. An allergy can also include sensitivity to certain chemicals, such as perfumes. The difficulty in these cases usually involves a question of how far employers must go to accommodate the allergy.

In one case, a Michigan employee brought an ADA action on the ground that she experienced a severe reaction to a co-employee's perfume, to a plug-in air freshener, and to potpourri in the bathroom.[182] The court agreed with the employee that her allergies interfered with a major life activity, namely, breathing. The court also said, however, that a scent-free workplace is an undue burden on the employer, but it noted that some other accommodation, such as a transfer to a different part of the building, might be reasonable. The case was ultimately settled without a trial in 2010, with the employer paying the employee a lump sum.

A similar case in Pennsylvania had a different result.[183] After an employee experienced severe allergic reactions to coworkers' perfume, the employer instituted a no-perfume policy. The employer also moved her desk, changed air filters, and gave her a desktop air filter and fan. The employer eventually fired her for poor performance because her attendance was erratic. Her ADA suit against the employer was dismissed on the ground that the employer met its accommodation obligations under the ADA. This case serves as another reminder for employers of the importance of having in place solid workplace rules that can be applied evenly to all employees.

Pregnancy and Postpartum

Under the ADA, pregnancy itself is not considered a disability. However, impairments that result from pregnancy, such as gestational diabetes, preeclampsia, or postpartum depression, may be considered disabilities under the ADA, even if they are temporary. An employer will, thus, need to provide reasonable accommodation. Accommodations may include additional leave; redistributing marginal or nonessential functions, such as occasional lifting; allowing an employee to work remotely; and purchasing or modifying equipment, such as a stool, to allow an employee to sit, even if the position usually requires that one stand.[184]

Additionally, the Pregnancy Discrimination Act (PDA),[185] an amendment to Title VII of the Civil Rights Act, requires that "women affected by pregnancy, childbirth, or related medical conditions shall be treated the same for all employment-related purposes . . . as other persons not so affected but similar in their ability or inability to work."[186] The PDA protects workers based on current, past, and potential pregnancy.[187] An employer may not discriminate because of a medical condition related to pregnancy.[188] For example, lactation is considered a pregnancy related medical condition and, therefore, an employer may not discriminate against an employee because of her or his breastfeeding schedule.[189] While an employer must provide reasonable accommodation, which may include additional time off, the employer may not compel an employee to take leave so long as the employee is able to perform her job.[190]

Postpartum depression is also protected under the ADA. In a 2018 case, *Hostettler v. College of Wooster*,[191] the Sixth Circuit Court of Appeals ruled that full-time, in-office attendance is not a per se "essential function" for the purposes of the ADA. Heidi Hostettler was hired as a HR generalist at the College of Wooster. When she was hired, Hostettler was pregnant and was promised 12 weeks of unpaid maternity leave. When it was time for Hostettler to return from her leave, she was diagnosed with "severe postpartum depression and separation anxiety," and she was cleared by her doctor only to return at a reduced schedule for the "foreseeable future." She negotiated to work five half-days per week. Though Hostettler "never failed to perform any responsibility or finish any assignment in a timely manner" and had been given a performance evaluation that "contained no negative feedback," she was fired when her supervisor concluded that the office was short-handed without her physical presence. The court rejected this argument, ruling that though her boss may have preferred that Hostettler be in the office 40 hours per week, "the ADA requires that employers reasonably accommodate employees with disabilities, including allowing modified work schedules."

Postpartum depression

"Postpartum" means the time after childbirth. Postpartum depression is a serious mental illness that involves the brain and affects your behavior and physical health. When a person who has recently given birth feels sad, hopeless, or empty for longer than two weeks, she or he may have postpartum depression. These feelings can interfere with day-to-day life and may leave the new parent feeling unconnected from the baby. These feelings may be mild to severe.

Gender Dysphoria

gender dysphoria
A condition in which a person experiences discomfort or distress because of a mismatch between their biological sex and gender identity. Sometimes known as gender incongruence.

Another area of growing concern for employers is the accommodation of people with **gender dysphoria** or other gender identity disorders. In a 2017 case, *Blatt v. Cabela's Retail, Inc.,*[192] a court in the Eastern District of Pennsylvania ruled that the ADA may cover gender dysphoria and other conditions related to gender identity disorder. The case was filed by a transgender woman, Kate Lynn Blatt, against her former employer, claiming that she had suffered disability discrimination and retaliation because of her gender dysphoria. The ADA explicitly excludes "gender identity disorders not resulting from physical impairments, or other sexual behavior disorders" from the ADA's definition of "disability."[193] However, Blatt argued that the ADA's exclusion of gender identity disorders violated her equal protection rights under the Constitution. In its ruling, the court relied on the legal "constitutional-avoidance canon," which requires the law to be interpreted in a way that avoids constitutional challenges. Thus, the court allowed the plaintiff to proceed with her discrimination claim to avoid constitutional questions, thereby paving the way for gender dysphoria to be protected under the ADA.[194]

Yet, in 2018, the district court in the Southern District of Ohio rejected the interpretation in *Blatt,* writing that "this court can find no support, textual or otherwise, for the *Blatt* court's interpretation." According to this court, "the exclusion plainly applies to all 'gender identity disorders not resulting from physical impairments,' without any regard to whether the gender identity disorder is disabling."[195] Similarly, in 2019, the Northern District of Alabama granted an employer's motion to dismiss ADA claims on the grounds that the employee's gender dysphoria is not protected by the ADA. According to that court, though the ADA does not explicitly list gender dysphoria in its exceptions, the statue excludes "gender identity disorders," which is synonymous with gender dysphoria.[196] At this time, no circuit courts have taken up this issue.

Service Animals

Scenario

Many people with disabilities use service animals to facilitate their participation in everyday life. For example, dogs can be used to provide stability for a person who has difficulty walking or to alert a person with hearing loss when someone is approaching from behind. Under the ADA, a service animal is defined as a "dog that has been individually trained to do work or perform tasks for an individual with a disability."[197] The animal must be trained to perform task(s) that directly assist the person with their disability.[198] Under the ADA, employers may not ban service animals in the workplace. If an employee brings a service dog, staff is permitted to ask only two questions about the animal: (1) Is the service animal required because of a disability? and 2) What work or task has the dog been trained to perform? Employers are not permitted to request for documentation, require that the dog demonstrate its task, or inquire further about the nature of the employee's disability.[199] Emotional support, therapy, comfort, or companion animals are not considered service animals.[200] Moreover, the ADA does not require that employers take action that would "fundamentally alter" the business to accommodate a service animal.[201]

- Never assume the physical or intellectual limitations of a worker or applicant with a disability. If you assume that someone cannot perform certain functions, you may be creating limitations where none actually exist.

- Review all job descriptions to make sure that the job requirements are actually required to complete the job; remove extraneous requirements that are not truly essential to job performance.

- Ensure that all decision makers understand what constitutes notice of a request for accommodation and what rights are triggered by that request. In some cases, offhand comments such as "I'm having a hard time pushing this cart" can constitute notice that an accommodation is needed.

- Be sure to explore all possible reasonable accommodations for otherwise qualified applicants or employees with a disability. Failure to do so might result not only in legal liability but also in costs connected with identifying and training alternative candidates. Often, a small accommodation will allow you to retain qualified and experienced individuals with disabilities.

- Engage in frank and open discussions. Determining the appropriate reasonable accommodation is a collaborative process. Candid communication is the key ingredient to success in handling ADA matters.

- Consult with the employee. Ask questions. Ask the employee to offer suggestions. Asking the employee to provide additional information will lead you to more opportunities for the most effective way to identify and to handle the accommodation.

- Document that dialogue. These are negotiations. They may or may not lead to litigation. Do not let the employee say that you remained silent once the employee asked for an accommodation if you did not. Confirm in writing your efforts to accommodate. This documentation is one of the best defenses against a possible failure in memory.

- Be proactive. Reasonable accommodation obligations require action and effort on the employer's part. Flexibility is critical to management's efforts.

- Negotiate. Make counterproposals. Be sure they are fair and reasonable. Remember, an employer is not required to provide the best accommodation, only a reasonable accommodation.

- Be clear on the rules for when medical examinations can be required of a disabled person. Pre-hiring examinations are never allowed. Post-hiring examinations are allowed, but only if all other employees are required to submit to the examination. Employees with disabilities can be subject to an individual, post-hiring examination in limited situations, such as where it relates to job performance or safety issues.

- Review all application materials to ensure that there are no inappropriate questions concerning irrelevant abilities.

- Since "disability" under the statutes includes someone who is perceived as being disabled, as well as those associated with individuals who are disabled, conduct training sessions with all management to educate them regarding what is actually a disability and what is not. All decision makers should understand that they can violate the ADA, even if the employee has no disability, if they *treat the employee as disabled.*

- You are not required to accommodate all disabilities. Consider all costs involved with providing accommodation and consider whether it would be an undue burden under the courts' precedents.
- If an employee is on leave, you may request documentation or a medical examination prior to her or his return to work. However, the request should only be made if you have a reasonable belief that the employee may be unable to perform her or his job or might pose a direct threat to herself, himself, or others. In addition, you may only ask about the employee's present ability to perform the work and to do so safely.
- Post information on the Genetic Information Nondiscrimination Act, which includes significant changes such as no longer asking employees about family medical history, including when they make FMLA leave requests or engage in a workplace wellness program. The EEOC publishes "EEO Is the Law" posters, which include up-to-date information on GINA, the ADAAA, and many federal laws in English, Arabic, Chinese, and Spanish.[202]
- All Equal Employment Opportunity statements and manuals should be amended to include references to genetic discrimination and the ADAAA.

Chapter Summary

- Statutory protections against disability discrimination in employment strike a balance between the right of individuals with disabilities to have job opportunities and the need of employers to have an "able" workforce. This balance is achieved by several measures. First, the determination of whether an individual has a disability is made on a case-by-case basis, examining whether the impairment substantially limits one or more of the individual's major life activities. "Major life activities" are defined as activities that have central importance to daily life. The definition of "substantially limited" has significantly been broadened under the ADAAA. An impairment need not "prevent, or severely or significantly restrict," a major life activity to consider that activity "substantially limited"; nor must it be present for a specified duration. Further, an employer may not consider "mitigating measures," other than ordinary eyeglasses or contact lenses, when determining the limitation.
- Not every impairment will lead to protection as a disability. However, those who have a record of such an impairment, who have been perceived as having such an impairment, and who are associated with individuals who are disabled also are protected. This prevents employers from defending discriminatory actions on the basis that the individual is not covered under the statute.
- The balance between employees' rights and employers' needs is further maintained by the concept of reasonable accommodation. An applicant or employee with a disability who meets the basic job requirements regarding education, experience, skills, and abilities may need accommodation to perform the essential job functions. The applicant or employee is required to notify the employer of the need for accommodation. If the accommodation places an undue hardship on the employer, the employer is not required to provide it. This determination is

fact intensive and case specific. Further, if the applicant or employee with a disability poses a direct threat to the health and safety of others that cannot be reasonably accommodated, then that individual is not "qualified" for the position.

• Employers are well advised to ensure that they fairly and equitably analyze these issues in addressing all disability-related situations arising in the workplace.

Chapter-End Questions

1. Eugene Stansberry managed Air Wisconsin's operations at the Kalamazoo Airport from 1999 until 2007, when he was terminated. His wife suffered from a rare autoimmune disorder throughout his employment period. Between February and May 2007, Stansberry failed to notify corporate headquarters about six security violations received by his subordinates and exchanged emails with his supervisor about his poor performance. Also during this same period, his wife's health deteriorated, and Air Wisconsin's health plan administrator informed him that it would no longer cover a treatment program that would improve her condition. In July 2007, Air Wisconsin fired Stansberry for poor performance, including his failure to stay within budget, failure to report security violations, and improper supervision of employees. Does Stansberry have a case under the ADA? [*Stansberry v. Air Wisconsin Airlines Corp.,* 651 F.3d 482 (6th Cir. 2011).]

2. Terri Kallail, a Type I insulin-dependent diabetic, worked at an Alliant Energy distribution dispatch center, where she monitored the distribution of electricity, gas, and steam throughout a service area and handled outages and other emergency situations. Coordinators worked in teams of two on nine-week schedules that rotate between 8- and 12-hour shifts and between day and night shifts, a requirement included in her job description. In 2004, she experienced increased difficulties managing her diabetes while working the rotating shifts, and her physician recommended that she work only day shifts. Alliant denied the request, stating that rotating shifts are an essential function of the coordinator position, and offered to permit her to apply for one of three vacant, noncoordinator positions with a straight day shift. Kallail initially considered accepting this offer but then rejected it after discovering that one position required walking, which she was unable to do; one paid less than her current position; and one would have required her to relocate or to commute a significant distance to work. After taking FMLA leave for surgery in 2005, Kallail was given a temporary light duty assignment. When this expired, Kallail's doctor again recommended that she be permanently limited to day shifts. Although Alliant offered her a number of other day shift positions, the jobs offered lower pay or required qualifications for which Kallail was not suited, and she refused them. Instead, she began to receive disability benefits and subsequently filed a complaint with the EEOC and then a lawsuit. Evaluate Alliant's liability under the ADA with regard to three factors: essential functions, reasonable accommodations, and the duty to engage in an interactive process. [*Kallail v. Alliant Energy Corp. Servs., Inc.,* 691 F.3d 925 (8th Cir. 2012).]

3. David Neely long suffered from sleeping problems. He claimed that he had sleep apnea and would sometimes get only two or three hours of restful sleep per night. Consequently, he experienced fatigue and would often fall into "micro sleeps" during the day. Though Neely saw a couple doctors about his condition, he never followed up with testing they ordered. Nearly two years after visiting the doctors, Neely was hired by Benchmark as a support specialist and was quickly promoted to support administrator. Shortly after his promotion, Benchmark noted that Neely was struggling with the technical aspects of his

job, general job performance, and attitude. Benchmark complained that Neely actively avoided new IT help tickets (a key aspect of his job), passed work to his supervisors before attempting to correct end user problems, and had work order response times that were nearly double those of his office peers. Benchmark also noted that Neely was "almost daily falling asleep at work." Benchmark demoted Neely. The week following the demotion, Neely's coworkers described his attitude as poor with regard to his supervisors and other staff members. Shortly thereafter, Neely was terminated. Neely sued Benchmark for discrimination under the ADA for failure to accommodate his disability. Does Neely have a case? [*Neely v. Benchmark Family Servs.,* 640 Fed. Appx. 429, 6th Cir. 2016.]

4. Marcus is the HR manager for United Airlines, an Illinois-based company. One of his employees has recently become disabled and is unable to fulfill the essential functions of his current position, even with accommodations. The employee has applied for another position for which he is qualified and where his disability can be accommodated. However, Marcus has also received an application from an external candidate with more experience in an equivalent position at a different company. Whom should Marcus hire? Might his decision be different if his company were based in Minnesota? [*EEOC v. United Airlines, Inc.,* 693 F.3d 760 (7th Cir. 2012).]

5. In 2007, Melissa Pennington had worked as a food truck operator at Churchill Downs for 10 years, employed by Wagner's Pharmacy, Inc. Pennington weighed 425 pounds and was 5 feet 4 inches tall. She suffered from diabetes, which caused pronounced dark circles under her eyes. On one of her off-duty days, she stopped by the office of her manager, Brenda Smyth, to pick up a paycheck. Pennington admits that she was between residences and was not looking her best but claims that her appearance on that day was not representative of how she looked at work. Soon afterward, Smyth instructed Pennington's supervisor, Martha Parrish, to terminate her employment due to her "personal appearance." Although Parrish did not specify to Pennington whether the termination was based upon her disheveled appearance on the off-duty visit or her morbid obesity, Parrish told two workers that she had been instructed by Smyth to fire Pennington because she was "dirty and overweight." Pennington filed suit, alleging that Wagner's had unlawfully discriminated against her due to her disability of morbid obesity. Wagner contested the allegation and won summary judgment. Pennington appealed the judgment, and the Kentucky state appellate court was faced with the task of determining whether morbid obesity constitutes a disability under the ADA. Does Pennington have a case? [*Pennington v. Wagner's Pharmacy, Inc.* (KY Ct. of App., July 12, 2013).]

6. An employee who suffers from fibromyalgia and degenerative disc and cervical disease worked as a Pulaski County juvenile detention officer from November 24, 2001, to May 21, 2013. Beginning in 2008, the employee obtained an annual Family Medical Leave Act certification from her doctor, allowing her to exercise unpaid intermittent leave. By February 2013, her conditions had deteriorated to the point that her doctor placed restrictions on her FMLA certification, which included "no sitting, standing, bending, and stooping for extended periods" and no lifting of more than 25 pounds. One of the requirements listed in the job description for the position of juvenile detention officer is the ability to lift and carry up to 40 pounds. The county eventually decided to terminate her employment because she could not meet the job requirement of lifting 40 pounds. In its termination letter, the county told the employee her employment was valuable and encouraged her to reapply if a change in circumstances allowed her to return to work. Does the employee have a claim under the ADA? [*Scruggs v. Pulaski Cty., Ark.,* 817 F.3d 1087, 1091 (8th Cir. 2016).]

7. A Vietnam War veteran diagnosed with post-traumatic stress disorder was employed at the post office. After missing significant time at work for depression related to the PTSD, he requested an accommodation. The post office refused the request on the ground that his condition did not prevent him from engaging in any major life activity as required by the Rehabilitation Act. Has the post office violated the Rehabilitation Act? Is the post office correct in asserting that the depression does not prevent the employee from engaging in any major life activity? [*Zeigler v. Potter,* 555 F. Supp. 2d 126 (D.D.C. 2008), *aff'd,*No. 09-5349, 2010 WL 1632965 (D.C. Cir. Apr. 1, 2010).]

8. Nair Parsons worked as a certified nursing assistant at Life Care Centers of America, a nationwide geriatric care provider. In June 2016, she informed supervisors of her pregnancy and requested light duty for the last part of her pregnancy. She provided a doctor's note supporting her request for a fifteen-pound lifting restriction. Life Care Centers informed her that it only provided light duty to those employees who were injured on the job. Parsons' supervisors denied her request and placed her on involuntary, unpaid leave. They told her when she was ready to return to unrestricted duty, she should reapply for her job. On what grounds would Parsons file a claim? Is the court likely to rule in her favor? Why or why not? [EEOC, *Life Care Centers of America Sued by EEOC For Pregnancy Discrimination* (September 25, 2018), https://www.eeoc.gov/eeoc/newsroom/release/9-25-18f.cfm (accessed January 6, 2020).]

9. In January 2012, Kimberly Lowe began working as a massage therapist at a Massage Envy located in Tampa, Florida. Lowe did not have a disability and was able to perform her job duties in a satisfactory manner. In September 2014, Lowe asked her supervisor for time off so she could visit her sister in Ghana, a country located in West Africa. Her supervisor initially approved the request. Three days before Lowe's scheduled departure, one of Massage Envy's owners informed Lowe that if she went ahead with her travel plans, she would be fired. The owner was concerned that she would contract the Ebola virus and would "bring it home to Tampa and infect everyone." Lowe refused to cancel her trip and was immediately fired. Lowe traveled to Ghana as planned. She did not contract the Ebola virus, as there was no Ebola outbreak in Ghana at the time of her visit. There was an Ebola epidemic is Guinea, Libera, and Sierra Leone, three other West African countries. When she returned to Florida, Lowe was not permitted to return to work or keep her clients. Does Lowe qualify for protection under the ADA? Does Lowe have an association discrimination claim under the ADA? Does it matter that her supervisor had incorrect information about where the Ebola outbreaks were? [*EEOC v. STME, LLC,* 938 F.3d 1305 (11th Cir. 2019).]

10. An employer hired Kristy Sones, a registered nurse, to work as a field nurse in Picayune, Mississippi, in 2006. Field nurses provide home health care to patients, and Sones estimated that she spent "probably a couple hours" traveling to see six to eight patients every day. In March 2009, Sones talked to her supervisor about being promoted to a team leader position, which would be more of a supervisory role, requiring fewer home visits. It was not clear whether this promotion actually went through.

On May 26, 2009, Sones had a grand mal seizure at work. An ambulance took her to a local hospital, and her treating physician released her to return to work two days later. She was restricted from driving for one year. When she returned to work, Sones discussed her medical condition with her supervisors, and they decided that Sones would get rides to work from her coworker and she could have her mother drive her to in-home visits.

Sones's new antiseizure medications left her feeling "very tired" and struggling with memory, so she asked her supervisor for "extra help" with the computer-related requirements of her job, including remembering her passwords and using the scheduling software. Sones testified that her supervisor responded to her request for help by simply walking away. After several weeks, management brought several problems to Sones's attention, including her subpar computer skills, errors she'd made while working with patients in the field, and communication and scheduling problems. Her employer also received a complaint from a patient who requested that Sones not be sent back to her home, so the employer decided to terminate Sones.

According to Sones's testimony, the employer said nothing about Sones's performance problems or driving restriction but rather stated: "We're going [to] have to let you go, because you're a liability to our company." Does Sones have a claim? Did the employer fail to accommodate Sones and discriminate against her on the basis of her disability? Does it matter if she had been promoted to team leader or was still a field nurse? [*E.E.O.C. v. LHC Grp., Inc.,* 773 F.3d 688, 692–93 (5th Cir. 2014).]

11. Melinda Crooke was a line worker for Herbruck Poultry Ranch, an egg farm located in Saranac, Michigan. After her supervisor learned about her disability-related symptoms, she was mocked regularly by her supervisor and coworkers because of those symptoms. Crooke reported the mocking nicknames and physical imitation of her symptoms, but her employer took no action. The harassment by her supervisor worsened, as the supervisor began following Crooke to the bathroom to time her breaks. On April 10, 2015, her supervisor followed her to the bathroom and shouted at her. Crooke reported the incidence to a person in human resources but was advised to return to her shift. Crooke found returning to the work environment to be unbearable, so she quit her job. Has the employer created a hostile work environment? To what extent is the employee required to notify her supervisor of her belief that the work environment is hostile? Even though Crooke quit, can she still file a complaint against her former employer? [EEOC, "Herbruck Poultry Ranch Sued by EEOC for Disability Harassment" (March 4, 2019), https://www.eeoc.gov/eeoc/newsroom/release/3-4-19.cfm (accessed January 6, 2020).]

End Notes

1. Centers for Disease Control and Prevention, "1 in 4 US Adults Live with a Disability," CDC press release (August 16, 2018), https://www.cdc.gov/media/releases/2018/p0816-disability.html (accessed October 9, 2020).

2. Bureau of Labor Statistics, "Persons with a Disability: Labor Force Characteristics Summary," BLS press release (February 26, 2019), http://www.bls.gov/news.release/disabl.nr0.htm (accessed October 9, 2020).

3. Institute on Disability/UCED, "2018 Annual Report on People with Disabilities in America," University of New Hampshire (2019), https://disabilitycompendium.org/sites/default/files/user-uploads/Annual_Report_2018_Accessible_AdobeReader-Friendly.pdf (accessed October 9, 2020).

4. Day, Jennifer Cheeseman, and Danielle Taylor, "Do People with Disabilities Earn Equal Pay?" U.S. Census Bureau (March 21, 2019), https://www.census.gov/library/stories/2019/03/do-people-with-disabilities-earn-equal-pay.html (accessed October 9, 2020).

5. Institute on Disability/UCED, "2018 Annual Report on People with Disabilities in America," University of New Hampshire (2019), https://disabilitycompendium.org/sites/default/files/user-uploads/Annual_Report_2018_Accessible_AdobeReader-Friendly.pdf (accessed October 9, 2020).

6. Social Security Administration, "Annual Statistical Report on the Social Security Disability Insurance Program" (2018), https://www.ssa.gov/policy/docs/statcomps/di_asr/2018/di_asr18.pdf (accessed October 9, 2020).

7. 41 C.F.R. § 60-741.1.

8. Office of Federal Contract Compliance Programs (OFCCP), "New Regulations: Section 503 of the Rehabilitation Act," https://www.dol.gov/ofccp/regs/compliance/section503.htm (accessed October 9, 2020).

9. 41 C.F.R. § 60-741.40.

10. Re-charting the Course: First Report of the Presidential Task Force on Employment of Adults with Disabilities, (November 15, 1998), http://digitalcommons.ilr.cornell.edu/cgi/viewcontent.cgi?artice = 1159&context = key_workplace (accessed October 8, 2020).

11. The task force recommended that President Clinton (1) increase the number of disabled adults working for the federal government, (2) increase the employment options for persons with psychiatric disabilities, and (3) support legislation allowing disabled adults to retain Medicare coverage when they return to work. See "Re-charting the Course: First Report of the Presidential Task Force on Employment of Adults with Disabilities" (November 15, 1998), https://digitalcommons.ilr.cornell.edu/key_workplace/157/ (accessed October 8, 2020).

12. The White House: President George W. Bush, "President's New Freedom Initiative," https://georgewbush-whitehouse.archives.gov/infocus/newfreedom/ (accessed October 8, 2020).

13. Somers, M., "Record Number of People with Disabilities in Federal Workforce," Federal News Radio (October 13, 2015), http://federalnewsradio.com/workforce/2015/10/record-number-people-disabilities-federal-workforce/ (accessed October 9, 2020.).

14. Shelby Hanssen, "Under Trump, Discrimination Complaints and Firing of Disabled Federal Workers Rise," NBC News (August 8, 2019), https://www.nbcnews.com/politics/donald-trump/under-trump-discrimination-complaints-firing-disabled-federal-workers-rise-n1036291 (accessed October 8, 2020.).

15. For example, the U.S. Supreme Court said in 2002 that the definition of disability should "be interpreted strictly to create a demanding standard for qualifying as disabled." *Toyota Motor Mfg. v. Williams,* 534 U.S. 184, 197 (2002).

16. Compare Colker, Ruth, "Winning and Losing under the Americans with Disabilities Act," *Ohio State Law Journal* 62 (2001), pp. 240–41, where an analysis of 720 appellate ADA employment discrimination cases reported that the employer–defendant was the successful party in 93 percent of trial cases and 84 percent of appeals, with the post–ADAAA case law reviewed in O'Brien-Heinzen, Tess, "The ADAAA: Key Changes to Disability Law," *Wisconsin Lawyer* 85, no. 5 (May 2012).

17. On March 25, 2011, the EEOC released final regulations on the ADAAA, "Regulations to Implement the Equal Employment Provisions of the Americans with Disabilities Act, as Amended," 29 CFR Part 1630 (2011), https://www.federalregister.gov/articles/2011/03/25/2011-6056/regulations-to-implement-the-equal-employment-provisions-of-the-americans-with-disabilities-act-as (accessed October 8, 2020).

18. The modifications enacted by the ADAAA were specifically extended to the Rehabilitation Act as well. EEOC, "Questions and Answers on the Final Rule Implementing the ADA Amendments Act of 2008," https://www.eeoc.gov/laws/regulations/ada_qa_final_rule.cfm (accessed October 8, 2020).

19. *Gogos v. AMS Mech. Sys., Inc.,* 737 F.3d 1170, 1172-3 (7th Cir. 2013).

20. Edmonds, Curtis D., "Lowering the Threshold: How Far Has the Americans with Disabilities Act Amendment Act Expanded Access to the Courts in Employment Litigation?" *Journal of Law and Policy* 26, no. 1 (2018).

21. The U.S. Supreme Court recognized that both types apply to ADA cases in *Raytheon v. Hernandez,* 540 U.S. 44 (2003).

22. *United States v. Nobel Learning Communities, Inc.,* 676 F. Supp. 2d 379 (E.D. Pa. 2009).

23. See *City of Moorpark v. Ventura County Superior Court,* 959 P.2d 752 (Cal. 1998), and *Dillard's v. Beckwith,* 989 P.2d 882 (Nev. 1999); see also Caroline Cournoyer, "How States Are Helping People With Disabilities Break Into Government Jobs," Governing (June 7, 2018), https://www.governing.com/topics/workforce/gov-disabled-state-government-workforce.html (accessed October 8, 2020).

24. 42 U.S.C. §§ 12102(1)-(2).

25. 480 U.S. 273 (1987).

26. 480 U.S. 273, 107 S. Ct. 1123 (1987).

27. 42 USC 12102.

28. *Adaire v. City of Muskogee,* 823 F.3d 1297, 1304 (10th Cir. 2016).

29. See, e.g., *Mancini v. City of Providence,* 909 F.3d 32 (1st Cir. 2018); EEOC v. BNSF Ry. Co., 902 F.3d 916 (9th Cir. 2018).

30. EEOC, "SoftPro to Pay $80,000 to Settle EEOC Disability Discrimination Suit," press release (August 16, 2019), https://www.eeoc.gov/eeoc/newsroom/release/8-16-19.cfm (accessed October 8, 2020).

31. 136 F. Supp. 3d 253, 261 (E.D.N.Y. 2015).

32. U.S. Equal Employment Opportunity Commission, "Questions and Answers about the Association Provision of the Americans with Disabilities Act," http://www.eeoc.gov/facts/association_ada.html (accessed October 9, 2020).

33. Ibid.

34. *Toyota Motor Mfg. v. Williams,* 534 U.S. 184, 198 (2002).

35. ADA Amendments Act §4(a)(2)(A).

36. ADA Amendments Act §4(a)(2)(B).

37. 58 F. Supp. 3d 446, 461 (M.D. Pa. 2014).

38. Id. at 461. See also *Angell v. Fairmount Fire Prot. Dist.,* 907 F. Supp. 2d 1242, 1250 (D. Colo. 2012); *Hoffman v. Carefirst of Fort Wayne, Inc.,* 737 F. Supp. 2d 976, 985–86 (N.D. Ind. 2010); *Chalfont v. U.S. Electrodes,* No. 10-2929, 2010 WL 5341846, at *9 (E.D. Pa. Dec. 28, 2010) (unpublished); and *Norton v. Assisted Living Concepts, Inc.,* 786 F. Supp. 2d 1173 (E.D. Tex. 2011).

39. 740 F.3d 325, 330 (4th Cir. 2014).

40. *Stephens v. Potter,* No. 3:06–CV–1290CFD, 2009 WL 2346771, at *4 (D.Conn. July 29, 2009) (holding that a reasonable juror could find that plaintiff's migraine condition constituted physical impairment that substantially limited major life activity of working).

41. 455 F. App'x 827 (10th Cir. 2011).

42. *Gaube v. Day Kimball Hosp.,* No. 3:13-CV-01845 VAB, 2015 WL 1347000, at *6 (D. Conn. Mar. 24, 2015); *Kinney v. Century Servs . Corp. II,* 2011 U.S. Dist. (S.D. Ind. Aug. 9, 2011); and *Holland v. Shinseki,* No. 3:10-CV-0908-B, 2012 U.S. Dist. (N.D. Tex. Jan. 18, 2012).

43. *Jacobs v. York Union Rescue Mission, Inc.,* No. 1:12-CV-0288, 2014 WL 6982618, at *10 (M.D. Pa. Dec. 10, 2014); and *Gibbs v. ADS Alliance Data Sys. Inc.,* U.S. Dist. (D. Kan. July 28, 2011).

44. *Lundy v. Phillips Staffing,* No. CIV.A. 7:13-0062-TMC, 2014 WL 811544, at *3 (D.S.C. Mar. 3, 2014); and *Horgan v. Simmons,* 704 F. Supp. 2d 814 (N.D. Ill. 2010).

45. *Myles v. University of Penn. Health Sys.,* No. 10-4118 (E.D. Penn. Dec. 12, 2011).

46. *Garcia-Hicks v. Vocational Rehab. Admin.,* 148 F. Supp. 3d 157 (D.P.R. 2015).

47. 2011 U.S. Dist. LEXIS 57537, 2011 WL 2119248 (W.D. Ky. 2011).

48. *Soileau v. Guilford of Maine, Inc.,* 105 F.3d 12, 15 (1st Cir. 1997).

49. *Weaving v. City of Hillsboro,* 763 F.3d 1106, 1112 (9th Cir. 2014).

50. See, e.g., *Bodenstab v. Cty. of Cook,* 569 F.3d 651, 655 (7th Cir. 2009); *Heisler v. Metro. Council,* 339 F.3d 622, 628 (8th Cir. 2003); and *Steele v. Thiokol Corp.,* 241 F.3d 1248, 1255 (10th Cir. 2001).

51. 534 U.S. 184, 198 (2002).

52. U.S. Equal Employment Opportunity Commission. ADA Amendments act of 2008 (PL 110-325 (S 3406).

53. ADA Amendments Act of 2008, sec. 2(b)(5).

54. 527 U.S. 471 (1999).

55. No.1:05cv794 (S.D. Ohio, June 20, 2007).

56. 455 F. App'x 827 (10th Cir. 2011).

57. *Allen v. SouthCrest Hosp.,* 455 F. App'x 827 (10th Cir. 2011).

58. *W. v. J.O. Stevenson, Inc.,* No. 7:15-CV-87-FL, 2016 WL 740431, at *13 (E.D.N.C. Feb. 24, 2016).

59. *Hennagir v. Utah Dep't of Corr.,* 587 F.3d 1255, 1262 (10th Cir. 2009).

60. *Hawkins v. Schwan's Home Serv., Inc.,* NO. CIV-12-0084-HE (W.D. Okla. May 28, 2013)

61. 524 U.S. 624 (1998).

62. 704 F. Supp. 2d 814 (N.D. Ill. 2010).

63. Department of Justice: Civil Rights Division, "Questions and Answers: The Americans with Disabilities Act and Persons with HIV/AIDS" (June 2012), https://www.ada.gov/hiv/ada_q&a_aids.pdf (accessed September 11, 2016).

64. Centers for Disease Control and Prevention, "U.S. Statistics" (last updated March 13, 2019), https://www.hiv.gov/hiv-basics/overview/data-and-trends/statistics (accessed December 17, 2019).

65. U.S. Equal Employment Opportunities Commission, "Suncup/Gregory Packaging to Pay $125,000 to Settle EEOC Disability Discrimination Lawsuit" (March 13, 2015), https://www.eeoc.gov/eeoc/newsroom/release/3-13-15.cfm (accessed November 2, 2020).

66. 137 F.3d 398 (6th Cir. 1998).

67. U.S. Equal Employment Opportunity Commission, "Christian Care Center of Johnson City to Pay $90,000 to Settle EEOC Disability Discrimination Suit," EEOC press release (May 9, 2014), https://www.eeoc.gov/eeoc/newsroom/release/5-9-14.cfm (accessed October 8, 2020).

68. EEOC, "What you should know about HIV/AIDS & Employment Discrimination," https://www1.eeoc.gov//eeoc/newsroom/wysk/hiv_aids_discrimination.cfm?renderforprint = 1 (accessed October 8, 2020).

69. 536 U.S. 73 (2002).

70. *Chevron USA v. Echazabal,* 226 F.3d 1063 (9th Cir. 2000).

71. 703 F.3d 918 (6th Cir. 2013).

72. Koeninger, Kevin, "County May Be Liable for Blocking Deaf Lifeguard," Courthouse News Service (January 18, 2013), http://www.courthousenews.com/county-may-be-liable-for-blocking-deaf-lifeguard/ (accessed October 8, 2020).

73. *Kees v. Wallenstein,* 161 F.3d 1196 (9th Cir. 1998).

74. 823 F.3d 1297 (10th Cir. 2016).

75. *Id.* at 1307 (citing 29 C.F.R. § 1630.2(n)(3)).

76. See Wich, Scott M., "Excessive Absenteeism Unprotected under FMLA and ADA," *SHRM* (October 9, 2018), https://www.shrm.org/resourcesandtools/legal-and-compliance/ employment-law/pages/court-report-excessive-absenteeism-unprotected.aspx (accessed October 8, 2020).

77. 782 F.3d 753 (6th Cir. 2015).

78. 430 F. Supp. 75 (M.D. Fla. 1977). See also *Olsen v. Capital Region Med. Ctr.,* 713 F.3d 1149 (8th Cir. 2013); *Ramos-Echevarria v. Pichis, Inc.,* 698 F. Supp. 2d 262 (D.P.R. 2010); and *Garavito v. City of Tampa,* 640 F. Supp. 2d 1374 (M.D. Fla. 2009).

79. Adapted from a successful accommodation described in Job Accommodation Network, "Workplace Accommodations: Low Cost, High Impact" (October 16, 2019), https://askjan.org/ publications/Topic-Downloads.cfm?pubid = 962628 (accessed October 8, 2020).

80. Adapted from a successful accommodation described in Job Accommodation Network, "Workplace Accommodations: Low Cost, High Impact" (October 16, 2019), https://askjan.org/publications/Topic-Downloads.cfm?pubid = 962628 (accessed December 17, 2019).

81. 855 F.3d 818 (7th Cir. 2017).

82. *Huber v. Wal-Mart Stores, Inc.,* 486 F.3d 480 (8th Cir. 2006).

83. *E.E.O.C. v. St. Joseph's Hospital, Inc.,* 842 F.3d 1333, 1346 (11th Cir. 2016).

84. *Arthur v. Am. Showa, Inc.,* 625 F. App'x 704, 711 (6th Cir. 2015).

85. 33 F. Supp. 2d 133 (N.D. N.Y. 1999), *vac'd on other grounds,* 205 F.3d 77 (2d Cir. 2000).

86. *Kilcullen v. New York State Department of Transportation*, 33 F. Supp. 2d 133 (N.D. N.Y. 1999), vac'd on other grounds, 205 F.3d 77 (2d Cir. 2000).

87. 42 U.S.C. §12111(10)(B).

88. 29 C.F.R. §1630.2(p)(2).

89. 432 U.S. 63 (1977).

90. *Trans World Airlines, Inc. v. Hardison,* 432 U.S. 63, 65 (1977).

91. *EEOC v. Convergys Customer Management Group, Inc.,* 2007 U.S. App. LEXIS 16019 (8th Cir. 2007).

92. See, e.g., id.; *Holly v. Clairson Indus., L.L.C.,* 492 F.3d 1247 (11th Cir. 2007).

93. (1990) "The Code of Federal Regulations of the United States of America," U.S. Government Printing Office.

94. See Ben Casselman, "In a Tight Labor Market, a Disability May Not Be a Barrier," *The New York Times* (September 5, 2019), https://www.nytimes.com/2019/09/05/business/ economy/recruiting-labor-force.html (accessed October 9, 2020).

95. EEOC, "EEOC Enforcement Guidance on the Application of the ADA to Contingent Workers Placed by Temporary Agencies and Other Staffing Firms" (December 22, 2010), https://www.eeoc.gov/policy/docs/guidance-contingent.html (accessed December 19, 2019).

96. IRS, "About Form 8826, Disabled Access Credit" (December 10, 2019), https://www. irs.gov/forms-pubs/about-form-8826 (accessed December 19, 2019).

97. IRS, "Tax Benefits for Businesses Who Have Employees with Disabilities" (May 10, 2019), https://www.irs.gov/businesses/small-businesses-self-employed/tax-benefits-for-businesses-who-have-employees-with-disabilities (accessed October 9, 2020).

98. Ibid.

99. IRS, "Work Opportunity Tax Credit" (July 29, 2019), https://www.irs.gov/businesses/small-businesses-self-employed/work-opportunity-tax-credit (accessed October 9, 2020).

100. 411 U.S. 792 (1973).

101. 826 F.3d 885 (6th Cir. 2016).

102 557 U.S. 167 (2009).

103. 591 F.3d 957 (7th Cir. 2010).

104. 689 F.3d 66 (1st Cir. 2012).

105. 681 F.3d 312 (6th Cir. 2012).

106. See *Silk v. Bd. of Trustees, Moraine Valley Cmty. Coll., Dist. No. 524,* 795 F.3d 698 (7th Cir. 2015).

107. *Figueroa Guzman v. WHM Carib, LLC,* 2016 U.S. Dist. LEXIS 33783, *8-9 (D.P.R. Mar. 14, 2016).

108. *Oehmke v. Medtronic, Inc.,* 844 F.3d 748 (8th Cir. 2016).

109. See, e.g., *Mendoza v. The Roman Catholic Archbishop of Los Angeles,* 824 F.3d 1148 (9th Cir. 2016); and *Anderson v. Consolidation Coal Co.,* 636 F. App'x 175 (4th Cir. 2016).

110. EEOC, "Enforcement Guidance: Reasonable Accommodation and Undue Hardship under the Americans with Disabilities Act" (October 2002), https://www.eeoc.gov/policy/docs/accommodation.html (accessed October 9, 2020).

111. See *McGinnis v. Wonder Chemical Co.,* 5 Am. Disabilities Cas. (BNA) 219 (E.D. Pa. 1995).

112. *E.E.O.C. v. Convergys Customer Mgmt. Grp., Inc.,* 491 F.3d 790 (8th Cir. 2007).

113. *Nebeker v. Nat'l Auto Plaza,* 643 F. App'x 817, 824 (10th Cir. 2016).

114. EEOC, "Enforcement Guidance on Reasonable Accommodation and Undue Hardship under the Americans with Disabilities Act" (October 17, 2002), https://www.eeoc.gov/policy/docs/accommodation.html (accessed December 19, 2019).

115. *Nebeker v. Nat'l Auto Plaza,* 643 F. App'x 817, 824 (10th Cir. 2016).

116. *E.E.O.C. v. Kohl's Dep't Stores, Inc.,* 774 F.3d 127 (1st Cir. 2014).

117. See *Gross v. FBL Fin. Servs., Inc.,* 557 U.S. 167 (2009). For more on the *Gross* decision, see Chapter 12.

118. 544 F.3d 328 (1st Cir. 2008).

119. *Deister v. Auto Club Ins. Ass'n,* 647 F. App'x 652 (6th Cir. 2016).

120. 42 U.S.C. §12111(9).

121. 42 U.S.C. §12113(a): "It may be a defense to a charge of discrimination . . . that an alleged application of qualification standards, tests, or selective criteria that screen out . . . an individual with a disability has been shown to be job-related and consistent with business necessity, and such performance cannot be accomplished by reasonable accommodation."

122. See *Bates v. United Parcel Service,* 511 F.3d 974 (9th Cir. 2007).

123. 42 U.S.C. §121112(a).

124. *Rorrer v. City of Stow,* 743 F.3d 1025, 1041 (6th Cir. 2014).

125. *Kroll v. White Lake Ambulance Auth.,* 763 F.3d 619 (6th Cir. 2014).

126. Ibid.

127. *Atkins v. Salazar,* 677 F.3d 667 (5th Cir. 2011).

128. Ibid.

129. Special Olympics, "What Is Intellectual Disability?," https://www.specialolympics.org/about/intellectual-disabilities/what-is-intellectual-disability (accessed January 25, 2020).

130. National Institute of Mental Health. Transforming the understanding and treatment of mental illnesses, February 2019.

131. EEOC, "Questions & Answers about Person's with Intellectual Disabilities in the Workplace and the American with Disabilities Act (ADA)," https://www.eeoc.gov/laws/types/intellectual_disabilities.cfm (accessed October 9, 2020).

132. Ibid.

133. Feldblum, Chai R., and Victoria A. Lipnic, "Select Task Force on the Study of Harassment in the Workplace," EEOC (June 2016), https://www.eeoc.gov/eeoc/task_force/harassment/report.cfm#_ftnref42 (accessed October 9, 2020).

134. National Institute of Mental Health. Transforming the understanding and treatment of mental illnesses, February 2019.

135. Ibid.

136. Allen Smith, "Accommodations for Mental Health Conditions Require Discretion, Flexibility," *SHRM* (January 6, 2017), https://www.shrm.org/resourcesandtools/legal-and-compliance/employment-law/pages/accommodations-mental-health-conditions.aspx (accessed January 25, 2020).

137. *Soileau v. Guildford of Maine, Inc.,* 105 F.3d 12 (1st Cir. 1997).

138. *McKane v. UBS Financial Services., Inc.,* 363 F. App'x 679 (11th Cir. 2010).

139. *Theilig v. United Tech Corp.,* 415 F. App'x 331 (2d Cir. 2011).

140. *McAlindin v. County of San Diego,* 192 F.3d 1226 (9th Cir. 1999).

141. *Head v. Glacier Northwest, Inc.,* 413 F.3d 1053 (9th Cir. 2005).

142. *Weaving v. City of Hillsboro,* 763 F.3d 1106 (9th. Cir. 2014).

143. OSH Act of 1970.

144. *Ford v. Marion Cty. Sheriff's Office,* 942 F.3d 839 (7th Cir. 2019); *Colon-Fontanez v. Municipality of San Juan,* 660 F.3d 17 (1st Cir. 2011); *Fox v. GMC,* 247 F.3d 169, (4th Cir. 2001).

145. Colon-Fontonez v. Municipality of San Juan, 660 F.3d 17, 44 (1st Cir. 2011).

146. *Vermont Dep't of Pub. Serv. v. United States,* 684 F.3d 149 (D.C. Cir. 2012).

147. *Schwarzkopf v. Brunswick Corp.,* 833 F. Supp. 2d 1106 (D. MN., 2011).

148. *Lowenstein v. Catholic Health E.,* 820 F. Supp. 2d 639 (E.D. Pa. 2011).

149. *EEOC v. Rite Aid Corp.,* 750 F. Supp. 2d 564 (D. Md. 2010).

150. 560 So. 2d 300 (Fla. Dist. Ct. App. 1990).

151. Ramada Inn Surfside v. Swanson, 560 So. 2d 300 (Fla. Dist. Ct. App. 1990).

152. Ibid.

153. Section 12203(a).

154. Section 12203(b).

155. EEOC Compliance Manual. Volume 2, Section 614.

156. See *Teutscher v. Woodson,* 659 F. App'x 930 (9th Cir. 2016); *Kovelesky v. First Data Corp.,* 534 F. App'x 811 (11th Cir. 2013); *Gowski v. Peake,* 682 F.3d 1299 (11th Cir. 2012); and *Kramer v. Banc. of Am. Sec.,* 335 F.3d 961 (7th Cir. 2004).

157. U.S National Library of Medicine, "What is genetic Testing?" (December 10, 2019), https://ghr.nlm.nih.gov/primer/testing/genetictesting (accessed October 9, 2020, 2019).

158. Center for Disease Control and Prevention, "Genomic Testing" (November 18, 2015), http://www.cdc.gov/genomics/gtesting/ (accessed September 20, 2016).

159. Ellis, Ashley, "Genetic Justice," *Texas Tech Law Review* 34 (2003), pp. 1071, 1074.

160. See, e.g., *EEOC v. Burlington Northern Santa Fe Railroad,* Cir. No. 01-4013 MWB (N.D. Iowa Apr. 23, 2001).

161. The EEOC removed the term "deliberate acquisition" from Section 1635.1 and explained that "a covered entity may violate GINA without a specific intent to acquire genetic information," http://www.federalregister.gov/articles/2010/11/09/2010-28011/regulations-under-the-genetic-information-nondiscrimination-act-of-2008#p-20 (accessed October 9, 2020).

162. *ARP v. United States EEOC,* 267 F. Supp. 3d 14 (D.D.C. 2017).

163. United States Department of Labor. Family and Medical Leave Act Advisor.

164. Emergency Family and Medical Leave Expansion Act, Division C of the Families First Coronavirus Response Act, H.R. 6210 (March 18, 2020), https://www.congress.gov/116/bills/hr6201/BILLS-116hr6201enr.pdf (accessed March 19, 2020).

165. U.S. Department of Labor, "Families First Coronavirus Response Act: Questions and Answers" (2020), https://www.dol.gov/agencies/whd/pandemic/ffcra-questions (accessed March 31, 2020); U.S. Department of Labor, "Families First Coronavirus Response Act: Employer Paid Leave Requirements" (2020), https://www.dol.gov/agencies/whd/pandemic/ffcra-employer-paid-leave (accessed March 31, 2020).

166. 92 F. Supp. 2d 424 (M.D. Pa. 2000).

167. Dobbs, R., C.Sawers, F. Thompson, J. Manyika, J. R. Woetzel, P. Child, S. McKenna, and A. Spatharou, *Overcoming Obesity: An Initial Economic Analysis.* Jakarta, Indonesia: McKinsey Global Institute, 2014.

168. See, e.g., *EEOC v. Watkins Motor Lines, Inc.,* 463 F.3d 436 (6th Cir. 2006); *Viscik v. Fowler Equipment Co., Inc.,* 800 A.2d 826, 173 N.J. 14 (2002).

169. *Shell v. Burlington Northern Santa Fe Ry.,* 941 F.3d 331 (7th Cir. 2019).

170. *Richardson v. Chicago Transit Authority,* No. 18-2199 (7th Cir. 2019).

171. See, e.g., *Morriss v. BNSF Ry. Co.,* 817 F.3d 1104 (8th Cir. 2016); *Valtierra v. Medtronic Inc.,* 934 F.3d 1089 (9th Cir. 2019).

172. *EEOC v. Resources for Human Development, Inc.,* F. Supp. 2d, 2011 WL 6091560 (E.D. La. Dec. 2011).

173. *Rodgers v. Lehman,* 869 F.2d 253 (4th Cir. 1989).

174. *Vandenbroek v. PSEG Power, CT LLC,* 356 F. App'x 457 (2d Cir. 2009).

175. *Teahan v. Metro-N. Commuter R.R.,* 951 F.2d 511, 513 (2d Cir. 1991).

176. *Kennedy v. Glen Mills School,* No. 10-7450 (November 15, 2011, Ed. PA).

177. See, for example, Texas, Georgia, Tennessee, and others. Texas does extend coverage to recovering alcoholics.

178. ProCon.org, "Legal Medical Marijuana States and DC" (July 24, 2019), https://medicalmarijuana.procon.org/legal-medical-marijuana-states-and-dc/ (accessed October 9, 2020).

179. *James v. City of Costa Mesa,* 700 F.3d 394 (9th Cir. 2012).

180. ProCon.org, "Legal Medical Marijuana States and DC" (July 24, 2019), https://medicalmarijuana.procon.org/legal-medical-marijuana-states-and-dc/ (accessed October 9, 2020).

181. Tom Angell, "Congress Votes to Block Feds From Enforcing Marijuana Laws in Legal States," *Forbes* (June 20, 2019), https://www.forbes.com/sites/tomangell/2019/06/20/congress-votes-to-block-feds-from-enforcing-marijuana-laws-in-legal-states/ (accessed October 9, 2020).

182. *McBride v. City of Detroit,* No. 07-12794, 2007 WL 4201134 (E.D. Mich. Nov. 28, 2007).

183. *Kaufmann v. GMAC Mortga*ge, 229 F. App'x 164 (3d Cir. 2007).

184. See EEOC, "Fact Sheet for Small Businesses: Pregnancy Discrimination," https://www.eeoc.gov/eeoc/publications/pregnancy_factsheet.cfm (accessed December 30, 2019); EEOC, "Pregnancy Discrimination," https://www.eeoc.gov/laws/types/pregnancy.cfm (accessed October 9, 2020).

185. Pregnancy sex discrimination, prohibition., 95 P.L. 555, 92 Stat. 2076 (October 31, 1978).

186. Ibid.

187. EEOC, "Fact Sheet for Small Businesses: Pregnancy Discrimination," https://www.eeoc.gov/eeoc/publications/pregnancy_factsheet.cfm (accessed October 9, 2020).

188. Ibid.

189. Ibid.

190. Ibid.

191. 895 F.3d 844 (6th Cir. 2018).

192. *Blatt v. Cabela's Retail, Inc.,* 2017 U.S. Dist. LEXIS 75665 (E.D. Pa. 2017).

193. U.S. Code § 12211.

194. *Blatt v. Cabela's Retail, Inc.,* 2017 U.S. Dist. LEXIS 75665 (E.D. Pa. 2017).

195. *Parker v. Strawser Constr., Inc.,* 307 F. Suff.3d 744 (S.D. Ohio 2018).

196. *Doe v. Northrop Grumman Sys. Corp.,* 2019 U.S. Dist. LEXIS 182435 (N.D. Ala. 2019).

197. U.S. Department of Justice, "Frequently Asked Questions about Service Animals and the ADA" (July 20, 2019), https://www.ada.gov/regs2010/service_animal_qa.html (accessed October 9, 2020).

198. Ibid.

199. Ibid.

200. Ibid.

201. Ibid.

202. EEOC, "'EEO Is the Law' Poster," http://www1.eeoc.gov/employers/poster.cfm (accessed October 9, 2020).

203. Gianni-paolo Ferrari v. Ford Motor Company (15-1479), June 23, 2016.

204. Equal Emp't Opportunity Comm'n v. M.G.H. Family Health Ctr., 230 F. Supp. 3d 796 (W.D. Mich. 2017).

205. *Daugherty v. Sajar Plastics*, 544 F.3d 696 (6th Cir. 2008).

206. Ibid.

207. Ibid.

208. *Whitfield*, 639 F.3d at 259.

209. Ibid.

210. *Romans v. Michigan Dep't of Human Servs.*, 668 F.3d 826 (6th Cir. 2012).

211. Perritt, Henry H., *Americans with Disabilities Act Handbook* (New York, NY: Aspen Publishers 2002).

212. *Deiters v. Donahoe*, NO. 3-13-0315 (M.D. Tenn. Nov. 17, 2014).

213. Gianni-paolo Ferrari v. Ford Motor Company, Defendant-Appellee (No. 15-1479), June 23, 2016.

214. *Ferrari v. Ford Motor Co.*, 826 F.3d 885 (6th Cir. 2016).

215. Ibid.

216. *Demyanovich v. Plating*, 747 F.3d 419 (6th Cir. 2014).

217. *Reeves [ex rel. Reeves v. Jewel Food Stores, Inc.*, 759 F.3d 698, 702 (7th Cir. 2014)].

218. *Malabarba [v. Chicago Tribune Co.*, 149 F.3d 690, 699 (7th. Cir. 1998).

219. Cf. *Emerson [v. Northern States Power Co.*, 256 F.3d 506, 515 (7th Cir. 2001)].

220. *Nguyen v. City & Cnty. of Denver*, Dec 21, 2017.

221. *Equal Employment Opportunity Commission v. Lee's Log Cabin, Inc.*, 546 F.3d 438 (7th Cir. 2008).

222. Amendment of Americans with Disabilities Act Title II and Title III Regulations to Implement ADA Amendments Act of 2008. United States Department of Justice.

223. (2012) "Code of Federal Regulations: 2000," U.S. General Services Administration.

224. 42 USC 12102: Definition of disability.

225. (2011) "Code of Federal Regulations: 2000," U.S. General Services Administration.

Cases

Ferrari v. Ford Motor Co., *826 F.3d 885 (6th Cir. 2016)*

Ford Motor Company hired Ferrari as an employee in 1996 to work in its assembly plant. After returning from medical leave due to a work-related neck injury, Ford accommodated Ferrari's restrictions for nine years by giving him light-work positions. During that time, Ferrari was granted leave four times under the FMLA, including two times in connection with his neck injury. Then Ferrari claimed that the final leave was the result of stress and depression caused by his immediate supervisor in the human resources department.

After that leave, Ferrari applied for an apprenticeship program. The program required that he climb ladders and Ferrari was rejected from the program in part because of evidence of opioid use during treatment of his prior injury. In addition, though Ferrari had been cleared "to work without restrictions from a physical perspective," the program supervisor concluded that he could not participate "[b]ecause having the ability to work overhead and climb ladders on a daily basis are essential to performing any RMI job." Further, "while an apprentice could, theoretically and occasionally, stay on the ground while a supervising journeyman climbed the ladder, the climbing of the ladder is essential to learning the task to be performed at the top of the ladder, which is also an essential function of the position, whether it be checking fluid levels, venting fluids, mixing chemicals, monitoring or repairing HVAC equipment, opening or closing a multitude of valves, sometimes on an emergency basis to prevent an explosion, or the like."[203] Instead of the apprenticeship, Ferrari was appointed to a machinist position. Ferrari sued Ford for violations of the ADA, among other statutes. The district court granted summary judgment for Ford, and Ferrari appealed.

Stranch, C. J.

***

1. Direct Method

Dr. Brewer's stated reason for imposing the February 2013 restrictions was Ferrari's continued use of opioids, and Ford based the temporary bypass decision on these restrictions. Ferrari does not present any other direct evidence regarding Dr. Brewer's restrictions or Ford's temporary bypass decision. To proceed under the direct method, then, Ferrari needed to show that opioid use is a disability under the ADA and that he was "otherwise qualified" for the RMI apprenticeship despite his continued opioid use. His claim fails at this first step.

Under the ADA, the term "disability" means a physical or mental impairment that substantially limits one or more major life activities of an individual; a record of such an impairment; or being regarded as having such an impairment. 42 U.S.C. § 12102(1). Ferrari contends that Ford regarded him as disabled because of his opioid use.

"The regarded-as-disabled prong of the ADA protects employees who are perfectly able to perform a job, but are rejected . . . because of the myths, fears and stereotypes associated with disabilities."[204] *Daugherty v. Sajar Plastics, Inc.* (quoting *Gruener v. Ohio Cas. Ins. Co.*). "Individuals may be regarded as disabled when (1) [an employer] mistakenly believes that [an employee] has a physical impairment that substantially limits one or more major life activities, or (2) [an employer] mistakenly believes that an actual, non-limiting impairment substantially limits one or more [of an employee's] major life activities." *Id.* at 704 (quoting *Gruener*). Major life activities include, but are not limited to, "[c]aring for oneself, performing manual tasks, seeing, hearing, eating, sleeping, walking, standing, sitting, reaching, lifting, bending, speaking, breathing, learning, reading, concentrating, thinking, communicating, interacting with others, and working." [205] 29 C.F.R. § 1630.2(i).

Ferrari does not specify which "major life activity" Ford believed was limited by his opioid use. He does challenge Ford's conclusion that the opioid use precluded him from working certain jobs. It would seem, then, that Ferrari is arguing that Ford mistakenly believed that his opioid use substantially limited him in the major life activity of "working."

In *Daugherty,* we considered a regarded-as-disabled claim in which the employer "believed that [the plaintiff's] back condition and current medication levels precluded him from performing the dangerous machinery functions required of [a] particular job,"[206] but informed the plaintiff that he would be considered for the job "if his medication levels were reduced or eliminated." 510 F.3d at 706. We observed that where the major life activity at issue is working,

> the statutory phrase "substantially limits" takes on special meaning . . . and imposes a stringent standard, requiring proof that the employer regarded the employee as significantly restricted in the ability to perform either a class of jobs or a broad range of jobs in various classes as compared to the average person having comparable training, skills and abilities.[207]

Id. at 704

Given this stringent standard, we held that the plaintiff had failed "to establish a *prima facie* regarded-as-disabled discrimination claim . . . that implicates the major life activity of working." *Id.* at 706. "The inability to perform a single, particular job," we explained, "does not constitute a substantial limitation in the major life activity of working." *Id.* at 704.

The present case is analogous to *Daugherty.* Ford concluded that Ferrari's opioid use restricted him from working jobs that required ladder climbing or working at heights. Ford cleared Ferrari to work in any job that did not require those activities, and in fact placed him in both clerical and assembly positions. Moreover, like the employer in *Daugherty,* Ford only barred Ferrari from a single, particular job—the RMI apprenticeship—and told Ferrari that he would be eligible for the job once he had weaned off opioids. Thus, as in *Daugherty,* the evidence does not show that Ford regarded Ferrari's opioid use as a substantial impairment on the major life activity of working. Ferrari's claim therefore fails under the direct method.

2. Indirect Method

As stated above, under the indirect method, Ferrari must first establish a *prima facie* case of discrimination by showing that (1) he is disabled, (2) he was otherwise qualified for the RMI position, with or without reasonable accommodation, (3) he suffered an adverse employment decision, (4) Ford knew or had reason to know of

his disability, and (5) the RMI apprenticeship remained open while Ford sought other applicants. *Monette,* 90 F.3d at 1186; *Whitfield* (reaffirming that "*Monette* states the proper test" under the indirect method). Establishing a *prima facie* case of discrimination under the indirect method is "not onerous." *Cline v. Catholic Diocese of Toledo* (quoting *Texas Dep't of Cmty. Affairs v. Burdine,* 450 U.S. 248, 253 (1981)). If Ferrari satisfies this burden, the burden shifts to Ford to offer a legitimate explanation for its decision to temporarily bypass Ferrari for the RMI apprenticeship. *Monette,* 90 F.3d at 1186. If Ford does so, the burden then shifts back to Ferrari, who "must introduce evidence showing that the proffered explanation is pretextual." *Id.*

In *Monette,* we unequivocally held that the above five-element test is the proper test for establishing a *prima facie* case under the indirect method. But despite *Monette,* some cases in this circuit appeared to use a three-element test instead of this five-element test. In *Whitfield,* we addressed this apparent inconsistency, holding that *Monette* "states the proper test." The line of cases using a three-element test, we explained, stemmed from a misreading of *Monette* in *Mahon v. Crowell.* Specifically, "*Monette* is cited for the formulation used in *Mahon,* and although *Monette* includes the three-element language, it is not used in the context of establishing a *prima facie* case for purposes of *McDonell Douglas,* but is rather in the context of what is required for *recovery* under the ADA." *Whitfield,* 639 F.3d at 259. "Because conflicts between published cases are resolved in favor of the earlier case, we adopt[ed] *Monette*'s five-element test for a *prima facie* case of employment discrimination under the ADA."[208] *Id.*

In most cases decided after *Whitfield,* panels in this circuit have used the five-element *Monette* test. In some cases, however, we have continued to cite the line of authority we rejected in *Whitfield.* These cases rely on *Mahon*'s misreading of our published precedent, *Monette,* an error we corrected in *Whitfield.* Since these cases use the three-element test from *Mahon,* they should not be cited for the *prima facie* test under the indirect method. The five-element test previously articulated in *Monette* remains the proper test.

As occurred in *Whitfield,* the district court here "used the incorrect *Mahon* formulation of a *prima facie* case" under the indirect method and, therefore, "[t]here [was] no decision below . . . on whether [the plaintiff] ha[d] made out a *prima facie* case of employment discrimination under the correct framework."[209] 639 F.3d at 261. And also like *Whitfield,* the district court here considered the defendant's legitimate, non-discriminatory reason for the adverse action (i.e., Ferrari's continued opioid use) at the *prima facie* case stage. *Id.* Faced with this situation in *Whitfield,* we assumed that the plaintiff "ha[d] made out a *prima facie* case" under the correct test and, finding that the plaintiff could not demonstrate a genuine dispute of material fact as to pretext, affirmed the district court's decision to grant summary judgment. *Id.* at 261–62. The same analysis is appropriate here. Assuming a *prima facie* case under the correct test, we affirm because Ferrari has not raised a genuine dispute of material fact as to pretext, as explained below.

Dr. Brewer's stated reason for imposing restrictions on Ferrari was his opioid use, and Ford temporarily bypassed Ferrari for the RMI position because of these restrictions. Ferrari's restrictions—and the medical condition underlying them—are a legitimate, nondiscriminatory explanation for Ford's adverse employment decision. The burden thus shifts to Ferrari, who "must introduce evidence showing that [Ford's] proffered explanation is pretextual." *Monette,* 90 F.3d at 1186.

To survive a motion for summary judgment, Ferrari need not definitively prove that Ford's reason is pretextual, but rather "must prove only enough to create a *genuine issue* as to whether the rationale is pretextual." *Whitfield,* 639 F.3d at 260. "Under the law of our circuit, a plaintiff can show pretext in three interrelated ways: (1) that the proffered reasons had no basis in fact, (2) that the proffered reasons did not actually motivate the employer's action, or (3) that they were insufficient to motivate the employer's action."[210] *Romans v. Mich. Dep't of Human Servs.*

This circuit has employed a version of the "honest belief" rule with regard to pretext. The formulation used provides that as long as the employer honestly believed the reason it gave for its employment action, an employee is not able to establish pretext even if the employer's reason is ultimately found to be mistaken. "[T]he focus of a discrimination suit is on the intent of the employer," so "[i]f the employer honestly, albeit mistakenly, believes in the non-discriminatory reason it relied upon in making its employment decision, then the employer arguably lacks the necessary discriminatory intent."[211] *Id.* But to prove that the offered, non-discriminatory basis for the employment action is "honestly held," "the employer must be able to establish its reasonable reliance on the particularized facts that were before it at the time the decision was made."[212] *Id.* at 807. Once the employer shows that it "made a reasonably informed and considered

decision before taking an adverse employment action," "the employee has the opportunity to produce proof to the contrary." *Id.* (internal quotation marks omitted).

Ferrari has failed to present evidence creating a dispute of material fact as to whether the RMI apprenticeship decisionmakers honestly believed that his restrictions reflected a reasonable medical judgment. Dr. Brewer imposed Ferrari's restrictions, but she was not the final decisionmaker with regard to the RMI apprenticeship. Rather, it was Ternan and Shaver who made this decision. Ferrari also failed to present evidence creating a dispute of material fact as to whether Dr. Brewer herself honestly believed that he was using opioids or honestly believed that the opioids could affect his performance, creating a danger to him and other employees. Dr. Brewer's evaluation of Ferrari's opioid use was thorough. She conducted two examinations of Ferrari, reviewed his medical history, obtained his most up-to-date medical records, ordered new tests, ordered an independent medical examination to resolve discrepancies in his medical record, and revised his restrictions based on this new information.

We are unpersuaded by Ferrari's arguments as to why Ford's explanation was pretextual. Ferrari claims that he had ceased using opioids when Dr. Brewer imposed restrictions, but he has not presented evidence creating a dispute of fact as to whether Dr. Brewer honestly believed he was using opioids. His medical record indicated that he was addicted to opioids and was still "actively" using them. Ferrari also does not provide sufficient evidence to challenge Dr. Friedman's independent medical examination, which the parties agreed was binding. That eleven-page report concluded (a) that the medical record did not substantiate Ferrari's claim to have weaned off opioids, and (b) that opioid use could affect his performance. Ferrari points to Dr. Kole's letter, which said that the opioids did not affect Ferrari's performance and concluded that Ferrari was "safely able to perform all functions listed in the RMI job description." But Dr. Kole's letter does not rise to the level of a material dispute because it lacks medical explanation, and Dr. Kole admitted in his testimony that "the only way [he] would know whether the opioids were impairing [Ferrari] either physically or mentally was if [Ferrari] told [him]."[213]

Ferrari also points to evidence outside his medical record that, he claims, shows that Ford's explanation was pretextual. He references the beginning of an email in which Dr. Brewer discusses an inquiry from workers' compensation about whether lifting restrictions would change his date of injury, seeking to imply that workers' compensation personnel were against lifting his neck-injury restrictions and that Dr. Brewer was sympathetic to those concerns. But the rest of Dr. Brewer's email explains the workers' compensation position differently, showing that such a conclusion is unwarranted. The email concludes, moreover, with Dr. Brewer's primary medical concern: the potential side effects of opioids on Ferrari's ability to perform the RMI trades position. Ferrari also challenges Ford as changing its explanation for the adverse employment decision, but Dr. Brewer revised Ferrari's restrictions *before* Ford made the adverse employment decision and, more importantly, she did so pursuant to the recommendation of an independent medical examination that the parties agreed was binding. Lastly, Ferrari claims that Dr. Brewer "hid" Ford's medical records from him because she did not release them immediately when they became available. Ford, however, had a policy of providing medical records within 15 days, and Ferrari does not allege that Ford exceeded this period.

Ferrari's evidence does not create a genuine dispute of material fact about whether Dr. Brewer relied on Dr. Friedman's binding medical examination, nor does it create a genuine dispute about whether Dr. Brewer honestly believed that Ferrari was using opioids or that opioid use could affect his performance. And without regard to

Dr. Brewer's medical evaluation, Ferrari's claim would fail for another reason: he has not presented any evidence that the RMI apprenticeship decisionmakers did not honestly believe that his restrictions reflected a reasonable medical judgment. Ferrari has thus failed to present sufficient evidence of pretext to survive summary judgment.

Case Questions

1. Under the direct method, what did Ferrari need to show to establish a disability under the ADA? Was he successful? Why or why not?

2. What must Ferrari establish to succeed under the indirect method? Is Ferrari able to establish a *prima facie* case of discrimination? Why or why not?

3. In your opinion, does Ford have enough evidence to show he is disabled? Does it matter that Ferrari's disability is a result of an on-the-job accident? What type of policy might you develop to deal with this sort of situation?

Case 2

Hostettler v. College of Wooster,
895 F.3d 844 (6th Cir. 2018)

Heidi Hostettler was hired as an HR Generalist by the College of Wooster in late summer 2013. At the time that she was interviewed and took the position, she was four-months pregnant. Throughout the hiring process, Hostettler was open about her pregnancy[, which the College of Wooster said they could be willing to accommodate]. For the first five months—before her maternity leave—Hostettler's employment seemed to be a mutually beneficial arrangement. [. . .]

Hostettler started her maternity leave at the beginning of February and took her full 12 weeks. She was slated to return to work at the end of April. But as the time to return to work approached, Hostettler experienced severe postpartum depression and separation anxiety. Hostettler's OB/GYN, Dr. David Seals, testified that "she had one of the worst cases of separation anxiety" that he had ever seen. Seals explained that she did not seem like herself and that she cried during almost every appointment with him. He prescribed her an antidepressant.

Seals also thought that it would be a bad idea for Hostettler to return to work right away, and testified that he believed that "it was medically necessary that [Hostettler] could work a reduced schedule." He suggested that she return to work on a part-time basis for the "foreseeable future.". . . Concerned that she could not return to work, Hostettler met with her direct supervisor, Marcia Beasley, and explained how she was doing and that she would need more time before coming back. According to Hostettler, Beasley was "sympathetic and understood." [. . .]

In the beginning of May, [w]hen Hostettler returned to work, Beasley recommended that. . . Hostettler work five half days a week [. . .] Wooster informed Hostettler that it would accommodate her part-time schedule until June 30, at which time she should submit an updated certification from her doctor. [. . .]

The parties disagree over what happened during the following two months. Hostettler continued to suffer from depression and anxiety. And if she had to work much later than noon—her modified stop time—she would have panic attacks, during which she would have difficulty breathing, thinking, and even walking. But with an accommodated schedule, Hostettler contends that she was able to do everything required of her position. [. . .]

Apparently, Beasley agreed with much of what Hostettler. . . concluded [and one of her colleagues confirmed]. [. . .] Throughout Hostettler's time at Wooster, there had been no complaints about her work or conduct. Beasley stated that Hostettler never failed to perform any responsibility or finish any assignment in a timely manner. And her first evaluation, done in June or July of 2014—shortly before Hostettler was fired—contained no negative feedback but instead concluded that "Heidi is a great colleague and a welcome addition to the HR team!"

At the same time, however, Beasley felt that Hostettler's modified schedule put a strain on Beasley and the rest of the department. She testified that during that time, Hostettler did not perform critical functions of her job, such as filling job openings, and leading trainings and lunch programs. As a result, Beasley was "just running from one thing to another to get things done" and was "really overwhelmed and left without anyone in the office to help with responsibilities and tasks that came up." She also contended that work in the department was left unfinished or ignored. And Beasley was concerned that an upcoming online benefits project would leave the HR team even more short-staffed. But when pressed to identify any specific responsibilities or assignments that were not completed, Beasley repeatedly was unable to name any. [. . .]

At the conclusion of the first two weeks of July, Seals submitted an updated medical certification, in which he explained that Hostettler should continue to work half-time and estimated that she might return to full-time employment at the beginning of September. Hostettler contends, however, that on the day after Seals submitted the medical certification, she followed up with Beasley, asking again about extending her hours from 8:00 a.m. to 2:00 p.m. Beasley never responded.

The next day, Beasley fired Hostettler. Beasley sent her a letter, stating that because her updated medical certification required her to work half-time, she was "unable to return to [her] assigned position of HR Generalist in a full time capacity" and was being terminated. A few weeks later, Beasley hired a temporary clerical employee to handle some of the administrative work in the department. But that employee did not do any of the tasks that the department required an HR Generalist to complete. As a result, Hostettler's firing left the department with fewer resources for employee relations, training, and hiring. It was not until October of that year that Wooster hired Hostettler's replacement—a man.

Hostettler sued Wooster, claiming violations of the ADA, the FMLA, Title VII's prohibition against sex discrimination, and corresponding Ohio state laws. Wooster moved for summary judgment on all claims and Hostettler moved for partial summary judgment on her ADA claim. The district court denied Hostettler's motion and granted Wooster's motion on all of Hostettler's claims.

Daughtrey, C.J.

***

Discussion

***

The Americans with Disabilities Act

The ADA forbids "discriminat[ion] against a qualified individual on the basis of disability" as it applies to hiring and firing. 42 U.S.C. § 12112(a). Prohibited discrimination also includes "not making reasonable accommodations," *id.* § 12112(b)(5)(A), such as "part-time or modified work schedules," 29 C.F.R. § 1630.2(o)(2)(ii) (2012). There are two ways that a litigant can prove discrimination—directly or indirectly—each with

its own test. *See Ferrari v. Ford Motor Co.,* 826 F.3d 885, 891 (6th Cir. 2016). "Distinguishing between cases that involve direct evidence of discrimination and those in which the plaintiff is not able to introduce direct evidence is vital because the framework for analyzing the two kinds of cases differs."[214] *Id.* at 892. [. . .]

Under the direct method of proof the plaintiff must show (1) that she is an individual with a disability, and (2) that she is otherwise qualified for her job despite the disability "(a) without accommodation from the employer; (b) with an alleged 'essential' job requirement eliminated; or (c) with a proposed reasonable accommodation."[215] *Ferrari,* 826 F.3d at 891. . . Claims that allege a failure to accommodate "necessarily involve direct evidence." *Kleiber*, 485 F.3d at 868. Inversely, then, termination for no reason other than alleged problems with an already-in-place accommodation should involve the same direct standard of proof. [. . .]

No inferences are required in this case. Beasley admitted that Hostettler was fired solely because the college determined that it no longer could accommodate her modified schedule. Indeed, when Beasley was asked whether, by referring to Hostettler's inability to work full-time, she was "pointing to [Hostettler's] need for a modified work schedule . . . and no other reason," Beasley readily agreed. [. . .] Because the resolution of the case revolves around the questions of the direct test, we apply it here.

Individual with a Disability

In the first step of the direct test, a plaintiff alleging an ADA violation must establish that she is an individual with a disability. The district court skipped this step, however, presumably because it presumed that Hostettler satisfied the definition of an individual with a disability. [. . .]

Under the post-2008 ADA law, Hostettler plainly is an individual with a disability. In keeping with the remedial purposes of the ADAAA, "[t]he definition of disability" under the ADA "shall be construed in favor of broad coverage." 42 U.S.C. § 12102(4)(A). That is because the primary concern of the ADA is "whether covered entities have complied with their obligations and whether discrimination has occurred," not whether an individual's impairment is a disability. 29 C.F.R. § 1630.2(j)(1)(iii). [. . .]

Wooster does not dispute that when Hostettler was experiencing her depression and anxiety she was substantially limited in her ability to care for herself, sleep, walk, or speak, among others. *See* 42 U.S.C. § 12102(2). That is enough for her to be considered an individual with a disability under the ADA.

Otherwise Qualified

The crux of this case is whether Hostettler was otherwise qualified for her position. The district court concluded that as a matter of law she was not. But both parties have presented sufficient evidence to raise genuine disputes of material fact that preclude summary judgment.

To show that she is otherwise qualified for a position—and thus meet her *prima facie* burden—an employee must show that she can perform the essential functions of a job with or without an accommodation. "A job function

is essential if its removal would fundamentally alter the position." *Mosby-Meachem v. Memphis Light, Gas & Water Div.*, 883 F.3d 595, 603 (6th Cir. 2018). [. . .] Put another way, essential functions are the core job duties, not the marginal ones. 29 C.F.R. § 1630.2 (n)(1).

This analysis does not lend itself to categorical rules—it is "highly fact specific." *Mosby-Meachem,* 883 F.3d at 605. . . [C]ourts must perform a fact-intensive analysis. In determining what functions are essential, courts may consider as evidence—among other things—the amount of time spent on a particular function; the employer's judgment; "written job descriptions prepared before advertising or interviewing" for the position; and the consequences of not requiring the employee to perform the particular function. 29 C.F.R. § 1630.2(n)(3). Although the employer's judgment receives some weight in this analysis, *see Williams v. AT&T Mobility Servs.*, 847 F.3d 384, 391–92 (6th Csr. 2017), it is not the end-all—*especially* when an employee puts forth competing evidence. *See id.* at 393. [. . .]

Hostettler presented evidence that she satisfied all the core tasks of her position. . . . What is more, statements by Wooster's representative (and the person who fired Hostettler), Marcia Beasley, support Hostettler's conclusion. Beasley gave Hostettler her employee review while Hostettler was working a part-time schedule. The review did not mention that Hostettler was needed on a full-time basis. Instead, it was very positive, praising Hostettler's work. [. . .] And during her deposition, Beasley explained that Hostettler never had failed to complete a task or meet a responsibility in a timely manner. Although Beasley contended that there were tasks that were not being completed, she was unable to name any specifically. In the end, Hostettler never received a performance improvement plan, discipline, written criticism, or even a single complaint about her work.

In many circumstances, that much evidence might be sufficient to grant summary judgment in an employee's favor. But here the record does contain some evidence that Hostettler was not completing all of her work during her part-time schedule. Beasley stated that she was overwhelmed as the only one in the office to handle employees who showed up unexpectedly to talk about an issue. And because there was no one in the office to help with the issues Beasley faced, some event-planning responsibilities "dropped through the cracks." Beasley further explained that Hostettler's absence was putting a strain on the department. The six-person department recently was down another employee on maternity leave. And two of the remaining employees were beginning an online benefits project in July, which would take up a significant amount of their time.

***

Wooster may have preferred that Hostettler be in the office 40 hours a week. And it may have been more efficient and easier on the department if she were. But those are not the concerns of the ADA: Congress decided that the benefits of gainful employment for individuals with disabilities—dignity, financial independence, and self-sufficiency, among others—outweigh simple calculations of ease or efficiency. To that end, the ADA requires that employers reasonably accommodate employees with disabilities, including allowing modified work schedules. An employer cannot deny a modified work schedule as unreasonable unless the employer can show *why* the employee is needed on a full-time schedule; merely stating that anything less than full-time employment is *per se* unreasonable will not relieve an employer of its ADA responsibilities.

[The court thus concludes that the district court improperly granted summary judgment in favor of the employer].

Failure to Engage in Interactive Process

Once an employee requests an accommodation, the employer has a duty to engage in an interactive process. Specifically, the employer must "identify the precise limitations resulting from the disability and potential reasonable accommodations that could overcome those limitations." *Mosby-Meachem,* 883 F.3d at 605–06 (citations omitted). Employers must engage in a "good faith" process and an "individualized inquiry" to determine whether a reasonable accommodation can be made. *Rorrer,* 743 F.3d at 1045 (citations omitted).

The district court ruled that Wooster satisfied this requirement because Beasley met with Hostettler four times in early July, and they discussed Hostettler's employment and the needs of both parties. The district court concluded that although the parties met and discussed accommodations, Hostettler was unwilling to accept anything less than her part-time schedule and "[t]he law does not require that the parties meet and that the employer concede to the employee's request."

But that conclusion is wrong for the same reason that the rest of the district court's ADA analysis is incorrect—it decides between competing facts, thus misapplying the summary-judgment standard. It is undisputed that Beasley and Hostettler met four times in early July. But what is unclear is what was discussed in those meetings. [. . .] In short, there is competing record evidence that makes it unclear whether, or how, Wooster was willing to engage in the interactive process. For this reason also, summary judgment was improper.

Title VII Sex/Pregnancy Discrimination Claim

The grant of summary judgment to Wooster on Hostettler's Title VII sex/pregnancy claim also was improper. Applying the *McDonnell Douglas* burden-shifting approach, the district court assumed that Hostettler satisfied her *prima facie* burden. But relying on its determination under the ADA that Hostettler could not satisfy an essential function of her job, the district court concluded that Wooster had a legitimate, nondiscriminatory reason to fire her. And, the court added, because Hostettler neither argued pretext nor pointed to any evidence that would support a finding of pretext, she could not carry her burden.

But, in fact, Hostettler *did* argue that Wooster's decision was pretextual. "Plaintiffs may show that an employer's proffered reasons for an adverse employment action are pretext for discrimination if the reasons '(1) have no basis in fact; (2) did not actually motivate the action; or (3) were insufficient to warrant the action.'"[216] *Demyanovich v. Cadon Plating & Coatings, L.L.C.,* 747 F.3d 419, 431 (6th Cir. 2014) (quoting *Seeger v. Cincinnati Bell Tel. Co.,* 681 F.3d 274, 285 (6th Cir. 2012).

Hostettler satisfied that burden. First, as described above, the district court wrongly concluded that full-time presence was an essential function of her position. Because there remain genuine disputes of material fact on that question, a jury could find that Wooster's proffered reason for firing Hostettler "ha[s] no basis in fact" or "did not actually motivate the action." *Demyanovich,* 747 F.3d at 431 (quoting *Seeger,* 681 F.3d at 285). Similarly, Hostettler pointed to two employees who received longer periods of medical leave for non-pregnancy conditions—one received 23 weeks of leave and another received 24 weeks of leave. That those employees were not fired is a circumstance sufficient to create a dispute of fact over whether Wooster's proffered explanation was insufficient to justify firing Hostettler. *See id.*

As with Hostettler's ADA claims, there remain disputes of material fact on Hostettler's Title VII claim. Thus, summary judgment was inappropriate.

***

Conclusion

Application of the proper summary-judgment standard answers the questions raised in this appeal. Each party has presented evidence supporting its conclusion on each contested issue. But instead of holding that these contradictory facts precluded summary judgment, the district court weighed the evidence against Hostettler and decided in favor of Wooster as a matter of law. In doing so, the district court misapplied both the summary-judgment standard and our ADA precedents. Repeating that error, the district court decided that the conclusion on Hostettler's ADA claim necessarily doomed her FMLA and Title VII sex/pregnancy claims as well. Because all of these errors involve improper factual determinations, we REVERSE the order of the district court and REMAND the matter for further proceedings consistent with this opinion.

Case Questions

1. Does Hostettler have a claim for relief under the ADA? According to the court, what is the appropriate test to prove discrimination in this case? Under this test, what then does Hostettler need to show?

2. Is full-time attendance an essential job function of Hostettler's position? Was Hostettler otherwise qualified for her position? If Hostettler was failing to fulfill her duties, what steps ought the College of Wooster have taken before firing Hostettler?

3. Do you believe the employer made a good-faith effort to reasonably accommodate the employee? Can you imagine a reasonable accommodation the College of Wooster otherwise might have been able to provide for Hostettler? Why might it be in the employer's best interest to provide reasonable accommodations to people with disabilities, regardless of whether there is a requirement to provide an accommodation?

Case 3

Brown v. Milwaukee Bd. of Sch. Dirs.,
855 F.3d 818 (7th Cir. 2017)

Sherlyn Brown was an assistant principal for defendant Milwaukee Public Schools until she badly injured her knee while restraining a student. When she returned to work following surgery, she and her doctor told Milwaukee Schools that she could not be "in the vicinity of potentially unruly students." Since virtually all students are "potentially" unruly, Milwaukee Schools understood that limit to bar virtually all contact with students. It repeatedly communicated that understanding to Brown as it tried to accommodate her disability by finding her a new position. When Brown's three-year leave of absence expired before a suitable position was found, Milwaukee Schools fired her. Brown sued under the Americans with Disabilities Act, claiming that her disability had never prevented interaction with students and that Milwaukee Schools failed to accommodate her disability. The district court granted summary judgment for Milwaukee Schools, and Brown has appealed.

Hamilton, C. J.

***

III. Analysis

Brown contends on appeal that Milwaukee Schools should have accommodated her disability by reinstating her as Assistant Principal or by reassigning her to any one of five vacant positions: Student Achievement Supervisor, Student Services Coordinator, Charter School Program Officer, GE Grant Administrator, and Title I Coordinator. Milwaukee Schools argues that because Brown could not be in the vicinity of potentially unruly students, she was not qualified to perform the essential functions of

either her Assistant Principal position or the first four vacant positions. It argues that the final vacant position would have been a promotion for which she was not the most qualified candidate. [. . .]

    A. *Qualified to Perform Essential Functions*

***

1. *Brown's Restrictions*

[I]dentifying reasonable accommodations for a disabled employee requires both employer and employee to engage in a flexible, interactive process. See *Stern [v. St. Anthony's Health Center,* 788 F.3d 276, 292 (7th Cir. 2015)]. The key principle for purposes of this case is that if the employee "does not provide sufficient information to the employer to determine the necessary accommodations, the employer cannot be held liable for failing to accommodate the disabled employee."[217] *Reeves [ex rel. Reeves v. Jewel Food Stores, Inc.,* 759 F.3d 698, 702 (7th Cir. 2014)]. [. . .]

Brown. . . repeatedly presented Milwaukee Schools with a broad restriction for a school system: she needed to avoid proximity to potentially unruly students. Essentially all students are *potentially* unruly. Milwaukee Schools was always clear about its understanding of her restrictions, and Brown never challenged that understanding [James Gorton, Milwaukee School's employment specialist,] repeatedly told Brown that she could not perform positions that required being "in the vicinity of potentially unruly students." He said that she was not qualified for a position because she would "need to be in the schools to interact with students and staff." In Brown's retelling of one meeting, Gorton told her (not surprisingly, we must add) that almost "every job in the district required individuals to work with students." Nowhere in the record did Brown tell him he had misunderstood her abilities and limitations. [. . .]

The undisputed facts show that Milwaukee Schools acted consistently with the restrictions imposed by Brown's doctors, which said that Brown simply could not work in the vicinity of potentially unruly students. To the extent Brown is arguing that her restrictions were less severe than Milwaukee Schools believed, the undisputed facts show that Brown "failed to hold up her end of the interactive process by clarifying the extent of her medical restrictions." *Steffes [v. Stepan Co.,* 144 F.3d 1070, 1073 (7th Cir. 1998)]. Milwaukee Schools accordingly cannot be held liable for failing to put her in a position it believed would exceed those restrictions.

2. *Essential Functions*

Brown argues that being in the vicinity of potentially unruly students was not an essential function of any of the positions she requested, for two reasons. First, she asserts, citing 29 C.F.R. § 1630.2(o)(1)(ii), that being in such proximity is a description of work environment, not a description of a job function. Second, she argues that such proximity is not an essential function according to any of the factors courts usually consider: it is not listed

on any job descriptions, for example, nor do any of the positions exist to perform it. See *Dunderdale v. United Airlines, Inc.,* 807 F.3d 849, 853–54 (7th Cir. 2015) (courts should examine several factors to determine essential functions, including the employer's judgment and the written job description), citing 42 U.S.C. § 12111(8) and 29 C.F.R. § 1630.2(n)(1)-(3).

Brown's rigid distinction between work environment and job functions is not realistic. Some job functions can be performed without regard to some aspects of work environment. In many office environments, for example, it may be possible to change the temperature, lighting, or desk arrangements to accommodate someone's needs. But sometimes a job function requires a specific work environment. Lawn maintenance cannot be performed indoors; a jockey must often work atop a horse; receptionists must be near office visitors. Section 1630.2(o)(1)(ii) does not say otherwise. It simply lists changes to work environment as one possible way of accommodating a disabled employee. Neither Brown's evidence nor her arguments suggest that the positions she wanted could have been modified to avoid student contact.

Brown's second argument is similarly artificial. She focuses on a narrow framing of her restriction, ignoring the logical consequences of that restriction. If Brown could not be near students, then she could not meet with students, could not walk down school hallways during the school day, could not sit in on classes, etc. Milwaukee Schools argues this means she could not perform: (1) the Assistant Principal position, because it would require her to be in schools overseeing their day-to-day operations; (2) the GE Grant Administrator position, because it would require her to attend and lead meetings at which students were present and in schools in which students were present; (3) the Student Achievement Supervisor position, because it would require her to conduct classroom observations and work daily in schools; (4) the Charter School Program Officer, because it would require in-school compliance checks and classroom observations; and (5) the Student Services Coordinator position, because it would require in-school meetings with students with serious disciplinary problems. To support these points, Milwaukee Schools relies on job descriptions, affidavits from human resources employees, and Brown's deposition testimony. Brown offers nothing to contradict these points, so we must agree with Milwaukee Schools. See *Hemsworth v. Quotesmith.com, Inc.,* 476 F.3d 487, 490 (7th Cir. 2007), *overruled on other grounds by*

Ortiz v. Werner Enterprises, Inc., 834 F.3d 760 (7th Cir. 2016) (non-moving party must identify "with reasonable particularity the evidence upon which the party relies"), citing *Johnson v. Cambridge Industries, Inc.,* 325 F.3d 892, 898 (7th Cir. 2003).

B. *Promotion*

Our discussion so far has eliminated from consideration four of the five positions Brown requested. The remaining position, the Title I Coordinator position, did not require proximity to students. Milwaukee Schools contends that it was a promotion and that Brown was not the most qualified candidate, and therefore it was not obligated to give her the position. See *Malabarba* [*v. Chicago Tribune Co.,* 149 F.3d 690, 699 (7th. Cir. 1998)] ("[A]n employer does not have to accommodate a disabled employee by promoting him or her to a higher level position."[218]). Brown does not contend that she was the most qualified candidate but instead argues that the position would not have been a promotion.

Milwaukee Schools advances three reasons that the Title I Coordinator position would have been a promotion: (1) Brown's pay grade would increase; (2) her salary would increase because of the pay grade change and because she would be working twelve months per year rather than ten; and (3) the position involved substantially increased responsibilities. Brown disagrees because she did not consider the position a promotion when she applied because the position's salary range included her salary as an assistant principal and because Milwaukee Schools had previously moved her between pay grades without classifying the change as a promotion.

[. . .] Whether a reassignment would be a promotion, demotion, or lateral transfer is not determined by the employee's perceptions. See *Gile v. United Airlines, Inc.,* 95 F.3d 492, 497 (7th Cir. 1996) ("Employers should reassign the individual to an equivalent position, in terms of pay, status, etc."), quoting 29 C.F.R. app. § 1630.2(o). And while Milwaukee Schools once moved Brown between pay grades without classifying the change as a promotion, her salary remained the same despite the change in grade. Brown does not explain why that happened, nor does she point to evidence that Milwaukee Schools could do that again. Most important, Brown does not dispute that her salary would have increased by about $20,000 per year if she had taken the Title I Coordinator position. Cf. *Office of the Architect of the Capitol v. Office of Compliance,* 361 F.3d 633, 640–41

(Fed. Cir. 2004) (finding substantial evidence that moving an employee into a position normally accorded a higher wage grade classification was not a promotion: the employer "frequently move[d] employees between positions without changing their pay or wage grade classification"). Brown does not deny that the Coordinator position involved twelve months of work rather than the Assistant Principal's ten. Cf. *Emerson* [*v. Northern States Power Co.,* 256 F.3d 506, 515 (7th Cir. 2001)] ("NSP did not simply transfer Emerson into the available full-time position because it would have been a promotion from part-time status to full-time status."[219]). Nor does she deny that the position involved increased responsibilities. A reasonable jury would be, and we are, forced to conclude that the Coordinator position would have been a promotion that the Americans with Disabilities Act did not require be offered to Brown.

This is an unusual case, and our holding is correspondingly narrow. If Milwaukee Schools, rather than Brown's doctor, had decided that she could not be near students, we would have a different case. So too if Milwaukee Schools had not communicated its understanding of Brown's restrictions to her or if it had not sought clarification when it received contradictory information. See *EEOC v. Sears, Roebuck & Co.,* 417 F.3d 789, 808 (7th Cir. 2005) (reversing summary judgment where employer "did not actively engage in the interactive process by suggesting possible accommodations or requesting information that would help it do so"[220]); *Bultemeyer v. Fort Wayne Community Schools,* 100 F.3d 1281, 1285 (7th Cir. 1996) (reversing summary judgment where employer could have called to clarify potentially ambiguous doctor's note but did not). But the undisputed facts show here Milwaukee Schools acted on the basis of restrictions imposed by Brown's doctors and that no reasonable accommodation of her disability was possible. The judgment of the district court is AFFIRMED.

Case Questions

1. Are you more persuaded by the analysis of the Seventh Circuit?

2. Does this case represent a clear win for the employer? What guidance would you give an employer after the holding in this case? What policies might be most effective?

3. What implications might this case have for determining the reasonableness of other forms of accommodation?

Gogos v. AMS Mechanical Systems,
737 F.3d 1170 (7th Cir. 2013)

In one of the first appellate court cases substantively to apply the ADA Amendments Act in an employment discrimination case, the Seventh Circuit offers helpful definitive language. In this case, the plaintiff, an individual with high blood pressure, was terminated from his position. The Seventh Circuit reversed and remanded the district court's order granting summary judgment and discussed the EEOC's regulatory language, episodic conditions, mitigating measures, and short-term conditions.

Specifically, the Seventh Circuit held that, even if the plaintiff's blood pressure spike and vision loss manifested themselves in an episodic way, episodic conditions are now covered by the ADA. It also found that short-term disabilities can be covered by the ADA, citing the appendix to the EEOC regulations. The Seventh Circuit held that the plaintiff's blood pressure spike and intermittent blindness could substantially limit two of his major bodily functions, eyesight and circulatory function. Finally, the Seventh Circuit explained that courts must disregard the ameliorative effects of mitigating measures when determining whether an individual has a disability under the ADA, and, thus, the ameliorative effects of the plaintiff's blood pressure medication must be disregarded.

Cudahy, Rovner, and Williams, C. J.

***

***

Gogos, a pipe welder with forty-five years experience, has taken medication to reduce his elevated blood pressure for more than eight years. He began working for AMS in December 2012 as a welder and pipe-fitter. The next month, his blood pressure spiked to "very high," and he experienced intermittent vision loss (sometimes for a few minutes at a time). Shortly after reporting to work on January 30, 2013, Gogos discovered that his right eye was red, and he requested and received from his supervisor leave to seek immediate medical treatment for his blood pressure and ocular conditions. As Gogos left the work site, he saw his general foreman and told him that he was going to the hospital because "my health is not very good lately." The foreman immediately fired him.

* * *

A claim for relief under Title I of the ADA, 42 U.S.C. § 12112(a), requires Gogos to allege facts showing that "(1) he is 'disabled'; (2) he is qualified to perform the essential function of the job either with or without reasonable accommodation; and (3) he suffered an adverse employment action because of his disability."[221] *E.E.O.C. v. Lee's Log Cabin, Inc.; Dargis v. Sheahan.* Since Gogos was discharged after January 1, 2009, the 2008 amendments to the ADA, which expanded the Act's coverage, apply to his claim.

Gogos alleged sufficient facts plausibly showing that he is disabled. The ADA defines "disability" as "(A) a physical or mental impairment that substantially limits one or more major life activities . . .; (B) a record of such an impairment; or (C) being regarded as having such an impairment. . . ." 42 U.S.C. § 12102(1). Under the 2008 amendments, a person with an impairment that substantially limits a major life activity, or a record of one, is disabled, even if the impairment is "transitory and minor" (defined as lasting six months or less). Likewise, "[a]n impairment that is episodic or in remission is a disability if it would substantially limit a major life activity when active."[222] 42 U.S.C. § 12102(4)(D).

Based on these provisions, Gogos's episode of a blood-pressure spike and vision loss are covered disabilities. He attributes both problems to his longstanding blood-pressure condition, and the ADA's implementing regulation lists hypertension as an example of an "impairment[] that may be episodic." Under the 2008 amendments, "[t]he fact that the periods during which an episodic impairment is active and substantially limits a major life activity may be brief or occur infrequently is no longer relevant to determining whether the impairment substantially limits a major life activity."[223] 29 C.F.R. Pt. 1630, App. at Section 1630.2(j)(1)(vii). Instead, the relevant issue is whether, despite their short duration in this case, Gogos's higher-than-usual blood pressure and vision loss substantially impaired a major life activity when they occurred. Construing the complaint generously and drawing reasonable inferences in Gogos's favor, we conclude that they did. Gogos alleges that his episode of "very high" blood pressure and intermittent blindness substantially impaired two major life activities: his circulatory function and eyesight. Accordingly, he has alleged a covered disability.

Moreover, Gogos's alleged chronic blood-pressure condition—for which he has taken medication for more than eight years—could also qualify as a disability. The amended ADA provides that when "determin[ing] whether an impairment substantially limits a major life activity[,] the ameliorative effects of mitigating measures such as . . . medication"[224] are not relevant. The interpreting regulation explains the new law by way of an example directly on point here: "[S]omeone who began taking medication for hypertension before experiencing substantial limitations related to the impairment would still be an individual with a disability if, without the medication, he or she would now be substantially limited in functions of the cardiovascular or circulatory system."[225] 29 C.F.R. Pt. 1630, App. at Section 1630.2(j)(1)(vi). Thus, even if Gogos had not experienced the episode of elevated blood pressure and vision loss, he could qualify as disabled due to his chronic blood-pressure condition.

Gogos alleges facts sufficient to satisfy the remaining elements necessary to state a claim for relief under Title I of the ADA. He alleges that he had forty-five years of experience as a pipe welder and that he worked for AMS as a welder and pipe fitter for more than a month before he was fired; thus, he adequately pleads that he was qualified to perform the essential functions of his job. *Peters v. City of Mauston.* And he alleges that he suffered an adverse employment action because of his disability: he asserts that immediately after he reported his medical conditions to his foreman at AMS, the foreman fired him.

We VACATE the dismissal and REMAND for further proceedings consistent with this opinion. On remand the district court should consider Gogos's application to proceed in *forma pauperis* and, in light of his limited education and English fluency, his request for counsel.

Case Questions

1. Are episodic conditions covered by the ADAAA? Would they have been covered if Gogos had experienced high blood pressure before 2008?

2. Does it matter whether Gogos's condition can be treated with medicine? If there is effective treatment available for a disability, is that person still protected under the ADAAA?

3. Was Gogos otherwise qualified for his job? Was he eligible to state a claim for relief? What form of relief might Gogos's employer offer? Can you imagine a situation in which Gogos would not be eligible for relief?

Part 3

Regulation of the Employment Environment

Chapter

14

The Employee's Right to Privacy and Management of Personal Information

Learning Objectives

joakimbkk/Getty Images

After completing this chapter, you should be able to:

LO1 Describe the nature of privacy as a fundamental right.

LO2 Explain the three general ways in which privacy is legally protected in the United States.

LO3 Define the legal concept of a "reasonable expectation of privacy" and its application to the workplace.

LO4 Identify and apply the standard for unreasonable searches and seizures under the Fourth Amendment.

LO5 Explain the distinctions between the protections for public and private sector privacy.

LO6 Describe the legal framework that applies to private sector privacy cases.

LO7 Identify and differentiate the *prima facie* cases for common-law claims of privacy invasions (intrusion into seclusion, public disclosure of private facts, publication in a false light, and breach of contract/defamation).

LO8 Explain the extent to which an employer can legally dictate the off-work acts of its employees.

LO9 Discuss how advances in technology have impacted employee privacy.

LO10 State the key business justifications for employee monitoring.

LO11 Explain the most effective means by which to design and implement a technology use policy.

LO12 Describe the legal environment that surrounds employee use of social media technologies.

Opening Scenarios

SCENARIO 1

1) Cherita runs a small family medical practice in rural Montana. She provides medical malpractice insurance to all five of her full-time physicians and is concerned about how much her insurance rates continue to skyrocket. She worries that her medical group would suffer a financial disaster if one of its workers inadvertently transferred a disease to a patient. Therefore, she wants to conduct confidential testing of each of her present employees and also all future applicants of several transmittable conditions, including HIV and COVID-19/coronavirus (and may add or change these choices, depending on existing health conditions at the time).

Cherita has several questions. First, what if a physician refuses to take one or any of the tests, claiming an invasion of privacy? Second, if any test returns a positive result, can Cherita refuse to hire that individual, or can she discharge an employee without violating federal laws protecting employees with disabilities? Third, if an employee's tests return with a negative result but Cherita decides to terminate the employee anyway, is she liable for the appearance that the employee is positive for any of these results and that Cherita terminated her or him as a consequence of the test results? Fourth, what is the most effective way for Cherita to ensure that the test results are kept confidential?

SCENARIO 2

2) Abraham, a real estate agent, has three children, two of whom are in college. In order to earn extra money to help with college tuition payments, Abraham (who studied modern dance during his college career) finds a job dancing during the evenings in a club that caters specifically to women. While not exactly erotic dancing (he keeps all of his clothes on), it is not ballroom dancing, either. Celebrating during a bachelorette party, one of the partners of the real estate firm for which Abraham works sees him dancing.

When he arrives at the office the next day, she calls him into her office and orders him to quit his night job. She claims that both existing clients and potential clients might see him there and he would lose all credibility as a real estate agent. Does she have a right to require Abraham to do this as a condition of continued employment? (Presume that he is an employee and not an independent contractor.)

SCENARIO 3

3) Kanani receives what appears to be a legitimate email asking her to click on an embedded link to learn more about new solar technologies. Though she does not recognize the name of the sender, she clicks on the link because she works at a solar panel installation company and is always excited to learn about the latest technology. She also is on several listservs, so it is not uncommon for her to receive emails such as this one.

Kanani finds herself looking at a website with photos of Leonardo DiCaprio that are "not safe/suitable for work" ("NSFW"). She is so annoyed by the original email and this website that she spends a few moments on the site trying to figure out how to unsubscribe from its list. After searching for several minutes with no luck, she leaves the website and returns to reading her email. She responds quickly to a question from her intern and then sends an email to her teenage daughter reminding her to pick up the dog from puppy day care on her way home from school. She then returns to preparing for her upcoming presentation.

A few days later, she receives a written warning from her manager reprimanding her for using employer-owned computer equipment for personal use, including looking at NSFW materials online and also for emailing her daughter. She learns that her manager was using a program that alerted him anytime an employee viewed certain inappropriate websites. He also was monitoring her work email account for key words, and her puppy day care was flagged. Kanani is furious at the invasion of her privacy posed by this computer monitoring. Does her employer have a right to monitor her computer use in this way, and how might you suggest she respond? If you were her manager, how might you separate your monitoring between appropriate technology use and inappropriate use, and was Kanani's use appropriate?

Are There Guarantees in Life?

Privacy is a surprisingly vague and disputed value in contemporary society. With the escalating use of technology in all aspects of our lives, we also have greater concerns for our personal privacy. Yet there is widespread confusion concerning the nature, extent, and value of privacy. Both philosophers and legal scholars have argued that our society cannot maintain its core values without simultaneously guaranteeing the privacy of the individual. For example, philosopher Immanuel Kant argues that the right to privacy imposes on us the duty not to intrude into the private activities of another person.[1] And Supreme Court Justice William O. Douglas wrote in his dissent of *Public Utilities Commission v. Pollak,* "The right to be let alone is indeed the beginning of freedom."[2]

New inventions and business processes are astonishing! Yet they also remind us that we have to pay attention to protecting that right "to be let alone." Instantaneous photographs, Twitter, and other forms of social media have invaded our sacred precincts of private and domestic life, and numerous technological devices threaten to make good the prediction that "what is whispered in the closet shall be proclaimed from the house-tops."[3]

Philosopher Chris MacDonald explains that privacy is about having a realm of personal control from which others can be excluded at will—by our choice. In other words, it has to do with freedom of action, freedom from the prying eyes of neighbors, governments, or employers. The more of this type of freedom that we have, the more privacy we have.[4]

As organizations face the increasing likelihood of worldwide pandemics, there are important implications for privacy at a global level. Privacy protections of employee data vary from country to country. Multinational corporations are advised to consider local laws on data privacy, which may be particularly strict in Europe and also in Asian countries such as China, Hong Kong, or Singapore.[5] During periods of pandemics, employers may have greater interests in investigating employees' close contacts, where they have traveled recently, or recent activities and also may be subject to different disclosure responsibilities. Employers must ensure compliance with these information-gathering and disclosure regulations in each jurisdiction in which they are doing business.

Yet while employers are trying to abide by the laws, technology increases their power, ability, and frequency to monitor their workers. Worldwide spending on security and computer monitoring software is expected to total $133.8 billion in 2022 compared to a total of $94.2 billion in 2018 (a 42 percent increase).[6] Perhaps due to the increase in monitoring, instances of employee-related theft in retail stores has come down slightly from a high in 2016 at an estimated average dollar lost per dishonest employee at $1,922.80 down to approximately $1,264.10 in 2018.[7] Apprehensions, terminations, prosecutions, and civil demands (demand from merchant for repayment in lieu of filing charges and/or prosecuting) all have gone down since 2015.

Europeans generally view employee rights from a different perspective than those living in the United States. While Americans view rights of employees in terms of the protection of their privacy, Europeans are more likely to perceive their protection with regard to human dignity and the employee's right to be free from embarrassment and humiliation.[8] As a practical application of this difference, in 2016, the European Parliament approved the very broad General Data Protection Regulation (GDPR) (discussed in greater detail later in this chapter). The GDPR was passed largely on arguments based on human dignity, stating specifically that its protections "shall include suitable and specific measures to safeguard the data subject's human dignity, legitimate interests and fundamental rights, with particular regard to the transparency of processing, the transfer of personal data within a group of undertakings, or a group of enterprises engaged in a joint economic activity and monitoring systems at the work place."[9] As a result of the GDPR, some U.S. firms that engage in business internationally have found themselves in violation of EU standards and therefore subject to hefty fines or worse, when they apply their privacy rules to employees who are located in the European Union.[10]

LO1 Describe the nature of privacy as a fundamental right.

The concept of privacy as a fundamental right certainly is not limited to the United States and Europe nor even to the legal environment. In the realm of religion, Islamic thought recognizes a fundamental right to privacy based in the Qur'an, which instructs: "Do not spy on one another" (49:12) and "Do not enter any houses except your own homes unless you are sure of their occupants' consent" (24:27). Hadiths (recorded sayings of the Prophet Mohammed) report that he instructed his followers that a man should not even enter his own house suddenly or surreptitiously.[11] Ancient Greece already had laws protecting privacy, and the Jewish Talmud considers privacy an aspect of one's sanctity, providing rules for protecting one's home. In fact, the Talmud contains reference to "harm caused by seeing" (*hezeq re'iyyah*) when one intrudes upon another.

Employers also may have legitimate business reasons for seeking seemingly private information about employees and about their activities *outside* work. The global economy is intensely competitive, so each employee is crucial to her or his employer, as a producer, as an income- and idea-generator, or for other contributions. When workers are distracted or unable to function effectively, they cost their employers money. Therefore, an employer may have a justification for its efforts to choose and retain the most qualified person for the job by learning as much as it can about each worker. However, that does not mean that every bit of information about the worker is fair game.

Consider that in 2019, there were an estimated 31.9 million users of illegal drugs who were aged 12 or older in the United States, and 13.4 million of those users were employed in some capacity.[12] Other sources estimate that approximately 8.8 percent of all full-time employees in the United States and 9.4 percent of part-time employees use illegal substances.[13] These numbers impact employers significantly; the National Safety Council (NSC) estimates that they lose anywhere from $25.6 billion to $53.4 billion in employee productivity due only to the misuse of prescription drugs.[14] The NSC also reports that workers who abuse alcohol and drugs are more likely to miss work than those who do not, are more likely to leave the organization, and are more likely to spend time in the emergency room or be admitted to the hospital. The average person who abuses opioids has annual health care costs that are 8.7 times higher than those of non-abusers.

These costs to the employer stem not only from lost productivity or absentee-ism. Failure to perform a drug test and perform an intensive reference and back-ground check of an applicant also may result in liability (or at least costs to defend claims) for negligent hiring. Employers therefore may consider the costs of testing versus the risk of not testing (see detailed discussion in Chapter 4). Even the use of social media on the job may represent a cost to employers in terms of lost produc-tivity. The average person spends an average of 2 hours and 16 minutes on social media during each 8-hour day,[15] and this access to social media during working hours costs employers $650 billion a year.[16]

The right to privacy not only is balanced with the arguably legitimate interests of the employer but also with the employer's responsibility to protect employees' and customers' personal information. Theft of computerized customer and employee records has increased dramatically over the past decade, and the costs associated can be enormous. Between 2017 and 2018, the average number of security breaches increased from 130 to 145 breaches (11 percent), and the average cost to an organi-zation of cyber-based crime increased by 12 percent ($1.4 million) to $13 million.[17] In July 2019, Capital One experienced a security breach in the United States when a hacker accessed 100 million credit card applications, including 140,000 social security numbers, 1 million social insurance numbers, and 80,000 bank accounts.[18] Capital One was later hit with a class action lawsuit by customers due to the data breach. In the first half of 2019 alone, data breaches exposed 4.1 billion records.[19] You can imagine that investment in cyber-security systems has become increasingly important to organizations.

Yet the fact that only the largest and most audacious data breaches are reported in the media means that we do not really know the true extent of the problem. A 2012 survey of over 1,200 U.S. small businesses (defined as those with annual revenues of less than $10 million) found that 55 percent had experienced a data breach, and of those, only 33 percent notified the people affected.[20] Yet all 50 states plus D.C., Guam, Puerto Rico, and the Virgin Islands require that indi-viduals are notified when their private information is exposed,[21] although many states allow exemptions from notification if an investigation determines there is no reasonable likelihood of harm to affected individuals.[22] In February 2018, a draft of a proposed federal Data Acquisition and Technology Accountability and Security Act was circulated. However, many state attorneys general feared that a federal law that was designed to preempt stronger state data breach laws would interfere with rather than enhance their states' laws. As of publication, there is no federal data breach law, and passage of one in the foreseeable future appears unlikely.[23]

The Ponemon Institute conducted research in 2017 of companies that had experienced data breaches and found that they experienced an average stock price decline of 5 percent immediately following the disclosure of their breach. It con-cluded that the more quickly a company responded to the data breach, the lower their costs, the more likely that their stock price would recover (an average of 7 days after the breach), and the more likely that their customers would remain with them, citing greater loyalty and trust.[24]

While erosion of at-will employment was considered one of the dominant issues in employment law at the end of the last century, scholars predicted that privacy would be the main theme for the next century. This chapter will address the employee's rights regarding personal information and the employer's responsibilities regarding that information as well as the employer's right to find out both job-related and non-related personal information about its employees. Chapter 4 previously addressed other issues regarding the legality of information gathering through testing procedures. This chapter will not address issues relating to consumer privacy since they fall outside the scope of the chapter's and the text's primary focus.

Privacy: U.S. Legal Framework

LO2 Explain the three general ways in which privacy is legally protected in the United States.

There are three ways in which privacy may be legally protected: by the Constitution (federal or state), by federal and/or state statutes, and by the common law. The U.S. Constitution does not actually mention privacy, but privacy has been inferred as a necessary adjunct of other constitutional rights we hold. The right to privacy was first recognized by the Supreme Court in *Griswold v. Connecticut,*[25] when the Court held that a Connecticut statute restricting a married couple's use of birth control devices unconstitutionally infringed on the right to marital privacy.

fundamental right
A right that is guaranteed by the Constitution, whether stated or not.

The Court held a constitutional guarantee of various zones of privacy as a part of the **fundamental rights** guaranteed by the Constitution, such as the right to free speech and the right to be free from unreasonable searches and seizures. The latter right is that on which many claims for privacy rights are based; the Court has held that under certain circumstances the required disclosure of certain types of personal information should be considered an unreasonable search. It has protected against the mandatory disclosure of personal papers, and it decided in favor of the right to make procreation decisions privately.

At first glance, one might argue that broad or baseless intrusions into one's personal sphere are inappropriate in the workplace. But the counterargument is that, if an employee does not want to offer a piece of information, maybe there is something that the employee is trying to hide. For example, why would an employee refuse to submit to a drug test if that employee is not abusing drugs? Do **private sector** employers have the right to ask their employees *any* question they choose and then take negative employment actions against the employee if she or he refuses to answer since they are not necessarily constrained by constitutional protections?

private sector
That segment of the workforce represented by private companies (companies that are not owned or managed by the government or one of its agencies).

While you might have one perspective on the question above, would your answer remain the same if your employer asked you for all of your social media passwords? What if that request were not limited to Facebook but included online dating sites like Tinder or others? (See Exhibit 14.1, "Realities about Employee Privacy Rights.")

Additionally, employees are concerned about the type of information gathered in the course of applying for and holding a job. Who has access to that information? What information may be deemed "confidential," and what does that mean to the employee? Evidently, employers perceive challenging issues among these and others

---

Exhibit 14.1   *Realities about Employee Privacy Rights*

1. Employees do not have an absolute right to privacy in their workplace.

2. It is not a breach of an employee's right to privacy for an employer to ask with whom the employee lives.

3. In the private sector, the Constitution does not protect employees' right to be free from unreasonable searches and seizures.

4. Without constitutional protection, employees are safeguarded to some extent by common-law protections against invasions of privacy.

5. Though an employee may give information to an employer, the employer is still bound to use that information only for the purpose for which it was collected.

---

with regard to privacy. In 2016, 54 percent of firms had a chief data officer; that number now is in excess of 67.9 percent.[26] Through the course of this chapter, we will address the wide range of privacy issues that employers and employees face.

Workplace Privacy, Generally

LO3 Define the legal concept of a "reasonable expectation of privacy" and its application to the workplace.

common law
Law made and applied by judges, based on precedent (prior case law).

Privacy protections in the workplace are a completely different animal than other types of workplace protections, such as protections against discrimination on the basis of gender, disability, and age. Simply put, employees in the private sector workplace in the United States do not have broad rights to personal privacy. Why? To begin, unlike the other areas, no *comprehensive* federal workplace privacy legislation exists. The protections that do exist, as discussed previously, arise from a motley collection of inferences from the Constitution, limited-purpose federal laws, assorted state laws, and some **common law** (court-created protections through case law).

Further, in almost every state, employees are hired at will, which means that employers can fire them for good reasons, for bad reasons, or for no reason at all, as long as it is not for an illegal reason, as we shall discuss in more detail later. By "bad reasons," we simply mean any reason that might not make sense to the employee. For instance, if the supervisor woke up on the wrong side of the bed, gets in an unfounded argument with the employee, and fires the worker, the worker has no claim.

If an employer legitimately can fire an employee for "bad reasons," you can see why an employee is not going to be successful in stating a case against the employer for violating the employee's privacy unless the employee can fit his or her complaint specifically into one of the protections guaranteed by the federal, state, and common laws, thus turning a "bad reason" into an "illegal reason."

Perhaps the most effective way to understand workplace privacy protections is to examine where the protections *do* exist. Courts have recognized an employee's right to privacy in the workplace where there is a "reasonable expectation of privacy."[27] However, contrary to, for instance, a bedroom, courts also have held that a work area is not a place of solitude or seclusion; therefore, employees should have no expectation of privacy in that environment.[28] In addition, employees should have no reasonable expectation of privacy surrounding anything that the employer provides to employees—a telephone, computer, desk, chair, or other business-related instrument—because those items also belong to the employer. Thus, *the content of emails, telephone calls, and computer activity conducted on employer-provided equipment also is considered not private.*

Is There *Any* Reasonable Expectation of Privacy in the Workplace?

Employees spend a third of their waking hours at work. As they go about their days, can they expect some semblance of privacy as they go about their work day? In short the answer is yes. There are three basic areas in which employees can reasonably expect their actions to be private.

First, employees have an expectation of privacy with regard to their body, including what they carry in their pockets. Their employer *generally* does not have the right to frisk them or to require them to disclose what they are carrying in their pockets, although, as we shall see later, there are situations in which such an invasion of privacy would be appropriate. This expectation of privacy extends to company-provided bathrooms, changing rooms, and showers. But should this expectation cover drug testing? We will explore that question later in this chapter. (See Exhibit 14.2, "'Reasonable' Areas in Which to Expect Privacy in the Workplace, Subject to Exceptions.")

Second, employees have an expectation of privacy in connection with items that are contained in other normally private locations, such as a purse or briefcase; however, these locations also are subject to exceptions under certain circumstances. For example, if an employee puts a purse in a company-provided desk drawer, the employer generally has the right to examine the desk drawer but likely not the contents of their purse. Similarly, employees have an expectation of privacy in the contents of their car that sits in the company parking lot, assuming that it is not a company car or that they are not using the car for company purposes other

---

Exhibit 14.2 *"Reasonable" Areas in Which to Expect Privacy in the Workplace, Subject to Exceptions*

1. One's body and physical space; one has a reasonable expectation to be free from a pat-down or body search.

2. Normally private locations, such as a purse or briefcase.

3. Personal information, accessed without permission.

than to go to and from work. Their employer generally cannot go and search an employee's car, with some exceptions.

Third, employees have an expectation of privacy in their personal (not "personnel") records and information. For example, they have the right to assume that their employer has no right to access their credit history, their driving record, or their family's medical records without their permission, but we can all imagine situations in which that rule may not apply or may be excepted. Their employer, for example, could reasonably expect to access their driving history if they were applying for a job operating a company vehicle, although the employer needs their permission to do so.

Workers usually have an expectation of privacy in the activities they choose to do in their free time, when they are away from work. We will discuss this topic in greater detail later in this chapter (see "Regulation of Employees' Off-Work Activities"). However, as you will see, this expectation is not quite as expansive as you might anticipate!

While the list may seem broad, the scope of workplace privacy rights is actually quite limited. The vast majority of the time during which employees are present at their employers' offices, they are subject to monitoring and other intrusions. Employers are free to monitor employees' movements, the keystrokes they make on their employer-provided computers, the time they spend communicating with coworkers, and even how much time they are away from their desks (as in, bathroom breaks!). Technological improvements not only have made the employer's task much easier but also have generated new ideas for intruding on employee privacy never before imagined (iris scans, voice prints, and face geometry, to name three).

Now we shall examine the specifics, first exploring public sector employee privacy and then moving on to private sector employee privacy.

Public Sector Employee Privacy

public sector
That segment of the workforce represented by governmental employers and governmental agency employers. In some situations, this term may include federal contractors.

With regard to the **public sector**, the Constitution protects individuals from wrongful invasions by the state or by anyone acting on behalf of the government. The personal privacy of federal, state, and local employees is therefore protected from governmental intrusion and excess. As we will see later in this chapter, private sector employees are subject to different—and often fewer—protections.

Constitutional Protection
The Fourth Amendment and Its Exceptions

For the Fourth Amendment's protection against unreasonable search and seizure to be applicable to a given situation, there must first exist a "search or seizure." The Supreme Court has liberally interpreted "search" to include a wide variety of activities such as the retrieval of blood samples and other bodily invasions, including urinalyses, as well as the collection of other personal information. One might imagine how the range of activities gets wider as technology advances.

LO4 Identify and apply the standard for unreasonable searches and seizures under the Fourth Amendment.

Case 1

For the search to violate the Fourth Amendment, that search must be deemed unreasonable, unjustified at its inception, and impermissible in scope. You will read in the seminal Supreme Court case *O'Connor v. Ortega,*[29] included at the end of the chapter, that a search is justified "at its inception" where the employer has reasonable grounds for suspecting that the search will turn up evidence that the employee is guilty of work-related misconduct or where the search is necessary for a non-investigatory, work-related purpose, such as to retrieve a file.

It is critical to review the *O'Connor* case at the end of the chapter to understand both the fundamental basis of public sector search and seizure law as it applies to the workplace and much of current case law today. The Court held that a search is permissible in scope where "the measures adopted are reasonably related to the objectives of the search and not excessively intrusive in light of . . . the nature of the misconduct being investigated."[30]

The U.S. Supreme Court addressed the privacy implications of global positioning systems ("GPS") in 2012 in *United States v. Jones.*[31] The Court held that placing a GPS tracking device on a suspect's car was a "search" under the Fourth Amendment. The concurring opinions in *Jones* also discussed the permissible scope of using GPS in an investigation with regard to the reasonable expectation of privacy standard. Despite an earlier holding that there is no reasonable expectation of privacy in one's location while traveling on public roads, the concurring opinions agreed that GPS tracking over an extended period of time (four weeks in this case) went beyond reasonable expectations of privacy under the Fourth Amendment. In addition, Justice Sotomayor noted that long-term GPS monitoring could reveal a wide range of personal information, including familial, political, professional, religious, and sexual associations. Though a growing number of employers are using GPS systems to track employee activity on the job (a topic discussed below), the effect of the Supreme Court's decision in the private sector remains unclear.[32] At this time, there has been no comprehensive federal legislation on GPS monitoring enacted into law.

Generally, all searches that are conducted without a judicially issued warrant based on a finding of reasonable cause are held to be unreasonable. But there are several exceptions to this rule, including searches that happen as part of an arrest, some automobile searches, pat-down searches with probable cause to believe the subject is armed, and administrative searches of certain regulated industries.

One example of an exception occurred in *Shoemaker v. Handel,*[33] where the Supreme Court found that a drug-related urine test of jockeys ordered by the State of New Jersey Racing Commission without a warrant was acceptable because it satisfied the court's two-pronged test. The Court held that the search does not violate the Fourth Amendment where:

1. There is a strong state interest in conducting the unannounced, warrantless search, and

2. The pervasive regulation of the industry reduces the expectation of privacy.

Similarly, in *Skinner v. Railway Labor Executives' Association,*[34] decided three years after *Shoemaker,* the Court again addressed the question of whether certain forms of drug and alcohol testing violate the Fourth Amendment. While this case is discussed earlier in this text in connection with testing, it also is relevant here for the Court's analysis of the privacy right challenged. In *Skinner,* the defendant justified testing railway workers based on safety concerns: "to prevent accidents and casualties in railroad operations that result from impairment of employees by alcohol or drugs." The Court held that "[t]he Government's interest in regulating the conduct of railroad employees to ensure safety, like its supervision of probationers or regulated industries, or its operation of a government office, school, or prison, likewise presents 'special needs' beyond normal law enforcement that may justify departures from the usual warrant and probable-cause requirements."[35]

It was clear to the Court that the governmental interest in ensuring the safety of the traveling public and of the employees themselves "plainly justifies prohibiting covered employees from using alcohol or drugs on duty, or while subject to being called for duty." The issue then for the Court was whether the means by which the defendant monitored compliance with this prohibition justified the privacy intrusion absent a warrant or individualized suspicion. In reviewing the justification, the Court focused on the fact that permission to dispense with warrants is strongest where "the burden of obtaining a warrant is likely to frustrate the governmental purpose behind the search" and recognized that "alcohol and other drugs are eliminated from the bloodstream at a constant rate and blood and breath samples taken to measure whether these substances were in the bloodstream when a triggering event occurred must be obtained as soon as possible."[36] In addition, the Court noted that the railway workers' expectations of privacy in this industry are diminished given its high scrutiny through regulation to ensure safety.

The Court therefore concluded that the railway's compelling interests outweigh privacy concerns since the proposed testing "is not an undue infringement on the justifiable expectations of privacy of covered employees." Consider the possible implications of this and related decisions on genetic testing in governmental workplaces or in employment in heavily regulated industries such as that involved in *Skinner.*

Related to issues of drug testing and privacy, is it acceptable for an employer to conduct a search of employee lockers? Under what circumstances would you consider this type of search to be acceptable? A search may constitute an invasion of privacy, depending on the nature of the employer and the purpose of the search. The reasonableness of a search is determined by balancing the extent of the invasion and the extent to which the employee should expect to have privacy in this area against the employer's interest in the security of its workplace, the productivity of its workers, and other job-related concerns.

Prior to any search of employer-owned property, such as desks or lockers, employees should be given formal written notice of the intent to search without their consent. If the employer seeks to search employee-owned property within the workplace, such as purses or wallets, consent should be obtained prior to the search, employees should be forewarned, and employees should be made well aware of the procedures involved.[37] Consent is recommended under these circumstances because an employee has a greater expectation of privacy in those personal areas. These rights are significantly diminished where the employer is not restrained by constitutional protections.

In an interesting combination of private and public workplace rights, the Ninth Circuit addressed these issues in the 2007 case *United States v. Ziegler.*[38] In that case, Ziegler worked for a private company that had a clear policy in technology use. It explained that equipment and software were company-owned, to be used for business purposes only, and that employees' emails would be monitored constantly. The FBI received a complaint from the firm's Internet provider that Ziegler had accessed child pornography from a company computer and requested access to his computer.[39] The employer consented to the request.

The *Ziegler* court held that the *employer* had the right to consent to the search because the computer was workplace property, the contents of Ziegler's hard drive were work-related items that contained business information, and those contents were provided to or created by the employee in the context of a business relationship. Ziegler's downloading of personal items (pornography) did not destroy the employer's common authority over the computer since the company had a policy that *informed employees that electronic devices were company-owned and subject to monitoring*—two key components necessary to the reasonable expectation element in any employment context.[40]

Ziegler had stored inappropriate files directly on a work computer. What would happen if the files were stored instead in the cloud rather than on the work computer? For instance, Dropbox is a common application where files are stored in the cloud. The application then synchronizes with an individual's hard drive in order to provide an access point for files stored remotely in the cloud. Should an employer with a policy such as that in *Ziegler* also have access to his Dropbox files?

In *Frankhouser v. Clearfield County Career and Technology Center,*[41] the judge denied summary judgment to Frankhouser's employer (CCCT) on her claim that her Fourth Amendment rights had been violated. CCCT gave Frankhouser permission to use her personal Dropbox account on her work computer. Frankhouser's supervisor knew where Frankhouser had stored her passwords, accessed her Dropbox account, and found personal pictures that the firm considered inappropriate. On the basis of those photos, Frankhouser was terminated. The plaintiff argued that she had a reasonable expectation of privacy since she did not view nor store the photos on her work computer, only in her private cloud account. The Court agreed with her based on three reasons: (1) She maintained her own private Dropbox account, (2) the account was password-protected, and (3) she never accessed or downloaded the pictures on the work computer. The parties settled out of court, leaving an open question whether cloud storage is considered private or subject to employer scrutiny when used on an employer's computer.

Carpenter v. United States[42] is also an important 2018 Supreme Court case that has implications for workplace privacy, particularly regarding tracking cell phone usage and location through cell phone history. Carpenter was involved with several individuals who were committing burglaries at RadioShack and T-Mobile locations in the Detroit area. Initially, Carpenter was not arrested, but one of those arrested handed over his phone to law enforcement so they could review calls he made in the period leading up to his arrest. The historical cell records enabled the government to track Carpenter's location for 127 days. They determined that he was within a two-mile radius of four of the incidents based on the cell tower records, and subsequently he was arrested.

The *Carpenter* court's decision was influenced by a number of important cases. *United States v. Knotts*[43] and *United States v. Jones*[44] both address a person's expectation of privacy in his physical location and movements. In *Knotts,* the officers planted a beeper in an item that Knotts's co-conspirators subsequently purchased. The officers then followed Knotts along the streets, with intermittent aerial assistance, to Knotts's cabin, where he was later apprehended. The Court concluded that tracking Knotts via beeper did not constitute a search because "a person traveling in an automobile on public thoroughfares has no reasonable expectation of privacy in his movements from one place to another."[45] As well, it believed that the Knotts case addressed a discrete event versus ongoing surveillance.

In *United States v. Jones,* the Court addressed more sophisticated surveillance but found that different principles applied. When FBI agents installed a GPS tracking devise on Jones's car, they conducted ongoing surveillance rather than a discrete event. GPS monitoring tracks movement constantly and thus constituted a violation of Jones's privacy.

In a second set of relevant cases cited in *Carpenter,* the Court explained the difference between the information that a person may keep private versus that which is shared with others. Under *Smith v. Maryland,*[46] once an individual hands over information to a third party, there is no longer a legitimate expectation of privacy. Recall that Carpenter was not the person who handed over his phone, it was his co-conspirator who did. Therefore, Carpenter did not give up his right to privacy in that context. *United States v. Miller* extended the conclusions in *Smith,* "even if the information is revealed on the assumption that it will be used only for a limited purpose."[47] Ultimately, the Court denied extension of *Smith* and *Miller,* holding that gathering phone numbers and bank records was not applicable to the novel circumstances that neither case could have foreseen in which a phone actually travels with the individual wherever they go. Because a cell phone's GPS can easily, cheaply, and efficiently gather detailed information about an individual's life, the Court concluded that Carpenter's Fourth Amendment rights had been violated. The majority explained,

> [S]eismic shifts in digital technology made possible the tracking of not only Carpenter's location but also everyone else's, not for a short period but for years and years. Sprint Corporation and its competitors are not your typical witnesses. Unlike the nosy neighbor who keeps an eye on comings and goings, they are ever alert, and their memory is nearly infallible. There is a world of difference between the limited types of personal information addressed in *Smith* and *Miller* and the exhaustive chronicle of location information casually collected by wireless carriers today.[48]

While this case does not directly speak to employment-related privacy issues, its implications for Fourth Amendment rights in a broad sense are important. This case will be addressed further in the discussion of monitoring employees at work.

Finally, when an employee is detained during a search, the employee may have a claim for *false imprisonment,* which is defined as a total restraint on an employee's freedom to move against her or his will, such as keeping an employee in one area of an office. The employee need not be "locked" into the confinement to be restrained, but when the employee remains free to leave at any time, there is no false imprisonment. Note that, even though a door may remain unlocked, a reasonable fear of consequences for leaving (such as losing one's job or physical harm) is sufficient to demonstrate imprisonment.

The Fifth and Fourteenth Amendments

The Fifth and Fourteenth Amendments also protect a government employee's right to privacy since the state may not restrict one's rights unless it is justified. For instance, the Supreme Court has consistently held that everyone has a fundamental right to travel, free of government intervention. Where the state attempts to infringe on anything that has been determined to be a fundamental right, that infringement or restriction is subject to the *strict scrutiny* of the courts. For the restriction to be allowed, the state must show that the restriction is justified by a *compelling state interest.* Moreover, the restriction must be the least intrusive alternative available.

On the other hand, for those interests not deemed by the courts to constitute fundamental rights, a state may impose any restrictions that can be shown to be *rationally related to a valid state interest,* a much more lenient test.

To determine whether the state may restrict or intrude on an employee's privacy rights, it must first be determined whether the claimed right is fundamental. Two tests are used to make this determination. First, the court may look to whether the right is "implicit in the concept of ordered liberty, such that neither liberty nor justice would exist if [the rights] were sacrificed." Second is whether the right is "deeply rooted in this Nation's history and tradition."[49]

While procreation, child rearing, education, marriage, and the right to refuse medical treatment have been held to be within the area of privacy protected by the Constitution, other issues have not yet been addressed or determined by the Court, including the right to be free from mandatory preemployment medical tests. Moreover, the Court has found *no* general right of the individual to be left alone.

The Privacy Act of 1974

See Chapter 2 to revisit key concepts.

Governmental intrusion into the lives of federal employees is also restricted by the Privacy Act of 1974. Much of the discussion in the area of employee privacy is framed by governmental response to the issue, both because of limitations imposed on the government regarding privacy and because of the potential for abuse. The Privacy Act of 1974 regulates the release of personal information about federal employees by federal agencies. Specifically, but for 12 stated exceptions, no federal agency may release information about an employee that contains the means for identifying that employee without the employee's prior written consent. (See Exhibit 14.3, "Privacy Act of 1974.")

There are four basic principles that underlie the Privacy Act:

1. To restrict disclosure of personally identifiable records maintained by agencies.
2. To grant individuals increased rights of access to agency records maintained on themselves.

Exhibit 14.3 *Privacy Act of 1974*

No Agency shall disclose any record which is contained in a system of records by any means of communication to any person, or to another agency, except pursuant to a written request by, or with the prior written consent of, the individual to whom the record pertains, unless disclosure of the record would be

1. To those officers and employees of the agency which maintains the record who have a need for the record in the performance of their duties.

2. Required under section 552 of this title; (*the Freedom of Information Act*). (*Note that this act does not apply to "personnel, medical, and similar files the disclosure of which would constitute a clearly unwarranted invasion of personal privacy."*)

3. For a routine use as defined in subsection (a)(7) of this section and described under subsection (e)(4)(D).

4. To the Bureau of the Census for purposes of planning or carrying out a census or survey or related activity. . . .

5. To a recipient who has provided the agency with advance adequate written assurance that the record will be used solely as a statistical research or reporting record, and the record is to be transferred in a form that is not individually identifiable.

6. To the National Archives and Records Administration as a record which has sufficient historical or other value to warrant its continued preservation by the United States

Government, or for evaluation by the Archivist of the United States or the designee of the Archivist to determine whether the record has such value.

7. To another federal agency or to an instrumentality of any government jurisdiction within or under the control of the United States for a civil or criminal law enforcement activity if the activity is authorized by law, and if the head of the agency or instrumentality has made a written request to the agency which maintains the record specifying the particular portion desired and the law enforcement activity for which the record is sought.

8. To a person pursuant to a showing of compelling circumstances affecting the health or safety of an individual if upon such disclosure notification is transmitted to the last known address of such individual.

9. To either House of Congress, or, to the extent of matter within its jurisdiction, any committee or subcommittee thereof, any joint committee of Congress or subcommittee of any such joint committee.

10. To the Comptroller General, or any of his authorized representatives, in the course of the performance of the duties of the Government Accountability Office.

11. Pursuant to the order of a court of competent jurisdiction.

12. To a consumer reporting agency in accordance with section 3711(e) of Title 31.

3. To grant individuals the right to seek amendment of agency records maintained on themselves upon a showing that the records are not accurate, relevant, timely, or complete.

4. To establish a code of "fair information practices" that requires agencies to comply with statutory norms for collection, maintenance, and dissemination of records.[50]

By affording the employee with these rights, Congress has effectively put the right of disclosure of personal information in the hands of the employee, at least when none of the 12 specified exceptions applies.

When one of the Privacy Act exceptions applies, the act dismisses the employee consent requirement, which gives the agency total control over the use of the file. The right to privacy is not absolute; the extent of protection varies with the extent of the intrusion, and the interests of the employee are balanced against the interests of the employer. Basically, the information requested under either the Privacy Act or the Freedom of Information Act is subject to a balancing test weighing the need to know the information against the employee's privacy interest.

The Ninth Circuit Court of Appeals has developed guidelines to assist in this balancing test. The court directs that the following four factors be looked to in reaching a conclusion relating to disclosure:

1. The individual's interest in disclosure of the information sought.
2. The public interest in disclosure.
3. The degree of invasion of personal privacy.
4. Whether there are alternative means of getting the information.[51]

Critics of the act suggest that it is enormously weakened as a result of one particular exemption that allows disclosure for "routine use" compatible with the reason the information was originally collected. In addition, certain specific agencies are exempted. For instance, in March 2003, the Department of Justice exempted the National Crime Information Center, which is a resource for 80,000 law enforcement agencies.

The Privacy Act grants employees two options for relief: criminal penalties and civil remedies, including damages and injunctive relief. The act also allows employees who are adversely affected by an agency's noncompliance to bring a civil suit against the agency in federal court.

Privacy Protection Study Commission

The Privacy Protection Study Commission was formed by Congress with the purpose of studying the possibility of extending the Privacy Act to the private sector. In 1977, the commission concluded that the Privacy Act should not be extended to private employers but that private sector employees should be given many new privacy protections. The suggested protections required a determination of current information-gathering practices and their reasons, a limitation on the information that may be collected to what is relevant, a requirement that the employer inform its employees to ensure accuracy, and a limitation on the usage of the information gathered both internally and externally.

The commission further found that certain issues demanded federal intervention and, for this reason, recommended that (1) the use of polygraph tests in employment-related issues be prohibited, (2) pretext interviews be prohibited, (3) the use of arrest or criminal records in employment decisions be prohibited except where otherwise allowed or required by law, (4) employers be required to use reasonable care in selection of their investigating agencies, and (5) the Federal Fair Credit Reporting Act provisions be strengthened. These recommendations have yet to be implemented by Congress, primarily due to private employers' vocal rejection of such an extension of federal law due to the cost of the implementation of the recommendations.

Federal Wiretapping—Title III

Title III of the Federal Wiretap Act,[52] as amended (particularly by the Electronic Communications Privacy Act of 1986, discussed below), provides privacy protection for and governs the interception of oral, wire, and electronic communications. Title III covers all telephone communications regardless of the medium, except that it does not cover the radio portion of a cordless telephone communication that is transmitted between the handset and base unit. The law authorizes the interception of oral, wire, and electronic communications by investigative and law enforcement officers conducting criminal investigations pertaining to serious criminal offenses or felonies, following the issuance of a court order by a judge. The Title III law authorizes the interception of particular criminal communications related to particular criminal offenses. In short, it authorizes the acquisition of evidence of crime. It does not authorize noncriminal intelligence gathering, nor does it authorize interceptions related to social or political views.

Forty-four states, plus the District of Columbia, the Virgin Islands, and Puerto Rico, have statutes permitting interceptions by state and local law enforcement officers for certain types of criminal investigations.[53] All of the state statutes are based upon Title III, from which they derive. These statutes must be at least as restrictive as Title III, and in fact, most are more restrictive in their requirements. In describing the legal requirements, we will focus on those for Title III since they define the baseline for all wiretaps performed by federal, state, and local law enforcement agencies.

In recent years, state statutes have been modified to keep pace with rapid technological advances in telecommunications. Thirty-nine states plus the District of Columbia have a "one-party consent" standard, which means that only one party to the conversation has to know the conversation is being recorded. The remaining 11 states have adopted "all-party consent," meaning that everyone involved in the conversation must consent to the recording prior to it occurring.[54]

Wiretaps are limited to the crimes specified in Title III and state statutes. Most wiretaps are large undertakings, requiring a substantial use of resources. In 2018, the average cost of installing a single instance of an intercept device and related monitoring communications was $66,807. The frequency of wiretap requests reached a high in 2015 at 4,148 requests but has since decreased to approximately 2,937 requests in 2018. Of the requests made in 2018 by both federal and states, only two wiretap applications were denied.[55]

Employers should be aware that office security systems, cell phones, and telephones used for conference calls might be considered eavesdropping devices.[56] Consider that Amazon's Alexa is known to record everything it hears after its name, as do Apple's Siri and Google's Assistant.[57] Even a seemingly harmless and helpful mechanism may fall under the category of an eavesdropping device, and employers should take precaution that they are complying with all applicable laws.

Electronic Communications Privacy Act (ECPA)

Title III was created to combat invasion by the government for eavesdropping, in large part due to the Watergate scandal in the 1970s. Originally the federal statutes targeted government eavesdropping on telephone discussions without the consent of the speakers. The federal statute required the government agents to obtain a warrant before they could intercept any oral discussions. In late 1986, Congress increased the coverage by broadening the range of electronic communications, resulting in the ECPA.

The ECPA covers all forms of digital communications, including transmissions of text and digitalized images, in addition to voice communications on the telephone. The law also prohibits unauthorized eavesdropping by all persons and businesses, not only by the government. However, U.S. courts have ruled that "interception" applies only to messages in transit and not to messages that have actually reached company computers. So that is not much help! The result is that the ECPA impacts electronic monitoring only by third parties and not by employers. Further, the ECPA allows interception where consent has been granted. Firms often will have employees consent to monitoring of all communications at the time of hire so they are immune from ECPA liability. They do not even need consent if the employer provided the service being monitored, such as the email system.[58]

Finally, the ECPA only covers electronic, voice, and wire communications, so many of the new ways in which employers might monitor employees were never contemplated by the act (e.g. GPS monitoring). Ultimately, under the act, employers are justified in intercepting email messages as long as they have a valid business reason for doing so (e.g., to ensure that the employee is not using work email to send personal messages or harass others).

Private Sector Employee Privacy

LO5 Explain the distinctions between the protections for public and private sector privacy.

Despite the fact that public and private employers often have a similar legitimate need for information about applicants and employees in order to make informed decisions about hiring, promotion, security, discipline, and termination, privacy rights in private sector employment are limited. An employee who is treated arbitrarily, but who is without a union agreement or contract, is generally left with *fewer* rights in the private sector environment.

Generally, employment actions by private employers do not trigger constitutional protections because the Constitution is designed mostly to curb government activities. The term used is *State action,* which includes actions by both state and federal governments. If no state action is involved, no constitutional protections are triggered.

Whether we are considering the right to privacy in either the public or the private sector, employers suggest that the employee has three choices when faced with objectionable intrusions by employers: quit, comply, or object (and risk being fired). Employees argue that they are defenseless because of their financial condition and that their privacy in the private sector is subject to greater abuse precisely because there are no protections and that the option to quit is, frankly, economically unrealistic.

One explanation offered for the difference between public and private sector privacy protections is compliance-related costs. The implementation of the Privacy Act throughout its agencies costs the government relatively little because it is regulating itself. By contrast, ensuring compliance within the private sector requires a separate administration of compliance and adjudication of violations. The Privacy Protection Study Commission found that requiring an employer to change its manner of maintaining and using records can drastically increase the cost of its operations.

These costs include the costs of changing employment record-keeping practices, removing relevant information from employment decisions, and implementing a social policy of employee privacy protection. Employers' concern for compliance costs may well be an unrealistic barrier to the development of regulations for privacy rights of private sector employees.

A second distinction between public and private sector employers that might explain the different privacy standards is that more stringent regulation is needed for government employees because it is common for federal agencies to be overzealous in surveillance and information gathering. Private sector employers, in contrast, do not generally have similar resources and, therefore, are unable to duplicate the more invasive activities at that same level of scrutiny.

Legal Framework for Employee Rights in the Private Sector

LO6   Describe the legal framework that applies to private sector privacy cases.

employment-at-will
Absent a particular contract or other legal obligation that specifies the length or conditions of employment, all employees are employed "at will." This means that, unless an agreement specifies otherwise, employees are free to leave the position at any time and for any reason. By virtue of the inherent imbalance of power in the relationship, this mutuality is often only in theory.

See Chapter 2 to revisit key concepts.

As discussed in Chapter 2, in every state but one (Montana),[59] employment in many contexts is considered to be "at-will." **Employment-at-will** means that the employee serves at the will of the employer. Barring a wrongful reason, such as discrimination, employers generally are permitted to fire an employee for reasons that some might consider valid (such as incompetence or insubordination) or for reasons that might seem preposterous. Perhaps the manager merely had a bad day and is taking it out on the worker.

In other words, in every state other than Montana, employers are permitted to create a relationship with their employees based on this at-will environment. But the issue is relevant to our discussion of privacy because an employer might discover some personal (i.e., otherwise private) information about an employee and choose to terminate the employment *on that basis.* Since employees often serve at the whim of the employer (when they are in an at-will relationship), understanding an employee's right to privacy in the private sector is important as they can become a legitimate defense when employers cross the line and use private information obtained about an employee.

In at-will states, employees have some rights and actually have some form of a "right to work" even if they work in an at-will state. Exhibit 14.4, "Protecting the Right to Work in the At-Will Employment Context" highlights four ways in which this occurs. First, as we have seen in other chapters, federal and state laws protect employees from certain employment actions, such as those based on discrimination against one of the protected classes, including gender or race.

There are several other bases to an employee's right to work. Second, an employee who signs an employment contract has the rights identified in the contract. As well, union employees have the protections guaranteed to them by the collective bargaining agreement between the employer and the union.

Exhibit 14.4 *Protecting the Right to Work in the At-Will Employment Context*

Four ways in which the Right to Work in the At-Will Employment Context are protected?

1. Federal and state statutory protections, such as antidiscrimination laws.

2. Employment contracts, where they exist.

3. Collective bargaining agreements, where applicable.

4. State law exceptions to employment-at-will, including violations of public policy, breaches of implied contracts, or other statutory exceptions.

Lastly, employment-at-will also is limited by certain exceptions created by either statute or case law. Some states recognize one or more exceptions, while others might recognize none at all. In addition, the definition of these exceptions may vary from state to state.

- Bad faith, malicious, or retaliatory termination in violation of *public policy.*
- Termination in breach of the *implied covenant of good faith and fair dealing.*
- Termination in breach of some other *implied contract term,* such as those that might be created by employee handbook provisions (in certain jurisdictions).
- Termination in violation of the doctrine of *promissory estoppel* (where the employee reasonably relied on an employer's promise, to the employee's detriment).
- Other exceptions as determined by *statutes* [such as the Worker Adjustment and Retraining Notification Act (WARN)].

See Chapter 2 to revisit key concepts.

If an employee wishes to recover against an employer in an at-will relationship, the employee must be able to point to a statute, court decision or common law, or contractual provision that protects her or him. In the area of privacy, given the absence of any comprehensive national privacy law, that task might be somewhat difficult. Thus understanding what privacy rights do exist can help employees mount a defense if they believe their privacy has been violated and they have been removed under the guise of an at-will employment relationship.

Bases for Right to Privacy in the Private Sector

Private sector employers are not bound by constitutional structures. On a state-by-state basis, however, private sector employees may have the protection of either common law or by statute. In addition, states provide common-law tort claims

tort
A private (civil) wrong
against a person or her
or his property.

to protect individual privacy, such as intrusion into seclusion. (A **tort** is a legal wrong, for which the law offers a remedy.) Various torts described below have developed to protect individual solitude, the publication of private information, and publications that present personal information in a false light.

Statutory Claims

State legislatures have responded to the issue of private sector employee privacy in one of four ways:

1. **Broad Legislation:** Enacting legislation mirroring federal law regarding the compilation and dissemination of information.
2. **State Constitutions:** Recognizing a constitutional right to privacy under their state constitutions, as in Alaska, Arizona, California, Florida, Hawaii, Illinois, Louisiana, Montana, New Hampshire, South Carolina, and Washington.[60] For example, California appellate courts have found that employees terminated for refusing to submit to drug tests were wrongfully discharged in violation of the state's constitutional guarantee of a right to privacy, which requires employers to demonstrate a compelling interest in invading an employee's privacy. In Pennsylvania, a court held that a drug test violates that state's policy against invasions of privacy where the methods used do not give due regard to the employee's privacy or if the test results disclose medical information beyond what is necessary. In all states except California, application of this provision to private sector organizations is limited, uncertain, or not included at all.
3. **Limited Legislation:** Protecting employees only in certain areas of employment, such as personnel records or the use of credit information.
4. **No State Protections:** Leaving private sector employees to fend for themselves while the federal laws and the Constitution afford protection to federal employees and those subject to state action.

Tort Law Protections/Common Law

As mentioned above, courts in almost all states have developed case law, "common law," which identifies certain torts in connection with private sector invasion of privacy. Georgia was the first jurisdiction whose courts recognized a common-law right to privacy. As the court explained in *Pavesich v. New England Life Ins. Co.,*[61] "a right of privacy is derived from natural law, recognized by municipal law, and its existence can be inferred from expressions used by commentators and writers on the law as well as judges in decided cases. The right of privacy is embraced within the absolute rights of personal security and personal liberty."[62] The torts of particular interest in this chapter include (1) intrusion into solitude or seclusion, (2) the publication of private information, (3) publication that places another in a false light, and (4) defamation.

Publication as used in these torts means not only publishing the information in a newspaper or other mass media but generally "bringing it to light" or disseminating the information. In addition, the concept of publication is defined slightly differently depending on the tort. Truth and absence of malice are generally not

LO7 Identify and differentiate the *prima facie* cases for common-law claims of privacy invasions (intrusion into seclusion, public disclosure of private facts, publication in a false light, and breach of contract/defamation).

acceptable defenses by an employer sued for invasion of an employee's privacy. They are acceptable, however, in connection with claims of defamation.

Intrusion into Seclusion The *prima facie* case for the tort of intrusion into seclusion is listed in Exhibit 14.5. (For a more detailed discussion of *prima facie* cases, please see Chapter 2.)

The intrusion may occur in any number of ways. An employer may:

- Verbally request information as a condition of employment.
- Require that its employees provide information in other ways such as through polygraphs, drug tests, or psychological tests.
- Require an annual medical examination.
- Ask others for personal information about its employees.
- Go into private places belonging to the employee.

Any of these methods may constitute a wrongful invasion that is objectionable to a reasonable person. On the other hand, if the employer can articulate a justifiable business purpose for the inquiry/invasion, the conduct may be deemed acceptable.

See Chapter 2
to revisit key
concepts.

The case of *Lawlor v. North American Corp. of Illinois*[63] provides an example of an objectionable intrusion. In this case, North American Corp. hired a private investigator to determine whether a former employee, Kathleen Lawlor, had breached her non-compete agreement when she left to work for a competitor company (see Chapter 1 for discussion of those related legal issues). North American asked the investigator to discover whether Lawlor had called its customers and tried to convince them to move their business to the competitor company and provided Lawlor's birth date and social security number. The investigator obtained information on her home phone and cell phone calls—including the date, time,

---

Exhibit 14.5 *The Prima Facie Case for the Tort of Intrusion into Seclusion*

To state a *prima facie* case for the tort of <u>intrusion into seclusion</u>, the plaintiff employee must show that

- The defendant employer intentionally intruded into a private area.

- The plaintiff was entitled to privacy in that area.

- The intrusion would be objectionable to a person of reasonable sensitivity.

duration, and numbers called—by contacting the phone companies and pretending to be Lawlor requesting her own records, using her personal information to "verify" their identity. Illinois's Supreme Court explained that "[o]ne who intentionally intrudes, physically or otherwise, upon the solitude or seclusion of another or his private affairs or concerns, is subject to liability to the other for invasion of his privacy, if the intrusion would be highly offensive to a reasonable person."[64]

Scenario

In connection with Opening Scenario 1, Cherita's decision in connection with any of the tests may be governed in part by the law relating to employment testing as discussed in Chapter 4 and in part by the law relating to disability discrimination as discussed in Chapter 13. The scenario indicates that Cherita already is considering testing for HIV, which is considered a disability under the Americans with Disabilities Act. At the time of our publication, there have been no court decisions in connection with temporary disability status relating to global pandemics such as COVID-19.

Cherita also might be concerned about her decision because the testing has implications with regard to intrusion into seclusion when one considers the disclosure of the test results. If Cherita discloses the results to anyone or, through her actions, leads someone to a belief about the employee's health status status, there could be potential liability. Yet she is located in Montana—perhaps that is relevant? Further, did you consider whether Cherita actually has a right to know her employee's testing status for each of the tests? With regard to the HIV test results, it is unlikely that this information would be job-related, even for physicians. (Can you imagine what employment position might warrant this type of information? Is there some job-related reason why an employer ever would need to know an employee's HIV status?) Can you argue both sides—in favor and against her right to know an employee's test results—in connection with a disease such as COVID-19 or something similar?

Public Disclosure of Private Facts   The *prima facie* case for the tort of public disclosure of private facts is listed in Exhibit 14.6.

The information disclosed must not already be publicized in any way, nor can it be information the plaintiff has consented to publish. Therefore, in *Pemberton v. Bethlehem Steel Corp.,*[65] publication of an employee's criminal record was not considered by the court to be public disclosure of private facts because the criminal record did not contain private facts; it was information that was already accessible by the public.

Disclosure can be either in writing or spoken. For example, in *Ignat v. Yum! Brands, Inc.*[66] Ignat's supervisor at Yum! Brands told everyone in her department that she had bipolar disorder. The trial court dismissed Ignat's case based on the fact that the disclosure was not in writing. However, the California Court of Appeals overturned the dismissal, concluding that "limiting liability or public disclosure of private facts to those recorded in writing is contrary to the tort's purpose, which has been since its inception to allow a person to control the kind of information about himself made available to the public—in essence, to define his public persona."[67]

As you will read in *Shoun v. Best Formed Plastics, Inc.,*[68] included at the end of the chapter, the publication also must be made public, which involves more than mere disclosure to a single third party. The public disclosure must be communication either to the public at large or to so many people that the matter must be regarded as substantially certain to become one of public knowledge or one of knowledge to

Exhibit 14.6 *The* Prima Facie *Case for the Tort of Public Disclosure of Private Facts*

To state a *prima facie* case for the tort of <u>public disclosure of private facts</u>, the plaintiff employee must show that

- There was an intentional or negligent public disclosure,

- Of private matters, and

- Such disclosure would be objectionable to a reasonable person of ordinary sensitivities.

a particular public whose knowledge of the private facts would be embarrassing to the employee. Therefore, publication to all of the employees in a company may be sufficient, while disclosure to a limited number of supervisors may not.

Several states have enacted legislation codifying this common-law doctrine under the rubric of "breach of confidentiality." Connecticut, for instance, has passed legislation requiring employers to maintain employee medical records separate from other personnel records.[69] Other states have limited an employer's ability to disclose personnel-related information or allowed a cause of action where, through the employer's negligent maintenance of personnel files, inaccurate employee information is communicated to a third party.

Publication in a False Light   The *prima facie* case of publication in a false light requires that there was a public disclosure of facts that place the employee in a false light before the public if the false light would be highly offensive to a reasonable person and the person providing the information had knowledge of or recklessly disregarded the falsity or false light of the publication.

Voluntary consent to publication of the information constitutes an absolute bar to a false-light action. This type of tort differs from defamation, where disclosure to even one other person than the employer or employee satisfies the requirements. The tort of publicizing someone in a false light requires that the general public be given a false image of the employee. In a false-light action, the damage for which the employee is compensated is the inability to be left alone, with injury to one's emotions and mental suffering, while defamation compensates the employee for injury to his or her reputation in the public's perception.

Note that any of the above claims may be waived by the employee if the employee also publishes the information or willingly or knowingly permits it to be published. For example, in *Cummings v. Walsh Construction Co.,*[70] the employee complained of public disclosure of embarrassing private facts, consisting of information relating to a sexual relationship in which she was engaged with her supervisor. The court held that, where the employee had informed others of her actions, she waived her right not to have her supervisor disclose the nature of their relationship.

As with defamation, an exception to this waiver exists in the form of compelled self-publication, where an employer provides the employee with a false reason as the basis for termination and the employee is compelled to restate this reason when asked by a future employer the basis of departure from the previous job. Therefore, where the employer intentionally misstates the basis for the discharge, that employer may be subject to liability for libel because it is aware that the employee will be forced to repeat (or "publish") that reason to others. An employee also may contest an invasion of privacy by her or his employer on the basis of a breach of contract. The contract may be an actual employment contract, collective bargaining agreement, or one found to exist because of promises in an employment handbook or a policy manual.

Defamation   *Libel* refers to defamation in a written document, while *slander* consists of defamation in an oral statement. Either may occur during the course of a reference process. And while the *prima facie* case of defamation requires a false statement, even a vague statement that casts doubt on the reputation of an individual by inference can cause difficulties for an employer if it cannot be substantiated.

The elements of a *prima facie* claim for defamation are included in Exhibit 14.7.

One cautious solution to this problem area is to request that all employees fill out an exit interview form that asks, "Do you authorize us to give a reference?" If the applicant answers yes, she or he should be asked to sign a release of liability for the company.

Exhibit 14.7   *The* Prima Facie *Claim for Defamation*

To state a *prima facie* case for the tort of defamation,
the plaintiff employee must show that

• There were false and defamatory words concerning the employee,

• Negligently or intentionally communicated to a third party without the employee's consent (publication), and

• Resulting harm to the employee defamed.

See Chapter 2 to revisit key concepts.

Ordinarily defamation arises from someone other than the defamed employee making defamatory statements about an employee, but can you imagine being in a situation where you have to defame yourself? One interesting form of defamation has evolved where an employee is given a false or defamatory reason for her or his discharge. In that case, the employee may be the one who is forced to publicize it to prospective employers when asked for the reason they were fired. These circumstances give rise to a cause of action for defamation, termed *compelled self-publication,* because the employee is left with no choice but to tell the prospective employer the defamatory reasons for her or his discharge. Barring this result, the employee would be forced to fabricate reasons different from those given by the former employer and run the risk of being reprimanded or terminated for not telling the truth. This cause of action has been recognized, however, only in Colorado, Minnesota, and California. (For a more detailed discussion, see Chapter 4.)

An employer may defend against an employee's claim of defamation by establishing the truth of the information communicated. While truth is a complete defense to defamation, it can be difficult to prove without complex paper management.

Employers also may be immune from liability for certain types of statements because of court-recognized privileges in connection with them. For example, in some states, an employer is privileged to make statements, even if defamatory, where the statement is made in the course of a judicial proceeding or where the statement is made in good faith by one who has a legitimate business purpose in making the communication (e.g., an ex-employer) to one who has a business interest in learning the information (e.g., a prospective employer).[71] This privilege would apply where a former employer offers a good-faith reference to an employee's prospective employer. (See additional discussion of liability for references, below.) "Good faith" means that the employer's statement, though defamatory, is not made with malice or ill will toward the employee.

Lastly, what one may think is defamation is not always the case. In a 2019 case, Allstate Insurance Company investigated suspicious trading on its equity desk and found evidence that four traders inflated their bonuses at the expense of their portfolios.[72] The traders were fired, sued for defamation, and initially won a $27 million settlement in damages. The Seventh Circuit vacated the award and ordered a dismissal of the case. The court held that the 10-K reports and internal memos mentioning the events (but not mentioning the plaintiffs' names) were not defamatory *per se* and that the plaintiffs' testimony that employers had declined to hire them was not supported by the evidence.

Regulation of Employees' Off-Work Activities

LO8 Explain the extent to which an employer can legally dictate the off-work acts of its employees.

Can your boss tell you what to do even when you are not at work? In the private sector, the answer generally is yes.

Employers may regulate the off-work or otherwise private activities of their employees when they believe that the off-work conduct affects the employee's performance at the workplace or when they believe that it otherwise could impact the workplace. This legal arena is a challenging one since, in the at-will environment,

See Chapter 2
to revisit key
concepts.

employers can generally impose whatever rules they wish. However, as discussed earlier in this chapter, they still have to be careful of common-law privacy protections and also state legislation protecting against discrimination on the basis of various off-work acts.

As just one example, New York's lifestyle discrimination statute prohibits employment decisions or actions based on four categories of off-duty activity: legal recreational activities, consumption of legal products, political activities, and membership in a union. Across the nation, there are other more detailed protections of off-work acts. For instance, 29 states and the District of Columbia have enacted protections specifically on the basis of consumption or use of *legal* products off the job, such as cigarettes.[73]

Tobacco Use

The Affordable Care Act permits employers to charge smokers up to 50 percent more for their premiums, effectively imposing a "tobacco surcharge."[74] Each state also is allowed to establish more restrictive limits on health insurance for smokers, and insurers can set tobacco surcharges at any level up to those limits. Further, states may choose to impose differential tobacco surcharges based on age. For example, in Nevada, New Hampshire, and Ohio, smokers pay insurance premium rates that are more than 25 percent higher than those paid by nonsmokers. In total, 15 states allow maximum surcharges of up to 50 percent. Other states such as Colorado, Kentucky, and Arkansas limit the maximum allowable surcharge to below 50 percent.[75] Conversely, several states, including California, Connecticut, New Jersey, New York, Massachusetts, Rhode Island, and Vermont, as well as the District of Columbia prohibit tobacco use surcharges for insurance plans.[76]

See Chapter 2
to revisit key
concepts.

You might be asking yourself, though, how do these firms know what employees are doing outside work? And what happens if employees *lie* about their habits? Alaska Airlines uses a preemployment urine screening and will not even hire candidates if they are smokers. (Yes, they can test your urine for that!) Some companies conduct "sniff tests" when employees enter the premises, while others require workers to sign an affidavit or take periodic urine tests. When 39 Whirlpool employees who claimed to be nonsmokers, and therefore did not pay the surcharge, were observed smoking in the firm's designated smoking areas, they were suspended for lying. Presumably, they also owed the surcharge. Since 2006, Weyco Inc., a Michigan-based medical benefits administrator, has extended its no-tobacco policy to include employees' spouses; workers whose husbands or wives refuse to take a test or come up positive are fined $1,000 a year until their loved one quits![77]

Weight and Wellness Programs

The issue of weight is handled slightly differently than smoking since weight can be impacted by an individual's disability. Therefore, employers may make decisions based on an employee's weight, but only if they are in compliance with the Americans with Disabilities Act (ADA) (see Chapter 13). If the individual's weight is the result of a disability, the employer will need to explore whether the worker is otherwise qualified for the position, with or without reasonable accommodation. If the individual cannot perform the essential functions of the position, the employer may continue with the adverse employment decision. However, employers should be cautious in this arena since the ADA also protects workers who are not disabled but who are *perceived* as being disabled, a category into which someone might fall based on her or his weight.

One recent trend with regard to weight and general health is to offer incentives to encourage healthy behavior. Some employers have adopted health plans with significantly lower deductibles for individuals who maintain healthier lifestyles (for instance, if an employee is not obese or does not smoke and has yearly physicals). In one audacious statement along these lines, a hospital in Indiana has begun to require its employees to pay as much as $30 every two weeks unless they meet certain company-determined weight, cholesterol, and blood-pressure guidelines.[78] Additionally, a handful of health insurance companies now offer discounts for employees who meet physical goals, such as walking a certain number of steps per day. Several health insurance companies also offer incentives to employers that encourage workers to use bands such as a Fitbit or Jawbone.[79]

There are a few considerations employers should consider when implementing wellness programs. First, in 2016 the EEOC issued a final rule on employer wellness programs and Title 1 of the ADA.[80] Of particular note to the topic of privacy, employers must provide a reasonable accommodation for employees with a disability so that they are able to participate in wellness programs and also must keep confidential any medical information gathered as part of the wellness program. Further, participation in wellness programs must be voluntary.

Second, a 2019 study might make employers think twice about implementing these incentives toward wellness. Researchers found that, while employees who were offered wellness programs were more likely to report engaging in healthy behaviors such as exercising more or managing their weight, those healthy behaviors did *not* result in improved health measures such as better blood sugar levels, lower health care costs, or reduced absenteeism. Job performance also remained the same.[81] While employers who engage in wellness monitoring may have positive intentions, it is important to balance privacy and discrimination issues with potential wellness and other outcomes.

Workplace and Off-Work Relationships

Laws that protect against discrimination based on marital status exist in just under half of the states. However, though a worker might be protected based on marital *status,* she or he is not necessarily protected against adverse action based on *the identity or gender of the person* to whom she or he is married. For instance, some companies might have an anti-nepotism policy under which an employer refuses to hire or terminates a worker based on the spouse working at the same firm or a conflict-of-interest policy under which the employer refuses to hire or terminates a worker whose spouse works at a competing firm. Some companies also may choose to terminate a worker who is married to someone of the same gender. While same-sex marriages have been permitted by law throughout the United States since 2015 (see Chapter 10), it was not until 2020 that the Supreme Court ruled in *Bostock v.*

Clayton County that discrimination on the basis of gender identity and sexual orientation was prohibited by Title VII. It remains to be seen how this decision will impact relationship privacy issues.

While survey data may underreport the reality, research shows that 48 percent of workers have dated an office colleague, so employment policies and attitudes on workplace dating may have a significant impact on one's decision to engage in a relationship with a coworker.[82] The #MeToo movement has shined a light (more than previously) on the inappropriate interpersonal conditions that individuals may encounter in the workplace—both women and men, though the numbers lean heavily toward inappropriate behavior toward women. As we discussed in Chapter 9, this behavior can range from what some might consider to be mild to microaggressions to extreme sexual harassment including assault. Accordingly, it is vital that organizations develop a policy to address workplace relationships, not only in order to have a structure in place but also to send a proactive message to all involved regarding what is unacceptable behavior or communications.[83]

For example, a 2019 study by the Society for Human Resource Management found that 42 percent of the employees surveyed said their company had a workplace romance policy on the books.[84] Yet policies certainly are only the first step and are often insufficient. Despite having a policy banning relationships with direct and indirect reports, McDonald's CEO Steve Easterbrook was fired in 2019 when it was revealed that he was in a consensual relationship with his subordinate.[85]

Even without a policy in place, a New York decision reaffirmed the employer's right to terminate a worker on the basis of romantic involvement. In *McCavitt v. Swiss Reinsurance America Corp.,*[86] the court held that an employee's dating relationship with a fellow officer of the corporation was not a "recreational activity" within the meaning of a New York statute that prohibited employment discrimination for engaging in such recreational activities. The employee contended that, even though "[t]he personal relationship between plaintiff and Ms. Butler has had no repercussions whatever for the professional responsibilities or accomplishments of either" and "Swiss Re . . . has no written anti-fraternization or anti-nepotism policy,"[87] he was passed over for promotion and then discharged from employment largely because of his dating. The court agreed with the employer and found that dating was not a recreational activity.

Workplace policies on dating coworkers are largely a function of the employer's corporate culture. Some have banned all interoffice dating, while others permit it. The historical arguments for a ban usually are based on (1) reduced productivity, centered on a belief that such forms of socialization distract the parties involved; (2) potential liability, based on a concern that soured romances may result in harassment charges; or (3) moralistic concerns, particularly in encouraging extramarital affairs. However, to the contrary, some studies suggest that romantically linked employees may be actually more productive.[88] The trend today is toward more openness and fewer bans. In fact, some legal analysts have recommended that employers ask couples to sign a "love contract." The contract outlines the voluntary, mutual, and non-coercive nature of the relationship, and both parties acknowledge that they understand the company policy on consensual relationships. The contract may (with emphasis on the *may*!) mitigate liability for harassment charges at a later date if the relationship goes sour.[89]

The Use of Marijuana

The legalization of both medical and recreational marijuana use also gives rise to privacy questions. Although marijuana still remains a Schedule 1 controlled substance[90] and therefore is illegal at the federal level, the environment for employers is complicated, particularly if firms have offices in multiple locations with differing state laws to consider. Currently, 12 states plus the District of Columbia have legalized marijuana use for both medical and recreational purposes and decriminalized its use, and it is either decriminalized or approved only for medical purposes in 30 additional states.[91] Eleven states remain with no provisions whatsoever for medical or recreational marijuana or CBD oil use.[92] The topic of medical marijuana was addressed in Chapter 4 in connection with testing. Also recall that the Americans with Disabilities Act does *not* protect individuals who use marijuana for medical purposes. For the purposes of this chapter, our concern is with the issue of an employee's privacy to engage in what is considered a legal activity in a majority of U.S. states.

The rapid change in laws relating to marijuana use over the past few years has left companies scrambling to respond with marijuana use policies that address the use of medical marijuana and the legality of recreational marijuana and also that protect the company from liability due to the potential for impairment on the job. For example, while it is relatively easy to test for impairment on the basis of alcohol, it is more difficult to test for impairment on the basis of marijuana. A positive drug test for marijuana could mean the individual used marijuana in some form minutes before or even days before they were tested.[93] Some companies are avoiding legal complications by supporting an outright ban on all marijuana use—on or off the job—until testing can be more accurate. While companies retain the right to impose restrictions, it is unclear how long that may last and under what conditions, since other controlled substances like alcohol and tobacco generally are deemed acceptable for use outside work. It also is uncertain how long marijuana will remain as a Schedule 1 controlled substance, with advocates arguing for its benefits in mitigating pain and chemotherapy side effects.[94]

Additional Considerations

See Chapter 2 to revisit key concepts.

A majority of states protect against discrimination on the basis of political involvement, though states vary on the type and extent of protection. Lifestyle discrimination also may be unlawful if the imposition of the rule treats one protected group differently from another. For instance, as discussed elsewhere, if an employer imposes a rule restricting the use of peyote in Native American rituals that take place during off-work hours, the rule may be suspect and may subject the employer to liability. Similarly, the rule may be unlawful if it has a disparate impact on a protected group. (For a more detailed discussion of disparate impact and disparate treatment, please see Chapter 2.)

This question of disparate impact arises surrounding the question of rules relating to one's hairstyle. Think about a workplace rule that prohibits individuals with naturally kinky hair (usually African Americans) from wearing their hair in its natural state, as an "afro," beyond a certain length or height. Would this rule have a disparate impact on individuals from particular races or national origins? In 2019, the New York City Commission on Human Rights issued guidelines that directed employers not to discriminate against individuals based on their hair or hairstyle. Specifically, it protects New York employees' right to maintain "natural hair, treated or untreated hairstyles such as locs, cornrows, twists, braids, Bantu knots, fades, Afros, and/or the right to keep hair in an uncut or untrimmed state."[95] In 2020, California became the first state in the nation to ban discrimination based on natural hairstyles.[96]

One's decision to express one's identity through this form of expression, therefore, is protected in these municipalities/states, and a job cannot be denied there because an employer believes that someone's hairstyle is not appropriate for a workplace. Historically, the hairstyles mentioned above have not always been deemed by a conservative U.S society to be appropriate in all workplaces, and in fact, students have been sent home from school for sporting some of these styles and refusing to change. For example, a student from Texas was told in 2020 that he would not be allowed to attend his high school graduation that year unless he cut his hair, which he had maintained in locs.[97] Yet, from a purely objective perspective, who is to dictate what haircut or style is "proper" for one environment or another? Why is long hair acceptable for women and not (traditionally) as acceptable for men, for instance?

Most statutes or common-law decisions, however, provide for employer defenses for their decisions or rules that (1) are reasonably and rationally related to the employment activities of a particular employee, (2) constitute a bona fide occupational requirement, or (3) are necessary to avoid a conflict of interest or the appearance of conflict of interest. For example, drug testing in positions that affect the public safety, such as bus driver, would not constitute an unlawful intrusion because the employer's interest in learning of that information is justified. Where the attempted employer control goes beyond the acceptable realm, courts have upheld an exception to the employment-at-will doctrine based on public policy concerns for personal privacy or, depending on the circumstances, intentional infliction of emotional distress.[98]

2 *Scenario*

In connection with Opening Scenario 2, does Abraham have to quit his nighttime dancing job? Recall that Abraham is an at-will employee, making the answer somewhat easier. Since he can be terminated for any reason, as long as it is not a wrongful reason, the real estate partner can impose this condition. But consider Abraham's arguments and the ethical as well as the legal implications. As long as Abraham can show that his dancing truly has no impact on his work (i.e., that the club is located in a different town from that of his clientele or that the club has an excellent reputation for beautiful, artistic dancing styles), then should he have to quit his night job? On the other hand, if Abraham's reputation is soiled by his connection with this club and his boss can show that his work has a negative impact on his ability to perform, then is she justified in her ultimatum?

See Chapter 2 to revisit key concepts.

In fact, in a case (albeit more extreme) from Arizona, a husband and wife who worked as nurses were fired from a hospital after hospital officials learned that they ran a pornographic website when not at work. The couple explained that they engaged in this endeavor in order to earn more money for their children's college education. "We thought we could just do this and it really shouldn't be a big deal," said the husband.[99] Though their dismissal attracted the attention of the American Civil Liberties Union for what it considered to be at-will gone awry, the nurses had no recourse. In another case in Ohio, a high school teacher resigned after it was discovered that she had participated in online video pornography. The teacher had been placed on administrative leave.[100]

In a third case, a police officer was refused three days of his pay when his wife posted nude pictures of herself on the Internet as a surprise to her husband. His employer justified the pay suspension in this case, arguing that police officers arguably are held to a higher standard of conduct than average citizens. What about individuals who previously worked in the pornography industry and then left the industry to seek work elsewhere? Many employers may refuse to hire someone who previously has engaged in that form of employment. Even if they no longer are working in the industry, their past employment history may cause some employers to discriminate against them on the basis of their prior job choices, creating a cycle that draws people back into that industry just to make a living.[101]

The *City of San Diego v. Roe* case,[102] provided at the end of this chapter, explores the controversial topic of regulation of private activities away from work. In this case, the employer, the San Diego Police Department, believed that an officer's off-duty activities reflected poorly on the department and therefore were entirely inappropriate. A critical component of the case was the fact that the officer's activities incorporated elements of his duties as a police officer. As you review the case, try to imagine where you would draw the line between appropriate and inappropriate behavior and whether you would have found the employer's actions proper, even if no such incorporation of police activities had been involved. For more information about this issue, see Exhibit 14.8, "Legal Restrictions on Off-Duty Behavior of Private Employees."

Managing Employee Information

In previous sections, we focused on the scope of the privacy rights of the employee in connection with what type of information is obtained. However, privacy can be invaded not only by a disclosure of certain types of information but also by the way in which that information was obtained. An employer may be liable for its *process* of information gathering, storing, or utilization. Inappropriate information gathering may constitute an invasion of privacy where the data is used inappropriately (for purposes other than those for which the information was collected), collected inappropriately, or disclosed inappropriately.

Exhibit 14.8   *Legal Restrictions on Off-Duty Behavior of Private Employees*

Off-Duty Behavior of Private Employee	Business Justification	State Statutory Restrictions on Employer Policy
Illicit drug use	Concern that worker may come to work impaired, jeopardizing the worker's safety and the safety of other workers Quality of work of impaired worker may affect the product or service provided by the company, which, in turn, can affect the business's reputation and profitability Conduct is illegal and not deserving of legal protection Medical and recreational marijuana, while legal in some states, is illegal at the federal level complicating discussions of privacy and usage.	All states allow for at least some testing for illicit drug use. Arizona and Delaware have laws.
Alcohol use	Same justifications as applied to those who use illicit drugs, except for the issue of legality	29 states have laws that prohibit employers from taking adverse action against an employee based on lawful off-duty activities, such as drinking.
Cigarette smoking	Smokers increase employer's healthcare costs and affect productivity by missing more work due to illness than nonsmokers	30 states have laws that prohibit employers from refusing to hire smokers, unless being a smoker goes against a specific job qualification.
Use of weight standards	Same justifications as apply to smokers	While there are pending bills, Michigan is the only state to prohibit employment discrimination on the basis of weight (note that some municipalities/cities do prohibit it).
Dating between employees	A romantic relationship between employees may affect their productivity The relationship could lead to sexual harassment charges against the employer, especially if one employee is a supervisor of the other Other employees may believe that an involved supervisor is showing favoritism and may then feel that they are victims of discrimination	Most states, with the exception of California, allow employers to regulate dating between employees.
Moonlighting	Working too many hours may impair worker's productivity Working for a competitor could jeopardize privacy of employer information	Most states allow employers to regulate at least some instances of moonlighting.
Social relationships with employees of a competitor	Concern that information could be exchanged that would cause harm to the business	Many states allow employers to regulate.

Source: Adapted with permission from John D. Pearce II and Dennis Kuhn, "The Legal Limits of Employees' Off-Duty Privacy Rights," Organizational Dynamics 32, no. 4 (2003), pp. 372–83, 376.

function creep

Function creep occurs where an individual voluntarily offers personal or otherwise private information—with consent—for a specific purpose and that information subsequently is used for purposes beyond the original consent.

When the data is used inappropriately, this is called **function creep** and may begin with a situation where someone voluntarily offers information and consents to its use for a specific purpose. However, that person's privacy is violated if her or his information is later used for other purposes beyond the scope of the original consent. For instance, an individual may offer personal information to her or his employer. The employer is engaging in function creep if it then shares more information than required with the Immigration and Naturalization Service. Similarly, information gathered during a preemployment physical for purposes of appropriate job placement may seem perfectly appropriate at the time, but the employee might have concerns if that information is later shared with her or his manager or coworkers for other purposes. Health information gathered during the time of a pandemic but then used by the employer for different purposes after the crisis would be another example of function creep.

The collection or retrieval of information may occur in a variety of ways, depending on the stage of employment and the needs of the employer. For example, an employer may merely make use of the information provided by an applicant on her or his application form, or it may telephone prior employers to verify the data provided by the applicant. One employer may feel confident about an employee's educational background when she sees the employee's diplomas hung on the office wall, while a different employer may feel the need to contact prior educational institutions to verify attendance and actual graduation. On the more lenient end of the spectrum, the employer may rest assured that the employee is all that he or she states that they are on the application form, while, in more extreme situations, an employer may subject its employees to polygraph analyses and drug tests.

As is covered extensively in other chapters, employers are limited in the questions that may be asked of a potential employee. For example, an employer may not ask an applicant whether she or he is married or plans to have children or the nature of her or his family's origin. These questions are likely to violate Title VII of the Civil Rights Act; in most cases, this is not because the employer should not have the information, literally, but instead because an employer is prohibited from reaching any employment decision on the basis of the answers. In addition, employers are limited in their collection of information through various forms of testing, such as polygraphs or medical tests. These are discussed further in Chapter 4, but employers are constrained by a business necessity and relatedness standard or, in the case of polygraphs, by a requirement of reasonable suspicion.

With regard to medical information specifically, employer's decisions are not only governed by the Americans with Disabilities Act but also restricted by the Health Insurance Portability and Accountability Act (HIPAA) (Public Law 104-191). HIPAA stipulates that employers cannot use "protected health information" in making employment decisions without prior consent. Protected health information includes all medical records or other individually identifiable health information. This becomes particularly salient if private health data is collected during a pandemic, as we saw in 2020. (See Exhibit 14.9, "Protecting Workers' Personal Data.")

Exhibit 14.9 *Protecting Workers' Personal Data*

In 1997, the International Labour Organization published a Code of Practice on the Protection of Workers' Personal Data. Though not binding on employers, it serves to help codify ethical standards in connection with the collection and use of employee personal information and is recognized as the standard among privacy advocates.[103] The code includes, among others, the following principles:

5. GENERAL PRINCIPLES

5.1 Personal data should be processed lawfully and fairly, and only for reasons directly relevant to the employment of the worker.

5.2 Personal data should, in principle, be used only for the purposes for which they were originally collected. . . .

5.4 Personal data collected in connection with technical or organizational measures to ensure the security and proper operation of automated information systems should not be used to control the behavior of workers.

5.5 Decisions concerning a worker should not be based solely on the automated processing of that worker's personal data.

5.6 Personal data collected by electronic monitoring should not be the only factors in evaluating worker performance. . . .

5.8 Workers and their representatives should be kept informed of any data collection process, the rules that govern that process, and their rights. . . .

5.10 The processing of personal data should not have the effect of unlawfully discriminating in employment or occupation. . . .

5.13 Workers may not waive their privacy rights.

6. COLLECTION OF PERSONAL DATA

6.1 All personal data should, in principle, be obtained from the individual worker.

6.2 If it is necessary to collect personal data from third parties, the worker should be informed in advance, and give explicit consent. The employer should indicate the purposes of the processing, the sources and means the employer intends to use, as well as the type of data to be gathered, and the consequences, if any, of refusing consent. . . .

6.5 An employer should not collect personal data concerning a worker's sex life; political, religious, or other beliefs; or criminal convictions. In exceptional circumstances, an employer may collect personal data concerning those in named areas above if the data are directly relevant to an employment decision and in conformity with national legislation.

6.6 Employers should not collect personal data concerning the worker's membership in a workers' organization or the worker's trade union activities, unless obliged or allowed to do so by law or a collective agreement.

6.7 Medical personal data should not be collected except in conformity with national legislation, medical confidentiality and the general principles of occupational health and safety, and only as needed to determine whether the worker is fit for a particular employment; to fulfill the requirements of occupational health and safety; and to determine entitlement to, and to grant, social benefits. . . .

6.10 Polygraphs, truth-verification equipment or any other similar testing procedure should not be used.

6.11 Personality tests or similar testing procedures should be consistent with the provisions of this code, provided that the worker may object to the testing.

6.12 Genetic screening should be prohibited or limited to cases explicitly authorized by national legislation.

6.13 Drug testing should be undertaken only in conformity with national law and practice or international standards.

Exhibit 14.9 *continued*

11. INDIVIDUAL RIGHTS

11.1 Workers should have the right to be regularly notified of the personal data held about them and the processing of that personal data.

11.2 Workers should have access to all their personal data, irrespective of whether the personal data are processed by automated systems or are kept in a particular manual file regarding the individual worker or in any other file which includes workers' personal data.

11.3 The workers' right to know about the processing of their personal data should include the right to examine and obtain a copy of any records to the extent that the data contained in the record includes that worker's personal data. . . .

11.9 Workers should have the right to demand that incorrect or incomplete personal data, and personal data processed inconsistently with the provisions of this code, be deleted or rectified. . . .

11.11 If the employer refuses to correct the personal data, the worker should be entitled to place a statement on or with the record setting out the reasons for that worker's disagreement. Any subsequent use of the personal data should include the information that the personal data are disputed and the worker's statement.

Source: International Labour Organization, "Protection of Workers' Personal Data" (1997), http://www.ilo.org/wcmsp5/groups/public/---ed_protect/---protrav/---safework/documents/normativeinstrument/wcms_107797.pdf (accessed March 9, 2020).

In connection with the storage of the information collected, employers must be careful to ensure that the information is stored in a way that ensures that it will not fall into the wrong hands. If an improper party has access to the personal information, the employer, again, may be subject to a defamation action by the employee based on the wrongful invasion of her or his personal affairs, as discussed above. For example, as of January 1, 2020, California employers are liable for statutory damages to employees if there is a data breach.[104]

The California Consumer Privacy Act of 2018 and its amendment, AB 25,[105] applies not only to customer data but also to employee data. The law protects, among many things, professional or employment-related information, education information, identifiers, characteristics of a protected category, biometric information, Internet activity, inferences drawn regarding a consumer's preferences, characteristics, psychological trends, predispositions, behavior, attitudes, intelligence, abilities, and attitudes as well as geolocation data. In short, if any employee information is breached, the law indicates three specific rights: (1) mandatory privacy notices and disclosures about the data collected and the purpose for collecting it, (2) statutory damages ranging from $100 to $750 if sensitive personal information is breached, and (3) the expanded right to request access/deletion of personal information. It is important to note that neither this law nor the European Union's GDPR (noted earlier) requires that a company be headquartered in California or Europe, respectively, for activities to be covered under those laws. Any organization doing business in those locations must comply with the relevant data security regulations.

In today's world of advanced computer data storage, new issues also arise in this arena that may not have been previously anticipated. For instance, when an item is stored in a computer, it may be crucial either to protect (or lock) the file to all except those who have a correct entry code or to delete private information from the file. Consider also the issue of cloud storage, as noted in *Frankhouser* earlier in the chapter.[106] Although that case eventually settled out of court, it leaves open the question of whether items stored in the cloud are the private domain of employees or, since it is in a shared-use environment, content in cloud storage space such as Dropbox is subject to employer scrutiny. Access to computer terminals throughout an office also creates vulnerability involving the sharing of private information and the control of access to files. The trend toward "bring your own device," or BYOD, which allows employees to use their personal smartphones, tablets, or laptops for business purposes rather than requiring them to use company-issued equipment, is complicating matters further (see detailed discussion below).[107]

Monitoring Employees at Work

While many predicted that privacy would become an increasingly central concern in employment law, little did anyone anticipate the range and scope of dilemmas that would arise as a result of advances in technologies over the past three decades. Who would have thought that the workday might begin with an employee placing a hand on a scanner or having his or her iris scanned to confirm her or his identity and time of arrival at work or that location-based technologies would allow employers to know an employee's whereabouts at all times?[108]

Although advances in the information-gathering capacities of 21st-century technologies appear monumental, these innovations actually are merely geometric rather than exponential. Employers have always sought out information about their employees. What has changed in recent decades is how that information is collected, not the underlying desire to collect it. For instance, Milton Hershey of Hershey's Chocolate used to tour Hershey, Pennsylvania, to see how well his employees maintained their homes and hired detectives to spy on Hershey Park dwellers in order to learn who threw trash on their lawns. Henry Ford used to condition wages on his workers' good behavior outside the factory, maintaining a Sociological Department of 150 inspectors to keep tabs on workers. The ethics of collecting this information aside, technological advances have dramatically increased the range and power of the ways in which to gather information about our employees.

LO9 Discuss how advances in technology have impacted employee privacy.

It is not only technological developments that are driving these changes but also transformations in social norms around communication and privacy as well as transformative external events. There is plenty of evidence that technology is altering how people relate to each other, and these changes are particularly pronounced among younger people. One study reveals that age has a significant effect on perceptions of workplace privacy, specifically in connection with technology.[109] Consider also the impact of September 11, 2001, on an employer's decision to share personal employee information with law enforcement. Private firms may be more willing to share private information today than they would have previously.

This willingness also is impacted by concerns about global pandemics; should we not share private health information about employees when it helps to combat the spread of a worldwide and deadly disease? Sorting through this tangle of old and new issues is challenging. Consider the implications of modern technology for some more traditional workplace challenges. (See Exhibit 14.2.)

New technologies are the primary force driving the emergence of what UCLA Law Professor Kathy Stone has called the "boundary-less workplace,"[110] in which the lines between personal and professional time, space, and equipment have become blurred. Email, remote access networks, cloud computing, and video conferencing allow for in-home offices and working remotely. Almost four million Americans, or 2.9 percent of the U.S. workforce, work from home at least half the time, while 25 percent of the workforce telecommutes on a part-time basis—and that number jumps to 70 percent on a global basis.[111] These numbers raise issues of safety as well as privacy, although efforts by OSHA in the late 1990s to impose workplace safety standards on home offices received a great deal of push-back. How can we guarantee that our work computers containing sensitive data are secure when they are not at our work places? What happens if there is a break-in at an employee's home and their work computer is stolen?[112]

In this context of a flexible workplace, what constitutes a "workday"—8 hours a day, 10 hours a day, 24 hours a day? When is enough, enough? Employers increasingly expect workers to be available outside normal business hours. For instance, workers often are expected to respond to emails at all hours using their company-provided smartphone. In return, employees expect to be able to conduct some of their personal tasks using the company-provided equipment or during the workday. How should these changing expectations be managed and the boundaries be drawn?

Increased monitoring and surveillance in the workplace not only provide the means to prevent or detect employee misconduct, they allow employers to raise the bar for all employees. Research suggests that monitoring may motivate behavioral changes that increase productivity, yet the full impact of these technologies on employee performance is only just beginning to be understood and is likely to have a downside.[113] Excessive exertion of power and authority over employees may actually lead to insecurity, feelings of being overwhelmed and powerless, and doubts about worthiness. Short-term productivity gains may be overshadowed by negative effects that accumulate over time. We will explore this further below.

Technology has greatly expanded the potential for both privacy invasions by employers and employee misconduct. Should the ability of employers to discover information make it relevant, particularly in the case of off-work activities, as noted earlier? As supervisors and coworkers increasingly connect on social media sites, how should an employer balance respect for employees' privacy against potentially competing responsibilities, such as preventing workplace harassment or bullying? In a world where smartphones and social media are pervasively integrated into everyday life and the personal and the professional are increasingly intertwined, the line between invasions of workers' privacy and defense of an employer's legitimate business interests is not always clear.

Courts have supported reasonable monitoring of employees in open areas as a method of preventing and addressing employee theft. For example, in *Sacramento County Deputy Sheriff's Association v. County of Sacramento,*[114] a public employer placed a silent video camera in the ceiling overlooking the release office counter-top in response to theft of inmate money. The California Court of Appeals determined that the county had engaged in reasonable monitoring because employee privacy expectations were "diminished (though not eliminated) where persons elect to work in a jail or prison setting."[115]

As we discussed earlier in this chapter, courts have sometimes recognized a wrongful intrusion into seclusion (and awarded significant damages to employee plaintiffs) in cases where employers have secretly videotaped employees in locations that are reasonably considered "inherently private"—such as locker rooms or changing rooms.[116] But a location does not have to be more obviously private, like a bathroom, to justify an employee's reasonable expectation of privacy. In *Bowyer v. Hi-Lad, Inc.,*[117] the West Virginia Supreme Court recognized that even surveillance of a space "open to the public" can wrongfully invade privacy interests. In that case, it upheld a jury verdict in favor of a hotel employee whose conversations with clients were recorded by a secret microphone. The court disagreed with the employer's argument that a front desk employee could have no reasonable expectation of privacy, stating that "most employees, even those working in 'public' spaces, have a reasonable expectation that their oral communications with other employees or with customers are not going to be recorded by hidden microphones."[118]

However, courts do not necessarily agree on how private break rooms should be. In *Brannen v. Kings Local Sch. Dist. Bd. of Edn.,*[119] because "other school employees at Kings had unfettered access to the break room, including the principal and most of the teachers,"[120] school custodians did not have a reasonable expectation of privacy in the break room. Courts have also found that police officers lacked a reasonable expectation of privacy in the locker room and that placement of a video recorder did not constitute a "search."[121]

Scenario

Employers now customarily provide many employees with personal computers that are linked either to the Internet or, at least, to an internal network. Employers can monitor the computer user's activities. For instance, employers may be able to determine which sites you visited, whether you were scrolling through the page or had it on in the background, and when you were away from your computer. While this information may not necessarily seem personal to some, consider the facts of Scenario 3. The employer in that case seems to be within its rights to monitor the use of its computers.

In a number of workplace privacy cases, courts have ruled in favor of employers that monitor employees' company emails and other workplace technology use.[122] In fact, experts estimate that monitoring responsibilities now take up at least 20 percent of an average information technology manager's time.[123] (See Exhibit 14.10, "What Do Employers Monitor?")

Blogs and social media sites like Facebook may initially seem to offer a platform for personal expression. Yet imagine the impact when an employee's blog post or status update venting about his or her employment situation or employer goes

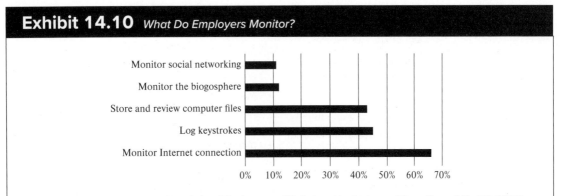

Exhibit 14.10 *What Do Employers Monitor?*

Source: American Management Association, "The Latest on Workplace Monitoring and Surveillance," (April 8, 2019), https://www.amanet.org/articles/the-latest-on-workplace-monitoring-and-surveillance/ (accessed March 9, 2020).

viral. Corporate reputations are at stake, and legal consequences can be severe. Consider some of the other ways that an employer's reputation is vulnerable.

Finally, intrusions may come from unexpected arenas. For instance, while employees perhaps are concerned about their rights with regard to employer monitoring in the workplace, they also should consider the possibility of intrusions from colleagues in addition to supervisors. For example, a 2016 lawsuit accused Google of violating its employees' rights to free speech by encouraging them to spy on each other and to report what coworkers say about anything that happened at work.[124] In a survey of more than 16,000 IT practitioners, almost two-thirds reported that they had intruded into another employee's personal computer without permission!

Given these developments, the International Labour Office assessment of the implications of the technology economy in its *World Employment Report* 2001 remains relevant, even years later:

> More and more, boundaries are dissolving between leisure and working time, the place of work and place of residence, learning and working. . . . Wherever categories such as working time, working location, performance at work and jobs become blurred, the result is the deterioration of the foundations of our edifice of agreements, norms, rules, laws, organizational forms, structures and institutions, all of which have a stronger influence on our behavioral patterns and systems of values than we are aware.[125]

See Exhibit 14.11, "Implications of New Technology."

The Legal Context of Employee Monitoring

Given the fast-paced evolution of technology, it is tough for employers and employees to keep up with the conditions and constraints placed on monitoring. While the U.S. Supreme Court first addressed the issue of employer monitoring in *City of Ontario v. Quon,*[126] the case was so specific and peculiar that the circuits have not really followed it since that time. In that case, the employees were assured by their

---

Exhibit 14.11 *Implications of New Technology*

Consider the implications of new technology on the following areas:

- Monitoring usage.
- Managing employee and employer expectations.
- Distinguishing between work use and personal use of technology.
- Managing flextime.
- Maintaining a virtual workplace.
- Protecting against medical concerns for telecommuters.
- Managing/balancing privacy interests.

- Monitoring use of the Web to spread information and misinformation.
- Managing fair use/disclosure.
- Responding to accessibility issues related to the digital divide.
- Managing temporary workforces.
- Adapting to stress and changing systems.
- Maintaining proprietary information.
- Measuring performance.
- Managing liability issues.

---

supervisor that their text messages on their city-issued devices would not be subject to an audit. However, the Court found for the city because it held that its reasons for the intrusion were reasonably "work-related." As a result, *Quon* suggests that, even where employees may have a reasonable expectation of privacy, employers are still entitled to monitor where there is a good business-related reason for doing so.

Yet *Quon* has not been extended to subsequent cases of employee monitoring. As one scholar notes, "[u]nder *Quon,* it remains unclear how much protection for electronic communications the Fourth Amendment will provide to employees, and in any event, those protections do not extend to the private sector."[127]

Recall our discussion of *Carpenter* earlier in this chapter.[128] While this case may seemingly not be related to employee-related monitoring issues, consider a situation where an employee may be on the road traveling and an employer wants to monitor their activities. Would this situation be different if the phone was the employer's or would the standards set in *Carpenter* still hold? Consider also that, under pandemic conditions, the U.S. government was in negotiation with social media companies like Facebook and Google to use location data to combat the spread of the novel coronavirus.[129] While this may have seemed justified in the moment, what if the data were not anonymized and reported in aggregate as the government reports? What if employers are then given access to sensitive information about employee whereabouts? Consider also what might happen if this practice is not stopped after the pandemic concerns have decreased (remember our discussion of function creep). As we enter into unprecedented arenas, employee privacy issues with respect to monitoring should be at the forefront of considerations.

Though courts do not, per se, *require* notice in order to find that no reasonable expectation of privacy exists and to therefore allow monitoring by employers, notice of monitoring is favored by the courts.[130] The court in *Thygeson v. U.S. Bancorp*[131] held that an employer's specific computer usage policy precluded an employee's reasonable expectation of privacy.

While, as stated earlier, there is little legislation that actually relates to these areas specifically, there is some statutory protection from overt intrusions, though the statute does not apply in all circumstances. The federal wiretapping statute, Title III of the Omnibus Crime Control and Safe Streets Act of 1968, as amended by the Electronic Communications Privacy Act of 1986,[132] protects private and public sector employees from employer monitoring of their telephone calls and other communications without a court order.

There are two exceptions to this general prohibition on overt intrusions. First, interception of phone calls and other communications is authorized where one of the parties to the communication has given prior consent. Second, the "business extension" provision creates an exception where the equipment used is what is used in the ordinary course of business. An employer must be able to state a legitimate business purpose, and there must be minimal intrusions into employee privacy such that they would not be objectionable to a reasonable person. It is by now well established that these exceptions enable an employer to conduct extensive electronic surveillance of employees' Internet usage on company computers, including communication via their work email account. Potential protections against computer monitoring in the workplace—including prohibitions on the interception of electronic communications in Title I of the ECPA and restrictions on accessing stored electronic communications in Title II of the ECPA (the Stored Communications Act)—have generally not been successful.[133]

Business Justifications for Monitoring Employees' Technology Use

There are three major business reasons why employers should monitor employees surfing on the Web: managing productivity, limiting liability risks due to employee behavior, and waste and cost of bandwidth. While these represent legitimate reasons to monitor employees, care must still be taken to protect employee privacy.[134]

LO10 State the key business justifications for employee monitoring.

See Chapter 2 to revisit key concepts.

Employers may choose to engage in electronic surveillance to increase employee productivity. Employers are particularly concerned about productivity loss due to time spent online—and with good reason. As we noted earlier in this chapter, the cost to organizations for non-job-related Internet surfing is upward of $650 billion annually.[135] (See Exhibit 14.12, "Surfing on the Job.") Strangely enough, even though employers are concerned about distractions at work impacting productivity, as seen in Exhibit 14.12, approximately 50 percent of workers use their own phone for surfing while at work and monitoring would have little impact on those employees.

Consider, however, what Kathy Joynes, a travel agent for American Express who works out of her own home, says about monitoring remote employees: "If [the employer] sees you doing something on the screen that they think you can do in a quicker way, they can tell you. They can even tell you ways to talk to people, or they can tell you ways to do things quicker to end your [customer service] call quicker."[136] Monitoring is a double-edged sword with both positive and negative implications for worker productivity and company culture.

Employers also may choose to monitor employees' technology usage in order to limit their liability in connection with potential legal concerns such as defamation,

Exhibit 14.12   *Surfing on the Job*

Time Distractions at Work:

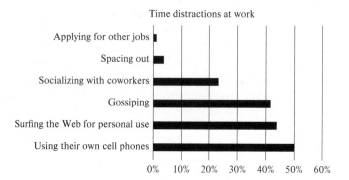

Time distractions at work

Sources: Schriever, N., "The Average Employee Wastes HOW Much Time Out of Every Work Day?" Blue Water Credit (December 10, 2018), https://bluewatercredit.com/the-average-employee-wastes-how-much-time-out-of-every-work-day/ (accessed March 22, 2020).

The most visited non-work sites are:

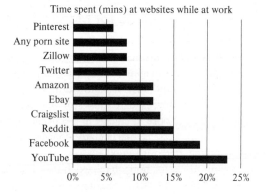

Time spent (mins) at websites while at work

Sources: Morris, C., "For a Workplace Productivity Boost, Ban These 10 Websites," CNBC (August 6, 2016), https://www.cnbc.com/2016/08/06/for-a-workplace-productivity-boost-ban-these-10-websites.html (accessed March 22, 2020).

copyright infringement, cyber attacks due to malware, sexual harassment, discrimination, theft, and obscenity. The guidelines that apply to a standard defamation claim apply in the same manner to communications on the Internet. However, some contend that the opportunity for harm is far greater because employees and employers can easily disseminate information to a broader range of media.

Further, firms are concerned about the potential for the inappropriate use of software by employees. This might happen when an employee downloads program files without compensating a creator or when an employee uses copyrighted information from the internet without giving credit to the original author. Additionally, when an employee downloads software programs from the Web, the employer's computer systems potentially could be compromised by viruses, malware, or even unauthorized access. As discussed earlier in this chapter, with a 12 percent increase in cyberattacks at a cost of over $13 million annually, managing employee Internet use is one way to minimize cyberattacks.

Sexual harassment and discrimination by employees via the Internet are governed by the same guidelines that are discussed in the chapters addressing sexual harassment and discrimination throughout the workplace. However, many employees believe that, once an email message is deleted, it is permanently removed from the system. This is not the case. All emails sent on company time, hardware and software may easily be discovered, both by the employer and by opposing parties to litigation against the employer.

Monitoring allows employers to uncover vulnerabilities and know what is happening within their own workplace environments. For example, in one case, female warehouse employees alleged that a hostile work environment was created in part by inappropriate emails and sought $60 million in damages in federal court. The case settled out of court.[137] In another case, *Zubulake v. UBS Warburg,* the plaintiff was awarded a jury verdict in the amount of $29.2 million.[138] The award ended up so large in part due to sanctions imposed by the trial judge as a result of the employer's failure to preserve emails for evidentiary purposes.

In another case in New York, the court found that an employer sending sexually offensive emails to both male and female employees could support a claim of a hostile work environment.[139] A District Court in Iowa found that a former human resources director for a medical practice stated plausible claims of retaliation for complaining about a sexually hostile work environment after the medical practice and the CEO subjected her to unwanted and unwelcome sexual comments, sexual questions, sexual conversations, sexual emails, sexual texts, and sexual jokes.[140]

An interesting question arises as to the extent of an employer's responsibilities once it begins monitoring. Paradoxically, since monitoring is done with the aim of limiting liability, the fact that the employer has collected and has access to certain data may by law impose responsibilities on that employer that, if not fulfilled, form the basis for liability. In other words, now that the employer knows if some inappropriate act is going on—as a result of the monitoring—the employer has a responsibility to do something about it. For example, where an employee harasses a coworker by sending sexually explicit messages or images over company email, an employer that has software that scans for sexually explicit material may be more likely to be liable for failing to take action to prevent a hostile work environment under Title VII.[141]

Employee monitoring also has had a tremendous impact on decreasing retail employee theft. As noted earlier in this chapter, retail theft has gone down over the past four years as monitoring has been increased. At the same time, however, employee theft and embezzlement remain a real concern with a huge price tag for employers, thus fueling justification for increased employee monitoring.

Finally, obscenity is an issue, which poses both legal and reputational risks when employees download pornographic images while at work. Consider this scenario. A customer service representative is using the store's computer to access a pornographic site and starts to laugh. A customer walks up behind the representative to see why the employee is laughing and sees the images. Certainly, the employer would be justified in blocking employees' access to a pornographic website. But is the employer equally justified in blocking the sites of an activist groups regarding sensitive issues such as abortion? Should an employer be allowed to block or restrict access to these sites as well?

If access may be restricted in order to promote efficiency and professionalism, then should employers also be permitted to limit access to other, arguably less controversial sites such as eBay or ESPN.com (though some readers may also find those controversial!)? Consider that surfing for personal reasons wastes an organization's bandwidth as well as results in unproductive work hours. This waste gets amplified if, while surfing, the employee inadvertently ends up introducing malware or viruses into the employer's network. According to research, the amount of time spent on surfing the Web at work varies by age. Those born between 1930 and 1949 are on the Internet for non-work reasons approximately a half hour each day, compared to those born between 1980 and 1985, who are online for non-work purposes almost 2 hours per day.[142] Should younger employees be limited but older workers given free rein?

Ultimately, by limiting or restricting access to websites, the employer may be creating an environment in which employees do not feel trusted and perhaps even feel inhibited about using the Internet for creative, work-related purposes because they fear being reprimanded for misusing access. As noted in the *Rescue Time* blog, "Many of these tools track productivity by taking regular screenshots while workers are on the clock. Not only does this make your team feel like you're invading their privacy but could also cause misleading assumptions. For example, you might assume an employee is wasting time by looking at Instagram when they're really doing research on social media marketing."[143]

Because of the overall potential liability for their employees' actions, employers should develop a formal policy or program regulating employee usage of the Internet. In addition to having a formal policy, employers may choose to establish a process of monitoring their employee's Internet usage. This may involve tracking websites visited and the amount of time spent at each site using software programs designed for that specific purpose. However, employers need to consider the employees' rights to free speech and privacy when developing such policies and systems. (See Exhibits 14.13, "Monitoring Employees' Technology Usage," and 14.14, "Allowable Monitoring.")

How Do Employers Monitor Employees?

Workplace surveillance using video cameras and audio recording equipment is a familiar and common form of monitoring. Employee theft and harassment, among other issues, have led both public and private employers to increase monitoring of employees by closed circuit video, which can be either recorded or watched live by

Exhibit 14.13   *Monitoring Employees' Technology Usage*

WHY DO FIRMS MONITOR TECHNOLOGY USAGE?

1. Managing the workplace:
   - Ensuring compliance with affirmative action.
   - Administering workplace benefits.
   - Placing workers in appropriate positions.
2. Ensuring effective, productive performance:
   - Preventing loss of productivity due to inappropriate technology use.
3. Protecting information and guarding against theft.
4. Protecting investment in equipment and bandwidth.
5. Protecting against legal liability, including possible:
   - Perceptions of hostile environments.
   - Violations of software licensing laws.
   - Violations regarding proprietary information or trade secrets.
   - Inappropriate gathering of competitive intelligence.
   - Financial fraud.
   - Theft.
   - Defamation/libel.
   - Discrimination.
6. Maintaining corporate records (including email, voice mail, and so on).
7. Investigating *some* personal areas.

ARGUMENTS IN FAVOR OF LIMITS ON MONITORING

1. Monitoring may create a suspicious and hostile workplace.
2. Monitoring constrains effective performance (employees claim that lack of privacy may prevent "flow").
3. It may be important to conduct *some* personal business at the office, when necessary.
4. Monitoring causes increased workplace stress and pressure, negatively impacting performance.
5. Employees claim that monitoring is an inherent invasion of privacy.
6. Monitoring does not always allow for workers to review and correct misinformation in the data collected.
7. Monitoring constrains the right to autonomy and freedom of expression.
8. Monitoring intrudes on one's right to privacy of thought. ("I use a company pen; does that mean the firm has a right to read my letter to my spouse?")

Source: Adapted by authors from data from the American Management Association, "2007 Electronic Monitoring & Surveillance Survey," March 13, 2008, http://www.amanet.org/training/articles/The-Latest-on-Workplace-Monitoring-and-Surveillance.aspx (accessed April 10, 2020).

management. Employee theft (often referred to as inventory shrinkage) alone cost retailers just under $50 billion in the United States,[144] and a quarter of employers claim that internal theft is much more of a priority now than in the past five years.[145]

Employers also are concerned about inappropriate Web surfing; approximately 66 percent monitor Internet usage, and 65 percent use software to block connections to inappropriate sites. This number represents a 27 percent increase since 2001 when the AMA/ePolicy Institute first surveyed electronic monitoring and surveillance policies and procedures.[146] Employers also report monitoring telephone and voice mail, email, theft/violence/sabotage through video, keystrokes, biometrics

Exhibit 14.14 *Allowable Monitoring*

Telephone calls	Monitoring is permitted in connection with quality control on the employer's phone. Notice to the parties to the call is often required by state law, though federal law allows employers to monitor work calls without notice. If the employer realizes that the call is personal, monitoring must cease immediately.
Email messages	Under most circumstances, employers may monitor employee emails on work accounts. Even in situations where the employer claims that it will not, its right to monitor has been held to persist. However, where the employee's reasonable expectation of privacy is increased (such as a private password-protected account), this may impact the court's decision, though it is not determinative.
Voice mail system messages	Though not yet completely settled, it appears that as long as employers have a work-related reason to question the content of voicemail, they may monitor the recording. May be difficult for an employer to prove no assumed privacy if the employer said they wouldn't monitor, gave employees a private voicemail access code, or allow employees to make or receive personal calls.
Internet use	Where the employer has provided the equipment and/or the access to the Internet, the employer may track, block, or review Internet use.

such as iris and finger print scans, SmartCard access to track movement, and global positioning systems (GPS) in vehicles. The AMA reports that 83 percent of surveyed employers notify their employees when they are being monitored.

Location Tracking

As GPS technology becomes more pervasive, some states have created new laws regulating GPS tracking. For instance, Illinois state statutes allow an employer to track the location of a company-owned vehicle used by its employees. The employer is permitted to track the vehicle because the employer is the vehicle's owner and therefore consents to the tracking. However, an employer may not install a GPS tracking device in an *employee-owned* vehicle without the employee's consent.[147] California's Consumer Privacy Act (effective as of July 1, 2020) explicitly protects GPS (geolocation) data.[148] Both Vermont and New York passed laws protecting the secondary use of GPS data by data brokers. A handful of states are considering legislation addressing GPS location data including Washington, Hawaii, Maryland, Massachusetts, New Mexico, and Rhode Island. Connecticut, Delaware, and Texas also have statutes that specifically apply to GPS tracking, specifically addressing notification if the employer will be using the GPS to track movements.[149]

Case law also may determine whether it is an invasion of privacy for an employer to use GPS tracking without an employee's knowledge or consent (on the basis of common law intrusion into seclusion). Court decisions in some states have found no basis for claims for invasion of privacy when employer-owned vehicles are involved, similar to the state statutes mentioned above.[150]

Another location tracking technology involves radio frequency identification devices (RFIDs), which are microchips that can be planted anywhere, including under the skin. In 2006, Citywatcher.com became the first U.S. firm to ask employees to accept RFID bodily implants and require those who refused the implant to carry a key chain with an RFID microchip. While one's first instinct might be a concern about privacy, consider the reasoning used by the attorney general in Mexico, who explained why he opted to implant the tiny devices under the skin of some of his workers. He wanted to be able to track them more effectively in case they were kidnapped because of their line of work. Can you think of a less intrusive solution for the attorney general?

In 2015, Epicenter, a Swedish office complex, offered about 400 employees a minuscule RFID chip. The chip was designed to provide various kinds of access to the employees, such as the ability to enter the building or use the copy machine. The chief disruption officer at the office block explained: "Today we need pin codes and passwords. Wouldn't it be easy to just touch with your hand? That's really intuitive."[151] Some employees refused to get a chip implanted.[152] States are concerned enough about the possibility of the widespread use of RFID implants that they have begun to act. In 2006, Wisconsin became the first state to ban mandatory implants. North Dakota, California, Missouri, and Oklahoma have since followed course, with other states considering similar regulations on the use of RFID implants.[153]

Hardware and Software Tracking

There are now hundreds of software and hardware solutions available on the market to monitor a vast array of activities through a variety of surveillance activities. For instance, there is software that employers can install on any employer-owned technology that can maintain a record of every key an employee hits at any moment along with every window that is open and what that person is looking at in those windows. It is even possible to re-create every deleted document because all of the original keystrokes have been recorded, including the "deletes."

Since all keystrokes are monitored and time-stamped, this surveillance also means that all staff downtime is also monitored. The employer is aware of all times when the technology is not in use, so breaks that stretch on for a bit too long can be flagged. Similar software alerts the employer to the installation and date of install of any applications, all files that have been opened, online chat (including content), and remote desktop usage.[154] Surveillance software also can track and screen employees' email for potentially offensive or inappropriate messages, as well as scan for keywords predetermined by the employer, automatically sending "flagged" websites or messages to an administrator. For example, an employer could scan employee emails for the names of competitors as keywords to monitor for theft or disclosure of proprietary information.

Artificial Intelligence

Artificial intelligence (AI) has the capacity to build a large database about the individual being monitored at a granular level.[155] A 2019 survey of employers[156] reported that 25 percent plan to use AI to screen résumés or applicants, and 11 percent will use it to identify hard-to-reach applicants (e.g., diverse, military retirees). An additional 9 percent will use it to analyze top performers in order to identify needed traits in applicants, and 8 percent each plan to use it to perform social media reviews of candidates and analyze applicant responses during interviews. Lastly, 7 percent plan to use it to reduce bias and facilitate more objective hiring decision, and 3 percent plan to use chatbots to obtain basic candidate information.

Chatbots are on the cutting edge of AI selection technology. A chatbot is a form of AI that can mimic human interaction during the beginning stages of the hiring process.[157] Chatbots can collect information from candidates such as their résumé and contact information; ask screening questions about candidates' experience, knowledge, and skills; rank candidates on metrics such as qualifications, engagement, or recent activity; answer FAQs about the job and the application process; and schedule an interview with a human recruiter.[158] While bots can save time for busy recruiters, their use could pose problems depending on the extent to which applicants are comfortable chatting with bot, and the AI may have difficulties discerning nonstandard communication such as texting shorthand or slang or may be unable to understand clearly applicants who are non-native English speakers. This could create potential non-job-related inequities for applicants but also poses questions about who owns and controls the information shared with the chatbot. Given the extent to which AI can gather and analyze applicant information, privacy laws may well be tested over the next few years.

Legal scholars Richard Bales and Katherine Stone attempt to address the issues surrounding who owns the employees' data, the company or the employee in their example of the real company HireVue.[159] HireVue is a real company that makes and analyzes pre-hire videos using AI to evaluate job candidates. When an applicant applies for a job, HireVue captures and then evaluates the interview video for initial screening. Because HireVue owns the video, the applicant can request that it be deleted, but the company does not necessarily have to honor that request. What happens if the candidate applies for another job for which HireVue screens? What if they just use the initial video; would that be acceptable? What if the applicant had a bad day and did not want the interview used; would the applicant be permitted to override that decision? Because of the high volume and great detail available from AI, larger questions of ownership over that data is important for the courts to address.

The use of AI has implication for both work and off-work behaviors of employees. A company named Slack uses AI to assess the speed at which workers perform tasks and monitors those who may be underperforming. AI can also be employed to listen to customer service calls. Amazon tracks worker movements on the job to assess productivity and accuracy through wristbands with tracking devices. A company called Humanyze requires employees to wear an ID badge that contains a microphone, Bluetooth, and infrared sensors to monitor breaks and conversations. Even off-work, employers may use AI to monitor online activities on social media. Instead of asking for social media passwords, a practice many states have outlawed, the AI conducts wide, perpetual sweeps of social media instead. These practices are at the cutting edge of technology and represent concerns for the privacy of employees.

Biometrics, Body-Scanning, and Future Advances

Biometrics continues to be on the cutting edge of identification technologies that include voice recognition, fingerprint verification, iris and retinal scanning, hand geometry analysis, and facial feature scanning. Biometrics has been widely adopted by the government for homeland security and border protection purposes. With increased availability of biometric technology, such as fingerprint and facial recognition, available in newer models of Apple's iPhone as well as an increasing number of Android handsets, there is a growing acceptance of this type of recognition technology. Ninety percent of businesses are expected to use some form of biometric authentication by the end of 2020.[160]

Despite some initial problems,[161] fingerprint scanning technology has become increasingly sophisticated. Organizations have been using the scanners to improve authentication and security, and iris scanning has become an increasingly popular form of authentication. For instance, the United Nations refugee program has used iris scanning to process refugees more efficiently and to help identify aid money fraud across the Middle East. Employers have been using iris scanning to prevent time loss by, for example, preventing employees from faking the time they were at work.[162] Those in favor of the technology contend that it will reduce the high economic and emotional costs of identity theft, among other benefits. Those opposed argue that it is subject to inaccuracies, provides more information than employers have a right to know, and is one additional way in which "big brother" can keep an eye on employees at all times.

In the near future, the biggest monitoring breakthroughs are likely to be productivity-related, as Big Data collection becomes a fixture of office life and increasingly sophisticated methods for analyzing and interpreting the data emerge. Sensors attached to lanyards or clothing can monitor the smallest movements, conversation patters, and even tone of voice. Some futurists predict that "wriggle monitors" will soon be used to measure employee focus, and some AI can track an employee's emotional state, such as the Spire,[163] which monitors stress levels! Employees may not be too excited about these changes. For instance, in January 2016, journalists at the *Daily Telegraph* found that individual sensors had been installed overnight that monitored when they were at their desks. The sensors appeared without notice or explanation. There was such an outcry that the *Telegraph* removed the sensors before the day's end.[164]

Expect more integrated monitoring that brings together voice and motion sensors, location tracking, and computer surveillance to enable fine-grained analysis of how employees actually work and interact in order to refine workflows and practices and improve office design. When Bank of America wanted to investigate the role of face time among call center workers, it conducted a study of 90 employees using sensors that monitored movement, location, and conversation patterns. The study revealed that workers in close-knit teams that interacted frequently were most productive. To promote employee interaction, the bank began scheduling workers for group breaks rather than solo ones, boosting productivity by 10 percent.[165]

Yet such intensive monitoring may reveal more than employers intend—or are comfortable with. Dr. Ben Waber, chief executive of Sociometric Solutions, a Boston start-up that conducts research like the Bank of America study, claims he can often predict from a worker's patterns of movement whether the worker is likely to leave the company or be promoted. As a result, Sociometric Solutions generally only provides employers with aggregate and unidentified data on team interaction, and while managers often want to see data on individual employees, they are prohibited from doing so (although employees get to see their own data). It seems unlikely that such privacy considerations will survive once this kind of monitoring goes mainstream.

Monitoring Employee Email

Email is the most common tool employees use to communicate to each other and to business associates, so we will take a more detailed look at this communication medium in particular.

Although neither federal nor state laws preclude an employer from monitoring email completely, an employer's right to monitor *private* communications from an employee is not absolute, regardless of what the company policy might say. Limits do exist. One is the privacy of communications subject to attorney–client privilege. For example, in *Stengart v. Loving Care Agency, Inc.,*[166] the New Jersey Supreme Court ruled that communications between an employee and her attorney sent through her personal email account, which involved potential employment discrimination claims by the employee against the employer, were not subject to monitoring by the employer. Monitoring of those password-protected communications violated both the employee's right of privacy and the attorney–client privilege.

However, where employees communicated with counsel via their work email (rather than a personal password-protected email or social media accounts such as Gmail, Snapchat, or Facebook), courts have been less willing to protect the privilege.[167] For example, in *Holmes v. Petrovich Dev. Co.,*[168] a California state court held that an employee who used her employer's computer and email system to communicate with her attorney had waived the attorney–client privilege. The court distinguished *Stengart* based on the fact that the employee in *Holmes* had used her work email account, not a password-protected Web-based account, and the company policy concerning monitoring specifically addressed communications on its email system.

In a Delaware case, the court found that the corporation's right of access to executives' work emails encouraged a finding that the executives had no reasonable expectation of privacy in those emails. The court noted that the executives' knowledge of the corporation's email policy supported the finding.[169]

An employer's need to monitor email must be weighed against an employee's right to privacy and autonomy. The employer is interested in ensuring that the email system is not being used in ways that offend others or harm morale or for disruptive purposes—a significant concern when one-third of employees admit to using their work email accounts to send personal emails.[170] Likewise, an employer may choose to review email in connection with a reasonable investigation of possible employee misconduct. Also, companies that maintain sensitive data may be concerned about disclosure of this information by disloyal or careless employees, apparently justifying this type of intrusion.

In one well-publicized 2012 incident, Harvard faculty members were outraged after *The Boston Globe* revealed that the administration had searched the work email accounts of 16 faculty deans to try to find the source of a media leak related to a cheating scandal. The search appeared to violate Harvard's privacy policy, which states that the administration may search employees' emails "in extraordinary circumstances such as legal proceedings and internal Harvard investigations" but also that employees must be notified either before or shortly after a search. However, in cases examining employer searches of employees' electronic communication, courts have repeatedly found that employees do *not* have a reasonable expectation of privacy when it comes to their work email accounts as long as the employer has a valid business-related purpose for conducting the search, *even where an employer's policy or a supervisor's comments suggest otherwise.*[171]

While monitoring email transmissions over telephone lines is forbidden by the ECPA, communications within a firm do not generally go over the phone lines and therefore may be legally available to employers, though interception of emails could still violate the Wiretap Act. In addition, there are numerous exceptions to the ECPA's prohibitions as discussed earlier in this chapter, including situations where one party to the transmission consents, where the provider of the communication service can monitor communications, or where the monitoring is done in the ordinary course of business. In order to satisfy the ECPA consent exception, however, the employer's interception must not exceed the scope of the employee's consent. Employers must be aware as well that an employee's knowledge that the employer is monitoring certain communications is insufficient to be considered implied consent. To avoid liability, employers must specifically inform employees of the extent and circumstances under which email communications will be monitored.

Despite the failure of federal legislative attempts to require employers to notify employees that their email is being monitored, employers are most protected if they do provide such notification, as described below. In addition, some states, including Delaware and Connecticut, have now imposed notice requirements before monitoring.

Developing Computer Use Policies

LO11 Explain the most effective means by which to design and implement a technology use policy.

An employer can meet its business necessity to monitor email, protect itself from liability, and, at the same time, respect the employees' legitimate expectation of privacy in the workplace in numerous ways. Moreover, research demonstrates that monitoring may be more acceptable to employees when they perceive that monitoring takes place within an environment of procedural fairness and one designed to ensure privacy.[172] Accordingly, employers should develop concise written policies and procedures regarding the use of company computers, specifically email.

The Society for Human Resource Management strongly encourages companies both to adopt policies that address employee privacy and to ensure that employees are notified of such policies.[173] Any email policy should be incorporated in the company policies and procedures manuals, employee handbooks, and instruction aids to ensure that the employee receives consistent information regarding the employer's rights to monitor employee email. Additionally, a company could display a notice each time an employee logs on to a company computer indicating that computers are to be used only for business-related communication or explaining that the employee has no reasonable expectation of privacy in the electronic messages. Employers also can periodically send memos reminding employees of the policy. For a sample email, voice mail, and computer systems policy, see Exhibit 14.15, "Sample Email, Voice Mail, and Computer Systems Policy."

Exhibit 14.15 *Sample Email, Voice Mail, and Computer Systems Policy*

Subject:	**Email, Voice Mail, and Computer Systems Policy**
Purpose:	To prevent employees from using the Company computer and voice mail systems for harassing, defamatory, or other inappropriate communications. To preserve the Company's right to monitor and retrieve employee communications. To prohibit excessive personal use of the company's electronic systems.
Related Policies:	Harassment Prevention, Rules of Conduct, Confidentiality of Company Information, Solicitations.
Background:	Inappropriate employee use of Company computer, email, and voice mail systems can subject the Company to significant legal exposure. Due to the effervescent nature of computer communications, employees will often say things in email that they would never put in writing. Thus, it is important that all employers have a policy which strongly prohibits the inappropriate use of the Company's electronic systems, and puts employees on notice that the employer reserves the right to monitor such use.
Policy:	The Company provides its employees with access to Company computers, network, Internet access, internal and external electronic mail, and voice mail to facilitate the conduct of Company business.

Company Property: All computers and data, information and software created, transmitted, downloaded, or stored on the Company's computer system are the property of Company. All electronic mail messages composed, sent, and received are and remain the property of Company. The voice mail system and all messages left on that system are Company property.

Business Use and Occasional Personal Use: The Company's computers, network, Internet access, electronic mail, and voice mail systems are provided to employees to assist employees in accomplishing their job responsibilities for the Company. Limited occasional personal use of such facilities is acceptable, provided such use is reasonable, appropriate, and complies with this policy. If you have any questions as to whether a particular use of such facilities is permissible, check with your supervisor before engaging in such use. The use of Company's computers, network, Internet access, electronic mail, and voice mail for personal use does not alter the facts that the foregoing remain Company property, and that employees have no reasonable expectation of privacy with respect to such use.

Exhibit 14.15 *continued*

Privacy: Employees shall respect the privacy of others. Except as provided below, messages sent via electronic mail are to be read only by the addressed recipient or with the authorization of the addressed recipient. The data, information and software created, transmitted, downloaded, or stored on the Company's computer system may be accessed by authorized personnel only. Employees should understand that the confidentiality of electronic mail cannot be ensured. Employees must assume that any and all messages may be read by someone other than the intended recipient. Personal passwords are not an assurance of confidentiality. *There is no reasonable expectation of privacy in any email, voice mail, and/or other use of Company computers, network, and systems.*

Prohibited Conduct:

- Employees may not use the Company's computers, network, Internet access, electronic mail, or voice mail to conduct illegal or malicious activities.
- Employees may not transmit or solicit any threatening, defamatory, obscene, harassing, offensive, or unprofessional material. Offensive content would include, but not be limited to, sexual comments or images, racial slurs, gender-specific comments or any comments that would offend someone on the basis of his or her race, religion, color, national origin, ancestry, disability, age, sex, marital status, sexual orientation, or any other class protected by any federal, state, or local law.
- Employees may not create, transmit, or distribute unwanted, mass, excessive or anonymous emails, electronic vandalism, junk email, or "spam."
- Employees may not access any website that is sexually or racially offensive or discriminatory.
- Employees may not display, download, or distribute any sexually explicit material.
- Employees may not violate the privacy of individuals by any means, such as by reading private emails or private communications, accessing private documents, or utilizing the passwords of others, unless officially authorized to do so.
- Employees may not represent themselves as being someone else, or send anonymous communications.
- Employees may not use the email, social networks, voice mail, or computer systems to solicit for religious causes, outside business ventures, or personal causes.
- Employees may not transmit any of Company's confidential or proprietary information including (without limitation) customer data, trade secrets, or other material covered by Company's policy in regard to Confidentiality of Company information.
- Employees may not install, run, or download any software (including entertainment software or games) not authorized by the Company.
- Employees may not disrupt or hinder the use of the Company computers or network, or infiltrate another computer or computing system.
- Employees may not damage software or propagate computer worms or viruses.

continued

Exhibit 14.15 *continued*

Only authorized employees may communicate on the Internet on behalf of the Company.

Monitoring: Company maintains the right to monitor and record employee activity on its computers, network, voice mail, and email systems. Company's monitoring includes (without limitation) reading email messages sent or received, files stored or transmitted, and recording websites accessed.

Archiving: It is Company's practice to archive (i.e., make backup copies) all electronic documents, files, and email messages incident to the Company's normal back-up procedures. Employees should therefore understand that even when a document, file, or message is deleted, it may still be possible to access that message. Management and law enforcement agencies have the right to access these archives.

Copyright Laws: Any software or other material downloaded into the Company's computers may be used only in ways consistent with the licenses and copyrights of the vendors, authors, and owners of the material. No employee shall make illegal or unauthorized copies of any software or data.

Violations of this Policy: Any violation of this policy may result in disciplinary action up to and including immediate termination. Any employee learning of any violation of this policy should notify his or her [e.g., immediate supervisor] immediately.

Lee T. Paterson, ed., Sample Personnel Policies (El Segundo, CA: Professionals in Human Resources Association [PIHRA], 2002).

Some experts advocate policies that restrict the use of email to business purposes only and explain that the employer may access the email both in the ordinary course of business and when business reasons necessitate. If the employer faithfully adheres to this policy 100 percent of the time, this process is certainly defensible. However, this is a standard that may be difficult to honor in every case, and the employer may be subject to claims of disparate treatment if applied inconsistently. Therefore, a more realistic approach—and one that is generally accepted in both the courts and common practice—suggests that employees limit their use of technology to reasonable personal access that does not unnecessarily interfere with their professional responsibilities or unduly impact the workplace financially or otherwise (referring to bandwidth, time spent online, impact on colleagues, and so on).

In addition, employers should be aware that developing a legitimate computer use policy and notifying employees of the policy on a frequent basis is not the whole story; it also matters how the policy is implemented and enforced. In a number of recent cases, the employer's enforcement of computer use policies has been found to violate existing laws. In particular, policies must not be enforced in a discriminatory manner or used selectively against employees for exercising their statutorily protected rights.

For example, in *Frankhouser v. Clearfield County Career and Technology Center,*[174] discussed earlier in this chapter, the employee submitted a claim against her employer for sexual harassment. Not long thereafter, she was fired for having what the employer considered to be an inappropriate photo in her personal Dropbox account (stored on her computer). The appeals court ruled in her favor, holding that her Dropbox folder was considered private, except for those files connected to her work.

A prior case, *Gorzynski v. JetBlue Airways Corp.,* alleged discriminatory enforcement of a technology policy based on age.[175] In addition to violating the policy, selective enforcement against members of a protected class may constitute an unlawful discriminatory action. Employees may also be protected where monitoring is undertaken in retaliation for engaging in a protected activity. For example, six staff doctors and scientists were permitted to sue the Food and Drug Administration (FDA) after discovering that the FDA accessed their personal Gmail accounts. This secret surveillance took place over a two-year period and only after the staffers had complained to Congress that the FDA was approving risky medical devices.[176]

Kevin Conlon, district counsel for the Communication Workers of America, suggests these additional guidelines that may be considered in formulating an accountable process for employee monitoring:

1. There should be no monitoring in highly private areas such as restrooms.
2. Monitoring should be limited to the workplace.
3. Employees should have full access to any information gathered through monitoring.
4. Continuous monitoring should be banned.
5. All forms of *secret* monitoring should be banned. Advance notice should be given.
6. Only information relevant to the job should be collected.
7. Monitoring should result in the attainment of some business interest.

These guidelines respect the personal autonomy of the individual worker by providing for personal space within the working environment, by providing notice of where that "personal" space ends, and by allowing access to the information gathered, all designed toward achievement of a personal and professional development objective.

As is apparent from the above discussion, it is possible to implement a monitoring program that is true to the values of the firm and accountable to those it impacts—the workers. Appropriate attention to the nature and extent of the monitoring, the notice given to those monitored, and the ethical management of the information obtained will ensure a balance of employer and employee interests.

Bring Your Own Device (BYOD)

Employees increasingly use their personal smartphones, tablets, or laptops for business purposes, either instead of or in addition to company-issued equipment.

While this can decrease company costs for devices, data, and IT support, it also poses a number of practical and legal risks. For example, according to research reported in Forbes, 61 percent of Gen Y and 50 percent of workers aged 30 and older believe the technology they use in their personal lives is more effective and productive than that provided by employers. As well, companies that allow employees to "bring your own device" (BYOD) have an annual savings of $350 per year per employee, and using portable devices for work tasks saves employees 58 minutes per day while increasing productivity by 34 percent. On the downside, BYOD users are the weakest link in a company's security chain. The risks associated with BYOD include cyberattacks, lost company information, or privacy violations.[177]

Companies that maintain a BYOD environment (in other words, those that do not have policies that prohibit these activities) may opt to integrate employees' smartphones, tablets, and other mobile devices in a number of different ways. A policy of *limited separation* that permits company information to be intermingled with personal information is extremely insecure and makes it difficult to balance protection of company data against respect for employee privacy. A slightly more secure *walled garden* approach separates company-owned data from personal data in a separate, secure application. The most secure approach is called *virtualization,* which provides remote access to company servers, so that employees can access and use the company's data, without actually downloading it or storing it on their device. Virtualization eliminates the risk that data will be lost if the device is misplaced or stolen. Whatever route they choose, employers that permit BYOD should develop clear and comprehensive policies and conduct regular employee training.[178]

Monitoring Social Media Activities

LO12 Describe the legal environment that surrounds employee use of social media technologies.

social media
User-created content, including text, video, audio, and other multimedia, published or otherwise communicated in an environment that enables scalable interactivity and dialogue, such as a blog, wiki, or other similar site.

Social media is dominating the way we interact and the way we conduct business and source potential employees and customers. Consider, for example, the question of employer access to employees' social media activity, a topic that has recently received a great deal of attention in the media as well as from state legislatures and courts (discussed further below). This issue raises two distinct questions. First, which social media sites should employers be permitted to access in order to obtain information about applicants and employees (and which are they able to access)? Second, to what extent lawfully can employers rely on information obtained from social media sites when making hiring and employment decisions? The first question does present employers with a novel and confusing landscape characterized by rapid technological innovation and a patchwork of new state legislation. The second question is hardly new, posing familiar anti-discrimination concerns that employers have faced offline for decades. These issues are discussed in more detail below.

As of early 2020, there were more than 500 million blogs out of 1.7 billion websites in the world, and their authors accounted for over 2 million blog posts daily.[179] To further illustrate the growth of blogs, in May 2011, Tumblr hosted approximately 17.5 million blogs; as of January 2020, that number has increased to 488.1 million blogs.[180] Social media is now the number one activity on the Web. At the time of publication, the worldwide number of social network users was 3.5 billion, representing a 45 percent penetration into the world population.[181] But individuals are not the only ones embracing social media. Research reports that 84 percent of companies use social media to recruit candidates, with an additional 9 percent stating they plan to use it.[182] As of 2020, 80 million small- and medium-sized businesses had Facebook pages, and 87 percent of U.S. marketers use Facebook marketing.[183]

Generally speaking, employers need permission from the employee to retrieve communications in most password-protected, non-work-related social media. The City of Bozeman, Montana, tried to require that all prospective employees disclose their user names and passwords for any profiles they have on Facebook, Twitter, Snapchat, Google, and YouTube.[184] However, the Montana legislature responded by enacting a law barring employers from delving into employees' and applicants' social media accounts, with a few exceptions. This statute prohibits employers from requiring employees or applicants to disclose any information about their social media accounts or to tell the employer their user names or passwords.[185]

Whether employers in other states can require potential or current employees to disclose the passwords to social media sites gained significant media and legislative attention for a period of time after the City of Bozeman actions. Maryland was the first state to pass a "social media password protection law" in April 2012, and by 2019, 26 states had passed special laws restricting access to personal media accounts of applicants and employers, and legislation is pending in at least five other states.[186]

A number of concerns have been raised about the laws. Some critics have questioned whether they are necessary, suggesting that the rash of legislation is a response to media hype rather than an actual problem. A 2012 survey of nearly 1,000 executives, corporate counsel, and human resource professionals from large corporations throughout the United States found that 99 percent of respondents denied that their organization had requested social media passwords as part of the hiring process.[187] In fact, there is a clear argument made that requesting passwords is bad HR policy for no other reason than it puts the employers at risk for being accused of illegal discrimination based on race, sex, and other characteristics easily discernible through social media posts.[188] Employers now find password protection laws unimportant in lieu of other issues such as AI and marijuana laws.[189]

Another concern raised by critics is that some state legislation may hamper employers' ability to deal with workplace violence or harassment. In some states (like California), the laws provide exemptions for legitimate business interests, including broad exceptions that permit asking employees to disclose social media content that is reasonably believed to be relevant to investigations of employee misconduct. Yet in other states (like Colorado, Illinois, Maryland, and New Jersey), social media privacy laws could potentially prevent an employer from requesting the password to a social media account from an employee whose coworker reported seeing a post like "I'm so angry I want to kill my boss." Given that it is not uncommon for perpetrators of violence to indicate their intentions online, this is hardly a hypothetical concern. Inconsistent state laws, which are particularly onerous for national companies, have led some commentators to suggest the need for federal legislation.

The enormous growth in blogging and other social media has created a dilemma for those businesses that have embraced these new technologies. While social media may offer new opportunities to reach a wider customer base in a variety of new ways, it also offers new arenas in which employees can harm the company image, share company information that should not be shared, harass fellow employees, or commit other acts that employers once worried about only with email. A 2016 study by the Ponemon Institute found that while only 23 percent of companies conducted an audit of their confidential documents, of those that did, 69 percent found security issues.[190]

For better or for worse, social media is here to stay. Social media advertising budgets increased worldwide from 2016 to 2020, going from $31 billion to $43 billion.[191] Though there is a near consensus that social content marketing is valuable and will continue to become more pervasive, measuring the exact value of social media marketing has been notoriously difficult.[192] Recent research has found it may take from one to two years to build social media engagement for a new business.[193] A 2009 report found a correlation between corporate profitability and engagement in social media, looking at 11 different online social media channels.[194] Generally, those that had a deeper involvement in social media saw revenues grow faster than those that did not. A 2013 study demonstrated that social media activities strengthen the bond between customers and businesses. Customers who engage with a firm through social media contribute 5.6 percent more revenue than those who do not.[195]

The challenge for employers now is to find the right balance between embracing social media and discouraging employee misuse. As with email, employers have the right to control what is sent out through the various social media channels they own. The difficult part is trying to control what employees send out on their own time and through their own social media channels.

In March 2019, a New Jersey sanitation worker named Sam Falcetano was fired when he expressed anger through Facebook about being required to clean up after a two-day outdoor concert. He followed these workplace complaints with additional negative posts about then President Obama, gays and lesbians, and New Jersey politics.[196] In another case, an employee of a car dealership posted comments criticizing the food served at a work event and negative comments about an accident involving a vehicle sold by the dealership. Getting "dooced"—being fired as a result of negative comments about one's company on a personal blog or social media site—has now entered the Internet lexicon.[197]

With the presence of the Internet and smartphones throughout our lives and the workplace, the NLRB has continued to expand the scope of how online communications are protected and has limited further the ability of employers to discipline their employees for work-related social media posts. For instance, in 2015 a long-time employee of Pier Sixty LLC, a New York catering company, used his iPhone to post a message to his Facebook page about his manager while he was on a break. His post read, "Bob is such a NASTY MOTHER F***ER . . . don't know how to talk to people!!!!! F**k his mother and his entire f***ing family!!!! What a LOSER!!!! Vote YES for the UNION!!!!!!!!!" The NLRB found that employee social media communications that relate to working conditions or unionization should tend to be protected. This is true even if the postings are offensive or obscene or attack individual members of management personally. Therefore, the employee's communications were protected communications, and discipline on this basis was prohibited.[198] Sadly, perhaps the fact that NLRA protection is the best that employees can hope for illustrates how few protections they have.

However, there are some limitations to free speech in online communications, especially when the employee is a public servant. A former police officer was fired after posting criticisms about her police chief's decision not to send department representatives to the funeral of a police officer who was killed in the line of duty a few towns away. In 2015, the Fifth Circuit held that the officer spoke as a citizen, rather than as a public employee, when she posted the comments. However, the court found that the city's "substantial interests in maintaining discipline and close working relationships and preventing insubordination within the department outweigh [the police officer's] minimal interest in speaking on a matter of public concern."[199]

Case 3

In a case included at the end of the chapter and discussed earlier, a San Diego police officer in his free time sold pornographic videos and other paraphernalia, including official police department uniforms, through an adults-only section of eBay. His superiors discovered the activity and ordered him to stop. When he did not, they dismissed him. He sued the department, alleging a violation of his First Amendment right to free speech. Although the appellate court accepted his argument, the U.S. Supreme Court reversed, concluding that the San Diego Police Department had legitimate and substantial interests of its own that were compromised by the employee's speech, especially because the police officer linked his videos to his work (the videos depicted the police officer in a simulated police uniform).[200] Speech by a public employee that involves "public concern" is entitled to a balancing test, but those that are outside of public concern are subject to tighter restrictions.

The general rule is that bloggers (and other social media users) enjoy First Amendment protections for comments made on blogs and elsewhere, but that protection is not absolute.[201] First, it does not extend to unprotected speech, such as defamation. Second, unless a termination violates an exception, it does not protect employees from the at-will employment doctrine.

The other thing to note is that government employees have even fewer First Amendment rights than private employees. As the Supreme Court said in *Roe,* "a governmental employer may impose certain restraints on the speech of its employees, restraints that would be unconstitutional if applied to the general public."[202]

Whether state laws that protect employees off-work activities (as noted in a previous section) can be extended to protect blogging activities conducted away from work seems unlikely but remains an open question. Some commentators have suggested that states amend their laws to incorporate protections for off-duty blogging.[203] Though Congress has not passed any national protections, some states, including California, Colorado, New York, and North Dakota, have passed laws that prohibit employers from discharging or otherwise discriminating against lawful conduct occurring during nonworking hours away from the workplace.[204] Until Congress or state legislatures step in, employers will continue to have wide latitude in managing off-duty blogging.

Several cases illustrate the point. Talia Jane, a customer service agent at Yelp!, was fired after she wrote an open letter to the company's CEO, imploring him to give employees a livable wage. In her letter, Jane described bread as a luxury she could not afford on her $367 per week salary in San Francisco.[205] Ellen Simonetti was fired in 2004 by Delta Air Lines for an online journal post showing a photograph of her in her Delta uniform. Jessica Cutler was fired in 2004 from her job as a congressional aide after posting blogs detailing her sexual adventures and criticizing her boss. Chez Pazienza was fired in 2008 by CNN for operating a blog without permission. Others have been fired by Starbucks, Microsoft, Wells Fargo, Google, Friendster, *The Washington Post,* and Kmart; and the list goes on. Many of those were fired even though they did not blog in their own name and did not have prior notice that what they were doing would subject them to punishment.

What is an employee to do? The Electronic Frontier Foundation maintains a tutorial on blogging that includes tips on how to avoid getting fired.[206] One key recommendation is to blog anonymously. The Delaware Supreme Court, for example, refused to compel discovery of the identity of an anonymous blogger who published allegedly defamatory comments about a Smyrna, Delaware, city councilman.[207] The ultimate fate of anonymity remains to be seen, but the court's assertions that "[b]logs and chat rooms . . . are not sources of facts or data upon which a reasonable person would rely" as well as "readers are unlikely to view messages posted anonymously as assertions of fact" already seem dated.[208]

In a another case, an appeals court in Texas held that the trial court did not have any authority to order disclosure of a blogger's identity.[209] However, in nonemployment situations, the Court has not always upheld the protection of anonymous bloggers.[210]

Until the legal boundaries become clearer, the best possible solution for employers and employees is probably a combination of a clear written policy, some tolerance of criticism, and more effective training. Companies that embrace social media need to find the right balance between encouraging employees to engage in open and honest communications with customers and protecting the company's interests. Therefore, a company social media policy should contain the following:[211]

- **Defined objectives that do not overreach.** A policy can range from restrictive—banning all employee comments on work-related matters, including on their own time—to permissive—allowing contact with customers but warning employees to avoid embarrassing the company.
- **A reminder that company policies apply.** Employers who embrace social media activities should remind employees that company policies continue to apply to

off-work social media-related activities, including those involving the sharing of company information, harassment, and discrimination.

- **Personal comment rules.** Employers should establish rules for employees who express opinions through social media; for example, employees who offer personal opinions may be required to identify themselves as employees of the company and provide a disclaimer that they have no authority to speak for the company and that the views are theirs, alone.

- **Disclosure reminders.** If the employer is publicly traded, the policy should include a reminder of the rules imposed by the Securities and Exchange Commission on information disclosures by publicly owned companies.

- **Monitoring reminders.** Employers should remind employees that they retain the right to monitor all social media activities, including the right to view Facebook and Twitter postings made while away from work; they may need to be reminded that content sent through social media channels is not private and cannot be recalled.

- **Copyright reminders.** Employers may want to include a reminder to respect copyright law; social media users often mistakenly believe that anything they see on the Internet is fair game for copying and reusing.

Employers who embrace social media will have to decide how much criticism they are willing to tolerate. Employers that have been willing to tolerate some internal criticisms have sometimes been rewarded for that tolerance with a reputation for open-mindedness and a progressive embrace of social media technologies.

Social media technologies have democratized opinion-giving. Once upon a time, employers could control their message rather effectively by training the few top executives who were authorized to speak for the company. Today, however, any employee with a cell phone or a personal computer can publish her or his opinion any number of ways. Putting such a public microphone in the hands of employees who are untrained in the dangers of misstatements can be disastrous, potentially exposing the company to legal liability and possibly damaging the stock price. The answer is better employee training of the dangers inherent in social media and a clear social media policy that sets forth the employer's expectations of those who intend to use the technologies, including the risks for those who misuse them.

YouTube is another popular social media outlet. Because many cell phones now have not only cameras but also video capabilities, and because many employees carry cell phones, it is a short step between something an employee sees at work and YouTube or another video-sharing site. Some employers, therefore, have implemented policies banning the use of cameras, cell phones, and any other devices used to take still pictures or video on the theory that employees may not fully appreciate the importance of not sharing the business's inner workings with the rest of the world. Although no cases exist that have challenged such bans, employers are likely within their rights to do so, especially if the ban is tied to a legitimate business reason. (See Exhibit 14.16, "Law Forbids Secret Videos of Factory Farms.")

Exhibit 14.16　*Law Forbids Secret Videos of Factory Farms*

The editorial excerpted below criticizes a new law passed in North Carolina that forbids "undercover recordings" of abuse at farms and slaughterhouses. (The law technically applies to other workplaces, too, but in practice the law is clearly aimed at protecting factory farms.) The criticism of this law is grounded upon the principle (and constitutional protection of) free speech. It is a good criticism.

We wonder, however, about something not mentioned in the editorial: a counterargument rooted in privacy and the sanctity of private property. When activists, for example, pose as employees to gain access and then secretly record wrongdoing, are they not effectively trespassing? This may well be morally justified, but legally it still seems plausibly subject to penalty. The question then becomes whether video illegally obtained could rightly be brought to light? Should a law forbid such video on the grounds that it was obtained by illegal means, or should the public's interest in knowing about bad behavior at slaughterhouses override such considerations?

　. . . The industry should welcome such scrutiny as a way to expose the worst operators. Instead, the industry's lobbyists have taken the opposite approach,

pushing for the passage of so-called "ag-gag" laws, which ban undercover recordings on farms and in slaughterhouses. These measures have failed in many states, but they have been enacted in eight. None has gone as far as North Carolina, where a new law that took effect Jan. 1 aims to silence whistle-blowers not just at agricultural facilities, but at all workplaces in the state. That includes, among others, nursing homes, day care centers, and veterans' facilities.

Anyone who violates the law—say, by secretly taping abuses of elderly patients or farm animals and then sharing the recording with the media or an advocacy group—can be sued by business owners for bad publicity and be required to pay a fine of $5,000 for each day that person is gathering information or recording without authorization. . . .

What do you think?

MacDonald, C., and A. Marcoux, "Law Forbids Secret Videos of Factory Farms," Business Ethics Highlights (February 6, 2016), https://businessethicshighlights.com/2016/02/06/law-forbids-secret-videos-of-factory-farms/, referring to "No Nore Exposés in North Carolina," New York Times (February 1, 2016), https://www.nytimes.com/2016/02/01/opinion/no-more-exposes-in-north-carolina.html. Business Ethics Highlights ©Christopher MacDonald, reprinted with permission.

Waivers of Privacy Rights

search
A physical invasion of a person's space, belongings, or body.

waiver
The intentional relinquishment of a known right.

On occasion, an employer may request that an employee waive her or his privacy rights as a condition of employment. For instance, the employer may request the waiver during a **search**. If valid, the **waiver** would mean that the employer is not liable to the employee for any violation of the employee's privacy rights. While a valid waiver must be given voluntarily, requiring a waiver as a condition of employment is a questionable approach. Employers are in a more powerful bargaining position from which to negotiate such an arrangement, so is it really "voluntary" if the employee is required to waive her or his rights in order to obtain or keep a job?

Waivers exist at all stages of employment, from preemployment medical screenings to a (Chapter 12) waiver of age discrimination claims when being bought out of one's job at a certain age. Courts are not consistent in their acceptance of these

contingent offer
An offer of employment that is based on compliance with specific conditions, such as a producing results of a successful medical exam, completing particular exams, or signing a waiver of claims. Not all contingent offers have been upheld as appropriate by the courts.

waivers, but one common link among those that are approved is that the employee receives some form of consideration (compensation or other value) in return for surrendering her or his rights.

When privacy or other waivers are requested by employers at the preemployment stage, courts have held that they are valid only when accompanied by an offer of employment. In the area of selection, this is called a **contingent offer**.[212] The job is offered and is contingent on successfully submitting to a search of some sort, such as a preemployment drug test or medical exam. If the candidate passes the test, the job offer no longer is contingent. No waiver that is given by an applicant prior to a job offer would be considered valid and enforceable. Courts also require that waivers be knowingly and intelligently given and that they be clear and unmistakable, in writing, and voluntary.

Privacy Rights Since September 11, 2001

The United States has implemented widespread modifications to its patchwork structure of privacy protections since the terrorist attacks of September 11, 2001. In particular, proposals for the expansion of surveillance and information-gathering authority were submitted and many, to the chagrin of some civil rights attorneys and advocates, were enacted.

The most public and publicized of these modifications was the adoption and implementation of the Uniting and Strengthening America by Providing Appropriate Tools Required to Intercept and Obstruct Terrorism Act of 2001 (USA PATRIOT Act).[213] The USA PATRIOT Act expanded states' rights with regard to Internet surveillance technology, including workplace surveillance and amending the Electronic Communications Privacy Act in this regard. The act also grants access to sensitive data with only a court order rather than a judicial warrant, among other changes, and imposes or enhances civil and criminal penalties for knowingly or intentionally aiding terrorists. In addition, the new disclosure regime increased the sharing of personal information between government agencies in order to ensure the greatest level of protection.

Title II of the act provides for the following enhanced surveillance procedures, among others, that have a significant impact on individual privacy and may impact an employer's effort to maintain employee privacy:

- Expanded authority to intercept wire, oral, and electronic communications relating to terrorism and to computer fraud and abuse offenses.

- Provided roving surveillance authority under the Foreign Intelligence Surveillance Act of 1978 (FISA) to track individuals. (FISA investigations are not subject to Fourth Amendment standards but are instead governed by the requirement that the search serve "a significant purpose.")

- Allowed nationwide seizure of voice mail messages pursuant to warrants (i.e., without the previously required wiretap order).

- Broadened the types of records that law enforcement may obtain, pursuant to a subpoena, from electronic communications service providers.

- Permitted emergency disclosure of customer electronic communications by providers to protect life and limb.

- Offered nationwide service of search warrants for electronic evidence.

Pursuant to these provisions, the government is now allowed to monitor anyone on the Internet simply by contending that the information is "relevant" to an ongoing criminal investigation. In addition, the act provides anti-money-laundering provisions designed to combat money-laundering activity or the funding of terrorist or criminal activity through corporate activity or otherwise. All financial institutions must now report suspicious activities in financial transactions and keep records of foreign national employees while also complying with anti-discrimination laws discussed throughout this text. It is a challenging balance, claim employers.

In March 2011, President Barack Obama signed the PATRIOT Sunsets Extension Act, which provided a four-year extension for three key provisions, including roving wiretaps and searches of business records, allowing authorities greater access to certain personal and business records.

The USA PATRIOT Act was not the only legislative response. Both federal and state agencies passed a number of additional pieces of legislation responding to terrorism. Not everyone was, or still is, comfortable with these pieces of legislation. For example, out of concern for the USA PATRIOT Act's permitted investigatory provisions, some librarians began warning computer users in their libraries that their computer use could be monitored by law enforcement agencies.[214] While there were a number of communities that passed anti–USA PATRIOT Act resolutions shortly after the Act's passage, acts of this nature have slowed down in the last few years.

On June 1, 2015, the USA PATRIOT Act expired. The next day, Congress enacted the USA Freedom Act,[215] which restored many modified provisions of the USA PATRIOT Act. The new act restored authorization for wiretaps but limits the bulk collection of telecommunication metadata on U.S. citizens by intelligence agencies, though critics point out that it still allows bulk collection of metadata by phone companies, which can be accessed by the National Security Agency.

In February 2020, Congress postponed a planned vote to reauthorize parts of the Foreign Intelligence Surveillance Act of 1978 (FISA). It may be reauthorized at a later date with no changes or have some of the privacy provisions narrowed to further limit government data collection.[216]

Employers have three choices in terms of their response to a governmental request for information. They may:

1. Voluntarily cooperate with law enforcement by providing, upon request (as part of an ongoing investigation), confidential employee information.

2. Choose not to cooperate and ask instead for permission to seek employee authorization to release the requested information.

3. Request to receive a subpoena, search warrant, or FISA order from the federal agency before disclosing an employee's confidential information.[217]

Management Considerations

Develop and publish policies that reserve your right to monitor, gain access to, or disclose all emails in your system. Notify employees of the policy and train all managers (see Exhibit 14.17, "Toward Appropriate Information Collection from Employees").

When developing an email policy, do not overlook instant messaging (IM). Ensure that any policy that applies to emails also applies to IMs. IMs can pose a greater security risk than email if the IMs sent to employees are not subject to virus-checking software.

The same warning applies for the so-called Web 2.0 technologies, such as blogs, social networking, wikis, and similar technologies. Ensure that the privacy policy accounts for these social media technologies and strikes the right balance between appropriate and inappropriate uses.

Exhibit 14.17 *Toward Appropriate Information Collection from Employees*

Though it appears that employee privacy might be a moving target, there are steps that employers may take to be respectful of employee information and personal privacy while also maintaining a balanced management of its workplace:

- **First, conduct an information audit** for the purpose of determining those areas of the company's practices and procedures that have the potential for invasion, including what type of information is collected, how that information is maintained, the means by which the information is verified, who has access to the information, and to whom the information is disclosed. The audit should cover all facets of the organization's activities, from recruitment and hiring to termination. In addition, it may be helpful to ascertain what type of information is maintained by different sectors of the organization.

- **Second, in connection with sensitive areas where the company maintains no formal policy, develop a policy** to ensure appropriate treatment of data. It is recommended that a policy and procedure be maintained in connection with the acquisition of information, the maintenance of that information, the appropriate contents of personnel files, the use of the information contained therein, and the conduct of workplace investigations. For instance, in connection with the maintenance of personnel files and the accumulation of personal information about company employees, the employer should request only information justified by the needs of the firm and relevant to employment-related decisions.

- **Third, the information collected should be kept in one of several files maintained on each employee:** (1) a personnel file, which contains the application, paperwork relating to hiring, payroll, and other nonsensitive data; (2) a medical file, which contains physicians' reports and insurance records; (3) evaluation files, which contain any evidence of job performance including, but not limited to, performance appraisals; and (4) a confidential file, which contains data relating to extremely sensitive matters that should not be disclosed except with express and specific authority, such as criminal records or information collected in connection with workplace investigations.

- **Fourth, information should be gathered from reliable sources** rather than sources of questionable repute such as hearsay and other subjective indicators. Irrelevant or outdated material should periodically be expunged from these records as well.

- **Fifth, publicize privacy policies and procedures, and educate employees** regarding their rights as well as their responsibilities.

The privacy policy should be clear that employees have no expectation of privacy in all employer-provided equipment. Clear policies reduce the likelihood of future disputes.

As an employer, you may search your employees' property where the employee does not have any expectation of privacy; the difficulty comes in determining where that expectation exists. Therefore, if you believe that searches are necessary, the policy should state clearly where the expectation of privacy ends and under what conditions searches will be permitted.

Monitoring policies should be clearly stated and should explain that use of technology is subject to review, notwithstanding password protection. They should explain that passwords are provided for the user's protection from external intrusion, as opposed to the creation of an expectation that email is actually private with regard to the employer.

In designing a monitoring process, avoid content-based and real-time monitoring as both give rise to subjective action rather than standardized procedures and may violate the Federal Wiretap Act.

Since many privacy protections exist on a state-by-state basis, be sure to investigate the specific protections for which you are responsible in the states in which you do business.

Your privacy policy should be targeted to protect your business interests. Therefore, consider prohibiting the following: (1) the use of cameras, cell phones, or other devices for taking pictures or making recordings on your property; (2) the use of emails for distributing illegal or improper content; (3) the use of company trademarks, logos, or other copyrighted material without permission; and (4) the disclosure of company materials to outside entities.

While it may appear reasonable for you to want to regulate certain off-work activities of your employees, be wary of overrestricting since courts do not look on these regulations positively. Policies regulating off-work activities that have been upheld are generally those that are targeted to protect legitimate business interests, such as the company's reputation.

On that note, if you do opt to regulate the off-work activities of your employees, you may wish to consider focusing the policy on the possible negative impact of off-duty conduct on the employer's business interests and on the public's perception of the employer, rather than on the specific off-duty conduct, in particular.

You are less likely to find problems with a waiver of privacy rights where the waiver is accompanied by an offer of employment.

Ensure that you comply with all privacy rules required by HIPAA, particularly involving the security of employee health records. Train the appropriate employees on those requirements.

When you do collect personal information about your employees, be sure to regulate access to this information since unwarranted disclosure might constitute an invasion of privacy even where the original collection of information is allowed.

Technology changes quickly. You should keep abreast of current developments and conduct periodic reviews of the privacy policy to ensure that emerging technologies are covered.

Ensure that the privacy rules are enforced consistently.

Chapter Summary

- Privacy is a fundamental right that has been recognized as deserving constitutional protection.
- Public employers are subject to greater scrutiny because their actions are considered to be State actions, thus triggering constitutional protections that generally do not apply to private sector employers.
- Employee privacy rights in the workplace originate from three sources: the Constitution, various state and federal laws, and the common law; those employees who have employment contracts, either individual or union-negotiated, also have whatever protections are provided in the contracts.
- Common law torts include intrusion into seclusion, public disclosure of private facts, publication in a false light, and defamation.
- Regulation of an employee's off-work activities is a controversial area, with the general rule being that employers have the right to regulate such activity as long as the regulation is connected to a legitimate business interest; some state legislatures have stepped in to limit what employers can regulate.
- Employers generally have the right to monitor employee activity while employees are on employer property; employers are generally on stronger footing if they develop a written policy, they notify employees of the policy, and they enforce the policy consistently.
- Technology is rapidly changing and has an impact on what is considered appropriate to monitor. The law is catching up to technological advances as we venture into unexpected and uncharted legal areas.

Chapter-End Questions

1. Can a government employee state a claim for a violation of the constitutional right to privacy when she was required, as a job applicant, to sign an affidavit stating that she had not used tobacco products for one year prior to the application date?

2. A gay employee files a claim for invasion of privacy against his employer who shared with coworkers the fact that the employee's male partner was listed on his insurance policy and pension plan as his beneficiary. Does he have a claim?

3. You learn that your employee is using medical marijuana to manage the side effects from chemotherapy, including nausea and pain. Medical marijuana is legal in your state, and this employee is an otherwise exemplary employee who performs high-quality work. The employee's performance has not suffered since she began treatment, but the company also has a zero tolerance policy on marijuana. Would you be within your legal rights to fire the employee? Would your answer be different if this worker were using marijuana for recreational purposes instead, even if she remained an exemplary employee with no performance issues? Presuming marijuana usage is legal in your state, how would you intend to navigate the boundary between off-work privacy and the impact on your organization?

4. Increasingly "smart products" such as Roombas, Fitbits, Alexas, refrigerators, thermostats and even fish tanks can be hacked, creating vulnerability for employee privacy and potential liability for employers. If we work at home, we likely do not have the same type of security that an organization might have through a strong cybersecurity system and its information technology infrastructure. Does the use of these types of products concern

See Chapter 2 to revisit key concepts.

you from a privacy perspective, or do you consider it just a cost of progress? How could we protect our privacy most effectively?

5. An employee submitted an expense report that included costs from a cell phone issued by his company. The company wanted to check the phone to verify information that the employee had provided, and because the employee was in the hospital, they obtained access to his office, as well as a key to his desk drawer, in order to look for the phone. Though they did not find the phone, they did find a pellet gun and ammunition. The employee was fired for violating the employer's weapons ban. Did the supervisors violate the employee's right to privacy? Is the fact that the employee shared the desk with other employees relevant? [*Ratti v. Serv. Mgmt. Sys., Inc.,* No. CIV. A. 06-6034 KSH, 2008 WL 4004256 (D.N.J. Aug. 25, 2008).]

6. Five employees were employed as cashiers at a supermarket chain. The employer noticed some losses in its products indicating possible theft and installed CCTV cameras as part of its investigation, both visibly within the store and also some hidden cameras at the checkout stations. Although customers and staff were aware that CCTV cameras operated on the premises, the employees were not aware of the concealed cameras. On review of the footage collected, the employer learned that the staff was involved in stealing items and these five employees were dismissed. They claimed unfair dismissal on the basis of unlawful surveillance. Though the employees did not know about the cameras at the checkout, the Court ruled the employer had the right to protect its property and thus the surveillance was justified. This particular case took place in Spain. What do you think the result would have been in the U.S. courts?[218]

7. A teacher claimed that she was diagnosed with adult attention deficit hyperactivity disorder (ADHD). She brought a claim against the school district alleging that the district had violated the Americans with Disabilities Act (ADA) and also a New York human rights law for discriminating against her on the basis of her ADHD, for retaliating against her for a complaint she filed with the New York State Division of Human Rights, and for failing to accommodate her ADHD. The teacher claimed that actions by the school district brought about emotional distress. Does the district have the right to compel the teacher to provide authorizations for the release of all records from her social networking accounts as part of its discovery during this case? [*Giacchetto v. Patchogue-Medford Union Free Sch. Dist.,* 293 F.R.D. 112, 115 (E.D.N.Y. 2013).]

8. Two female employees of a 24-hour residential facility for abused and neglected children discovered video recording equipment hidden on a bookshelf in an office that they shared. They were able to lock the door and close the blinds to the office, and one of the women regularly changed clothes there. The California Supreme Court upheld the placement of the hidden video equipment by their employer, even though neither woman was suspected of any wrongdoing. How is that possible? Under what set of facts do you imagine that an employer could permissibly monitor employees who are not suspected of wrongdoing? [*Hernandez v. Hillsides, Inc.,* 47 Cal. 4th 272 (2009).]

9. Ashley Johnson worked at Brixx Pizza in Charlotte, North Carolina. During one of her lunch shifts, a couple stayed for three hours, forcing Ashley to remain past her scheduled hours. They left her a tip of only $5.00, much lower than would be expected for the total bill that they incurred. Ashley was quite upset and, when she got home, vented on Facebook by calling them cheap and also mentioning the restaurant by name. Two days later, Ashley was confronted by her employer about the post. Despite her having few Facebook friends and strong privacy settings, Brixx had learned about the rant. They fired her based on two components of company policy: (1) speaking disparagingly about

customers and (2) casting the restaurant in a negative light on social networks. Was the employer within its legal right to terminate her employment? Is the termination a violation of Ashley's privacy?

10. During her employment with Verizon, Sandi Lazette was issued a company-owned Blackberry device, which she was allowed to use for personal as well as professional business. When Lazette left Verizon in October 2010, she attempted to delete her personal Gmail account prior to returning the device to her former boss, Chris Kulmatycki. She believed that the device would be "recycled" and given to another employee. Unbeknownst to Lazette, the Gmail deletion was unsuccessful. Over the next 18 months, Kulmatycki accessed over 48,000 emails from Lazette's personal Gmail account, including "communications about family, career, financials, health, and other personal matters." Lazette filed suit, asserting that Kulmatycki had invaded her privacy, among other claims. Kulmatycki and Verizon sought to have the case dismissed, arguing that Kulmatycki could not violate Lazette's privacy by accessing a company-owned device in his capacity as a company employee. Whose claim prevailed? [*Lazette v. Kulmatycki,* 949 F. Supp. 2d 748 (N.D. Ohio 2013).]

11. Jason Harrington worked at Chicago's O'Hare International Airport for the Transportation Safety Administration (TSA) screening luggage. Stating that it was for his own protection, his employer had Jason followed and also video-recorded his activities. TSA explained that, for example, if an item were reported stolen, the video would then be able to demonstrate that Jason was not responsible for the missing item. Jason learned that his employer was also using the video recordings to identify more minor infractions and these infractions were listed on his permanent employment record. They included, for instance, violations of TSA regulations such as chewing gum on the job or unauthorized trips to the bathroom that were otherwise not reported. Does the employer have the right to use the monitoring for purposes beyond those for which they notified Jason: to protect him from theft allegations? What are the trade-offs for monitoring at this level? What are the advantages, and what are the disadvantages?

12. In May 2015, a woman sued her employer after she was fired for uninstalling a GPS tracking app from a company-issued smartphone. Does she have a case for wrongful termination? What about a violation of privacy? Does it matter if the employer requires that employees leave their smartphones on at all times? Would it make a difference if the employees were told at the beginning of their employment that the employer would monitor their off-duty activity? [*Arias v. Intermex Wire Transfer,* 15-cv-01101 (E.D. CA, 2015).]

End Notes

1. Velasquez, M., C. Andre, T. Shanks, and M. J. Meyer, "Rights" (August 8, 2014), https://www.scu.edu/ethics/ethics-resources/ethical-decision-making/rights/ (accessed February 26, 2020).

2. *Public Utilities Commission v. Pollak,* 343 U.S. 451, 467 (1952) (dissenting).

3. Warren, Samuel D., and Louis D. Brandeis, "The Right to Privacy," *Harvard Law Review* 4, no. 193 (1890).

4. MacDonald, C., "Why Privacy Matters," *Management Ethics* (Fall/Winter 2010), http://www.ethicscentre.ca/EN/resources/Management_Ethics_FW10_dh.pdf (accessed March 10, 2020).

5. Wang, D., et al., "Worldwide: Data Privacy Issues In Connection with the Novel Coronavirus Outbreak: Requirements on Employee Personal Data Differ in China, Hong Kong and Singapore," *Mondaq Business Briefing* (February 7, 2020), https://www.mondaq.com/uk/

Privacy/891630/Data-Privacy-Issues-In-Connection-With-The-Novel-Coronavirus-Outbreak-Requirements-On-Employee-Personal-Data-Differ-In-China-Hong-Kong-And-Singapore (accessed March 21, 2020).

6. IDC, "Worldwide Spending on Security Solutions Forecast to Reach $103.1 Billion in 2019, According to a New IDC Spending Guide" (March 20, 2019), https://www.idc.com/getdoc.jsp?containerId=prUS44935119 (accessed February 26, 2020).

7. National Retail Federation, "2019 National Retail Security Survey" (June 6, 2019), https://nrf.com/research/national-retail-security-survey-2019 (accessed February 26, 2020).

8. See, for example, Levin, A. "Dignity in the Workplace: An Enquiry into the Conceptual Foundation of Workplace Privacy Protection Worldwide," *ALSB Journal of Employment and Labor Law* 11, no. 1 (Winter 2009), p. 63.

9. Council of the European Union, General Data Protection Regulation, Article 88, "Processing in the Context of Employment" (April 27, 2016), https://datagrc.co.uk/legislation/gdpr.php (accessed March 9, 2020).

10. Finley, K., "EU Privacy Law Snares Its First Tech Giant: Google," *Wired* (January 22, 2019), https://www.wired.com/story/eu-privacy-law-snares-first-tech-giant-google/ (accessed March 8, 2020).

11. Hayat, M. A., "Privacy and Islam: From the Quran to Data Protection in Pakistan," *Information & Communications Technology Law* (October 22, 2007), http://www.tandfonline.com/doi/abs/10.1080/13600830701532043?journalCode=cict20 (accessed March 10, 2020).

12. Buddy T., "Rates of Illicit Drug Abuse in the U.S" (September 26, 2019), https://www.verywellmind.com/rates-of-illicit-drug-abuse-in-the-us-67027 (accessed February 26, 2020).

13. Ibid.

14. National Safety Council, "Implications of Drug and Alcohol Use for Employers," http://www.nsc.org/work-safety/safety-topics/drugs-at-work/substances (accessed February 26, 2020).

15. Statusbrew, "100 Social Media Statistics for Marketers in 2020" (November 19, 2019), http://statusbrew.com/insights/social-media/statistics-2020 (accessed February 26, 2020).

16. Kuligowski, K., "Distracted Workers Are Costing You Money," *Business News Daily* (May 7, 2019), http://www.businessnewsdaily.com/267-distracted-workforce-costs-businesses-billions.html (accessed February 26, 2020).

17. Bissell, K., R. M. Lasalle, and P. Dal Cin, "Ninth Annual Cost of Cybercrime Study" (March 6, 2019), http://www.accenture.com/us-en/insights/security/cost-cybercrime-study (accessed February 27, 2020).

18. McLean, Rob, "A Hacker Gained Access to 100 Million Capital One Credit Card Applications and Accounts," *CNN Business* (July 30, 2019), https://edition.cnn.com/2019/07/29/business/capital-one-data-breach/index.html (accessed March 9, 2020); Dellinger, AJ, "Capital One Hit with Class-Action Lawsuit Following Massive Data Breach," *Forbes* (July 30, 2019), https://www.forbes.com/sites/ajdellinger/2019/07/30/capital-one-hit-with-class-action-lawsuit-following-massive-data-breach/#5dc2d4406b1a (accessed March 9, 2020).

19. Sobers, R., "110 Must-Know Cybersecurity Statistics for 2020" (January 9, 2020), http://www.varonis.com/blog/cybersecurity-statistics/ (accessed February 27, 2020).

20. Milewski, D., "Survey Shows Small Businesses Have Big Data Breach Exposure" (March 6, 2013), https://www.businesswire.com/news/home/20130306005904/en/Survey-Shows-Small-Businesses-Big-Data-Breach (accessed March 25, 2020).

21. Limpscomb, K., and P. McDaniel, "Data Breach Laws on the Books in Every State; Federal Data Breach Law Hangs in the Balance" (April 30, 2018), https://www.securityprivacybytes.com/2018/04/data-breach-laws-om-the-books-in-every-state-federal-data-breach-law-hangs-in-the-balance/ (accessed March 7, 2020).

22. IT Governance, "Data Breach Notification Laws by State" (July 2018), https://www.itgovernanceusa.com/data-breach-notification-laws (accessed March 7, 2020).

23. Limpscomb, K., and P. McDaniel, "Data Breach Laws on the Books in Every State; Federal Data Breach Law Hangs in the Balance" (April 30, 2018), https://www.securityprivacybytes.com/2018/04/data-breach-laws-om-the-books-in-every-state-federal-data-breach-law-hangs-in-the-balance/ (accessed March 7, 2020).

24. Ponemon Institute LLC, "The Impact of Data Breaches on Reputation & Share Value" (May 2017), https://www.centrify.com/media/4737054/ponemon_data_breach_impact_study.pdf (accessed March 7, 2020).

25. 381 U.S. 479 (1965).

26. Bean, R., "Chief Data Officers Struggle to Make a Business Impact," *Forbes* (June 24, 2019), http://www.forbes.com/sites/ciocentral/2019/06/24/chief-data-officers-struggle-to-make-a-business-impact/#204fae9ff1a4 (accessed February 27, 2020).

27. See, for example, *Smyth v. Pillsbury,* 914 F. Supp. 97 (E.D. Penn. 1996). The standard was first enunciated by the U.S. Supreme Court in *Katz v. U.S.,* 389 U.S. 347 (1967), a Fourth Amendment search and seizure case involving a public telephone booth.

28. See *Ulrich v. K-Mart,* 858 F. Supp. 1087 (D. Kan. 1994).

29. 480 U.S. 709 (1987).

30. *O'Connor v. Ortega,* 480 U.S. 709 (1987).

31. 132 S. Ct. 945 (2012).

32. Sommers, L., "Is It Legal to Track Employees Using GPS" (2019), https://www.timesheets.com/blog/2019/08/is-it-legal-to-track-employees-using-gps/ (accessed March 10, 2020).

33. 795 F.2d 1136, 1141 (3d Cir. 1986).

34. 109 S. Ct. 1402 (1989).

35. *Skinner v. Railway Labor Executives Association*, 109 S. Ct. 1402 (1989).

36. Ibid.

37. *U.S. v. Slanina,* 283 F.3d 670 (5th Cir. 2002); and *Leventhal v. Knapek,* 266 F.3d 64 (2d Cir. 2001).

38. 474 F.3d 1184 (9th Cir. 2007).

39. As an interesting side note, though U.S. law considers child pornography illegal, most states have no legal obligation to report it. Only Arkansas, Missouri, Oklahoma, South Carolina, and South Dakota have laws that require workers in the information technology arena to report child pornography when it is found on workers' computers. Harbert, T., "Dark Secrets and Ugly Truths: When Ethics and IT Collide," *Computerworld* (September 12, 2007), http://www.computerworld.com/article/2540961/it-careers/dark-secrets-and-ugly-truths--when-ethics-and-it-collide.html (accessed March 10, 2020). Fifteen states—Delaware, Florida, Idaho, Kentucky, Maryland, Mississippi, Nebraska, New Hampshire, New Mexico, North Carolina, Oklahoma, Rhode Island, Tennessee, Texas, and Utah—require reporting of suspected child abuse or neglect. As a result, by extension, anyone in these states is obligated to report any child pornography encountered. See Child Welfare Information Gateway, "Mandatory Reporters of Child Abuse and Neglect," *Children's Bureau* (April 2019), https://www.childwelfare.gov/pubPDFs/

manda.pdf (accessed March 10, 2020). Internet service providers, and by extension their employees, also have an obligation under 18 USC §2258A to report to the National Center of Missing or Exploited Children when they have knowledge of facts or circumstances involving sexual exploitation of children, selling or buying of children, production or distribution of child pornography, and websites designed to trick minors into viewing pornography or other obscene material. See DiGiacomo, John, "Internet Server Provider Requirements to Report Child Pornography," *Revision Legal* (December 7, 2018), https:// revisionlegal.com/internet/report-child-pornography/ (accessed March 10, 2020).

40. *Ziegler,* 474 F.3d at 1199.

41. *Frankhouser v. Clearfield County Career and Technology Center,* No. 3:18-cv-00180 (D.Ct. WD Pa. March 19, 2019).

42. *Carpenter v. United States,* No. 16-402, 585 U.S. ___(2018).

43. 460, U.S. 276 (1983).

44. 132 S. Ct. 945 (2012).

45. *United States v. Jones,* 132 S. Ct. 945 (2012).

46. 442 U.S. 735 (1979).

47. 425 U.S. 435, 443 (1976).

48. *Carpenter v. United States,* No. 16-402, 585 U.S. ___, 138 S. Ct. 2206, slip opinion p.15 (2018), https://www.supremecourt.gov/opinions/17pdf/16-402_h315.pdf (accessed April 11, 2020).

49. *Washington v. Glucksberg,* 521 U.S. 702 (1997).

50. U.S. Department of Justice, Overview of the Privacy Act of 1974: 2015 Edition, https:// www.justice.gov/opcl/file/793026/download (accessed March 10, 2020).

51. *Dobronski v. F.C.C.,* 17 F.3d 275 (9th Cir. 1994).

52. 18 U.S.C. §§ 2510–2521.

53. United States Courts, "Wiretap Report 2018" (December 31, 2018), http://www. uscourts.gov/statistics-reports/wiretap-report-2018 (accessed March 8, 2020).

54. These states include California, Delaware, Florida, Illinois, Maryland, Massachusetts, Montana, Nevada, New Hampshire, Pennsylvania, and Washington. See Pauley, E. M., "Conflicts among Federal and State Wiretap Statutes Present Practical Challenges for Businesses," *The National Law Review* (September 26, 2018), https://www. natlawreview.com/article/conflicts-among-federal-and-state-wiretap-statutes-present-practical-challenges (accessed March 8, 2020).

55. United States Courts, "Wiretap Report 2018," *op. cit.*

56. Pauley, E. M., "Conflicts Among Federal and State Wiretap Statutes Present Practical Challenges for Businesses," *The National Law Review* (September 26, 2018), https:// www.natlawreview.com/article/conflicts-among-federal-and-state-wiretap-statutes-present-practical-challenges (accessed March 8, 2020).

57. Fowler, G. A., "Alexa Has Been Eavesdropping on You This Whole Time," *The Washington Post* (May 6, 2019), https://www.washingtonpost.com/technology/2019/05/06/alexa-has-been-eavesdropping-you-this-whole-time/ (accessed March 8, 2020).

58. *Fraser v. National Mutual Insurance,* 352 F.3d 107 (3d Cir. 2003). See also *United States v. Steiger,* 318 F.3d 1039 (11th Cir. 2003); *Konop v. Hawaiian Airlines, Inc.,* 302 F.3d 868 (9th Cir. 2002); and *Steve Jackson Games, Inc. v. U.S. Secret Serv.,* 36 F.3d 457 (5th Cir. 1994).

59. Montana is the one exception. Employees can be fired only for good cause under the Wrongful Discharge from Employment Act, Mont. Code Ann. §39-2-901, et seq.

(2008); see also Better Team, "At-Will Employment" (July 29, 2019), https://www.better team.com/at-will-employment (accessed April 14, 2020).

60. National Conference of State Legislatures, "Privacy Protections in State Constitutions" (November 7, 2018), https://www.ncsl.org/research/telecommunications-and-information-technology/privacy-protections-in-state-constitutions.aspx (accessed March 8, 2020).

61. 50 S.E. 68 (Ga. 1905).

62. *Pavesich v. New England Life Ins. Co.,* 50 S.E. 68 (Ga. 1905).

63. *Lawlor v. N. Am. Corp. of Illinois,* 2012 IL 112530, ¶ 40, 983 N.E.2d 414, 426.

64. Ibid.

65. 66 Md. App. 133, 502 A.2d 1101 (1986).

66. *Ignat v. Yum! Brands, Inc.,* 214 Cal. App. 4th 808, 154 Cal. Rptr. 3d 275 (2013).

67. Ibid.

68. 28 F. Supp. 3d 786 (N.D. Ind. 2014).

69. *Connecticut Personnel Files Act,* Conn. Gen. Stat. § 31-128a et seq.

70. 561 F. Supp. 872 (S.D. Ga. 1983).

71. Certain states, however, provide no statutory protection, including Alabama, Mississippi, New Jersey, New York, and Vermont.

72. *Rivera v. Allstate Insurance Co.,* No. 17-1649 (7th Cir. 2019).

73. As of publication, these states included California; Colorado; Connecticut; District of Columbia; Illinois; Indiana; Kentucky; Louisiana; Maine; Minnesota; Mississippi; Missouri; Montana; Nevada; New Hampshire; New Jersey; New Mexico; New York; North Carolina; North Dakota; Oklahoma; Oregon; Rhode Island; South Carolina; South Dakota; Tennessee; Virginia; West Virginia; Wisconsin; and Wyoming. ComplyRight, "Can You Discipline Employees for Conduct Outside the Workplace? Nine Common Scenarios," (January 15, 2019), https://www.complyright.com/policies/can-you-discipline-employees-for-conduct-outside-of-the-workplace (accessed March 8, 2020).

74. ObamaCare Facts, "ObamaCare and Smokers" (July 2, 2015), http://obamacarefacts.com/obamacare-smokers/ (accessed March 8, 2020).

75. Kansas Health Institute, "States Vary on Higher Premiums Paid by Tobacco Users under the ACA" (2015), https://www.khi.org/assets/uploads/news/13870/tobaccosurcharge_final.pdf (accessed March 8, 2020).

76. Crist, Carolyn, "Employee Health Plans Charge Smokers Extra but Don't Help Them Quit," *Reuters* (March 16, 2018), https://www.reuters.com/article/us-health-insurance-smokers/employee-health-plans-charge-smokers-extra-but-dont-help-them-quit-idUSKCN1GS1Y5 (accessed March 8, 2020).

77. Wechsler, P. "Companies Get Tougher with Employees Who Smoke," *Business Week* (June 30, 2011), http://www.bloomberg.com/news/articles/2011-06-30/companies-get-tougher-with-employees-who-smoke (accessed March 8, 2020); Moraff, C. "Four Extreme Ways Companies Have Restricted Smoking on the Job," *Philadelphia* (April 11, 2013), http://www.phillymag.com/news/2013/04/11/smoking-at-work-health-insurance-smokers-obamacare/ (accessed March 8, 2020); Sammer, J., "Employer Incentives Encourage Employees to Quit Smoking," Society for Human Resource Management (October 29, 2018), https://www.shrm.org/hr-today/news/hr-magazine/1118/pages/employer-incentives-encourage-employees-to-quit-smoking.aspx (accessed March 8, 2020).

78. Costello, D., "Workers Are Told to Shape Up or Pay Up," *Los Angeles Times* (July 29, 2007), https://www.latimes.com/archives/la-xpm-2007-jul-29-fi-obese29-story.html (accessed April 14, 2020).

79. Khan, A., "Can a Fitness Tracker Save You Money on Health Insurance?" *U.S. News* (October 3, 2014), http://health.usnews.com/health-news/health-wellness/articles/2014/10/03/can-a-fitness-tracker-save-you-money-on-health-insurance (accessed April 14, 2020).

80. United States, Equal Employment Opportunity Commission, "Regulations under the ADA" *29 CFR Part 1630* (2016).

81. Appleby, J., "How Well Do Workplace Wellness Programs Work?" *National Public Radio* (April 16, 2019), https://www.npr.org/sections/health-shots/2019/04/16/713902890/how-well-do-workplace-wellness-programs-work (accessed March 8, 2020).

82. Chinery, A., "Workplace Study: Office Romance Statistics for 2019," *Reboot* (November 5, 2019), https://www.rebootonline.com/blog/study-office-romances-2019/ (accessed March 8, 2020).

83. Elsesser, K., "These 6 Surprising Office Romance Stats Should Be a Wake-Up Call for Organizations," *Forbes* (February 14, 2019), https://www.forbes.com/sites/kimelsesser/2019/02/14/these-6-surprising-office-romance-stats-should-be-a-wake-up-call-to-organizations/#6f0dba6323a2 (accessed March 8, 2020).

84. Heathfield, S. M., "Tips for Dealing with Romantic Relationships in the Workplace" (December 3, 2019), https://www.thebalancecareers.com/tips-about-dating-sex-and-romance-at-work-1916861 (accessed March 8, 2020).

85. Bote, J., "Should You Date Your Boss or Coworker? How an Office Relationship Might End Your Career," *USA Today* (November 4, 2019), https://www.usatoday.com/story/news/nation/2019/11/04/mcdonalds-ceo-firing-should-you-date-your-boss-absolutely-not/4155917002/ (accessed March 8, 2020).

86. 237 F.3d 166 (2d Cir. 2001).

87. *McCavitt v. Swiss Reinsurance America Corp.*, 237 F.3d 166 (2d Cir. 2001).

88. "The True Secret to Workplace Productivity? Dating a Coworker," *Working Mother* (February 22, 2018), https://www.workingmother.com/true-secret-to-workplace-productivity-dating-coworker-study-shows (accessed March 10, 2020).

89. Betts, J., "Love at Work: 5 Things for Employers to Know," *The National Law Review* (February 11, 2020), https://www.natlawreview.com/article/love-work-5-things-employers-to-know (accessed March 8, 2020).

90. Title 21 United States Code, Controlled Substances Act, 21 U.S.C.§801.

91. As of March 8, 2020, states where marijuana is fully legal include Alaska, California, Colorado, Illinois, Maine, Massachusetts, Michigan, Nebraska, Nevada, Oregon, Vermont, Washington, and the District of Columbia. See DISA Global Solutions, "Map of Marijuana Legality by State" (April 2020), https://disa.com/map-of-marijuana-legality-by-state (accessed on April 15, 2020).

92. These states include Alabama, Idaho, Kansas, Mississippi, Nebraska, North Carolina, South Carolina, South Dakota, Tennessee, Wisconsin, and Wyoming. See *ibid.*

93. Uzialko, A. C., "Cannabis at Work: How Employers Are Reacting to the Legalization of Marijuana," *Business News Daily* (February 1, 2019), https://www.businessnews-daily.com/9386-legal-marijuana-employment-practices.html (accessed March 8, 2020).

94. Grinspoon, P., "Medical Marijuana," *Harvard Health Publishing* (June 25, 2019), https://www.health.harvard.edu/blog/medical-marijuana-2018011513085 (accessed March 9, 2020).

95. Stowe, S., "New York City to Ban Discrimination Based on Hair," The New York Times (February 18, 2019), https://www.nytimes.com/2019/02/18/style/hair-discrimination-new-york-city.html (accessed April 10, 2020).

96. Chavez, N., and F. Karimi, "California Becomes the First State to Ban Discrimination Based on Natural Hairstyles," *CNN* (July 3, 2019), https://www.cnn.com/2019/07/03/us/california-hair-discrimination-trnd/index.html (accessed March 8, 2020).

97. Griffith, J., "Black Texas Teen Told to Cut His Dreadlocks to Walk at Graduation," *NBC News* (January 23, 2020), https://www.nbcnews.com/news/us-news/black-texas-teen-told-cut-his-dreadlocks-order-walk-graduation-n1120731 (accessed March 8, 2020).

98. Gabel, J. T. A., and N. R. Mansfield, "The Information Revolution and Its Impact on the Employment Relationship: An Analysis of the Cyberspace Workplace," *American Business Law Journal* 40 (2003), pp. 301–51.

99. Brunker, M., "Cyberporn Nurse: I Feel Like Larry Flynt," *MSNBC* (July 16, 1999), http://www.zdnet.com/article/cyberporn-nurse-i-feel-like-larry-flynt/ (accessed March 8, 2020).

100. Parry, H., "Ohio Band Teacher Quits after School Is tipped Off to Her Secret Life as an Internet Porn Star," *Daily Mail* (September 17, 2015), http://www.dailymail.co.uk/news/article-3238643/Ohio-band-teacher-quits-school-tipped-secret-life-internet-porn-star.html (accessed April 10, 2020).

101. Dickson, E. J., "Fired for Doing Porn: The New Employment Discrimination," *Salon* (October 1, 2013), https://www.salon.com/2013/09/30/fired_for_doing_porn_the_new_employment_discrimination/ (accessed March 8, 2020).

102. 543 U.S. 77 (2004).

103. Electronic Privacy Information Center, "Workplace Privacy" (2010), http://epic.org/privacy/workplace/ (accessed March 9, 2020).

104. Phillips, J., and J. Gross, "Employee Privacy by Design: Guidance for Employers Beginning to Comply with the California Consumer Privacy Act," *Sheppard Mullin Labor and Employment Law Blog* (September 20, 2019), https://www.laboremploymentlawblog.com/2019/09/articles/privacy/employee-privacy-by-design-guidance-for-employers-beginning-to-comply-with-the-california-consumer-privacy-act/ (accessed March 9, 2020).

105. California Civ. Code § 1798.100; AB 25 amendment to § 1798.130 and 1798.145.

106. *Frankhouser v. Clearfield County Career and Technology Center,* No. 3:18-cv-00180 (D.Ct. WD Pa. March 19, 2019).

107. Bullock, L., "The Future of BYOD: Statistics, Predictions and Best Practices to Prep for the Future," *Forbes* (January 21, 2019), https://www.forbes.com/sites/lilachbullock/2019/01/21/the-future-of-byod-statistics-predictions-and-best-practices-to-prep-for-the-future/#14098091f307 (accessed March 9, 2020).

108. See, for example, Newman, D., "Will Iris Scanning Become the New Login?" *Forbes* (October 4, 2016), http://www.forbes.com/sites/danielnewman/2016/10/04/will-iris-scanning-become-the-new-login/#4f24f7d95942 (accessed March 9, 2020); and Herbert, W., and A. Tuminaro, "The Impact of Emerging Technologies in the Workplace: Who's Watching the Man (Who's Watching Me)?" *Hofstra Labor & Employment Law Journal* 25 (2009), p. 355.

109. Auxier, B., L. Rainie, M. Anderson, A. Perrin, M. Kumar, and E. Turner, "Americans and Privacy: Concerned, Confused and Feeling Lack of Control over Their Personal Information," *Pew Research Center* (November 15, 2019), https://www.pewresearch.org/internet/2019/11/15/americans-and-privacy-concerned-confused-and-feeling-lack-of-control-over-their-personal-information/ (accessed March 9, 2020).

110. Cited in Levinson, Ariana R., "Workplace Privacy and Monitoring: The Quest for Balanced Interests," 59 *Clev. St. L. Rev.* 377 (2011).

111. Guta, Michael, "3.9 Million Americans—Including Freelancers—Now Work from Home at Least Half the Week," *Small Business Trends* (April 2, 2018), https://smallbiztrends.com/2018/04/2018-remote-work-statistics.html (accessed March 10, 2020); Guta, Michael, "Up to 25% of Americans Now Work Occasionally from Home Even at Small Businesses," *Small Business Trends* (March 7, 2018), https://smallbiztrends.com/2018/03/2017-virtual-vocations-year-end-report-and-telecommuting-statistics.html (accessed March 10, 2020); Browne, Ryan, "70% of People Globally Work Remotely at Least Once a Week," *CNBC* (May 30, 3018), https://www.cnbc.com/2018/05/30/70-percent-of-people-globally-work-remotely-at-least-once-a-week-iwg-study.html (accessed March 10, 2020).

112. Perkins, B., "9 Hidden Risks of Telecommuting Policies," *CIO* (March 15, 2018), https://www.cio.com/article/3261950/hidden-risks-of-telecommuting-policies.html (accessed March 9, 2020).

113. Anteby, M., and C. K. Chan, "Why Monitoring Your Employees' Behavior Can Backfire," HBR.org (April 25, 2018), https://hbr.org/2018/04/why-monitoring-your-employees-behavior-can-backfire (accessed March 9, 2020).

114. 59 Cal. Rptr. 2d 834 (Cal. Ct. App. 1996).

115. Ibid., at 842.

116. See, e.g., *Doe by Doe v. B.P.S. Guard Services, Inc.,* 945 F.2d 1442 (8th Cir. 1991); *Liberti v. Walt Disney World Co.,* 912 F. Supp. 1494 (M.D. Fla. 1995); and *Trujillo v. City of Ontario,* 428 F. Supp. 2d 1094 (C.D. Cal. 2006).

117. *Bowyer v. Hi-Lad, Inc.,* 216 W. Va. 634 (2004).

118. Ibid.

119. 144 Ohio App. 3d 620 (2001).

120. *Brannen v. Kings Local Sch. Dist. Bd. of Edn.,* 144 Ohio App. 3d 620 (2001).

121. See *DeVittorio v. Hall,* 589 F. Supp. 2d 247 (S.D.N.Y. 2008), *aff'd,* 347 F. App'x 650 (2d Cir. 2009).

122. See, e.g., *Smyth v. Pillsbury Co.,* 914 F. Supp. 97 (E.D. Pa. 1996); *Falmouth Fire Fighters' Union Local 1497 v. Town of Falmouth,* No. BACV200900517, 2011 WL 7788014 (Mass. Super. Feb. 2, 2011); and *In re Reserve Fund Sec. & Derivative Litig.,* 275 F.R.D. 154 (S.D.N.Y. 2011).

123. Harbert, T., "Employee Monitoring: When IT Is Asked to Spy," *Computerworld* (June 16, 2010), http://www.computerworld.com/s/article/9177981/Employee_monitoring_When_IT_is_asked_to_spy?taxonomyId=17&pageNumber=1 (accessed March 28, 2020).

124. Bhattacharya, A., "A Lawsuit Accuses Google of Encouraging Employees to Spy on Each Other," *Quartz* (December 24, 2016), https://qz.com/871345/a-lawsuit-accuses-google-of-encouraging-employees-to-spy-on-each-other/ (accessed March 9, 2020).

125. Klotz, U., "The Challenges of the New Economy," (October 1999), cited in World Employment Report 2001: Life at Work in the Information Economy, p. 145 (Geneva: International Labour Office, 2001).

126. 560 U.S. 746 (2010).

127. Levinson, Ariana, "Toward a Cohesive Interpretation of the Electronic Communications Privacy Act for the Electronic Monitoring of Employees," West Virginia Law Review 114 (Winter 2012), pp. 461–530, 469.

128. *Carpenter v. United States,* No. 16-402, 585 U.S. ___(2018).

129. Romm, T., E. Dwoskin, and C. Timberg, C., "U.S. Government, Tech Industry Discussing Ways to Use Smartphone Location Data to Combat Coronavirus," *The Washington Post* (March 17, 2020), https://www.washingtonpost.com/technology/2020/03/17/white-house-location-data-coronavirus/ (accessed March 24, 2020).

130. Reed, Lisa, and Barry Freidman, "Workplace Privacy: Employee Relations and Legal Implications of Monitoring Employee Email Use," *Employee Responsibilities and Rights Journal* 19, no. 2 (June 2007), pp. 75–83.

131. 2004 U.S. Dist. LEXIS 18863 (D. Or. 2004).

132. 18 U.S.C. §§ 2510–2520.

133. Nord, G., T. McCubbins, and J. Nord, "E-monitoring in the Workplace: Privacy, Legislation, and Surveillance Software," *Communications of the ACM 49,* no. 8 (2006), pp. 73–77.

134. Rutherford, R., "Why Do Companies Need to Control Internet Access?" *QuoStar* (November 4, 2019), https://www.quostar.com/blog/why-do-companies-need-to-control-internet-access/ (accessed March 22, 2020).

135. Kuligowski, K., "Distracted Workers Are Costing You Money," *Business News Daily (*May 7, 2019), http://www.businessnewsdaily.com/267-distracted-workforce-costs-businesses-billions.html (accessed February 26, 2020).

136. Charles, Dan, "High-Tech Equipment in the Workplace," All Things Considered, National Public Radio, April 1, 1996.

137. *Harley v. McCoach,* 928 F. Supp. 533 (E.D. Pa. 1996).

138. 217 F.R.D. 309, 312 (S.D.N.Y. 2003); see also "Jury Awards $29.2 Million in Damages to Discharged Equities Saleswoman," *Daily Labor Report* (BNA) (April 13, 2005), p. 449.

139. *Hernandez v. Kaisman,* 103 A.D.3d 106, 957 N.Y.S.2d 53 (2012).

140. *Robertson v. Siouxland Cmty. Health Ct*r., 938 F. Supp. 2d 831, 836 (N.D. Iowa 2013).

141. Riedy, Marian K., and Joseph H. Wen, "Electronic Surveillance of Internet Access in the American Workplace: Implications for Management," *Information & Communications Technology Law* 19, no. 1 (March 2010).

142. Schriever, N., "The Average Employee Wastes HOW Much Time Out of Every Work Day?" Blue Water Credit (December 10, 2018), https://bluewatercredit.com/the-average-employee-wastes-how-much-time-out-of-every-work-day/ (accessed March 22, 2020).

143. Matthews, K., "Privacy vs. Productivity: How employee monitoring software backfires (and what to use instead)," Rescue Time Blog (July 18, 2019), https://blog.rescuetime.com/employee-monitoring-privacy-vs-productivity/ (accessed March 23, 2020).

144. DeAngelis, S., "Retail Inventory Shrinkage Remains a Problem" (June 25, 2019), https://www.enterrasolutions.com/blog/retail-inventory-shrinkage-remains-a-problem/ (accessed April 15, 2020).

145. National Retail Foundation, "National Retail Security Survey 2019" (June 2019), https://cdn.nrf.com/sites/default/files/2019-06/NRss%202019.pdf (accessed March 9, 2020).

146. American Management Association, "The Latest on Workplace Monitoring and Surveillance" (April 8, 2019), https://www.amanet.org/articles/the-latest-on-workplace-monitoring-and-surveillance/ (accessed March 9, 2020).

147. "Electronic Tracking Devices Prohibited," 720 Ill. Comp. Stat. Ann. 5/21-2.5, http://ilga.gov/legislation/ilcs/documents/072000050K21-2.5.htm. See, e.g., *Cunningham v. New York State Dept. of Labor,* 21 N.Y.3d 515 (NY Ct. App., 2013) (finding that

installing a GPS device on the personal vehicle of a state employee who was suspected of falsifying time records was an unreasonable search).

148. Boshell, P. M., "The Power of Place: Geolocation Tracking and Privacy," American Bar Association Business Law Section (March 25, 2019), https://businesslawtoday.org/2019/03/power-place-geolocation-tracking-privacy/ (accessed March 9, 2020).

149. Austermuehle, E., "Monitoring Your Employees through GPS: What Is Legal, and What Are Best Practices?" (February 18, 2016), https://www.greensfelder.com/business-risk-management-blog/monitoring-your-employees-through-gps-what-is-legal-and-what-are-best-practices (accessed March 9, 2020).

150. See, e.g., *Elgin v. Coco-Cola Bottling Co.,* 2005 WL 3050633 (E.D. Mo. 2005); and *Tubbs v. Wynne Transport,* 2007 WL 1189640 (S.D. Texas, 2007).

151. Colgrass, Neal, "Office Inserts Microchips in Workers' Skin," USA Today (February 2, 2015), http://www.usatoday.com/story/news/2015/02/02/swedish-office-workers-microchip-inserted-hands/22737875/ (accessed March 10, 2020).

152. Ibid.

153. Fowler, M. C. C., "Chipping Away Employee Privacy: Legal Implications of RFID Microchip Implants for Employees," *The National Law Review* (October 10, 2019), https://www.natlawreview.com/article/chipping-away-employee-privacy-legal-implications-rfid-microchip-implants-employees (accessed March 9, 2020).

154. American Management Association, "The Latest on Workplace Monitoring and Surveillance" (April 8, 2019), https://www.amanet.org/articles/the-latest-on-workplace-monitoring-and-surveillance/ (accessed March 9, 2020).

155. Bales, R. A., and K. V. W. Stone, "The Invisible Web of Work: The Intertwining of A-I, Electronic Surveillance, and Labor Law," *Berkeley Journal of Labor and Employment Law* 41 (2020), p. 1, https://ssrn.com/abstract=3410655 (accessed March 10, 2020).

156. Littler Mendelson, *The Littler Annual Employer Survey* (May 2019), https://www.littler.com/files/2019_littler_employer_survey.pdf (accessed March 11, 2020).

157. Ideal, "A How-To Guide for Using a Recruitment Chatbot" (2020), https://ideal.com/recruitment-chatbot/ (accessed March 11, 2020).

158. Ibid.

159. Bales, R. A., and K. V. W. Stone, "The Invisible Web of Work: The Intertwining of A-I, Electronic Surveillance, and Labor Law," *Berkeley Journal of Labor and Employment Law, v.* 41 (2020), p. 1, https://ssrn.com/abstract=3410655 (accessed March 10, 2020).

160. Poza, D., "3 Critical Trends in Biometric Authentication in 2019" (March 21, 2019), https://auth0.com/blog/3-critical-trends-in-biomeric-authentication-in-2019/ (accessed March 9, 2020).

161. Arthur, Charles, "iPhone 5S Fingerprint Sensor Hacked by Germany's Chaos Computer Club," *The Guardian* (September 23, 2013), http://www.theguardian.com/technology/2013/sep/22/apple-iphone-fingerprint-scanner-hacked (accessed March 28, 2020).

162. Ballard, B., "What You Need to Know about Biometric Security," *betanews* (2016), https://betanews.com/2016/02/15/what-you-need-to-know-about-biometric-security/ (accessed March 9, 2020).

163. See Spire Health at https://spirehealth.com/pages/stone (accessed on April 8, 2020).

164. Zillman, Claire, "Here's Yet Another Way Your Boss Can Spy on You," *Fortune* (January 13, 2016), http://fortune.com/2016/01/13/employee-surveillance-motion-sensors/ (accessed March 10, 2020).

165. Silverman, R. "Tracking Sensors Invade the Workplace," *The Wall Street Journal* (March 7, 2013), http://online.wsj.com/news/articles/SB10001424127887324034804578344303429080678 (accessed March 28, 2020).

166. 201 N.J. 300 (March 30, 2010).

167. See *Long v. Marubeni Am. Corp.,* No. 05 Civ. 639, 2006 US Dist. LEXIS 76594 (S.D.N.Y. Oct. 19, 2006); *Scott v. Beth Israel Med. Ctr. Inc.,* 847 N.Y.S.2d 436, 444 (N.Y. Sup. Ct. 2007).

168. *Holmes v. Petrovich Dev. Co., LLC,* 191 Cal. App. 4th 1047 (Cal. App. 2011).

169. *In re Info. Mgmt. Servs., Inc. Derivative Litig.,* 81 A.3d 278 (Del. Ch. 2013).

170. Kelleher, D., "Survey: 81% of U.S. Employees Check Their Work Mail outside Work Hours," GFI Tech Talk (May 20, 2013), https://techtalk.gfi.com/survey-81-of-u-s-employees-check-their-work-mail-outside-work-hours/ (accessed April 10, 2020).

171. Anderson, Lisa, "Can Your Boss Read Your Email?" *Slate* (March 11, 2013), http://www.slate.com/articles/news_and_politics/explainer/2013/03/harvard_email_search_scandal_can_your_employer_read_your_private_messages.html (accessed April 10, 2020).

172. See Heathfield, S., "Electronic Surveillance of Employees: Pros of Electronic Surveillance of Employees," *The Balance* (updated December 5, 2019), https://www.thebalance.com/electronic-surveillance-of-employees-1919262 (accessed April 10, 2020).

173. Society for Human Resource Management, "Managing Workplace Monitoring and Surveillance," *SHRM* (March 13, 2019), https://www.shrm.org/resourcesandtools/tools-and-samples/toolkits/pages/workplaceprivacy.aspx (accessed April 9, 2020).

174. *Frankhouser v. Clearfield County Career and Technology Center,* No. 3:18-cv-00180 (D.Ct. WD Pa. March 19, 2019).

175. *Gorzynski v. JetBlue Airways Corp.,* 596 F.3d 93, 2010 US App. LEXIS 3424 (2d Cir. Feb. 19, 2010).

176. Nakashima, Ellen, and Lisa Rein, "FDA Staffers Sue Agency over Surveillance of Personal E-mail," *The Washington Post* (January 29, 2012), https://www.washingtonpost.com/world/national-security/fda-staffers-sue-agency-over-surveillance-of-personal-e-mail/2012/01/23/gIQAj34DbQ_story.html?utm_term=.9fdabf1025f3 (accessed April 10, 2020).

177. Bullock, L., "The Future of BYOD: Statistics, Predictions and Best Practices to Prep for the Future," *Forbes.com* (January 21, 2019), https://www.forbes.com/sites/lilachbullock/2019/01/21/the-future-of-byod-statistics-predictions-and-best-practices-to-prep-for-the-future/#19b8f81f3077 (accessed April 10, 2020).

178. Larose, Cynthia, and Narges Kakalia, "Integrating Employees' Smart Devices into the Workplace," *New York Law Journal* 248, no. 114 (December 13, 2012).

179. Hosting Tribunal, "How Many Blogs Are There? We Counted Them All!" *HostingTribunal.com* (2020), https://hostingtribunal.com/blog/how-many-blogs/#gref (accessed April 10, 2020).

180. Clement, Jason, "Cumulative Total of Tumblr Blogs from May 2011 to January 2020," *statista* (January 13, 2020), https://www.statista.com/statistics/256235/total-cumulative-number-of-tumblr-blogs/ (accessed April 10, 2020).

181. Kemp, Simon, "Digital Trends 2019: Every Single Stat You Need to Know about the Internet," *TNW* (January 30, 2019), https://thenextweb.com/contributors/2019/01/30/

digital-trends-2019-every-single-stat-you-need-to-know-about-the-internet/ (accessed April 10, 2020).

182. Kunsman, T., "17 Social Recruiting Statistics and the Impact on Hiring Top Talent," *Everyone Social* (February 12, 2020), https://everyonesocial.com/blog/social-recruiting-statistics/ (accessed April 10, 2020).

183. Newberry, C., "33 Facebook Stats That Matter to Marketers in 2020," *Hootsuite* (November 4, 2019), https://blog.hootsuite.com/facebook-statistics/#business (accessed April 10, 2020).

184. See Fromer, D., "Montana Town Demands Job Applicants' Facebook Passwords," B*usiness Insider* (June 19, 2009), https://www.businessinsider.com/montana-town-demands-job-applicants-facebook-passwords-2009-6 (accessed March 23, 2020).

185. Cadrain, Diane, "Mont.: Law Bars Employers from Employee Social Media Information," Society for Human Resource Management (June 10, 2015), https://www.shrm.org/resourcesandtools/legal-and-compliance/state-and-local-updates/pages/mont-employee-social-media.aspx (accessed December 19, 2016).

186. "Access to Social Media Usernames and Passwords," *National Conference of State Legislatures* (March 15, 2019), http://www.ncsl.org/research/telecommunications-and-information-technology/employer-access-to-social-media-passwords-2013.aspx (accessed March 11, 2020).

187. Littler Mendelson, *Executive Employer Survey Report* (June 2012), http://www.littler.com/files/press/pdf/Littler-Mendelson-Executive-Employer-Survey-Report-June-2012.pdf (accessed March 11, 2020).

188. Hyman, J., "NBC Reignites Privacy Debate by Requiring Job Seekers' Social Media Passwords," *Workforce.com* (August 1, 2017), https://www.workforce.com/news/nbc-reignites-privacy-debate-requiring-job-seekers-social-media-passwords (accessed March 11, 2020).

189. Employers see little concern over acquiring social media passwords; see Littler Mendelson, *Executive Employer Survey Report* (July 2014), http://www.littler.com/files/2014_Littler_Executive_Employer_Survey.pdf (accessed March 11, 2020). The 2019 report has no mention of concern over acquiring social media passwords; Littler Mendelson, "The Littler Annual Employer Survey" (May 2019), https://www.littler.com/files/2019_littler_employer_survey.pdf (accessed March 11, 2020).

190. Korolov, Maria, "Study: Most Companies Can't Protect Confidential Documents," *CSO* (June 13, 2016), http://www.csoonline.com/article/3082557/data-protection/study-most-companies-cant-protect-confidential-documents.html (accessed April 10, 2020).

191. Cooper, P., "140+ Social Media Statistics That Matter to Marketers in 2020," *Hootsuite* (February 20, 2020), https://blog.hootsuite.com/social-media-statistics-for-social-media-managers/#advertising (accessed April 10, 2020).

192. Schaefer, M., "What Is the True Business Value of Social Media Engagement?" Schaefer Marketing Solutions (March 11, 2019), https://businessesgrow.com/2019/03/11/business-value-of-social-media-engagement/ (accessed April 10, 2020).

193. Ibid.

194. "New Study Indicates Social Media Pays; Wetpaint and Altimeter Group Find Correlation between Brands' Social Media Efforts and Financial Performance," *PR Newswire* (July 20, 2009), https://www.socialmediatoday.com/content/new-study-deep-brand-engagement-correlates-financial-performance (accessed April 10, 2020).

195. Rishika, R. et al. "The Effect of Customers' Social Media Participation on Customer Visit Frequency and Profitability: An Empirical Investigation," *Information Systems Research* (March 2013).

196. Lee, E., "Maplewood DPW Worker Fired after Facebook Comments Spark Fury, Officials Mum on Reason" (March 30, 2019), https://www.nj.com/essex/2013/07/maplewood_dpw_employee_fired_for_anti-liberal_anti-gay_facebook_comments_sparks_controversy.html (accessed March 9, 2020).

197. "Dooced," *Urban Dictionary,* http://www.urbandictionary.com/define.php?term=dooced (accessed April 10, 2020).

198. *In Pier Sixty, LLC,* 362 NLRB 59 (March 31, 2015).

199. *Graziosi v. City of Greenville Miss.,* 775 F.3d 731, 741 (5th Cir. 2015).

200. *City of San Diego v. Roe,* 543 U.S. 77 (2004).

201. See, e.g., Watson, T., and E. Piro, "Bloggers Beware: A Cautionary Tale of Blogging and the Doctrine of At-Will Employment," *Hofstra Labor & Employment Law Journal* 24 (August 30, 2007), p. 358.

202. *City of San Diego, supra* note 200.

203. See, e.g., Levinson, Arianna R., "Industrial Justice: Privacy Protection for the Employed," *Cornell Journal of Law and Public Policy* 18 (2009), p. 609.

204. Ballman, D. "States with Pro-Employee Laws: No Firing for Legal Off-Duty Activity," LexisNexis (December 18, 2014), https://www.lexisnexis.com/legalnewsroom/labor-employment/b/labor-employment-top-blogs/archive/2014/12/18/states-with-pro-employee-laws-no-firing-for-legal-off-duty-activity.aspx (accessed April 10, 2020).

205. Palma Markus, B., "Silicon Valley Tech Worker Fired after Blogging about Starving while Working at Billion-Dollar Food Delivery Firm," *Rawstory* (February 20, 2016), https://www.rawstory.com/2016/02/silicon-valley-tech-worker-fired-after-blogging-about-starving-while-working-at-billion-dollar-food-delivery-firm/ (accessed April 10, 2020).

206. Electronic Frontier Foundation, "How to Blog Safely (About Work or Anything Else)" (April 11, 2005), https://www.eff.org/wp/blog-safely (accessed April 10, 2020).

207. *Doe v. Cahill,* 884 A.2d 451 (Del. 2005).

208. Ibid.

209. In re Does 1-10, 242 S.W.3d 805 (Tex. App. 2007).

210. See, e.g., *Cohen v. Google, Inc.,* 25 Misc. 3d 945, 887 N.Y.S.2d 424 (Sup. Ct. 2009).

211. Adapted from Barnes, Robert, and Darya V. Pollak, "Employees Online: Protecting Company Interests in a Web 2.0 World," Bloomberg Finance L.P. (November 10, 2008). For an example of a sample blogging and social networking policy, see one produced by the International Public Management Association for Human Resources. See IMPA, "Sample Blogging and Social Networking Policy," https://www.ipma-hr.org/docs/default-source/public-docs/importdocuments/sample-blogging-and-social-networking-policy (accessed April 10, 2020).

212. Thompson, J., "What Is a Conditional Letter of Employment?" (May 14, 2019), https://smallbusiness.chron.com/conditional-letter-employment-42585.html (accessed March 11, 2020).

213. Public Law 107-56.

214. Glaser, A., "Long before Snowden, Librarians Were Anti-Surveillance Heroes," *Slate* (June 3, 2015), https://slate.com/technology/2015/06/usa-freedom-act-before-snowden-librarians-were-the-anti-surveillance-heroes.html (accessed March 8, 2020).

215. Pub.L. 114–23.

216. Robertson, A., "Congress Postponed a Vote to Extend Patriot Act Surveillance Programs," *The Verge* (February 27, 2020), https://www.theverge.com/2020/2/27/21155185/congress-house-judiciary-committee-postpone-fisa-patriot-act-zoe-lofgren-amendments (accessed March 8, 2020).

217. Knapp, V., "The Impact of the Patriot Act on Employers" (2003), https://www.mondaq.com/unitedstates/Employment-and-HR/22891/The-Impact-Of-The-Patriot-Act-On-Employers (accessed March 8, 2020).

218. Sanders, A., "Covert Monitoring in the Workplace—Impact on an Employee's Privacy," *Data Protection Report* (November 8, 2019), https://www.dataprotectionreport.com/2019/11/covert-monitoring-in-the-workplace-impact-on-an-employees-privacy/ (accessed April 16, 2020).

Cases

Case 1

O'Connor v. Ortega, *480 U.S. 709 (1987)*

The respondent, Dr. Ortega, was a physician and psychiatrist and an employee of a state hospital who had primary responsibility for training physicians in the psychiatric residency program. Hospital officials became concerned about possible improprieties in his management of the program. In particular, the officials thought that Dr. Ortega may have misled the hospital into believing that the computer had been donated when, in fact, the computer had been financed by the possibly coerced contributions of residents. Hospital officials were also concerned about charges that Dr. Ortega had sexually harassed two female hospital employees, and that he had taken inappropriate disciplinary action against a resident.

While he was on administrative leave pending investigation of the charges, hospital officials, allegedly in order to inventory and secure state property, searched Dr. Ortega's office and took personal items from his desk and file cabinets that later were used in administrative proceedings resulting in his discharge. The employee filed an action against the hospital officials, alleging that the search of his office violated the Fourth Amendment. The trial court found that the search was proper in order to secure state property. The court of appeals held that the employee had a *reasonable expectation of privacy* in his office and thus the search violated the Fourth Amendment. The Supreme Court explains that a search must be reasonable both from its inception and in its scope and remands the case to the district court for review of the reasonableness of both of those questions.

O'Connor, J.

***

Because the reasonableness of an expectation of privacy, as well as the appropriate standard for a search, is understood to differ according to context, it is essential first to delineate the boundaries of the workplace context. The workplace includes those areas and items that are related to work and are generally within the employer's control. At a hospital, for example, the hallways, cafeteria, offices, desks, and file cabinets, among other areas, are all part of the workplace. These areas remain part of the workplace context even if the employee has placed personal items in them, such as a photograph placed in a desk or a letter posted on an employee bulletin board.

Not everything that passes through the confines of the business address can be considered part of the workplace context, however. . . . The appropriate standard for a workplace search does not necessarily apply to a piece of closed personal luggage, a handbag or a briefcase that happens to be within the employer's business address.

***

Given the societal expectations of privacy in one's place of work, we reject the contention made by the Solicitor General and petitioners that public employees can never have a reasonable expectation of privacy in their place of work. Individuals do not lose Fourth Amendment rights merely because they work for the government instead of a private employer. The operational realities of the workplace, however, may make some employees' expectations of privacy unreasonable when an intrusion is by a supervisor rather than a law enforcement official. Public employees' expectations of privacy in their offices, desks, and file cabinets, like similar expectations of employees in the private sector, may be reduced by virtue of actual office practices and procedures, or by legitimate regulation. The employee's expectation of privacy must be assessed in the context of the employment relation. An office is seldom a private enclave free from entry by supervisors, other employees, and business and personal invitees. Instead, in many cases offices are continually entered by fellow employees and other visitors during the workday for conferences, consultations, and other work-related visits. Simply put, it is the nature of government offices that others—such as fellow employees, supervisors, consensual visitors, and the general public—may have frequent access to an individual's office. . . .

The undisputed evidence discloses that Dr. Ortega did not share his desk or file cabinets with any other employees. Dr. Ortega had occupied the office for 17 years and he kept materials in his office, which included personal correspondence, medical files, correspondence from private patients unconnected to the Hospital, personal financial records, teaching aids and notes, and personal gifts and mementos. The files on physicians in residency training were kept outside Dr. Ortega's office. Indeed, the only items found by the investigators were apparently personal items because, with the exception of the items seized for use in the administrative hearings, all the papers and effects found in the office were simply placed in boxes and made available to Dr. Ortega. Finally, we note that there was no evidence that the Hospital had established any reasonable regulation or policy discouraging employees such as Dr. Ortega from storing personal papers and effects in their desks or file cabinets, although the absence of such a policy does not create an expectation of privacy where it would not otherwise exist.

On the basis of this undisputed evidence, we accept the conclusion of the Court of Appeals that Dr. Ortega had a reasonable expectation of privacy at least in his desk and file cabinets.

Having determined that Dr. Ortega had a reasonable expectation of privacy in his office, . . . we must determine the appropriate standard of reasonableness applicable to the search. A determination of the standard of reasonableness applicable to a particular class of searches requires "balanc[ing] the nature and quality of the intrusion on the individual's Fourth Amendment interests against the importance of the governmental interests alleged to justify the intrusion." In the case of searches conducted by a public employer, we must balance the invasion of the employees' legitimate expectations of privacy against the government's need for supervision, control, and the efficient operation of the workplace.

***

The governmental interest justifying work-related intrusions by public employers is the efficient and proper operation of the workplace. Government agencies provide myriad services to the public, and the work of these agencies would suffer if employers were required to have probable cause before they entered an employee's desk for the purpose of finding a file or piece of office correspondence. Indeed, it is difficult to give the concept of probable cause, rooted as it is in the criminal investigatory context, much meaning when the purpose of a search is to retrieve a file for work-related reasons. Similarly, the concept of probable cause has little meaning for a routine inventory conducted by public employers for the purpose of securing state property. To ensure the efficient and proper operation of the agency, therefore, public employers must be given wide latitude to enter employee offices for work-related, noninvestigatory reasons.

We come to a similar conclusion for searches conducted pursuant to an investigation of work-related employee misconduct. Even when employers conduct an investigation, they have an interest substantially different from "the normal need for law enforcement." Public employers have an interest in ensuring that their agencies operate in an effective and efficient manner, and the work of these agencies inevitably suffers from the inefficiency, incompetence, mismanagement, or other work-related misfeasance of its employees. Indeed, in many cases, public employees are entrusted with tremendous responsibility, and the consequences of their misconduct or incompetence to both the agency and the public interest can be severe. . . . Public employers have a direct and overriding interest in ensuring that the work of the agency is conducted in a proper and efficient manner. In our view, therefore, a probable cause requirement for searches of the type at issue here would impose intolerable burdens on public employers. The delay in correcting the employee misconduct caused by the need for probable cause rather than reasonable suspicion will be translated into tangible and often irreparable damage to the agency's work, and ultimately to the public interest. Additionally, while law enforcement officials are expected to "schoo[l] themselves in the niceties of probable cause," no such expectation is generally applicable to public employers, at least when the search is not used to gather evidence of a criminal offense. It is simply unrealistic to expect supervisors in most government agencies to learn the subtleties of the probable cause standard. . . .

Balanced against the substantial government interests in the efficient and proper operation of the workplace are the privacy interests of government employees in their place of work which, while not insubstantial, are far less than those found at home or in some other contexts. . . . The employer intrusions at issue here "involve a relatively limited invasion" of employee privacy. Government offices are provided to employees for the sole purpose of facilitating the work of an agency. The employee may avoid exposing personal belongings at work by simply leaving them at home.

. . . We hold . . . that public employer intrusions on the constitutionally protected privacy interests of government employees for noninvestigatory, work-related purposes, as well as for investigations of work-related misconduct, should be judged by the standard of reasonableness under all the circumstances. Under this reasonableness standard, both the inception and the scope of the intrusion must be reasonable:

> Determining the reasonableness of any search involves a twofold inquiry: first, one must consider "whether the . . . action was justified at its inception," second, one must determine whether the search as actually conducted "was reasonably related in scope to the circumstances which justified the interference in the first place."

Ordinarily, a search of an employee's office by a supervisor will be "justified at its inception" when there are reasonable grounds for suspecting that the search will turn up evidence that the employee is guilty of work-related misconduct, or that the search is necessary for a noninvestigatory work-related purpose such as to retrieve a needed file. Because petitioners had an "individualized suspicion" of misconduct by Dr. Ortega, we need not decide whether individualized suspicion is an essential element of the standard of reasonableness that we adopt today. The search will be permissible in its scope when "the measures adopted are reasonably related to the objectives of the search and not excessively intrusive in light of . . . the nature of the [misconduct]."

***

On remand, therefore, the District Court must determine the justification for the search and seizure, and evaluate the reasonableness of both the inception of the search and its scope.

Accordingly, the judgment of the Court of Appeals is REVERSED and the case is REMANDED to that court for further proceedings consistent with this opinion.

Case Questions

1. Do you think the standard of the search articulated in this opinion is the correct standard for determining whether a search violates the Fourth Amendment? Think of arguments for both perspectives—the employer and employee.

2. How can an employer protect itself from a claim of an unreasonable search conducted in the workplace? Note the court stated that a policy regarding this issue was not a determinative factor in determining the constitutionality of the search.

3. What could you do as an employee to protect yourself from a company search?

Shoun v. Best Formed Plastics, Inc.,
Case 2
28 F. Supp. 3d 786 (N.D. Ind. 2014)

In March 2012, George Shoun fell and injured his shoulder while on the job at Best Formed Plastics and spent several months away from work recovering. Jane Stewart, who processed workers' compensation claims for the company, prepared an accident report for the incident and notified the company's insurer. Mr. Shoun says that between March and August 2012, Ms. Stewart monitored his medical treatment for the company and so learned the nature and extent of his injury.

In February 2013, Ms. Stewart posted the following on her Facebook page: "Isn't [it] amazing how Jimmy experienced a 5 way heart bypass just one month ago and is back to work, especially when you consider George Shoun's shoulder injury kept him away from work for 11 months and now he is trying to sue us." Mr. Shoun claims Ms. Stewart's Facebook page is linked to her business email address and available to the business communities in northeastern Indiana and southern Michigan. The quoted statement remained on Ms. Stewart's Facebook page for 76 days.

Mr. Shoun asserts that Ms. Stewart's posting of the statement was a "deliberate disclosure of [his] medical condition to other persons" in violation of the Americans with Disabilities Act. He claims, too, that Ms. Stewart "acted with the intent to expose him to public scorn and ridicule and to blacklist him among prospective employers within her broad network." Mr. Shoun seeks compensatory and punitive damages, pre-judgment interest, attorney fees, and costs.

Best Formed Plastics moves to dismiss Mr. Shoun's complaint because, first, the company can't be liable for violating the ADA's confidentiality provisions when Mr. Shoun voluntarily disclosed his medical condition to the public and, second, Mr. Shoun hasn't alleged any tangible injury that resulted from the alleged ADA violation.

Miller, J.

***

Discussion

Section 102 of the Americans with Disabilities Act provides that any information relating to a medical condition of an employee obtained by an employer during "voluntary medical examinations, including voluntary work histories, which are part of an employee health program available to employees at that work site," must be "collected and maintained on separate forms and in separate medical files and [be] treated as a confidential medical record." To state a claim for violation of the ADA's confidentiality provisions, a plaintiff must allege that his employer obtained his medical information through employment-related medical examinations and inquiries, the information obtained through such means was disclosed by the employer rather than treated as confidential (unless that information falls under one of the exceptions found in 42 U.S.C. § 12112(d)(3)(B)(i), (ii), (iii), none of which are alleged here), and he suffered a tangible injury as a result of the disclosure.

Best Formed Plastics argues that Mr. Shoun's amended complaint should be dismissed because Mr. Shoun voluntarily and publicly disclosed his medical condition in the complaint he filed in the Elkhart Superior Court before Ms. Stewart's alleged disclosure of that same information. The company asks the court to take judicial notice of Mr. Shoun's state court complaint, a request to which Mr. Shoun hasn't objected. "Taking judicial notice of matters of public record need not convert a motion to dismiss into a motion for summary judgment" if the facts are "readily ascertainable from the public court record and not subject to reasonable dispute." *Ennenga v. Starns.* Mr. Shoun's complaint meets those requirements. Because the state court complaint "is offered to show what was stated to the court rather [than] for the truth of the matter asserted," *Felty v. Driver Solutions* (internal quotation and citation omitted), the court grants the motion to take judicial notice of Mr. Shoun's Elkhart Superior Court complaint.

Best Formed Plastics notes that Mr. Shoun filed his state court complaint on February 14, 2013, and Ms. Stewart posted her comment on her Facebook page five days after Mr. Shoun's public disclosure of his medical condition. Thus, the company says, Mr. Shoun voluntarily publicized his medical condition outside the context of an authorized employment-related medical examination or inquiry prior to Ms. Stewart's Facebook comment, so Ms. Stewart's alleged disclosure was nothing more than a mere recitation of facts previously disclosed to the public by Mr. Shoun. Best Formed Plastics concludes that based on Mr. Shoun's voluntary disclosure, the company can't be liable for violating the ADA's confidentiality provisions, and Mr. Shoun isn't entitled to the relief he seeks.

The cases relied on by Best Formed Plastics support the company's argument that an employee's voluntary disclosure of medical information outside the context of an authorized employment-related medical examination or inquiry can render the confidentiality requirements of the ADA inapplicable to the employer, but in those cases the plaintiff-employees volunteered their medical information to their employer or a co-employee.

Neither side has alleged or argued that Mr. Shoun voluntarily disclosed his medical information to Ms. Stewart or anyone else at Best Formed Plastics; instead, Mr. Shoun alleges that Ms. Stewart acquired information about his medical condition through an employment-related medical inquiry by the company and then wrongfully disclosed that information. Whether Ms. Stewart gained knowledge of Mr. Shoun's medical condition solely within the context of his employment-related medical examination is a question of fact not appropriate for resolution in a motion

to dismiss. Mr. Shoun has set forth facts sufficient to allege a violation of the confidentiality provisions of the ADA and the motion of Best Formed Plastics to dismiss for failure to state a claim will be denied.

Best Formed Plastics also moves to dismiss the amended complaint based on its claim that Mr. Shoun hasn't alleged any tangible injury. The court can't agree. Mr. Shoun has alleged that as a result of Ms. Stewart's actions, "prospective employers refused to hire him," and he suffered emotional injury, both of which have been recognized as tangible injuries under the ADA. Dismissal on this basis is inappropriate.

Based on the foregoing, the court GRANTS the renewed motion to take judicial notice and DENIES the motion to dismiss the amended complaint.

SO ORDERED.

Case Questions

1. Should Best Formed Plastics' motion to dismiss have been granted? Why or why not?

2. Assume that Ms. Stewart had only two Facebook friends who could see her post: Mr. Shoun and Mr. Shoun's boss (who already had signed off on his medical leave and was aware of Mr. Shoun's condition). Would the judge have ruled differently?

3. If you were the owner of Best Formed Plastics, what rules and procedures might you put in place to ensure that you are not faced with a similar lawsuit in the future?

Case 3

City of San Diego v. Roe, *543 U.S. 77 (2004)*

The City of San Diego terminated a police officer for selling homemade, sexually explicit videotapes and related activities. Using an adults-only section of eBay, the officer sold not only videotapes of himself in a police uniform but also official San Diego Police Department uniforms and other police equipment. The officer sued the city, alleging a violation of his First Amendment right to free speech. The trial court found for the city on the ground that the speech was not entitled to protection because it was not of "public concern." The Ninth Circuit, however, reversed the trial court, finding that his conduct fell within the protected category of citizen commentary on matters of public concern because it took place off-duty, it was away from the employer's premises, and it did not involve a workplace grievance. The U.S. Supreme Court reversed.

Per Curiam

***

A government employee does not relinquish all First Amendment rights otherwise enjoyed by citizens just by reason of his or her employment. On the other hand, a governmental employer may impose certain restraints on the speech of its employees, restraints that would be unconstitutional if applied to the general public. The Court has recognized the right of employees to speak on matters of public concern, typically matters concerning government policies that are of interest to the public at large, a subject on which public employees are uniquely qualified to comment. Outside of this category, the Court has held that when government employees speak or write on their own time on topics unrelated to their employment, the speech can have First Amendment protection, absent some governmental justification "far stronger than mere speculation" in regulating it. *United States v. Treasury Employees* (NTEU). We have little difficulty in concluding that the City was not barred from terminating Roe under either line of cases.

In concluding that Roe's activities qualified as a matter of public concern, the Court of Appeals relied heavily on the Court's decision in NTEU. In NTEU it was established that the speech was unrelated to the employment and had no effect on the mission and purpose of the employer. The question was whether the Federal Government could impose certain monetary limitations on outside earnings from speaking or writing on a class of federal employees. The Court held that, within the particular classification of employment, the Government had shown no justification for the outside salary limitations. The First Amendment right of the employees sufficed to invalidate the restrictions on the outside earnings for such activities. The Court noted that throughout history public employees who undertook to write or to speak in their spare time had made substantial contributions to literature and art, and observed that none of the speech at issue "even arguably [had] any adverse impact" on the employer.

The Court of Appeals' reliance on NTEU was seriously misplaced. Although Roe's activities took place outside the workplace and purported to be about subjects not related to his employment, the SDPD demonstrated legitimate and substantial interests of its own that were compromised by his speech. Far from confining his activities to speech unrelated to his employment, Roe took deliberate steps to link his videos and other wares to his police work, all in a way injurious to his employer. The use of the uniform, the law enforcement reference in the website, the listing of the speaker as "in the field of law enforcement," and the debased parody of an officer performing indecent acts while in the course of official duties brought

the mission of the employer and the professionalism of its officers into serious disrepute.

The Court of Appeals noted the City conceded Roe's activities were "unrelated" to his employment. In the context of the pleadings and arguments, the proper interpretation of the City's statement is simply to underscore the obvious proposition that Roe's speech was not a comment on the workings or functioning of the SDPD. It is quite a different question whether the speech was detrimental to the SDPD. On that score the City's consistent position has been that the speech is contrary to its regulations and harmful to the proper functioning of the police force. The present case falls outside the protection afforded in NTEU. The authorities that instead control, and which are considered below, are this Court's decisions in *Pickering, Connick,* and the decisions which follow them.

To reconcile the employee's right to engage in speech and the government employer's right to protect its own legitimate interests in performing its mission, the Pickering Court adopted a balancing test. It requires a court evaluating restraints on a public employee's speech to balance "the interests of the [employee], as a citizen, in commenting upon matters of public concern and the interest of the State, as an employer, in promoting the efficiency of the public services it performs through its employees."

Underlying the decision in *Pickering* is the recognition that public employees are often the members of the community who are likely to have informed opinions as to the operations of their public employers, operations which are of substantial concern to the public. Were they not able to speak on these matters, the community would be deprived of informed opinions on important public issues. The interest at stake is as much the public's interest in receiving informed opinion as it is the employee's own right to disseminate it.

Pickering did not hold that any and all statements by a public employee are entitled to balancing. To require Pickering balancing in every case where speech by a public employee is at issue, no matter the content of the speech, could compromise the proper functioning of government offices. This concern prompted the Court in *Connick* to explain a threshold inquiry (implicit in *Pickering* itself) that in order to merit Pickering balancing, a public employee's speech must touch on a matter of "public concern."

In *Connick,* an assistant district attorney, unhappy with her supervisor's decision to transfer her to another division, circulated an intraoffice questionnaire. The document solicited her co-workers' views on, inter alia, office transfer policy, office morale, the need for grievance committees, the level of confidence in supervisors, and whether employees felt pressured to work in political campaigns.

Finding that—with the exception of the final question—the questionnaire touched not on matters of public concern but on internal workplace grievances, the Court held no Pickering balancing was required. To conclude otherwise would ignore the "common-sense realization that government offices could not function if every employment decision became a constitutional matter." *Connick* held that a public employee's speech is entitled to Pickering balancing only when the employee speaks "as a citizen upon matters of public concern" rather than "as an employee upon matters only of personal interest."

Although the boundaries of the public concern test are not well-defined, *Connick* provides some guidance. It directs courts to examine the "content, form, and context of a given statement, as revealed by the whole record" in assessing whether an employee's speech addresses a matter of public concern. In addition, it notes that the standard for determining whether expression is of public concern is the same standard used to determine whether a common-law action for invasion of privacy is present. That standard is established by our decisions in *Cox Broadcasting Corp. v. Cohn,* and *Time, Inc. v. Hill.* These cases make clear that public concern is something that is a subject of legitimate news interest; that is, a subject of general interest and of value and concern to the public at the time of publication. The Court has also recognized that certain private remarks, such as negative comments about the President of the United States, touch on matters of public concern and should thus be subject to Pickering balancing.

Applying these principles to the instant case, there is no difficulty in concluding that Roe's expression does not qualify as a matter of public concern under any view of the public concern test. He fails the threshold test and Pickering balancing does not come into play.

Connick is controlling precedent, but to show why this is not a close case it is instructive to note that even under the view expressed by the dissent in *Connick* from four

Members of the Court, the speech here would not come within the definition of a matter of public concern. The dissent in *Connick* would have held that the entirety of the questionnaire circulated by the employee "discussed subjects that could reasonably be expected to be of interest to persons seeking to develop informed opinions about the manner in which . . . an elected official charged with managing a vital governmental agency, discharges his responsibilities." No similar purpose could be attributed to the employee's speech in the present case. Roe's activities did nothing to inform the public about any aspect of the SDPD's functioning or operation. Nor were Roe's activities anything like the private remarks at issue in *Rankin,* where one co-worker commented to another co-worker on an item of political news. Roe's expression was widely broadcast, linked to his official status as a police officer, and designed to exploit his employer's image.

The speech in question was detrimental to the mission and functions of the employer. There is no basis for finding that it was of concern to the community as the Court's cases have understood that term in the context of restrictions by governmental entities on the speech of their employees.

Case Questions

1. In your opinion, does the Ninth Circuit's conclusion that Roe's activities were protected by the First Amendment have merit?

2. Where do you think the line would have been drawn on Roe's free speech rights by the Supreme Court had he not tied his activities to the police department? What if Roe did not wear a police uniform but still sold police-related paraphernalia? What if he wore a police uniform but did not sell police-related paraphernalia?

3. Is the "public concern" requirement from the *Pickering* case a fair balancing of the rights involved? How might it be improved?

Chapter

15

Labor Law

Source: Library of Congress Prints and Photographs Division [LC-USZC2-837]

Learning Objectives

After completing this chapter, you should be able to:

LO1 Discuss the history of unions in the United States.

LO2 Identify the Norris–LaGuardia Act of 1932 and what it covers.

LO3 Identify the National Labor Relations Act of 1935 (Wagner Act) and what it requires.

LO4 List and explain several collective bargaining agreement clauses.

LO5 Explain unfair labor practices and give examples.

LO6 Describe the Taft–Hartley Act of 1947 and its requirements.

LO7 Define the Landrum–Griffin Act of 1959 (Labor Management Reporting and Disclosure Act) and its provisions.

LO8 Discuss collective bargaining in the public sector and how it differs from the private sector.

Opening Scenarios

Statutory Basis

Employees shall have the right to self-organization, to form, join, or assist labor organizations, to bargain collectively through representatives of their own choosing, and to engage in other concerted activities for the purpose of collective bargaining or other mutual aid or protection, and shall also have the right to refrain from any or all such activities. [National Labor Relations Act of 1935, 29 U.S.C. §§ 151–169, § 157, section 7.]

Coming Together on Issues

Think labor law doesn't affect you? Thank goodness we're not back at the 2008 television season. If we were, you would probably have missed your favorite TV shows. The airwaves were full of reruns and lame substitute shows put on in their place. The reason was that television writers were on strike. The 13,500-member Writers Guild of America wanted a share of profits from the increasingly popular new technological outlets for their shows, such as the Internet. The 100-day strike ended just before the Academy Awards were to be telecast—much to the relief of everyone. But the Writers Guild of America is hardly alone. The NFL has certainly seen its share of being locked in rancorous collective bargaining negotiations with the NFL players, up to and including resorting to litigation.

The years 2018 and 2019 had a record number of U.S. workers on strike because of labor disputes with employers, indicating they are unhappy with their employer. (As you will see in the chapter, there can be strikes for other reasons.)[1] There were 20 major strikes in 2018, involving 485,000 employees in work stoppages, the highest number since 1986.[2] In 2017, the number was 25,000.[3] It has been suggested that this frustration comes, at least in part, from workers not experiencing the economic growth candidate Trump touted in his campaign. Workers saw the economy expanding and profits growing (until the COVID-19 pandemic hit) but did not see an accompanying change in their paychecks.[4] The strikes, work stoppages, work slowdowns, and lockouts boosted wages for thousands of employees. Is it any wonder there has also been a strong anti-union effort during this administration? Major strikes surged again in 2019. And these strikes were up 257 percent in the past two years at a time when labor membership was down.[5]

Recent events include the following:

- Beginning in February 2018, teachers all over the United States went on strike in 2018 and on through 2019 for pay, funding cuts, and other issues. However, the strike that began in West Virginia ended in March but inspired strikes in several other states, including Colorado, Kentucky, Arizona, Oklahoma, and North Carolina, as well as a school bus driver strike in Georgia and adjunct professors at Virginia Commonwealth University. More than 110,000 teachers were on strike during the year.[6]

- In January 2019, the nation's second largest school system, Los Angeles, CA, saw teachers go on strike for more than a week, seeking raises and smaller class sizes. Denver teachers protested the large fluctuations in their bonus-based yearly salaries and failure of their wages to keep up with the cost of living.[7]

- In Chicago, where rules require teaching assistants to live in the city, their pay starts at around $36,000 per year, and teachers went on strike, in part, because the wages do not allow them to live in the high-cost city.[8]

- At a time when the company was making record earnings, the largest hotel strike in U.S. history took place, when 6,000 Marriott hotel employees went on strike for two months for higher wages and increased benefits, losing a total of 215,000 work days. In San Francisco, 75 Marriott workers were arrested for blocking the street outside the hotel during their protests.[9]

- In January 2014, for the first time in the history of college sports, athletes asked to be represented by a labor union and took formal steps to begin the National Labor Relations Board (NLRB) process to be recognized as employees by submitting the appropriate form at the regional NLRB office in Chicago. In March 2014, the NLRB determined that Northwestern football players receiving grants-in-aid were employees and granted them the right to hold a representation election. Northwestern appealed and sixteen months later the NLRB declined to grant employee status to the players, thus denying them the right to unionize.[10]

- Hundreds of McDonald's minimum-wage employees around the country went on strike for higher wages, including workers in New York, Boston, Chicago, and Detroit.[11]

- Baked confection Twinkies maker Hostess Brands, Inc. closed after a strike left it without enough workers to operate.[12] The good news for fans was that the brand was bought by two private equity firms and Twinkies were again available by July 2013, with a shelf life 26 days longer than under Hostess.[13]

- A slim 51 percent of the machinists' union agreed to a pension freeze and higher health care expenses in order to save thousands of jobs by Boeing keeping the manufacture of the 777X jet in Washington state rather than moving it to South Carolina.[14]

- In the traditionally nonunion South, students joined forces to raise awareness and mobilize students in support of workers' right to organize and form a union by having the Mississippi Student Justice Alliance and the Georgia Student Justice Alliance present Bernie Sanders and actor and humanitarian Danny Glover (who has previously been arrested at labor protests) as a speaker as part of the Concerned Students for a Better Nissan College Tour.[15]

- Harley-Davidson wrapped up its labor negotiations with employees throughout its operations, including making an agreement in Pennsylvania to cut nearly 50 percent of jobs in exchange for the company's commitment to invest $90 million in the plant. In New York, the company threatened to move to a new plant in Kentucky if the contract was rejected.[16]

- Concerned about being too taxed with extra responsibilities to do their jobs well, nurses have walked out at least 750 times in recent decades, making nursing the most strike-prone job in the country. A study published by the National Bureau of Economics shows that during 50 strikes at New York state hospitals between 1984 and 2004, patients were almost 20 percent more likely to die (about 140 patients).[17]

- After New Yorkers braced for a walkout by apartment building doormen, a strike was averted when a deal was reached.[18]

- The NBA "avoids the apocalypse" by reaching an interim labor agreement, thereby narrowly avoiding a walkout.[19]

- The National Hockey League lost its season to labor disputes, angering thousands of loyal fans; baseball lockouts threaten to cost revenues and crowds.[20]

- Disgruntled private-sector lawyers unionize over pay and working conditions for the first time.[21]

Though they have lost much of the numbers and clout that they once had, maybe even because in some ways they have done their job too well (compared to how things were when unions got started in the 1930s), as you can see from these recent issues, unions are still an important part of the American workplace landscape. (See Exhibit 15.1, "Who's in Unions?")

Labor law is actually a very different and discrete part of the law from employment law, but given its far-reaching impact on the workplace, it is important to be familiar with its basic history and provisions in order to have a more complete knowledge of issues in the workplace environment. Labor law involves **collective bargaining** between employers and employees about issues in the workplace. Rather than each employee entering into his or her own individual agreement with the employer covering his or her employment, the law now permits employees to do so in an organized and collective way. This was not always so. The agrarian nature of the economy in the United States was such that until the middle of the 19th century, the majority of working Americans worked on farms. In 1820, only about 12 percent of workers were employed in manufacturing. When the industrial

collective bargaining
Negotiations and agreements between management and labor about wages, hours, and other terms and conditions of employment.

Exhibit 15.1 *Who's in Unions?*

According to the 2019 report of the U.S. Department of Labor's Bureau of Labor Statistics, released in January 2020:

- In 2019, the number of union members was down 0.2 percent from 2018.
- 16.4 million employees are represented by a union in the United States. 14.6 million are union members, while the rest (1.8 million) are not union affiliated but have jobs covered by union contracts.
- 10.3 percent of wage and salary workers are union members, down from 20.1 percent in 1983, the first year such figures were kept.
- The median weekly earning for union members is $1,094; for nonunion workers, $892.
- Men are more likely to be union members (10.8 percent) than women (9.7 percent); when records were first kept in 1983, the gap between men and women was 10 points, but men's union membership declined more rapidly than women's and narrowed the gap.
- Blacks (11.2 percent) are more likely to be in a union than whites (10.3 percent), Asians (8.8 percent), or Hispanics (8.9 percent).
- Workers 45 to 54 (12.6 percent) and 55 to 64 (12.7 percent) are more likely to be union members than younger workers. The 45–54 group stayed about the same from 2018, but the age group of 55–64 declined by 0.6 percent.
- Full-time workers are twice as likely to be union members (11.2 percent) than part-time workers (5.5 percent).
- All states in the Middle Atlantic and Pacific divisions have membership rates above the national average.

- All states in the East South Central and West South Central have rates below the national average.
- The state with the highest membership rate is New York (23.5 percent).
- The state with the lowest union membership rate is South Carolina (2.2 percent).
- About 1.8 million employees are represented by a union but are not members of the union.
- Union membership rate has steadily declined from a high of 20.1 percent in 1983, the first year the data were available.
- 7.5 million (6.2 percent) private industry employees are union members (less than half of what it was in 1983), but 7.1 million (33.6 percent) of public employees are in a union. Of the government workers, 39.4 percent are in local government, the group with the highest representation.
- Two occupational groups have the highest unionization rates: protective service occupations such as police and firefighters (33.8 percent) and education, training, and library occupations (33.1 percent).
- In the private sector, utilities have the highest rate of union membership (23.4 percent), followed by transportation and warehousing (16.1 percent) and telecommunications (14.1 percent). Finance is lowest at 1.1 percent union membership, with insurance, professional and technical services, and food services and drinking places following closely at 1.4 percent.

Source: U.S. Department of Labor, Bureau of Labor Statistics, *Union Members Summary,* https://www.bls.gov/news.release/union2.nr0.htm.

revolution ended in about 1860, that number had increased to about 18 percent, and the location of manufacturing had shifted from private homes to factories. As this trend continued to grow, so did the size of the non-farm labor class, and the basis for modern labor issues was created. Compounding the competitive nature of industry during this time were several things, including the simultaneous improvement of the transportation system. This served to allow products from other markets to compete with local products, thus decreasing the local demand and the profit margin of production. This was often offset by decreasing the wage of the worker. It was in this atmosphere that the earliest labor strife leading to what most of us know as workers refusing to work unless their grievances are addressed—strikes—took place.

A Historical Accounting

LO1   Discuss the history of unions in the United States.

Labor law has a long and somewhat acrimonious history in this country. Central to an understanding of the struggle between labor and management is understanding the role the courts played in shaping labor policy before the U.S. Congress enacted legislation that forms the basis for labor relationships today. There were four weapons of choice that business used to control early unionizing efforts: criminal conspiracy laws, injunctions, antitrust laws, and constitutional challenges. A brief examination of these early antiunion efforts helps to explain how the balance between workers' rights and management's rights was ultimately reached.

Criminal Conspiracy Laws

What you take for granted today as simply part of the workplace landscape was not always that way. Remember that because of the industrial revolution's agrarian roots, we were moving away from individual efforts to make a living by farming or skilled labor, to working in factories. Workers in factories eventually came to realize they were working in dangerous or unhealthy situations for very low pay while factory owners and industrialists lived the privileged life of the wealthy. It was a time of major industrialists and "robber barons." These groups of employees often saw this, and their observations turned to workplace grumbling over lunch breaks and from there to conversations between increasingly disaffected workers. While in the much smaller agrarian culture individuals were on their own to speak with the land owner about their wages, conditions, and terms of employment, they now worked with many other workers. These discussions often turned into conversations about concerted activity to address these common workplace issues.

In the 1800s, many courts considered concerted activity by workers such as striking and picketing to be common-law criminal conspiracies. Workers were convicted for trying to improve working conditions through collective efforts. As early as 1806, employers in the shoemaking industry in Philadelphia discovered that they could enlist the aid of the courts by charging their unionized employees with criminal conspiracy. Thus, if a group of employees attempted to exert pressure on an employer to increase wages, they would be charged with criminal conspiracy and, if convicted, subject to imprisonment. Generally, the penalties imposed were fines rather than jail, but along with them came the threat of harsher sentences upon subsequent convictions. This acted to discourage and even eliminate concerted activity. This practice continued until 1842 when the landmark case of *Commonwealth v. Hunt,* included at the end of the chapter, severely criticized the use of criminal conspiracy charges to discourage unionization.

Despite *Commonwealth v. Hunt,* the criminal conspiracy trials retained some vitality until the 1890s. During this time, conspiracy trials were losing steam because of difficulty in getting juries to side with employers. Another method of discouraging unions was being developed that would prove equally difficult for labor.

Injunctions

injunction
A court order requiring individuals or groups of persons to refrain from performing certain acts that the court has determined will do irreparable harm.

Employers sought the use of **injunctions** to gain immediate relief from workers' attempted collective bargaining activities. This legal action was encouraged and proliferated after 1895. In that year, the U.S. Supreme Court issued a decision that upheld the constitutionality of the labor injunction.[22] Armed with this potent legal support, judges were quick to apply this remedy to quash strikes and protests. Judges often committed abuses by wielding their power in personal ways. For example, when an injunction was sought, a judge would have to decide whether a union's objectives were lawful or unlawful. Judges outlawed many union activities this way. This was not always an issue of improper motivation; judges were left without legislative directives and, in their absence, were free to use their own beliefs, attitudes, and prejudices to reach conclusions. Given the antilabor sentiment among the business class, which was the background of a good many judges of this period, the rulings were overwhelmingly against labor's attempt to organize.

This method came to a head in the case of *Hitchman Coal Company v. Mitchell*,[23] in which the Supreme Court declared that a labor injunction could be used to enforce a **yellow dog contract**. The yellow dog contract was a device used by antiunion employers to stop the progress of the union movement. It was the promise of a worker not to join a labor union while in the hire of an employer. Yellow dog contracts, used sparingly before *Hitchman,* proliferated afterward. Employees, often faced with no alternative employment options, were forced to sign yellow dog contracts. Later, if their employer was faced with a unionizing campaign, the employer could receive an injunction that would restrain anyone from encouraging these workers to join a union. This decision's hostile view toward organized labor dealt a harsh blow to workers seeking to organize. Its effects were felt until 1932, when yellow dog contracts were outlawed by Congress.

yellow dog contract
Agreement employers require employees to sign stating they do not belong to a union and will not join one; now illegal.

Antitrust Attacks

The early part of the 20th century saw declining competition and mammoth growth of industrialization. By 1930, nonagricultural occupations accounted for about 80 percent of the labor force. Business leaders saw the advantage of cooperation and began to establish price agreements, trusts, pools, and trade associations. These devices were intended to stamp out competition between rivals. Elimination of competition meant growth of huge and powerful corporations whose purpose was to monopolize an area. Once competition was eliminated, it was easy to control prices and make them whatever the corporation wanted them to be. Of course, this was a disaster for consumers, who were at the mercy of the monopolies.

Congress enacted the Sherman Antitrust Act in 1890 to eliminate monopolistic control of the nation's economy. After its passage, labor unions learned that the law limited a variety of their activities. Unions were prosecuted under various provisions that were interpreted to include them under the provisions that prohibited "every contract, combination . . . or conspiracy, in restraint of trade. . . ." When unions challenged the application of the Sherman Antitrust Act to their activities, the Supreme Court, in 1908,[24] held that the Sherman Act applied to labor unions, giving business a new weapon to combat unionism. In addition, the Court held that individual union members were responsible for the actions of their officers, making the rank and file liable for judgments against the union, and outlawed **secondary boycotts**. In response, unions organized themselves into a strong political force and in 1912 helped to elect Woodrow Wilson (who had pledged his support to the American Federation of Labor) as well as other Democratic candidates. The Democratic Party soon fulfilled its promise to organized labor, and in October 1914 the Clayton Act became law. Section 6 of that act provided that "nothing contained in the antitrust laws shall be construed to forbid the existence and operation of labor organizations" nor shall labor unions be held to be "illegal combinations or conspiracies in restraint of trade under the antitrust laws."

secondary boycott
Union pressure on management created by getting others who do business with management to cease.

More importantly, the Clayton Act regulated the procedure by which a federal court could issue an injunction against labor. Some of the most important gains from labor's perspective were the requirement that an injunction not be issued without notice to the union, absent emergency circumstances; the requirement that a jury trial be held for those members who were charged with a violation under the injunction; the requirement that a bond be posted by the party seeking the injunction and indemnifying the union if they were found to have acted lawfully; and the requirement that specific acts be enjoined and not just the activity of the union wholesale.

Constitutional Challenges to Early Congressional Enactments

Early efforts by federal and state legislators to support organized labor were thwarted by the courts as a whole. Many state laws were declared unconstitutional by state supreme courts. Congress continued to recognize the rights of labor organizations and in 1898 passed the Erdman Act. The objective of the act was to set up a procedure by which conflicts in the railroad industry could be handled. Among other rights, it gave the railroad workers the right to self-organization and collective bargaining and outlawed the yellow dog contract. At this time, Congress targeted railroad workers for protection largely because of the Pullman strike, which had disrupted service in 1894. Feeling the need to ensure against further disruptions that had the effect of paralyzing the nation's transportation system, Congress thought it had found a way to make this issue one of constitutional dimension by making it one of interstate commerce. However, when confronted with the issue of whether Congress could regulate industry by regulating employer–employee relations in this way, the Supreme Court held that Congress could not and struck down this critical law. The Court was not partial to any laborers in particular. In 1918 and 1923, the Court struck down congressional laws that would have controlled the use of child laborers and legislation that would have given women a minimum wage when employed in industry.

Out of Necessity Comes Change

The start of World War I saw the first real movement away from antiunion sentiment. The need for uninterrupted production and for preventing wartime strikes was seen as critical for the greater national interest. President Woodrow Wilson formed the National War Labor Board for the purpose of peacefully resolving labor disputes. This precursor to the National Labor Relations Board (NLRB) embodied many of the tenets that were eventually adopted by the NLRB. While the war acted to create a moratorium on attacks on organized labor, it also served to show that peaceful efforts aimed at resolving labor disputes were possible. After World War I, the National War Labor Board was dismantled, but the unmistakable effect was that it was a stepping stone toward recognition of the organized labor movement.

Congress continued to enact piecemeal legislation aimed at limited pockets of laborers, but in 1932, responding to the harsh effects of the Depression, Congress enacted the National Industrial Recovery Act (NIRA). This law put business in charge of regulating prices and production. Because the regulation of the market in this way was a clear violation of the Sherman Antitrust Act, the NIRA exempted any price control measure (called "codes") from the reach of the Sherman Act. In addition, the NIRA established a minimum wage and gave workers collective bargaining and other rights. Under the NIRA, the ranks of organized labor began to increase. It was under the umbrella of the NIRA that President Roosevelt created the National Labor Board in 1933 and bolstered its enforcement provisions in 1934. Both the NIRA and the board operated successfully until a dispute with the automobile industry, which it could not settle, undermined labor's confidence in the board to such an extent that it was effectively dismantled. In 1935, the NIRA was declared unconstitutional by the Supreme Court because, the Court held, neither the president of the United States nor any private group (such as the business entities given the power under the NIRA to control prices) had the constitutional authority to do what was required of them under the act.

It is against this backdrop that the modern labor movement was born. After this, Congress was able to enact legislation that has formed the basis of what we know as organized labor. Through a series of enactments that have shifted the balance of power first to the unions and then to employers, the balance that has been created is subject today only to refinement. (See Exhibit 15.2, "Union Role in Services Expanding.")

Exhibit 15.2 *Union Role in Services Expanding*

In a 1990 *New York Times* article on the sharp decline of union membership in the 1980s, the conclusion was that unions had to evolve or die. Suggestions for evolving included unions providing social and financial services such as drug and alcohol abuse prevention, reduced-fee credit cards, checking accounts, and so forth. It noted that the "Union, yes" television campaign to attract workers and the AFL-CIO's creation of a new membership category had been put in place to address these issues, but low private-sector unionization numbers weakened the union's bargaining position. Many experts were guardedly optimistic that unions would be revitalized, but with the downward decline in numbers, we can now see, a few decades later, this has not been realized.

At one point, labor unions enjoyed great popularity in the United States. According to the U.S. Department of Labor's Bureau of Labor Statistics, in 2019, about 10.3 percent of the workforce (about 14.6 million) were unionized, a decrease from former years, such as 1983, the first year for which comparable union data are available, when the number was 20.1 percent (17.7 million). In just the one-year period from 2009 to 2010, union representation went from 12.3 percent to 11.9 percent, a loss of 612,000 members. By contrast, it rose by 311,000 from 2006 to 2007.

Due in part to such factors as the reduction in the labor force of traditionally heavily unionized industries such as steel manufacturing, international competition, aggressive nonunionizing campaigns by employers, union concessions during downturns in the economy, the enactment of legislation such as the North American Free Trade Agreement (NAFTA), and the loss of jobs to other countries with cheaper labor, the percentage has steadily decreased since the 1970s. (See Exhibit 15.3, "Maquiladoras: Mexico's Cheap Labor Lures Firms.") The economic downturn in the past few years, including the housing bust, accounted for heavy losses in areas like the construction industry and trades.

Exhibit 15.3 *Maquiladoras: Mexico's Cheap Labor Lures Firms*

See an example of why labor complains about managements' moving jobs out of the United States.

TAKING JOBS SOUTH

In 1965 Mexico introduced the concept of maquiladoras as a way of encouraging foreign investment. They are plants just across the Mexican border to which U.S. companies such as Maytag, Nokia, Eaton, General Motors, and Zenith deliver raw materials and/or parts and receive finished goods. About 1 million Mexicans work at about 3,000 plants in Mexico. Not only are taxes and customs fees almost nonexistent because of the North American Free Trade Agreement (NAFTA), but Mexican workers work cheaper. Some employers may pay as much as $1 or $2 per hour for skilled labor, but most pay less—as little as 50 cents per hour—up to 10 hours per day, six days per week. Ten Mexican workers can be hired for the price of one American worker. There are virtually no unions for employers to worry about, and working conditions required by American laws such as the Occupational Safety and Health Act in the United States do not apply. Some employees may have air-conditioned, modern workplaces and employer-provided cheap lunches, health services, and housing aid, but that is generally not the case. Most maquiladoras are more like sweatshops that expose workers to dangerous conditions or chemicals without any of the protections they would have in the United States. Maquiladoras are also responsible for industrial pollution that would not be allowed if the company were operating just across the border in the United States. Because of foreign competition, American companies have used maquiladoras to stay competitive or even to remain in business at all. In recent years, due in large part to globalization, Mexico has been losing maquiladoras to places like Central America, China, and Taiwan. China, in particular, has been giving Mexican maquiladoras stiff competition and is trying hard to become the world's cheapest assembly destination. Maquiladoras still account for 45 percent of Mexico's exports and $51 billion in imports of parts, however.

Yet with 14.6 million members, labor unions remain an important part of the workplace. In 2019, nonunion members made only 81 percent of the salary of union members. The median weekly income of full-time wage and salary union members was $1094 and that of nonunion members was $892 (although union membership does not totally account for the difference). You can therefore see at least some of the reason why unions still play an important part in the workplace landscape. One of the issues we may well see developing more frequently in the near future is unions increasing their membership by getting involved in issues such as low wages or immigrant workers. In the South, which is traditionally low in union membership, this occurred in the Koch Foods and Gold Kist poultry plants in Tennessee and Alabama. When employers engage in practices like refusing to allow employees to leave the processing line to go to the bathroom; heavy, unrealistic work quotas; wages so low that even employees working for 10 years can only make a maximum of $7.55 per hour; and abusive treatment such as screaming, cursing, or not allowing sick employees to leave, even traditionally nonunion workplaces run the risk of workers uniting and resorting to collective bargaining. In this chapter, we will discuss the basic laws addressing collective bargaining, what the laws require, and how to lessen the likelihood of an employer running into union troubles.

Labor Laws

Four main federal laws constitute the statutory basis for labor law and unionization. The legislation initiating a move toward collective bargaining in the United States began with restricting court responses to union activity and establishing the right of employees to form labor organizations and to be protected against unfair labor practices at the hands of employers.

Until the Norris–LaGuardia Act of 1932 and the Wagner Act of 1935 (generally referred to as the National Labor Relations Act of 1935), employers had held virtually all the power. However, once that right to bargain collectively was created and unions were established, the matter took some rather sinister twists. Unions started feeling their power and often went overboard in using it.

This resulted in two other legislative measures to address the evolution of collective bargaining. The Taft–Hartley Act (also known as the Labor Management Relations Act) amended the Wagner Act in 1947 to establish unfair *union* practices, and the Landrum–Griffin Act of 1959 gave certain civil rights to union members and addressed corruption of union officials.

The Norris–LaGuardia Act of 1932

LO2 Identify the Norris–LaGuardia Act of 1932 and what it covers.

The Norris–LaGuardia Act was the first major labor law statute enacted in the United States. The opening section of the Norris–LaGuardia Act established that government recognized that the job is more important to a worker than a worker is to a corporation. It recognized that the only real power workers had was in impacting employers through numbers. An employer may not be disturbed when one worker walks out, but most certainly will be when all or most workers do so. The Norris-LaGuardia Act endorsed collective bargaining as a matter of public policy. To implement this policy, Congress sharply curbed the power of the courts to intervene in labor disputes, including curtailing use of the injunction. Norris-LaGuardia did not give labor unions any new legal rights; rather, it allowed them more freedom to operate free from court control and interference. This greatly facilitated labor unions acting as effective collective bargaining agencies.

Section 4 of the act declares that no federal court has the power to issue any form of injunctive relief in any case involving a labor dispute if that injunction would prohibit any person who was participating in such a dispute from doing certain acts. Judges cannot restrain any strike, regardless of its objective, and cannot restrain picketing activities. A labor union can provide relief funds to its strikers and publicize its labor disputes, and workers can urge other employees to join the conflict. Norris-LaGuardia allows a union to act in defense of a person prosecuted for his or her actions or to prosecute an action under the worker's contract. A union can conduct meetings to promote the interests of workers. Norris-LaGuardia protected any "labor dispute" even though parties did not stand as employer–employee with each other, further encouraging collective bargaining.

Most importantly, while it did not directly outlaw yellow dog contracts, the act declared that yellow dog contracts were inconsistent with U.S. public policy and not enforceable in any court in the United States. Later, the NLRB held that an employer engaged in an unfair labor practice if it demanded that an employee execute such an agreement.

The act also had a significant impact in curbing prosecution under the antitrust laws. In its statement of purpose, Congress claimed that the intent of the act was to give labor what it thought it had received under the Clayton Act. Given the broadly stated purpose of the act, the Supreme Court has broadly construed it, providing unions with the opportunity to engage in activities calculated to affect the collective bargaining process. When Norris-LaGuardia limited the enforcement of yellow dog contracts and removed the impediments of workers to organize in a concerted fashion, the way was paved for enactment of the National Labor Relations Act three years later.

The National Labor Relations Act of 1935 (Wagner Act)

LO3 Identify the National Labor Relations Act of 1935 (Wagner Act) and what it requires.

Of the four pieces of seminal labor legislation, it is the National Labor Relations Act (NLRA) that most people consider to be the mainstay of union activity since it established the right of employees to form unions, to bargain collectively, and to strike. Recall that, at one time, it had been illegal—in fact, criminal—for employees to join together in an effort to collectively bargain with employers.

The National Labor Relations Act

In order to avoid the unconstitutional delegation of legislative power, Congress, in enacting the NLRA, placed the administration of the act in the hands of the National Labor Relations Board (NLRB), an independent federal administrative agency, rather than in the hands of an industrial group; set up standards to govern the exercise of power delegated to that administrative agency; and provided for the judicial enforcement of the orders of that agency. The board was empowered to issue remedial orders, enforceable in the courts, to prevent commission of unfair labor practices. Five such unfair practices were outlined in section 8 of the act. Under this section, it is an unfair labor practice to

- Interfere with, restrain, or coerce employees in the exercise of their rights.
- Interfere with the formation of a labor organization.
- Discriminate in the hiring or tenure of employment or discourage membership in a labor organization.
- Retaliate for filing charges or testifying under the act.
- Refuse to bargain with the representatives of the employees.

Notably absent from this act are unfair labor practices that might be committed by unions, although there were unfair labor practices listed that might be committed by employers. In the political climate that prevailed in 1935, the government placed its weight on the side of laborers because of the imbalance between corporate power and the labor market. The act was government's attempt to guarantee workers the right to organize so they would be able to bargain on a more equal basis with employers.

As you can imagine, given the history we discussed, creation of the NLRB did not rest well with business. For the first few years of its existence, the board survived a well-organized and concerted attack challenging its constitutionality and the scope of its authority. Finally, in 1937 and 1938, the U.S. Supreme Court brought the avalanche of injunction suits against the NLRB to a halt in a series of rulings that found the authority of the board to determine whether an employer had engaged in an unfair labor practice to be exclusive, subject only to subsequent judicial review after the board had issued its decision, and that detailed the scope of the NLRB's legal powers. These decisions form the foundations of the NLRB that are still effective today.

With the constitutionality of the NLRB settled and the injunctions halted, the judicial proceedings during the third year of the board's existence concerned the correctness of the NLRB's decisions and the power of the board to fashion remedies. Certain principles of law were established, including that employees on strike are still employees; that employees striking because of an unfair labor practice are entitled to reinstatement, even if reinstatement makes it necessary to discharge employees hired to replace them; and that threatened economic loss does not justify the commission of an unfair labor practice. From 1935 to 1947, the courts developed a vast body of law dealing with labor issues.

The National Labor Relations Board

The NLRB is the independent federal agency that enforces labor laws in the private sector. Once sufficient interest has been indicated by the employees (usually by signing union authorization cards), the NLRB conducts elections to determine what union, if any, will represent the employees in collective bargaining. The NLRB also decertifies unions that employees no longer wish to have represent them, issues labor regulations, hears unfair labor practice cases at the agency level, brings enforcement proceedings for unfair labor practice cases, and otherwise administers the NLRA. The board itself is composed of five members who, among other things, hear appeals from administrative law judge decisions of the agency on issues of unfair labor practices and union elections.

An interesting, unusual issue arose a few years ago with far-ranging legal impact. Due to expiration of member terms and political stalemates in D.C., the National Labor Relations Board was down by three members for 27 months, beginning in January 2008 and lasting until President Obama's recess appointment on March 27, 2010. The two-member board issued nearly 600 decisions during that time, acting as a quorum of a three-member board delegated the power to do so. In June 2010, the U.S. Supreme Court held, in *New Process Steel, L.P. v. NLRB*,[25] that the board lacked the authority to issue decisions during this 27-month period. This effectively invalidated the nearly 600 cases addressed by the two-member board, leaving unclear how they would be resolved by the fully functioning board. At the very least, the board had to reissue decisions in the 74 cases pending before the federal courts in which the losing party challenged the board's authority to act with only two members.[26]

community of interests
Factors employees have in common for bargaining purposes.

bargaining unit
The group of employees in a workplace that have the legal right to bargain with the employer.

In collective bargaining, employees with a **community of interests**—that is, similar workplace concerns and conditions—come together as a **bargaining unit** that the union will represent. The community of interests is based on such factors as similarity of the jobs the employees perform, similar training or skills, and so on. While the general rule is that at least two employees must be in a bargaining unit, an employer may agree to a one-person unit, such as for an on-site craftworker (e.g., a carpenter who belongs to a carpenter's union being employed at a worksite as the only carpenter).

Scenario

Employees may unionize either by signing a sufficient number of authorization cards, by voting in a union during a union representation election, or, in some cases, by the NLRB ordering the employer to bargain with a union. The NLRB supervises the union election and certifies the results. The employer cannot interfere in any way with the employees' efforts to form a union, as was done in Opening Scenario 1.

Concerted Activity

Section 7 of the NLRA guarantees employees the right to engage in concerted activities for mutual aid or protection. Typical protected concerted activities include union organizing, the discussion of unionization among employees, and the attempt by one employee to solicit union support from another employee. But concerted activity need not involve a union. Activities by groups of employees unaffiliated with a union to improve their lot in their workplace are deemed protected concerted activities.

Concerted activity also covers activity by a single employee, even if no other employee joins him or her. The reasoning is that the protected status of such activity should not turn on whether another employee decides to join the activity. Not all concerted activity is protected, however. Acts or threats of violence are not protected.

Unions

Unions are composed of nonsupervisory or non-managerial employees, including part-time workers. Specifically excluded from the NLRA are agricultural and domestic workers, independent contractors, and those employed by their spouse or parent. As we discussed in the chapter on affirmative action, agricultural and domestic workers were excluded from the law because these were the primary occupations to which Blacks were consigned. The law was passed during the Jim Crow era of segregation as southern legislators refused to have Blacks on par with whites.

The issue of supervisory employee inclusion in bargaining units has become heated recently. During the Bush administration, the definition of supervisor was clarified in *Oakwood Health Care, Inc.*[27] The terms *assign, responsible to direct,* and *independent judgment* in section 2(11) of the law were interpreted in a way that made it easier for an employer to consider an employee as a supervisory employee excluded from a bargaining unit for collective bargaining purposes. Unions were upset by this.

The Re-empowerment of Skilled and Professional Employees and Construction Tradeworkers (RESPECT) Act[28] was introduced in Congress in 2007 but has not been enacted into law. The law would essentially greatly increase the number of managers who could qualify to be a part of a bargaining unit. The law would remove from the definition of supervisor the duties of assigning the responsibility to direct other employees and would require that supervisors "hire, transfer, suspend, lay off, recall, promote, discharge, reward or discipline other employees" for a majority of their work time. This would have the effect of greatly reinvigorating unions, an idea of great concern to business. President Obama supported the law, but he had a Republican Congress, and under President Trump passage is unlikely anytime soon.

The union's **shop steward**, elected by the members, is the intermediary generally between the union and the employer. He or she may collect dues and recruit new workers, and, if a union member feels the **collective bargaining agreement** has been violated in some way or an unfair labor practice has been committed, the shop steward is usually the first to contact the employer and discuss the issue, hopefully having it resolved.

Unions may be organized by industry or craft/trade. If all employees of a particular industry organize into a union, such as autoworkers, regardless of the job the members hold, this is an **industrial union**. The value of an industrial union from an employee's point of view is the solidarity and strength in a comprehensive group of workers—especially important in the event of a strike. Rather than being organized by industry, unions also may be organized around a particular craft or trade such as carpenters, sheet metal workers or pipefitters. These are **craft unions**. The value of a craft union is that the members all have the same issues specific to their craft or trade. Craft union members' interests are represented by a **business agent** of the craft union. You can imagine that management generally has an easier time trying to negotiate with one industrial union rather than a union for each craft/trade involved in management's enterprise. However, each type of union has its own advantages and disadvantages.

shop steward
Union member chosen as an intermediary between union members and employers.

collective bargaining agreement
Negotiated contract between labor and management.

industrial union
Union organized across an industry, regardless of members' job type.

craft unions
Unions organized by the employee's craft or trade.

business agent
The representative of a union, usually a craft union.

An interesting phenomenon in the past decade or so has been the unionization or attempted unionization of groups traditionally nonunion. For instance, since the early 1990s, registered nurses across the country sought to unionize and did so in record numbers. Before that time, nurses had considered unions to be for blue-collar workers, while nurses were considered professionals. One of the first projects President Clinton undertook when he came into office was to ask his wife, Hillary Rodham Clinton, to head up efforts to make health care more accessible and affordable to all. The health industry's response was unprecedented restructuring, and the resulting downsizing, among other things, displaced registered nurses. Registered nurses' perception of unions as being only for blue-collar workers changed, and they began to seek a collective voice purportedly to protect their profession and patient safety.

Even private attorneys are getting into the act. District attorneys had for some time been unionized in the public sector, but in 2003, in what is believed to be a first in the private legal profession, lawyers at the Phoenix office of the Los Angeles law firm of Parker Stanbury, which subcontracts with Pre-Paid Legal Service to provide easily accessible legal services, voted to unionize. Citing a lack of response by their employer to their complaints about low pay, few research materials, no law library, limited Internet access, hourly performance quotas, and working in open cubicles, they voted in representation by the local Teamsters union, which also represents truckers, grocery workers, bakery drivers, and UPS employees. There were allegations that management frequently tried to block the organizing effort, but the unionized lawyers said they were contacted by several other private attorneys interested in exploring unionizing.

There also have been organizing efforts for other nontraditional groups such as graduate students, college football players, medical interns and residents, and congressional researchers. In 2019, Harvard graduate students went on strike after a year of negotiations with the administration proved fruitless. They wanted higher pay, better health benefits, and protection from harassment and discrimination. They vowed not to administer exams, grade papers, or complete research until their demands were taken seriously.[29]

The strike was called off 27 days later, without reaching an agreement, with the graduate students agreeing to return to work at the beginning of the semester. The students said negotiations would resume, but the administration said there was no timeline provided.[30]

We cannot leave the area of organizing efforts without touching on another topic important to that area: the rise of the use of labor management consulting firms and the other methods used to thwart efforts at unionization. These organizations (often known as *union busters*) arose in the 1970s as primarily only a handful of law firms. Today, such firms have grown into a very sophisticated, billion-dollar industry. By 1989, employers had hired antiunion consultants in 76 percent of all union organizing campaigns. To the extent that employers can stop organizing efforts by hiring help regarding how to discourage employees from voting to have union representation, they would consider the money spent as well worth the price. (See Exhibit 15.4, "Why Employers Don't Want Unions.")

Exhibit 15.4 *Why Employers Don't Want Unions*

Union busting is big business. You might wonder why a business would pay to have an organization come in to the workplace and stop employees' efforts to unionize. Here are a few of the reasons.

- Businesses generally prefer to make their own decisions, without the input of employees.

- Having to consult with the union means business is less likely to be able to make quick decisions.

- Bottom-line decisions such as outsourcing, subcontracting, or relocating to take advantage of cheaper labor or other costs would require union negotiation, thus making it less likely to be done smoothly, quickly, and efficiently.

- Due to the long history of contention between labor and management, being unionized often gives the workplace a feeling of "us versus them," which can adversely impact morale and productivity.

- Union contracts requiring grievance proceedings and arbitration can be inefficient though they are certainly less costly and time-consuming than litigation.

- Striking by workers, work stoppages, or slowdowns are a possible costly risk.

- The collective bargaining process is usually an adversarial affair, which does not help workplace morale.

- An employer looking to sell his or her business looks less appealing if a union is in place. This can lead to a lowering of the potential selling price for the business.

The consulting firms' efforts may be successful in keeping unions out, but the employers may pay in other ways. For instance, nurses at Long Beach Memorial Hospital ran an organizing campaign to have the nurses join the California Nurses Association. A consulting firm was brought in to help keep the union out. The vote was eventually 591 to 581 to not have the nurses represented by a union, but the NLRB issued a complaint against the hospital alleging 26 violations of federal labor law. Many tactics are used to thwart unions during organizing efforts, some legal and some not. (See Exhibit 15.5, "Antiunionizing Tactics.") The best strategy is to have

Exhibit 15.5 *Antiunionizing Tactics*

Below is a list of tactics used by employers over the years, both legal and illegal, to keep their employees from voting for union representation. As you will see, this is an extremely creative process, so the list is not exhaustive.

- Utilize scare tactics, including additional security guards and guard dogs, to create an atmosphere of fear and intimidation.

- Direct managers to disseminate misinformation about the union.

- Direct managers to disseminate antiunion flyers—one company passed out over 100 different flyers!

- Run newspaper ads against the union.

- Create antiunion videos and deliver them to employees' homes.

- Offer enticements such as improved working conditions and pay increases and imply that they will not come about if the union is voted in.

- Plead for more time to try to make things better.

(continued)

- Have supervisors interrogate employees to find out how they intend to vote.
- Pressure supporters not to talk to other employees about the union.
- Place managers in employee hangouts such as lounges, cafeterias, or break rooms to inhibit employees' discussion of the union vote.
- Have supervisors write letters to individual employees telling them things like the supervisor will lose his or her job if the union is voted in.
- Ignore and isolate pro-union employees.
- Use ethnicity as a wedge between various ethnic groups.
- Have supervisors call daily mandatory meetings.
- Have supervisors engage employees in one-on-one conversations about the union as much as possible.
- Disseminate antiunion buttons, flyers, posters, videos, bumper stickers, and T-shirts.

- Have an antiunion website.
- Install locked, glass-covered bulletin boards all over the workplace and post antiunion material on them.
- Make supervisors think they will lose their jobs if they do not get the employees to vote against the union.
- Have a few employees run an antiunion campaign.
- Spring last-minute surprises on employees, such as rumors of possible workplace shutdowns, bonuses, or pay raises.
- Have payroll send out checks with an amount equal to union dues taken out, tell employees this is what their paychecks will look like if the union is voted in, and then put the money back in their next paychecks.
- Shut down part or all of operations and allege that the shutdown is because of union costs.

a workplace in which employees feel no need for a union because their reasonable needs are taken care of by the employer. However, if employers choose to make use of management consulting firms to keep unions out of the workplace, they should keep in close touch with the consultants and their tactics in order to avoid being left with the liability when the NLRB alleges unfair management practices.

Good-Faith Bargaining

mandatory subject of bargaining
Wages, hours, and other conditions of employment, which, by law, must be negotiated between labor and management.

permissive subjects of bargaining
Nonmandatory subjects that can be negotiated between labor and management.

closed shop
Employer hires only union members.

Under the NLRA, an employer is required to bargain in good faith with union representatives about wages, hours, and terms and conditions of employment. These are **mandatory subjects of bargaining**. While employers may actually bargain about other matters (**permissive subjects**), only a refusal to bargain about mandatory subjects of bargaining may form the basis of an unfair labor practice. (See Exhibit 15.6, "Selected Collective Bargaining Agreement Clauses.")

At times, management and labor may differ on whether a particular matter is a mandatory subject of bargaining. If this disagreement is legitimate, it can form the basis of an unfair labor practice—for instance, a union may allege management has committed an unfair labor practice by refusing to bargain over a mandatory subject of bargaining such as wage increases. In one case, the union demanded negotiations on the issue of the agency's new smoking ban.[31]

If the matter proposed for negotiation is illegal, such as a proposal to have a **closed shop**, it is bad-faith bargaining even to bring it up as a proposal, and management's refusal to bargain cannot be the basis of an unfair labor practice.

The law requires only that the parties bargain in good faith about appropriate matters, not that one party necessarily agree with the other's position and include

Exhibit 15.6 *Selected Collective Bargaining Agreement Clauses*

LO4 List and explain several collective bargaining agreement clauses.

List and explain several collective bargaining agreement clauses.

Wages—including cost-of-living increases, production increases, learners' and apprentices' overtime.

Benefits—including vacations, sick pay, holidays, insurance.

Hours—including overtime and determinations about assignment.

Seniority—setting forth how employee seniority is determined and used.

Management security—employers may make their own decisions about how to run the business as long as they are not contrary to the collective bargaining agreement or law.

Union security—the union's legal right to exist and to represent the employees involved.

Job security—how employees will maintain employment, including procedures for layoffs, downsizing, work sharing, and so on.

Dues checkoff—right of a union to have the employer deduct union dues from employees' wages and turn them over to the union.

Union shop—requires all employees to join the union within a certain time of coming into the bargaining unit.

Modified union shop—requires that all new employees must join the union after an agreement

becomes effective, as must any employees who were already union members; but those already working who were not union members and do not wish to join need not do so.

Maintenance-of-membership—employees who voluntarily join a union may leave only during a short window period prior to agreement expiration.

Agency shop—requires all employees of the bargaining unit to pay union dues, whether union members or not.

Grievances—sets forth the basis for grievances regarding conflicts over the meaning of the collective bargaining agreement and procedures for addressing them.

Exclusive representation—the union representative will be the only party who can negotiate with the employer about matters affecting bargaining unit employees.

Arbitration—the matters that cannot be otherwise resolved will be submitted to arbitration to be resolved by a neutral third party whose decision is usually binding.

Midterm negotiations—permits agreed-on topics to be reopened to negotiation prior to contract expiration.

No-strike, no lockout—parties agree that the employees will not strike or will only do so under limited circumstances and that employers will not engage in lockouts. Instead, the grievance procedure will be used to handle labor disputes.

it in the collective bargaining agreement. The intent is to prevent management from unilaterally instituting workplace policies that closely affect workers without at least getting employee input and negotiating the matter. The fact that one side or the other does not receive what it wants in the contract is not just cause for an unfair labor practice. As long as good-faith bargaining takes place, there has been compliance with the statute.

A case of bargaining in bad faith might occur when, for instance, management comes to the bargaining table and denies a raise to employees without offering any evidence whatever as to why and simply continues to reject the union's wage proposals. The 2011 National Football League negotiations with the National Football League Players Association experienced a stalemate where negotiation impasses and failure to agree on a new contract threatened to interrupt the start of the football season. Despite more than $9 billion in league revenues, owners asserted that stadium construction and other investments had driven their profits down to the single digits. They proposed that players should take 18 percent off the pool of money used to calculate salary caps. The players wanted to see league financial statements justifying the owners' claims, but the owners were reluctant to share.[32] Fortunately, an agreement was reached and the season salvaged.

Bargaining in bad faith also could occur if one side rejects proposals out of hand without making counterproposals to the other side. Missing scheduled negotiation sessions without a valid reason and setting forth unsupported proposals could lead to an unfair labor practice charge. Of course, failing to show up for negotiations or refusing to sign the written agreement to which the parties orally agreed also would be bad-faith bargaining. The *Gimrock Construction, Inc. v. International Union of Operating Engineers, Local 487* case, provided at the end of the chapter for your review, demonstrates how extreme an employer can be in failing or refusing to bargain in good faith. Since 1999, Gimrock refused to bargain with the employees' union representative on the first collective bargaining agreement or to provide the union with requested relevant information. The 11th Circuit Court of Appeals upheld and enforced two earlier board decisions finding a refusal to bargain. Finally, the NLRB general counsel took the extraordinary step of requesting remedies that included requiring the employer to bargain for a minimum of 16 hours per week and also to send written bargaining progress reports to the NLRB regional director every 30 days. Twelve years later, in a 2011 decision, the NLRB agreed that because of the employer's extended reluctance, the remedies were appropriate. Delaying negotiating for 12 years gives you some idea of the resistance some employers have to unions and the lengths to which they will go to avoid unions in the workplace.

The duty to bargain in good faith over terms and conditions of employment does not require agreement between the parties. As with the NFL negotiations, if agreement is not reached with the union after good-faith bargaining is conducted, the union may then be free to advance to other alternatives it can exercise, up to and including strikes. These are not activities exclusive to management. Unions are also capable of engaging in refusals to bargain or bargaining in bad faith.

Duty of Fair Representation

Frequently, when union members do not like the contract that results from collective bargaining negotiations, they will allege the union has breached its duty of fair representation. This duty, not formally defined in the statute and often used as a catchall allegation, requires the union to represent all employees fairly and non-discriminatorily. If employees feel that one group has come out better than another in a contract, they will use the duty of fair representation as a basis for challenging the contract. The U.S. Supreme Court spoke to this issue in *Air Line Pilots Association International v. O'Neill,*[33] when it held that since the final outcome was not "wholly irrational or arbitrary," the union had done its statutory job of upholding its duty of fair representation even though some members may not have liked the outcome.

Collective Bargaining Agreements

If all goes well, bargaining between labor and management results in a collective bargaining agreement. This is the term for the contract that is reached between the employer and the union about workplace issues. There is no set form that this agreement must take, and it may be any length and contain any provisions the parties decide. (See Exhibit 15.6, "Selected Collective Bargaining Agreement Clauses.") Job and union security are the main issues for employees, while freedom from labor strife such as strikes, slowdowns, and work stoppages is paramount for employers. Management will often wish to include a **management security clause**, stating that it has the power to run its business and make business decisions as long as it is not in violation of the collective bargaining agreement or the law.

Toward that end, in addition to wages and hours, collective bargaining agreements often also contain provisions regarding strikes, arbitration of labor disputes, seniority, benefits, employment classifications, and so on. Because things change, the agreement is in effect only for a specified period. Prior to expiration of that period, the parties will negotiate a new contract to take effect when the old one expires. As you know from NFL negotiations discussed above, that does not always occur. The collective bargaining agreement between the NFL and the NFL Players Association expired on March 4, 2011, but that date came and went through summer 2011 with no agreement. Two extensions were agreed to, but to no avail. In fact, the NFLPA decertified its union on March 11, 2011, and was no longer represented by a union at the bargaining table. The NFLPA filed an antitrust suit against the NFL, and the NFL responded with a lockout of the players on March 12, 2011.[34] This first NFL work stoppage since 1987, of course, put the 2011 season in jeopardy as the situation moved from negotiation to litigation. On April 25, 2011, a federal judge granted the players' request for an injunction stopping the lockout.[35]

The collective bargaining agreement also may include a clause permitting **midterm negotiations**. These are negotiations agreed to and scheduled during the life of the contract, rather than immediately prior to its expiration, about matters on which the parties have agreed they will permit interim negotiations. The parties may not be able to agree on a particular provision and, rather than allow it to hold up the entire contract, will agree to come back together later to negotiate it. Alternatively, the parties may agree to midterm negotiations because the contract may cover a fairly long period and the provision subject to midterm negotiation is one that may change quickly and need to be reviewed before the contract's expiration date.

Unfair Labor Practices

Refusal to bargain in good faith is not the only unfair labor practice that an employer can commit. Others include engaging in activities that would tend to attempt to control or influence the union or to interfere with its affairs and discriminating against employees who join or assist unions. Actual interference by the employer need not be proved for it to be considered an unfair labor practice. Rather, the question is whether the activity *tends* to interfere with, restrain, or coerce employees who are exercising rights protected under the law. (See Exhibit 15.7, "Management Unfair Labor Practices.") The *Columbia Portland Cement Co. v.*

management security clause
Parties agree that management has the right to run the business and make appropriate business decisions as long as applicable laws are complied with.

midterm negotiations
Collective bargaining negotiations during the term of the contract rather than at its expiration.

LO5 Explain unfair labor practices and give examples.

Case 3

Exhibit 15.7   *Management Unfair Labor Practices*

- Trying to control the union or interfering with union affairs, such as trying to help a certain candidate get elected to a union office.
- Discriminating against employees who join a union or are in favor of bringing in a union or who exercise their rights under the law (e.g., terminating, demoting, or giving poor working schedules to such employees).

- Interfering with, coercing, or restraining employees exercising their rights under the labor law legislation (e.g., telling employees they cannot have a union or they will be terminated if they do).
- Refusal to bargain or refusal to bargain in good faith.

National Labor Relations Board case, which is provided at the conclusion of the chapter and is the basis for Opening Scenario 2, indicates the extent of possible unfair labor practices when the employer refused to reinstate striking employees and gave a unilateral wage increase without consulting the union.

As mentioned previously, some employers are more aggressive in interfering with their employees' unionizing efforts. In *Davis Supermarkets, Inc. v. National Labor Relations Board,*[36] the company interfered with its employees' organizing efforts and even terminated some of its employees. The court found these acts to be unfair labor practices that violated the NLRA.

Sometimes, even though the employer may have the best of intentions, its other actions may amount to a violation of law. In *Electromation v. National Labor Relations Board,* included at the end of the chapter, what may have appeared to the company to be legitimate negotiations with nonunion employees was held to violate the NLRA. The nonunion employer attempted to resolve labor issues through "employee participation" or "employee–management" focus groups. When the court determined that the groups actually constituted labor organizations and were dominated by management, who had too much of a hand in administering these groups, it held that the employer's actions constituted an unfair labor practice. *Electromation* is the basis for Opening Scenario 3.

In Exhibit 15.5, "Antiunionizing Tactics," we listed many of the antiunion organizing tactics that have been used by management over the years to thwart union efforts to organize, and in Exhibit 15.7, "Management Unfair Labor Practices," we listed some unfair labor practices. In Exhibit 15.8, "Cans and Can'ts during Union Campaigns," we list some specific acts employers can and cannot engage in during organizing efforts. It would be wise for employers to use these lists as guides in order to avoid unfair labor practice complaints.

Strikes and Lockouts

The NLRA permits certain strikes by employees as a legitimate bargaining approach that leverages economic and public pressure. (See Exhibit 15.9, "Types of Strikes.") When a union strikes, union members do not work but, instead,

Exhibit 15.8   *Cans and Can'ts during Union Campaigns*

Often referred to as "NO TIPS" (threats, interrogation promises, or spying, along with several other things an employer cannot do), during a unionizing campaign, the employer *can't*

- Threaten to fire an employee for joining a union.
- Try to help the employees form a union.
- Lay off or terminate employees who support the union.
- Allow employees to copy antiunion leaflets at work and pass them out.
- Let employees hold antiunion meetings at work.
- Email, post, or circulate threatening or intimidating letters or leaflets.
- Try to question employees about their support of (or opposition to) the union.
- Terminate, discipline, transfer, or reassign union supporters to less desirable shifts, duties, or locations without some legitimate business cause other than their union support.
- Ask about union meetings or union activities.
- Spy on union activities or union supporters.
- Isolate all union supporters so that they cannot speak with other employees.

- Promise wage increases or other benefits if employees don't join the union.
- Threaten to take away job benefits if employees vote in a union.
- Ban pro-union buttons if such things are generally permitted.

During a unionizing campaign, an employer *can*

- Send letters to employees' homes.
- Establish a suggestion box or complaint process.
- Give pay raises or benefits overall, not just to union supporters. (This can be limited after the union applies for its certificate or gives notice to bargain its first agreement.)
- Hold meetings in an effort to address or solve problems it becomes aware of.
- Tell employees how good the company is.
- Tell employees how good the company's benefits and working conditions are.
- Address issues that it may become aware of during the unionizing process.

Exhibit 15.9   *Types of Strikes*

- *Economic strike*—used to exert pressure on the employer regarding economic issues. Also used for strikes resulting from any other reason than an unfair labor practice. Protected activity.
- *Unfair labor practice strike*—called by union because of an employer's unfair labor practice. Protected activity.
- *Sympathy strike*—union not involved in strike also strikes to show solidarity and support for striking union.

- *Sitdown strike*—employees illegally take possession of workplace during strike. Not protected activity.
- *Wildcat strike*—strike not authorized by union. Generally not protected activity, but may be.
- *Intermittent strike*—strikes that occur from time to time and are not announced. Not protected activity.
- *Slowdown*—employees remain on the job and generally do not produce as much. Not protected activity.

picketing
Union members carrying signs in front of the employer's business that tell of an unfair labor practice or strike.

generally gather outside the employer's place of business and carry signs about the nature of the strike (**picketing**) and chant slogans. Engaging in such activity is for purposes of pressuring management to concede, bringing attention to the strikers' demands, gathering public support, and discouraging others who may support the employer. For instance, a picket line may encourage shoppers going into a grocery store not to patronize the store where the clerks are on strike because wages are too low. This has occurred at various McDonald's locations across the country for several years as employees go on strike for higher wages.

Legitimate strikes may be called by the union either for economic reasons or because of unfair labor practices. For instance, the employees may strike when a collective bargaining agreement expires without a new one to take its place or if the employees are attempting to force economic concessions from the employer. If employees strike for legally recognized reasons, their actions are protected under the NLRA, and they retain their status as employees. Strikes not authorized by the union are called **wildcat strikes** and are illegal if they force the employer to deal with the employees rather than the union or impose the will of the minority rather than the majority. They have been found not to be unlawful if they are merely to make a statement.

wildcat strike
A strike not sanctioned by the union.

Since strikes correctly engaged in are perfectly legal, if the employer replaces the strikers with new employees, then once the strike is over, the strikers have a right to reinstatement if they offer an unconditional offer to return to work. If their jobs are occupied by replacement workers, then unfair labor practice strikers are entitled to be reinstated, but economic strikers are not.

lockout
Management does not allow employees to come to work.

Just as employees can stop working if they feel the need to strike to make their point, the employer can close the premises to employees and engage in a **lockout**. In a lockout, the employer curtails employment by either shutting down the plant or bringing in temporary nonunion employees after laying off striking workers. Under the NLRA, the employer may engage in lockouts not as a way of avoiding bargaining or unionizing but rather, as with strikes, to bring pressure to bear on the other side for legitimate purposes. The pressure position is probably why the NFL chose to announce a lockout of the NFL players on March 11, 2011, effective at midnight that night.

no-strike, no-lockout clause
Labor and management agree that labor will not strike and management will not stage a lockout.

Many collective bargaining agreements contain **no-strike, no-lockout clauses**, which either prohibit or limit the availability of this action and instead call for the use of the grievance process to handle issues. In 2002, baseball commissioner Bud Selig pledged not to lock out players throughout the season and the World Series. His statement left open the possibility that team owners would come up with new work rules after that. Because the players' union had been working without a labor contract since November 7, 2001, they interpreted the commissioner's statement as a "veiled threat" to impose vast economic changes as soon as the postseason ended. In 1994, in its eighth walkout since 1972, the baseball players' union struck in order to fight management's plan to implement changes that included a salary cap. The walkout lasted 232 days and resulted in the cancellation of the World Series for the first time since 1904. In 2002, after fighting for months over changes imposed by club owners, the players entered into a new contract on August 30, avoiding the strike deadline by only hours.

In 2004–2005, there was the unfortunate National Hockey League fiasco where differences between the owners and players, primarily over the issue of salary caps, resulted in a five-month lockout by the owners and, eventually, cancellation of the entire season by the NHL commissioner—an event many hockey fans still think back on with much dismay. It was the first time a major North American professional sports league lost an entire season to a labor dispute.[37] The last time the NHL's Stanley Cup was not awarded was in 1919 because of a flu pandemic. The year before, the Boston Red Sox had won the World Series. Coincidentally, this time around, when the cup wasn't awarded because of labor disputes canceling the season, the Red Sox had once again, after over 80 years, won the World Series the year before.

In *Local 825, Int'l Union of Operating Engineers v. National Labor Relations Board,*[38] the union challenged the lockout and hiring of temporary workers as unfair labor practices, but the court held that the practices did not violate the law. The court discussed legitimate purposes for which an employer can stage a lockout and what happens if the workers are replaced with temporary employees during the lockout. It said that "if the adverse effect of the discriminatory conduct on employee rights is 'comparatively slight' an anti-union motivation must be proved to sustain the charge if the employer has come forward with evidence of legitimate and substantial business justifications for the conduct." Thus, the "slight" impact on employee rights (to organize, etc.) that the conduct at issue arguably had is negated if the employer has established a legitimate and substantial business justification for its conduct.

The Taft–Hartley Act of 1947

LO6 Describe the Taft–Hartley Act of 1947 and its requirements.

With the enactment of the NLRA and the subsequent gains made in unionism, the Taft–Hartley Act of 1947 was enacted as an amendment to the NLRA to curb excesses by unions. Most importantly, the Taft–Hartley Act changed the policies of the NLRA. No longer were all employers legislatively determined to be frustrating the organizational rights of their employees. Congress recognized that unions had grown so strong and powerful over the years that their activities required federal regulation. As such, unions were to have certain limitations placed on their activity. Congress wanted employers, employees, and labor organizations to recognize one another's legitimate rights and made the rights of all three subordinate to the public's health, safety, and interests.

Section 7 was rewritten to recognize the right of an employee to refrain from concerted activity, including union activity. Like section 8 of the Wagner Act, which enumerates unfair labor practices that could be committed by employees, section 8 of the Taft–Hartley Act spells out six unfair labor practices that could be committed by organized labor (see Exhibit 15.10, "Union Unfair Labor Practices"), thereby bringing unions under the regulation of the federal law. Under this section, it is an unfair labor practice for unions to

1. Restrain or coerce employees in the exercise of their rights or employers in the selection of their representatives for collective bargaining.
2. Cause an employer to discriminate against an employee.

Exhibit 15.10 *Union Unfair Labor Practices*

- Refusing to bargain or bargaining in bad faith— that is, not attending bargaining sessions, not providing proposals, not providing necessary information.
- Coercing or restraining employees in exercising their rights to join (or not join) a union. This is not a problem if the union and employer have a provision in their collective bargaining agreement that states a nonunion member coming into the bargaining unit must join the union within a certain amount of time.
- Charging discriminatory or very high dues or entrance fees for admittance into the union.

- Threatening, encouraging, or influencing employees to strike in an effort to pressure the employer to join an employer organization, to get the employer to recognize an uncertified union, or to stop doing business with an employer because of the employer not doing so.
- Influencing employers to discriminate against or otherwise treat differently employees who do not belong to the union or are denied union membership for some reason other than nonpayment of union dues or fees.

---

3. Refuse to bargain with an employer.

4. Engage in jurisdictional or secondary boycotts.

5. Charge excess or discriminatory initiation fees or dues.

6. Cause an employer to pay for goods or services that are not provided.

In an interesting case from 2014, the NLRB refused to find social media statements made to employees who worked during a strike to be violations of law. On the union's Facebook page, union members verbally and physically threatened employees who refused to participate in the strike. One union member even posted that he found out the addresses of the members who crossed the line, and another commented: "Can we bring Molotov Cocktails?" One of the employees filed an unfair labor practice charging the union was obligated to disavow such statements because they coerced or restrained employees in the exercise of their right to engage in concerted activity in crossing the picket line. The NLRB determined that the comments were not threats that violated the law and the union was not responsible for them because the members making them were not agents of the union.[39]

Before closed shops (where the employee must become a member of the union in order to obtain a job) were outlawed by the Taft–Hartley Act, states enacted right-to-work laws. (See Exhibit 15.11, "Right-to-Work States.") This was done in response to the use of closed shops by unions to control dissenters by severing their union membership, without which they could not work in a closed shop. The

right-to-work laws
Permits employees to choose not to become a part of the union.

NLRA permits states to have **right-to-work laws**, and as of 2017, 28 of them do. In a right-to-work state, employment cannot be conditioned on union membership. Despite some employees' nonparticipation in the union, and thus their not being required to pay union dues, the union must still represent these employees as a part of the bargaining unit. If a state is not a right-to-work state, the union and employer

union shop
Union and management agree that employees must be members of the union.

union shop clause
Provision in a collective bargaining agreement allowing a union shop.

may have as a part of their collective bargaining agreement union security device a provision for a **union shop**. This provision, called a **union shop clause**, requires the employer to have all members or potential members of the bargaining unit agree that they will join the union within a certain amount of time (not less than 30 days) after becoming employed.

The issues involved in states having right-to-work laws versus not having them arose recently in the state of Michigan, which, with 19.6 percent of its workforce belonging to a union, is the fourth largest union membership state in the country. It is also the birthplace and home of the United Auto Workers union. Though job losses have decreased UAW membership from 1.5 million in 1979 to about 390,000 now, the union has been so successful in Michigan that even white-collar workers admit that their salaries would not be as high and their benefits as good if it were not for the unions. Due to union negotiations, among other things, union members enjoy good wages, extra days off, and rights such as the auto manufacturers' job bank preserving hourly workers' jobs even if there is nothing for them to do (earning UAW the nickname "U Ain't Working"). At the same time, for the past several years, Michigan has been losing jobs (336,000 from 2000 to 2006 alone) to places like Mexico, with its lower wages. In June 2007, at 7.2 percent, Michigan's unemployment rate was the highest in the nation. In an effort to attract more business to the state, in 2007, Michigan Republican Rep. Jack Hoogendyk introduced a right-to-work bill for the state to change its closed shop

Exhibit 15.11 *Right-to-Work States*

According to the National Right To Work Committee, the following states and territories had right-to-work laws in effect as of May 29, 2017:

Alabama	8/28/1953	Missouri	2/24/1954
Arizona	11/5/1946	Missouri	2/6/2017 effec 8/28/2017
Arkansas	11/7/1944	Nebraska	12/11/1946
Florida	11/7/1944	Nevada	12/4/1952
Georgia	3/27/1947	N Carolina	3/18/1947
Guam	5/15/2000	N Dakota	6/28/1948
Idaho	1/31/1985	Oklahoma	9/2/2001
Indiana	2/1/2012	S Carolina	3/19/1954
Iowa	4/28/1947	S Dakota	7/1/1947
Kansas	11/4/1958	Tennessee	2/21/1947
Kentucky	1/7/2017	Texas	9/5/1947
Louisiana	7/9/1976	Utah	5/10/1955
Michigan	3/8/2013	Virginia	1/12/1947
Mississippi	2/24/1954	W Virginia	2/12/2016
		Wisconsin	3/9/2015
		Wyoming	2/8/1963

Source: http://www.nrtw.org/d/rtws.htm.

laws, which require that if there is a union in the workplace, employees must join, to an open shop where employees can decide for themselves if they wish to do so.

In the view of some, the closed shop law in Michigan makes Michigan less attractive to businesses contemplating moving there because it means that the work environment is not employer-friendly. On the other hand, unions say such laws lead to lower wages and benefits and, because Michigan is such a strong union state, dismissed the idea of such legislation, saying they would fight any such moves. Michigan passed the law in December 2012. The governor, who, during campaigning, said it was not a priority for him, shocked national observers by quickly signing the bill. In his mind, the law made Michigan more attractive to new industry and no longer automatically crossed it off the list when businesses sought a new home because of the state now permitting employees to choose whether to join a union. Since job creation was a priority for him, if the law would attract new business to the state, it made sense, he said in an interview in February 2014.[40]

Oklahoma had the same fight before it passed its law in 2001 becoming effective in 2003. Since Oklahoma's law became effective, the impact has been "minimal," according to researchers. Personal income grew 7.6 percent in 2006, the third highest in the United States, but according to the Department of Commerce, that was because of growth in the preexisting oil and gas industry. On the minus side, several manufacturing plants closed, including General Motors, Bridgestone Firestone, and Wrangler jeans, which moved to Mexico. Union membership went from 8 percent to 5.4 percent.

A study from the Fraser Institute, a leading Canadian think tank, found that since 2009, right-to-work states created four times as many jobs as other states. In Oklahoma, data suggests the faster manufacturing growth after passage was due in substantial degree to passing the law because businesses looking to invest and expand no longer dismissed the state as a possibility. Holding other factors steady, right-to-work states increase states' economic growth by about 1.8 percent versus 1 percent in states without such laws.[41] At the same time, an Economic Policy Institute analysis of Bureau of Labor Statistics data on the unemployment rate for Oklahoma with its right-to-work law and six other nearby states without it from 2001 to 2010 showed little difference in the unemployment rates (1.4 for Oklahoma versus 1.3 for surrounding states), indicating that the law did not necessarily create the jobs and improve the employment situation as it was touted to do.[42] It should be noted that a national right-to-work law was introduced in Congress in 2017 and since. Such laws have been introduced before, but with the present political climate weakening unions in several other ways, it is entirely possible that it could pass. If it does, the impact would be to weaken unions by decreasing the chance that they have the money needed to conduct their business. They will be pressed to represent even more employees who see no benefit in joining a union and paying dues when, by law, they must be represented as part of a bargaining unit anyway. The idea of being a "freeloader" who uses the union's resources and protection but does not pay their fair share would not be as socially unacceptable as it may once have been—except, of course, to other members of the bargaining unit who are dues-paying members of the union.

agency shop clause
Requires nonunion members to pay union dues without having to be subject to the union rules.

free riders
Bargaining unit employees who do not pay union dues but whom the union is still obligated to represent.

It is also permissible for the collective bargaining agreement to contain an **agency shop clause**, which requires nonunion members to pay to the union the usual union dues and fees without joining the union and thereby becoming subject to union rules. Some right-to-work laws do not allow this and, instead, permit nonunion employees of the bargaining unit to be **free riders**—that is, to receive union benefits without having to pay union dues or fees. In *National Football League Players Association v. Pro Football, Inc.,* the court addressed the issue of pro football players who did not want to pay union dues. The decision turned on whether the state law of the place where they played their games or the place where they held their practices would govern. Virginia, where they primarily practiced, is a right-to-work state, while Washington, DC, where they played their games, is not. The court held that their primary workplace was in Virginia, and since it is a right-to-work state, the players were not required to pay union dues.

A frequent bone of contention with union members is the use of union dues for activities with which the members do not agree. This is a particularly interesting question when it involves the agency shop since employees who do not want to belong to the union must still pay to the union an amount equal to the union dues (often called a *service fee*). This is, of course, to prevent the problem of free riders who benefit from union activity but do not contribute to the union's resources.

In 1991, the U.S. Supreme Court addressed the issue of what the union could use this money for. In *Lehnert v. Ferris Faculty Association,*[43] the court determined that unions could use nonmember service fees for political activities. It said that that "chargeable activities must (1) be 'germane' to collective-bargaining activity; (2) be justified by the government's vital policy interest in labor peace and avoiding 'free riders,' and (3) not significantly add to the burdening of free speech that is inherent in the allowance of an agency or union shop." It used these guidelines to decide if the specific programs being challenged were within these rules.

In 2007, the Court addressed the agency shop nonmember funds' use issue when a public employee union asserted that Washington state's law prohibiting labor unions from using the agency shop fees of nonmembers for election-related purposes unless the nonmember affirmatively consents was an unconstitutional burden on the union's First Amendment right to free speech. In *Davenport v. Washington Education Association,*[44] the union asserted that the law was unconstitutionally restrictive of free speech because it put the burden on the union to find out if the nonmember objected to the use of the funds for election-related purposes. The Court said that the public employee union being able to receive agency shop fees from government employees was much like the union being able to tax government employees for having a job. Under these circumstances, if the state of Washington wished to put the burden on the union to find out if the nonmembers wanted their funds used for election-related purposes, the Court did not think that was an unconstitutionally high price to pay.

In 2008, the U.S. Supreme Court further refined the issue decided in *Lehnert* and addressed whether service fees could be used for litigation activities far removed from the workplace, a question upon which the Court had not reached a consensus in *Lehnert*. In *Locke v. Karass,*[45] the Court allowed such a use by the union for national union affairs such as litigation.

One of the other powers in the Taft–Hartley Act rarely comes into play, but it is an important provision when needed. The act gives the president of the United States the authority to halt a strike or lockout if it would imperil national health or safety. Under the act, the president can seek an injunction that would require an 80-day "cooling-off period" for the parties during which, hopefully, they would reach an agreement. If the union rejects management's terms after the cooling-off period, then the union can strike.

In the fall of 2002, not long after the tragic events of September 11, 2001, the 10,500 West Coast dockworkers of the International Longshore and Warehouse Union (ILWU) threatened to strike over issues involving the introduction of labor-saving technology and the outsourcing of union jobs. The 29 ports from San Diego to Seattle handled about 50 percent of all ocean-borne cargo entering the United States. This was $300 billion in goods (about 7 percent of the gross domestic product). They did so at the rate of $1 billion per day, supporting about 1.4 million U.S. jobs and at least 45 retailing giants like Walmart, Home Depot, Target, and The Gap. These retailers represent over $1 trillion in annual sales and 100,000, manufacturing, distribution, and retail centers. Given the seriousness of the matter and the issues at stake, the retailers and ports lobbied President George W. Bush to avert a strike or slowdown. President Bush certainly thought the matter was serious. He promised to use any means necessary to make sure troops received what they needed. Options floated included using U.S. Navy personnel to run the ports, trying to break up the union's coastwide bargaining unit, or introducing legislation that would restrict the union's ability to call a strike.

Management instituted a lockout after deciding the workers had engaged in a work slowdown. After eight days of the lockout, President Bush declared a national emergency, asserting the strike's potentially crippling effect on the national economy. On October 8, the U.S. Department of Justice took the case to a federal court in San Francisco to halt the lockout and requested a temporary restraining order under the Taft–Hartley Act. On behalf of President Bush they argued that the order was necessary to protect the economy because some businesses were reportedly running low on inventories and supplies and the strike was also jeopardizing the war on terrorism. Defense Secretary Donald Rumsfeld gave a sworn statement that the port dispute threatened to "degrade military readiness, hinder the department's ability to prosecute the global war on terrorism, and undercut other defense needs and worldwide commitments." The judge granted the restraining order and called an immediate halt to the lockout, ordering the West Coast ports to reopen immediately. More than 200 ships waited in the waters outside the ports, with an estimated unloading time of eight to nine weeks. On November 1, 2002, the union and management announced an agreement regarding the central technology issue.

The Landrum–Griffin Act of 1959

Also known as the Labor Management Reporting and Disclosure Act, this legislation was enacted in response to congressional investigations into union corruption from 1957 to 1959. After finding evidence of such corruption, Congress passed the legislation. Based on the investigative findings, the purpose of the law

Exhibit 15.12   *Union Members' Bill of Rights*

Among other things, the Landrum–Griffin Act provides that

- Union members have the right to attend union meetings, vote on union business, and nominate candidates for union elections.
- Members may bring an agency or court action against the union after exhausting union procedures.

- Certain procedures must be followed before any dues or initiation fee increases.
- Except for the failure to pay dues, members must have a full and fair hearing when being disciplined by the union.

LO7 Define the Landrum–Griffin Act of 1959 (Labor Management Reporting and Disclosure Act) and its provisions.

is to establish basic ways of unions operating to ensure a democratic process, to provide union members with a minimum bill of rights attached to union membership, and to regulate the activities of union officials and the use of union funds. (See Exhibit 15.12, "Union Members' Bill of Rights.")

The act provides a bill of rights for union members. Looking at some of the provisions of the bill of rights, one might think that they are so simplistic as to be taken as givens for an organization. However, keep in mind that the bill of rights was enacted in response to union abuses actually found during the two-year congressional investigation.

The Landrum-Griffin Act also set forth specific procedures to be followed when unions hold elections, including voting for officers by secret ballot, holding elections at least every three years (other times for different levels of the union, such as international officers), candidates being able to see lists of eligible voters, and procedures for having an election declared improper. Provisions also were enacted to safeguard union funds. Under the act, unions cannot use union funds for anything except benefiting the union or its members. Funds cannot be used to support union office candidates, and union officials, agents, employees, and so on, cannot acquire financial interests that conflict with the union's. The law made stealing or embezzling union funds a federal crime.

Labor Relations in the Public Sector

LO8 Discuss collective bargaining in the public sector and how it differs from the private sector.

Much of what has been discussed relates to the private sector. Of more recent vintage is the matter of collective bargaining in the public sector.

Federal Employees

Historically, there has been little legislation affecting the labor relations of public employees (federal, state, and local government employees). The NLRA has always exempted these employees. There was no uniform federal policy on public labor-management relations. Currently, however, over half of the 50 states and the District of Columbia have collective bargaining statutes covering most, if not all, public employees.

Over time, federal employees formed associations, but only postal workers were not powerless to influence their workplace. In 1962, President Kennedy established the right of federal employees to form and join unions. Since that time, union ranks have increased in the public sector.

Federal restrictions prevent federal unions from conducting direct bargaining over wages and benefits and from striking. The Civil Service Reform Act of 1978 established the Federal Labor Relations Authority (FLRA) to administer federal sector labor law. This agency may be thought of as the federal counterpart to the private sector's National Labor Relations Board (NLRB).

State, County, and Municipal Public Employees

Collective bargaining in the public sector is an important aspect of labor law. One of the most heavily unionized sectors of public employment is that of teachers, police officers, and firefighters, who are generally state, county, or municipal employees. Most public employee organizations at the state, county, and municipal levels can be divided into three major categories: professional associations, craft unions, and industrial-type unions. *Professional associations* are composed of a wide variety of professionals. The largest professional employee organization is the National Education Association (NEA). This organization of school teachers has over 3 million members from kindergarten to college and, in addition to teachers, consists of principals, administrators, and other school specialists. The Fraternal Order of Police does not consider itself a union, but many local lodges engage in collective bargaining, handle grievances, and represent the interests of their members to their employers.

Craft unions consist of such groups as the International Association of Firefighters (IAFF), which is an affiliate of the AFL-CIO. Another teachers union that considers itself to be a craft union is the American Federation of Teachers (AFT), which limits its membership to classroom teachers only. While craft unions are too numerous to list, many of them are familiar and have been in existence for nearly a century, such as the United Mine Workers and International Brotherhood of Electrical Workers.

The union that typifies the *industrial-type union* is the American Federation of State, County, and Municipal Employees (AFSCME), an affiliate of the AFL-CIO. These local unions may represent an entire city or county, or they may represent a smaller unit of government, such as a department or a group of employees that cuts across many departments.

The AFL-CIO assists public workers' unions that affiliate with it through its Public Employees Department. This department, formed in 1974, has 33 affiliated unions that represent millions of federal, state, and local government employees. These unions represent workers in schools, courts, regulatory agencies, hospitals, transportation networks, police, and fire departments. The AFL-CIO believes that state and local employees are the only workers in the United States who do not enjoy the basic right to enter into collective bargaining agreements with their employers. That is, there is no national legislation that gives these workers the right to enter into collective bargaining agreements. If they have the right, it is because the state in which they operate has enacted state legislation that permits it.

To many, the most important difference between public and private collective bargaining is that federal legislation and most state statutes do not contain the right of public employees to strike. This prohibition is grounded in the need to protect public health and safety (i.e., to prevent police officers or firefighters from

Management Tips

Dealing with unions can be an uncomfortable situation for an employer. The very idea is antithetical to many business owners who feel the business is theirs, and since they are taking all the risks and putting up all the money, they should have full control. Giving over any control to employees through the unions and the collective bargaining process is not easy for them. Like it or not, however, collective bargaining is the law. Following the tips below can help avoid problems resulting in liability for violating labor laws:

- If employees decide they wish to unionize, do not try to negatively influence the decision in impermissible ways.
- Do not assume any employee you speak to for the purpose of persuading him or her not to unionize will keep the conversation confidential.
- Know the kinds of things the employer can legally do to influence the unionizing decision, and do only those things that are permissible.
- Once the union is in place, conduct all negotiations only with the union representatives. Avoid making side deals with individual employees.
- Treat the collective bargaining process as you would any business activity. Do not invite unfair labor practice charges by engaging in activity that could be deemed a refusal to bargain in good faith.
- Know what the law requires—the employer need not do any more than the law requires in permitting the union to conduct its business. Know well what the employer can and need not do.
- Keep the lines of communication open between labor and management.
- Try to keep the "us versus them" mentality from having a negative impact on the collective bargaining process. It can be difficult to avoid, but if you can, it helps negotiations stay on an even keel without letting egos get in the way.
- Play hardball without setting management up for an unfair labor practice charge.

being out on strike while crime rises or buildings burn) as well as the sovereignty doctrine deeming striking against a governmental employer as inconsistent with the government being the sovereign or highest authority.

State and federal employees have not always honored the prohibition on striking. While many ignored the prohibition, probably the most famous example occurred when the federal air traffic controllers, represented by the Professional Air Traffic Controllers Organization (PATCO), went on strike in 1981. One of the reasons the strike was so memorable was undoubtedly because newly elected President Ronald Reagan took a hard line and terminated 11,000 striking employees. The air traffic controllers were sued for their action in *United States v. Professional Air Traffic Controllers Organization.*[46]

There are also differences between the private and public sector about what may be negotiated. While the U.S. postal workers may do so, generally federal employees cannot bargain over wages, hours, or benefits. On the other hand, they can bargain about the numbers, types, and grades of positions; procedures for performing work or exercising authority; the use of technology; and alternatives for employees harmed by management decisions.

Chapter Summary

- The four main labor law statutes form a framework within which employers and employees may address workplace issues with some modicum of predictability.
- Laws paved the way for unionism by preventing courts from prohibiting union activity. They also provided a statutory basis, with the Wagner or National Labor Relations Act, and they fine-tuned and addressed union abuses, with the Taft–Hartley Act and the Landrum–Griffin or Labor Management Recording and Disclosure Act.
- Private employers and employees are free to negotiate upon mandatory as well as permissive terms of bargaining to determine matters of wages, hours, and other terms and conditions of employment.

Chapter-End Questions

1. After a bitter strike and boycott that included strike-related violence and the use of "scabs" to replace workers in the walnut industry, a returning worker who had been a quality control supervisor prior to the strike was placed in a seasonal packing position, a job with less status, because the employer was afraid that the replacement workers, some of whom were still on the job, would try to instigate violence against the returning workers. The workers claimed that the employer refused to place them in their prior positions as retaliation for striking. After a strike, does the employer have an obligation to place striking workers back in their prestrike position if there might be violence aimed at them? [*Diamond Walnut Growers Inc. v. NLRB*, 113 F.3d 1259 (DC Cir. 1997).]

2. Bloom was hired to perform clerical work for Group Health Incorporated Office and Professional Employees International Union Local 12. Group Health had negotiated a collective bargaining agreement that contained a union security clause that stated employees must be "members in good standing," which Bloom interpreted as requiring that he pay union dues. Upon filing a grievance with the NLRB, what is the likely outcome? [*Bloom v. NLRB*, 30 F.3d 1001 (8th Cir. 1994).]

3. C. Tyler Williams Co. set up a committee called the Employee-Owners' Influence Council (EOIC). All employees were encouraged to become members. Of 150 employees who applied, 30 of Tyler Williams' 8,000 employees were selected by the company. They discussed such issues as medical insurance benefits, the Employee Stock Ownership Plan, and family and medical leave. Is this organization in violation of the NLRA? [*Polaroid v. NLRB*, 329 NLRB No. 47 (Oct. 6, 1999).]

4. In its employee handbook, an employer stated that it would do "*everything possible* to maintain the company's union-free status for the benefit of both our employees and [the Company]." Is this an unfair labor practice under the NLRB? [*Aluminum Casting & Engineering Co. v. NLRB*, 328 NLRB No. 2 (Apr. 9, 1999).]

5. A truck driver who refused to drive a truck because he "smelled fumes" informed his co-worker of this fact. When the employee was disciplined for refusing to take the truck, he alleged that he was engaged in "concerted activity." What basis does he have for alleging this? [*NLRB v. PALCO*, 163 F.3d 662 (1st Cir. 1998).]

6. An employer was hiring employees after a strike. On employment applications, the employer asked potential employees whether they belonged to a union. Was the employer engaged in an unfair labor practice? [*Mathews Readymix, Inc. v. NLRB*, 165 F.3d 74 (DC. Cir. 1999).]

7. The employer engaged in the practice of photographing an employee engaged in picket-line activity. Is this illegal surveillance, even though the activity was "open and obvious," no action was taken against the employee, and the employer was preparing a defense regarding potential illegal secondary activity? [*Clock Electric, Inc. v. NLRB,* 162 F.3d 907 (6th Cir. 1998).]

8. What are the most important differences between public- and private-sector collective bargaining?

9. During contract negotiations, employer and union exchange information on the union's proposal for pay raises. The employer rejects the proposal. The employer is adamant and refuses to agree to the raises. The union alleges that this is an unfair labor practice in that the employer is not bargaining in good faith. Is it?

10. The union strikes the employer in an effort to receive higher wages. The employer brings in workers to replace the striking employees. Agreement is finally reached between the employer and employees. Must the employer dismiss the replacement workers?

End Notes

1. "20 major work stoppages in 2018 involving 485,000 workers," Bureau of Labor Statistics, February 2, 2019, https://www.bls.gov/opub/ted/2019/20-major-work-stoppages-in-2018-involving-485000-workers.htm.

   "Strikes are 257% up in 2 years, even though labor union membership is down–why more workers are taking a stand," Market Watch, Andrew Keshner, February 13, 2020, https://www.marketwatch.com/story/strikes-are-up-but-union-membership-is-down-and-that-could-be-a-good-sign-for-the-economy-2020-02-13.

2. "A record number of US workers went on strike in 2018," Vox, Alexia Fernández Campbell, 2/13/2019, https://www.vox.com/platform/amp/policy-and-politics/2019/2/13/18223211/worker-teacher-strikes-2018-record.

3. "Strikes are 257% up in 2 years, even though labor union membership is down–why more workers are taking a stand," Market Watch, Andrew Keshner, February 13, 2020, https://www.marketwatch.com/story/strikes-are-up-but-union-membership-is-down-and-that-could-be-a-good-sign-for-the-economy-2020-02-13.

4. Ibid.

5. Ibid.

6. "Year of the Strike," *The National Review,* Frederick M. Hess, 10/11/2018, https://www.nationalreview.com/magazine/2018/10/29/year-of-the-strike/.

7. Medina, Jennifer, and Dana Goldstein, "Los Angeles Teacher's Strike to End as Deal Reached," *The New York Times* (January 22, 2019), https://www.nytimes.com/2019/01/22/us/la-teacher-strike-deal.html.

8. Hauck, Grace, "Chicago School Strike Is for Aides Living Off Less Than $36,000 per Year, Union Members Say," *USA Today* (October 18, 2019), https://www.usatoday.com/story/news/education/2019/10/18/cps-strike-chicago-public-schools-closed-teacher-aides-union-seiu/3997887002/.

9. Campbell, Alexis Fernández, "Marriott Workers Just Ended the Largest Hotel Strike in US History," *Vox* (December 4, 2018), https://www.vox.com/policy-and-politics/2018/12/4/18125505/marriott-workers-end-strike-wage-raise.

10. "Here's the Road Ahead for College Athletes After Union Setback," *Time* magazine, Sean Gregory, 8/18/2015. https://time.com/4002245/after-union-setback-heres-the-road-ahead-for-college-athletes/

11. "Fast-Food Workers Strike Nationwide in Protest against Wages," Fox News (August 29, 2013), http://www.foxnews.com/us/2013/08/29/fast-food-workers-to-strike-nationwide-over-wages/.

12. Torres, Jeanette, "Hostess Maker Will Close after Strike," ABC News (November 16, 2012), http://abcnews.go.com/Business/twinkies-maker-hostess-liquidate-company-strike/story?id=17736898.

13. "Twinkie's Make Early Return at WalMart Stores," *USA Today* (July12, 2013), http://www.usatoday.com/story/money/business/2013/07/12/twinkies-make-early-return-walmart/2511927/.

14. "Boeing's Machinists Union OKs Benefit Cuts to Keep 777X," WITN-NBC (January 4, 2014), http://www.witn.com/home/headlines/Boeings-Machinists-Union-OKs-Benefit-Cuts-To-Keep-777X-238703321.html.

15. "March on Mississippi: Danny Glover, Bernie Sanders Are Taking on Nissan," NBC News, Tory N. Parrish, 3/14/2017.

16. Kell, John, "Harley-Davidson Wraps Up Labor Negotiations," *The Wall Street Journal* (February 28, 2011), http://online.wsj.com/article/SB10001424052748704615504576172851667284040.html.

17. Dokoupil, Tony, "When Nurses Strike in New York," *Newsweek* (May 3, 2010), p. 8.

18. McGeehan, Patrick, "Deal Reached That Averts a Walkout by Doormen," *The New York Times* (April 21, 2010), http://community.nytimes.com/comments/www.nytimes.com/2010/04/21/nyregion/21strike.html; Sulzberger, A. G., "New Yorkers Brace for Doorman Strike," *The New York Times* (April 18, 2010), http://www.nytimes.com/2010/04/19/nyregion/19strike.html.

19. Beck, Howard, and Liz Robbins, "Pro Basketball; NBA and Players Union Agree to a Six-Year Deal," *The New York Times* (June 22, 2005), http://query.nytimes.com/gst/fullpage.html?res=9401EED9103EF931A15755C0A9639C8B63.

20. "Lockout over Salary Caps Shuts Down NHL," ESPN NHL (February 16, 2005), http://sports.espn.go.com/nhl/news/story?id=1992793.

21. Baldas, Tresa, "Lawyers Unionize, Vote to Join the Teamsters," *The National Law Journal* (April 8, 2003), http://www.judicialaccountability.org/articles/lawyersunionize.htm.

22. *In re Debs,* 158 U.S. 564 (1895).

23. 245 U.S. 229 (1917).

24. *Loewe v. Lawlor* (a.k.a. the *Danbury Hatters* case), 208 U.S. 274 (1908).

25. 130 S. Ct. 2635 (2010).

26. http://www.jonesday.com/new_process_steel/.

27. 348 NLRB No. 37; Case 7-RC-22141 (September 29, 2006).

28. H.R. 1622/S. 969 (110th Cong.).

29. Douglas-Gabriel, Danielle, "Harvard Graduate Students Strike after Year-Long Contract Negotiations with the University," *The Washington Post* (December 30, 2019), https://www.washingtonpost.com/education/2019/12/03/harvard-graduate-students-strike-after-year-long-contract-negotiations-with-university/.

30. Johnson, Katie, "Harvard Graduate Students Call Off Strike," *The Boston Globe* (December30, 2019), https://www.bostonglobe.com/metro/2019/12/30/harvard-grad-students-call-off-strike/uemx6YCHygDA06fuTvW70J/story.html.

31. *Department of Health and Human Services v. Federal Labor Relations Authority,* 920 F.2d 45 (DC. Cir 1990).

32. Kaplan, Daniel, "NFL Labor Negotiations: The Issues," *Sports Business Journal* (April 25, 2011), http://aol.sportingnews.com/nfl/feed/2010-09/nfl-labor-talks/story/nfl-labor-negotiations-the-issues:http://sports.espn.go.com/nfl/news/story?id=6205936.

33. 499 U.S. 65 (1991).

34. Fendrich, Howard, "NFLPA Decertifies as Talks Break Down," CBS Boston (March 11, 2011), http://boston.cbslocal.com/2011/03/11/report-nflpa-plans-to-decertify/.

35. Battista, Judy, "Judge Grants Injunction to End N.F.L. Lockout Pending Appeal," *The New York Times* (April 25, 2011), http://www.nytimes.com/2011/04/26/sports/football/26nfl.html?_r=1&emc=na.

36. 2 F.3d 1162 (D.C.Cir. 1993).

37. "Lockout over Salary Cap Shuts Down NHL," Associated Press, ESPN-NHL (February 16, 2005), http://sports.espn.go.com/nhl/news/story?id=1992793; "NHL Lockout Chronology," *USA Today*(July 13, 2005), http://www.usatoday.com/sports/hockey/nhl/2005-07-13-lockout-chronology_x.htm.

38. 829 F.2d 458 (3rd Cir. 1987).

39. Amalgamated Transit Union, Local Union No. 1433, AFL-CIO and Charles Weigand, No. 28-CB-078377 (February 12, 2014).

40. Woods, Ashley, "Rick Snyder Claims Michigan Is 'Absolutely' Better with Right-to-Work," *The Huffington Post* (February 8, 2014), http://www.huffingtonpost.com/2014/02/08/rick-snyder-right-to-work_n_4751896.html.

41. Keating, Frank, and Brandon Dutcher, "Right-to Work Laws Help States Like Oklahoma Shine," *Forbes* (October 8, 2013), http://www.forbes.com/sites/realspin/2013/10/08/right-to-work-laws-help-states-like-oklahoma-shine/.

42. "Right-to-Work Law Did Not Help Oklahoma's Labor Market," Economic Policy Institute (March 3, 2011), http://www.epi.org/publication/right-to-work_law_did_not_help_oklahomas_labor_market/.

43. 500 U.S. 501 (1991).

44. 127 S. Ct. 2372 (2007).

45. 129 S. Ct. 798 (2008).

46. 653 F.2d 1134 (7th Cir. 1981).

47. Following the Court's enforcement of the Board's Orders in December 2006, the Board's Regional Office advised the Respondent of its remedial obligations, including the obligation to meet and bargain with the Union. Thereafter, and continuing through March 2008, the Union repeatedly requested bargaining with the Respondent pursuant to the terms of the court-enforced Order, sending five letters to the Respondent requesting that it provide dates to meet and bargain. The Union also requested the Respondent to furnish it with the requested information required under the terms of the Board's Order. The Respondent did not respond to any of these requests.

Cases

Commonwealth v. Hunt 45 Mass.,
(4 Metc.) 111 (Mass. 1842)

A lower court found a group of seven shoemakers who belonged to a union guilty of conspiracy because they refused to work for an employer who hired a shoemaker who was not a member of their union. The Supreme Judicial Court of Massachusetts, in reversing the convictions, found not only that it was not an unlawful activity to unionize but that the object of unions may be "highly meritorious and public spirited."

Shaw, J.

***

Without attempting to review and reconcile all the cases, we are of the opinion, that as a general description, though perhaps not a precise and accurate definition, a conspiracy must be a combination of two or more persons, by some concerted action, to accomplish some criminal or unlawful purpose, or to accomplish some purpose, not in and of itself criminal or unlawful, by criminal or unlawful means. We use the terms criminal or unlawful, because it is manifest that many acts are unlawful, which are not punishable by indictment or other public prosecution; and yet there is no doubt, we think, that a combination by numbers to do them would be an unlawful conspiracy, and punishable by indictment.

Several rules upon the subject seem to be well established, to wit, that the unlawful agreement constitutes the gist of the offence, and therefore that it is not necessary to charge the execution of the unlawful agreement.

Another rule is a necessary consequence of the former, which is, that the crime is consummate and complete by the fact of unlawful combination, and, therefore, that if the execution of the unlawful purpose is averred, it is by way of aggravation, and proof of it is not necessary to conviction; and therefore the jury may find the conspiracy, and negative the execution, and it will be a good conviction.

And it follows, as another necessary legal consequence, from the same principle, that the indictment must—by averring the unlawful purpose of the conspiracy, or the unlawful means by which it is contemplated and agreed to accomplish a lawful purpose—set out an offense complete in itself; and that an illegal combination, imperfectly and insufficiently set out in the indictment, will not be aided by averments of acts done in pursuance of it.

From this view of the law respecting conspiracy, we think it an offence which especially demands the application of that wise and humane rule of the common law, that an indictment shall state, with as much certainty as the nature of the case will admit, the facts which constitute the crime intended to be charged. This is required, to enable the defendant to meet the charge and prepare for his defence, and, in case of acquittal or conviction, to show by the record the identity of the charge, so that he may not be indicted a second time for the same offence. It is also necessary, in order that a person, charged by the grand jury for one offence, may not be substantially convicted, on his trial, of another.

From these views of the rules of criminal pleading, it appears to us to follow, as a necessary legal conclusion, that when the criminality of a conspiracy consists in an unlawful agreement of two or more persons to compass or promote some criminal or illegal purpose, that purpose must be fully and clearly stated in the indictment; and if the criminality of the offence, which is intended to be charged, consists in the agreement to compass or promote some purpose, not of itself criminal or unlawful, by the use of fraud, force, falsehood, or other criminal or unlawful means, such intended use of fraud, force, falsehood, or other criminal or unlawful means, must be set out in the indictment.

We are here carefully to distinguish between the confederacy set forth in the indictment, and the confederacy or association contained in the constitution of the Boston Journeymen and Bootmakers' Society, as stated in the little printed book, which was admitted as evidence on the trial. Because, though it was thus admitted as evidence, it would not warrant a conviction for anything not stated in the indictment. It was proof, as far as it went to support the averments in the indictment. If it contained any criminal matter not set forth in the indictment, it is of no avail.

Now, it is to be considered, that the preamble and introductory matter in the indictment—such as unlawfully and deceitfully designing and intending unjustly to extort great sums, etc.—is mere recital, and not traversable, and therefore cannot aid an imperfect averment of the facts constituting the description of the offence. The same may be said of the concluding matter, which follows the averment, as to the great damage and oppression not only of their said masters, employing them in said art and occupation, but also of divers other workmen in the same art, mystery and occupation, to the evil example, &c. If the facts averred constitute the crime, these are properly stated as the legal inferences to be drawn from them. If they do not constitute the charge of such an offence, they cannot be aided by these alleged consequences.

Stripped then of these introductory recitals and alleged injurious consequences, and of the qualifying epithets attached to the facts, the averment is this: that the defendants and others formed themselves into a society, and agreed not to work for any person, who should employ any journeyman or other person, not a member of such society, after notice given to discharge such workman.

The manifest intent of the association is to induce all those engaged in the same occupation to become members of it. Such a purpose is not unlawful. It would give them a power which might be exerted for useful and honorable purposes, or for dangerous and pernicious ones. If the latter were the real and actual object, and susceptible of proof, it should have been specially charged. Such an association might be used to afford each other assistance in times of poverty, sickness and distress; or to raise their intellectual, moral, and social condition; or to make improvement in their art; or for other proper purposes. Or the association might be designed for purposes of oppression and injustice. But in order to charge all those, who become members of an association, with the guilt of a criminal conspiracy, it must be averred and proved that the actual, if not the avowed object of the association, was criminal. An association may be formed, the declared objects of which are innocent and laudable, and yet they may have secret articles, or an agreement communicated only to the members, by which they are banded together for purposes injurious to the peace of society or the rights of its members. Such would undoubtedly be a criminal conspiracy, on proof of the fact, however meritorious

and praiseworthy the declared objects might be. The law is not to be hoodwinked by colorable pretenses. It looks at truth and reality, through whatever disguise it may assume. But to make such an association, ostensibly innocent, the subject of prosecution as a criminal conspiracy, the secret agreement, which makes it so, is to be averred and proved as the gist of the offence. But when an association is formed for purposes actually innocent, and afterwards its powers are abused by those who have the control and management of it, to purposes of oppression and injustice it will be criminal in those who thus misuse it, or give consent thereto, but not in the other members of the association.

Nor can we perceive that the objects of this association, whatever they may have been, were to be attained by criminal means. The means which they proposed to employ, as averred in this count, and which, as we are now to presume, were established by the proof, were, that they would not work for a person, who, after due notice, should employ a journeyman not a member of their society. Supposing the object of the association to be laudable and lawful, or at least not unlawful, are these means criminal? The case supposes that these persons are not bound by contract, but free to work for whom they please, or not to work, if they so prefer. On this state of things, we cannot perceive, that it is criminal for men to agree together to exercise their own acknowledged rights, in such a manner as best to subserve their own interests.

Suppose a baker in a small village had the exclusive custom of his neighborhood, and was making large profits by the sale of his bread. Supposing a number of those neighbors, believing the price of his bread too high, should propose to him to reduce his prices, or if he did not, that they would introduce another baker; and on his refusal, such other baker should, under their encouragement, set up a rival establishment, and sell his bread at lower prices; the effect would be to diminish the profit of the former baker, and to the same extent to impoverish him. And it might be said and proved, that the purpose of the associates was to diminish his profits, and thus impoverish him, though the ultimate and laudable object of the combination was to reduce the cost of bread to themselves and their neighbors. The same thing may be said of all competition in every branch of trade and industry; and yet it is through that competition, that the best interests of trade and industry are promoted. It is scarcely necessary to allude to the familiar instances of opposition lines of conveyance, rival hotels, and the thousand other instances, where each strives to gain custom to himself, by which he may lessen the price of commodities, and thereby diminish the profits of others.

We think, therefore, that associations may be entered into, the object of which is to adopt measures that may have a tendency to impoverish another, that is, to diminish his gains and profits, and yet so far from being criminal or unlawful, the object may be highly meritorious and public spirited. The legality of such an association will therefore depend upon the means to be used for its accomplishment. If it is to be carried into effect by fair or honorable and lawful means, it is, to say the least, innocent; if by falsehood or force, it may be stamped out with the character of conspiracy. REVERSED.

Case Questions

1. Why do you think it was necessary to dissolve the relationship between criminal conspiracy and the labor movement? What was the relationship given by the court between criminal acts and employees' rights to control their environment at work?

2. Why do you think the court found that there was some good in organizing to affect the employer's policies? Explain.

3. Do you agree with the court's analysis in this case? Explain.

Case 2

Gimrock Construction, Inc., and International Union of Operating Engineers, Local 487,

356 NLRB No. 83 (January 28, 2011)

After repeatedly rejecting the union's request to engage in negotiations to create its first collective bargaining agreement, the board ordered the employer to engage in collective bargaining. The employer again refused, and the board eventually issued this order for the employer to engage in very specific activity in order to bargain collectively in good faith.

By Chairman Liebman and Members Pearce and Hayes

***

For context, pursuant to a Stipulated Election Agreement, the International Union of Operating Engineers, Local 487, AFL-CIO (the Union) won an election on March 3, 1995, and was certified on March 20, 1995, as the bargaining representative of Respondent's equipment operators, oiler/drivers, and equipment mechanics employed in Miami-Dade and Monroe counties, Florida (the two counties). The Respondent's bargaining obligation arose from the Board's June 30, 2005 decision, finding that the Respondent violated Section 8(a)(5) and (1) of the Act by refusing—since October 27, 1999—to meet and bargain with the Union and provide it with requested relevant information. The board's order was enforced by the 11th Circuit on December 27, 2006. As explained in the judge's decision, the Respondent thereafter failed to respond to numerous requests to meet and bargain with the Union and to furnish it with the requested information.

In view of the Respondent's continuing refusal—over a period of years—to comply with the Board's bargaining

order, the institution of a bargaining schedule and the submission of progress reports are necessary to ensure that (and gauge whether) the Respondent meaningfully complies with its bargaining obligations as set forth under the terms of the court-enforced Order. Because the General Counsel specifically sought these requirements in the compliance specification, we reject the Respondent's argument that it was denied due process.[47]

Further, as of September 2007, the Respondent had not posted the required notices to employees, and its failure to post was one of the subjects of a proceeding in the United States District Court for the Southern District of Florida, wherein the Board sought to enforce certain investigative subpoenas requiring the Respondent to (a) demonstrate that it had posted the required notices, and (b) furnish requested information necessary to calculate the amount of back pay due under the terms of the Order in 344 NLRB 1033 (2005). By Order dated September 13, 2007, the District Court directed the Respondent to comply with the investigative subpoenas, and thereafter the Respondent posted the notices and provided certain payroll records to the Board's Regional Office.

Order

The National Labor Relations Board adopts the recommended Supplemental Order of the administrative law judge and orders that the Respondent, Gimrock Construction, Inc., Hialeah Gardens, Florida, its officers, agents, successors, and assigns, shall take the action set forth in the Order, including the payment to backpay claimants of the amounts set forth below, plus interest accrued to the date of payment minus tax and withholdings by Federal and State laws.

Murray R. Chinners $74,583.12

Alfred K. Duey $125,057.47

Joseph G. MacNeil $10,367.77

Joseph T. Robinson $580.83

Barney Sims $92,243.40

James K. Wilkerson $37,208.66

James L. Wolf $14,311.31

TOTAL $354,352.56

IT IS HEREBY ORDERED that Respondent Gimrock Construction, within 21 days of the Board's issuance of its Supplemental Decision in this matter, bargain upon request with the Union; meet and bargain for a minimum of 16 hours per week until an agreement is reached, the parties agree to a hiatus in bargaining, or they reach a lawful impasse; and prepare written bargaining progress reports every 30 days, submitting them to the Regional Director and serving copies on the Union to provide it with an opportunity to reply. The Administrative Law Judge's order is AFFIRMED.

Case Questions

1. Do you think the court made the right decision in this case?

2. Given that there is a statutory duty to bargain in good faith, why do you think management chose to do what it did?

3. Given how strict the final order to bargain was on the employer, does the employer's strategy make sense to you?

Columbia Portland Cement Co. v. National Labor Relations Board, *979 F.2d 460 (6th Cir. 1992)*

The employer engaged in unfair labor practices that eventually led employees to engage in an unfair labor practice strike. After the union gave an unconditional request for reinstatement to the employer, the employer refused to reinstate them and also unilaterally gave a wage increase without consulting the union. The court found both to be unfair labor practices by the employer.

Contie, J.

***

Petitioner, Columbia Portland Cement Company (the "Company"), operates a limestone shale quarry and cement production facility in Zanesville, Ohio. Since at least September 1, 1984, Local Lodge D24 of the Cement, Lime, Gypsum & Allied Workers Division of the International Brotherhood of Boilermakers, Iron Shipbuilders, Blacksmiths, Forgers and Helpers, AFL-CIO (the "Union"), has represented the Company's employees. The most recent

collective-bargaining contract between the Union and the Company's predecessor expired on May 1, 1984, but the predecessor company and the Union agreed to extend that contract during negotiations for a new contract.

The Company purchased the facility from the predecessor on August 28, 1984. The Company notified the Union on August 29, 1984, that it intended to terminate the extended contract and desired to negotiate a new one.

The parties failed to reach agreement on a new contract, however, and on October 28, 1984, the Company unilaterally implemented the last offer it had made. On May 8, 1985, the employees went out on strike.

By letter dated April 29, 1987, the Union made an offer to return to work on behalf of the striking employees. The letter stated that the employees "unconditionally offer to return to work immediately." In response, the Company sent a letter dated May 7, 1987, informing the Union that, "with regard to [the] unconditional offer to return to work," the Company would not reinstate the striking employees. The Company contended that some of the employees had been lawfully terminated, and that the remainder were permanently replaced economic strikers who would be kept on a list for future vacancies.

On April 20, 1988, the Company offered reinstatement, without back pay, to 62 of the striking employees; 33 eventually returned to work.

"A strike which is caused in whole or in part by an employer's unfair labor practices *is* an unfair labor practice strike." Employees who go out on strike in response to an employer's unfair labor practices may not be permanently replaced by other employees. Unfair labor practice strikers are entitled to immediate reinstatement by the employer upon their unconditional offer to return to work. Refusing to reinstate striking employees after their unconditional offer to return to work violates section 8(a)(3) and (1) of the Act.

The Company granted employees a wage increase of 20 cents per hour; replaced the retirement plan with a 401(k) plan; and changed the grievance procedure to bypass the union and deal directly with the grievant. These actions all violate the employer's duty to bargain with the employees' exclusive bargaining agent in contravention of section 8(a)(5) and (1). Accordingly, the Board's decision must be AFFIRMED.

Case Questions

1. Why do you think the employer refused to rehire the strikers after they gave an unconditional promise to return?

2. Do you think it is fair that employees striking because of an unfair labor practice are entitled to reinstatement? Explain.

3. Do you think the new owner of the business took this hard line in dealing with the union in order to try to initially establish its dominance over the union? Explain.

Electromation v. National Labor Relations Board,
35 F.3d 1148 (7th Cir. 1993)

A nonunion company negotiated with its workers to resolve labor issues through employee participation or employee–management focus groups rather than a union. The court held that these committees constituted labor organizations and were dominated by the employer, thus constituting an unfair labor practice.

Will, J.

***

At the time of the events which gave rise to this suit, Electromation's approximately 200 employees, most of whom were women, were not represented by any labor organization. To minimize the financial losses it was experiencing at the time, the company in late 1988 decided to cut expenses by revising its employee attendance policy and replacing the 1989 scheduled wage increases with lump sum payments based on the length of each employee's service at the company.

In January 1989, the company received a handwritten request signed by 68 employees expressing their dissatisfaction with and requesting reconsideration of the revised attendance bonus/wage policy. After meeting with the company's supervisors, the company President, John Howard, decided to meet directly with employees to discuss their concerns. Accordingly, on January 11, 1989, the company met with eight employees—three randomly selected high-seniority employees, three randomly selected low-seniority employees, and two additional employees who had requested that they be included—to discuss a number of matters, including wages, bonuses, incentive pay, tardiness, attendance programs, and bereavement and sick leave policy, all normal collective bargaining issues.

Following this meeting, Howard met again with the supervisors and concluded that management had "possibly made a mistake in judgment in December in deciding what we ought to do" . . . [and] "that the better course of action would be to involve the employees in coming up with solutions to these issues." The company determined that "action committees" would be an appropriate way to involve employees in the process. Accordingly, on January 18, 1989, the company met again with the same eight employees and proposed the creation of action committees to "meet and try to come up with ways to resolve these problems; and that if they came up with solutions that we believed were within budget concerns and they generally felt would be acceptable to the employees, that we would implement these suggestions or proposals." At the employees' suggestion, Howard agreed that, rather than having a random selection of employee committee members, sign-up sheets for each action committee would be posted.

On the next day, the company posted a memorandum to all employees announcing the formation of the following five action committees: (1) Absenteeism/Infractions; (2) No Smoking Policy; (3) Communication Network; (4) Pay Progression for Premium Positions; and (5) Attendance Bonus Program. Sign-up sheets were also posted at this time.

On February 13, 1989, the International Brotherhood of Teamsters, Local Union No. 1049 (the "union") demanded recognition from the company. Until then, the company was unaware that any organizing efforts had occurred at the plant. In late February, Howard informed Employee Benefits Manager Loretta Dickey of the union's demand for recognition. Upon the advice of counsel, Dickey announced at the next meeting of each committee that, due to the union demand, the company could no longer participate in the committees, but that the employee members could continue to meet if they so desired.

Finally, on March 15, 1989, Howard formally announced to the employees that "due to the union's campaign, the Company would be unable to participate in the [committee] meetings and could not continue to work with the committees until after the [union] election." The

union election took place on March 31, 1989; the employees voted 95 to 82 against union representation. On April 24, 1989, a regional director of the National Labor Relations Board (Board) issued a complaint alleging that Electromation had violated the Act by refusing to meet.

Section 2(5) of the Act defines a labor organization as:

> any organization of any kind, or any agency or employee representation committee or plan, in which employees participate and which exists for the purpose, in whole or in part, of dealing with employers concerning grievances, labor disputes, wages, rates of pay, hours of employment, or conditions of work.

Under this statutory definition, the action committees would constitute labor organizations if: (1) the Electromation employees participated in the committees; (2) the committees existed, at least in part, for the purpose of "dealing with" the employer; and (3) these dealings concerned "grievances, labor disputes, wages, rates of pay, hours of employment, or conditions of work."

With respect to the first factor, there is no question that the Electromation employees participated in the action committees. Turning to the second factor, which is the most seriously contested on appeal, the Board found that the activities of the action committees constituted "dealing with" the employer. We agree with the Board that the action committees can be differentiated only in the specific subject matter with which each dealt. Each committee had an identical relationship to the company: the purpose, structure, and administration of each committee was essentially the same. We note, in addition, that even if the committees are considered individually, there exists substantial evidence that each was formed and existed for the purpose of "dealing with" the company. It is in fact the shared similarities among the committee structures which compels unitary treatment of them for the purposes of the issues raised in this appeal.

Given the Supreme Court's holding that "dealing with" includes conduct much broader than collective bargaining, the Board did not err in determining that the Electromation action committees constituted labor organizations within the meaning of Sections 2(5) and 8(a) (2) of the Act.

Finally, with respect to the third factor, the subject matter of that dealing—for example, the treatment of employee absenteeism and employee bonuses—obviously concerned conditions of employment. The purpose of the action committees was not limited to the improvement of company efficiency or product quality, but rather that they were designed to function and in fact functioned in an essentially representative capacity. Accordingly, given the statute's traditionally broad construction, there is substantial evidence to support the Board's finding that the action committees constituted labor organizations.

Section 8(a)(2) declares that it shall be an unfair labor practice for an employer: to dominate or interfere with the formation or administration of any labor organization or contribute financial or other support to it: Provided, that subject to rules and regulations made and published by the Board pursuant to Section 6, an employer shall not be prohibited from permitting employees to confer with him during working hours without loss of time or pay. Section 8(a)(1) provides that it shall be an unfair labor practice for an employer: to interfere with, restrain or coerce employees in the exercise of the rights guaranteed in section 157 of this title. Section 7 in turn provides that: [e]mployees shall have the right to self-organization, to form, to join, or assist labor organizations, to bargain collectively through representatives of their own choosing, and to engage in other concerted activities for the purpose of collective bargaining or other mutual aid or protection, and shall also have the right to refrain from any and all such activities except to the extent that such right may be affected by an agreement requiring membership in a labor organization as a condition of employment as authorized in section 158(a)(3) of this title.

Electromation argues that the Board's ruling in this case implies that an employer violates Section 8(a)(2) whenever it proposes a structure whereby the employees and employer "cooperate," or meet together to discuss topics of mutual concern. The company thus asserts that the Board may find a violation of Section 8(a)(2) only where it finds that the employer has actually undermined the free and independent choice of the employees.

The company played a pivotal role in establishing both the framework and the agenda for the action committees. Electromation unilaterally selected the size, structure, and procedural functioning of the committees; it decided the number of committees and the topic(s) to be addressed by each. The company unilaterally drafted the action committees' purposes and goal statements, which identified from the start the focus of each committee's work. Also, despite the fact that the employees were seriously concerned about the lack of a wage increase, no action committee was designated to consider this specific issue. In this way, Electromation actually controlled which issues received attention by the committees and which did not.

Although the company acceded to the employees' request that volunteers form the committees, it unilaterally determined how many could serve on each committee, decided that an employee could serve on only one committee at a time, and determined which committee certain employees would serve on, thus exercising significant control over the employees' participation and voice at the committee meetings. Also, although it never became a significant issue because so few employees signed up for the committees, the initial sign up sheets indicated that the employer would decide which six employees would be chosen as committee members where more than six expressed interest in a particular committee. Ultimately, the company limited membership to five and determined the five to serve. Also, the company designated management representatives to serve on the committees. Employee Benefits Manager Dickey was assigned to coordinate and serve on all committees. In the case of the Attendance Bonus Program Committee, the management representative—Controller Mazur—reviewed employee proposals, determined whether they were economically feasible, and further decided whether they would be presented to higher management. This role of the management committee members effectively put the employer on both sides of the bargaining table, an avowed proscription of the Act.

Finally, the company paid the employees for their time spent on committee activities, provided meeting space, and furnished all necessary supplies for the committees' activities. While such financial support is clearly not a violation of Section 8(a)(2) by itself, in the totality of the circumstances in this case such support may reasonably be characterized to be in furtherance of the company's domination of the action committees. We therefore conclude that there is substantial evidence to support the Board's finding of unlawful employer domination and interference in violation of Section 8(a)(2) and (1). NLRB ORDER ENFORCED.

Case Questions

1. Did the employer seem to intentionally violate the law? Explain.
2. What do you think would motivate an employer to prefer to deal directly with an employee participation group rather than a union?
3. Do you think it's harmful to put the employer on "both sides of the bargaining table"? Explain the pros and cons.

Chapter 16

Selected Employment Benefits and Protections

Learning Objectives

After completing this chapter, you should be able to:

LO1 List the matters regulated by the Fair Labor Standards Act.

LO2 Discuss the requirements of the minimum wage laws and to whom they apply.

LO3 Explain the Family Medical Leave Act, including to whom it applies and under what circumstances.

LO4 Explain contributory negligence, assumption of risk, and the fellow servant rule, and their roles in the regulation of safety in the workplace and determine how OSHA impacted this regulatory environment.

LO5 Set forth what OSHA requires of employers to create a safer workplace and how it is enforced.

LO6 Describe the reporting responsibilities of employers under the OSH Act.

LO7 Explain the purposes of ERISA and identify who and what type of entities are covered.

LO8 Describe the minimum ERISA standards for employee benefit plans.

Opening Scenarios

SCENARIO 1

1
Scenario

Fenwick, a new MBA graduate, is hired into a management position at $125,000 per year. It is Fenwick's first job as a professional. After several months, Fenwick finds he is leaving work later and later. Fenwick begins to resent that he works late, putting in more and more hours, and is not receiving any more than the originally agreed-upon salary. He is contemplating legal action against his employer for violation of the Fair Labor Standards Act. Will it be worth his while to pursue this?

SCENARIO 2

2
Scenario

Carly and Carl live with their two children and Carl's mom, who is in the advanced stages of Alzheimer's. Carly works in pharmaceutical sales and has a lot of job flexibility. Carl is the chief financial officer for an investment firm, and his job is very demanding. Carl's mom takes a turn for the worse and will need extra care for a few weeks. Carly knows she has the flexibility and time, so she goes to her supervisor and requests time off under the Family and Medical Leave Act to take care of her ailing mother-in-law. Will it be granted?

SCENARIO 3

3
Scenario

Singhie, an employee of Carterez, a contractor, is hospitalized due to the large number of cement particles she inhaled while Bartow, a subcontractor, was laying the cement foundation for a structure. Carterez is cited by OSHA for violation of the protective gear requirements. Who is liable, Carterez, the contractor, or Bartow, the subcontractor?

Introduction

Beyond those laws that we have discussed in previous chapters, there are several other laws that do not contain antidiscrimination provisions but nevertheless significantly impact the workplace; this chapter will introduce you to some of them. These include the Fair Labor Standards Act of 1938 (FLSA), the Family and Medical Leave Act of 1993 (FMLA), the Occupational Safety and Health Act of 1970 (OSHA), and the Employee Retirement Income Security Act of 1974 (ERISA). Each is an important aspect of the workplace landscape.

Fair Labor Standards Act of 1938

Statutory Basis

Every employer shall pay to each of his employees who in any workweek is engaged in commerce or in the production of goods for commerce, or is employed in an enterprise engaged in commerce or in the production of goods for commerce, wages at the following rates: . . . not less than $6.55 an hour beginning July 24, 2008; and $7.25 per hour effective July 24, 2009. [Sec. 6(a), Fair Labor Standards Act of 1938, as amended, 29 U.S.C. § 201 et seq.]

. . . No employer shall employ any of his employees for a workweek longer than forty hours unless such employee receives compensation for his employment in excess of the hours above specified at a rate not less than one and one-half times the regular rate at which he is employed. [Sec. 7(a)(1), Fair Labor Standards Act of 1938, as amended, 29 U.S.C. § 201 et seq.]

Introduction: Show Me the Money!

Face it. If we were all rich and didn't have to work, many of us would not do so. Since we do have to work, we want to make sure that we get all that is coming to us. We don't want to have to work for whatever meager wages our employer wants to pay us, compete with 10-year-olds for our job, or work whatever number of hours our employer decides they want us to work without them paying us extra for it. Under the broad constitutional powers that Congress has to regulate interstate commerce, in 1938 it passed a law to regulate pay and hours worked in order to address just such issues. Now amended several times, the law is called the Fair Labor Standards Act (FLSA). The act set standards for the minimum age for workers, **minimum wages** they can make, and the rate at which they must be paid if they work over a certain amount of time during a workweek. Much like the Equal Pay Act and Title VII, the act also prohibits pay differentials based solely on gender.

A 2015 *Washington Post* headline was "Why Wage and Hour Litigation Is Sky-rocketing."[1] It wasn't the first time the headline showed up, nor was it the last. In more recent years these cases have been class action suits rather than individual cases, and thus have cost employers millions of dollars. Federal wage and hour suits have increased by more than 400 percent since 2000.[2] It is one of the main areas of companies' legal concerns.[3] And for good reason. In fiscal year 2019, the Wage and Hour Division, which enforces the law, recovered a record-setting $322 million for employees. But the Wage and Hour Division is not just suing for back wages. It also set a record for the most educational outreach events (3,700) to help those who create jobs understand their responsibilities under the law. Another reason companies should be concerned is that in October 2019, the Wage and Hour Division launched its new office of Enterprise Data and Analytics "to ensure the use of the most cutting-edge tools and data sources available to guide decision-making and secure the largest possible impact."[4]

Again, the FLSA is administered by the U.S. Department of Labor's Wage and Hour Division, which has authority to investigate, gather information, issue regulations, and enforce FLSA provisions. States also have wage and hour provisions administered by comparable state agencies. Violations, if willful, are crimes punishable by fines of up to $10,000, with second convictions resulting in possible imprisonment. Child labor violations carry civil penalties. The FLSA contains antiretaliation provisions to protect employees who use the FLSA when they do such things as filing a complaint or participating in an FLSA proceeding.[5]

As you can see, if an employer violates the FLSA by underpaying employees, the employees may recover back wages. Again, the federal government recovered more than $322 million in back wages in fiscal year 2019 alone.[6]

As an interesting—and, in all probability, surprising—example of wage issues, in 2014, one of the Oakland Raiders cheerleaders filed a lawsuit on her own behalf and that of the 40 other cheerleaders, alleging that at $125 per home game or $1,250 per season, the Raiders did not pay the Raiderettes minimum wages for the work they are required to do both on and off the field. In her estimation, they were

minimum wages
The least amount a covered employee must be paid in hourly wages.

LO1 List the matters regulated by the Fair Labor Standards Act.

paid less than $5 per hour. In addition to the 10 eight-hour-shift home games, the cheerleaders must do 10 charity events, a team rally, Fan Day, and the swimsuit calendar photo shoot. They must pay the costs of travel to these events; their suits; accessories such as tights, false eyelashes, and a yoga mat; and a team-elected hair-stylist who costs several hundred dollars.[7]

Team administration basically took the position that the cheerleaders were not employees and thus not subject to the FLSA. Although evidence showed that like employees, team administration had virtually complete control over the women's interactions with the organization for which they cheered, including controlling significant aspects of their life off the field. One of the repercussions of the suits being filed was that for the first time, fans had a chance to see what the environment was really like for the women they saw smiling and cheering along the sides during the games. It was not the glamorous life it appeared to be. And while they may not have appreciated the distraction of the lawsuits, few wanted anyone to have to work for less than minimum wages, as was the case with the cheerleaders.

Once the suit was brought, several cheerleaders from other professional teams followed suit and painted the same picture. There were cheerleaders who resented those who filed the suits, opining that they knew what they were getting into and cheering for a professional team is often a means of going on to greater things like modeling, movies, television, or more.

In what some thought of as quite intentional timing since more and more FLSA lawsuits were being brought against teams, the 2018 NFL season opened with both the L.A. Rams and the New Orleans Saints having hired the first male cheerleaders in NFL history in August 2018.[8] The thought was that this might well work to blunt the argument that team administration was paying the cheerleaders less because they were women. The claims have begun to take hold and gain ground, and some of the teams have begun to resolve the issues that led to them, often through settlements with claimants rather than litigated cases. In 2015, in the aftermath of a settlement in a wage suit brought by the Raiderettes, California passed legislation classifying professional cheerleaders as employees rather than independent contractors, thus bringing them within the minimum wage laws. A law mirroring California's was introduced in New York.[9] A Change.org petition urging the NFL to pay their cheer-leaders at least minimum wage garnered over 181,144 signatures before closing.[10] Legislators in New York, Illinois, Ohio, Texas, Pennsylvania, and Maryland called on the NFL to pay cheerleaders a fair wage.[11]

There have been many other interesting pay issues in the past several years.

When Congress would not allow passage of a raise in the minimum wage, President Obama did all that he could under the circumstances and issued an executive order requiring that all new contracts with those who do business with the federal government were required to include provisions for paying the employees of the federal contractors at least $10.10 per hour.[12] Between February 12, 2014, and the effective date of January 1, 2015, "agencies were strongly encouraged to take all steps that are reasonable and legally permissible to ensure that individuals working pursuant to those contracts and contract-like instruments are paid an hourly wage of at least $10.10."[13]

In January 2014, the U.S. Supreme Court gave guidance in a case in which the issue was whether employees must be paid for the time they spent "donning and doffing" clothing required for their jobs.[14] The Court said that employees were not covered for this time because their collective bargaining agreement provision covering the issue said it must be negotiated, and it had not been.

In February 2014, Hibachi Grill and Supreme Buffet paid $2 million in wage and hour violations.[15]

In 2008, Walmart paid $54.25 million to settle a lawsuit alleging Walmart cut Walmart and Sam's Club employees' break times short and worked employees while off the clock without paying them. The decision involved about 100,000 current and former hourly employees in Minnesota over the past decade.[16] The fines could have been much higher since Minnesota law allows a $1,000 fine to be imposed for each violation and the state district judge found that Walmart had violated the law more than 2 million times. Walmart has faced similar suits in at least 35 states but rarely settles as it did this time.

The Obama administration was quite aggressive in making sure wage and hour laws were complied with and employees got what they had bargained for. It is expected that enforcement will become even more vigorous, with additional funding for agencies to handle the increased enforcement.[17] For instance, the Department of Labor proposed a rule designed to better protect children under 16 working in agricultural vocations, especially from injuries. The agency withdrew the proposed rule, however, after thousands of comments about its negative impact on family farms.[18] In September 2013, pursuant to an executive order, the Department of Labor announced that nearly 2 million direct care workers who provide essential home care assistance to the ill, the elderly, and those with injuries and disabilities as home health care aides, personal caretakers, and certified nursing assistants would now be included in minimum wage and overtime protection.[19] The agency has also undertaken a Misclassification Initiative by which it signed agreements with several states and their attorneys general to make sure they do not misclassify employees as independent contractors and thereby avoid paying proper minimum wages. States who have signed such agreements include California, Colorado, Connecticut, Hawaii, Illinois, Iowa, Louisiana, Maryland, Massachusetts, Minnesota, Missouri, Montana, New York, Utah, and Washington. In the past two years, the agency has recovered $18.2 million, a 97 percent increase, in back wages for more than 19,000 employees where the primary reason for violations was misclassified employees.[20]

One of the issues that has seen growing interest has been unpaid student internships. The U.S. Department of Labor has said it is cracking down on firms that do not properly pay interns and increasing their education in the area to make employers aware of the law.[21] It issued new guidance to employers in 2010. (See Exhibit 16.1, "Fact Sheet on Internships under the Fair Labor Standards Act.") A June 2013 decision, *Glatts v. Fox Searchlight Pictures,*[22] involving unpaid interns working on the film *Black Swan* for Searchlight Pictures, ruled that unpaid interns were employees and should receive minimum wage. The court rejected Fox's argument that it should rely on a balancing test weighing who received the primary benefit of the internship because

Exhibit 16.1   *Fact Sheet on Internships under the Fair Labor Standards Act*

(April 2010) Fact Sheet #71: Internship Programs under the Fair Labor Standards Act

This fact sheet provides general information to help determine whether interns must be paid the minimum wage and overtime under the Fair Labor Standards Act for the services that they provide to "for-profit" private-sector employers.

BACKGROUND

The Fair Labor Standards Act (FLSA) defines the term *employ* very broadly as including to "suffer or permit to work." Covered and nonexempt individuals who are "suffered or permitted" to work must be compensated under the law for the services they perform for an employer. Internships in the "for-profit" private sector will most often be viewed as employment, unless the test described below relating to trainees is met. Interns in the for-profit private sector who qualify as employees rather than trainees typically must be paid at least the minimum wage and overtime compensation for hours worked over forty in a workweek.*

THE TEST FOR UNPAID INTERNS

There are some circumstances under which individuals who participate in for-profit private sector internships or training programs may do so without compensation. The Supreme Court has held that the term *suffer or permit to work* cannot be interpreted so as to make a person whose work serves only his or her own interest an employee of another who provides aid or instruction. This may apply to interns who receive training for their own educational benefit if the training meets certain criteria. The determination of whether an internship or training program meets this exclusion depends upon all of the facts and circumstances of each such program.

The following six criteria must be applied when making this determination:

The internship, even though it includes actual operation of the facilities of the employer, is similar to training which would be given in an educational environment;

The internship experience is for the benefit of the intern;

The intern does not displace regular employees, but works under close supervision of existing staff;

The employer that provides the training derives no immediate advantage from the activities of the intern; and on occasion its operations may actually be impeded;

The intern is not necessarily entitled to a job at the conclusion of the internship;

The employer and the intern understand that the intern is not entitled to wages for the time spent in the internship.

If all of the factors listed above are met, an employment relationship does not exist under the FLSA, and the Act's minimum wage and overtime provisions do not apply to the intern. This exclusion from the definition of employment is necessarily quite narrow because the FLSA's definition of "employ" is very broad. Some of the most commonly discussed factors for for-profit private-sector internship programs are considered below.

SIMILAR TO AN EDUCATION ENVIRONMENT AND THE PRIMARY BENEFICIARY OF THE ACTIVITY

In general, the more an internship program is structured around a classroom or academic experience as opposed to the employer's actual operations, the more likely the internship will be viewed as an extension of the individual's educational experience (this often occurs where a college or university exercises oversight over the internship program and provides educational credit). The more the internship provides the individual with skills that can be used in multiple employment settings, as opposed to skills particular to one employer's operation, the more likely the intern would be viewed as receiving training. Under these circumstances the intern does not perform the routine work of the business on a regular and recurring basis, and the business is not dependent upon the work of the intern. On the other hand, if the interns are engaged in the operations of the employer or are performing productive work (for example, filing, performing other clerical work, or assisting customers), then the fact that they may be receiving some benefits in the form of a new skill or improved work habits will not exclude them from the FLSA's minimum wage and overtime requirements because the employer benefits from the interns' work.

DISPLACEMENT AND SUPERVISION ISSUES

If an employer uses interns as substitutes for regular workers or to augment its existing workforce during specific time periods, these interns should be paid at least the minimum wage and overtime compensation for hours worked over forty in a workweek. If the employer would have hired additional employees or required existing staff to work additional hours had the interns not performed the work, then the interns will be viewed as employees and entitled compensation under the FLSA. Conversely, if the employer is providing job shadowing opportunities that allow an intern to learn certain functions under the close and constant supervision of regular employees, but the intern performs no or minimal work, the activity is more likely to be viewed as a *bona fide* education experience. On the other hand, if the intern receives the same level of supervision as the employer's regular workforce, this would suggest an employment relationship, rather than training.

JOB ENTITLEMENT

The internship should be of a fixed duration, established prior to the outset of the internship. Further,

unpaid internships generally should not be used by the employer as a trial period for individuals seeking employment at the conclusion of the internship period. If an intern is placed with the employer for a trial period with the expectation that he or she will then be hired on a permanent basis, that individual generally would be considered an employee under the FLSA.

WHERE TO OBTAIN ADDITIONAL INFORMATION

This publication is for general information and is not to be considered in the same light as official statements of position contained in the regulations.

For additional information, visit our Wage and Hour Division website: http://www.wagehour.dol.gov and/or call our toll-free information and helpline, available 8 a.m. to 5 p.m. in your time zone, 1-866-4USWAGE (1-866-487-9243).

*The FLSA makes a special exception under certain circumstances for individuals who volunteer to perform services for a state or local government agency and for individuals who volunteer for humanitarian purposes for private non-profit food banks. WHD also recognizes an exception for individuals who volunteer their time, freely and without anticipation of compensation for religious, charitable, civic, or humanitarian purposes to non-profit organizations. Unpaid internships in the public sector and for non-profit charitable organizations, where the intern volunteers without expectation of compensation, are generally permissible. WHD is reviewing the need for additional guidance on internships in the public and non-profit sectors.

Source: U.S. Department of Labor, http://www.dol.gov/whd/regs/compliance/whdfs71.htm.

it was subjective and unworkable for employers, as often the intern would not even know this until the end of the internship. Instead, the court used the factors in the DOL fact sheet in Exhibit 16.1 and made the determination. There have been several moves to address unpaid internships, including more than 20 lawsuits filed and the Fair Pay Campaign whose purpose is to end unpaid internships. The common assumption is that unpaid interns are privileged college kids, but a 2012 study showed they are mostly middle or working class and often hold down second jobs to pay the bills. They are also 77 percent more likely to be female. Interestingly, a survey of 20,000 students conducted by the National Association of Colleges and Employers found that unpaid interns have no advantage in the job market and no higher starting salaries than students who did not have internships.[23]

According to the National Association of Colleges and Employers, the number of graduating students who have held internships rose from 9 percent in 1992 to 83 percent in 2008,[24] so it is an area of increasing concern. Since most students want the experience, connections, and job possibilities that come from holding an internship, they are less likely to complain if they are unpaid or are used as a temporary employee, thus making them likely targets for exploitation. The good thing about the cases and pushback activity from interns is that it has caused employers to take a look at their policies and see how they can better comply with the law.

Another recent active area of concern in wages is lactation time for nursing mothers. Keep in mind that we discussed in the gender chapter that the FLSA was amended by the Patient Protection and Affordable Care Act to require that an employer provide reasonable unpaid breaks for nursing mothers to express milk for up to a year from the birth of their child. If the expressing is done during a regular paid break, the break is paid time. Unless the employer has fewer than 50 employees and it would cause an undue hardship to do so, the employer must also provide a private place other than a restroom in which the new mother can express her milk. The law does not preempt state laws requiring that such breaks be paid.

Another area of growing concern has been that of payment of employees' time for "donning and doffing" protective gear—that is, time spent before and after work putting on and taking off protective covering or equipment that is necessary for work. Generally, if the clothing and equipment are necessary for work, the time must be paid. As we mentioned in the opening information of the chapter, the U.S. Supreme Court determined that it can, however, be negotiated otherwise in a collective bargaining agreement if employees wish to trade off something else with the employer, for instance, a higher hourly wage.

The Fifth Circuit in *Allen v. McWane, Inc.,*[25] joining the Third and Eleventh Circuits, held that if an employer has a custom and practice of not paying for time spent donning and doffing protective equipment and the employees never discussed it during collective bargaining negotiations, it is not a basis for claims of violation under the FLSA. In the court's view, "as long as there was a company policy of non-compensation for time spent changing for a prolonged period of time—allowing the court to infer that the union had knowledge of and acquiesced to the employer's policy—and a CBA existed, the parties need not have explicitly discussed such compensation when negotiating the CBA. McWane 'only need prove that the parties had a 'custom or practice' of non-compensation under the agreement.'"

Covered Employees

Since the FLSA was enacted pursuant to the powers of Congress to regulate interstate commerce, that requirement forms, in part, a basis for determining coverage. Actually, there are two types of coverage in the FLSA: individual coverage and enterprise coverage. If the individual employee's job involves interstate commerce directly, such as an over-the-road truck driver traveling from state to state, or moving or preparing goods for interstate commerce, including phoning and using the mail, then the individual is covered. For enterprise coverage, all employees of a business will be covered if the business is engaged in interstate commerce or in producing goods for interstate commerce and meets a minimum gross annual income requirement of $500,000. The law applies to both part-time and full-time employees. Federal, state, and local employees are also covered by the law, though there are some specific provisions for certain state and local employees.

If an employee works for certain types of businesses, the $500,000 minimum does not apply. That is, employees will be covered even if their employer does not make at least $500,000 per year. These organizations include hospitals and other institutions primarily engaged in the care of the sick, aged, mentally ill, or disabled who reside on the premises; schools for children who are mentally or physically disabled or gifted; preschools, elementary and secondary schools, and institutions of higher education; and federal, state, and local government agencies. The law also covers domestic service workers such as day workers, housekeepers, chauffeurs, cooks, valets, or full-time babysitters (defined as other than those babysitting on a casual basis; typically requiring at least 20 hours per week). State laws also may apply, and when both cover a situation, the law setting the higher standards must be the one used.

The FLSA contains exemptions from these rules for several groups, which vary depending on the area of the FLSA being addressed. As can be seen from *Reich v. Circle C Investment, Inc.,* given at the end of the chapter, even the threshold decision as to who is covered by the act is not always an easy one. In *Reich* the court was faced with deciding whether topless dancers who only received tips were, in fact, employees for purposes of the Fair Labor Standards Act provisions on minimum wages, overtime, and record-keeping requirements.

Minimum Wages

The minimum wage law was passed in 1938, nine years after the Wall Street crash of 1929, in hopes that it would prevent another Depression. The advocates of the law, primarily unions and other workers, believed that a minimum wage would provide everyone with sufficient money on which to live without causing economic harm to business owners. With the growing income gap, the issue of minimum wages has been of great interest lately as businesses like McDonald's and Walmart have come under fire for their low wages for entry-level employees. Demonstrations and strikes have been held and social media campaigns engaged in to try to raise the minimum wage for these workers to a living wage that is, in the view of some, more realistic. It probably did not help matters when Walmart came under fire for setting up food donation collection bins for its employees at Thanksgiving (Walmart said it was for helping employees who may have undergone a misfortune such as a home fire or spouse's loss of a job)[26] or McDonald's posted on its company website for employees its Practical Money Skills Budget Journal with tips for coping with low wages.[27]

LO2 Discuss the requirements of the minimum wage laws and to whom they apply.

Under the FLSA, employers are required to pay covered employees a certain minimum hourly wage. On July 24, 2007, pursuant to the Fair Minimum Wage Act signed by President George W. Bush on May 25, 2007, the minimum wage rose from $5.15 per hour, where it had been since September 1, 1997, to $5.85 per hour. On July 24, 2008, the minimum wage increased to $6.55, and on July 24, 2009, it increased to $7.25. In 1938, when the FLSA was enacted, it was 25 cents per hour.

We are presently in the longest period in which the federal government has not raised the minimum wage. That should seem odd since it is worth 17 percent less than it was when that law was passed 11 years ago, and until the COVID-19 pandemic hit, the economy was said to have been doing so well. On June 16, 2019, "lawmakers set a new record . . . by leaving the federal minimum wage untouched since July 24, 2009, the year of former President Barack Obama's first term. The rate hasn't been increased from $7.25 in a whopping 3,615 days, making it the longest dry spell since the federal minimum wage was enacted under President Franklin Delano Roosevelt in 1938."[28] As mentioned earlier, in 2014, President Obama signed an executive order requiring federal contractors to pay their employees a minimum of $10.10 per hour. As president, it was all he could do since in refusing to support his efforts to do so, Republicans in Congress made him the first president since Ronald Reagan to not sign off on a minimum wage bill.

There has been an ongoing call in some quarters to raise the minimum wage. The Raise Wage Act of 2019, with 190 cosponsors (all Democrats), was passed by the U.S. House of Representatives on July 18, 2019. If signed into law, the bill would amend the FLSA by raising the federal minimum wage to $15 per hour by 2025 for 33.5 million employees (including regular, tipped, and newly hired employees less than 20 years old) and automatically set it to update automatically each year based on median wage growth. It was introduced in the Senate by Bernie Sanders on January 16, 2019, and read a second time on July 22, 2019, but has not been taken up for debate in the Senate. At this time, 26 states and D.C. as well as some local governments raised their state minimum wages on their own to become effective in 2020.[29]

State wage laws, passed by individual state's legislators, may have higher minimums than the federal law. (See Exhibit 16.2, "Consolidated Minimum Wage Table.") If a state law is more than the federal minimum wage, state law prevails, but if it is less, federal minimum wage law prevails.

Wage rates may be lower if, in accordance with appropriate regulations, an industry wage order makes them so in Puerto Rico, the Virgin Islands, or American Samoa. The Fair Minimum Wage Act of 2007 provided for a 50-cent-per-hour industry-based increase in wages for American Samoa until the wage rate was generally the same as for the United States. If the covered employee is an apprentice, learner, or disabled worker, then, under certain circumstances, she or he may receive less than the minimum wage if the employer obtains a certificate issued by the Department of Labor's wage and hour administrator.

Tipped employees (defined in the regulations as those who regularly receive more than $30 a month in tips) may be paid direct wages of $2.13 per hour, but the employer must make up the difference if the tips do not equal the usual minimum wage.[30] The Raise Wage bill, if passed, eliminates this distinction between tipped and non-tipped employees. In *Kilgore v. Outback Steakhouse of Florida, Inc.,*[31] the

Exhibit 16.2 *Consolidated Minimum Wage Table*

Applicable to Nonsupervisory NONFARM Private Sector Employment Under State and Federal Laws[1]

Consolidated State Minimum Wage Update Table (Effective Date: 07/01/2020)

Greater than federal MW	Equals federal MW of $7.25	Greater than federal MW	No MW required
AK $10.19	CNMI	MT $8.65	PR
AR $10.00	GA	NE $9.00	
AZ $12.00	IA	NJ $11.00	
CA $12.00	ID	NM $9.00	
CO $12.00	IN	NV $9.00/8.00[2]	
CT $11.00	KS	NY $11.80	
DC $15.00	KY	OH $8.70	
DE $9.25	NC	OR $12.00	
FL $8.56	ND	RI $10.50	
HI $10.10	NH	SD $9.30	
IL $10.00	OK	VT $10.96	
MA $12.75	PA	WA $13.50	
MD $11.00	TX	WV $8.75	
ME $12.00	UT	WV $8.75	
MI $9.65	VA	VI $10.50	
MN $10.00	WI	GU $8.25	
MO $9.45	WY		
29 States + DC, GU, & VI	**16 States + PR, CNMI**	**5 States**	

[1]Like the federal wage and hour law, State law often exempts particular occupations or industries from the minimum labor standard generally applied to covered employment. Some states also set subminimum rates for minors and/or students or exempt them from coverage, or have a training wage for new hires. Additionally, some local governments set minimum wage rates higher than their respective state minimum wage. Such differential provisions are not identified in this table. Users are encouraged to consult the laws of particular States in determining whether the State's minimum wage applies to a particular employment. This information often may be found at the websites maintained by State labor departments. Links to these websites are available at www.dol.gov/agencies/whd/state/contacts.

[2]On July 1, 2020, the minimum wage for employees with health insurance will increase to $8.00. The minimum wage for employees without health insurance will increase to $9.00.

(continued)

Exhibit 16.2 *continued*

The state minimum wage rate requirements, or lack thereof, are controlled by legislative activities within the individual states.

Federal minimum wage law supersedes state minimum wage laws where the federal minimum wage is greater than the state minimum wage. In those states where the state minimum wage is greater than the federal minimum wage, the state minimum wage prevails.

There are 4 states than have a minimum wage set lower than the federal minimum wage. There are 21 states (plus DC) with minimum wage rates set higher than the federal minimum wage. There are 20 states that have a minimum wage requirement that is the same as the federal minimum wage requirement. The remaining 5 states do not have an established minimum wage requirement.

The State of Washington has the highest minimum wage at $9.32/hour. The states of Georgia and Wyoming have the lowest minimum wage ($5.15) of the 45 states that have a minimum wage requirement.

Note: There are 10 states (AZ, CO, FL, MO, MT, NV, OH, OR, VT, and WA) that have minimum wages that are linked to a consumer price index. As a result of this linkage, the minimum wages in these states are normally increased each year, generally around January 1. Effective January 1, 2014, 9 of the 10 states increased their respective minimum wages. The exception was Nevada, which adjusts in the month of July each year.

Source: Division of Communications, Wage and Hour Division, U.S. Department of Labor, http://www.dol.gov/whd/minwage/america.htm.

court wrestled with the issue of whether it was permissible for an employer to require servers who receive tips to pool their tips and split them with other employees who do not receive tips. The court held that this was permissible for the employer to do. In 2008, a San Francisco superior court held that Starbucks would have to pay $100 million ($86 million plus interest) to its 120,000 baristas (coffee servers) statewide because it had been Starbucks' policy to allow shift supervisors to share the tips received by the baristas, resulting in an average hourly wage of $1.71 for the baristas.[32] The California Court of Appeals, however, reversed the decision, saying that no law or court ruling prevents a service employee from sharing a collective tip.[33]

Employees may be paid on a piece rate rather than an hourly rate as long as they receive the equivalent of the minimum wage. (See Exhibit 16.3, "Exemptions from Both Minimum Wage and Overtime Pay," and Exhibit 16.4, "Other FLSA Exemptions," for wage and overtime exemptions.) As mentioned, the FLSA has exemptions, so not everyone is covered under the statute. However, some states cover FLSA-exempted employees under their state laws.

The following are the primary exemptions from both the wage and the overtime provisions of the FLSA. Note that under the FLSA, some employees are exempt from the overtime provisions but not the minimum wage provisions (see Exhibit 16.4, "Other FLSA Exemptions").

1. Outside salespeople; executive, administrative, and professional employees, including teachers, academic administrative employees in elementary and secondary schools; and certain employees in computer-related occupations if they are paid at least $27.63 per hour. (This is why it would not be worth Fenwick's time to pursue a claim in Opening Scenario 1; more below.)

Exhibit 16.3 *Exemptions from Both Minimum Wage and Overtime Pay*

Most employers must pay the majority of their employees minimum wage and overtime pursuant to the Fair Labor Standards Act (FLSA). However, there are some categories of employees that qualify for Fair Labor Standards Act exemptions. Section 213(a) of the Fair Labor Standards Act provides for several exemptions from both its minimum wage and overtime requirements. 29 USC 213(a); 29 CFR 541 (*See also Overtime only exemptions*) Each exemption has its own requirements that must be met for an employee to qualify. The most common categories of employees that qualify for the Fair Labor Standards Act exemptions for both minimum wage and overtime requirements include:

MOST COMMON EXEMPTIONS

- Administrative Employees
- Computer Employees
- Executive Employees
- Highly Compensated Employees
- Creative Professional Employees
- Learned Professional Employees
- Teaching Professional Employees
- Outside Salesperson

Additional categories of exemptions from both the minimum wage and overtime requirements of the FLSA are:

ADDITIONAL MINIMUM WAGE AND OVERTIME EXEMPTIONS

- Amusement and recreational establishments
- Fishing operations
- Agricultural employees
- Special certificate exemption
- Small newspapers
- Switchboard operators
- Seamen
- Babysitter exemption
- Domestic service employees companionship services exemption
- Criminal investigators

Source: https://www.employmentlawhandbook.com/federal-employment-and-labor-laws/flsa/exemptions/

---

2. Employees of certain individually owned and operated small retail or service establishments not part of a covered enterprise.

3. Employees of certain seasonal amusement or recreational establishments, messengers, full-time students, employees of certain small newspapers, switchboard operators of small telephone companies, sailors employed on foreign vessels, and employees engaged in fishing operations.

4. Farm workers employed by anyone who used no more than 500 person-days of farm labor in any calendar quarter of the preceding calendar year.

5. Casual babysitters and people employed as companions to the elderly.

1)
Scenario

The FLSA overtime regulations underwent a major overhaul in 2004 regarding their exemption for white-collar professionals, that is, primarily those in executive,

Exhibit 16.4 *Other FLSA Exemptions*

As you can see from the following list, there are many exemptions to the FLSA provisions. These do not include state exemptions that may exist.

(MW = minimum wage; OT = overtime; CL = child labor)

- Aircraft salespeople—OT
- Airline employees—OT
- Amusement/recreational employees in national parks/forests/wildlife refuge system— OT
- Babysitters on a casual basis—MW & OT
- Boat salespeople—OT
- Buyers of agricultural products—OT
- Companions for the elderly—MW & OT
- Country elevator workers (rural)—OT
- Disabled workers—MW
- Domestic employees who live in—OT
- Farm implement salespeople—OT
- Federal criminal investigators—MW & OT
- Firefighters working in small (less than five firefighters) public fire departments—OT
- Fishing—MW & OT
- Forestry employees of small (less than nine employees) firms—OT
- Fruit & vegetable transportation employees—OT
- Homeworkers making wreaths—MW, OT, & CL
- Houseparents in nonprofit educational institutions—OT
- Livestock auction workers—OT
- Local delivery drivers and drivers' helpers—OT
- Lumber operations employees of small (less than nine employees) firms—OT
- Motion picture theater employees—OT
- Newspaper delivery—MW, OT, & CL
- Newspaper employees of limited-circulation newspapers—MW & OT
- Police officers working in small (less than five officers) public police departments—OT
- Radio station employees in small markets—OT
- Railroad employees—OT
- Seamen on American vessels—OT
- Seamen on other than American vessels—MW & OT
- Sugar processing employees—OT
- Switchboard operators—MW & OT
- Taxicab drivers—OT
- Television station employees in small markets—OT
- Truck and trailer salespeople—OT
- Youth employed as actors or performers—CL
- Youth employed by their parents—CL

Source: http://www.dol.gov/elaws/esa/flsa/screen75.asp.

administrative, and professional jobs. This matter had been debated for years and was accomplished under President George W. Bush. These rules are extremely important since they determine who must be paid overtime for working more than 40 hours per week. The general rule was that white-collar employees in the above categories were not entitled to overtime pay. Determinations as to who fit into these categories were made using a salary test and a duties test.

Prior to the rule change, the salary levels used in the wage and hour rules had not been updated for nearly 30 years. Under the old rules, the FLSA exempted from overtime pay workers who made more than $155 per week, or $8,060 per year, and who met certain other requirements that had been criticized as convoluted and confusing. For instance, the employee also had to devote at least 80 percent of his or her time to "exercising discretion" or other "intellectual" tasks that cannot be "standardized in . . . a given period of time." The new rules were designed to simplify application of the regulations to white-collar exemptions.

Under the new regulations, which required businesses to review their pay levels and jobs to make sure employees were being paid correctly under the new rules, employees earning up to $23,660 per year, or $455 per week, are automatically entitled to over-time pay, regardless of whether they are hourly or annual salaried employees. That is, regardless of the classification of the job, if the salary is at or below a certain level ($23,660 per year or $455 per week), the employee is entitled to overtime pay. For the most part, executive employees would be exempt if they manage two or more employees; if they have hiring, firing, and promotion authority or significant input; or if they have advanced degrees or similar training and work in a specialized field or the operations, finance, and auditing areas of a business. It was speculated that the jobs that would be most affected by the new overtime regulations would be assistant managers in stores, restaurants, and bars. Under the new regulations, an employer could boost salaries (that is, pay an employee more than $23,660) in order to avoid the new rules requiring overtime to be paid to those who earn up to $23,660.

Scenario

Employees who earn at least $100,000 per year and perform some executive, professional (either learned or creative), or administrative job duties are automatically exempt from the overtime provisions of the FLSA. That is why in Opening Scenario 1, Fenwick would not be entitled to more pay for the additional hours he finds himself putting in. As with the prior regulations, the Department of Labor can collect back wages for overtime violations, and companies not in compliance run the risk of costly lawsuits by employees. Retaliation against employees filing claims or reporting an employer's violations is a separate violation of the law. Because FLSA class action lawsuits have increased by 70 percent since 2000 and the regulations may change employees' status from what it was before the new regulations, employers would do well to give considerable attention to these matters.

Overtime Provisions

In addition to minimum wages, covered employees working over 40 hours per week are entitled to overtime pay of at least time and a half—at least one and one-half times the covered employee's regular hourly wage rate. Contrary to popular belief, FLSA does not limit the hours employees work but, rather, sets standards for the hours constituting a normal workweek for wage purposes. The statute then sets wage rates for hours worked over and above the normal week. It is a common misconception that the law prohibits an employer from requiring employees to work over 40 hours per week. The law does not dictate hours but merely states that if an employee works over 40 hours, he or she must be paid time and a half for the time worked in excess of 40 hours. (See Exhibit 16.5, "Full and Partial Overtime Pay Exemptions.") CALNET, Inc., and two of its subcontractors were ordered to pay $1,060,554 in back wages for failing to pay employees for time that they were on call.[34] Domestic workers who live in the employer's home permanently or for an extended period of time who are employed by an individual, family, or household are not entitled to overtime pay, but they must earn at least federal minimum wage. They can enter into agreements to exclude certain time from compensable hours worked, such as sleep time, meal time, and other periods of freedom from work duties. Employers must maintain accurate work records and may require employees to record and submit their hours worked to the employer.

Exhibit 16.5 *Full and Partial Overtime Pay Exemptions*

EXEMPTIONS FROM OVERTIME PAY ONLY

Certain commissioned employees of retail or service establishments; auto, truck, trailer, farm implement, boat, or aircraft salesworkers; or parts-clerks and mechanics servicing autos, trucks, or farm implements who are employed by nonmanufacturing establishments primarily engaged in selling these items to ultimate purchasers.

Employees of railroads and air carriers, taxi drivers, certain employees of motor carriers, seamen on American vessels, and local delivery employees paid on approved trip-rate plans. Announcers, news editors, and chief engineers of certain nonmetropolitan broadcasting stations.

Domestic service workers living in the employer's residence.

Employees of motion picture theaters.

Farm workers.

PARTIAL EXEMPTIONS FROM OVERTIME PAY

Partial overtime pay exemptions apply to employees engaged in certain operations on agricultural commodities and to employees of certain bulk petroleum distributors.

Hospitals and residential care establishments may adopt, by agreement with their employees, a 14-day work period instead of the usual 7-day workweek, if the employees are paid at least time and one-half their regular rates for hours worked over 8 in a day or 80 in a 14-day work period, whichever is the greater number of overtime hours.

Employees who lack a high school diploma, or who have not attained the educational level of the 8th grade, can be required to spend up to 10 hours in a workweek engaged in remedial reading or training in other basic skills without receiving time and one-half overtime pay for these hours. However, the employees must receive their normal wages for hours spent in such training, and the training must not be job specific.

Source: http://www.dol.gov/esa/wpd.

Retaliation

The FLSA prohibits employers from retaliating against any employee who exercises his or her rights under the act, such as by filing suit to collect benefits wrongfully withheld. As we will see in *Mullins v. City of New York,* reproduced at the end of the chapter, retaliation can include acts of intimidation that fall short of firing or disciplining someone for exercising lawfully held rights.

Child Labor Laws

The FLSA sets minimum age standards for allowing children to work. Under the law, most cannot work before age 16, with 18 being the minimum age for hazardous jobs. The Department of Labor publishes a list of such occupations. Children between the ages of 14 and 16 may work at certain types of jobs that do not interfere with their health, education, or well-being. Certain agricultural work also is permitted. States may have child labor laws even stricter than the federal law, and, if so, the stricter rules apply. In 2008, as a part of the Genetic Information Nondiscrimination Act of 2008, the FLSA was amended to increase the civil penalties for child labor violations resulting in death or serious bodily injury.

The Family and Medical Leave Act of 1993

Statutory Basis

Leave Requirement

a. (1) Entitlement to leave—an eligible employee shall be entitled to a total of 12 workweeks of leave during any 12-month period for one or more of the following:

   A. Because of the birth of a son or daughter of the employee and in order to care for such son or daughter.

   B. Because of the placement of a son or daughter with the employee for adoption or foster care.

   C. In order to care for the spouse, or a son, daughter, or parent, of the employee, if such spouse, son, daughter, or parent has a serious health condition.

   D. Because of a serious health condition that makes the employee unable to perform the functions of the position of such employee. [The Family and Medical Leave Act of 1993, 29 U.S.C. § 2601 et seq.]

Introduction: It's All in the Family

The FMLA was previously in the gender chapter because it was enacted primarily in response to female employees' concerns about keeping their job or being demoted or losing benefits after the birth or arrival of a child. Since its passage, however, the law has evolved into a much broader piece of legislation. With baby boomers playing such a large part in the national conscience and policies, it was inevitable that since the law also covers taking time off to care for parents, this would become a fertile area under the law.

General Provisions

LO3 Explain the Family Medical Leave Act, including to whom it applies and under what circumstances.

Scenario

On February 5, 1993, President Clinton signed into law the first piece of legislation of his administration: the Family and Medical Leave Act (FMLA). The act guarantees employees who have been on the job at least a year up to 12 weeks of unpaid leave per year for a birth; an adoption; or care of sick children, spouses, or parents (or their own serious illness) and the same or an equivalent job upon their return. This is why, in Opening Scenario 2, Carly will not be granted the FMLA leave she requests. She wishes to take time off for her husband's parent, not her own. This is not covered by the act. In January 2008, President George W. Bush signed into law an FMLA amendment that would allow an eligible employee to take up to 26 weeks unpaid leave in a 12-month period to care for a returning war veteran seriously injured in the line of duty. In addition, the National Defense Authorization Act for FY 2008 (NDAA)[35] allows eligible employees to take up to 12 weeks of unpaid leave to deal with exigencies caused by a spouse, son, daughter, or parent either being called to active duty or being on active duty. The FMLA applies to employers with 50 or more employees within a 75-mile radius. Employees must have worked for their employer for at least one year and for at least 1,250 hours during the 12 months preceding the time off. They must give the employer at least 30 days' notice when practical (such as for a birth).

In 2010, the Department of Labor expanded leave rights under the FMLA and extended the right to care for a sick child to an employee who is acting as a parent, even if the employee does not have a legal or biological relationship to the child. In announcing the new guidance, Hilda Solis, Secretary of Labor, stated:

> No one who loves and nurtures a child day-in and day-out should be unable to care for that child when he or she falls ill. No one who steps in to parent a child when that child's biological parents are absent or incapacitated should be denied leave by an employer because he or she is not the legal guardian. No one who intends to raise a child should be denied the opportunity to be present when that child is born simply because the state or an employer fails to recognize his or her relationship with the biological parent. These are just a few of many possible scenarios. The Labor Department's action today sends a clear message to workers and employers alike: All families, including LGBT families, are protected by the FMLA.[36]

Employers may require employees to first use vacation or other leave before applying for the unpaid leave, but employees must be compensated for the vacation days as they normally would be. Where both members of the couple work for the same employer, the employer can restrict the couple to a total of 12 weeks' leave per year. Employers must continue to provide employees with health insurance during their leave and may exclude the highest-paid 10 percent of their employees from FMLA coverage.

Employers also can require medical confirmation of an illness, which the U.S. Department of Labor defines as requiring at least one night in the hospital. Complaints may be filed with the Wage and Hour Division of the Labor Department, or the employee can file a lawsuit if he or she feels the employer violated the act.

In 1997, Congress declined to grant President Clinton's request to extend the FMLA to permit employees to take up to 24 hours of unpaid leave each year to fulfill certain family obligations such as attending parent-teacher conferences, taking a child to the doctor, finding child care, or caring for elderly relatives. Societal impediments also can be a factor, such as men feeling they will be viewed as disloyal if they take a leave of absence under the FMLA.

However, the greatest impediment to full use of the law is the fact that the leave is unpaid. In 2002, California became the first state to provided that employees be paid 55 percent of their salary for up to six weeks of FMLA leave (in addition to whatever other leave employees may have). It has been joined by New Jersey and New York, with Rhode Island, Oregon, and Massachusetts considering it. Other than those states, the United States is in the unique position of being the only industrially similar nation that does not provide at least some type of paid parental leave. This may, in fact, be remedied at some future point. In April 2008, the House Committee on Government Oversight and Reform passed a bill to provide federal employees at least a percentage of their income for four weeks when leave is taken to have or adopt a child.[37] The bill, never passed, proposed that employees and employers pay into a fund that will provide the source of the paid leave. Such legislation has been introduced before without success even though both parents work in about 76 percent of American working households and all other similar countries have such legislation.

The FMLA has been the subject of a great deal of uncertainty ever since its passage. The law, particularly the Department of Labor's regulations, has been a constant source of confusion for employers. There have been questions as to how serious an illness must be for the employee to qualify for the leave, assessment of eligibility requirements for the leave, what to do about intermittent leave, reinstatement after taking leave, and notification and certification requirements for leave, just to name a few issues.

These issues have resulted in a steadily increasing number of FMLA claims, causing it to develop into one of the most active areas of employment law. A survey by the Society for Human Resource Management (SHRM) found that nearly 40 percent of human resource professionals reported that confusion over implementation of the FMLA has led to illegitimate leave being granted.[38] Two of the most challenging FMLA-related activities identified by organizations are tracking/administering intermittent FMLA leave and determining the overall costs incurred while complying with the requirements of the FMLA. According to the survey, many HR professionals noted that the timing of intermittent FMLA leave requests (e.g., around weekends, holidays, pleasant weather) raised suspicions of abuse.

The Wage and Hour Division of the Department of Labor heard these comments and on November 17, 2008, announced the first major overhaul of the FMLA in 10 years. The new regulations became effective on January 16, 2009, and provided clarification and detailed new leave entitlements for the military, as mentioned earlier.[39] When the agency posted a request for comments on its proposed changes, over 15,000 were received.

If you think about the problems that can be presented for an employer if found to be in violation of the FMLA and the many ways in which the law can be violated, you can see how the law would be such a frustrating one for employers. It doesn't help matters when employees take FMLA leave and then post photos on social media showing them vacationing, including participating in strenuous physical activity despite having said they were taking the leave because they were ill. A 7th Circuit case involved what it meant for a daughter to take FMLA leave to "care for" for her parent dying of cancer. The daughter took FMLA leave to grant her dying-of-cancer mother's wish to go to Las Vegas, where they engaged in gambling and other Las Vegas activities such as dining on the strip and shopping. The daughter helped her mother take medication, but the trip did not include medical care, therapy, or treatment for the mother's cancer.[40] The court said this was permissible under the FMLA. Then there are other issues of vagueness. For instance, the *Spangler v. Federal Home Loan Bank of Des Moines*[41] case demonstrates why employers have such a problem with this law. A bank employee had a long history of depression that caused her to miss days of work. She had been given notice about her excessive absences and put on probation about her absenteeism, and yet she still took time off. She was terminated after calling in and leaving a voicemail message saying that she would not be in because of "depression again." The issue was whether this statement was sufficient to put the employer on notice that the employee was invoking the FMLA and taking FMLA leave. The court determined it well could be sufficient notice of a serious health condition as required by the FMLA because of the employer's extensive history with the employee taking absences because of depression. It did not mean the employer would be required to keep her on despite her absences, but it at least put the employer on notice that the employee was absent for FMLA reasons.

On the other hand, in *Righi v. SMC Corporation of America*,[42] the court upheld the termination of an employee who, discovering his mother had a medical emergency, emailed his supervisor that he would need the next couple of days off to arrange for her care. He was gone for nine days and during that time did not contact the employer to inform him of what was going on. When the employer repeatedly called the employee, there was no answer. The court said that under the FMLA the employee had a duty to comply with the employer's policies for taking FMLA leave, including notifying the employer of plans to take such leave. Avoiding the employer's calls and not contacting the employer relieved the employer of liability for the termination.

In *Terwilliger v. Howard Memorial Hospital*,[43] the court said the employee's FMLA rights were interfered with when the employee, a hospital housekeeper off for back surgery, kept receiving phone calls from her supervisor asking when she was returning to work. The employee had already requested and been granted FMLA leave for her serious medical condition but felt pressured to return to work by the calls continually made to her by her supervisor during recuperation.

As you can see, there seem to be as many ways to violate the FMLA as there are employees, so it is in an employer's best interest to know the FMLA requirements and comply with them.

Occupational Safety and Health Act

Statutory Basis

Occupational Safety and Health Act

§ 654 (§ 5) Duties

   a. Each employer—
     1. shall furnish to each of his employees employment and a place of employment which are free from recognized hazards that are causing or are likely to cause death or serious physical harm to his employees;
     2. shall comply with occupational safety and health standards promulgated under this Act.
   b. Each employee shall comply with occupational safety and health standards and all rules, regulations and orders issued pursuant to this Act which are applicable to his own actions and conduct.

Introduction: Safety at Work

Workplace safety seems like it might not be such a big deal—that is, of course, until you slip on spilled salad dressing in the kitchen of the restaurant for which you work and you cannot continue to pay your tuition. Workplace safety is often perceived as the bailiwick of angry-looking union reps or blue-collar "working stiffs" who carry lunch pails to work. But it is a workplace issue that affects us all. In 2012, 4,383 workers were killed on the job.[44] That is an average of nearly 12 deaths each day, and more than 96,700 violations of the Occupational Safety and Health Act's standards were found in 2010 across tens of thousands of work sites and 3 million suffer nonfatal workplace injuries costing millions of dollars. In its 2012 Workplace Safety Index, Liberty Mutual found that disabling workplace injuries and illnesses cost employers a total of nearly $1 billion per week in direct workers' compensation costs,[45] making health and safety one of the most vital workplace issues facing employers today. (See Exhibit 16.6, "The Top Six Ethics-Related Global Workplace Issues.")

On December 29, 1970, President Richard Nixon signed into law the Occupational Safety and Health Act, attempting to ensure safe and healthful working conditions for all employees and to preserve the human resources of the United States. Since 1971, OSHA claims that the act has helped to cut workplace fatalities by more than 65 percent and injury/illness rates by 67 percent; at the same time, U.S. employment has nearly doubled.[46] More than 100,000 workers who might have died on the job did not because of improved safety and health.

Exhibit 16.6   *The Top Six Ethics-Related Global Workplace Issues*

The following issues were named by the American Management Association in 2006 as the "Top Six Ethics-Related Global Workplace Issues" that would face firms in 2015. Did the AMA get them right, and are they currently our most pressing issues today?

1. Forced labor, child labor, working hours
2. Health and safety in the workplace, working conditions
3. Discrimination, harassment
4. Financial malfeasance
5. Fraud, theft
6. Gift giving, bribes

In 2014, Kirk Hanson, executive director of the Markkula Center for Applied Ethics at Santa Clara University, identified six ethical dilemmas that *every* professional faces. Do you see some overlaps or contrasts?

1. What Is Worthwhile Work? ("What is worthwhile spending the majority of my waking time on for the next year—or 30 years?")
2. Work vs. Family

3. Going Along with the Crowd (will you go along even if you disagree with the crowd?)
4. When Leaders Mislead (what do you do in the face of inappropriate authority?)
5. Are You a Change Agent?
6. Careers and the Common Good (will you apply your knowledge for the benefit of others?)

Sources: American Management Association, *The Ethical Enterprise: Doing the Right Things in the Right Ways, Today and Tomorrow* (New York: American Management Association/Human Resources Institute, 2006), http://www.amanet.org; Hanson, Kirk O., "The Six Ethical Dilemmas Every Professional Faces," Verizon Visiting Professorship in Business Ethics, Bentley University (February 3, 2014), http://www.bentley.edu/sites/www.bentley.edu.centers/files/2014/10/22/Hanson%20VERIZON%20Monograph_2014-10%20Final%20(1).pdf (accessed February 25, 2016).

OSHA specifically requires that an employer provide a safe and healthy workplace "to each of *its* employees. . . ." Does that language limit the liability of the employer only to those individuals who are actually employees of the employer? Under a concept called the "multiemployer doctrine," on multiemployer worksites, an employer who creates a safety hazard can be liable under the OSHA, regardless of whether the employees threatened are its own or those of another employer on the site. In Opening Scenario 3, Carterez could be found liable due to the multiemployer doctrine. An employer is liable as long as the government can show that the employee at a worksite was exposed to the risk by the contractor's safety violations. In Scenario 3, if it can be shown that Singhie was exposed to the cement dust due to the contractor's safety violation by not providing the mask, Carterez can be held liable and would be the responsible party to handle the OSHA violation.

While the Occupational Safety and Health Review Commission ruled that the multiemployer worksite policy does not apply to a general contractor if the general contractor's own employees were not exposed to the hazard, the Eighth Circuit reversed that interpretation, ruling that the multiemployer worksite policy makes the general contractor, in effect, the guarantor of all construction work as long as it has employees present, regardless of whether they are similarly exposed.[47]

General Provisions

LO4 Explain contributory negligence, assumption of risk, and the fellow servant rule, and their roles in the regulation of safety in the workplace and determine how OSHA impacted this regulatory environment.

contributory negligence
A defense to a negligence action based on the injured party's failure to exercise reasonable care for her or his own safety.

assumption of risk
A defense to a negligence action based on the argument that the injured party voluntarily exposed herself or himself to a known danger created by the other party's negligence.

LO5 Set forth what OSHA requires of employers to create a safer workplace and how it is enforced.

OSHA requires that an employer provide a safe workplace. Prior to passage of OSHA, there was no comprehensive national legislation about workplace safety, and state laws varied greatly. Employers could locate their workplaces in states with lax safety laws providing little protection for workers. Under such laws, employees were often limited in the damages they could recover due to injuries arising from the employer's unsafe workplace.

Several defenses were available to employers to escape liability for providing an unsafe work environment. **Contributory negligence** allowed the employer to defend against the employee's injury suit by claiming that the employee contributed to the injury through the employee's own negligence. The **assumption of risk** defense precluded the employee from recovering when the employee knew of a risk involved in the workplace, chose to chance not being injured, and was in fact injured. The **fellow servant rule** permitted the employer to escape liability when the negligence was the fault of an employee rather than the employer. As you can imagine, injured workers did not find much protection under these laws requiring that the employer provide a safe working environment.

Workers' compensation laws, however, are generally **no-fault**, which means that workers injured on the job are entitled to recover for their injuries without having to prove who is at fault. The defenses became irrelevant. The trade-off for employers, in agreeing to be bound by a no-fault system, is that the injured workers are limited in their financial recovery to what they can obtain under workers' compensation laws.

Section 5(a) of the act imposes two basic requirements on all employers—regardless of size—to accomplish the goal of a safer workplace. First, the employer must comply with all the safety and health standards dictated by the Department

fellow servant rule
An employer's defense to liability for an employee's injury where the injury occurred on the job and was caused by the negligence of another employee.

no-fault
Liability for injury imposed regardless of fault.

of Labor, generally called the "compliance" requirements. Second, the employer must "furnish to each of [its] employees employment and a place of employment which are free from recognized hazards that are causing or are likely to cause death or serious physical harm." This broad requirement is called the "general duty" clause, and the traditional employer defenses noted above are not often available. The only exceptions to the reach of the act are self-employed people, family members employed by family farms, state and local government employees (except under an OSHA-approved plan), and work environments that are regulated by other federal agencies (such as mining or nuclear energy).

In furtherance of workplace safety, OSHA creates certain specific regulatory standards of safety (for example, how much flour dust is permitted to be in a wheat-processing plant) in addition to its general duty clause, which applies in the absence of specific standards. The law applies to any employer that has employees and is in a business affecting commerce (most employers!). In order to accomplish its mission of workplace safety, OSHA provides several tools, including unannounced workplace inspections by OSHA compliance officers, citations and penalties for violations, and continual safety training requirements. Complaints to OSHA may arise from employees, grievances filed by other sources, or reports of fatal or multiple injuries. OSHA protects from retaliation employees who file such complaints by prohibiting employers from discharging or discriminating against employees who exercise rights afforded by the act. OSHA also provided for the creation of the National Institute for Occupational Safety and Health (NIOSH), the research arm of OSHA, which conducts research on workplace health and safety and makes recommendations to the secretary of labor that, if approved, may become the standards of conduct in a certain industry.

Routine inspections in certain high-risk industries also are conducted by OSHA. The employer may consent to the inspection or may demand that the OSHA representatives obtain a search warrant. There may be reasons to use one strategy or the other that lie outside the scope of this text, so it is advisable to consult with legal counsel. The inspection is likely to proceed in either scenario. To ensure that the inspectors are viewing the workplace in the same condition as that experienced by the employees, inspections are conducted without prior notice to an employer. In fact, anyone giving unauthorized advance notice of the inspection to the employer can be punished by a fine of up to $1,000. The inspector will arrive at the worksite, ask to see the safety and accident records of the employer, conduct a "walk around" to visually inspect the site, and discuss with the employer any violations or concerns, as well as possible solutions to the problems. Because OSHA cannot inspect the more than 8 million worksites covered by the act, it has established an inspection priority system in order to have the most significant impact. Under this system, the agency inspects situations of imminent danger, catastrophes and fatal accidents, employee complaints involving serious harm, referrals, or planned inspections.

LO6 Describe the reporting responsibilities of employers under the OSH Act.

Penalties and "abatement orders" are assessed in connection with the inspection officer's report. A nonserious or a serious violation may require payment of a penalty ranging from $0 to $7,000, while repeated and/or willful violations have a price tag of up to $70,000 per violation or up to $500,000 plus prison time if the violation was willful and involved a fatality. Criminal sanctions and even higher fines are also possible where the employer acts willfully and causes the death of an employee. (See Exhibit 16.7, "Seven Main Categories of OSHA Violations and Resulting Penalties.") Congress has contemplated raising these fines several times. In fact, in 2008, it did so for child labor injuries. However, the main penalty categories have not been reformed in decades. Though a bill was introduced in 2013 that would significantly increase penalties in many categories, it is considered unlikely to pass.[48]

As long as an employer is covered by the act, has more than 10 employees, and is not subject to one of the few exceptions (certain low-hazard industries in the

---

Exhibit 16.7 *Seven Main Categories of OSHA Violations and Resulting Penalties*

1. **Other than serious violation:** A violation that has a direct relationship to job safety and health, but probably would not cause death or serious physical harm. A proposed penalty of up to $7,000 for each violation is discretionary.

2. **Serious violation:** A violation where there is substantial probability that death or serious physical harm could result and the employer knew, or should have known, of the hazard. A mandatory penalty of up to $7,000 for each violation is proposed.

3. **Willful violation:** A violation that the employer knowingly commits or commits with plain indifference to the law. Penalties of up to $70,000 may be proposed for each willful violation, with a minimum penalty of $5,000 for each violation. If an employer is convicted of a willful violation of a standard that resulted in the death of an employee, the offense is punishable by a court-imposed fine or by imprisonment for up to six months, or both. A fine of up to $250,000 for an individual, or $500,000 for a corporation, may be imposed for a criminal conviction.

4. **Repeated violation:** A violation of any standard, regulation, rule, or order where, upon reinspection, a substantially similar violation can bring a fine of up to $70,000 for each such violation. The original violation must be final in order to be the basis for a repeated citation.

5. **Failure to abate prior violation:** Failure to abate a prior violation may bring a civil penalty of up to $7,000 for each day the violation continues beyond the prescribed abatement date.

6. ***De minimis* violation:** Violations of standards that have no direct or immediate relationship to safety or health.

7. **Additional violations:** Examples include falsifying records, reports, or applications; violations of posting requirements; assaulting a compliance officer; or otherwise resisting, opposing, intimidating, or interfering with a compliance officer while engaged in the performance of her or his duties.

Due to the expenses associated with these violations and considering the fact that each day represents a separate violation, employers often request variances in order to prevent citations or penalties. Employers may ask OSHA for a variance from a standard or regulation if they cannot fully comply by the effective date, due to shortages of materials, equipment, or professional or technical personnel, or can prove their facilities or methods of operation provide employee protection "at least as effective" as that required by OSHA. Employers can request a temporary variance, a permanent variance, an interim order, or an experimental variance in order to remain in compliance with OSHA standards. Variances are not retroactive, so an employer who has been cited for a standards violation may not seek relief from that citation by applying for a variance.

Source: OSHA Training Institute, OSHA Directorate of Training and Education, "Introduction to OSHA, Instructor Guide" (April 2011), https://www.osha.gov/dte/outreach/intro_osha/intro_to_osha_guide.html (accessed September 17, 2017).

retail, finance, insurance, real estate, and service sectors), it must maintain certain records for OSHA compliance. Where the injury or illness is work-related and meets the general recording criteria or falls into specific categories, reporting is mandated. Employers must report injuries and fatalities without delay—within eight hours for fatalities and within twenty-four hours for in-patient hospitalizations.[49] It must be reported as long as it is an illness, a death, or an injury that involves (1) medical treatment, (2) loss of consciousness, (3) restriction of work or motion, or (4) transfer to a different position. Employers also must report workplace injuries due to assaults by family members or ex-spouses as a part of their record-keeping requirements. The records must contain the following information, must be reported on OSHA Form 300,[50] and must be posted for the employees to see (i.e., it need not be filed with the government but, instead, must be kept throughout the year and compiled for the February posting): case number, employee's name, job title, date of injury or onset of illness, where the event occurred, description of the event, classification of the case, and number of days away from work.[51]

Employees must be informed of their OSHA rights by their employer. This requirement may be met by displaying an OSHA poster in the workplace, but displaying this poster is not mandatory. Employee rights also include requesting and participating in inspections, notice of an employer's violations or citations, access to monitoring procedures and results, and access to medical information. Employees who provide information to OSHA are protected from discharge and/or discrimination by the employer in retaliation for the reporting.

Responsibility for enforcing OSHA rests with the Department of Labor's Occupational Safety and Health Administration (OSHA). If an employer seeks to challenge a citation or penalty imposed, as opposed to simply demanding a warrant from the inspector to come onto the premises, it may submit an appeal to the Occupational Safety and Health Review Commission (OSHRC), an independent federal agency functioning as an administrative court created to decide issues of citations or penalties resulting from OSHA inspections.

An example of a relatively large penalty for willful violations would be the *Cintas* case in 2007, where OSHA proposed a penalty of $2.78 million after an inspection following the death of a worker who fell into a dryer while clearing a wet laundry jam.[52] Cintas, the largest industrial laundry company in the United States, was subject to 42 willful, instance-by-instance citations for violations of the OSHA lockout/tagout standard, including the failures to shut down and to lock out power to the equipment before clearing jams. Cintas eventually settled with OSHA a year and a half later for $2.76 million, along with commitments to improve site safety. However, related unions claimed that the agreement had no teeth since Cintas was given two years to correct the severe safety violations and no follow-up inspections were planned. "On its way out the door, the Bush Labor Department has granted serial offender Cintas a despicable pardon for their failure to protect its workers from hazardous machinery," said Congressman Phil Hare (D-IL). Hare also noted that, as part of the settlement agreement, "the Department of Labor modified the willful citations to 'unclassified citations,' despite the fact that Cintas knew about these hazards and OSHA originally found the company to be negligent. There is nothing in the law that even allows unclassified citations and we are determined to take legislative action to prohibit the declassification of willful citations."[53]

Actually, the question of willfulness is one that remains somewhat open in the courts. It is an important one to answer because fines can be significantly increased where willfulness is shown. OSHA defines a willful violation as "a violation that the employer intentionally and knowingly commits or a violation that the employer commits with plain indifference to the law. The employer either knows that what he or she is doing constitutes a violation, or is aware that a hazardous condition existed and made no reasonable effort to eliminate it." In addition, the OSHRC has also interpreted willfulness to include a violation the employer should have known.

In November 2010, the OSH Act (OSHA) launched the Severe Violator Enforcement Program (SVEP) in order to "more effectively focus enforcement efforts on recalcitrant employers who demonstrate indifference to the health and safety of their employees through willful, repeated, or failure-to-abate violations of the OSH Act."[54] Evaluating the program after its initial 18 months, OSHA found that targeting "recalcitrant" employers led to increased follow-up inspections and enhanced settlements from repeat offenders. Critics of the program have charged that businesses may find themselves on the SVEP list prematurely and face high barriers in getting off the list.[55]

Specific Regulations

Certain specific regulations seem to apply across the board to all types of employment environments. For instance, a number of specific requirements involve the physical layout of the worksite including proper ventilation, adequate means of emergency exit, safety nets, guard rails, and so on. Employees must be trained and informed (through classes, labels, signs) regarding protective measures, for everything from wearing protective devices, such as masks, to the proper use of chemicals. Medical examinations must be provided by the employer where an employee has been exposed to toxic substances.

OSHA can set standards on its own initiative or in response to petitions from other parties. If it is determined that a specific standard is needed, any of several advisory committees may be called upon to develop recommendations. Recommendations for standards also may come from NIOSH. Once OSHA has developed plans for a standard, it publishes them in the *Federal Register* as a "Notice of Proposed Rulemaking." A recent example is OSHA's recommendations to lower worker exposure to crystalline silica, a deadly dust that needlessly kills hundreds of workers and sickens thousands more each year.[56] Exposure to airborne silica dust occurs in operations involving cutting, sawing, drilling, and crushing of concrete, brick, block, and other stone products and in operations using sand products, such as in glass manufacturing, foundries, and sand blasting. In preparing the recommendations, OSHA reviewed existing practices and programs as well as available scientific information on silica dust and cancer, and solicited comments from representatives of trade and professional associations, labor organizations, individual firms, and other interested parties. The final recommendations were announced in August 2013. The employer may be held liable for workplace hazards under the general duty clause even if specific regulations do not exist (see discussion of the general duty clause below).

Finalizing a new standard can be a time-consuming process. A 2012 report by the Government Accountability Office (GAO) found that between 1981 and 2010, the time it took OSHA to develop and issue safety and health standards ranged from 15 months to 19 years and averaged more than seven years.[57] Though rarely used, the secretary of labor may establish **emergency temporary standards** that will be effective immediately on publication in the *Federal Register* without having to go through the lengthy rule-making process otherwise required by the act where he or she "determines (a) that employees are exposed to grave danger from exposure to substances or agents determined to be toxic or physically harmful or from new hazards, and (b) that such emergency standard is necessary to protect employees from such danger." The emergency standard is effective until regular standards are approved through the regular procedures or for six months, whichever is shorter.

One of the most burdensome requirements on employers is the **continual-training requirement**. OSHA requires that employers adopt a program of continual workplace safety training of employees. An employer is required to provide safety training every time an employee is hired or transferred into a new position, even if for just a day. This is generally the most frequently cited type of violation under the statute. As a result, OSHA has made an effort to simplify the requirement and now supplies employers with material safety data sheets regarding various types of chemicals and the surrounding hazards associated with them.

General Duty Clause

The **general duty clause** protects employees against hazards in the workplace, *where no other OSHA standard would address the condition.* The general duty clause stems from the act's provision that "Each employer . . . shall furnish to each of his employees employment and a place of employment which are free from recognized hazards that are causing or are likely to cause death or serious physical harm to his employees." For instance, once it is found that a certain chemical used in an employer's manufacturing process causes reproductive harm or perhaps damage to the employee's skin, then under the general duty clause the employer must take steps to protect employees and to provide a workplace free from this hazard. It is the employer's responsibility to be aware of these workplace hazards and to ensure that all employees are equally protected. A recognized hazard also may take the form of actual knowledge when the employer actually knows of the hazard or the form of constructive knowledge if the industry recognizes the hazard even if the employer does not actually know of the hazard.

It is not always easy for an employer to determine what constitutes a recognized hazard because we are constantly improving our knowledge; so, what we may think is all right today may prove harmful later. Whereas smokers were once free to puff away in the workplace, today OSHA has classified secondhand smoke as a potential cancer-causing agent. In fact, 36 states, along with the District of Columbia, American Samoa, the Northern Mariana Islands, Puerto Rico, and the U.S. Virgin Islands, have regulations on the provision of smoke-free working conditions.[58]

---

emergency temporary standards
Standards are imposed by OSHA without immediately going through the typical process where an employee is exposed to grave danger from exposure to substances and the standards are necessary to protect employees from the danger.

continual-training requirement
OSHA requires that the employer provide safety training to all new employees and to all employees who have been transferred into new positions.

general duty clause
A provision of the act requiring that employers furnish to each employee employment and a place of employment free from recognized hazards that cause or are likely to cause death or serious physical harm to the employee.

And what does the general duty clause's term *likely* mean in connection with those risks that an employer must protect against? If there is a chance that 1 person in 1,000 may be harmed, does that mean that the risk is likely, or must 5 people out of 10 be at risk for harm to be likely? The OSHRC has stated that the harm need not be likely but possible. In fact, the commission has said that "the proper question is not whether an accident is likely to occur, but whether, if an accident does occur, the result is likely to be death or serious physical harm."

Under OSHA, there are times when an employer or an employee may not comply with workplace rules or safety regulations and no violation results. For instance, where, based on a reasonable apprehension of death or serious injury and a reasonable belief that no less drastic alternative is available, an employee believes that the employer has violated its general duty to provide a safe working environment, the employees may refuse to work in that environment and the employer cannot punish them for doing so.

In *Whirlpool Corporation v. Marshall,*[59] the U.S. Supreme Court upheld an OSHA regulation protecting employees against retaliation for refusing to work under dangerous conditions. Two employees at a Whirlpool plant refused to perform maintenance work that would require them to walk on elevated mesh screens less than two weeks after a coworker fell to his death through the screens. The employees were sent home, and written reprimands were placed in their personnel files. The Court held that Whirlpool had illegally retaliated against the employees.

As an example of the application of the general duty clause as well as the enormous expense of pursuing the defense of an OSHA claim for an employer, consider the case of a Walmart employee in Valley Stream, Long Island, Jdimytai Damour, who was trampled to death in a Black Friday sales stampede early on the morning after Thanksgiving in 2008. OSHA determined that Walmart had committed a "serious violation" of the general duty clause. It ruled, in effect, that Walmart's failure to properly control the crowd, which had been foreseeable given previous Black Friday sales events, created a workplace hazard that was likely to cause death or serious physical injury to the employee. Although the proposed fine was only $7,000, the retail giant fought OSHA's citation in court—spending, so far, more than $2 million in legal fees—presumably because of the citation's future implications for any retailer when faced with large, unpredictable crowd surges. Although OSHA's fine was upheld in court and upheld on appeal to the OSHRC, Walmart appealed the ruling to the full body of the OSHRC in 2011. There has been no progress on the case since that point, as the OSHRC is short a member and is not therefore a "full" body. President Obama nominated a third commissioner to the OSHRC in November 2013, but the nomination awaits Senate confirmation.[60] Meanwhile, no criminal penalties were ever brought against anyone at Walmart (Walmart settled the criminal case by agreeing to pay money to a victims' fund and to institute crowd management techniques), but a wrongful death suit brought against Walmart by Damour's family was still pending.

On the other hand, there may be workplace hazards or injuries for which the employer will *not* be held responsible under OSHA. The three most common of these circumstances include the following:

recklessness

Conscious disregard for safety; conscious failure to use due care.

greater hazard defense

An employer may use the greater hazard defense to an OSHA violation where the hazards of compliance are greater than the hazards of noncompliance, where alternative means of protection are unavailable, and where a variance was not available.

1. Where the harm is the result of **reckless** behavior by an employee.
2. Where it is physically or economically impossible for the employer to comply with a safety requirement.
3. Where compliance with a requirement presents a greater harm than not complying (**greater hazard defense**).

If any of the above three conditions exist, there will be no OSHA violation imposed on the employer. For example, a citation was issued because a construction company failed to install a cable railing on the perimeter of the top of a building it was constructing. The employer presented evidence that the risk involved in constructing the railing would subject its employees to a greater risk than if the railing were not there. To assert this defense, however, an employer must show

- The hazards of compliance with the standard are greater than the hazards of noncompliance.
- Alternative means of protection are unavailable.
- A variance from the secretary of labor was unavailable or inappropriate.

In *Horne Plumbing and Heating Co. v. OSHRC*,[61] the employer had taken precautionary measures, but two employees ignored the employer's instructions and warnings from coworkers, worked in an unsafe area of the site anyway, and were killed. The court noted: "[a] hazard consisting of conduct by employees, such as equipment riding, cannot be totally eliminated. A willfully reckless employee may on occasion circumvent the best conceived and most vigorously enforced safety regime. Congress intended to require elimination only of preventable hazards." The court found that the employer did everything possible to ensure compliance with the law, short of remaining at the worksite and directing the operations itself. This is slightly different from willfulness because it is simply whether a reasonable person would have recognized the hazard. Was this final effort required to protect the employee? The court responded that (citing a separate case):

> While close supervision may be required in some cases to avoid accidents, it is unrealistic to expect an experienced and well-qualified [worker] to be under constant scrutiny. Such a holding by the Commission, requiring that each employee be constantly watched by a supervisor, would be totally impractical and in all but the most unusual circumstances, an unnecessary burden.

Finally, if the injury or illness does not result from a work-related cause, no report need be made. An illness or injury is considered work-related if (1) it occurred on the employer's premises, (2) it occurred as a result of work-related activities, (3) the employee was required to be there by the employer, or (4) the employee was traveling to work or to a place he or she was required to be by the employer. If the activity does not fit into one of these categories, it was not work-related, and no report needs to be made. Accidents occurring in a telecommuting employee's home are not covered, but those occurring in an employer's car are. According to OSHA, "An employer is responsible for ensuring that its employees have a safe and healthful workplace, not a safe and healthful home." However, the employer is not without any responsibility toward telecommuting workers. OSHA clarifies this responsibility as follows: "The employer is responsible only for preventing or correcting hazards to which employees may be exposed in the course of their work. For example: if work is performed in the basement space of a residence and the stairs leading to the space are unsafe, the employer could be liable if the employer knows or reasonably should have known of the dangerous condition."[62]

Intentional Acts

Although workers' compensation is the exclusive remedy available to injured employees, an exception exists for "intentional acts." If the workplace injury is caused by the employer's willful act, including the willful disregard of known dangers, the employee can sue the employer for compensatory (to compensate the injured party) and punitive (to punish the employer) damages.

Violence in the Workplace

Workplace violence is an often-overlooked component of on-the-job injuries, though it has been among the top four causes of workplace death for over 15 years.[63] A 2011 government report found that in 2009 alone there were 572,000 reported occurrences of nonfatal workplace violence and 521 homicides in the workplace.[64] Under the OSH Act, an employer is required to protect employees against "recognized" workplace safety and health hazards that are likely to cause serious injury or death. OSHA takes the position that employers who do not take reasonable steps to prevent or abate a recognized workplace violence hazard could be found to be in violation of the general duty clause.

Although workplace violence is most often associated with a current or former disgruntled employee, it can also arise from customers, spouses, or relatives. To respond most effectively to potential violence and to head off any potential claim that the employer has failed in its duty to protect its employees, employers should develop a workplace violence policy that includes the following features:

- A "zero tolerance" policy toward threats or acts of violence.
- An established complaint process for employees to be able to warn the employer of potential violence.
- An established process for investigating complaints.
- A consistent application of disciplinary actions in response to violent acts.
- Training for managers and employees to recognize workplace violence.
- A requirement that employees provide the employer (usually HR or Security) with any protective or restraining order that lists the workplace as a protected area. (This circumstance actually comes up with some frequency for large employers, unfortunately.)

The establishment of firm antiviolence policies and consistent application of those policies do not solve all the potential difficulties with workplace violence. Employers must also remember that perpetrators of the violence may also have rights. For example, the Americans with Disabilities Act protects an employee with an emotional impairment that qualifies as a disability under the ADA who is *otherwise qualified for the position.* An employer may be restricted from taking certain employment actions against the protected individual with mental or emotional impairments and instead might need to consider the possibility of accommodations. However, "[n]othing in the ADA prevents an employer from maintaining a workplace free of violence or threats of violence."[65] An employer never has to condone threats or actual violence, *even if* a disability caused the threats or violence.[66]

Bullying

Many workplace acts of violence are easy to recognize. Others, however, are subtler and harder to detect. Bullying, which has been defined as "the tendency of individuals or groups to use persistent aggressive or unreasonable behavior against a coworker," is a prime example.

Workplace bullying is a serious problem affecting over 60 million workers each year. A 2017 study by the Workplace Bullying Institute (WBI) (yes, there is such a place) found that almost a quarter of Americans have directly experienced bullying in the workplace, an additional 19 percent have witnessed bullying, and in 63 percent of the cases, the bullies are one's bosses.[67] Thirty-three percent of the bullies were peers with the same rank as the targets. Seventy percent of the perpetrators are male, and two-thirds of targeted workers are female. When workers who have experienced bullying are asked what made the behavior stop, the WBI reports that the consistent answer is quitting the job or being terminated.[68]

Bullying can rise to the level of harassment and discrimination, and the creation of a hostile work environment, which can be especially difficult to prevent if the manager responsible for ensuring a safe work environment is the bully. In 2008, in *Raess v. Doescher,* the Indiana Supreme Court reinstated a $325,000 verdict in favor of an employee who was verbally assaulted by a surgeon during an altercation in the hospital's operating room. The decision is noteworthy because liability depended directly on the act of bullying rather than on any hostile work environment or antidiscrimination law. The decision, therefore, appears to have created a common-law tort of workplace bullying, making Indiana the first such state with this tort, but probably not the last. Since 2003, 26 states have proposed legislation that would prohibit bullying in the workplace, though no such laws have yet been enacted.[69]

Bullying can be difficult to detect. In addition to acts commonly associated with bullying, such as humiliating comments, intimidation, overly harsh criticism, excessive yelling, belittling remarks, and even physical assault, bullying can also involve setting impossible deadlines, undermining work productivity, and failing to give credit. Bullying can even be nonverbal and covert.

The *Raess* case is a warning to employers to get their workplace bullies under control. The fact that bullying may not involve serious physical harm or constitute harassment and discrimination does not mean that a workplace bully is not causing irreparable damage to the workplace, including high turnover costs and bad public relations, as well as creating serious legal liability, including higher workers' compensation costs.

Retaliation

Section 11(c) of the OSH Act prohibits retaliation against whistleblowers. To establish retaliation, an employee needs to prove (1) that he or she engaged in a protected activity (i.e., whistleblowing), (2) that the employer knew about that activity, (3) that the employer subjected him or her to an adverse action (which can include intimidation or threats), and (4) that the protected activity contributed to the adverse action. In 2015, 3,288 whistleblower complaints were filed with OSHA. In addition to the OSH Act antiretaliation provision, federal whistleblowing provisions exist to protect 19 specific industries, including airline, commercial motor carrier, consumer product, environmental, financial reform, health care reform, nuclear, pipeline, public transportation agency, railroad, maritime, and securities laws. OSHA administers all 20 provisions. In December 2013, OSHA announced its intention to launch an online complaint system to report whistleblower retaliation. If the proposed online system is approved, the streamlined process is expected to result in an increase in complaints.[70]

Employee Benefits—ERISA, COBRA, and HIPAA

Statutory Basis

Employee Retirement Income Security Act (ERISA)

§ 1132. Civil Enforcement.
  a. A civil action may be brought—
    1. By a participant or beneficiary—
      (B) to recover benefits due to him under the terms of his plan, to enforce his rights under the terms of the plan, or to clarify his rights to future benefits under the terms of the plan.

§ 1140. Interference with protected rights.

It shall be unlawful for any person to discharge, fine, suspend, expel, discipline, or discriminate against a participant or beneficiary for exercising any right to which he is entitled under the provisions of an employee benefit plan, or for the purpose of interfering with the attainment of any right to which such participant may become entitled under the plan.

Introduction: Will It Be There When I Retire?

Although not required to provide such benefits, many firms offer employees retirement plans, health care, and other employee benefits. In most cases, through their employers, employees invest a portion of their salary in a plan that provides funding for the employee's retirement. But if the employer goes bankrupt or the employee switches jobs, what happens to all of the money the employee paid into that plan? Or assume an employee has excellent medical benefits with his present company, benefits that he often takes advantage of; is he tied to that company and discouraged from leaving because he is concerned that he will not find those benefits on his own or elsewhere? What about an employee who pays into a retirement fund through her employer only to find there are insufficient funds for her to receive the benefits when she retires?

Enron, WorldCom, Global Crossing, and United Airlines all filled the headlines of major newspapers in recent years with reports on their bankruptcies and accounting scandals. But Enron and WorldCom also contributed significantly to employee benefits law by adversely impacting the retirement benefits and health benefits of their employees as well as the investments of other companies' and entities' retirement plans. For example, Enron employees whose retirement plans were heavily invested in Enron stock lost their retirement savings, the University of California lost $145 million when Enron's stock collapsed, and the Florida State Board of Administration and New York City pension funds lost a combined $444 million.[71]

LO7 Explain the purposes of ERISA and identify who and what type of entities are covered.

In 1974, as a result of concerns regarding the protection of pension benefits of workers who lost their jobs prior to retirement, Congress enacted the Employee Retirement Income Security Act (ERISA), a federal law that governs certain administrative aspects of employee benefit and retirement plans and that is enforced by the Department of Labor (DOL). Congress was concerned about the millions of employees and their dependents who were affected by employee benefit plans. ERISA was designed to encourage cautious, careful management of retirement funds by employers who were receiving tax benefits for doing so. As we will see, ERISA coverage is not restricted to merely retirement plans but covers many types of promised employee benefits. ERISA is a complex act that is multifaceted, and you will only be introduced to it in this text. (See Exhibit 16.8, "Realities about ERISA.")

General Provisions

LO8 Describe the minimum ERISA standards for employee benefit plans.

An employer that offers welfare benefits (e.g., health, life, disability, or accident insurance) or retirement plans to its employees is subject to certain requirements under ERISA, which covers most private-sector employee benefit plans. In general, ERISA does not cover plans established or maintained by governmental entities or churches, plans maintained outside the United States primarily for the benefit of nonresident aliens, or plans maintained for nonemployees such as a director or independent contractors. The Department of Labor enforces the reporting and disclosure, as well as fiduciary requirements of ERISA. Individual plaintiffs may file actions based on ERISA violations, and ERISA preempts all state laws that relate to employee benefit plans, whether or not the situation contemplated by the state law is actually covered specifically in ERISA.

Exhibit 16.8 *Realities about ERISA*

1. Your pension plans are not protected against the trustees who administer them.
2. Even if you put money into a retirement plan, it might not be there when you retire.
3. Even if your employer puts money into your retirement plan, depending on the type of plan, it might not be there when you retire.
4. ERISA applies beyond simply retirement or pension funds.

employee benefit plan (or plans)
A contractual obligation either through a plan, fund, or arrangement by which an employer or an employee organization such as a labor union agrees to provide retirement benefits or welfare benefits to employees and their dependents and beneficiaries.

retirement or pension plan
A plan that provides for compensation at retirement or deferral of income to periods beyond termination of employment.

defined contribution
Retirement plan where the benefits payable to a participant are based on the amount of contributions and earnings on such contributions.

defined benefit
Retirement plan where the benefit payable to a participant is defined up front by a formula, the funding of which is determined actuarially.

ERISA technically applies to **employee benefit plans** and covers two basic types of plans. The first type of plan ERISA covers is welfare plans. A *welfare plan* is any plan, program, or fund that the employer maintains to provide the following: medical, surgical, or hospital care; benefits for sickness, accident, disability, or death; unemployment benefits; vacation benefits; apprenticeship and training programs; day care centers; scholarship funds; prepaid legal services; or severance pay. However, payroll practices from the employer's general assets are not welfare benefit plans covered by ERISA.

The other type of plan ERISA covers is **retirement** or **pension plans**. There are two general forms of *pension plans:* those with **defined contributions** and those with **defined benefits**. The former involves plans in which each employee has her or his own account and the benefits received at retirement are based solely on the principal and income contributed. Contributions and defined contribution plans can come from employees, the employer, or both. Defined benefit plans comprise all other plans but generally refer to plans where the amount the employee receives at retirement is specifically designated at the time the employee enters the plan. Contributions to defined benefit plans generally only come from the employer, although some old plans also allow employee contributions. In defined contribution plans, the security comes from knowing the amount of principal that will be invested, while the security in defined benefit plans comes from knowing exactly how much will be paid in the end.

ERISA imposes the following requirements on a plan to ensure that employee benefit plans are created and maintained in a fair and financially sound manner:

- It must be in writing and communicated to all employees in a language they will understand within a specified period of time. Employees also must be notified in writing of plan changes.
- The assets of a plan must be held in trust.
- A plan must be for the exclusive benefit of the employees and their beneficiaries. An employer may have assets of the plan returned only after all plan liabilities have been satisfied.
- It must satisfy certain minimum participation, vesting, and distribution requirements.
- A plan may only be established and maintained by an employer, although funding of the plan may be from employer or employee contributions or both.

Also, ERISA establishes requirements for managing and administering pension and welfare plans. There are two main important issues arising from ERISA compliance: (1) fiduciary duties and (2) reporting and disclosure.

Fiduciary Duty

Prior to the enactment of ERISA, plan coordinators routinely abused the funds entrusted to them, often at the expense of the employees. For instance, the funds may have been offered as loans to selected people, with little or no interest in return and little or no security for the loans, thereby interfering with employees' ability to earn income from the otherwise proper investment of funds.

fiduciary
Someone who has discretionary authority over the investment or management of plan assets of others.

ERISA established a number of requirements, called *fiduciary standards,* to prevent these abuses. Those authorized to make decisions about the placement and investment of the pension plan or those who offer the plan investment advice are considered **fiduciaries** and are subject to the following fiduciary requirements:

- *Loyalty*—Fiduciaries must discharge their duties *solely in the interests of plan participants.* Although fiduciaries may have other concerns, they must ignore those concerns when making fiduciary decisions. They must have undivided loyalty to the participants in the plan.

- *Exclusive purpose*—Fiduciaries when making decisions must make them with the exclusive purpose of providing benefits under the plan and defraying the reasonable expenses under the plan. Accordingly, fiduciaries may not act for their personal benefit or for the benefit of their employer or any other party.

- *Prudence*—A fiduciary must exercise the care and judgment one would expect from a prudent person pursuing similar objectives under the same circumstance. In some instances, this requires a fiduciary to rely on the judgment of advisors, provided that such advisors are prudently selected and supervised. Prudence is determined at the time the investment decision is made and not retroactively with 20/20 hindsight.

- *Diversification*—When investing plan assets, a fiduciary must do so in a diversified manner so as to avoid large losses. This *diversification* standard is intended to limit the investment risk of a plan. The *prudence* standard generally would require that a fiduciary managing the investments of a plan maintain a diversified portfolio. However, the *diversification* standard in effect creates a presumption that an undiversified portfolio is not prudent.

- *Compliance with plan documents*—A fiduciary is required to administer the plan in a manner that is consistent with its governing documents.

If fiduciaries of retirement plans are required to diversify the plan's assets and act prudently, why did Enron, WorldCom, Global Crossing, and other large corporations have a significant concentration of plan assets in the company's stock? ERISA provides an exception to the fiduciary requirements for "individual account plans" that allow participants to direct the investment of their accounts. Individual account plans are defined contribution plans like popular 401(k) plans. However, the fiduciary is still responsible for selecting the menu of investment alternatives and providing adequate information concerning these choices. One such investment is often the employer's stock. Whether the employer's stock should be an investment and whether the amount of investment in employer stock should be limited is a question of prudence and diversification, as Enron, WorldCom, and Global Crossing have proven. In reaction to Enron, WorldCom, Global Crossing, and other instances where the value of employer stock has dropped, causing losses in retirement plans, Congress amended ERISA in 2006 to require public companies that allow for investment of employee contributions into an employer stock fund to notify them of their right to diversify into other nonemployer stock investments. In addition, public companies that match employee contributions in company stock must allow participants who have more than three years of service to diversify out of such investment and must provide for at least three alternative investments. Such companies also must provide notice of such diversification rights. Until employees are allowed to diversify out of employer stock, continued investment in such employer stock will be subject to the general fiduciary requirements of ERISA. *Varity Corp. v. Howe,* parts of which are reproduced at the end of this chapter, explores the nature of these fiduciary duties.

Certain transactions between an employee benefit plan and "parties in interest," which include the employer, fiduciaries, and others who may be in a position to exercise improper influence over the plan, are prohibited by ERISA and may suffer penalties. Most of these types of transactions also are prohibited by the tax code. However, there are some statutory exemptions from the prohibited transaction rules, and the DOL and IRS can authorize such exemptions through regulatory and individual exemptive procedures.

One holding that seems to be gaining steam as the dominant standard is the "presumption of prudence" approach, which is typified in this statement by the Third Circuit in *Moench v. Robertson.*[72] It *"essentially shields the fiduciaries from such claims where the plan expressly authorizes employer stock as an investment unless the company and/or its stock value had been placed at extreme risk."*[73] The standard is supported in the Second, Third, Fifth, Seventh, Ninth, and Eleventh Circuits.[74] The Sixth Circuit has also supported the standard. However, in a 2012 stock drop case, this court broke with the other circuits in refusing to apply this standard at the pleading stage, a ruling that lowers the burden for plaintiffs.[75] In 2014, the Sixth Circuit case went to the Supreme Court, which rejected the presumption of prudence approach based on the language in ERISA and held, to the contrary, that all ERISA plan fiduciaries are subject to a similar duty of prudence.[76]

Reporting and Disclosure

ERISA requires the employer or plan administrator to provide information to each participant and beneficiary about retirement plans and welfare plans; this information also must be provided to the federal government under certain circumstances. The required information includes a summary plan description (SPD), identifying in understandable terms the plan participants' eligibility for participation and benefits under the plan. Plan changes must be communicated in a timely manner through either a new SPD or a summary of material modification. The SPD is required to be furnished to each participant eligible for benefits under the plan as well as other beneficiaries. The SPD is not required to be filed with the DOL, but it must be furnished when requested. An annual report must be filed with the DOL containing financial and other information concerning the operation of the plan. Plan administrators also must furnish participants and beneficiaries with a summary of the information contained in the annual report. Certain plans may be exempt for the annual report requirement. For instance, the reporting and disclosure laws do not apply to insured welfare plans with fewer than 100 participants.

ERISA was amended by the Pension Protection Act (PPA) of 2006 to address the perceived abuses of Enron and WorldCom and the risks of having retirement investments heavily weighted in employer stock. Since Enron, participants in individually directed account plans have the following rights and must be notified of such rights:

- Participants must be notified in advance of any period in which they will be prohibited from trading in their plan accounts, or so-called blackout periods.
- Participants in defined contribution plans that invest in publicly traded stock of their employer must be allowed to diversify their accounts into at least three other investment options and must be notified of such rights.

Courts have taken ERISA's specific disclosure rules and crafted a broader and more general duty to disclose information. For example, as discussed in the *Varity Corp. v. Howe* case, provided at the end of the chapter, the Supreme Court ruled that a fiduciary has the duty not to mislead participants regarding their benefits. Many lower courts also have addressed cases alleging an affirmative duty to disclose information that may impact a participant's decisions regarding her or his benefits.

For example, several cases address whether a company has an affirmative duty to disclose to retiring employees whether enhanced early retirement benefits may be offered in the future. Claimants in these cases argue that the fiduciary had the duty to provide more or better information to the plaintiff regarding benefits. The stock drop cases addressed whether ERISA requires an affirmative duty to disclose. The *Enron* court in particular found that such a duty might exist if there are "special circumstances" with a potentially "extreme impact" on the "plan as a whole." The next wave of ERISA litigation also hinges on this affirmative duty to disclose and has been focused on disclosure of plan fees and expenses. This duty-to-disclose issue continues to be litigated and to develop, and ERISA fiduciaries might be wise to overdisclose rather than underdisclose information that may be relevant to plan participants.

The Department of Labor issued new rules, in 2012, that expand the disclosure responsibilities of ERISA plan providers, particularly in the area of fee disclosures. Under the amended disclosure rules, "[r]etirement plan providers are required to disclose fee and service information to plan sponsors, in order to help them fulfill their fiduciary duties."[77]

The DOL summarized the new rule as requiring "that certain service providers to employee pension benefit plans disclose information to assist plan fiduciaries in assessing the reasonableness of contracts or arrangements, including the reasonableness of the service providers' compensation and potential conflicts of interest that may affect the service providers' performance. These disclosure requirements are established as part of a statutory exemption from ERISA's prohibited transaction provisions. This regulation will affect employee pension benefit plan sponsors and fiduciaries and certain service providers to such plans."[78]

The Supreme Court has determined that ERISA fiduciaries must consider the conflict of interest that may arise from the dual role of paying out plans and determining eligibility for benefits.[79] In *Metropolitan Life Insurance Company v. Glenn* (2008):

> "Metropolitan Life Insurance Company (MetLife) is an administrator and the insurer of Sears, Roebuck & Company's long-term disability insurance plan, which is governed by the Employee Retirement Income Security Act of 1974 (ERISA). The plan gives MetLife (as administrator) discretionary authority to determine the validity of an employee's benefits claim and provides that MetLife (as insurer) will pay the claims. Respondent Wanda Glenn, a Sears employee, was granted an initial

24 months of benefits under the plan following a diagnosis of a heart disorder. MetLife encouraged her to apply for, and she began receiving, Social Security disability benefits based on an agency determination that she could do no work. But when MetLife itself had to determine whether she could work, in order to establish eligibility for extended plan benefits, it found her capable of doing sedentary work and denied her the benefits. Glenn sought federal-court review under ERISA, but the District Court denied relief. In reversing, the Sixth Circuit . . . considered it a conflict of interest that MetLife both determined an employee's eligibility for benefits and paid the benefits out of its own pocket. Based on a combination of this conflict and other circumstances, it set aside MetLife's benefits denial."

In upholding the employee's claim, the Court found that although the structural conflict of interest within the fiduciary's role is permissible, it must be weighed when considering discretionary abuse in denial of benefits. Emphasizing that this consideration must be made on the basis of the particular facts in each case, the *Glenn* ruling enlarges the scope of discovery in denial of benefits cases and shifts the burden of proof to the fiduciary to show that discretionary power was not abused. Recent lower court decisions have contested the degree of discovery required by *Glenn,* however, and produced varying interpretations of the conflict of interest consideration it requires.[80]

Eligibility and Vesting Rules

ERISA and the tax code require that all employees age 21 or over who have completed one year of employment must be covered by their employer's pension plan. **Vesting** means acquiring rights that cannot be taken away. ERISA and the tax code provide that an employee's right to her or his pension benefit becomes 100 percent nonforfeitable after three years of employment or gradually nonforfeitable over six years (20 percent per year, beginning in the second year). In either case, the employee's right is vested, but the employee may not obtain the money or use it until retirement. Once an employee's rights in the plan are vested, the employee cannot lose the pension benefits, even if she or he switches employers. Regardless of vesting schedules with regard to pension benefits for contributions by employers on behalf of employees, employees are *always* 100 percent vested in their *own* contributions, though there are variable tax penalties for early withdrawal.

vesting
Becoming legally entitled to receive a benefit where the benefit cannot be forfeited if employment is terminated.

Funding Requirements for Defined Benefit Plans

To ensure that adequate funds are available under defined benefit plans to pay employees on their retirement, ERISA establishes minimum standards on how those plans should be funded throughout the years. Such standards require that employers fund the costs associated with accruals of benefits based on service in each year and amortize any prior service or actuarial gains or losses on investment over a set period of years.

In addition, employers with defined benefit plans must purchase insurance from the Pension Benefit Guarantee Corporation (PBGC) to cover potential losses of benefits if the plan is terminated without sufficient funds to pay all promised benefits. The PBGC was established by ERISA and is similar to the FDIC in that it acts to insure pensions to a certain guaranteed limit in the event that the plan and the employer are unable to pay all promised benefits. The pensions of retired workers generally are insured for the full amount owed, while the pensions of vested but still employed workers are covered only to the extent that their vested interests have accrued at the time the plan terminates, but only to a level guaranteed by the PBGC. Accordingly, workers can lose promised and accrued benefits. This result is what happened to workers at United Airlines, for instance, when their pension plans were terminated in its bankruptcy proceedings.

When a firm considers modifying a retirement plan for its employees, it must be wary since the employees may have been making decisions in reliance on the original benefit plan. Even if a proposed plan offers greater benefits than those originally included, an employer has a fiduciary duty to notify all employees of the changes that might take effect once the employer gives the proposal "serious consideration." Consider the perspective of someone who is about to retire but who might have greater benefits if she simply waits a month or two until a new plan is implemented. She would prefer to know about the possibility, wouldn't she?

Where a plan is being given serious consideration, managers must truthfully and forthrightly offer the information to all employees. If notice of the possible changes is not given to employees, the firm should make eligibility for plan participation retroactive to the date of serious consideration. (See Exhibit 16.9, "Employee Benefit Plans Overview," for an overview of benefit plans, and Exhibit 16.10, "What Everyone Should Know about ERISA," for ERISA provisions.)

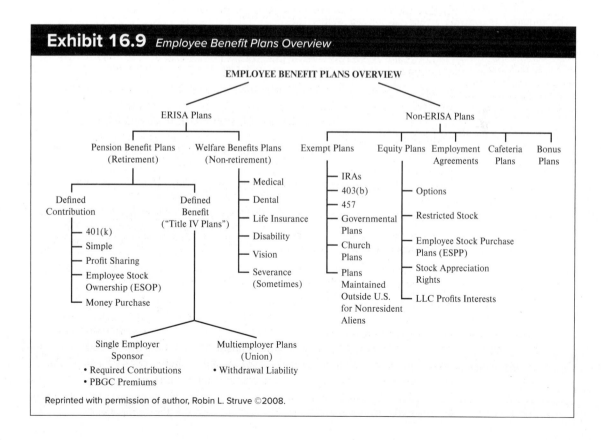

Exhibit 16.9 *Employee Benefit Plans Overview*

EMPLOYEE BENEFIT PLANS OVERVIEW

ERISA Plans — Non-ERISA Plans

Pension Benefit Plans (Retirement) — Welfare Benefits Plans (Non-retirement) — Exempt Plans — Equity Plans — Employment Agreements — Cafeteria Plans — Bonus Plans

Defined Contribution
- 401(k)
- Simple
- Profit Sharing
- Employee Stock Ownership (ESOP)
- Money Purchase

Defined Benefit ("Title IV Plans")

Welfare Benefits:
- Medical
- Dental
- Life Insurance
- Disability
- Vision
- Severance (Sometimes)

Exempt Plans:
- IRAs
- 403(b)
- 457
- Governmental Plans
- Church Plans
- Plans Maintained Outside U.S. for Nonresident Aliens

Equity Plans:
- Options
- Restricted Stock
- Employee Stock Purchase Plans (ESPP)
- Stock Appreciation Rights
- LLC Profits Interests

Single Employer Sponsor
• Required Contributions
• PBGC Premiums

Multiemployer Plans (Union)
• Withdrawal Liability

Reprinted with permission of author, Robin L. Struve ©2008.

Exhibit 16.10 *What Everyone Should Know about ERISA*

REPORTING AND DISCLOSURE

Participants

- *Summary Plan Descriptions (SPD)*—within 90 days after an employee becomes a participant in a plan, or 120 days after a plan becomes subject to ERISA. Updated SPD must be provided every 5 years if amendments made to plan or 10 years if no amendments made.
- *Summary of Material Modifications*—210 days after the end of the plan year in which the modification or change was adopted. If change is a "material reduction in covered services or benefits" under a group health plan then within 60 days after the change is adopted.
- *Summary Annual Reports*—within 9 months after the close of the plan year. Model notice available.
- *Annual Funding Notice*—Defined benefit plans required to provide notice of funded status within 120 days after the end of each plan year. Model notice available.
- *Benefit Statements*—Annually, except defined contribution plans if the participant has the right to direct investments, then quarterly.
- *COBRA Notices*
- *Blackout Period Notices*—30-day advance notice, with limited exceptions.
- Plan documents upon request.

IRS/DOL

- Form 5500

PBGC

- Premiums—defined benefit plans only

Penalties

- Daily penalties for failure to file required reports or provide required disclosure.
- Penalties for failure to provide required participant disclosure generally $110/day per participant.
- DOL/IRS penalties range for $25 per day to $110 per day for delinquencies.

- Criminal penalties can apply.
- DOL delinquent filer program available with reduced set penalties.

FIDUCIARY DUTIES

- Plan assets held exclusively for the purposes of providing benefits to participants and beneficiaries
- Prudent Person rule
- Investment diversification
- Must abide by plan document
- Participant directed accounts
- Plan assets must be transmitted into trust as soon as possible, but no later than 15 business days after the end of the month in which payroll withholding occurs.
- Prohibited Transactions
  - Loans
  - Sales/Purchases
  - Providing services
  - Using Plan assets for own account
- Breach of fiduciary duty is a personal liability.

GENERAL WELFARE PLAN ISSUES

- *Severance Plans*—ERISA plans if have "administrative scheme." If not, then no.
- *Cafeteria Plans*—Not ERISA plans but still subject to IRS Form 5500 reporting (waived at this time). Cafeteria plan contributions not subject to FICA.
- *Disability*—When is an employee no longer "employed" once on disability? ADA concerns.

GENERAL PENSION PLAN ISSUES

- *401(k) Plans*—nondiscrimination/plan operation issues. Investments in employer stock. Fees regarding administration and investment management.
- *Defined Benefit Pension Plans*—Funding and cost of administration issues.

ERISA Litigation

The collapse of Enron was the impetus behind many legal and regulatory reforms in the area of corporate governance. It also contributed to substantial litigation involving complex ERISA issues regarding fiduciary liability. Although, ultimately, the Enron ERISA litigation settled out of court, the few judicial decisions and the briefs that DOL filed in the *Enron* case influenced many cases claiming breach of fiduciary duty when the value of employer stock in retirement plans declined suddenly.[81] The outcomes of these "stock drop" cases differ, with some being decided during the pleading stage, before the case goes to the jury, and most of them settling out of court. However, such cases provide insight into who is or is not a fiduciary as well as whether such fiduciaries have an affirmative duty to disclose information that may be relevant to a participant regarding his or her benefits. Generally, these cases find that a fiduciary will be *anyone who has functional discretionary control over the plan.* In addition, these cases generally hold that fiduciaries have a duty to be truthful, under the *Varity* standard discussed earlier, but may not always have an affirmative duty to disclose all financial details of the company merely due to the ability of participants to invest in company stock.[82]

The plaintiffs in the cases found in the notes all alleged that the fiduciaries of the plans breached their fiduciary duties under ERISA in one of the following ways:

- Allowing the plan to continue to acquire and hold employer stock after the defendants knew or should have known it was an imprudent investment,
- Failing to disclose to plan participants facts that would have enabled them to make an informed judgment regarding their continued acquisition and holding of employer stock, and/or
- Affirmatively inducing participants to continue to invest in employer stock after the defendants knew or should have known it was an imprudent investment.

Some of the more interesting claims in the stock drop cases surround the issue of who are the fiduciaries of the plan. Most of these plans gave fiduciary responsibility either to the company or to an administrative committee made up of individual employees appointed by the company.

ERISA declares that a person is a plan fiduciary "to the extent that" he or she exercises discretionary authority over plan management or plan administration, regardless of whether the person is a named fiduciary. Until Enron and its progeny, courts tended to interpret this functional definition of a fiduciary narrowly and held that individuals acting in the scope of their employment were not personally liable for actions of the corporation. For example, the Third Circuit in *Confer v. Custom Engineering Co.*[83] held that "when an ERISA plan names a corporation as a fiduciary, the officers who exercise discretion on behalf of the corporation are not fiduciaries within the meaning of [ERISA] unless it can be shown that these officers have individual discretionary roles as to plan administration." But other courts, such as the Fifth Circuit in *Musmeci v. Giant Super Markets, Inc.,*[84] have adopted an expanded interpretation of the functional approach to determining fiduciary status, where the court held officers and employees performing fiduciary acts on behalf of a corporation that is a fiduciary will be fiduciaries themselves.

This broad functional approach is the position taken by the Department of Labor and by the *Enron* court when it wrote, "[i]n view of the broad language [and] the functional and flexible definition of 'fiduciary' . . . this Court agrees with those courts which reject a per se rule of non-liability for corporate officers acting on behalf of the corporation and instead make a functional, fact-specific inquiry to assess 'the extent of responsibility and control exercised by the individual with respect to the Plan' to determine if a corporate employee . . . has exercised sufficient discretionary authority and control to be deemed an ERISA fiduciary and thus personally liable for a fiduciary breach."[85] Most of the stock drop cases followed a similar approach.

The Department of Labor has sought to broaden the definition of a fiduciary under ERISA. In April 2016, the DoL's Employee Benefits Security Administration issued a final regulation defining who is a "fiduciary" of an employee benefit plan under ERISA, which also applies to the Internal Revenue Code. The 2016 regulation "treats persons who provide investment advice or recommendations for a fee or other compensation with respect to assets of a plan or IRA as fiduciaries in a wider array of advice relationships."[86] The rule eliminates many regulations limiting fiduciary duties. For example, the definition no longer requires investment advice to be given on a regular basis for the advisor to be considered a fiduciary; just one instance of advising will suffice.

The financial crisis that hit the United States in the 2000s caused pension plan losses that have been estimated at $2 trillion.[87] Most of those losses were the result of drops in the value of stocks held by pension plans. Not surprisingly perhaps, ERISA-based lawsuits to recover pension plan losses have skyrocketed.[88] Paving the way to more lawsuits was a 2008 decision by the U.S. Supreme Court, *LaRue v. DeWolff, Boberg & Associates,*[89] in which the Court ruled that individuals can sue the plan trustee under ERISA for individual losses to their retirement plans. ERISA §502(a)(2) allows recovery against the trustee for "losses to the plan." The question for the Court was whether "losses to the plan" meant that the suit against the trustee must be filed by the plan itself or if one person could bring suit for his or her individual losses. Provided that the plan is a defined contribution plan, such as a 401(k) plan, which has individual accounts, individuals are allowed to file suit under ERISA to recover damages resulting from the trustee's breach of his or her fiduciary duty. In the *LaRue* case, the individual contended that his retirement account lost $150,000 because the trustee failed to carry out his investment orders.

In response to the financial crisis in 2008, the Bush administration passed the Worker, Retiree, and Employer Recovery Act, which amended several features of ERISA and the PPA.[90] The law clarifies that employers "are required to allow non-spouse rollovers and provide direct rollover notices as a condition of plan qualification."[91] Previously, pension providers were permitted, but not required, to allow non-spouses who are designated to receive participant death benefits to "roll over" the funds into an inherited IRA. Another provision permits "smoothing" in the calculation of the value of a pension plan's assets, protecting ERISA plans from market volatility by averaging value over a two-year period. Other measures ease the transition to PPA funding rules by lowering the required funding threshold for plans that fail to meet expected annual earnings.

Since the passage of the Affordable Care Act in 2010, there have been concerns about potential conflicts between the ACA and ERISA. One issue has attracted particular attention as a possible area of new litigation. It is likely that some employers will be tempted to reduce employees to part-time status, to avoid the costs of providing ACA-mandated health insurance coverage to full-time employees. However, employers who do so risk violating Section 510 of ERISA. This section provides that, "It shall be unlawful for any person to discharge, fine, suspend, expel, discipline, or discriminate against a participant or beneficiary for exercising any right to which he is entitled under the provisions of an employee benefit plan or for the purpose of interfering with the attainment of any right to which such participant may become entitled under the plan."[92] For example, under Section 510, an employer is prohibited from terminating an employee days before the employee's pension vests, in order to prevent the employee from accessing her or his full benefits. The health insurance benefits that the ACA requires employers to provide to their full-time employees may be covered by ERISA as an element of employee benefit plans. Employers who reduce employee hours to part-time status to avoid funding their health insurance coverage therefore may be vulnerable to charges of violating this provision of ERISA.[93]

Consolidated Omnibus Budget Reconciliation Act of 1985 (COBRA)

The problem of an employee losing workplace health care coverage when the employee stopped working or switched jobs was addressed by the Consolidated Omnibus Budget Reconciliation Act of 1985 (COBRA) and was codified in ERISA and the tax code.[94] COBRA applies to group health plans provided by employers with 20 or more employees on a typical working day in the previous calendar year. COBRA gives participants and beneficiaries the right to maintain, at their own expense, coverage under their health plan that would be lost due to a change in circumstance such as termination of employment or divorce. However, many states have similar laws governing smaller employers. A small employer should not assume that it does not have continuation requirements if it is otherwise not covered by COBRA.

If a worker's employment terminates or she or he loses benefit coverage due to a reduction in hours, COBRA requires that employers extend employee health insurance coverage for up to 18 months and may charge up to 102 percent of the rates originally charged while the individual was still working for the employer. While the coverage is paid for by the employee, COBRA provides guaranteed coverage for an employee who leaves employment for a relatively short time where that person may have difficulty obtaining coverage. COBRA also requires employers to extend coverage to dependents who would otherwise lose coverage due to divorce or ceasing to be a dependent. General notice informing the covered individuals must be given informing them of their rights under COBRA and describing the law.

There are questions regarding the ongoing relevance of COBRA as the provisions of the Affordable Care Act are implemented. The ACA does not replace or reform COBRA provisions, and those eligible for COBRA coverage may choose to use the program. However, many expect that the rates available on the new state insurance exchanges mandated by the ACA will be lower than the rates offered by COBRA. "As soon as the law was passed, the question among employers and benefits people was: Is there still going to be a reason for COBRA?" said Steve Wojcik, vice president of public policy for the National Business Group on Health, an employer group. Offered a choice between heavily subsidized coverage in the health act's insurance exchanges or paying full price under COBRA, he said, "most people are going to choose the exchange."[95]

The Health Insurance Portability and Accountability Act (HIPAA)

The Health Insurance Portability and Accountability Act (HIPAA) is a federal law that amended ERISA in 1996 to promote standardization and efficiency in the health care industry.[96] HIPAA accomplishes several goals including protecting individuals from discrimination based on their health status because it restricts exclusion from coverage due to preexisting medical conditions (employers are prohibited from denying coverage or charging more for coverage based on an individual's past or present poor health); it created a uniform system for processing, retaining, and securing health care information by encouraging the use of electronic technology, mandating standardization of health-related transactions, and promoting security precautions to maintain the privacy of health information; and perhaps, most importantly, it protects the privacy of individuals with respect to their health care data, and the sharing of such data. Other HIPAA protections relate to the portability of medical coverage by individuals who experience a job loss or job change. When such an event occurs, HIPAA may increase the ability to obtain or maintain health coverage for oneself or one's dependents if the election is made within a certain time frame.

HHS delegated responsibility for enforcing HIPAA's privacy rules to the HHS Office for Civil Rights (OCR). HIPAA does not provide a private right of action for individuals to sue covered entities for alleged violations. However, covered entities may be subject to private lawsuits borne under tort or other legal theories. For example, individual state laws may offer relief that can be invoked by private plaintiffs. Further, some situations may be governed by ERISA, which would allow participants and beneficiaries to sue for enforcement of the applicable plan document.

In 2009, the Health Information Technology for Economic and Clinical Health Act (HITECH Act) was enacted to promote and expand the adoption of health information technology.[97] The HITECH Act extends new responsibilities to HIPAA covered entities regarding data breaches and other privacy issues. To implement various provisions of the HITECH Act, HHS published a major set of reforms to HIPAA, referred to as the HIPAA Omnibus Rule, which went into effect in September 2013.[98] In addition to expanding protections of personal health information, the Omnibus Rule strengthens the capacity of the HHS to respond to patient complaints, in part by instituting a new penalty structure for HIPAA violations.

HIPAA violations are subject to civil and criminal sanctions enforced by the Department of Justice. The 2013 reforms created a tiered system of civil penalties, depending upon the level of culpability of the violator. For instance, HHS may impose civil monetary penalties on a covered entity of $100 to $50,000 per failure to comply with HIPAA's privacy rules, with a calendar year limit of $1.5 million for identical violations. The maximum penalty of $50,000 per violation is mandated in instances of "willful neglect," defined as the "conscious, intentional failure or reckless indifference to the obligations to comply," where the violation goes uncorrected for more than 30 days. The criminal penalties can include up to 10 years of imprisonment if the wrongful conduct involves the intent to sell, transfer, or use individually identifiable health information for personal gain, or malicious reasons.

HIPAA does not preempt all state privacy laws. Furthermore, there are no provisions in HIPAA that exempt an employer from complying with other federal laws such as ERISA, ADA, and FMLA. In jurisdictions where the state privacy laws are more stringent than HIPAA, those laws or the relevant portions thereof are preserved and should be applied instead of HIPAA.[99] Therefore, a state privacy law that provides more privacy protections or greater individual rights than provided by the federal HIPAA privacy rules will generally govern the situation. Employers should initially determine whether and to what extent they are required to follow state law (including local statutes and regulations) instead of the requirements of HIPAA. The HHS website, http://www.hhs.gov, contains numerous links and technical assistance on HIPAA-related topics.

HIPAA Privacy Rules

HIPAA's privacy rules specifically address the permitted and prohibited use(s) and disclosure(s) of health information by organizations subject to them.[100] A covered entity is generally permitted (but not required) to use and disclose protected health information, *without* an individual's authorization, for the following purposes or situations: to the individual for "treatment," "payment," and "health care operations" as defined in the rule; to certain governmental authorities if abuse, neglect, or domestic violence is at issue; for many law enforcement activities pursuant to court orders and/or subpoenas; to funeral directors, coroners, or medical examiners to identify a deceased person or to determine the cause of death; and to the U.S. Department of Health and Human Services (HHS) when it is undertaking a compliance investigation, review, or enforcement action.

Generally, covered entities may use or disclose protected health information only if the use or disclosure is permitted or required by these privacy rules.[101] In very general terms, a group health plan may use protected health information internally or disclose it externally only under the limited circumstances and for the specific purposes articulated in the privacy rules. Otherwise, group health plans may use or disclose protected health information only with the specific permission of the individual who is the subject of the protected health information. Such permission is manifested in the form of a signed, valid authorization form. No doubt, you have signed at least one such form in the past couple of years if you have visited a doctor. Such forms must be written in plain language and they must include a number of elements, including the following:[102]

- A description of the protected health information to be used and disclosed.
- The person(s) authorized to make the use or disclosure.
- The person(s) to whom the covered entity may make the disclosure.
- An expiration date or event.
- The purpose for which the information may be used or disclosed.
- A notice of the individual's right to revoke the authorization.

In some circumstances, it may be necessary to include additional information for the authorization to be valid. There are special rules, for instance, that apply to psychotherapy notes and the use of health information for marketing purposes. The validity of an authorization also may be subject to various state laws and may be further varied depending on the subject of the health information that is being used or disclosed. Additional privacy requirements may be imposed by state law in jurisdictions where the state law provides greater protections for health information.

These privacy rules attempt to strike a balance between permitting important uses of information and protecting the privacy of people who seek medical treatment. The rule is supposedly flexible and comprehensive enough to cover the variety of uses and disclosures that need to be addressed while still promoting high-quality health care.

HIPAA applies to any entity that is a health care provider that conducts certain transactions in electronic form, a health care clearinghouse, or a health plan. Entities that fall within one or more of these categories are referred to as *covered entities.* Many varied organizations (in addition to hospitals) *may* be considered a covered entity due to the activities they conduct. For instance, a university might be considered a covered entity if it has a student health center or a mental health center that provides health care. A grocery store may be considered a covered entity if it has a group health plan managed by the benefits office for its employees. In addition, the 2013 Omnibus Rule revises the definition and clarifies the responsibilities of "business associates" of HIPAA-covered entities. A business associate, under the rule, is a person or entity that creates, receives, maintains, or transmits protected health information (PHI) in fulfilling certain functions or activities for a HIPAA-covered entity. Health information organizations, records storage facilities, and subcontractors are examples of business associates under the Omnibus Rule.

General Obligations of Covered Entities

In general, HIPAA requires covered entities to notify patients of their privacy rights and to explain how their personal health information can be used or disclosed by the organization or its business associates. To this end, they must prepare and distribute a Notice of Privacy Practices to their patients or employees depending on the activities that they regularly conduct.

Covered entities are required to adopt and implement privacy policies and procedures. These policies should be widely publicized and distributed to all individuals within the organization. Individuals who work closely with health information or who are responsible for securing this information should receive detailed training on the organization's established policies and procedures.

All covered entities should make an effort to prevent unauthorized viewing or access to (electronic and paper) health records in their care. To this end, administrative, physical, and technical safeguards should be implemented. Specific protective steps may include the establishment of regular and ongoing training sessions for new and current employees who handle health information; documentation of office procedures for managing health information; creation of firewalls between departments to shield those departments that maintain health information from, for example, individuals who make human resources decisions; addition of locks to file cabinets that house medical information; and use of passwords and timed screen savers on all computers of individuals whose jobs require them to regularly come into contact with health information.

Organizations also must designate a privacy officer who has responsibility for ensuring that the above steps are adopted and followed, and that complaints regarding privacy violations are addressed through the organization's established procedures. The privacy officer should use a monitoring plan to randomly check on the effectiveness of the organization's privacy practices. (See Exhibit 16.11, "Sample Monitoring Plan.")

Enforcement of ERISA

Employers have the right to reduce or modify employee benefits (unless prohibited by contractual obligations), as long as similarly situated plan participants are treated alike. For instance, the employer may not reduce benefits for one full-time employee without similarly reducing the benefits for all similar employees. In order to prevail on a claim of a violation of Section 510 of the act, in the case of discharge, the employee must prove that the employer terminated her or his employment with the "specific intent" to interfere with her or his benefit rights.

In *Owens v. Storehouse, Inc.,*[103] the court was asked to consider the employer's (Storehouse) choice to limit coverage for specific types of claims, a choice that could adversely impact certain employees. Specifically, the employer's insurance company notified Storehouse that it intended to cancel the firm's policy because of the high incidence of AIDS in the retail industry generally, and among Storehouse's employees specifically (five employees had AIDS at the time). Eventually, Storehouse convinced the company to continue the contract, but there was now a $75,000 deductible for AIDS-related claims, while other coverage began at $25,000. As it looked for another insurer, Storehouse considered placing a $25,000 lifetime cap on all AIDS-related claims. Owens, an employee, sued, claiming that this modification lowering the cap violated ERISA. The court held that there is no "vested" interest in the type of coverage an employer provides, even once someone begins to take advantage of that coverage, as long as the employer reserves the right to change or terminate its terms. As there was no specific intent to violate ERISA (i.e., denial of coverage in retaliation for exercising an ERISA right), the employer prevailed. (Note: This type of arrangement would now be prohibited by the ADA as it would be discriminatory against someone with a disability.)

Exhibit 16.11 *Sample Monitoring Plan*

Specific Risk (1)	Operating Control (2)	Monitoring Control (3)	Evidence of Control	Oversight Control (4)	Evidence of Oversight Control
Complaint of inappropriate use/disclosure of their PHI.	HIPAA policy forbids this action by personnel.	Violations of HIPAA policy are subject to disciplinary action.	Policy that supports disciplinary action for violation of HIPAA policy.	Complaint procedure, as outlined in university HIPAA policy.	Periodic check by component areas of complaints logged by privacy office.
New employees in component areas are not trained on HIPAA protocol.	Policy officials within each component area should train new employees in their respective areas.	Written training procedures developed by departments that handle PHI.	Training attendance forms signed by training participants once training is completed.	Training attendance forms are returned to privacy officer once training has been completed.	Training attendance forms are filed in privacy office.
Notice of privacy practices is not distributed in accordance with HIPAA.	Component areas set up procedures that govern the designated times and manner notice is to be distributed.	Random (annual), periodic auditing/monitoring by privacy office of organization's privacy practices.	Schedule of random/periodic monitoring.	Complaint procedure, as outlined in university HIPAA policy.	Periodic check by complaints logged by privacy office.
"Business associates" are not bound by agreement with the organization before they access PHI.	Component areas identify vendors and any others who may have access to PHI and provide this information to privacy officer.	Privacy officer contacts vendor and memorializes terms of agreement.	Business associate agreements.	Business associate agreements are cataloged in organization's database.	Random audits of database.
PHI is not protected by administrative, physical, and technical safeguards.	Component areas set up procedures that determine the minimum necessary disclosures to make pursuant to valid requests; in addition, component areas have to identify physical safeguards to protect PHI locks on file cabinets, passwords on computers.	Review departmental procedures and establish random, periodic auditing/monitoring by privacy officer.	Schedule of random/periodic monitoring.	Complaint procedure, as outlined in HIPAA policy.	Periodic check by component areas of complaints logged by privacy office.

Management Tips

- Ensure that all employees are correctly classified so that the appropriate FLSA provisions are applied.
- Be sure to include all appropriate time in wages, such as donning and doffing time.
- Know that the Obama administration tightened up enforcement of wage laws, so make sure the laws are handled appropriately.
- Check the status of employees carefully before granting or denying FMLA leave.
- Be aware that the Obama administration clarified coverage of sick child laws to gays and lesbians caring for children of the relationship.
- Note that the Bush administration extended FMLA laws to better cover members of the military and their families being cared for during deployment or after returning with an injury.
- Make sure that all of your communications about your benefit plans are clear and written in a way that a reasonable person would understand. If you make any changes, those need to be communicated in writing to all affected employees.
- Under the Pension Protection Act (PPA) of 2006, you may have an additional communication requirement if you are a public company. If you allow for investment of employee contributions into your stock fund, you will need to notify employees of their right to diversify into other stock investments outside of your fund. There are other requirements along these lines, as well; so public companies need to be especially careful and diligent with respect to notification to employees.
- Individuals acting as officers and employees who are performing fiduciary acts on behalf of a corporation that is a fiduciary should be aware of the potential for a broad-scale adoption of an expanding definition of fiduciary that is tending to include them.

In *Central Laborers' Pension Fund v. Heinz,* provided for your review at the end of the chapter, the Supreme Court evaluated a similar claim with regard to the amendment of a pension plan that expanded the definition of disqualifying employment and resulted in a suspension of early retirement benefits to some participants, in possible violation of ERISA's prohibition against reducing an accrued right or benefit under a pension plan (the "anti-cutback" rule), an issue not addressed in *Owens* because those benefits were welfare benefits not protected by ERISA's accrual rule.

It should be noted that some ERISA claims also may be asserted under the Age Discrimination in Employment Act (ADEA). For instance, since benefits are more likely to become vested as a worker gains seniority and as seniority may be more likely with advancing age, employers attempting to avoid paying benefits may be more likely to terminate older workers, giving rise to a claim under both ERISA and the ADEA.

949

Chapter Summary

We have covered a lot of ground in this chapter.

- Employers must be aware that employees have certain rights due to them under various statutes, including the right to a minimum wage and to be paid time and a half for hours worked over 40.

- Children below a certain age may not be employed except as specified by law, and there are only certain hours they can work and certain jobs they can do.

- By law, employees who have worked for an employer for at least 12 months are entitled to take up to 12 weeks' unpaid leave for illness or to care for their children, parents, or a returning war veteran without fear that their job will be taken from them or that their benefits or seniority will suffer.

- In addition, employees have a right to a safe workplace. Employers have a general duty to provide a safe workplace for their employees, in addition to any specific workplace safety regulations that have been developed by OSHA. OSHA inspectors have the authority to conduct unannounced inspections of a workplace, either without a warrant if the employer agrees or with a warrant if the employer insists upon one. Employers may be fined for violations of the safety regulations.

- While employers are not required to provide workplace benefits and retirement plans for their employees, if they choose to do so, they must carefully follow the applicable laws, including allowing employees to have interim coverage if they leave the job and protecting any medical information the employer may have for the employee. In providing benefits, the employer is under a duty to disclose relevant facts to employees, including contemplated changes, and to safeguard the employees' contributions from unethical or illegal interference.

- An awareness of these workplace rules is a must for an employer who wishes to avoid federal and state liability for violations.

Chapter-End Questions

1. No employer intends to harm its employees. How would you define the term *willful* that would give rise to penalties of up to $70,000?

2. The range of dangerous conditions in which employees have been forced to work has been well documented, at least since Upton Sinclair's *The Jungle*. But, what if the danger is the condition of the workplace building itself? Do the OSH Act protections extend to dangers created by, for example, a decrepit building? [*Cascades Boxboard Group,* http://www.osha.gov/pls/oshaweb/owadisp.show_doucment?p_table=NEWS_RELEASES&p_id=17393 (January 30, 2009).]

3. A police officer is eligible for two hours of additional leave bonus if he does not take more than 40 hours of sick leave during a year. If he loses the bonus as a result of taking FMLA leave, have his rights been violated because he has not been restored to an equivalent position before he left? Does it matter how he chooses to take his FMLA leave (i.e., as sick leave versus some other type of leave)? [*Chubb v. City of Omaha,* No. 05-1172, Eighth Circuit (September 27, 2005).]

4. Allbright finds that Benito, Juana, and Lao Tsu, three of his employees, were the cause of the discovery of FLSA violations. As a result, he terminates them. Do the employees have any recourse? Explain.

5. Sasha is employed as the Winstons' babysitter when they must occasionally stay over in town because of their jobs. Sasha is becoming increasingly discontented with her wages, which are below minimum wage. What relief does the FLSA provide for Sasha?

6. A Christmas tree grower used seasonal help to assist in harvesting Christmas trees and did not pay them overtime wages since the growers deemed the employees as engaged in agriculture, which is exempted from the overtime provisions. The DOL argued that the planting, fertilizing, and all other tasks relevant to growing the trees were performed by others who were agricultural workers exempted from the overtime provisions. However, they argued, since the seasonal employees only harvested the trees, they were not engaged in agriculture but rather in forestry and lumbering, which requires the payment of overtime wages. Which view prevails? [*DOL v. N.C. Tree Growers Association, Inc.,* 377 F.3d 345 (4th Cir. 2004).]

7. In a construction project, a company built an 18-foot-by-20-foot trench that had to be lined with a special fabric. When the workers had trouble stretching the fabric over the trench, an employee volunteered to go into the trench and fix the problem. His supervisor stopped him, saying it was too dangerous because the walls of the trench had not been properly supported. After several additional failed attempts to stretch the fabric, the supervisor relented and told the employee to go into the trench. Within five minutes, he was seriously injured when the trench collapsed. Does the supervisor's initial statement constitute an intentional act of injury by the employer, thus removing the case from the limits set by the workers' compensation statutes? Is it relevant to a jury's decision if OSHA issues a citation for a willful violation in this case before it goes to trial? [*Van Dunk v. Reckson Associates Realty Corp.,* Superior Court of NJ, Appellate Div., No. A-3548-08T2 (August 30, 2010).]

8. A tenured professor falls down the stairs at her university, suffers a brain injury, and is unable to work. She is told by the university that in order to be in compliance, she must apply for FMLA leave. She refuses to do so because she believes she would receive her salary if she did not file. The university suspends her salary. If she sues the university for interfering with her FMLA rights, will she win? [*Keselyak v. Curators of the University of Missouri,* 200 F. Supp. 3d 814 (W.D. Mo. 2016).]

9. Jared requested FMLA time off from his job to care for his partner, Samuel, who was suffering from a particularly acute case of adult mumps. Is the leave likely to be granted?

10. Nine months after coming to work for Gaggle, Inc., Sarah was diagnosed with breast cancer. The prognosis was not good. Sarah underwent surgery and a chemotherapy regimen that physically depleted her. When Sarah's sick leave was used up, Sarah asked her employer for 12 weeks of FMLA leave. Will Sarah be likely to receive the requested FMLA leave?

End Notes

1. DePillis, Lydia, "Why Wage and Hour Litigation Is Skyrocketing," *The Washington Post* (November 25, 2015), https://www.washingtonpost.com/.

2. Seyfarth & Shaw, LLP.

3. "5 Key Trends in Workplace Class Action Litigation for 2019: Trend #1 Class Certification Trends in 2019," JD SUPRA (January 21, 2020), https://www.jdsupra.com/legalnews/5-key-trends-in-workplace-class-action-59769/.

4. "USDOL Delivers Record $322 Million in Recovered Wages for Workers in Fiscal Year 2019" (October 28, 2019), https://www.dol.gov/newsroom/releases/whd/whd20191028.

5. The federal regulations of the Wage and Hour Division can be found at 29 C.F.R. chapter V, http://www.dol.gov/esa/whd/flsa/index.htm.

6. "USDOL Delivers Record $322 Million in Recovered Wages for Workers in Fiscal Year 2019," https://www.dol.gov/newsroom/releases/whd/whd20191028.

7. Egelko, Bob, "Raiders Cheerleader Sues, Says Pay Is Less Than $5 an Hour," *San Francisco Gate* (January 22, 2014), http://www.sfgate.com/raiders/article/Raiders-cheerleader-sues-says-pay-is-less-than-5165922.php.

8. Warner, Ralph, "Male Cheerleaders Set to Make NFL History in 2018," *NFL News* (August 6, 2018), http://www.nfl.com/news/story/0ap3000000945403/article/male-cheerleaders-set-to-make-nfl-history-in-2018.

9. "Rozic Bill Ensures Fair Pay for Professional Cheerleaders Employed by New York Teams," NY Assembly woman Nily Rozic's webpage (June 3, 2015), https://nyassembly.gov/mem/Nily-Rozic/story/63939.

10. Todd, Diane, "In the News: #NFLCheerPay: This Super Bowl, Let's Remember the Ultimate Wage Gap," Change.org (February 3, 2018), https://www.change.org/p/roger-goodell-nfl-commissioner-petition-to-provide-nfl-cheerleaders-with-a-livable-salary.

11. "Lawmakers Call on NFL to Give Cheerleaders a Fair Wage," *The Guardian* (September 13, 2015), https://www.theguardian.com/sustainable-business/2015/sep/13/nfl-roger-goodell-cheerleaders-minimum-wage.

12. "Obama Signs Order to Raise Minimum Wage for Federal Contractors," Reuters (February 12, 2014), https://www.reuters.com/article/us-usa-obama-wages/obama-signs-order-to-raise-minimum-wage-for-federal-contractors-idUSBREA1B0PZ20140212.

13. "Executive Order: The Minimum Wage for Contractors," White House press release (February 12, 2014), http://www.whitehouse.gov/the-press-office/2014/02/12/executive-order-minimum-wage-contractors.

14. *Sanifer v. U.S. Steel Corp.,* (No. 12-417, January 27, 2014).

15. "DOL Serves Hibachi Grill & Supreme Buffet a $2 Million Wage/Hour Bill," HR Daily Advisor (February 13, 2014), http://hrdailyadvisor.blr.com/2014/02/13/dol-serves-hibachi-grill-supreme-buffet-a-2-million-wagehour-bill/#more-5683.

16. Randolph, Toni, "Wal-mart to Pay $54.25 M to Settle Minnesota Lawsuit," MPRNews (December 9, 2008), http://minnesota.publicradio.org/display/web/2008/12/09/wall_mart_suit/.

17. "The Labor Department—which has set new records for aggressive Wage and Hour enforcement—now has strong new standards in place to better protect workers' pay," http://www.dol.gov/elaws/overtime.htm; Stamer, Cynthia, "The DOL's announcement of the recovery of more than $1.5 million in back pay under these two settlements in less than a week highlights the rising risks U.S. employers run if their overtime, wage and hour, worker classification or recordkeeping practices don't comply with the Fair Labor Standards Act or other federal wage and hour laws" (January 24, 2011), http://cynthiastamer.com/get_docID2a.asp?fileID=7PB1gVYd7l1hpbBzI5MEOVY8u.

18. U.S. Department of Labor, "Labor Department Statement on Withdrawal of Proposed Rule Dealing with Children Who Work in Agricultural Vocations," press release (April 26, 2013), http://www.dol.gov/whd/media/press/whdpressVB3.asp?pressdoc=national/20120426.xml.

19. U.S. Department of Labor, "Minimum Wage, Overtime Protections Extended to Direct Care Workers by US DOOL," press release (September 17, 2013), http://www.dol.gov/whd/media/press/whdpressVB3.asp?pressdoc=national/20130917.xml.

20. U.S. Department of Labor, "US Labor Department Signs Agreements with New York Labor Department, New York Attorney General's Office to Reduce Misclassification of Employees," press release (November 18, 2013), http://www.dol.gov/opa/media/press/whd/WHD20132180.htm.

21. Greenhouse, Steve, "Growth of Unpaid Internships May Be Illegal, Official Says," *The New York Times* (April 2, 2010), http://nytimes.com/2010/04/03/business/03intern.html.

22. 11 Civ. 6784 (WHP) (SDNY 6/11/13).

23. Aronowitz, Nona, "'No One Should Have to Work for Free': Is This the End of the Unpaid Internship?" NBC News (September 2, 2013), http://www.nbcnews.com/news/us-news/no-one-should-have-work-free-end-unpaid-internship-v20262899.

24. CollegeRecruiters.com (September 24, 2015).

25. 593 F.3d 449 (5th Cir. 2010).

26. Kim, Eun Kyung, "Walmart Defends Controversial Food Drive for Its Employees," *Today* (November 18, 2013), http://www.today.com/news/wal-mart-defends-controversial-food-drive-employees-2D11618754.

27. Langfield, Amy, "McDonald's Finance Guide 'Insulting' to Low-Wage Workers," NBCNews (July 16, 2013), http://www.nbcnews.com/business/personal-finance/mcdonalds-finance-guide-insulting-low-wageworkers-f6C10653604.

28. "Monday's Mini-Report," MSNBC, Steve Benen, 6/17/2019.

29. "Minimum Wages Will Increase in Majority of U.S. States in 2020," Business Facilities.com (December 30, 2019), https://businessfacilities.com/2019/12/minimum-wage-will-increase-in-majority-of-u-s-states-in-2020/.

30. For a list of state minimum wage laws regarding tipping, see the Wage and Hour Division of the Department of Labor's information at http://www.dol.gov/whd/state/tipped.htm.

31. 160 F.3d 294 (6th Cir. 1998).

32. *Chou v. Starbucks,* No. GIC 836925 (Cal. Super. Ct. Mar. 19, 2008).

33. http://www.courtinfo.ca.gov/opinions/archive/D053491.pdf.

34. U.S. Department of Labor, "U.S. Department of Labor recovers more than $1M in overtime wages for employees of U.S. Army contractor in Southern California: Back wages paid to 864 employees working at Ft. Irwin," press release (January 13, 2011), http://www.dol.gov/whd/media/press/whdpressVB3.asp?pressdoc=Western/20110113.xml.

35. www.dol.gov/esa/whd/fmla/ndaa_fmla.htm.

36. U.S. Department of Labor, "U.S. Department of Labor Clarifies FMLA Definition of Son and Daughter: Interpretation Is a Win for All Families No Matter What They Look Like," press release (June 22, 2010), http://www.dol.gov/opa/media/press/WHD/WHD20100877.htm.

37. http://oversight.house.gov/story.asp?ID=1878.

38. Society for Human Resource Management, "FMLA and Its Impact on Organizations," *HR News* (July 2007), http://www.shrm.org/Publications/HRNews/Pages/CMS_022292.aspx.

39. U.S. Department of Labor, "U.S. Department of Labor Final Rule Will Expand FMLA for Military Families and Clarify Rules for Workers and Employers," press release (November 17, 2008), http://www.dol.gov/opa/media/press/esa/archive/esa20081703.htm.

40. *Ballard v. Chicago Park District* (7th Cir. 1/28/2014).

41. 278 F.3d 847 (8th Cir. 2002).

42. No. 09-1775 (7th Cir. 2/14/11).

43. No. 09-CV-4055 (W.D. Ark. 1/27/2011).

44. U.S. Department of Labor, "Occupational Safety & Health Administration: Commonly Used Statistics" (2014), http://www.osha.gov.

45. "2012 Liberty Mutual Workplace Safety Index," Liberty Mutual Insurance Company (2012), http://www.libertymutualgroup.com.

46. USDL, "OSHA: Commonly Used Statistics."

47. *Solis v. Summit Contractors, Inc.,* No. 07-2191, Feb. 26, 2009, Eighth Circuit. In February 2014, the Utah Supreme Court rejected the "multiemployer doctrine" as incompatible with the Utah Occupational Safety and Health Act (UOSH Act). *Hughes General Contractors, Inc. v. Utah Labor Commission* UT 3 (2014). Applying only to the UOSH Act the Hughes decision does not affect federal OSHA jurisprudence. However, the ruling does provide a road map that may prove enticing to future federal challengers to the doctrine.

48. H.R. 1649: Protecting America's Workers Act, introduced April 18, 2013, govtrack.us.

49. As of January 1, 2015.

50. http://www.osha.gov/recordkeeping/new-osha300form1-1-04.pdf.

51. In November 2013, OSHA proposed a rule change that requires employers to file all workplace injury, health, and safety records electronically with the government in order to better track data. Employers' groups, such as the U.S. Chamber of Commerce, are opposed to the proposed rule change, arguing that it would expose confidential business records to the public without proper context. Public comment on the rule change closed in March 2014, and a decision was expected later in that year. For more information, please see Maurer, Roy, "Proposal to Submit Injury Reports Meets Opposition," Society for Human Resource Management (November 11, 2013), http://www.shrm.org.

52. U.S. Department of Labor, "U.S. Department of Labor's OSHA Proposes $2.78 Million Fine against Cintas Corp.," press release (August 16, 2007), http://www.osha.gov/pls/oshaweb/owadisp.show_document?p_table-NEWS_RELEASE&p_id-14397.

53. OSHA, "U.S. Dept. of Labor, Cintas Settle Pending Federal OSHA Cases," OSHA trade news release (December 18, 2008), http://www.osha.gov/pls/oshaweb/owadisp. show_document?p_table=NEWS_RELEASES&p_id=17213; U.S. House of Representatives, Committee on Education and Labor, "Woolsey, Hare Assail Cintas Settlement," press release (December 19, 2008), http://www.house.gov/apps/list/speech/edlabor_dem/1219Cintas.html.

54. OSHA, "Severe Violator Enforcement Program," White Paper (January 2013), http://www.osha.gov.

55. Conn, Eric J., "Analysis: OSHA's Severe Violators Program Prematurely Punishes Employers," Society for Human Resource Management (May 28, 2013), http://www.shrm.org/hrdisciplines/safetysecurity/articles/pages/osha-svep-punishes-employers.aspx (May 28, 2013).

56. U.S. Department of Labor, Occupational Safety and Health Administration, "Crystalline Silica Notice of Proposed Rulemaking," Statement of Dr. David Michaels, Assistant Secretary of Labor, Press Release (August 23, 2013), https://www.osha.gov/pls/oshaweb/owadisp.show_document?p_table=NEWS_RELEASES&p_id=24615.

57. "Multiple Challenges Lengthen OSHA's Standard Setting," GAO-12-602T (April 19, 2012), http://www.gao.gov/products/GAO-12-602T.

58. "Overview List—How Many Smokefree Laws?" American Nonsmokers' Rights Foundation (2014), http://www.no-smoke.org/pdf/mediaordlist.pdf.

59. 445 U.S. 1 (1980).

60. Hosier, Fred, "Five Years Later, Walmart Still Hasn't Paid Trampling Death OSHA Fine," Safety News Alert (December 6, 2013), http://www.safetynewsalert.com/5-years-later-wal-mart-still-hasnt-paidtrampling-death-osha-fine/.

61. 528 F.2d 54 (5th Cir. 1976).

62. "OSHA Advisory Opinion. Re: Application of OSHA Rules to People Who Work at Home," *Tech Law Journal* (November 15, 1999), http://www.techlawjournal.com/agencies/labor/telework/19991115.htm.

63. OSHA, "Enforcement Procedures for Investigating or Inspecting Workplace Violence Incidents," Directive No. CPL 02-01-052 (September 8, 2011), https://www.osha.gov/OshDoc/Directive_pdf/CPL_02-01-052.pdf.

64. Harrell, Erika, "Workplace Violence, 1993–2009," Department of Justice, NCJ 233231, March 29, 2011, http://www.bjs.gov/index.cfm?ty=pbdetail&iid=2377.

65. EEOC Guidance No. 915.002 (03/25/97) at pg. 29.

66. See, e.g.,*Calef v. Gillette,* 322 F.3d 75 (1st Cir. 2003). (The court held "the ADA does not require that an employee whose unacceptable behavior threatens the safety of others be retained, even if the behavior stems from a mental disability.")

67. Namie, G., "2017 Workplace Bullying Institute U.S. Workplace Bullying Survey" (2017), http://workplacebullying.org/multi/pdf/2017/2017-WBI-US-Survey.pdf (accessed September 17, 2017).

68. Ibid.

69. See "The Healthy Workplace Bill," a website that maintains a record of all such legislative efforts, at http://www.healthyworkplacebill.org/states.php.

70. See, for example, Still, Kyle R., "OSHA Whistleblower Claims Expected to Increase due to Online Complaint System," Ward and Smith, P. A. (February 28, 2014), http://www.wardandsmith.com/blog/osha-whistleblower-claims-expected-to-increase-due-to-online-complaint-system.

71. See Milford, Maureen, "UC Takes Charge of Enron Suit," *National Law Journal* (March 7, 2002).

72. *Moench v. Robertson,* 62 F.3d 553 (3d Cir. 1995).

73. Rosenberg, Stephen, "The Ninth Circuit Adopts Moench and Why It Matters," Boston ERISA & Insurance Litigation Blog (October 8, 2010), http://www.bostonerisalaw.com/archives/401k-plans-the-ninth-circuit-adopts-moench-and-why-it-matters.html.

74. *Dudenhoeffer v. Fifth Third Bancorp,* 692 F.3d 410 (6th Cir. 2012).

75. *Fifth Third Bancorp v. Dudenhoeffer,* No. 12–751.

76. *Fifth Third Bank Corp. v. Dudenhoeffer,* No. 12-751 (S. Ct., June 25, 2014), https://www.supremecourt.gov/opinions/13pdf/12-751_d18e.pdf.

77. Andrus, Danielle, "To Aid with Compliance of DOL's ERISA Rules, Principal Releases White Paper," *Advisor One* (January 11, 2011), http://www.advisorone.com/article/aid-compliance-dols-erisa-rules-principal-releases-white-paper.

78. Department of Labor, 29 CFR Part 2550, Reasonable Contract or Arrangement under Section 408(b)(2)—Fee Disclosure; Interim Final Rule.

79. 128 S. Ct. 2343 (2008).

80. See *Cardoza v. United of Omaha Life Insurance Company,* 708 F.3d 1196 (10th Cir. 2013); *Todd v. CP Kilco, et al.,* 2011 WL 838848 (E.D. Oka. Mar. 1, 2011); *Tillotson v.*

Life Ins. Co. of N. Am., 2011 WL 285815 (D. Utah Jan. 28, 2011); *Murphy v. Deloitte & Touche Group Ins. Plan,* 619 F.3d 1151 (10th Cir. 2010); and *Crosby v. La. Health Serv. & Indem. Co.,* Case No. 10-30043, 2010 WL 5356498 (5th Cir. Dec. 29, 2010).

81. See *In re WorldCom Inc. ERISA Litig.,* 263 F. Supp. 2d 745 (S.D. N.Y. 2003); *In re Polaroid ERISA Litig.,* 362 F. Supp. 2d 461 (S.D. N.Y. 2005); *In re McKesson HBOC, Inc. ERISA Litig.,* 291 F. Supp. 2d 812 (N.D. Cal. 2005); *In re Goodyear Tire & Rubber Co. ERISA Litig.,* 438 F. Supp. 2d 783 (N.D. Ohio 2006); *DiFelice v. US Airways,* 436 F. Supp. 2d 756 (E.D. Va. 2006); *In re Electronic Data Systems Corp. "ERISA" Litig.,* 305 F. Supp. 2d 658 (E.D. Tex. 2004); *In re Sears Roebuck & Co. ERISA Litig.,* No. 02 C 8324, 2004 U.S. Dist. LEXIS 3241 (N.D. Ill. Mar. 3, 2004); and *In re Tyco Int'l Ltd., Multidistrict Litig.,* 2004 U.S. Dist. LEXIS 24272 (D.N.H. Dec. 2, 2004).

82. See *Kelley v. Household International, Inc.,* 312 F. Supp. 2d 1165 (N.D. Ill. 2004), and *Hill v. Bellsouth Corp.,* 313 F. Supp. 2d 1361 (N.D. Ga 2004).

83. 952 F.2d 34 (3d Cir. 1991).

84. 332 F.3d 339, 350–52 (5th Cir. 2003).

85. *Title v. Enron Corp.,* 2003 WL 22245394 at 85 (S.D. Tex. September 30, 2003).

86. 29 CFR Parts 2509, 2510, and 2550, Federal Register Rules and Regulations, Vol. 81, No. 68 (April 8, 2016), https://webapps.dol.gov/federalregister/PdfDisplay.aspx? DocId=28806.

87. Caggeso, Mike, "Retirement Blues: Financial Crisis Pulls Billions from Pension Plans, Crimping Consumers' Dreams and Corporate Profits," *Money Morning* (January 29, 2009), http://www.moneymorning.com/2009/01/29/pension-plans.

88. See, for example, Driscoll, Sean F., "More Retirement Plan Lawsuits Filed as Stock Market Slumps," *Rockford Register Star* (December 11, 2010), http://www.rrstar.com/businessrockford/x1757258400/More-pension-fund-lawsuits-filed-as-stock-market-falls.

89. 128 S. Ct. 1020 (2008).

90. Worker, Retiree, and Employer Recovery Act of 2008. H.R. 7327 (December 23, 2008).

91. McCurdy, Keith, "Worker, Retiree and Employer Recovery Act Changes Required Minimum Distributions," *Employee Benefits Legal Blog* (December 22, 2008), http://employeebenefits.foxrothschild.com.

92. 29 U.S.C. § 1140.

93. American Bar Association, "The Patient Protection and Affordable Care Act, ERISA § 510 and the Next Generation of Benefits Litigation Concerns," *Employee Benefits Committee Newsletter* (Spring 2013), http://www.americanbar.org/content/newsletter/groups/labor_law/ebc_newsletter/13_spr_ebcnews/ppaca.html.

94. Consolidated Omnibus Budget Reconciliation Act of 1985, Pub. Law No. 99-272 (April 7, 1986).

95. Hancock, Jay, "Swapping COBRA for Obamacare Likely to Be Windfall for Big Business," *Kaiser Health News* (September 23, 2013), http://www.kaiserhealthnews.org/stories/2013/september/24/obamacare-cobra-businesses-marketplaces-exchanges.aspx.

96. Health Insurance Portability and Accountability Act of 1996, Pub. Law No. 104-191 (August 21, 1996).

97. Health Information Technology for Economic and Clinical Health (HITECH) Act, Title XIII of Division A and Title IV of Division B of the American Recovery and Reinvestment Act of 2009 (ARRA), Pub. L. No. 111-5, 123 Stat. 226.

98. "Modifications to the HIPAA Privacy, Security, Enforcement, and Breach Notification Rules under the Health Information Technology for Economic and Clinical Health Act and the Genetic Information Nondiscrimination Act; Other Modifications to the HIPAA Rules; Final Rule," *Federal Register* 78, no. 17 (January 25, 2013), http://www.gpo.gov/fdsys/pkg/FR-2013-01-25/pdf/2013-01073.pdf.

99. For instance, Illinois has more stringent requirements regarding use and disclosure of genetic health information. See 410 Ill. Comp. Stat. 513/15 et seq.–the Genetic Information Privacy Act–regarding the use and disclosure of mental health information. See also 740 Ill. Comp. Stat. 110/1 et seq., the Mental Health and Developmental Disabilities Confidentiality Act.

100. Though certain information may be released pursuant to permitted uses and disclosures, the amount of released information should be limited to the "minimum necessary" that is needed to accomplish the intended purpose of the use, disclosure, or request, as defined in the rules.

101. See 45 C.F.R. § 164.502(a).

102. See 45 C.F.R. § 164.508.

103. 984 F.2d 394 (11th Cir. 1993).

Cases

Reich v. Circle C Investments, Inc.,
998 F.2d 324 (5th Cir. 1993)

The court analyzes whether topless nightclub dancers who received no compensation except tips from customers are employees subject to FLSA or "business women renting space, stages, music, dressing rooms and lights from the club," not subject to the law. The court determined that they were, in fact, employees for FLSA purposes.

Reavley, J.

***

The secretary of labor alleges that a topless nightclub has improperly compensated its dancers, waitresses, disc jockeys, bartenders, doormen, and "housemothers" and has failed to keep accurate records of the hours worked by its employees. The district court determined that the topless dancers and other workers are "employees" under the FLSA and that the club willfully violated its minimum wage, overtime and record-keeping provisions.

The dancers receive no compensation from the club. Their compensation is derived solely from the tips they receive from customers for performing on stage and performing private "table dances" and "couch dances." At the end of each night, the dancers must pay the club a $20 "tip-out," regardless of how much they make in tips. The club characterizes this tip-out as stage rental and argues that the dancers are really tenants. According to the club, the dancers are neither employees nor independent contractors, but are business women renting space, stages, music, dressing rooms, and lights from the club.

To determine employee status under the FLSA, we focus on whether the alleged employee, as a matter of economic reality, is economically dependent upon the business to which she renders her services, or in business for herself. To make this determination, we must analyze five factors.

The first factor is the degree of control exercised by the alleged employer. The district court found that the club exercises a great deal of control over the dancers. They are required to comply with weekly work schedules, which the club compiles with input from the dancers. The club fines the dancers for absences or tardiness. It instructs the dancers to charge at least $10 for table dances and $20 for couch dances. The dancers supply their own costumes, but the costumes must meet standards set by the club. The dancers can express a preference for a certain type of music, but they do not have the final say in the matter. The club has many other rules concerning the dancers' behavior; for example, no flat heels, no more than 15 minutes at one time in the dressing room, only one dancer in the restroom at a time, and all dancers must be "on the floor" at opening time. The club enforces these rules by fining infringers.

The club attempts to de-emphasize its control by arguing that most of the rules are directed at maintaining decorum or keeping the club itself legal. The club explained that it publishes the minimum charge for table and couch dances at the request of the dancers to prevent dancers from undercutting each others' prices. Finally, it stresses the fact that it does not control the dancers' routines. We believe, however, that the record fully supports the district court's findings of significant control.

The second factor is the extent of relative investments of the worker and alleged employer. The district court found that a dancer's investment is limited to her costumes and a padlock. The amount spent on costumes varies from dancer to dancer and can be significant. The club contends that we should also consider as an investment each dancer's nightly tip-out, which it characterizes as rent. The district court rejected this argument, and so do we. It is the economic realities that control our determination of employee status.

Third, we must look at the degree to which the workers' opportunity for profit and loss is determined by the alleged employer. Once customers arrive at the club, a dancer's initiative, hustle and costume significantly contribute to the amount of her tips. But the club has a significant role in drawing customers. Given its control over determinants of customer volume, the club exercises a high degree of control over a dancer's opportunity for "profit." Dancers are far more closely akin to wage earners toiling for a living than to independent entrepreneurs seeking a return on their risky capital investments.

The fourth factor is the skill and initiative required in performing the job. Many of the dancers did not have any prior experience with topless dancing before coming to work at the club. They do not need long training or highly developed skills to dance at the club. A dancer's initiative is essentially limited to decisions involving costumes and dance routines. This does not exhibit the skill or initiative indicative of persons in business for themselves.

Finally, we must analyze the permanency of the relationship. The district court found that most dancers have short-term relationships with the club. Although not determinative, the impermanent relationship between the dancers and the club indicates non-employee status.

Despite the lack of permanency, on balance, the five factors favor a determination of employee status. A dancer has no specialized skills and her only real investment is in her costumes. The club exercises significant control over a dancer's behavior and the opportunity for profit. The transient nature of the workforce is not enough here to remove the dancers from the protections of the FLSA. AFFIRMED.

Case Questions

1. Does any of the case surprise you? Explain.
2. If you were the club owner and did not want the dancers to be employees, after receiving this decision, how would you change things?
3. Do you think the dancers should have been considered employees? Why or why not?

Mullins v. City of New York, *626 F.3d 47 (2nd Cir. 2010)*

A group of police officers sued their police department for violations of the FLSA, specifically for failing to pay them for overtime. In the course of that lawsuit, the police department took depositions of some of the police officers. Following those depositions, the police department ordered its Internal Affairs Bureau to become involved in the lawsuit, both by collecting various documents and by attending future depositions. The officers claimed that IAB's involvement constituted retaliation, which is prohibited by the FLSA, and they sought a preliminary injunction stopping all such intimidation. The trial court granted the injunction, and the police department appealed to the Second Circuit.

Pooler, J.

***

Plaintiff-Appellees are approximately 4300 current and former New York City police sergeants who filed suit against the City of New York (the "City") and the New York City Police Department ("NYPD") on April 19, 2004, claiming systematic violations of their overtime rights under the Fair Labor Standards Act of 1938 ("FLSA"). Because of the sheer volume of plaintiffs, the parties agreed in May of 2005 to limit depositions to "test plaintiffs"—individuals from seventeen job categories, who would be organized into three groups.

The record reflects that, at some point in January 2006, NYPD's outside counsel, Seyfarth Shaw LLP, met with Charles Campisi, Chief of the "Internal Affairs Bureau" ("IAB"), as well as other high level IAB officials and NYPD lawyers regarding the "topic of deposition testimony." On January 19, 2006, Seyfarth Shaw sent transcripts from depositions of the first group of test plaintiffs to Appellants. The next day, the NYPD ordered lieutenants from IAB to collect command logs, memo books, activity reports, overtime slips, and requests for leave reports from all of the test plaintiffs as well as individuals who worked with them. Some of the IAB document collectors were plaintiffs in this lawsuit—they were promoted to lieutenants after the action was filed. The pool of plaintiffs from whom documents were collected included both those who had been deposed and those who had not.

Counsel for the test plaintiffs immediately objected to the use of IAB to collect documents on the ground that certain plaintiffs understood IAB's involvement to mean they were under investigation. Sergeant Paul Capotosto, Citywide Secretary of the Sergeants Benevolent Association, described the document collection process as a "raid." During his testimony at the preliminary injunction hearing, Sergeant Capotosto chronicled at least a dozen phone calls he received from worried plaintiffs, who expressed concern to him that the NYPD was retaliating against them for their participation in the lawsuit. Among these callers was IAB Lieutenant Ed Heim, a plaintiff in this action, who described being "forced" to collect documents from other plaintiffs and communicated his apprehension to Sergeant Capotosto about the NYPD's approach. Another sergeant referred to IAB's actions as "goon tactics."

Testimony at the preliminary injunction hearing about the unusual nature of the process used to collect documents confirmed that plaintiffs' concerns were not unfounded. Sergeant Anthony Lisi of the Emergency Services Unit of the NYPD testified that document collection is typically conducted by Administrative Lieutenants or Integrity Control Officers assigned to a particular command. In addition, Sergeant Brian Coughlan, Sergeant Supervisor of Detectives in the Bomb Squad, testified that IAB is involved in most cases only when an officer is being arrested or removed from his post.

In March 2006, shortly after the document collection, IAB sent an Integrity Control Officer to attend the deposition of Sergeant Edward Scott. As of his deposition date, Sergeant Scott, who was a plaintiff in the lawsuit against the City and NYPD, had given no testimony in connection with the action. Sergeant Scott, who testified by affidavit at the preliminary injunction hearing, explained that Integrity Control Officers do not normally attend depositions, and he was, therefore, "surprised and concerned" by the officer's presence. He also testified that he found the officer's presence to be "intimidating." When Sergeant Scott's retirement was administratively deferred pending resolution of an unspecified "disciplinary matter" some months later, it came to light that he was under investigation for testimony he had given during his deposition. Sergeant Scott stated that, at the time, "I believed that if I withdrew from this FLSA lawsuit, the City would close its investigation into my deposition testimony."

FLSA provides that it is "unlawful for any person . . . to discharge or in any other manner discriminate against any employee because such employee has filed any complaint or instituted or caused to be instituted any proceeding under [FLSA]." 29 U.S.C. § 215(a)(3). FLSA retaliation claims are subject to the three-step burden-shifting framework established by *McDonnell Douglas Corp. v. Green,* 411 U.S. 792 (1973). Thus, a plaintiff alleging retaliation under FLSA must first establish a *prima facie* case of retaliation by showing (1) participation in protected activity known to the defendant, like the filing of a FLSA lawsuit; (2) an employment action disadvantaging the plaintiff; and (3) a causal connection between the protected activity and the adverse employment action. An employment action disadvantages an employee if "it well might have 'dissuaded a reasonable worker from making or supporting [similar] charge[s]. . . .'" Although the application of pre-existing disciplinary policies to a plaintiff "without more, does not constitute adverse employment action," a causal connection between an adverse action and a plaintiff's protected activity may be established "through evidence of retaliatory animus directed against a plaintiff by the defendant," or "by showing that the protected activity was closely followed in time by the adverse action."

Regarding the causal connection between the NYPD's actions and Appellees' participation in this lawsuit, we think the link is self-evident, and the district court did not err in concluding as much—IAB investigated the veracity of testimony given by the sergeants as part of the lawsuit. Moreover, the sequence, timing and nature of events only reinforces the connection. The day after the NYPD received transcripts from the depositions of certain test plaintiffs, IAB was dispatched to collect documents from the first group of plaintiffs. As testimony indicated, this was unusual in and of itself, because such documents are typically collected by Administrative Lieutenants or other officers in the individual precincts—not IAB. For the foregoing reasons, we AFFIRM the order of the district court.

Case Questions

1. Do you agree with the court that IAB's involvement constituted retaliation? Why or why not?

2. To what extent did the police department culture play a role in this decision?

3. What steps could the police department have taken to prevent these actions from constituting retaliation?

Case 3

Varity Corp. v. Howe, *516 U.S. 489 (1996)*

At the time employer Varity Corporation transferred its money-losing divisions in its subsidiary Massey-Ferguson, Inc., to Massey Combines, a separate firm (it called the transfer "Project Sunshine"), it held a meeting to persuade its employees of these failing divisions to change benefit plans. Varity conveyed the impression that the employees' benefits would remain secure when they transferred. In fact, Massey Combines was insolvent from the day it was created, and by the end of its receivership, the employees who had transferred lost all of their nonpension benefits. The employees sued under ERISA, claiming that Varity breached its fiduciary duty in leading them to withdraw from their old plan and to forfeit their benefits. The district court held for the employees, and the court of appeals affirmed.

Breyer, J.

*** *

. . . The second question—whether Varity's deception violated ERISA-imposed fiduciary obligations—calls for a brief, affirmative answer. ERISA requires a "fiduciary" to "discharge his duties with respect to a plan solely in the interest of the participants and beneficiaries." To participate knowingly and significantly in deceiving a plan's beneficiaries in order to save the employer money at the beneficiaries' expense, is not to act "solely in the interest of the participants and beneficiaries."

As other courts have held, "[l]ying is inconsistent with the duty of loyalty owed by all fiduciaries and codified in section 404(a)(1) of ERISA."

Because the breach of this duty is sufficient to uphold the decision below, we need not reach the question of whether ERISA fiduciaries have any fiduciary duty to disclose truthful information on their own initiative, or in response to employee inquiries.

We recognize, as mentioned above, that we are to apply common-law trust standards "bearing in mind the special nature and purpose of employee benefit plans." But we can find no adequate basis here, in the statute or otherwise, for any special interpretation that might insulate Varity, acting as a fiduciary, from the legal consequences of the kind of conduct (intentional misrepresentation) that often creates liability even among strangers.

We are aware, as Varity suggests, of one possible reason for a departure from ordinary trust law principles. In arguing about ERISA's remedies for breaches of fiduciary obligation, Varity says that Congress intended ERISA's fiduciary standards to protect only the financial integrity of the plan, not the individual beneficiaries. This intent, says Varity, is shown by the fact that Congress did not provide remedies for individuals harmed by such breaches; rather, Congress limited relief to remedies that would benefit only the plan itself. This argument fails, however, because, in our view, Congress did provide remedies for individual beneficiaries harmed by breaches of fiduciary duty.

Case Questions

1. What should Varity have done in order to avoid liability under ERISA?

2. How can an employee ensure that she or he knows all of the facts relevant to a question such as the one present in this case?

3. Why do you think Varity handled this in the way that it did?

Central Laborers' Pension Fund v. Heinz,
541 U.S. 739 (2004)

Retirees who had been receiving early retirement benefits from a multiemployer pension fund sued the fund under ERISA's anti-cutback rule after their plan was amended to expand which types of postretirement employment triggered suspension of such benefits. Heinz understood that, if he were to work as "a union or non-union construction worker" ("disqualifying employment"), his pension would be suspended during that time. However, he also understood that his benefits would not be suspended if he chose to work in a supervisory capacity. Heinz therefore took a job in central Illinois in 1996, after retiring, as a construction supervisor, and the plan continued to pay out his monthly benefit.

In 1998, the plan's definition of disqualifying employment was expanded by amendment to include any job "in any capacity in the construction industry (either as a union or non-union construction worker)." The plan took the amended definition to cover supervisory work and warned Heinz that if he continued on as a supervisor, his monthly pension payments would be suspended. Heinz kept working, and the plan stopped paying.

Heinz sued to recover the suspended benefits on the ground that applying the amended definition of disqualifying employment so as to suspend payment of his accrued benefits violated ERISA's anti-cutback rule. The District Court granted judgment for the plan, only to be reversed by a divided panel of the Seventh Circuit, which held that imposing new conditions on rights to benefits already accrued was a violation of the anti-cutback rule. The Supreme Court granted certiorari in order to resolve the resulting Circuit Court split and affirms the Seventh Circuit in favor of the retirees.

Souter, J.

***

With few exceptions, the "anti-cutback" rule of the Employee Retirement Income Security Act of 1974 (ERISA) prohibits any amendment of a pension plan that would reduce a participant's "accrued benefit." The question is whether the rule prohibits an amendment expanding the categories of postretirement employment that triggers suspension of payment of early retirement benefits already accrued. We hold such an amendment prohibited.

II.

A.

There is no doubt about the centrality of ERISA's object of protecting employees' justified expectations of receiving the benefits their employers promise them. "Nothing in ERISA requires employers to establish employee benefits plans. Nor does ERISA mandate what kind of benefits employers must provide if they choose to have such a plan. ERISA does, however, seek to ensure that employees will not be left empty-handed once employers have guaranteed them certain benefits. . . . [W]hen Congress enacted ERISA, it wanted to . . . mak[e] sure that if a worker has been promised a defined pension benefit upon retirement—and if he has fulfilled whatever conditions are required to obtain a vested benefit—he actually will receive it."

ERISA's anti-cutback rule is crucial to this object, and (with two exceptions of no concern here) provides that "[t]he accrued benefit of a participant under a plan may not be decreased by an amendment of the plan. . . ." After some initial question about whether the provision addressed early retirement benefits, a 1984 amendment made it clear that it does. Now § 204(g) provides that "a plan amendment which has the effect of . . . eliminating or reducing an early retirement benefit . . . with respect to benefits attributable to service before the amendment shall be treated as reducing accrued benefits."

Hence the question here: did the 1998 amendment to the Plan have the effect of "eliminating or reducing an early retirement benefit" that was earned by service before the amendment was passed? The statute, admittedly, is not as helpful as it might be in answering this question; it does not explicitly define "early retirement benefit," and it rather circularly defines "accrued benefit" as "the individual's accrued benefit determined under the plan. . . ." Still, it certainly looks as though a benefit has suffered under the amendment here, for we agree with the Seventh Circuit that, as a matter of common sense, "[a] participant's benefits cannot be understood without reference to the conditions imposed on receiving those benefits, and an amendment placing materially greater restrictions on the receipt of the benefit 'reduces' the benefit just as surely as a decrease in the size of the monthly benefit payment." Heinz worked and accrued retirement benefits under a plan with terms allowing him to supplement retirement income by certain employment, and he was being reasonable if he relied on those terms in planning his retirement. The 1998 amendment undercut any such reliance, paying retirement income only if he accepted a substantial curtailment of his opportunity to do the kind of work he knew. We simply do not see how, in any practical sense, this change of terms could not be viewed as shrinking the value of Heinz's pension rights and reducing his promised benefits.

B.

The Plan's responses are technical ones, beginning with the suggestion that the "benefit" that may not be devalued is actually nothing more than a "defined periodic benefit the plan is legally obliged to pay," so that §204(g) applies only to amendments directly altering the nominal dollar amount of a retiree's monthly pension payment. A retiree's benefit of $100 a month, say, is not reduced by a post-accrual plan amendment that suspends payments, so long as nothing affects the figure of $100 defining what he would be paid, if paid at all. Under the Plan's reading, § 204(g) would have nothing to say about an amendment that resulted even in a permanent suspension of payments. But for us to give the anti-cutback rule a reading that constricted would take textual *force majeure,* and certainly something closer to irresistible than the provision quoted in the Plan's observation that accrued benefits are ordinarily "expressed in the form of an annual benefit commencing at normal retirement age."

The Plan also contends that, because § 204(g) only prohibits amendments that "eliminat[e] or reduc[e] an early retirement benefit," the anti-cutback rule must not apply to mere suspensions of an early retirement benefit. This argument seems to rest on a distinction between "eliminat[e] or reduc[e]" on the one hand, and "suspend" on the other, but it just misses the point. No one denies that some conditions enforceable by suspending benefit payments are permissible under ERISA: conditions set before a benefit accrues can survive the anti-cutback rule, even though their sanction is a suspension of benefits.

Because such conditions are elements of the benefit itself and are considered in valuing it at the moment it accrues, a later suspension of benefit payments according to the Plan's terms does not eliminate the benefit or reduce its value. The real question is whether a new condition may be imposed after a benefit has accrued; may the right to receive certain money on a certain date be limited by a new condition narrowing that right? In a given case, the new condition may or may not be invoked to justify an actual suspension of benefits, but at the moment the new condition is imposed, the accrued benefit becomes less valuable, irrespective of any actual suspension.

***

This is not to say that § 203(a)(3)(B) does not authorize some amendments. Plans are free to add new suspension provisions under § 203(a)(3)(B), so long as the new provisions apply only to the benefits that will be associated with future employment. The point is that this section regulates the contents of the bargain that can be struck between employer and employees as part of the complete benefits package for future employment.

The judgment of the Seventh Circuit is AFFIRMED.

Justice Breyer, with whom the Chief Justice, Justice O'Connor, and Justice Ginsburg join, CONCURRING.

Case Questions

1. Notwithstanding the law as applied, do you believe an employer should be able to change the terms of pension plan qualifications once individuals have begun to avail themselves of the benefits? Can you think of *any* circumstances where you might be persuaded that the employer should be able to modify the plan in this regard?

2. The Court does not seem to be persuaded at all by the plan's arguments, though the district court found in its favor. Are you persuaded by *any* of the plan's arguments?

Glossary

A

ADA and Rehabilitation Act protection   As long as an individual with a disability is otherwise qualified for a position, with or without reasonable accommodation, the employer may not make an adverse employment decision solely on the basis of the disability.

adverse employment action   Any action or omission that takes away a benefit, opportunity, or privilege of employment from an employee.

affirm   Reviewing court upholds lower court decision.

affirmative action   Intentional inclusion of women and minorities in the workplace based on a finding of their previous exclusion.

affirmative action plan   A government contractor's plan containing placement goals for inclusion of women, minorities, veterans, and disabled individuals in the workplace and timetables for accomplishing the goals.

Age Discrimination in Employment Act   Prohibits discrimination in employment on the basis of age; applies to individuals who are at least 40 years old. Individuals who are not yet 40 years old are not protected by the act and *may* be discriminated against on the basis of their age.

agency shop clause   Requires nonunion members to pay union dues without having to be subject to the union rules.

Americans with Disabilities Act   Extends Rehabilitation Act protection to employees in the private sector, with few modifications.

antifemale animus   Negative feelings about women and/or their ability to perform jobs or functions, usually manifested by negative language and actions.

appellant   Party who brings an appeal.

appellee   Party against whom an appeal is brought.

assumption of risk   A defense to a negligence action based on the argument that the injured party voluntarily exposed herself or himself to a known danger created by the other party's negligence.

at-will employment   An employment relationship where there is no contractual obligation to remain in the relationship; either party may terminate the relationship at any time, for any reason, as long as the reason is not prohibited by law, such as for discriminatory purposes.

availability   Minorities and women in a geographic area who are qualified for a particular position.

B

back pay   Money awarded for time an employee was not working (usually due to termination) because of illegal discrimination.

bargaining unit   The group of employees in a workplace that have the legal right to bargain with the employer.

bona fide occupational qualification (BFOQ)   Permissible discrimination if legally necessary for an employer's particular business.

business agent   The representative of a union, usually a craft union.

business necessity   Defense to a disparate impact case based on the employer's need for the policy as a legitimate requirement for the job.

C

"cat's paw" theory of liability   An employer may be liable for discrimination if it takes an adverse action against an employee based on what appears to be a reasonable factor, but the decision actually is grounded in bias and/or a discriminatory motive. Liability attaches even if a decision has a legitimate non-discriminatory reason but is influenced by a biased third party.

cause of action   Right provided by law for a party to sue for remedies when certain legal rights are violated.

claimant or charging party   The person who brings an action alleging violation of Title VII.

closed shop   Employer hires only union members.

collective bargaining   Negotiations and agreements between management and labor about wages, hours, and other terms and conditions of employment.

collective bargaining agreement   Negotiated contract between labor and management.

common law   Law made and applied by judges, based on precedent (prior case law).

common-law agency test   A test used to determine employee status; the employer must merely have the right or ability to control the work for a worker to be classified as an employee.

community of interests   Factors employees have in common for bargaining purposes.

comparable worth   A Title VII action for pay discrimination based on gender, in which jobs held mostly by women are compared with comparable jobs held mostly by men in regard to pay to determine if there is gender discrimination.

compelled self-publication   Occurs when an ex-employee is forced to repeat the reason for her or his termination and thereby makes a claim for defamation.

compensatory damages   Money a court orders to be paid by one who harmed another to compensate for the harm done.

compensatory damages   Money damages ordered by a court to be given to a party to compensate for direct losses due to an injury suffered.

conciliation   Attempting to reach agreement on a claim through discussion without resort to litigation.

constructive discharge   Occurs when the employee is given no reasonable alternative but to end the employment relationship; considered an *involuntary* act on the part of the employee.

contingent offer   An offer of employment that is based on compliance with specific conditions, such as a producing results of a successful medical exam, completing particular exams, or signing a waiver of claims. Not all contingent offers have been upheld as appropriate by the courts.

continual-training requirement   OSHA requires that the employer provide safety training to all new employees and to all employees who have been transferred into new positions.

contributory negligence   A defense to a negligence action based on the injured party's failure to exercise reasonable care for her or his own safety.

corporate management compliance evaluation   Evaluations of mid- and senior-level employee advancement for artificial barriers to advancement.

covenant of good faith and fair dealing   Implied contractual obligation to act in good faith in the fulfillment of each party's contractual duties.

craft unions   Unions organized by the employee's craft or trade.

D

de novo review   Complete new look at an administrative case by the reviewing court.

debar   Prohibit a federal contractor from further participation in government contracts.

defendant   One against whom a case is brought.

defined benefit   Retirement plan where the benefit payable to a participant is defined up front by a formula, the funding of which is determined actuarially.

defined contribution   Retirement plan where the benefits payable to a participant are based on the amount of contributions and earnings on such contributions.

disability   A physical or mental impairment that substantially limits one or more major life activities (sometimes referred to in the regulations as an "actual disability"), or a record of a physical or mental impairment that substantially limited a major life activity ("record of"), or when an employer takes an action prohibited by the ADA because of an actual or perceived impairment that is not both transitory and minor ("regarded as"). *42 U.S.C. §§ 12102(1)-(2).*

disparate treatment   Treating a similarly situated employee differently because of prohibited Title VII or other employment discrimination law factors.

disparate/adverse impact   Deleterious effect of a facially neutral policy on a Title VII group.

duty to reasonably accommodate   The employer's Title VII duty to try to find a way to avoid conflict between workplace policies and an employee's religious practices or beliefs.

E

economic realities test   A test to determine whether a worker qualifies as an employee. Courts use this test to determine whether a worker is economically dependent on the business or is in business for himself or herself. To apply the test, courts look to the degree of control exerted by the alleged employer over the worker, the worker's opportunity for profit or loss, the worker's investment in the business, the permanence of the working relationship, the degree of skill required by the worker, and the extent to which the work is an integral part of the alleged employer's business.

EEO investigator   Employee of the EEOC who reviews Title VII complaints for merit.

eligibility testing   Tests an employer administers to ensure that the potential employee is capable and qualified to perform the requirements of the position.

emergency temporary standards   Standards are imposed by OSHA without immediately going through the typical process where an employee is exposed to grave danger from exposure to substances and the standards are necessary to protect employees from the danger.

employee benefit plan (or plans)   A contractual obligation either through a plan, fund, or arrangement by which an employer or an employee organization such as a labor union agrees to provide retirement benefits or welfare benefits to employees and their dependents and beneficiaries.

employment-at-will   Absent a particular contract or other legal obligation that specifies the length or conditions of employment, all employees are employed "at will." This means that, unless an agreement specifies otherwise, employers are free to leave the position at any time and for any reason. By virtue of the inherent imbalance of power in the relationship, this mutuality is often only in theory.

equitable relief   Relief that is not in the form of money damages, such as injunctions, reinstatement, and promotion. Equitable relief is based on concepts of justice and fairness.

essential functions of a position   Those tasks that are fundamental, not marginal or unnecessary, to the fulfillment of the position's objectives. The employer may not take an adverse employment action against a disabled employee based on the disability where the individual can perform the essential functions of the position.

exhaustion of administrative remedies   Going through the EEOC administrative procedure before being permitted to seek judicial review of an agency decision.

F

facially neutral policy   Workplace policy that applies equally to all appropriate employees.

fellow servant rule   An employer's defense to liability for an employee's injury where the injury occurred on the job and was caused by the negligence of another employee.

fetal protection policies   Policies an employer institutes to protect the fetus or the reproductive capacity of employees.

fiduciary   Someone who has discretionary authority over the investment or management of plan assets of others.

forum selection clauses   A clause in a contract that identifies the state law that will apply to any disputes that arise under the contract.

four-fifths or 80 percent rule   The minority group must perform at least four-fifths (80 percent) as well as the majority group under a screening device or a presumption arises that the screening device has a disparate impact on the minority group and must be shown to serve a legitimate business necessity for the employer.

free riders   Bargaining unit employees who do not pay union dues but whom the union is still obligated to represent.

front pay   Equitable remedy of money awarded to a claimant when reinstatement is not possible or feasible.

function creep   Function creep occurs where an individual voluntarily offers personal or otherwise private information—with consent—for a specific purpose and that information subsequently is used for purposes beyond the original consent.

fundamental right   A right that is guaranteed by the Constitution, whether stated or not.

G

gender dysphoria   A condition in which a person experiences discomfort or distress because of a mismatch between their biological sex and gender identity. Sometimes known as gender incongruence.

"gender-plus" discrimination   Employment discrimination based on gender and some other factor such as marital status or children.

gender identity   How one identifies for male/female purposes, based on a combination of genetics and environment, including, among other things, transgender.

gender stereotypes   The assumption that most or all members of a particular gender must act a certain way.

general duty clause   A provision of the act requiring that employers furnish to each employee employment and a place of employment free from recognized hazards that cause or are likely to cause death or serious physical harm to the employee.

genetic testing   Investigation and evaluation of an individual's biological predispositions based on the presence of a specific disease-associated gene on the individual's chromosomes.

Gig work   Generally refers to temporary work or work as an independent contractor. More recently, refers to work in the "gig economy," where there is an abundance of short-term "gigs"—odd jobs— available on a part-time basis. While these positions may be seen as entrepreneurial and have the potential to springboard careers, they also have the downside of offering no health insurance or other benefits.

greater hazard defense   An employer may use the greater hazard defense to an OSHA violation where the hazards of compliance are greater than the hazards of noncompliance, where alternative means of protection are unavailable, and where a variance was not available.

Guidelines on Discrimination Because of Religion or National Origin   Federal guidelines that apply only to federal contractors or agencies and that impose on these employers an affirmative duty to prevent discrimination.

H

homophily   A theory in sociology that people tend to form connections with others who are similar to them in characteristics such as socioeconomic status, values, beliefs, or attitudes.

hostile environment sexual harassment   Sexual harassment in which the harasser creates an abusive, offensive, or intimidating environment for the harassee.

hostile work environment   A work environment in which harassment of an employee exists to such an extent that a reasonable employee would dread or fear going to work.

I

impairment   "Any physiological disorder or condition . . . affecting one or more of the following body systems: neurological; musculoskeletal; special sense organs; respiratory, including speech organs; cardiovascular; reproductive; digestive; genitourinary; hemic and lymphatic; skin; and endocrine; or any mental or psychological disorder" that substantially limits one of life's major activities. [From the EEOC regulations.]

implied contract   A contract that is not expressed but, instead, is created by other words or conduct of the parties involved.

independent contractor   Generally, a person who contracts with a principal to perform a task according to her or his own methods and who is not under the principal's control regarding the physical details of the work.

industrial union   Union organized across an industry, regardless of members' job type.

inevitable disclosure   Theory under which a court may prohibit a former employee from working for an employer's competitor if the employer can show that it is inevitable that the former employee will disclose a trade secret by virtue of her or his position.

injunction   A court order requiring individuals or groups of persons to refrain from performing certain acts that the court has determined will do irreparable harm.

intersectionality   Experiencing more than one type of discrimination at a time, e.g., that of being Black and female.

IRS 20-factor analysis   List of 20 factors to which the IRS looks to determine whether someone is an employee or an independent contractor. The IRS compiled this list from the results of judgments of the courts relating to this issue.

J

job analysis   Information regarding the nature of the work associated with a job and the knowledge, skills, and abilities required to perform that work.

job group analysis   Combines job titles with similar content, wage rates, and opportunities.

judicial affirmative action   Affirmative action ordered by a court as a remedy for discrimination found by the court to have occurred rather than affirmative action arising from Executive Order 11246.

judicial review   Court review of an agency's decision.

L

law reporter   Book in which court opinions are placed.

legal precedent   Court opinions from cases that have already been decided that are used to determine similar cases later.

liquidated damages   Liquidated damages limit awards to a predetermined amount. As used in the ADEA, liquidated damages are equal to the unpaid wage and are available in cases involving "willful violations" of the statute.

lockout   Management does not allow employees to come to work.

M

major life activities   "[F]unctions such as caring for one's self, performing manual tasks, walking, seeing, hearing, speaking, breathing, learning and working" as well as "the operation of a major bodily function." [From the EEOC regulations.]

make-whole relief   Attempt to put a claimant in the position he or she would have been in had there been no discrimination.

management security clause   Parties agree that management has the right to run the business and make appropriate business decisions as long as applicable laws are complied with.

mandatory arbitration agreement   Agreement an employee signs as a condition of employment, requiring that workplace disputes be arbitrated rather than litigated.

mandatory retirement   Employee must retire upon reaching a specified age. Deemed illegal by the 1986 amendments to the ADEA, with few exceptions.

mandatory subject of bargaining   Wages, hours, and other conditions of employment, which, by law, must be negotiated between labor and management.

Microtargeting   Microtargeting is a form of marketing in which advertisers target a particular age demographic and show tailored advertisements to each age category. The term also may be used for other forms of extremely tailored marketing based on groups.

midterm negotiations   Collective bargaining negotiations during the term of the contract rather than at its expiration.

minimum wages   The least amount a covered employee must be paid in hourly wages.

motion for summary judgment   Defendant's request for the court to rule on the plaintiff's case based on the documents submitted, alleging that there are no triable issues of fact to be decided.

motion to dismiss   Request by a defendant for the court to dismiss the plaintiff's case.

N

national origin   Individual's, or her or his ancestor's, place of origin (as opposed to citizenship) or physical, cultural, or linguistic characteristics of an origin group.

National origin discrimination   Defined by EEOC Guidelines on Discrimination as "discrimination because an individual (or his or her ancestors) is from a certain place or has the physical, cultural, or linguistic characteristics of a particular national origin group." Note that national origin discrimination can include discrimination by members of the same national origin group against each other.

national origin discrimination protection   It is unlawful for an employer to limit, segregate, or classify employees in any way on the basis of national origin that would deprive them of the privileges, benefits, or opportunities of employment.

negligence   The omission or failure to do something in the way that a reasonable or prudent person would have done the same thing or doing something that a reasonable or prudent person would not have done. Failing to raise one's standard of care to the level of care that a reasonable person would use in a given situation. In order to prove negligence, one must show that these acts or omissions resulted in damage to another person or property.

negligent hiring   Employment of a person who causes harm that could have been prevented if the employer had conducted a reasonable and responsible background check on the employee. The standard against which the decision is measured is when the employer knew or should have known that the worker was not fit for the job.

no reasonable cause   EEOC finding that evidence indicates no reasonable basis to believe Title VII was violated.

no-fault   Liability for injury imposed regardless of fault.

no-strike, no-lockout clause   Labor and management agree that labor will not strike and management will not stage a lockout.

non-compete agreement (or covenant not to compete)   An agreement signed by the employee agreeing not to disclose the employer's confidential information or enter into competition with the employer for a specified period of time and/or within a specified region.

O

organizational profile   Staffing patterns showing organizational units; their relationship to each other; and gender, race, and ethnic composition.

P

per curiam   Short decision by a court issued without a judge's name.

performance appraisal   A periodic assessment of an employee's performance, usually completed by her or his immediate supervisor and reviewed, at times, by others in the company.

permissive subjects of bargaining Nonmandatory subjects that can be negotiated between labor and management.

petitioner Party who appeals a case to the Supreme Court.

picketing Union members carrying signs in front of the employer's business that tell of an unfair labor practice or strike.

placement goal Percentage of women and/or minorities to be hired to correct underrepresentation, based on availability in the geographic area.

plaintiff One who brings a civil action in court.

polygraph A lie-detecting device that measures biological reactions in individuals when questioned.

Postpartum depression "Postpartum" means the time after childbirth. Postpartum depression is a serious mental illness that involves the brain and affects your behavior and physical health. When a person who has recently given birth feels sad, hopeless, or empty for longer than two weeks, she or he may have postpartum depression. These feelings can interfere withday-to-day life and may leave the new parent feeling unconnected from the baby. These feelings may be mild to severe.

preemployment testing Testing that takes place before hiring, or sometimes after hiring but before employment in connection with such qualities as integrity, honesty, drug and alcohol use, HIV status, or other characteristics.

prima facie **case** The evidence that fits each requirement of a cause of action is present to conclude that the party alleging the violation has met all the requirements of the cause of action.

private sector That segment of the workforce represented by private companies (companies that are not owned or managed by the government or one of its agencies).

public policy A legal concept intended to ensure that no individual lawfully does that which has a tendency to be injurious to the public or against the public good. Public policy is undermined by anything that harms a sense of individual rights.

public sector That segment of the workforce represented by governmental employers and governmental agency employers. In some situations, this term may include federal contractors.

punitive damages Money ordered by a court to be paid by harming party to harmed party, above the actual loss suffered, for purposes of punishing the one doing the harm and to send a message to society that the activity is not to be done.

punitive damages Money over and above compensatory damages, imposed by a court to punish a defendant for willful acts and to act as a deterrent.

Q

qualification standards The EEOC regulations define qualification standards as "the personal and professional attributes, including the skill, experience, education, physical, medical, safety and other requirements established . . . as requirements which an individual must meet in order to be eligible for the position held or desired."

qualified for the position Able to meet the employer's legitimate job requirements.

quid pro quo sexual harassment Sexual harassment in which the harasser requests sexual activity from the harassee in exchange for workplace benefits.

R

reasonable accommodation An accommodation to the individual's disability that does not place an undue burden or hardship (courts use the language interchangeably) on the employer. The reasonableness of the accommodation may be determined by looking to the size of the employer, the cost to the employer, the type of employer, and the impact of the accommodation on the employer's operations. It is important to understand that each case will be determined by looking to the *particular* job responsibilities as they are impacted by the employee's or applicant's *particular* disability. Courts have referred to this inquiry as one that is "fact intensive and case specific."

reasonable cause EEOC finding that Title VII was violated.

reasonable factor other than age (RFOA) A defense to a *prima facie* claim of age discrimination, offered by employers. May include any requirement that does not have an adverse impact on older workers as well as those factors that do adversely affect this protected class but are shown to be job-related. For example, if an employee is not performing satisfactorily and is terminated, her failure to meet reasonable performance standards would constitute a reasonable factor other than age.

reasonable person standard   Viewing the harassing activity from the perspective of a reasonable person in society at large (generally tends to be the male view).

reasonable victim standard   Viewing the harassing activity from the perspective of a reasonable person experiencing the harassing activity including gender-specific sociological, cultural, and other factors.

rebuttable presumption   Legal determination arising from proven evidence that can be refuted by facts to the contrary.

recklessness   Conscious disregard for safety; conscious failure to use due care.

record keeping and reporting requirements   Title VII requires that certain documents must be maintained and periodically reported to the EEOC.

remand   Reviewing court orders lower court to take further action on a case in accordance with the reviewing court's opinion.

respondent or responding party   Party against whom a case is appealed to the Supreme Court.

retirement or pension plan   A plan that provides for compensation at retirement or deferral of income to periods beyond termination of employment.

retroactive seniority   Seniority that dates back to the time the claimant was treated illegally.

reverse   Reviewing court does not uphold the lower court's decision.

reverse discrimination   Claim brought by a majority member who feels adversely affected by the use of an employer's affirmative action plan.

right-to-sue letter   Letter given by the EEOC to claimants, notifying them of the EEOC's no-cause finding and informing them of their right to pursue their claim in court.

right-to-work laws   Permits employees to choose not to become a part of the union.

S

706 agency   State agency that handles EEOC claims under a work-sharing agreement with the EEOC.

screening device   Factor used to weed out applicants from the pool of candidates.

search   A physical invasion of a person's space, belongings, or body.

secondary boycott   Union pressure on management created by getting others who do business with management to cease.

Section 503 of the Rehabilitation Act   Prohibits discrimination against otherwise-qualified individuals with disabilities by any program or activity receiving federal assistance. Requires affirmative action on the part of federal contractors and agencies to recruit, hire, and train disabled workers.

severe and/or pervasive activity   Harassing activity that is more than an occasional act or is so serious that it is the basis for liability.

sexual orientation   Whom one is attracted to for personal and intimate relationships.

shop steward   Union member chosen as an intermediary between union members and employers.

social media   User-created content, including text, video, audio, and other multimedia, published or otherwise communicated in an environment that enables scalable interactivity and dialogue, such as a blog, wiki, or other similar site.

stare decisis   Latin for "to stand by a decision." Process of a court using prior decisions to determine the decision for the case before it.

substantially limited   An individual does not need to have an impairment that prevents or severely or significantly restricts a major life activity to be considered to be "substantially limited," nor does the impairment need to last for a set period of time. Multiple impairments that, together, substantially restrict a major life activity may also constitute a disability.

T

tort   A private (civil) wrong against a person or her or his property.

U

under color of state law   Government employee is illegally discriminating against another during performance of his or her duties.

underrepresentation or underutilization   Significantly fewer minorities or women in the workplace than relevant statistics indicate are available or their qualifications indicate they should be working at better jobs.

undue hardship   A burden imposed on an employer, by accommodating an employee's religious conflict, that would be too onerous for the employer to bear.

union shop   Union and management agree that employees must be members of the union.

union shop clause   Provision in a collective bargaining agreement allowing a union shop.

unjust dismissal   Employee terminated from a job for a reason the law will not support. Used interchangeably with the term wrongful termination.

V

validation   Evidence that shows a test evaluates what it says it evaluates.

valuing diversity   Learning to accept and appreciate those who are different from the majority and value their contributions to the workplace.

vesting   Becoming legally entitled to receive a benefit where the benefit cannot be forfeited if employment is terminated.

vicarious liability   The imposition of liability on one party for the wrongs of another. Liability may extend from an employee to the employer on this basis if the employee is acting within the scope of her or his employment at the time the liability arose.

W

waiver   The intentional relinquishment of a known right.

wildcat strike   A strike not sanctioned by the union.

wrongful termination   Employee dismissed from a job for reasons the law will not support. Used interchangeably with the term unjust dismissal.

Y

yellow dog contract   Agreement employers require employees to sign stating they do not belong to a union and will not join one; now illegal.

Case Index

Subject Index

Marijuana, medical, 195-196, 737
Marijuana, use of, 797
Marital privacy, 773
Marital status, 158, 795
Market rates, 437
Marshall, Thurgood, 319, 320, 424
Martinez, Alicia, 425
Martinez, Maria, 480
Martin, Trayvon, 312
Mass layoffs, 71
Master and servant, 6
Material facts, 159
Maternity leave policies, 442
Mayer, Marissa, 405
McCall, Harry, 403
McDonald's, 465, 909
Mediation, 133-134, 496
Medical compensatory damages, 88
Medical examinations, 731, 926
Medical leave laws, 729
Medical records, 720, 776
Medical tests, 188-189, 781, 801
Medicare, 8
Medication, 731
Medication-assisted treatment
  (MAT), 698
Melting pot diversity theory, 348-351
Men
  hair of, 590
  as sexual harassment victims, 480
  standard for, 487
  work of, 488
Mental health professionals, 517
Mental illness, 720-721
  defined, 720
Merrill Lynch, 407
#MeToo movement, 467-468, 471,
  485, 796
Micro-aggression, 269
Microsoft, 686
Microtargeting, 637
Middle Eastern discrimination,
  361-362
Midterm negotiations, 877
Migraine headaches, 701
Mine workers, 688
Minimum age standards, 916
Minimum wages
  exceptions from, 251, 911
  Fair Labor Standards Act, 8, 251
  federal contractors, 903
  history of, 909
  independent contractors and, 905
  for low entry-level employees, 909
  provisions for, 917
  state levels for, 910
  U.S. laws, 5
Ministerial exception, 585
Minnesota Multiphasic Personality
  Indicator test, 187
Minorities. See also Affirmative
  action; Ethnicity; Gender
  discrimination; National
  origin discrimination; Race
  and color discrimination;
  specific minority groups
  categories, 257

credit histories, 122
employee discrimination, 122
employment by word-of-mouth
  network, 246
employment level, 117
glass ceiling, 319, 415
hiring, 237
history of, 248
internal promotions, 162
job interviews and, 167
job qualifications of, 142
job statistics for, 252-253
negative views about, 245
underrepresentation of, 254
written exams for, 84
Misclassification initiative, 905
Misconduct. See Conduct
Misrepresentation, 158-159
Mississippi Sovereignty Commission,
  114, 249-250
Mixed-motives cases, 714
Mommy track, 433
Money-laundering activity, 732
Monitoring of employees
  about, 809-812
  allowable monitoring, 814
  for defamation, 809
  email, 809, 814-815
  purpose of, 813-814
  as retaliation, 823
  right to privacy and, 804-818
Monitoring reminders, 829
Monopolies, 863
Moonves, Leslie, 465
Moore, Roy S., 578
Morbid obesity, 733-734
Morgan, Mary, 526
Motion for summary judgment, 56
Motion to dismiss, 56
Motivating factor, 639
Motive to falsify, 493
Multiculturalism, 269
Multiemployer doctrine, 922
Muslims, 124, 361-362, 577, 586-587,
  597. See also Religious
  discrimination
Myerson, Bess, 331
"The Myth of the Ideal Worker"
  study, 405

N

NAACP, 259, 319
NAFTA (North American Free Trade
  Agreement), 866
Names, 325, 577, 582
Nassar, Dr., 640
National Academy of Sciences, 198
National Association for Law
  Placement, 408
National Association of Colleges and
  Employers, 908
National Basketball Association (NBA),
  418, 860

National Bureau of Economics, 860
National Coming Out Day, 530
National Crime Information
  Center, 783
National Defense Authorization Act
  (NDAA) of 2008, 917
National Education Association
  (NEA), 888
National Football League (NFL),
  875, 877
National Hockey League, 860
National Industrial Recovery Act
  (NIRA), 865
National Institute for Mental
  Health, 720
National Institute for Occupational
  Safety and Health
  (NIOSH), 923
National Labor Relations Act of 1935
  (Wagner Act), 9-10, 365,
  728, 868-881
National Labor Relations Board
  (NLRB), 765, 859, 870, 888
National Law Journal, 473
National origin
  country of citizenship *vs.,* 351
  ethnicity *vs.,* 351
  Hispanics and, 305-307
  race questions and, 306
National origin discrimination,
  376-398
  adverse employment action and
    dissimilar treatment,
    357-358
  alternative basis for, 374-375
  buy American and hire American
    government policy and,
    363-365
  cases, 386-398
  EEOC guidance on, 305, 311
  federal contractors, guidelines for,
    360-361
  harassment and, 311, 358-360
  Immigration Reform and Control
    Act, 363-374
  legislation prohibiting,
    overview, 349
  management tips, 376
  melting pot diversity theory,
    348-351
  Middle Eastern discrimination,
    361-362
  national origin discrimination
    guidelines, 360-361
  protected classes, 351-352
  qualifications and BFOQs, 352-357
  race discrimination and, 310
  realities about, 351
  regulatory overview, 351-358
  religious discrimination guidelines,
    360-361
  remedies, 89
  statutory basis, 348
National Pay Equity Task Force, 435
National War Labor Board, 865
Native Americans, 124, 515, 597

Unions. *See also* Labor law
  antiunionization tactics, 872
  benefit plans, 934
  bill of rights for, 887
  collective bargaining agreements,
    875, 877
  craft unions, 871, 888
  decertification, 877
  dues for, 599
  duty of fair representation, 876
  employees and, 786, 871
  employers against, 872–873
  examples, 858–860
  First Amendment rights, 885
  funds for, 887
  good-faith bargaining, 874–876
  history of, 862–864
  management tips, 889
  mandatory arbitration agreements, 135
  nonconforming, 262
  of nurses, 872
  quotas and, 262
  religious beliefs and, 598, 599
  role in services, 865
  in the South, 251
  statistics on, 861
  strikes and lockouts, 878–881
  Title VII of the Civil Rights Act and,
    128, 140
  unfair labor practices, 877–878,
    880–881
Union shop, 883
Union shop clause, 883
United Auto Workers, 883
United Nations, 689
Uniting and Strengthening America by
    Providing Appropriate Tools
    Required to Intercept and
    Obstruct Terrorism (USA
    PATRIOT) Act, 831–832
Universities, recruitment, 157, 163
Unjust dismissal, 70
Unpaid internships, 905–907
Unprotected speech, 827
Unreasonable searches, 184, 204, 773
Unsafe working conditions, 725, 920–922
Urinalyses, 195
USA PATRIOT Act, 831–832
U.S. Constitution
  Eleventh Amendment, 141, 631
  Fifth Amendment, 532, 781
  First Amendment, 517, 532, 588,
    597, 599, 827
  Fourteenth Amendment, 141, 189,
    409, 532, 588, 631, 781
  Fourth Amendment, 184, 195,
    777–780, 808
  function of, 189
  private-sector employee privacy, 786
  promise of, 116
  protected activities, termination
    and, 66
  religious freedom in, 579, 584
  Thirteenth Amendment, 138
U.S. Department of Health and Human
    Services (HHS), 945

U.S. Department of Homeland Security
    (DHS), 366, 372
U.S. Department of Justice (DOJ), 733,
    783, 886
U.S. Department of Labor (DOL), 10,
    199, 688, 732, 903, 915,
    919, 933, 937, 942. *See
    also* Occupational Safety
    and Health Administration
    (OSHA)
U.S. Government Accounting Office, 532
U.S. Merit Systems Protection Board
    (MSPB), 473
U.S. Supreme Court
  decisions, 54, 136, 266, 640, 656
  determinations, 443, 631, 640, 908
  justices, 55, 87, 300, 319–320, 405,
    482, 491, 629, 777
  reversals, 704, 827
  rulings, 89, 206, 480, 517, 540,
    651, 937
U.S. Supreme Court Reporter, 55
UTSA (Uniform Trade Secrets Act), 33

V

Vacation time, 918
Validation of tests, 185–186, 205
Valuing diversity, 269–282
Varity standard, 941
Venue recruiting, 163
Verbal conduct, 463
Vesting, 939
Vicarious liability, 9
Victim assistance, 497
Victims of domestic violence, 411
Vinson, Mechelle, 483
Violation of policy, 822
Violation of public policy, 60, 62–63
Violence in workplace, 930–931
Virtualization, 824
Vision impairment, 701, 718
Vocational Rehabilitation Act of 1973,
    157, 200, 684, 687–688, 695
Vogue (magazine), 277
Voice mail system messages, 721
Voluntariness, 649
Voluntary affirmative action, 260–261,
    264–266
Voluntary retirement plans, 643
Volunteers, 17–18
Voter registration, 300
Voting in a union, 870
Voting Rights Act of 1965, 316

W

Waber, Ben, 817
Wages. *See also* Minimum wages;
    Pay gap
  apprentice, 910

back pay, 88, 373, 905
  discrimination and, 131
  Fair Labor Standards Act and, 903,
    905–906
  gender and, 122, 405–406, 416
  pay cuts in lieu of termination, 648
  people with disabilities and,
    684–685
  theft of, 128
Wagner Act of 1935. *See* National
    Labor Relations Act of 1935
Waivers, 654–657, 830–831
Walgreens, 686
Walk-in applicants, 163
Walkouts, 880
Walled garden approach, 824
Waller, Bill, 250
Wall Street, 407
Wall Street Journal, 313, 538
Walmart, 405, 518, 905, 909, 928
WARN (Worker Adjustment and
    Retraining Notification) Act,
    71–72, 787
WARN Act notices, 71–72
Warrant
  before action, 785
  obtaining, 778
  requirements of, 778
  search, 831, 923
Washington Post, 466, 828
Wasson, Greg, 685
Watergate scandal, 785
Websites leading employers not to hire, 175
Weight. *See also* Obese employees
  discrimination policy, 428
  of employees, 794–795
  issues, 420–421
  restriction policy, 428
  and wellness programs, 794–795
Weinstein, Harvey, 465, 468
Welfare benefits, 933
Welfare plan, 934
Welfare plan issues, 940
Wellness programs, 730, 794–795
Westlaw (database), 55, 90
Weyco, Inc., 794
Wheelchairs, 718
Whistleblowing, 63–64, 932
White buffalo (sexual harassment class
    action trials), 469
White Citizen Council, 115
White House Commission on Women
    and Girls, 413
Whiteness, preference for, 330
Whites, discrimination against, 321
"Whites Only" sign, 313
White-sounding names, 165, 325, 577
Wildcat strike, 879
Willful violation, 926
Williams, Vanessa, 330
Wilson, Woodrow, 864–865
Winfrey, Oprah, 299
Wiretaps, 784
Witness testimony, 493
Wojcik, Steve, 944
Womack, Paul, 423
Woman standard, 487